Product Liability Desk Reference
A Fifty-State Compendium

2015 Edition

Morton F. Daller

Editor-in-Chief

This edition supersedes the 2014 Edition and all other previous editions.

Wolters Kluwer

This publication is designed to provide accurate and authoritative information in regard to the subject matter covered. It is sold with the understanding that the publisher and the author(s) are not engaged in rendering legal, accounting, or other professional services. If legal advice or other professional assistance is required, the services of a competent professional should be sought.

> — From a *Declaration of Principles* jointly adopted by a Committee of the American Bar Association and a Committee of Publishers and Associations

Copyright © 2015 Morton F. Daller. All Rights Reserved.

No part of this publication may be reproduced or transmitted in any form or by any means, including electronic, mechanical, photocopying, recording, or utilized by any information storage or retrieval system, without written permission from the publisher. For information about permissions or to request permissions online, visit us at *http://www.wklawbusiness.com/footer-pages/permissions*, or a written request may be faxed to our permissions department at 212-771-0803.

Published by Wolters Kluwer in New York.

Wolters Kluwer serves customers worldwide with CCH, Aspen Publishers and Kluwer Law International products.

ISBN 978-1-4548-4391-7
ISSN 1528-7173

Printed in the United States of America

1 2 3 4 5 6 7 8 9 0

About Wolters Kluwer Law & Business

Wolters Kluwer Law & Business is a leading global provider of intelligent information and digital solutions for legal and business professionals in key specialty areas, and respected educational resources for professors and law students. Wolters Kluwer Law & Business connects legal and business professionals as well as those in the education market with timely, specialized authoritative content and information-enabled solutions to support success through productivity, accuracy and mobility.

Serving customers worldwide, Wolters Kluwer Law & Business products include those under the Aspen Publishers, CCH, Kluwer Law International, Loislaw, ftwilliam.com and MediRegs family of products.

CCH products have been a trusted resource since 1913, and are highly regarded resources for legal, securities, antitrust and trade regulation, government contracting, banking, pension, payroll, employment and labor, and healthcare reimbursement and compliance professionals.

Aspen Publishers products provide essential information to attorneys, business professionals and law students. Written by preeminent authorities, the product line offers analytical and practical information in a range of specialty practice areas from securities law and intellectual property to mergers and acquisitions and pension/benefits. Aspen's trusted legal education resources provide professors and students with high-quality, up-to-date and effective resources for successful instruction and study in all areas of the law.

Kluwer Law International products provide the global business community with reliable international legal information in English. Legal practitioners, corporate counsel and business executives around the world rely on Kluwer Law journals, looseleafs, books, and electronic products for comprehensive information in many areas of international legal practice.

Loislaw is a comprehensive online legal research product providing legal content to law firm practitioners of various specializations. Loislaw provides attorneys with the ability to quickly and efficiently find the necessary legal information they need, when and where they need it, by facilitating access to primary law as well as state-specific law, records, forms and treatises.

ftwilliam.com offers employee benefits professionals the highest quality plan documents (retirement, welfare and non-qualified) and government forms (5500/PBGC, 1099 and IRS) software at highly competitive prices.

MediRegs products provide integrated health care compliance content and software solutions for professionals in healthcare, higher education and life sciences, including professionals in accounting, law and consulting.

Wolters Kluwer Law & Business, a division of Wolters Kluwer, is headquartered in New York. Wolters Kluwer is a market-leading global information services company focused on professionals.

WOLTERS KLUWER SUPPLEMENT NOTICE

This product is updated on a periodic basis with supplements and/or new editions to reflect important changes in the subject matter.

If you would like information about enrolling this product in the update service, or wish to receive updates billed separately with a 30-day examination review, please contact our Customer Service Department at 1-800-234-1660 or email us at: *customer.service@wolterskluwer.com*. You can also contact us at:

> Wolters Kluwer
> Distribution Center
> 7201 McKinney Circle
> Frederick, MD 21704

Important Contact Information

- To order any title, go to *www.wklawbusiness.com* or call 1-800-638-8437.
- To reinstate your manual update service, call 1-800-638-8437.
- To contact Customer Service, e-mail *customer.service@wolterskluwer.com*, call 1-800-234-1660, fax 1-800-901-9075, or mail correspondence to: Order Department—Wolters Kluwer, PO Box 990, Frederick, MD 21705.
- To review your account history or pay an invoice online, visit *www.aspenpublishers.com/payinvoices*.

Contents

Introduction	vii
Contributing Editors	ix
Alabama	1
Alaska	11
Arizona	29
Arkansas	57
California	75
Colorado	99
Connecticut	125
Delaware	143
District of Columbia	159
Florida	173
Georgia	195
Hawaii	227
Idaho	241
Illinois	261
Indiana	279
Iowa	305
Kansas	317
Kentucky	335
Louisiana	355
Maine	369
Maryland	385
Massachusetts	423
Michigan	463
Minnesota	477
Mississippi	489
Missouri	499
Montana	513
Nebraska	539
Nevada	561
New Hampshire	577
New Jersey	589
New Mexico	613
New York	643
North Carolina	671
North Dakota	693
Ohio	703
Oklahoma	733
Oregon	757
Pennsylvania	777
Rhode Island	799
South Carolina	811

South Dakota	851
Tennessee	863
Texas	877
Utah	903
Vermont	917
Virginia	935
Washington	951
West Virginia	971
Wisconsin	991
Wyoming	1011

INTRODUCTION

The *Product Liability Desk Reference*, 2015 Edition, is designed to provide a succinct summary of the product liability laws of the 50 states and the District of Columbia and is a handy first stop practice tool for:

- the attorney handling product liability litigation in more than one state;
- the corporate in-house counsel, litigation management professional, or risk manager who is overseeing product liability cases in more than one state;
- and the outside risk manager and insurance professional where policies may cover product liability claims.

This book, used in conjunction with the *Tort Law Desk Reference* and *Business Torts, A Fifty-State Guide* also published annually by Wolters Kluwer, should provide such users with helpful summaries of the substantive law involved in a great many of the lawsuits or claims that cross their desk. Please note that each state's summary is completed some time prior to the date of this Introduction. Please be careful to update any citation from this book prior to relying upon it.

Each summary is designed to provide an overview. In order to be useful, each summary must therefore be brief, which is, of course, very difficult. The summaries are not designed as full-scale research tools, but rather as starting points for assessing the merits or pitfalls of litigation in a particular jurisdiction.

During the past year, there have been significant changes in the product liability laws of a number of states.

A quite significant change in the product liability law of Pennsylvania occurred in November, 2014 when the Supreme Court of Pennsylvania overruled longstanding precedent and held the question as to whether a product was unreasonably dangerous would no longer be determined by the court rather than the jury. Confounding many predictions the court declined to adopt the provisions of Restatement (Third) of Torts. Rather, the court adopted a standard of proof premised upon alternative consumer expectations or risk utility balancing tests.

Also in Pennsylvania, all strict liability claims have been disallowed in cases involving prescription drugs and prescription medical devices. However, such claims sounding in negligence have been permitted.

The New York Court of Appeals recently refused to recognize a judicially created, independent cause of action for medical monitoring, but the court noted that plaintiffs who have established an actionable tort may still obtain the remedy of medical monitoring.

In New Jersey, when a manufacturer requires the use of a component part, the manufacturer has a duty to warn of reasonably anticipated damages posed by that component even as to replacement parts manufactured by others. The Ohio Supreme Court has ruled that a manufacturer who makes a product in an unassembled state and is not involved in the design or assembly of the integrated product or system cannot be held liable for a defect introduced by a third party.

There is a recent split of authority in California concerning the liability for injuries to employees of the product manufactured caused by raw materials used during the manufacturing process. One line of cases holds the supplier of the raw materials is not liable for such injuries but more recent authority holds the component parts doctrine does not bar liability on the part of such a supplier of raw materials. In California, those who sell their services to others in the development of a product, e.g., engineers or designers, but do not participate in bringing a product to market are not subject to strict product liability, but they may still be subject to liability for negligence.

A Texas Appellate Court recently held that resale of a used good does not automatically terminate remaining implied warranty obligations and a subsequent buyer of used goods may sue the manufacturer of the used goods for a breach of the implied warranty of merchantability.

The Maine Supreme Court recently adopted Section 3(b) of the Restatement (Third) of Torts which provides that, even without proof of a specific defect, evidence that an injury was not solely the result of causes other than a product defect existing at the time of sale or distribution can lead to an inference that a product was defective.

Although the independent intervening cause doctrine is rather limited in New Mexico, the New Mexico Court of Appeals recently held that such an instruction should have been given in a wrongful death case where there was evidence the plaintiff had committed suicide and there was a dispute as to whether the decedent's death was a foreseeable result of the defendant's alleged negligence.

I am indebted to my son, Nicholas G. Daller, for assisting me in editing this book.

On behalf of all the contributing editors, I hope all users of the 2015 Edition of *Product Liability Desk Reference* will find the book to be a useful and practical tool.

Morton F. Daller
Editor-in-Chief
Cell Phone: 215-738-3800
Email: mort.daller@gmail.com

Nicholas G. Daller
Cell Phone: 215-264-8665
Email: ngdaller@syr.edu

November, 2014

CONTRIBUTING EDITORS

ALABAMA
John E. Goodman, Esquire
R. Thomas Warburton, Esquire
Bradley Arant Boult Cummings LLP
One Federal Place
1819 Fifth Avenue North
Birmingham, Alabama 35203
(205) 521-8000/(205) 521-8800 (Fax)
www.babc.com

ALASKA
John B. Thorsness, Esquire
Liam J. Moran, Esquire
Clapp, Peterson, Tiemessen,
Thorsness & Johnson, LLC
711 H Street, Suite 620
Anchorage, Alaska 99501-3454
(907) 272-9272/(907) 272-9586 (Fax)
www.akcplaw.com

ARIZONA
Patrick X. Fowler, Esquire
Kelly Wilkins MacHenry, Esquire
Snell & Wilmer L.L.P.
One Arizona Center
400 East Van Buren Street
Phoenix, Arizona 85004-2202
(602) 382-6000/(602) 382-6070 (Fax)
www.swlaw.com

ARKANSAS
Kathryn Bennett Perkins, Esquire
Rose Law Firm
120 East Fourth Street
Little Rock, Arkansas 72201-2893
(501) 375-9131/(501) 375-1309 (Fax)
www.roselawfirm.com

CALIFORNIA	Arnold D. Larson, Esquire Mary P. Lightfoot, Esquire Darren M. Ballas, Esquire Drew Larson, Esquire Larson, Garrick & Lightfoot, LLP 801 South Figueroa Street, Suite 1750 Los Angeles, California 90017-5504 (213) 404-4100/(213) 404-4123 (Fax) www.lgl-law.com
COLORADO	Thomas B. Quinn, Esquire Greg S. Hearing, Esquire Gordon & Rees LLP 555 Seventeenth Street, Suite 3400 Denver, Colorado 80202 (303) 534-5160/(303) 534-5161 (Fax) www.gordonrees.com
CONNECTICUT	Donald E. Frechette, Esquire Aubrey E. Blatchley, Esquire Edwards Wildman Palmer LLP 20 Church Street Hartford, CT 06103 (860) 525-5065/(860) 527-4198 (Fax) www.edwardswildman.com
DELAWARE	Frederick L. Cottrell, III, Esquire Anthony Flynn, Jr. Richards, Layton & Finger One Rodney Square P.O. Box 551 Wilmington, Delaware 19899 (302) 651-7700/(302) 651-7701 (Fax) www.rlf.com
DISTRICT OF COLUMBIA	Robert N. Kelly, Esquire Jackson & Campbell, P.C. 1120 20th Street, NW Suite 300-South Washington, D.C. 20036 (202) 457-1600/(202) 457-1678 (Fax) www.jackscamp.com

FLORIDA Alvin F. Lindsay, Esquire
James L. VanLandingham, Esquire
Hogan Lovells US LLP
600 Brickell Avenue, Suite 2700
Miami, Florida 33131
(305) 459-6633/(305) 459-6550 (Fax)
www.hoganlovells.com

GEORGIA John F. Yarber, Esquire
Kacy G. Romig, Esquire
Jesika S. Wehunt, Esquire
Jones Day
1420 Peachtree Street, N.E., Suite 800
Atlanta, Georgia 30309-3053
(404) 581-3939/(404) 581-8330 (Fax)
www.jonesday.com

HAWAII Joachim P. Cox, Esquire
Robert K. Fricke, Esquire
Kamala S. Haake, Esquire
Cox Fricke LLP
500 Ala Moana Boulevard, Suite 3-499
Honolulu, Hawaii 96813
(808) 585-9440/(808) 524-3838 (Fax)
www.cfhawaii.com

IDAHO Jed W. Manwaring, Esquire
Judy L. Geier, Esquire
Evans Keane, LLP
1161 West River Street, Suite 100
P.O. Box 959
Boise, Idaho 83701-0959
(208) 384-1800/(208) 345-3514 (Fax)
www.evanskeane.com

ILLINOIS Colin Smith, Esquire
Thomas R. Woodrow, Esquire
Troy D. Hoyt, Esquire
Laura E. Atherstone, Esquire
Holland & Knight, LLP
131 South Dearborn Street, 30th Floor
Chicago, Illinois 60603
(312) 263-3600/(312) 578-6666 (Fax)
www.hklaw.com

INDIANA	Mark J. R. Merkle, Esquire Marc T. Quigley, Esquire Krieg DeVault LLP One Indiana Square, Suite 2800 Indianapolis, Indiana 46204-2079 (317) 636-4341/(317) 636-1507 (Fax) www.kriegdevault.com
IOWA	Bradley C. Obermeier, Esquire Joseph G. Gamble, Esquire Duncan, Green, Brown & Langeness, P.C. 400 Locust Street, Suite 380 Des Moines, Iowa 50309 (515) 288-6440/(515) 288-6448 (Fax) www.duncangreenlaw.com
KANSAS	Thomas P. Schult, Esquire Sharon A. Stallbaumer, Esquire Kenneth J. Duvall, Esquire Berkowitz Oliver Williams Shaw & Eisenbrandt, LLP 2600 Grand Blvd., Suite 1200 Kansas City, Missouri 64108 (816) 561-7007/(816) 561-1888 (Fax) www.berkowitzoliver.com
KENTUCKY	John L. Tate, Esquire J. Brittany Cross Carlson, Esquire Stites & Harbison, PLLC 400 West Market Street, Suite 1800 Louisville, Kentucky 40202 (502) 587-3400/(502) 587-6391 (Fax) www.stites.com
LOUISIANA	Darnell Bludworth Sher Garner Cahill Richter Klein & Hilbert 909 Poydras St. 28th Floor New Orleans, Louisiana 70112 Telephone (504) 299-2114 dbludworth@shergarner.com

MAINE

Bernard J. Kubetz, Esquire
Jeremy S. Grant, Esquire
Eaton Peabody
80 Exchange Street
P.O. Box 1210
Bangor, Maine 04402-1210
(207) 947-0111/(207) 942-3040 (Fax)
www.eatonpeabody.com

MARYLAND

Daniel R. Lanier, Esquire
Michael J. Halaiko, Esquire
Christopher R. Daily, Esquire
Leianne S. McEvoy, Esquire
Miles & Stockbridge
100 Light Street
Baltimore, Maryland 21202-1487
(410) 385-3651/(410) 385-3700 (Fax)
www.milesstockbridge.com

MASSACHUSETTS

David R. Geiger, Esquire
Jeffrey S. Follett, Esquire
Matthew C. Baltay, Esquire
Foley Hoag LLP
155 Seaport Boulevard
Boston, Massachusetts 02210
(617) 832-1000/(617) 832-7000 (Fax)
www.foleyhoag.com

MICHIGAN

James E. Wynne, Esquire
Phillip C. Korovesis, Esquire
Daniel R. Rustmann, Esquire
John C. Valenti, Esquire
William J. Kliffel, Esquire
James F. Gehrke, Esquire
Bernard J. Fuhs, Esquire
Paul M. Mersino, Esquire
Brian E. McGinty, Esquire
Butzel Long
150 West Jefferson, Suite 100
Detroit, Michigan 48226-4430
(313) 225-7000/(313) 225-7080 (Fax)
www.butzel.com

MINNESOTA	George W. Soule, Esquire Soule & Stull LLC Eight West 43rd Street, Suite 200 Minneapolis, Minnesota 55409 (612) 353-6491/ (612) 573-6484 (Fax) E-mail: gsoule@soulestull.com
MISSISSIPPI	Lewis W. Bell, Esquire Watkins & Eager, PLLC The Emporium Building, Suite 300 400 East Capitol Street P.O. Box 650 Jackson, Mississippi 39205 (601) 965-1977/(601) 965-1901 (Fax) Email: lbell@watkinseager.com www.watkinseager.com
MISSOURI	K. Christopher Jayaram, Esquire Robert A. Horn, Esquire Horn Aylward & Bandy, LLC 2600 Grand Boulevard, Suite 1100 Kansas City, Missouri 64108 (816) 421-0700/(816) 421-0899 (Fax) www.hab-law.com
MONTANA	Kristi Blazer, Esquire Missouri River Law Office P.C. 145 Bridge Street, Suite B Craig, Montana 59648 (406) 235-4000/(406) 235-4082 (Fax) www.missouririverlaw.com
NEBRASKA	Anne Marie O'Brien, Esquire Sarah F. Macdissi, Esquire Lamson, Dugan and Murray, LLP 10306 Regency Parkway Drive Omaha, Nebraska 68114-3743 (402) 397-7300/(402) 397-7824 (Fax) www.ldmlaw.com
NEVADA	Wayne Shaffer, Esquire Holly Parker, Esquire Laxalt & Nomura 9600 Gateway Drive Reno, NV 89521 (775) 297-44535

NEW HAMPSHIRE	Fred J. Desmarais, Jr., Esquire Desmarais, Ewing & Johnston, P.L.L.C. 175 Canal Street Manchester, New Hampshire 03101 (603) 623-5524/(603) 623-6383 (Fax) www.dejlawfirm.com
NEW JERSEY	Gerhard P. Dietrich, Esquire Amy L. Hansell, Esquire Ward Greenberg Heller & Reidy LLP 701 East Gate Drive, Suite 220 Mt. Laurel, New Jersey 08054 (856) 866-8920/(856) 866-8761 (Fax) www.wardgreenberg.com
NEW MEXICO	Alex C. Walker, Esquire Modrall, Sperling, Roehl, Harris & Sisk 500 Fourth Street, N.W., Suite 1000 P.O. Box 2168 Albuquerque, New Mexico 87103-2168 (505) 848-1800/(505) 848-1882 (Fax) www.modrall.com
NEW YORK	Thomas E. Reidy, Esquire Tony R. Sears, Esquire Ward Greenberg Heller & Reidy LLP 300 State Street Rochester, New York 14614 (585) 454-0700/(585) 423-5910 (Fax) www.wardgreenberg.com
NORTH CAROLINA	William F. Womble, Jr., Esquire Womble Carlyle Sandridge & Rice, L.L.P. One West Fourth Street Winston-Salem, North Carolina 27101 (336) 721-3600/(336) 721-3660 (Fax) Frederick W. Rom, Esquire Womble Carlyle Sandridge & Rice, L.L.P. 150 Fayetteville Street, Suite 2100 Raleigh, North Carolina 27601 (919) 755-2100/(919) 755-2150 (Fax) www.wcsr.com

NORTH DAKOTA   Patrick W. Durick, Esquire
                           Larry L. Boschee, Esquire
                           Zachary E. Pelham, Esquire
                           Pearce & Durick
                           314 East Thayer Avenue
                           P.O. Box 400
                           Bismarck, North Dakota 58502
                           (701) 223-2890/(701) 223-7865 (Fax)
                           www.pearce-durick.com

OHIO   David B. Alden, Esquire
                           Katrina L. S. Caseldine, Esquire
                           Jones Day
                           North Point
                           901 Lakeside Avenue
                           Cleveland, Ohio 44114
                           (216) 586-3939/(216) 579-0212 (Fax)
                           www.jonesday.com

OKLAHOMA   John C. Niemeyer, Esquire
                           Linda G. Alexander, Esquire
                           Niemeyer, Alexander & Phillips, P.C.
                           Three Hundred North Walker
                           Oklahoma City, Oklahoma 73102-1822
                           (405) 232-2725/(405) 239-7185 (Fax)
                           www.niemeyerfirm.com

OREGON   Elizabeth A. Schleuning, Esquire
                           Andrew J. Lee, Esquire
                           Schwabe Williamson & Wyatt, P.C.
                           Pacwest Center
                           1211 S.W. Fifth Avenue, Suite 1900
                           Portland, Oregon 97204-3795
                           (503) 222-9981/(503) 796-2900 (Fax)
                           www.schwabe.com

PENNSYLVANIA   Morton F. Daller, Esquire
                           (215) 738-3800 (cell phone)
                           Mort.Daller@gmail.com

                           Gerhard P. Dietrich, Esquire
                           Paul D. Lux, Esquire
                           Ward Greenberg Heller & Reidy LLP
                           1835 Market Street, Suite 650
                           Philadelphia, PA 19103
                           (215) 836-1100/(215) 836-2845 (Fax)
                           www.wardgreenberg.com

RHODE ISLAND	Gordon P. Cleary, Esquire Vetter & White Center Place 50 Park Row West—Suite 109 Providence, Rhode Island 02903 (401) 421-3060/(401) 272-6803 (Fax) www.vetterandwhite.com
SOUTH CAROLINA	James T. Irvin, III, Esquire Jay T. Thompson, Esquire Jessica Peters Goodfellow, Esquire Nelson Mullins Riley & Scarborough LLP Meridian, Suite 1700 1320 Main Street Columbia, South Carolina 29201 (803) 799-2000/(803) 256-7500 (Fax) www.nelsonmullins.com
SOUTH DAKOTA	James E. Moore, Esquire James A. Power, Esquire Woods, Fuller, Shultz & Smith P.C. 300 South Phillips Avenue, Suite 300 Sioux Falls, South Dakota 57117-5027 (605) 336-3890/(605) 339-3357 (Fax) www.woodsfuller.com
TENNESSEE	W. Kyle Carpenter, Esquire J. Ford Little, Esquire Woolf, McClane, Bright, Allen & Carpenter, PLLC Suite 900, Riverview Tower P.O. Box 900 Knoxville, Tennessee 37901 (865) 215-1000/(865) 215-1001 (Fax) www.wmbac.com
TEXAS	Walter Lynch, Esquire Paige S. Goodwin, Esquire Baker Botts, L.L.P. One Shell Plaza 910 Louisiana Houston, Texas 77002-4995 (713) 229-1234/(713) 229-1522 (Fax) www.bakerbotts.com

UTAH	Rick L. Rose, Esquire Kristine M. Larsen, Esquire Ray, Quinney & Nebeker 36 South State Street, Suite 1400 P.O. Box 45385 Salt Lake City, Utah 84145-0385 (801) 532-1500/(801) 532-7543 (Fax) www.rqn.com
VERMONT	Karen McAndrew, Esquire Wm. Andrew MacIlwaine, Esquire N. Joseph Wonderly, Esquire Dinse, Knapp & McAndrew, P.C. 209 Battery Street P.O. Box 988 Burlington, Vermont 05402-0988 (802) 864-5751/(802) 862-6409 (Fax) www.dinse.com
VIRGINIA	Michael W. Smith, Esquire R. Braxton Hill, IV, Esquire S. Perry Coburn, Esquire Christian & Barton, LLP 909 East Main Street, Suite 1200 Richmond, Virginia 23219-3095 (804) 697-4100/(804) 697-4112 (Fax) www.cblaw.com
WASHINGTON	John D. Dillow, Esquire Kate Reddy, Esquire Perkins Coie, LLP 1201 Third Avenue, Suite 4900 Seattle, Washington 98101-3099 (206) 359-8000/(206) 359-9000 (Fax) www.perkinscoie.com
WEST VIRGINIA	J. David Bolen, Esquire Alexis B. Mattingly, Esquire Huddleston Bolen, LLP 611 Third Avenue P.O. Box 2185 Huntington, West Virginia 25722-2185 (304) 529-6181/(304) 522-4312 (Fax) www.huddlestonbolen.com

WISCONSIN   Eric W. Matzke, Esquire
                         Patrick S. Nolan, Esquire
                         Quarles & Brady LLP
                         411 East Wisconsin Avenue
                         Milwaukee, Wisconsin 53202
                         (414) 277-5000/(414) 271-3552 (Fax)
                         www.quarles.com

WYOMING   James C. Worthen, Esquire
                         Murane & Bostwick, LLC
                         201 North Wolcott
                         Casper, Wyoming 82601
                         (307) 234-9345/(307) 237-5110 (Fax)
                         www.murane.com

ALABAMA

A. NEGLIGENCE

Contributory negligence in the use of the product, misuse of the product, and assumption of the risk are complete defenses to negligence claims.[1] The statute of limitations for negligence actions is two years.[2]

B. STRICT LIABILITY

Alabama's version of strict liability, known as the Alabama Extended Manufacturer's Liability Doctrine (AEMLD), was judicially created in 1976.[3] While incorporating much of the lexicon of and rationale underlying Section 402A of the Restatement (Second) of Torts, AEMLD purports to retain the "fault" concept of a negligence action.[4] While an AEMLD claim does not subsume a common law negligence claim, the Alabama Supreme Court has noted the commonality between such claims.[5]

1. Plaintiff's Prima Facie Case

An AEMLD plaintiff must prove he suffered injury or damages to himself or his property by one who sold a product in a defective condition unreasonably dangerous to the plaintiff as the ultimate user or consumer if (a) the seller was engaged in the business of selling such a product and (b) the product was expected to, and did, reach the user or consumer without substantial change in the condition in which it was sold. If such showing is made, the seller is negligent as a matter of law, even though he may have exercised all possible care in the preparation and sale of the product.[6] In cases alleging a design defect, plaintiff must prove that a safer, practical, alternative design was available to the manufacturer at the time the product was manufactured, the utility of which outweighed the utility of the design actually used, in light of a variety of factors.[7] The fact that the product failed in furthering or performing its intended use, or the fact of an injury, is not itself sufficient to prove liability.[8] Ordinarily, expert testimony is required to prove defectiveness and causation.[9] The fact that a product has been modified by the buyer does not necessarily relieve the manufacturer or seller of liability, but the plaintiff in such an instance must show that the injury was not caused by the change, or that the alteration or modification was reasonably foreseeable to the defendant.[10]

2. "Defect"

The jury in an AEMLD case is instructed that a product is defective if it is "unreasonably dangerous," or is not fit for the ordinary purposes for which it was intended, or does not meet the reasonable expectations of an ordinary consumer as to its safety. Plaintiff does not have to prove the specific negligent conduct that caused the defective condition, but he must prove a defective condition in the product and that the defect proximately caused his injury.[11]

3. **Defenses Under AEMLD**

   a. **No Causal Relation**

   The defendant may show that there is no causal relation in fact between her activities in connection with handling the product and its defective condition. This defense is not available to a manufacturer where the defect is in a component made by a third party or to a defendant who distributes a product under its own trade name, nor to a defendant who has an opportunity to inspect the product, or knowledge of it, superior to that of the consumer.[12]

   b. **Assumption of the Risk**

   The defendant may show that any danger associated with its product was either apparent to the consumer or was adequately warned against by the defendant. If the user or consumer discovered the defect and was aware of the danger, and nevertheless proceeded unreasonably to make use of the product and was injured, he is barred from recovery.[13]

   c. **Contributory Negligence and Product Misuse**

   Contributory negligence is a defense in AEMLD actions, and is defined as the plaintiff's failure to use reasonable care with regard to the product.[14] Product misuse is a related but distinct defense, defined as the plaintiff's use of the product not intended or foreseen by the manufacturer or seller.[15]

4. **Crashworthiness**

   A plaintiff can recover on a claim that a defect in a product (usually an automobile) was not the proximate cause of a collision but nonetheless enhanced the injury sustained in the collision. To do so, the plaintiff must show the existence of a safer, practical alternative design that would have reduced or eliminated the plaintiff's injuries, the utility of which design outweighed the utility of the design actually used in light of a variety of factors.[16] All AEMLD defenses are available to the defendant.

5. **Successor Liability**

   A successor corporation that purchases the assets of its predecessor is liable for the defects in the predecessor's products if (1) there was an express agreement to assume such obligations, (2) the transaction amounts to a de facto merger or consolidation, (3) the transaction is a fraudulent attempt to evade liability, or (4) the asset transferee's business is a "mere continuation" of the transferor's business.[17]

6. **Failure to Warn**

   A manufacturer owes a duty to warn if he knows, or reasonably should know, that his product is unreasonably dangerous when put to its reasonably intended use.[18] Products that are "unavoidably unsafe" are nonetheless not defective or unreasonably dangerous if they are accompanied by adequate warnings and instructions.[19] A plaintiff who fails to read an allegedly inadequate warning cannot maintain a failure-to-warn claim unless the alleged inadequacy is such that it prevents her from reading it.[20] A manufacturer cannot be held liable for failure to warn the ultimate consumer where the manufacturer did relay an adequate warning to an intermediate party and the intermediate party failed to pass on the warning.[21] A product is not defective under AEMLD if the manufacturer fails to warn of open and obvious dangers associated with it.[22]

7. **State of the Art and Industry Standards**

   That a product was or was not "state of the art" is neither a part of the plaintiff's prima facie AEMLD case nor an affirmative defense, but rather goes to whether the product is unreasonably dangerous and thus defective.[23] Evidence that a product complied with, or did not comply with, regulatory or industry standards is admissible.[24]

8. **Nonsale Transactions**

   AEMLD applies to any transaction whereby a product is placed in the stream of commerce, including by sale, lease, free sample, or demonstration.[25] However, the supplier must be in the business of supplying the product and not merely involved in isolated or occasional sales or leases of it.[26]

9. **Statute of Limitations**

   The Alabama statute of limitations for personal injuries not arising out of contract, which includes AEMLD and negligence actions, is two years.[27]

10. **Spoliation of Evidence**

    Failure by a party to preserve material evidence in a product liability case can warrant sanctions, up to and including dismissal or default.[28] The Alabama Supreme Court has recognized a "spoliation of evidence" cause of action sounding in negligence, though only against a third party (one not alleged to have committed the underlying tort as to which the lost or destroyed evidence related).[29]

C. BREACH OF WARRANTY

1. **Nature of the Cause of Action**

   Breach of warranty is a viable product liability theory in Alabama. Although there is no warranty cause of action for wrongful death (see Section D, *infra*), a breach of warranty action can be maintained for compensatory damages, including pain and suffering, between the time of the accident and death.[30] In such an action, no compensatory damages are recoverable for the loss or worth of the life of the decedent. In a warranty action, a seller's warranty, whether express or implied, extends to any natural person if it is reasonable to expect that such person may use, consume, or be affected by the goods and who is injured in person by breach of the warranty.[31] Thus, lack of privity is not a defense in personal injury cases.[32] The proof required in a non-death warranty product claim is essentially the same as that required in an AEMLD claim. Punitive damages are not recoverable in a breach of warranty action.[33]

2. **Statute of Limitations and Miscellaneous**

The statute of limitations for a breach of warranty action is four years.[34] In cases of personal injury caused by consumer goods, the statute begins to run when the plaintiff's cause of action accrues, that is, when the plaintiff first suffers injury.[35] In the case of nonconsumer goods, the statute of limitations begins to run from the date of sale, unless the warranty sued upon expressly extends to future performance of the goods.[36] Notice of any breach by the buyer to the seller is a condition precedent to recovery under a warranty theory, even in personal injury actions.[37] However, a warranty beneficiary (as opposed to the buyer) need not give such notice.[38]

D. WRONGFUL DEATH

1. **Nature of the Claim and Nature of Damages**

Under Alabama's wrongful death statute,[39] as interpreted, the *only* damages recoverable by the plaintiff are punitive damages, their amount depending on the nature of the defendant's act, his degree of culpability, and the need for deterring the defendant and others from committing similar wrongful conduct.[40] The product liability wrongful death plaintiff need not show wanton, reckless, or intentional conduct, but merely the same proof required to make out a standard negligence or AEMLD claim. Evidence of loss of earnings, loss of enjoyment of life, and contributions to family are inadmissible because they are irrelevant. As noted in Section C, *supra*, a wrongful death plaintiff can also bring a claim (or a separate action) in warranty for compensatory damages incurred during the period of time between accident and death.[41] In addition, an action by a personal injury plaintiff survives his or her death, meaning that representatives of such a plaintiff may pursue the existing personal injury action (for recovery of exclusively compensatory damages) *and also* pursue a wrongful death claim (for recovery of exclusively punitive damages).[42]

2. **Proper Capacity of Plaintiff**

The decedent's "personal representative" is the proper party plaintiff in a wrongful death action.[43] In the usual case this is the administrator or executor of the decedent's estate.[44] However, if the dependents of a decedent, as defined in Alabama's worker's compensation act, have a statutory right to bring suit for workers' compensation benefits against the decedent's employer, such dependents (rather than the "personal representative") also have the right to bring a wrongful death action against a third party potentially liable for the decedent's death.[45]

3. **Foreign Application of the Wrongful Death Statute**

The statute requires that all actions arising under it be brought in Alabama courts; courts in other states have, however, applied the statute to actions brought in those states.[46] The Alabama statute cannot be used to support an action brought in Alabama where the wrongful act was committed in another state.[47]

4. **Statute of Limitations**

All actions for wrongful death must be commenced within two years of the death of the decedent.[48] This limitations period is contained within the wrongful death statute itself, and is thus considered a part of the plaintiff's prima facie case rather than an affirmative defense.[49]

E. CONTRIBUTION AND INDEMNITY

If the separate acts of more than one defendant proximately result in one indivisible injury to the plaintiff, all defendants are jointly and severally liable for the entire damage, although the plaintiff is entitled to only one recovery.[50] Contribution or indemnity among joint tortfeasors is not allowed, except when an agreement exists between the liable parties clearly indicating indemnity of the type of conduct in question.[51] A further, very limited exception to the no-contribution rule exists (though its applicability is not entirely clear) when the party seeking indemnity is totally without fault but is held liable solely because of an absolute nondelegable duty to the injured plaintiff.[52] In general, proof of facts sufficient to establish a right to indemnity will also establish a no-causal relation defense to liability under AEMLD.

F. FICTITIOUS PARTY PRACTICE

A product liability plaintiff may designate a fictitious defendant in her complaint if the defendant's true name is not known.[53] When the true name is discovered it may be substituted, and the substitution will relate back to the time of original filing for statute of limitations purposes, so long as the fictitious party's true identity was not known to the plaintiff at the time of filing and the plaintiff has exercised reasonable diligence in discovering the fictitious defendant's true identity.[54] The presence of fictitious defendants is disregarded for purposes of removal to federal court.[55]

G. MISCELLANEOUS

1. Collateral Source Rule

In cases in which the plaintiff claims medical expenses that have been or will be reimbursed as an element of damages, the product manufacturing defendant can introduce evidence that these expenses have been or will be paid.[56]

2. Substantial Evidence Rule

Motions for summary judgment and directed verdict are governed by the "substantial evidence" standard, meaning evidence of such quality and weight that reasonable persons exercising impartial judgment could reach different conclusions about the existence of a fact to be proved.[57]

3. Punitive Damages

Except in wrongful death actions, punitive damages are by statute not recoverable unless the plaintiff proves by "clear and convincing evidence" that the defendant consciously or deliberately engaged in oppression, fraud, wantonness, or malice with regard to the plaintiff.[58] Punitive damages in cases not involving physical injury have been legislatively capped at three times compensatory damages or $500,000, whichever is greater.[59] In physical injury cases, punitive damages are capped at three times compensatory damages or $1.5 million, whichever is greater.[60] There are lower caps in cases involving small business defendants.[61] None of the caps apply in class actions, or in cases involving wrongful death or intentional infliction of physical injury.[62]

The following language is included pursuant to Rule 7.2 of the Alabama State Bar Rules of Professional Conduct:

No representation is made that the quality of the legal services to be performed is greater than the quality of legal services performed by other lawyers.

John E. Goodman
R. Thomas Warburton
Bradley Arant Boult Cummings LLP
One Federal Place
1819 Fifth Avenue North
Birmingham, Alabama 35203
(205) 521-8000
(Fax) (205) 521-8800

Endnotes - Alabama

1. *E.g., General Motors Corp. v. Saint*, 646 So. 2d 564 (Ala. 1994); *Campbell v. Cutler Hammer, Inc.*, 646 So. 2d 573 (Ala. 1994); *Williams v. Delta Int'l Mach. Corp.*, 619 So. 2d 1330 (Ala. 1993); *Brown v. Piggly-Wiggly Stores*, 454 So. 2d 1370, 1372 (Ala. 1984); *Rivers v. Stihl, Inc.*, 434 So. 2d 766, 773 (Ala. 1983).

2. Ala. Code § 6-2-38(l) (2005 Repl. Vol.).

3. *Casrell v. Altec Indus.*, 335 So. 2d 128 (Ala. 1976); *Atkins v. American Motors Corp.*, 335 So. 2d 134 (Ala. 1976).

4. *Casrell*, 335 So. 2d at 132; *Atkins*, 335 So. 2d at 137.

5. *McMahon v. Yamaha Motor Corp., USA*, 95 So. 3d 769 (Ala. 2012).

6. *Atkins*, 355 So. 2d at 141; Alabama Pattern Jury Instructions (Civil) § 32.08 (2d ed. 1993) (hereinafter APJI).

7. *Beech v. Outboard Marine Corp.*, 584 So. 2d 447 (Ala. 1991); *Elliott v. Brunswick Corp.*, 903 F.2d 1505 (11th Cir. 1990), *cert. denied*, 498 U.S. 1048 (1991); APJI § 32.08 (2009 Supp.).

8. *Sears, Roebuck & Co., Inc. v. Haven Hills Farm, Inc.*, 395 So. 2d 991, 995 (Ala. 1981); *Townsend v. General Motors Corp.*, 642 So. 2d 411 (Ala. 1994).

9. *Sears, Roebuck & Co.*, 395 So. 2d 991, 995; *Townsend*, 642 So. 2d 411.

10. *Sears, Roebuck and Co. v. Harris*, 630 So. 2d 1018 (Ala. 1993); *McDaniel v. French Oil Mach. Co.*, 623 So. 2d 1146 (Ala. 1993).

11. *Taylor v. General Motors Corp.*, 707 So. 2d 198 (Ala. 1997); *Atkins*, 335 So. 2d at 142; APJI § 32.12.

12. *Atkins*, 335 So. 2d at 143; APJI § 32.16; *Foremost Ins. Co. v. Indies House Inc.*, 602 So. 2d 380, 381-82 (Ala. 1992); *Dillard v. Pittway Corp.*, 719 So. 2d 188 (Ala. 1998).

13. *Atkins*, 335 So. 2d at 143; APJI, §§ 32.17, 32.18.

14. *General Motors Corp. v. Saint*, 646 So. 2d 564 (Ala. 1994).

15. *Saint*, 646 So. 2d 564; *Kelly v. M. Trigg Enters., Inc.*, 605 So. 2d 1185 (Ala. 1992).

16. *Flemister v. General Motors Corp.*, 723 So. 2d 25 (Ala. 1998); *General Motors Corp. v. Edwards*, 482 So. 2d 1176, 1191-92 (Ala. 1985); APJI § 32.22.

17. *Colonial Bank of Ala. v. Coker*, 482 So. 2d 286, 292 (Ala. 1985); *Rivers*, 434 So. 2d at 771.

18. *Gurley v. American Honda Motor Co., Inc.*, 505 So. 2d 358, 361 (Ala. 1987); *Rivers*, 434 So. 2d at 773.

19. *Purvis v. PPG Indus., Inc.*, 502 So. 2d 714, 718 (Ala. 1987); *Stone v. Smith, Kline & French Labs.*, 447 So. 2d 1301 (Ala. 1984).

20. *E. R. Squibb & Sons, Inc. v. Cox*, 477 So. 2d 963, 971 (Ala. 1985).

21. *Purvis*, 502 So. 2d at 719.

22. *Entrekin v. Atlantic Richfield Co.*, 519 So. 2d 447, 450 (Ala. 1987); *Ford Motor Co. v. Rodgers*, 337 So. 2d 736 (Ala. 1976).

23. *E.g., General Motors v. Edwards*, 482 So. 2d 1176. See also *Elliott v. Brunswick Corp.*, 903 F.2d 1505 (11th Cir. 1990), cert. denied, 498 U.S. 1028 (1991) (applying Alabama law).

24. *E.g., General Motors*, 482 So. 2d at 1198; *Dunn v. Wixom Bros.*, 493 So. 2d 1356 (Ala. 1986).

25. *First Nat'l Bank of Mobile v. Cessna Aircraft Co.*, 365 So. 2d 966, 968 (Ala. 1978).

26. *Baugh v. Bradford*, 529 So. 2d 996, 999 (Ala. 1988).

27. Ala. Code § 6-2-38(l) (1993 Repl. Vol.).

28. *Capitol Chevrolet, Inc. v. Smedley*, 614 So. 2d 439 (Ala. 1993). See also *Campbell v. Williams*, 638 So. 2d 804, 817 n.9 (Ala.), cert. denied, 115 S. Ct. 188 (1994) (jury can be instructed that spoliation is sufficient to support an inference of negligence).

29. *Smith v. Atkinson*, 771 So. 2d 429 (Ala. Feb. 4, 2000).

30. *Benefield v. Aquaslide 'N' Dive Corp.*, 406 So. 2d 873, 875-76 (Ala. 1981).

31. Ala. Code § 7-2-318 (1993 Repl. Vol.).

32. *Bishop v. Sales*, 336 So. 2d 1340, 1345 (Ala. 1976).

33. *E.g., Geohagen v. General Motors Corp.*, 291 Ala. 167, 279 So. 2d 436, 438 (1973).

34. Ala. Code § 7-2-725(1) (1993 Repl. Vol.).

35. Ala. Code § 7-2-725(2) (1993 Repl. Vol.); *Moon v. Harco Drugs, Inc.*, 435 So. 2d 218, 220 (Ala. 1983).

36. *E.g., Simmons v. Clemco Indus.*, 368 So. 2d 509, 510 (Ala. 1979); *Stephens v. Creel*, 429 So. 2d 278, 282 (Ala. 1983).

37. Ala. Code § 7-2-607 (1993 Repl. Vol.); *Simmons*, 368 So. 2d at 513.

38. Ala. Code § 7-2-318 (1993 Repl. Vol.); *Simmons*, 368 So. 2d at 513.

39. Ala. Code § 6-5-410 (1993 Repl. Vol.); *see also* Ala. Code § 6-5-391 (1993 Repl. Vol.) (wrongful death of minor).

40. *E.g., Deaton, Inc. v. Burroughs*, 456 So. 2d 771, 776 (Ala. 1984).

41. *Benefield*, 406 So. 2d at 875-76.

42. *King v. National Spa and Pool Inst.*, 607 So. 2d 1241 (Ala. 1992).

43. Ala. Code § 6-5-410 (1993 Repl. Vol.).

44. *Downtown Nursing Home v. Pool*, 375 So. 2d 465, 466 (Ala. 1979), *cert. denied*, 445 U.S. 930 (1980).

45. Ala. Code § 25-5-11 (1993 Repl. Vol.); *Baggett v. Webb*, 46 Ala. App. 666, 248 So. 2d 275, 282, *cert. denied*, 287 Ala. 725, 248 So. 2d 284 (1971).

46. *E.g., Stevens v. Pullman, Inc.*, 388 So. 2d 580 (Fla. App. 1980); *Spriggs v. Dredge*, 140 N.E.2d 45 (Ohio App. 1955).

47. *E.g., Spencer v. Malone Freight Lines, Inc.*, 292 Ala. 582, 584, 298 So. 2d 20, 22 (1974).

48. Ala. Code § 6-5-410 (1993 Repl. Vol.).

49. *Downtown Nursing Home*, 375 So. 2d at 466.

50. *E.g., General Motors*, 482 So. 2d at 1195.

51. *Crigler v. Salac*, 438 So. 2d 1375, 1385-86 (Ala. 1983).

52. *Consolidated Pipe & Supply Co., Inc. v. Stockham Valves & Fittings, Inc.*, 365 So. 2d 968, 970 (Ala. 1978).

53. Ala. R. Civ. P. 9(h).

54. Ala. R. Civ. P. 15(c); *Kinard v. C. A. Kelly & Co.*, 468 So. 2d 133, 135 (Ala. 1985); *Ex parte Klemawesch*, 549 So. 2d 62, 64 (Ala. 1989); *Ex parte Noland Hosp. Montgomery, LLC*, __ So. 3d __, 2012 WL 3241971 (Ala. 2012).

55. 28 U.S.C. § 1441(a) (1988).

56. Ala. Code § 6-5-522 (1993 Repl. Vol.); § 12-21-45; *Marsh v. Green*, 782 So. 2d 223 (Ala. 2000); *McCormick v. Bunting*, 99 __ So. 3d 1248 (Ala. Civ. App. 2012).

57. Ala. Code § 12-21-12 (1995 Supp.); *West v. Founders Life Assurance Co. of Fla.*, 547 So. 2d 870, 871 (Ala. 1989).

58. Ala. Code § 6-11-20(a) (1993 Repl. Vol.).

59. Ala. Code § 6-11-21(a) (1999).

60. Ala. Code § 6-11-21(d) (1999).

61. Ala. Code § 6-11-21(c) (1999).

62. Ala. Code §§ 6-11-21(h), (j) (1999).

ALASKA

A. CAUSES OF ACTION

Product liability actions may include causes of action for (1) strict liability, (2) negligence, or (3) breach of an express or implied warranty. Most commonly, the actions are brought as one or more forms of negligence and strict liability. Specifically, the claims most likely assert that the product is defectively designed and/or manufactured, and/or it does not contain adequate warnings.

B. STATUTES OF LIMITATION

Causes of action for personal injury[1] and wrongful death[2] are subject to a two-year statute of limitation. The time period does not begin to run until plaintiff "discovers, or reasonably should discover, the existence of all elements of his cause of action."[3] This has also been defined as the time at which the plaintiff should have begun an inquiry to protect his rights, whether or not he knew of the technical cause of the defect.[4] It is enough that the plaintiff knew that the product malfunctioned and an accident ensued.[5] It is not necessary that the plaintiff suffer all of his damages or even know the full extent of his damages before the cause of action accrues and the statute begins to run.[6] Strict liability or negligence claims asserting only damage to personal property are governed by a two-year statute of limitations.[7] Claims based on breach of an express warranty must be brought within four years of the breach, or, in the case of a warranty that explicitly extends to future performance of goods, within four years of the date the defect is or should have been discovered, provided that that day is still within the warranty period.[8] Claims based on a breach of an implied warranty, such as merchantability or fitness for a particular purpose, must be brought within four years from the date of purchase, since implied warranties never extend to future performance.[9] A ten-year statute of repose applies to certain actions for personal injury, death, or property damage, subject to the limitations set forth in AS 09.10.055(b).[10] "Defective product" claims are specifically excluded from this statute.[11]

C. STRICT LIABILITY

1. The Standard

Alaska's theory of strict product liability is as follows: "A manufacturer is strictly liable in tort when an article he places on the market, knowing that it is to be used without inspection for defects, proves to have a defect that causes injury to a human being."[12] Strict liability in tort can also be imposed in cases where a product defect "creates a situation potentially dangerous to persons or other property" and then in fact does cause personal injury or property damage. In an action based on strict liability where no personal injury is involved, the plaintiff must show "(1) that the loss was a proximate result of the dangerous defect and (2) that the loss occurred under the kind of circumstances that made the product a basis for strict liability."[13]

A plaintiff in Alaska need not prove that there is a practical and feasible, safer design alternative in order to succeed in a design defect claim. The plaintiff need only prove that the product's design proximately caused injury. The burden then falls upon the defendant manufacturer to prove, in light of the relevant factors, that on balance the benefits of the challenged design outweigh the risk of danger inherent in such design.[14] The "relevant factors" include, but are not limited to, "the gravity of the danger posed by the challenged design, the likelihood that such danger would occur, the mechanical feasibility of a safer alternative design, the financial cost of an improved design, and the adverse consequences to the product and to the consumer that would result from an alternative design."[15]

2. "Defect"

The focus in a strict products liability action is on the product itself, not on the conduct of the manufacturer.[16] A product may be defective because of a manufacturing defect, a design defect, or a failure to contain adequate warnings.[17]

A product is defective in design if (1) the plaintiff proves that the product failed to perform as safely as an ordinary consumer would expect when used in an intended or reasonably foreseeable manner, or (2) the plaintiff proves that the product's design proximately caused injury, and the defendant fails to prove, in light of the relevant factors, that on balance, the benefits of the challenged design outweigh the risk of danger inherent in such design.[18] The expectation of the ordinary consumer is an objective test.[19] A design defect will be the legal or proximate cause of a plaintiff's injury if the product's defect was more likely than not a substantial factor in bringing about the plaintiff's injury.[20]

A product may also be defective if its reasonably foreseeable use involves a substantial danger that would not be readily recognized by the ordinary user of the product, and the manufacturer fails to give adequate warning of such danger.[21]

3. **Causation**

As a general rule, Alaska follows the "substantial factor" test when evaluating causation.[22] But in all cases in Alaska, there are two prongs to the concept of legal cause: (1) actual causation; and (2) a more intangible legal policy element.[23] In most cases, the "but for" test is the appropriate test for actual causation.[24] As for the legal policy prong, the question is "whether the conduct has been so significant and important a cause that the defendant should be legally responsible."[25] A valid instruction on legal causation must include both these elements.[26]

Alaska's "substantial factor test," derived from the Restatement (Second) of Torts § 431 (1965), encompasses both the actual and legal prongs of legal causation, and states: conduct is a legal cause of harm to another if: (a) it is a substantial factor in bringing about the harm, and (b) there is no rule of law relieving the actor from liability.[27]

4. **Contributory Negligence/Assumption of Risk**

Alaska is a "pure" comparative negligence state.[28] In a product liability suit, the comparative negligence, or fault, of a plaintiff is considered by the trier of fact.[29] Contributory negligence and assumption of risk are not complete defenses; such evidence is admissible only to prove a plaintiff's comparative fault.[30] As clarified by the Alaska Supreme Court, in strict product liability cases, the comparative negligence defense "applies in two types of cases: knowing product misuse where misuse is a proximate cause of injuries, or assumption of the risk by a plaintiff who is aware of the product's defect."[31]

Alaska statutory law requires that the trier of fact allocate "fault" among all named parties to the lawsuit, and in so doing the "trier of fact shall consider both the nature of the conduct of each person at fault, and the extent of the causal relation between the conduct and the damages claimed."[32] Statutory law defines "fault" to include breach of warranty, unreasonable assumption of risk, misuse of a product, and the unreasonable failure to avoid an injury or mitigate damages.[33] The fact finder may not allocate fault to nonparties and may only allocate fault to parties to the action, including third-party defendants and settling or released parties.[34]

The trier of fact may allocate fault to a nonparty who was responsible for damages but who the other parties did not have a reasonable opportunity to join as a party to the action.[35] The Alaska Supreme Court has held that a third-party defendant can be sued for apportionment of fault under AS 09.17.080 after the statute of limitations has run on the plaintiff's claim and can be held liable to the plaintiff for any money damages allocated to the third-party defendant.[36]

5. **Sale or Lease**

Strict products liability applies to sellers, manufacturers, wholesale or retail dealers, and distributors.[37] Strict liability in tort is not confined to sales transactions, but extends equally to commercial leases and bailments.[38] No sale exists, and strict liability does not attach, where a product is merely serviced or repaired.[39] However, an overhauler/repairer of an engine has been held strictly liable for selling and installing a used defective component part that was extensively repaired, inspected and tested, then billed as a separate item.[40]

6. **Inherently Dangerous Products**

   A product may be defective despite warnings of obvious dangers if the product is so dangerous that such warnings would not protect the "inadvertent plaintiff."[41]

7. **Successor Liability**

   The Alaska Supreme Court has adopted the "mere continuation" and "continuity of enterprise" theories of successor liability.[42] The court declined to consider whether to adopt the "product line" theory of successor liability based on the facts of the case in dispute. The Alaska Supreme Court characterized successor liability in the products liability setting as a tort and applied tort choice-of-law rules, rather than contract choice-of-law rules, in holding Alaska law applied to the issue of successor liability.

8. **Market Share Liability**

   There are no Alaska decisions in this area.

9. **Privity**

   Alaska does not require vertical privity of contract between a consumer and a manufacturer where the injuries claimed consist of more than pure economic loss,[43] either in cases based on strict liability in tort[44] or in cases based on breach of warranty.[45] It remains unclear whether lack of horizontal privity is a defense.[46]

10. **Failure to Warn**

    A faultlessly manufactured and designed product may nonetheless be defective if it lacks an adequate warning of how to safely use the product.[47] Manufacturers must warn of dangers not readily recognized by the ordinary consumer. However, there is no duty to warn of open and obvious dangers.[48] In most cases, for a warning to be adequate, it should (1) clearly indicate the scope of the risk or danger posed by the product; (2) reasonably communicate the extent or seriousness of harm that could result from the risk or danger; and (3) be conveyed in such a manner as to alert the reasonably prudent person.[49]

    Plaintiff carries a "more likely than not" burden of proving a causal relationship between the alleged failure-to-warn and the injury; the failure must be a substantial factor in bringing about the injury.[50] A factor is considered substantial only when it can be shown that (1) the accident would not have happened "but for" the failure-to-warn, and (2) that such failure-to-warn was so important in bringing about the injury that a reasonable person would regard it as a cause and attach responsibility.[51]

11. **Post-Sale Duty to Warn/Remedial Measures**

    A manufacturer has a post-sale duty in accordance with the Restatement (Third) of Torts: Products Liability § 10 (1998) to inform consumers of its product of dangers that become apparent after sale when the danger is potentially life-threatening.[52] Suppliers of hazardous materials, such as propane, who have acquired actual or constructive knowledge by inspection or otherwise of the dangerous condition of an appliance owned by a customer, *e.g.*, a defective propane tank, have a duty to warn their customers.[53]

Subsequent design changes relevant to a plaintiff's allegation of defect are admissible in a product liability action to prove the existence of a defective condition.[54]

12. Learned Intermediary Doctrine

A prescription drug manufacturer satisfies the duty to warn if it provides adequate warnings to the prescribing physician.[55]

13. Substantial Change/Product Misuse

For liability to attach, a plaintiff has the burden of demonstrating (1) that the product was defective as marketed and (2) that the defect existed at the time it left the manufacturer's possession or control.[56] A substantial alteration or change in a product after it leaves the manufacturer, that is shown to have proximately caused plaintiff's injury, will ordinarily defeat a claim based on strict tort liability.[57] However, the plaintiff must first demonstrate that a defect existed at the time the product left the manufacturer, before the burden shifts to the manufacturer to demonstrate that the injury resulted from the alteration and not from the defect in the product.[58]

The Alaska Supreme Court has affirmed that in strict liability cases misuse of a product by the plaintiff may constitute comparative negligence and a partial defense to strict liability.[59] To establish a plaintiff's comparative negligence based on misuse of the product, the defendant must establish that the plaintiff knowingly misused the product and that such misuse was a proximate cause of plaintiff's injuries.[60]

14. State of the Art

State of the art, or conformity with industry-wide practices, will not insulate a manufacturer from liability,[61] but the jury may consider such evidence to determine the existence of a defect,[62] the feasibility of other designs,[63] or to consider whether the defect was scientifically knowable to the manufacturer.[64]

15. Malfunction

There are no Alaska cases on this issue.

16. Standards

Compliance with industry standards is not a defense and is considered to have little probative value, but it may be considered by a jury to determine the existence of a defect[65] or the feasibility of alternative designs.[66]

17. **Other Accidents**

    Evidence of prior or subsequent accidents may be introduced to demonstrate the existence of a product defect or notice of defect, provided that the incidents took place under substantially similar circumstances and conditions.[67] Even relevant evidence, however, may be excluded if its probative value is outweighed by the danger of unfair prejudice, confusion of the issues, or misleading the jury, or by considerations of undue delay, waste of time, or needless presentation of cumulative evidence.[68]

18. **Misrepresentation**

    Alaska has not judicially adopted the Restatement (Second) of Torts Section 402B and has not decided any misrepresentation cases outside of those cited in the breach of warranty context, discussed in Section E, *infra*.

19. **Spoliation or Concealment of Evidence**

    In cases in which records are destroyed or wrongfully withheld through the intentional or negligent act of the adverse party, a court may apply a rebuttable presumption that the missing documents would have established facts unfavorable to the adverse party. The spoliation of evidence doctrine requires that the aggrieved litigant establish that the absence of the records hinders his ability to establish a prima facie case.[69]

    Alaska also recognizes the tort of intentional spoliation of evidence.[70] The tort requires a viable underlying cause of action.[71] When the element of intent is not borne out, "the remedy for the alleged spoliation would be appropriate jury instructions as to permissible inferences, not a separate and collateral action."[72] Alaska recognizes a cause of action in tort for intentional third-party spoliation of evidence. Liability for intentional spoliation of evidence is predicated upon an intent to disrupt the underlying litigation; third parties will thus not be liable if the missing evidence simply has been discarded or misplaced in the ordinary course of events.[73]

    In cases in which evidence is not destroyed but is intentionally concealed until after entry of judgment and expiration of the period allowed for seeking relief from judgment, and no other remedy is available, Alaska recognizes the tort of fraudulent concealment of evidence.[74]

20. **Economic Loss**

    A litigant may recover economic loss under a strict products liability theory if the "defective product creates a situation potentially dangerous to persons or other property, and loss occurs as a result of that danger. . . ."[75]

21. Crashworthiness Doctrine

The Alaska Supreme Court "explicitly endorse[d] the crashworthiness doctrine as a valid theory of recovery" in strict liability.[76] The crashworthiness doctrine declares that a "manufacturer has a duty to design and manufacture its product so as reasonably to reduce the foreseeable harm that may occur in an accident brought about by causes other than a product defect."[77] The court adopted the theory despite the plaintiff's non-traditional crashworthiness claim that the allegedly defective product "caused all, rather than part, of her significant injuries."[78]

D. NEGLIGENCE

In order to prevail on a negligence claim, a party must prove "a duty, a breach of that duty, and an injury which was proximately caused by the breach."[79]

Several factors, known as the *D.S.W.* factors, are considered in determining whether a duty exists: (1) foreseeability of harm to plaintiff; (2) degree of certainty that plaintiff suffered injury; (3) closeness of connection between defendant's conduct and injury suffered; (4) moral blame attached to defendant's conduct; (5) policy for preventing future harm; (6) extent of burden to defendant and consequences to community by imposing a duty to exercise care, with resulting liability for breach; and (7) availability, cost and prevalence of insurance for the risk involved.[80]

E. BREACH OF WARRANTY

Breach of warranty as a basis for a product liability claim is, in most cases, merely an alternative form of relief.[81] However, in cases involving solely economic harm, the warranty remedies of the Uniform Commercial Code provide the only basis for a product liability claim.[82]

F. DAMAGES

1. Punitive Damages

Punitive damages are appropriate in product cases only where the defendant's conduct "(1) was outrageous, including acts done with malice or bad motives; or (2) evidenced reckless indifference to the interests of another person."[83] Punitive damages may not be awarded unless plaintiff proves such conduct by clear and convincing evidence.[84] An award of punitive damages must be set aside where errors made by the trial court "may have increased . . . [the defendant's] culpability in the jury's eyes by diminishing the culpability of other potential wrongdoers."[85] Punitive damages are capped at the greater of three times compensatory damages or $500,000. If there is proof that the conduct was motivated by financial gain, the cap is the greater of four times compensatory damages, four times the amount of the financial gain, or $7 million.[86] One half of any punitive damages award must be paid to the state of Alaska.[87]

2. **Contribution**

There is no right of contribution against a co-tortfeasor in Alaska. Alaska is a pure comparative negligence state and the trier of fact must allocate liability in relation to each party's comparative fault.[88] In the absence of contribution, equitable apportionment is available as a means of bringing other tortfeasors into the lawsuit.[89]

3. **Pain and Suffering**

Awards for noneconomic damages, including awards for pain and suffering, are limited to the greater of $400,000, or the injured person's life expectancy in years multiplied by $8,000.[90] If the injured person suffers from a "severe permanent physical impairment or severe disfigurement[,]" the noneconomic damage award is limited to the greater of $1,000,000, or the person's life expectancy multiplied by $25,000.[91] To be compensable, pain and suffering must be consciously experienced.[92] Pain and suffering experienced contemporaneously with death is not compensable.[93]

4. **Minor's Right to Sue for Loss of Consortium**

A minor child is entitled to loss of consortium damages when his or her parent is tortiously injured.[94] Similarly, a parent is entitled to recover for the loss of a child's society when the child is tortiously injured by a third party.[95]

5. **Emotional Distress**

Sensory perception or contemporaneous observance of an accident is not required for one to recover for emotional distress.[96] Instead, the test for recovery is reasonable foreseeability that the claimant would suffer emotional harm.[97] Damages for emotional distress where there has been no physical injury are ordinarily restricted to instances involving intentional or reckless conduct of an extreme or outrageous nature.[98] Plaintiff may recover for negligent infliction of emotional distress without physical injury only where there is a pre-existing relationship that establishes a duty to refrain from activity that presents a foreseeable and unreasonable risk of causing emotional harm.[99] In the case of a bystander claim, only damages for severe or serious emotional distress may be recovered.[100] These noneconomic damages are limited by the cap described in Section F.3 on Pain and Suffering, *supra*.

6. **Implied Indemnity**

An innocent supplier of a defective product found liable on a theory of strict liability is entitled to a defense and indemnity from the manufacturer of the defective product.[101] Even if no liability is found, the innocent supplier may nonetheless be entitled to recover its reasonable actual attorney's fees and costs in defending the action from the manufacturer.[102] However, a supplier who is independently negligent is completely barred from recovery under the theory of implied indemnity.[103]

7. Apportionment of Damages/Enhanced Injury

The issue of apportionment of damages arises where the plaintiff alleges that the product defect was a contributing, but not the sole, cause of a single injury, such as a crashworthiness case in which the plaintiff alleges her resulting paraplegia was caused by both the product defect and the severity of the crash, which are referred to as enhanced and non-enhanced injuries, respectively.[104] If the defendant maintains that apportionment of the plaintiff's injury is possible, *i.e.*, does not stipulate that plaintiff's injuries are not apportionable, the trial court may properly give an apportionment instruction.[105] Such an instruction informs the jury that, once the plaintiff proves the defective design was a substantial factor in causing the plaintiff's injury, it must hold the defendant liable for all of the plaintiff's damages, unless the defendant proves a basis for distinguishing enhanced from non-enhanced injuries.[106]

G. PRE- AND POST-JUDGMENT INTEREST

The rate of interest on judgments, including pre-judgment interest, is "three percentage points above the 12th Federal Reserve District discount rate in effect on January 2 of the year in which the judgment or decree is entered. . . ."[107]

H. EMPLOYER IMMUNITY FROM SUIT

Under the Alaska Workers' Compensation Act, an employee is barred from suing the employer who has paid workers' compensation benefits for the employee's work-related injuries.[108] Workers' compensation is the exclusive remedy.[109] The employee is compensated irrespective of fault.[110] Receiving benefits does not preclude an employee from seeking damages from a third party who was at fault or otherwise negligent.[111] The employer may seek recovery from the third party in order to recover any amounts paid by the employer.[112]

An exception to the exclusivity doctrine exists in cases of intentional torts committed by the employer or fellow employee.[113] Further, a jury may still allocate a percentage of fault to an employer, regardless of the inability to recover money damages from the employer.[114]

I. COLLATERAL ESTOPPEL

Collateral estoppel has barred a defendant in a subsequent action from relitigating a finding that its concealment of a manufacturing defect constituted outrageous conduct and a reckless disregard of the rights of others.[115]

J. STATUTES

Statutes relevant to product liability actions in Alaska include the statutes of limitations,[116] limitations on liability,[117] and, in cases where breach of warranty is alleged, the Uniform Commercial Code.[118]

K. SEVERAL LIABILITY

A unique and significant feature in Alaska's law of products liability is that liability is determined on the basis of several liability only. In such cases, each defendant's liability, including settling or released parties, is limited to that percentage of fault allocated to it by the jury.[119] This system of fault allocation applies to strict liability as well as to negligence claims.[120] As discussed in Section C.4, *supra*, a jury may allocate fault only to parties, including third-party defendants and settling or released parties, and nonparties whom the other parties did not have a reasonable opportunity to join as parties.[121]

John B. Thorsness
Liam J. Moran
Clapp, Peterson, Tiemessen,
Thorsness & Johnson, LLC
711 H Street, Suite 620
Anchorage, Alaska 99501-3454
(907) 272-9272
(Fax) (907) 272-9586

Endnotes - Alaska

1. Alaska Stat. § 09.10.070(a).

2. Alaska Stat. § 09.55.580(a).

3. *Alaska Interstate Constr., LLC v. Pacific Diversified Invs., Inc.*, 279 P.3d 1156, 1178 n.131 (Alaska 2012); *Cameron v. State*, 822 P.2d 1362, 1365-68 (Alaska 1991); *Hanebuth v. Bell Helicopter Int'l*, 694 P.2d 143, 144 (Alaska 1984); *Greater Area Inc. v. Bookman*, 657 P.2d 828, 829 (Alaska 1982).

4. *Yurioff v. Am. Honda Motor Co., Inc.*, 803 P.2d 386, 389 (Alaska 1990); *Mine Safety Appliances v. Stiles*, 756 P.2d 288, 291-92 (Alaska 1988).

5. *Yurioff*, 803 P.2d 386, 389; *Mine Safety Appliances*, 756 P.2d 288, 291-92.

6. *Sopko v. Dowell Schlumberger, Inc.*, 21 P.3d 1265, 1272 (Alaska 2001).

7. *Kodiak Elec. Ass'n, Inc. v. Delaval Turbine, Inc.*, 694 P.2d 150, 154-56 (Alaska 1984); Alaska Stat. § 09.10.070(a).

8. *Kodiak Elec. Ass'n*, 694 P.2d at 156-57; *Anderson v. Fairchild Hiller Corp.*, 358 F. Supp. 976 (D. Alaska 1973); Alaska Stat. § 45.02.725.

9. *Armour v. Alaska Power Auth.*, 765 P.2d 1372, 1375 (Alaska 1988).

10. Alaska Stat. § 09.10.055.

11. Alaska Stat. § 09.10.055(b)(1)(E).

12. *Clary v. Fifth Ave. Chrysler Ctr., Inc.*, 454 P.2d 244, 247 (Alaska 1969) (quoting *Greenman v. Yuba Power Prods., Inc.*, 377 P.2d 897, 900 (Cal. 1962)).

13. *Northern Power & Eng'g Corp. v. Caterpillar Tractor Co.*, 623 P.2d 324, 329 (Alaska 1981) (footnotes omitted).

14. *Colt Indus. Operating Corp. v. Frank W. Murphy Mfr. Inc.*, 822 P.2d 925, 929 (Alaska 1991); *Caterpillar Tractor Co. v. Beck*, 593 P.2d 871, 885-86 (Alaska 1979).

15. *Caterpillar Tractor Co.*, 593 P.2d at 886.

16. *Caterpillar Tractor Co. v. Beck*, 593 P.2d 871, 883 (Alaska 1979), *appeal after remand*, 624 P.2d 790 (Alaska 1981).

17. *Caterpillar Tractor Co.*, 593 P.2d 871, 879 n.15.

18. *Caterpillar Tractor Co.*, 593 P.2d 871, 884-85.

19. *Keogh v. W. R. Grasle, Inc.*, 816 P.2d 1343, 1352 (Alaska 1991). The Alaska Supreme Court reaffirmed the general validity of the consumer expectations test of product defectiveness in *General Motors Corp. v. Farnsworth*, 965 P.2d 1209, 1220-21 (Alaska 1998). In *Farnsworth*, a crashworthiness case involving allegations of defective seat belt design, the defendant argued the trial court erred in instructing the jury on the consumer expectations test because, due to the complexity of the design issues raised by the plaintiff's claims, the ordinary consumer lacked a basis for forming, or likely had uninformed or unreasonable, expectations concerning how a vehicle should perform in a serious accident. *Farnsworth*, 965 P.2d at 1220. Rejecting this argument, the Alaska Supreme Court agreed with *Soule v. General Motors Corp.*, 882 P.2d 298 (Cal. 1994), and held that "consumers can form reasonable and educated expectations about how certain products should perform." *Farnsworth*, 965 P.2d at 1221. The court reasoned that a "seat belt is a familiar product whose basic function is well understood by the general population." *Farnsworth*, 965 P.2d at 1221. Nonetheless, the Alaska Supreme Court acknowledged the possibility that the consumer expectations test might be "inappropriate under certain facts," *i.e.*, where it can be shown that the ordinary consumer lacked life experiences that would provide a reasonable basis for forming educated expectations concerning a particular product. *Farnsworth*, 965 P.2d at 1221 n.16.

20. *Dura Corp. v. Harned*, 703 P.2d 396, 406 (Alaska 1985); see discussion at section C.3, *supra*.

21. *Prince v. Parachutes, Inc.*, 685 P.2d 83, 88 (Alaska 1984).

22. *Ennen v. Integon Indem. Corp.*, 268 P.3d 277, 290 (Alaska 2012) ("The central question [in proximate cause analysis] is 'whether the conduct has been so significant and important a cause that the defendant should be legally responsible.'"); *Winschel v. Brown*, 171 P.3d 142, 148 (Alaska 2007); *Vincent by Staton v. Fairbanks Memorial Hosp.*, 862 P.2d 847, 851 (Alaska 1993) (citing *Morris v. Farley Enter., Inc.*, 661 P.2d 167, 169 (Alaska 1983)); *Yukon Equip., Inc. v. Gordon*, 660 P.2d 428, 433 (Alaska 1983).

23. *Howarth v. State, Public Defender Agency*, 925 P.2d 1330, 1333 (Alaska 1996); *Staton*, 862 P.2d at 851.

24. *See Staton*, 862 P.2d at 851.

25. *Howarth*, 925 P.2d at 1333; *Staton*, 862 P.2d at 851 (quoting W. Page Keeton, et al., Prosser and Keeton on Torts § 42, at 273 (5th ed. 1984)).

26. *See Staton*, 862 P.2d at 851.

27. *See Staton*, 862 P.2d at 851.

28. *Kaatz v. State*, 540 P.2d 1037, 1049 (Alaska 1975).

29. *Butaud v. Suburban Marine & Sporting Goods, Inc.*, 555 P.2d 42, 45-46 (Alaska 1976).

30. *Kaatz*, 540 P.2d at 1049; *Dura Corp.*, 703 P.2d at 404-06 (Alaska 1985).

31. *Farnsworth*, 965 P.2d at 1215 n.6 (discussing *Dura Corp.*, 703 P.2d at 403-04 and rejecting the contention that the comparative negligence defense was limited to assumption of risk-type contexts). Presumably, because the court did not address the question in *Farnsworth*, the Alaska Supreme Court regards the determination of whether a plaintiff was comparatively negligent (in a manner cognizable in strict liability, as clarified by *Farnsworth*) as distinct from, and consistent with, Alaska statutory law, Alaska Stat. § 09.17.080(a), (b), governing the fact finder's allocation of fault, discussed *infra*. Cf. *Kaatz v. State*, 572 P.2d 775, 782 (Alaska 1977) (explaining that in making a comparative fault determination, "[t]here is no requirement that the party who is negligent in more ways, or for whom a greater number of individual negligent acts can be found, must be assigned the higher percentage" of fault).

32. Alaska Stat. § 09.17.080(a), (b); *Ogle v. Craig Taylor Equip. Co.*, 761 P.2d 722, 724 (Alaska 1988) (citing 1986 SLA ch. 139, Sec. 9, 11).

33. Alaska Stat. § 09.17.900.

34. *Benner v. Wichman*, 874 P.2d 949, 958 (Alaska 1994).

35. Alaska Stat. § 09.17.080(a). The court held Alaska Stat. § 09.17.080 constitutional in *Evans v. State of Alaska*, 56 P.3d 1046, 1070 (Alaska 2002).

36. *Alaska Gen. Alarm, Inc. v. Grinnell*, 1 P.3d 98, 104 (Alaska 2000).

37. *Burnett v. Covell*, 191 P.3d 985, 987-88 (Alaska 2008).

38. *Bachner v. Pearson*, 479 P.2d 319, 327 (Alaska 1970).

39. *Kodiak Elec. Ass'n*, 694 P.2d at 154; *Swenson Trucking & Excav., Inc. v. Truckweld Equip. Co.*, 604 P.2d 1113, 1116-17 (Alaska 1980).

40. *Bell v. Precision Airmotive Corp.*, 42 P.3d 1071, 1072 (Alaska 2002).

41. *Sturm, Ruger & Co., Inc. v. Day*, 594 P.2d 38, 44 (Alaska 1979), *modified on other grounds*, 615 P.2d 621 (Alaska 1981), *cert. denied*, 454 U.S. 894 (1981), *overruled in part on other grounds*, *Dura Corp. v. Harned*, 703 P.2d 396, 405 n.5 (Alaska 1985).

42. *Savage Arms, Inc. v. Western Auto Supply Co.*, 18 P.3d 49, 55-58 (Alaska 2001).

43. *State v. Tyonek Timber, Inc.*, 680 P.2d 1148, 1151 (Alaska 1984).

44. *Clary*, 454 P.2d at 247-48.

45. *Morrow v. New Moon Homes, Inc.*, 548 P.2d 279, 288-89 (Alaska 1976).

46. *Morrow*, 548 P.2d 279, 288 n.25.

47. *Prince*, 685 P.2d at 87.

48. *Prince*, 685 P.2d at 88-89; *Ross Labs. v. Thies*, 725 P.2d 1076, 1078-79 (Alaska 1986).

49. *Shanks v. Upjohn Co.*, 835 P.2d 1189, 1200 (Alaska 1992).

50. *Alvey v. Pioneer Oilfield Servs., Inc.*, 648 P.2d 599, 600 (Alaska 1982).

51. *Ennen*, 268 P.3d at 290; *Sharp v. Fairbanks North Star Borough*, 569 P.2d 178, 181 (Alaska 1977); *State v. Abbott*, 498 P.2d 712, 727 (Alaska 1972). *See* discussion at section C.3, *supra*.

52. *Jones v. Bowie Industries, Inc.*, 282 P.3d 316, 335 (Alaska 2012). The court in *Jones* explicitly did not hold that there is a duty to warn of technological improvements or to recall a defective product. *Jones*, 282 P.3d at 335 n.70.

53. *Robles v. Shoreside Petroleum, Inc.*, 29 P.3d 838, 843-44 (Alaska 2001). Be sure to read the dissent as well, which begins on page 846 of the opinion.

54. *See* Alaska Rule of Evidence 407; *Caterpillar Tractor Co. v. Beck*, 624 P.2d 790, 793-94 (Alaska 1981); *Bachner*, 479 P.2d at 329.

55. *Shanks*, 835 P.2d at 1200.

56. *Hiller v. Kawasaki Motors Corp., U.S.A.*, 671 P.2d 369, 372 (Alaska 1983) (citing *Caterpillar Tractor Co.*, 593 P.2d at 879 & 886 n.52).

57. *Hiller*, 671 P.2d at 372 (citing *Caterpillar Tractor Co.*, 624 P.2d at 793).

58. *Hiller*, 671 P.2d at 372 (citing *Caterpillar Tractor Co.*, 624 P.2d at 793).

59. *Farnsworth*, 965 P.2d at 1215 nn.6-7.

60. *Farnsworth*, 965 P.2d at 1215 nn.6-7.

61. *Caterpillar Tractor Co.*, 593 P.2d at 887.

62. *Sturm, Ruger*, 594 P.2d at 45.

63. *Caterpillar Tractor Co.*, 593 P.2d at 887.

64. *Heritage v. Pioneer Brokerage & Sales, Inc.*, 604 P.2d 1059, 1063-64 (Alaska 1979).

65. *Sturm, Ruger*, 594 P.2d at 45.

66. *Caterpillar Tractor Co.*, 593 P.2d at 887.

67. *Caterpillar Tractor Co.*, 624 P.2d at 794; *Harned v. Dura Corp.*, 665 P.2d 5, 8 n.8 (Alaska 1983); *Johnson v. State*, 636 P.2d 47, 57 (Alaska 1981).

68. *See* Alaska Rule of Evidence 403; *Johnson*, 636 P.2d at 57-58.

69. *Doubleday v. State, Commercial Fisheries Entry Comm'n*, 238 P.3d 100, 106 (Alaska 2010); *Sweet v. Sisters of Providence in Washington*, 895 P.2d 484, 491 (Alaska 1995); *Nayokpuk v. United States*, 2012 WL 1906533 (D. Alaska 2012).

70. *Allstate Ins. Co. v. Dooley*, 243 P.3d 197, 200-01 (Alaska 2010); *Hazen v. Municipality of Anchorage*, 718 P.2d 456, 463 (Alaska 1986).

71. *Allstate*, 243 P.3d at 201-02; *Estate of Day v. Willis*, 897 P.2d 78, 81 (Alaska 1995).

72. *Sweet*, 895 P.2d at 493 (quoting *Miller v. Montgomery County*, 494 A.2d 761, 768 (Md. Spec. App. 1985)).

73. *Allstate*, 243 P.3d at 201; *State v. Carpenter*, 171 P.3d 41, 64 (Alaska 2007); *Hibbits v. Sides*, 34 P.3d 327, 328-30 (Alaska 2001).

74. *Allstate*, 243 P.3d at 203-05.

75. *Northern Power & Eng'g Corp. v. Caterpillar Tractor Co.*, 623 P.2d 324, 329 (Alaska 1981).

76. *Farnsworth*, 965 P.2d at 1212 n.1.

77. *Farnsworth*, 965 P.2d at 1212 n.1.

78. *Farnsworth*, 965 P.2d at 1212 n.1.

79. *Richey v. Oen*, 824 P.2d 1371, 1374 (Alaska 1992).

80. *R.E. v. State*, 878 P.2d 1341, 1346 (Alaska 1994) (citing *D.S.W. v. Fairbanks N. Star Borough Sch. Dist.*, 628 P.2d 554, 555-56 (Alaska 1981)).

81. *Clary*, 454 P.2d at 248-49.

82. *Tyonek Timber*, 680 P.2d at 1151-54; *Morrow*, 548 P.2d at 285-86.

83. Alaska Stat. § 09.17.020(b); *Sturm, Ruger*, 594 P.2d at 46.

84. Alaska Stat. § 09.17.020(b).

85. *Farnsworth*, 965 P.2d at 1222 (setting aside award of punitive damages where the trial court erred in not instructing the jury on the plaintiff's comparative negligence and in not instructing the jury as a matter of law that a person convicted of criminal negligence in connection with accident contributed to plaintiff's injuries).

86. Alaska Stat. § 09.17.020(f), (g). The damages caps in Alaska Stat. § 09.17.020 were found to be constitutional by the Alaska Supreme Court in *Evans v. State of Alaska*, 56 P.3d 1046, 1070 (Alaska 2002).

87. Alaska Stat. § 09.17.020(j).

88. Alaska Stat. § 09.17.080.

89. *Benner*, 874 P.2d at 956-57; Alaska Stat. § 09.17.080; Alaska Rule of Civil Procedure 14(c).

90. Alaska Stat. § 09.17.010(b).

91. Alaska Stat. § 09.07.010(c).

92. *Northern Lights Motel, Inc. v. Sweaney*, 561 P.2d 1176, 1190 (Alaska 1977).

93. *Northern Lights Motel*, 561 P.2d 1176, 1190.

94. *Hibpshman v. Prudhoe Bay Supply, Inc.*, 734 P.2d 991, 997 (Alaska 1987).

95. *Gillispie v. Beta Constr. Co.*, 842 P.2d 1272, 1273-74 (Alaska 1992).

96. *Croft by Croft v. Wicker*, 737 P.2d 789, 792 (Alaska 1987); *Tommy's Elbow Room, Inc. v. Kavorkian*, 727 P.2d 1038, 1043 (Alaska 1986).

97. *Croft by Croft*, 737 P.2d 789, 792; *Tommy's Elbow Room*, 727 P.2d 1038, 1043.

98. *Hancock v. Northcutt*, 808 P.2d 251, 258 (Alaska 1991); *Dietzmann v. City of Homer*, 2010 WL 4684043, at *25 (D. Alaska 2010).

99. *Mattingly v. Sheldon Jackson College*, 743 P.2d 356, 365-66 (Alaska 1987); *Chizmar v. Mackie*, 896 P.2d 196, 204-05 (Alaska 1995). However, in *Southern Alaskan Carpenters Health & Sec. Trust Fund v. Jones*, 177 P.3d 844, 856 (Alaska

2008), the court held that, even in the absence of a pre-existing relationship between a nonunion employee and an employee benefits trust fund, the employee and his wife would be relieved of the requirement of showing physical injury in order to recover damages for emotional distress which was foreseeably caused by the trust fund's negligent misrepresentation to the employee and his then-pregnant wife that they would be covered, and later that they were covered, by health insurance through the trust fund.

100. *Chizmar*, 896 P.2d at 204.

101. *Ross Labs.*, 725 P.2d at 1081.

102. *Heritage*, 604 P.2d 1059.

103. *Koehring Mfg. Co. v. Earthmovers of Fairbanks, Inc.*, 763 P.2d 499, 503-04 (Alaska 1988); *Ross Labs.*, 725 P.2d at 1081.

104. *Farnsworth*, 965 P.2d at 1218.

105. *Farnsworth*, 965 P.2d at 1218-19.

106. *Farnsworth*, 965 P.2d at 1218-20 (holding "it should be the proven wrongdoer who must bear the burden of limiting its liability").

107. Alaska Stat. § 09.30.070(a).

108. Alaska Stat. § 23.30.055.

109. *See* Alaska Stat. § 23.30.055.

110. Alaska Stat. § 23.30.045(b).

111. Alaska Stat. § 23.30.015(a).

112. Alaska Stat. § 23.30.050.

113. *Fenner v. Municipality of Anchorage*, 53 P.3d 573, 576 (Alaska 2002); *Van Biene v. ERA Helicopters, Inc.*, 779 P.2d 315, 318 (Alaska 1989).

114. Alaska Stat. §§ 09.17.080, 23.30.015(g); *State Farm Mut. Auto. Ins. Co. v. Wilson*, 199 P.3d 581, 588 (Alaska 2008).

115. *Borg-Warner Corp. v. Avco Corp. (Lycoming Div.)*, 850 P.2d 628, 636 (Alaska 1993).

116. *See* discussion at section B, *supra*.

117. Alaska Stat. §§ 09.17.010-900.

118. Alaska Stat. § 45.02.101, *et seq.*

119. Alaska Stat. § 09.17.080.

120. Alaska Stat. § 09.17.080.

121. *Benner*, 874 P.2d at 958; Alaska Stat. § 09.17.080(a).

ARIZONA

A. THEORIES OF LIABILITY

Arizona statutes broadly define a product liability action as any action brought against a manufacturer or seller of a product for damages, bodily injury, death, or property damage caused by or resulting from the manufacture, construction, design, formula, installation, preparation, assembly, testing, packaging, labeling, sale, use, or consumption of any product, the failure to warn or protect against a danger or hazard in the use or misuse of the product, or the failure to provide proper instructions for the use or consumption of any product.[1]

In Arizona, a product liability action can be pursued under theories of strict liability, negligence, and breach of warranty.[2] The strict liability theory is rooted in the Restatement (Second) of Torts, § 402(A).[3] The negligence theory is an outgrowth of the traditional negligence tort, although the plaintiff is still required to prove the product is unreasonably dangerous.[4] The breach of *implied* warranty theory has been merged into strict liability, but the breach of express warranty theory is still available.[5]

Arizona courts traditionally follow the Restatement when not inconsistent with Arizona statutes or public policy. Arizona courts have clearly adopted Section 402A of Restatement (Second) of Torts[6] and have generally recognized and approved of the Restatement (Third) approach to product liability issues.[7]

B. STATUTE OF LIMITATIONS; NO STATUTE OF REPOSE

In Arizona, product liability actions based on negligence, strict liability, and breach of warranty that seek damages for personal injury, property damage, or wrongful death, must be commenced within two years after the cause of action accrues.[8] Arizona courts have held that a cause of action for personal injury "accrues" when a plaintiff discovers, or by the exercise of reasonable diligence should have discovered, that the injury was related to a defendant's conduct or a defective product.[9]

There is no statute of repose in Arizona for product liability claims, and prior statutes have been ruled unconstitutional by the Arizona courts.[10]

C. POTENTIALLY LIABLE PARTIES

Potentially liable parties include manufacturers, other entities in the chain of distribution, and commercial lessors.

1. **Manufacturer**

   A "manufacturer" is a person or entity that designs, assembles, fabricates, produces, constructs, or otherwise prepares a product or component part of a product prior to its sale to a user or consumer, including a seller owned in whole or significant part by the manufacturer, or a seller owning the manufacturer in whole or significant part.[11]

2. **Sellers or Others in the Chain**

   A "seller" includes a person or an entity, including a wholesaler, distributor, retailer, or lessor in the business of leasing any product or in the business of selling any product for consumption, use, or resale.[12] Although Arizona courts have defined "seller" broadly, they have excluded from liability entities that do not participate significantly in the stream of commerce and do not have the right to control the incidents of manufacture or distribution.[13] Product distribution facilitators, such as parties who advertise or finance products are not strictly liable.[14]

   Auctioneers are not sellers.[15] The term "seller" is not strictly construed in that a sale in the technical sense of the word is not necessarily required.[16] No privity of contract is required.[17] Sellers of used products may be potentially liable.[18] Under certain circumstances, even a trademark licensor can be held strictly liable for personal injuries caused by a defective product put into the stream of commerce by a trademark licensee.[19] While not all licensors would be subject to strict liability, the courts closely examine the degree of control possessed by the trademark licensor in deciding whether to apply strict liability to a licensor.[20]

   As discussed in Section E.1, *infra*, Arizona's comparative fault system applies to entities in the product's chain of distribution. In practice, comparing the fault of an "innocent" seller of a defective product to the manufacturer may limit and possibly eliminate the seller's liability.[21]

3. **Successor Liability**

   Arizona follows the general rule that a successor corporation is not liable for product liability arising from products manufactured by a predecessor corporation, unless certain conditions are met. Those conditions are: (1) there is an express or implied agreement of assumption by the successor corporation of liabilities of the predecessor corporation; (2) the transaction amounts to a consolidation or merger of the two corporations; (3) the purchasing corporation is a mere continuation (or reincarnation) of the seller; or (4) the transfer of assets to the purchaser is for the fraudulent purpose of escaping liability for the seller's debts.[22] Arizona courts have not adopted the "product line" exception to successor non-liability.[23]

D. PRODUCT LIABILITY-RELATED CAUSES OF ACTION

There are three general types of defects that form the basis for most product liability actions in Arizona—"manufacturing defects," "design defects," and "information defects." Each of these alleged defects can be presented under either a negligence or a strict liability theory.[24]

A defective product is one that is not reasonably fit for the ordinary purposes for which such products are sold and used.[25] A product in a "defective condition unreasonably dangerous" is one in a condition not contemplated by the ultimate consumer that will be unreasonably dangerous to him or her.[26] A defendant can be held liable despite its best efforts to make or design a safe product.[27] To determine whether a product is defective and unreasonably dangerous, the courts have developed two models of inquiry: the "risk/benefit" test and the "consumer expectation" test; *see* Sections D.3 and D.4, *infra*.

1. Manufacturing Defect

A product has a manufacturing defect if it "contains a danger which the manufacturer did not intend and the customer did not expect."[28] Typically, a manufacturing defect claim involves a flaw in the product as the result of something that went wrong in the manufacturing process and thus does not meet the manufacturer's design specifications.[29] The focus is on the quality of manufacture of the individual product at issue, rather than on the reasonableness of the design of the entire model line.[30]

2. Design Defect

A defectively designed product is one that is made as the manufacturer intended but that is unreasonably dangerous.[31] Thus, the focus in this situation is on the reasonableness of the design of the product or component.[32] The determination of whether a product has a defective and unreasonably dangerous design is based on the application of the "risk/benefit" analysis or the "consumer expectation" test.[33]

a. Strict Liability

In a strict liability design case, the knowledge revealed by the accident and other evidence discovered through the time of trial may be imputed to the manufacturer, and the risk/benefit factors are applied in "hindsight" to decide whether it was reasonable for a manufacturer with this knowledge to have put the product on the market.[34] Recently, the "hindsight" test has been criticized by Arizona courts as being inconsistent with the Restatement (Third) of Torts, Product Liability, but it remains in effect in Arizona.[35]

b. Negligence

The focus in negligent design cases is whether the manufacturer's *conduct* was unreasonable in light of the foreseeable risk of injury.[36]

In a negligent design case, the risk/benefit test factors are used to assess the reasonableness of the manufacturer's choice of design in light of the knowledge available at the time of design or manufacture.[37] Under the negligence standard, the design is evaluated based on the knowledge known at the time of manufacture, unlike the evaluation under the strict liability standard, where the design is evaluated with all of the knowledge available up through and including the time of trial.

3. **The "Risk/Benefit" Test**

The "risk/benefit" test has been expressly approved for design defect cases.[38] The "risk/benefit" test asks the jury to decide whether the benefits of the design outweigh the risk of danger in the design. If the risks outweigh the benefits, then the design is defective and unreasonably dangerous.[39]

In evaluating the reasonableness of a product's design, the jury is permitted to consider the following factors: (1) the usefulness and desirability of the product; (2) the availability of other and safer products to meet the same need; (3) the likelihood of injury and its probable seriousness; (4) the obviousness of the danger; (5) common knowledge and normal public expectations of the danger; (6) the avoidability of injury by care in use of the product, including the effect of instructions or warnings; and (7) the ability to eliminate the danger without seriously impairing the usefulness of the product or making it unduly expensive.[40]

4. **The "Consumer Expectation" Test**

The "consumer expectation" test is less widely used, predominantly in manufacturing defect cases. It analyzes the safety of the product based on the expectations of the "average consumer." This test of defectiveness provides that the product is defective and unreasonably dangerous if it fails to perform as safely as an ordinary consumer would expect when the product is used in a reasonably foreseeable manner.[41] Where the minimum safety of a product is within the common knowledge of lay jurors, expert witnesses may not be used to demonstrate what an ordinary consumer would or should expect.[42]

Arizona courts have noted that the "consumer expectation" test works well in manufacturing defect cases because consumers have developed safety expectations from using properly manufactured products of the same general design. In design defect cases, however, the "consumer expectation" test has limited utility because the consumer does not know what to expect since he would have no idea how safe a product could be made.[43] The "consumer expectation" test may also be used in cases when the ordinary consumer, through use of a product, has developed an expectation regarding the performance safety of the product.[44]

5. **Information Defects**

   A manufacturer has a duty to warn if, without the warning, the use of the product for its intended or reasonably foreseeable use causes the product to be dangerous to an extent beyond that contemplated by the ordinary consumer possessing the knowledge common to the community of the product's characteristics.[45] The product may be found to be defective, even though faultlessly made, if the product is unreasonably dangerous to sell without a suitable warning.[46] However, a manufacturer may not be required to provide a warning for clearly obvious hazards.[47] The "hindsight" test does not apply to information defect claims.[48]

   Arizona courts are among the more liberal courts in extending liability in warning cases. A defendant may be liable even if the evidence indicates that a warning would not have been read and heeded by the injured plaintiff, if there is evidence that warning might have caused some other person (such as the plaintiff's employer) to take action that would have lessened the danger to the plaintiff.[49]

6. **Post-Sale Duty to Warn**

   Under Arizona law, if a product was not defective when sold, the manufacturer has no duty to notify past customers about subsequent safety improvements, particularly when the manufacturer no longer services or maintains the product.[50] The case with this holding made its analysis in the context of a strict liability claim.

   However, a recent medical device case from the Ninth Circuit, applying Arizona law, suggested that under a negligence theory, a manufacturer may have a continuing duty to warn that applies to dangers the manufacturer discovers after sale.[51] In dicta and when discussing an added negligence claim, the court stated, "The manufacturer of a product must warn of dangers which he knows or should know are inherent in its use. This duty may be a continuing one applying to dangers the manufacturer discovers after sale." The Ninth Circuit went on to discuss that under Arizona law, a warning to a third party satisfies a manufacturer's duty if, given the nature of the warning and the relationship of the third party, there is "reasonable assurance that the information will reach those whose safety depends on their having it." Thus, negligence might provider a broader duty to warn than strict liability.

7. **Crashworthiness**

   The crashworthiness doctrine is recognized in Arizona. It has been recognized in cases involving automobiles as well as motorcycles.[52] In a crashworthiness case in which an alleged manufacturing or design defect did not cause the accident, a manufacturer is liable only for enhancement damages comprised of "that portion of the damage or injury caused by the defective design over and above the damage or injury that probably would have occurred as a result of the impact or collision absent the defective design."[53] In a crashworthiness case involving an indivisible injury, a plaintiff fulfills her burden of proof by showing that the defective design caused injuries over and above those caused by the original impact. The burden then shifts to the defendant to show that the damages that arose from the enhanced injury are apportionable.[54]

8. Breach of Warranty

A claim for breach of express warranty may be brought under a contract or under the Uniform Commercial Code. Privity within the chain of distribution is required to maintain a contract-based breach of warranty claim.[55]

Arizona does not recognize a separate cause of action for breach of implied warranty in the product liability context because the theory of liability under implied warranty has been merged into the doctrine of strict liability.[56] Implied warranties that arise from contract are still separate claims.[57] Privity is not required to maintain a tort action under the theory of strict liability.[58]

E. DEFENSES

1. Comparative Fault

Comparative fault reduces, but does not bar, a plaintiff's recovery in Arizona. A plaintiff's recovery is reduced by the percentage of fault allocated to him by the jury.[59] Each defendant is allocated a percentage of fault from 0% to 100%. Each defendant is liable only for its percentage of fault. The damages for which each defendant is responsible is calculated by multiplying the total amount of damages awarded to the plaintiff by the defendant's percentage of fault.[60]

In apportioning fault, the fault of all persons who may have contributed to the alleged injury, death, or damage to property is considered.[61] "Fault" means an actionable breach of legal duty, act, or omission proximately causing or contributing to injury or damages sustained by a person seeking recovery, including negligence in all of its degrees, contributory negligence, assumption of risk, strict liability, breach of express or implied warranty of a product, products liability and misuse, modification, or abuse of a product.[62] Where any of those were a contributing cause of the harm, such fault will be apportioned by the jury.[63]

A defendant may file a written notice of potential nonparties at fault to identify nonparties that it may intend at trial to argue and present evidence that the nonparties caused or partially caused the harm.[64] Such a notice may be filed even in crashworthiness cases.[65] The notice must be filed within 150 days after the defendant's answer and must meet the requirements of Ariz. R. Civ. P. 26(b)(5).[66] When filing a notice of nonparty that asserts that a healthcare professional was at fault or did not meet the standard of care, the designating party must serve a preliminary expert opinion affidavit with the notice.[67] Fault may be apportioned among defendants and nonparties without distinguishing between negligent and intentional conduct and without requiring that a minimum percentage of responsibility be assigned to an intentional tortfeasor.[68]

Comparative fault principles apply to all the entities in the chain of distribution of an allegedly defective product, even if one or more are insolvent or full collection on a judgment is not possible.[69] In strict product liability actions, the various participants in the chain of distribution are liable not for the actions of others, but for their own actions in distributing the defective product.[70] In indivisible injury cases, fault is apportioned under the statute as in any other tort action; the defendants bear the burden of proving that damages should be apportioned.[71]

Plaintiffs often attempt to challenge the application of comparative fault in strict liability cases. The Arizona Supreme Court has repeatedly held that comparative fault is compatible with, and should be applied in, strict product liability cases.[72]

2. **State of the Art**

By statute, a product's status as "state of the art" is an absolute defense to an Arizona product liability case. A defendant is not liable if it proves that the plans or designs for the product or the methods and techniques of manufacturing, inspecting, testing, and labeling the product conformed with the state of the art at the time the product was first sold by the defendant.[73]

"State of the art" is further defined by statute to mean "the technical, mechanical and scientific knowledge of manufacturing, designing, testing labeling the same or similar products that was in existence and reasonably feasible for use at the time of manufacture."[74] Thus, a product is state of the art if nothing better is in existence and reasonably feasible at the time it is manufactured.[75] If a defendant can show that no better product existed, or that no better product was reasonably feasible, then by definition its own product was state of the art. If a defendant can show that the alternative design offered by the plaintiff was not feasible, then defendant's product is state of the art.[76]

The judge determines whether the particular case is one in which the defense can be raised at trial.[77] If a jury rejects a strict liability design defect claim based on a manufacturer's state of the art defense, it is inconsistent for the jury to hold the manufacturer liable for negligent design.[78]

3. **Modification and Misuse**

A manufacturer is not responsible for injuries caused by unreasonable and unforeseeable alterations or modifications of the product made after the initial sale by someone other than the manufacturer.[79] A manufacturer is also not responsible for injuries caused by unreasonable and unforeseeable misuse of the product.[80] Misuse can also be used as a defense in strict liability cases as part of the jury's allocation of comparative fault.[81]

4. **Assumption of Risk**

   Assumption of the risk is an affirmative defense to a product liability action in Arizona.[82] However, defendants must pass a very high threshold to establish the defense. To prove that a plaintiff "assumed the risk," the defendant must establish that the plaintiff had knowledge of the specific defect at issue and that the plaintiff appreciated the risk of injury from using the product in its defective condition.[83] Assumption of the risk is always a question of fact for the jury, even in cases where there is an express contractual release or waiver.[84]

5. **Seat Belt Defense**

   Arizona recognizes the seat belt defense, which allows a plaintiff's non-use of a seat belt to be considered in apportionment of fault.[85] The defendant must prove a causal relationship between the non-use of the seat belt and plaintiff's injuries.[86]

6. **Inherently Dangerous Products**

   Arizona follows the approach of comment *k* to Section 402A of the Restatement (Second) of Torts, which, under certain circumstances, immunizes the producers of some unavoidably unsafe products.[87] Courts have interpreted comment *k* to mean that for experimental drugs, the manufacturer must clearly advise that the drug is experimental and must warn of known risks and those risks that should be known through the exercise of reasonable care.[88]

7. **Learned Intermediary Doctrine**

   In some circumstances, a proper warning given to a "learned intermediary" or a "sophisticated user" of the product may be deemed adequate as to the end user.[89] Arizona follows Section 388 of the Restatement (Second) of Torts, which is a fact-based determination of particular factors such as the likelihood and nature of harm and burden of giving the warning to the end user.[90] The manufacturer's duty to warn is ordinarily satisfied if a proper warning is given to the specialized class of people that may prescribe or administer the product.[91] For example, drug manufacturers have been found to discharge their duty to the public if they properly warn the administering physician of the contraindications and possible side effects of the drug.[92] The doctrine applies to failure-to-warn and strict liability claims.[93]

8. **Intoxication or Drug Use**

   In any civil action, a defendant may be found not liable if the defendant proves that the plaintiff was under the influence of an intoxicating liquor or drug and, as a result of that influence, the plaintiff was at least 50 percent responsible for the accident or event that caused the plaintiff's injury.[94] This is not a bar to a cause of action, but rather remains a jury question. It permits, but does not require, the jury to find in a defendant's favor.[95]

9. **Criminal Acts**

   A defendant is not liable for damages that the plaintiff incurs if the plaintiff is harmed while the plaintiff is attempting to commit, committing, or fleeing from a felony criminal act and as a result of that act, attempted act, or flight, the plaintiff (or his decedent) was at least 50 percent responsible for the accident or event that caused the harm.[96] The same is true for harms committed during misdemeanors, so long as the plaintiff was at least 50 percent responsible for the accident or event.[97] This statute was revised in 2009 to address prior constitutional concerns.

10. **Disclaimer of Warranty**

    Warranties may be disclaimed or limited if certain conditions are met. To exclude or modify the implied warranty of merchantability or any part of it, the language must mention merchantability and in the case of a writing, it must be conspicuous.[98] To exclude or modify any implied warranty of fitness, the exclusion must be in writing and be conspicuous.[99]

    The limitation or exclusion will not be upheld if it is found unconscionable.[100] A disclaimer of warranty obligations has no effect on a seller's tort liability. Regardless of what a seller disclaims by contract, it remains subject to tort liability, which is imposed by law.[101]

11. **Destruction or Loss of Evidence**

    Arizona does not recognize a distinct cause of action for spoliation.[102] However, the court will undertake a case-specific evaluation to decide whether an adverse inference instruction, dismissal, or other sanctions are warranted.[103]

F. **EVIDENCE AND PROCEDURAL RULES**

1. **Industry Standards**

   Evidence of industry standards, customs, and practices is admissible, as is evidence of compliance with federal and other regulatory standards, to assist in determining the "state of the art."[104] Such evidence may also be considered on the issue of whether a product is in a defective condition unreasonably dangerous to the user. However, without more, such evidence does not necessarily establish the state of the art.[105]

2. **Other Accidents/Incidents**

   Evidence of other incidents or accidents is inadmissible unless the plaintiff can show that the circumstances of those incidents are "substantially similar to the conditions resulting in the accident at issue."[106] The substantial similarity requirement applies regardless of the proponent's theory of relevance. Substantial similarity requires that the accidents be closely related in time and character to the subject accident. Evidence of other incidents has typically only been properly admitted in premises liability cases in which the other incidents occurred at exactly the same location.[107]

3. **Post-Sale Changes**

   Evidence of advancements or changes in the state of the art after the product was first sold by the defendant, or any change made in the design or methods of manufacturing or testing of the product or any similar product subsequent to the time the product was first sold, is not admissible as direct evidence of a defect.[108] Subsequent remedial measures are not admissible to prove negligence but may be admissible when offered for another purpose.[109]

4. **Product Safety Analysis Privilege**

   Evidence of a company's own product safety analyses or reviews, and any reasonable remedial measures taken pursuant to such analyses or reviews, are inadmissible to prove negligence, that the product was defective or unreasonably dangerous, or other culpable conduct. A plaintiff may not use such evidence to prove punitive damages unless the product safety analyses or reviews or reasonable remedial measures were done in bad faith or solely to affect litigation.[110] A plaintiff may use the same evidence for other purposes such as feasibility or impeachment.[111] The product safety analyses are generally discoverable unless they involve trade secrets or competitively sensitive information.

   A "product safety analysis or review" is any investigation, inquiry, review, evaluation, or other means by which a person or entity seeks to determine, calculate, predict, estimate, evaluate, or report the safety or health effects of the use of any of its products, systems, services, or processes.[112] Analyses or reviews of component parts by a component manufacturer are included. "Reasonable remedial measures" are actions, including recalls and changes in quality assurance procedures, taken as a result of a product safety analysis or review and intended to improve safety or to lessen the likelihood of safety-related accidents.[113]

5. **Generally No Joint and Several Liability**

   There is no joint and several liability in Arizona in most standard product liability cases. Joint and several liability has been abolished except where the tortfeasors acted in concert to commit an intentional tort or where one acted as the agent or servant of the other. Arizona follows the doctrine of "pure" comparative fault instead and has adopted the Uniform Contribution Among Tortfeasors Act.[114] There are generally no rights to a credit or set-off for settlements by co-defendants.

In the limited circumstances where joint and several liability is found, there is a right to contribution among joint tortfeasors, except none for a tortfeasor found to have acted intentionally, willfully, or wantonly.[115] A defendant who is jointly and severally liable for an intentional tort with a co-tortfeasor is entitled to have an adverse judgment reduced by the amount of any settlement reached with the settling co-tortfeasor.[116]

6. Statutory Indemnification

Arizona has a strong and specific statute about indemnification and tenders of defense by a seller to a product manufacturer.[117] The indemnification statute generally entitles a downstream seller[118] to tender its defense to an upstream manufacturer and is intended to place the burden and costs of defending products on their manufacturers.[119] Such indemnification may even be required where there is a conflict of interest between the manufacturer and seller.[120]

In the event of an adverse judgment, a seller can recover a judgment plus its reasonable attorneys' fees and costs for defending the action.[121] In the event of a settlement, a seller may be able to recover its defense costs and fees against the manufacturer, although the statute does not give the right to recover the amount paid in settlement.[122] Indemnification is not conditioned on the seller having diligently defended the product or the manufacturer's interests, particularly if the manufacturer has rejected the seller's tender of defense.[123]

Indemnification is not required where either of two exceptions apply: (1) if the seller had knowledge of a defect in the product, or (2) if the seller, without the manufacturer's authorization, altered, modified, or installed the product, and the alteration was a substantial cause of the resulting injury.[124] The manufacturer is not relieved of its indemnity obligation to the final seller where some party in the chain of distribution, other than the final seller, might have known of the defect or might have altered, modified, or installed the product.[125]

The statute does not specifically state what the tender of defense must contain, nor does it prescribe any time limits for making or responding to a tender. A tender of defense was held to be proper when it detailed the substance of plaintiff's allegations, enclosed a copy of the complaint, and cited the statute.[126] A written response of some type is well advised.[127]

A seller may be required to indemnify the manufacturer if the seller provided the product plans or specifications and those plans and specifications were a substantial cause of the product's alleged defect.[128] A manufacturer cannot obtain indemnification from the seller, however, if the manufacturer had knowledge or, with the exercise of reasonable and diligent care should have had knowledge, of a defect in the product.[129]

7. **Employer Immunity Under Workers' Compensation**

Under the exclusive remedy provisions of Arizona's Workers' Compensation Act, employers who comply with its provisions are not subject to suit by an employee injured by a job-connected accident,[130] with two exceptions: (1) when the injury is caused by the employer's willful misconduct, an act knowingly and purposely done with the direct object of injuring another,[131] and (2) when the employee rejects the compensation provided by workers' compensation and, as the law permits, retains the right to sue the employer.[132]

If the employee is injured by a third party, other than the employer or a co-worker, the employee may file suit against the third party, provided the employee brings such action within one year of the date of injury.[133] During the second year after injury, the employee can still sue but only if she first gets a reassignment of rights from the workers' compensation insurer.[134] If an employee sues a third party, the employee still is entitled to workers' compensation benefits, but the insurer has a lien on the employee's net recovery to the extent of its payments.[135]

A nonparty employer's fault can be considered in the apportionment of fault (see D.1, *supra*), even though the employer is immune from liability and cannot be made a party under the exclusive remedy provisions.[136]

A "lent employee" becomes the employee of a "special employer" when: "(1) the employee has made a contract of hire, express or implied, with the special employer; (2) the work being done is essentially that of the special employer; and (3) the special employer has the right to control the details of the work."[137] When all three factors are met, the special employer is liable for workers' compensation and entitled to the benefits of workers' compensation immunity.[138]

A manufacturer who has manufactured equipment for an employer pursuant to the employer's design specifications is barred by the Workers' Compensation Act from seeking indemnification from the employer in a product liability suit by an employee against the manufacturer that asserts a design defect in the equipment.[139] Nor is a manufacturer entitled to statutory indemnification from the employer under these circumstances.[140]

8. **Survival and Wrongful Death Actions**

Arizona does not allow for a decedent's pain and suffering damages to be recovered in a survival action. Thus if an injured person dies, his representatives cannot recover for the injured person's own pre-death conscious pain and suffering, either actual or perceived.[141] Evidence of pre-death pain and suffering has been held irrelevant and inadmissible.[142] If the manner of the decedent's death increases the survivor's mental anguish, however, it is arguably relevant to damages and may be admitted under a balancing test of relevance as compared to prejudice.[143]

Wrongful death actions are brought by the surviving spouse, child, or parents on behalf of all statutory beneficiaries. If there are no surviving statutory beneficiaries, then a wrongful death action may be maintained by the decedent's estate, and any recovery will be distributed to other beneficiaries under the laws of intestate succession.[144] Either parent may maintain the action for the death of a child, and a guardian may do so for the death of a ward.[145] Damages are distributed to the statutory beneficiaries in proportion to their damages.[146] A child unborn at the time of the death of the parent is included in the term "children" for whose benefit a wrongful death action may be maintained.[147]

9. **Expert Admissibility Standard**

Arizona follows the *Daubert* standard. Effective January 1, 2012, the Arizona Supreme Court modified Ariz. R. Evid. 702 to track the equivalent federal rule and, thus, adopted by implication the *Daubert* standard for the admissibility of expert opinion testimony. A witness who is qualified as an expert by knowledge, skill, experience, training, or education may testify in the form of an opinion or otherwise if: (a) the expert's scientific, technical, or other specialized knowledge will help the trier of fact to understand the evidence or to determine a fact in issue; (b) the testimony is based on sufficient facts or data; (c) the testimony is the product of reliable principles and methods; and (d) the expert has reliably applied the principles and methods to the facts of the case.[148]

10. **Noteworthy Rules—Arizona Rules of Civil Procedure**

   a. **Rule 5(f). Sensitive Data**

   When making a filing with the court, a person should refrain from including social security numbers and financial account numbers in all pleadings or other documents.[149] The responsibility for redacting this sensitive data rests solely with the person making the filing.[150] For violation of this rule, the court may impose sanctions against counsel of the parties to ensure future compliance.[151]

   b. **Rule 45.1. Interstate Depositions and Discovery**

   Arizona adopted the Interstate Depositions and Discovery Act effective January 1, 2013.

   To request issuance of a subpoena, a party must present a foreign subpoena to a clerk of court in the county in which the discovery is sought to be conducted in Arizona.[152] The foreign subpoena must include the following phrase below the case number: "For the Issuance of an Arizona Subpoena Under Ariz. R. Civ. P. 45.1."[153] Upon presentation, the clerk shall promptly issue a blank subpoena to the requesting party to be completed prior to service.[154]

Prior to service, the subpoena must state the name of the Arizona court issuing it; contain the caption and case number of the out-of-state case to which it relates; identify the discovery requested; contain or be accompanied by the names, addresses, and telephone numbers of all counsel of record and any party not represented by counsel; comply with the form specified in Rule 45(a)(1); and not request discovery beyond what is authorized by Rule 45.[155]

G. DAMAGES

1. No Statutory Cap on Damages

Arizona has no statutory caps on either compensatory or punitive damages.

2. Punitive Damages

Punitive damages generally are available for claims sounding in tort, such as strict liability and negligence, only if "something more" than the mere commission of the tort is shown.[156] To justify the award of punitive damages, more than "gross negligence" must be proven.[157] The plaintiff must prove, by clear and convincing evidence, both aggravated and outrageous conduct on the part of the defendant and that the defendant acted with an "evil mind," which means the defendant either intended to injure the plaintiff or "consciously pursued a course of conduct knowing that it created a substantial risk of significant harm to others."[158] Punitive damages are not allowed in actions based on breach of warranty, sounding exclusively in contract.[159]

Punitive damage claims are subject to both state and federal constitutional safeguards. Punitive damage awards are ultimately reviewable by the United States Supreme Court, which in recent years has repeatedly demonstrated its concern over the constitutionality of large punitive damage awards.[160]

a. Punitive Damages Limits for Government-Approved Products

Arizona has statutory exemptions for punitive damages for virtually any kind of product that was government-approved or that complied with government regulations. First, there is a long-standing statute related to drugs (Ariz. Rev. Stat. § 12-701). Manufacturers or sellers of drugs are not liable for exemplary or punitive damages if the drug alleged to cause the harm was manufactured and labeled in accordance with the terms of an approval or license issued by the Federal Food and Drug Administration or is generally recognized as safe and effective pursuant to conditions established by the FDA and applicable regulations.[161] A subsection of the law that allowed an exception for misrepresentation to the FDA was found unconstitutional on the basis of preemption.[162]

Second, another similar statute (Ariz. Rev. Stat. § 12-689) became effective on August 1, 2012. This expanded to virtually any kind of product the exemption for government-approved products or products in compliance with regulations. The exemption applies if the product at issue was designed/manufactured/sold according to the terms of government approval, or the product complied with all state or U.S. government regulations when the product left the control of the manufacturer/seller, or the act or transaction forming the basis of the claim involves practices authorized by or in compliance with government regulations. The exemption from punitive damages does not apply if the product was sold after the government ordered the product removed from market, or withdrew or substantially altered its approval, or if the government later found the manufacturer/seller knowingly violated applicable regulations requiring reporting of risks of harm. It does not apply if illegal payments were made to the government to gain approval, or if the manufacturer/seller intentionally and in violation of regulations withheld from or misrepresented relevant information to the government.

b. Punitive Damages Unavailable for "Illegal Aliens"

Pursuant to the Arizona Constitution, punitive damages may not be recovered "by a person who is present in this state in violation of federal immigration law related to improper entry by an alien."[163]

3. Loss of Consortium

Either spouse may maintain an action for loss of the other's consortium or harm to the marital relationship due to injuries caused by the defendant's fault.[164] Arizona also allows parents to sue for the loss of an injured minor or adult[165] child's consortium.[166] In order for a parent to maintain this cause of action, the child must suffer a "severe, permanent, and disabling injury that substantially interferes with the child's capacity to interact with the parents in a normally gratifying way."[167] Although evidence of a significant interference in the parent-child relationship must exist, an injury need not be the functional equivalent of death, nor even be catastrophic.[168] Children can also maintain an action for the loss of an injured parent's consortium. In order for a child to recover, the parent's injury must be severe, permanent, or disabling and the resulting impairment must leave the parent-child relationship destroyed or nearly destroyed.[169]

4. Hedonic Damages

Damages for pain and suffering must be reasonably certain and cannot be predicated upon conjecture and speculation.[170] Rather, it is "'necessary to show by the evidence either that the pain and suffering actually did exist, or that the injuries were of such a nature that it would presumably follow therefrom.'"[171] The Arizona Court of Appeals has recognized the right of recovery for the loss of enjoyment of life, or hedonic damages, which is the participation in life's activities to the quality and extent normally enjoyed before the injury.[172] In the same opinion, the court reaffirmed that damages for disability and disfigurement may be awarded where appropriate.[173]

5. **Emotional Distress**

A claim for negligent infliction of emotional distress requires a showing of bodily harm. To maintain an action for emotional distress damages, a plaintiff must show either a physical injury or a long-term physical illness or mental disturbance.[174]

6. **Economic Loss Rule**

Arizona recognizes the economic loss rule. The economic loss rule bars a party from recovering purely economic damages in tort unless accompanied by physical harm, either in the form of personal injury or secondary property damage.[175] In the absence of personal injury or property damage, parties are limited to contractual remedies for purely economic loss.[176] In order to determine whether a particular cause of action sounds in tort or contract, a court must consider the facts of the case while bearing in mind that tort law is designed to promote the safety of persons and property, whereas contract law is designed to protect the parties' expectations.[177]

7. **Pre- and Post-Judgment Interest**

In Arizona, pre-judgment interest is generally not available in a standard product liability tort action. "Because non-economic tort damages are not subject to exact computation, such damages are not liquidated until a trier of fact determines the amount to be awarded."[178] Interest on unliquidated claims typically does not begin until judgment is entered.[179] However, pre-judgment on a liquidated claim is a matter of right.[180] Damages are liquidated if "the evidence furnishes data which, if believed, makes it possible to compute the amount with exactness, without reliance upon opinion or discretion."[181] Costs and interest on the verdict from the time it was rendered are included in a judgment.[182] Interest on a judgment is at the rate of 10 percent per year, or at any rate expressly agreed to by the parties in writing.[183] A satisfaction of judgment stops the accrual of post-judgment interest.[184]

Patrick X. Fowler
Kelly Wilkins MacHenry
Snell & Wilmer L.L.P.
One Arizona Center
400 East Van Buren Street
Phoenix, Arizona 85004-2202
(602) 382-6000
E-mail: pfowler@swlaw.com
kmachenry@swlaw.com

ENDNOTES - ARIZONA

1. Ariz. Rev. Stat. § 12-681(5).

2. *Readenour v. Marion Power Shovel*, 149 Ariz. 442, 452 n.4, 719 P.2d 1058, 1061 n.4 (Ariz. 1986).

3. *See Lunt v. Brady Mfg. Corp.*, 13 Ariz. App. 305, 306-07, 475 P.2d 964, 965-66 (1970).

4. *See Mather v. Caterpillar Tractor Corp.*, 23 Ariz. App. 409, 411, 533 P.2d 717, 719 (1975).

5. *Hearn v. R.J. Reynolds Tobacco Co.*, 279 F. Supp. 2d 1096, 1103 (D. Ariz. 2003) (citing *Scheller v. Wilson Certified Foods*, 114 Ariz. 159, 559 P.2d 1074 (Ct. App. 1976)); *see also Salt River Project Agric. Improvement & Power Dist. Corp. v. Westinghouse Electric Corp.*, 143 Ariz. 368, 694 P.2d 198 (1984).

6. *Sullivan v. Green Mfg. Co.*, 118 Ariz. 181, 186, 575 P.2d 811, 816 (Ct. App. 1977) (citing *O.S. Stapley Co. v. Miller*, 103 Ariz. 556, 447 P.2d 248 (1968)).

7. *See, e.g., Golonka v. General Motors*, 204 Ariz. 575, 584 n.3, 65 P.3d 956 n.3 (2003) (citing Restatement (Third) of Torts, Product Liability § 2 cmt. n); *see also Winsor v. Glasswerks PHX, L.L.C.*, 204 Ariz. 303, 308, 63 P.3d 1040, 1045 (2003) (recognizing the consistency between Arizona law on successor liability and Restatement (Third) of Torts, Product Liability § 12).

8. Ariz. Rev. Stat. §§ 12-542 and 12-551. *See also Gates v. La Belle's Distrib. of Ariz., Inc.*, 147 Ariz. 23, 25, 708 P.2d 114, 116 (Ct. App. 1985) (in evaluating whether to apply two-year product liability statute of limitations or four-year UCC statute of limitations to breach of warranty claim, the focus is on type of damages sought).

9. *Lawhon v. L.B.J. Inst. Supply, Inc.*, 159 Ariz. 179, 183, 765 P.2d 1003, 1007 (Ct. App. 1988).

10. *Hazine v. Montgomery Elevator Co.*, 176 Ariz. 340, 344, 861 P.2d 625, 629 (1993); *see also Cronin v. Sheldon*, 195 Ariz. 531, 539, 991 P.2d 231, 239 (1999) (explaining the *Hazine* decision).

11. Ariz. Rev. Stat. § 12-681(3).

12. Ariz. Rev. Stat. § 12-681(9); *see also Sequoia Mfg. Co. v. Halec Constr. Co., Inc.*, 117 Ariz. 11, 570 P.2d 782 (Ct. App. 1977) (applying strict liability to a lessor of a product).

13. *Grubb v. Do It Best Corp.*, 279 P.3d 626, 627-28 (Ariz. Ct. App. 2012) (granting summary judgment for defendant that did not "participate significantly in the stream of commerce" as to the product at issue).

14. *Grubb*, 279 P.3d at 627-28 (quoting Restatement (Third) of Torts: Product Liability § 20 cmt. g (1998)).

15. *Antone v. Greater Ariz. Auto Auction, Inc.*, 214 Ariz. 550, 551-52, 155 P.3d 1074, 1075-76 (Ct. App. 2007) (finding strict liability policies are not satisfied when the entity only plays a "passive role in contributing to the product's presence in the stream of commerce.").

16. *Gaston v. Hunter*, 121 Ariz. 33, 45-46, 588 P.2d 326, 338-39 (Ct. App. 1978) (seller includes donor of a pharmaceutical product).

17. *Nastri v. Wood Bros. Homes, Inc.*, 142 Ariz. 439, 445, 690 P.2d 158, 164 (Ct. App. 1984) *overruled on other grounds by Flagstaff Affordable Hous. Ltd. P'ship v. Design Alliance, Inc.*, 223 Ariz. 320, 223 P.3d 664 (2010).

18. *Jordan v. Sunnyslope Appliance Propane & Plumbing Supplies Co.*, 135 Ariz. 309, 314, 660 P.2d 1236, 1241 (Ct. App. 1983) ("a dealer engaged in the business of selling used goods . . . may be held strictly liable under the terms of the Restatement rule.").

19. *See Torres v. Goodyear Tire & Rubber Co., Inc.*, 163 Ariz. 88, 92, 786 P.2d 939, 943 (1990) (applying strict liability to a trademark licensor under the facts of the case).

20. *Torres*, 163 Ariz. at 92, 786 P.2d at 943 (finding the trademark licensor fell within the class of those "in the business of placing products in the stream of commerce" and thus subject to the doctrine of strict liability).

21. *See State Farm Ins. Cos. v. Premier Manufactured Sys., Inc.*, 217 Ariz. 222, 229, 172 P.3d 410, 417 (2007) ("It may, of course, be difficult in some circumstances for the finder of fact to allocate statutory fault among the various participants in the chain of distribution of a defective product.").

22. *Winsor*, 204 Ariz. at 307, 63 P.3d at 1044 (citing *A.R. Teeters & Assocs., Inc. v. Eastman Kodak Co.*, 172 Ariz. 324, 329, 836 P.2d 1034, 1039 (1992)).

23. *Winsor*, 204 Ariz. at 309-10, 63 P.3d at 1046-47.

24. *Gosewisch v. American Honda Motor Co., Inc.*, 153 Ariz. 400, 403, 737 P.2d 376, 379 (1987); *see also* Ariz. Rev. Stat. § 12-681(5) (defining "product liability action").

25. *Bailey v. Montgomery Ward & Co.*, 6 Ariz. App. 213, 218, 431 P.2d 108, 113 (1967); *see also Dietz v. Waller*, 141 Ariz. 107, 112, 685 P.2d 744, 749 (1984) (stating that breach of implied warranty has "virtually the same elements" as strict liability).

26. *Dart v. Wiebe Mfg. Inc.*, 147 Ariz. 242, 244, 709 P.2d 876, 878 (1985) (quoting Restatement (Second) of Torts § 402A).

27. *Golonka*, 204 Ariz. at 581, 65 P.3d at 962 (citing *Mather*, 23 Ariz. App. 409, 411, 533 P.2d 717, 719 (1975)).

28. *Dart*, 147 Ariz. at 244, 709 P.2d at 878 (citing *Brady v. Melody Homes Mfr.*, 121 Ariz. 253, 256, 589 P.2d 896, 899 (1978)).

29. *Gomulka v. Yavapai Mach. & Auto Parts, Inc.*, 155 Ariz. 239, 241-42, 745 P.2d 986, 988-89 (1987).

30. *See, e.g., Brady*, 121 Ariz. at 256, 589 P.2d at 898 (overruled on other grounds).

31. *Gomulka*, 155 Ariz. at 242, 745 P.2d at 989.

32. *See Brady*, 121 Ariz. at 256, 589 P.2d at 898 (overruled on other grounds).

33. *See Golonka*, 204 Ariz. at 581, 65 P.3d at 962 (citing *Dart*, 147 Ariz. at 244-45, 709 P.2d at 878-79).

34. *Golonka*, 204 Ariz. at 582, 65 P.3d at 963.

35. *Powers v. Taser Int'l, Inc.*, 217 Ariz. 398, 403-04, 174 P.3d 777, 782-83 (Ct. App. 2007).

36. *Golonka*, 204 Ariz. at 582, 65 P.3d at 963.

37. *Golonka*, 204 Ariz. at 582, 65 P.3d at 963.

38. *Dart*, 147 Ariz. at 244-45, 709 P.2d at 878-79.

39. *Dart*, 147 Ariz. at 244-45, 709 P.2d at 878-79.

40. *Golonka*, 204 Ariz. at 581 n.2, 65 P.3d at 962 n.2.

41. *See Gomulka*, 155 Ariz. at 242, 745 P.2d at 989 (citing *Dart*, 147 Ariz. at 244, 709 P.2d at 878); *see also Golonka*, 204 Ariz. at 581, 65 P.3d at 962.

42. *Long v. TRW Vehicle Safety Sys.*, 796 F. Supp. 2d 1005, 1010 (D. Ariz. 2011) (applying consumer expectation test to seat belts and noting that "[w]hen a seat belt, designed to be an instrument of protection, becomes an instrument of life-threatening injury, a consumer is justified in concluding that it did not perform as safely as promised.") (citations omitted).

43. *Gomulka*, 155 Ariz. at 243, 745 P.2d at 990.

44. *Brethauer v. General Motors Corp.*, 221 Ariz. 192, 199, 211 P.3d 1176, 1183 (Ct. App. 2009).

45. *Kavanaugh v. Kavanaugh*, 131 Ariz. 344, 348, 641 P.2d 258, 262 (Ct. App. 1981); *see also Brown v. Sears, Roebuck & Co.*, 136 Ariz. 556, 563, 667 P.2d 750, 757 (Ct. App. 1983).

46. *Piper v. Bear Med. Sys., Inc.*, 180 Ariz. 170, 177, 883 P.2d 407, 414 (Ct. App. 1993) (citing *Brown*, 136 Ariz. at 563, 667 P.2d at 757).

47. *Raschke v. Carrier Corp.*, 146 Ariz. 9, 12, 703 P.2d 556, 559 (Ct. App. 1985); *Brown*, 136 Ariz. at 561, 667 P.2d at 755.

48. *Powers*, 217 Ariz. at 405, 174 P.3d at 784.

49. *See Tucson Indus., Inc. v. Schwartz*, 108 Ariz. 464, 468-69, 501 P.2d 936, 940-41 (1972).

50. *Wilson v. United States Elevator Corp.*, 193 Ariz. 251, 257, 972 P.2d 235, 241 (Ct. App. 1998).

51. *Wilson v. United States Elevator Corp.*, 193 Ariz. 251, 257, 972 P.2d 235, 241 (Ct. App. 1998).

52. *See, e.g., Larsen v. General Motors Corp.*, 391 F.2d 495 (8th Cir. 1968) (original case adopting crashworthiness doctrine); *Cota v. Harley Davidson, a Division of AMF, Inc.*, 141 Ariz. 7, 12-14, 684 P.2d 888, 893-95 (Ct. App. 1984) (adopting crashworthiness theory enunciated in *Larsen* and applying it to motorcycles).

53. *Czarnecki v. Volkswagen of Am.*, 172 Ariz. 408, 412 n.2, 837 P.2d 1143, 1147 n.2 (Ct. App. 1991).

54. *Czarnecki*, 172 Ariz. at 413, 837 P.2d at 1148.

55. *Flory v. Silvercrest Indus., Inc.*, 129 Ariz. 574, 578, 633 P.2d 383, 387 (1981); *Seekings v. Jimmy GMC, Inc.*, 130 Ariz. 596, 601, 638 P.2d 210, 215 (1981).

56. *Hearn*, 279 F. Supp. 2d at 1103 (citing *Scheller*, 114 Ariz. at 161, 559 P.2d at 1076); *see also Flory*, 129 Ariz. at 576, 633 P.2d at 385; *Seekings*, 130 Ariz. at 601, 638 P.2d at 215.

57. *Woodward v. Chirco Constr. Co.*, 141 Ariz. 514, 515-16, 687 P.2d 1269, 1270-71 (1984).

58. *Flory*, 129 Ariz. at 579, 633 P.2d at 388.

59. Ariz. Rev. Stat. § 12-2506.

60. Ariz. Rev. Stat. § 12-2506(A).

61. Ariz. Rev. Stat. § 12-2506(B).

62. Ariz. Rev. Stat. § 12-2506(F)(2).

63. *See* Ariz. Rev. Stat. §§ 12-2505, 12-2506, and 12-2509; *see also Jimenez v. Sears, Roebuck & Co.*, 183 Ariz. 399, 402, 904 P.2d 861, 864 (1995) ("We begin by distinguishing misuse from contributory negligence and assumption of the risk, defenses that have been subject to the rules of comparative fault since UCATA's original enactment in 1984.").

64. Ariz. Rev. Stat. § 12-2506(B).

65. *Zuern v. Ford Motor Co.*, 188 Ariz. 486, 492, 937 P.2d 676, 692 (Ct. App. 1996) (affirming trial court's ruling to allow evidence of nonparty's intoxication and criminal conviction).

66. *Scottsdale Ins. Co. v. Cendejas*, 220 Ariz. 281, 286-87, 205 P.3d 1128, 1133-34 (Ct. App. 2009).

67. Ariz. Rev. Stat. § 12-2603. The constitutionality of this statute was reviewed and upheld in *Jilly v. Rayes*, 221 Ariz. 40, 42-43, 209 P.3d 176, 178-79 (2009).

68. *Strawberry Water Co. v. Paulsen*, 220 Ariz. 401, 410, 207 P.3d 654, 663 (Ct. App. 2008).

69. *Premier Manufactured Sys., Inc.*, 217 Ariz. at 229, 172 P.3d at 417 (2007).

70. *Young v. Beck*, 227 Ariz. 1, 5 (Ariz. 2011) (citing *Premier Manufactured Sys.*, 217 Ariz. at 226, 172 P.3d.

71. *Piner v. Superior Ct.*, 192 Ariz. 182, 189, 962 P.2d 909, 916 (1998); *Salica v. Tucson Heart Hosp. – Carondelet, L.L.C.*, 224 Ariz. 414, 418-19, 231 P.3d 946, 950-51 (Ct. App. 2010).

72. *Jimenez*, 183 Ariz. at 404-05, 904 P.2d at 865; *Zuern*, 188 Ariz. at 491, 937 P.2d at 676.

73. Ariz. Rev. Stat. § 12-683(1); *Piper*, 180 Ariz. at 178-79, 883 P.2d at 415-16.

74. Ariz. Rev. Stat. § 12-681(10).

75. *See Golonka*, 204 Ariz. at 593, 65 P.3d at 974.

76. *Gosewisch*, 153 Ariz. 289, 394, 737 P.2d 365, 370 (1985) (vacated in part by 153 Ariz. 400, 737 P.2d 376).

77. Rev. Ariz. J. Inst. 4th Product Liab. 7, at n.1.

78. *Golonka*, 204 Ariz. at 584, 65 P.3d at 965.

79. Ariz. Rev. Stat. § 12-683(2); *Anderson v. Nissei ASB Mach. Co.*, 197 Ariz. 168, 173-74, 3 P.3d 1088, 1093-94 (Ct. App. 1999); *Piper*, 180 Ariz. at 175-76, 883 P.2d at 412-13.

80. Ariz. Rev. Stat. § 12-683(3); *Jimenez*, 183 Ariz. at 403, 904 P.2d at 865.

81. Ariz. Rev. Stat. § 12-683(3); *Jimenez*, 183 Ariz. at 403, 904 P.2d at 865.

82. *Jimenez*, 183 Ariz. at 402, 904 P.2d at 864 (citing *O.S. Stapley Co.*, 103 Ariz. at 561, 447 P.2d at 253).

83. *Jimenez*, 183 Ariz. at 402, 904 P.2d at 864.

84. *Phelps v. Firebird Raceway, Inc.*, 210 Ariz. 403, 410, 111 P.3d 1003, 1010 (2005).

85. *Law v. Superior Ct.*, 157 Ariz. 147, 157, 755 P.2d 1135, 1145 (1988); *see also Warfel v. Cheney*, 157 Ariz. 424, 427-30, 758 P.2d 1326, 1329-32 (Ct. App. 1988) (evidence of motorcycle helmet non-use may be admissible to show that a plaintiff could have reduced injuries, and is case-specific determination).

86. *Law*, 157 Ariz. at 157, 755 P.2d at 1145.

87. *See Gaston*, 121 Ariz. at 46-47, 588 P.2d at 339-40.

88. *Gaston*, 121 Ariz. at 46-47, 588 P.2d at 339-40.

89. *Dole Food Co. v. North Carolina Foam Indus.*, 188 Ariz. 298, 302-05, 935 P.2d 876, 880-83 (Ct. App. 1996).

90. *Dole Food Co.*, 188 Ariz. at 302-05, 935 P.2d at 880-83.

91. *Piper*, 180 Ariz. at 178 n.3, 883 P.2d at 415 n.3.

92. *Gaston*, 121 Ariz. at 47, 588 P.2d at 340; *Dyer v. Best Pharmacal*, 118 Ariz. 465, 468, 577 P.2d 1084, 1088 (Ct. App. 1978).

93. *Dole Food Co.*, 188 Ariz. at 301 n.7, 935 P.2d at 881 n.7.

94. Ariz. Rev. Stat. § 12-711.

95. *Romero v. Southwest Ambulance*, 211 Ariz. 200, 205, 119 P.3d 467, 472 (Ct. App. 2005) (*corrected for case citation by* 2005 Ariz. App. LEXIS 120 (Ct. App. Sept. 12, 2005).

96. Ariz. Rev. Stat. § 12-712(A).

97. Ariz. Rev. Stat. § 12-712(B).

98. Ariz. Rev. Stat. § 47-2316; *Nomo Agroindustrial SA DE CV v. Enza Zaden N. Am., Inc.*, 492 F. Supp. 2d 1175, 1181 (D. Ariz. 2007).

99. Ariz. Rev. Stat. § 47- 2316; *Nomo Agroindustrial*, 492 F. Supp. 2d at 1181.

100. Ariz. Rev. Stat. § 47-2719.

101. *Salt River Project*, 143 Ariz. at 382, 694 P.2d at 212.

102. *Lips v. Scottsdale Healthcare Corp.*, 224 Ariz. 266, 229 P.3d 1008 (2010) (affirming no recognition of independent tort of first-party spoliation or negligent third-party spoliation). The Arizona Supreme Court has hinted that it may recognize a tort of intentional third-party spoliation, if presented on applicable facts. *Id.* at 269, 229 P.3d at 1011.

103. *Strawberry Water Co.*, 220 Ariz. 401, 411, 207 P.3d 654, 664; *Smyser v. City of Peoria*, 215 Ariz. 428, 438-40, 160 P.3d 1186, 1196-98 (Ct. App. 2007).

104. Ariz. Rev. Stat. § 12-683(1); *Piper*, 180 Ariz. at 178-79, 883 P.2d at 415-16.

105. *Piper*, 180 Ariz. at 178-79, 883 P.2d at 415-16.

106. *Burgbacher v. Mellor*, 112 Ariz. 481, 483, 543 P.2d 1110, 1112 (1975).

107. *Slow Dev. Co. v. Coulter*, 88 Ariz. 122, 125, 353 P.2d 890 (1960) (witness's fall in same location occurred under substantially similar conditions to plaintiff's accident); *Johnson v. Tucson Estates, Inc.*, 140 Ariz. 531, 533, 683 P.2d 330 (Ct. App. 1984) (two falls in same location occurred under almost identical conditions to plaintiff's accident).

108. Ariz. Rev. Stat. § 12-686; *Readenour*, 149 Ariz. at 444-45, 719 P.2d at 1060-61.

109. Ariz. R. Evid. 407; *Johnson v. State*, 224 Ariz. 554, 559, 233 P.3d 1133, 1138 (2010).

110. Ariz. Rev. Stat. § 12-687.

111. *Baroldy v. Ortho Pharm. Corp.*, 157 Ariz. 574, 585, 760 P.2d 574, 585 (Ct. App. 1988).

112. Ariz. Rev. Stat. § 12-681(6).

113. Ariz. Rev. Stat. § 12-681(6).

114. Ariz. Rev. Stat. §§ 12-2501 through 12-2509.

115. Ariz. Rev. Stat. §§ 12-2501(A)-(C), 12-2506(E).

116. *Bishop v. Pecanic*, 193 Ariz. 524, 525, 975 P.2d 114, 115 (Ct. App. 1998).

117. Ariz. Rev. Stat. § 12-684.

118. Ariz. Rev. Stat. § 12-681(9) (defining "seller" as a person or entity, including a wholesaler, distributor, retailer, or lessor, engaged in the business of leasing any product or selling any product for resale, use, or consumption).

119. *Desert Golf Cars v. Yamaha Motor Co.*, 198 Ariz. 103, 106, 7 P.3d 112, 115 (Ct. App. 2000).

120. *See Bridgestone/Firestone N. Am. Tire, L.L.C. v. A.P.S. Rent-A-Car & Leasing, Inc.*, 207 Ariz. 502, 510-11, 88 P.3d 572, 580-81 (Ct. App. 2004).

121. Ariz. Rev. Stat. § 12-684(A).

122. *See* Ariz. Rev. Stat. § 12-684(A); *see also McIntyre Refrigeration, Inc. v. Mepco Electra*, 165 Ariz. 560, 563, 799 P.2d 901, 904 (Ct. App. 1990) (citing *Hellebrandt v. Kelley Co. Inc.*, 153 Ariz. 429, 430, 737 P.2d 405, 406 (Ct. App. 1987)).

123. *Bridgestone/Firestone*, 207 Ariz. at 512, 88 P.3d at 582.

124. Ariz. Rev. Stat. § 12-684(A)(1) and (2).

125. *Bridgestone/Firestone*, 207 Ariz. at 515-16, 88 P.3d at 585-86.

126. *Bridgestone/Firestone*, 207 Ariz. at 509, 88 P.3d at 579.

127. A manufacturer that received a tender of defense from a seller but did not respond was later held in the seller's indemnity action to be 30% responsible for the judgment. *Bridgestone/Firestone*, 207 Ariz. at 510-11, 88 P.3d at 580-81.

128. Ariz. Rev. Stat. § 12-684(C).

129. Ariz. Rev. Stat. § 12-684(C).

130. Ariz. Rev. Stat. § 23-906(A).

131. Ariz. Rev. Stat. § 23-1022(A).

132. Ariz. Rev. Stat. § 23-906(B), (C).

133. Ariz. Rev. Stat. § 23-1023.

134. Ariz. Rev. Stat. § 23-1023(B); *Stephens v. Textron, Inc.*, 127 Ariz. 227, 230, 619 P.2d 736, 739 (1980).

135. Ariz. Rev. Stat. § 23-1023(C).

136. *Dietz v. General Elec. Co.*, 169 Ariz. 505, 511, 821 P.2d 166, 172 (1991).

137. *Wiseman v. DynAir Tech of Ariz., Inc.*, 192 Ariz. 413, 415, 966 P.2d 1017, 1019 (Ct. App. 1998).

138. *Wiseman*, 192 Ariz. at 415, 966 P.2d at 1019.

139. *Unique Equip. Co. v. TRW Vehicle Safety Sys., Inc.*, 197 Ariz. 50, 55, 3 P.3d 970, 975 (Ct. App. 1999).

140. *Unique Equip.*, 197 Ariz. at 56, 3 P.3d at 976.

141. Ariz. Rev. Stat. § 14-3110.

142. *Girouard v. Skyline Steel, Inc.*, 215 Ariz. 126, 131-32, 158 P.3d 255, 260-61 (Ct. App. 2007).

143. *Girouard*, 215 Ariz. at 131-32, 158 P.3d at 260-61.

144. Ariz. Rev. Stat. § 12-612; *see also Solomon v. Harman*, 107 Ariz. 426, 429-30, 489 P.2d 236, 239-40 (1971).

145. Ariz. Rev. Stat. §§ 12-612(B) and 12-641.

146. Ariz. Rev. Stat. § 12-612(C).

147. *Hurt v. Superior Ct.*, 124 Ariz. 45, 48, 601 P.2d 1329, 1332 (1979) (*en banc*).

148. *Sandretto v. Payson Healthcare Mgmt., Inc.*, 234 Ariz. 351, 322 P.3d 168 (Ct. App. 2014).

Endnotes - Arizona

149. Ariz. R. Civ. P. 5(f)(1).

150. Ariz. R. Civ. P. 5(f)(2).

151. Ariz. R. Civ. P. 5(f)(3).

152. Ariz. R. Civ. P. 45.1(b)(1).

153. Ariz. R. Civ. P. 45.1(b)(1).

154. Ariz. R. Civ. P. 45.1(b)(2).

155. Ariz. R. Civ. P. 45.1(b)(3)(A)-(F).

156. *See generally Rawlings v. Apodaca*, 151 Ariz. 149, 162, 726 P.2d 565, 578 (1986) (quoting W. Prosser & W. Keeton, *Law of Torts* § 2, at 9-10 (5th ed. 1984)).

157. *Volz v. Coleman Co., Inc.*, 155 Ariz. 567, 570-71, 748 P.2d 1191, 1194-95 (1987); *Smith v. Chapman*, 115 Ariz. 211, 215, 564 P.2d 900, 904 (1977).

158. *Thompson v. Better-Bilt Aluminum Prods. Co., Inc.*, 171 Ariz. 550, 557, 832 P.2d 203, 210 (1992); *Rawlings*, 151 Ariz. at 162, 726 P.2d at 578.

159. *Richards v. Powercraft Homes, Inc.*, 139 Ariz. 264, 266, 678 P.2d 449, 451 (Ct. App. 1983), *vacated on other grounds*, 139 Ariz. 242, 678 P.2d 427 (1984).

160. *See generally Exxon Shipping Co. v. Baker*, 554 U.S. 471, 128 S. Ct. 2605 (2008); *Philip Morris USA v. Williams*, 549 U.S. 346, 127 S. Ct. 1057 (2007); *State Farm Mut. Auto. Ins. Co. v. Campbell*, 538 U.S. 408, 123 S. Ct. 1513 (2003); *Cooper Indus., Inc. v. Leatherman Tool Group, Inc.*, 532 U.S. 424, 121 S. Ct. 1678 (2001).

161. Ariz. Rev. Stat. § 12-701(A).

162. *Kobar v. Novartis Corp.*, 378 F. Supp. 2d 1166 (D. Ariz. 2005).

163. Ariz. Const. Art. II, § 35 (2011).

164. *Barnes v. Outlaw*, 192 Ariz. 283, 285-86, 962 P.2d 484, 486-87 (1998) (finding physical injury not required to maintain claim for loss of spousal consortium).

165. *See* Ariz. Rev. Stat. § 1-215(3) (defining "adult" as a person who has attained the age of 18 years).

166. *Howard Frank, M.D., P.C. v. Superior Ct.*, 150 Ariz. 228, 231-34, 722 P.2d 955, 958-61 (1986) (en banc).

167. *Pierce v. Casas Adobes Baptist Church*, 162 Ariz. 269, 272, 782 P.2d 1162, 1165 (1989).

168. *Pierce*, 162 Ariz. at 272, 782 P.2d at 1165.

169. *Villareal v. State, Dept. of Transp.*, 160 Ariz. 474, 480, 774 P.2d 213, 219 (1989).

170. *Nunsuch v. United States*, 221 F. Supp. 2d 1027, 1035 (D. Ariz. 2001) (citing *Allen v. Devereaux*, 5 Ariz. App. 323, 326, 426 P.2d 659, 662 (1967)).

171. *Nunsuch*, 221 F. Supp. 2d at 1035 (quoting *Olsen v. Mading*, 45 Ariz. 423, 432, 45 P.2d 23, 26 (1935)).

172. *Nunsuch*, 221 F. Supp. 2d at 1035 (citing *Ogden v. J.M Steel Erecting, Inc.*, 201 Ariz. 32, 31 P.3d 806 (Ct. App. 2001)).

173. *Nunsuch*, 221 F. Supp. 2d at 1035 (citing *Ogden*, 201 Ariz. at 31 P.3d 806).

174. *Monaco v. Healthpartners of S. Arizona*, 196 Ariz. 299, 303, 995 P.2d 735, 739 (Ct. App. 1999) (emotional distress damages supported by evidence of long-term emotional disturbances); *Gau v. Smitty's Super Valu*, 183 Ariz. 107, 109, 901 P.2d 455, 457 (Ct. App. 1995) (disallowing emotional distress damages for "[t]ransitory physical phenomena such as weeping and insomnia" where symptoms cleared in a matter of months and without medical treatment).

175. *Carstens v. City of Phoenix*, 206 Ariz. 123, 75 P.3d 1081, 1083-84 (Ct. App. 2003) *overruled on other grounds by Flagstaff Affordable Hous. Ltd. P'ship v. Design Alliance, Inc.*, 223 Ariz. 320, 223 P.3d 664 (2010); *see also Salt River Project*, 143 Ariz. at 379, 694 P.2d at 209 ("where economic loss . . . is the plaintiff's only loss, the policies of the law will generally be best served by leaving the parties to their commercial remedies.").

176. *Cook v. Orkin Exterminating Co.*, 227 Ariz. 331, 335, 258 P.3d 149, 153 (Ct. App. 2011).

177. *Cook*, 227 Ariz. at 335, 258 P.3d at 153.

178. *Canal Ins. Co. v. Pizer*, 183 Ariz. 162, 164, 901 P.2d 1192, 1194 (Ct. App. 1995).

179. Ariz. Rev. Stat. § 12-347; *Pizer*, 183 Ariz. at 164, 901 P.2d at 1194.

180. *Fleming v. Pima County*, 141 Ariz. 149, 155, 685 P.2d 1301, 1307 (1984) ("A good faith dispute over liability will not defeat a recovery of pre-judgment interest on a liquidated claim.").

181. *Arizona Title Ins. & Trust Co. v. O'Malley Lumber Co.*, 14 Ariz. App. 486, 496, 484 P.2d 639, 649 (1971); *see also Paul R. Peterson Constr., Inc. v. Arizona State Carpenters Health & Welfare Trust Fund*, 179 Ariz. 474, 485, 880 P.2d 694, 705 (Ct. App. 1994) ("The fact that the amount of damages claimed differs from the amount ultimately awarded does not preclude an award of pre-judgment interest.").

182. Ariz. Rev. Stat. § 12-347.

183. Ariz. Rev. Stat. § 44-1201.

184. *Brewer v. Gerson*, 190 Ariz. 164, 165, 945 P.2d 1295, 1296 (1997).

ARKANSAS

A. CAUSES OF ACTION

A "product liability action" includes all actions brought for or on account of personal injury, death, or property damage caused by or resulting from the manufacture, construction, design, formula, preparation, assembly, testing, service, warning, instruction, marketing, packaging, or labeling of any product.[1]

B. STATUTES OF LIMITATION

All product liability actions must be commenced within three years after the date the death, injury, or damage occurred.[2] Accrual is established by reference to a claimant's awareness of injury and the probable causal connection between the injury and the product's use—in essence, the time when an individual would have sufficient knowledge and understanding of an injury to initiate a lawsuit.[3] The Arkansas Supreme Court has adopted the "discovery rule" in product liability actions, holding that the statute of limitations does not commence until the plaintiff knew or, by the exercise of reasonable diligence, should have discovered the causal connection between the product and the injuries suffered.[4] The trier of fact resolves any issues as to when the discovery of the causal connection should have occurred.[5] It is not necessary for the full extent of the injury to be manifested for the period to start running.[6] The general limitations period found in Arkansas's version of the UCC states that breach of warranty claims must be brought within four years from the date of sale and delivery unless a warranty explicitly extends to future performance of the goods, in which case discovery of the breach must await the time of such performance and the cause accrues when the breach is or should have been discovered.[7] However, the Eighth Circuit affirmed the holding of a district court sitting in Arkansas that breach-of-warranty actions seeking damages for personal injury are product liability actions under Arkansas law and that, consequently, the three-year statute of limitations found in the Product Liability Act governs a breach-of-warranty suit when damages for personal injury are sought.[8] In product liability actions against a hospital for use of a defective product, the medical malpractice statute of limitations of two years, rather than the three-year product liability statute, controls.[9] There is no discovery rule in such cases.[10] An action timely filed and later nonsuited may be refiled within one year even though otherwise barred by the statute of limitations.[11]

C. STRICT LIABILITY

1. The Standard

Arkansas's consumer protection statute contains the following provision:

Arkansas

(a) A supplier of a product is subject to liability in damages for harm to a person or to property if:

(1) the supplier is engaged in the business of manufacturing, assembling, selling, leasing, or otherwise distributing the product;

(2) the product was supplied by him in a defective condition which rendered it unreasonably dangerous; and

(3) the defective condition was a proximate cause of the harm to person or to property.

(b) The provisions of subsection (a) of this section apply although the claiming party has not obtained the product from or entered into any contractual relation with the supplier.

(1) Any licensee under Section 17-42-103(10) who is only providing brokerage and sales services under his or her license shall not be considered a supplier under this section.

(A) Except as provided in subdivisions (c)(2)(B) and (C) of this section, real estate and improvements located on real estate shall not be considered a product under this section.

(B) Any tangible object or good produced that is affixed to, installed on or incorporated into real estate or any improvement on real estate shall be considered a product under this section.

(C) If environmental contaminants exist or have occurred in an improvement on real estate, the improvement on real estate shall be considered a product under this section.[12]

The Arkansas Product Liability Act defines these terms.[13]

2. **Definition of "Defect"**

"Defective condition" is defined as a condition that renders a product unsafe for reasonably foreseeable use and consumption.[14] Proof of a specific defect is not required when common experience teaches that the accident or damage would not have occurred in the absence of a defect.[15]

The Arkansas courts use a subjective consumer expectations test to determine whether a product is reasonably safe.[16]

3. **Causation**

Proximate cause is defined as that which in a natural and continuous sequence, unbroken by any efficient intervening cause, produces the injury, and without which the result would not have occurred.[17] Proximate cause is usually a question for the jury, but it becomes a question of law if reasonable minds could not differ.[18] Proximate cause may be established by circumstantial or direct evidence if the proven facts are of such a nature and are sufficiently connected and related to each other that the conclusion can be inferred.[19] The evidence must tend to eliminate other causes that may fairly arise from the evidence, and the jury must use more than speculation and conjecture in deciding between two equally probable possibilities.[20] The actual discharge of a firearm or ammunition is deemed to be the proximate cause of injury, damage, or death in product liability actions.[21] Therefore, the "mere placement" of firearms or ammunition into the stream of commerce by manufacturers, distributors, or importers does not constitute proximate cause.[22] However, proof that a firearm or ammunition is defective or was defectively designed may constitute proximate cause.[23]

4. **Contributory Negligence/Assumption of Risk**

Arkansas has adopted comparative fault by statute.[24] "Fault" is defined to include any act, omission, conduct, risk assumed, breach of warranty, or breach of any legal duty that is a proximate cause of any damage sustained by a party.[25] Thus, a plaintiff's negligence that was a proximate cause of his own injury may be compared with a defendant's fault in supplying an unreasonably dangerous product.[26] The fault of a claiming party does not bar recovery unless it equals or exceeds in degree any fault on the part of a party or parties from whom a recovery is sought. On the other hand, if the fault of a claiming party is of less degree, his damages are reduced in proportion to the degree of his own fault.[27] In cases in which there are multiple defendants, a plaintiff can recover if his relative fault is less than the combined fault of all defendants.[28] A plaintiff may recover from an individual defendant in a multiple defendant case even though the negligence of the individual defendant is less than that of the plaintiff.[29] The fault of the plaintiff is compared with the fault of only the party or parties from whom he seeks to recover, that is, the fault of a third party defendant should not be combined with the fault of the defendant(s) in the absence of an amended complaint by the plaintiff seeking recovery from the third party defendant.[30] Comparative fault is used even in so-called enhanced injury cases.[31] The doctrine of assumption of the risk is no longer applicable in Arkansas as a separate theory.[32] Failure to wear a seat belt is admissible in a civil action to show causation if the claim is timely asserted and is not based on an alleged failure of a seat belt.[33]

5. **Sale or Lease/Persons Liable**

"Supplier" means any individual or entity engaged in the business of selling a product, whether the sale is for resale, or for use or consumption. "Supplier" includes a retailer, wholesaler, or distributor, and it also includes a lessor or bailor engaged in the business of leasing or bailment of a product.[34] Strict liability applies to property damage in a house sold by a builder-vendor,[35] but a street designed and built by a residential developer is not a product within the meaning of the statute.[36] The provision of personal services does not constitute the sale of a product under the statute.[37] A commercial lease of an industrial building is not a product under the Arkansas strict liability statute.[38] A supplier of a defectively manufactured product has a cause of action for indemnity from the manufacturer.[39]

6. **Inherently Dangerous Products**

Comment k to Section 402A of the Restatement (Second) of Torts (unavoidably unsafe products) has been adopted as an affirmative defense in certain prescription pharmaceutical cases when a design defect is alleged. There must be no feasible alternative design that accomplishes the product's purposes at lesser risk, and the product must be used under the direction of a prescribing physician with adequate warning of the potential dangers inherent in its intended or foreseeable uses.[40]

7. **Successor Liability**

A corporation that purchases the assets of another corporation does not succeed to the liability of the selling corporation except (1) where the transferee assumes the debts of the transferor by express or implied agreement; (2) where there is a consolidation or merger of the two corporations; (3) where the transaction is fraudulent or lacking in good faith; and (4) where the purchasing corporation is a mere continuation of the selling corporation.[41] Arkansas courts have not yet had occasion to consider adoption of the more liberal "product line" exception.[42]

8. **Market Share Liability/Enterprise Liability**

The Arkansas courts have not adopted the concepts of market share or enterprise liability.[43] Instead, in all cases the plaintiff must show that the defendant's conduct constituted a substantial contributing factor in causing the plaintiff's injuries.[44] Similarly, a plaintiff must demonstrate that the actual product manufactured or distributed by the defendant caused injury to the plaintiff.[45] This concept has been applied to determine that a manufacturer of a brand name prescription drug may not be held liable for injuries arising from the use of another manufacturer's generic equivalent of the drug.[46]

In a somewhat related issue, it appears that the Arkansas Supreme Court has favorably discussed, if not adopted, the component-parts doctrine, which provides that the suppliers of inherently safe component parts are not responsible for accidents that result when the parts are integrated into a larger system that the component-part supplier did not design or build. If the component-parts manufacturer does not participate in the integration of the component into the finished product, it is not liable for defects in the final product if the component itself is not defective.[47]

9. **Privity**

   Strict liability applies although the claiming party has not obtained the product from or entered into any contractual relation with the supplier.[48]

10. **Failure to Warn**

    A failure to warn or the giving of an inadequate warning may be relevant to an action based on strict liability, negligence, or breach of warranty.[49] There is no duty, however, to warn a user of obvious dangers or those known to him or those that he should reasonably discover for himself.[50] Once a plaintiff proves the lack of an adequate warning or instruction, a presumption arises that the user would have read and heeded adequate warnings or instructions. This presumption may be rebutted by evidence that persuades the trier of fact that an adequate warning or instruction would have been futile under the circumstances.[51] The alleged defect, whether resulting from a failure to warn or otherwise, must constitute a proximate cause of the injury.[52]

11. **Post-Sale Duty to Warn and Remedial Measures**

    Arkansas appellate courts have had no occasion to decide whether there are any circumstances when a manufacturer has a duty to warn of a danger in the use of a product learned subsequent to its sale.[53]

12. **Learned Intermediary Doctrine**

    Arkansas has addressed and adopted the learned intermediary doctrine pursuant to which a drug manufacturer may rely on the physician to warn the patient of the risks of a prescription drug.[54] The Arkansas Supreme Court has extended this doctrine to pharmacists.[55] Generally pharmacies have no common-law or statutory duty to warn customers of the risks associated with the prescription drugs they purchase, and the learned intermediary doctrine precludes holding pharmacists or pharmacies strictly liable for failing to warn consumers who purchase prescription drugs. The duty to warn, instead, belongs to the consumer's physician.[56]

13. **Design Defects**

    Arkansas law makes clear that a defective design can be established without proof of a safer alternative design.[57] Under Arkansas law, the existence, practicality, and technological feasibility of an alternative safe design are not necessary elements of the plaintiff's cause of action, but rather are merely factors that may be considered by the jury in determining whether a product was supplied in a defective condition that rendered it unreasonably dangerous.[58] In applying Arkansas law, the Eighth Circuit has recognized that when a plaintiff's sole proof of a defective design is the designer's choice not to pursue a safer design, the evidentiary burden is on the plaintiff to show that the safer alternative design he advocates actually exists.[59] It is unclear whether

Arkansas has a cause of action for design defect cases involving generic prescription drugs.[60]

14. **Substantial Alteration/Abnormal Use**

    The fact that a product was made unreasonably dangerous by subsequent unforeseeable alteration, change, improper maintenance, or abnormal use may be considered as evidence of fault on the part of the user.[61] The supplying of a product by a distributor after the anticipated expiration of life date placed on the product as required by law is a defense to a claim brought by the distributor against the manufacturer. Use of a product beyond its anticipated life by a consumer who knows or should have known the anticipated life of the product is evidence of fault on the part of the consumer.[62]

15. **State of the Art**

    Compliance by a manufacturer or supplier with any federal or state statute or administrative regulation, existing at the time a product was manufactured and prescribing standards of design, inspection, testing, manufacturing, labeling, warning, or instructions for use of a product, is evidence that the product was not in an unreasonably dangerous condition in regard to the matters covered by the standards.[63] On the other hand, a reasonable jury can conclude that a machine was negligently designed despite evidence that the machine complied with applicable industry standards in place at the time of manufacture and that the machine was as safe as other similar machines manufactured at the same time.[64] Compliance with industry customs is not a defense to a negligence action.[65]

    In some situations, the existing statutory and regulatory framework can preempt any common-law tort claims. In 2007, the Arkansas Supreme Court held that the statutory and regulatory framework governing the specifications for school bus design in Arkansas preempted any common-law tort claims against school bus manufacturers that have complied with the Department of Education's design specifications, which the Arkansas General Assembly has stated must be a part of every school bus contract in Arkansas.[66]

16. **Malfunction**

    A defect may be inferred by the fact finder if the injury or damage would not have occurred in the absence of some defect.[67] Proof of existence of a defect may be by circumstantial evidence.[68] However, if direct proof is lacking, a plaintiff must negate other possible causes of the accident by a preponderance of the probabilities.[69]

17. **Standards and Governmental Regulation**

    See Section 15, State of the Art, *supra*.[70]

18. **Other Accidents**

    Evidence of other accidents involving the same product may be admissible to demonstrate existence of a defect, notice to the defendant, or causation, but to be probative and admissible, the accidents must be sufficiently similar in time, place, or circumstances.[71]

19. **Misrepresentation**

    Arkansas has not adopted Restatement (Second) of Torts Section 402B, but it recognizes claims for damages based on deceit.[72]

20. **Destruction or Loss of Product**

    Arkansas has endorsed the minority rule allowing recovery in instances in which the only damages are for economic loss or to the product itself.[73]

21. **Economic Loss**

    See Section 20, Destruction or Loss of Product, *supra*.

22. **Crashworthiness**

    The Eighth Circuit, applying Arkansas law in a product liability case, discussed the "crashworthiness theory," or the duty of vehicle manufacturers to design their vehicles to be "crashworthy," which means that they must be capable of preventing "enhanced injuries" resulting from an accident.[74] The lower court in that case, a district court in Arkansas, determined that the Arkansas Supreme Court would likely adopt the reasoning that, in a strict liability crashworthiness case, evidence of seat-belt non-use is admissible. The Eighth Circuit did not reach the issue because it determined that the plaintiff had failed to prove that she was prejudiced by the admission of the seat-belt evidence.[75] The Arkansas Court of Appeals has stated that evidence of comparative fault is admissible in enhanced injury cases.[76]

D. NEGLIGENCE

A prima facie case of negligence requires the plaintiff to prove that he or she sustained damages, that the defendant was negligent, and that such negligence was a proximate cause of the damages.[77] To constitute negligence, an act must be one from which a reasonably careful person would foresee such an appreciable risk of harm to herself or others as to cause her not to do the act or to do it in a more careful manner.[78] To constitute actionable negligence, it is not necessary that the actor foresee the particular injury that occurred, but only an appreciable risk of harm.[79]

E. BREACH OF WARRANTY

A breach of warranty action does not arise unless there is an actual sale or a transaction analogous to a sale, such as a lease.[80] Lack of privity is not a defense as long as the injured party was a person whom the manufacturer or seller might reasonably have expected to use, consume, or be affected by the goods.[81] Reasonable notice of the breach given to the seller must be alleged and proved.[82] To some degree, the strict liability statute has rendered the personal injury action in warranty obsolete. The required proof of defectiveness and the defenses are identical.[83]

F. PUNITIVE DAMAGES

Punitive damages are recoverable in product liability actions.[84] Punitive damages are not recoverable unless compensatory damages are also awarded.[85] When punitive damages are claimed against more than one defendant, the right to introduce evidence of the financial condition of any of the defendants is waived.[86]

The Arkansas legislature put limitations on the recovery of punitive damages for all causes of action accruing on or after March 25, 2003, in any action for injury, damage, or death.[87] In 2011, however, the Arkansas Supreme Court ruled the measure unconstitutional.[88] The Court held that the limitation on punitive damages was only permissible in matters arising between employer and employee.[89]

G. PRE- AND POST-JUDGMENT INTEREST

Pre-judgment interest is awarded as a matter of law when there is a method of determining the value of the property at the time of the injury.[90]

Post-judgment interest is awarded by statute.[91] Interest on any judgment entered on a contract bears interest at the greater of the rate provided in the contract or 10 percent per year; all other judgments unless specifically excluded bear interest at 10 percent per year.[92] The amount of interest awarded on all judgments is limited by the maximum rate of interest permitted by the Arkansas Constitution, Article 19, Section 13.[93] The trial court has no discretion to lower the rate of interest.[94] Judgments rendered against counties in the state on county warrants or other indebtedness are excluded from bearing post-judgment interest.[95]

H. EMPLOYER IMMUNITY FROM SUIT

Under the exclusive remedy provisions in the Arkansas Workers' Compensation Act, a contributorily negligent employer cannot be held liable for contribution by a third-party joint tortfeasor.[96] However, an employer can be held liable to a third party joint tortfeasor under an indemnity contract.[97] An employer may also be liable to a third party joint tortfeasor for implied indemnity based on a special relationship between the employer and the third party arising by operation of law.[98]

I. STATUTES

Arkansas has adopted a product liability act.[99] The age of majority in Arkansas is 18.[100]

J. JOINT AND SEVERAL LIABILITY

For causes of action accruing prior to March 25, 2003, Arkansas does not require that joint tortfeasors act in concert to result in joint and several liability.[101] When there is a single injury, it is irrelevant that the acts of the individual defendants would not have caused the ultimate result.[102] In other words, "when concurrent negligent acts result in a single injury, each tortfeasor is jointly and severally liable."[103] Joint and several liability may also be found if the tortfeasors are liable on different theories of recovery, *i.e.*, joint and several liability may be found if one defendant has committed negligent acts and another defendant has committed intentional acts.[104] In addition, joint tortfeasors may be jointly and severally liable for punitive damages.[105]

For all causes of action accruing on or after March 25, 2003, the liability of each defendant for either compensatory or punitive damages is several only and not joint.[106] Each defendant is generally liable only for the amount of damages allocated to that defendant based on that defendant's percentage of fault.[107] The maximum amount of damages recoverable against a defendant usually is the total amount of damages recoverable multiplied by the percentage of the particular defendant's fault.[108] Upon a determination by the court that a several judgment against one or more defendants is not reasonably collectible, the court may increase the percentages of the several shares of the remaining defendants.[109] This provision does not apply to an award of punitive damages.[110] A defendant may be held responsible for the fault of another if the defendant was acting in concert with another person or entity, or if the other person or entity acted as an agent or servant of the defendant.[111] Acting in concert means acting pursuant to a conscious agreement in order to commit an intentional tort, based on a common plan or design to commit the intentional tort, and actively taking part in the commission of the intentional tort.[112] Acting in concert does not include negligent conduct.[113]

Arkansas has adopted the 1939 version of the Uniform Contribution Among Tortfeasors Act (UCATA).[114] This Act is applicable only to persons liable for torts.[115] The act provides that a right of contribution exists among "joint tortfeasors," which are defined as "two (2) or more entities who may have joint or several liability in tort for the same injury to person or property, whether or not judgment has been recovered against all or some of them."[116] As the right of contribution includes money damages, a tortfeasor is also provided an allocation of fault among all joint tortfeasors.[117] However, a joint tortfeasor cannot recover contribution from another tortfeasor unless he has by payment discharged the common liability or has paid more than his pro rata share of the common liability.[118] Furthermore, a joint tortfeasor who settles his claim with the injured person cannot seek contribution from a joint tortfeasor whose liability was not extinguished by the settlement.[119] A release obtained by one tortfeasor from the injured party does not discharge any other tortfeasors unless specifically stated in the release.[120] Similarly, a joint tortfeasor is not relieved from liability to make contribution to another joint tortfeasor merely because he obtains a release.[121] Such a release reduces the injured party's claim against the other tortfeasors by the amount paid for the release, the pro rata share of the released tortfeasor's responsibility for the injured party's damages, or any amount by which the release provides that the total claim shall be reduced.[122]

Kathryn Bennett Perkins
Rose Law Firm
120 East Fourth Street
Little Rock, Arkansas 72201-2893
(501) 375-9131
(Fax) (501) 375-1309
E-mail: kperkins@roselawfirm.com

ENDNOTES - ARKANSAS

1. Ark. Code Ann. § 16-116-102(5).

2. Ark. Code Ann. § 16-116-103.

3. *Uhiren v. Bristol-Myers Squibb Co.*, 346 F.3d 824 (8th Cir. 2003) (applying Arkansas law).

4. *Martin v. Arthur*, 339 Ark. 149, 3 S.W.3d 684 (1999); *Uhiren*, 346 F.3d 824.

5. *Martin*, 339 Ark. 149, 3 S.W.3d 684; *Uhiren*, 346 F.3d 824.

6. *Spickes v. Medtronic, Inc.*, 275 Ark. 421, 631 S.W.2d 5 (1982); *Martin*, 339 Ark. 149, 3 S.W.3d 684.

7. Ark. Code Ann. § 4-2-725.

8. *Follette v. Wal-Mart Stores, Inc.*, 41 F.3d 1234 (8th Cir. 1994), *supp. opinion on reh'g*, 47 F.3d 311 (8th Cir. 1995), *cert. denied*, 516 U.S. 814 (1995).

9. *Wages v. Johnson Reg'l Med. Ctr.*, 916 F. Supp. 2d 900 (W.D. Ark. 2013).

10. *Shepherd v. Baptist Health*, 916 F. Supp. 2d 891 (E.D. Ark. 2012).

11. Ark. Code Ann. § 16-56-126(a)(1); *Bakker v. Ralston*, 326 Ark. 575, 932 S.W.2d 325 (1996).

12. Ark. Code Ann. § 4-86-102.

13. *See* Ark. Code Ann. § 16-116-102.

14. Ark. Code Ann. § 16-116-102(4).

15. *Lakeview Country Club, Inc. v. Super. Prods.*, 325 Ark. 218, 926 S.W.2d 428 (1996); *Ruminer v. Gen. Motors Corp.*, 483 F.3d 561 (8th Cir. 2007).

16. *Mason v. Mitcham*, 2011 Ark. App. 189, 382 S.W.3d 717 (2011).

17. *Anslemo v. Tuck*, 325 Ark. 211, 924 S.W.2d 798 (1996).

18. *Anslemo*, 325 Ark. 211, 924 S.W.2d 798.

19. *Newberg v. Next Level Events Inc.*, 82 Ark. App. 1, 110 S.W.3d 332 (2003).

20. *St. Paul Fire & Marine Co. v. Brady*, 319 Ark. 301, 891 S.W.2d 351 (1995).

21. Ark. Code Ann. § 16-116-201(a).

22. Ark. Code Ann. § 16-116-201(b).

23. Ark. Code Ann. § 16-116-203.

24. Ark. Code Ann. § 16-64-122.

25. Ark. Code Ann. § 16-64-122(c).

26. Ark. Code Ann. § 16-64-122(a); *Skinner v. R.J. Griffin & Co.*, 313 Ark. 430, 855 S.W.2d 913 (1993); *Elk Corp. of Ark. v. Jackson*, 291 Ark. 448, 725 S.W.2d 829 (1987).

27. Ark. Code Ann. § 16-64-122(a)-(b).

28. Ark. Code Ann. § 16-64-122(b)(1).

29. *Hiatt v. Mazda Motor Corp.*, 75 F.3d 1252 (8th Cir. 1996).

30. *Hiatt*, 75 F.3d 1252; *see also E-Ton Dynamics Indus. Corp. v. Hall*, 83 Ark. App. 35, 115 S.W.3d 816 (2003); *Johnson v. Rockwell Automation, Inc.*, 2009 Ark. 241, 308 S.W.3d 135 (2009); *ProAssurance Indem. Co., Inc. v. Metheny*, 2012 Ark. 461, 425 S.W.3d 689 (2012).

31. *Bishop v. Tariq, Inc.*, 2011 Ark. App. 445, 384 S.W.3d 659 (2011).

32. *Ouachita Wilderness Inst. v. Mergen*, 329 Ark. 405, 947 S.W.2d 780 (1997); *Dawson v. Fulton*, 294 Ark. 624, 745 S.W.2d 617 (1988).

33. Ark. Code Ann. § 27-37-703(a)(2) (Supp. 1995).

34. Ark. Code Ann. §§ 16-116-102(6), 4-86-102(a)(1); *Parker v. Seaboard Coastline R.R.*, 573 F.2d 1004 (8th Cir. 1978).

35. *Blagg v. Fred Hunt Co.*, 272 Ark. 185, 612 S.W.2d 321 (1981).

36. *Milam v. Midland Corp.*, 282 Ark. 15, 665 S.W.2d 284 (1984), *overruled on other grounds by Suneson v. Holloway Constr. Co.*, 337 Ark. 571, 992 S.W.2d 79 (1999).

37. *Mason v. Jackson*, 323 Ark. 252, 914 S.W.2d 728 (1996).

38. *McMichael v. United States*, 856 F.2d 1026 (8th Cir. 1988).

39. Ark. Code Ann. § 16-116-107.

40. *West v. Searle & Co.*, 305 Ark. 33, 806 S.W.2d 608 (1991). For further definition of "unavoidably unsafe," *see* Joanne Rhoton Galbreath, *Products Liability: What Is an "Unavoidably Unsafe" Product*, 70 A.L.R. 4th 16 (1989 & Supp. 2009). *See also Hill v. Searle Labs.*, 884 F.2d 1064 (8th Cir. 1989); Ian Birkett, Note, *Arkansas Adopts Comment k as an Affirmative Defense in Prescription Drug Actions*, 14 U. Ark. Little Rock L.J. 199 (1992).

41. *Swayze v. A.O. Smith Corp.*, 694 F. Supp. 619 (E.D. Ark. 1988); *Ford Motor Co. v. Nuckolls*, 320 Ark. 15, 894 S.W.2d 897 (1995); *Granjas Aquanova S.A. de C.V. v. House Mfg. Co., Inc.*, 3:07CV00168 BSM, 2010 WL 2243673 (E.D. Ark. June 4, 2010).

42. *Swayze*, 694 F. Supp. 619.

43. *Jackson v. Anchor Packing Co.*, 994 F.2d 1295 (8th Cir. 1993); *see also Bell v. Pfizer, Inc.*, 716 F.3d 1087 (8th Cir. 2013).

44. *Jackson*, 994 F.2d 1295; *see also Bell*, 716 F.3d 1087.

45. *Fields v. Wyeth, Inc.*, 613 F. Supp. 2d 1056 (W.D. Ark. 2009).

46. *Neal v. Teva Pharms. USA, Inc.*, 2010 WL 2640170 (W.D. Ark. July 1, 2010).

47. *See Davis v. Goodyear Tire & Rubber Co.*, 2010 WL 1710001 (E.D. Ark. Apr. 26, 2010); *Wagner v. General Motors Corp.*, 370 Ark. 268, 258 S.W.3d 749 (2007).

48. Ark. Code Ann. § 4-86-102(b).

49. *Hill*, 884 F.2d 1064.

50. *Hergeth, Inc. v. Green*, 293 Ark. 119, 733 S.W.2d 409 (1987); *see* Arkansas Model Jury Instructions 1002 and 1005.

51. *Bushong v. Garman Co.*, 311 Ark. 228, 843 S.W.2d 807 (1992).

52. *Flippo v. Mode O'Day Frock Shops of Hollywood*, 248 Ark. 1, 449 S.W.2d 692 (1970).

53. *See Campbell v. Davol, Inc.*, 620 F.3d 887 (8th Cir. 2010).

54. *West*, 305 Ark. 33, 806 S.W.2d 608.

55. *Kowlaski v. Rose Drugs of Dardanelle, Inc.*, 2011 Ark. 44, 378 S.W.3d 109 (2011).

56. *Kowlaski*, 2011 Ark. 44, 378 S.W.3d 109.

57. *French v. Grove Mfg. Co.*, 656 F.2d 295 (8th Cir. 1981); *Boerner v. Brown & Williamson Tobacco Corp.*, 260 F.3d 837 (8th Cir. 2001).

58. *French*, 656 F.2d 295; *Boerner*, 260 F.3d 837.

59. *Dancy v. Hyster Co.*, 127 F.3d 649 (8th Cir. 1997); *Boerner*, 260 F.3d 837.

60. *Fullington v. Pfizer, Inc.*, 720 F.3d 739 (8th Cir. 2013).

61. Ark. Code Ann. § 16-116-106.

62. Ark. Code Ann. § 16-116-105(b)-(c).

63. Ark. Code Ann. § 16-116-105(a).

64. *Buchanna v. Diehl Mach., Inc.*, 98 F.3d 366 (8th Cir. 1996).

65. *Forest City Mach. Works v. Aderhold*, 273 Ark. 33, 616 S.W.2d 720 (1981).

66. *Price v. Thomas Built Buses*, 370 Ark. 405, 260 S.W.3d 300 (2007).

67. *Harrell Motors, Inc. v. Flanery*, 272 Ark. 105, 612 S.W.2d 727 (1981); *Ruminer v. Gen. Motors Corp.*, 483 F.3d 561 (8th Cir. 2007).

68. *Petrus Chrysler-Plymouth v. Davis*, 283 Ark. 172, 671 S.W.2d 749 (1984).

69. *Yielding v. Chrysler Motor Co.*, 301 Ark. 271, 783 S.W.2d 353 (1990); *Pilcher v. Suttle Equip. Co.*, 365 Ark. 1, 223 S.W.3d 789 (2006).

70. Ark. Code Ann. § 16-116-105(a).

71. *Thomas v. Chrysler Corp.*, 717 F.2d 1223 (8th Cir. 1983); *Firestone Tire & Rubber Co. v. Little*, 276 Ark. 511, 639 S.W.2d 726 (1982); *Lockley v. Deere & Co.*, 933 F.2d 1378 (8th Cir. 1991).

72. *Lancaster v. Schilling Motors, Inc.*, 299 Ark. 365, 772 S.W.2d 349 (1989).

73. *Farm Bureau Ins. Co. v. Case Corp.*, 317 Ark. 467, 878 S.W.2d 741 (1994); *Alaskan Oil, Inc. v. Central Flying Serv., Inc.*, 975 F.2d 553 (8th Cir. 1992).

74. *Lovett ex rel. Lovett v. Union Pacific R.R. Co.*, 201 F.3d 1074 (8th Cir. 2000).

75. *Lovett ex rel. Lovett*, 201 F.3d 1074.

76. *Bishop v. Tariq, Inc.*, 2011 Ark. App. 445, 384 S.W.3d 659 (2011).

77. *Mason v. Jackson*, 323 Ark. 252, 914 S.W.2d 728 (1996); *Mangrum v. Pigue*, 359 Ark. 373, 198 S.W.3d 496 (2004).

78. Ark. Model Jury Instruction 302.

79. *Coca-Cola Bottling Co. v. Gill*, 352 Ark. 240, 100 S.W.3d 715 (2003).

80. *Sawyer v. Pioneer Leasing Corp.*, 244 Ark. 943, 428 S.W.2d 46 (1968), *amended on reh'g*, 5 UCC Rep. Serv. 841 (Ark. 1968).

81. Ark. Code Ann. § 4-86-101.

82. Ark. Code Ann. § 4-2-607(3)(a); *Adams v. Wacaster Oil Co.*, 81 Ark. App. 150, 98 S.W.3d 832 (2003); *Gatlin v. Cooper Tire & Rubber Co.*, 252 Ark. 839, 481 S.W.2d 338 (1972); *L.A. Green Seed Co. of Ark. v. Williams*, 246 Ark. 463, 438 S.W.2d 717 (1969).

83. Henry Woods, *The Personal Injury Action in Warranty—Has the Arkansas Strict Liability Statute Rendered It Obsolete?*, 28 Ark. L. Rev. 335 (1974).

84. *Forrest City Mach. Works, Inc. v. Aderhold*, 273 Ark. 33, 616 S.W.2d 720 (1981); *Airco, Inc. v. Simmons First Nat'l Bank*, 276 Ark. 486, 638 S.W.2d 660 (1982).

85. *Takeya v. Didion*, 294 Ark. 611, 745 S.W.2d 614 (1988).

86. *Berkeley Pump Co. v. Reed-Joseph Land Co.*, 279 Ark. 384, 653 S.W.2d 128 (1983).

87. Ark. Code Ann. § 16-55-208, *invalidated by Bayer Cropscience LP v. Schafer*, 2011 Ark. 518, 385 S.W.3d 822 (2011).

88. *See Bayer Cropscience LP v. Schafer*, 2011 Ark. 518, 385 S.W.3d 822 (2011).

89. *Bayer Cropscience*, 2011 Ark. 518; 385 S.W.3d 822.

90. *Pro-Comp Mgmt., Inc. v. R.K. Enters.*, 372 Ark. 190, 272 S.W.3d 91 (2008); *Warren v. State Farm Fire & Cas. Co.*, 2007 WL 936354 (E.D. Ark. Mar. 26, 2007); *Mitcham v. First State Bank of Crossett*, 333 Ark. 598, 970 S.W.2d 267 (1998).

91. Ark. Code Ann. § 16-65-114.

92. Ark. Code Ann. § 16-65-114(a).

93. *Hartford Fire Ins. Co. v. Sauer*, 358 Ark. 89, 186 S.W.3d 229 (2004).

94. *Chambers v. Manning*, 315 Ark. 369, 868 S.W.2d 64 (1993).

95. Ark. Code Ann. § 16-65-114(b).

96. *W.M. Bashlin Co. v. Smith*, 277 Ark. 406, 643 S.W.2d 526 (1982); *Robertson v. Norton Co.*, 148 F.3d 905 (8th Cir. 1998).

97. *C. & L. Rural Elec. Co-op. Corp. v. Kincaid*, 221 Ark. 450, 256 S.W.2d 337 (1953). *See also Oaklawn Jockey Club, Inc. v. Pickens-Bond Constr. Co.*, 251 Ark. 1100, 477 S.W.2d 477 (1972).

98. *Smith v. Paragould Light & Water Comm'n*, 303 Ark. 109, 793 S.W.2d 341 (1990).

99. Ark. Code Ann. § 16-116-101 *et seq.*

100. Ark. Code Ann. § 9-25-101 (Repl. 1998).

101. *Boatmen's Nat'l Bank of Ark. v. Cole*, 329 Ark. 209, 947 S.W.2d 362 (1997).

102. *McGraw v. Weeks*, 326 Ark. 285, 930 S.W.2d 365 (1996).

103. *Boatmen's Nat'l Bank*, 329 Ark. 209, 947 S.W.2d 362.

104. *Boatmen's Nat'l Bank*, 329 Ark. 209, 947 S.W.2d 362.

105. *Allred v. Demuth*, 319 Ark. 62, 890 S.W.2d 578 (1994).

106. Ark. Code Ann. § 16-55-201(a).

107. Ark. Code Ann. § 16-55-201(b)(1).

108. Ark. Code Ann. § 16-55-201(c).

109. Ark. Code Ann. § 16-55-203(a)(2).

110. Ark. Code Ann. § 16-55-203(b).

111. Ark. Code Ann. § 16-55-205(a).

112. Ark. Code Ann. § 16-55-205(b)(1).

113. Ark. Code Ann. § 16-55-205(b)(2).

114. Ark. Code Ann. § 16-61-201 *et seq.*

115. *Roberts & Co. v. Sergio*, 22 Ark. App. 58, 733 S.W.2d 420 (1987).

116. Ark. Code Ann. §§ 16-61-201 to -202(a).

117. Ark. Code Ann. § 16-61-202(c).

118. Ark. Code Ann. § 16-61-202(b).

119. Ark. Code Ann. § 16-61-202(d).

120. Ark. Code Ann. § 16-61-204(a).

121. Ark. Code Ann. § 16-61-204(b).

122. Ark. Code Ann. § 16-61-204(c).

CALIFORNIA

A. CAUSES OF ACTION

Product liability lawsuits commonly include causes of action for strict liability, negligence, and breach of warranty.

B. STATUTES OF LIMITATION

1. Personal Injury and Wrongful Death

Two years.[1] Under the discovery rule applicable to the statute of limitations for actions for personal injury, the statute begins to run when a plaintiff has knowledge of injury, and knowledge of facts creating, or which in any reasonable person would create, a suspicion of wrongdoing on the part of someone, even if plaintiff is unable to identify the wrongdoer.[2] A wrongful death action must be commenced within two years of the decedent's death.[3]

2. Property Damage (Real or Personal)

Three years.[4]

3. Breach of Warranty

Four years.[5]

4. Asbestos Exposure

Either within one year after the date of plaintiff's initial disability (or the decedent's death) or within one year after plaintiff knew, or through the exercise of reasonable diligence should have known, that the disability (or death) was caused or contributed to by asbestos exposure, whichever is later.[6]

C. STRICT LIABILITY

1. The Standard

Under California law, "a manufacturer is strictly liable in tort when an article he placed on the market, knowing that it is to be used without inspection for defects, proves to have a defect that causes injury to a human being."[7]

The essential elements for imposing strict liability are that plaintiff was harmed by a product distributed, manufactured, and/or sold by a defendant that contained a manufacturing defect, was defectively designed, and/or did not include sufficient instructions or warning of potential safety hazards,[8] and that the product was used or misused in a reasonably foreseeable manner,[9] regardless of the actual manner in which the accident occurred.[10]

California's standard is less restrictive than the Restatement (Second) of Torts § 402A and those other jurisdictions that have adopted the "unreasonably dangerous standard," which involves a two-pronged test requiring the product to be found both "defective" and "unreasonably dangerous."[11] California requires only that the plaintiff demonstrate that the product was "defective."[12]

2. **Definition of "Defect"**

California allows strict product liability claims based upon defect in manufacture, design, and failure to provide adequate warning.[13]

a. **Defect in Manufacture**

A manufacturing defect exists if the product deviates from the manufacturer's intended result or from other seemingly identical products from the manufacturer's same product line.[14] A manufacturer's failure to comply with its own design specifications can constitute a manufacturing defect.[15]

b. **Defect in Design**

California uses two alternative tests to establish the existence of a design defect. A product is defective in design if (1) it fails to perform as safely as an ordinary consumer would expect when used in an intended or reasonably foreseeable manner, or (2) the risk of danger inherent in the challenged design outweighs the benefits of such design.[16]

The consumer expectation test applies only where the everyday experience of a product's users permits the conclusion that the product's design violated minimum safety assumptions, and not where an expert *must* balance the benefits of design against the risk of danger.[17] A judge makes the determination as to whether the consumer expectation test applies under the facts of the case.[18] In determining whether the product failure is within the common experience of ordinary consumers, the judge considers whether evidence presented by the plaintiff establishes (1) his or her use of the product; (2) the circumstances surrounding the injury; and (3) the objective features of the product *which are relevant to an evaluation of its safety.*[19] The test is that of a hypothetical reasonable consumer, not the expectation of the particular plaintiff in the case.[20] Unless the facts permit an inference that the product did not meet minimum safety expectations, the jury must be instructed solely on the alternative risk-benefit theory of design defect.[21]

Under California's risk-benefit test for design defect, after the plaintiff makes an initial showing that the injury was proximately caused by the product's design, the burden of proof shifts to the manufacturer to prove, in light of relevant factors, that the benefits of the challenged design outweigh the risks of danger inherent in the design.[22] "Relevant factors" may include, but are not limited to, the gravity of the danger posed by the challenged design, the likelihood that such danger would occur, the mechanical feasibility of a safer alternative design, the financial cost of an improved design, and the adverse consequences to the product and to the consumer that would result from an alternative design.[23] Compliance with government specifications is not a factor to be considered in determining that a design was not defective.[24] However, prescription drugs and implanted medical devices have been exempted from strict liability for design defects.[25]

c. **Defect Based Upon "Failure to Warn"**

Inadequate warnings or a failure to warn can constitute a defect in a strict product liability action.[26] Manufacturers and distributors may be subject to strict liability if a reasonably foreseeable use of the product involves a particular risk not readily recognizable to an ordinary consumer, and the manufacturer or distributor fails to adequately warn of the particular risk which was known or knowable given the accepted scientific knowledge at the time of distribution.[27] However, the duty to warn does not extend to products manufactured or distributed by others.[28] There is no duty to warn of an obvious or known danger.[29]

The requisite warnings can either instruct the consumer how to use the product, or inform the consumer of potential risks that could be associated with foreseeable use of the product.[30]

The "sophisticated user defense" applies to failure to warn causes of action in California. Under this doctrine, a manufacturer is not liable to a sophisticated user of its product for failure to warn of risk, harm, or danger, if the sophisticated user knew or should have known of that risk, harm, or danger.[31] To establish the defense, a defendant must (1) identify the relevant risk, (2) show that sophisticated users are already aware of the risk, and (3) demonstrate that the plaintiff is a member of the group of sophisticated users.[32]

3. **Causation**

Imposition of liability for a defective product requires a showing that defendant's product caused the plaintiff's injuries.[33] A manufacturer is liable if a defect in its product was a legal cause[34] or substantial factor[35] in producing the injury.

4. **Comparative Fault/Assumption of Risk**

California applies comparative fault principles to strict liability and negligence actions, and requires a comparison of fault attributable to the plaintiff's conduct and that attributable to the defendant's product.[36] Plaintiff's recovery is reduced in direct proportion to his or her fault.[37]

Assumption of risk is an affirmative defense, which requires knowledge of the particular risk and appreciation of its magnitude.[38] Primary assumption of the risk, when applicable, involves a determination that in particular situations the defendant did not owe a duty to plaintiff in the context of the activity in which they were engaged, and serves to completely bar a plaintiff's recovery.[39] On the other hand, the doctrine of secondary assumption of the risk is merged with the comparative fault scheme, and involves situations where the trier of fact is permitted to consider the relative fault of all of the parties when apportioning the loss resulting from the injury.[40]

5. **Persons Liable**

Strict product liability extends to those enterprises that place defective products in the stream of commerce, including manufacturers, suppliers, retailers, and distributors.[41] Persons who are in a class that is intended to be protected by the doctrine of strict liability, such as an ultimate consumer, are not liable.[42] Strict liability can also apply to commercial lessors and bailors,[43] as well as to licensors and franchisors.[44] Residential landlords are not strictly liable if they are not involved in the manufacturing or marketing of the defective product that causes injury.[45] Those who sell their services to others in the development of a product, *e.g.*, engineers or designers, but do not participate in bringing a product to market, are not subject to strict products liability. They may still be subject to liability for negligence.[46]

6. **Inherently Unsafe Products**

A manufacturer or seller is not liable for an inherently unsafe product if (1) the product is one that is known to be inherently unsafe by the ordinary consumer; and (2) the product is a common consumer product intended for personal consumption, such as sugar, castor oil, alcohol, and butter.[47]

The California Legislature has removed the statutory bar against tobacco-related tort claims against tobacco manufacturers and their successors-in-interest.[48] However, retailers and distributors of tobacco products are still exempt from such claims.[49]

California also has repealed the special immunity privileges previously granted to gun manufacturers stating that, "The design, distribution, or marketing of firearms and ammunition is not exempt from the duty to use ordinary care and skill that is required by [California law]."[50]

7. **Successor Liability**

A successor corporation does not assume the predecessor's liabilities unless (1) there is an agreement of assumption; (2) there is a consolidation or merger of the two corporations; (3) the successor corporation is a continuation of the predecessor; or (4) the transfer of assets to the successor corporation is fraudulent.[51] A successor corporation can be liable even when it did not continue the predecessor's identical product line.[52] A parent corporation is not liable for damages caused by a product of a wholly owned subsidiary where the parent corporation only acquired stock of the subsidiary, and not assets.[53]

8. **Market Share Liability/Enterprise Liability**

Under the market share doctrine, the burden of proof shifts to the defendant when various defendants produced an identical product and the plaintiff, through no fault of his or her own, is unable to establish the identity of the manufacturer of the defective product.[54] "Enterprise liability," whereby liability for a product of unknown origin is imposed upon a defendant due to defendant's adherence to an industry-wide standard, has been rejected in California.[55]

9. **Privity**

Privity is not required in California product liability actions based on negligence or strict liability.[56] Claims for strict product liability can be brought by heirs of a decedent killed by a defective product[57] and by third parties or mere bystanders who did not purchase or use the defective product.[58] Sophisticated commercial purchasers are precluded from recovery in strict liability.[59] Privity of contract is not required in actions based upon express warranty.[60] Privity remains a requirement in actions involving implied warranties,[61] except where the product is food[62] or a food container,[63] the injured person is a member of the purchaser's family,[64] or the injured person is a worker whose employer was in privity with the manufacturer.[65] In one case, the court found no privity requirement where the product, a gun, was an inherently dangerous instrumentality.[66]

10. **Post-Sale Duty to Warn and Remedial Measures**

California Evidence Code § 1151, which makes evidence of subsequent remedial or precautionary measures inadmissible to prove negligent or culpable conduct, does not apply to strict product liability claims.[67]

11. **Learned Intermediary Doctrine**

There is no duty by a drug manufacturer to ensure that the warning reaches the patient for whom the drug is prescribed; the duty to warn runs to the physician, not to the patient.[68] As with other products, actual or constructive knowledge of potential risks or dangers associated with prescription drugs is required before strict liability for failure to warn is imposed.[69]

12. **Substantial Alteration/Abnormal Use**

The manufacturer of a product is not liable for damages arising from a misuse that is not reasonably foreseeable,[70] or a substantial change[71] to a product after it leaves the manufacturer's possession. California law imposes a duty on the manufacturer to foresee careless behavior by the user of its product.[72] Alteration may constitute an affirmative defense.[73]

13. **State of the Art**

    Evidence of "the state of the art" may be admitted in a failure to warn case to show that the particular risk was neither known nor knowable by the application of scientific knowledge available at the time of manufacture or distribution.[74] Evidence that a product's design was "state of the art" is relevant to the feasibility and cost of alternative designs.[75]

14. **Malfunction**

    A malfunction, along with other circumstantial evidence such as a lack of abnormal use or a reasonable secondary cause, constitutes proof of defect.[76]

15. **Combined Use/Component Parts Doctrine**

    Courts in California have recently begun to assign liabilities in situations where the products of different suppliers are used together and an injury occurs. One line of cases involves the consumer's combined use of finished products of different suppliers where the finished product of one of the suppliers caused injury. A supplier may not be held liable in strict liability (design, manufacturing or warning defect) or negligence for harm caused by another supplier's product unless the supplier's own product contributed substantially to the harm that occurred while the two products were used together (*e.g.*, a valve manufacturer is not liable for the harm caused by asbestos packing materials used around the valve by an injured party's employer).[77] On the other hand, a supplier of a finished product may be liable even though another supplier's product was the actual injury causing instrument where it participated substantially in creating a harmful combined use of the product with other products (*e.g.*, a grinder manufacturer may be liable where the grinder is used as intended with grinding attachments that are ingested by the plaintiff during use).[78]

    The other line of cases involves the liability of a supplier of a component part or raw material that is integrated into a finished product by another manufacturer. A manufacturer is liable for component parts supplied by others that it then integrates into a finished product in the event that any of the component parts prove to be defective.[79] However, the "component parts doctrine" precludes the liability of a supplier of a component part or raw material for injuries caused by the finished product unless the component or raw material is itself contaminated or otherwise defective and causes harm.[80] Further, suppliers of components and raw materials will not be held liable to the ultimate consumers where they sell their product in bulk to a sophisticated buyer who then changes the component or raw material during the manufacturing process, unless the component or raw material supplier plays a significant role in developing or designing the end product.[81] Some "basic raw materials" such as sand, gravel, or kerosene can never be defectively designed.[82] Within this line of cases, there is a recent split of authority regarding liability for injury caused by raw materials used during the manufacturing process: one branch of authority holds that suppliers of certain raw materials will not be held liable to employees of manufacturers who sustain injuries while using the raw materials during their employer's manufacturing of finished products.[83] More recent authority holds that the component parts doctrine does not bar liability against a manufacturer or supplier of materials that cause injury to an employee while the materials are used in the manufacturing process.[84]

The component parts doctrine precludes liability of a component or raw materials supplier for strict liability (design, manufacturing, or warning defect) and negligence.[85]

16. **Standards and Governmental Regulation**

Evidence of industry custom and usage is not permitted to establish that a product is not defective.[86]

Where a field is highly regulated (*e.g.*, warnings in prescription drug cases), and a manufacturer's conduct is mandated by a legislative or regulatory scheme, California courts may be inclined to adopt the statutory or regulatory scheme as the applicable standard of care, and in doing so, the courts acknowledge the superior "procedure and resources" of legislative and administrative entities that make "relevant inquiries" in developing the standards.[87]

The California Supreme Court has held that design defect claims for use of asbestos in locomotive design[88] and failure to warn claims regarding the adequacy of pesticide labels[89] are pre-empted by federal statute. The U.S. Supreme Court has ruled that makers of medical devices are immune from liability for personal injuries as long as the Food and Drug Administration (FDA) approved the device before it was marketed and the device meets the FDA's specifications that it is reasonably safe and effective for human use, thus preempting state law remedies including product liability, breach of warranty, and negligent design.[90] California has carved out its own exception to strict liability for design defects for prescription drugs and implanted medical devices.[91] A Department of Transportation safety standard for automobiles may preempt state product liability claims if the tort action would interfere with a significant regulatory objective of the federal requirement.[92]

17. **Other Accidents**

Evidence regarding the absence of prior similar accidents in cases based on negligence or strict product liability is admissible, depending upon the purpose of such evidence and a showing of foundational requirements.[93] Such evidence tends to be more relevant in negligence cases because of the "foreseeability of harm" issue in such cases.[94] At a minimum, such evidence should be proffered by a witness who is familiar with product safety surveys or safety records concerning the product.[95] An even stronger showing is made by a witness in a product safety department or division which has kept records of the safety performance of the product.[96]

18. **Misrepresentation**

California has adopted Section 402B of the Restatement (Second) of Torts.[97]

19. **Destruction or Loss of Product**

There is no tort cause of action for first-party intentional spoliation of evidence when the spoliation is or reasonably should have been discovered before the conclusion of the underlying litigation.[98] Remedies for first-party spoliation are available through evidentiary inferences[99] and sanctions for abuse of discovery.[100]

There is also no tort cause of action against a third party for intentional[101] or for negligent[102] spoliation of evidence.

20. **Commercial or Economic Loss**

Recovery of commercial or economic loss (the diminished value of a defective product that does not meet the consumer's needs as well as a non-defective product) is not allowed in California under a strict product liability claim.[103] Such damages might be recoverable in California under an express warranty or misrepresentation claim.[104]

21. **Crashworthiness**

Manufacturers have a duty to design crashworthy, not crash-proof, vehicles because accidents, although not an intended use, are a foreseeable consequence of vehicle use.[105] A vehicle must be designed and constructed to forestall particular crash injuries.[106] To this extent, an automobile manufacturer has a legal duty to design and manufacture its vehicles to provide for the safety of the occupants in a vehicular accident.[107]

22. **Government Contractor Defense**

The government contractor defense is available to non-military manufacturers in product liability actions where (1) the United States itself would be immune from liability, (2) the contractor can show that the United States established or approved reasonably precise specifications, (3) the specifications were followed by the manufacturer, and (4) the supplier warned the United States about errors or dangers associated with the specifications.[108]

D. NEGLIGENCE

1. The Standard

A plaintiff establishes a prima facie case of negligence by showing duty, breach, proximate causation and injury.[109]

2. Breach of Duty

A products claim based on negligence focuses on the conduct of the defendant instead of the condition of the product.[110]

3. Duty to Inspect/Test

The scope of the duty to inspect and test a product depends on what the manufacturer knows or should know about the intended use of the product.[111] Negligent failure to test, when the defendant has a duty to test, can provide a basis for liability even where the product is not defective.[112]

E. BREACH OF WARRANTY

In California, a product liability claim based upon breach of warranty is governed by three statutory schemes.[113] Recovery can be based on express warranty,[114] implied warranty of merchantability,[115] or implied warranty of fitness for a particular purpose.[116]

While disclaimers of liability are not valid in strict liability and negligence claims,[117] it is possible under California law for a seller to negate implied warranties and preclude warranty liability for economic loss,[118] and possibly consequential damages.[119]

F. PUNITIVE DAMAGES

California law permits recovery of punitive damages in product liability actions.[120] Plaintiff is required to prove, by clear and convincing evidence, that the defendant is guilty of malice, oppression, or fraud.[121] "Malice" is defined as "despicable conduct . . . with a willful and conscious disregard of the rights and safety of others."[122] Conscious disregard can be established by consumer complaints, similar products, failure to test, and adequacy of testing.[123]

Punitive damages are not recoverable pursuant to a wrongful death cause of action[124] but may be recoverable in wrongful life actions.[125] Punitive damages that the decedent would have been entitled to recover, had he or she lived, are recoverable in a survival action, which may be brought on behalf of a decedent's estate.[126]

Mere negligence, even gross negligence, is not sufficient to justify an award of punitive damages.[127] Punitive damages are also not recoverable in claims based on breach of contract or breach of warranty.[128]

A corporate defendant is liable for punitive damages where an officer, a director or a managing agent of the corporation (1) knew of an employee's unfitness, yet employed him or her anyway in "conscious disregard of the rights and safety of others;" (2) authorized or ratified the wrongful conduct for which punitive damages are sought; or (3) is personally guilty of oppression, fraud, or malice.[129]

Punitive damages must bear a reasonable relation to the amount of actual or compensatory damages sustained.[130] There are three factors considered in determining the amount of punitive damages:[131] (1) the financial condition of the defendant,[132] including the wealth or net worth, or otherwise, the ability of the defendant to pay a punitive damages award;[133] (2) the amount of compensatory damages;[134] and (3) the reprehensibility of the defendant's conduct.[135]

G. PRE- AND POST-JUDGMENT INTEREST

Pre-judgment interest is awarded in the discretion of the trier of fact in noncontractual claims,[136] cases where "oppression, fraud, or malice" is shown,[137] and in personal injury actions where statutory settlement offers[138] are rejected and the offeree fails to obtain a "more favorable" judgment.[139] Interest on non-contractual obligations generally accrues at the rate of 7 percent per annum.[140] However, one exception is pre-judgment interest awarded in personal injury suits to a prevailing plaintiff who has made a statutory settlement offer that has been rejected by a defendant who fails to obtain a "more favorable" judgment, which accrues at the rate of 10 percent per annum from the date of the rejected offer until the judgment is satisfied.[141] In cases involving "oppression, fraud or malice," pre-judgment interest is first computed on the entire judgment, without deduction or offset for amounts paid by a settling joint tortfeasor.[142] The plaintiff may then recover (1) prejudgment interest from the non-settling tortfeasor on the total judgment up to the date of the settlement; and (2) pre-judgment interest after the date of the settlement only on the judgment balance remaining after being reduced by the amount of the paid settlement.[143]

Plaintiff is entitled to interest from the date of entry of a money judgment.[144] If a money judgment is payable in installments, interest begins to accrue as to each installment on the date the installment is due.[145] Post-judgment interest accrues on a money judgment at the rate of 10 percent per annum.[146] The 10 percent limit also applies to stipulated judgments.[147] Post-judgment interest is not compounded, although compounding is authorized when the judgment is renewed, which can occur once every five years.[148] A plaintiff who is awarded 10 percent interest from the date of a statutory offer may not also recover 10 percent post-judgment interest under the separate post-judgment interest statute.[149]

H. EMPLOYER IMMUNITY FROM SUIT

Under California's Workers' Compensation Act, an employee is generally prohibited from joining the employer as a party to an action for the employee's injuries under the "exclusive remedy provision."[150] California has also eliminated the dual capacity doctrine as a basis for a tort action against employers, except in limited circumstances.[151] One such exception allows an action against the employer where injury or death is caused by a defective product that is (1) manufactured by the employer and (2) sold, leased or otherwise transferred for valuable consideration to an independent third party and thereafter provided for the employee's use by a third party.[152] Another exception to the exclusive remedy rule authorizes an action against an employer where the injury or death is caused by the employer's knowing removal of or failure to provide a guard on a power press.[153] An employer who designs, manufactures, and installs its own power presses for use by its employees is subject to potential liability as a third-party tortfeasor.[154]

I. STATUTES

The relevant statutes for a product liability action are the statutes of limitations, the Commercial Code, and Civil Code §§ 1790-1795.4. The Business and Professions Code sections pertaining to unfair and fraudulent business acts or practices,[155] and unfair, deceptive, untrue, or misleading advertising[156] may also have some application in product liability actions.

Uninsured motorists and drunk drivers are precluded from recovering non-economic damages in an action arising out of the operation or use of a motor vehicle.[157] However, this limit on the recovery of non-economic damages does not apply to a product liability action brought by an uninsured motorist.[158]

The age of majority in California is 18 years of age.[159]

J. JOINT AND SEVERAL LIABILITY

In California, actions based on comparative fault, liability for economic damages is joint and several,[160] while liability for noneconomic damages is limited to the proportion of such damages that is equal to the defendant's percentage of fault.[161] Damages are apportioned among the "universe of tortfeasors," including non-joined tortfeasors.[162]

California's limitation on joint and several liability for noneconomic damages is applicable to a strict products liability action.[163] However, an exception to the limitation on recovery of noneconomic damages exists where a defendant's liability is based on being a supplier in the chain of distribution of a single product that allegedly caused the injury.[164] In such a case, noneconomic damages are not apportioned between other defendants in the chain.

A joint tortfeasor who settles with the plaintiff may obtain an adjudication that the settlement is in "good faith," which bars any further claims against the settling tortfeasor for equitable contribution or indemnity.[165] A non-settling joint tortfeasor is only entitled to a set-off as to a money judgment against it in an amount equal to the economic portion of another tortfeasor's settlement with plaintiff.[166] The non-settling tortfeasor has the burden of showing the percentage of the jury award that is attributable to economic damages.[167]

Where a settlement is not deemed to have been made in "good faith" by the court, the non-settling tortfeasor may seek contribution from the settling tortfeasor for the full amount of the settling tortfeasor's proportionate share of liability, minus an offset for the amount paid by the settling tortfeasor.[168]

Arnold D. Larson
alarson@lgl-law.com
Mary P. Lightfoot
mlightfoot@lgl-law.com
Darren M. Ballas
dballas@lgl-law.com
Drew Larson
drewlarson@lgl-law.com
Larson, Garrick & Lightfoot, LLP
801 South Figueroa Street, Suite 1750
Los Angeles, California 90017-5504
(213) 404-4100/(Fax) (213) 404-4123

ENDNOTES - CALIFORNIA

1. Cal. Civ. Proc. Code § 335.1.

2. *Jolly v. Eli Lilly & Co.*, 44 Cal. 3d 1103, 245 Cal. Rptr. 658 (1988); *Bernson v. Browning-Ferris Indus.*, 7 Cal. 4th 926, 931, 30 Cal. Rptr. 2d 440 (1994).

3. Cal. Civ. Proc. Code § 335.1.

4. Cal. Civ. Proc. Code § 338(b) (real property); Cal. Civ. Proc. Code § 338(c) (personal property).

5. Cal. U. Com. Code § 2725.

6. Cal. Civ. Proc. Code § 340.2; *Hamilton v. Asbestos Corp., Ltd.*, 22 Cal. 4th 1127, 95 Cal. Rptr. 2d 701 (2000).

7. *Greenman v. Yuba Power Prods., Inc.*, 59 Cal. 2d 57, 27 Cal. Rptr. 697 (1963); *Vandermark v. Ford Motor Co.*, 61 Cal. 2d 256, 37 Cal. Rptr. 896 (1964).

8. 6 Witkin, *Summary of Cal. Law*, (10th ed. 2005), Ch. IX Torts, § 1430-1435; *Cronin v. J.B.E. Olson Corp.*, 8 Cal. 3d 121, 104 Cal. Rptr. 433 (1972); California Civil Jury Instructions ("CACI") No. 1200-1205.

9. *See, Soule v. General Motors Corp.*, 8 Cal. 4th 548, 560, 34 Cal. Rptr. 2d 607 (1994).

10. *Soule*, 8 Cal. 4th at 560, 34 Cal. Rptr. 2d 607.

11. *Cronin*, 8 Cal. 3d 121; *Barker v. Lull Eng'g Co.*, 20 Cal. 3d 413, 143 Cal. Rptr. 225 (1978).

12. *Cronin*, 8 Cal. 3d 121; *Barker*, 20 Cal. 3d 413, 143 Cal. Rptr. 225; CACI Nos. 1201, 1202; 6 Witkin, Summary of Cal. Law (10th ed. 2005), Ch. IX, Torts §§ 1435, 1436.

13. *Greenman*, 59 Cal. 2d 57; *Thomas v. General Motors Corp.*, 13 Cal. App. 3d 81, 91 Cal. Rptr. 301 (1970); *DeLeon v. Commercial Mfg. & Supply Co.*, 148 Cal. App. 3d 336, 195 Cal. Rptr. 867 (1983).

14. *Barker*, 20 Cal. 3d 413; *Lewis v. American Hoist & Derrick Co.*, 20 Cal. App. 3d 570, 97 Cal. Rptr. 798 (1971); *Campbell v. GMC*, 32 Cal. 3d 112, 123, 184 Cal. Rptr. 891 (1982); CACI Nos. 1201, 1202.

15. *Lewis*, 20 Cal. App. 3d 570.

16. *Barker*, 20 Cal. 3d 413; CACI Nos. 1203, 1204.

17. *Soule v. General Motors Corp.*, 8 Cal. 4th 548, 567 (1994); *Stephen v. Ford Motor Co.*, 134 Cal. App. 4th 1363, 1371, 37 Cal. Rptr. 3d 9, 15, n.6 (2005); *Akers v. Kelley Co.*, 173 Cal. App. 3d 633, 650 (1985) ("There are certain kinds of accidents—even where fairly complex machinery is involved—which are so bizarre that the average juror, upon hearing the particulars might reasonably think: *'Whatever the user may have expected from that contraption, it certainly wasn't that.'*") (emphasis added).

18. *Soule*, 8 Cal. 4th at 568-69.

19. *Mansur v. Ford Motor Co.*, 197 Cal. App. 4th 1365, 1375, 129 Cal. Rptr. 3d 200, 208 (2011).

20. *Mansur*, 197 Cal. App. 4th at 1375.

21. *Soule*, 8 Cal. 4th at 568 ("[T]he jury may not be left free to find a violation of ordinary consumer expectations whenever it chooses. Unless the facts actually permit an inference that the product's performance does not meet the minimum safety expectations of its ordinary consumers, the jury must engage in the balancing of risks and benefits required by the second prong of *Barker*.").

22. *Barker*, 20 Cal. 3d at 431-32; *Lunghi v. Clark Equip. Co., Inc.*, 153 Cal. App. 3d 485, 497-88, 200 Cal. Rptr. 387 (1984).

23. *Barker*, 20 Cal. 3d at 431, *Gonzalez v. Autoliv ASP, Inc.*, 154 Cal. App. 4th 780, 786, 64 Cal. Rptr. 3d 908 (2007).

24. *McLaughlin v. Sikorsky Aircraft*, 148 Cal. App. 3d 203, 195 Cal. Rptr. 764 (1983).

25. *Garrett v. Howmedica Osteonics Corp.*, 214 Cal. App. 4th 173, 183-84, 153 Cal. Rptr. 3d 693 (2013).

26. *Anderson v. Owens-Corning Fiberglas Corp.*, 53 Cal. 3d 987, 281 Cal. Rptr. 528 (1991).

27. *Anderson*, 53 Cal. 3d 987, 281 Cal. Rptr. 528; CACI No. 1205.

28. *Taylor v. Elliott Turbomachinery Co., Inc.*, 171 Cal. App. 4th 564, 90 Cal. Rptr. 3d 414 (2009).

29. *Rosburg v. Minnesota Mining & Mfg. Co.*, 181 Cal. App. 3d 726, 226 Cal. Rptr. 299 (1986).

30. *Finn v. G.D. Searle & Co.*, 35 Cal. 3d. 691, 200 Cal. Rptr. 870 (1984).

31. *Johnson v. American Standard, Inc.*, 43 Cal. 4th 56, 74 Cal. Rptr. 3d 108 (2008). However, the sophisticated user defense does not bar a design defect cause of action under a risk benefit theory. *Chavez. v. Glock, Inc.*, 207 Cal. App. 4th 1283, 1313-14, 144 Cal. Rptr. 3d 326 (2012).

32. *Buckner v. Milwaukee Elec. Tool Corp.*, 222 Cal. App. 4th 522, 535, 166 Cal. Rptr. 3d 202 (2013).

33. *Sindell v. Abbott Labs.*, 26 Cal. 3d 588, 598, 163 Cal. Rptr. 132, *cert. denied*, 449 U.S. 912 (1980).

34. *Soule*, 8 Cal. 4th 548.

35. *Mitchell v. Gonzales*, 54 Cal. 3d 1041, 1 Cal. Rptr. 2d 913 (1991); *Sindell v. Abbott Labs.*, 26 Cal. 3d 588, 163 Cal. Rptr. 132, *cert. denied*, 449 U.S. 912 (1980).

36. *Daly v. General Motors Corp.*, 20 Cal. 3d 725, 144 Cal. Rptr. 380 (1978); *Fluor Corp. v. Jeppesen & Co.*, 170 Cal. App. 3d 468, 216 Cal. Rptr. 68 (1985).

37. *Daly*, 20 Cal. 3d 725, 144 Cal. Rptr. 380; *Fluor Corp.*, 170 Cal. App. 3d 468, 216 Cal. Rptr. 68.

38. *Allabach v. Santa Clara County Fair Ass'n*, 46 Cal. App. 4th 1007, 1012, 54 Cal. Rptr. 2d 330 (1996).

39. *Knight v. Jewett*, 3 Cal. 4th 296, 308, 11 Cal. Rptr. 2d 2 (1992).

40. *Knight*, 3 Cal. 4th at 308.

41. *Greenman*, 59 Cal. 2d 57; *Barth v. B.F. Goodrich Tire Co.*, 265 Cal. App. 2d 228, 71 Cal. Rptr. 306 (1968) (including component part manufacturers); *Jenkins v. T&N PLC*, 45 Cal. App. 4th 1224, 53 Cal. Rptr. 2d 642 (1996); *Vandermark*, 61 Cal. 2d 256. However, retailers who sell to dealers will not be held liable. *Fruehauf Corp. v. Lakeside Chevrolet Co.*, 117 Cal. App. 3d 783, 173 Cal. Rptr. 55 (1981).

42. *Ramsey v. Marutamaya Ogatsu Fireworks Co.*, 72 Cal. App. 3d 516, 140 Cal. Rptr. 247 (1977).

43. *Price v. Shell Oil Co.*, 2 Cal. 3d 245, 85 Cal. Rptr. 178 (1970); *Fakhoury v. Magner*, 25 Cal. App. 3d 58, 101 Cal. Rptr. 473 (1972); *Golden v. Conway*, 55 Cal. App. 3d 948, 128 Cal. Rptr. 69 (1976).

44. *Garcia v. Halsett*, 3 Cal. App. 3d 319, 82 Cal. Rptr. 420 (1970); *Kasel v. Remington Arms Co.*, 24 Cal. App. 3d 711, 101 Cal. Rptr. 314 (1972).

45. *Peterson v. Superior Court*, 10 Cal. 4th 1185, 43 Cal. Rptr. 2d 836 (1995).

46. *Romine v. Johnson Controls, Inc.*, 224 Cal. App. 4th 990, 1008, 169 Cal. Rptr. 3d 208 (2014).

47. Cal. Civ. Code § 1714.45. Where a manufacturer or seller has statutory immunity under Section 1714.45, it is not subject to an indirect assignment of comparative fault for noneconomic damages under California's joint and several liability law ("Proposition 51"). *Richards v. Owens-Illinois, Inc.*, 14 Cal. 4th 985, 60 Cal. Rptr. 2d 103 (1997).

48. Cal. Civ. Code § 1714.45(b).

49. Cal. Civ. Code § 1714.45(b).

50. Cal. Civ. Code § 1714.

51. *Ray v. Alad Corp.*, 19 Cal. 3d 22, 136 Cal. Rptr. 574 (1977).

52. *Rawlings v. D.M. Oliver, Inc.*, 97 Cal. App. 3d 890, 159 Cal. Rptr. 119 (1979).

53. *Potlatch Corp. v. Superior Court*, 154 Cal. App. 3d 1144, 1150-51, 201 Cal. Rptr. 750 (1984).

54. *Sindell*, 26 Cal. 3d 588.

55. *Sindell*, 26 Cal. 3d 588.

56. *Greenman*, 59 Cal. 2d 57; *Vandermark*, 61 Cal. 2d 256; *Klein v. Duchess Sandwich Co., Ltd.*, 14 Cal. 2d 272, 93 P. 2d 799 (1939).

57. *Barrett v. Superior Court*, 222 Cal. App. 3d 1176, 272 Cal. Rptr. 304 (1990).

58. *Elmore v. American Motors Corp.*, 70 Cal. 2d 578, 75 Cal. Rptr. 652 (1969).

59. *International Knights of Wine, Inc. v. Ball Corp., Inc.*, 110 Cal. App. 3d 1001, 168 Cal. Rptr. 301 (1980).

60. *Hauter v. Zogarts*, 14 Cal. 3d 104, 115, n.8, 120 Cal. Rptr. 681, 688 (1975).

61. *Hauter*, 14 Cal. 3d at 115, n.8, 120 Cal. Rptr. at 688; *Rodriguez v. Campbell Indus.*, 87 Cal. App. 3d 494, 500, 151 Cal. Rptr. 90, 93 (1978).

62. *Klein*, 14 Cal.2d at 282-84.

63. *Vassallo v. Sabatte Land Co.*, 212 Cal. App. 2d 11, 16-17, 27 Cal. Rptr. 814, 817 (1963).

64. *Hauter*, 14 Cal. 3d at 115, n.8.

65. *Jones v. ConocoPhillips*, 198 Cal. App. 4th 1187, 1201, 130 Cal. Rptr. 2d 571, 581-82 (2011).

66. *Chavez*, 207 Cal. App. 4th at 1315.

67. *Ault v. International Harvester Co.*, 13 Cal. 3d 113, 117 Cal. Rptr. 812 (1974); *Schelbauer v. Butler Mfg. Co.*, 35 Cal. 3d 442, 198 Cal. Rptr. 155 (1984); *Burke v. Almaden Vineyards, Inc.*, 86 Cal. App. 3d 768, 150 Cal. Rptr. 419 (1978); Cal. Evid. Code § 1151.

68. *Carlin v. Superior Court*, 13 Cal. 4th 1104, 1116, 56 Cal. Rptr. 2d 162 (1996).

69. *Carlin*, 13 Cal. 4th at 1110, citing *Brown v. Superior Court*, 44 Cal. 3d 1049, 245 Cal. Rpt. 412 (1988).

70. *Horn v. General Motors Corp.*, 17 Cal. 3d 359, 131 Cal. Rptr. 78 (1976); *Campbell v. Southern Pac. Co.*, 22 Cal. 3d 51, 148 Cal. Rptr. 596 (1978); *Chavez*, 207 Cal. App. 4th 1283, 1308, 144 Cal. Rptr. 3d 326 (A misuse that absolves the tortfeasor is one that is so highly extraordinary as to be unforeseeable; however, except where the facts leave no room for doubt, foreseeability is a question for the jury.).

71. *Moerrer v. Ford*, 57 Cal. App. 3d 114, 129 Cal. Rptr. 112 (1976).

72. *Bates v. John Deere Co.*, 148 Cal. App. 3d 40, 195 Cal. Rptr. 637 (1983).

73. *Williams v. Beechnut Nutrition Corp.*, 185 Cal. App. 3d 135, 229 Cal. Rptr. 605 (1986).

74. *Anderson*, 53 Cal. 3d 987; *Vermeulen v. Superior Ct.*, 204 Cal. App. 3d 1192, 251 Cal. Rptr. 805 (1988).

75. *McLaughlin*, 148 Cal. App. 3d 203.

76. *Hinckley v. La Mesa R.V. Ctr., Inc.*, 158 Cal. App. 3d 630, 205 Cal. Rptr. 22 (1984).

77. *O'Neil v. Crane Co.*, 53 Cal. 4th 335, 342, 349-50, 366, 135 Cal. Rptr. 3d 288 (2012); *Taylor v. Elliott Turbomachinery Co., Inc.*, 171 Cal. App. 4th 564, 575, 90 Cal. Rptr. 3d 414 (2009) (duty to warn limited to dangerous propensities in manufacturer's own products even where product to be used in conjunction with another product that causes harm).

78. *O'Neil*, 53 Cal. 4th at 342, 361-62; *Tellez -Cordova v. Campbell-Hausfeld/Scott Fetzger Co.*, 129 Cal. App. 4th 577, 585, 28 Cal. Rptr. 3d 744 (manufacturer of grinder liable for dust associated with use of grinding material); *but cf. Sanchez v. Hitachi Koki Co., LTD.*, 217 Cal. App. 4th 948, 158 Cal. Rptr. 3d 907

(2013) (manufacturer of grinder not liable where grinder was not intended to be used with saw blade improvidently attached by plaintiff).

79. *Vandemark v. Ford Motor Co.*, 61 Cal. 2d 256, 261, 37 Cal. Rptr. 896 (1964).

80. *O'Neil*, 53 Cal. 4th at 355; *Maxton v. Western States Metals*, 203 Cal. App. 4th 81, 85, 136 Cal. Rptr. 3d 630 (2012).

81. *Artiglio v. General Elec. Co.*, 61 Cal. App. 4th 830, 837-39, 71 Cal. Rptr. 2d 817 (1998); *Maxton*, 203 Cal. App. 4th at 88.

82. *Maxton*, 203 Cal. App. 4th at 90.

83. *Maxton*, 203 Cal. App. 4th at 85.

84. *Uriarte v. Scott Sales Co.*, 226 Cal. App. 4th 1396, __ 172 Cal. Rptr. 3d 886, 889 (2014); *but see also Ramos v. Brewing Specialties*, 224 Cal. App. 4th 1239, 1255, 169 Cal. Rptr. 3d 513 (2014), which held similarly to *Uriarte*, but which is no longer citable as valid legal authority because the California Supreme Court has granted review.

85. *Maxton*, 203 Cal. App. 4th 85, 90.

86. *Grimshaw v. Ford Motor Co.*, 119 Cal. App. 3d 757, 174 Cal. Rptr. 348 (1981).

87. *Rodriguez v. Plough*, 6 Cal. 4th 539, 553, 25 Cal. Rptr. 2d 97 (1994).

88. *Scheiding v. General Motors Corp.*, 22 Cal. 4th 471, 93 Cal. Rptr. 2d 342 (2000), *cert. denied*, 531 U.S. 958 (Oct. 30, 2000).

89. *Etcheverry v. Tri-Ag Serv., Inc.*, 22 Cal. 4th 316, 93 Cal. Rptr. 2d 36 (2000); *but see Bates v. Dow Agrosciences LLC*, 544 U.S. 431, 447, 125 S. Ct. 1788, 1800 (2005), in which the U.S. Supreme Court held that design and manufacturing defect claims were not preempted by federal pesticide labeling statutes, and that it would remand that case back to the lower courts to decide whether the applicable state common law failure to warn requirements were inconsistent with federal labeling statutes.

90. *Riegel v. Medtronic, Inc.*, 128 S. Ct. 999, 169 L. Ed. 2d 829 (2008); followed recently by California courts finding preemption in *Robinson v. Endovascular Techs., Inc.*, 190 Cal. App. 4th 1490, 1499-500, 119 Cal. Rptr. 3d 158, 164-65 (2010); *McGuan v. Endovascular Techs., Inc.* 182 Cal. App. 4th 974, 106 Cal. Rptr. 3d 277 (2010).

91. *Garrett v. Howmedica Osteonics Corp.*, 214 Cal. App. 4th 173, 183-84, 153 Cal. Rptr. 3d 693 (2013).

92. *See Geier v. Am. Honda Motor Co., Inc.*, 529 U.S. 861, 120 S. Ct. 913 (2000) (District of Columbia tort law as applied to airbags conflicted with objective of Department of Transportation to allow manufacturers freedom to develop airbag technologies); *but cf. Williamson v. Mazda Motor of Am., Inc.*, 562 U.S.____, 131 S. Ct. 1131 (2011) (The Department of Transportations' providing of an option to use lap belts or lap-and-shoulder belts for rear middle passengers was not intended to achieve a significant regulatory objective, and, therefore, did not preempt California product liability law.).

93. *Benson v. Honda Motor Co.*, 26 Cal. App. 4th 1337, 1344, 32 Cal. Rptr. 322 (1994).

94. *Benson*, 26 Cal. App. 4th at 1345.

95. *Benson*, 26 Cal. App. 4th at 1346.

96. *Benson*, 26 Cal. App. 4th at 1346.

97. *Hauter*, 14 Cal. 3d 104; Restatement (Second) of Torts § 402B provides: "One engaged in the business of selling chattels who, by advertising, labels, or otherwise, makes to the public a misrepresentation of a material fact concerning the character or quality of a chattel sold by him is subject to liability for physical harm to a consumer of the chattel caused by justifiable reliance upon the misrepresentation, even though, (a) it is not made fraudulently or negligently, and, (b) the consumer has not bought the chattel from or entered into any contractual relation with the seller."

98. *Cedars-Sinai Med. Center v. Superior Ct.*, 18 Cal. 4th 1, 74 Cal. Rptr. 2d 248 (1998).

99. Cal. Evid. Code § 413.

100. Cal. Civ. Proc. Code §§ 2023.010 and 2023.030.

101. *Temple Cmty. Hosp. v. Superior Ct.*, 20 Cal. 4th 464, 84 Cal. Rptr. 2d 852 (1999).

102. *Farmers Ins. Exch. v. Superior Ct.*, 79 Cal. App. 4th 1400, 95 Cal. Rptr. 2d 51 (2000).

103. *Seely v. White Motor Co.*, 63 Cal. 2d 9, 45 Cal. Rptr. 17 (1965).

104. *Seely*, 63 Cal. 2d 9, 45 Cal. Rptr. 17.

105. *McGee v. Cessna Aircraft Co.*, 139 Cal. App. 3d 179, 189, 188 Cal. Rptr. 542 (1983).

106. *Doupnik v. General Motors Corp.*, 225 Cal. App. 3d 849, 859, 275 Cal. Rptr. 715 (1990).

107. *Doupnik*, 225 Cal. App. 3d at 859, 275 Cal. Rptr. 715.

108. *McLaughlin*, 148 Cal. App. 3d 203; *Vermeulen*, 204 Cal. App. 3d 1192.

109. 6 Witkin, *Summary of Cal. Law* (10th Ed. 2005) Ch. IX Torts, § 835; CACI No. 408.

110. *Finn*, 35 Cal. 3d 691.

111. *Warner v. Santa Catalina Island Co.*, 44 Cal. 2d 310, 282 P.2d 12 (1955).

112. *Hasson v. Ford Motor Co.*, 19 Cal. 3d 530, 138 Cal. Rptr. 705 (1977).

113. Cal. U. Com. Code §§ 2101-2725. The Song-Beverly Consumer Warranty Act, Cal. Civ. Code §§ 1790-1795.8; Magnuson-Moss Warranty Act, 15 U.S.C. §§ 2301-2312.

114. Cal. U. Com. Code § 2313(1); Cal. Civ. Code § 1791.2(a).

115. Cal. U. Com. Code § 2314(1); *Hauter*, 14 Cal. 3d 104; Cal. Civ. Code § 1792.

116. Cal. U. Com. Code § 2315; Cal. Civ. Code §§ 1791.1(b) (defining implied warranty of fitness in consumer goods context); 1792.1 (warranty by manufacturer); and 1792.2 (warranty by retailer or distributor).

117. *Greenman*, 59 Cal. 2d 57; *Southern Cal. Edison Co. v. Harnischfeger Corp.*, 120 Cal. App. 3d 842, 175 Cal. Rptr. 67 (1981).

118. Cal. U. Com. Code § 2316(2) and (3); *Seely*, 63 Cal. 2d 9.

119. Cal. U. Com. Code § 2719(3).

120. Cal. Civ. Code § 3294.

121. Cal. Civ. Code § 3294.

122. Cal. Civ. Code § 3294(c)(1).

123. *West v. Johnson & Johnson Prods., Inc.*, 174 Cal. App. 3d 831, 220 Cal. Rptr. 437 (1986); *Hilliard v. A.H. Robins Co.*, 148 Cal. App. 3d 374, 196 Cal. Rptr. 117 (1983).

124. Cal. Civ. Proc. Code § 377.61; Cal. Civ. Proc. Code § 377.34.

125. *Curlender v. Bio-Science Labs., Inc.*, 106 Cal. App. 3d 811, 831, 165 Cal. Rptr. 477, 490 (1977).

126. Cal. Civ. Proc. Code § 377.34; *Grimshaw*, 119 Cal. App. 3d 757.

127. Cal. Civ. Code § 3294; Cal. U. Com. Code §§ 2314-2315.

128. *Ebaugh v. Rabkin*, 22 Cal. App. 3d 891, 99 Cal. Rptr. 706 (1972).

129. Cal. Civ. Code § 3294(b).

130. *Vallbona v. Springer*, 43 Cal. App. 4th 1525, 1536, 51 Cal. Rptr. 2d 311, 318 (1996). While there is no fixed ratio between the amount of compensatory and punitive damages prescribed by law, the U.S. Supreme Court stated in *State Farm Mut. Auto. Ins. Co. v. Campbell*, 538 U.S. 408, 123 S. Ct. 1513 (2003), that ordinarily a punitive damage award should not exceed a compensatory award by more than a single digit ratio. In California, several reviewing courts post-*Campbell* have lowered punitive damage awards as a result. See *Textron Fin. Corp. v. National Union Fire Ins. Co. of Pittsburgh, Pa.*, 118 Cal. App. 4th 1061, 1085, 13 Cal. Rptr. 3d 586, 605 (2004); *Romo v. Ford Motor Co.*, 113 Cal. App. 4th 738, 764, 6 Cal. Rptr. 3d 793, 812-13 (2003); *Diamond Woodworks, Inc. v. Argonaut Ins. Co.*, 109 Cal. App. 4th 1020, 1056-57, 135 Cal. Rptr. 2d 736, 761-62 (2003). However, in *Johnson v. Ford Motor Company*, 35 Cal. 4th 1191, 1206-07, 29 Cal. Rptr. 3d 401 (2005), the California Supreme Court suggested that a defendant's recidivism and the scale of its violation to the public may at times call for an award of punitive damages which is proportionately greater than compensatory damages by more than single digits. *See also Bullock v. Phillip Morris U.S.A., Inc.*, 198 Cal. App. 4th 543, 554-61 (2011) (upholding a punitive damages ratio of 16 to 1 where relatively small amount of compensatory damages was awarded in comparison to company's ability to pay); *See also Simon v. San Paulo U.S. Holding Co., Inc.*, 109 Cal. App. 4th 1020, 1182-83, 29 Cal. Rptr. 3d 370 (2005), warning that the single-digit ratio provides the outer limits of constitutionality in many cases, but is not binding in all instances.

131. *Stevens*, 49 Cal. App. 4th 1645, 1658, 57 Cal. Rptr. 2d 525 (1996).

132. *Bertero v. National Gen. Corp.*, 13 Cal. 3d 43, 65, 118 Cal. Rptr. 184 (1974); *Adams v. Murakami*, 54 Cal. 3d 105, 110, 284 Cal. Rptr. 318 (1991); *Richmond v. Allstate Ins. Co.*, 897 F. Supp. 447 (S.D. Cal. 1995); *Kenly v. Ukegawa*, 16 Cal. App. 4th 49, 56, 19 Cal. Rptr. 2d 771, 775 (1993); *Chodos v. Insurance Co. of N. Am.*, 126 Cal. App. 3d 86, 103, 178 Cal. Rptr. 831 (1981). Since the Supreme Court's decision in *State Farm Mut. Auto. Ins. Co. v. Campbell*, 538 U.S. 408, 123 S. Ct. 1513 (2003), there has been some uncertainty in California courts as to whether the defendant's financial condition should be considered in a punitive damages award. One California case, *Romo*, 113 Cal. App. 4th 738,

753, indicated that consideration of the defendant's wealth is no longer permissible, while another, *Bardis v. Oates*, 119 Cal. App. 4th 1, 25-26, 14 Cal. Rptr. 3d 89, 108 (2004), took the defendant's financial condition into account while being "mindful of *Campbell's* admonition that the wealth of a defendant will not by itself compensate for a lack of other factors." *Romo* was substantially criticized by the California Supreme Court in *Johnson v. Ford Motor Co.*, 35 Cal. 4th 1191, 1207, 29 Cal. Rptr. 3d 401 (2005), which acknowledged that a consideration of the "reasonableness of the award" is influenced by the "frequency and profitability of the defendant's prior or contemporaneous similar conduct."

133. *See Bankhead v. ArvinMeritor, Inc.*, 205 Cal. App. 4th 68, 78-80, 139 Cal. Rptr. 3d 849 (2012) (Net worth is just one factor a court may consider in determining whether a defendant is financially able to pay a punitive damages award; since net worth calculations can be manipulated, even a defendant with negative net worth may have cash flow or cash reserves sufficient to pay a punitive damages award.)

134. *Little v. Stuyvesant Life Ins. Co.*, 67 Cal. App. 3d 451, 469, 136 Cal. Rptr. 653, 663 (1977). (*See infra* text accompanying note 149.)

135. *Walker v. Signal Cos., Inc.*, 84 Cal. App. 3d 982, 997-98, 149 Cal. Rptr. 119, 126-28 (1978).

136. Cal. Civ. Code § 3288.

137. Cal. Civ. Code § 3288.

138. Cal. Civ. Proc. Code § 998.

139. Cal. Civ. Code § 3291.

140. Cal. Const. art. XV, § 1; *May Dep't Stores Co. v. City of Los Angeles*, 204 Cal. App. 3d 1368, 1378, 251 Cal. Rptr. 873, 880 (1988).

141. Cal. Const. art. XV, § 1; *May Dep't Stores*, 204 Cal. App. 3d 1368, 1378, 251 Cal. Rptr. 873, 880.

142. *Newby v. Vroman*, 11 Cal. App. 4th 283, 289-90, 14 Cal. Rptr. 2d 44, 48 (1992).

143. *Newby*, 11 Cal. App. 4th at 289-90, 14 Cal. Rptr. 2d at 48.

144. Cal. Civ. Proc. Code § 685.020(a).

145. Cal. Civ. Proc. Code § 685.020(b).

146. Cal. Civ. Proc. Code § 685.010(a).

147. *John Siebel Assocs. v. Keele*, 188 Cal. App. 3d 560, 233 Cal. Rptr. 231 (1986).

148. *OCM Principal Opportunities Fund v. CIBC World Mkts. Corp.*, 168 Cal. App. 4th 185, 200, 85 Cal. Rptr. 3d 350, 361 (2008).

149. *Mendez v. Kurten*, 170 Cal. App. 3d 481, 215 Cal. Rptr. 924 (1985).

150. Cal. Lab. Code § 3602(a).

151. Cal. Lab. Code § 3602(a); *Perry v. Heavenly Valley*, 163 Cal. App. 3d 495, 501, 209 Cal. Rptr. 171 (1985).

152. Cal. Lab. Code§ 3602(b)(3).

153. Cal. Lab. Code § 4558; *but see, LeFiell Mfg. Co. v. Superior Court*, 55 Cal. 4th 275, 285 (2012) (while an injured employee may bring a concurrent action in Superior Court to augment recovery under a workers' compensation claim, Cal. Lab. Code § 4558 does not authorize spouses to bring actions outside the workers' compensation system against the injured worker's employer, *e.g.*, an action for loss of consortium).

154. *Flowmaster v. Superior Court*, 16 Cal. App. 4th 1019, 1030, 20 Cal. Rptr. 2d 666 (1993).

155. Cal. Bus. & Prof. Code § 17200 *et seq.* (unfair business practices).

156. Cal. Bus. & Prof. Code § 17500 *et seq.* (false and misleading advertising).

157. Cal. Civ. Code § 3333.4.

158. *Hodges v. Superior Court*, 21 Cal. 4th 109, 86 Cal. Rptr. 2d 884 (1999).

159. Cal. Fam. Code § 6500.

160. Cal. Civ. Code § 1431.2(a). California's joint and several liability law is also known as "Proposition 51."

161. Cal. Civ. Code § 1431.2(a).

162. *Roslan v. Permea, Inc.*, 17 Cal. App. 4th 110, 21 Cal. Rptr. 2d 66 (1993); *Vollaro v. Lispi*, 224 Cal. App. 4th 93, 100, 168 Cal. Rptr. 3d 323 (2014); *Romine v. Johnson Controls, Inc.*, 224 Cal. App. 4th 990, 1008-09, 169 Cal. Rptr. 3d 208 (2014).

163. *Arena v. Owens Corning*, 63 Cal. App. 4th 1178, 74 Cal. Rptr. 2d 580 (1998).

164. *Wimberly v. Derby Cycle Corp.*, 56 Cal. App. 4th 618, 626, 65 Cal. Rptr. 2d 532 (1997).

165. Cal. Civ. Proc. Code § 877.6.

166. *Conrad v. Ball*, 24 Cal. App. 4th 439, 29 Cal. Rptr. 2d 441 (1994).

167. *Conrad*, 24 Cal. App. 4th 439, 29 Cal. Rptr. 2d 441.

168. *Leung v. Verdugo Hills Hosp.*, 55 Cal. 4th 291, 308, 145 Cal. Rptr. 3d 553 (2012).

COLORADO

A. CAUSES OF ACTION

In Colorado, the Product Liability Act of 1977 covers product liability actions.[1] Under the Product Liability Act, actions may be based on strict liability,[2] negligence,[3] breach of warranty,[4] or misrepresentation.[5] No product liability action is available if misuse of the product was the cause of the injury.[6] The Product Liability Act limits the scope of actions that can be brought under it by mandating that strict liability actions can only be maintained against manufacturers.[7] In actions involving breach of warranty, the Uniform Commercial Code (UCC) provides a unified statutory scheme directed to the sale of goods with detailed provisions governing express and implied warranties.[8]

B. STATUTES OF LIMITATION AND REPOSE

1. Statutes of Limitation

In Colorado, the applicable limitations period for a products liability action varies depending upon the cause of the action alleged. Breach of warranty claims governed by the UCC must be brought within three years after the cause of action accrues.[9] Claims for breach of warranty accrue upon the discovery of the breach or on the date when, in the exercise of reasonable diligence, the breach should have been discovered.[10] All other product liability actions against a manufacturer or seller must be brought within two years after the claim for relief accrues.[11] Colorado follows the "discovery rule" for determining when a cause of action accrues; that rule provides that "a cause of action for injury to [a] person . . . shall be considered to accrue on the date both the injury and its cause are known or should have been known by the exercise of reasonable diligence."[12] Therefore, "[a] claim for relief 'does not accrue until the plaintiff knows, or should know, in the exercise of reasonable diligence, all material facts essential to show the elements of that cause of action.'"[13]

2. Statute of Repose

A statute of repose governs product liability actions against manufacturers, sellers, and lessors of new manufacturing equipment.[14] A statute of repose may bar a claim before an injury occurs.[15] The statute of repose governing new manufacturing equipment provides that no product liability action may be brought on a claim arising more than seven years after the equipment was first used.[16] There are four enumerated exceptions to the statute of repose for claims arising from: (1) hidden defects; (2) prolonged exposure to hazardous material; (3) intentional misrepresentation; or (4) fraudulent concealment.[17] The

Colorado Supreme Court has held that for a product to contain a "hidden defect" it must "have a defect that creates an unreasonably dangerous condition which is not readily apparent."[18] The Colorado Supreme Court has not considered the other three exceptions under the statute of repose.

C. STRICT LIABILITY

1. Restatement (Second) Torts, Section 402A

Colorado has adopted the Restatement (Second) Torts, Section 402A (Section 402A), to govern strict product liability cases.[19] Under Section 402A, the plaintiff must prove each element of a claim for relief by a preponderance of the evidence.[20] This includes proving that the product was in a defective condition and unreasonably dangerous.[21] However, a plaintiff does not have to demonstrate that the defendant was negligent in manufacturing or selling the product.[22]

2. Basic Elements

A products liability action may be brought against a manufacturer or seller of a product for injury, death, or property damage resulting from the "manufacture, construction, design, formula, installation, preparation, assembly, testing, packaging, labeling, or sale of any product. . . ."[23] Colorado courts apply the strict liability principles set forth in Section 402A.[24] Strict liability actions can be based on a failure-to-warn, design defect, or manufacturing defect.[25] Relying on Section 402A, the Colorado Supreme Court has held that a plaintiff's prima facie case premised upon strict liability requires proof of each of the following elements: (1) the product was in a defective condition unreasonably dangerous to the user or consumer; (2) the product was expected, and did, reach the consumer without substantial change in the condition in which it was sold; (3) the defect caused the plaintiff's injury; (4) the defendant sold the product and is engaged in the business of selling products; and (5) the plaintiff sustained damages.[26] Whether something is a "product" is a question of law for the court to answer.[27]

3. Defective Condition Unreasonably Dangerous

Under Section 402A, a plaintiff is required to demonstrate that the product was defective and unreasonably dangerous.[28] Although this is only one element in the plaintiff's prima facie case, it is probably the most important, and the other four elements may be established using ordinary principles of tort law.[29] A product may be unreasonably dangerous due to a manufacturing defect, design defect, or a failure-to-warn.[30] In a manufacturing defect case, a product is "unreasonably dangerous" if it was not produced in conformity with the manufacturer's specifications.[31] In a design defect case, the Colorado Supreme Court will use a risk-benefit analysis to determine whether a product is "unreasonably dangerous."[32] In failure-to-warn case, a product is "unreasonably dangerous" if a particular risk is known or knowable in light of the generally recognized prevailing scientific and technical knowledge available at the time of manufacture and distribution.[33] Colorado courts will not use the consumer contemplation test in determining whether a product is unreasonably dangerous.[34]

4. The Product Liability Act of 1977

Strict liability is imposed on every manufacturer and seller in the chain of distribution of a product under Section 402A.[35] In response to the Restatement's broad imposition of liability on manufacturers and sellers the Colorado legislature enacted the Product Liability Act of 1977 (Act).[36] The Act only allows actions in strict liability against manufacturers.[37] However, an exception allows a plaintiff to maintain a products liability action against the manufacturer's principal seller or distributor if jurisdiction cannot be obtained over the manufacturer.[38] The Act broadly defines a manufacturer as "a person or entity who designs, assembles, fabricates, produces, constructs, or otherwise prepares a product or a component part of a product prior to the sale of the product to a user or consumer."[39] Colorado courts have liberally interpreted this statutory definition to allow product liability actions in contexts that only appear to involve sellers.[40] In addition, a plaintiff in a products liability action may assert claims for negligence, breach of warranty, and misrepresentation notwithstanding the Products Liability Act.

5. The Crashworthiness Doctrine

Colorado has adopted the "crashworthiness" or "second collision" doctrine.[41] The doctrine applies to automobile and motorcycle manufacturers.[42] Under the crashworthiness doctrine, a "motor vehicle manufacturer may be liable in negligence or strict liability for injuries sustained in a motor vehicle accident where a manufacturing or design defect, though not the cause of the accident, caused or enhanced the injuries."[43] The critical issue in a crashworthiness case is "whether, under all of the surrounding circumstances, a manufacturer has created an unreasonable risk of increasing the harm in the event of the statistically inevitable. . . ."[44] The doctrine does not require the manufacturer to provide absolute safety; rather, it requires the manufacturer to provide some measure of reasonable and cost-effective safety for the foreseeable use of the product.[45]

D. NEGLIGENCE

Negligence requires that a defendant's conduct fall below an acceptable standard of care; hence, in a products liability action based on negligence the plaintiff must prove the defendant's fault.[46] In contrast to strict liability claims, which require proof of the nature of the dangerous product rather than the fault of the defendant, negligence claims are premised upon the general duty manufacturers and sellers have to consumers or users of their products.[47] The basic elements of a product liability negligence claim are: (1) the product was in a defective condition unreasonably dangerous; (2) the defect resulted from the defendant's breach of a duty owed to the plaintiff; (3)

the defect caused injury to the plaintiff; and (4) the plaintiff suffered damages.[48] Each element will be discussed seriatim.

As in strict liability cases, the plaintiff must prove the product was defective and unreasonably dangerous.[49] This can be done by using the same standards as in strict liability cases.[50] Under the second element, a manufacturer or seller of a product has a duty to "act reasonably in the design, manufacture, and sale of the product."[51] This includes the duty to adequately warn the user or consumer.[52] An important factor in the determination of the duty to warn is the extent to which the danger is open and obvious.[53] If a danger is open and obvious there is no duty to warn unless there is a substantial likelihood that the proposed warning would have prevented injury to the ordinary user.[54] With respect to the last two elements, they may be established using ordinary principles of tort law.[55]

E. BREACH OF WARRANTY

A products liability action for breach of warranty is governed by the UCC.[56] An action for breach of warranty may be brought on the basis of either express or implied warranties.[57] To state a cause of action for breach of warranty, a plaintiff must show: (1) that timely notice was provided to the defendant; (2) if the action is based on breach of an express warranty, that an express warranty was actually made and that she relied on the warranty in purchasing the product; and (3) that a warranty was breached.[58] A seller's warranties, whether express or implied, extend to any person who may reasonably be expected to use, consume, or be affected by the goods and who is injured by the breach of the warranty.[59] A seller may not exclude or limit the operation of this rule.[60]

F. MISREPRESENTATION

A cause of action for misrepresentation is predicated upon an express warranty by advertising rather than on a defective or unreasonably dangerous product.[61] The Colorado Supreme Court has adopted the Restatement (Second) Torts, Section 402B (Section 402B), for misrepresentation claims.[62] As adopted, Section 402B imposes strict liability upon a manufacturer for product misrepresentation.[63] To establish a prima facie case for a strict liability action under Section 402B, three elements must be satisfied: (1) there must be a misrepresentation of a material fact concerning the character or quality of a chattel; (2) the misrepresentation must be made to the public; and (3) physical harm must have resulted to a consumer from justifiable reliance upon the misrepresentation.[64] The third element, justifiable reliance, is the critical element and is determined based upon the reasonable objective belief of the purchaser or user.[65]

G. DEFENSES

Certain affirmative defenses are available to the product liability defendant. Most defenses serve only to reduce the percentage of the damages for which the defendant is liable.

1. **Comparative Fault**

    In Colorado, comparative fault is an affirmative defense for a manufacturer or seller in a product liability action; that is, comparative fault is a damage diminution remedy governed by the Product Liability Act.[66] Comparative fault concepts apply to all product liability causes of action, including breach of express and implied warranty.[67] A defendant in a product liability action who is less negligent than the plaintiff is only required to pay damages in proportion to her pro rata share of causal fault.[68] In other words, the products liability statute "requires the trier of fact in any products liability action to reduce a plaintiff's recovery by a percentage representing the amount of fault attributable to a plaintiff's own conduct."[69] If the injured person's misuse of the product is the sole cause of damages it will bar the plaintiff's recovery.[70]

2. **Assumption of Risk**

    The Colorado Supreme Court has adopted assumption of risk as an affirmative defense to a products liability action under Section 402A.[71] Assumption of risk requires a showing of more than ordinary contributory negligence.[72] The plaintiff must have voluntarily and unreasonably proceeded to encounter a known danger arising from the use of the defendant's product, the specific hazards of which the plaintiff had actual knowledge.[73] Thus, the defendant must establish that the plaintiff had actual knowledge of the specific danger posed by the defect and not just a general knowledge that the product could be dangerous.[74] The party asserting the defense has the burden of establishing its elements.[75] This defense reduces, but does not bar, recovery.

3. **Misuse**

    In the advent of the 2003 legislative changes dealing with misuse, it is unclear whether the legislature has changed the misuse defense to an element of liability which must be disproved by the plaintiff. Misuse has been considered an affirmative defense to a product liability action under Section 402A if the consumer's misuse of the product was unforeseeable by the manufacturer.[76] The usual situation in which the defense is asserted is where the product is being used in a way other than intended, which was not reasonably anticipated by the manufacturer.[77] A defendant who could reasonably foresee the possibility of misuse is not entitled to the defense.[78] Misuse is a question of causation.[79] Regardless of the product's defective condition, the misuse defense can bar recovery if the defendant can show: (1) the plaintiff misused the product; (2) the misuse caused the injury; and (3) the misuse was unforeseeable.[80] In sum, "misuse by an injured party which cannot reasonably be anticipated by the manufacturer can be utilized as a defense in a products liability case by showing that the conduct of the user, and not the alleged defect in a product, actually caused the accident."[81]

4. **Unavoidably Unsafe Product**

Under Section 402A, if a product is determined to be unavoidably unsafe the manufacturer cannot be held liable.[82] The defense was intended for manufacturers of prescription drugs and medical products.[83] In Colorado, transfused blood has been held to be unavoidably unsafe[84] while other products, such as motorcycles, have not been deemed unavoidably unsafe.[85] The manufacturer has the burden of demonstrating four factors to be entitled to the "unavoidably unsafe" defense: (1) the product's utility must greatly outweigh the risk created by its use; (2) the risk must be a known one; (3) the product's benefits must not be achievable in another manner; and (4) the risk must be unavoidable under the present state of knowledge.[86] For the defendant to successfully assert the defense, the product should carry a profound benefit that extends to the vast majority of the users of the product.[87] The manufacturer must know the risk associated with the product at the time of distribution and demonstrate that at the time the product was marketed the state of the art had not progressed to a point where the risk was no longer unavoidable.[88]

5. **Open and Obvious**

In failure-to-warn products liability cases, the manufacturer may assert that a risk is open and obvious as a partial defense.[89] It is the trial court's obligation to determine if the defendant had a duty to warn.[90] Whether the danger is open and obvious is a factor the court will consider in determining if the manufacturer had a duty to warn.[91] A Colorado Court of Appeals explained that:

> [i]n determining whether a defendant had a duty to warn an ordinary user in the plaintiff's position, the trial court should consider the obviousness of the danger and the efficacy of the proposed warning. If a danger is open and obvious, there is no duty to warn unless there is a substantial likelihood that the proposed warning would have prevented injury to the ordinary user.[92]

The partial defense cannot be asserted, even if the danger is open and obvious, if a warning would have made the product safer or if there was an actual defect in the product.[93]

6. **Learned Intermediary Doctrine**

While the Colorado Supreme Court has not expressly adopted the learned intermediary doctrine, courts have applied the rule; in a product liability case, a prescription drug manufacturer's duty to warn is owed to the physician.[94] A warning is adequate when it explains to the physician the dangers and risks that the plaintiff alleges caused her injuries from the drug.[95] The physician has the responsibility, as the learned intermediary, to assess the risks and benefits of a particular drug and to prescribe a course of treatment.[96]

7. **Successor Corporations**

In Colorado, strict products liability does not attach to a corporate successor for the defective product of a predecessor corporation.[97] Generally, a corporation that acquires the assets of another corporation does not become liable for the debts of the selling corporation.[98] This rule is not absolute and successors have been held liable where: (1) the purchaser expressly or impliedly agrees to assume the debts of the selling corporation; (2) the transaction amounts to a consolidation or merger of the seller and purchaser; (3) the purchasing corporation is merely a continuation of the selling corporation; or (4) the transaction is entered into fraudulently in order to escape liability.[99] However, under the Product Liability Act[100] a successor corporation does not fall within the statutory definition of a manufacturer; hence, it cannot be held strictly liable under Section 402A.[101] Colorado courts have expressly rejected exceptions to the general rule against successor nonliability in products liability actions such as the "product line doctrine" and the "continuity of enterprise" exception.[102]

8. **Release**

However, in Colorado a defendant may not rely on an exculpatory agreement purporting to release a manufacturer from a strict products liability claim as a defense.[103] In 2010, the Colorado Supreme Court held that such agreements necessarily violate public policy in this jurisdiction.[104] The Court previously held that exculpatory agreements purporting to release a party from negligence claims are not necessarily void, and articulated a four-factor public policy test for courts to use in determining whether such an agreement is valid.[105] But the Court made clear that strict products liability is an entirely different matter, to which this public policy test does not apply.[106]

H. FIREARMS

In Colorado, a product liability action involving a firearm can only be based upon "an actual defect in the design or manufacture of such firearm or ammunition. . . ."[107] In a design defect case involving a firearm the plaintiff must prove, in addition to any other elements, that: (1) the actual design was defective; (2) the defective design was the proximate cause; (3) of injury, damage, or death.[108] In a manufacturing defect case the plaintiff must prove the firearm or ammunition was manufactured at variance from its design and that this was the proximate cause of her injuries, damages, or death.[109] In both design and manufacturing defect product liability cases proximate cause is defined as the actual discharge of the firearm or ammunition.[110] A product liability action cannot be based upon the inherent danger of a firearm or ammunition to cause injury or death.[111] In addition, a Colorado court has held that the failure to adequately warn concerning the experience, maturity, and knowledge of the potential users of firearms cannot render the firearm defective and unreasonably dangerous.[112]

I. **FOOD**

In Colorado, the Commonsense Consumption Act[113] was enacted to limit the civil liability of a food provider for claims arising from "weight gain, obesity, a health condition associated with weight gain or obesity, or other injury caused from the long-term consumption of food."[114] The Act declares that individuals remain ultimately responsible for the choices they make regarding their bodies, and excessive litigation restricts the range of choices available to individuals who consume products responsibly.[115] This Act does not preclude civil liability of a food provider in cases involving injury caused by a material violation of a composition, branding, or labeling standards prescribed by state or federal law.[116] In a food product liability case involving a violation of a standard prescribed by state or federal law, the plaintiff must state with particularity in the complaint: (1) actual injury; (2) knowledge and willfulness; and (3) proximate cause.[117]

J. **PRESUMPTIONS**

1. **State-of-the-Art Presumption of Non-Defectiveness**

    Under Section 402A, evidence that a product conformed to the level of scientific and technical knowledge considered to be state-of-the-art at the time of manufacture is admissible to determine if a product is defective or unreasonably dangerous in failure-to-warn and design defect strict product liability actions.[118] State-of-the-art is defined as "the point of scientific and technological advancement with respect to a given product at the time of the product's manufacture and design."[119] In a negligence products liability action, the defendant's state-of-the-art evidence is one factor to consider in assessing the manufacturer's due care.[120] In Colorado, it is rebuttably presumed that the product which caused the injury was not defective if the manufacturer conformed to the state of the art applicable to the product at the time of sale.[121] The presumption, however, does not apply in the case of a product that is claimed to be unavoidably unsafe.[122] A plaintiff can rebut the state-of-the-art presumption by demonstrating by a preponderance of the evidence that the product did not conform to the scientific and technological state-of-the-art at the time of manufacture or design.[123]

2. **Presumption of Non-Defectiveness for Compliance with Government Codes**

    In a products liability action, if the product complied with any applicable government code, standard, or regulation at the time of sale then there is a rebuttable presumption that the product was not defective.[124] Thus, although it does not conclusively establish due care by the manufacturer, evidence of compliance with applicable federal regulation is admissible to show the product was not defective.[125] Compliance with federal and state codes will raise this presumption; however, compliance with local codes is not sufficient to raise the presumption.[126] Conversely, if the product violated a government code, standard, or regulation at the time of sale it is rebuttably presumed that the product was defective.[127] If the court determines by a preponderance of the evidence that all of the established facts give rise to a presumption, the court will instruct the jury concerning the presumption.[128]

3. Ten-Year Presumption of Non-Defectiveness

A rebuttable presumption arises that a product was not defective and contained adequate warnings if there are no injuries for ten years after the product was first sold.[129] Colorado Revised Statute, Section 13-21-403(3), which creates the presumption, is not a statute of repose that insulates a defendant from liability if the product was sold, used, or consumed more than ten years prior to injury; rather, it creates only a presumption that will prevail in the absence of evidence to the contrary.[130] Once a court determines by a preponderance of the evidence that the necessary facts giving rise to a presumption have been established, the court shall instruct the jury concerning the presumption.[131]

K. EVIDENTIARY ISSUES

Under the Product Liability Act,[132] evidence of scientific or technological advancement that occurred after the product was sold is not admissible to show that the product was defective.[133] However, under the Product Liability Act evidence of post-sale advancements in scientific or technological knowledge may be admitted to demonstrate that the manufacturer had a duty to warn.[134] Pursuant to Colorado Rule of Evidence 407, evidence of subsequent remedial measures is generally precluded if it is introduced to prove negligence or culpable conduct.[135] The Colorado Supreme Court has held that Rule 407 does not apply to strict liability design defect cases.[136] Nevertheless, evidence of subsequent remedial measures must still be relevant and pass the Rule 403 balancing test to be admissible.[137] Although never directly addressing the issue, the Colorado Supreme Court has strongly hinted that Rule 407 does, however, apply to strict liability cases premised on a failure to warn.[138]

L. DAMAGES

1. Generally

Subject to certain statutory limits, in any products liability action a plaintiff will be entitled to recover the same damages as a general personal injury plaintiff.[139] Hence, a plaintiff in a products liability action can recover lost earnings and profits, lost earning capacity, lost time, medical expenses, special damages, loss of consortium, pain and suffering, loss of enjoyment of life, emotional distress, and interest.

2. Noneconomic Damages

The Colorado legislature, however, has imposed a statutory cap on noneconomic damages.[140] A Colorado court of appeals has upheld the constitutionality of the statutory cap on noneconomic damages.[141] Pursuant to the statutory language, in a products liability action the plaintiff's recovery for noneconomic losses cannot exceed $468,010 unless the court finds clear and convincing evidence that the award should exceed $468,010; however, in no event can recovery exceed $936,030.[142] In addition, the trial court is not required to make a special finding of clear and convincing evidence.[143] Derivative noneconomic loss damages cannot be awarded unless the court finds clear and convincing evidence that they should be awarded, and if awarded, the amount cannot exceed $468,010.[144] These statutory limits on damages do not apply to compensatory damages for physical impairment or disfigurement.[145]

The statutory cap on noneconomic damages applies to the liability share of each defendant in a case and does not cap the total amount a plaintiff can recover from several defendants.[146] Therefore, if a plaintiff proves the liability of multiple defendants she will be allowed the maximum amount of recovery under the statutory cap against each defendant.[147]

In wrongful death actions, noneconomic losses cannot exceed $436,070 in any case unless the act causing death constituted a felonious killing.[148] However, subject to the cap, surviving plaintiffs are expressly allowed to recover for grief, loss of companionship, pain and suffering, and emotional distress.[149]

3. **Economic Loss Rule**

The Economic Loss Rule prohibits a negligence claim when the duty is contractual and the harm incurred is the "result of failure of the purpose of the contract."[150] In order to determine whether the rule applies, the court must "focus on the source of the duty alleged to have been violated."[151] The Colorado Supreme Court recognized in *Town of Alma v. Azco Construction, Inc.* that some relationships "by their nature automatically trigger an independent duty of care that supports a tort action even when the parties have entered into a contractual relationship."[152] Strict products liability imposes a duty on the manufacturer of a product, outside any contractual duty, to act reasonably in the design, manufacture, and sale of a product.[153] Therefore, because a product manufacturer has the independent duty to act reasonably in the design, manufacture, and sale of a product, the Economic Loss Rule does not serve to preclude a plaintiff's tort claims.[154]

4. **Punitive or Exemplary Damages**

In Colorado, reasonable exemplary damages can be awarded only pursuant to statute.[155] A claim for exemplary damages may not be included in an initial claim for relief, it is only allowed by an amendment to the pleadings after the exchange of initial disclosures pursuant to Rule 26 of the Colorado Rules of Civil Procedure and after the plaintiff establishes prima facie proof of a triable issue; the court may then use its discretion to allow additional discovery on the issue of exemplary damages as the court deems appropriate.[156] In order to recover exemplary damages, the plaintiff must demonstrate beyond a reasonable doubt that the defendant engaged in willful and wanton misconduct.[157] Exemplary damages are allowed to punish the wrongdoer and deter similar conduct in the future rather than compensate the injured party for the wrong done.[158] Under Colorado's Exemplary Damage Statute the amount of exemplary damages awarded shall not exceed the amount of actual damages awarded to the injured party.[159] However, the statutory scheme permits a court to treble the exemplary damages if during the pendency of the action the defendant continued his injurious behavior.[160] Moreover, an award of exemplary damages remains in the discretion of the trier of fact even if the plaintiff has established that such damages are permissible.[161]

M. EMPLOYER IMMUNITY FROM SUIT

The Colorado Workers' Compensation Act[162] provides the exclusive remedy for a worker injured on the job and an employee may not bring an action against their employer for typical work-related injuries.[163] This litigation bar extends to protect actual employers and independent contractors who perform essential functions of the employer's business.[164] Despite the Workers' Compensation bar, an employer may bear ultimate financial responsibility for a defective product which causes injury if the employer has a contractual duty to indemnify the manufacturer of the product. The Colorado Supreme Court has also indicated that nonparties who are immune because of the statutory bar of the Workers' Compensation Act may nevertheless be designated as nonparties at fault under Colorado Revised Statute, Section 13-21-111.5.[165]

N. THE LIABILITY APPORTIONMENT STATUTE

1. Generally

Colorado has abolished the common law doctrine of joint and several liability[166] and adopted a several liability scheme that only holds a tortfeasor responsible for the portion of damages that she caused.[167] Joint and several liability was abolished to reduce unfair burdens placed on defendants.[168] Under Colorado's pro rata liability apportionment statute ("Section 13-21-111.5") liability is apportioned among the parties according to their relative degree of fault.[169] Further, under Section 13-21-111.5, plaintiffs and defendants may designate nonparties as being wholly or partially at fault and the finder of fact is authorized to consider a percentage of the nonparty's negligence or fault in apportioning ultimate liability.[170] If nonparties are designated the defendant is liable only for that fault apportioned to it by the jury.[171] However, a designated nonparty who is at fault is not liable for the judgment amount apportioned to it.[172] Likewise, the designated nonparty is not bound by the determination of liability or the amount of damages in a subsequent action against it.[173]

2. Statutory Language

Section 13-21-111.5 provides in pertinent part:

(1) In an action brought as a result of a death or an injury to person or property, no defendant shall be liable for an amount greater than represented by the degree or percentage of the negligence or fault attributable to such defendant that produced the claimed injury, death, damage or loss, except as provided in subsection (4) of this section.

(2) The jury shall return a special verdict . . . determining the percentage or negligence or fault attributable to each of the parties an[d] any persons not parties to the action of whom notice has been given . . . to whom some negligence or fault is found and determining the total amount of damages sustained by each claimant . . .

(3)(a) Any provision of the law to the contrary notwithstanding, the finder of fact in a civil action may consider the degree or percentage of negligence or fault of a person not a party to the action, based upon evidence thereof, which shall be admissible, in determining the degree or percentage of negligence or fault of those persons who are parties to such action. . . .

3. **Causes of Action Effected by Section 13-21-111.5**

Section 13-21-111.5 applies to both negligence and strict liability actions.[174] The statute allows apportionment of fault between parties and nonparties to the action without regard to whether the tortfeasor acted intentionally or negligently.[175] However, in actions based on breach of fiduciary duty or duty of loyalty, joint and several liability has not been abrogated.[176] Likewise, joint and several liability is applicable when evidence demonstrates a course of conduct by the defendants from which a tacit agreement to act in concert can be implied.[177] The tort of negligent entrustment can be deemed a "tortious act" in order to establish joint and several liability.[178]

4. **Common Issues Under Section 13-21-111.5**

Several common issues reoccur under Section 13-21-115.5, including the effect of settlements on being designated as a nonparty, joint and several liability for partnerships, and contribution/indemnity issues. Each will be discussed in turn.

a. **Settlement Issue**

Pursuant to Section 13-21-111.5, the court can consider the negligence or fault of a nonparty who settled with the plaintiff when it apportions damages.[179] Therefore, a defendant who has settled with the plaintiff may be designated as a nonparty under the statute.[180] However, the nonparty must still owe the plaintiff a duty in order to apportion fault to it.[181] Apportioning fault to a nonparty that settled with the plaintiff has been held constitutional as long as the procedural safeguards in Section 13-21-111.5(3)(b) are followed.[182] Section 13-21-111.5(3)(b) requires that before the fault of a nonparty may be considered the defending party must give notice that a nonparty was at fault within 90 days following commencement of the action unless the court grants a longer period.[183]

b. Partnership Issues

Colorado follows the well-established rule that partners are jointly and severally liable for the wrongs of the partnership.[184] Although this rule is arguably in conflict with Colorado's pro rata liability statute, a federal district court applying Colorado law held that "section 13-21-111.5 does not abrogate the well-established Colorado rule that partners are jointly and severally liable for the wrongs of the partnership."[185] Therefore, an individual partner can be held vicariously liable for the wrongful acts or omissions of a partner in the ordinary course of partnership business.[186]

c. Contribution and Indemnity Issues

Contribution is the right to demand that a party bear its share of the liability on a concurrently caused injury and is "based on the equitable notion that one tortfeasor should not be required to pay sums to an injured party in excess of that tortfeasor's proportionate share of the responsibility for the injuries."[187] Section 13-21-111.5 has been integrated with the Uniform Contribution Among Tortfeasors Act.[188] This gives the defendant the right to seek contribution from a joint tortfeasor for the amount the defendant paid in excess of her pro rata share of liability for the plaintiff's injuries.[189] Thus, the pro rata liability statute does not abrogate the defendant's right to contribution from joint tortfeasors.[190]

Indemnity is "grounded in the legal principle that one joint tortfeasor, as indemnitor, may owe a duty of care to another joint tortfeasor, which duty is unrelated to any duty of care owed by the tortfeasors to the injured party."[191] When such duty is established, the indemnitor may be liable to the indemnitee.[192] In Colorado, "the doctrine of indemnity insofar as it requires one of two joint tortfeasors to reimburse the other for the entire amount paid by the other as damages to a party injured as a result of the negligence of both tortfeasors is . . . abolished."[193] A federal district court has extended this rationale by holding that Section 13-21-111.5 applies in strict product liability actions; hence, extending the Colorado Supreme Court's reasoning to situations where the party seeking indemnity is not at fault.[194]

O. PRE- AND POST-JUDGMENT INTEREST

In Colorado, pre- and post-judgment interest is determined by statute.[195] Colorado's general interest statute provides in pertinent part that "[i]n all actions brought to recover damages for personal injuries, . . . it is lawful for the plaintiff in the complaint to claim interest on the damages alleged from the date said suit is filed; and, interest on the damages claimed from the date the action accrued."[196] If the judgment debtor appeals the trial court's final judgment, pre- and post-judgment interest is determined by using a market-determined interest rate, which is amended annually.[197] Conversely, if the judgment debtor does not appeal the trial court's final judgment, the statute requires a 9 percent interest rate on personal injury money judgments.[198] Colorado's general interest statute does not distinguish between future and past damages when awarding interest.[199] However, there are two major limitations on Colorado's general interest statute: (1) property damage is not considered within the purview of the statute because it does not constitute a "personal injury" for purposes of awarding interest;[200] and (2) the authorized pre-judgment interest does not apply to punitive damages.[201]

Thomas B. Quinn, Esquire
Greg S. Hearing, Esquire
Gordon & Rees LLP
555 Seventeenth Street, Suite 3400
Denver, Colorado 80202
(303) 534-5160
(Fax) (303) 534-5161
tquinn@gordonrees.com
ghearing@gordonrees.com

ENDNOTES - COLORADO

1. Colo. Rev. Stat. §§ 13-21-401 to 13-21-406 (2011).

2. *Union Supply Co. v. Pust*, 583 P.2d 276, 282-83 (Colo. 1978); *see also Barton v. Adams Rental, Inc.*, 938 P.2d 532, 536-37 (Colo. 1997).

3. *Persichini v. Brad Ragan, Inc.*, 735 P.2d 168, 174 (Colo. 1987).

4. *Persichini*, 735 P.2d at 176.

5. *Am. Safety Equip. Corp. v. Winkler*, 640 P.2d 216, 220-21 (Colo. 1982).

6. Colo. Rev. Stat. § 13-21-402.5 (2011).

7. Colo. Rev. Stat. § 13-21-402(1) (2011); *but see* Colo. Rev. Stat. § 13-21-401(1) (2011) (defining "manufacturer" broadly).

8. Colo. Rev. Stat. §§ 4-2-313 to 4-2-318 (2011).

9. Colo. Rev. Stat. § 13-80-101(1)(a) (2011).

10. Colo. Rev. Stat. § 13-80-108(6) (2011); *see Hersch Cos. Inc. v. Highline Village Assocs.*, 30 P.3d 221, 224-25 (Colo. 2001); *see also Stiff v. BilDen Homes, Inc.*, 88 P.3d 639, 642 (Colo. App. 2003).

11. Colo. Rev. Stat. § 13-80-106(1) (2011).

12. Colo. Rev. Stat. § 13-80-108(1) (2011).

13. *Miller v. Armstrong World Indus., Inc.*, 817 P.2d 111, 113 (Colo. 1991) (quoting *City of Aurora v. Bechtel Corp.*, 599 F.2d 382, 389 (10th Cir. 1979)).

14. Colo. Rev. Stat. § 13-80-107 (2011).

15. *Anderson v. M.W. Kellogg Co.*, 766 P.2d 637, 640 (Colo. 1988).

16. Colo. Rev. Stat. § 13-80-107(1)(b).

17. Colo. Rev. Stat. § 13-80-107(1)(b)-(c).

18. *Anderson*, 766 P.2d at 643 (emphasis, citations, and quotations omitted); *see also Urban v. Beloit Corp.*, 711 P.2d 685, 687 (Colo. 1985).

19. *Hiigel v. Gen. Motors Corp.*, 544 P.2d 983, 989 (Colo. 1975); *Town of Alma v. Azco Constr., Inc.*, 10 P.3d 1256, 1260-61 (Colo. 2000).

20. *Mile Hi Concrete, Inc. v. Matz*, 842 P.2d 198, 205 (Colo. 1992).

21. *Mile Hi Concrete*, 842 P.2d at 205.

22. *See* Restatement (Second) of Torts § 402A(2)(a) (1965). While some jurisdictions require a plaintiff to show that a practical and feasible, safer alternative exists to succeed on a design defect claim, Colorado does not require such a showing.

23. Colo. Rev. Stat. § 13-21-401(2) (2011).

24. *Barton*, 938 P.2d 532, 536-37.

25. *Fibreboard Corp. v. Fenton*, 845 P.2d 1168, 1173 (Colo. 1993).

26. *Barton*, 938 P.2d at 536-37.

27. *Smith v. Home Light & Power Co.*, 695 P.2d 788, 789 (Colo. App. 1984), *aff'd*, 734 P.2d 1051 (Colo. 1987).

28. *Fenton*, 845 P.2d at 1175.

29. *See Fenton*, 845 P.2d at 1173-75; *Barton*, 938 P.2d at 536-39.

30. *Camacho v. Honda Motor Co. Ltd.*, 741 P.2d 1240, 1247 (Colo. 1987).

31. *Camacho*, 741 P.2d at 1247.

32. *Barton*, 938 P.2d at 537. To determine whether the risks outweigh the benefits, the finder of fact must consider various factors including: (1) the usefulness and desirability of the product—its utility to the user and to the public as a whole; (2) the safety aspects of the product—the likelihood that it will cause injury and the probable seriousness of the injury; (3) the availability of a substitute product which would meet the same need and not be as unsafe; (4) the manufacturer's ability to eliminate the unsafe character of the product without impairing its usefulness or making it too expensive to maintain its utility; (5) the user's ability to avoid danger by the exercise of care in the use of the product; (6) the user's anticipated awareness of the dangers inherent in the product and their avoidability because of general public knowledge of the obvious condition of the product, or of the existence of suitable warnings or instructions; (7) the feasibility, on the part of the manufacturer, of spreading the loss by setting the price of the product or carrying liability insurance. *Barton*, 938 P.2d at 537.

33. *Fenton*, 845 P.2d at 1175.

34. *Camacho*, 741 P.2d at 1245 ("[The consumer contemplation test] is not the appropriate standard in Colorado for measuring whether a particular product is in a defective condition unreasonably dangerous to the consumer or user."). Under the consumer contemplation test a manufacturer is not liable if the article sold is not dangerous to an extent beyond that which would be contemplated by the ordinary consumer who purchases it. *See* Restatement (Second) of Torts § 402A cmt. i (1965).

35. W. Page Keeton, et al., Prosser & Keeton on Torts § 100, at 704-07 (5th ed. 1984).

36. Colo. Rev. Stat. §§ 13-21-401 to 13-21-406 (2010).

37. Colo. Rev. Stat. § 13-21-402(1) (2011).

38. Colo. Rev. Stat. § 13-21-402(2). *See also Halter v. Waco Scaffolding & Equip. Co.*, 797 P.2d 790, 793 (Colo. App. 1990).

39. Colo. Rev. Stat. § 13-21-401(1).

40. *See Miller v. Solaglas Cal., Inc.*, 870 P.2d 559, 565 (Colo. App. 1993) (declining to reverse a jury's finding that a corporation that installed windshields was a manufacturer under the Product Liability Act); *see also Ruiz v. ExCello Corp.*, 653 P.2d 415, 417 (Colo. App. 1982) (reversing summary judgment on grounds that corporate rule of successor liability as applied to manufacturer raised a genuine issue of material fact).

41. *Roberts v. May*, 583 P.2d 305, 307 (Colo. App. 1978); *Camacho*, 741 P.2d at 1242-43.

42. *Roberts*, 583 P.2d at 307; *Camacho*, 741 P.2d at 1243.

43. *Camacho*, 741 P.2d at 1242-43.

44. *Roberts*, 583 P.2d at 308.

45. *Camacho*, 741 P.2d at 1243.

46. *Lui v. Barnhart*, 987 P.2d 942, 945 (Colo. App. 1999).

47. *Lui*, 987 P.2d at 945.

48. *See Mile Hi Concrete*, 842 P.2d 198, 202.

49. *Mile Hi Concrete*, 842 P.2d at 205.

50. *See supra* notes 26-32 and accompanying text.

51. *Halliburton v. Pub. Serv. Co.*, 804 P.2d 213, 216-17 (Colo. App. 1990).

52. *Halliburton*, 804 P.2d at 216-17.

53. *Armentrout v. FMC Corp.*, 842 P.2d 175, 181 (Colo. 1992).

54. *White v. Caterpillar, Inc.*, 867 P.2d 100, 107 (Colo. App. 1993).

55. *See Union Supply Co. v. Pust*, 583 P.2d 276, 283 (Colo. 1978).

56. *Persichini v. Brad Ragan, Inc.*, 735 P.2d 168, 176 (Colo. 1987); *see also* Colo. Rev. Stat. §§ 4-2-313 to 4-2-318 (2011).

57. Colo. Rev. Stat. § 4-2-313 (2011) (express warranties); Colo. Rev. Stat. § 4-2-314 (2011) (implied warranty of merchantability); Colo. Rev. Stat. § 4-2-315 (2011) (implied warranty of fitness for a particular purpose).

58. *Palmer v. A.H. Robins Co. Inc.*, 684 P.2d 187, 205-08 (Colo. 1984).

59. Colo. Rev. Stat. § 4-2-318 (2011).

60. Colo. Rev. Stat. § 4-2-318 (2011).

61. *Am. Safety Equip. Corp. v. Winkler*, 640 P.2d 216, 219 (Colo. 1982).

62. *Am. Safety Equip. Corp.*, 640 P.2d at 220.

63. *Am. Safety Equip. Corp.*, 640 P.2d at 221.

64. *Am. Safety Equip. Corp.*, 640 P.2d at 222.

65. *Am. Safety Equip. Corp.*, 640 P.2d at 222. *See also* Restatement (Second) of Torts § 402B cmt. j (1965).

66. Colo. Rev. Stat. § 13-21-406(1) (2011).

67. *Loughridge v. Goodyear Tire & Rubber Co.*, 207 F. Supp. 2d 1187, 1189 (D. Colo. 2002), *rev'd on other grounds*, 431 F.3d 1268 (10th Cir. 2005).

68. *Mountain Mobile Mix, Inc. v. Gifford*, 660 P.2d 883, 889-90 (Colo. 1983).

69. *Miller v. Solaglas Cal., Inc.*, 870 P.2d 559, 565 (Colo. App. 1993).

70. *States v. R.D. Werner Co., Inc.*, 799 P.2d 427, 430 (Colo. App. 1990).

71. *Jackson v. Harsco Corp.*, 673 P.2d 363, 366 (Colo. 1983).

72. *Camacho*, 741 P.2d at 1245 n.6.

73. *Camacho*, 741 P.2d at 1245 n.6.

74. *Littlejohn v. Stanley Structures, Inc.*, 688 P.2d 1130, 1133 (Colo. App. 1984).

75. *Jackson*, 673 P.2d at 366.

76. *See Jackson*, 673 P.2d at 367; *see also Uptain v. Huntington Lab., Inc.*, 723 P.2d 1322, 1325 (Colo. 1986), *overruled on other grounds by Wagner v. Case Corp.*, 33 F.3d 1253, 1256 (10th Cir. 1994).

77. *Jackson*, 673 P.2d at 367.

78. *Schmutz v. Bolles*, 800 P.2d 1307, 1316 (Colo. 1990).

79. *Uptain*, 723 P.2d at 1325.

80. *Uptain*, 723 P.2d at 1324-26.

81. *Jackson*, 673 P.2d at 367.

82. *Belle Bonfils Mem'l Blood Bank v. Hansen*, 665 P.2d 118, 122 (Colo. 1983). *See also* Restatement (Second) of Torts § 402A cmt. k (1965); *but see United Blood Servs. v. Quintana*, 827 P.2d 509, 522 n.9 (Colo. 1992) (noting that *Hansen* was decided prior to the Colorado legislature's enactment of Colo. Rev. Stat. § 13-22-104).

83. *Belle Bonfils Mem'l Blood Bank v. Hansen*, 665 P.2d 118, 122 (Colo. 1983). *See also* Restatement (Second) of Torts § 402A cmt. k (1965); *but see United Blood Servs. v. Quintana*, 827 P.2d 509, 522 n.9 (Colo. 1992) (noting that *Hansen* was decided prior to the Colorado legislature's enactment of Colo. Rev. Stat. § 13-22-104).

84. *Hansen*, 665 P.2d at 127.

85. *Camacho*, 741 P.2d at 1244 n.5 (Colo. 1987).

86. *Hansen*, 665 P.2d at 122-23; *Ortho Pharm. Corp. v. Heath*, 722 P.2d 410, 415 (Colo. 1986); *but see Armentrout v. FMC Corp.*, 842 P.2d 175, 183-84 (Colo. 1992) (overruling *Heath* to the extent it holds that the burden of proving a product's benefits outweigh its inherent risks rests with the manufacturer).

87. *Hansen*, 665 P.2d at 123.

88. *Hansen*, 665 P.2d at 123.

89. *Anderson*, 766 P.2d 637, 643 (Colo. 1988).

90. *White v. Caterpillar, Inc.*, 867 P.2d 100, 107 (Colo. App. 1993).

91. *Armentrout v. FMC Corp.*, 842 P.2d 175, 181 (Colo. 1992).

92. *White*, 867 P.2d at 107.

93. *Armentrout*, 842 P.2d at 181.

94. *Hamilton v. Hardy*, 549 P.2d 1099, 1109-10 (Colo. App. 1976), *overruled on other grounds by State Bd. of Med. Exam'rs v. McCroskey*, 880 P.2d 1188, 1192 (Colo. 1994).

95. *Caveny v. CIBA-GEIGY Corp.*, 818 F. Supp. 1404, 1406 (D. Colo. 1992). *See also O'Connel v. Biomet, Inc.*, 250 P.3d 1278, 1281-82 (Colo. App. 2010) (extending the learned intermediary rule to "medical devices installed operatively when it is available only to physicians and obtained by prescription, and the doctor is in a position to reduce the risks of harm in accordance with the instructions or warnings.").

96. *Caveny v. CIBA-GEIGY Corp.*, 818 F. Supp. 1404, 1406 (D. Colo. 1992). *See also O'Connel v. Biomet, Inc.*, 250 P.3d 1278, 1281-82 (Colo. App. 2010) (extending the learned intermediary rule to "medical devices installed operatively when it is available only to physicians and obtained by prescription, and the doctor is in a position to reduce the risks of harm in accordance with the instructions or warnings."); *see also Bowman v. Songer*, 820 P.2d 1110, 1114 (Colo. 1991).

97. *Johnston v. Amsted Indus., Inc.*, 830 P.2d 1141, 1143-44 (Colo. App. 1992).

98. *Alcan Aluminum Corp. v. Elec. Metal Prods., Inc.*, 837 P.2d 282, 283 (Colo. App. 1992).

99. *Ruiz v. ExCello Corp.*, 653 P.2d 415, 416 (Colo. App. 1982).

100. Colo. Rev. Stat. §§ 13-21-401 to 13-21-406 (2011).

101. *Johnston*, 830 P.2d at 1143-44.

102. *Johnston*, 830 P.2d at 1146-47.

103. *Boles v. Sun Ergoline, Inc.*, 223 P.3d 724 (Colo. 2010).

104. *Boles*, 223 P.3d at 728.

105. *Jones v. Dressel*, 623 P.2d 370, 376 (Colo. 1981).

106. *Boles*, 223 P.3d at 726-27.

107. Colo. Rev. Stat. § 13-21-501(1) (2011).

108. Colo. Rev. Stat. § 13-21-503(2)(a) (2011).

109. Colo. Rev. Stat. § 13-21-503(b).

110. Colo. Rev. Stat. § 13-21-504(1) (2011).

111. Colo. Rev. Stat. § 13-21-503(3).

112. *Hilberg v. F.W. Woolworth Co.*, 761 P.2d 236, 240-42 (Colo. App. 1988), *overruled on other grounds by Casebolt v. Cowan*, 829 P.2d 352, 360 (Colo. 1992).

113. Colo. Rev. Stat. §§ 13-21-1101 to 13-21-1106 (2011).

114. Colo. Rev. Stat. § 13-21-1104(1) (2011).

115. Colo. Rev. Stat. § 13-21-1102(1)(b)-(c) (2011).

116. Colo. Rev. Stat. § 13-21-1104(2) (2011).

117. Colo. Rev. Stat. § 13-21-1105 (2011).

118. *Fenton*, 845 P.2d 1168, 1172 (failure to warn); *Roberts*, 583 P.2d 305, 307 (design defect).

119. *Hansen*, 665 P.2d at 124; *see also supra* note 2.

120. *Hansen*, 665 P.2d at 124 n.10.

121. Colo. Rev. Stat. § 13-21-403(1)(a) (2011).

122. *Hansen*, 665 P.2d at 126 n.14.

123. *Tafoya v. Sears Roebuck & Co.*, 884 F.2d 1330 (10th Cir. 1989) (It should be noted that upon careful analysis, this case remains good law but has been questioned directly on point by *Wagner v. Case Corp.*, 33 F.3d 1253, 1257 (10th Cir. 1994)).

124. Colo. Rev. Stat. § 13-21-403(1)(b).

125. *Blueflame Gas, Inc. v. Van Hoose*, 679 P.2d 579, 591-92 (Colo. 1984).

126. Colo. Rev. Stat. § 13-21-403(1)(b).

127. Colo. Rev. Stat. § 13-21-403(2).

128. Colo. Rev. Stat. § 13-21-403(4).

129. Colo. Rev. Stat. § 13-21-403(3).

130. *Mile Hi Concrete*, 842 P.2d 198, 204.

131. Colo. Rev. Stat. § 13-21-401(4) (2011); *see also Kokins v. Teleflex, Inc.*, 621 F.3d 1290, 1306 (10th Cir. 2010).

132. Colo. Rev. Stat. §§ 13-21-401 to 13-21-406.

133. Colo. Rev. Stat. § 13-21-404 (2011).

134. Colo. Rev. Stat. § 13-21-404 (2011).

135. Colo. R. Evid. 407. Rule 407 provides: "When after an event, measures are taken which, if taken previously, would have made the event less likely to occur, evidence of the subsequent measures is not admissible to prove negligence or culpable conduct in connection with the event. This rule does not require the exclusion of evidence of subsequent measures when offered for another purpose, such as proving ownership, control, or feasibility of precautionary measures, if controverted, or impeachment."

136. *Forma Scientific, Inc. v. BioSera, Inc.*, 960 P.2d 108, 118 (Colo. 1998).

137. *Forma Scientific*, 960 P.2d at 118. *See also* Colo. R. Evid. 401, 403.

138. *Forma Scientific*, 960 P.2d at 118; *see also Uptain*, 723 P.2d 1322, 1328.

139. *See generally Seaward Constr. Co., Inc. v. Bradley*, 817 P.2d 971 (Colo. 1991).

140. Colo. Rev. Stat. § 13-21-102.5(3) (2011).

141. *Scharrel v. Wal-Mart Stores Inc.*, 949 P.2d 89, 95-96 (Colo. App. 1997).

142. Colo. Rev. Stat. § 13-21-102.5(3)(a). However, the statutory caps are allowed to rise over time to reflect inflation and practitioners should check to determine what the actual statutory cap is in any given year; *see* Secretary of State of Colorado, Adjusted Limitation on Damages Certificate, *available at* http://www.sos.state.co.us/pubs/info_center/certificates.html.

143. *Colwell v. Mentzer Invs., Inc.*, 973 P.2d 631, 639 (Colo. App. 1998).

144. Colo. Rev. Stat. § 13-21-102.5(3)(b).

145. Colo. Rev. Stat. § 13-21-102.5(5).

146. *General Elec. Co. v. Niemet*, 866 P.2d 1361, 1368 (Colo. 1994).

147. *General Elec. Co.*, 866 P.2d at 1368.

148. Colo. Rev. Stat. § 13-21-203(1) (2011); *see also Aiken v. Peters*, 899 P.2d 382, 385 (Colo. App. 1995).

149. Colo. Rev. Stat. § 13-21-203(1).

150. *Town of Alma v. Azco Constr., Inc.*, 10 P.3d 1256, 1263 (Colo. 2000) (citing references omitted); *see also Grynberg v. Agri Tech, Inc.*, 10 P.3d 1267 (Colo. 2000).

151. *Town of Alma*, 10 P.3d at 1263; *see also BRW, Inc. v. Dufficy & Sons, Inc.*, 99 P.3d 66 (Colo. 2004).

152. *Town of Alma*, 10 P.3d at 1263.

153. *Halliburton v. Pub. Serv. Co. of Colo.*, 804 P.2d 213 (Colo. App. 1990).

154. *Loughridge v. Goodyear Tire & Rubber Co.*, 192 F. Supp. 2d 1175 (D. Colo. 2002), *rev'd on other grounds*, 431 F.3d 1268 (10th Cir. 2005).

155. Colo. Rev. Stat. § 13-21-102 (2011); *see also Corbetta v. Albertson's, Inc.*, 975 P.2d 718, 721 (Colo. 1999); *Peterson v. McMahon*, 99 P.3d 594, 597 (Colo. 2004).

156. Colo. Rev. Stat. § 13-21-102(1.5)(a).

157. Colo. Rev. Stat. § 13-21-102(1)(a); *see also Pizza v. Wolf Creek Ski Dev. Corp.*, 711 P.2d 671, 684 (Colo. 1985).

158. *Bradley*, 817 P.2d at 974.

159. Colo. Rev. Stat. § 13-21-102(1)(a). *See also Kirk v. Denver Publ'g Co.*, 818 P.2d 262, 266 (Colo. 1991).

160. Colo. Rev. Stat.§ 13-21-102(3)(a)-(b).

161. *Bradley*, 817 P.2d at 975.

162. Colo. Rev. Stat. § 8-40-101 *et seq.* (2011).

163. *Frohlick Crane Serv. Inc. v. Mack*, 510 P.2d 891 (Colo. 1973).

164. *See* Colo. Rev. Stat. § 8-41-101(1) (2011); *see also Finlay v. Storage Tech. Corp.*, 764 P.2d 62 (Colo. 1988); *Newsom v. Frank M. Hall & Co.*, 101 P.3d 1107 (Colo. App. 2004). *But see Frank M. Hall v. Newsom*, 125 P.3d 444 (Colo. 2005).

165. *Miller v. Byrne*, 916 P.2d 566, 577 (Colo. App. 1995). *See also Williams v. White Mountain Constr. Co., Inc.*, 749 P.2d 423 (Colo. 1988).

166. *But see supra* notes 164-65, *infra* note 179, and accompanying text.

167. Colo. Rev. Stat. § 13-21-111.5 (2011). *See also Slack v. Farmers Ins. Exch.*, 5 P.3d 280, 284 (Colo. 2000).

168. *Slack*, 5 P.3d at 286.

169. *Harvey v. Farmers Ins. Exch.*, 983 P.2d 34, 37 (Colo. App. 1998), *aff'd and remanded by Slack*, 5 P.3d 280.

170. *Barton*, 938 P.2d 532, 535.

171. *Harvey*, 983 P.2d at 37.

172. *Harvey*, 983 P.2d at 37.

173. *Harvey*, 983 P.2d at 37.

174. *Barton*, 938 P.2d at 536 n.4, citing *Miller*, 916 P.2d at 578. *See also O'Quinn v. Wedco Tech., Inc.*, 746 F. Supp. 38, 39 (D. Colo. 1990).

175. *Slack*, 5 P.3d at 283.

176. *Resolution Trust Corp. v. Heiserman*, 898 P.2d 1049 (Colo. 1995).

177. Colo. Rev. Stat. § 13-21-111.5(4) (2011).

178. *Schneider v. Midtown Motor Co.*, 854 P.2d 1322, 1327 (Colo. App. 1992).

179. Colo. Rev. Stat. § 13-21-111.5(2)-(3).

180. Colo. Rev. Stat. § 13-21-111.5(2)-(3); *Harvey*, 983 P.2d at 37.

181. *Miller v. Byrne*, 916 P.2d 566, 577-78 (Colo. App. 1995).

182. *Salazar v. Am. Sterilizer Co.*, 5 P.3d 357, 371-72 (Colo. App. 2000).

183. *Salazar*, 5 P.3d at 371.

184. Colo. Rev. Stat. § 7-60-115(1) (2011).

185. *Bank of Denver v. SE Capital Group, Inc.*, 763 F. Supp. 1552, 1560 (D. Colo. 1991).

186. *Hughes v. Johnson*, 764 F. Supp. 1412, 1413 (D. Colo. 1991).

187. *Brochner v. W. Ins. Co.*, 724 P.2d 1293, 1295 (Colo. 1986).

188. Colo. Rev. Stat. § 13-50.5-101 *et seq.* (2011).

189. *Graber v. Westaway*, 809 P.2d 1126 (Colo. App. 1991).

190. *Brochner*, 724 P.2d at 1298 ("Joint tortfeasors are now subject to contribution among themselves based upon their relative degrees of fault.").

191. *Brochner*, 724 P.2d at 1295.

192. *Brochner*, 724 P.2d at 1295.

193. *Brochner*, 724 P.2d at 1299. The Colorado Supreme Court, however, did not answer the question of whether the common law doctrine of indemnity should be preserved or abolished in situations where the party seeking indemnity is vicariously liable or is without fault. *Brochner*, 724 P.2d at 1298 n.6.

194. *O'Quinn v. Wedco Tech., Inc.*, 746 F. Supp. 38, 39 (D. Colo. 1990).

195. Colo. Rev. Stat. § 13-21-101 (2011); *but see Sperry v. Field*, 186 P.3d 133 (Colo. App. 2008) (holding post-judgment interest accrues from the date original judgment was entered, rather than the date the action accrued), *aff'd*, 205 P.3d 365 (Colo. 2009).

196. Colo. Rev. Stat. § 13-21-101(1).

197. Colo. Rev. Stat. § 13-21-101(2)(a), (3)-(4).

198. Colo. Rev. Stat. § 13-21-101(1).

199. *Stevens ex rel. Stevens v. Humana of Del., Inc.*, 832 P.2d 1076, 1080 (Colo. Ct. App. 1992). *See also Scott v. Matlack, Inc.*, 1 P.3d 185, 191 (Colo. App. 1999), *rev'd on other grounds by* 39 P.3d 1160 (Colo. 2002).

200. *Miller v. Carnation Co.*, 564 P.2d 127, 132 (Colo. App. 1977).

201. *Bradley*, 817 P.2d at 979.

CONNECTICUT*

A. THE PRODUCTS LIABILITY ACT

In Connecticut, the Products Liability Act[1] (the Act) creates the exclusive remedy for all claims of injury and property damage allegedly caused by defective products.[2] Although the Act generally has no effect on the substantive theories of traditional product liability law—strict liability, negligence, and warranty—it does establish uniform procedural rules governing those claims.

B. PRODUCT SELLERS

A product liability claim may be brought against any person or entity engaged in the business of selling an allegedly defective product, including lessors or bailors.[3]

C. THEORIES AND ELEMENTS OF LIABILITY

1. Strict Liability

a. The Standard

The Connecticut Supreme Court has recognized that all product liability claims are essentially strict liability claims.[4] Connecticut has adopted the Restatement (Second) of Torts § 402A (1965). "[T]o recover under the doctrine of strict liability . . . the plaintiff must prove that: (1) the defendant was engaged in the business of selling the product; (2) the product was in a defective condition unreasonably dangerous to the consumer or user;[5] (3) the defect caused the injury [or damage]; (4) the defect existed at the time of the sale; and (5) the product was expected to and did reach the consumer without substantial change in condition."[6] A dispute exists as to whether the strict liability standard is applicable to sellers of used products.[7] Because the Connecticut Supreme Court declined to require a plaintiff prove the existence of a reasonable alternative design, a product manufacturer may be strictly liable for a design defect even in the absence of a safer alternative.[8]

b. Definition of "Defect"

Connecticut courts consider a product to be "unreasonably dangerous" when it is "dangerous to an extent beyond that which would be contemplated by the ordinary consumer who purchases it, with

---

* This chapter was originally written by Francis H. Morrison III and James Rotondo of Day, Berry & Howard LLP. Since 2005, the chapter has been updated by Donald E. Frechette of Edwards Wildman Palmer LLP.

the ordinary knowledge common to the community as to its characteristics."[9] This definition has its roots in comment (i) § 402A.[10] Connecticut courts utilize a modified consumer expectation test when determining whether a product is unreasonably dangerous.[11] The ordinary consumer expectation test is appropriate when the everyday experience of a particular product user permits the inference that a product does not meet minimum safety standards.[12] In situations involving complex product design, however, the consumer expectation test is modified, and involves the balancing of different risk utility factors: including: (1) relative cost of the product, (2) severity of potential harm from the claimed defect, (3) cost and feasibility of eliminating or minimizing the risk, (4) usefulness of the product, (5) the likelihood and severity of the danger imposed by the design, (6) feasibility of an alternative design, (7) financial cost of an improved design, (8) the ability to reduce the product's danger without impairing usefulness or making it too expensive, and (9) feasibility of spreading the loss by increasing a product's price.[13] The trial court is responsible for "determin(ing) whether an instruction based on the ordinary consumer expectation test or the modified consumer expectation test, or both, is appropriate in light of evidence presented" at trial.[14]

c. **Evidence Admissible to Prove Defect**

In addition to the factors identified above, the existence of a defect may also be shown through direct evidence or reference to: (1) "prior or contemporaneous design features";[15] (2) subsequent design modifications;[16] (3) learned treatises establishing the feasibility of alternative design;[17] (4) other "similar" accidents;[18] (5) OSHA regulations;[19] (6) state of the art;[20] (7) "unspecified dangerous condition"; and (8) *res ipsa loquitur*.

In certain cases, a plaintiff does not need to establish the presence of a specific defect, and may proceed on a theory of an "unspecified dangerous condition" where "other identifiable causes are absent,"[21] or under the doctrine of *res ipsa loquitur*. A jury may be instructed on *res ipsa loquitur* when two prerequisites are satisfied: (1) the situation, condition or apparatus causing the injury must be such that in the ordinary course of events no injury would have occurred unless someone had been negligent, *and* (2) at the time of the injury, both inspection and operation must have been in the control of the party charged with neglect.[22] Two recent decisions have addressed *res ipsa loquitor* within the products liability context. Both cases argue that, technically speaking, *res ipsa loquitor* is not applicable within the products liability context. Instead, they rely on a corollary doctrine to *res ipsa loquitor*, the "malfunction doctrine."[23]

d. No Substantial Change in Condition

One of the elements of Section 402A of the Restatement (Second) of Torts is that "the product [is] expected to and [does] reach the . . . consumer without substantial change in . . . condition."[24] The Act provides that product sellers are not liable for harm occurring because of a modification or alteration of the product by a third party, unless such modification was specified by the seller, made with the seller's consent or could have been reasonably anticipated by the seller.[25]

The Connecticut Supreme Court has determined that the Act is consistent with the common-law requirement that the plaintiff must prove the product arrived without a substantial change in condition.[26] While not an affirmative defense, the defendant may claim that modification or alteration was the sole proximate cause of a plaintiff's injury, after the plaintiff has established, as part of its prima facie case, that the product reached the ultimate consumer without substantial change.[27] The plaintiff then bears the burden of disproving the alleged substantial change, by showing "the harm would have occurred notwithstanding the alteration or modification,"[28] or by establishing that the alteration or modification was made at the seller's instruction, with its consent, or reasonably should have been anticipated.[29]

2. Negligence

Plaintiffs often plead negligence as an alternative theory of liability. In addition to the strict liability requirements that the product seller sold the product in question, that it was defective, and that it caused the injuries, plaintiffs pursuing a negligence cause of action must also prove the existence of a duty and subsequent breach of duty by the defendant, resulting in the defective design, manufacture or warning.[30]

3. Breach of Warranty

Plaintiffs may bring claims for breach of warranty under the Act, but they may not recover "commercial losses"—such as lost profits—unless they prevail on a claim under the Uniform Commercial Code.[31] Plaintiffs do not need to establish privity to prevail on a breach of warranty claim under the Act.[32] There is a split of authority among the trial courts on the issue of whether privity is required in a breach of warranty claim under the Uniform Commercial Code.[33]

4. Failure to Warn

a. The Standard

A plaintiff must prove that "the product was defective in that adequate warnings or instructions were not provided" and that "if adequate warnings . . . had been provided, the [plaintiff] would not have suffered harm."[34] Product sellers have a duty to warn of dangers they know or should know about, but they are not obligated to warn of obvious dangers.[35]

The Act, like recent case law adopting a modified consumer expectation standard, employs a "risk-utility" standard for determining the adequacy of warnings and instructions.[36] Under this standard, the trier of fact considers "(1) [t]he likelihood that the product would cause the harm suffered by the claimant; (2) the ability of the product seller to anticipate at the time of manufacture that the expected product user would be aware of the product risk, and the nature of potential harm; and (3) the technological feasibility and cost of warnings."[37]

Under a failure to warn theory, a product may be defective only "because a manufacturer or seller fail[s] to warn of the product's unreasonably dangerous propensities."[38] Warnings are presumptively inadequate if the trier of fact determines that they were not devised to communicate to the person best able to take precaution against the harm.[39] Courts have stated that even though the statute indicates that liability may be imposed for a failure to warn "whether negligent or innocent,"[40] "in practical terms, there is no difference between the statutory strict liability of section 52-572q and negligence with respect to the law of warnings."[41]

b. **State of the Art**

Evidence on the issue of the state of the art is a factor for the jury to consider, both under the modified and the ordinary consumer expectation tests, and is admissible on the issue of failure to warn.[42]

c. **Continuing Duty**

In Connecticut, product sellers have a continuing duty to warn.[43] The continuing duty to warn ends, however, when the plaintiff becomes aware of the problem.[44] There is some question as to the necessity of the continuing duty to warn doctrine. The doctrine was developed in response to the general tort statute of limitations which ran three years from the seller's act or omission, potentially barring a cause of action before the accident giving rise to the claim occurred.[45] Unlike the general tort statute of limitations, however, the current statute of limitations governing product liability cases begins to run from the date the injury is sustained or discovered, eliminating the need for a continuing duty to warn.[46]

d. **Learned Intermediary Doctrine**

Connecticut recognizes the learned intermediary doctrine with respect to prescription drugs and prescription medical devices. Under this doctrine, a prescription drug or prescription medical device seller satisfies its duty to warn of the risks inherent in the use of a product by warning the prescribing physician. The courts have reasoned that prescribing physicians are in the best position to weigh the potential medical risks associated with the use of these products against the needs and susceptibilities of their patients.[47]

Connecticut courts treat this doctrine as a question of law, not as a question of fact.

e. Sophisticated User

While not an affirmative defense, the Act allows the trier of fact to consider the impact of a purchaser's sophistication and knowledge.[48] Depending on the purchaser's degree of knowledge and sophistication, and the seller's knowledge thereof, warnings may not be mandated.[49]

5. Causation

a. Actual and Proximate Cause

Plaintiffs must prove not only that the product was defective but also that the defect was the actual and proximate cause of their injuries.[50] To establish a causal connection between the defect and the plaintiff's damages, a plaintiff must prove that the defect was a "substantial factor" in producing its damages.[51]

b. Superseding Cause

Connecticut is a comparative negligence jurisdiction and allows for apportionment among negligent defendants. Connecticut courts analyze subsequent and/or multiple acts of negligence in terms of proximate cause rather than allow defendants to raise the defense of superseding cause.[52] Accordingly, Connecticut has done away with the doctrine of superseding cause where a defendant claims that its tortious conduct is superseded by a subsequent negligent act or when there are multiple acts of negligence.[53]

c. Causation in Warning Cases

In product liability cases based on lack of adequate warnings, the claimant must prove only that the issuance of adequate warnings would have prevented the harm to the claimant.[54] A product seller may not be held liable for failure to warn the user of dangers of which he was already aware.[55] Additionally, proximate cause is not presumed simply because there is a finding of failure to provide adequate warnings.[56] The issue of causation in failure to warn cases is generally reserved for the trier of fact.[57]

6. Third-Party and Cross Claims

Product sellers may bring third-party actions for contribution against other product sellers and nonproduct sellers.[58] In Connecticut, a party is entitled to indemnification only upon proof that the party against whom indemnification is sought "either dishonored a contractual provision or engaged in some tortious conduct."[59] Where all potential defendants are parties to the suit, however, courts do not permit cross claims.[60]

A question remains as to whether product sellers may bring common law indemnity actions against employers of individuals who have brought product liability actions for injuries sustained in the course of employment.[61]

D. DEFENSES

1. Assumption of Risk

Assumption of risk may be a proper special defense under the Act (see discussion on "knowing use," *infra*).[62] However, there is no appellate authority to support this concept, and Connecticut does not recognize the doctrine of assumption of risk as a common law affirmative defense.

2. Comparative Responsibility

Even if the plaintiff establishes that the defendant is legally responsible, the jury may reduce the amount of any award if the defendant establishes that plaintiff contributed to the injuries or damage through misuse, negligence, or knowingly using the product in a defective condition.[63] The Act establishes a system of pure comparative responsibility, so that plaintiff may recover as long as it demonstrates that any defendant is partly responsible for the accident.[64] Under this system, even if a jury determines that the plaintiff was 99 percent responsible for causing his own injury, the plaintiff may still recover 1 percent of any compensatory damages proximately caused by any of the defendants.[65] When determining the percentage of responsibility for each party, the trier of fact shall consider the "nature and quality" of the conduct of the parties, including plaintiff.[66]

The Act is silent on the issue of whether a plaintiff has a duty to mitigate its damages; however, a plaintiff's failure to mitigate damages is a form of comparative fault and operates to reduce recovery if proven at trial.[67]

3. Statutes of Limitation and Repose

Claims made under the Act must be brought "within three years from the date when the injury . . . is first sustained or discovered or in the exercise of reasonable care should have been discovered,"[68] except for claims alleged to be caused by exposure to asbestos. Claims for personal injury or death due to alleged exposure to asbestos are barred by the Act if brought more than sixty years from the date of the claimant's last exposure, and for asbestos claims for property damage the Act's limit is thirty years.[69] The Act also establishes a statute of repose barring all claims arising out of workplace accidents brought more than ten years after the date the seller parted with possession of the product.[70] Indemnity actions must be brought within three years of the date on which the underlying action is settled or adjudicated.[71]

4. Government Contractor Defense

In Connecticut, a supplier of military equipment to the United States government may not be held liable for design defects when the United States approved reasonably precise specifications, the equipment conformed to those specifications, and the supplier warned the United States about the dangers in the use of the equipment that were known to the supplier but not to the United States.[72] Additionally, the government contractor defense may function as an affirmative defense to a failure to warn claim, but a failure to warn claim is not automatically precluded by the government contractor defense.[73]

5. Misuse of Product and Knowing Use of Defective Product

Misuse of a product or knowing use of a defective product are valid defenses in Connecticut.[74]

6. Spoliation

A trier of fact may draw a negative inference from the intentional spoliation of evidence. In such a situation, the trier of fact may infer, but is not required to infer, that the destroyed evidence would have been unfavorable to the party that destroyed it.[75] An adverse inference may be drawn against a party who has destroyed evidence only if three conditions are established: (1) the spoliation must have been intentional, and not inadvertent; (2) the destroyed evidence must be relevant to the issue or matter for which the party seeks the inference; and (3) he or she must act with due diligence toward the evidence, for example, the spoliator must have been put on notice that the evidence should be preserved.[76] In addition to the negative inference that may be drawn, intentional spoliation is a recognized tort in Connecticut.[77]

7. Disclaimer of Liability

The Act is silent on the issue of disclaimers of liability. However, the Connecticut Commercial Code states that disclaimers of liability for personal injury are prima facie unconscionable and invalid. Courts have upheld disclaimers for property damage or commercial loss only when the parties entered into an agreement voluntarily and with equal bargaining power.[78]

E. DAMAGES

1. Workers' Compensation Offset

The provisions of the Act concerning workers' compensation issues such as offset were repealed on July 1, 1993.[79] Connecticut now allows the employer or its workers' compensation insurance carrier to place a lien against any judgment or settlement received by an injured employee from a product defendant.[80]

2. **Joint and Several Liability**

The doctrine of joint and several liability is applicable to product sellers.[81] Notwithstanding the Act's provision for pure comparative fault, discussed *supra*, a court will enter judgment against any liable party based upon common law joint and several liability principles.[82] Accordingly, a plaintiff may recover an entire judgment from one liable defendant, and if that defendant pays more than its proportionate share, it may pursue an action for contribution against the remaining liable defendants, if they have failed to pay their respective proportionate shares of the damages.

3. **Market Share Liability**

No Connecticut appellate court has addressed the issue of market share liability in a product liability case. However, at least one trial court has found that a prior manufacturer of the same product—not the actual product at issue—may not be held liable under the Act.[83]

4. **Punitive Damages and Sanctions**

The Act allows for punitive damages when the seller acts with reckless disregard for the safety of product users, consumers or others who were injured by the product.[84] A plaintiff must introduce evidence permitting a jury to find that the seller's conduct was "outrageous."[85] The trier of fact determines whether punitive damages should be awarded and the trial court determines the amount, but the award may not exceed twice the amount of compensatory damages.[86] Punitive damages are not allowed for property damage claims[87] or subrogation cases.[88] The Act also allows for attorney's fees for bringing a frivolous claim or asserting a frivolous defense.[89]

Donald E. Frechette
Aubrey E. Blatchley
Edwards Wildman Palmer LLP
20 Church Street
Hartford, Connecticut 06103
(860) 525-5065
(Fax) (860) 527-4198

ENDNOTES - CONNECTICUT

1. Conn. Gen. Stat. §§ 52-240a, 52-240b, 52-572m to 52-572q, and 52-577a (2013).

2. Conn. Gen. Stat. § 52-572n; *Winslow v. Lewis-Shepard, Inc.*, 212 Conn. 462, 471, 562 A.2d 517, 521 (1989) ("[P]roducts liability act [is] an exclusive remedy for claims falling within its scope."); *Daily v. New Britain Mach. Co.*, 200 Conn. 562, 571, 512 A.2d 893, 899 (1986) (the Act provides exclusive remedy and by asserting claims under the Act, the plaintiff is precluded from also bringing common law claims); *Gajewski v. Pavelo*, 36 Conn. App. 601, 611, 652 A.2d 509, 514 (1994) ("[the Act] was intended to merge the various common law theories of products liability in one cause of action"), *aff'd*, 236 Conn. 27, 670 A.2d 318 (1996); *but see Lynn v. Haybuster Mfg., Inc.*, 226 Conn. 282, 292, 627 A.2d 1288, 1293 (1993) (the Act did not abolish common law loss of consortium claims); *Lutes, et al. v. Kawasaki Motors Corp., U.S.A., et al.*, No. 3:10cv1549 (WWE), 2011 U.S. Dist. LEXIS 39990 (D. Conn. Apr. 13, 2011) (recognizing ability to bring a derivative bystander emotional distress claim).

3. Conn. Gen. Stat. §§ 52-572n and 52-572m(a); *see also Svege v. Mercedes-Benz Credit Corp.*, 329 F. Supp. 2d 272, 278 (D. Conn. 2004); *Ferrucci v. Atlantic City Showboat, Inc.*, 51 F. Supp. 2d 129 (D. Conn. 1999) (holding no bailment relationship existed between hotel and guest as to bed in guest's room, and that therefore hotel was not a "product seller"); *Massey v. Yale Univ.*, No. CV 030475250S, 2005 Conn. Super. LEXIS 2043 (Conn. Super. Aug. 9, 2005) (discussing whether use of a golf cart at a golf course is a bailment within context of a product liability claim); *Peloquin v. Stop & Shop Holdings, Inc.*, No. CV 970082759, 1998 Conn. Super. LEXIS 1511 (Conn. Super. May 27, 1998) (holding the Act does not cover all bailments by business entities but only by those entities whose business consists of bailment of products and that therefore Stop & Shop was not engaged in business of bailment of shopping carts).

4. *Allard v. Liberty Oil Equip. Co.*, 253 Conn. 787, 804, 756 A.2d 237, 247 (2000).

5. *See Bifolck v. Philip Morris, Inc.* No. 3:06cv1768 (SRU), 2014 WL 585325, 6 (D. Conn. Feb. 14, 2014) (order certifying to Connecticut Supreme Court question of whether the requirement under § 402A of the Restatement (Second) of Torts (1965) that a product be "unreasonably dangerous" and Comment i's definition of that term apply in a CPLA claim grounded in negligence).

6. *Vitanza v. The Upjohn Co.*, 257 Conn. 365, 373-74, 778 A.2d 829, 835 (2001) conformed to 271 F.3d 89 (2d Cir. 2001); *Giglio v. Conn. Light & Power Co.*, 180 Conn. 230, 234, 429 A.2d 486, 488 (1980); *Rossignol v. Danbury Sch. of*

Aeronautics, Inc., 154 Conn. 549, 559, 227 A.2d 418, 423 (1967); *Garthwait v. Burgio*, 153 Conn. 284, 289-90, 216 A.2d 189, 192 (1965).

7. *Compare Stanton v. Carlson Sales, Inc.*, No. 356371, 1998 Conn. Super. LEXIS 2936, at *2 (Conn. Super. Oct. 21, 1998) (applying doctrine of strict liability to seller of used products), *with King v. Damiron Corp.*, 113 F.3d 93 (7th Cir. 1997) (applying Connecticut law and holding that strict liability does not apply to a seller of used products).

8. *Potter v. Chicago Pneumatic Tool Co.*, 241 Conn. 199, 215-19, 694 A.2d 1319, 1331-34 (1997).

9. *Giglio*, 180 Conn. at 234, 429 A.2d at 488; *Slepski v. Williams Ford, Inc.*, 170 Conn. 18, 23, 364 A.2d 175, 178 (1975) (both quoting Restatement (Second) of Torts § 402A, cmt. i (1965)).

10. *Potter*, 241 Conn. at 214, 694 A.2d at 1330.

11. *Potter*, 241 Conn. at 219-21, 694 A.2d at 1333.

12. *Potter*, 241 Conn. at 211-13, 694 A.2d at 1328-29; *Giglio*, 180 Conn. at 234, 429 A.2d at 488; *Slepski*, 170 Conn. at 23, 364 A.2d at 178.

13. *Potter*, 241 Conn. at 219-21, 694 A.2d at 1332-34.

14. *Potter*, 241 Conn. at 223, 694 A.2d at 1334.

15. *Hartmann v. Black & Decker Mfg. Co.*, 16 Conn. App. 1, 14, 547 A.2d 38, 45 (1988); *Ames v. Sears, Roebuck & Co.*, 8 Conn. App. 642, 645-47, 514 A.2d 352, 354-55 (1986) *cert. denied* 201 Conn. 809, 515 A.2d 378 (1986).

16. *See Wagner v. Clark Equip. Co.*, 243 Conn. 168, 192-98, 700 A.2d 38, 51-54 (1997); *Sanderson v. Steve Snyder Enters., Inc.*, 196 Conn. 134, 147-48, 491 A.2d 389, 396 (1985). *But see Fish v. Georgia-Pac. Corp.*, 779 F.2d 836, 839-40 (2d Cir. 1985); *Cann v. Ford Motor Co.*, 658 F.2d 54, 59-60 (2d Cir. 1981).

17. *Ames*, 8 Conn. App. at 650-51, 514 A.2d at 357.

18. *Hall v. Burns*, 213 Conn. 446, 452-53, 569 A.2d 10, 16 (1990), (citing *Wray v. Fairfield Amusement Co.*, 126 Conn. 221, 226, 10 A.2d 600, 603 (1940)) (the party attempting to offer evidence of prior accidents or of the experience of others bears the burden of establishing "that the circumstances were substantially the same as those under which the plaintiff was injured, and that the use by others was substantially similar to that of the plaintiff."); *Facey v. Merkle*, 146 Conn. 129, 136, 148 A.2d 261, 265 (1959); *Pickel v. Automated Waste Disposal, Inc.*, 65 Conn. App. 176, 185, 782 A.2d 231, 237 (2001).

19. *Wagner*, 243 Conn. at 186-92, 700 A.2d at 48-52 (OSHA regulations are admissible in action against a product seller if the regulation addresses the safety of a product; evidence of industry standards and compliance with federal regulations with respect to product safety may also be admissible on the issue of defect).

20. State of the art, defined as "relevant, scientific, technological and safety knowledge existing and reasonably feasible at the time of the design and rather than merely industry custom," is admissible and probative with respect to expectations of a reasonable consumer and with respect to the risk utility factors of alternative design features relating to safety. It does not, however, constitute an affirmative defense to a design defect claim. *See Potter*, 241 Conn. at 248-53, 694 A.2d at 1346-49.

21. *Standard Structural Steel Co. v. Bethlehem Steel Corp.*, 597 F. Supp. 164, 183 (D. Conn. 1984); *Living & Learning Ctr., Inc. v. Griese Custom Signs, Inc.*, 3 Conn. App. 661, 664, 491 A.2d 433, 435 (1985); *Liberty Mut. Ins. Co. v. Sears, Roebuck & Co.*, 35 Conn. Supp 687, 691, 406 A.2d 1254, 1256-57 (1979).

22. *Boone v. William W. Backus Hosp.*, 272 Conn. 551, 576, 864 A.2d 1, 19 (2005); *Barretta v. Otis Elevator Co.*, 242 Conn. 169, 173-74, 698 A.2d 810, 812-13 (1997) (holding plaintiff was not entitled to a jury charge on the doctrine of *res ipsa*, in a negligent maintenance action where plaintiff claimed to have sustained injuries when an escalator came to a sudden stop); *Giles v. City of New Haven*, 228 Conn. 441, 455, 636 A.2d 1335, 1341-42 (1994).

23. *Hartford Fire Ins. Co. v. Dent X Int'l, Inc.*, No. 3:05cv1019 (TPS), 2007 U.S. Dist. LEXIS 20858 (D. Conn. Mar. 23, 2007) (discussing the "malfunction doctrine"); *Fallon v. The Matworks*, 50 Conn. Supp. 207, 918 A.2d 1067 (Conn. Super. 2007) (articulating the "malfunction doctrine" as a three-part test: "[A] product defect may be inferred by circumstantial evidence that (1) the product malfunctioned, (2) the malfunction occurred during proper use, and (3) the product had not been altered or misused in a manner that probably caused the malfunction.").

24. *Prokolkin v. Gen. Motors Corp.*, 170 Conn. 289, 299-301, 365 A.2d 1180, 1185 (1976); *Rossignol*, 154 Conn. at 559, 227 A.2d at 423; *Spencer v. Star Steel Structures, Inc.*, 96 Conn. App. 142, 145; 900 A.2d 42, 44 (2006).

25. Conn. Gen. Stat. § 52-572p(b) defines alteration or modification to include changes in the design, formula, function or use of the product from that originally designed, tested or intended by the product seller. *See also Elliot v. Sears, Roebuck & Co.*, 229 Conn. 500, 507, 642 A.2d 709, 712 (1994).

26. *Potter*, 241 Conn. at 236, 694 A.2d at 1340.

27. *Potter*, 241 Conn. at 236, 694 A.2d at 1340.

28. *Whitbeck v. Jones Mfg. Co.*, No. 3:01cv750 (AHN), 2003 U.S. Dist. LEXIS 6275, at *14 (D. Conn. Jan. 3, 2003); *Potter*, 241 Conn. at 237, 694 A.2d at 1341.

29. *Whitbeck*, 2003 U.S. Dist. LEXIS 6275, at *14-15; *Elliot*, 229 Conn. at 508, 642 A.2d at 713.

30. *LaMontagne v. E.I. Du Pont de Nemours & Co.*, 41 F.3d 846, 856-58 (2d Cir. 1994); *Coburn v. Lenox Homes, Inc.*, 186 Conn. 370, 372, 441 A.2d 620, 622 (1982); *see Bifolck, supra,* 2014 WL 585325, at *6 (order certifying question regarding appropriate standard in products liability claims grounded in negligence to Connecticut Supreme Court).

31. Conn. Gen. Stat. §§ 52-572m(d), 52-572n(c).

32. Conn. Gen. Stat. § 52-572n(b); *see also Rossignol*, 154 Conn. at 561, 227 A.2d at 424.

33. *Compare Ferguson v. Sturn, Ruger & Co.*, 524 F. Supp. 1042, 1048 (D. Conn. 1981) (imposing a privity requirement) *with Quadrini v. Sikorski Aircraft, Div.*, 505 F. Supp. 1049, 1051 (D. Conn. 1981) (dispensing with privity requirement where other remedy not available); *see also TD Props., LLC v. VP Bldgs., Inc.*, 602 F. Supp. 2d 351, 363 (D. Conn. 2009) (discussing Connecticut case law regarding privity).

34. Conn. Gen. Stat. § 52-572q(a), (c); *see also Haesche v. Kissner*, 229 Conn. 213, 640 A.2d 89 (1994) (upholding trial court's entry of summary judgment where the defendant's alleged failure to warn could not have proximately caused plaintiff's injuries); *Sharp v. Wyatt, Inc.*, 31 Conn. App. 824, 834, 627 A.2d 1347, 1353 *cert. granted, in part,* 228 Conn. 904, 634 A.2d 298 (1993), *aff'd,* 230 Conn. 12, 644 A.2d 871 (1994) (the issues of the existence and adequacy of warnings are typically factual issues for the trier of fact). *But see Battistoni v. Weatherking Prods., Inc.*, 41 Conn. App. 555, 676 A2d 890 (1996) (summary judgment in favor of the defendant reversed where the appellate court found a material issue of fact based upon the plaintiff's testimony that she did not understand the *consequences* of her action).

35. *Basko v. Sterling Drug, Inc.*, 416 F.2d 417, 426 (2d Cir. 1969); *LaMontagne*, 41 F.3d at 859-60; *Gajewski*, 36 Conn. App. at 617, 652 A.2d at 517; *Haesche*, 229 Conn. at 217, 640 A.2d at 91.

36. *Potter*, 241 Conn. at 219-21, 694 A.2d at 1333.

37. Conn. Gen. Stat. § 52-572q(b).

38. *Oliva v. Bristol-Myers Squibb Co.*, No. 3:05cv486 (JCH), 2005 U.S. Dist. LEXIS 35881, at *23-24 (D. Conn. Dec. 15, 2005); *Gajewski*, 36 Conn. App. at 604 n.2, 652 A.2d at 511 n.2; *Sharp*, 31 Conn. App. at 833, 627 A.2d at 1353.

39. Conn. Gen. Stat. § 52-572q(d).

40. Conn. Gen. Stat. § 52-572m(b).

41. *Kosmynka v. Polaris Indus., Inc.*, 462 F.3d 74 (2d Cir. 2006); *Gajewski*, 36 Conn. App. at 612, 652 A.2d at 515; *Sharp*, 31 Conn. App. at 848, 627 A.2d at 1360.

42. *Potter*, 241 Conn. at 253, 694 A.2d at 1348-49; Conn. Gen. Stat. § 52-572q(b)(3); *Tomer v. American Home Prods. Corp.*, 170 Conn. 681, 687-88, 368 A.2d 35, 38-39 (1976); *Greenwood v. Eastman-Kodak Co.*, No. CV-92-0452919S, 1994 Conn. Super. LEXIS 851, at *8-10 (Conn. Super. Mar. 25, 1994); *Sylvain v. Madison's Inc.*, No. CV-92-0449656S, 1992 Conn. Super. LEXIS 3230, at *5-6 (Conn. Super. Nov. 10, 1992).

43. *Giglio*, 180 Conn. at 241, 429 A.2d at 491 (quoting *Handler v. Remington Arms Co.*, 144 Conn. 316, 321, 130 A.2d 793, 795 (1957)); *see also Densberger v. United Tech. Corp.*, 297 F.3d 66, 71-72 (2d Cir. 2000) (noting failure to warn liability persists post-sale); *Savage v. Scripto-Tokai Corp.*, 266 F. Supp. 2d 344, 351 (D. Conn. 2003).

44. *Beckenstein v. Potter & Carrier, Inc.*, 191 Conn. 150, 162, 464 A.2d 18, 24-25 (1983).

45. Conn. Gen. Stat. § 52-577 (2005); *see also Prokolkin v. General Motors Corp.*, 170 Conn. 289, 365 A.2d 1180 (1976).

46. Conn. Gen. Stat. § 52-577a(a); *Zielinski v. Kotsoris*, 279 Conn. 312, 330, 901 A.2d 1207, 1219 (2006).

47. *See Hurley v. The Heart Physicians, P.C.*, 278 Conn. 305, 317, 898 A.2d 777 (2006) (applying the learned intermediary doctrine to prescription medical devices); *see also Moss v. Wyeth, Inc.*, No. 3:04cv1511 (SRU), 2012 U.S. Dist. LEXIS 72569 (D. Conn. May 24, 2012) (discussing learned intermediary doctrine in the context of a design defect claim involving prescription drugs); *Basko*, 416 F.2d at 426 (applying Connecticut law and addressing the learned intermediary doctrine); *Allen v. Mentor*, No. 3:04cv642 (PCD), 2006 U.S. Dist. LEXIS 14914, at *16 (D. Conn. Mar. 31, 2006); *Oliva*, 2005 U.S. Dist. LEXIS 35881, at *26 (the learned intermediary doctrine is an affirmative defense); *Goodson v. Searle Labs.*, 471 F. Supp. 546, 548 (D. Conn. 1978) (applying the learned intermediary doctrine to enter summary judgment for drug manufacturer); *Vitanza*, 257 Conn. 365, 778 A.2d 829 (answering certified question from Second Circuit and holding that learned intermediary doctrine applies in Connecticut and that it is to be applied as a matter of law), *aff'd*, 271 F.3d 89 (2d Cir. 2001) (affirming summary judgment for drugmaker where decedent with known steroid allergy died after taking sample of prescription medication given to his wife by her physician without warning inserts).

48. Conn. Gen. Stat. § 52-572q; *Sharp*, 31 Conn. App. at 847-48, 627 A.2d at 1359-60; *see also Vitanza, v. Upjohn* Co., 271 F.3d 89, 92 (2d Cir. 2001) (noting appellate authority for the proposition that sophisticated user doctrine not bar to liability but a defense for jury to consider).

49. *Sharp*, 31 Conn. App. at 847-48, 627 A.2d at 1359-60.

50. *Marko v. Stop & Shop, Inc.*, 169 Conn. 550, 553, 364 A.2d 217, 219 (1975).

51. *See Mahoney v. Beatman*, 110 Conn. 184, 195-98, 147 A. 762, 767-68 (1929) (establishing the "substantial factor" standard); *Wierzbicki v. W.W. Grainger, Inc.*, 20 Conn. App. 332, 334, 566 A.2d 1369, 1370 (1989) (plaintiff satisfied burden of proving proximate cause by providing expert testimony that "it was highly probable that the defects caused the plaintiff's fall"). Although language in *Champagne v. Raybestos-Manhattan, Inc.* and *Sharp v. Wyatt, Inc.* seems to suggest that Connecticut courts would not strictly adhere to the "substantial factor" standard in cases in which product identification is at issue, close analysis of these opinions reveals that neither court specifically decided this issue. *Champagne v. Raybestos-Manhattan, Inc.*, 212 Conn. 509, 530, 562 A.2d 1100, 1112 (1989) (finding sufficient evidence for product); *Sharp*, 31 Conn. App. at 842, 627 A.2d at 1357 (holding there was sufficient evidence to establish that the defendant's products significantly contributed to the dangerous condition and therefore summary judgment was inappropriate).

52. *Barry v. Quality Steel Prod. Inc.*, 263 Conn. 424, 442, 820 A.2d 258, 269 (2003), *aff'd on reh'g*, 280 Conn. 1, 905 A.2d 55 (2006).

53. *Barry*, 263 Conn. at 436, 820 A.2d at 266-67 (abrogating doctrine of superseding cause when defendant claims that a subsequent negligent act by a third party cuts off its own liability for the plaintiff's injury, because Connecticut statutes allow for apportionment among negligent defendants). *See* Conn. Gen. Stat. § 52-572h.

54. Conn. Gen. Stat. § 52-572q(c); *Sharp*, 31 Conn. App. at 835-37, 627 A.2d at 1354-55.

55. *Beckenstein*, 191 Conn. at 161-62, 464 A.2d at 24-25; *see also Haesche*, 229 Conn. at 219-20, 640 A.2d at 92.

56. *Danise v. Safety-Kleen Corp.*, 17 F. Supp. 2d 87, 95 (D. Conn. 1998); *DeJesus v. Craftsman Mach. Co.*, 16 Conn. App. 558, 574, 548 A.2d 736, 744 (1988).

57. *Battistoni*, 41 Conn. App. at 563, 676 A.2d at 894-95; *Sharp*, 31 Conn. App. at 845, 627 A.2d at 1358.

58. Conn. Gen. Stat. § 52-577a(b); *Burkert v. Petrol Plus of Naugatuck, Inc.*, 216 Conn. 65, 73, 579 A.2d 26, 31 (1990); *Malerba v. Cessna Aircraft Co.*, 210 Conn.

189, 194, 554 A.2d 287, 289 (1989); *Ives v. NMTC, Inc.*, No. CV 970073322S, 1999 Conn. Super. LEXIS 2002 (Conn. Super. July 26, 1999).

59. *Burkert*, 216 Conn. at 74, 579 A.2d at 31. The Act does not contain an express provision authorizing indemnification in product actions; however, contractual claims for indemnity have been allowed in products cases. *See Sivilla v. Phillips Med. Sys. of N. Am., Inc.*, 46 Conn. App. 699, 700 A.2d 1179 (1997). The continued viability of indemnification in products cases remains in question, and practitioners should be aware that this area of the law is somewhat unstable.

60. *Kyrtatas v. Stop & Shop, Inc.*, 205 Conn. 694, 701, 535 A.2d 357, 360 (1988).

61. On July 1, 1993, the legislature repealed Conn. Gen. Stat. § 52-572r, which prohibited product sellers from bringing such third-party claims. Public Acts 1993, No. 228, § 34. According to two unreported trial court decisions, however, section 52-572r still governs product actions involving injuries sustained before July 1, 1993. The repeal, moreover, did not disturb established precedent holding that, in negligence actions, a special defense of the employer's contributory negligence cannot be asserted. *Durniak v. August Winter & Sons, Inc.*, 222 Conn. 775, 781-82, 610 A.2d 1277, 1280 (1992). *Durniak* was applied in a product liability action by an unreported trial court decision. *Crutchfield v. The Stanley Works*, No. X03CV054022228S, 2006 Conn. Super. LEXIS 1252, at *5-6 (Conn. Super. Apr. 27, 2006). The Connecticut Supreme Court recently held that a defendant is "entitled to assert, under a *general denial*, that the negligence of an employer *who is not a party to the action* is the sole proximate cause of the plaintiff's injuries." *Archambault v. Soneco/Northeastern, Inc., et al.*, 287 Conn. 20, 37 (2008) (emphases added). In *Archambault*, the Court clarified dicta from *Durniak* establishing that the employer must not be a party to an action to permit the introduction of evidence regarding the employer's liability. *Archambault*, 287 Conn. at 38.

62. *Martens v. Wild Bill Surplus Inc.*, No. CV 94-539091S, 1995 Conn. Super. LEXIS 1870, at *2-4 (Conn. Super. June 20, 1995); *see also Norrie v. Heil Co.*, 203 Conn. 594, 525 A.2d 1332 (1987) (observing that knowingly using a product in a defective condition is narrower than the common law defense of assumption of risk). *But see Stevenson v. Kettler Int'l, Inc.*, No. FSTCV055000357, 2006 Conn. Super. LEXIS 2416, at *12-13 (Conn. Super. Aug. 14, 2006) (granting the plaintiff's motion to strike defendant's special defense of assumption of risk in products liability action).

63. *Champagne*, 212 Conn. at 541, 562 A.2d at 1117 (reducing compensatory and punitive awards in asbestosis case based on plaintiff's own conduct); *Norrie*, 203 Conn. at 600-01, 525 A.2d at 1335 (jury entitled to consider defense that plaintiff knowingly used product in defective condition).

64. Conn. Gen. Stat. § 52-572o; *see Elliot*, 229 Conn. at 500, 642 A.2d at 709 (holding that the bar created by § 52-572p applies only where a third party,

and not the plaintiff, has made the alteration); *see also Mohan v. B.V. Unitron Mfg., Inc.*, 284 Conn. 645, 656-57 (2007) (holding that Conn. Gen. Stat. § 52-572o incorporates the idea of pure comparative responsibility into Connecticut's product liability law). *But see Petrol Plus, Inc. v. D'Onofrio, Inc.*, No. CV93 035 17 00S, 1995 Conn. Super. LEXIS 2651 (Conn. Super. Sept. 19, 1995); *Greenwood*, 1994 Conn. Super. LEXIS 851 (reasoning that comparative responsibility under the Act only diminishes plaintiff's recovery and is not an appropriate special defense); *Sterling v. Vesper Corp.*, No. 060771, 1993 Conn. Super. LEXIS 2353 (Conn. Super. Aug. 30, 1993).

65. Conn. Gen. Stat. § 52-572o(b).

66. Conn. Gen. Stat. § 52-572o(c).

67. Conn. Gen. Stat. § 52-572o.

68. Conn. Gen. Stat. § 52-577a(a); *see Fenton v. United Techs. Corp.*, 204 F. Supp. 2d 367, n. 1 (D. Conn. 2002); *Champagne*, 212 Conn. at 521, 526 A.2d at 1107-08; *Peerless Ins. Co. v. Tucciarone*, 48 Conn. App. 160, 167, 708 A.2d 611, 614 (1998); *see also Catz v. Rubenstein*, 201 Conn. 39, 43, 513 A.2d 98, 100 (1986).

69. Conn. Gen. Stat. § 52-577a(e).

70. Conn. Gen. Stat. § 52-577a(c); *see Baxter v. Sturm, Ruger & Co.*, 230 Conn. 335, 644 A.2d 1297 (1994) (reviewing criteria for determining whether statute of repose is procedural or substantive for choice of law purposes).

71. Conn. Gen. Stat. § 52-598a (2005).

72. *Miller v. United Tech. Corp.*, 233 Conn. 732, 660 A.2d 810 (1995); *see Boyle v. United Techs. Corp.*, 487 U.S. 500 (1999).

73. *Miller*, 233 Conn. at 782, 660 A.2d at 835-36; *Densberger*, 297 F.3d 66 (holding that government contractor defense does not apply unless the government itself dictated the content of warnings and limited the ability of contractors to warn end users of the product).

74. Conn. Gen. Stat. § 52-572l (2005); *Norrie*, 203 Conn. at 600, 525 A.2d at 1335.

75. *Beers v. Bayliner Marine Corp.*, 236 Conn. 769, 675 A.2d 829 (1996); *Surrells v. Belinkie*, 95 Conn. App. 764, 898 A.2d 232 (2006) (applying *Beers* to a medical malpractice case).

76. *Beers*, 236 Conn. 769, 675 A.2d 829; *see Surrells*, 95 Conn. App. at 771, 898 A.2d at 236-37 (following *Beers*, the court declined to draw a negative inference when spoliation occurred before defendant had any reason to anticipate subsequent litigation); *Rizzuto v. Davidson Ladders, Inc., et al.*, 280 Conn. 225, 243, 905 A.2d 1165 (2006); *MacLauchlin v. Gen. Motors., Corp.*, No.

CV94 533959S, 1996 Conn. Super. LEXIS 1725 (Conn. Super. July 3, 1996) (following *Beers*, the court declined to impose sanctions for spoliation and enter default against the defendant, which was never put on notice by the plaintiff that evidence was to be preserved, and had not acted in bad faith in destroying damaged warranty items in accordance with company policy).

77. *Rizzuto*, 280 Conn. at 243-48, 905 A.2d 1165, 1178-81 (recognizing the tort of intentional spoliation under Connecticut law).

78. Conn. Gen. Stat. § 42a-2-719 (2002); *McKernan v. United Techs. Corp. Sikorsky Aircraft Div.*, 717 F. Supp. 60, 69 (D. Conn. 1989).

79. P.A. 93-228, § 34.

80. Conn. Gen. Stat. § 31-293(a) (2003).

81. Conn. Gen. Stat. § 52-572o; *Marko*, 169 Conn. at 556, 364 A.2d at 220.

82. Conn. Gen. Stat. § 52-572o(d).

83. *Barbour v. Dow Corning Corp.*, 2002 Conn. Super. LEXIS 1316 (Conn. Super. Apr. 19, 2002).

84. Conn. Gen. Stat. § 52-240b (2013); *Bifolck, supra,* 2014 WL 585325, at *6 (order certifying to Connecticut Supreme Court the question of whether "Connecticut's common law rule of punitive damages, as articulated in *Waterbury Petroleum Prods., Inc. v. Canaan Oil & Fuel Co.*, 193 Conn. 208, 477 A.2d 988 (1984), apply to an award of statutory punitive damages pursuant to Conn. Gen. Stat. § 52-240b, the punitive damages provision of the CPLA?).

85. *Ames*, 8 Conn. App. at 654-55, 514 A.2d at 359; *Kerrigan v. Kerrigan*, No. CV0540073595, 2006 Conn. Super LEXIS 1527, at *27 (Conn. Super. May 24, 2006).

86. Conn. Gen. Stat. § 52-240b.

87. *Sacred Heart Church v. F.F. Hitchcock Co.*, No. 123104, 1995 Conn. Super. LEXIS 1397 (Conn. Super. May 9, 1995).

88. *Utica Mut. Ins. Co. v. Denwat Corp.*, 778 F. Supp. 592, 594 (D. Conn. 1991); *accord Colorado Farm Bureau Mut. Ins. Co. v. CAT Cont'l, Inc.*, 649 F. Supp. 49, 52 (D. Colo. 1986); *Colonial Penn Ins. Co. v. Ford*, 172 N.J. Super. 242, 243, 411 A.2d 736, 737 (1979); *Maryland Cas. Co. v. Brown*, 321 F. Supp. 309, 312 (N.D. Ga. 1971); *Bituminous Fire & Marine Ins. Co. v. Culligan Fyrprotexion, Inc.*, 437 N.E. 2d 1360, 1371 (Ind. Ct. App. 1982); *see also Cont'l Ins. Co. v. Connecticut Natural Gas Corp.*, 5 Conn. App. 53, 60, 497 A.2d 54, 59 (1985) (a subrogee's rights can rise no higher than those of a subrogor).

89. Conn. Gen. Stat. § 52-240a (2005).

DELAWARE

A. CAUSES OF ACTION

Product liability lawsuits commonly include causes of action for negligence and breach of warranty under the Uniform Commercial Code as adopted in Delaware. The doctrine of strict liability in tort has been rejected by the Delaware Supreme Court as inconsistent with the Delaware version of the UCC.[1]

B. STATUTES OF LIMITATION

An action for personal injury due to negligence is subject to a two-year statute of limitations.[2] The statute of limitations may be tolled for an "inherently unknowable injury"[3] or when "fraudulent concealment" of the cause of action is present.[4] An action for wrongful death or for injury to personal property is also subject to a two-year statute of limitations.[5] The statute of limitations may be tolled in a wrongful death action when an "inherently unknowable injury" was involved, but the statute of limitations begins to run when a qualifying survivor is chargeable with knowledge of a potential cause of action.[6] Most other actions are subject to a three-year statute of limitations.[7] Parties may write into a contract valued at over $100,000 a provision extending the statute of limitations to up to 20 years.[8] An action for breach of contract for a sale arising under the Uniform Commercial Code must be commenced within four years after the cause of action has accrued.[9] Under a product liability action arising from breach of the implied warranties of merchantability and fitness for a particular purpose, a four-year statute of limitations applies from the date of delivery.[10] A party's lack of knowledge of a breach of warranty does not toll the applicable statute of limitations,[11] although the statute may be tolled due to the presence of other factors including fraudulent concealment of the cause of action.[12]

C. STRICT LIABILITY

Strict liability is not a recognized cause of action in Delaware for product liability claims.[13] A party seeking recovery must proceed under either negligence or under the UCC for breach of an implied warranty.[14] The only exceptions are for a lease-bailment transaction and defective products which are distributed in non-sale, promotional transactions.[15]

D. NEGLIGENCE

A plaintiff seeking to recover under a negligence theory must establish that the manufacturer failed to exercise the care of a reasonably prudent manufacturer under all the circumstances.[16]

1. **Definition of "Defect"**

    A product is defective in design if it is not reasonably fit for its intended purpose.[17] Some evidence of the existence of a defect at the time of delivery is an essential element of a cause of action for the breach of the implied warranty of merchantability.[18] Identification of a defect is also required in products liability actions based solely in negligence.[19]

2. **Comparative Negligence/Assumption of the Risk**

    Delaware has adopted a comparative negligence statute that precludes recovery if a plaintiff is more than 50 percent negligent under the facts of the case and diminishes plaintiff's recovery in proportion to any negligence less than or equal to 50 percent of defendant's negligence.[20] In order for the negligence of a third party to absolve a negligent defendant, such negligence must be the sole proximate cause of the accident.[21]

    Assumption of the risk is also an affirmative defense in a product liability action when there is a finding of liability.[22] Delaware courts have divided assumption of the risk into two categories: primary assumption of the risk and secondary implied assumption of the risk.[23] Primary assumption of the risk refers to cases in which the plaintiff expressly relieves the defendant from all legal duty. Secondary implied assumption of the risk refers to cases in which the plaintiff's deliberate and unreasonable choice to encounter a risk created another's breach of duty.[24] Moreover, in Delaware, the doctrine of secondary implied assumption of risk is subsumed within a comparative fault analysis.[25] Therefore, a plaintiff is not necessarily barred from recovery if he assumed the risk under this category.[26]

3. **Sale or Lease**

    A sale of a product is governed by provisions of the UCC as adopted in Delaware.[27] However, the doctrine of strict liability may apply to a lease-bailment transaction.[28]

4. **Inherently Dangerous Products**

    A product is inherently dangerous when it poses a threat of serious physical harm if it proves to be defective.[29]

5. **Successor Liability**

    The general rule is that, when one company sells or transfers all of its assets to another, the purchaser does not become liable for the debts and liabilities, including torts, of the transferor.[30] There are four exceptions to this rule: (1) the purchaser expressly or impliedly assumes such obligations; (2) the transaction amounts to a consolidation or merger of the seller into the purchaser; (3) the purchaser is merely a continuation of the seller; or (4) the transaction has been entered into fraudulently.[31]

6. **Privity**

    There is no privity requirement in post-UCC warranty cases. A manufacturer may be liable to those it should expect to be endangered by the probable use of the product.[32] However, third-party beneficiary recovery under an express or implied warranty is limited to natural persons.[33]

7. **Failure to Warn**

    A product, although virtually faultless in design, material, and workmanship, may nevertheless be deemed defective where the manufacturer fails to discharge a duty to warn.[34] However, a supplier should normally be able to rely on a knowledgeable purchaser/employer to warn its employees of the hazards of a product.[35] A manufacturer also has no duty to warn if it reasonably perceives that the potentially dangerous condition of the product is readily apparent.[36]

8. **Post-Sale Duty to Warn**

    A rule of law imposing successor liability based on a continuing duty to warn has not been expressly adopted in Delaware.[37]

9. **Substantial Change/Abnormal Use**

    Post-manufacturing alterations may relieve the manufacturer of liability if the alterations rendered the product defective and were the actual and proximate cause of the injury.[38]

10. **State of the Art**

    Evidence of a nationally accepted standard is admissible in a design failure case.[39]

11. **Other Accidents**

    Evidence of other accidents may be used to show knowledge on the part of the manufacturer.[40]

12. **Misrepresentation**

    Misrepresentation consists of (1) a false representation, usually one of fact, made by the defendant; (2) the defendant's knowledge or belief that the representation was false, or was made with reckless indifference to the truth; (3) an intent to induce the plaintiff to act or to refrain from acting; (4) the plaintiff's action or inaction taken in justifiable reliance on the representation; and (5) damage to the plaintiff as a result of such reliance.[41] Misrepresentation may be raised in a product liability case, although Delaware law generally requires a relationship between the parties that imposes upon them a duty of honesty and candor.[42] For example, it requires a fiduciary or confidential relationship such as a corporate fiduciary or physician-patient relationship.[43]

13. **Economic Loss**

    Under Delaware law, the economic loss doctrine is a complete bar to the recovery of economic loss caused by qualitatively defective products, notwithstanding the presence of privity of contract.[44] An exception to the economic loss rule is a claim for negligent misrepresentation that may allow recovery in tort for economic loss.[45] Moreover, the economic loss doctrine allows a party to recover in tort only if losses are accompanied by bodily harm or property damage, and, therefore, prevents recovery in tort for purely economic losses.[46]

14. **Crashworthiness**

    The crashworthiness doctrine, also known as the "second collision" or "enhanced injury" doctrine,[47] is an extension of the principle that an automobile manufacturer has a duty to design its products to be safe for normal use.[48] Under the doctrine, a manufacturer of automobiles must consider accidents as among the normal uses of its product and has a legal duty to use reasonable care to design its automobiles to be reasonably safe in the event of a collision.[49]

    In a crashworthiness action, the plaintiff alleges that there was an initial collision unrelated to any design defect.[50] Next, the plaintiff alleges that there was a second impact, during which some design defect caused an exacerbated injury that would not have otherwise occurred as a result of the original collision.[51] The "enhanced injury" for which the plaintiff seeks compensation is the amount of injury over and above the injury that would have occurred as a result of the second collision absent the defect.[52] Therefore, the plaintiff in a crashworthiness action does not seek compensation for all injuries suffered in an accident;[53] the plaintiff seeks compensation for those enhanced or additional injuries caused by the design defect.[54] To prove that the defect was the proximate cause of the additional injuries, the plaintiff must offer some evidence of the injuries that would not have occurred had the automobile been properly designed.[55]

15. **Res Ipsa Loquitur**

    Res ipsa loquitur is a rule of circumstantial evidence that may be invoked in a product liability suit and permits, but does not require, the trier of fact to draw an inference of negligence from the occurrence of an accident, provided that certain elements are established.[56] Because *res ipsa loquitur* acts only to permit an inference of negligence, it does not affect a plaintiff's burden of proof or create a presumption of negligence.[57] When *res ipsa loquitur* is potentially applicable in a product liability suit, trial courts are required to employ the requirements set out in the Delaware Rules of Evidence under § 304(b).[58] Rule 304(b) contains four requirements: (1) the accident that occurred would not normally happen in the ordinary course of events but for some type of negligence; (2) the facts warranted an inference of negligence of such force as to call for an explanation or rebuttal from the defendant; (3) the thing or instrumentality that caused the injury was under the control of the defendant at the time the negligence likely occurred; and (4) where the injured person participated in the events leading up to the accident, he must not have contributed to the negligence that caused his injury.[59] Contributory negligence under the fourth requirement does not mean any degree of negligence, but only a degree of negligence that is greater than that of the defendants.[60] In Delaware, exclusive control is not required for the third requirement.[61] Moreover, although under Rule 304(b), the applicability of *res ipsa loquitur* should be decided at the close of the plaintiff's evidence, Delaware courts recognize that the stage at which a court should apply the *res ipsa loquitur* doctrine should be determined on a case-by-case basis after considering the nature of the contentions, the sufficiency of the parties' factual showings, and the doctrine's applicable standards.[62]

16. **Expert Testimony Requirement**

Delaware has adopted the *Daubert* trilogy[63] in its entirety in determining the admissibility of expert testimony.[64] A cause of action for negligence for personal injuries sustained from a product generally requires expert testimony from the plaintiff to establish the existence of a defect in the product as a prerequisite to proceed with trial.[65] However, where the product is a common household item that has no mechanical parts or sophisticated design, the existence of any potential defect in the product is within an average juror's scope of knowledge, and no expert testimony is required to establish the existence of a defect.[66]

E. **BREACH OF WARRANTY**

Warranty actions may involve an implied warranty of merchantability[67] and an implied warranty of fitness for a particular purpose.[68] The elements of the merchantability cause of action are (1) that a merchant sold goods that (2) were not merchantable at the time of sale, (3) injury and damages resulted to the claimant or his property (4) that were proximately and in fact caused by the defective nature of the goods, and (5) notice was given to the seller of the injury.[69] When a purchaser knows of the dangers of a product, or where that danger is obvious, there is no duty to warn either the purchaser or the purchaser's employees and no implied warranty of merchantability arises.[70] The crucial element in an implied warranty of fitness for a particular purpose is that the buyer relies on the seller's skill or judgment to select or furnish suitable goods.[71] A seller's warranty extends to any natural person who may reasonably be expected to use, consume, or be affected by the goods and who is injured by breach of the warranty.[72] Moreover, a plaintiff is not required to show that an alternative, safer design is feasible and available in order to succeed in a design defect cause of action.[73]

F. **WRONGFUL DEATH**

An action for wrongful death may be brought by the wife, husband, parent, child, or sibling of the deceased or, if these persons do not exist, by "any person related to the deceased person by blood or marriage."[74]

G. **PUNITIVE DAMAGES**

Punitive damages may be awarded in a product liability case, but only when outrageous conduct is present.[75] The imposition of punitive damages may be sought for persistent distribution of an inherently dangerous product with knowledge of its injury-causing effect among the consuming public.[76] Mere negligence is not enough to warrant punitive damages.[77]

H. **PRE- AND POST-JUDGMENT INTEREST**

Pre-judgment interest is available in Delaware as a matter of right.[78] Such interest accumulates from the date liability accrues.[79] When there is no express contract rate, pre-judgment interest will be awarded at the legal rate of 5 percent over the Federal Reserve discount rate including any surcharge as of the time from when payment was due to the plaintiff.[80] Although a plaintiff has the right to pre-judgment interest, it is not self-executing and a plaintiff must request, at least by way of a general allegation of damages, that interest be awarded.[81] Furthermore, the court may, in its discretion, reduce the amount of interest awarded to a plaintiff who unreasonably delays the prosecution of his claim.[82] No element of bad faith or economic benefit is required to show that a plaintiff's delay was unreasonable.[83]

Historically, Delaware did not allow for the recovery of pre-judgment interest in actions based upon bodily harm.[84] Additionally, pre-judgment interest was not a proper element of damages in actions brought under the wrongful death or survival statutes.[85] Currently, however, in a tort action seeking monetary relief for bodily injuries, death or property damage, pre-judgment interest shall be awarded if, prior to trial, the plaintiff extended to the defendant a written settlement offer valid for a minimum of 30 days, in an amount less than the award of damages when judgment was entered.[86]

Plaintiffs have a right to post-judgment interest from the date judgment is entered.[87] Post-judgment interest is awarded at the legal rate of 5 percent over the Federal Reserve discount rate including any surcharge as of the time from which interest is due.[88]

I. **EMPLOYER IMMUNITY FROM SUIT**

The Delaware Workers' Compensation Law provides an employer immunity from claims for work-related injures which fall within the coverage of the law.[89] An employer who is also the supplier of products used by its employees, acting in a dual capacity, still enjoys immunity from common law liability.[90] In the context of asbestos litigation, immunity extends to each employer in the chain of employment, whether or not such employer responded to a claim for benefits.[91] Furthermore, when an employee is injured by the combined negligence of his employer and another, the joint tortfeasor cannot hold the employer liable for contribution.[92] However, an employer, even though it has paid workers' compensation benefits, may be held contractually liable to a third party if the employer agreed to indemnify the third party from claims arising out of the employer's own negligence.[93]

J. STATUTES

Relevant statutes for product liability actions are the statutes of limitations and the UCC provisions when a breach of warranty is alleged.[94] The age of majority in Delaware is 18 years of age.[95]

K. JOINT AND SEVERAL LIABILITY

Under the theory of joint and several liability, an injured person is entitled to recover the sum of his damages from any or all of the joint tortfeasors, regardless of comparative fault, subject to the limitation that his total recovery may not exceed the full amount of his damage.[96] Joint tortfeasors are defined under Delaware law as "2 or more persons jointly or severally liable in tort for the same injury to person or property, whether or not judgment has been recovered against all or some of them."[97] Joint tortfeasor status may be established by admission or determined judicially by the trier of fact.[98] An agreement to pay for damages and a release of liability is not itself an admission of joint tortfeasor status.[99] Joint tortfeasors who pay all or more than their proportionate share of a judgment may seek contribution from other joint tortfeasors.[100] A release by the injured person of one joint tortfeasor does not discharge the liability of other joint tortfeasors unless the release so provides.[101] However, the claim against the other joint tortfeasors is reduced by the amount of consideration paid for the release.[102] Delaware recognizes the collateral source rule which provides that a tortfeasor has no right to mitigate damages because of compensation received by the injured person from an independent source.[103] Thus, the liability of joint tortfeasors is not reduced by insurance payments[104] or through settlement agreements between the injured person and non-joint tortfeasors.[105]

L. CHOICE OF LAW

Local law of the state with the most significant relationship to the occurrence and the parties, rather than the law of the state of the occurrence (lex loci delicti), governs tort suits.[106] Delaware courts usually recognize a valid choice of law provision in a contract if the jurisdiction selected has some material relationship with the transaction.[107] In the absence of a contract between the parties specifying the choice of law, the court must apply the law of the state with the most significant relationship to the controversy.[108] In determining which state has the most significant relationship, a court will consider the following factors: (1) the place of contracting or place of injury; (2) the place where the contract was negotiated or the place where conduct causing injury occurred; (3) the place where the parties are resident and/or domiciled; and (4) the place where the relationship between the parties is centered.[109]

M. "CAUSE" TEST

For cases involving continuous acts and multiple injuries where the question of the "number of occurrences" involved is an issue, Delaware recognizes and follows the "cause" test for determining the "number of occurrences" in products liability cases.[110] This test often arises in liability insurance coverage cases. Under this test, where there are losses to more than one person or entity, the number of occurrences should be determined by looking at the underlying cause of the liability. The number of occurrences is determined by the cause or source of the damaging condition or the place of its creation, and not by the number of injuries or claims.[111] Under the causal analysis, if there is one proximate, uninterrupted, and continuing cause that resulted in all of the damages, it will be deemed a single occurrence even if the damages are widespread in both time, place, and effect.[112] The proper focus is on production and dispersal of the product, and not on the location of the injury or the specific means by which the injury occurred.[113]

Frederick L. Cottrell, III
Anthony Flynn, Jr.
Richards, Layton & Finger
One Rodney Square
P.O. Box 551
Wilmington, Delaware 19899
(302) 651-7700
(Fax) (302) 651-7701

ENDNOTES - DELAWARE

1. *Cline v. Prowler Indus. of Md., Inc.*, 418 A.2d 968 (Del. 1980); *Hervey v. Leisure World Corp.*, C.A. No. 90C-JL-14, 1991 WL 113427 (Del. Super. June 18, 1991); *Amoroso v. Joy Mfg. Co.*, 531 A.2d 619 (Del. Super. 1987).

2. Del. Code Ann. tit. 10, § 8119.

3. *Collins v. Pittsburgh Corning Corp. (In re Asbestos Litig.)*, 673 A.2d 159 (Del. 1996); *Bendix Corp. v. Stagg*, 486 A.2d 1150 (Del. 1984); *McClements v. Kong*, 820 A.2d 377 (Del. Super. 2002); *Brown v. E.I. Dupont de Nemours & Co.*, 820 A.2d 362 (Del. 2003).

4. *Resources Ventures, Inc. v. Resources Mgmt. Int'l, Inc.*, 42 F. Supp. 2d 423 (D. Del. 1999); *Walls v. Abdel-Malik*, 440 A.2d 992 (Del. 1982); *Muscelli v. Dean Witter Reynolds, Inc.*, C.A. No. 84C-FE-43, 1989 WL 63966 (Del. Super. June 2, 1989).

5. Del. Code Ann. tit. 10, § 8107.

6. *Collins*, 673 A.2d 159; *McClements*, 820 A.2d 377; *Brown*, 820 A.2d 362; *In re Asbestos Litig. West Trial Group*, 622 A.2d 1090 (Del. Super. 1992).

7. Del. Code Ann. tit. 10, § 8106.

8. Del. Code Ann. tit. 10, § 8106(c).

9. Del. Code Ann. tit. 6, § 2-725.

10. *Addison v. Emerson Elec. Co.*, C.A. No. 96-146, 1997 WL 129327 (D. Del. Feb. 24, 1997); *Amoroso*, 531 A.2d 619.

11. Del. Code Ann. tit. 6, § 2-725(2).

12. Del. Code Ann. tit. 6, § 2-725(4); *Sellon v. Gen. Motors Corp.*, 571 F. Supp. 1094 (D. Del. 1983); *Lecates v. Hertrich Pontiac Buick Co.*, 515 A.2d 163 (Del. Super. 1986).

13. *Cline*, 418 A.2d 968; *Miley v. Harmony Mill Ltd. P'ship*, 803 F. Supp. 965 (D. Del. 1992); *Hervey*, 1991 WL 113427; *Hammond v. Colt Indus. Oper. Corp.*, 565 A.2d 558, 562-63 (Del. Super. 1989).

14. *See Cline*, 418 A.2d 968.

15. *Martin v. Ryder Truck Rental, Inc.*, 353 A.2d 581 (Del. 1976); *Beattie v. Beattie*, 786 A.2d 549 (Del. Super. 2001); *Golt v. Sports Complex, Inc.*, 644 A.2d 989(Del. Super. 1994). *But see Baylis v. Red Lion Group, Inc.*, C.A. No. 06-1010, 2007 WL 188879 (3d Cir. Jan. 24, 2007).

16. *Franchetti v. Intercole Automation, Inc.*,529 F. Supp. 533 (D. Del. 1982); *Brower v. Metal Indus., Inc.*, 719 A.2d 941 (Del. 1998); *Massey-Ferguson, Inc. v. Wells*, 383 A.2d 640 (Del. 1978).

17. *Dillon v. Gen. Motors Corp.*, 315 A.2d 732 (Del. Super. 1974).

18. *Reybold Group, Inc. v. Chemprobe Techs., Inc.*, 721 A.2d 1267 (Del. 1998); *Brink v. Ethicon, Inc.*, C.A., No. 02C-01-030, 2003 WL 23277272 (Del. Super. Dec. 9, 2003, revised Dec. 16, 2003); *Towe v. Justis Bros., Inc.*, 290 A.2d 657 (Del. Super. 1972).

19. *Farm Family Mut. Ins. Co. v. Perdue, Inc.*, 608 A.2d 726, 1992 WL 21141 (Del. 1992); *Hartford Accident & Indem. Co. v. Anchor Hocking Glass Corp.*, 55 A.2d 148, 151 (Del. Super. 1947); *see also In re Benzene Litig.*, C.A. Nos. 05C-09-020, 06C-05-295, 2007 WL 625054 (Del. Super. Feb. 26, 2007) (noting heightened pleading requirements for toxic torts product liability actions).

20. Del. Code Ann. tit. 10, § 8132; *In re Asbestos Litig. Pusey Trial Group*, 669 A.2d 108 (Del. 1995); *Culver v. Bennett*, 588 A.2d 1094, 1098 (Del. 1991).

21. *Lynch v. Athey Prods. Corp.*, 505 A.2d 42 (Del. Super. 1985).

22. *Spencer v. Wal-Mart Stores East, LP*, 930 A.2d 881, 885 (Del. 2007).

23. *Spencer*, 930 A.2d at 885.

24. *Spencer*, 930 A.2d at 885.

25. *Spencer*, 930 A.2d at 885.

26. *Massey-Ferguson*, 383 A.2d 640; *North v. Owens-Corning Fiberglas Corp.*, 704 A.2d 835, 839 (Del. 1997).

27. *Martin*, 353 A.2d 581; Del. Code Ann. tit. 6, § 2-102.

28. *Martin*, 353 A.2d 581; *Golt*, 644 A.2d 989.

29. *Franchetti*, 529 F. Supp. 533; *Graham v. Pittsburgh Corning Corp.*, 593 A.2d 567 (Del. Super. 1990).

30. *Elmer v. Tenneco Resins, Inc.*,698 F. Supp. 535 (D. Del. 1988); *Stalvey v. Haveg Indus. Inc. (In re Asbestos Litig.)*, C.A. No. 92C-10-100, 1994 WL 89643 (Del. Super. Feb. 4, 1994).

31. *Elmer*, 698 F. Supp. 535; *Stalvey*, 1994 WL 89643.

32. *Martin*, 353 A.2d 581; *Nacci v. Volkswagen of Am., Inc.*, 325 A.2d 617 (Del. Super. 1974).

33. Del. Code Ann. tit. 6, § 2-318.

34. *Betts v. Robertshaw Controls Co.*, C.A. No. 89C-08-028, 1992 WL 436727 (Del. Super. Dec. 28, 1992); *In re Asbestos Litig. (Mergenthaler)*, 542 A.2d 1205 (Del. Super. 1986); *Wilhelm v. Globe Solvent Co.*, 373 A.2d 218 (Del. Super. 1977), *aff'd in part and rev'd in part*, 411 A.2d 611 (Del. 1979).

35. *In re Asbestos Litig. (Mergenthaler)*, 542 A.2d 1205; *Bishop v. Thermotech Sys. Corp.*, C.A. No. 92C-10-130, 1997 WL 817859 (Del. Super. Oct. 17, 1997).

36. *Macey v. AAA-1 Pool Builders & Serv. Co.*, C.A. No. 88C-JN-10, 1993 WL 189481, at *3 (Del. Super. Apr. 30, 1993).

37. *See supra* note 30; *Smith v. DaimlerChrysler Corp.*, C.A. No. 94C-12-002-JEB, 2002 WL 31814534 (Del. Super. Nov. 20, 2002).

38. *Lynch v. Athey Prods. Corp.*, 505 A.2d 42 (Del. Super. 1985).

39. *Slover v. Fabtek, Inc.*, 517 A.2d 293 (Del. Super. 1986).

40. *Delmarva Power & Light Co. v. King*, 608 A.2d 726, 1992 WL 53413 (Del. 1992); *Firestone Tire & Rubber Co. v. Adams*, 541 A.2d 567 (Del. 1988).

41. *Stephenson v. Capano Dev., Inc.*, 462 A.2d 1069 (Del. 1983); *Atamian v. Nemours Health Clinic*, C.A. No. 01C-07-038, 2001 WL 1474819 (Del. Super. Nov. 14, 2001); *Homan v. Turoczy*, C.A. No. 19220, 2005 WL 2000756 (Del. Ch. Aug. 12, 2005).

42. *Nicolet, Inc. v. Nutt*, 525 A.2d 146 (Del. 1987); *Zerby v. Allied Signal Inc.*, C.A. No. 00C-07-068, 2001 WL 112052 (Del. Super. Feb. 2, 2001).

43. *Zerby*, 2001 WL 112052, at *7.

44. *Danforth v. Acorn Structures, Inc.*, 608 A.2d 1194, 1198 (Del. 1992); superseded by statute as it applied to actions for negligence in the construction and/or improvement to property used as a residence, *Marcucilli v. Boardwalk Builders, Inc.*, C.A. No. 99C-02-007, 1999 WL 1568612 (Del. Super. Dec. 22, 1999); Del. Code Ann. tit. 6, § 3652.

45. *Guardian Constr. Co. v. Tetra Tech Richardson, Inc.*, 583 A.2d 1378 (Del. Super. 1990).

46. *Kuhn Constr. Co. v. Ocean & Coastal Consultants, Inc.*, 844 F. Supp. 2d 519, 526 (D. Del. 2012).

47. *Meekins v. Ford Motor Co.*, 699 A.2d 339 (Del. Super. 1997).

48. *Mazda Motor Corp. v. Lindahl*, 706 A.2d 526 (Del. 1998).

49. *Mazda Motor Corp.*, 706 A.2d 526.

50. *Meekins*, 699 A.2d 339.

51. *Meekins*, 699 A.2d 339.

52. *Gen. Motors Corp. v. Wolhar*, 686 A.2d 170 (Del. 1996); *Meekins*, 699 A.2d 339.

53. *Gen. Motors Corp.*, 686 A.2d 170.

54. *Gen. Motors Corp.*, 686 A.2d 170.

55. *Lindahl*, 706 A.2d 526.

56. *Gen. Motors Corp. v. Dillon*, 367 A.2d 1020 (Del. 1976); *State Farm Fire & Cas. Co. v. Middleby Corp.*, C.A. Nos. 09C-08-216 PLA, 09C-08-217 PLA, 2011 WL 1632341 (Del. Super. Apr. 12, 2011); *Gebelein v. Hopkins Trucking, Inc.*, C.A. No. 92C-02-121, 1993 WL 543981 (Del. Super. Dec. 14, 1993); *Smigelski v. Smith*, C.A. No. 86C-SE-148, 1990 WL 161242 (Del. Super. Nov. 30, 1990).

57. *Harris v. Cochran Oil Co.*, No. 282,2010, 2011 WL 3074419, at *1, *4 (Del. July 26, 2011).

58. *Moore v. Anesthesia Servs. P.A.*, 966 A.2d 830, 839 (Del. Super. 2008).

59. *Moore*, 966 A.2d at 837, 839-40; *State Farm Fire & Cas. Co.*, 2011 WL 1632341, at *4.

60. *Dillon v. Gen. Motors Corp.*, 315 A.2d 732, 737 (Del. Super. 1974) (citing *Phillips v. Delaware Power & Light Co.*, 202 A.2d 131, 133 (Del. Super. 1964)).

61. *Dillon*, 315 A.2d at 840.

62. *State Farm Fire & Cas. Co.*, 2011 WL 1632341 at *4 (citing *Orsini v. K-Mart Corp.*, 1997 WL 528034, at *4 (Del. Super. Feb. 25, 1997)).

63. The *Daubert* trilogy consists of a series of three U.S. Supreme Court decisions on the admissibility of expert witness testimony: *Daubert v. Merrell Dow Pharms.*, 509 U.S. 579 (1993); *Gen. Electric Co. v. Joiner*, 522 U.S. 136 (1997); and *Kuhmo Tire Co. v. Charmichael*, 526 U.S. 137 (1999).

64. *M.G. Bancorporation, Inc. v. Le Beau*, 737 A.2d 513 (Del. 1999).

65. *Brown v. Dollar Tree Stores, Inc.*, C.A. No. 07C-07-092, 2009 WL 5177162 (Del. Super. Dec. 9, 2009).

66. *Brown*, 2009 WL 5177162, at *7–8.

67. Del. Code Ann. tit. 6, § 2-314.

68. Del. Code Ann. tit. 6, § 2-315.

69. *Hyatt v. Toys R Us, Inc.*, 930 A.2d 928, 2007 WL 1970075 (Del. 2007); *Reybold Group, Inc. v. Chemprobe Tech., Inc.*, 721 A.2d 1267 (Del. 1998) (citing *Neilson Bus. Equip. Ctr., Inc. v. Monteleone*, 524 A.2d 1172, 1175 (Del. 1987)).

70. *In re Asbestos Litig. (Mergenthaler)*, 542 A.2d 1205.

71. *In re Asbestos Litig. (Mergenthaler)*, 542 A.2d 1205.

72. Del. Code Ann. tit. 6, § 2-318.

73. Del. Code Ann. tit. 10, §§ 3721-3725.

74. *See Bell Sports, Inc. v. Yarusso*, 759 A.2d 582, 594 (Del. 2000); *Mazda Motor Corp. v. Lindahl*, 706 A.2d 526, 531 (Del. 1998).

75. *Conway v. A. C. & S. Co.*, C.A. No. 82C-AP-77, 1987 WL 16785 (Del. Super. Aug. 13, 1987); *Sheppard v. A. C. & S. Co.*, 484 A.2d 521 (Del. Super. 1984).

76. *Jardel Co. v. Hughes*, 523 A.2d 518 (Del. 1987); *Greenlee v. Imperial Homes Corp.*, C.A. No. 91C-01-021, 1994 WL 465556 (Del. Super. July 19, 1994).

77. *Jardel Co.*, 523 A.2d 518; *Greenlee*, 1994 WL 465556.

78. *Moskowitz v. Mayor & Council of Wilmington*, 391 A.2d 209 (Del. 1978); *American Gen. Corp. v. Continental Airlines Corp.*, 622 A.2d 1 (Del. Ch. 1992); *Janas v. Biedrzycki*, C.A. No. 97C-08-060, 2000 WL 33114354 (Del. Super. Oct. 26, 2000); *Getty Oil Co. v. Catalytic, Inc.*, 509 A.2d 1123 (Del. Super. 1986).

79. *Lewis v. State Farm Mut. Auto. Ins. Co.*, C.A. No. 04C-09-238, 2007 WL 1651960 (Del. Super. May 29, 2007); *Summa Corp. v. Trans World Airlines, Inc.*, 540 A.2d 403 (Del. 1988); *Moskowitz*, 391 A.2d 209; *Boyer v. Wilmington Materials, Inc.*, 754 A.2d 881 (Del. Ch. 1999).

80. Del. Code Ann. tit. 6, § 2301; *Moskowitz*, 391 A.2d 209; *Hercules Inc. v. Aetna Cas. & Sur. Co.*, C.A. Nos. 92C-10-105, 90C-FE-195-1, 1998 WL 962089 (Del. Super. Sept. 30, 1998); *rev'd on other grounds*, 784 A.2d 481 (Del. 2001); *Rollins Envtl. Servs., Inc. v. WSMW Indus., Inc.*, 426 A.2d 1363 (Del. Super. 1980).

81. *Brandywine 100 Corp. v. New Castle Cnty.*, 541 A.2d 598 (Del. 1988); *Collins v. Throckmorton*, 425 A.2d 146 (Del. 1980).

82. *Summa*, 540 A.2d 403; *Moskowitz*, 391 A.2d 209; *Wacht v. Continental Hosts, Ltd.*, C.A. No. 7954, 1994 WL 728836 (Del. Ch. Dec. 23, 1994).

83. *Getty Oil*, 509 A.2d 1123.

84. *Harris v. Capano Holdings, Inc.*, C.A. No. 80C-FE-120, 1981 WL 1724 (Del. Super. Nov. 17, 1981).

85. *Harris*, 1981 WL 1724.

86. Del. Code Ann. tit. 6, § 2301(d).

87. *Knapp v. Shepherd*, 741 A.2d 1026, 1999 WL 1254559 (Del. 1999); *Moffitt v. Carroll*, 640 A.2d 169 (Del. 1994); *Moskowitz*, 391 A.2d 209; *Process Indus., Inc. v. Del. Ins. Guar. Ass'n*, C.A. No. 92C-11-7, 1994 WL 680122 (Del. Super. Sept. 27, 1994).

88. Del. Code Ann. tit. 6, § 2301; *Home Ins. Co. v. Concors Supply Co.*, 618 A.2d 90, 1992 WL 397455 (Del. 1992).

89. Del. Code Ann. tit. 19, § 2304; *Precision Air, Inc. v. Standard Chlorine of Del., Inc.*, 654 A.2d 403 (Del. 1995).

90. *Farrall v. Armstrong Cork Co.*, 457 A.2d 763 (Del. Super. 1983).

91. *Farrall*, 457 A.2d 763; *Mergenthaler v. Asbestos Corp. of Am., Inc.*, 534 A.2d 281 (Del. Super. 1987).

92. *Diamond State Tel. Co. v. University of Del.*, 269 A.2d 52 (Del. 1970).

93. *Precision Air*, 654 A.2d 403.

94. Del. Code Ann. tit. 10, §§ 8106, 8107, 8119, and tit. 6, §§ 2-314, 2-315, 2-318, 2-725.

95. Del. Code Ann. tit. 1, § 701.

96. *Ikeda v. Molock*, 603 A.2d 785 (Del. 1991).

97. Del. Code Ann. tit. 10, § 6301.

98. *Med. Ctr. of Del., Inc. v. Mullins*, 637 A.2d 6 (Del. 1994).

99. *Med. Ctr. of Del.*, 637 A.2d 6.

100. Del. Code Ann. tit. 10, § 6302.

101. Del. Code Ann. tit. 10, § 6304.

102. Del. Code Ann. tit. 10, § 6304.

103. *Estate of Farrell v. Gordon*, 770 A.2d 517 (Del. 2001); *State Farm Mut. Auto Ins. Co. v. Nalbone*, 569 A.2d 71 (Del. 1989); *Yarrington v. Thornburg*, 205 A.2d 1 (Del. 1964).

104. *Saienni v. Anderson*, 669 A.2d 23 (Del. 1995).

105. *Mullins*, 637 A.2d 6.

106. *Travelers Indem. Co. v. Lake*, 594 A.2d 38 (Del. 1991); *Pittman v. Maldania, Inc.*, C.A. No. 00C-01-029, 2001 WL 1221704 (Del. Super. July 31, 2001); *Lagrone v. American Mortell Corp.*, Nos. 04C-10-116-ASB, 07C-12-019-JRS, 2008 WL 4152677, at *5 (Del. Super. Sept. 4, 2008); *Viking Pump, Inc. v. Century Indem. Co.*, No. 1465-VCS, 2009 WL 3297559, at *6-8 (Del. Ch. Oct. 14, 2009).

107. *See Annan v. Wilmington Trust Co.*, 559 A.2d 1289 (Del. 1989).

108. *Lagrone*, 2008 WL 4152677, at *5.

109. *Lagrone*, 2008 WL 4152677, at *5.

110. *E.I. Du Pont De Nemours & Co. v. Stonewall Ins. Co.*, C.A. No. 99C-12-253 (JTV), 2009 WL 1915212, at *4-6 (Del. Super. June 30, 2009).

111. *E.I. Du Pont De Nemours*, 2009 WL 1915212, at *4-6.

112. *E.I. Du Pont De Nemours*, 2009 WL 1915212, at *5.

113. *E.I. Du Pont De Nemours*, 2009 WL 1915212, at *6.

DISTRICT OF COLUMBIA

A. CAUSES OF ACTION

Causes of action in product liability lawsuits include strict liability, negligence, and warranty.[1] The District of Columbia courts construe an action for strict products liability and breach of the implied warranties of merchantability as a single tort.[2] Indeed, "[b]reach of implied warranty and strict liability in tort are expressions of a single basic public policy as to liability for defective products."[3]

As a general matter, it should be noted that District of Columbia courts look to Maryland case law for guidance in the absence of District of Columbia law on point.[4] For this reason, Maryland law is cited herein when District of Columbia courts have yet to decide an issue.

B. STATUTES OF LIMITATION

Suits for recovery of damages for injuries to real or personal property must be brought within three years.[5] A three-year statute of limitations also applies to personal injury claims sounding in tort, whether based on strict liability, negligence, or warranty.[6] Although ordinary contract actions are also subject to a three-year statute of limitations,[7] a four-year statute of limitations applies to breach of warranty claims that arise under the Uniform Commercial Code (UCC) as adopted by the District of Columbia.[8] Various intentional torts rarely if ever implicated in product liability actions are subject to a one-year statute of limitations.[9]

What constitutes the accrual of a cause of action is a question of law for the court, but when accrual actually occurred in a particular case is a question of fact.[10]

Tort causes of action generally accrue at the time of injury,[11] although an exception is recognized for continuing torts.[12] A "discovery" rule of accrual is also recognized.[13] Although the discovery rule arose in the context of medical malpractice[14] and has been most frequently applied in professional malpractice cases,[15] it has not been confined to this context[16] and has been applied in product liability actions.[17]

Actions arising out of death or injury caused by exposure to asbestos must be brought within the usual three years from the time the cause of action arises, though by statute the limitation period is extended to one year after the plaintiff suffered disability and knew, or in the exercise of reasonable diligence should have known, that it was caused or contributed to by exposure to asbestos.[18] This limitation period has been held to govern in product liability cases.[19]

The District of Columbia's UCC provides that actions for breach of implied and express warranty accrue at the time a product is tendered for delivery,[20] unless the warranty explicitly extends to future performance.[21] The discovery rule is inapplicable to cases arising under this statute.[22]

C. STRICT LIABILITY

1. The Standard

In the District of Columbia, a merchant who sells a defective and unreasonably dangerous product to a consumer is liable for resultant injuries, regardless of fault or privity of contract.[23]

A plaintiff in a product liability action must prove the element of causation connecting plaintiff's alleged injuries to a specific product manufactured and sold by specific persons or companies, but in appropriate cases (such as asbestos claims) proof of causation may be proved by circumstantial evidence, deriving the benefits of all reasonable inferences. In such cases, lest the jury stray too far, it is the duty of the trial court to withdraw the case from the jury when the necessary inference is so tenuous that it rests merely upon speculation and conjecture.[24]

2. "Defect"

Strict liability is imposed when a product leaves a seller's hands in a condition that is unreasonably dangerous to the consumer. Courts in the District of Columbia apply a "risk/utility" analysis in design defect cases. For example, the United States District Court for the District of Columbia has applied a "risk-utility balancing test" in a medical device product liability case.[25] Similarly, the District of Columbia Court of Appeals has applied a "risk/utility" analysis in a design defect case involving heavy machinery[26] but has implied that the choice between the "risk/utility" analysis and a "consumer expectation" test should be made on a case-by-case basis.[27]

A plaintiff in a products liability action may proceed on a "general defect theory," that is, solely on circumstantial evidence of an unspecified defect—conceptually a products liability version of the tort doctrine of *res ipsa loquitur*. To prevail, a plaintiff must present evidence that would negate causes for an accident other than a defect in the product and proof that whatever defect may have existed was introduced into the product by the defendant.[28] However, it has been held that this doctrine does not apply to design defect cases.[29]

3. Contributory Negligence/Assumption of Risk

Contributory negligence is not a defense to a strict liability claim,[30] whereas assumption of the risk is.[31] To establish an assumption of risk, the defendant must show that the plaintiff knew of the specific defect in the product and was aware of the danger arising from it, but nevertheless voluntarily and unreasonably proceeded to use the product.[32]

Unlike contributory negligence, the assumption of risk analysis focuses on the plaintiff's actual knowledge: the plaintiff must know subjectively of the existence of the risk and appreciate its unreasonable character.[33]

4. **Sale or Lease**

A consumer has a cause of action against all who participated in placing the product into the stream of commerce,[34] including manufacturers and intermediate sellers.[35] While District of Columbia courts have yet to address the issue, in Maryland strict liability is not applicable to lessors of products.[36]

5. **Inherently Dangerous Products**

A product that can never be made completely safe for all users is not unreasonably dangerous if it is accompanied by an adequate warning.[37]

6. **Successor Liability**

Adopting Maryland law in the absence of settled District of Columbia law on point, the federal district court in the District of Columbia predicted that the law of the District of Columbia would be that a corporation which acquires all or a part of the assets of another corporation generally is not responsible for the unliquidated tort liabilities or debts of its predecessor corporation.[38] Liability for dangerous or defective products may be imposed on a successor corporation, however, where (1) there has been an express or implied assumption of liability; (2) the predecessor has effectively consolidated with or merged into the successor; (3) the successor is a "mere continuation or reincarnation" of the predecessor entity; or (4) the transfer of assets to the successor was fraudulent, not made in good faith, or made without sufficient consideration.[39]

7. **Market Share Liability/Enterprise Liability**

The District of Columbia has not to date adopted the theory of market share liability.[40] It has suggested that the theory might apply in an appropriate case.[41] To the extent that a defendant's market share exceeds 50 percent, however, statistical evidence might be sufficient to prove that a plaintiff's injuries were more likely than not caused by that defendant's product.[42]

8. **Privity**

Strict liability for defective products does not depend on any contractual relationship between the manufacturer and the ultimate user or consumer.[43]

9. **Design Defects**

To prove the existence of a design defect, a plaintiff must show that the magnitude of the danger from the product outweighs the cost of avoiding that danger.[44] Thus, the plaintiff must show that a safer alternative design was commercially feasible at the time the product at issue was manufactured.[45] However, the plaintiff need not show that such alternative was commercially available.[46]

An adequate warning by itself does not immunize a manufacturer from liability for a defectively designed product; adequacy of a warning is a consideration, but not the sole consideration, in the "risk/utility" analysis that determines whether a product is defective.[47]

10. **Failure to Warn**

Manufacturers and sellers have a duty to warn consumers of attendant risks associated with normal use of their products and to provide specific instructions for safe use.[48] Compliance with governmental regulatory labeling requirements are probative of whether due care was exercised, but it does not itself preclude a finding that additional warnings should have been given.[49] A plaintiff may seek damages for negligent failure to warn or based on strict liability arising from the same failure.[50]

11. **Post-Sale Duty to Warn**

A manufacturer may have a post-sale duty to warn consumers about the dangerous propensities of its products where the manufacturer acquires knowledge or has a reasonable opportunity to learn about a defect.[51] No District of Columbia or Maryland courts have ordered product recall or replacement on the basis of strict liability.

12. **Learned Intermediary Doctrine**

Manufacturers of prescription drugs and medical prostheses need only warn prescribing physicians of risks associated with their product. The manufacturer is not under a duty to warn individual patients.[52] Any alleged inadequacy of a warning becomes moot because the chain of causation is broken by the learned intermediary's decision, made independently of the manufacturer's warning, to recommend or prescribe the use of the product.[53]

13. **Substantial Change/Abnormal Use**

Manufacturers are not liable for injuries caused by misuse or by a substantial alteration of their products except where reasonably foreseeable.[54]

14. **State of the Art**

"State of the art" can be a defense in strict liability tort cases where failure to warn is the alleged wrong.[55]

15. **Malfunction**

Unexplained malfunctioning of a product and absence of fault on the part of an accident victim is evidence tending to show a product defect. In appropriate cases the doctrine of *res ipsa loquitur* is applied, such that a specific defect need not be proven.[56]

16. **Standards and Government Regulations**

   Industry-wide custom influences, but does not conclusively determine, applicable standards of care for the manufacturer. Evidence of conformity to industry and legal standards may be conclusive if the claimant offers no contrary evidence that the product, as designed, created an unreasonable danger.[57]

17. **Other Accidents**

   Evidence of substantially similar accidents may be admitted to show the existence of a design defect or notice of such defect, but the trial judge has broad discretion to exclude such evidence if it is overly prejudicial or likely to confuse the factfinder.[58] The requisite degree of "substantial similarity" varies with the proponent's theory of proof. If the claimant seeks to prove that a design defect and dangerousness are at issue, a high degree of similarity is essential.[59] If, however, an accident is offered to prove notice, a lack of similarity will not necessarily result in exclusion, as long as the accident was of a kind that should have served to warn the defendant.[60] The burden is on the party seeking admission to prove that substantially similar circumstances exist.[61]

18. **Misrepresentation**

   District of Columbia cases have yet to address Restatement (Second) of Torts Section 402B or the issue of strict liability for misrepresentation.

19. **Economic Loss**

   District of Columbia courts have yet to rule on the economic loss doctrine in the context of product liability cases,[62] but Maryland courts generally deny tort claims for purely economic losses,[63] and the U. S. District Court for the District of Columbia applying District of Columbia law has twice refused to allow damages for economic loss under both negligence and strict liability theories.[64] A plaintiff suffering only economic loss because of a defective product is usually limited to contract causes of action, including breach of implied and express warranties, and in the case of fraud, to an action for deceit.[65] However, Maryland recognizes an exception to the economic loss rule: when a defect creates a substantial and unreasonable risk of death or personal injury, the plaintiffs may recover the reasonable cost of correcting the condition.[66]

D. **NEGLIGENCE**

Comparative negligence is not recognized by District of Columbia courts.[67] Contributory negligence[68] and assumption of the risk[69] are recognized as complete bars to recovery in negligence.

E. **BREACH OF WARRANTY**

District of Columbia courts have generally regarded strict liability and tort-based warranty as a single co-extensive tort.[70] However, warranty claims may be governed by tort law or the UCC, and there are significant differences between the two. These differences range from the applicable statute of limitations to the relevance of privity to the effect of contractual limitations on liability to the categories of damages available.[71] A breach of warranty claim is not actionable in coordination with a product liability claim.[72]

F. JOINT AND SEVERAL LIABILITY

The District of Columbia recognizes the principle of joint liability, whereby two or more tortfeasors that contribute to the harm of a plaintiff are each potentially liable for the entire harm.[73] Because the District does not recognize the doctrine of comparative negligence, the "allowance of contribution under our rules is premised upon each tortfeasor being responsible for a single injury and sharing equally in making the injured party whole."[74]

G. PRE- AND POST-JUDGMENT INTEREST

By statute, pre-judgment interest is available in contract actions.[75] Pre-judgment interest in tort actions "is neither authorized nor forbidden by statute" and has been awarded in an action for conversion "to the extent . . . needed to make the injured party whole."[76] Post-judgment interest is available and begins to run from the date of the judgment or the date of the verdict, whichever is earlier.[77]

Unless fixed by contract, the rate of interest on judgments (except those against the district government itself, which is fixed at 4 percent) shall be 70 percent of the rate of interest set by the Secretary of the United States Treasury for underpayments of tax to the Internal Revenue Service.[78] For purposes of post-judgment interest, this rate is not fixed at the date of judgment but fluctuates with the market during the period between entry of judgment and satisfaction of the judgment.[79] A lower rate of interest is allowed by statute for good cause shown or upon a showing that the judgment debtor in good faith is unable to pay the judgment.[80]

H. EMPLOYER IMMUNITY FROM SUIT

The District of Columbia's Workers' Compensation Act's "exclusive remedy provision" exempts employers from tort liability for harms to employees injured in the workplace, except for intentional torts by the employer.[81]

I. PUNITIVE DAMAGES

Punitive damages are recoverable upon "clear and convincing evidence that the act was accompanied by conduct and a state of mind evincing malice or its equivalent."[82] Punitive damages cannot be awarded absent a verdict assessing compensatory damages,[83] although nominal damages are sufficient to meet this standard.[84] The trial court has discretion to bifurcate compensatory and punitive damages proceedings.[85]

J. **STATUTES, INCLUDING APPLICABLE "TORT REFORM" STATUTES**

Relevant statutes for product liability actions are those providing statutes of limitation[86] and the commercial code sections when a breach of warranty is alleged.[87]

Robert N. Kelly
Jackson & Campbell, P.C.
1120 20th Street, NW
Suite 300-South
Washington, DC 20036
www.jackscamp.com
(202) 457-1600
(Fax) (202) 457-1678

ENDNOTES - DISTRICT OF COLUMBIA

1. *Payne v. Soft Sheen Prods.*, 486 A.2d 712, 719-23 (D.C. 1985).

2. *Wainwright v. Washington Metro. Area Transit Auth.*, 903 F. Supp. 133, 140 (D.D.C.1995).

3. *Wainwriight*, 903 F. Supp. at 140, citing *Fisher v. Sibley Mem'l Hosp.*, 403 A.2d 1130, 1133 (D.C. 1979).

4. *See Conesco Indus., Ltd. v. Conforti & Eisele, Inc., D.C.*, 627 F.2d 312, 315-16 (D.C. Cir. 1980) (discussing evolution of District of Columbia common law); *Hoehn v. United States*, 217 F. Supp. 2d 39, 47 (D.D.C. 2002); *Hull v. Eaton Corp.*, 825 F.2d 448, 453-54 (D.C. Cir. 1987); *Kreuzer v. George Washington Univ.*, 896 A.2d 238, 243 & n.3 (D.C. 2006), citing *Walker v. Independence Fed. Sav. & Loan Ass'n*, 555 A.2d 1019, 1022 (D.C. 1989).

5. D.C. Code § 12-301(3) (2001).

6. D.C. Code § 12-301(8) (2001). *See Dawson v. Eli Lilly & Co.*, 543 F. Supp. 1330, 1332 (D.D.C. 1982); *Grigsby v. Sterling Drug, Inc.*, 428 F. Supp. 242, 243 (D.D.C. 1975).

7. D.C. Code § 12-301(7) (2001); *Medhin v. Hailu*, 26 A.3d 307 (D.C. 2011).

8. D.C. Code § 28:2-725(1) (2001). *See Hull*, 825 F.2d at 456; *Long v. Sears Roebuck & Co.*, 877 F. Supp. 8, 13-14 (D.D.C. 1995). This statute of limitations applies to contract actions involving "transactions in goods." D.C. Code § 28:2-102 (2001). *See also Bowler v. Stewart-Warner Corp.*, 563 A.2d 344, 346 (D.C. 1989); *Jenkins v. Washington Metro Area Transit Auth.*, 793 F. Supp. 2d 133 (D.D.C. 2011) (differentiating between warranty claims brought in tort and those brought under the UCC).

9. *See* D.C. Code § 12-301 (4), which applies to libel, slander, assault, battery, mayhem, wounding, malicious prosecution, and false arrest or false imprisonment. There is some authority for including the tort of intentional infliction of emotional distress within this list. *See Dawson v. Eli Lilly & Co.*, 543 F. Supp. 1330, 1332 (D.D.C. 1982).

10. *Diamond v. Davis*, 680 A.2d 364, 370 (D.C. 1996).

11. *Shehyn v. District of Columbia*, 392 A.2d 1008, 1013 (D.C. 1978) (negligent supervision, but speaking of tort in general); *Morton v. National Med. Enters., Inc.*, 725 A.2d 462, 468 (D.C. 1999) (negligent treatment at psychiatric

hospital); *Prouty v. National R.R. Passenger Corp.*, 572 F. Supp. 200, 205 (D.D.C. 1982) (negligent maintenance of employment records).

12. *Beard v. Edmonson & Gallagher*, 790 A.2d 541, 547-48 (D.C. 2002) (noting elements needed to establish existence of continuing tort); *Rochon v. FBI*, 691 F. Supp. 1548, 1563-64 (D.D.C. 1988) (applying "continuing tort" doctrine in racial discrimination case); *Morton v. D.C. Housing Auth.*, 720 F. Supp. 2d 1 (D.D.C. 2010) (discrimination based on disability). *See also Perkins v. Nash*, 697 F. Supp. 527, 533-34 (D.D.C. 1988) (concluding fraudulent loan was not a continuing tort).

13. An action accrues when a plaintiff has knowledge of, or through the exercise of reasonable diligence should have knowledge of, (1) the existence of the injury, (2) its cause in fact, and (3) some evidence of wrongdoing. *Diamond v. Davis*, 680 A.2d 364, 389 (D.C. 1996); *Ling Yuan Hu v. George Washington Univ.*, 766 F. Supp. 2d 236 (D.D.C. 2011).

14. *See Burns v. Bell*, 409 A.2d 614 (D.C. 1979) (extending applicability of "foreign object" discovery rule to medical malpractice in general); *Morton*, 725 A.2d at 468 (declining to extend applicability of discovery rule).

15. *See Burns*, 409 A.2d at 614, *Morton*, 725 A.2d at 468 (medical malpractice); *Stager v. Schneider*, 494 A.2d 1307, 1316-17 (D.C. 1985) (same); *Bussineau v. President & Dirs. of Georgetown Coll.*, 518 A.2d 423, 425 (D.C. 1986) (dental malpractice action, in which court clarified that cause of action does not accrue until plaintiff has (or should know of) some evidence of wrongdoing); *Knight v. Furlow*, 553 A.2d 1232, 1234 (D.C. 1989) (extending rule to legal malpractice); *Seed Co. v. Westerman*, 840 F. Supp. 2d 116 (D.D.C. 2012) (same).

16. *See Shamloo v. Lifespring, Inc.*, 713 F. Supp. 14, 17 (D.D.C. 1989) (discovery rule not limited to licensed professionals); *Fearson v. Johns-Manville Sales Corp.*, 525 F. Supp. 671, 674 (D.D.C. 1981) (discovery rule extended to latent occupational disease).

17. *See, e.g., Grigsby*, 428 F. Supp. at 243; *Dawson*, 543 F. Supp. at 1333. *See also Bussineau*, 518 A.2d at 428 (approving of *Dawson's* application of discovery rule to product liability cases).

18. D.C. Code § 12-311 (2012).

19. *Owens-Corning Fiberglas Corp. v. Henkel*, 689 A.2d 1224 (D.C. 1996).

20. D.C. Code § 28:2-725(2) (2001). *See also Hull*, 825 F.2d at 456; *Long*, 877 F. Supp. at 14.

21. D.C. Code § 28:2-725(2) (2001). *See Hunt v. DePuy Orthopaedics, Inc.*, 636 F. Supp. 2d 23, 27 (D.D.C. 2009).

22. *See* D.C. Code § 28:2-725(2) (2001); *Hunt*, 636 F. Supp. 2d at 27. *See also Hull*, 825 F.2d at 456-57; *Long*, 877 F. Supp. at 14.

23. *See, e.g., McNeal v. Hi-Lo Powered Scaffolding, Inc.*, 836 F.2d 637 (D.C. Cir. 1988); *Young v. Up-Right Scaffolds, Inc.*, 637 F.2d 810, 812-13 (D.C. Cir. 1980); *Payne*, 486 A.2d 712, 719-20.

24. *Claytor v. Owens-Corning Fiberglas Corp.*, 662 A.2d 1374, 1384 (D.C. 1995).

25. *Webster v. Pacesetter, Inc.*, 259 F. Supp. 2d 27, 31-34 (D.D.C. 2003); *see also Rollins v. Wackenhut Servs.*, 802 F. Supp. 2d 111 (D.D.C. 2011) (pharmaceutical products).

26. *Warner Fruehauf Trailer Co., Inc. v. Boston*, 654 A.2d 1272, 1276 (D.C. 1995); *Rogers v. Ingersoll-Rand Co.*, 144 F.3d 841, 843-45 (D.C. Cir. 1998).

27. *Warner Fruehauf*, 654 A.2d at 1276 n.9; *see Wilson Sporting Goods Co. v. Hickox*, 59 A.3d 1267, 1274-75 (D.C. 2013).

28. *Zanganeh v. BMW of N. Am., Inc.*, 962 F.2d 1076 (D.C. Cir. 1992).

29. *Pappas v. Ford Motor Co.*, 7 F. Supp. 2d 22, 26 (D.D.C. 1998).

30. *Jarrett V. Woodward Bros.*, 751 A.2d 972 (D.C.2000); *Payne*, 486 A.2d at 722 n.9; *East Penn Mfg. Co. v. Pineda*, 578 A.2d 1113, 1118-19 (D.C. 1990).

31. *Warner Fruehauf*, 654 A.2d at 1274; *East Penn*, 578 A.2d at 1118-19.

32. *Warner Fruehauf*, 654 A.2d at 1274-75.

33. *Jarrett v. Woodward Bros.*, 751 A.2d 972 (D.C. App. 2000); *Sinai v. Polinger Co.*, 498 A.2d 520, 524 (D.C. 1985).

34. *Berman v. Watergate West, Inc.*, 391 A.2d 1351, 1352 (D.C. 1978).

35. *Stewart v. Ford Motor Co.*, 553 F.2d 130, 137 (D.C. Cir. 1977).

36. *Bona v. Graefe*, 285 A.2d 607, 611 (Md. 1972).

37. *Payne*, 486 A.2d at 722.

38. *LeSane v. Hillenbrand Indus., Inc.*, 791 F. Supp. 871, 873-74 (D.D.C. 1992), adopting the reasoning and holdings of *Nissen Corp. v. Miller*, 594 A.2d 564, 565-66 (Md. 1991) (rejecting the continuity of enterprise theory of successor corporate liability and adhering to the general rule of nonliability of corporate successors).

39. *LeSane*, 791 F. Supp. at 874; *Nissen Corp.*, 594 A.2d at 566.

40. *Claytor v. Owens-Corning Fiberglas Corp.*, 662 A.2d 1374, 1383 & n.10 (D.C. 1995) (requiring asbestos claimants to "identify and prove which manufacturers of allegedly hazardous products caused their injuries," and noting that "market share" liability has been rejected in several other jurisdictions). See also *Tidler v. Eli Lilly & Co.*, 851 F.2d 418, 424 (D.C. Cir. 1988); *District of Columbia v. Beretta U.S.A. Corp.*, 2002 WL 31811717 at *56 (D.C. Super. Dec. 16, 2002), *rev'd on other grounds*, 872 A.2d 633 (D.C. 2005).

41. *Bly v. Tri-Cont'l Indus.*, 663 A.2d 1232, 1241-44 (D.C. 1995).

42. *Galvin v. Eli Lilly & Co.*, 488 F.3d 1026, 1034-35 (D.C. Cir. 2007).

43. *Bowler*, 563 A.2d 344, 346; *Payne*, 486 A.2d at 719-20; *Picker X-Ray Corp. v. General Motors Corp.*, 185 A.2d 919, 923 (D.C. 1962).

44. *Warner Fruehauf*, 654 A.2d at 1276; *Hull*, 825 F.2d at 453.

45. *Warner Fruehauf*, 654 A.2d at 1277; *Artis v. Corona Corp. of Japan*, 703 A.2d 1214, 1217 (D.C. 1997).

46. *Artis*, 703 A.2d at 1217.

47. *Warner Fruehauf*, 654 A.2d at 1278; *Rogers*, 144 F.3d at 844.

48. *Burch v. Amsterdam Corp.*, 366 A.2d 1079, 1085-86 (D.C. 1976).

49. *Burch*, 366 A.2d at 1085-86.

50. *East Penn Mfg. Co.*, 578 A.2d at 1118; *Russell v. G.A.F. Corp.*, 422 A.2d 989, 991 (D.C. 1980).

51. *Owens-Illinois, Inc. v. Zenobia*, 601 A.2d 633, 645-46 (Md. 1992).

52. The "learned intermediary" doctrine was first acknowledged by the District of Columbia Court of Appeals in *Payne*, 486 A.2d at 722 n.10. See *Patterson v. AstraZeneca, LP*, 876 F. Supp. 2d 27, 33 (D.D.C. 2012).

53. *Mampe v. Ayerst Labs.*, 548 A.2d 798, 802 (D.C. 1988).

54. *Young*, 637 F.2d at 815; *Payne*, 486 A.2d at 720 n.6, 725-26.

55. *Lohrmann v. Pittsburgh Corning Corp.*, 782 F.2d 1156, 1164 (4th Cir. 1986) (applying Maryland law); see *Claytor v. Owens-Corning Fiberglas Corp.*, 662 A.2d 1374, 1382 (D.C. 1995).

56. *Stewart*, 553 F.2d at 136, 141; *Hall v. General Motors Corp.*, 647 F.2d 175, 178 (D.C. Cir. 1980).

57. *Sledd v. Washington Metro. Area Transit Auth.*, 439 A.2d 464, 469 (D.C. 1981); *Westinghouse Elec. Corp. v. Nutt*, 407 A.2d 606, 610 (D.C. 1979).

58. *Brooks v. Chrysler Corp.*, 786 F.2d 1191, 1195 (D.C. Cir. 1986).

59. *Exum v. General Elec. Co.*, 819 F.2d 1158, 1162-63 (D.C. Cir. 1987).

60. *Exum*, 819 F.2d at 1162-63.

61. *Nakajima v. General Motors Corp.*, 857 F. Supp. 100, 102 (D.D.C. 1994).

62. *Bowler*, 563 A.2d at 355 ("We have not decided whether economic loss is recoverable under strict liability, as well as breach of warranty theory.").

63. *United States Gypsum Co. v. Mayor & City Council of Baltimore*, 647 A.2d 405, 410 (Md. 1994); *but see Council of Co-Owners Atlantis Condo., Inc. v. Whiting-Turner Contracting Co.*, 517 A.2d 336, 338 (Md. 1986) (economic damages recoverable where alleged construction defect created a threat to the safety and welfare of condominium owners and occupants).

64. *Potomac Plaza Terraces, Inc. v. QSC Products, Inc.*, 868 F. Supp. 346 (D.D.C. 1994); *RLI Ins. Co. v. Pohl, Inc. of America*, 468 F. Supp. 2d 91, 94 (D.D.C. 2006).

65. *United States Gypsum Co.*, 647 A.2d at 410.

66. *United States Gypsum Co.*, 647 A.2d at 410-11; *Council of Co-Owners Atlantis Condo., Inc. v. Whiting-Turner Contracting Co.*, 517 A.2d 336, 345 (Md. 1986); *United States Gypsum Co.*, 647 A.2d at 410-11.

67. *See, e.g., Estate of Kurstin v. Jordan*, 25 A.3d 54, 63 (D.C. 2011); *District of Columbia v. C.F. & B., Inc.*, 442 F. Supp. 251, 257 (D.D.C. 1977); *National Health Labs., Inc. v. Ahmadi*, 596 A.2d 555, 561 (D.C. 1991); *D.C. Transit Sys., Inc. v. Garman*, 301 F.2d 568, 570 (D.C. Cir. 1962).

68. *Grogan v. General Maint. Serv. Co.*, 763 F.2d 444, 448 (D.C. Cir. 1985); *Elam v. Ethical Prescription Pharmacy, Inc.*, 422 A.2d 1288, 1289 & n.2 (D.C. 1980); *Scoggins v. Jude*, 419 A.2d 999, 1004 (D.C. 1980); *Brown v. Clancy*, 43 A.2d 296, 298 (D.C. 1945).

69. *Scoggins*, 419 A.2d at 1004.

70. *Bowler*, 563 A.2d at 347-48; *Payne*, 486 A.2d at 720; *Cottom v. McGuire Funeral Serv., Inc.*, 262 A.2d 807, 808 (D.C. 1970).

71. *Bowler*, 563 A.2d at 353-54 (Ferren, J., concurring).

72. *Dyson v. Winfield*, 113 F. Supp. 2d 35, 42 (D.C. Cir. 2000); *Webster*, 259 F. Supp. 2d at 38.

73. *Nat'l Health Labs.*, 596 A.2d at 557; *Hubbard v. Chidel*, 790 A.2d 558, 569-70 (D.C. 2002).

74. *Estate of Kurstin*, 25 A.3d at 63, quoting from *District of Columbia v. Washington Hosp. Ctr.*, 722 A.2d 332, 339 (D.C. 1998).

75. D.C. Code § 15-109 (2001). To the extent that the judgment is on a liquidated amount and interest is payable on that debt by contract, law or usage, pre-judgment interest is mandatory. D.C. Code § 15-108 (2001).

76. *Duggan v. Keto*, 554 A.2d 1126, 1140 (D.C. 1989).

77. D.C. Code § 15-109 (2001); *Bell v. Westinghouse Elec. Co.*, 507 A.2d 548, 556 (D.C. 1986).

78. D.C. Code § 28-3302.

79. *Burke v. Groover, Christie & Merritt, P.C.*, 26 A.3d 292, 300 (D.C. 2011).

80. D.C. Code § 28-3302(c). *See Burke, supra*, 26 A.3d at 301.

81. D.C. Code §§ 32-1504(a), 36-301(12) ("by definition, injuries to an employee that are intended by the employer fall outside of the WCA's exclusivity provisions, even though they are work-related, because they are nonaccidental") (2001); *Grillo v. National Bank of Washington*, 540 A.2d 743, 747-48 (D.C. 1988); *Clark v. District of Columbia Dep't of Employment Servs.*, 743 A.2d 722, 727 (D.C. 2000) (employer may be liable under the Workers' Compensation Act for the intentional tort of a third party if the injury arose out of and occurred in the course of employment).

82. *Jonathan Woodner, Co. v. Breeden*, 665 A.2d 929, 938 (D.C. 1995); *Wesley Theological Seminary of the United Methodist Church v. United States Gypsum Co.*, 876 F.2d 119, 124 (D.C. Cir. 1989) (warranty); *Raynor v. Richardson-Merrell, Inc.*, 643 F. Supp. 238, 245 (D.D.C. 1986) (strict liability and negligence).

83. *Franklin Inv. Co., Inc. v. Smith*, 383 A.2d 355, 358 (D.C. 1978); *Maxwell v. Gallagher*, 709 A.2d 100, 104 (D.C. 1998).

84. *Ayala v. Washington*, 679 A.2d 1057, 1070 (D.C. 1996).

85. *Cf., Merrell Dow Pharms., Inc. v. Oxendine*, 593 A.2d 1023 (D.C. 1991).

86. D.C. Code §§ 12-301, 28:2-725(1) (2001).

87. D.C. Code §§ 28:2-313 to 2-318 (2001).

FLORIDA

A. CAUSES OF ACTION

Product liability lawsuits commonly include causes of action for strict liability, negligence, breach of warranty, and wrongful death.

B. STATUTES OF LIMITATION

A product liability action based on strict liability, negligence, or breach of implied warranty must be brought within four years or it is barred.[1] An action based on breach of express warranty has a five-year statute of limitations.[2] An action for wrongful death must be brought within the two-year statute of limitations.[3] The limitations period runs from the time the defect is discovered or should have been discovered with the exercise of due diligence.[4] Florida's statute of repose, however, generally bars product liability claims brought more than 12 years after delivery of the product to the original purchaser.[5]

C. STRICT LIABILITY

1. The Standard

Florida has expressly adopted Section 402A of the Restatement (Second) of Torts,[6] and requires that the plaintiff establish the following three elements:

a. the defendant's relationship to the product;

b. the defective and unreasonably dangerous condition of the product; and

c. the causal connection between the product's condition and the plaintiff's injuries.[7] Several courts have also required that the defect exist at the time of the accident and when the product was in the possession of the defendant.[8]

2. "Product"

A "Product" is property entered into the stream of commerce that can be sold for a profit to consumers.[9]

3. "Defect"

"In the byzantine world of products liability, there are three basic families of defects that may be the subject of strict product liability: manufacturing defects, design defects, and failures to warn."[10] A product may be "defective" when risks exceed a reasonable buyer's expectations (the consumer-expectation test),[11] although at least one district court in Florida has rejected this test.[12] A product may also be

Florida

defective when the foreseeable risks of harm posed by the product could have been reduced or avoided by the adoption of a reasonable alternative design and its omission renders the product not reasonably safe (the risk-utility test).[13] A reasonable buyer should expect the product to contain parts which require inspection and maintenance.[14] The *Cassisi* inference allows a jury to infer, under Florida law, that a product is defective when it (a) malfunctions (b) under normal use.[15]

4. **Sale or Lease/Persons Liable**

   The plaintiff must allege a sale or other commercial transaction of the product by the defendant.[16]

   Strict liability applies to any seller in the chain of a product's distribution.[17] Lessors also may be held strictly liable.[18] A single sale or lease of a product, however, by a person not ordinarily in the business of distributing such products does not support a strict-liability action.[19]

5. **Market-Share Liability/Enterprise Liability**

   Market-share liability and enterprise liability are two theories of liability that relax the traditional requirement of tort law that plaintiffs identify a specific tortfeasor as causing the injury.[20] The Supreme Court of Florida, in a DES case, adopted a hybrid market-share theory of liability that was initially formulated by the Supreme Court of Washington.[21] This theory, however, is limited to actions sounding in negligence and is not available in conjunction with allegations of fraud, breach of warranty, or strict liability.[22]

6. **Privity**

   Any consumer, user, or bystander injured by a defective product has standing to bring a product liability action.[23] Privity is not required.[24]

7. **Failure to Warn**

   In the failure-to-warn context, an "otherwise safe product" may be defective solely by virtue of an inadequate warning.[25] The rules of strict liability require a plaintiff to prove only that the defendant did not adequately warn of a particular risk that was known or knowable in light of the generally recognized and prevailing best scientific and medical knowledge available at the time of manufacture and distribution.[26] To warn adequately, the product label must make apparent the potential harmful consequences. The warning should be of such intensity as to cause a reasonable person to exercise his or her own safety caution commensurate with the potential danger.[27] There is no duty, however, to warn of an obvious danger.[28] Moreover, manufacturers are not required to warn of every risk that might be remotely suggested by any obscure knowledge, but only of those risks that are discoverable in light of the "generally recognized and prevailing best" knowledge available.[29] Further, a plaintiff's failure to read a warning label extinguishes proximate cause in a failure-to-warn claim.[30]

8. **Post-Sale Duty to Warn**

   The issue of whether a manufacturer has a duty to warn of defects discovered after sale of the product in question is not clearly addressed in published Florida case law.

9. **Crashworthiness Doctrine**

   The crashworthiness doctrine states that automobile manufacturers have to design and construct their automobiles so that they are crashworthy. The doctrine, in other words, rejects the argument that an automobile does not have to be crashworthy because its "intended use" does not include "crashes." Florida courts have adopted the crashworthiness doctrine and applied it against automobile manufacturers as well as motorcycle manufacturers.[31] This doctrine is available in strict-liability actions, as well as in negligence and breach-of-warranty actions.[32] In crashworthiness actions, comparative fault is not tried because it is always presumed that the negligence of others caused the basic vehicular collision.[33]

D. NEGLIGENCE

A negligence action to recover for injuries caused by a defective product requires:

(1) the defendant's duty of reasonable care in manufacturing or distributing the product;

(2) a breach of the duty;

(3) injury to the party seeking relief as a result; and

(4) damages.[34]

Unlike strict liability, the plaintiff must prove the defendant had actual or constructive knowledge of the defect.[35]

The "patent-danger" doctrine is rejected in Florida, but may otherwise reduce recovery through comparative fault.[36]

An adjunct to a negligence claim may be based on the manufacturer's or the distributor's "failure to warn" of the product defect or the foreseeable manner in which the product could be used.[37]

E. BREACH OF WARRANTY

Unlike strict liability and negligence, a breach-of-warranty action requires "privity" of the parties.[38]

An action for breach of warranty is subject to both the Florida Uniform Commercial Code and Florida common law.[39]

F. **DEFENSES**

1. **Comparative Negligence**

   Florida is a comparative-negligence state.[40] The comparative fault of either the plaintiff[41] or a non-party,[42] misuse,[43] change of the product's condition,[44] and the "military contractor's defense"[45] are defenses to a strict-liability action.[46] Comparative fault in the sense of a failure to discover a defect, or to guard against the possibility of its existence, however, is not a defense.[47]

2. **Inherently Dangerous Products**

   A supplier of products will not be held strictly liable simply because the product is inherently dangerous. The court must evaluate the product based on the factors enumerated in Section 402A of the Restatement (Second) of Torts.[48] An unavoidably dangerous product cannot be made safe for its intended and ordinary use; however, if accompanied by sufficient directions and warnings, it will not be considered unreasonably dangerous.[49] Some courts have applied the risk-utility test to this determination.[50]

3. **Used Products**

   A seller of used products will ordinarily not be strictly liable for a defective product if the defects are latent and not discoverable with reasonable care.[51]

4. **Learned Intermediary Doctrine**

   A "learned intermediary" is one who has the knowledge of the danger and whose position, vis-à-vis the manufacturer and consumer, confers a duty to convey the requisite warnings to the consumer.[52] When a warning is designed to inform a learned intermediary, a manufacturer can more readily establish the adequacy of the warning because it will be read and considered by a trained expert.[53]

5. **Standards and Government Regulations**

   Compliance with industry standards and government regulation may be used as evidence that a product is not defective.[54] The manufacturer's compliance with such standards does not, however, constitute an absolute defense.

6. **Economic Loss**

   The economic-loss rule is a court-created doctrine that prohibits the extension of tort recovery to cases in which a product has damaged only itself and there is no personal injury or damage to other property, and the losses or damage are purely economic.[55] This rule applies only in product liability cases. The Florida Supreme Court recently determined that the economic-loss rule no longer applies outside the product liability context.[56]

7. Harmless Products

Under tort law, a plaintiff may not recover damages incurred solely because a harmless product does not work.[57] Similarly, a manufacturer is not strictly liable for damages incurred through a product's normal wear and tear.[58]

8. Successor Liability

Florida law does not impose the debts and obligations of a predecessor upon a successor corporation unless: (1) the successor expressly or impliedly assumes obligations of the predecessor; (2) the transaction is a de facto merger; (3) the successor is a mere continuation of the predecessor; or (4) the transaction is a fraudulent effort to avoid liabilities of the predecessor.[59]

9. Idiosyncratic-Reaction Defense

The idiosyncratic-reaction defense is not clearly addressed in Florida case law. Courts in other jurisdictions that construe the defense hold that it involves a two-step process. *First*, a defendant must produce evidence that the plaintiff's injury is the result of an allergic response from the use of a product. *Second*, after the defendant has produced such evidence, the plaintiff bears the burden of proving that the reaction, rather than being idiosyncratic, could be experienced by an identifiable class of consumers.[60]

G. INTERNATIONAL PRODUCT LIABILITY CASES

Product liability cases are taking on more of an international aspect given increasing globalization. As such, litigants are frequently required to deal with issues concerning the proper forum. Forum non conveniens is a common law doctrine that permits a court to decline jurisdiction over a case where there is a more convenient forum for the case to be litigated.[61] This doctrine is frequently invoked in product liability cases, when the manufacturer of the allegedly defective product resides outside Florida.[62] As such, Florida courts will consider, among other things, the location of the witnesses and where the product was researched, designed, manufactured, and marketed.[63]

H. SUNSHINE-IN-LITIGATION STATUTE

In 1991, the Florida legislature enacted the Sunshine in Litigation Act.[64] The Act states that courts may not enter any order or judgment with the "purpose or effect of concealing a public hazard or any information concerning a public hazard, nor shall the court enter an order or judgment which has the purpose or effect of concealing any information which may be useful to members of the public in protecting themselves from injury which may result from the public hazard."[65] The term "public hazard" is defined as "an instrumentality, including but not limited to any device, instrument, person, procedure, product, or a condition of a device, instrument, person, procedure or product, that has caused and is likely to cause injury."[66]

I. **ADMISSIBILITY OF EXPERT TESTIMONY**

For ninety years Florida courts used the test set forth in *Frye v. United States*, 293 F. 1013 (D.C. Cir. 1923) to determine the admissibility of expert witness testimony. Florida was one of the last states to continue using that standard after the 1993 United States Supreme Court decision in *Daubert v. Merrell Dow Pharmaceuticals, Inc.*, 509 U.S. 579 (1993). In 2013, however, Florida abolished the *Frye* test and adopted a standard patterned after both the arguably more demanding federal *Daubert* standard and Federal Rule of Evidence 702. The new law, incorporated into Florida's Evidence Code, states as follows:

> If scientific, technical, or other specialized knowledge will assist the trier of fact in understanding the evidence or in determining a fact in issue, a witness qualified as an expert by knowledge, skill, experience, training, or education may testify about it in the form of an opinion or otherwise, if:
>
> (1) The testimony is based upon sufficient facts or data;
> (2) The testimony is the product of reliable principles and methods; and
> (3) The witness has applied the principles and methods reliably to the facts of the case.[67]

Although the statute itself mentions neither *Daubert* nor *Frye*, legislative history makes clear that the amendment "provide[s] a standard that is more closely related to *Daubert* and the Federal Code of Evidence than *Frye*. . . . [and] appl[ies] the *Daubert* standard to all proposed expert testimony, including pure opinion testimony. . . ."[68]

J. **WRONGFUL-DEATH STATUTE**

Florida's Wrongful Death Act gives a right of action to certain statutory beneficiaries for the recovery of damages suffered by reason of the death of the party killed.[69]

K. **DAMAGES**

Strict-liability and negligence actions permit recovery of damages for personal injury and injury to property. Breach-of-contract damages are recoverable only in warranty actions.[70]

Florida law requires that a judgment against a party found liable must be entered in proportion to that party's percentage of fault.[71] Thus, comparative fault operates to apportion damages.[72]

Punitive damages may not be alleged unless there is a reasonable showing by evidence in the record or proffered by the claimant that would provide a reasonable basis for recovery of such damages.[73] Punitive damages must bear some relationship to the defendant's ability to pay and not result in economic castigation or bankruptcy to the defendant.[74] Moreover, the amount of compensatory damages must be determined in advance of a determination of amount of punitive damages awardable, if any, so that the relationship between the two may be reviewed for reasonableness.[75]

In 1999, Florida enacted the Florida Tort Reform Act, which provided sweeping changes to a number of areas of concern in product liability actions. In addition to the imposition of the twelve-year statute of repose, discussed *supra*, the Act, among other things: revised and limited statutory provisions with respect to claims for punitive damages in civil actions; and provided for the apportionment of damages on the basis of joint-and-several liability when a party's fault exceeds a certain percentage. Importantly, however, in 2006 the Florida legislature repealed the former joint-and-several liability provisions and, for negligence cases (including strict liability, products liability, and professional malpractice), enacted a comparative-fault standard, whereby courts shall enter judgments against any party on the basis of the party's percentage of fault "and not on the basis of the doctrine of joint and several liability."[76]

L. PRE- AND POST-JUDGMENT INTEREST

In contract cases, pre-judgment interest is available from the date the debt is due.[77] In tort cases, when a jury verdict liquidates damages on a plaintiff's out-of-pocket pecuniary losses, the plaintiff is entitled to pre-judgment interest at the statutory rate from the date of that loss.[78] An unliquidated claim becomes liquidated and, thus, susceptible of bearing pre-judgment interest, when a jury verdict has the effect of fixing the amount of damages.[79] At that point, the court simply computes pre-judgment interest at the same rate as post-judgment interest from the jury verdict to the date of judgment.[80] Historically, plaintiffs in personal-injury cases have not been entitled to pre-judgment interest, and there is no entitlement to post-verdict prejudgment interest.[81]

Florida Rule of Appellate Procedure 9.340(c) requires that, upon reversal of a trial court order depriving a plaintiff of the full benefit of a jury verdict, the trial court enter judgment as of the date of the verdict.[82]

M. EMPLOYER IMMUNITY FROM SUIT

Section 440.11(1), Florida Statutes (2014), provides, with few exceptions, that workers' compensation is the exclusive remedy for an employee injured on the job.[83] This exclusive remedy extends to claims against fellow employees.[84]

N. AGE OF MAJORITY

In Florida, the age of majority is 18.[85]

Alvin F. Lindsay
James L. VanLandingham
Hogan Lovells US LLP
600 Brickell Avenue
Suite 2700
Miami, Florida 33131
(305) 459-6633
(Fax) (305) 459-6550
Alvin.Lindsay@HoganLovells.com
James.VanLandingham@HoganLovells.com

Endnotes - Florida

1. Fla. Stat. § 95.11(3)(a), (e), (k) (2014).

2. Fla. Stat. § 95.11(2)(b) (2014).

3. Fla. Stat. § 95.11(4)(d) (2014). Notably, an action for medical malpractice shall be commenced within two years from the time the incident giving rise to the action occurred or within two years from the time the incident is discovered or should have been discovered with the exercise of due diligence up to a maximum of four years from the incident; except that the four-year period shall not bar an action on behalf of a minor on or before the minor's eighth birthday. Fla. Stat. § 95.11(4)(b) (2014).

4. Fla. Stat. § 95.031(2) (2014); *see also Carter v. Brown & Williamson Tobacco Corp.*, 778 So. 2d 932, 934 (Fla. 2000) (holding that in a product liability cause of action involving a latent or "creeping" disease, the cause of action accrues when the accumulated effects of the deleterious substance manifest themselves to the plaintiff in a way that supplies some evidence of a causal relationship to the manufactured product); *American Optical Corp. v. Spiewak*, 73 So. 3d 120, 126 (Fla. 2011); *Frazier v. Philip Morris USA Inc.*, No. 3D11-580, 2012 WL 1192076, at *9 (Fla. 3d DCA 2012) ("the 'manifestations' that are pertinent are symptoms or effects that actually disclose that the prospective claimant is suffering from a disease or medical condition").

5. Fla. Stat. § 95.031(2)(b), (c) & (d) state:

    (b) An action for products liability under s. 95.11(3) [the four-year limitation period for actions founded, inter alia, upon: negligence; the design, manufacture, distribution of personal property; statutory liability; fraud; and contracts not founded on a written instrument] must be begun within the period prescribed in this chapter, with the period running from the date that the facts giving rise to the cause of action were discovered, or should have been discovered with the exercise of due diligence, rather than running from any other date prescribed elsewhere in s. 95.11(3), except as provided within this subsection. Under no circumstances may a claimant commence an action for products liability, including a wrongful death action or any other claim arising from personal injury or property damage caused by a product, to recover for harm allegedly caused by a product with an expected useful life of 10 years or less, if the harm was caused by exposure to or use of the product more than 12 years after delivery of the product to its first purchaser or lessee who was not engaged in the business of selling or leasing the product or of using the product as a component in the manufacture of another product. All products, except those included within subparagraph 1. or subparagraph 2., are conclusively presumed to have an expected useful life of 10 years or less.

1. Aircraft used in commercial or contract carrying of passengers or freight, vessels of more than 100 gross tons, railroad equipment used in commercial or contract carrying of passengers or freight, and improvements to real property, including elevators and escalators, are not subject to the statute of repose provided within this subsection.

2. Any product not listed in subparagraph 1., which the manufacturer specifically warranted, through express representation or labeling, as having an expected useful life exceeding 10 years, has an expected useful life commensurate with the time period indicated by the warranty or label. Under such circumstances, no action for products liability may be brought after the expected useful life of the product, or more than 12 years after delivery of the product to its first purchaser or lessee who was not engaged in the business of selling or leasing the product or of using the product as a component in the manufacture of another product, whichever is later.

3. With regard to those products listed in subparagraph 1., except for escalators, elevators, and improvements to real property, no action for products liability may be brought more than 20 years after delivery of the product to its first purchaser or lessor who was not engaged in the business of selling or leasing the product or of using the product as a component in the manufacture of another product. However, if the manufacturer specifically warranted, through express representation or labeling, that the product has an expected useful life exceeding 20 years, the repose period shall be the time period warranted in the representations or label.

(c) The repose period prescribed in paragraph (b) does not apply if the claimant was exposed to or used the product within the repose period, but an injury caused by such exposure or use did not manifest itself until after expiration of the repose period.

(d) The repose period prescribed within paragraph (b) is tolled for any period during which the manufacturer through its officers, directors, partners, or managing agents had actual knowledge that the product was defective in the manner alleged by the claimant and took affirmative steps to conceal the defect. Any claim of concealment under this section shall be made with specificity and must be based upon substantial factual and legal support. Maintaining the confidentiality of trade secrets does not constitute concealment under this section.

Fla. Stat. § 95.031(2)(b), (c) & (d) (2014).

Note that the delayed-discovery portion of the statute applies only to product liability actions under § 95.11(3), not wrongful-death actions which are governed by the two-year limitations period pursuant to § 95.11(4)(d). The statute-of-repose portion of this statute, however, expressly applies also to wrongful-death actions. *See Raie v. Cheminova, Inc.*, 336 F.3d 1278, 1281 (11th Cir. 2003).

6. *See Ligett Group, Inc. v. Davis*, 973 So. 2d 467 (Fla. 4th DCA 2007), *appeal dismissed*, 997 So. 2d 400 (2008); *Samuel Friedland Family Enter. v. Amoroso*, 630

So. 2d 1067, 1068 (Fla. 1994); *West v. Caterpillar Tractor Co., Inc.*, 336 So. 2d 80, 87 (Fla. 1976).

7. *West*, 336 So. 2d at 87; *Cintron v. Osmose Wood Preserving, Inc.*, 681 So. 2d 859, 861 (Fla. 5th DCA 1996).

8. *See, e.g., Diversified Prods. Corp. v. Faxon*, 514 So. 2d 1161, 1162 (Fla. 1st DCA 1987); *Cassisi v. Maytag Co.*, 396 So. 2d 1140 (Fla. 1st DCA 1981); *Florida Ins. Guar. Ass'n v. Nat'l Presto Indus., Inc.*, 6:12-CV-160-ORL-31, 2013 WL 3786636, at *2 (M.D. Fla. July 18, 2013).

9. *Edward M. Chadbourne, Inc. v. Vaughn*, 491 So. 2d 551, 553 (Fla. 1986). *See also Pamperin v. Interlake Cos., Inc.*, 634 So. 2d 1137, 1140 (Fla. 1st DCA 1994) (storage-rack system installed on a building, which was capable of being dismantled and resold, is a product and not a permanent improvement to real property).

10. *Force v. Ford Motor Co.*, 879 So. 2d 103, 106 (Fla. 5th DCA 2004) (citing E. Wertheimer, *Calabresi's Razor: A Short Cut to Responsibility*, 28 Stetson L. Rev. 105, 113 (1998)).

11. *See generally Force*, 879 So. 2d 103 (Fla. 5th DCA 2004) (discussion and analysis of consumer-expectation and risk-utility tests, concluding that there may be products too complex for a logical application of the consumer-expectation test); *see also Tran v. Toyota Motor Corp.*, 420 F.3d 1310, 1313 (11th Cir. 2005) ("We emphasize that we do not hold that the consumer expectations test jury instruction is required in all product liability cases. We merely hold, like the court in *Force*, that the instruction is proper as an independent basis for liability under Florida law when the product in question is one about which an ordinary consumer could form expectations."); *Bearint v. Johnson Controls, Inc.*, No. 8:04-cv-1714-T-17MAP, 2006 WL 1890186, at *5 (M.D. Fla. July 10, 2006) ("There is a split of authority as to when liability should be imposed. Florida has used the Restatement Third of Torts, Prods. Liab. § 5, as instructive on what creates defective product liability.... Additionally, Florida has expressly adopted the consumer expectation standard.... However, *Force* did not expressly reject using Restatement Third of Torts, Prods. Liab. § 5, and has still left open the possibility of using other tests for 'products that are too complex for a logical application of the consumer-expectation standard.' "); *McConnell v. Union Carbide Corp.*, 937 So. 2d 148 (Fla. 4th DCA 2006) (plaintiff entitled to "consumer expectations" jury instruction); *Standard Jury Instructions—Civil Cases*, 872 So. 2d 893, 893-94 (Fla. 2004); *Cassisi*, 396 So. 2d at 1144-45 ("Were the ordinary consumer's expectations frustrated by the product's failure to perform under the circumstances in which it failed?").

12. Although many courts interpreting Florida law have held that the state recognizes both the consumer-expectations test and the risk-utility test (requiring the demonstration of an adequate available design), Florida's

Third District Court of Appeal (covering Miami-Dade county) recently rejected the consumer-expectations test. *See Agrofollajes, S.A. v. E.I. Du Pont de Nemours & Co, Inc.*, 48 So. 3d 976, 996 (Fla. 3d DCA 2010) ("The Restatement (Third) of Torts: Products Liability rejects the 'consumer expectations test' as an independent basis for finding a design defect. . . . Accordingly, we reverse on this issue because in giving the instruction, the trial court permitted the jury to make the finding that Benalte was defective under an inappropriate test."). *Compare Agrofollajes, S.A.*, 48 So. 3d 976, 996 (Fla. 3d DCA 2010) *with Tran*, 420 F.3d 1310, 1312 (11th Cir. 2005) (Under Florida law "we must conclude that the court erred in not instructing the jury that it could find for Tran under a consumer expectations theory."), *Liggett Group, Inc.*, 973 So. 2d 467, 475 (Fla. 4th DCA 2007) ("We find no case which holds that a plaintiff is required to show a safer alternative design in order to prevail on a strict liability design defect claim. Rather, it appears to be one factor which can be demonstrated and argued to the jury."), *Standard Jury Instructions—Civil Cases*, 872 So. 2d 893, 895 (Fla. 2004) (Florida supreme court approving jury instruction defining the term "unreasonably dangerous" by two alternative tests, the consumer-expectation test and the risk-utility test), *and Force*, 879 So. 2d 103, 109 (Fla. 5th DCA 2004) ("[W]e hold that Mr. Force was entitled to submit his case to the jury on both the risk-utility test and the consumer-expectation test, and, therefore, reverse and remand for a new trial.").

13. *Edic v. Century Prods. Co.*, 364 F.3d 1276, 1280 n.2 (11th Cir. 2004) (quoting *Scheman-Gonzalez v. Saber Mfg. Co.*, 816 So. 2d 1133, 1139 (Fla. 4th DCA 2002)); *Hernandez v. Altec Envtl. Prods., LLC*, 10-80532-CIV, 2013 WL 836870, at *1 (S.D. Fla. Mar. 16, 2013). *See also Murray v. Traxxas Corp.*, 78 So. 3d 691, 693-94 (Fla. 2d DCA 2012) (presence of actual product involved in the accident unnecessary so long as its condition was documented and plaintiff could still potentially prove that "Traxxas and Powermaster were negligent for not equipping the fuel can with . . . a readily available device" that "would have prevented the incident").

14. *Perez v. National Presto Indus., Inc.*, 431 So. 2d 667, 669 (Fla. 3d DCA 1983).

15. *Cassisi*, 396 So. 2d at 1148 ("[W]hen a product malfunctions during normal operation, a legal inference, which is in effect a mirror reflection of the Restatement's standard of product defectiveness, arises, and the injured plaintiff thereby establishes a prima facie case for jury consideration."). *See also United Fire & Cas. Co. v. Whirlpool Corp.*, 704 F.3d 1338, 1343 (11th Cir. 2013) (application of *Cassisi* inference was sufficient to defeat summary judgment); *Nelson v. Freightliner, LLC*, 154 F. App'x 98, 105-06 (11th Cir. 2005) ("Under Florida law, a plaintiff in a products liability action may prove his case by 'creating a legal inference that the product was defective both at the time of the injury and at the time it was within the control of the supplier.' ").

16. *See Williams v. Nat'l Freight, Inc.*, 455 F. Supp. 2d 1335, 1337 (M.D. Fla. 2006) ("Under Florida law, strict liability actions are 'based on the essential requirement that the responsible party is in the business of and gains profits from distributing or disposing of the 'product' in question through the stream of commerce.'"); *see also Adoro Mktg., Inc. v. Da Silva*, 623 So. 2d 542, 543 (Fla. 3d DCA 1993); *Johnson v. Supro Corp.*, 498 So. 2d 528, 529 (Fla. 3d DCA 1986).

17. *Johnson*, 498 So. 2d at 529. *Dorsch v. Pilatus Aircraft Ltd.*, No.8:11-CV-441-T-17MAP, 2012 WL 1565447, at *1 (M.D. Fla. May 2, 2012) ("strict liability applies to any supplier, distributor, or retailer"). *See also Rivera v. Baby Trend, Inc.*, 914 So. 2d 1102, 1104-05 (Fla. 4th DCA 2005) (fact that company that never possessed the product during its journey through the distribution chain does not preclude a strict-liability claim when the company was responsible for placing the product in the stream of commerce and had the ability to control the product's design). *See also Barnes v. Bayside Orthopaedics, Inc.*, No. 8:11-cv-2827-T-30EAJ, 2012 WL 162368, at *2 (M.D. Fla. Jan. 19, 2012) ("Entities that play an active role in promoting a particular product within the chain of distribution to the general public are strictly liable for any defect in the product" regardless of whether they "placed the product in the stream of commerce" or were "in the position to control the risk of harm that [the product] may cause."). *But see Cataldo v. Lazy Days R.V. Ctr., Inc.*, 920 So. 2d 174, 177-80 (Fla. 2d DCA 2006) (Seller of a used product is not strictly liable for a design defect that ultimately injures the purchaser.).

18. *See Samuel Friedland Family Enter.*, 630 So. 2d at 1071 (the doctrine of strict liability applies to commercial lease transactions just as it does to sales).

19. *Samuel Friedland Family Enter.*, 630 So. 2d at 1071.

20. *Conley v. Boyle Drug Co.*, 570 So. 2d 275, 279 (Fla. 1990).

21. *Conley*, 570 So. 2d at 286; *Martin v. Abbott Lab.*, 102 Wash. 2d 581, 689 P.2d 368 (1984).

22. *Conley*, 570 So. 2d at 286; *Guarino v. Wyeth, LLC*, 719 F.3d 1245, 1252 (11th Cir. 2013).

23. *See, e.g., West*, 336 So. 2d at 89; *Cedars of Lebanon Hosp. Corp. v. European X-Ray Distribs.*, 444 So. 2d 1068, 1070 (Fla. 3d DCA 1984).

24. *See Easterday v. Masiello*, 518 So. 2d 260, 261 (Fla. 1988).

25. In Florida, the only difference between a negligent failure to warn and failure to warn under a strict-liability theory is that a prima facie case of strict liability failure to warn does not require a showing of negligence. Thus, under either theory, both duty and causation must be established. *Brewer v. Stop Stick, Ltd.*, No. 2:04-CV-613FTM33DNF, 2005 WL 2614537, at *2

(M.D. Fla. Oct. 14, 2005). *See also Veliz v. Rental Serv. Corp., USA Inc.*, 313 F. Supp. 2d 1317 (M.D. Fla. 2003); *Brown v. Glade & Grove Supply, Inc.*, 647 So. 2d 1033, 1035 (Fla. 4th DCA 1994).

26. *Thomas v. Bombardier Recreational Prods., Inc.*, 682 F. Supp. 2d 1297, 1300 (M.D. Fla. 2010) (citing *Ferayorni v. Hyundai Motor Co.*, 711 So. 2d 1167, 1172 (Fla. 4th DCA 1998)). *See also Griffin v. KIA Motors Corp.*, 843 So. 2d 336, 338 (Fla. 1st DCA 2003).

27. *Manion v. General Elec. Co.*, No. 3:06cv9/MRC/MD, 2007 WL 2565979, at *5 (N.D. Fla. Aug. 31, 2007); *Pinchinat v. Graco Children's Prods., Inc.*, 390 F. Supp. 2d 1141, 1146 (M.D. Fla. 2005); *Scheman-Gonzalez v. Saber Mfg. Co.*, 816 So. 2d 1133, 1139 (Fla. 4th DCA 2002). *See also Humphreys v. General Motors Corp.*, 839 F. Supp. 822, 829-30 (N.D. Fla. 1993); *Johns-Manville Sales Corp. v. Janssens*, 463 So. 2d 242, 248-49 (Fla. 1st DCA 1984); *Farias v. Mr. Heater, Inc.*, No.11-10405, 2012 WL 2354369, at *3-4 (11th Cir. 2012).

28. *See Insua v. JD/BBJ, LLC*, 913 So. 2d 1262, 1264 (Fla. 4th DCA 2005) (no duty to warn electrician of inherent danger of working on wires in an electrically charged panel); *see also Siemens Energy & Automation, Inc. v. Medina*, 719 So. 2d 312, 314 (Fla. 3d DCA 1998).

29. *Faddish v. Buffalo Pumps*, 881 F. Supp. 2d 1361, 1369-70 (S.D. Fla. 2012), *Griffin v. Kia Motors Corp.*, 843 So. 2d 336, 339 (Fla. 1st DCA 2003) (citing *Ferayorni v. Hyundai Motor Co.*, 711 So. 2d 1167, 1172 (Fla. 4th DCA 1998)).

30. *Cooper v. Old Williamsburg Candle Corp.*, 653 F. Supp. 2d 1220, 1225 (M.D. Fla. 2009); *Pinchinat v. Graco Children's Prods., Inc.*, 390 F. Supp. 2d 1141, 1148 (M.D. Fla. 2005); *Lopez v. Southern Coatings, Inc.*, 580 So. 2d 864, 865 (Fla. 3d DCA 1991).

31. *Ford Motor Co. v. Evancho*, 327 So. 2d 201 (Fla. 1976) (automobiles); *Nicolodi v. Harley-Davidson Motor Co., Inc.*, 370 So. 2d 68 (Fla. 2d DCA 1979) (motorcycles).

32. *Nicolodi*, 370 So. 2d at 72-73.

33. *See General Motors Corp. v. McGee*, 867 So. 2d 1244, 1245 (Fla. 4th DCA 2004) (citing *D'Amario v. Ford Motor Co.*, 806 So. 2d 424 (Fla. 2001)); *see also Griffin v. KIA Motors Corp.*, 843 So. 2d 336, 338 (Fla. 1st DCA 2003).

34. *See Cintron v. Osmose Wood Preserving, Inc.*, 681 So. 2d 859, 861 (Fla. 5th DCA 1996); *Westchester Exxon v. Valdes*, 524 So. 2d 452, 454 (Fla. 3d DCA 1988); *Stahl v. Metropolitan Dade County*, 438 So. 2d 14, 17 (Fla. 3d DCA 1983).

35. *Carter v. Hector Supply Co.*, 128 So. 2d 390, 392 (Fla. 1961); *Jackson v. H.L. Bouton Co., Inc.*, 630 So. 2d 1173, 1176 (Fla. 1st DCA 1994); *Kessler v. Gumenick*, 358 So. 2d 1167 (Fla. 3d DCA 1978).

36. *Auburn Mach. Works Co., Inc. v. Jones*, 366 So. 2d 1167, 1172 (Fla. 1979). Thus, a patent danger only bars liability when the negligence is solely in the lack of a warning. *See Mosher v. Speedstar Div. of AMCA Int'l*, 979 F.2d 823, 826 (11th Cir. 1992).

37. *See E.R. Squibb & Sons, Inc. v. Fames*, 697 So. 2d 825, 827 (Fla. 1997).

38. *See Rees v. Engineered Controls Int'l, Inc.*, No. 6:06-cv-1558-ORL-19JGG, 2006 WL 3162834, at *2 (M.D. Fla. Nov. 2, 2006); *Kramer v. Piper Aircraft Corp.*, 520 So. 2d 37, 39 n.4 (Fla. 1988); *T.W.M. v. Am. Med. Sys., Inc.*, 886 F. Supp. 842, 844 (N.D. Fla. 1995); *Williams v. Bear Stearns & Co.*, 725 So. 2d 397 (Fla. 5th DCA 1998); Fla. Stat. § 672.318 (2014).

39. *See* Fla. Stat. § 672.313 (2014) (express warranty); Fla. Stat. § 672.314 (2014) (implied warranty of merchantability); Fla. Stat. § 672.315 (2014) (implied warranty of fitness for particular purpose).

40. *Hoffman v. Jones*, 280 So. 2d 431 (Fla. 1973) (abolishing the doctrine of contributory negligence).

41. *See West*, 336 So. 2d at 90; *Alderman v. Wysong & Miles Co.*, 486 So. 2d 673, 678 (Fla. 1st DCA 1986); *see also Goulah v. Ford Motor Co.*, 118 F.3d 1478, 1485 (11th Cir. 1997) (defendant may argue that plaintiff's action was the "sole legal cause" of the accident, even after withdrawal of comparative-negligence defense). In *Philip Morris USA, Inc. v. Arnitz*, 933 So. 2d 693 (Fla. 2d DCA 2006), the court held that the fact that a cigarette manufacturer withdrew its affirmative defense of comparative negligence did not preclude the plaintiff from pleading his comparative negligence.

42. *Nash v. Wells Fargo Guard Servs., Inc.*, 678 So. 2d 1262, 1264 (Fla. 1996) (to apportion fault to a non-party, defendant must plead it as an affirmative defense and "specifically identify the non-party"). *Clark v. Polk County*, 753 So. 2d 138 (Fla. 2d DCA 2000) (suggesting that a defendant may be able to apportion fault to a nonparty by identifying a specific tortious act by a specific person, albeit a person whose name is unknown). *But see R.J. Reynolds Tobacco Co. v. Grossman ex rel. Grossman*, No. 4D10-2993, 2012 WL 2400887, at *2 (Fla. 4th DCA June 27, 2012) ("A nonparty defendant . . . may not be included on the verdict form until a defendant has proven the nonparty's negligence at trial. . . . [W]e find the argument that Jan created a 'zone of risk' to be unpersuasive under the facts of this case.").

43. *High v. Westinghouse Elec. Corp.*, 610 So. 2d 1259, 1262 (Fla. 1992); *Tri-County Truss Co. v. Leonard*, 467 So. 2d 370, 371 (Fla. 4th DCA 1985). In other words, strict liability only applies if the product is used for the purpose for which it was intended when produced. *High*, 610 So. 2d 1262. *See also Liberty Mut. Fire Ins. Co. v. A.O. Smith Corp.*, No. 4:04CV371SPMAK, 2006 WL 897616, at *2 (N.D. Fla. Mar. 31, 2006) (applying *High*); *Martin v. JLG Indus., Inc.*, No. 8:06-CV-234-T-24TBM, 2007 WL 2320593, at *3 (M.D. Fla. Aug. 10, 2007).

44. *Cintron v. Osmose Wood Preserving, Inc.*, 681 So. 2d 859, 861 (Fla. 5th DCA 1996).

45. *Hercules, Inc. v. United States*, 516 U.S. 417 (1996); *Dorse v. Armstrong World Indus., Inc.*, 513 So. 2d 1265, 1269 (Fla. 1987).

46. Res judicata may also apply against others in the chain of distribution. *See West v. Kawasaki Motors Mfg. Corp.*, 595 So. 2d 92, 96-97 (Fla. 3d DCA 1992) (previous unsuccessful product liability claim against one party in the chain of distribution bars a subsequent claim, based on the same allegations, against another party in the same distribution chain).

47. *West*, 336 So. 2d at 90.

48. *Radiation Tech., Inc. v. Ware Constr. Co.*, 445 So. 2d 329, 331 (Fla. 1983); *Liggett Group*, 2007 WL 2935236, at *12 (applying *Radiation Tech*); *Hernandez v. Altec Envtl. Prods., LLC*, 903 F. Supp. 2d 1350, 1358 (S.D. Fla. 2012).

49. *See Buckner v. Allergan Pharms., Inc.*, 400 So. 2d 820, 822-23, n.4 (Fla. 5th DCA 1981); *Beale v. Biomet, Inc.*, 492 F. Supp. 2d 1360, 1365-66 (S.D. Fla. 2007).

50. *Adams v. G.D. Searle & Co., Inc.*, 576 So. 2d 728, 733 (Fla. 2d DCA 1991); *Bailey v. Janssen Pharmaceutica, Inc.*, 288 Fed. Appx. 597, 607 (11th Cir. 2008) (citing *Adams*).

51. *Keith v. Russell T. Bundy & Assocs., Inc.*, 495 So. 2d 1223, 1228 (Fla. 5th DCA 1986).

52. *Hayes v. Spartan Chem. Co., Inc.*, 622 So. 2d 1352, 1354 (Fla. 2d DCA 1993).

53. *Hayes*, 622 So. 2d at 1354.

54. *See Kidron, Inc. v. Carmona*, 665 So. 2d 289, 291 n.1 (Fla. 3d DCA 1995), overruled on other grounds, *D'Amario v. Ford Motor Co.*, 806 So. 2d 424 (Fla. 2001); *Jackson v. H.L. Bouton Co., Inc.*, 630 So. 2d 1173, 1175 (Fla. 1st DCA 1994) ("[C]ompliance with industry standards is merely evidence that a product was not defective.").

55. *Turbomeca, S.A. v. French Aircraft Agency, Inc.*, 913 So. 2d 714 (Fla. 3d DCA 2005) (holding that the economic-loss rule barred helicopter owner from recovering from engine manufacturer on negligence theory for loss of helicopter in crash).

56. *Tiara Condo. Ass'n, Inc. v. Marsh & McLennan Co.*, 110 So. 3d 399, 407 (Fla. 2013) (holding that the "economic loss rule applies only in the products liability context" and the court "recede[s] from our prior rulings to the extent that they have applied the economic loss rule to cases other than products liability").

57. *Monsanto Agric. Prod. Co. v. Edenfield*, 426 So. 2d 574, 575-76 (Fla. 1st DCA 1982).

58. *Perez v. Nat'l Presto Indus. Inc.*, 431 So. 2d 667, 669 (Fla. 3d DCA 1983); *Beauregard v. Cont'l Tire N. Am., Inc.*, 695 F. Supp. 2d 1344, 1356 (M.D. Fla. 2010) ("The law does not require a manufacturer to be a lifetime guarantor of its product").

59. *Bernard v. Kee Mfg. Co., Inc.*, 409 So. 2d 1047 (Fla. 1982); *Corporate Exp. Office Prods. Inc. v. Phillips*, 847 So. 2d 406, 412 (Fla. 2003); *Coral Windows Bahamas, LTD v. Pande Pane, LLC*, 11-22128-CIV, 2013 WL 321584, at *3 (S.D. Fla. Jan. 28, 2013) (applying *Bernard*).

60. *Knight v. Just Born, Inc.*, No. CV-99-606-ST, 2000 WL 924624, at *8 (D. Or. Mar. 28, 2000) (citing *Jones v. General Motors Corp.*, 139 Or. App. 244, 262-65, 911 P.2d 1243, 1254-55 (1996)).

61. *Kinney Sys., Inc. v. Cont'l Ins. Co.*, 674 So. 2d 86 (Fla. 1996) (setting forth the factors applicable to a forum non conveniens analysis).

62. *Ciba-Geigy Ltd. v. Fish Peddler, Inc.*, 691 So. 2d 1111 (Fla. 4th DCA 1997) (dismissing case under the doctrine of forum non conveniens where the defendants were foreign corporations and the alleged negligence occurred outside of Florida).

63. *Fihe v. Rexall Sundown, Inc.*, 966 So. 2d 415, 420 (Fla. 4th DCA 2007); *Scotts Co. v. Hacienda Loma Linda*, 942 So. 2d 900 (Fla. 3d DCA 2006) (holding that dismissal was warranted under the forum non conveniens doctrine where "the evidence and the vast majority of the witnesses in this case are located in Panama").

64. Fla. Stat. § 69.081 (2014).

65. Fla. Stat. § 69.081(3) (2014).

66. Fla. Stat. § 69.081(2) (2014).

67. Fla. Stat. § 90.702 (2014).

68. *See* House of Representatives' Final Bill Analysis for HB 7015, at 3, found at http://www.myfloridahouse.gov/Sections/Documents/loaddoc.aspx?FileName=h7015z1.CJS.DOCX&DocumentType=Analysis&BillNumber=7015&Session=2013 (last visited July 30, 2014); *Perez v. Bell S. Telecommunications, Inc.*, 138 So. 3d 492, 497 (Fla. 3d DCA 2014) ("In 2013, the Florida legislature amended section 90.702 of the Florida Evidence Code to adopt the standards for expert testimony in the courts of this state as provided in *Daubert*").

69. Fla. Stat. §§ 768.16 *et seq.* (2014); *Toombs v. Alamo Rent-A-Car, Inc.*, 833 So. 2d 109, 111-18 (Fla. 2002).

70. *Casa Clara Condo. Ass'n, Inc. v. Charley Toppino & Sons*, 620 So. 2d 1244, 1247 (Fla. 1993), *receded from on other grounds, Tiara Condo. Ass'n, Inc. v. Marsh & McLennan Co.*, 110 So. 3d 399, 407 (Fla. 2013); *GAF Corp. v. Zack Co.*, 445 So. 2d 350, 351-52 (Fla. 3d DCA 1984).

71. Fla. Stat. § 768.81 (2014); *see also Y.H. Investments, Inc. v. Godales*, 690 So. 2d 1273, 1278 (Fla. 1997) (party may add negligent tortfeasor on jury verdict form regardless of immunity, provided there is sufficient evidence of fault).

72. *Nash v. Wells Fargo Guardo Servs., Inc.*, 678 So. 2d 1262, 1263 (Fla. 1996); *see also Merrill Crossings Assocs. v. McDonald*, 705 So. 2d 560, 562 (Fla. 1997).

73. *Ross Dress for Less Virginia, Inc. v. Castro*, 134 So. 3d 511, 524 (Fla. 3d DCA 2014); *Simeon, Inc. v. Cox*, 671 So. 2d 158, 160 (Fla. 1996); and Fla. Stat. § 768.72 (2014). Section 768.72 states:

>   (1) In any civil action, no claim for punitive damages shall be permitted unless there is a reasonable showing by evidence in the record or proffered by the claimant which would provide a reasonable basis for recovery of such damages. The claimant may move to amend her or his complaint to assert a claim for punitive damages as allowed by the rules of civil procedure. The rules of civil procedure shall be liberally construed so as to allow the claimant discovery of evidence which appears reasonably calculated to lead to admissible evidence on the issue of punitive damages. No discovery of financial worth shall proceed until after the pleading concerning punitive damages is permitted.
>
>   (2) A defendant may be held liable for punitive damages only if the trier of fact, based on clear and convincing evidence, finds that the defendant was personally guilty of intentional misconduct or gross negligence. As used in this section, the term:
>
>   (a) "Intentional misconduct" means that the defendant had actual knowledge of the wrongfulness of the conduct and the high probability that injury or damage to the claimant would result and, despite that knowledge, intentionally pursued that course of conduct, resulting in injury or damage.
>
>   (b) "Gross negligence" means that the defendant's conduct was so reckless or wanting in care that it constituted a conscious disregard or indifference to the life, safety, or rights of persons exposed to such conduct.
>
>   (3) In the case of an employer, principal, corporation, or other legal entity, punitive damages may be imposed for the conduct of an employee or agent only if the conduct of the employee or agent meets the criteria specified in subsection (2) and:
>
>   (a) The employer, principal, corporation, or other legal entity actively and knowingly participated in such conduct;

(b) The officers, directors, or managers of the employer, principal, corporation, or other legal entity knowingly condoned, ratified, or consented to such conduct; or

(c) The employer, principal, corporation, or other legal entity engaged in conduct that constituted gross negligence and that contributed to the loss, damages, or injury suffered by the claimant.

(4) The provisions of this section shall be applied to all causes of action arising after the effective date of this act.

Fla. Stat. § 768.72 (2014).

Fla. Stat. § 768.725 provides that:

In all civil actions, the plaintiff must establish at trial, by clear and convincing evidence, its entitlement to an award of punitive damages. The "greater weight of the evidence" burden of proof applies to a determination of the amount of damages.

Fla. Stat. § 768.725 (2014).

And Fla. Stat. § 768.73 limits the amount of punitive damages:

(1)(a) Except as provided in paragraphs (b) and (c), an award of punitive damages may not exceed the greater of:

1. Three times the amount of compensatory damages awarded to each claimant entitled thereto, consistent with the remaining provisions of this section; or

2. The sum of $500,000.

(b) Where the fact finder determines that the wrongful conduct proven under this section was motivated solely by unreasonable financial gain and determines that the unreasonably dangerous nature of the conduct, together with the high likelihood of injury resulting from the conduct, was actually known by the managing agent, director, officer, or other person responsible for making policy decisions on behalf of the defendant, it may award an amount of punitive damages not to exceed the greater of:

1. Four times the amount of compensatory damages awarded to each claimant entitled thereto, consistent with the remaining provisions of this section; or

2. The sum of $2 million.

(c) Where the fact finder determines that at the time of injury the defendant had a specific intent to harm the claimant and determines that the defendant's conduct did in fact harm the claimant, there shall be no cap on punitive damages.

(d) This subsection is not intended to prohibit an appropriate court from exercising its jurisdiction under s. 768.74 in determining the reasonableness of an award of punitive damages that is less than three times the amount of compensatory damages.

(2)(a) Except as provided in paragraph (b), punitive damages may not be awarded against a defendant in a civil action if that defendant establishes, before trial, that punitive damages have previously been awarded against that defendant in any state or federal court in any action alleging harm from the same act or single course of conduct for which the claimant seeks compensatory damages. For purposes of a civil action, the term "the same act or single course of conduct" includes acts resulting in the same manufacturing defects, acts resulting in the same defects in design, or failure to warn of the same hazards, with respect to similar units of a product.

(b) In subsequent civil actions involving the same act or single course of conduct for which punitive damages have already been awarded, if the court determines by clear and convincing evidence that the amount of prior punitive damages awarded was insufficient to punish that defendant's behavior, the court may permit a jury to consider an award of subsequent punitive damages. In permitting a jury to consider awarding subsequent punitive damages, the court shall make specific findings of fact in the record to support its conclusion. In addition, the court may consider whether the defendant's act or course of conduct has ceased. Any subsequent punitive damage awards must be reduced by the amount of any earlier punitive damage awards rendered in state or federal court.

(3) The claimant attorney's fees, if payable from the judgment, are, to the extent that the fees are based on the punitive damages, calculated based on the final judgment for punitive damages. This subsection does not limit the payment of attorney's fees based upon an award of damages other than punitive damages.

(4) The jury may neither be instructed nor informed as to the provisions of this section.

(5) The provisions of this section shall be applied to all causes of action arising after the effective date of this act.

Fla. Stat. § 768.73 (2014).

74. *Bould v. Touchette*, 349 So. 2d 1181, 1186 (Fla. 1977); *Philip Morris USA Inc. v. Cohen*, 102 So. 3d 11, 16 (Fla. 4th DCA 2012).

75. *Engle v. Liggett Group, Inc.*, 945 So. 2d 1246, 1264 (Fla. 2006); *R.J. Reynolds Tobacco Co. v. Webb*, 93 So. 3d 331, 339 (Fla. 1st DCA 2012) (applying *Engle*).

76. The text of Florida's comparative fault statute, Fla. Stat. § 768.81, is set forth below:

(1) DEFINITION.—As used in this section, the term:

(a) "Accident" means the events and actions that relate to the incident as well as those events and actions that relate to the alleged defect or injuries, including enhanced injuries.

(b) "Economic damages" means past lost income and future lost income reduced to present value; medical and funeral expenses; lost support and services; replacement value of lost personal property; loss of appraised fair market value of real property; costs of construction repairs, including labor, overhead, and profit; and any other economic loss that would not have occurred but for the injury giving rise to the cause of action.

(c) "Negligence action" means, without limitation, a civil action for damages based upon a theory of negligence, strict liability, products liability, professional malpractice whether couched in terms of contract or tort, or breach of warranty and like theories. The substance of an action, not conclusory terms used by a party, determines whether an action is a negligence action.

(d) "Products liability action" means a civil action based upon a theory of strict liability, negligence, breach of warranty, nuisance, or similar theories for damages caused by the manufacture, construction, design, formulation, installation, preparation, or assembly of a product. The term includes an action alleging that injuries received by a claimant in an accident were greater than the injuries the claimant would have received but for a defective product. The substance of an action, not the conclusory terms used by a party, determines whether an action is a products liability action.

(2) EFFECT OF CONTRIBUTORY FAULT.—In a negligence action, contributory fault chargeable to the claimant diminishes proportionately the amount awarded as economic and noneconomic damages for an injury attributable to the claimant's contributory fault, but does not bar recovery.

(3) APPORTIONMENT OF DAMAGES.—In a negligence action, the court shall enter judgment against each party liable on the basis of such party's percentage of fault and not on the basis of the doctrine of joint and several liability.

(a) 1. In order to allocate any or all fault to a nonparty, a defendant must affirmatively plead the fault of a nonparty and, absent a showing of good cause, identify the nonparty, if known, or describe the nonparty as specifically as practicable, either by motion or in the initial responsive pleading when defenses are first presented, subject to amendment any time before trial in accordance with the Florida Rules of Civil Procedure.

2. In order to allocate any or all fault to a nonparty and include the named or unnamed nonparty on the verdict form for purposes of apportioning damages, a defendant must prove at trial, by a preponderance of the evidence, the fault of the nonparty in causing the plaintiff's injuries.

(b) In a products liability action alleging that injuries received by a claimant in an accident were enhanced by a defective product, the trier of fact shall consider the fault of all persons who contributed to the accident when apportioning fault between or among them. The jury shall be appropriately instructed by the trial judge on the apportionment of fault in products liability actions where there are allegations that the injuries received by the claimant in an accident were enhanced by a defective product. The rules of evidence apply to these actions.

(4) APPLICABILITY.—This section does not apply to any action brought by any person to recover actual economic damages resulting from pollution, to any action based upon an intentional tort, or to any cause of action as to which application of the doctrine of joint and several liability is specifically provided by chapter 403, chapter 498, chapter 517, chapter 542, or chapter 895.[1]

(5) MEDICAL MALPRACTICE.—Notwithstanding anything in law to the contrary, in an action for damages for personal injury or wrongful death arising out of medical malpractice, whether in contract or tort, if an apportionment of damages pursuant to this section is attributed to a teaching hospital as defined in s. 408.07, the court shall enter judgment against the teaching hospital on the basis of such party's percentage of fault and not on the basis of the doctrine of joint and several liability.

[1]Note.—Contains no readily apparent specific reference to joint and several liability.

Fla. Stat. § 768.81 (2014).

77. *Lumbermens Mut. Cas. Co. v. Percefull*, 653 So. 2d 389, 390 (Fla. 1995); *Parker v. Brinson Constr. Co.*, 78 So. 2d 873, 874 (Fla. 1955).

78. *Argonaut Ins. Co. v. May Plumbing Co.*, 474 So. 2d 212, 215 (Fla. 1985); *Bosem v. Musa Holdings, Inc.*, 46 So. 3d 42, 44-46 (Fla. 2010) (reaffirming *Argonaut*).

79. *Palm Beach County Sch. Bd. v. Montgomery*, 641 So. 2d 183, 184 (Fla. 4th DCA 1994).

80. *Palm Beach County Sch. Bd.*, 641 So. 2d at 184 (citing *Argonaut*, 474 So. 2d at 215).

81. *Amerace Corp. v. Stallings*, 823 So. 2d 110, 112-13 (Fla. 2002) (noting that "the proper procedure . . . would have been to request that the court enter a judgment promptly after the verdict").

82. *Green v. Rety*, 616 So. 2d 433, 435 (Fla. 1993).

83. Fla. Stat. § 440.11 (2014); *Locke v. SunTrust Bank*, 484 F.3d 1343, 1347 (11th Cir. 2007). *But see Connelly v. Arrow Air, Inc.*, 568 So. 2d 448 (Fla. 3d DCA 1990) (holding that employer was not entitled to summary judgment under workers' compensation law where employer routinely overloaded and improperly maintained airplane, and withheld this information from its pilot).

84. Fla. Stat. § 440.11 (2014); *Oppenheim v. Reliance Ins. Co.*, 804 F. Supp. 305, 307 (M.D. Fla. 1991) (holding that fellow employees are immune from suit unless the acts are committed with "willful and wanton disregard, unprovoked physical aggression, or gross negligence when such acts result in injury").

85. Fla. Stat. § 1.01(13) (2014).

Georgia

A. CAUSES OF ACTION

Product liability lawsuits may proceed on theories of strict liability, negligence, or breach of warranty.[1] Relevant statutes for product liability actions are the statute of limitations, the sections of the commercial code for breach of warranty claims, and the statutes governing product liability actions.[2] In Georgia, the substantive law in effect at the time of the injury controls the ensuing litigation.[3]

B. STATUTES OF LIMITATION

Negligence and strict liability actions must be brought within two years of the date of accrual for bodily injury[4] and within four years for property damage.[5] The discovery rule applies only to bodily injuries[6] and acts to toll the running of the statute of limitations until the injured knew or should have discovered, through the exercise of reasonable diligence, both (1) the nature of his injury and (2) the causal connection between the injury and the alleged conduct of the defendant.[7]

Georgia has enacted a statute of repose that bars filing tort actions more than ten years after the date of the first sale for use or consumption of the product causing the injury.[8] Georgia courts have interpreted first sale for use or consumption to require more than static retention.[9] Instead, the first sale means a sale of "a finished product . . . sold as new to the intended consumer who is to receive the product."[10] The statute of repose does not apply to negligent failure to warn claims.[11] The statute of repose also does not apply to (1) actions in negligence against a manufacturer for products that cause a disease or birth defect, and (2) actions against manufacturers arising out of conduct that manifests a willful, reckless, or wanton disregard for life and property.[12] Willful conduct entails an actual intent to cause harm or injury, and wanton conduct is that which is so reckless or so indifferent to consequences that it is equivalent in spirit to actual intent.[13] An after-the-fact opinion that a product was defective is insufficient to create a jury question on the issue of wantonness when the product satisfied the government and industry standards existing at the time of manufacturing or design.[14]

In cases alleging damage to property, the discovery rule does not apply. Instead, the statute of limitations begins to run at the time of substantial completion, and ignorance of damage does not toll the statute.[15] Damage to property arising out of construction is generally considered to occur at the time of the contractor's substantial completion of the project, and a subsequent purchaser who discovers the damages more than four years after substantial completion is barred by the statute of limitations.[16] However, the statute of limitations does not bar claims by the initial purchaser against the builder-seller until four years after the sale of the property, even if the substantial completion by the contractor occurred more than four years before the discovery of the damages.[17]

Warranty causes of action generally must be brought within four years of the tender of delivery of the good,[18] but this four-year statute of limitations does not apply to personal injury actions grounded on breach of warranty.[19] This period may be reduced by agreement to not less than a year but may not be extended.[20] If a written express warranty does not come within the Uniform Commercial Code, the statute of limitations for breach of warranty is six years.[21]

C. STRICT LIABILITY

1. The Standard

Rather than relying on common law or Section 402A of the Restatement (Second) of Torts, Georgia has adopted a statutory standard for strict liability. A manufacturer will be liable in strict liability if its product when sold "was not merchantable and reasonably suited to the use intended, and its condition when sold is the proximate cause of the injury sustained."[22] This means that the product must be defective when sold.[23] The existence of a defect is critical because a manufacturer "is not an insurer against all risks of injury associated with its product."[24] In Georgia, a product need not be unreasonably dangerous before imposition of strict liability.[25] A product is defective if it fails to perform in a manner reasonably expected in light of its nature and intended function.[26]

2. Basic Elements

a. Sale or Lease

Under the Georgia strict liability provision, an action may be brought for "any personal property sold as new property directly or through a dealer or any other person."[27] It is not necessary for the purchase price to have been paid and a product's title to have passed to be considered "sold" for the purposes of the statute.[28] Rather, "sold" has been construed to mean "placed in the stream of commerce."[29] However, a product does not pass in the stream of commerce until the manufacturer "put[s] the product in the hands of and under the control of a consumer."[30] Thus, to effectuate the purposes of the statute, it appears that Georgia courts will continue to apply a flexible, case-by-case approach in determining which transactions fall within the ambit of strict liability.[31]

b. Product Does Not Have to Be in Use

The product does not have to be in use at the time of injury for a defendant to be held liable for defective design under theories of strict liability, negligence, or failure to warn.[32] Liability extends not only to those who may use the product, but also to those persons who consume the product or are reasonably affected by it.[33]

c. **Privity**

No privity is required for an individual plaintiff to sue a manufacturer.[34] However, corporate plaintiffs must still establish privity.[35]

d. **Inherently Dangerous Products**

There is no strict liability cause of action simply because an item is inherently dangerous.[36] However, if a product is so inherently dangerous that it requires a particular warning as to that characteristic, there may be a strict liability action for failure to warn.[37]

e. **Liable Parties**

 i. **Manufacturers and Product Sellers**

Only manufacturers may be strictly liable in tort. A manufacturer is one who "sells a product and has input or is actively involved in the design, concept, or specifications of the product."[38] Product sellers have been excluded from strict liability actions.[39] A "product seller" is defined as "a person who, in the course of a business conducted for the purpose leases or sells and distributes; installs; prepares; blends; packages; labels; markets; or assembles pursuant to a manufacturer's plan, intention, design, specifications, or formulation; or repairs; maintains; or otherwise is involved in placing a product in the stream of commerce."[40] "A defendant can be both a manufacturer and a seller simultaneously; in such a case, it is not entitled to the protections afforded a mere product seller."[41]

 ii. **Successor Liability**

A purchasing corporation does not assume the liabilities of a seller unless (1) there is an agreement to assume liabilities; (2) the transaction is a merger; (3) the transaction is a fraudulent attempt to avoid liabilities; or (4) the purchaser is a mere continuation of the predecessor corporation.[42] To be a continuation, there must be some identity of ownership[43] and continuation of the design and manufacture of the predecessor corporation's product.[44]

 iii. **Joint and Several Liability**

In 2005, the Georgia legislature enacted "tort reform" legislation specifically addressing, among other topics, joint and several liability. The legislature eliminated joint and several liability and adopted an apportionment scheme of liability in cases involving injury to person or property. Under O.C.G.A. § 51-12-33, "the trier of fact must 'apportion its award of damages among the persons who are liable according to the percentage of fault of each person' even if the plaintiff is not at fault for the injury or damages claimed."[45] The revised statute now requires the jury to consider together all of the tortfeasors who may be liable to the plaintiff so that their respective responsibilities for harm can be determined.[46] Fault for the same tortious incident can be apportioned to both negligent and intentional tortfeasors.[47] After determination of the fault of all parties, including the plaintiff, O.C.G.A. § 51-12-33 requires the amount of damages awarded to the plaintiff to be first reduced by a percentage equal to the level of fault attributed to her.[48] Then, the remaining amount is apportioned "among the persons who are liable according to the percentage of fault of each person."[49] The fault of nonparties may be taken into consideration.[50] The fault or negligence of a nonparty, however, shall be considered only if a defendant gives notice "not later than 120 days prior to the date of trial that a nonparty was wholly or partially at fault," or if the plaintiff entered into a settlement agreement with a nonparty.[51] Fault may be assigned to a nonparty even if the nonparty is immune from suit.[52] Apportionment as to settled nonparties is not automatic, rather the defendant must still show that the nonparty "'contributed to the alleged injury or damages' before its fault can be assessed by the trier of fact."[53] A finding of fault assessed against a nonparty for the purpose of apportionment will not subject a nonparty to liability in the action and may not be introduced as evidence of liability in any action.[54]

Despite initial speculation to the contrary,[55] Georgia appellate courts have confirmed that apportionment under O.C.G.A. § 51-12-33 is not undermined by the retention of the contribution statutes because those statutes, O.C.G.A. § 51-12-31 and O.C.G.A. § 51-12-32, are expressly limited by O.C.G.A. § 51-12-33.[56] Additionally, the Georgia Supreme Court recently confirmed the constitutionality of this apportionment scheme.[57]

iv. **Market Share Liability/Enterprise Liability**

Georgia has not adopted the theory of market share liability.[58]

v. **Employer Immunity from Suit**

Georgia's Workers' Compensation Law is the exclusive remedy for injuries sustained by employees arising out of and in the course of employment, exempting employers from liability and from being joined as a party to an action for an employee's injuries.[59]

Georgia has rejected the "dual capacity doctrine," which would allow an employee to sue an employer when the employer is acting in a capacity outside the employer-employee relationship,[60] but has adopted the more narrow "dual persona doctrine" exception, which makes an employer vulnerable to a tort suit by an employee "if—and only if—he possesses a second persona so completely independent from and unrelated to his status as employer that by established legal standards the law recognizes it as a separate legal person."[61]

3. **Types of Defects**

In Georgia, a plaintiff may establish a "defect" by showing (1) an inadequate warning or marketing defect;[62] (2) a design or engineering defect;[63] (3) a manufacturing or construction defect;[64] or (4) a "semi-warranty" defect—that the product was not merchantable and not fit for use.[65] To recover under a theory of strict liability, the plaintiff must show that a defect existed in the product at the time it was sold to him or otherwise came under his control.[66] Georgia cases demonstrate that expert testimony, though generally required, is not always necessary to establish whether a product was defective.[67]

a. **Design Defect**

i. **The Standard**

Georgia applies a risk-utility standard in design defect cases,[68] rather than a reasonable foreseeability standard.[69] Under the new standard, a design defect is present where "the risks inherent in a product design [outweigh] the utility of the product so designed."[70] The factors that can be considered in weighing the risks against the utility of the product include:

- the usefulness of the product;
- the gravity and severity of the danger posed by the design;
- the likelihood of that danger;
- the avoidability of that danger (i.e., the user's knowledge of the product, publicity surrounding the danger, or the efficacy of warnings, as well as common knowledge and the expectation of danger);
- the user's ability to avoid danger;
- the state of the art at the time the product is manufactured;
- the ability to eliminate danger without impairing the usefulness of the product or making it too expensive;
- the feasibility of spreading the loss in the setting of the product's price or by purchasing insurance;
- the feasibility of an alternative design;

- the availability of an effective substitute for the product which meets the same need but is safer;
- the financial cost of the improved design;
- the adverse effects from the alternative; and
- the manufacturer's proof of compliance with federal regulations.[71]

The heart of a design defect case is the reasonableness of choosing from alternative product designs and adopting the safest feasible one because "it is only at their most extreme that design defect cases reflect the position that a product is simply so dangerous that it should not have been made available at all."[72]

Whether a product has a "defect" is decided on a case-by-case basis, and is usually a jury question.[73] The plaintiff is not required to specify precisely the nature of the defect, but must only show that the product failed to perform as intended and that this failure proximately caused his injury.[74]

ii. **"Open and Obvious" Rule in Design Defect Cases**

The "open and obvious" rule does not bar design defect claims. Rather, the obviousness of the danger is merely one factor to be considered in applying the risk-utility test.[75]

iii. **Risk-Utility Test and Comment K to 402A of the Restatement Second of Torts**

Pharmaceutical manufacturers are not exempt from liability for design defect claims.[76] Design defect claims against pharmaceutical manufacturers are evaluated under a risk-utility analysis. Once a prima facie case for design defect is established, a pharmaceutical manufacturer will be relieved from strict liability only when the manufacturer proves that "(1) the product is properly manufactured and contains adequate warnings, (2) its benefits justify its risks, and (3) the product was at the time of manufacture and distribution incapable of being made more safe."[77]

iv. **Crashworthiness**

A manufacturer must use reasonable care in its design to avoid subjecting product users to enhanced injuries,[78] including enhanced injuries based on failure to warn.[79] Once the plaintiff proves that a design defect was a substantial factor in producing damages over and above those that were probably caused as a result of the original impact or collision, the burden of proof shifts to the manufacturer to demonstrate a rational basis for apportioning liability for the injuries.[80]

b. Manufacturing Defect

Manufacturers are liable for product defects which proximately cause injury to individuals.[81] A manufacturer is liable if its product "when sold . . . was not merchantable and reasonably suited to the use intended and its condition when sold is the proximate cause of the injury sustained."[82] A manufacturing defect is present where the product is "defective in its manufacture, its packaging, or the failure to adequately warn of its dangerous propensities."[83] A plaintiff is not required to specify the precise nature of the manufacturing defect.[84]

The product's design is presumed to be safe in this context[85] and the key inquiry is whether "the product would have been safe for consumer use had it been manufactured in accordance with the design."[86] Unlike design defects, manufacturing defects are judged objectively.[87] The defective product is compared to properly manufactured items from the same product line.[88] Circumstantial evidence may be used to establish a manufacturing defect in certain situations[89] and may be necessary where the product has been consumed or destroyed.[90]

4. Common Evidentiary Rules

a. Product Malfunction

Georgia has not adopted the theory that a malfunction alone is sufficient to establish a defect.[91]

b. Evidence of Government Standards and Regulations

Compliance with industry-wide practices, state of the art, or federal regulations does not eliminate conclusively a manufacturer's liability for its design of allegedly defective products.[92] Compliance with federal regulations is a factor to be considered,[93] however, and punitive damages are generally improper when a manufacturer has adhered to applicable industry standards and federal regulations.[94]

c. State of the Art

The state of the art is not a defense, but a factor to be considered in assessing whether a design defect exists.[95]

d. Evidence of Other Accidents

Evidence of other similar accidents or lack thereof is admissible to demonstrate the manufacturer's knowledge of the alleged defect, to show the existence of a dangerous condition, and for punitive damages provided there is a showing of substantial similarity between the nature and causes of the other claims and the claim at issue.[96] The showing of substantial similarity must include a showing of similarity as to causation.[97] The degree of substantial similarity necessary to admit such evidence is a matter left to the sound discretion of the trial court.[98] Such evidence is not admissible to prove that a product was defective.[99]

e. Evidence of Subsequent Remedial Measures

Evidence of subsequent remedial measures appears to be admissible in strict liability actions.[100]

5. Causation

a. Proximate Cause

To show proximate cause, the plaintiff must present sufficient evidence that she was specifically exposed to the defendant's product.[101] A manufacturer "has the absolute right to have his strict liability for *injuries* adjudged on the basis of the design of his own marketed product and not that of someone else."[102] Unless the manufacturer's defective product can be shown to be the proximate cause of the injuries, the manufacturer is not liable.[103]

b. Substantial Alteration/Abnormal Use

A manufacturer may not be held strictly liable for injuries resulting from a substantial change in or an abnormal use of a product.[104] Manufacturers are liable only for foreseeable misuses of property, which means those uses that are objectively reasonable to expect, not merely what might occur.[105]

6. Defenses

a. Contributory Negligence/Assumption of Risk

Contributory negligence is not a defense to strict liability claims.[106] Assumption of risk is a defense.[107] Two types of assumption of risk may be present: (1) assumption of risk of the product defect; or (2) assumption of risk of the physical injuries incurred.[108] To establish assumption of the risk and be entitled to a jury instruction, the defendant must establish that the plaintiff (1) had knowledge of the danger; (2) understood and appreciated the risks associated with such danger; and (3) voluntarily exposed himself to those risks.[109] To show that the plaintiff had knowledge of the risk, the defendant must show that the plaintiff had actual and subjective knowledge of the specific, particular risk of harm associated with the product.[110]

b. Destruction or Loss of Product

Georgia courts have recognized that sanctions are appropriate for the spoliation of evidence, i.e. when one party destroys or significantly and meaningfully alters the evidence.[111] The factors the court should consider in determining the appropriate sanction include: (1) whether the party was prejudiced as a result of the spoliation of the evidence; (2) whether the prejudice could be cured; (3) the practical importance of the evidence; (4) whether the party that caused the destruction or alteration acted in good or bad faith; and (5) the potential for abuse if expert testimony about the evidence is not excluded.[112] Appropriate sanctions can include excluding testimony about the evidence, or dismissing the case entirely.[113] When determining whether the "severe sanction of dismissal should be imposed," the "party's degree of fault is an important factor" for the court to consider.[114] Nevertheless, a court may determine that dismissal is appropriate even in the absence of malice. "Dismissal may be necessary if the prejudice to the defendant is extraordinary, denying it the ability to adequately defend its case."[115] Therefore, in determining whether sanctions for spoliation are warranted, the court must weigh the prejudice to the opposing party against the degree of the spoliator's culpability.[116]

Georgia does not recognize a separate tort for the spoliation of evidence.[117]

7. **Damages**

   a. **Collateral Source Rule**

   The common law rule generally enforced in Georgia permits an injured party to recover damages from a manufacturer regardless of any compensation he may have received from others.[118] A litigant's insurance policy is therefore thought to be inadmissible because of its prejudicial nature.[119] Nevertheless, the Georgia Court of Appeals appears to limit the scope of the collateral source rule, holding that insurance policies are relevant to determining damages to be paid by a party, even though they are inadmissible in the liability phase of the trial.[120] The court reasoned that this application of the rule prevents a plaintiff from receiving a double recovery from both his insurer and from the defendant tortfeasor for the same item of damages, while still providing the protections afforded by the collateral source rule.[121]

   b. **Economic Loss**

   Recovery is generally only permitted for personal injuries or damage to property other than to the allegedly defective product.[122] Recovery for solely economic loss may only be brought as a contract warranty action.[123]

   However, Georgia courts have created two exceptions to this general rule:

   (1) Under the "accident exception," a plaintiff can recover in tort for solely economic loss "when there is a sudden and calamitous event that not only causes damages to the product but poses an unreasonable risk of injury to persons and other property."[124]

   (2) Under the "misrepresentation exception," "one who supplies information during the course of his business, profession,

employment, or in any transaction in which he has a pecuniary interest has a duty of reasonable care and competence to parties who rely upon the information in circumstances in which the maker was manifestly aware of the use to which the information was to be put and intended that it be so used. This liability is limited to a foreseeable person or limited class of persons for whom the information was intended, either directly or indirectly."[125] In other words, a plaintiff can recover for economic loss if the defendant provided false information to a foreseeable person (the plaintiff) that the defendant was manifestly aware would use the information, and on which the plaintiff detrimentally relied.[126]

c. **Punitive Damages**

In Georgia, punitive damages may be recovered only where "it is proven by clear and convincing evidence that the defendant's actions showed willful misconduct, malice, fraud, wantonness, oppression, or that entire want of care which would raise the presumption of conscious indifference to consequences."[127] The statute also provides that only one award of punitive damages may be awarded against a defendant for any act or omission[128] and requires 75 percent of the award to go to the state.[129] These two provisions have been declared constitutional by the Georgia Supreme Court and have been found not to create an arbitrary and unreasonable classification between product liability plaintiffs and other tort plaintiffs.[130]

d. **Pre- and Post-Judgment Interest**

In Georgia, pre-judgment interest is provided for under the "Unliquidated Damages Interest Act."[131] A plaintiff can recover pre-judgment interest only if (1) she gives "written notice by registered or certified mail or statutory overnight delivery to a person against whom claim is made" before trial of a demand for an amount of unliquidated damages, (2) the person against whom the claim is made fails to pay that demand within 30 days, and (3) at trial "the judgment is for an amount not less than the amount demanded."[132] The interest is calculated "at an annual rate equal to the prime rate . . . on the thirtieth day following the date of the mailing of the last written notice plus 3 percent" and will accrue from the "thirtieth day following the date of the mailing or delivering of the written notice until the date of judgment."[133] If the person against whom the claim and demand is made offers to pay the amount demanded with interest within 30 days of the plaintiff's demand, and the plaintiff rejects the offer, the plaintiff will no longer be entitled to pre-judgment interest.[134] Failure to follow the procedures set forth under the Act precludes recovery of pre-judgment interest.[135]

In a case where plaintiff provides written notice of settlement to multiple defendants, the amounts demanded from each defendant will be aggregated in determining whether the judgment is for an amount not less than the amount demanded, unless the payment of the requested amount from one defendant will end the litigation against all remaining parties.[136]

Post-judgment interest "shall apply automatically to all judgments in this state and such interest shall be collectable as a part of each judgment whether or not such judgment specifically reflects the entitlement to such interest."[137] The interest shall accrue on the principal amount of the judgment, but not on any pre-judgment interest, at a rate of 12 percent per year.[138]

D. NEGLIGENCE

1. The Standard

In negligence actions, "the duty imposed is the traditional one of reasonable care, and the *manufacturer* need not provide . . . a product incapable of producing injury."[139] The essential elements of a cause of action for negligence are (1) a legal duty; (2) a breach of this duty; (3) an injury; and (4) a causal connection between the breach and the injury.[140] In cases asserting negligent design, the risk-utility analysis applies to determine whether the manufacturer is liable.[141]

2. Basic Elements

a. Liable Parties

Although sellers of products are exempted from strict liability, they can still be found liable for negligence. If the seller knows of no defect in the product, however, the seller is entitled to assume that the product was properly manufactured and not defective when placed on the market by the manufacturer.[142] In addition, when a manufacturer has already warned consumers of the particular dangers of a product, a seller is entitled to assume that the manufacturer has fulfilled its duty to warn and the seller's duty to warn the consumers of that particular danger may be extinguished.[143] A seller still has a duty to warn of any known dangers either not communicated by the manufacturer or substantively different from dangers the manufacturer has included on its warning labels.[144] Further, when a seller knows, or should know, of the danger that may result from a particular use of a product, it has a duty to give an adequate warning of the danger.[145]

3. Evidentiary Issues

a. *Res Ipsa Loquitur*

Georgia recognizes *res ipsa loquitur* as a theory that plaintiffs can rely on to show negligence.[146] *Res ipsa loquitur* will only be applied with caution and in extreme cases, and is not applicable in cases where there is an intermediary cause which could have produced the injury.[147] It is also inapplicable to mechanical devices because they can become out of working order and dangerous without anyone's negligence.[148] If the defendant manufacturer does not have exclusive control of the product before it reaches the plaintiff, the plaintiff cannot rely on *res ipsa loquitur*.[149]

b. Evidence of Government Standards and Regulations

In negligence actions, evidence as to industry standards is admissible and relevant as to whether an ordinary, prudent manufacturer would act in accordance with the standard.[150]

c. Evidence of Subsequent Remedial Measures

Unlike with claims of strict liability, evidence of subsequent remedial measures is generally inadmissible to prove negligence.[151]

4. Causation

Intervening acts may prevent a negligent manufacturer from being liable.[152] Unforeseeable negligence of another person is an intervening cause that negates the liability of the manufacturer for an allegedly defective product.[153]

5. Defenses

Contributory and comparative negligence are defenses to a product liability suit under a negligence theory.[154] A plaintiff's contributory negligence bars any recovery whatsoever if his failure to use ordinary care for his own safety is the sole proximate cause of his injuries, even though such negligence concurs with the negligence of the defendant.[155] The Georgia comparative negligence standard permits a plaintiff to recover only if her negligence is less than that of the defendant.[156] A jury may award zero damages to the plaintiff even if it finds the manufacturer is negligent.

Assumption of the risk is a complete defense in negligence actions if (1) the plaintiff had some actual knowledge of the danger; (2) she understood and appreciated the risk; and (3) she voluntarily exposed herself to the risk.[157] The plaintiff must subjectively possess the knowledge of the specific, particular risk of harm associated with the activity or condition that proximately causes injury.[158] Whether the party assumed the risk is usually a question for the jury unless the defense is conclusively established by "plain, palpable and undisputed evidence."[159]

E. FAILURE TO WARN

1. The Standard

A manufacturer has a duty to give adequate warning where it has reason to believe that a use of the product may cause harm. This duty to warn can arise even if the product is not found to be otherwise defectively designed, manufactured, or assembled.[160] If the product does not contain an adequate warning, the product is defective.[161]

Manufacturers of component parts also have a duty to warn of a danger that may result from a reasonably foreseeable use of the component part.[162]

A manufacturer has no duty to warn of an obvious or generally known danger.[163] Whether a peril is obvious is determined under the objective "open and obvious" rule.[164] Likewise, actual knowledge of the dangers of a product by the person claiming to be entitled to a warning precludes a duty to provide a warning.[165] Further, a duty to warn extends only to the manufacturer's reasonably contemplated and anticipated use of the product,[166] and does not extend to unexpected modifications or alterations.[167]

A distributor's liability is more limited. A distributor has a duty to warn only if it had actual or constructive knowledge of the potential danger at the time of sale.[168]

Whether a warning is adequate is a question for the jury.[169] Questions used in determining whether a warning was adequate are as follows: (1) Was there a danger that required a warning or instruction? (2) Was any warning or instruction given? (3) Was the warning or instruction read? (4) Was the warning label effective for those who would foreseeably be affected by the product? and (5) Did the label give adequate instructions on how to safely use the product?[170]

The lack or inadequacy of warning must be the proximate cause of the injury. If the plaintiff did not read the allegedly inadequate warning, there is no proximate causation.[171] A plaintiff is not required to show bodily harm to maintain a claim for negligent failure to warn.[172]

2. **Post-Sale Duty**

A manufacturer is under a duty to warn consumers of danger arising from the use of a product based on knowledge acquired after the product is sold.[173] Because this duty may arise decades after the date the product was sold, negligent failure to warn claims are not barred by the statute of repose.[174]

A seller's duty to warn is limited to only those dangers actually and constructively known when the product is sold; a seller does not have a post-sale duty to warn of dangers that become known after the sale.[175] If a dealer, distributor, or other intermediary voluntarily agrees to notify consumers of a defect, he may be found negligent for failure to perform.[176]

3. **Learned Intermediary**

In a negligence action, the learned intermediary doctrine may relieve a manufacturer of its duty to warn the end consumer of its product when the product is first sold to, and ultimately supplied to the consumer by, a "learned intermediary."[177] This circumstance most often arises in the context of medical devices and prescription drugs. Under this doctrine, a manufacturer of prescription drugs or medical devices has a duty to warn only the doctor of the potential dangers related to the drug or device. The physician then acts as the "learned intermediary" between the manufacturer and the consumer.[178] For the learned intermediary doctrine to apply, a manufacturer's warning to a doctor must be adequate or reasonable under the circumstances.[179] Thus, a court must first find that the manufacturer's warning to a doctor was adequate and reasonable as a matter of law before granting summary judgment to a manufacturer under the learned intermediary doctrine.[180] Nevertheless, a plaintiff may still be barred from recovering regardless of the sufficiency of the warning.[181] "Where a learned intermediary has actual knowledge of the substance of the alleged warning and would have taken the same course of action even with the information the plaintiff contends should have been provided," the learned intermediary breaks the causal link and precludes plaintiff from recovering.[182]

Outside of the medical profession, Georgia courts have narrowly applied the learned intermediary doctrine. In most cases, Georgia courts will strictly apply a five-part balancing test to determine whether a manufacturer's duty to warn a consumer is discharged by the knowledge of an intermediary regarding the potential product risks. This test balances (a) the burden of requiring a warning; (b) the likelihood that the intermediary will provide a warning; (c) the likely efficacy of such a warning; (d) the degree of danger posed by the absence of such a warning; and (e) the nature of the potential harm.[183] In certain cases, however, where a product is vended to a particular group or profession, Georgia courts have not required the manufacturer to warn against risks generally known to such group or profession.[184] Nevertheless, where the danger involved is great and the means of disclosure are not unduly burdensome, the learned intermediary doctrine does not apply and a manufacturer must supply product warnings directly to the consumer.[185]

F. BREACH OF WARRANTY

A breach of warranty occurs when a product is not fit for the ordinary purposes for which such goods are used.[186] Breach of warranty claims require privity.[187] There is, however, an exception for a natural person in the family or household of the buyer or a guest in the home where the warranty extends to the identifiable third person.[188] A person may not effectively assign a warranty to a subsequent purchaser of a product.[189]

If a purchaser fails to follow directions provided by a manufacturer, there can be no liability for breach of warranty.[190]

For breach of warranty claims, Georgia continues to distinguish between a "sale" and a "lease." However, the characteristics of an agreement, not its name, determine its treatment. Only if a "lease" is essentially a sale may the lessee be treated as an owner.[191] If an express warranty provides the manufacturer with a right to repair defects, a breach of warranty does not occur unless and until the manufacturer has been given an opportunity to repair.[192]

G. MISREPRESENTATION

Georgia has not adopted Restatement (Second) of Torts Section 402B dealing with misrepresentation. However, the courts have created a misrepresentation action as an exception to the economic loss rule. *See* Economic Loss, *supra*.

John F. Yarber
Kacy G. Romig
Jesika S. Wehunt
Jones Day
1420 Peachtree Street, N.E., Suite 800
Atlanta, Georgia 30309-3053
(404) 581-3939
(Fax) (404) 581-8330

Endnotes - Georgia

1. *See generally Bodymasters Sports Indus., Inc. v. Wimberley*, 232 Ga. App. 170, 501 S.E.2d 556 (1998) (proceeding on a theory of strict liability); *Barger v. Garden Way, Inc.*, 231 Ga. App. 723, 499 S.E.2d 737 (1998) (proceeding on a theory of strict liability for defective design, and failure to warn as well as theories of negligent design, and negligent failure to warn); *Corbin v. Farmex, Inc.*, 227 Ga. App. 620, 490 S.E.2d 395 (1997) (proceeding on a theory of strict liability), *rev'd on other grounds by Farmex, Inc. v. Wainwright*, 269 Ga. 548, 501 S.E.2d 802 (1998); *Ogletree v. Navistar Int'l Transp. Corp.*, 194 Ga. App. 41, 390 S.E.2d 61 (1989) (proceeding on a theory of negligence), *overruled on other grounds by Weatherby v. Honda Motor Co.*, 195 Ga. App. 169, 393 S.E.2d 64 (1990), *overruled on other grounds by Ogletree v. Navistar Int'l Transp. Corp.*, 269 Ga. 443, 500 S.E.2d 570 (1998), *rev'd on other grounds by Ogletree v. Navistar Int'l Transp. Corp.*, 271 Ga. 644, 522 S.E.2d 467 (1999).

2. O.C.G.A. §§ 9-3-30, *et seq.*, 11-2-312, *et seq.*, 51-1-11, 51-11-7, 51-12-1, *et seq.*

3. *L.P. Gas Indus. Equip. Co. v. Burch*, 306 Ga. App. 156, 701 S.E.2d 602 (2010).

4. O.C.G.A. § 9-3-33.

5. O.C.G.A. §§ 9-3-30, 9-3-31. O.C.G.A. § 9-3-30(b) now provides that causes of action for recovery of damages to a dwelling due to the manufacture of or the negligent design or installation of synthetic exterior siding shall accrue when the damage to the dwelling is discovered or, in the exercise of reasonable diligence should have been discovered, whichever first occurs, but all causes of action are still subject to the ten-year statute of repose.

6. *Corp. of Mercer Univ. v. Nat'l Gypsum Co.*, 258 Ga. 365, 368 S.E.2d 732 (1988), *cert. denied*, 493 U.S. 965 (1989); *Mitchell v. Contractors Specialty Supply, Inc.*, 247 Ga. App. 628, 544 S.E.2d 533 (2001); *but see Smith v. Branch*, 226 Ga. App. 626, 487 S.E.2d 35 (1997) (distinguishing the application of the discovery rule from the commencement of the statute of limitations for continuing torts).

7. *Welch v. Celotex Corp.*, 951 F.2d 1235 (11th Cir. 1992) (applying Georgia law); *Anderson v. Sybron Corp.*, 165 Ga. App. 566, 353 S.E.2d 816, *aff'd*, 251 Ga. 593, 310 S.E.2d 232 (1983); *King v. Seitzingers, Inc.*, 160 Ga. App. 318, 287 S.E.2d 252 (1981).

8. O.C.G.A. § 51-1-11(b)(2).

9. *Pafford v. Biomet*, 264 Ga. 540, 448 S.E.2d 347 (1994).

10. *Campbell v. Altec Indus., Inc.*, 288 Ga. 535, 535, 707 S.E.2d 48, 48-49 (2011).

11. O.C.G.A. § 51-1-11(c); *Chrysler Corp. v. Batten*, 264 Ga. 723, 450 S.E.2d 208 (1994); *see also Parks v. Hyundai Motor Am., Inc.*, 258 Ga. App. 876, 575 S.E.2d 673 (2002) (holding that the statute of repose does not provide an absolute bar to claims for negligent failure to warn).

12. O.C.G.A. § 51-1-11(c); *Vickery v. Waste Mgmt. of Ga., Inc.*, 249 Ga. App. 659, 549 S.E.2d 482 (2001).

13. *Vickery*, 249 Ga. App. at 660-61, 549 S.E.2d at 484.

14. *Ivy v. Ford Motor Co.*, 646 F.3d 769 (11th Cir. 2011) (applying Georgia law).

15. *Corp. of Mercer Univ. v. Nat'l Gypsum Co.*, 258 Ga. 365, 368 S.E.2d 732 (1988), *cert. denied*, 493 U.S. 965 (1989); *Dekalb County v. C.W. Matthews Contracting Co.*, 254 Ga. App. 246, 562 S.E.2d 228 (2002); *see also Dryvit Sys., Inc. v. Stein*, 256 Ga. App. 327, 568 S.E.2d 569 (2002) (holding that tort actions for damage to realty must be brought within four years of substantial completion regardless of knowledge of any alleged defects). *But see Travis Pruitt & Assoc., P.C. v. Bowling*, 238 Ga. App. 225, 518 S.E.2d 453 (1999) (holding the statute of limitations does not begin to run until the defendant's negligent act damages the plaintiff's property).

16. *Colormatch Exteriors, Inc. v. Hickey*, 275 Ga. 249, 569 S.E.2d 495 (2002); *Corp. of Mercer Univ.*, 258 Ga. at 366, 368 S.E.2d at 733.

17. *Colormatch Exteriors, Inc.*, 275 Ga. at 250, 569 S.E.2d at 496.

18. O.C.G.A. § 11-2-725(1).

19. *Adair v. Baker Bros., Inc.*, 185 Ga. App. 807, 808, 366 S.E.2d 164, 165 (1988) (noting that an action "to recover for personal injuries is, in essence, a personal injury action, and, regardless of whether it is based upon an alleged breach of an implied warranty or is based upon an alleged tort, the limitations statute governing actions for personal injuries is controlling.").

20. O.C.G.A. § 11-2-725(1).

21. O.C.G.A. § 9-3-24.

22. O.C.G.A. § 51-1-11(b)(1); *see Carmical v. Bell Helicopter Textron, Inc.*, 117 F.3d 490, 494 (11th Cir. 1997) (applying Georgia law) (holding that "[t]o prevail in a Georgia products liability action, whether based on negligence or strict liability, a plaintiff must show that the proximate cause of the injury was a defect which existed when the product was sold."); *Trickett v. Advanced*

Neuromodulation Sys., Inc., 542 F. Supp. 2d 1338 (S.D. Ga. 2008); *but see Haynes v. Cyberonics, Inc.*, No. 1:09-CV-2700-JEC, 2011 U.S. Dist. LEXIS 99738, at *16-17 (N.D. Ga. Sept. 6, 2011) (stating that manufacturing defect claims under O.C.G.A. § 51-1-11(b)(1) are preempted by the Medical Device Amendment to the federal Food, Drug and Cosmetic Act as to Class III medical devices).

23. *Giordano v. Ford Motor Corp.*, 165 Ga. App. 644, 299 S.E.2d 897 (1983) (quoting *Ctr. Chem. Co. v. Parzini*, 234 Ga. 868, 218 S.E.2d 580 (1975)); *see also Wheat v. Sofamor, S.N.C.*, 46 F. Supp. 2d 1351 (N.D. Ga. 1999) ("A manufacturer can be held strictly liable for manufacturing defects, marketing/packaging defects and inadvertent design defects only if the plaintiff shows the product sold was defective.").

24. *Giordano*, 165 Ga. App. at 645, 299 S.E.2d at 899.

25. *Parzini*, 234 Ga. at 870, 218 S.E.2d at 582, *overruled in part by Banks v. ICI Americas, Inc.*, 264 Ga. 732, 450 S.E.2d 671 (1994) (overruling *Parzini* to the extent it requires one standard for all types of product liability cases).

26. *Jonas v. Isuzu Motors Ltd.*, 210 F. Supp. 2d 1373, 1380 (M.D. Ga. 2002) (applying Georgia law).

27. O.C.G.A. § 51-1-11(b)(1); *but see Haynes*, 2011 U.S. Dist. LEXIS 99738, at *16-17 (stating O.C.G.A. § 51-1-11(b)(1) is preempted by the Medical Device Amendment to the Federal Food, Drug and Cosmetic Act as to Class III medical devices).

28. *Robert F. Bullock, Inc. v. Thorpe*, 256 Ga. 744, 353 S.E.2d 340 (1987).

29. *Thorpe v. Robert F. Bullock, Inc.*, 179 Ga. App. 867, 872, 348 S.E.2d 55, 59 (1986) *aff'd by Robert F. Bullock, Inc. v. Thorpe*, 256 Ga. 744 (1987).

30. *Robert F. Bullock, Inc.*, 256 Ga. at 745, 353 S.E.2d at 342; *see also Monroe v. Savannah Elec. & Power Co.*, 267 Ga. 26, 471 S.E.2d 854 (1996) (finding that in determining whether electricity had been placed in the stream of commerce for purposes of strict liability, the relinquishment of control over the electricity and/or the marketable condition of that electricity were essential factors); *Tyler v. Pepsico, Inc.*, 198 Ga. App. 223, 400 S.E.2d 673 (1990) (applying the stream-of-commerce analysis in assessing liability of component manufacturers for damages caused by the end product).

31. *See, e.g., Monroe*, 267 Ga. at 28-29, 471 S.E.2d at 856-57; *Robert F. Bullock, Inc.*, 256 Ga. at 745, 353 S.E.2d at 341-42 (finding the manufacturer of a new product that offers use of product on trial basis with the hope of ultimate sale subject to strict liability); *Jenkins v. GMC*, 240 Ga. App. 636, 636-37, 524 S.E.2d 324, 325 (1999) (applying strict liability to a truck purchased through lease financing arrangement).

32. *Jones v. NordicTrack, Inc.*, 274 Ga. 115, 550 S.E.2d 101 (2001).

33. *Jones*, 274 Ga. at 117, 550 S.E.2d at 102; *see also* O.C.G.A. § 51-1-11(b)(1).

34. O.C.G.A. § 51-1-11(a).

35. *Chem Tech Finishers, Inc. v. Paul Mueller Co.*, 189 Ga. App. 433, 375 S.E.2d 881 (1988); *see also Gen. Motors Corp. v. Halco Instruments, Inc.*, 124 Ga. App. 630, 185 S.E.2d 619 (1971) (denying recovery due to a lack of privity).

36. *Blood Balm Co. v. Cooper*, 83 Ga. 457, 10 S.E. 118 (1889).

37. *Pepper v. Selig Chem. Indus., Inc.*, 161 Ga. App. 548, 288 S.E.2d 693 (1982).

38. *Karoly v. Kawasaki Motors Corp.*, 259 Ga. App. 225, 227, 576 S.E.2d 625, 627 (2003).

39. O.C.G.A. § 51-1-11.1(b); *see, e.g., Dean v. Toyota Indus. Equip. Mfg.*, 246 Ga. App. 255, 540 S.E.2d 233 (2000) (holding trial court erred in granting summary judgment to defendant based on its status as a mere product seller); *Robinson v. Williamson*, 245 Ga. App. 17, 537 S.E.2d 159 (2000) (holding pharmacy and pharmacist are product sellers, not manufacturers); *Ream Tool Co. v. Newton*, 209 Ga. App. 226, 433 S.E.2d 67 (1993) (holding a mail vendor was merely a product seller).

40. O.C.G.A. § 51-1-11.1(a). *See Freeman v. United Cities Propane Gas Inc.*, 807 F. Supp. 1533, 1540 (M.D. Ga. 1992) (applying Georgia law); *Farmex, Inc. v. Wainwright*, 269 Ga. 548, 501 S.E.2d 802 (1998). *But see English v. Crenshaw Supply Co.*, 193 Ga. App. 354, 387 S.E.2d 628 (1989) (applying strict liability to a non-manufacturing seller who represents to purchasers that it manufactured the product).

41. *Dean*, 246 Ga. App. at 257, 540 S.E.2d at 235; *see also* O.C.G.A. §§ 51-1-11.1(a), (b).

42. *Bullington v. Union Tool Corp.*, 254 Ga. 283, 328 S.E.2d 726 (1985).

43. *Bullington*, 254 Ga. 283, 328 S.E.2d at 727.

44. *Farmex, Inc.*, 269 Ga. at 549-50, 501 S.E.2d at 803-04.

45. *McReynolds v. Krebs*, 290 Ga. 850, 852, 725 S.E.2d 584, 587 (2012) (quoting O.C.G.A. § 51-12-33(b)); *see also Barnett*, 308 Ga. App. at 362, 707 S.E.2d at 573; *Cavalier Convenience v. Sarvis*, 305 Ga. App. 141, 699 S.E.2d 104 (2010) (holding the trier of fact shall apportion damages among persons liable according to percentage of fault).

46. O.C.G.A. § 51-12-33; *see Couch v. Red Roof Inns, Inc.*, 291 Ga. 359, 729 S.E.2d 378 (2012).

47. *Couch*, 291 Ga. at 359, 729 S.E.2d at 379 (interpreting O.C.G.A. § 51-12-33 as displacing the common law rule preventing apportionment to intentional tortfeasors).

48. O.C.G.A. § 51-12-33(a).

49. O.C.G.A. § 51-12-33(b).

50. O.C.G.A. § 51-12-33(c); *see also Union Carbide Corp. v. Fields*, 315 Ga. App. 554, 726 S.E.2d 521 (2012), *cert. granted*, No. S12C1417, 2013 Ga. LEXIS 248 (Feb. 4, 2013).

51. O.C.G.A. § 51-12-33(d)(1)-(2); *see also Union Carbide Corp.*, 315 Ga. App. at 558-59, 726 S.E.2d at 524-25.

52. *Barnett v. Farmer*, 308 Ga. App. 358, 362, 707 S.E.2d 570, 574 (2011) (holding the jury could consider the fault of the plaintiff's husband even though he was protected from suit by the interspousal tort immunity doctrine).

53. *Union Carbide Corp.*, 315 Ga. App. at 558-59, 726 S.E.2d at 526.

54. O.C.G.A. § 51-12-33(f)(1)-(2).

55. *See* Jason Crawford, *Trial Practice and Procedure*, 57 MERCER L. REV. 381, 384 (2005) (questioning whether the language of O.C.G.A. § 51-12-31 preserved joint and several liability by allowing a plaintiff to "recover damages for an injury caused by any of the defendants against only the defendant or defendants liable for the injury" because "[a] defendant who is five percent responsible for an indivisible injury is still, indisputably, 'liable for the injury'" and, thus, a plaintiff may recover fully from that defendant. *See also* Lonnie T. Brown, Jr. et al., *Joint Liability Rules in Georgia's New Battleground: Five Georgia Law Professors Examine the State's New Tort Legislation*, 39 GA. L. ADVOC. 18 (Spring/Summer 2005) (arguing that O.C.G.A. § 51-12-32 would be a "nullity" if joint and several liability is no longer a viable theory of recovery); *Reasoner v. Schwartz*, No. 08A92811-3 (Ga. St. Ct. July 30, 2009) (stating the statute would be "meaningless" if joint and several liability were abolished); *Spina v. Henry County, et al.*, No. 08SV02639 (Ga. St. Ct. Oct. 21, 2009) (same); Crawford, at 385 (stating the statute would be "mere surplusage" if joint and several liability were abolished).

56. *McReynolds*, 290 Ga. at 852, 725 S.E.2d at 587; *Barnett*, 308 Ga. App. at 362, 707 S.E.2d at 573-74; *see also Murray v. Patel*, 304 Ga. App. 253, 696 S.E.2d 97 (2010) (stating that the purposes of the contribution and apportionment statutes are not incompatible). *But see Dist. Owners Ass'n v. AMEC Envtl. & Infrastructure, Inc.*, 2013 Ga. App. LEXIS 595 (Ga. Ct. App. July 8, 2013) (questioning *Murray's* continued precedential value given the Georgia Supreme Court's adjustment of the common law right of apportionment in *Couch*, *see supra* note 46).

57. *See Couch v. Red Roof Inns, Inc.*, 291 Ga. 359, 729 S.E.2d 378 (2012) (holding that the right to jury trial was not violated by the introduction of apportioned fault because the jury still retained the same abilities it had under the joint and several liability scheme—assessing liability, determining the amount of damages, etc. Plaintiff's due process and equal protection arguments similarly failed because the statute was not unconstitutionally vague, preserved the right to pursue a judgment, and passed rational basis scrutiny); *GFI Mgmt. Servs. v. Medina*, 291 Ga. 741. 733 S.E.2d 329 (2012) (following *Couch*).

58. *Starling v. Seaboard Coast Line R. Co.*, 533 F. Supp. 183 (S.D. Ga. 1982) (applying Georgia law).

59. O.C.G.A. § 34-9-1, *et seq.*; *see also Hadsock v. J.H. Harvey Co.*, 212 Ga. App. 782, 442 S.E.2d 892 (1994) (stating that the "exclusivity provisions" of the Workers' Compensation Act provided immunity because the incident arose out of and in the course of employment); *Porter v. Beloit Corp.*, 194 Ga. App. 591, 391 S.E.2d 430 (1990) (rejecting adoption of the dual capacity doctrine).

60. *Porter*, 194 Ga. App. at 593, 391 S.E.2d at 432.

61. *Doggett v. Patrick*, 197 Ga. App. 420, 421, 398 S.E.2d 770, 770-71 (1990) (citing *Porter*, 194 Ga. App. 591, 391 S.E.2d 430).

62. *See, e.g., Chrysler Corp. v. Batten*, 264 Ga. 723, 450 S.E.2d 208 (1994); *Wells v. Ortho Pharm. Corp.*, 615 F. Supp. 262 (N.D. Ga. 1985) (applying Georgia law), *aff'd in part, modified on other grounds in part*, 788 F.2d 741 (11th Cir.), *cert. denied*, 479 U.S. 950 (1986).

63. *Barnes v. Harley-Davidson Co., Inc.*, 182 Ga. App. 778, 357 S.E.2d 127 (1987).

64. *See, e.g., Whirlpool Corp. v. Hurlbut*, 166 Ga. App. 95, 303 S.E.2d 284 (1983); *Firestone Tire & Rubber Co. v. Pinyan*, 155 Ga. App. 343, 270 S.E.2d 883 (1980).

65. *Ctr. Chem. Co. v. Parzini*, 234 Ga. 868, 218 S.E.2d 580 (1975).

66. *Jenkins v. Gen. Motors Corp.*, 240 Ga. App. 636, 524 S.E.2d 324 (1999); *see also Miller v. Ford Motor Co.*, 287 Ga. App. 642, 653 S.E.2d 82 (2007) (holding that summary judgment in favor of defendant was proper because the plaintiffs failed to present evidence that there was a defect when it left the manufacturer).

67. *See, e.g., Williams v. Mast Biosurgery USA, Inc.*, 644 F.3d 1312 (11th Cir. 2011) (applying Georgia law); *see also McDonald v. Mazda Motors of Am., Inc.*, 269 Ga. App. 62, 603 S.E.2d 456 (2004) ("Breach of implied warranty may be proven without expert testimony to show that a product is defective and that the defect existed from the time of manufacture."); *Williams v. Am. Med.*

Sys., 248 Ga. App. 682, 548 S.E.2d 371 (2001) ("It is not necessary for the plaintiff to specify precisely the nature of the defect.").

68. *Hunt v. Harley-Davidson Motor Co., Inc.*, 147 Ga. App. 44, 248 S.E.2d 15 (1978).

69. *Banks v. ICI Americas*, 264 Ga. 732, 450 S.E.2d 671 (1994); *Trickett v. Advanced Neuromodulation Sys., Inc.*, 542 F. Supp. 2d 1338 (S.D. Ga. 2008).

70. *Banks*, 264 Ga. at 735, 450 S.E.2d at 674.

71. *Banks*, 264 Ga. at 736 n.6, 450 S.E.2d at 675 n.6; *Trickett*, 542 F. Supp. 2d at 1347 n.10.

72. *Banks*, 264 Ga. at 736, 450 S.E.2d at 674; *compare Jones v. NordicTrack, Inc.*, 274 Ga. 115, 550 S.E.2d 101 (2001) *and Jonas v. Isuzu Motors, Ltd.*, 210 F. Supp. 2d 1373 (M.D. Ga. 2002) *with Volkswagen of Am., Inc. v. Gentry*, 254 Ga. App. 888, 564 S.E.2d 733 (2002) (holding that the trial court did not err in failing to charge the jury that plaintiff had to offer proof of a safer feasible alternate design because such a charge reflects only one factor of the balancing test and is therefore an incomplete statement of law).

73. *Dean v. Toyota Indus. Equip. Mfg.*, 246 Ga. App. 255, 540 S.E.2d 233 (2000) (summary judgment generally improper where any factor is disputed); *SK Hand Tool Corp. v. Lowman*, 223 Ga. App. 712, 479 S.E.2d 103 (1996); *Ctr. Chem Co v. Parzini*, 234 Ga. 868, 218 S.E.2d 580 (1975).

74. *Williams v. Am. Med. Sys.*, 248 Ga. App. 682, 548 S.E.2d 371 (2001).

75. *Ogletree v. Navistar Int'l Transp. Corp.*, 269 Ga. 443, 500 S.E.2d 570 (1998); *Barger v. Garden Way, Inc.*, 231 Ga. App. 723, 499 S.E.2d 737 (1998); *see also Cornish v. Byrd Welding Serv., Inc.*, 252 Ga. App. 793, 557 S.E.2d 432 (2001) (It is not error for the trial court to instruct the jury to consider the open and obvious danger in a product as one of the factors for determining design defect under the risk-utility test.).

76. *Bryant v. Hoffmann-La Roche Inc.*, 262 Ga. App. 401, 585 S.E.2d 723 (2003).

77. *Bryant*, 262 Ga. App. at 406, 585 S.E.2d at 728.

78. *Friend v. Gen. Motors Corp.*, 118 Ga. App. 763, 165 S.E.2d 734 (1968).

79. *Ford Motor Co. v. Gibson*, 283 Ga. 398, 659 S.E.2d 346 (2008).

80. *Polston v. Boomershine Pontiac-GMC Truck, Inc.*, 262 Ga. 616, 423 S.E.2d 659 (1992); *see also Owens v. Gen. Motors Corp.*, 272 Ga. App. 842, 613 S.E.2d 651 (2005) (holding that burden-shifting applies only in design defect cases, not manufacturing defect cases).

81. *Kersey v. Dolgencorp, LLC*, No. 1:09-CV-898-RWS., 2011 U.S. Dist. LEXIS 47249, at *3 (N.D. Ga. May 03, 2011); *see also* O.C.G.A. § 51-1-11(b)(1) ("The manufacturer of any personal property sold as new property directly or through a dealer or any other person shall be liable in tort, irrespective of privity, to any natural person who may use, consume, or reasonably be affected by the property and who suffers injury to his person or property because the property when sold by the manufacturer was not merchantable and reasonably suited to the use intended, and its condition when sold is the proximate cause of the injury sustained.").

82. *Ctr. Chem. Co. v. Parzini*, 234 Ga. 868, 869, 218 S.E.2d 580, 582 (1975), *overruled in part by Banks v. ICI Americas, Inc.*, 264 Ga. 732, 450 S.E.2d 671 (1994) (overruling *Parzini* to the extent it requires one standard for all types of product liability cases); *Owens v. Gen. Motors. Corp.*, 272 Ga. App. 842, 846, 613 S.E.2d 651, 654 (2005).

83. *Parzini*, 234 Ga. at 871, 218 S.E.2d at 583.

84. *Trickett v. Advanced Neuromodulation Sys., Inc.*, 542 F. Supp. 2d 1338 (S.D. Ga. 2008).

85. *Banks*, 264 Ga. at 733-34, 450 S.E.2d at 673.

86. *Kersey*, 2011 U.S. Dist. LEXIS 47249, at *11.

87. *Banks*, 264 Ga. at 734 n.2, 450 S.E.2d at 673 n.2.

88. *Banks v. ICI Americas, Inc.*, 264 Ga. 732, 734, 450 S.E.2d 671, 673 (1994).

89. *Firestone Tire & Rubber Co. v. Hall*, 152 Ga. App. 560, 565, 263 S.E.2d 449, 453 (1979).

90. *See Lang v. Federated Dep't Stores*, 161 Ga. App. 760, 763, 287 S.E.2d 729, 731-32 (1982) (allowing introduction of circumstantial evidence to prove a manufacturing defect where the hair cream relaxer at issue was entirely consumed); *Hall*, 152 Ga. App. at 562, 263 S.E.2d at 451 (allowing introduction of circumstantial evidence to prove a manufacturing defect where the tire at issue was destroyed during the blowout).

91. *See Dorminey v. Harvill Mach., Inc.*, 141 Ga. App. 507, 508, 233 S.E.2d 815, 817 (1977) ("The appellant's requested charge on malfunction as a defect, building on an earlier charge based on strict liability, was inaccurate as a statement of law.").

92. *Doyle v. Volkswagenwerk Aktiengesellschaft*, 267 Ga. 574, 481 S.E.2d 518 (1997); *Gentry v. Volkswagen of Am., Inc.*, 238 Ga. App. 785, 521 S.E.2d 13 (1999).

93. *Banks*, 264 Ga. at 736, 450 S.E.2d at 675; *Duren v. Paccar, Inc.*, 249 Ga. App. 758, 549 S.E.2d 755 (2001); *Dean v. Toyota Indus. Equip. Mfg.*, 246 Ga. App. 255, 540 S.E.2d 233 (2000).

94. *Stone Man, Inc. v. Green*, 263 Ga. 470, 435 S.E.2d 205 (1993); *Barger v. Garden Way, Inc.*, 231 Ga. App. 723, 499 S.E.2d 737 (1998).

95. *Doyle*, 267 Ga. at 574, 481 S.E.2d at 519; *Banks*, 264 Ga. at 736 n.6, 450 S.E.2d at 675 n.6.

96. *Cooper Tire & Rubber Co. v. Crosby*, 273 Ga. 454, 455, 543 S.E.2d 21,23-24 (2001); *Shasta Beverages, Inc. v. Tetley USA, Inc.*, 248 Ga. App. 381, 385, 546 S.E.2d 800, 804 (2001); *Ray v. Ford Motor Co.*, 237 Ga. App. 316, 317, 514 S.E.2d 227, 230 (1999); *Dep't of Transp. v. Brown*, 218 Ga. App. 178, 183, 460 S.E.2d 812, 817 (1995); *Mack Trucks, Inc. v. Conkle*, 263 Ga. 539, 544, 436 S.E.2d 635, 640 (1993); *Jackson v. Int'l Harvester Co.*, 190 Ga. App. 765, 766-67,380 S.E.2d 306, 308 (1989); *Skil Corp. v. Lugsdin*, 168 Ga. App. 754, 755, 309 S.E.2d 921, 922-23 (1983).

97. *Cooper Tire*, 273 Ga. at 455, 543 S.E.2d at 23-24; *Colp v. Ford Motor Co.*, 279 Ga. App. 280, 281, 630 S.E.2d 886, 887 (2006); *Stovall v. DaimlerChrysler Motors Corp.*, 270 Ga. App. 791, 793,608 S.E.2d 245, 247 (2004).

98. *Stovall*, 270 Ga. App. at 791-92, 608 S.E.2d at 247.

99. *Skil Corp.*, 168 Ga. App. at 754-55, 309 S.E.2d at 922.

100. *Gen. Motors Corp. v. Moseley*, 213 Ga. App. 875, 881, 447 S.E.2d 302, 309 (1994), *abrogated on other grounds by Webster v. Boyett*, 269 Ga. 191, 496 S.E.2d 459 (1998).

101. *Hoffmann v. AC&S, Inc.*, 248 Ga. App. 608, 610, 548 S.E.2d 379, 382 (2001) (findingproximate cause was not established where plaintiff could not prove she was exposed to Defendant's asbestos products as opposed to those made by another manufacturer); *see also Williams v. Flintkote Co.*, 256 Ga. App. 205, 208, 568 S.E.2d 106, 108 (2002) (stating a plaintiff must present evidence that he or she was in proximity to the harm-causing product during its use to survive summary judgment).

102. *Talley v. City Tank Corp.*, 158 Ga. App. 130, 135, 279 S.E.2d 264, 269 (1981); *see also Carmical v. Bell Helicopter Textron, Inc.*, 117 F.3d 490, 494 (11th Cir. 1997) (explaining that Georgia relies on risk-utility analysis, where risks inherent in the manufacturer's product design are balanced against utility).

103. *Jonas v. Isuzu Motors, Ltd.*, 210 F. Supp. 2d 1373, 1376-77 (M.D. Ga. 2002); *Talley*, 158 Ga. App. at 135, 279 S.E.2d at 269.

104. *Giordano v. Ford Motor Co.*, 165 Ga. App. 644, 644, 299 S.E.2d 897, 897 (1983); *Greenway v. Peabody Int'l Corp.*, 163 Ga. App. 698, 703-04 294 S.E.2d 541, 547 (1982); *Talley*, 158 Ga. App. at 137, 279 S.E.2d at 271; *Jonas*, 210 F. Supp. 2d at 1377 (applying Georgia law).

105. *Jonas*, 210 F. Supp. 2d 1373, 1377.

106. *Patterson v. Long*, 321 Ga. App. 157, 160, 741 S.E.2d 242, 247 (2013); *Ray v. Ford Motor Co.*, 237 Ga. App. 316, 319,514 S.E.2d 227, 231 (1999); *Cont'l Research Corp. v. Reeves*, 204 Ga. App. 120, 128, 419 S.E.2d 48, 56 (1992); *Deere & Co. v. Brooks*, 250 Ga. 517, 520, 299 S.E.2d 704, 707 (1983).

107. *Deere & Co.*, 250 Ga. at 520, 299 S.E.2d at 707; *Hunt v. Harley-Davidson Motor Co., Inc.*, 147 Ga. App. 44, 45, 248 S.E.2d 15, 16 (1978).

108. *Deere & Co.*, 250 Ga. at 520, 299 S.E.2d at 707; *Rubin v. Cello Corp.*, 235 Ga. App. 250, 252,510 S.E.2d 541, 543 (1998).

109. *Bowen v. Cochran*, 252 Ga. App. 457, 458, 556 S.E.2d 530, 531-32 (2001); *Cotton v. Bowen*, 241 Ga. App. 543, 543, 524 S.E.2d 737,738 (1999); *Bodymasters Sports Indus., Inc. v. Wimberly*, 232 Ga. App. 170, 174-75, 501 S.E.2d 556, 560 (1998); *Barrash v. DeWalt Indus. Tool Co.*, 1999 WL 1486278 (N.D. Ga. Sept. 27, 1999).

110. *Cotton*, 241 Ga. App. at 544, 524 S.E.2d at 738.

111. *Chicago Hardware & Fixture Co. v. Letterman*, 236 Ga. App. 21, 23, 510 S.E.2d 875, 877 (1999); *Sharpnack v. Hoffinger Indus.*, 231 Ga. App. 829, 830, 499 S.E.2d 363, 364 (1998).

112. *Letterman*, 236 Ga. App. at 23, 510 S.E.2d at 877.

113. *Letterman*, 236 Ga. App. at 23, 510 S.E.2d at 877; *Chapman v. Auto Owners Ins. Co.*, 220 Ga. App. 539, 539-40, 469 S.E.2d 783, 783-84 (1996).

114. *Letterman*, 236 Ga. App. at 25, 510 S.E.2d at 878.

115. *Bridgestone/Firestone N. Am. Tire v. Campbell*, 258 Ga. App. 767, 770, 574 S.E.2d 923, 927 (2002) (quoting *Silvestri v. Gen. Motors Corp.*, 271 F.3d 583, 593 (4th Cir. 2001)).

116. *Bridgestone/Firestone N. Am. Tire*, 258 Ga. App. at 770, 574 S.E.2d at 927.

117. *Owens v. Am. Refuse Sys., Inc.*, 244 Ga. App. 780, 780, 536 S.E.2d 782, 784 (2000) (expressly declining to recognize an independent tort for spoliation of evidence); *Gardner v. Blackston*, 185 Ga. App. 754, 755, 365 S.E.2d 545, 546 (1988).

118. *Denton v. Con-Way S. Express, Inc.*, 261 Ga. 41, 42-43, 402 S.E.2d 269, 270-71 (1991), *overruled on other grounds by Grissom v. Gleason*, 262 Ga. 374, 418 S.E.2d 27 (1992); *Amalgamated Transit Union Local 1324 v. Roberts*, 263 Ga. 405, 407-08, 434 S.E.2d 450, 452 (1993); *Bennett v. Haley*, 132 Ga. App. 512, 522, 208 S.E.2d 302, 310 (1974) (extending the collateral source rule to exclude Medicaid payments from the calculation of damages); *Chambers v. Gwinnett Comm. Hosp., Inc.*, 253 Ga. App. 25, 26, 557 S.E.2d 412, 415 (2001); *but see McGlohon v. Ogden*, 251 Ga. 625, 628,308 S.E.2d 541, 543 (1983) (holding the collateral source rule inapplicable because plaintiff's no-fault insurer was entitled to subrogation).

119. *Chambers*, 253 Ga. App. at 26, 557 S.E.2d at 415; *Roberts*, 263 Ga. at 405, 434 S.E.2d at 451-52.

120. *Andrews v. Ford Motor Co.*, 310 Ga. App. 449, 451-52, 713 S.E.2d 474, 477-78 (2011).

121. *Andrews*, 310 Ga. App. at 451-52, 713 S.E.2d at 477-78.

122. *Busbee v. Chrysler Corp.*, 240 Ga. App. 664, 666, 524 S.E.2d 539, 541 (1999); *Advanced Drainage Sys., Inc. v. Lowman*, 210 Ga. App. 731, 733-34, 437 S.E.2d 604, 605 (1993).

123. *Lowman*, 210 Ga. App. at 733, 437 S.E.2d at 607.

124. *Lowman*, 210 Ga. App. at 734, 437 S.E.2d at 607; *see also Vulcan Materials Co. v. Driltech, Inc.*, 251 Ga. 383, 388, 306 S.E.2d 253, 257 (1983).

125. *Robert & Co. Assoc. v. Rhodes-Haverty P'ship*, 250 Ga. 680, 681-82, 300 S.E.2d 503, 504 (1983); *see also Lowman*, 210 Ga. App. at 734, 437 S.E.2d at 607 (explaining the misrepresentation exception is an exception to the general rule that absent injury to person or property, a cause of action for allegedly defective products may only be brought as a contract warranty action).

126. *City of Cairo v. Hightower Consulting Eng'rs, Inc.*, 278 Ga. App. 721, 727, 629 S.E.2d 518, 524 (2006).

127. O.C.G.A. § 51-12-5.1(b).

128. O.C.G.A. § 51-12-5.1(e)(1).

129. O.C.G.A. § 51-12-5.1(e)(2).

130. *Mack Trucks, Inc. v. Conkle*, 263 Ga. 539, 544-45, 436 S.E.2d 635, 639 (1993); *State v. Moseley*, 263 Ga. 680, 689, 436 S.E.2d 632, 634 (1992), *cert. denied*, 511 U.S. 1107 (1994); *but see McBride v. Gen. Motors Corp.*, 737 F. Supp. 1563, 1584 (M.D. Ga. 1990) (finding the one-award provision of O.C.G.A. § 51-12-5.1(e)(1) and all of section (e)(2) unconstitutional, null, and void).

131. O.C.G.A. § 51-12-14; *Williams v. Runion*, 173 Ga. App. 54, 59, 325 S.E.2d 441, 447 (1984).

132. O.C.G.A. § 51-12-14(a); *see Kuhl v. Shepard*, 226 Ga. App. 439, 440, 487 S.E.2d 68, 70 (1997) (plaintiff not entitled to pre-judgment interest unless a judgment is entered by the trial court). For notices served on or after July 1, 2000, statutory overnight delivery is now an acceptable method of service. For notices served prior to July 1, 2000, notice was only properly served by registered or certified mail. O.C.G.A § 51-12-14(a) (citing statutory notes).

133. O.C.G.A. § 51-12-14(c).

134. O.C.G.A. § 51-12-14(a).

135. *Kuhl*, 226 Ga. App. at 440, 487 S.E.2d at 70; *Resnik v. Pittman*, 203 Ga. App. 835, 835-36, 418 S.E.2d 116, 117 (1992).

136. *Compare White v. Jensen*, 257 Ga. App. 560, 561, 571 S.E.2d 544, 546 (2002) (where plaintiff sent different settlement letters to two different defendants without any indication that payment by one would end the litigation in its entirety, the amount requested from both defendants was aggregated for determining whether the judgment was not less than the amount demanded) *and Wolf Camera, Inc. v. Royter*, 253 Ga. App. 254, 261, 558 S.E.2d 797, 803 (2002) (same) *with Kniphfer v. Memorial Health Univ. Med. Ctr., Inc.*, 256 Ga. App. 874, 876-77, 570 S.E.2d 16, 17-18 (2002) (where plaintiff sent settlement demands to two different defendants requesting the identical amount from each and indicated that payment of the requested settlement amount by either party would have ended the litigation, the amounts requested were not aggregated for determining whether the judgment was not less than the amount demanded).

137. O.C.G.A. § 7-4-12(c).

138. O.C.G.A. § 7-4-12(c) (citing statutory notes); *Williams v. Reunion*, 173 Ga. App. 54, 60-61, 325 S.E.2d 441, 448 (1984).

139. *Ream Tool Co. v. Newton*, 209 Ga. App. 226, 228, 433 S.E.2d 67, 71 (1993) (emphasis in original).

140. *Persinger v. Step By Step Infant Dev. Ctr.*, 253 Ga. App. 768, 769, 560 S.E.2d 333, 335 (2002).

141. *Jones v. NordicTrack, Inc.*, 274 Ga. 115, 117, 550 S.E.2d 101, 103 (2001); *Ogletree v. Navistar Int'l Transp. Corp.*, 271 Ga. 644, 645, 522 S.E.2d 467, 469 (1999).

142. *Hester v. Human*, 211 Ga. App. 351, 353, 439 S.E.2d 50, 53 (1993); *Battersby v. Boyer*, 241 Ga. App. 115, 118, 526 S.E.2d 159, 162-63 (1999); *see also Federal Ins. Co. v. Farmer's Supply Store, Inc.*, 252 Ga. App. 17, 19, 555 S.E.2d 238, 240

(2001) (explaining vendors who purchase and sell articles in the usual course of trade may assume the manufacturer properly constructed the article); *but see Crowley v. Lane Drug Stores, Inc.*, 54 Ga. App. 859, 860, 189 S.E. 380, 381 (1936) (stating a retailer may be liable if it handles ice cream containing a shard of glass by removing it from the original container and scooping it into a cone or dish before providing it to the consumer); *Albany Coca-Cola Bottling Co. v. Shiver*, 67 Ga. App. 359, 364-65, 20 S.E.2d 181, 184-85 (1942) (stating a retailer may be liable where the beverage product is contained in clear glass and would allow detection of the presence of the defect).

143. *Farmer v. Brannan Auto Parts*, 231 Ga. App. 353, 355, 498 S.E.2d 583, 585 (1998); *Hester*, 211 Ga. App. at 353-54, 439 S.E.2d at 53; *Battersby*, 241 Ga. App. at 118, 526 S.E.2d at 162.

144. *Farmer*, 231 Ga. App. at 354, 498 S.E.2d at 585 (citing *Beam v. Omark Indus.*, 143 Ga. App. 142, 237 S.E.2d 607 (1977); *Bishop v. Farhat*, 227 Ga. App. 201, 206, 489 S.E.2d 323, 328 (1997)).

145. *Boyce v. Gregory Poole Equip. Co.*, 269 Ga. App. 891, 896, 605 S.E.2d 384, 389 (2004).

146. *Ballard v. S. Reg'l Med. Ctr.*, 216 Ga. App. 96, 99, 453 S.E.2d 123, 125 (1995); *S. Bell Tel. & Tel. Co. v. LaRoche*, 173 Ga. App. 298, 299, 325 S.E.2d 908, 910 (1985).

147. *Sams v. Wal-Mart Stores, Inc.*, 228 Ga. App. 314, 316, 491 S.E.2d 517, 519 (1997); *see also Persinger*, 253 Ga. App. 768, 770-71, 560 S.E.2d 333, 336-37 (2002) (explaining *res ipsa loquitor* should be applied with caution and only in circumstances where the evidence presented shows, to an appreciable degree, the conclusion claimed).

148. *Miller v. Ford Motor Co.*, 287 Ga. App. 642, 645, 653 S.E.2d 82, 84 (2007).

149. *Williams v. Am. Med. Sys.*, 248 Ga. App. 682, 689, 548 S.E.2d 371, 374 (2001); *see also Persinger*, 253 Ga. App. at 770, 560 S.E.2d at 336.

150. *Ogletree v. Navistar Int'l Transp. Corp.*, 194 Ga. App. 41, 41-47, 390 S.E.2d 61, 66 (1989) (*overruled on other grounds, see supra* note 1).

151. *McCorkle v. Dept. of Transp.*, 257 Ga. App. 397, 398-99, 571 S.E.2d 160, 163 (2002) (citing *Thomas v. Dept. of Transp.*, 232 Ga. App. 639, 502 S.E.2d 748 (1998)); *see also Gen. Motors Corp. v. Moseley*, 213 Ga. App. 875, 882, 447 S.E.2d 302, 310 (1994), *abrogated on other grounds by Webster v. Boyett*, 269 Ga. 191, 496 S.E.2d 459 (1998) (stating subsequent remedial measures may be admitted in a negligence action "when the subsequent repair, change, or modification tends to prove some fact of the case on trial (other than belated awareness of negligence, of course), to show contemporary knowledge of

the defect, causation, a rebuttal of a contention that it was impossible for the accident to happen in the manner claimed, and so on.").

152. *Pepper v. Selig Chem. Indus.*, 161 Ga. App. 548, 551, 288 S.E.2d 693, 696 (1982); *Union Carbide Corp. v. Holton*, 136 Ga. App. 726, 729, 222 S.E.2d 105, 108-09 (1975).

153. *Jonas v. Isuzu Motors Ltd.*, 210 F. Supp. 2d 1373, 1379 (M.D. Ga. 2002).

154. *Union Carbide Corp*, 136 Ga. App. at 730-32, 222 S.E.2d at 109-11.

155. *Bossard v. Atlanta Neighborhood Dev. P'ship, Inc.*, 254 Ga. App. 799, 800, 564 S.E.2d 31, 34 (2002); *Bowen v. Cochran*, 252 Ga. App. 457, 459, 556 S.E.2d 530, 532 (2001); *N. Ga. Elec. Membership Corp. v. Webb*, 246 Ga. App. 316, 319, 540 S.E.2d 271, 275 (2000).

156. O.C.G.A. § 51-11-7; *Union Camp Corp. v. Helmy*, 258 Ga. 263, 264, 367 S.E.2d 796, 797 (1988).

157. *Prillaman v. Sark*, 255 Ga. App. 781, 782, 567 S.E.2d 76, 77 (2002); *Desai v. Silver Dollar City*, 229 Ga. App. 160, 164-65, 493 S.E.2d 540, 544 (1997).

158. *Rubin v. Cello Corp.*, 235 Ga. App. 250, 252, 510 S.E.2d 541, 543 (1998); *Prillaman*, 255 Ga. App. at 782, 567 S.E.2d at 77 (citing *Rubin*).

159. *Rubin*, 235 Ga. App. at 252, 510 S.E.2d at 543; *Prillaman*, 255 Ga. App. at 782, 567 S.E.2d at 77 (citing *Rubin*).

160. *Battersby v. Boyer*, 241 Ga. App. 115, 116, 526 S.E.2d 159, 161 (1999), citing *Yaeger v. Stith Equip. Co.*, 177 Ga. App. 835, 341 S.E.2d 492 (1986).

161. *Hunt v. Harley Davidson Motor Co., Inc.*, 147 Ga. App. 44, 45, 248 S.E.2d 15, 16 (1978).

162. *Parker v. Brush Wellman, Inc.*, Nos. 1:04-CV-606-RWS, 1:08-CV-02725-RWS, 2010 U.S. Dist. LEXIS 88355, at *19 (N.D. Ga. Aug. 25, 2010) (citing *Tomlinson v. Resqline, Inc.*, 2006 U.S. Dist. LEXIS 30348 (N.D. Ga. Apr. 24, 2006)) (applying Georgia law).

163. *Vickery v. Waste Mgmt. of Ga.*, 249 Ga. App. 659, 661, 549 S.E.2d at 482, 484; *Moore v. ECI Mgmt.*, 246 Ga. App. 601, 606,542 S.E.2d 115, 121 (2000); *Fluidmaster, Inc. v. Severinsen*, 238 Ga. App. 755, 756, 520 S.E.2d 253, 255 (1999) (finding that it was obvious that internal component parts of a device such as a toilet would wear out over time and therefore the manufacturer had no duty to warn); *Vax v. Albany Lawn & Garden Ctr.*, 209 Ga. App. 371, 372, 433 S.E.2d 364, 366 (1993); *but see Raymond v. Amada Co. Ltd.*, 925 F. Supp. 1572, 1576-77 (N.D. Ga. 1996) (applying Georgia law) (stating the "open and obvious" rule is no longer an absolute defense).

164. *Weatherby v. Honda Motor Co., Ltd.*, 195 Ga. App. 169, 171, 393 S.E.2d 64, 66 (1990) (*overruled on other grounds, see supra* note 1).

165. *Weatherby*, 195 Ga. App. at 173, 393 S.E.2d at 68; *Royal v. Ferrellgas, Inc.*, 254 Ga. App. 696, 705, 563 S.E.2d 451, 459 (2002) ("When the injured party is aware of the danger, failure to warn of that danger cannot be the proximate cause of the injury.").

166. *Talley*, 158 Ga. App. at 137, 279 S.E.2d at 271.

167. *Giordano v. Ford Motor Co.*, 165 Ga. App. 644, 644 299 S.E.2d 897, 898-99 (1983).

168. *Askew v. DC Med. LLC*, No. 1:11-cv-1245-WSD, 2011 U.S. Dist. LEXIS 50817, at *12 (N.D. Ga. May 12, 2011) (citing *Bishop v. Farhat*, 227 Ga. App. 201, 489 S.E.2d 323 (1997)).

169. *Dorsey Trailers Se., Inc. v. Brackett*, 185 Ga. App. 172, 175, 363 S.E.2d 779, 782 (1987); *Omark Indus., Inc. v. Alewine*, 171 Ga. App. 207, 208-09, 319 S.E.2d 24, 25-26 (1984).

170. *Cobb Heating & Air Conditioning Co. v. Hertron Chem. Co.*, 139 Ga. App. 803, 804, 229 S.E.2d 681,682 (1976); *Dorsey Trailers Se.*, 185 Ga. App. at 175, 363 S.E.2d at 782.

171. *Cobb Heating*, 139 Ga. App. at 804, 229 S.E.2d at 682; *but see Wilson Foods Corp. v. Turner*, 218 Ga. App. 74, 75, 460 S.E.2d 532, 534 (1995) (failure to read a warning does not bar recovery where plaintiff is challenging manufacturer efforts to communicate warnings and is merely circumstantial evidence of the inadequacy of the warning).

172. *Johnson v. Ford Motor Co.*, 281 Ga. App. 166, 173, 637 S.E.2d 202, 207 (2006), *overruled on other grounds by Campbell v. Altec Indus., Inc.*, 288 Ga. 535, 707 S.E.2d 48 (2011).

173. *DeLoach v. Rovema Corp.*, 241 Ga. App. 802, 804, 527 S.E.2d 882, 883 (2000); *Chrysler Corp. v. Batten*, 264 Ga. 723, 724, 450 S.E.2d 208, 211 (1994); O.C.G.A. § 51-1-11(c).

174. *Hunter v. Werner Co.*, 258 Ga. App. 379, 383-84, 574 S.E.2d 426, 431 (2002).

175. *DeLoach*, 241 Ga. App. at 804, 527 S.E.2d at 883.

176. *McGinty v. Goldens' Foundry & Mach. Co.*, 208 Ga. App. 248, 249, 430 S.E.2d 185, 187 (1993); *Blossman Gas Co. v. Williams*, 189 Ga. App. 195, 198, 375 S.E.2d 117, 120 (1988).

177. *Freeman v. United Cities Propane Gas of Ga.*, 807 F. Supp. 1533, 1537-38 (M.D. Ga. 1992) (applying Georgia law).

178. *Williams v. Am. Med. Sys.*, 248 Ga. App. 682, 685, 548 S.E.2d 371, 375 (2001); *Wheat v. Sofamor S.N.C.*, 46 F. Supp. 2d 1351, 1364 (N.D. Ga. 1999; *Presto v. Sandoz Pharms. Corp.*, 226 Ga. App. 547, 548, 487 S.E.2d 70, 73 (1997); *Hawkins v. Richardson-Merrell, Inc.*, 147 Ga. App. 481, 482-83, 249 S.E.2d 286, 287-88 (1978); *see also Chamblin v. K-Mart Corp.*, 272 Ga. App. 240, 244, 612 S.E.2d 25, 28 (2005) (discharging a pharmacist's duty to warn consumer based on the learned intermediary doctrine); *Lance v. Am. Edwards Lab.*, 215 Ga. App. 713, 716, 452 S.E.2d 185, 187 (1994) (extending the learned intermediary doctrine to distributors of medical devices).

179. *McCombs v. Synthes*, 277 Ga. 252, 253, 587 S.E.2d 594, 595 (2003).

180. *McCombs v. Synthes*, 266 Ga. App. 304, 304, 596 S.E.2d 780, 780 (2004) (affirming trial court's finding that warning was adequate and reasonable under the circumstances of the case).

181. *Wheat*, 46 F. Supp. 2d at 1365.

182. *Wheat*, 46 F. Supp. 2d at 1363.

183. *Stuckey v. N. Propane Gas Co.*, 874 F.2d 1563, 1568 (11th Cir. 1989) (applying Georgia law); *Long v. Amada Mfg. Am., Inc.*, No. 1:02-CV-1245, 2004 U.S. Dist. LEXIS 30708, at *60 (N.D. Ga. 2004); *Carter v. E.I. DuPont de Nemours & Co., Inc.*, 217 Ga. App. 139, 143,456 S.E.2d 661, 664 (1995).

184. *Exxon Corp. v. Jones*, 209 Ga. App. 373, 375, 433 S.E.2d 350, 353 (1993) (applying doctrine to gas company); *Brown v. Apollo Indus.*, 199 Ga. App. 260, 263, 404 S.E.2d 447, 450 (1991) (applying doctrine to manufacturer of cleaning supplies); *Eyster v. Borg-Warner Corp.*, 131 Ga. App. 702, 704-05, 206 S. E.2d 668, 670 (1974) (applying doctrine to manufacturer of heating and air conditioning units).

185. *Stuckey*, 874 F.2d at 1568 (applying Georgia law).

186. O.C.G.A. § 11-2-314(2)(c).

187. *Best Canvas Prods. & Supplies, Inc. v. Ploof Truck Lines, Inc.*, 713 F.2d 618, 620 (Ga. Ct. App. 1983); *Evershine Prods., Inc. v. Schmitt*, 130 Ga. App. 34, 35, 202 S.E.2d 228, 231 (1973).

188. O.C.G.A. § 11-2-318; *Ellis v. Rich's, Inc.*, 233 Ga. 573, 575-76, 212 S.E.2d 373, 375 (1975).

189. *Decatur N. Assoc., Ltd. v. Builders Glass, Inc.*, 180 Ga. App. 862, 864, 350 S.E.2d 795, 797 (1986).

190. *See EvershineProds.*, 130 Ga. App. at 36, 202 S.E.2d at 231 ("[A]n express warranty by implication, arising out of the words on the label . . . could only apply if the article was used . . . according to the directions on the label."); *see also Dryvit Sys., Inc. v. Stein*, 256 Ga. App. 327, 328, 568 S.E.2d 569, 570 (2002) (holding that a manufacturer is entitled to summary judgment on a breach of warranty claim where a consumer fails to comply with a mandatory notice provision in the manufacturer's warranty).

191. *See Advanced Computer Sales, Inc. v. Sizemore*, 186 Ga. App. 10, 10, 366 S.E.2d 303, 304-05 (1988); *Citicorp Indus. Credit, Inc. v. Rountree*, 185 Ga. App. 417, 420, 364 S.E.2d 65, 68 (1987).

192. *DeLoach v. Gen. Motors*, 187 Ga. App. 159, 159, 369 S.E.2d 484, 485 (1988).

HAWAII

A. **CAUSES OF ACTION**

Hawaii recognizes actions for strict liability, negligence, and breach of warranty.

B. **STRICT LIABILITY**

1. **The Standard**

    Hawaii courts had long followed the definition given in Restatement (Second) of Torts Section 402A (1965) with one exception: Section 402A specifies a defective product that is unreasonably dangerous, while Hawaii omitted the term "unreasonably."[1] However, case law defines "defect" as an "unreasonably dangerous" condition.[2] Accordingly, to make out a prima facie case of strict products liability, a plaintiff must prove (1) a defect in the product that rendered it unreasonably dangerous for its intended or reasonably foreseeable use; and (2) a causal connection between the defect and the plaintiff's injuries.[3] The plaintiff must also show that the seller or distributor of the defective product is engaged in the business of selling or distributing such product.[4]

2. **"Product"**

    Whether an object is a product for purposes of strict liability should be determined on a case-by-case basis.[5] An escalator in a commercial building accessible to the general public constitutes a product for purposes of a strict liability claim against the manufacturer or distributor of the escalator but not as to the premises owner.[6]

3. **"Defect"**

    A product is dangerously defective if it does not meet the reasonable expectations of the ordinary consumer or user as to its safety when the product is used in its intended or reasonably foreseeable manner.[7]

    A product may be defective under one of three general theories: defective manufacture, defective design, or insufficient warning.[8] The manufacturer's failure to equip its product with a safety device may constitute a design defect[9] although a manufacturer is not subject to an independent continuing duty to "retrofit" its product with aftermarket manufacturer safety equipment.[10] There are two tests to determine whether a product is defective: the consumer expectation test and the risk-utility test.[11] Under the consumer expectation test, the plaintiff must show that the product failed to perform as safely as an ordinary consumer would expect when the product was used in its intended or reasonably foreseeable manner.[12] Under the risk-utility test, design defect may be found if the plaintiff demonstrates that the product's design was a legal cause of the injuries[13] and the defendant fails to prove, in light of the relevant factors, that the benefits of the design outweigh the risk of danger inherent in the design.[14] The relevant factors a fact finder may consider under the risk-utility test are: (1) the usefulness and desirability of the product; (2) the safety aspects of the product; (3) the availability of a substitute product that would meet the same need and not be unsafe; (4) the manufacturer's ability to eliminate the unsafe character of the product without impairing its usefulness or making it too expensive to maintain its utility; (5) the user's ability to avoid danger by the exercise of care in the use of the product; (6) the user's anticipated awareness of the dangers inherent in the product and their avoidability, because of general public knowledge of the obvious condition of the product, or of the existence of suitable warnings or instructions; and (7) the feasibility, on the part of the manufacturer, of spreading the loss by setting the price of the product or carrying liability insurance.[15] Evidence of a specific defect through expert testimony is not required.[16]

Circumstantial evidence is sufficient,[17] and plaintiff need not produce the specific instrumentality involved.[18] In implied warranty cases, malfunction is not a prerequisite to establishing defect.[19]

4. **Contributory Negligence/Assumption of Risk**

Strict liability[20] and warranty[21] claims are subject to a pure comparative negligence analysis. Express assumption of risk is available as a complete bar to liability in tort and warranty strict product liability actions.[22] Primary implied assumption of risk is abolished; however, secondary implied assumption of risk, which is a form of contributory negligence, is preserved in and subsumed by comparative fault analysis.[23]

5. **Sale or Lease**

Occasional sellers who are engaged in isolated sales of products are not liable for strict liability, unlike manufacturers who are in the business of producing such products.[24]

6. **Inherently Dangerous Products**

Hawaii courts recognize asbestos[25] and chlorine[26] as inherently dangerous. It is obvious to all that swimming pools are dangerous to young children.[27]

7. **Privity**

All persons in the chain of distribution for component parts or final products are strictly liable for harm caused by products defectively designed or manufactured.[28] No privity is required; any consumer or ultimate user of the product may bring an action for product liability.[29]

8. **Failure to Warn**

   A manufacturer must give appropriate warning of any known dangers that the users of its product would not ordinarily discover.[30] The duty to warn consists of two duties: a duty to give adequate instruction for safe use and a duty to give warning as to the dangers inherent in improper use.[31]

   A manufacturer has no duty to warn of open and obvious dangers, such as riding unrestrained in the bed of a pickup truck.[32]

9. **Substantial Change/Abnormal Use**

   In a product liability action, the product must have reached the consumer or ultimate user without substantial change or modification with respect to the alleged defect.[33] The defendant bears the initial burden of showing that a substantial change has been made, after which the burden shifts to the plaintiff to disprove the point.[34]

10. **State of the Art**

    State of the art is not a defense to a strict liability action.[35] Such evidence may be admissible in a negligence action, however, to show that the seller knew or reasonably should have known of the dangerousness of his or her product.[36]

11. **Standards**

    Evidence of industry practices is relevant to, but not determinative of, the negligence issue of due care in the design of a product.[37] Nor is compliance with government regulations an absolute defense in strict liability cases involving inherently dangerous products.[38] A trial court must view a videotape before ruling on its admissibility.[39] Videotapes offered to illustrate the principles used in forming an opinion do not require strict adherence to the facts of the case and are admissible provided they are not misleading and make it clear that they are offered only as illustrations of the principles involved.[40]

12. **Other Accidents**

    Evidence of prior accidents may be admissible to show notice if there is sufficient similarity of circumstances to the subject accident.[41] Evidence of prior accidents may be admissible to show negligence, that the condition was dangerous, or that there was a defect only if there is substantial similarity between the accidents.[42]

13. **Subsequent Remedial Measures**

    Hawaii Rules of Evidence Rule 407 specifically allows evidence of subsequent remedial measures for the purpose of proving dangerous defect in product liability cases.[43]

C. NEGLIGENCE

A person who manufactures or designs a product that injures someone is liable for negligence if he fails to take reasonable measures to protect against foreseeable dangers that pose an unreasonable risk of harm.[44] Among the factors to be considered in determining whether the manufacturer acted reasonably are: (1) balancing the likelihood and gravity of the potential harm against the burden of precautions that would effectively avoid the harm; (2) the style, type, and particular purpose of the product; (3) the cost of an alternative design, since the product's marketability may be adversely affected by a cost factor that greatly outweighs the added safety of the product; and (4) the price of the product itself.[45] The product must include adequate safety devices and warnings.[46] The duty to warn extends to manufacturers that discover a danger concerning the product subsequent to the sale and delivery of the product, even though the danger was not known at the time of sale.[47]

A plaintiff can invoke *res ipsa loquitur* to prove negligence or strict liability where the accident was: (1) one that ordinarily does not occur absent someone's negligence; (2) caused by an agency or instrumentality within the exclusive control of the defendant; and (3) not due to any voluntary action or contribution on the part of the plaintiff.[48]

A plaintiff whose negligence exceeds 50 percent is precluded from recovering under a negligence theory.[49]

A plaintiff may assert a market share theory of liability against a defendant even where the identity of the specific defendant is unknown.[50]

Although physical injury, overt symptoms of emotional distress and actually witnessing the tortious event are not prerequisites to a claim for negligent infliction of emotional distress, the presence or absence of these factors may be relevant to establishing such a claim. The question is not whether serious emotional distress might have resulted, but whether it actually resulted.[51]

D. BREACH OF WARRANTY

Merchant sellers are liable to all consumers and users who are injured if a product fails to meet its express warranties, the implied warranty of merchantability, or the implied warranty of fitness for a particular purpose.[52]

In a breach of the implied warranty of merchantability claim, a plaintiff must prove (1) the seller is a merchant of such goods, and (2) the product was defective or unfit for the ordinary purpose for which it is used.[53] For pleading purposes, it is sufficient for a consumer to plead a cognizable loss under a benefit of the bargain theory—*i.e.*, that the consumer contracted for a safe product but received a defective product—even if the product has not yet caused any external damage.[54]

In a breach of the implied warranty of fitness for a particular purpose claim, a plaintiff must prove (1) plaintiff desired a product for a particular purpose,

(2) defendant had reason to know about this purpose, and (3) the product sold to plaintiff failed to meet that purpose.[55] The implied warranty of fitness may be disclaimed if it is in writing and conspicuous.[56]

Implied warranty claims based on strict liability can be maintained against the merchant seller even though the defect was not detectable by the seller.[57] A plaintiff may recover for emotional distress in tort and implied warranty strict liability actions.[58]

In a breach of express warranty claim, a plaintiff must prove that (1) defendant made an affirmation of fact or promise regarding the product, (2) that statement became part of the basis of the bargain, and (3) the product failed to perform according to the statement.[59] Reliance is not an essential element of a breach of express warranty claim.[60]

E. DAMAGES

The "economic loss rule" applies to bar claims for relief based on either a negligence or strict products liability theory for economic loss stemming from injury only to the product itself.[61] Where the product causes damage to other property, the economic loss doctrine does not apply.[62] To determine what constitutes "the product" and what constitutes "other property," the court must analyze the "object of the bargain" between the parties.[63] Generally, the economic loss rule applies where "the defective product is a component of an integrated system/structure because the damage is to the defective product itself, not 'other property.'"[64] As such, some courts have extended the economic loss rule to preclude "purely economic losses including 'consequential damages' to property other than the allegedly defective product."[65]

The economic loss rule also bars claims for relief based on possible future injury.[66]

F. PUNITIVE DAMAGES

Punitive damages are allowed in product liability cases.[67] Hawaii requires clear and convincing proof of such damages.[68] The Hawaii Tort Reform Act provides that punitive damages are not covered by liability insurance policies unless specifically provided.[69] In reviewing the several decisions of the United States Supreme Court on the issue of punitive damages, the Ninth Circuit Court of Appeals concluded that its constitutional sensibilities were not offended by a 9-to-1 ratio of punitive damages in relation to the actual harm caused, thereby greatly reducing ratios awarded at the trial level that were well in excess of single digits.[70]

G. PRE- AND POST-JUDGMENT INTEREST

Hawaii statute confers upon courts significant discretion to award prejudgment interest.[71] The statute allows the court to designate the commencement date of interest in order to correct injustice when a judgment is delayed for a long period of time for any reason, including litigation delays.[72] The statute is also intended to discourage recalcitrance and unwarranted delays in cases.[73]

Pre-judgment interest is essentially compensatory in nature.[74] The commencement date of the interest period is fixed according to the circumstances of each case, provided that the earliest commencement date in tort cases is when the injury first occurred, and in contract cases, when the breach first occurred.[75] Pre-judgment interest may be awarded for any substantial delay in the proceedings, and no purposeful delay on the part of the non-moving party is required.[76] It may appropriately be denied where (1) the defendant's conduct did not cause any delay in the proceedings; (2) the plaintiff has caused or contributed to the delay in bringing the action to trial; or (3) an extraordinary damage award has already compensated plaintiff.[77] Pre-judgment interest may not be awarded on punitive damages.[78]

Post-judgment interest is fixed by statute at the rate of 10 percent per year.[79]

H. EMPLOYER IMMUNITY

Under the Hawaii Workers' Compensation Act, an employer may not be held liable to an employee in an action for personal injury arising out of and in the course of the employment.[80] Nor may an employer be held liable for contribution to a third-party tortfeasor. There is a statutory exception for claims of sexual harassment or sexual assault and for related emotional distress and invasion of privacy.[81] An employer may also be held liable for indemnity to a third-party tortfeasor based on a contract of indemnity or an independent duty.[82] Employer immunity does not bar suits against coemployees based on willful or wanton misconduct,[83] and it does not bar suits based on non-work injuries.[84]

I. STATUTES

Relevant statutes for product liability actions are the statutes of limitation[85] and the comparative negligence statute.[86] Hawaii's workers' compensation laws permit an action for indemnity based on an express agreement or on the existence of an independent duty.[87] Age of majority is 18.[88]

J. JOINT AND SEVERAL LIABILITY

Effective June 28, 2001, Hawaii amended its Joint Tortfeasor Law.[89] The new Joint Tortfeasor Release Statute, including rights of contribution, repeals the prior Joint Tortfeasor Release Statute and Right of Contribution Statute and enacts a Good Faith Settlement law for joint tortfeasors and co-obligors.[90] Hawaii law is now similar to California's good faith settlement law.[91]

Hawaii's amended Joint Tortfeasor Statute: (1) does not discharge co-defendants from liability; (2) reduces claims against co-defendants by the amount agreed; (3) discharges all liability of the settling defendant, unless there is an express, written agreement to apportion liability; (4) protects the terms of confidential settlements; and (5) places the burden on the party contesting good faith determination.[92]

Joachim P. Cox
Robert K. Fricke
Kamala S. Haake
Cox Fricke LLP
500 Ala Moana Boulevard,
Suite 3-499
Honolulu, Hawaii 96813
(808) 585-9440
(Fax) (808) 524-3838

Endnotes - Hawaii

1. *Brown v. Clark Equip. Co.*, 62 Haw. 530, 541-42, 618 P.2d 267, 274-75 (1980).

2. *Wagatsuma v. Patch*, 10 Haw. App. 547, 564, 879 P.2d 572, 583 (1994), *cert. denied*, 77 Haw. 373, 884 P.2d 1149 (1994); *Tabieros v. Clark Equip. Co.*, 85 Haw. 336, 354, 944 P.2d 1279, 1297 (1997); *Rodriguez v. Gen. Dynamics Armament*, 696 F. Supp. 2d 1163, 1171 (D. Haw. 2010), *rev'd on other grounds*, 510 F. App'x 675 (9th Cir. 2013).

3. *Tabieros*, 85 Haw. at 354, 944 P.2d at 1297.

4. *Nielsen v. Am. Honda Motor Co., Inc.*, 92 Haw. 180, 190 n.14, 989 P.2d 264, 274 (Ct. App. 1999).

5. *Leong v. Sears Roebuck & Co.*, 89 Haw. 204, 207, 211, 970 P.2d 972, 975, 979 (1998). At least one Hawaii court has held that a scuba diving program "constitutes a 'service' rather than a 'product' for the purpose of strict liability." *Isham v. Padi Worldwide Corp.*, Civ. Nos. 07-00382, 07-00386, 2007 U.S. Dist. LEXIS 62419 (D. Haw. Aug. 23, 2007). Hawaii courts have also held that travel guides are not "products" for purposes of strict liability. *Birmingham v. Fodor's Travel Publ'ns*, 73 Haw. 359, 375, 833 P.2d 70, 79 (1992).

6. *Leong*, 89 Haw. at 211, 970 P.2d at 979.

7. *Ontai v. Straub Clinic & Hosp. Inc.*, 66 Haw. 237, 241, 659 P.2d 734, 739 (1983). This is also known as the "consumer expectation" test. *Wagatsuma*, 10 Haw. App. at 566, 879 P.2d at 584.

8. *Wagatsuma*, 10 Haw. App. at 564, 879 P.2d at 583 (citing Ontai, 66 Haw. 237, 659 P.2d 734).

9. *Id.* (citing *Ontai*).

10. *Tabieros*, 85 Haw. at 358, 944 P.2d at 1301.

11. *Wagatsuma*, 10 Haw. App. at 566, 879 P.2d at 584.

12. *Wagatsuma*, 10 Haw. App. at 566, 879 P.2d at 584.

13. Hawaii adopts the "substantial factor" test in determining legal cause. *Knodle v. Waikiki Gateway Hotel, Inc.*, 69 Haw. 376, 390, 742 P.2d 377, 386 (1987).

14. *Masaki v. Gen. Motors Corp.*, 71 Haw. 1, 24, 780 P.2d 566, 579 (1989); *see also Wagatsuma*, 10 Haw. App. at 566-68, 879 P.2d at 584.

15. *Wagatsuma*, 10 Haw. App. at 566-67, 879 P.2d at 584.

16. *Stewart v. Budget Rent-A-Car*, 52 Haw. 71, 76, 470 P.2d 240, 243 (1970).

17. *Stewart*, 52 Haw. at 76, 470 P.2d at 243; *Rodriguez*, 696 F. Supp. 2d at 1179.

18. *Beerman v. Toro Mfg. Corp.*, 1 Haw. App. 111, 115, 615 P.2d 749, 753 (1980).

19. *Larsen v. Pacesetter Sys., Inc.*, 74 Haw. 1, 25-26, 837 P.2d 1273, 1286 (1992).

20. *Hao v. Owens-Illinois, Inc.*, 69 Haw. 231, 236, 738 P.2d 416 (1987).

21. *Larsen*, 74 Haw. at 33, 837 P.2d at 1289-90; *Armstrong v. Cione*, 69 Haw. 176, 180-83, 738 P.2d 79, 82-83 (1987).

22. *Larsen*, 74 Haw. at 36, 837 P.2d at 1291.

23. *Larsen*, 74 Haw. at 37-39, 837 P.2d at 1291-92.

24. *Kaneko v. Hilo Coast Processing*, 65 Haw. 447, 459, 654 P.2d 343, 351 (1982).

25. *Nobriga v. Raybestos-Manhattan, Inc.*, 67 Haw. 157, 161, 683 P.2d 389, 392 (1984), *recon. denied*, 57 Haw. 683, 744 P.2d 779 (1984).

26. *Kajiya v. Dep't of Water Supply*, 2 Haw. App. 221, 225, 629 P.2d 635, 639 (1981).

27. *Wagatsuma*, 10 Haw. App. at 570, 879 P.2d at 585.

28. *Stewart*, 52 Haw. at 75, 470 P.2d at 243; *Rodriguez*, 696 F. Supp. 2d at 1180.

29. *Chapman v. Brown*, 198 F. Supp. 78, 118 (D. Haw. 1961).

30. *Ontai*, 66 Haw. at 248, 659 P.2d at 743.

31. *Ontai*, 66 Haw. at 248, 659 P.2d at 743.

32. *Josue v. Isuzu Motors Am., Inc.*, 87 Haw. 413, 418, 958 P.2d 535, 540 (1998).

33. *Stewart*, 52 Haw. at 75, 470 P.2d at 243.

34. *Stender v. Vincent*, 92 Haw. 355, 373, 992 P.2d 50, 68 (2000).

35. *In re Haw. Fed. Asbestos Cases*, 665 F. Supp. 1454, 1460 (D. Haw. 1986).

36. *Johnson v. Raybestos-Manhattan, Inc.*, 69 Haw. 287, 288 n.2, 740 P.2d 548, 549 n.2 (1987).

37. *Brown*, 62 Haw. at 537, 618 P.2d at 272.

38. *Nobriga*, 67 Haw. at 161-62, 683 P.2d at 392.

39. *Tabieros*, 85 Haw. at 377, 944 P.2d at 1320.

40. *Tabieros*, 85 Haw. at 377, 944 P.2d at 1320.

41. *Warshaw v. Rockresorts, Inc.*, 57 Haw. 645, 652, 562 P.2d 428, 434 (1977).

42. *American Broadcasting v. Kenai Air of Haw.*, 67 Haw. 219, 226-27, 686 P.2d 1, 6 (1984).

43. Haw. R. Evid. 407. In contrast, Federal Rule of Evidence 407 provides that subsequent remedial measures are not admissible to prove "a defect in a product or its design." Fed. R. Evid. 407 (2011).

44. *Ontai*, 66 Haw. at 247, 659 P.2d at 742; *Wagatsuma*, 10 Haw. App. at 565, 879 P.2d at 583. Similarly, a lessor is required to exercise reasonable care to inspect the leased property before turning it over to the lessee. *See Durham v. County of Maui*, No. 08-00342, 2010 U.S. Dist. LEXIS 4807, at *27-28 (D. Haw. Jan. 21, 2010) (quoting Restatement (Second) of Torts § 408, cmt. a). Where the lessor purchased the property from a maker who has a high reputation for the quality of its product, the lessor has a duty to inspect only to the same extent as any other purchaser. *Durham*, 2010 U.S. Dist. LEXIS 4807, at *27-28.

45. *Wagatsuma*, 10 Haw. App. at 565, 879 P.2d at 583.

46. *Brown*, 62 Haw. at 539-40, 618 P.2d at 273.

47. *Tabieros*, 85 Haw. at 355, n.11, 944 P.2d 1298, n.11.

48. *Windward Aviation, Inc. v. Rolls-Royce Corp.*, No. 10-00542, 2011 U.S. Dist. LEXIS 72608, at *72 (D. Haw. July 6, 2011) (citing *Carlos v. MTL, Inc.*, 77 Haw. 269, 277-78, 280, 883 P.2d 691, 699-700, 702 (Ct. App. 1994)).

49. Haw. Rev. Stat. § 663-31 (1984).

50. *Smith v. Cutter Biological, Inc.*, 72 Haw. 416, 437, 823 P.2d 717, 729 (1991).

51. *Tabieros*, 85 Haw. at 361-62, 944 P.2d at 1304-05.

52. *See Ontai*, 66 Haw. at 249-52, 659 P.2d at 744.

53. *Nielsen v. Am. Honda Co., Inc.*, 92 Haw. 180, 190, 989 P.2d 264, 274 (Ct. App. 1999).

54. *Baker v. Castle & Cooke Homes Haw., Inc.*, Civ. No. 11-00616, 2012 U.S. Dist. LEXIS 57954, at *42-47 (D. Haw. Apr. 25, 2012) (declining to dismiss breach of implied warranty of merchantability claim where plaintiffs alleged that the yellow brass fittings defendant manufactured were inherently defective, will result in damage, and violate the Honolulu Plumbing Code). Hawaii courts have not adopted the custom product exception. *See Keahole Point Fish LLC v. Skretting Canada Inc.*, 971 F. Supp. 2d 1017, 1035 (D. Haw. 2013).

55. *Nielsen*, 92 Haw. at 191, 989 P.2d at 275.

56. Haw. Rev. Stat. § 490:2-316(2); *see also Keahole Point Fish*, 971 F. Supp. 2d at 1037 (finding disclaimer not "conspicuous" where the disclaiming language was located at the bottom of the product sheet, in the same font as the main text though in a smaller font size, and there was no heading separating the disclaimer from the main text).

57. *See Ontai*, 66 Haw. at 249-52, 659 P.2d at 744.

58. *Larsen*, 74 Haw. at 43, 837 P.2d at 1294.

59. *Nielsen*, 92 Haw. at 190-91, 989 P.2d at 274-75.

60. *Torres v. Northwest Eng'g Co.*, 86 Haw. 383, 392, 949 P.2d 1004, 1013 (1997).

61. *State by Bronster v. U.S. Steel Corp.*, 82 Haw. 32, 919 P.2d 294 (1996); *Windward Aviation*, 2011 U.S. Dist. LEXIS 72608, at *18-19.

62. *Windward Aviation*, 2011 U.S. Dist. LEXIS 72608, at *18.

63. *Windward Aviation*, 2011 U.S. Dist. LEXIS 72608, at *19.

64. *Keahole Point Fish*, 971 F. Supp. 2d at 1029 (quoting *Ass'n of Apartment Owners of Newtown Meadows v. Venture 15*, 115 Haw. 232, 167 P.3d 225 (2007)).

65. *Id.* (quoting *Burlington Ins. Co. v. United Coatings Mfg. Co., Inc.*, 518 F. Supp. 2d 1241, 1254 (D. Haw. 2007)). The court in *Keahole Point Fish* found that, at least in the context of fish feed, even though allegedly defective fish feed caused damage to plaintiff's fish (*i.e.*, "other property"), the economic loss rule nonetheless barred plaintiff's damages for lost revenue, actual feed cost incurred, and additional costs incurred because such damages were purely economic in nature and did not seek damages for injury to the fish. 971 F. Supp. 2d at 1030-31.

66. *Baker*, 2012 U.S. Dist. LEXIS 57954, at *22-31.

67. *Beerman*, 1 Haw. App. at 118-19, 615 P.2d at 755.

68. *Masaki*, 71 Haw. at 16, 780 P.2d at 575.

69. Haw. Rev. Stat. § 431:10-240 (1987).

70. *Planned Parenthood of the Columbia/Williamette, Inc. v. American Coalition of Life Activists*, 422 F.3d 949 (9th Cir. 2005).

71. Haw. Rev. Stat. § 636-16 (1993).

72. *Page v. Domino's Pizza, Inc.*, 80 Haw. 204, 209, 908 P.2d 552, 557 (Ct. App. 1995).

73. *Page*, 80 Haw. at, 209, 908 P.2d at 557; *Ditto v. McCurdy*, 86 Haw. 93, 114, 947 P.2d 961, 982 (Ct. App. 1997) ("[O]ne of the purposes of pre-judgment interest is to cut delays in litigation, and to undo substantial injustice caused by such delays"), *rev'd in part on other grounds*, 86 Haw. 84, 947 P.2d 952 (1997).

74. *Roxas v. Marcos*, 89 Haw. 91, 153, 969 P.2d 1209, 1271, *recon. denied*, 1999 Haw. LEXIS 95 (Haw. Jan. 28, 1999).

75. Haw. Rev. Stat. § 636-16 (1993); *Eastman v. McGowan*, 86 Haw. 21, 946 P.2d 1317 (1997).

76. *Ditto*, 86 Haw. 93, 113-14, 947 P.2d 961, 981-82.

77. *Roxas*, 89 Haw. 91, 153, 969 P.2d 1209, 1271; *see also Weite v. Momohara*, 124 Haw. 236, 266, 240 P.3d 899, 929 (Ct. App. 2010) (citing *Page*, 80 Haw. at 209, 908 P.2d at 557).

78. *Ditto*, 86 Haw. 93, 114, 947 P.2d 961, 982.

79. Haw. Rev. Stat. § 478-3 (1993).

80. Haw. Rev. Stat. § 386-5 (1993).

81. Haw. Rev. Stat. § 386-5 (1993).

82. *Kamali v. Hawaiian Elec. Co., Inc.*, 54 Haw. 153, 504 P.2d 861 (1972); *Keawe v. Hawaiian Elec. Co., Inc.*, 65 Haw. 232, 649 P.2d 1149, *recon. denied*, 65 Haw. 682 (1982).

83. Haw. Rev. Stat. § 386-8 (1993).

84. *Hough v. Pac. Ins. Co., Ltd.*, 83 Haw. 457, 927 P.2d 858 (1996) (exclusive remedy provision of workers' compensation statutes does not preclude a worker from bringing an action against the workers' compensation insurer for a separate claim of intentional torts and bad faith in processing the workers' compensation claim, resulting in additional injury to the worker).

85. *See, e.g.*, Haw. Rev. Stat. § 657-7 (1972) (two years for property damage and personal injury actions); § 490:2-725 (1965) (four years for breach of implied warranty of merchantability).

86. Haw. Rev. Stat. § 663-31 (1984); *see also Suzuki v. Castle & Cooke Resorts*, 124 Haw. 230, 232-33, 239 P.3d 1280, 1282 (Ct. App. 2010).

87. *Kamali*, 54 Haw. at 159, 504 P.2d at 865.

88. Haw. Rev. Stat. § 577-1 (1975).

89. Haw. Rev. Stat. § 663-15.5 (2002).

90. Haw. Rev. Stat. § 663-15.5 (2002).

91. *See* Cal. Civ. Proc. § 877.6.

92. *See Troyer v. Adams*, 102 Haw. 399, 77 P.3d 83 (2003).

IDAHO

A. **CAUSES OF ACTION**

Under Idaho law, litigation arising from the use of a product may include causes of action for strict liability under Restatement (Second) of Torts Section 402A (1964); common law negligence; breach of warranty, including Uniform Commercial Code implied and express warranties;[1] the Idaho Consumer Protection Act;[2] and Idaho's Motor Vehicle Express Warranties Act (Lemon Law).[3] Product liability actions are governed by the Idaho Products Liability Reform Act (IPLRA).[4] The IPLRA modified previously existing product liability law to the extent that it was inconsistent with the Act.[5]

B. **STATUTES OF LIMITATION**

An action for personal injuries based on negligence, strict liability, or breach of warranty must be brought within two years after the cause of action accrues.[6] Generally, a cause of action accrues at the time of wrongdoing, rather than the time of discovery of a wrongful act.[7] However, in cases where damages arise from concealed acts, from a foreign object left in the body of a person, or in cases of professional malpractice, the cause of action arises when some damage relating to the wrongful act or omission becomes "objectively ascertainable," such that objective proof would support the existence of actual injury.[8]

Actions brought under IPLRA must be commenced within the two years after the claim accrues, provided damages do not arise from a breach of express or implied warranty.[9] A cause of action for property damage arising from the breach of an express or implied warranty must be commenced within four years after the breach occurs.[10] Parties may contract to reduce the period of limitations for express warranties to not less than one year but cannot agree to extend the period of limitations to more than four years.[11]

IPLRA bars product liability actions after the expiration of the product's "useful safe life," unless the manufacturer expressly warrants otherwise.[12] A manufacturer may prove the expiration of the product's useful safe life by a preponderance of the evidence.[13] Alternatively, a manufacturer may rely on a rebuttable presumption that, ten years after the initial sale of a product, the useful safe life of the product has expired.[14] This rebuttable presumption is statutorily characterized as a "statute of repose" and has survived constitutional challenge.[15] The Idaho Supreme Court has held that there are two ways to overcome this presumption: (1) by establishing the product at issue falls within a class of products that have a useful safe life in excess of the presumptive period; or (2) by establishing that the particular product was operating within its useful safe life.[16] To be qualified as an expert as to useful safe life, a witness must be shown to have experience in actually assessing the useful safe life—span of products similar to the one at issue.[17] This experience may be obtained through academic training, practical experience, and or specialized knowledge.[18] At trial, the presumption may only be rebutted by clear and convincing evidence.[19] Exceptions to the useful safe life defense include express warranties exceeding the ten-year period, hidden defect, and fraudulent concealment.[20]

A six-year statute of repose applies to tort actions arising out of the design or construction of improvements to real property.[21] A cause of action accrues when damages are suffered or six years after the completion of the construction, whichever occurs first.[22] Idaho courts have applied this statute of repose to bar a product liability action stemming from an alleged defect in a control switch on equipment installed in a factory.[23] The court ruled that the equipment was a fixture and therefore an improvement to real property.[24] The limitation of action on improvements to real property has survived constitutional challenge.[25]

C. STRICT LIABILITY

1. The Standard

Idaho has adopted the Restatement (Second) of Torts Section 402A,[26] which gives rise to a cause of action for strict liability if a product is defective *and* is unreasonably dangerous to person or property. A product is unreasonably dangerous if it is more dangerous than would be expected by an ordinary person who may reasonably be expected to use it.[27] For example, whether irrigation equipment was defective and unreasonably dangerous should be viewed from the perspective of a farmer or qualified maintenance person.[28] A plaintiff may establish that a product was defectively designed and unreasonably dangerous by presenting evidence of a feasible alternative design available to the manufacturer, at the time of manufacturing, that would have reduced the risk associated with the product.[29]

2. The Defect

A product may be defective due to a defect in design, a defect in the manufacturing process, or inadequate warnings accompanying the product at the time of sale.[30] A product is not necessarily defective and unreasonably dangerous merely because it poses some danger from its contemplated use; the danger posed by the product must be an unreasonable risk of physical injury.[31] A defect may be proved either by direct evidence or from circumstantial evidence and inferences arising therefrom.[32] The occurrence of a malfunction is circumstantial evidence of a defect.[33] This evidence may also be used to prove that the product defect is unreasonably dangerous.[34] If a plaintiff relies on circumstantial evidence, the plaintiff must exclude the possibility of other reasonably likely causes of the accident, but is not required to exclude every likely cause.[35] Plaintiff must prove that the product was defective when it left the control of the manufacturer.[36]

3. **Causation**

Whether a cause of action is based on warranty, negligence, or strict products liability, the plaintiff has the burden of alleging and proving that (1) he/she was injured by the product, (2) the injury was the result of a defective or unsafe product, and (3) the defect existed when the product left the control of the manufacturer.[37] Causation involves both proximate cause and actual cause; proximate cause being the legal policy behind whether responsibility will be extended to the consequences of conduct that has occurred and actual cause being whether the antecedent factors produced a particular consequence.[38]

4. **Contributory Negligence/Assumption of Risk**

Comparative negligence is a defense, but not a complete bar, to a product liability action sounding in negligence; instead liability is apportioned between the parties based on the degree of fault attributed among them.[39] Comparative responsibility is a defense to a product liability action under IPLRA.[40] Assumption of risk is not a valid defense, except in instances of express written or oral consent.[41] Idaho applies a modified comparative fault standard that precludes recovery by a plaintiff if that plaintiff is *as* comparatively responsible as, or *more* comparatively responsible than, the defendant; for example, if a plaintiff is 50 percent at fault and a defendant is 50 percent at fault, the plaintiff does not recover. A plaintiff's comparative responsibility must be less than a particular defendant's comparative responsibility in order to recover from that defendant. For example, if plaintiff is 20 percent at fault, defendant No. 1 is 70 percent at fault, and defendant No. 2 is 10 percent at fault, plaintiff recovers 70 percent of assessed damages from defendant No. 1, but plaintiff does not recover from defendant No. 2.[42] Comparative responsibility that does not bar a plaintiff's recovery results in a *pro rata* reduction in damages.[43]

Under IPLRA, comparative responsibility includes use of a product with an obviously defective condition, use of a product with knowledge of a defective condition, misuse of a product, and alteration of a product.[44]

A claimant's failure to inspect a product to discover a defect will not serve to reduce a plaintiff's award of damages.[45] Similarly, a nonclaimants's failure to observe an obviously defective condition will not serve to reduce a plaintiff's award of damages.[46]

5. **Sale or Lease/Persons Liable**

IPLRA defines "product sellers" as persons or entities engaged in the business of selling products, whether for resale use or consumption, including manufacturers, wholesalers, distributors, and lessors.[47] IPLRA excludes from the definition of product sellers providers of professional services, some providers of nonprofessional services, commercial sellers of used products, and financial lessors.[48] Freight forwarders, parties that arrange for transportation of an allegedly defective product from manufacturer to seller, also are not subject to imputed liability under the IPLRA because their activities are merely related to coordinating and documenting delivery of the product.[49]

Product sellers, other than manufacturers, who neither warrant a product nor have a reasonable opportunity or expertise to perform an inspection of a product that would or should reveal a defect are not liable for injuries caused by the product.[50] This statutory limitation of liability does not apply if (1) the seller knew about the defect; (2) an alteration, modification, or installation of the product by the seller caused plaintiff's injuries; (3) the product design was provided by the seller and was a cause of plaintiff's injuries; (4) the seller is a wholly owned subsidiary of the manufacturer or vice versa; or (5) the product was sold after an expiration date placed on the product by the manufacturer.[51]

These defenses are not available to a non-manufacturer product seller if the plaintiff is unable to pursue a claim against the manufacturer because of insolvency, inability to obtain service of process on the manufacturer, or a judicial determination that a judgment could not be collected against the manufacturer.[52] A product seller may be considered a manufacturer if it holds itself out as the manufacturer.[53]

A product seller entitled to the liability limitation of IPLRA is also entitled to indemnification from the manufacturer for the costs of defense of the action if the manufacturer rejects the product seller's tender of defense.[54]

6. **Inherently Dangerous Products**

Idaho has adopted comment k to the Restatement (Second) of Torts Section 402A (1964), which exempts manufacturers from strict product liability if the product sold is determined to be "unavoidably unsafe."[55] A product may be deemed "unavoidably unsafe" if there were no feasible alternatives available and the product is one which is useful and desirable to society.[56] Knowledge of the product's risks is imputed to the manufacturer.[57] In order for the exemption to strict liability to apply, the product must have been properly prepared and accompanied by proper directions and warnings.[58]

7. **Successor Liability**

Idaho does follow generally a policy of free transferability of assignments of causes of action.[59] Regarding successor liability, Idaho has not expressly addressed the potential liability of a successor corporation for products manufactured by its predecessor. Idaho's Supreme Court recently issued a certified opinion holding that "while legal malpractice claims are generally not assignable, where [a] legal malpractice claim is transferred to an assignee in a commercial transaction along with other business assets and liabilities, such a claim is assignable."[60] Idaho law also recognizes that a cause of action for personal injury caused by wrongful acts or negligence survives the death of either the wrongdoer or the injured party.[61]

8. **Market Share Liability/Enterprise Liability**

The Idaho appellate courts have not specifically addressed market share liability. However, Idaho has adopted comment c to the Restatement (Second) of Torts Section 492 (1965), which recognizes a commercial or business characterization of a joint enterprise.[62]

9. **Privity**

Privity of contract is not required to maintain a cause of action for personal injuries arising from the use of a product.[63] However, the Idaho courts have held the economic loss rule prohibits recovery of purely economic losses in a negligence action because there is no duty to prevent purely economic loss to another.[64] Privity is necessary to maintain an action for economic damages stemming from a breach of warranty [65] or the Idaho Consumer Protection Act.[66]

10. **Failure to Warn**

A cause of action may be maintained in Idaho for failure to warn of dangers that are not open and obvious.[67] The "open and obvious" doctrine is not an absolute bar to recovery in Idaho but rather its applicability is limited by statute.[68] The duty to warn extends to dangers that arise during known or reasonably foreseeable uses of the product.[69]

Whether a danger is open and obvious giving rise to a duty to warn is a question of fact to be decided by a jury.[70] The causal relationship between the alleged failure to warn and plaintiff's injury should not be decided as a matter of law notwithstanding plaintiff's admission that he/she was aware of the hazard that caused his/her injury.[71]

11. **Post-Sale Duty to Warn and Remedial Measures**

IPLRA recognizes the existence of a duty to warn of known defects discovered after a product is designed and manufactured.[72] However, evidence of changes in warnings or instructions is not admissible to prove that a product is defective, but may be used for other purposes upon the court's determination of the probative value of the evidence.[73]

12. **Learned Intermediary**

There are no Idaho cases directly adopting the learned intermediary doctrine. However, the Idaho Supreme Court has made approving reference to the doctrine in dicta.[74]

13. **Substantial Change/Abnormal Use**

   Under IPLRA, "misuse" and "alteration" are defined as conduct affecting comparative responsibility.[75] Misuse occurs when a product is used in a manner that would not be expected of an ordinary reasonably prudent person using the product under similar circumstances.[76] A finding of misuse results in a reduction in the plaintiff's damage award to the extent that the misuse was the proximate cause of the harm.[77]

   Alteration or modification occurs when the design, construction, or formula of a product is changed or when the accompanying warnings or instructions are altered after sale by a party other than the seller.[78] Alteration or modification is not a defense if the alteration was made in accordance with the manufacturer's instructions, was made with the express or implied consent of the manufacturer, or could reasonably be anticipated.[79] Product alteration or modification results in a reduction of the claimant's damages to the extent that the alteration or modification was the proximate cause of the harm.[80]

14. **State of the Art**

   Evidence of changes in a product's design, warning, technological feasibility, or the state of the art is not admissible to prove a product defect if such changes occurred after the product was delivered to a purchaser other than intermediary seller.[81] Such evidence may be admitted for other relevant purposes such as impeachment or to prove ownership or control.[82] Before such evidence can be admitted, the court must determine, outside the presence of the jury, that the probative value of the evidence outweighs its prejudicial effect.[83] Of course, the state of the art of product design or manufacture is admissible to show what was technologically feasible *at the time* a product was manufactured, such evidence being relevant to the question of a defect.[84]

15. **Malfunction**

   Malfunction of a product is circumstantial evidence of a defective condition.[85] When relying on the occurrence of a malfunction as circumstantial evidence of a defect, the plaintiff must exclude other reasonably likely causes of the accident.[86]

16. **Standards and Governmental Regulation**

   Evidence that a product did or did not comply with industry standards is admissible, but not conclusive.[87] Products that are manufactured in compliance with standards set by federal law or regulation are not defective absent evidence of some other nonregulated defect.[88]

17. **Other Accidents**

   Evidence of other accidents is admissible to show the existence of a particular physical condition or defect and, in the case of prior accidents, notice to the manufacturer of a dangerous condition.[89] The trial court in its discretion may exclude evidence of other accidents if they are not substantially similar to the subject case, if the admission of evidence regarding other accidents will raise collateral issues, or if the evidence of the other accidents will tend to confuse the jurors.[90]

18. **Misrepresentations**

Idaho has not expressly recognized a cause of action for misrepresentation under Section 402B of the Restatement (Second) of Torts (1965). Idaho does recognize a common law cause of action for fraud and fraudulent misrepresentation.[91] Negligent misrepresentation claims are narrowly confined to the accountant-client relationship.[92]

19. **Destruction or Loss of Product**

Even though Idaho has not expressly adopted spoliation of evidence as separate tort action, it has recognized that spoliation of evidence is a tort that is closely aligned with the already recognized claim of intentional interference with prospective civil action by spoliation of evidence.[93] Spoliation, or "intentional interference with prospective civil action by spoliation of evidence," requires a state of mind that shows plan or premeditation.[94] Idaho does recognize spoliation of evidence as an evidentiary rule, allowing a negative inference to arise from the destruction.[95]

20. **Economic Loss**

Absent personal injuries or property damage, breach of warranty is the sole remedy for recovery of purely economic damages.[96] The difference between property damage and economic loss is that "[p]roperty damage encompasses damage to property other than that which is the subject of the transaction. Economic loss includes costs of repair and replacement of defective property which is the subject of the transaction, as well as commercial loss for inadequate value and consequent loss of profits or use."[97]

Economic loss may be recoverable in tort under one of the three exceptions to the "economic loss rule": (1) as a loss parasitic to an injury to person or property, (2) where unique circumstances require a different allocation of the risk, or (3) where a "special relationship" exists between the parties.[98] The special relationship exception has been applied in only two situations such as where a professional or quasi professional has performed personal services and where one party has held itself out to the public as having expertise regarding a specialized function and thereby induces reliance on that representation of expertise.[99]

21. **Crashworthiness**

In a crashworthiness case, the plaintiff bears the burden of proving that the vehicle was defective and unreasonably dangerous and that the vehicle's defectiveness enhanced or intensified the injuries rather than caused the accident itself.[100] Idaho recognizes the doctrine of crashworthiness creates a duty on a manufacturer to eliminate unreasonable risks of injury in the event of a collision.[101] A claim under this doctrine arises when evidence shows that the defect enhanced or intensified a party's injuries.[102]

D. NEGLIGENCE

Strict product liability and negligence are not mutually exclusive theories; an injury may give rise to claims that can be asserted under either principle.[103] Failure to prove one of the theories does not preclude the other.[104] To prevail under a cause of action for negligence, a plaintiff must show: (1) a duty or obligation of defendant to protect plaintiff from injury; (2) failure to discharge that duty; and (3) injury resulting from the failure.[105] Whether an action is in negligence, strict liability or breach of warranty, to prevail under a cause of action arising from the use of a product, a plaintiff must show that (1) he/she was injured by the product, (2) the injury was the result of a defective or unsafe product, and (3) the defect existed when the product left the manufacturer's control.[106] Idaho courts have ruled that one who provides a product owes a duty to provide the product in a nondefective condition.[107]

E. BREACH OF WARRANTY

The Idaho Supreme Court has held that implied warranty and strict liability are coextensive causes of action except for the defenses of privity and disclaimer of warranty.[108] In a product liability-personal injury setting, the breach of implied warranty standard is most frequently stated as a failure of the goods to be fit for the ordinary purposes for which such goods are used (*i.e.*, the goods are not merchantable).[109]

An implied warranty of fitness for a particular purpose arises at the time of purchase if the seller knows or has reason to know of a particular purpose for which the products will be used and that the buyer is relying on the seller's skill or judgment to select and furnish goods.[110] Implied warranties may be disclaimed if the disclaimer is a basis of the bargain.[111]

Even though an express affirmation of fact is not conveyed in the transaction, an express warranty may arise from a description of the goods conveyed in prior dealings.[112]

A nonprivity breach of warranty action brought against a manufacturer or seller to recover for personal injuries from a defective product is not governed by the UCC but is governed by tort law.[113] Whether a breach of warranty claim sounds in tort law or is governed by the UCC is a question of law determined by the Court based on whether the plaintiff seeks damages for personal injuries or for economic losses.[114] Such an action finds support in comment m of Section 402A of the Restatement (Second) of Torts (1965). The cause of action is for strict liability in tort and is subject to the common law and the IPLRA.[115]

F. PUNITIVE DAMAGES

Punitive damages may be recovered in actions for strict liability, negligence, and breach of an implied warranty.[116] Punitive damages are defined by statute as noncompensatory damages that serve the public policy of punishing and deterring outrageous conduct.[117] In order to support an award for punitive damages, clear and convincing evidence must show that the defendant acted in a manner that was an extreme deviation from reasonable standards of conduct, such as fraud, malice, oppression, or gross negligence, and that the defendant had an understanding of or disregard for the consequences of his act.[118] Punitive damages may not initially be pled as an element of damages in a complaint. A claim for punitive damages may be added by amendment after the plaintiff presents evidence to the court that there is a "reasonable likelihood" of proving facts at trial sufficient to support an award of punitive damages.[119] Punitive damages are limited to the greater of $250,000 or three (3) times the compensatory damages award.[120]

Punitive damages may be awarded, in the discretion of the court, in cases of repeated or flagrant violations of the Idaho Consumer Protection Act.[121] The statutory "repeated or flagrant" standard is independent of the common law standards.[122]

G. PRE- AND POST-JUDGMENT INTEREST

Pre-judgment interest is allowable only if the amount of liability is liquidated, or if it is readily capable of ascertainment by mathematical process or by a legal or recognized standard.[123] Pre-judgment interest is also allowable when a pretrial or prior offer of settlement was not accepted but the prevailing claimant obtained a judgment that equaled or exceeded the unaccepted offer.[124] Post-judgment interest is automatic at a rate which is recalculated yearly.[125]

H. EMPLOYER IMMUNITY FROM SUIT

The Idaho Worker's Compensation Act's "exclusive remedy provision" exempts the plaintiff's direct employer from tort liability for injuries suffered by the employee in the course and scope of employment.[126] The Idaho Supreme Court has not expressly adopted, or rejected, the "dual capacity doctrine," pursuant to which an employee may sue the employer for tortious conduct arising from a non-employer capacity.[127] A so-called "statutory" (*i.e.*, non-direct) employer who is not liable for the provision of benefits under the Idaho Worker's Compensation Act is not exempt from tort liability.[128]

I. STATUTES

A private right of action exists under the Idaho Consumer Protection Act.[129] The Act declares unfair methods of competition and unfair or deceptive acts or practices in the conduct of any trade or commerce with respect to goods or services to be unlawful.[130] Violation of the Act occurs when a person knows, or in the exercise of due care should know, that he/she has in the past, or is presently engaging in, one of the enumerated proscribed acts or "in any act or practice which is otherwise misleading, false, or deceptive to the consumer."[131] The "due care" language has been suggested to imply a negligence standard.[132] Ascertainable loss of money or property is a prerequisite to private recovery under the Act.[133]

Generally, attorney's fees are not recoverable in actions based upon the traditional strict liability, negligence, and warranty theories.[134] Attorney's fees may be awarded, however, if the gravamen of the lawsuit is the commercial transaction of the parties and constitutes the basis upon which the party is attempting to recover.[135] Attorney's fees may be recoverable in cases involving less than $35,000 or in actions for personal injury where the claim for damages does not exceed $25,000.[136] Attorney's fees are recoverable under the Idaho Consumer Protection Act.[137] Noneconomic damages are limited to a 2003 base of $250,000, adjusted annually.[138] The cap is an individual cap, not an aggregate applicable to all claimants.[139] The limitation does not violate the Idaho constitution.[140]

The age of majority in Idaho is 18.[141]

J. JOINT AND SEVERAL LIABILITY

The doctrine of joint and several liability has been abolished except as to tortfeasors acting as an agent or servant of another party or acting in concert to commit an intentional or reckless act.[142] A joint tortfeasor who settles with plaintiff is not entitled to contribution from another joint tortfeasor whose liability is not extinguished.[143] The settling joint tortfeasor is not released from contribution to the other joint tortfeasors unless the release provides a *pro rata* reduction for the benefit of the non-settling joint tortfeasor.[144] A non-settling joint tortfeasor's liability is not released by another's settlement, unless the release so provides, but is entitled to a reduction of the claim.[145]

Jed W. Manwaring
Judy L. Geier
Evans Keane, LLP
1161 West River Street, Suite 100
P.O. Box 959
Boise, Idaho 83701-0959
(208) 384-1800
(Fax) (208) 345-3514
jmanwaring@evanskeane.com
jgeier@evanskeane.com

ENDNOTES - IDAHO

1. Idaho Code Ann. §§ 28-2-313 to 28-2-318.

2. Idaho Code Ann. §§ 48-601 to 48-619.

3. Idaho Code Ann. §§ 48-901 to 48-913.

4. Idaho Code Ann. §§ 6-1401 to 6-1410.

5. Idaho Code Ann. § 6-1401.

6. Idaho Code Ann. § 5-219(4).

7. Idaho Code Ann. § 5-219(4). *See also Reynolds v. Trout Jones*, 154 Idaho 21, 24, 293 P.3d 645, 648 (2013); *Cosgrove v. Merrell Dow Pharm.*, 117 Idaho 470, 475, 788 P.2d 1293, 1298 (1989); and *Wing v. Martin*, 107 Idaho 267, 270, 688 P.2d 1172, 1175 (1984).

8. *Stuard v. Jorgenson*, 150 Idaho 701, 704-708, 249 P.3d 1156, 1159-1163 (2011); *Blahd v. Richard B. Smith, Inc.*, 141 Idaho 296, 108 P.3d 996 (2005); *Conway v. Sonntag*, 141 Idaho 144, 106 P.3d 470 (2005); *Brennan v. Owens-Corning Fiberglas Corp.*, 134 Idaho 800, 10 P.3d 749 (2000); *Fairway Dev., Co. v. Peterson, Moss, Olsen*, 124 Idaho 866, 865 P.2d 957 (1993); *Chicoine v. Bignall*, 122 Idaho 482, 835 P.2d 1293 (1992); *Griggs v. Nash*, 116 Idaho 228, 775 P.2d 120 (1989).

9. Idaho Code Ann. § 6-1403(2)(b) and (3). *See also Cosgrove v. Merrell Dow Pharm.*, 117 Idaho 470, 475, 788 P.2d 1293, 1298 (1989); and *Wing v. Martin*, 107 Idaho 267, 270, 688 P.2d 1172, 1175 (1984).

10. Idaho Code Ann. § 28-2-725(1).

11. Idaho Code Ann. § 28-2-725(1).

12. Idaho Code Ann. § 6-1403(1)(a) and (b).

13. Idaho Code Ann. § 6-1403(1)(a).

14. Idaho Code Ann. § 6-1403(2)(a).

15. *Olsen v. J. A. Freeman Co.*, 117 Idaho 706, 791 P.2d 1285 (1990).

16. Idaho Code Ann. § 6-1403(2)(a). *See also West v. Sonke*, 132 Idaho 133, 141, 968 P.2d 228, 236 (1998).

17. *West v. Sonke*, 132 Idaho 133, 139, 968 P.2d 228, 235 (1998).

18. *State v. Konechny*, 134 Idaho 410, 414, 3 P.3d 535, 539 (Ct. App. 2000).

19. Idaho Code Ann. § 6-1403(2)(a); *West v. Sonke*, 132 Idaho 133, 139, 968 P.2d 228, 235 (1998); *Oats v. Nissan Motor Corp.*, 126 Idaho 162, 879 P.2d 1095 (1994).

20. Idaho Code Ann. § 6-1403(2)(b).

21. Idaho Code Ann. § 5-241.

22. Idaho Code Ann. § 5-241(a).

23. *West v. El Paso Prods. Co.*, 122 Idaho 133, 137, 832 P.2d 306, 310 (1992).

24. *West v. El Paso Prods. Co.*, 122 Idaho 133, 136, 832 P.2d 306, 309 (1992).

25. *West v. El Paso Prods. Co.*, 122 Idaho 133, 137, 832 P.2d 306, 310 (1992).

26. *Shields v. Morton Chem. Co.*, 95 Idaho 674, 676, 518 P.2d 857, 859 (1974).

27. *Rojas v. Lindsay Mfg. Co.*, 108 Idaho 590, 592, 701 P.2d 210, 212 (1985) (distinguished *on other grounds by Robertson v. Richards*, 115 Idaho 628 (1987)).

28. *Rojas v. Lindsay Mfg. Co.*, 108 Idaho 590, 591, 701 P.2d 210, 211 (1985).

29. *Wilson v. Amneal Pharm., LLC*, 2013 U.S. Dist. LEXIS 181953,*22 (D. Idaho 2013); *Nepanuseno v. Hansen*, 140 Idaho 942, 946, 104 P.3d 984, 988 (Ct. App. 2004).

30. *Brown v. Miller Brewing Co.*, 2014 U.S. Dist. LEXIS 7628, *14 (D. Idaho 2014); *Rindlisbacker v. Wilson*, 95 Idaho 752, 759, 519 P.2d 421, 428 (1974); *Bryant v. Technical Research Co.*, 654 F.2d 1337 (9th Cir. 1981).

31. *Wilson v. Amneal Pharm., LLC*, 2013 U.S. Dist. LEXIS 181953,*22 (D. Idaho 2013); *Puckett v. Oakfabco, Inc.*, 132 Idaho 816, 821, 979 P.2d 1174, 1179 (1999).

32. *Massey v. Conagra Foods, Inc.*, 2014 Idaho LEXIS 151, *8 (2014); *Doty v. Bishara*, 123 Idaho 329, 332, 848 P.2d 387, 389 (1992) remanded by *Truck Ins. Exch. v. Bishara*, 128 Idaho 550, 916 P.2d 1275 (1996); *Farmer v. Int'l Harvester Co.*, 97 Idaho 742, 553 P.2d 1306 (1976).

33. *Doty v. Bishara*, 123 Idaho 329, 332, 848 P.2d 387, 389(1992) remanded by *Truck Ins. Exch. v. Bishara*, 128 Idaho 550, 916 P.2d 1275 (1996); *Farmer v. Int'l Harvester Co.*, 97 Idaho 742, 553 P.2d 1306 (1976).

34. *Westfall v. Caterpillar, Inc.*, 120 Idaho 918, 921, 821 P.2d 973, 975 (1991).

35. *Hurtado v. Land O' Lakes, Inc.*, 153 Idaho 13, 18-19, 278 P.3d 415, 420-421 (2012); *Mortensen v. Chevron Chem. Co.*, 107 Idaho 836, 693 P.2d 1038 (1984).

36. *Westfall v. Caterpillar, Inc.*, 120 Idaho 918, 921, 821 P.2d 973, 975 (1991).

37. *Massey v. Conagra Foods, Inc.*, 2014 Idaho LEXIS 151, *8 (2014).

38. *Massey v. Conagra Foods, Inc.*, 2014 Idaho LEXIS 151, *8 (2014).

39. Idaho Code Ann. § 6-801 (negligence); *Roundtree v. Boise Baseball, LLC*, 154 Idaho 167, 175, 296 P.3d 373, 381 (2013); *Woodburn v. Manco Prods., Inc.*, 137 Idaho 502, 50 P.3d 997 (2002) (negligence of decedent imputed to heirs).

40. Idaho Code Ann. § 6-1404 (product liability).

41. *Roundtree v. Boise Baseball, LLC*, 154 Idaho 167, 174-175, 296 P.3d 373, 380-381 (2013).

42. Idaho Code Ann. §§ 6-801, *et seq.*; *Adams v. Krueger*, 124 Idaho 74, 75, 856 P.2d 864, 865 (1993); *Ross v. Coleman Co., Inc.*, 114 Idaho 817, 761 P.2d 1169 (1988).

43. Idaho Code Ann. §§ 6-801 *et seq.* and 6-1404.

44. Idaho Code Ann. § 6-1405.

45. Idaho Code Ann. § 6-1405(1)(a), (1)(c).

46. Idaho Code Ann. § 6-1405(1)(c).

47. Idaho Code Ann. § 6-1402(1).

48. Idaho Code Ann. § 6-1402(1)(a)-(c).

49. *Delgadillo v. Unitrons Consolidated, Inc.*, 191 Fed. Appx. 547 (9th Cir. 2006) (unpublished opinion).

50. Idaho Code Ann. § 6-1407(1); *Crandall v. Seagate*, 2011 U.S. Dist. LEXIS 7174,*6 (D. Idaho 2011); *Hawks v. EPI Prods. USA*, 129 Idaho 281, 287, 923 P.2d 988, 994 (1996); *Hoopes v. Deere & Co.*, 117 Idaho 386, 390, 788 P.2d 201, 205 (1990).

51. Idaho Code Ann. § 6-1407(1)(a)-(e).

52. Idaho Code Ann. § 6-1407(4).

53. *Hawks v. EPI Prods. USA*, 129 Idaho 281, 286, 923 P.2d 988, 993 (1996).

54. Idaho Code Ann. § 6-1407(2).

55. *Toner v. Lederle Labs., a Div. of Am. Cyanamid Co.*, 112 Idaho 328, 336, 732 P.2d 297, 305 (1987), *answer to certification question conformed*, 828 F.2d 510 (9th Cir. 1987), *cert. denied*, 485 U.S. 942 (1988).

56. *Nepanuseno v. Hansen*, 140 Idaho 942, 946, 104 P.3d 984, 988 (Ct. App. 2004).

57. *Major v. Sec. Equip. Corp.*, 155 Idaho 199, 203, 307 P.3d 1225, 1229 (2013).

58. *Toner v. Lederle Labs.*, 112 Idaho 328, 336, 732 P.2d 297, 305 (1987).

59. *United Heritage Prop. & Cas. Co. v. Farmers Alliance Mut. Ins. Co.*, 2012 U.S. Dist. LEXIS 17592, at *11, 2012 WL. 442881 (D. Idaho 2012)(*citing to Purco Fleet Servs., Inc., v. Idaho State Dep't of Finance*, 140 Idaho 121, 126, 90 P.3d 346 (2004)).

60. *St. Luke's Magic Valley Reg'l Med. Ctr. v. Luciani*, (In re Order Certifying Question to Idaho Supreme Court), 154 Idaho 37, 43, 292 P.3d 661, 667 (2013). *See also St. Luke's Magic Valley Reg'l Med. Ctr. v. Luciani*, 2013 U.S. Dist. LEXIS 143020, 2013 WL 5486863 (D. Idaho 2013).

61. Idaho Code Ann. § 5-327.

62. *Maselli v. Ginner*, 119 Idaho 702, 705, 809 P.2d 1181, 1184 (Ct. App. 1991); *Easter v. McNabb*, 97 Idaho 180, 182, 541 P.2d 604, 606 (1975).

63. *See generally, Brian & Christie, Inc.*, 150 Idaho 22, 244 P.3d 166 (2010).

64. *Blahd v. Richard B. Smith, Inc.*, 141 Idaho 296, 300, 108 P.3d 996, 1000 (2005).

65. *Puckett v. Oakfabco, Inc.*, 132 Idaho 816, 825, 979 P.2d 1174, 1183 (1999).

66. *Duspiva v. Fillmore*, 154 Idaho 27, 35, 293 P.3d 651, 659 (2013); *Taylor v. McNichols*, 149 Idaho 826, 846, 243 P.3d 642, 662 (2010).

67. *Massey v. Conagra Foods, Inc.*, 2014 Idaho LEXIS 151, at *20 (2014); *Liberty Northwest Ins., Co. v. Spudnik Equip. Co. LLC*, 155 Idaho 730, 734, 316 P.3d 646, 650 (2013); *Puckett v. Oakfabco*, 132 Idaho 816, 823-824, 979 P.2d 1174, 1181 (1999).

68. *Watson v. Navistar Int'l Transp. Corp.*, 121 Idaho 643, 660, 827 P.2d 656, 673 (1992). *See also* Idaho Code Ann. § 6-801 and Idaho Code Ann. §6-1405.

69. *Sliman v. Aluminum Co. of Am.* 112 Idaho 277, 280, 731 P.2d 1267, 1270 (1986); *Robinson v. Williamsen Idaho Equip. Co.*, 94 Idaho 819, 827, 498 P.2d 1292, 1300 (1972) (*citing* Restatement (Second) of Torts §§ 388, 497 (1965)).

70. *Watson v. Navistar Int'l Transp. Corp.*, 121 Idaho 643, 661-662, 827 P.2d 656, 674-675 (1992) (*distinguished on this issue by Chapman v. Chapman*, 147 Idaho 756, 761, 215 P.3d 476 (2009)).

71. *Watson v. Navistar Int'l Transp. Corp.*, 121 Idaho 643, 662, 827 P.2d 656, 675 (1992).

72. Idaho Code Ann. § 6-1406(1).

73. Idaho Code Ann. § 6-1406(1) and (2).

74. *Sliman v. Aluminum Co. of Am.*, 112 Idaho 277, 280-284, 731 P.2d 1267, 1270-1274 (1986) (*distinguished by Adams v. United States*, 449 Fed. Appx. 653, 659, 2011 U.S. App. LEXIS 18707, **11 (9th Cir. 2011).

75. Idaho Code Ann. § 6-1405(3) and (4).

76. Idaho Code Ann. § 6-1405(3)(a).

77. Idaho Code Ann. § 6-1405(3)(b).

78. Idaho Code Ann. § 6-1405(4)(a).

79. Idaho Code Ann. § 6-1405(4)(b)(1)-(3).

80. Idaho Code Ann. § 6-1405(4)(b).

81. Idaho Code Ann. § 6-1406(1)(a)-(d); Idaho Rule of Evidence 407.

82. Idaho Code Ann. § 6-1406(2).

83. Idaho Code Ann. § 6-1406(2).

84. *Toner v. Lederle Labs, a Div. of Am. Cyanamid Co.*, 112 Idaho 328, 335-342, 732 P.2d 297, 304-311(1987) (adopting comment k to Restatement (Second) of Tort § 402A (1965) and applying the principles stated therein to product defect cases sounding in strict liability, but declining to extend them to negligence actions, holding instead that similar principles articulated in Sections 291-293 of the Restatement (Second) of Torts (1965) apply). *Edwards v. Conchemco, Inc.*, 111 Idaho 851, 852, 727 P.2d 1279, 1281 (1986) ("*In Farmer v. International Harvester Co.*, 97 Idaho 742, 553 P.2d 1306 (1976), our Supreme Court held that a product defect may be established by circumstantial evidence"). *See generally Fouche v. Chrysler Motors Corp.*, 107 Idaho 701, 692 P.2d 345 (1984).

85. *Toner v. Lederle Labs., a Div. of Am. Cyanamid Co.*, 112 Idaho 328, 337, 732 P.2d 297, 306 (1987), *answer to certification question conformed*, 828 F.2d 510 (9th Cir. 1987), *cert. denied*, 485 U.S. 942 (1988). *Farmer v. Int'l Harvester Co.*, 97 Idaho 742, 553 P.2d 1306 (1976). *See generally, Fouche v. Chrysler Motors Corp.*, 107 Idaho 701, 692 P.2d 345 (1984).

86. *Farmer v. Int'l Harvester Co.*, 97 Idaho 742, 747, 553 P.2d 1306, 1311 (1976).

87. *Westfall v. Caterpillar, Inc.*, 120 Idaho 918, 921, 821 P.2d 973, 976 (1991). *See generally, Tuttle v. Sudenga Indus.*, 125 Idaho 145, 868 P.2d 473 (1994).

88. *See generally Marchand v. JEM Sportwear, Inc.*, 143 Idaho 458, 147 P.3d 90 (2006) (cotton t-shirt manufactured in compliance with standards set by the Flammable Fabrics Act is not defective).

89. *Hawks v. EPI Prods. USA, Inc.*, 129 Idaho 281, 287, 923 P.2d 988, 994 (1996); *Sliman v. Aluminum Co. of Am.*, 112 Idaho 277, 280-284, 731 P.2d 1267, 1270-1274 (1986) cert. denied, 486 U.S. 1031, 100 L. Ed. 2d 601, 108 S. Ct. 2013 (1988).

90. *Hawks v. EPI Prods. USA, Inc.*, 129 Idaho 281, 287, 923 P.2d 988, 994 (1996); *Sliman v. Aluminum Co. of Am.*, 112 Idaho 277, 280-284, 731 P.2d 1267, 1270-1274 (1986) cert. denied, 486 U.S. 1031, 100 L. Ed. 2d 601, 108 S. Ct. 2013 (1988).

91. *Faw v. Greenwood*, 101 Idaho 387, 389, 613 P.2d 1338, 1340 (1980).

92. *Duffin v. Idaho Crop Improvement Ass'n*, 126 Idaho 1002, 1010, 895 P.2d 1195, 1203 (1995).

93. *Cook v. State Dep't of Transp.*, 133 Idaho 288, 298, 985 P.2d 1150, 1160 (1999) (*citing to* Yoakum v. Hartford Fire Ins. Co., 129 Idaho 171, 177, 923 P.2d 416, 422 (1996).

94. *Ricketts v. Eastern Idaho Equip. Co., Inc.*, 137 Idaho 578, 582, 51 P.3d 392, 396 (2002).

95. *Waters v. All Phase Constr.*, 322 P.3d 992, 996 (2014); *Courtney v. Big O Tires, Inc.*, 139 Idaho 821, 823, 87 P.3d 930, 932 (2003) (*citing to Bromley v. Garey*, 132 Idaho 807, 812, 979 P.2d 1165, 1170 (1999)).

96. *Aardema v. U.S. Dairy Sys., Inc.*, 147 Idaho 785, 790, 215 P.3d 505, 510 (2009); *Ramerth v. Hart*, 133 Idaho 194, 196-197, 983 P.2d 848, 850-851 (1999); *Clark v. Int'l Harvester Co.*, 99 Idaho 326, 332-333, 581 P.2d 784, 790-791 (1978).

97. *Brian & Christie, Inc. v. Lieshman Electric, Inc.*, 150 Idaho 22, 26, 244 P.3d 166, 170 (2010) (*quoting Salmon River Sportsman Camps, Inc. v. Cessna Aircraft*, 97 Idaho 348, 544 P.2d 306 (1975).

98. *Aardema Dairy*, 147 Idaho 785, 792, 215 P.3d 505, 508 (2009); *Duffin v. Idaho Crop Improvement Ass'n*, 126 Idaho 1002, 1007-1008, 895 P.2d 1195, 1199-1201 (1995).

99. *Blahd v. Richard B. Smith, Inc.*, 141 Idaho 296, 301, 108 P.3d 996, 1001 (2005); *Duffin v. Idaho Crop Improvement Ass'n*, 126 Idaho 1002, 1008, 895 P.2d 1195, 1201(1995).

100. *Jensen v. Am. Suzuki Motor Corp.*, 136 Idaho 460, 463, 35 P.3d 776 (2001) (*citing to Johnson v. Pischke*, 108 Idaho 397, 403, 700 P.2d 19, 25 (1985)). *See generally, Fouche v. Chyrsler Motor Corp.*, 107 Idaho 701, 692 P.2d 345 (1984).

101. *Jensen v. Am. Suzuki Motor Corp.*, 136 Idaho 460, 463, 35 P.3d 776 (2001) (*citing to Johnson v. Pischke*, 108 Idaho 397, 403, 700 P.2d 19, 25 (1985)).

102. *Jensen v. Am. Suzuki Motor Corp.*, 136 Idaho 460, 463, 35 P.3d 776 (2001) (*citing to Johnson v. Pischke*, 108 Idaho 397, 403, 700 P.2d 19, 25 (1985)). *See generally, Fouche v. Chyrsler Motor Corp.*, 107 Idaho 701, 692 P.2d 345 (1984).

103. *Chancler v. American Hardware Mut. Ins. Co.*, 109 Idaho 841, 846, 712 P.2d 542, 547 (1985).

104. *Chancler v. Am. Hardware Mut. Ins. Co.*, 109 Idaho 841, 846, 712 P.2d 542, 547 (1985) (*distinguish but on other grounds by Market Int'l Ins. Co. v. Erekson*, 153 Idaho 107, 279 P.3d 93 (2012)).

105. *Reardon v. Union Pac. R.R.*, 93 Idaho 833, 834, 475 P.2d 370, 371 (1970) (*citing to H.J. Wood Co. v. Jevons*, 88 Idaho 377, 400 P.2d 287 (1965) and Prosser, Law of Torts, § 30, p. 146 (3d ed. 1964)).

106. *Henderson v. Cominco Am.*, 95 Idaho 690, 696, 518 P.2d 873, 879 (1973). *See generally Fitting v. Dell, Inc.*, 2008 U.S. Dist. LEXIS 41946, 2008 WL 2152233 (D. Idaho 2008).

107. *Bromley v. Garey*, 132 Idaho 807, 979 P.2d 1165 (1999); *Metz v. Haskell*, 91 Idaho 160, 161-162, 417 P.2d 898, 899-900 (1966).

108. *Robinson v. Williamsen Idaho Equip. Co.*, 94 Idaho 819, 824. 498 P.2d 1292, 1297 (1972).

109. Idaho Code Ann. § 28-2-314(2)(c).

110. Idaho Code Ann. § 28-2-315.

111. *Duffin v. Idaho Crop Improvement Ass'n*, 126 Idaho 1002, 1012, 895 P.2d 1195, 1205 (1995) .

112. *Duffin v. Idaho Crop Improvement Ass'n*, 126 Idaho 1002, 1011, 895 P.2d 1195, 1204(1995).

113. *Wilson v. Amneal Pharms. LLC*, 2013 U.S. Dist. LEXIS 181953, at *42-46 (D. Idaho 2013); *Oats v. Nissan Motor Corp. in the United States*, 126 Idaho 162, 168-170, 879 P.2d 1095, 1101-1103 (1994).

114. *Wilson v. Amneal Pharms. LLC*, 2013 U.S. Dist. LEXIS 181953, at *42-46 (D. Idaho 2013); *Oats v. Nissan Motor Corp. in the United States*, 126 Idaho 162, 168-170, 879 P.2d 1095, 1101-1103 (1994).

115. *Wilson v. Amneal Pharms. LLC*, 2013 U.S. Dist. LEXIS 181953, at *42-46 (D. Idaho 2013); *Oats v. Nissan Motor Corp. in the United States*, 126 Idaho 162, 168-170, 879 P.2d 1095, 1101-1103 (1994).

116. *Brown v. Fritz*, 108 Idaho 357, 359-364, 669 P.2d 1371, 1373-1378 (1985) (*distinguished by Roper v. State Farm Mut. Auto. Ins. Co.*, 131 Idaho 459, 958 P.2d 1145 (1998) and *questioned by Walston v. Monumental Life Ins. Co.*, 129 Idaho 211, 923 P.2d 456 (1996)); *Cheney v. Palos Verdes Inv. Corp.*, 104 Idaho 897, 903-906, 665 P.2d 661, 667-670 (1983); *Hatfield v. Max Rouse & Sons, Northwest*, 100 Idaho 840, 851-854, 606 P.2d 944, 955-958 (1980).

117. Idaho Code Ann. § 6-1601(9).

118. Idaho Code Ann. § 6-1604 (1).

119. Idaho Code Ann. § 6-1604 (2).

120. Idaho Code Ann. § 6-1604 (3).

121. Idaho Code Ann. § 48-608(1).

122. *Mac Tools, Inc. v. Griffin*, 126 Idaho 193, 197-198, 879 P.2d 1126, 1130-1131 (1994) (discussing common law standards for punitive awards versus the applicability of the general standard found in I.C. § 6-1604 and specific standards found in other statutes such as I.C. § 48-608, but ultimately upholding a punitive damage award in excess of 26 times the compensatory award). *See also, Wiggins v. Peachtree Settlement Funding (In re Wiggins)*, 273 B.R. 839, 881-882, (Bankr. D. Idaho 2001). Also note, I.C. § 6-1604 was amended in 2003 to require a clear and convincing proof standard for establishing punitive damages and to establish a monetary damage cap of $250,000 or an amount equal to three times the compensatory damage award, whichever is greater.

123. Idaho Code Ann. § 28-22-104; *Child v. Blaser*, 111 Idaho 702, 727 P.2d 893 (Ct. App. 1986).

124. Idaho Code Ann. § 12-301(c).

125. Idaho Code Ann. § 28-22-104.

126. Idaho Code Ann. § 72-211. *See also Rhodes v. Sunshine Mining Co.*, 113 Idaho 162, 164, 742 P.2d 417, 419 (1987).

127. *Rhodes v. Sunshine Mining Co.*, 113 Idaho 162, 168, 742 P.2d 417, 423 (1987) (rejecting the application of the dual capacity doctrine to a joint venture arrangement). *See generally Gavin v. Busch Agric. Resources*, 1993 U.S. App. LEXIS 30536 (9th Cir. 1993) and *Fagundes for Fagundes v. Soloy Conversions, Ltd.*, 1990 U.S. App. LEXIS 18826 (9th Cir. 1990).

128. Idaho Code Ann. § 72-223; *Robison v. Bateman-Hall, Inc.*, 139 Idaho 207, 210-212, 76 P.3d 951, 954-956 (2003) (*distinguished by Liberty Northwest Ins. Corp. v. United States*, 2011 U.S. Dist. LEXIS 138291 (D. Idaho 2011)).

129. Idaho Code Ann. § 48-608(1).

130. Idaho Code Ann. § 48-603.

131. Idaho Code Ann. § 48-603 (17).

132. William J. Batt, *Litigation Under the Idaho Consumer Protection Act*, 20 Idaho L. Rev. 63 (1984).

133. Idaho Code Ann. § 48-608(1).

134. *Northwest Bec-Corp. v. Home Living Serv.*, 136 Idaho 835, 842, 41 P.3d 263, 270 (2002); *Property Mgmt. West, Inc. v. Hunt*, 126 Idaho 897, 894 P.2d 130 (1995); *Chenery v. Agri-Lines Corp.*, 106 Idaho 687, 690, 682 P.2d 640, 643 (Ct. App. 1984).

135. Idaho Code Ann. § 12-120; *Brower v. E.I. DuPont De Nemours & Co.*, 117 Idaho 780, 792 P.2d 345 (1990); *Walker v. Am. Cyanamid Co.*, 130 Idaho 824, 948 P.2d 1123 (1997) (breach of warranty).

136. Idaho Code Ann. § 12-120(1) and (4).

137. Idaho Code Ann. § 48-608(4) and/or subject to 12-month wage increase or decrease set for in Idaho Code Ann. § 72-409(2).

138. Idaho Code Ann. § 6-1603(1).

139. *Carillo v. Boise Tire Co.*, 152 Idaho 741, 751, 274 P.3d 1256, 1266 (2012); *Horner v. Sani-Top, Inc.*, 143 Idaho 230, 235, 141 P.3d 1099, 1104 (2006).

140. *Kirkland v. Blaine County Med. Ctr.*, 134 Idaho 464, 467, 4 P.3d 1115, 1118 (2000).

141. Idaho Code Ann. § 32-101.

142. Idaho Code Ann. § 6-803 (3) and (5).

143. Idaho Code Ann. § 6-803(2).

144. Idaho Code Ann. § 6-806.

145. Idaho Code Ann. § 6-805(1).

Illinois

A. CAUSES OF ACTION

Product liability lawsuits commonly include causes of action for strict liability, negligence, and breach of warranty.[1]

B. STATUTES OF LIMITATIONS AND REPOSE

Generally, a cause of action for personal injuries must be brought within two years of its accrual,[2] while any action for property damage must be brought within five years of its accrual.[3] The limitations period starts to run when the plaintiff knows, or reasonably should know, (1) that he has suffered an injury, and (2) that the injury was wrongfully caused.[4] A cause of action for damages arising from a breach of warranty, however, must be brought within four years after tender of delivery, unless an express warranty extends to future performance beyond the four-year limitations period.[5]

Strict product liability actions are subject to a statute of repose in addition to any other applicable limitations period.[6] Under the statute of repose, the action must be commenced within the shorter of (1) ten years from the date of first sale, delivery, or lease to the initial user, consumer, or other non-seller; or (2) twelve years from the date of any first sale, lease, or delivery of possession by a seller.[7] This time period may be extended if the defendant has expressly promised or warranted the product for a longer period of time.[8] An exception to this statute allows a plaintiff to bring suit within two years from the date plaintiff knew or should have known of the injury, provided that the injury occurred within the repose period and no more than eight years have passed since the injury occurred.[9] A ten-year statute of repose also applies to improvements to real property.[10]

If an individual is legally disabled or under the age of 18 when his cause of action accrues, he may bring an action within two years after the removal of the disability or the date the individual turns 18 years of age, whichever applicable.[11] As long as the injury occurred during the repose period, the strict product liability statute of repose will begin to run at that time as well.[12]

C. STRICT LIABILITY

1. Standard for Liability

Illinois has adopted the strict liability doctrine set forth in Section 402A of the Restatement (Second) of Torts (1965).[13] Under this doctrine, strict liability arises if the product left the defendant's control with a condition making it "unreasonably dangerous."[14] A product is "unreasonably dangerous" if there is "a physical defect in the product itself, a defect in the product's design, or a failure of the manufacturer to warn of the danger or to instruct on the proper use of the product."[15]

In the case of an alleged design defect, a plaintiff may prove that the product was unreasonably dangerous by means of either the "consumer-expectation test" or the "risk-utility test."[16] Under the consumer-expectation test, a product is defectively designed if "'the product failed to perform as safely as an ordinary consumer would expect when used in an intended or reasonably foreseeable manner.'"[17] Under the risk-utility test, the inquiry is whether "'on balance the benefits of the challenged design outweigh the risk of danger inherent in such designs.'"[18]

In a recent decision, the Illinois Supreme Court reaffirmed the validity of both the consumer-expectation test and the risk-utility test in cases involving design defects.[19] The court went on to set forth an "integrated" version of the risk-utility test, under which a number of factors—including consumer expectations—are taken into account in weighing a design's risk against its utility.[20]

Where the evidence presented by either or both parties supports its application, the jury should be instructed as to the risk-utility test.[21] But if the parties frame their evidence "entirely in terms of consumer expectations," the jury should only be instructed as to the consumer-expectation test.[22]

2. **Causation**

To recover under strict liability in tort, a plaintiff bears the burden to show that his injury was proximately caused by the product defect.[23] Proximate cause exists when the defect, in the "natural or probable sequence," produced the injury in question.[24]

3. **Contributory Negligence—Assumption of Risk/Misuse**

Although a plaintiff's contributory negligence is not an absolute defense to strict liability,[25] it is a damage-reducing factor and a complete defense if the plaintiff is more than 50 percent at fault.[26]

A plaintiff's assumption of risk or misuse of the product no longer constitutes an absolute defense to a strict liability action, but is treated as a factor reducing the plaintiff's recovery.[27] In this context, a plaintiff assumes the risk of injury if he is subjectively aware of the unreasonably dangerous condition, but proceeds in the face of that danger.[28] Misuse occurs where the plaintiff used the product for a purpose neither intended nor reasonably foreseeable by the defendant.[29]

4. **Sale or Lease**

Strict liability applies to any entity in a product's chain of distribution,[30] so long as that entity is in the business of supplying such products.[31] Subject to certain conditions, a non-manufacturer defendant can be dismissed from a strict liability action if the manufacturer is amenable to suit.[32]

Generally, strict liability applies to commercial lessors in the business of supplying products.[33]

5. **Successor Liability**

A successor company that purchases the assets of a predecessor is generally not responsible for injuries arising from the predecessor's products.[34] Exceptions are made to this general rule if (1) the successor expressly or impliedly agrees to assume liability; (2) the transfer amounts to a consolidation or merger of the purchaser and seller; (3) the purchaser is a mere continuation of the seller; or (4) if the transaction is for the fraudulent purpose of escaping liability.[35]

6. **Market Share Liability**

The Illinois courts have rejected market share liability[36] as a theory "unworkable under existing Illinois law."[37] In rejecting market share liability, the Illinois Supreme Court noted, among other things, the lack of "reliable information . . . to establish the defendants' percentages of the market," the "tremendous cost" the market share theory would impose on the courts, and the unfairness inherent in the likelihood "that the defendant who actually sold the product is not before the court."[38]

7. **Privity**

No privity is required for a strict liability action; a plaintiff may sue a manufacturer even if he did not buy the product directly from that manufacturer.[39]

8. **Failure to Warn**

A product may be deemed defective solely because "the manufacturer or seller fails to adequately warn of the potential risks or hazards associated with its use."[40] A manufacturer or seller has a duty to warn if it knew or should have known of the danger presented by the product at the time of its production,[41] unless the plaintiff knew or should have known of that danger.[42]

9. **Post-Sale Duty to Warn, Retrofit, or Recall**

The manufacturer of a product is "under no duty to issue post-sale warnings or to retrofit its products to remedy defects first discovered after a product has left its control."[43] Similarly, no Illinois court has yet recognized a duty on the part of a manufacturer to recall a product after it has left the manufacturer's control.[44]

10. **Learned Intermediary Doctrine**

The learned intermediary doctrine constitutes "an exception to the general rule that a failure to warn of a product's dangerous propensities may serve as a basis for holding a manufacturer strictly liable in tort."[45] Under this doctrine, "manufacturers of prescription drugs have a duty to warn prescribing physicians of a drug's known dangerous propensities and . . . physicians, in turn, using their medical judgment, have a duty to convey any relevant warnings to their patients."[46] As a result, "there is no duty on the part of the manufacturer of prescription drugs to directly warn patients."[47]

11. **Third-Party Alterations to Product**

A manufacturer is not responsible for injuries caused by a third party's substantial alteration of the product after the initial sale unless the alteration was reasonably foreseeable.[48]

12. **State of the Art**

"State of the art" evidence—evidence of an alternative product design that is effective, practical, and economical—is admissible but inconclusive as to the existence of a design defect.[49] Thus, while a plaintiff is not required to demonstrate the "availability and feasibility of alternate designs at the time of the product's manufacture," it is one factor that courts consider in determining whether a defect exists.[50]

13. **Malfunction**

A product's malfunction absent "abnormal use or reasonable secondary causes" is *prima facie* evidence of a defect,[51] but only if the product is of a type that would not otherwise be expected to malfunction in normal use.[52]

14. **Customary, Industry, and Government Standards**

Evidence that the product complied with customary, industry, or government standards is admissible but not conclusive.[53]

15. **Other Accidents**

Evidence of other accidents is admissible if the plaintiff proves that the accidents occurred under substantially similar conditions and are of a common cause.[54] Defendants seeking to admit evidence of the absence of prior accidents must establish a foundation of substantial similarity, as well.[55]

16. **Subsequent Remedial Measures**

The Illinois courts are divided regarding the admissibility of subsequent remedial measures to prove the existence of a defect.[56]

17. **Destruction or Loss of Product**

The Illinois courts have held that potential litigants are under "a duty to take reasonable measures to preserve the integrity of relevant and material evidence."[57] Accordingly, a variety of discovery sanctions may be imposed when the product at issue has been altered, lost, or destroyed.

The destruction or alteration of evidence does not automatically entitle a party to a specific sanction, however.[58] Rather, Illinois courts consider the unique factual circumstances of each case to determine the particular sanction to be imposed.[59] Sanctions may include dismissal,[60] exclusion of evidence,[61] or the issuance of an adverse jury instruction.[62] While the preservation of the product is of the utmost importance, the product's absence is not necessarily "fatal to a plaintiff's cause of action."[63]

18. **Economic Loss**

The Illinois Supreme Court has described economic loss as "'damages for inadequate value, costs of repair and replacement of the defective product, or consequent loss of profits-without any claim of personal injury or damage to other property.'"[64] A product liability plaintiff cannot recover solely economic loss on the grounds of strict liability,[65] negligence,[66] or innocent misrepresentation.[67] Illinois courts recognize three exceptions to this rule:

> (1) where the plaintiff sustained damage, *i.e.*, personal injury or property damage, resulting from a sudden or dangerous occurrence; (2) where the plaintiff's damages are proximately caused by a defendant's intentional, false representation, *i.e.*, fraud; and (3) where the plaintiff's damages are proximately caused by a negligent misrepresentation by a defendant in the business of supplying information for the guidance of others in their business transactions.[68]

19. **Crashworthiness**

Under the "crashworthiness doctrine," a manufacturer's liability "may extend in motor vehicle cases to situations in which the defect did not cause the accident or initial impact, but rather increased the severity of the injury over that which would have occurred absent the defective design."[69] This doctrine "recognizes that the foreseeable and intended use of a motor vehicle encompasses the inevitability of collisions and requires the manufacturer to design a vehicle reasonably safe for those foreseeable risks."[70] "It does not, however, place the manufacturer in the position of insurer, but merely extends a manufacturer's duties while invoking the same requirements of liability as in other products liability actions."[71] Thus, a plaintiff is still required "to prove that his injury resulted from a condition of the product, that the condition was an unreasonably dangerous one, and that the condition existed at the time the product left the defendant's control."[72]

Under the crashworthiness doctrine, also known as the "second collision" theory of liability,[73] a plaintiff must prove "only that the design defect was a 'substantial factor' in producing damages over and above those which were probably caused as a result of the original impact or collision."[74] If this has been proven and the injury to the plaintiff is indivisible, "then 'absent a reasonable basis to determine which wrongdoer actually caused the harm, the defendants should be treated as joint and several tortfeasors.'"[75]

While a plaintiff's showing under the crashworthiness doctrine is similar to that necessary in strict product liability actions,[76] the Illinois Supreme Court has observed that this doctrine has been treated as theory of negligence, as well as an amalgamation of negligence and strict liability.[77]

D. NEGLIGENCE

Negligence product liability case law in Illinois generally follows the common law.[78] Some defenses available in a strict liability claim may be unavailable in a claim based on negligence.[79]

By Illinois statute, contributory fault applies to reduce a plaintiff's damages in proportion to the degree to which he is at fault for his injuries, unless the plaintiff is more than 50 percent at fault, in which case recovery is barred.[80]

E. BREACH OF WARRANTY

In Illinois, a plaintiff may bring a product liability action based upon a breach of an express or implied warranty regarding the product.[81]

Generally, a plaintiff must establish privity with the defendant to state a cause of action for breach of implied warranty.[82] Privity need not be shown in personal injury actions, but must be established in actions based on damage to property.[83]

With respect to the statute of limitations, the cause of action accrues upon tender of delivery, regardless of whether the plaintiff knows of the breach.[84]

To maintain a warranty action, a plaintiff must plead and prove that he gave the defendant notice of the alleged breach within a reasonable time after the breach was discovered.[85]

F. FRAUDULENT, NEGLIGENT, AND FALSE MISREPRESENTATIONS

Under Illinois law, a defendant may be held liable for fraudulent or negligent misrepresentations regarding a product.[86] To state a cause of action for fraudulent misrepresentation, a plaintiff must show

> (1) a false statement of material fact, (2) knowledge or belief of the falsity by the party making it, (3) intention to induce the other party to act, (4) action by the other party in reliance on the truth of the statements, and (5) damage to the other party resulting from such reliance.[87]

The elements of negligent misrepresentation are similar, except that the plaintiff must show that the defendant owed a duty to the plaintiff to provide accurate information, and then need only prove the defendant's "carelessness or negligence" in ascertaining the truth of the representation.[88]

At least when a negligent misrepresentation causes physical injury, the Illinois Supreme Court has held that the plaintiff need not show that the defendant was in the business of supplying information, following Section 311 of the Restatement (Second) of Torts.[89]

Some Illinois appellate courts have recognized a cause of action for strict liability, or "innocent," misrepresentation against those "engaged in the business of selling chattels," under Section 402B of the Restatement (Second) of Torts.[90]

G. JOINT AND SEVERAL LIABILITY

In 1995, the Illinois General Assembly passed the Civil Justice Reform Amendments of 1995 in an attempt to, among other things, eliminate joint and several liability.[91] The Illinois Supreme Court, however, invalidated those Amendments in their entirety in 1997.[92] As a result, joint and several liability, with one narrow statutory exception described below, is alive and well in Illinois.

By statute, in negligence and strict product liability actions that result in death, bodily injury, or damage to property, "all defendants found liable are jointly and severally liable for plaintiff's past and future medical and medically related expenses."[93]

While all defendants are jointly and severally liable for medical expenses, an individual defendant's liability for non-medical expenses is dependent on his degree of fault, so long as each defendant's liability can be legally apportioned.[94] If the defendant's fault "is less than 25% of the total fault attributable to the plaintiff, the defendants sued by the plaintiff, and any third party defendant except the plaintiff's employer," that defendant is only severally liable for such non-medical expenses.[95] However, if the defendant's fault "is 25% or greater than the fault attributable to the plaintiff, the defendants sued by the plaintiff, and any third party defendants except the plaintiff's employer," the defendant is jointly and severally liable for those expenses.[96] Defendants who have settled in good faith are not included in this apportionment of fault or on the verdict form.[97]

H. PRE- AND POST-JUDGMENT INTEREST

"Judgments recovered in any court shall draw interest at the rate of 9% per annum from the date of the judgment until satisfied or 6% per annum when the judgment debtor is a unit of local government. . . . "[98] Interest continues to accrue while an appeal is pending.[99] However, "[t]he judgment debtor may by tender of payment of judgment, costs and interest accrued to the date of tender, stop the further accrual of interest on such judgment notwithstanding the prosecution of an appeal, or other steps to reverse, vacate or modify the judgment."[100] "Illinois statutes do not authorize pre-judgment interest in tort cases."[101]

I. EMPLOYER IMMUNITY FROM SUIT

The exclusivity provision of the Illinois Workers' Compensation Act bars all other statutory or common law causes of action brought by a covered employee against his employer for injuries received in the course of his employment.[102] When an injured employee files a lawsuit against another party—such as a manufacturer or an independent contractor—for a work-related accident, the defendant may sue the employer as a third-party defendant and obtain contribution from the employer.[103] However, such contribution may not exceed the employer's liability under the Illinois Workers' Compensation Act.[104]

An employer may contractually waive the cap on its contribution liability,[105] and may waive its workers' compensation lien even after the return of a jury's verdict.[106]

J. PUNITIVE DAMAGES

Punitive damages are recoverable in product liability actions if the defendant acted willfully or with such gross negligence as to indicate a wanton disregard of others' rights.[107] A plaintiff may not request punitive damages in his original complaint, however, and any such request may be added by amendment only pursuant to pretrial motion and after the plaintiff establishes at a hearing "a reasonable likelihood of proving facts at trial sufficient to support an award of punitive damages."[108]

Evidence of other accidents involving the product does not by itself establish a sufficient basis for punitive damages.[109] Punitive damages are not allowed in warranty actions unless the breach amounts to an independent, willful tort.[110]

K. STATUTES

Relevant statutes for product liability actions are the statutes of limitations[111] and, when a breach of warranty is alleged, the applicable commercial code sections.[112] The age of majority, for purpose of suit, is eighteen.[113]

Colin Smith
Thomas R. Woodrow
Troy D. Hoyt
Laura E. Atherstone
Holland & Knight, LLP
131 South Dearborn Street, 30th Floor
Chicago, Illinois 60603
(312) 263-3600
(Fax) (312) 578-6666

ENDNOTES - ILLINOIS

1. *Werckenthein v. Bucher Petrochemical Co.*, 248 Ill. App. 3d 282, 289, 618 N.E.2d 902, 907 (1st Dist. 1993) ("For injuries caused by defective products, a plaintiff may have four theories of recovery available: express warranty, implied warranty, negligence, and strict liability.").

2. 735 Ill. Comp. Stat. 5/13-202 (2010).

3. 735 Ill. Comp. Stat. 5/13-205 (2010).

4. *Witherell v. Weimer*, 85 Ill. 2d 146, 156, 421 N.E.2d 869, 874 (1981).

5. 810 Ill. Comp. Stat. 5/2-725 (2010).

6. 735 Ill. Comp. Stat. 5/13-213(b)-(d) (1994).

7. 735 Ill. Comp. Stat. 5/13-213(b).

8. 735 Ill. Comp. Stat. 5/13-213(b).

9. 735 Ill. Comp. Stat. 5/13-213(d); *see also Davis v. Toshiba Mach. Co.*, 186 Ill. 2d 181, 186, 710 N.E.2d 399, 401-02 (1999) (exception applies to both latent injuries and immediately discoverable injuries).

10. 735 Ill. Comp. Stat. 5/13-214(b) (2010). The statute expressly allows a plaintiff to bring suit within four years of the discovery of the act or omission on which the suit is based, provided that the act or omission was discovered or should have been discovered within the period of repose. 735 Ill. Comp. Stat. 5/13-214(b).

11. 735 Ill. Comp. Stat. 5/13-211 (2010).

12. 735 Ill. Comp. Stat. 5/13-213(d); *Thornton v. Mono Mfg. Co.*, 99 Ill. App. 3d 722, 728-29, 425 N.E.2d 522, 526-27 (2d Dist. 1981).

13. *Calles v. Scripto-Tokai Corp.*, 224 Ill. 2d 247, 254, 864 N.E.2d 249, 254 (2007); *Korando v. Uniroyal Goodrich Tire Co.*, 159 Ill. 2d 335, 343, 637 N.E.2d 1020, 1024 (1994); *Suvada v. White Motor Co.*, 32 Ill. 2d 612, 619-22, 210 N.E.2d 182, 186-87 (1965), *abrogated on other grounds by Frazer v. A.F. Munsterman, Inc.*, 123 Ill. 2d 245, 262, 527 N.E.2d 1248, 1255 (1988).

14. Ill. Pattern Jury Instr.-Civil § 400.02 (West. Supp. 2008).

15. *Mikolajczyk v. Ford Motor Co.*, 231 Ill. 2d 516, 525, 901 N.E.2d 329, 335 (2008).

16. *Mikolajczyk*, 231 Ill. 2d at 532, 901 N.E.2d at 339.

17. *Mikolajczyk*, 231 Ill. 2d at 526, 901 N.E.2d at 336 (quoting *Lamkin v. Towner*, 138 Ill. 2d 510, 529, 563 N.E.2d 449, 457 (1990)).

18. *Mikolajczyk*, 231 Ill. 2d at 526-27, 901 N.E.2d at 336 (quoting *Lamkin*, 138 Ill. 2d at 529, 563 N.E.2d at 457). Although *Lamkin* appeared to adopt a burden-shifting scheme in regard to the risk-utility test, the Illinois Supreme Court has distanced itself from that proposition. *See Mikolajczyk*, 231 Ill. 2d at 536, 901 N.E.2d at 341 ("[The] burden-shifting formulation of the risk-utility test comes from [*Lamkin*], but was not a part of the holding in that case. . . . [N]o decision of this court has expressly adopted [the] burden-shifting formulation of the risk-utility test.").

19. *Mikolajczyk*, 231 Ill. 2d at 541, 901 N.E.2d at 344.

20. *Mikolajczyk*, 231 Ill. 2d at 555, 901 N.E.2d at 352 ("[T]he risk-utility balance is to be determined based on consideration of a 'broad range of factors,' including 'the magnitude and probability of the foreseeable risks of harm, the instructions and warnings accompanying the product, and the nature and strength of consumer expectations regarding the product, including expectations arising from product portrayal and marketing,' as well as 'the likely effects of the alternative design on production costs; the effects of the alternative design on product longevity, maintenance, repair, and esthetics; and the range of consumer choice among products.'" (quoting Restatement (Third) of Torts: Products Liability § 2, cmt. f, at 23 (1998)) (emphasis removed)).

21. *Mikolajczyk*, 231 Ill. 2d at 555, 901 N.E.2d at 352.

22. *Mikolajczyk*, 231 Ill. 2d at 555-56, 901 N.E.2d at 352.

23. Ill. Pattern Jury Instr.-Civil § 400.02.

24. Ill. Pattern Jury Instr.-Civil § 400.04 (West 2006); *see also* Ill. Pattern Jury Instr.-Civil § 15.01 (West Supp. 2008). Illinois courts do not differentiate between strict liability and negligence products liability when evaluating proximate cause. *Kleen v. Homak Mfg. Co.*, 321 Ill. App. 3d 639, 641, 749 N.E.2d 26, 29 (1st Dist. 2001).

25. *Williams v. Brown Mfg. Co.*, 45 Ill. 2d 418, 426, 261 N.E.2d 305, 310 (1970), *overruled on other grounds by Coney v. J.L.G. Indus., Inc.*, 97 Ill. 2d 104, 119, 454 N.E.2d 197, 204 (1983).

26. 735 Ill. Comp. Stat. 5/2-1116 (1994); *see also Coney*, 97 Ill. 2d at 119, 454 N.E.2d at 204 ("Once defendant's liability is established, and where both the

defective product and plaintiff's misconduct contribute to cause the damages, the comparative fault principle will operate to reduce plaintiff's recovery by that amount which the trier of fact finds him at fault.").

27. *See Coney*, 97 Ill. 2d at 119, 454 N.E.2d at 204 ("[T]he defenses of misuse and assumption of the risk will no longer bar recovery. Instead, such misconduct will be compared in the apportionment of damages.").

28. *Thomas v. Kaiser Agric. Chems.*, 81 Ill. 2d 206, 213, 407 N.E.2d 32, 35 (1980) ("A plaintiff assumes the risk of a defective product only if he is actually aware of the defective nature of the product and appreciates its unreasonably dangerous character, but chooses voluntarily to act in disregard of such known danger."); *Betts v. Manville Pers. Injury Settlement Trust*, 225 Ill. App. 3d 882, 904, 588 N.E.2d 1193, 1207 (4th Dist. 1992) ("The test is subjective in that it is plaintiff's knowledge, understanding, and appreciation of the danger which must be assessed, rather than that of the reasonably prudent person. The defense applies only if the plaintiff is actually aware of the defective nature of the product and appreciates its unreasonably dangerous character, but chooses voluntarily to act in disregard of the known danger.").

29. *J.I. Case Co. v. McCartin-McAuliffe Plumbing & Heating, Inc.*, 118 Ill. 2d 447, 460, 516 N.E.2d 260, 266 (1987); *see Williams*, 45 Ill. 2d at 425-26, 261 N.E.2d at 309.

30. *Hammond v. N. Am. Asbestos Corp.*, 97 Ill. 2d 195, 206, 454 N.E.2d 210, 216 (1983); *Crowe v. Pub. Bldg. Comm'n*, 74 Ill. 2d 10, 13, 383 N.E.2d 951, 952 (1978); *Prompt Air, Inc. v. Firewall Forward, Inc.*, 303 Ill. App. 3d 126, 129, 707 N.E.2d 235, 238 (1st Dist. 1999).

31. *Timm v. Indian Springs Recreation Ass'n*, 187 Ill. App. 3d 508, 511-12, 543 N.E.2d 538, 541 (4th Dist. 1989); *Keen v. Dominick's Finer Foods, Inc.*, 49 Ill. App. 3d 480, 482, 364 N.E.2d 502, 504 (1st Dist. 1977).

32. 735 Ill. Comp. Stat. 5/2-621 (1994).

33. *Crowe*, 74 Ill. 2d at 14-15, 383 N.E.2d at 953.

34. *Green v. Firestone Tire & Rubber Co.*, 122 Ill. App. 3d 204, 209, 460 N.E.2d 895, 898 (2d Dist. 1984).

35. *Green*, 122 Ill. App. 3d at 209, 460 N.E.2d at 898-99.

36. "Market share liability" is a theory of liability applied in some states when a harmful product "cannot be traced to any specific producer." *Smith v. Eli Lilly*, 137 Ill. 2d 222, 237, 560 N.E.2d 324, 330 (1990). Under this theory of liability, "the plaintiff must first join as defendants the manufacturers of a 'substantial share' of the [product] and must prove a *prima facie* case on

every element except identification of the direct tortfeasor. . . . [T]he burden of proof [then] shifts to defendants to demonstrate that they could not have manufactured the [product]. If a defendant fails to meet this burden, the court. . . . apportion[s] damages. . . . by holding each defendant liable for the proportion of the judgment represented by its share of that market." *Smith*, 560 N.E.2d at 330-31.

37. *Millar-Mintz v. Abbott Labs.*, 268 Ill. App. 3d 566, 572, 645 N.E.2d 278, 283 (1st Dist. 1994); *see also Smith*, 137 Ill. 2d at 251, 560 N.E.2d at 337 ("[M]arket share liability is not a sound theory, [and] is too great a deviation from our existing tort principles. . . .").

38. *Smith*, 137 Ill. 2d at 251-55, 560 N.E.2d at 337-38.

39. *Hammond v. N. Am. Asbestos Corp.*, 97 Ill. 2d 195, 208, 454 N.E.2d 210, 217 (1983) (citing *Suvada*, 32 Ill. 2d at 617, 210 N.E.2d at 185).

40. *Hammond*, 97 Ill. 2d at 206, 454 N.E.2d at 216; *Ill. State Trust Co. v. Walker Mfg. Co.*, 73 Ill. App. 3d 585, 589, 392 N.E.2d 70, 73 (5th Dist. 1979) ("It is now clear under Illinois law that a product may be defective solely by its failure to warn of dangers attending its use."); *see also Mikolajczyk v. Ford Motor Co.*, 231 Ill. 2d 516, 525, 901 N.E.2d 329, 335 (2008); *Skonberg v. Owens-Corning Fiberglas Corp.*, 215 Ill. App. 3d 735, 741, 576 N.E.2d 28, 31 (1st Dist. 1991).

41. *Smith*, 137 Ill. 2d at 266, 560 N.E.2d at 344.

42. *See Proctor v. Davis*, 291 Ill. App. 3d 265, 277, 682 N.E.2d 1203, 1211 (1st Dist. 1997); *McColgan v. Envtl. Control Sys., Inc.*, 212 Ill. App. 3d 696, 700, 571 N.E.2d 815, 817 (1st Dist. 1991) ("[I]njuries are not compensable under strict liability law if they are caused by those inherent propensities of a product which are obvious to all who come in contact with the product.").

43. *Modelski v. Navistar Int'l Transp. Corp.*, 302 Ill. App. 3d 879, 890, 707 N.E.2d 239, 247 (1st Dist. 1999); *see Collins v. Hyster Co.*, 174 Ill. App. 3d 972, 977, 529 N.E.2d 303, 306 (3d Dist. 1988) ("Certainly the law does not contemplate placing the onerous duty on manufacturers to subsequently warn all [foreseeable] users of products based on increased design or manufacture expertise that was not present at the time the product left its control."). In a recent case, the Illinois Supreme Court reaffirmed that a manufacturer is under "no duty to issue postsale warnings or to retrofit its products to remedy defects first discovered after a product has left its control." *Jablonski v. Ford Motor Co.*, 2011 IL 110096, ¶ 112 (citing *Modelski*, 302 Ill. App. 3d at 890, 707 N.E.2d at 274). However, the court refused to "foreclose the possibility that a postsale duty to warn could be recognized in the future in Illinois." *Jablonski*, 2011 IL 110096, ¶ 118.

44. *Modelski*, 302 Ill. App. 3d at 890, 707 N.E.2d at 274.

45. *Martin ex rel. Martin v. Ortho Pharm. Corp.*, 169 Ill. 2d 234, 238, 661 N.E.2d 352, 354 (1996).

46. *Martin*, 169 Ill. 2d at 238, 661 N.E.2d at 354 (citing *Kirk v. Michael Reese Hosp. & Med. Ctr.*, 117 Ill. 2d 507, 517, 513 N.E.2d 387, 392 (1987)).

47. *Martin*, 169 Ill. 2d at 238-39, 661 N.E.2d at 354.

48. *Davis v. Pak-Mor Mfg. Co.*, 284 Ill. App. 3d 214, 220, 672 N.E.2d 771, 775 (1st Dist. 1996); *Woods v. Graham Eng'g Corp.*, 183 Ill. App. 3d 337, 341, 539 N.E.2d 316, 318-19 (2d Dist. 1989).

49. *See Rucker v. Norfolk & W. Ry. Co.*, 77 Ill. 2d 434, 437-38, 396 N.E.2d 534, 536 (1979) ("[A] plaintiff in a design defect case [may] attempt to prove such a defect by introducing evidence of feasible alternative designs. . . ."); *Kerns v. Engelke*, 76 Ill. 2d 154, 162-63, 390 N.E.2d 859, 863 (1979) ("'[A] manufacturer's product can hardly be faulted if safer alternatives are not feasible. . . . [F]easibility includes not only the elements of economy, effectiveness and practicality but also *the technological possibilities viewed in the present state of the art*.'" (quoting *Sutkowski v. Universal Marion Corp.*, 5 Ill. App. 3d 313, 319, 281 N.E.2d 749, 753 (3d Dist. 1972) (emphasis added))); *see also Jablonski v. Ford Motor Co.*, 2011 IL 110096, ¶ 102 ("It is not sufficient that the alternative design would have reduced or prevented the harm suffered by the plaintiff if it would also have introduced into the product other dangers of equal or greater magnitude." (quoting Restatement (Third) of Torts: Products Liability § 2, cmt. f)).

50. *Jablonski*, 2011 IL 110096, ¶ 85.

51. *Tweedy v. Wright Ford Sales, Inc.*, 64 Ill. 2d 570, 574, 357 N.E.2d 449, 452 (1976).

52. *See Shramek v. Gen. Motors Corp.*, 69 Ill. App. 2d 72, 78, 216 N.E.2d 244, 247 (1st Dist. 1966) ("The mere fact of a tire blowout does not . . . tend to establish that the tire was defective. Blowouts can be attributed to myriad causes, including not only the care with which the tires are maintained, but the conditions of the roads over which they are driven and the happenstance striking of damaging objects.").

53. *Moehle v. Chrysler Motors Corp.*, 93 Ill. 2d 299, 304-05, 443 N.E.2d 575, 577-78 (1982); *Rucker*, 77 Ill. 2d at 439, 396 N.E.2d at 536-37; *see also Jablonski*, 2011 IL 110096, ¶ 92 ("[E]vidence of industry standards is a factor to be considered in the balance and has always been relevant to determining whether a defendant has exercised reasonable care in designing a product. . . . It is well settled that conformance to industry standards is relevant, but not dispositive on the issue of negligence.").

54. *Rucker*, 77 Ill. 2d at 440-41, 396 N.E.2d at 537-38; *Gowler v. Ferrell-Ross Co.*, 206 Ill. App. 3d 194, 202, 564 N.E.2d 773, 778 (1st Dist. 1990).

55. *Schaffner v. Chi. & N.W. Transp. Co.*, 129 Ill. 2d 1, 40, 541 N.E.2d 643, 660 (1986); *Balsley v. Raymond Corp.*, 232 Ill. App. 3d 1028, 1030, 600 N.E.2d 424, 425 (1st Dist. 1992).

56. *Compare Brown v. Ford Motor Co.*, 306 Ill. App. 3d 314, 318, 714 N.E.2d 556, 559 (1st Dist. 1999) (evidence of subsequent design change inadmissible to show negligence or willful and wanton conduct in product liability action), *and Davis v. Int'l Harvester Co.*, 167 Ill. App. 3d 814, 823, 521 N.E.2d 1282, 1288 (2d Dist. 1988) (post-occurrence change admissible only to establish feasible alternative design), *with Burke v. Ill. Power Co.*, 57 Ill. App. 3d 498, 514, 373 N.E.2d 1354, 1369 (1st Dist. 1978) (subsequent remedial measures admissible in strict liability case).

57. *Shimanovsky v. Gen. Motors Corp.*, 181 Ill. 2d 112, 121, 692 N.E.2d 286, 290 (1998) (considering appropriate discovery sanction for pre-suit destructive testing of allegedly defective product). *But see Boyd v. Travelers Ins. Co.*, 166 Ill. 2d 188, 652 N.E.2d 267 (1995) (holding that, in the context of a cause of action for negligent spoliation, "[t]he general rule is that there is no duty to preserve evidence; however a duty to preserve evidence may arise through an agreement, a contract, a statute . . . or another special circumstance.").

58. *Shimanovsky*, 181 Ill. 2d at 127, 692 N.E.2d at 292 ("[A] party is not automatically entitled to a specific sanction just because evidence is destroyed or altered.").

59. *Shimanovsky*, 181 Ill. 2d at 124, 692 N.E.2d at 291 (stating that trial courts should consider "(1) the surprise to the adverse party; (2) the prejudicial effect of the proffered . . . evidence; (3) the nature of the testimony or evidence; (4) the diligence of the adverse party in seeking discovery; (5) the timeliness of the adverse party's objection to the testimony or evidence; and (6) the good faith of the party offering the testimony or evidence. Of these factors, no single factor is determinative." (citation omitted)).

60. *See, e.g., Allstate Ins. Co. v. Sunbeam Corp.*, 53 F.3d 804, 806-07 (7th Cir. 1995) (applying Illinois law in affirming dismissal based on spoliation); *Shimanovsky*, 181 Ill. 2d at 128, 692 N.E.2d at 293 (indicating that dismissal may be appropriate if "sufficient evidence is [not] available to both parties . . . to establish their case or defense.").

61. *Shelbyville Mut. Ins. Co. v. Sunbeam Leisure Prods. Co.*, 262 Ill. App. 3d 636, 643, 634 N.E.2d 1319, 1324 (5th Dist. 1994) (affirming grant of motion to exclude evidence based on inadvertent disposal of part of cooking grill); *Graves v. Daley*, 172 Ill. App. 3d 35, 38-39, 526 N.E.2d 679, 681-82 (3d Dist. 1988) (affirming order barring presentation of evidence regarding defect in furnace as sanction for destruction of furnace).

62. *Braverman v. Kucharik Bicycle Clothing Co.*, 287 Ill. App. 3d 150, 158-59, 678 N.E.2d 80, 85-86 (1st Dist. 1997) (noting availability of instruction allowing

jury to infer that missing evidence would be unfavorable to party responsible for spoliation).

63. *Braverman*, 287 Ill. App. 3d at 154, 678 N.E.2d at 83. *But see, e.g., Scott v. Fruehauf Corp.*, 602 F. Supp. 207, 209 (S.D. Ill. 1985) (granting summary judgment in tire rim defect case where rim was unavailable); *Shramek v. Gen. Motors Corp.*, 69 Ill. App. 2d 72, 80, 216 N.E.2d 244, 248 (1st Dist. 1966) (same).

64. *Moorman Mfg. Co. v. Nat'l Tank Co.*, 91 Ill. 2d 69, 82, 435 N.E.2d 443, 449 (1982) (quoting Note, *Economic Loss in Products Liability Jurisprudence*, 66 Colum. L. Rev. 917, 918 (1966)). Economic loss has also been defined as "diminution in the value of the product because it is inferior in quality and does not work for the general purposes for which it was manufactured and sold." *Moorman Mfg.*, 91 Ill. 2d 69, 82, 435 N.E.2d 443, 449 (quoting Comment, *Manufacturers' Liability to Remote Purchasers for "Economic Loss" Damages—Tort or Contract ?*, 114 U. Pa. L. Rev. 539, 541 (1966)).

65. *Moorman Mfg.*, 91 Ill. 2d at 81, 435 N.E.2d at 448.

66. *Moorman Mfg.*, 91 Ill. 2d at 87, 435 N.E.2d at 450.

67. *Moorman Mfg.*, 91 Ill. 2d at 91, 435 N.E.2d at 453.

68. *In re Chicago Flood Litig.*, 176 Ill. 2d 179, 199, 680 N.E.2d 265, 275 (1997) (emphasis removed) (citations omitted).

69. *Kutzler v. AMF Harley-Davidson*, 194 Ill. App. 3d 273, 283-84, 550 N.E.2d 1236, 1243 (1st Dist. 1990) (Buckley, P.J. dissenting); *see Buehler v. Whalen*, 70 Ill. 2d 51, 61, 374 N.E.2d 460, 464-65 (1977) ("[T]he manufacturer's duty is to use reasonable care in the design and manufacture of its product, bearing in mind that the intended and actual use of automobiles results in collisions."). Somewhat surprisingly, Illinois law does not contemplate the extension of this doctrine beyond the vehicle's passengers. *See Rennert v. Great Dane Ltd. P'ship*, 543 F.3d 914, 916 (7th Cir. 2008) (applying Illinois law to deny manufacturer's liability for death resulting from defect in trailer with which plaintiff's car collided); *Mieher v. Brown*, 54 Ill. 2d 539, 544, 301 N.E.2d 307, 309 (1973) (rejecting extension of doctrine to injuries sustained by collision with defective vehicle).

70. *Kutzler*, 194 Ill. App. 3d at 284, 550 N.E.2d at 1243 (Buckley, P.J., dissenting).

71. *Kutzler*, 194 Ill. App. 3d at 284, 550 N.E.2d at 1243.

72. *Kutzler*, 194 Ill. App. 3d at 284, 550 N.E.2d at 1243 (citing *Suvada*, 32 Ill. 2d at 623, 210 N.E.2d at 188).

73. "Second collision" refers not to an additional collision between vehicles, but "to the collision between a passenger and an interior part of the vehicle following the initial impact." *Bean v. Volkswagenwerk Aktiengesellschaft of Wolfsburg, Germany*, 109 Ill. App. 3d 333, 336, 440 N.E.2d 426, 428 (5th Dist. 1982).

74. *Oakes v. Gen. Motors Corp.*, 257 Ill. App. 3d 10, 23, 628 N.E.2d 341, 349 (1st Dist. 1993).

75. *Oakes*, 257 Ill. App. 3d at 23, 628 N.E.2d at 349 (quoting *Mitchell v. Volkswagenwerk, AG*, 669 F.2d 1199, 1206 (8th Cir. 1982)).

76. *See Kutzler*, 194 Ill. App. 3d at 284, 550 N.E.2d at 1243 (citing *Suvada*, 32 Ill. 2d at 623, 210 N.E.2d at 188).

77. *Buehler*, 70 Ill. 2d at 61-62, 374 N.E.2d at 464-65 (describing cases adopting crashworthiness doctrine as "predicated on negligence, [or] both negligence and the wholly dissimilar strict liability in tort doctrine").

78. *See Calles v. Scripto-Tokai Corp.*, 224 Ill. 2d 247, 270, 864 N.E.2d 249, 263 (2007) ("A product liability action asserting a claim based on negligence, such as negligent design, falls within the framework of common law negligence.").

79. *E.g., Blue v. Envtl. Eng'g, Inc.*, 215 Ill. 2d 78, 97, 828 N.E.2d 1128, 1142 (2005) (stating that the risk-utility test is inapplicable in negligence) (plurality opinion). *But see Calles*, 224 Ill. 2d at 269-70, 864 N.E.2d at 269 (noting that *Blue* was non-binding precedent).

80. 735 Ill. Comp. Stat. 5/2-1116 (1994); *see* 735 Ill. Comp. Stat. 5/2-1107.1 (1994); Ill. Pattern Jury Instr.-Civil § B10.03 (West 2006).

81. *See, e.g., Werckenthein v. Bucher Petrochemical Co.*, 248 Ill. App. 3d 282, 289, 618 N.E.2d 902, 907 (1st Dist. 1993).

82. *Bd. of Educ. v. A, C & S, Inc.*, 131 Ill. 2d 428, 461, 546 N.E.2d 580, 595 (1989).

83. *Bd. of Educ.*, 131 Ill. 2d at 461, 546 N.E.2d at 595.

84. 810 Ill. Comp. Stat. 5/2-725(2) (2010).

85. 810 Ill. Comp. Stat. 5/2-607(3)(a) (2010); *see also Bd. of Educ.*, 131 Ill. 2d at 462, 546 N.E.2d at 596.

86. *Bd. of Educ.*, 131 Ill. 2d at 452, 546 N.E.2d at 591.

87. *Bd. of Educ.*, 131 Ill. 2d at 452, 546 N.E.2d at 591.

88. *Bd. of Educ.*, 131 Ill. 2d at 452, 546 N.E.2d at 591.

89. *Bd. of Educ.*, 131 Ill. 2d at 454-55, 546 N.E.2d at 592-93.

90. *See Hollenbeck v. Selectone Corp.*, 131 Ill. App. 3d 969, 971, 476 N.E.2d 746, 747 (3d Dist. 1985); *Pitler v. Michael Reese Hosp.*, 92 Ill. App. 3d 739, 743, 415 N.E.2d 1255, 1258 (1st Dist. 1980).

91. Pub. Act 89-7, eff. March 9, 1995.

92. *Best v. Taylor Mach. Works*, 179 Ill. 2d 367, 467, 689 N.E.2d 1057, 1104 (1997). After finding certain "core provisions" of the Amendments unconstitutional, the court held the remainder of the Amendments void on the grounds of non-severability. *Best*, 179 Ill. 2d 367, 467, 689 N.E.2d 1057, 1104. The court then invited the legislature to reenact any non-severable provision of the Amendments that the legislature deemed "desirable or appropriate." *Best*, 179 Ill. 2d at 471, 689 N.E.2d at 1106. Where the legislature has not done so, the pre-1995 version of that particular statute is currently in effect.

93. 735 Ill. Comp. Stat. 5/2-1117 (2010).

94. *Woods v. Cole*, 181 Ill. 2d 512, 520, 693 N.E.2d 333, 337 (1998) ("Section 2-1117 requires, as a threshold matter, that the liability of the tortfeasors which is at issue be capable of being legally apportioned. If the liability cannot be legally apportioned, then section 2-1117 never comes into play.").

95. 735 Ill. Comp. Stat. 5/2-1117.

96. 735 Ill. Comp. Stat. 5/2-1117; *see Woods*, 181 Ill. 2d at 513, 693 N.E.2d at 334 ("If a defendant's fault is determined to be 25% or more, then the defendant shall be jointly and severally liable for any nonmedical damages.").

97. *Ready v. United/Goedecke Servs., Inc.*, 232 Ill. 2d 369, 905 N.E.2d 725 (2008); *see Heupel v. Jenkins*, 395 Ill. App. 3d 689, 691, 919 N.E.2d 378, 380 (1st Dist. 2009) (holding that *Ready* "applies equally" to the current version of 735 Ill. Comp. Stat. 5/2-1117).

98. 735 Ill. Comp. Stat. 5/2-1303 (2010).

99. *Shuster v. Brantley*, 238 Ill. App. 3d 770, 772, 606 N.E.2d 612, 613 (1st Dist. 1992).

100. 735 Ill. Comp. Stat. 5/2-1303.

101. *N. Trust Co. v. Cnty. of Cook*, 135 Ill. App. 3d 329, 336, 481 N.E.2d 957, 962 (1st Dist. 1985).

102. 820 Ill. Comp. Stat. 305/5(a) (1994).

103. *Doyle v. Rhodes*, 101 Ill. 2d 1, 14, 461 N.E.2d 382, 388 (1984); *see also Kotecki v. Cyclops Welding Corp.*, 146 Ill. 2d 155, 158, 585 N.E.2d 1023, 1024 (1991) ("While recognizing that the Workers' Compensation Act gives an employer immunity from tort actions by its employees, this court, in *Doyle*, found that there is no bar to a claim for contribution from that employer by a defendant held liable to that employee.").

104. *Kotecki*, 146 Ill. 2d. at 164-65, 585 N.E.2d at 1027-28.

105. *Braye v. Archer-Daniels-Midland Co.*, 175 Ill. 2d 201, 218, 676 N.E.2d 1295, 1304 (1997).

106. *LaFever v. Kemlite Co.*, 185 Ill. 2d 380, 399-405, 706 N.E.2d 441, 451-54 (1998).

107. *J.I. Case Co. v. McCartin-McAuliffe Plumbing & Heating, Inc.*, 118 Ill. 2d 447, 453, 516 N.E.2d 260, 263 (1987); *Proctor v. Davis*, 291 Ill. App. 3d 265, 285, 682 N.E.2d 1203, 1216 (1st Dist. 1997).

108. 735 Ill. Comp. Stat. 5/2-604.1 (1994).

109. *See Loitz v. Remington Arms Co.*, 138 Ill. 2d 404, 419-20, 563 N.E.2d 397, 404 (1990).

110. *McGrady v. Chrysler Motors Corp.*, 46 Ill. App. 3d 136, 141, 360 N.E.2d 818, 822 (4th Dist. 1977).

111. 735 Ill. Comp. Stat. 5/13-202, 13-203, 13-204, 13-205, 13-211, 13-214 (2010); 735 Ill. Comp. Stat. 5/13-213 (1994).

112. 810 Ill. Comp. Stat. 5/2-313 to 2-318 (2010).

113. 735 Ill. Comp. Stat. 5/13-211.

INDIANA

A. CAUSES OF ACTION

In Indiana, product liability lawsuits were historically based upon theories of negligence and strict liability. In 1978, Indiana adopted the Indiana Product Liability Act (IPLA) which governed actions against a seller of a defective product.[1] Causes of action for breach of implied warranty sounding in tort were deemed to be identical to strict liability imposed by the IPLA but negligence and breach of express warranty actions were governed not by the IPLA but by Indiana's common law,[2] the Comparative Fault Act[3] (CFA), and Indiana's commercial code.[4] Effective July 1, 1995, the Indiana legislature passed legislation amending the IPLA, the CFA, and statutes on punitive damages so that the IPLA is no longer limited to strict liability claims.[5] The IPLA, the CFA, and the statutes on punitive damages were recodified in 1998.[6]

As amended, the IPLA now governs all actions against a manufacturer or seller for physical harm caused by a product regardless of the theories upon which the action is brought.[7]

B. STATUTES OF LIMITATION

1. Two-Year Statute of Limitation

A product liability action must be commenced within two years of the date the cause of action accrues. This statute of limitations applies regardless of minority or legal disability.[8] The two-year statute of limitation begins to run when the plaintiff knew or, in the exercise of ordinary diligence, could have discovered that an injury had been sustained as a result of the act of another.[9] The duty to investigate commences once a plaintiff is on notice of a possible cause of his injury, not when all confusion or doubt has dissipated.[10] Suspicion or speculation that another's product caused the injury is insufficient to trigger the statute of limitations. The plaintiff must gather information that changes speculation of a causal link into "reasonable possibility if not a probability."[11] In cases that fall under the IPLA and the Indiana Wrongful Death Act, plaintiffs must file their lawsuits within the limitations period of each statute.[12] The statute of limitations for the Wrongful Death Act, which is two years from the date of death, may provide an earlier time bar than the IPLA.[13]

2. Statute of Repose

The IPLA contains a statute of repose.[14] Under this statute a cause of action based on negligence or strict liability must be commenced within two years of accrual or within ten years after the delivery of the product to the initial user or consumer.[15] If the cause of action accrues at least eight years but less than ten years after initial delivery, the action may be commenced at any time within two years after accrual.[16] The statute of repose is implicated only if the complained-of defect was present at or before the time the product was delivered to the initial user or consumer.[17] The statute of repose applies regardless of minority or legal disability of the plaintiff.[18] The statute of repose cannot be circumvented by claiming that the manufacturer "continued its negligence after the initial sale by failing to warn customer of known dangers."[19]

Delivery under the statute of repose occurs when the product is delivered to the first "consuming entity."[20] The ten-year period may recommence "when a product has been reconditioned, altered, or modified to the extent that a 'new' product has been introduced into the stream of commerce."[21] However, a simple repair or maintenance of the product, which does not materially alter the product, does not recommence the running of the period of repose.[22] A cause of action accrues when all of the elements necessary for recovery are met.[23] Accrual does not necessarily occur merely because the plaintiff is aware that he has suffered physical harm, but it does accrue when the plaintiff knew or should have known that the alleged product defect caused his physical harm.[24]

The Indiana Supreme Court has repeatedly upheld the constitutionality of the IPLA's statute of repose as it applies to products.[25] Subject to the discussion below, the statute of repose under the IPLA may apply when the injury is caused by a disease contracted because of protracted exposure to an inherently dangerous foreign substance, such as asbestos.[26]

3. **Asbestos-Related Injuries**

The IPLA has a separate statute of limitation for certain asbestos-related injuries. Any cause of action resulting from an initial exposure to asbestos must be commenced within two years after the cause of action accrues. The cause of action accrues when the injured person knows that she has an asbestos-related injury. This section on its face with its specific statute of limitation applies only to product liability actions against persons who mined *and* sold commercial asbestos and to actions which seek to recover from certain bankruptcy funds that have been created for payment of asbestos-related claims.[27]

For many years there was a split in the Indiana Courts of Appeals on whether this section of the IPLA applied to sellers of products containing asbestos which was mined by others. Despite the apparent clarity of the section requiring the seller to have mined the asbestos, decisions had ignored the conjunctive "and" and found the special limitations period applied to manufacturers that sold asbestos containing products. The Indiana Supreme Court has recently clarified the application of this section and the statute of limitations as it applies to asbestos actions.[28]

The Indiana Supreme Court has held that the exception to the general two year statute of limitations and ten (10) year statute of repose only applies to claims against entities that both mined and sold commercial asbestos.[29] In addition, the Indiana Supreme Court clarified the definition of "commercial asbestos" to exclude asbestos-containing products, and to only refer to either raw or processed asbestos that is incorporated into other products.[30] Thus, asbestos plaintiffs who wish to bring suit against an entity that did not both mine and sell commercial asbestos, must bring suit under the general statute of limitations and are subject to the ten year statute of repose.[31] With respect to asbestos claims brought under the general statute of repose, "a cause of action accrues at that point at which a physician who is reasonably experienced at making such diagnosis could have diagnosed the individual with an asbestos-related illness or disease."[32]

C. CLAIMS UNDER THE IPLA

1. The Standard

Prior to passage of the IPLA, Indiana recognized strict liability in tort as embodied in Section 402A of the Restatement (Second) of Torts.[33] Strict liability actions have been replaced by the IPLA and its definitions.[34] Pursuant to the IPLA, a person who places into the stream of commerce a product in a defective condition unreasonably dangerous to any consumer is subject to liability for the physical harm caused by the product to the consumer or his property if: (1) the consumer is in the class of persons that the seller should reasonably foresee as being subject to the harm caused by the defective condition; (2) the seller is engaged in the business of selling the product; and (3) the product is expected to and does reach the user or consumer without substantial alteration in the condition in which the product is sold by the person sought to be held liable.[35] "Unreasonably dangerous" refers to situations in which the use of a product exposes the user or consumer to "a risk of physical harm to an extent beyond that contemplated by the ordinary consumer who purchases the product with the ordinary knowledge about the product's characteristics common to the community of consumers."[36] "The requirement that the product be in a defective condition focuses on the product itself while the requirement that the product be unreasonably dangerous focuses on the reasonable expectations of the consumer."[37] Generally, the issue of defect is a question of fact.[38]

2. "Defect"

A product is defective if, at the time it is conveyed by the seller to another party, it is in a condition (a) not contemplated by reasonable persons among those considered expected users or consumers of the product and (b) that will be unreasonably dangerous to the expected user or consumer when used in reasonably expectable ways of handling or consumption. A product defect can take the form of a manufacturing defect, a design defect, or the lack of adequate instructions and warnings.[39]

A product is not defective if it is safe for reasonably expectable handling and consumption. If an injury results from handling, preparation for use, or consumption that is not reasonably expectable, the seller is not liable. A product is not defective if it is incapable of being made safe for its reasonably expectable use when manufactured, sold, handled, and packaged properly.[40] The "mere existence of a safer product" is not sufficient to establish liability.[41]

A party claiming that a product is defective by design or because of inadequate warnings must establish that the manufacturer failed to exercise reasonable care in designing the product or in providing warnings.[42] Thus, the IPLA "departs from strict liability" and applies a negligence standard in these areas.[43]

There is uncertainty in the law regarding whether adequate warnings can be used as a defense to design defect claims if there is a reasonable, safer design available. In *Marshall v. Clark Equipment Co.*, the Indiana Court of Appeals held that "a manufacturer may avoid liability by placing adequate warnings on a product even when there is evidence of a 'safer' alternative design."[44] In *Weigle v. SPX Corp.*, the Seventh Circuit Court of Appeals held that if the Indiana Supreme Court addressed this issue, it would disagree with the *Marshall* decision.[45] The *Weigle* court stated that it is "unreasonable to omit from a product an easily installed and inexpensive safeguard that would prevent potentially fatal accidents and rely simply on the users' ability and willingness to read, comprehend, and follow all instructions and warnings on all occasions."[46] The *Weigle* court criticized and distinguished a footnote in the Indiana Supreme Court's decision in *TRW Vehicle Safety Systems, Inc. v. Moore*, that arguably could be read to support the *Marshall* decision.[47] Until the Indiana Supreme Court directly addresses these conflicting decisions, there will be uncertainty in the law in this area and the forum of the lawsuit could dictate the result.

3. **Causation**

The proximate cause rules which apply in negligence cases are also applicable to cases brought under the IPLA.[48] For proximate cause to exist, the plaintiff's injury must be "a natural and probable consequence of the defendant's act or omission 'which was, or should have been, reasonably foreseen or anticipated in light of attendant circumstances.'"[49]

4. **Contributory Negligence/Assumption of Risk**

Prior to July 1, 1995, contributory negligence or comparative fault was not a defense in product liability actions based on strict liability.[50] Effective July 1, 1995, comparative fault applies to all product liability actions that accrue subsequent to June 30, 1995. The fault of the person suffering the physical harm and the fault of all others who caused the harm are to be allocated in accordance with the provisions of the CFA.[51]

In an action based on fault (negligence), any contributory fault chargeable to the claimant diminishes proportionately the amount awarded as compensatory damages for an injury attributable to the claimant's contributory fault. Generally, the claimant may be barred from recovery if his contributory fault is greater than the fault of all persons whose fault proximately contributed to the claimant's damages.[52] Incurred risk bars a product liability claim when the evidence is undisputed that the plaintiff had actual knowledge of the specific risk and understood and appreciated the risk.[53]

5. **Manufacturer**

A manufacturer is a person or entity who designs, assembles, fabricates, produces, constructs, or otherwise prepares a product or a component part of a product before the sale of the product to a user or consumer.[54] A manufacturer also includes a seller who:

(1) has actual knowledge of a defect in a product;

(2) creates and furnishes a manufacturer with specifications relevant to the alleged defect for producing the product or who otherwise exercises some significant control over all or a portion of the manufacturing process;

(3) alters or modifies the product in any significant manner after the product comes into the seller's possession and before it is sold to the ultimate user or consumer;

(4) is owned in whole or significant part by the manufacturer; or

(5) owns in whole or significant part the manufacturer.[55]

A seller who discloses the name of the actual manufacturer of a product is not a manufacturer under this section merely because the seller places or has placed a private label on a product.[56] Where an entity reconditions, alters, or modifies a product or raw material to the extent that a new product has been introduced into the stream of commerce, the entity is a manufacturer and provider of the products under the IPLA.[57] However, an entity will not be subject to liability under the IPLA for a defective product that it did not sell, lease, or put into the stream of commerce.[58] Indiana does not recognize "apparent manufacturers" who merely put out products as their own which are manufactured by someone else.[59] If the court is unable to hold jurisdiction over the actual manufacturer of an allegedly defective product, then the manufacturer's principal distributor or seller over whom the court may hold jurisdiction shall be considered the manufacturer of the product.[60] If a manufacturer is a party to a product liability action and then files for bankruptcy, "the trial court still holds jurisdiction for the purposes of the IPLA."[61] Accordingly, in such circumstances, the principal distributor will not be considered the manufacturer.

Trademark licensors have responsibility for defective products placed in the stream of commerce bearing their marks relative to their role in the design, advertising, manufacturing, and distribution of the products.[62]

6. **User or Consumer**

The user or consumer of the product is one "who might foreseeably be harmed by a product at or after the point of its retail sale or equivalent transaction with a member of the consuming public."[63] This includes family members, employees, or guests of the consuming public.[64] The intended use of a product includes foreseeable maintenance and clean-up activities.[65] Assembly or installation of a product can also constitute use, "but only if the product is 'expected to reach the ultimate user or consumer' in an unassembled or uninstalled form."[66] A products liability claim will not be sustained where the manufacturer has yet to complete its obligation to assemble or install the product.[67]

7. **Product vs. Service**

The IPLA applies only to physical harm caused by a product.[68] A product is defined as "any item or good that is personalty at the time it is conveyed by the seller to another party."[69] The term "does not apply to a transaction that, by its nature, involves wholly or predominantly the sale of a service rather than a product."[70] Where a transaction involves both products and services, a court must determine whether the "predominate thrust" of the transaction was the rendition of service or the sale of a product.[71] The repair or refurbishing of a product is considered a service, while the reconditioning or reconstruction of a product creates a new product.[72]

Electricity may be a product under the IPLA.[73]

8. **Sale or Lease**

While a technical and complete sales transaction is the most easily recognizable commercial type of transaction, it is not the only transaction within the purview of the IPLA.[74] The plaintiff need only show that defendant placed the product into the stream of commerce.[75] Strict liability is not imposed on the occasional seller of food or other such products who is not engaged in that activity as part of her business.[76]

9. **Inherently Dangerous Products**

A product is not defective if it is incapable of being made safe for its reasonably expectable use when manufactured, sold, handled, and packaged properly.[77] It is a defense to an action that the user or consumer bringing the action knew of the defect, was aware of the danger and nevertheless proceeded to make use of the product and was injured.[78] Whether the dangerous condition of the product was open and obvious is a factor to be considered in strict liability cases in determining whether or not a product is defective and unreasonably dangerous.[79]

10. **Successor Liability**

Whether a successor corporation assumed a duty to a person injured by a product may be a jury question. An agreement between the successor and the predecessor absolving the successor of liability is not dispositive of whether the successor owed such a duty.[80] When the predecessor corporation remains in business, the predecessor will remain liable and the successor will not be liable. Conversely, where the predecessor has ceased to exist and the successor is a mere continuation of the first through a sale, liability may be imposed on the successor.[81]

11. **Market Share Liability/Enterprise Liability**

The above theories are not recognized under the laws of the State of Indiana.

12. **Privity**

Lack of privity between plaintiff and defendant does not bar plaintiff's personal injury claim sounding in strict liability or negligence.[82] The user or consumer need not have bought the product from or entered into any contractual relation with the seller.[83] A consumer may sue a manufacturer for economic losses based on the implied warranty of merchantability even if the consumer purchased the product from an intermediary in the distribution chain. There is no longer a requirement of "vertical" privity for such a claim.[84]

13. **Failure to Warn**

As set forth above, under the IPLA, "inadequate-warnings claims are to be governed by negligence principles rather than strict liability."[85] A product is deemed defective if the seller fails to properly package or label the product to provide adequate instructions for safe use and to provide warnings as to dangers inherent to improper use.[86] The rule applies when the seller, by exercising reasonable diligence, could have made such warnings or instructions available to the user or consumer.[87] The adequacy of warnings is generally a question of fact.[88] The warning should be of such intensity as to cause a reasonable person to exercise for his or her own safety caution commensurate with the potential danger.[89] A warning's adequacy is measured by its factual content, the manner in which it is expressed, and the method of conveying these facts.[90] A party is not required to provide a "physics lesson" regarding the operation of a product.[91] A manufacturer must only warn of reasonably foreseeable dangers.[92] There is no duty to warn of open and obvious dangers.[93] Where the manufacturer has provided adequate warnings regarding its product and the seller has passed the warnings onto the buyer, the seller has no duty to provide additional warnings to the buyer.[94] In the context of warnings on prescription drugs, the IPLA is not expressly preempted by the Federal Food, Drug, and Cosmetic

Act.[95] The Federal Insecticide, Fungicide, and Rodenticide Act preempts failure to warn claims under IPLA against pesticide manufactures; however, failure to warn claims against pesticide applicators is not preempted.[96] In the context of automobile airbag warnings, the safety standards promulgated under the National Traffic and Motor Vehicle Safety Act ("Safety Act") do not preempt failure-to-warn claims.[97] The regulations for airbag warnings under the Safety Act provide a floor, not a ceiling, for the warnings to be included in the owner's manual.[98]

As noted above, the IPLA expressly requires proof that the manufacturer failed to act with reasonable care in a product liability case predicated on lack of warnings.[99] A manufacturer's warnings will not render a product with a manufacturing defect non-defective, regardless of whether compliance with the warning would have rendered the product safe.[100]

14. **Post-Sale Duty to Warn**

As stated above, the IPLA provides that a product is defective if the seller fails to properly package or label the product to give reasonable warnings of danger about the product or instructions on proper use. It is possible that a post-sale duty to warn exists in limited circumstances. For instance, in a case involving a drug product, the Indiana Court of Appeals held that the duty to warn is limited to what the manufacturer knew during the period that the plaintiff took the drug in question.[101] Furthermore, dicta from a 1981 Indiana Supreme Court case left open the possibility of the existence of a post-sale duty to warn.[102] Any such claims would be subject to the IPLA's ten-year statute of repose.[103] However, the Seventh Circuit Court of Appeals applying Indiana law, recently held that "although the Indiana legislature did not expressly exclude a manufacturer's post-sale duty to warn from the IPLA, the statute does not expressly proscribe or define any cause of action arising from a post-sale duty to warn."[104] Therefore, the court concluded that plaintiff's claim for post-sale duty to warn failed.[105]

15. **Learned Intermediary**

The learned intermediary doctrine, the sophisticated user exception, and the sophisticated intermediary doctrine are all exceptions to the statutory duty to warn. The IPLA codified the sophisticated user exception.[106] The learned intermediary exception is limited to prescription drugs and medical devices. Under this exception, the manufacturer only has the duty to warn the intermediary rather than the user.[107] The duty to warn is also limited to the intermediary under the "knowledgeable" or "sophisticated intermediary exception."[108] This exception is applicable if the product is sold to an intermediary with knowledge or sophistication equal to that of the manufacturer, the manufacturer adequately warns this intermediary, and the manufacturer can reasonably rely on the intermediary to warn the ultimate consumer.[109]

16. **Substantial Alteration/Abnormal Use**

    The IPLA provides only three defenses: modification, incurred risk, and misuse.[110] The defense of modification provides that a manufacturer is not liable when a substantial change has occurred to the product between the time the product left the manufacturer's hands and the time of the accident if the change was not reasonably foreseeable.[111] A substantial alteration is a change to the product that increases the likelihood of a product malfunction.[112] Misuse of the product is also a defense if the misuse was not reasonably foreseeable at the time the product was sold or conveyed.[113] Misuse is defined as a use for a purpose or in a manner not foreseeable by the manufacturer.[114] If the injured person is reckless with regard to his own safety in using the product, recovery against even a reckless manufacturer may be barred.[115] The Seventh Circuit Court of Appeals has interpreted the misuse defense to be merely an aspect of comparative fault, rather than a complete defense.[116]

17. **State-of-the Art**

    Prior to July 1, 1995, the IPLA provided a defense if the design, manufacture, inspection, packaging, warnings, or labeling of the product conformed with the generally recognized state of the art at the time the product was designed, manufactured, packaged, and labeled.[117]

    The July 1, 1995 amendments to the IPLA deleted the former state of the art defense and created a rebuttable presumption that a product was not defective and the manufacturer or seller was not negligent if, before the sale, the product:

    1. was in conformity with the generally recognized state of the art applicable to the safety of the product; or

    2. complied with codes, standards, regulations, or specifications of the United States, Indiana, or their agencies.[118]

    A manufacturer or seller attempting to invoke a rebuttable presumption must introduce state of the art evidence that is relevant to the risk at issue in the case. "The fact that a product may be in conformity with the generally recognized state of the art applicable to a particular risk does not make it state of the art for all purposes."[119]

    The rebuttable presumption does not shift the burden of persuasion, but it does impose upon the plaintiff a burden of producing evidence.[120] Even after the plaintiff produces evidence, the rebuttable presumption does not drop from the case, but is given continuing effect and may be considered by the jury.[121]

18. **Malfunction**

    Evidence of a malfunction is insufficient to make a prima facie case that the alleged defective condition was attributable to the defendant manufacturer.[122] Any alteration by the user or consumer that increases the likelihood of a malfunction is a substantial change that may bar recovery under the IPLA.[123]

19. Standards and Governmental Regulation

Standards set by the industry do not define the standard of reasonable care against which the conduct of a manufacturer in such industry is measured in a negligence case.[124] Standards and government regulations are relevant to the presumption described in paragraph 17 above. A claim under the IPLA may, in some instances, be preempted by federal law where allowing such a claim could upset a careful, comprehensive regulatory scheme established by federal law.[125]

20. Other Accidents

In a product liability action, evidence of prior accidents may be admissible. However, the proponent of such evidence must lay a proper foundation by demonstrating sufficient similarity of circumstances and conditions between the other accidents and the one in issue.[126] Evidence of prior accidents may also be admissible as proof in determining the issue of punitive damages.[127]

21. Misrepresentation

The above theory has no separate existence apart from fraud under the laws of the State of Indiana.

22. Destruction or Loss of Product

"In Indiana, the exclusive possession of facts or evidence by a party, coupled with the suppression of the facts or evidence by that party, may result in an inference that the production of the evidence would be against the interest of the party which suppresses it."[128] The rule applies both to situations in which a party actively prevents the disclosure of the evidence as well as when the parties simply failed to produce the evidence.[129] Further, the rule applies "where the party spoliates evidence prior to the commencement of a lawsuit that the party knew or should have known was imminent."[130]

The Indiana Court of Appeals has ruled that if an expert for one of the parties has control of a piece of evidence and that evidence disappears, the expert should not be allowed to testify at trial as to any test on the evidence which the other party was unable to duplicate.[131] This rule applies even if the result is that the first party's case "would be severely hampered, if not rendered impossible."[132]

23. Economic Loss/Damage

The IPLA subjects a seller of a defective product to liability for physical harm caused by that product to the user or consumer or to his property. In general, there is no liability in tort for "pure economic loss caused unintentionally."[133] Where a claim is based upon the failure of a product to perform as expected and the plaintiff incurs only "pure" economic damages, the plaintiff's remedy is under contract law, not the IPLA.[134] "Pure" economic loss is defined as "pecuniary harm not resulting from an injury to the plaintiff's person or property.[135] However, the economic loss doctrine does not preclude a plaintiff from pursuing a remedy for breach of contract and a "tort action for a loss that is not purely economic and not covered in the contract,"—*i.e.*, for personal injury or damages to property under the IPLA.[136] In order to recover damages, the defective product must cause damage to other property or cause an injury to a person.[137] A consumer or user may not maintain a cause of action for damage to the product itself.[138] The economic loss rule does not bar recovery for damage that a separately acquired defective product or service causes to other portions of a larger product into which the former has been incorporated.[139] Furthermore, recovery for damages to property can be had under the IPLA only if the injury results in sudden, major damage to property; gradually evolving damage to property and economic losses incurred on account of such gradual damage are not recoverable under the IPLA. The Indiana Supreme Court instructed courts to recognize the economic loss doctrine as a "*general* rule" and to be "open to appropriate exceptions, such as (for illustration only) lawyer malpractice, breach of a duty of care owed to a plaintiff by a fiduciary, breach of a duty to settle owed by a liability insurer to the insured, and negligent misstatement."[140] However, in the same decision, the Court refused to make an exception for engineers and design professionals.[141]

Additionally, the IPLA does not recognize damages for mental or emotional distress since such a claim does not fit the definition of "physical harm" under the IPLA.[142] However, a plaintiff may have a cause of action under the IPLA for mental or emotional distress if the claimant can prove that some "physical manifestation of [his or her] emotional distress" arose out of an injury related to the defective product.[143]

24. Enhanced Injury/Crashworthiness

Indiana recognizes the enhancement of injury theory of liability under the IPLA.[144] In the context of claims involving crashworthiness, a court will apply the general principles of negligence when determining whether there is a product defect.[145] The manufacturer is not required to make an injury-proof vehicle, but instead, merely has to ensure the design does not create an unreasonable risk of injury.[146] Juries are to apply the comparative fault of the plaintiff in enhanced injury claims and "shall apportion fault" to the plaintiff if that fault is a proximate cause of the harm for which damages are being sought.[147] A question exists as to whether or not the theory would apply outside of the motor vehicle context to other products.[148]

25. **Bystander**

A bystander injured by a product who would reasonably be expected to be in the vicinity of the product during its reasonably expected use may recover.[149] The bystander is not required to sustain bodily injury to be able to maintain an action under the IPLA for damage to his property.[150] The Indiana Supreme Court recently reversed a court of appeals decision to hold that the wife of a worker who brought asbestos dust home on his clothes was a bystander under the IPLA.[151] The normal expected use of asbestos products entails contact with its migrating residue and the cleansing of this residue from one's person and clothing.[152]

D. NEGLIGENCE

As noted above, the IPLA was amended effective July 1, 1995, to make its provisions applicable to all product liability actions against a manufacturer regardless of the legal theory utilized for recovery.[153] This includes theories of fraud.[154] The IPLA "departs from strict liability" and applies a negligence standard to design defect and inadequate warnings claims.[155] To establish negligence, the plaintiff must prove the following to recover on a claim of negligence under the IPLA: (1) a duty owed by the defendant to the plaintiff; (2) a breach of that duty; and (3) an injury to the plaintiff proximately caused by the breach.[156]

E. BREACH OF WARRANTY

As noted above, the IPLA governs all product liability actions, whether the theory of recovery is strict liability or negligence in tort. Claims for breach of implied warranty sounding in tort are duplicative with strict liability claims and are subsumed by the IPLA.[157] However, breach of warranty claims alleged under Indiana's UCC are independent from claims under the IPLA.[158] Contract disclaimers that purport to limit a seller's liability for "any claim of any kind" are unenforceable as to strict liability claims.[159] One court described the relationship between tort claims under the IPLA and contract claims under the UCC as "still evolving in Indiana law."[160] The court noted that the recovery of consequential damages for injuries to person or property under the UCC "looks very much like a product claim in tort."[161]

F. PUNITIVE DAMAGES

Punitive damages may be recovered in a product liability suit based on negligence or strict liability.[162] To support a claim for punitive damages, there must be clear and convincing evidence that the tortious conduct was committed oppressively, fraudulently, or with malice or gross negligence.[163]

Effective July 1, 1995, the Indiana legislature enacted certain punitive damages statutes which provide that punitive damages awards may not be more than the greater of: (1) three times the amount of compensatory damages; or (2) fifty thousand dollars. In most cases the person who received the punitive damage award will be paid 25 percent of the award and the state treasurer will be paid 75 percent of the award for deposit in the violent crimes compensation fund.[164]

G. PRE- AND POST-JUDGMENT INTEREST

1. Pre-Judgment Interest

As a part of the judgment, a court may award pre-judgment interest.[165] By statute, limitations have been placed on pre-judgment interest awards.[166] Pre-judgment interest is not available from the Patient's Compensation Fund, for awards of punitive damages, nor against the state or a political subdivision.[167] Pre-judgment interest is disallowed if either the plaintiff or defendant fails to make a settlement offer that meets the specifications of the statute.[168] The amount of interest is to be set by the court at a rate of simple interest between six and ten percent per year.[169] Pre-judgment interest begins to accrue at a statutorily defined period which cannot exceed forty-eight months.[170] Pre-judgment interest is only appropriate in situations where "the injury and consequent damages are complete and must be ascertained as of a particular time and in accordance with fixed rules of evidence and known standards of value" rather than based on the best judgment of the court.[171] Therefore, pre-judgment interest requires that the value of the liability be predetermined such that the only question for the trier of fact is the existence of liability.[172]

2. Post-Judgment Interest

Post-judgment interest on judgments for money begins to accrue from the date of the return of the verdict or finding of the court. The rate of interest is the rate agreed upon in the original contract sued upon, but may not exceed an annual rate of 8 percent. If either there is no contract or no agreement in the contract, the annual rate of 8 percent shall be charged by the court.[173] With regard to medical malpractice judgments, the plaintiff is entitled to post-judgment interest from the health care provider and from the Patient's Compensation Fund.[174] Each is held liable for the interest.[175] In addition, the statute only provides for the accrual of interest on the judgment and not for the accrual of interest on the interest on the judgment; therefore, the creditor cannot recover compound interest, but rather simple interest is calculated only on the outstanding principal balance.[176] For each payment, the principal is reduced by the amount of the payment that is in excess of the interest accrued.[177]

H. EMPLOYER IMMUNITY FROM SUIT

With few exceptions, employers are immune from suit under the exclusive remedy provision of the Indiana Worker's Compensation Act.[178] To be covered by the Act, the injury must be by accident and within the course of employment. The phrase "by accident" means that the injury was intended by neither the victim-employee nor by the employer.[179] With regard to acts of co-employees, if the injured employee was actively participating in horseplay or other non job-related activities, then the exclusive remedy provision does not apply. However, if the injured employee is merely an innocent victim of another's prank, the exclusivity provision does apply.[180] Therefore, intentional acts of a co-worker fall within the definition of "by accident."[181] However, intentional torts of the employer are beyond the reach of the exclusivity provision, but the employer rather than his agent must harbor the intent.[182] If the employer is a corporation rather than an individual, the plaintiff must show that the corporation is the tortfeasor's alter ego or that injuries were the intended product of corporate policy.[183] For the exclusive remedy provision to apply, the injury must not only be by accident, but also arise out of employment or arise in the course of employment.[184] To determine whether or not an act was "in the course of employment," the time, place and circumstances surrounding the act will be evaluated.[185] If the act directly or indirectly advances the interests of the employer, even if it occurs at an employer sponsored party, it will most likely be found to be within "the course of employment."[186] If an employee has an action that could stand in tort and falls outside of the Act, but accepts compensation under the Act, then the courts will lack subject matter jurisdiction to hear the claim.[187] Finally, the exclusivity provision of the Worker's Compensation Act does not prevent an employee from maintaining an action against a third-party tortfeasor if the third party is not in the same employ as the plaintiff.[188]

I. STATUTES

As noted in the preceding sections, statutes other than the IPLA that may be relevant to product liability actions include the Uniform Commercial Code sections applicable to breach of warranty claims and the CFA, which applies to negligence actions.[189]

J. JOINT AND SEVERAL LIABILITY

Joint and several liability has been abolished by law in Indiana in a product liability action so each defendant cannot be held liable for more than the amount of fault attributable to that defendant.[190] Under the CFA, there is no right of contribution among tortfeasors.[191] However, rights of indemnity are not precluded. Contribution differs from indemnity in that contribution involves partial reimbursement of one who discharged common liability whereas indemnity is total reimbursement of the amount of liability based on contract or on the constructive liability of the indemnified party.[192] However, if there was any negligence on the part of the party seeking indemnification, it will not be granted.[193]

Mark J. R. Merkle
Marc T. Quigley
Krieg DeVault LLP
One Indiana Square, Suite 2800
Indianapolis, Indiana 46204-2079
(317) 636-4341
(Fax) (317) 636-1507

ENDNOTES - INDIANA

1. *See Masterman v. Veldman's Equip., Inc.*, 530 N.E.2d 312 (Ind. Ct. App. 1988), *superseded by statute*, 1999 Technical Corrections Bill, Pub. L. No. 1-1999, Ind. Code § 34-20-8-1, *as recognized in Green v. Ford Motor Co.*, 942 N.E.2d 791 (Ind. 2011).

2. *See Miller v. Todd*, 551 N.E.2d 1139, 1143 (Ind. 1990), *superseded by statute*, 1999 Technical Corrections Bill, Pub. L. No. 1-1999, Ind. Code § 34-20-8-1, *as recognized in Green v. Ford Motor Co.*, 942 N.E.2d 791, 791 (Ind. 2011).

3. *See* Ind. Code § 34-6-2-45 (2014), Ind. Code § 34-51-2 (2014), Ind. Code § 34-20-1-1 (2014), Ind. Code § 34-20-2-1 (2014).

4. *See* Ind. Code § 26-1-2-103 (2014); *see also Insul-Mark Midwest, Inc. v. Modern Materials, Inc.*, 612 N.E.2d 550, 554 (Ind. 1993).

5. IPLA: Ind. Code § 34-20 (2014)(previously Ind. Code §§ 33-1-1.5-1 to -10); CFA: Ind. Code § 34-51-2 (2014) (previously Ind. Code §§ 34-4-33-2 to -14); Punitive Damages: Ind. Code § 34-51-3 (2014) (previously Ind. Code §§ 34-4-34-3 to -6).

6. *See* Ind. Code § 34-20-1 (2014), Ind. Code § 34-20-2 (2014), Ind. Code § 34-6-2-29 (2014), Ind. Code § 34-6-2-45 (2014), Ind. Code § 34-6-2-77 (2014), Ind. Code § 34-6-2-105 (2014), Ind. Code § 34-6-2-114 (2014); Ind. Code § 34-6-2-115 (2014); Ind. Code § 34-6-2-136 (2014); Ind. Code § 34-6-2-146 (2014); Ind. Code § 34-51-2 (2014); Ind. Code § 34-51-3-3 (2014), Ind. Code § 34-51-3-4 (2014), Ind. Code § 34-51-3-5 (2014), Ind. Code § 34-51-3-6 (2014).

7. Ind. Code § 34-20-1-1; *Stegemoller v. ACandS, Inc.*, 767 N.E.2d 974, 976 (Ind. 2002); 729 F.3d 724, 734 (7th Cir. 2013) (addressing history of IPLA and theories of recovery, and noting that "[a] product can be defective because of a manufacturing defect, a design defect, or a lack of adequate instructions and warnings.").

8. Ind. Code § 34-20-3-1 (2014).

9. *Degussa Corp. v. Mullens*, 744 N.E.2d 407, 410 (Ind. 2001); *Dorman v. Osmose, Inc.*, 782 N.E.2d 463, 466 (Ind. Ct. App. 2003).

10. *Degussa Corp. v. Mullens*, 744 N.E.2d 407, 411 (Ind. 2001); *Dorman v. Osmose, Inc.*, 782 N.E.2d 463, 467 (Ind. Ct. App. 2003).

11. *Degussa Corp. v. Mullens*, 744 N.E.2d 407, 411 (Ind. 2001).

12. *Technisand, Inc. v. Melton*, 898 N.E.2d 303, 306 (Ind. Ct. App. 2008).

13. *Technisand, Inc. v. Melton*, 898 N.E.2d 303, 306 (Ind. Ct. App. 2008).

14. Ind. Code § 34-20-3-1 (2014).

15. Ind. Code § 34-20-3-1 (2014).

16. Ind. Code § 34-20-3-1 (2014).

17. *Stump v. Ind. Equip. Co.*, 601 N.E.2d 398, 401-02 (Ind. Ct. App. 1992).

18. *See* Ind. Code § 34-20-3-1 (2014).

19. *Land v. Yamaha Motor Corp.*, 272 F.3d 514, 518 (7th Cir. 2001) (citing *Dague v. Piper Aircraft Corp.*, 418 N.E.2d 207 (Ind. 1981)).

20. *Whittaker v. Fed. Cartridge Corp.*, 466 N.E.2d 480, 482 (Ind. Ct. App. 1984).

21. *Wenger v. Weldy*, 605 N.E.2d 796, 798 (Ind. Ct. App. 1993).

22. *Florian v. GATX Rail Corp.*, 930 N.E.2d 1190, 1201-02 (Ind. Ct. App. 2010).

23. *Wojcik v. Almase*, 451 N.E.2d 336, 341 (Ind. Ct. App. 1983).

24. *Barnes v. A.H. Robins Co., Inc.*, 476 N.E.2d 84, 87-88 (Ind. 1985); *Wojcik v. Almase*, 451 N.E.2d 336, 341 (Ind. Ct. App. 1983).

25. *See McIntosh v. Melroe Co.*, 729 N.E.2d 972, 984 (Ind. 2000).

26. *See Sears Roebuck and Co. v. Noppert*, 705 N.E.2d 1065, 1068 (Ind. Ct. App. 1999).

27. Ind. Code § 34-20-3-2 (2014).

28. *Allied Signal, Inc. v. Ott*, 785 N.E.2d 1068 (Ind. 2003).

29. *Allied Signal, Inc. v. Ott*, 785 N.E.2d 1068, 1073 (Ind. 2003).

30. *Allied Signal, Inc. v. Ott*, 785 N.E.2d 1068, 1073 (Ind. 2003).

31. *Allied Signal, Inc. v. Ott*, 785 N.E.2d 1068, 1073 (Ind. 2003); *Jurich v. Garlock, Inc.*, 785 N.E.2d 1093 (Ind. 2003); *Harris v. A.C. & S., Inc.*, 785 N.E.2d 1087 (Ind. 2003).

32. *Allied Signal, Inc. v. Ott*, 785 N.E.2d 1068, 1075 (Ind. 2003).

33. *See Reed v. Cent. Soya Co., Inc.*, 621 N.E.2d 1069, 1072 (Ind. 1993), *modified on reh'g*, 644 N.E.2d 84 (Ind. 1994).

34. *Reed v. Cent. Soya Co., Inc.*, 621 N.E.2d 1069, 1073 (Ind. 1993).

35. Ind. Code § 34-20-2-1 (2014).

36. Ind. Code § 34-6-2-146 (2014).

37. *Cole v. Lantis Corp.*, 714 N.E.2d 194, 198-99 (Ind. Ct. App. 1999) (citing *Welch v. Scripto-Tokai Corp.*, 651 N.E.2d 810, 814 (Ind. Ct. App. 1995)).

38. *Corbin v. Coleco Indus., Inc.*, 748 F.2d 411, 419 (7th Cir. 1984).

39. *Weigle v. SPX Corp.*, 729 F.3d 724, 734 (7th Cir. 2013).

40. Ind. Code § 34-20-4-4 (2014); *Peters v. Judd Drugs, Inc.*, 602 N.E.2d 162, 164 (Ind. Ct. App. 1992).

41. *Bourne v. Marty Gilman, Inc.*, 452 F.3d 632, 638 (7th Cir. 2006).

42. Ind. Code § 34-20-2-2 (2014).

43. *TRW Vehicle Safety Sys., Inc. v. Moore*, 936 N.E.2d 201, 209, 214 (Ind. 2010) (citing Ind. Code § 34-20-2-2).

44. *Marshall v. Clark Equip. Co.*, 680 N.E.2d 1102, 1106 (Ind. Ct. App. 1997).

45. *Weigle v. SPX Corp.*, 729 F.3d 724, 737 (7th Cir. 2013).

46. *Weigle v. SPX Corp.*, 729 F.3d 724, 738 (7th Cir. 2013).

47. *Weigle v. SPX Corp.*, 729 F.3d 724, 734 n.2 (7th Cir. 2013) (analyzing *TRW Vehicle Safety Sys., Inc. v. Moore*, 936 N.E.2d 201, 209 n.2 (Ind. 2010)).

48. *See U-Haul Int'l, Inc. v. Nulls Mach. & Mfg. Shop*, 736 N.E.2d 271, 281-85 (Ind. Ct. App. 2000); *Marshall v. Clark Equip. Co.*, 680 N.E.2d 1102, 1108 (Ind. Ct. App. 1997); *Schooley v. Ingersoll Rand, Inc.*, 631 N.E.2d 932, 937 (Ind. Ct. App. 1994).

49. *Schooley v. Ingersoll Rand, Inc.*, 631 N.E.2d 932, 937 (Ind. Ct. App. 1994) (quoting *Montgomery Ward & Co. v. Gregg*, 554 N.E.2d 1145, 1156 (Ind. Ct. App. 1990)).

50. *See Jarrell v. Monsanto Co.*, 528 N.E.2d 1158, 1167 (Ind. Ct. App. 1988).

51. Ind. Code § 34-20-8-1 (2014).

52. Ind. Code § 34-20-8-1 (2014), Ind. Code § 34-51-2-5 (2014), Ind. Code § 34-51-2-6 (2014); Elizabeth M. Behnke, Note, *Partial Settlement of Multiple Tortfeasor Cases Under the Indiana Comparative Fault Act*, 22 Ind. L. Rev. 939 (1989).

53. *Coffman v. PSI Energy, Inc.*, 815 N.E.2d 522, 527-28 (Ind. Ct. App. 2004).

54. Ind. Code § 34-6-2-77 (2014).

55. Ind. Code § 34-6-2-77 (2014).

56. Ind. Code § 34-6-2-77 (2014).

57. *R.R. Donnelley & Sons Co. v. N. Tex. Steel Co., Inc.*, 752 N.E.2d 112, 122 (Ind. Ct. App. 2001) (quoting *Lenhardt Tool & Die Co. v. Lumpe*, 703 N.E.2d 1079, 1085 (Ind. Ct. App. 1998)).

58. *Williams v. REP Corp.*, 302 F.3d 660, 665 (7th Cir. 2002); *accord Watson v. Covance*, No. 3:10-cv-99-RLY-WGH, 2010 WL 5058391, at *2 (S.D. Ind. Dec. 6, 2010) (holding that drugs administered during clinical trials, while a "product" within the construct of the IPLA, are not "sold, leased, or otherwise placed into the stream of commerce" precluding recovery under IPLA).

59. *Duncan v. M & M Auto Serv., Inc.*, 898 N.E.2d 338, 342 (citing Restatement (Second) of Torts § 400 (1965)).

60. Ind. Code § 34-20-2-4 (2014); *see also Kennedy v. Guess, Inc.*, 806 N.E.2d 776, 781 (Ind. 2004).

61. *Warriner v. DC Marshall Jeep*, 962 N.E.2d 1263, 1268 (Ind. Ct. App. 2012).

62. *Kennedy v. Guess, Inc.*, 806 N.E.2d 776, 786 (Ind. 2004).

63. *Butler v. City of Peru*, 733 N.E.2d 912, 919 (Ind. 2000) (quoting *Thiele v. Faygo Beverage*, Inc., 489 N.E.2d 562, 586 (Ind. Ct. App. 1986)).

64. *Butler v. City of Peru*, 733 N.E.2d 912, 919 (Ind. 2000).

65. *Vaughn v. Daniels Co. (W. Va.), Inc.*, 841 N.E.2d 1133, 1140 (Ind. 2006).

66. *Vaughn v. Daniels Co. (W. Va.), Inc.*, 841 N.E.2d 1133, 1141 (Ind. 2006) (citing *Kaneko v. Hilo Coast Processing*, 654 P.2d 343, 350 (Haw. 1982)).

67. *Vaughn v. Daniels Co. (W. Va.), Inc.*, 841 N.E.2d 1133, 1142 (Ind. 2006).

68. Ind. Code § 34-6-2-115 (2014).

69. Ind. Code § 34-6-2-114 (2014).

70. Ind. Code § 34-6-2-114 (2014).

71. *See Dow Chem. Co. v. Ebling*, 723 N.E.2d 881, 904-05 (Ind. Ct. App. 2000) (asserting that the primary thrust of a pest control transaction was for the pest control service and not the sale of pesticide products), *aff'd in part, vacated in part, Dow Chem. Co. v. Ebling ex rel. Ebling*, 753 N.E.2d 633 (Ind. 2001).

72. *Baker v. Heye-America*, 799 N.E.2d 1135, 1140-41 (Ind. Ct. App. 2003).

73. *Butler v. City of Peru*, 733 N.E.2d 912, 919 (Ind. 2000).

74. Ind. Code § 34-20-1-1 (2014), Ind. Code § 34-20-1-2 (2014), Ind. Code § 34-20-1-3 (2014), Ind. Code § 34-20-1-4 (2014), Ind. Code § 34-20-2-1 (2014); *Link v. Sun Oil Co.*, 312 N.E.2d 126, 130 (Ind. Ct. App. 1974).

75. *Link v. Sun Oil Co.*, 312 N.E.2d 126, 130 (Ind. Ct. App. 1974).

76. *Lucas v. Dorsey Corp.*, 609 N.E.2d 1191, 1202 (Ind. Ct. App. 1993).

77. Ind. Code § 34-20-4-4 (2014); *see also* John W. Wade, *A Conspectus of Manufacturers' Liability for Products*, 10 IND. L. REV. 755, 767-68 (1977).

78. Ind. Code § 34-20-6-3 (2014).

79. *Johnson v. Kempler Indus., Inc.*, 677 N.E.2d 531, 538 (Ind. Ct. App. 1997).

80. *See Lucas v. Dorsey Corp.*, 609 N.E.2d 1191, 1200-01 (Ind. Ct. App. 1993).

81. *Guerrero v. Allison Engine Co.*, 725 N.E.2d 479, 483-87 (Ind. Ct. App. 2000).

82. *Peters v. Forster*, 804 N.E.2d 736, 741 (Ind. 2004); *Gen. Elec. Co. v. Drake*, 535 N.E.2d 156, 158-59 (Ind. Ct. App. 1989).

83. Ind. Code § 34-20-2-2 (2014); *McClellon v. Thermo King Corp.*, No. 1:11-cv-01337-SEB-MJD, 2013 WL 6571946, at *4 (S.D. Ind. Dec. 13, 2013).

84. *Hyundai Motor Am., Inc. v. Goodin*, 822 N.E.2d 947, 960 (Ind. 2005), *abrogating Candlelight Homes, Inc. v. Zornes*, 414 N.E.2d 980 (Ind. Ct. App. 1981), *Martin Rispens & Son v. Hall Farms, Inc.*, 621 N.E.2d 1078 (Ind. 1993), *Lane v. Barringer*, 407 N.E.2d 1173 (Ind. Ct. App. 1980), and *Richards v. Goerg Boat & Motors Co.*, 384 N.E.2d 1084 (Ind. Ct. App. 1979).

85. *Weigle v. SPX Corp.*, 729 F.3d 724, 737 (7th Cir. 2013) (citing Ind. Code § 34-20-2-2).

86. Ind. Code § 34-20-4-2 (2014); *Coffman v. PSI Energy, Inc.*, 815 N.E.2d 522, 527 (Ind. Ct. App. 2004).

87. *McClain v. Chem-Lube Corp.*, 759 N.E.2d 1096, 1103 (Ind. Ct. App. 2001), *disapproved of by Schultz v. Ford Motor Co.*, 857 N.E.2d 977 (Ind. 2006).

88. *Jarrell v. Monsanto Co.*, 528 N.E.2d 1158, 1162 (Ind. Ct. App. 1988).

89. *Weigle v. SPX Corp.*, 729 F.3d 724, 731 (7th Cir. 2013) *(citing Jarrell v. Monsanto Co.*, 528 N.E.2d 1158, 1162 (Ind. Ct. App. 1988)).

90. *Weigle v. SPX Corp.*, 729 F.3d 724, 731 (7th Cir. 2013).

91. *Weigle v. SPX Corp.*, 729 F.3d 724, 733 (7th Cir. 2013).

92. *Wingett v. Teledyne Indus., Inc.*, 479 N.E.2d 51, 56 (Ind. 1985), *overruled on other grounds by Douglas v. Irvin*, 549 N.E.2d 368 (Ind. 1990).

93. *First Nat'l Bank & Trust Corp. v. Am. Eurocopter Corp.*, 378 F.3d 682, 690 (7th Cir. 2004).

94. *Ford Motor Co. v. Rushford*, 868 N.E.2d 806, 811 (Ind. 2007).

95. *Bell v. Lollar*, 791 N.E.2d 849, 854 (Ind. Ct. App. 2003).

96. *Dow Chem. Co. v. Ebling ex rel. Ebling*, 753 N.E.2d 633, 639 (Ind. 2001).

97. *Cook v. Ford Motor Co.*, 913 N.E.2d 311, 320-26 (Ind. Ct. App. 2009).

98. *Cook v. Ford Motor Co.*, 913 N.E.2d 311, 325 (Ind. Ct. App. 2009).

99. Ind. Code § 34-20-2-2 (2014).

100. *Chapman v. Maytag Corp.*, 297 F.3d 682, 689 (7th Cir. 2002).

101. *Ortho Pharm. Corp. v. Chapman*, 388 N.E.2d 541, 558 (Ind. Ct. App. 1979).

102. *Dague v. Piper Aircraft Corp.*, 418 N.E.2d 207, 212 (Ind. 1981).

103. *Dague v. Piper Aircraft Corp.*, 418 N.E.2d 207, 212 (Ind. 1981).

104. *Tober v. Graco Children's Prods.*, 431 F.3d 572, 579 (7th Cir. 2005).

105. *Tober v. Graco Children's Prods.*, 431 F.3d 572, 579 (7th Cir. 2005).

106. Ind. Code § 34-20-6-3 (2014).

107. *Ortho Pharm. Corp. v. Chapman*, 388 N.E.2d 541, 548-49 (Ind. Ct. App. 1979).

108. *Natural Gas Odorizing, Inc. v. Downs*, 685 N.E.2d 155, 163 (Ind. Ct. App. 1997).

109. *First Nat'l Bank & Trust Corp. v. Am. Eurocopter Corp.*, 378 F.3d 682, 691 (7th Cir. 2004).

110. *Weigle v. SPX Corp.*, 729 F.3d 724, 738 (7th Cir. 2013) (citing Ind. Code § 34-20-6-3, Ind. Code § 34-20-6-4, and Ind. Code § 34-20-6-5).

111. *Bishop v. Firestone Tire & Rubber Co.*, 814 F.2d 437, 440-44 (7th Cir. 1987).

112. *Tober v. Graco Children's Prods., Inc.*, No. 1:02-CV-1682-LJM-WTL, 2004 WL 1987239, at *6 (S.D. Ind. July 28, 2004) (unpublished), *aff'd*, 431 F.3d 572 (7th Cir. 2005).

113. Ind. Code § 34-20-6-4 (2014); *Morgen v. Ford Motor Co.*, 797 N.E.2d 1146, 1150 (Ind. 2004).

114. *Tober v. Graco Children's Prods., Inc.*, No. 1:02-CV-1682-LJM-WTL, 2004 WL 1987239, at *8 (S.D. Ind. July 28, 2004) (unpublished), *aff'd*, 431 F.3d 572 (7th Cir. 2005).

115. *Koske v. Townsend Eng'g Co.*, 526 N.E.2d 985, 991 (Ind. Ct. App. 1988) (citing *Davis v. Stinson*, 508 N.E.2d 65, 67-68 (Ind. Ct. App. 1987)), *aff'd in part, vacated on other grounds*, 551 N.E.2d 437 (Ind. 1990).

116. *Weigle v. SPX Corp.*, 729 F.3d 724, 739 (7th Cir. 2013) (citing *Chapman v. Maytag Corp.*, 297 F.3d 682, 689 (7th Cir. 2002)); *cf. Morgen v. Ford Motor Co.*, 797 N.E.2d 1146, 1148 n.3 (Ind. 2003) (declining to decide whether misuse is a complete defense).

117. Ind. Code § 33-1-1.5-4 (1995), *repealed by* Civil Procedure-General Amendments, 1998 Ind. Pub. L. No. 1-1998, § 221 (amended 2004); *see also FMC Corp. v. Brown*, 526 N.E.2d 719, 729 (Ind. Ct. App. 1988), *aff'd on other grounds*, 551 N.E.2d 444 (Ind. 1990).

118. Ind. Code § 34-20-5-1 (2014); *Stuhlmacher v. Home Depot U.S.A., Inc.*, No. 2:10-CV-00467-JTM, 2013 WL 3201572 (N.D. Ind. June 21, 2013).

119. *Wade v. Terex-Telelect, Inc.*, 966 N.E.2d 186, 193 (Ind. Ct. App. 2012).

120. *Schultz v. Ford Motor Co.*, 857 N.E.2d 977, 984 (Ind. 2006).

121. *Schultz v. Ford Motor Co.*, 857 N.E.2d 977, 985 (Ind. 2006).

122. *Cornette v. Searjeant Metal Prods., Inc.*, 258 N.E.2d 652 (Ind. Ct. App. 1970).

123. *See Cornette v. Searjeant Metal Prods., Inc.*, 258 N.E.2d 652, 657 (Ind. Ct. App. 1970).

124. *Thiele v. Faygo Beverage, Inc.*, 489 N.E.2d 562, 575 (Ind. Ct. App. 1986).

125. *Roland v. Gen. Motors Corp.*, 881 N.E.2d 722, 726 (Ind. Ct. App. 2008), abrogated by *Williamson v. Mazda Motor of Am., Inc.*, 131 S. Ct. 1131 (2011).

126. *Ind. State Highway Comm'n v. Fair*, 423 N.E.2d 738, 740 (Ind. Ct. App. 1981).

127. *See Sipes v. Osmose Wood Preserving Co. of Am.*, 546 N.E.2d 1223, 1225-26 (Ind. 1989).

128. *Porter v. Irvin's Interstate Brick & Block Co., Inc.*, 691 N.E.2d 1363, 1364-65 (Ind. Ct. App. 1998) (citing *Westervelt v. Nat'l Mfg. Co.*, 69 N.E. 169, 172 (Ind. Ct. App. 1903)).

129. *Porter v. Irvin's Interstate Brick & Block Co., Inc.*, 691 N.E.2d 1363, 1365 (Ind. Ct. App. 1998) (citing *Morris v. Buchanan*, 44 N.E.2d 166, 169 (Ind. 1942)).

130. *Porter v. Irvin's Interstate Brick & Block Co., Inc.*, 691 N.E.2d 1363, 1365 (Ind. Ct. App. 1998).

131. *Columbian Rope Co. v. Todd*, 631 N.E.2d 941, 944 (Ind. Ct. App. 1994).

132. *Columbian Rope Co. v. Todd*, 631 N.E.2d 941, 944 (Ind. Ct. App. 1994).

133. *Indianapolis-Marion Cnty. Pub. Library v. Charlier Clark & Linard, P.C.*, 929 N.E.2d 722, 736 (Ind. 2010).

134. *Indianapolis-Marion Cnty. Pub. Library v. Charlier Clark & Linard, P.C.*, 929 N.E.2d 722, 728 (Ind. 2010) (citing *Martin Rispens & Son v. Hall Farms, Inc.*, 621 N.E.2d 1078, 1089-90 (Ind.1993); *Reed v. Central Soya Co., Inc.*, 621 N.E.2d 1069, 1075 (Ind.1993)).

135. *Indianapolis-Marion Cnty. Pub. Library v. Charlier Clark & Linard, P.C.*, 929 N.E.2d 722, 731 (Ind. 2010).

136. *Thalheimer v. Halum*, 973 N.E.2d 1145, 1152 (Ind. Ct. App. 2012) (citing *Fleetwood Enters., Inc. v. Progressive N. Ins. Co.*, 749 N.E.2d 492, 495 (Ind. 2001)).

137. *Progressive Ins. Co. v. Gen. Motors Corp.*, 749 N.E.2d 484, 486 (Ind. 2001).

138. *Fleetwood Enter., Inc. v. Progressive N. Ins. Co.*, 749 N.E.2d 492, 493-94 (Ind. 2001); *I/N Tek v. Hitachi, Ltd.*, 734 N.E.2d 584, 587-88 (Ind. Ct. App. 2000).

139. *Gunkel v. Renovations, Inc.*, 822 N.E.2d 150, 156 (Ind. 2005).

140. *Indianapolis-Marion Cnty. Pub. Library v. Charlier Clark & Linard, P.C.*, 929 N.E.2d 722, 736 (Ind. 2010).

141. *Indianapolis-Marion Cnty. Pub. Library v. Charlier Clark & Linard, P.C.*, 929 N.E.2d 722, 734-36 (Ind. 2010).

142. *Doerner v. Swisher Int'l, Inc.*, 272 F.3d 928, 932 (7th Cir. 2001).

143. *Doerner v. Swisher Int'l, Inc.*, 272 F.3d 928, 932 (7th Cir. 2001); *see also Barker v. Carefusion 303, Inc.*, No. 1:11-cv-00938-TWP-, 2012 WL 5997494, at *2 (S.D. Ind. Nov. 30, 2012).

144. *Green v. Ford Motor Co.*, 942 N.E.2d 791, 793 (Ind. 2011); *Rogers v. Ford Motor Co.*, 952 F. Supp. 606 (N.D. Ind. 1997); *Miller v. Todd*, 551 N.E.2d 1139, 1143 (Ind. 1990), *superseded by statute*, 1999 Technical Corrections Bill, Pub. L. No. 1-1999, Ind. Code § 34-20-8-1, *as recognized in Green v. Ford Motor Co.*, 942 N.E.2d 791, 791 (Ind. 2011).

145. *Stamper v. Hyundai Motor Co.*, 699 N.E.2d 678, 689 (Ind. Ct. App. 1998).

146. *Guerrero v. Allison Engine Co.*, 725 N.E.2d 479, 482 (Ind. Ct. App. 2000); *Stamper v. Hyundai Motor Co.*, 699 N.E.2d 678, 689 (Ind. Ct. App. 1998) (citing *Larsen v. Gen. Motors Corp.*, 391 F.2d 495 (8th Cir. 1968)).

147. *Green v. Ford Motor Co.*, 942 N.E.2d 791, 796 (Ind. 2011).

148. *Moss v. Crosman Corp.*, 945 F. Supp. 1167 (N.D. Ind. 1996).

149. Ind. Code § 34-6-2-29 (2014), Ind. Code § 34-6-2-147 (2014).

150. *Gen. Elec. Co. v. Drake*, 535 N.E.2d 156, 159 (Ind. Ct. App. 1989).

151. *Stegemoller v. ACandS, Inc.*, 767 N.E.2d 974, 976 (Ind. 2002).

152. *Stegemoller v. ACandS, Inc.*, 767 N.E.2d 974, 976 (Ind. 2002).

153. Ind. Code § 34-20-1-1 (2014); *Stegemoller v. ACandS, Inc.*, 767 N.E.2d 974, 976 (Ind. 2002); *Weigle v. SPX Corp.*, 729 F.3d 724, 731 (7th Cir. 2013) (addressing history of IPLA and theories of recovery, and noting that "[a] product can be defective because of a manufacturing defect, a design defect, or a lack of adequate instructions and warnings.").

154. *Ryan ex rel. Estate of Ryan v. Philip Morris USA, Inc.*, No. 1:05 CV 162, 2006 WL 449207 (N.D. Ind., Feb. 22, 2006).

155. *TRW Vehicle Safety Sys., Inc.*, 936 N.E.2d 201, 209 (citing Ind. Code § 34-20-2-2).

156. See *Kovach v. Alpharma, Inc.*, 890 N.E.2d 55, 67 (Ind. Ct. App. 2008) *vacated on other grounds, Kovach v. Caligor Midwest*, 913 N.E.2d 193 (Ind. 2009).

Endnotes - Indiana

157. *The Cincinnati Ins. Cos. v. Hamilton Beach/Proctor-Silex, Inc.*, No. 4:05 CV 49, 2006 WL 299064, at *3 (N.D. Ind. Feb. 7, 2006).

158. *The Cincinnati Ins. Cos. v. Hamilton Beach/Proctor-Silex, Inc.*, No. 4:05 CV 49, 2006 WL 299064, at *3 (N.D. Ind. Feb. 7, 2006).

159. *See McGraw-Edison Co. v. Ne. Rural Elec. Membership Corp.*, 678 N.E.2d 1120, 1122-25 (Ind. 1997); *Guerrero v. Allison Engine Co.*, 725 N.E.2d 479, 482 (Ind. Ct. App. 2000).

160. *Collins v. Pfizer, Inc.*, No. 1:08-cv-0888, 2009 WL 126913, at *2 (S.D. Ind. Jan. 20, 2009).

161. *Collins v. Pfizer, Inc.*, No. 1:08-cv-0888, 2009 WL 126913, at *2 (S.D. Ind. Jan. 20, 2009).

162. *See Sipes v. Osmose Wood Preserving Co. of Am.*, 546 N.E.2d 1223, 1223 (Ind. 1989).

163. *Ragsdale v. K-Mart Corp.*, 468 N.E.2d 524, 527 (Ind. Ct. App. 1984) (citing *Travelers Indem. Co. v. Armstrong*, 442 N.E.2d 349 (Ind. 1982)), *superseded by statute, as stated by Koske v. Townsend Eng'g Co.*, 551 N.E.2d 437, 441 (Ind. 1990).

164. Ind. Code § 34-51-3-6 (2014).

165. Ind. Code § 34-51-4-7 (2014).

166. *See* Ind. Code § 34-51-4 (2014).

167. Ind. Code § 34-51-4-2 (2014), Ind. Code § 34-51-4-3 (2014), Ind. Code § 34-51-4-4 (2014).

168. Ind. Code § 34-51-4-5 (2014), Ind. Code § 34-51-4-6 (2014).

169. Ind. Code § 34-51-4-9 (2014).

170. Ind. Code § 34-51-4-8 (2014).

171. *Eden United, Inc. v. Short*, 653 N.E.2d 126, 133 (Ind. Ct. App. 1995) (citing *N.Y.C., Chi. & St. Louis Ry. Co. v. Roper*, 96 N.E. 468, 472-73 (Ind. 1911)).

172. *Eden United, Inc. v. Short*, 653 N.E.2d 126, 133 (Ind. Ct. App. 1995).

173. Ind. Code § 24-4.6-1-101 (2014).

174. *Poehlman v. Feferman*, 717 N.E.2d 578, 583-84 (Ind. 1999).

175. *Poehlman v. Feferman*, 717 N.E.2d 578, 584 (Ind. 1999).

176. *Nesses v. Kile*, 656 N.E.2d 546, 547 (Ind. Ct. App. 1995).

177. *See Nesses v. Kile*, 656 N.E.2d 546, 547 (Ind. Ct. App. 1995).

178. Ind. Code § 22-3-2-6 (2014).

179. *Williams v. Delta Steel Corp.*, 695 N.E.2d 633, 635 n.5 (Ind. Ct. App. 1998) (citing *Perry v. Stitzer Buick GMC, Inc.*, 637 N.E.2d 1282, 1287 (Ind. 1994)). Ind. Code § 5-2-6.1-1 details compensation for victims or survivors of victims of violent crimes. Ind. Code § 5-2-6.1 (2014).

180. *Weldy v. Kline*, 616 N.E.2d 398, 402 n.2 (Ind. Ct. App. 1993). Courts have applied this distinction in a very fact sensitive matter and the herein cited case provides a good discussion of this principle.

181. *Baker v. Westinghouse Elec. Corp.*, 637 N.E.2d 1271, 1275 n.6 (Ind. 1994).

182. *See Lawson v. Raney Mfg., Inc.*, 678 N.E.2d 122, 125 (Ind. Ct. App. 1997), *disapproved of by GKN Co. v. Magness*, 744 N.E.2d 397 (Ind. 2001).

183. *Lawson v. Raney Mfg., Inc.*, 678 N.E.2d 122, 125 (Ind. Ct. App. 1997).

184. *Williams v. Delta Steel Corp.*, 695 N.E.2d 633, 635 (Ind. Ct. App. 1998).

185. *Weldy v. Kline*, 616 N.E.2d 398, 404 (Ind. Ct. App. 1993).

186. *Weldy v. Kline*, 616 N.E.2d 398, 404-05 (Ind. Ct. App. 1993).

187. *See Williams v. Delta Steel Corp.*, 695 N.E.2d 633, 636 (Ind. Ct. App. 1998).

188. *Williams v. Delta Steel Corp.*, 695 N.E.2d 633, 636 (Ind. Ct. App. 1998).

189. Ind. Code § 26-1-2 (2014), Ind. Code § 34-6-2-45 (2014), Ind. Code § 34-51-2 (2014).

190. Ind. Code § 34-20-7-1 (2014).

191. Ind. Code § 34-51-2-12 (2014).

192. *Mullen v. Cogdell*, 643 N.E.2d 390, 400 n.3 (Ind. Ct. App. 1994).

193. *Mullen v. Cogdell*, 643 N.E.2d 390, 400 n.3 (Ind. Ct. App. 1994).

IOWA

A. STATUTES OF LIMITATION

Causes of action for personal injuries must be brought within two years, whether based in contract or tort.[1] Causes of action founded on unwritten contracts, such as breach of implied warranty,[2] must be brought within five years.[3] Causes of action founded on written contracts, such as breach of warranty, must be brought within ten years.[4] When determining the date of injury or breach, the discovery rule is applied by Iowa courts.[5] Where a cause of action accrues while a person is a minor, the statute of limitations for the claim is extended one year following their attainment of the age of majority, which is eighteen.[6]

There is a fifteen-year statute of repose limited to causes of action founded on personal injury or death that arise from a product.[7] The statute begins to run on the date the product was "first purchased, leased, bailed or installed for use or consumption," unless the product is expressly warranted for a period of time longer then fifteen years.[8] For injuries caused by exposure to harmful products, the statute does not begin to run until the plaintiff discovers the injury and its cause or at such a time when the plaintiff should have discovered the injury and its cause.[9] Further, it will not function to bar a claim where the manufacturer of a product intentionally misrepresents facts about a product or fraudulently conceals information regarding the product, and the conduct was a substantial cause of the harm suffered by a plaintiff.[10] The time limit does not apply to a defendant's claims for contribution or indemnification against a person "whose actual fault caused a product to be defective."[11]

B. CAUSES OF ACTION

A product liability lawsuit "encompasses three separate and distinct theories of liability: negligence, strict liability, and breach of warranty."[12] The theories behind each of these causes of action are ordinarily concerning "improper design, inadequate warnings, or mistakes in manufacturing."[13] Less commonly, a product liability lawsuit includes actions alleging misrepresentation and violation of federal or state statutes.

C. THE STANDARD

In 2002, the Iowa Supreme Court abandoned the "unreasonably dangerous" standard found in Section 402A of the Restatement (Second) of Torts: Product Liability, which it had previously used, and adopted Sections 1 and 2 of the Restatement (Third) of Torts: Product Liability, for product defect cases.[14] The Restatement (Third) of Torts provides that a "product is defective when at the time of sale or distribution, it contains a manufacturing defect, is defective in design, or is defective because of inadequate instructions or warning. A product:

(a) Contains a manufacturing defect when the product departs from its intended design even though all possible care was exercised in the preparation and marketing of the product;

(b) Is defective in design when the foreseeable risks of harm posed by the product could have been reduced or avoided by the adoption of a reasonable alternative design by the seller or other distributor, or a predecessor in the commercial chain of distribution, and the omission of the alternative design renders the product not reasonably safe; and

(c) Is defective because of inadequate instructions or warnings when the foreseeable risks of harm posed by the product could have been reduced or avoided by the provision of reasonable instructions or warnings by the seller or other distributor, or a predecessor . . . , and the omission of the instructions or warnings renders the product not reasonably safe."[15]

The Iowa Supreme Court noted that the Restatement (Third) of Torts declined to place labels such as strict liability or negligence on defective design claims and questioned the need or usefulness of such "traditional doctrinal label[s]" with regards to these types of claims.[16] In a comment to Section 2 of the Restatement (Third) of Torts, the authors noted that "claims based on product defect . . . must meet the requisites set forth in Subsection (a), (b), or (c) . . . [a]s long as these requisites are met, doctrinal tort categories such as negligence or strict liability may be utilized in bringing the claim."[17]

To prevail on a products liability claim based on a manufacturing defect, a plaintiff must demonstrate the following elements: (1) that the defendant sold or distributed the product; (2) that defendant was engaged in the business of selling or distributing the product; (3) that the product contained a manufacturing defect or defects that departed from the product's intended design at the time it left the defendant's control; (4) that the manufacturing defect was a proximate cause of plaintiff's damages; and (5) the amount of damages.[18] When a product remained in the condition intended by the manufacturer, a claim based on defective design is inappropriate.[19]

A plaintiff bringing a products liability claim based on defective design must establish the existence of nine factors, which include a showing that: (1) the defendant sold or distributed the product; (2) the defendant was engaged in the business of selling or distributing the product; (3) the way or ways in which the product was in a defective condition at the time it left the defendant's control; (4) a reasonable alternative safer design could have been practically adopted at the time of sale or distribution; (5) the alternative design would have reduced or avoided the foreseeable risks of harm posed by the products; (6) the omission of the alternative design rendered the product not reasonably safe; (7) the alternative design would have reduced or prevented the plaintiff's harm; (8) the design defect was a proximate cause of plaintiff's damage; and (9) the amount of damages.[20] When asserting a claim based on defective design, a plaintiff is advancing the argument that although a product complied with the manufacturer's design specifications, those specifications in and of themselves, created an unreasonable risk of harm.[21] In the absence of an alternative design, a plaintiff can attempt to argue that the design was "manifestly unreasonable" and, therefore, no safe alternative exists.[22] However, the Supreme Court of Iowa has ruled that this exception to the required showing of an alternative design should be "sparingly applied."[23]

Finally, a successful products liability suit based on inadequate instructions or warnings depends on the plaintiff's ability to show: (1) that the defendant sold or distributed the product; (2) that the defendant was engaged in the business of selling or distributing the product; (3) the ways in which the foreseeable risks of harm posed by the product could have been reduced or avoided by the provision of reasonable instructions or warnings; (4) that the omission of the instructions or warnings rendered the product not reasonably safe; (5) that the risk to be addressed by the instructions or warnings was not obvious to, or generally known by, foreseeable product users; (6) that the omission of the instructions or warnings was a proximate cause of the plaintiff's damages; and (7) the amount of damages.[24]

D. LIABILITY

1. Sale or Lease

A products liability claim grounded in the theory of strict liability can be brought against the seller of a product when the following factors occur: (1) the defendant sold the product; (2) the product was in a defective condition; (3) the defective condition was unreasonably dangerous to the user or consumer when used in a reasonably foreseeable manner; (4) the seller was engaged in the business of manufacturing such a product; (5) said product was expected to and did reach the user without substantial change in condition, *i.e.*, the defect existed at the time of the sale; (6) said product was the proximate cause of personal injuries or property damage suffered by the user or consumer; and (7) damages suffered by the user or consumer.[25] The same factors are used to establish liability for claims brought against the manufacturer of the product at issue.[26] A defendant who "is not the assembler, designer, or manufacturer, and who wholesales, retails, distributes, or otherwise sells a product" is immune to any lawsuit brought on the theory of strict liability in tort or breach of implied warranty if the suit arises solely from an alleged defect in the design or manufacturing of the product, and there is no causal relationship between the nonmanufacturer and the injury suffered.[27] Iowa no longer recognizes the common carrier exception to strict liability.[28]

2. Successor Liability

In general, when a company sells or transfers assets to another company, the purchasing company is not liable for debts or liabilities of the transferring company.[29] However, Iowa recognizes four exceptions to this rule.[30] A successor corporation may be liable for the debts and liabilities of the predecessor corporation if there is an agreement to assume such debts or liabilities, there is a consolidation of the two corporations, the purchasing corporation is a mere continuation of the selling corporation, or the transaction is fraudulent in fact.[31] The Iowa Supreme Court has declined to adopt the "product line" exception which holds that a "party which acquires a manufacturing business and continues the output of its line of products . . . assumes strict tort liability for defects in units of the same product line previously manufactured and distributed by the entity from which the business was acquired."[32]

3. **Failure to Warn**

A manufacturer's duty to warn of potential dangers depends upon the possession of superior knowledge regarding the product, and the duty exists "when one may reasonably foresee a danger of injury or damage to one less knowledgeable unless an adequate warning is given."[33] To determine whether or not a duty existed, the inquiry is focused on what the manufacturer knew or should have known about the danger of the product, in light of accepted scientific knowledge.[34] Whether a warning should have been given is generally a question for the trier of fact.[35] Suppliers of goods do not have a duty to warn of potential dangers where the probability of injury is "remote, slight, or inconsequential."[36] Moreover, manufacturers and suppliers do not have a duty to warn where the potential danger of a product is known and obvious.[37]

4. **Post-Sale Duty to Warn**

After the sale of a product, a manufacturer may have a duty to warn concerning subsequently acquired knowledge of a defect or dangerous condition that would render the product unreasonably dangerous for its foreseeable use, depending on the circumstances.[38] A post-sale duty to warn may affect a product seller's ability to raise the state-of-the-art defense—that defense applies only to strict liability claims and not the negligence claims of failure to warn pre-and post-sale.[39]

5. **Reasonably Foreseeable Use/Misuse**

A plaintiff who is injured by misuse of a product, and is able to demonstrate that consumer misuse of that product was "reasonably foreseeable" by a manufacturer, may be able to show the product was defective in spite of the misuse.[40] A plaintiff attempting to impose strict liability against a manufacturer must demonstrate their injury was a result of reasonably foreseeable use, which also includes reasonably foreseeable misuse of the product.[41] A plaintiff whose misuse of a product results in injury is not barred from recovery for strict liability; the plaintiff's misuse of a product is a matter of comparative fault to be determined by the trier of fact.[42]

6. Crashworthiness/Enhanced Injury

Iowa follows the doctrine of enhanced injury or, in the case of vehicles, crashworthiness.[43] Enhanced injury claims are subject to the principles of Iowa's comparative fault statute.[44] To prevail on a claim of this nature a plaintiff must first demonstrate a design defect, and then establish the following factors: "(1) the existence of a safer, practicable, alternative design, (2) the extent of the injuries the plaintiff would have suffered had the alternative design been used, and (3) some method of establishing the extent of enhanced injuries attributable to the defective design."[45]

E. AVAILABLE REMEDIES AND THE ECONOMIC LOSS DOCTRINE

When determining the appropriate remedy in a product defect case, Iowa courts look to the nature of the injury suffered. Although personal injury claims can be submitted under both tort and breach of contract theories, a plaintiff cannot recover under a tort claim if the loss suffered is purely economic.[46] Without personal property injury, a plaintiff is limited to a claim brought under breach of contract or warranty.[47] However, lack of personal injury is not determinative of whether or not a plaintiff can assert a tort or contract claim.[48] Rather, the court will review a number of related factors "such as the nature of the defect, the type of risk and the manner in which the injury arose."[49] At the very minimum, a plaintiff must demonstrate damage to something beyond the alleged defective product to prevail in a tort action.[50] The Iowa Supreme Court explained the difference between tort and contract remedies by stating "[w]hen . . . the loss relates to a consumer or user's disappointed expectations due to deterioration, internal breakdown or non-accidental cause, the remedy lies in contract. Tort theory . . . is generally appropriate when the harm is a sudden or dangerous occurrence, frequently involving some violence or collision with external objects, resulting from a genuine hazard of the product defect."[51]

F. DEFENSES TO PRODUCTS LIABILITY CLAIMS

1. State of the Art Defense

Iowa's comparative fault statute allows for a defendant in a products liability claim to assert a so-called "state of the art" defense, stating "a percentage of fault shall not be assigned to [the defendant] if they plead and prove that the product conformed to the state of the art in existence at the time the product was designed, tested, manufactured, formulated, packaged, provided with a warning or labeled."[52] Iowa recognizes a distinction between "custom in the industry" and what is "state of the art."[53] While custom "refers to what was being done in the industry . . . state of the art refers to what feasibly could have been done."[54] Feasibility in this context refers to a product design that is "practically, as well as technically sound."[55] This approach to the state of the art defense allows a defendant to prevail even where the allegedly defective product design did not incorporate the most current technology, so long as the design reflected what could reasonably be done given the circumstances.[56]

2. **Assumption of Risk**

This defense requires the jury to determine whether or not a plaintiff in a products liability case acted "unreasonably in assuming a particular risk."[57] Iowa recognizes two separate definitions of assumption of risk, primary and secondary.[58] Primary assumption of risk is not an affirmative defense, rather it is a way of expressing that no duty was owed or none breached.[59] Secondary assumption of risk can be asserted as an affirmative defense and may serve to bar a plaintiff's claim if the plaintiff knew that the defect or dangerous condition was present, understood the nature of the danger to himself or herself, and yet fully and voluntarily used the product and such use was the proximate cause of plaintiff's injury.[60] However, unreasonable assumption of risk caused by misuse of a product will not otherwise bar the injured party's recovery, but rather will subject the claim to that party's comparative fault.[61] Assumption of risk is not available as a separate defense where the defense of contributory negligence can be raised.[62]

3. **Contributory Negligence**

Contributory negligence is not a complete defense under the Iowa Comparative Fault Act.[63] Iowa has adopted a comparative fault statute, identified as Iowa Code, ch. 668. The statute applies to strict liability actions. While this is not a complete defense, a plaintiff who is found to be more than fifty percent at fault for the injury suffered is barred from recovery.[64]

G. **ADMISSABILITY OF EVIDENCE**

Evidence of subsequent remedial or precautionary measures is admissible in strict liability and breach of warranty for limited purposes.[65] Evidence of subsequent remedial measures is not admissible to prove negligence or culpable conduct, but it may be used for the purpose of proving ownership, control, feasibility of precautionary measures, if controverted, or impeachment.[66]

Evidence of similar accidents is admissible for a number of reasons, such as demonstrating the existence and nature of the alleged defect, causation purposes, notice to the defendant, and impeachment or rebuttal of witnesses.[67] A requirement of substantial similarity between the accident at issue and other accidents is a matter of relevance to be decided in the discretion of the trial judge.[68] Other occurrence evidence also is admissible to prove lack of adequate warning, notice of defect, and punitive damages.[69]

H. **BREACH OF WARRANTY**

In the product liability setting, a cause of action for breach of warranty and a cause of action for strict liability are not mutually exclusive.[70] Each cause of action may be brought if supportable under the facts.[71] The "discovery rule" does not apply to implied warranty of fitness claims.[72]

I. **PUNITIVE DAMAGES**

Punitive damages are recoverable in actions in strict liability[73] and negligence[74] when defendant's conduct amounts to willful and wanton disregard for the rights or safety of another (actual or legal malice).[75] Punitive damages are not recoverable in actions for breach of warranty unless the breach amounts to an independent, willful tort where actual or legal malice is shown.[76]

J. **STATUTES**

Relevant statutes for product liability actions are the statutes of limitation, the Iowa Comparative Fault Act, and the commercial code sections when a breach of warranty is alleged.[77]

Bradley C. Obermeier
Joseph G. Gamble
DUNCAN, GREEN, BROWN & LANGENESS, P.C.
400 Locust Street, Suite 380
Des Moines, Iowa 50309
(515) 288-6440
Fax (515) 288-6448
bobermeier@duncangreenlaw.com
jgamble@duncangreenlaw.com

Endnotes - Iowa

1. Iowa Code § 614.1(2).

2. Iowa Code §§ 554.2725, 614.1(5); *Fell v. Kewanee Farm Equip. Co.*, 457 N.W.2d 911 (Iowa 1990).

3. Iowa Code § 614.1(4).

4. Iowa Code §§ 614.1, 554.2725, 614.1(5).

5. *Buechel v. Five Star Quality Care, Inc.*, 745 N.W.2d 732 (Iowa 2008); *Sparks v. Metalcraft, Inc.*, 408 N.W.2d 347 (Iowa 1987).

6. Iowa Code § 614.8.

7. Iowa Code §§ 614.2A and 614.1(11).

8. Iowa Code § 614.1(2A).

9. Iowa Code § 614.1(2A).

10. Iowa Code § 614.1(2A).

11. Iowa Code § 614.1(2A).

12. *Lovick v. Wil-Rich*, 588 N.W.2d 688, 698 (1999).

13. *Lovick*, 588 N.W.2d 688, 698.

14. *Wright v. Brooke Grp. Ltd.*, 652 N.W.2d 159, 169 (Iowa 2002).

15. Restatement (Third) of Torts: Prod. Liab. § 2 (1998).

16. *Wright*, 652 N.W.2d 159, 169.

17. Restatement (Third) of Torts: Prod. Liab. § 2 cmt. n (1998).

18. Iowa Civil Jury Instructions, No. 1000.1 (Oct. 2004); *see also Wright*, 652 N.W.2d at 178.

19. *Wright*, 652 N.W.2d 159, 178.

20. Iowa Civil Jury Instructions, No. 1000.2 (Oct. 2004); *see also Wright*, 652 N.W.2d 159, 168-69.

21. *Parish v. Jumpking, Inc.*, 719 N.W.2d 540, 543 (Iowa 2006).

22. *Parish.*, 719 N.W.2d 540, 543.

23. *Parish.*, 719 N.W.2d 540, 544.

24. Iowa Civil Jury Instructions, No. 1000.3 (Oct. 2004); *see also Wright*, 652 N.W.2d 159, 169-71; Restatement (Third) of Torts: Prod. Liab. §§ 1, 2(c), cmts. i, j.

25. *Kleve v. Gen. Motors Corp.*, 210 N.W.2d 568, 570-571 (Iowa 1973).

26. *Osborn v. Massey Ferguson, Inc.*, 290 N.W.2d 893, 901 (Iowa 1980).

27. Iowa Code § 613.18.

28. *National Steel Serv. Ctr., Inc. v. Gibbons*, 319 N.W.2d 269, 273 (Iowa 1982).

29. *DeLapp v. Xtraman*, 417 N.W.2d 219, 220 (Iowa 1987).

30. *DeLapp*, 417 N.W.2d 219, 220.

31. *DeLapp*, 417 N.W.2d 219, 220.

32. *DeLapp*, 417 N.W.2d 219, 220-21.

33. *Beeman v. Manville Corp. Asbestos Fund*, 496 N.W.2d 247, 252 (Iowa 1993); *Lakatosh v. Diamond Alkali Co.*, 208 N.W.2d 910, 913 (Iowa 1973).

34. *Mercer v. Pittway Corp.*, 616 N.W.2d 602, 623-24 (Iowa 2000).

35. *Beeman*, 496 N.W.2d 247, 252.

36. *Henkel v. R and S Bottling Co.*, 323 N.W.2d 185, 188 (Iowa 1982).

37. *Olson v. Prosoco, Inc.*, 522 N.W.2d 284, 291 (Iowa 1994); *Nichols v. Westfield Indus., Inc.*, 380 N.W.2d 392, 401 (Iowa 1985).

38. Iowa Code § 668.12.

39. *Huber v. Watson*, 568 N.W.2d 787, 792 (Iowa 1997).

40. *Henkel*, 323 N.W.2d 185; *Cooley v. Quick Supply Co.*, 221 N.W.2d 763, 765-66 (Iowa 1974).

41. *Henkel*, 323 N.W.2d 185; *Cooley*, 221 N.W.2d 763, 765-66.

42. *Fell*, 457 N.W.2d 911; *Slager v. H.W.A. Corp.*, 435 N.W.2d 349 (Iowa 1989); Iowa Code § 668.1.

43. *Jahn v. Hyundai Motor Co.*, 773 N.W.2d 550 (Iowa 2009); *Hillrichs v. Avco Corp.*, 478 N.W.2d 70 (Iowa 1991).

44. *Jahn*, 773 N.W.2d 550, 560.

45. *Jahn*, 773 N.W.2d 550, 554.

46. *Wright*, 652 N.W.2d 159, 181.

47. *Mercer*, 616 N.W.2d 602, 621.

48. *Tomka v. Hoechst Celanese Corp.*, 528 N.W.2d 103, 106 (Iowa 1995).

49. *Determen v. Johnson*, 613 N.W.2d 259, 262 (Iowa 2000).

50. *Determen*, 613 N.W.2d 259, 262.

51. *Determen*, 613 N.W.2d 259, 262.

52. Iowa Code § 668.12.

53. *Chown v. USM Corp.*, 297 N.W.2d 218, 221 (Iowa 1980).

54. *Chown*, 297 N.W.2d 218, 221.

55. *Hughs v. Massey-Ferguson, Inc.*, 522 N.W.2d 294, 296 (Iowa 1994).

56. *Hughs*, 522 N.W.2d 294, 296.

57. *Nichols v. Westfield Ind., Ltd.*, 380 N.W.2d 392, 399 (Iowa 1985); *see also Rosenau v. City of Estherville*, 199 N.W.2d 125, 131 (Iowa 1972).

58. *Nichols*, 380 N.W.2d 392, 399; *see also Rosenau*, 199 N.W.2d 125, 131.

59. *Nichols*, 380 N.W.2d 392, 399; *see also Rosenau*, 199 N.W.2d 125, 131.

60. *Speck v. Unit Handling Div., Litton Sys.*, 366 N.W.2d 543 (Iowa 1995).

61. Iowa Code § 668.1(1).

62. *Rosenau*, N.W.2d 125, 133.

63. *Speck*, 366 N.W.2d 543.

64. Iowa Code § 668.3.

65. *Bandstra v. Int'l Harvester Co.*, 367 N.W.2d 282, 287-88 (1985); Iowa R. Evid. 5.407.

66. *Bandstra*, 367 N.W.2d 282, 287-88; Iowa R. Evid. 5.407.

67. *Lovick*, 588 N.W.2d 688, 697; *Rattenborg v. Montgomery Elevator Co.*, 438 N.W.2d 602 (Iowa 1989).

68. *Lovick*, 588 N.W.2d 688, 697; *Rattenborg*, 438 N.W.2d 602.

69. *Lovick*, 588 N.W.2d 688, 697; *Rattenborg*, 438 N.W.2d 602; *Fell*, 457 N.W.2d 911.

70. *Hawkeye Sec. Ins. Co. v. Ford Motor Corp.*, 199 N.W.2d 373 (Iowa 1972).

71. *Hawkeye Sec. Ins. Co.*, 199 N.W.2d 373.

72. *City of Carlisle v. Fetzer*, 381 N.W.2d 627 (Iowa 1986); Iowa Code § 554.2725.

73. *Beeck v. Aquaslide 'N' Dive Corp.*, 350 N.W.2d 149 (Iowa 1984).

74. *Cedar Falls Bldg. Ctr., Inc. v. Vietor*, 365 N.W.2d 635 (Iowa 1985).

75. Iowa Code § 668A.1.

76. *Parks v. City of Marshalltown*, 440 N.W.2d 377 (Iowa 1989).

77. Iowa Code §§ 554.2725; 613.18; 614.1(2); (4), (5), (11); 668.1 *et seq.*; 668A.1.

Kansas

A. CAUSES OF ACTION

Product liability actions as defined under the Kansas Product Liability Act (KPLA) include claims based on: strict liability; negligence; breach of express or implied warranty; breach of, or failure to discharge, a duty to warn or instruct, whether negligent or innocent; misrepresentation, concealment, or nondisclosure, whether negligent or innocent; or under any other substantive legal theory.[1] Thus, the KPLA "consolidates all product liability actions, regardless of theory, into one basis for liability."[2] The KPLA is loosely based upon the Model Uniform Product Liability Act (MUPLA).[3] However, the Kansas Legislature omitted some phrases and sections of MUPLA when it enacted the KPLA.[4] Thus, "[w]hen it comes to setting out the responsibilities and potential liabilities of a 'product seller,' the KPLA is silent. This legislative approach leaves this court [the Supreme Court of Kansas] and other courts no choice but to look to the substantive rights and liabilities recognized under Kansas common law for each type of product liability action."[5] In Kansas, strict liability and implied warranty claims are recognized only at the time of the sale of the product.[6] In the post-sale context, a negligence analysis is more appropriate than an application of strict liability.[7]

B. STATUTES OF LIMITATION

A product liability action for personal injuries, death, or property damage must be brought within two years of the date of substantial injury or the date such injury becomes reasonably ascertainable, whether in negligence, strict liability, or breach of warranty.[8]

The KPLA includes a "useful safe life" statute of repose. A product seller is not liable if it proves by a preponderance of the evidence that the harm was caused after the product's useful safe life has expired.[9] Relevant factors to determine whether a product's useful safe life has expired include: the amount of wear and tear; the effect of deterioration from natural causes; the normal practices of the user as to the product's use, repair, renewal, and replacement; any representations, instructions or warnings made concerning maintenance and use of the product; and any modification or alteration to the product.[10]

Where the harm was caused more than ten years after delivery of the product, it is presumed that the harm was caused after the expiration of the product's useful safe life.[11] This presumption may only be rebutted by clear and convincing evidence.[12] The Kansas general statute of repose, which purports to state a ten-year statute of repose for all tort cases,[13] has been held not to apply to cases brought under the KPLA.[14]

C. STRICT LIABILITY

1. The Standard

The Kansas strict liability standard is modeled after Section 402A of the Restatement (Second) of Torts.[15] The plaintiff must prove that the injury resulted from an unreasonably dangerous condition of the product that existed at the time the product left the defendant's control.[16] Thus, "[t]he plaintiff, to present a prima facie strict liability case, must produce proof of three elements: (1) the injury resulted from a condition of the product; (2) the condition was an unreasonably dangerous one; and (3) the condition existed at the time it left the defendant's control."[17] Kansas follows the consumer expectation test. An unreasonably dangerous product is one that is dangerous to an extent beyond that which would be contemplated by the ordinary consumer who purchases it, with the ordinary knowledge common to the community as to its characteristics.[18] Evidence of a feasible alternative design is admissible in design defect cases, though Kansas courts have not required it in all cases.[19] "While evidence of a safer alternative design is not required in all cases, there must be a specific claim concerning what aspect of the design was defective for a plaintiff to prevail on a strict liability design defect claim."[20] To succeed on a product liability claim involving an unavoidably unsafe product, plaintiff must prove a safer, cost-effective alternative.[21] If defendant does not claim its product was unavoidably unsafe, such proof is not required.[22]

2. Definition of "Defect"

The plaintiff must prove a specific defect to recover in strict liability.[23] The product is considered defective if it leaves the manufacturer's or seller's hands in a condition unreasonably dangerous to the ordinary user. The defect may be in the product's manufacturing or design, in its container or packaging, or in the instructions or warnings necessary for the product's safe use.[24]

3. Causation

Proof that a defect in the product caused the injury is a prerequisite to recovery in a product liability case.[25] Plaintiffs must establish a specific defect to prevail on a defective product claim.[26] Proof of injury during use of a product is not sufficient to establish causation.[27] "[A] strict liability claim may be proven inferentially, by either direct or circumstantial evidence."[28] Proof of intervening negligent acts can break the causal chain between negligence of manufacturer and harm caused.[29]

4. Contributory Negligence/Assumption of Risk

Contributory negligence is not a complete defense to a claimant's recovery.[30] Assumption of the risk remains an absolute bar to recovery, but applies only in limited circumstances involving employer-employee relationships.[31]

The comparative fault doctrine governs product liability cases in negligence, strict liability, and breach of implied warranty.[32] Under Kansas comparative fault principles, recovery is barred only if the claimant's fault is greater than the combined causal negligence of all the defendants.[33]

If the plaintiff's fault is less than that of the defendants, the jury may attribute fault to the plaintiff, the defendants, and any other entity whose causal negligence is claimed to have contributed to the plaintiff's damages.[34] Each party is liable only for that percentage of the total damages attributed to it.[35] The negligence of any entity, whether joined as a party or not, may be compared if supported by the evidence, even if recovery against that entity is barred.[36]

5. Sale or Lease/Persons Liable

The plaintiff must show that a defendant had some relationship to the allegedly defective product, for example, as a manufacturer, retailer, or distributor.[37] A lessor may contractually limit its liability to the lessee for negligence in the manufacture of a product.[38] The KPLA limits a seller's liability arising from an alleged defect when certain enumerated conditions are met.[39] The enumerated conditions are not listed as alternatives, and a seller must satisfy all five of the conditions in order to limit liability.[40]

The liability of the seller of a used product is very limited under the KPLA.[41] Remanufacturers and sellers in the chain of distribution after remanufacture can be subject to strict liability.[42] However, when a repair of a product does not take place in the context of a "sale," a repairer is not subject to liability under theories of strict liability or implied warranty of merchantability, even if the repair is comprehensive enough to amount to a remanufacture or complete overhaul.[43]

6. Inherently Dangerous Products

Kansas recognizes the unavoidably unsafe product exception to strict liability for products that have been properly prepared and accompanied by proper directions and warnings.[44]

7. Successor Liability

To establish the liability of a successor entity for failure to warn, there must be some basis of benefit to the successor in the successor's relationship with the predecessor entity's customers, and the successor must be aware of the defective condition of the product.[45] This is a very narrow exception to the traditional rule of successor nonliability.

8. Market Share Liability/Enterprise Liability

Kansas courts have not adopted either market share liability or alternative liability.

9. **Privity**

Privity is not required to recover in tort. Liability for a defective product extends to those individuals to whom injury from that product may reasonably be foreseen and then only where the product is being used for the purpose for which it was intended or for which it is reasonably foreseeable that it may be used.[46]

10. **Failure to Warn**

A manufacturer or seller that knows or should know that a product is potentially dangerous to users has a duty to give adequate warnings of such danger where injury to a user can be reasonably anticipated if an adequate warning is not given.[47] To be adequate, a warning must be comprehensible to the average user and convey to the mind of a user a fair indication of the nature and extent of the danger.[48] Under the KPLA, however, the duty does not extend to warnings, protecting against or instructing with regard to those safeguards, precautions, and actions which a reasonable user or consumer of the product, with the training, experience, education, and any special knowledge the user or consumer did, should or was required to possess under all the facts and circumstances.[49] A defendant owes no duty to warn of dangers of which the plaintiff is actually aware.[50]

Manufacturers have a duty to research and test their products to establish a basis for warning consumers.[51] Kansas recognizes a rebuttable presumption that an adequate warning will be heeded and that an inadequate warning caused the injury.[52] Conversely, Kansas recognizes a rebuttable presumption of causation if the warning is inadequate.[53] As a practical matter, the adequacy of a warning is determined by application of a negligence standard. An adequate warning is one that is reasonable under the circumstances.[54] The KPLA addresses situations in which there is some legislative or administrative regulatory safety standard relating to warnings or instructions.[55] The determination whether a warning is adequate is a question of fact.[56]

There is no duty to warn when the user already knows of the danger or where the danger is open and obvious.[57] However, although the fact that the danger is open and obvious may be a factor in determining whether plaintiff contributed to his own injuries, it does not bar a finding that the product is defective.[58] Kansas has rejected the portion of comment j to the Restatement (Second) of Torts, Section 402A, which provides that a product which is safe to use if its warning is followed is not defective or unreasonably dangerous, and comment l to the Restatement (Third) of Torts, Section 2, which provides that an adequate warning does not foreclose a finding that a product is defectively designed.[59]

The duty to warn is commensurate with the seriousness of the danger.[60]

11. Post-Sale Duty to Warn and Remedial Measures

A manufacturer has a post-sale duty to warn ultimate consumers who purchased the product who can be readily identified or traced when a defect that originated at the time the product was manufactured and was unforeseeable at the point of sale is discovered to present a life-threatening hazard. Determining the nature of the duty to warn and the persons to whom the warning should be given involves a case-by-case analysis.[61] Where a successor corporation has a relationship with its predecessor's customers and knows of a defective condition in the predecessor's product, it too may incur a post-sale duty to warn.[62]

Kansas law imposes no duty to recall or retrofit a product not defective at the time of sale.[63]

Evidence relating to technological advancements or changes made, learned, or placed into common use subsequent to the time the product in use was designed, formulated, tested, manufactured, or sold by the manufacturer is inadmissible unless such evidence is offered to impeach a witness who has expressly denied the feasibility of such advancements or changes.[64]

12. Learned Intermediary Doctrine

Kansas courts have applied the learned intermediary doctrine in cases involving prescription drugs and medical devices.[65] Under the doctrine, a manufacturer's duty to warn is satisfied when the prescribing doctor is informed of the product's inherent risks.[66]

13. Substantial Alteration/Abnormal Use

Kansas courts instruct jurors that a consumer must exercise ordinary care with reference to those obvious defects and dangerous conditions about which he does or should know and understand.[67] The consumer also has a duty to use a product in accordance with adequate instructions and warnings and to use the product in a normal manner.[68] A manufacturer may be relieved of liability for a defective design if the product has been modified in a manner that the manufacturer could not reasonably have foreseen.[69] Failure to fulfill any of these duties constitutes negligence on the part of the consumer, which the jury may consider in determining the comparative fault of the parties.[70]

14. State of the Art

Evidence of advancements in knowledge or theories of design, manufacturing, testing or instructions learned or placed into common use after the product in issue was designed, manufactured, tested or sold is not admissible for any purpose except to rebut a denial of feasibility.[71]

15. **Malfunction**

    A malfunction occurs when a product performs other than as expected. It is more likely to indicate a manufacturing defect than a design defect. Inferring a defect from the fact of the injury is inappropriate.[72]

16. **Standards and Governmental Regulation**

    The KPLA allocates evidentiary burdens according to whether the product was in compliance with legislative or administrative regulatory standards at the time of manufacture.[73]

    When the injury-causing aspect of the product complied with legislative or administrative safety standards at the time of manufacture, the product is deemed not defective unless the plaintiff proves that a reasonably prudent seller could and would have taken added precautions.[74] When the injury-causing aspect of the product did not comply with existing standards, the product is deemed defective unless the seller proves its failure to comply was reasonably prudent under the circumstances.[75] Compliance with voluntary industry standards does not give rise to the presumption.[76]

17. **Other Accidents**

    Evidence of other accidents is admissible, pursuant to a strict liability theory, to establish notice (relevant in punitive cases only) or the existence of a defect, or to refute testimony by a defense witness that a given product was safely designed.[77] Admission of testimony regarding other accidents is usually predicated on a showing that the circumstances are substantially similar to those involved in the present case.[78]

18. **Misrepresentation**

    A seller's misrepresentation may give rise to a cause of action for breach of implied or express warranty.[79]

19. **Destruction or Loss of Product**

    Kansas has not recognized an independent tort of spoliation.[80] Kansas has further rejected creation of the tort of spoliation between co-defendants or potential co-defendants in an underlying product liability case.[81] However, sanctions are sometimes available for spoliation.[82]

20. **Economic Loss**

    A buyer of defective goods cannot recover in strict liability or negligence for purely economic loss.[83] Injury to the allegedly defective product itself is considered economic loss,[84] as are loss of bargain damages, repair and replacement costs, loss of profits, loss of goodwill, and loss of business reputation.[85] The type of risk involved is not the determinative factor. Instead, regardless of how the loss occurs, damage that is limited to the defective product itself is economic loss, not recoverable in tort.[86] This rule applies to both commercial and consumer purchasers.[87]

21. Crashworthiness

The crashworthiness or second collision recovery doctrine has yet to be adopted by any Kansas state court.[88] Federal courts in Kansas, however, have predicted the doctrine will be accepted and have applied it.[89] The crashworthiness doctrine renders a manufacturer liable for damages caused by the defect over and above those damages that likely would have resulted from the accident absent the defect.[90]

D. NEGLIGENCE

To recover for negligence, plaintiffs must prove the existence of a duty, breach of that duty, injury, and a causal connection between the duty breached and the injury suffered.[91] A plaintiff must establish that there was a defect in the product.[92] Proof that a better design might have been possible is not enough to prevail on a negligent design claim.[93] "Whether expert testimony is necessary to prove negligence is dependent on whether, under the facts of a particular case, the trier of fact would be able to understand, absent expert testimony, the nature of the standard of care required of defendant and the alleged deviation from the standard."[94]

A manufacturer has a duty to use reasonable care in designing its products so that they will be reasonably safe for their intended use.[95] Jurors are instructed that negligence is the lack of ordinary care under the existing circumstances.[96]

E. BREACH OF WARRANTY

The KPLA governs product liability actions in warranty, as well as those in strict liability and negligence.[97]

F. PUNITIVE DAMAGES

Punitive damages may be awarded when the plaintiff proves by clear and convincing evidence that the defendant acted with fraud, malice, gross negligence, or oppression. An award of punitive damages is to be viewed in light of the actual damages sustained, the actual damage award, the circumstances of the case, the evidence presented, the relative positions of the plaintiff and the defendant, and the defendant's financial worth.[98]

Under Kansas law, the jury determines whether punitive damages are to be awarded, and the court determines the amount of such damages.[99] Kansas statutes cap the amounts that can be awarded for punitive damages.[100]

G. PRE-AND POST-JUDGMENT INTEREST

Pre-judgment interest is available only when the amount in question is liquidated[101] or for money due and withheld by an "unreasonable and vexatious delay."[102]

Post-judgment interest is added after entry of a valid judgment at a rate determined by the statutory formula.[103]

H. EMPLOYER IMMUNITY FROM SUIT

The Kansas Workers' Compensation Act exempts the plaintiff's employer from liability for any injury for which compensation is available under the Act.[104]

I. STATUTES

Relevant statutes for product liability actions are the statutes of limitation,[105] the comparative negligence statute,[106] the commercial code sections (when a breach of warranty is alleged),[107] the KPLA,[108] statutes placing caps on amounts to be awarded for punitive damages and non-economic losses,[109] and the Kansas Workers' Compensation Act.[110]

The period of minority in Kansas extends to the age of 18.[111]

J. JOINT AND SEVERAL LIABILITY

The concept of joint and several liability does not apply in comparative negligence actions in Kansas.[112]

Thomas P. Schult
Sharon A. Stallbaumer
Kenneth J. Duvall
Berkowitz Oliver Williams Shaw & Eisenbrandt, LLP
2600 Grand Boulevard, Suite 1200
Kansas City, Missouri 64108
(816) 561-7007
(Fax) (816) 561-1888
E-mail: tschult@berkowitzoliver.com
E-mail: sstallbaumer@berkowitzoliver.com
E-mail: kduvall@berkowitzoliver.com
www.berkowitzoliver.com

ENDNOTES - KANSAS

1. Kan. Stat. Ann. § 60-3302(c); *see, e.g., Gaumer v. Rossville Truck & Tractor Co., Inc.*, 292 Kan. 749, 752, 257 P.3d 292, 295 (2011); *Patton v. Hutchinson Wil-Rich Mfg. Co.*, 253 Kan. 741, Syl. 2, 756, 861 P.2d 1299, Syl. 2, 1311 (1993); *Gonzalez v. PepsiCo., Inc.*, 489 F. Supp. 2d 1233, 1241-42 (D. Kan. 2007) (Kansas Product Liability Act does not foreclose claims under the UCC or Kansas Consumer Protection Act for economic damage caused by defective products).

2. *David v. Hett*, 293 Kan. 679, 685, 270 P.3d 1102, 1106 (2011) (citing *Patton v. Hutchinson Wil-Rich Mfg. Co.*, 253 Kan. 741, 756, 861 P.2d 1299 (1993)); *see also Mattos v. Eli Lilly & Co.*, 2012 WL 1893551, at *3 (D. Kan. May 23, 2012) (rejecting plaintiff's claims seeking redress for harm caused by prescription drug's design or warnings because plaintiff's strict liability, negligence, warranty and misrepresentation claims (but not Kansas Consumer Protection Act claim) are merged into and subsumed by single claim under the KPLA).

3. *Gaumer*, 292 Kan. at 753, 257 P.3d at 296.

4. *Gaumer*, 292 Kan. at 753, 257 P.3d at 296.

5. *Gaumer*, 292 Kan. at 756, 257 P.3d at 298.

6. *Hoskinson v. High Gear Repair, Inc.*, 982 F. Supp. 2d 1210, 1225 (D. Kan. 2013) (citing *Patton v. Hutchinson Wil–Rich Mfg. Co.*, 253 Kan. 741, 755, 861 P.2d 1299, 1310-11 (1993) (other citation omitted)).

7. *Hoskinson v. High Gear Repair, Inc.*, 982 F. Supp. 2d 1210, 1225 (citing *Patton*, 253 Kan. at 755, 861 P.2d at 1301-11).

8. Kan. Stat. Ann. § 60-513; *Grey v. Bradford-White Corp.*, 581 F. Supp. 725, 728 (D. Kan. 1984).

9. Kan. Stat. Ann. § 60-3303(a)(1). *See* Pattern Instructions Kansas (Civil) (Fourth) §§ 128.20, 128.21 (2010).

10. Kan. Stat. Ann. § 60-3303(a)(1); Pattern Instructions Kansas (Civil) (Fourth) § 128.20 (2010).

11. Kan. Stat. Ann. § 60-3303(b)(1). *See* Pattern Instructions Kansas (Civil) (Fourth) § 128.21 (2010).

12. Kan. Stat. Ann. § 60-3303(b)(1); *Grider v. Positive Safety Mfg. Co.*, 887 F. Supp. 251, 252 (D. Kan. 1995); *Noll v. Bridgestone Americas Tire Operations, LLC*, 2011

WL 4526775, at *3 (D. Kan. Sept. 28, 2011) (plaintiff may rebut the statutory presumption by clear and convincing evidence that the product had not exceeded its useful safe life).

13. Kan. Stat. Ann. § 60-513(b).

14. *Speer v. Wheelabrator Corp.*, 826 F. Supp. 1264, 1272 (D. Kan. 1993); *Kerns v. G.A.C., Inc.*, 255 Kan. 264, 272, 875 P.2d 949, 957 (1994); *Baumann v. Excel Indus., Inc.*, 17 Kan. App. 2d 807, 814, 845 P.2d 65, 71 (1993).

15. *Wessinger v. Vetter Corp.*, 716 F. Supp. 537, 539 (D. Kan. 1989); *Brooks v. Dietz*, 218 Kan. 698, 702, 545 P.2d 1104, 1108 (1976).

16. *Jenkins v. Amchem Prods., Inc.*, 256 Kan. 602, 630, 886 P.2d 869, 886 (1994), *cert. denied*, 516 U.S. 820 (1995); *see also* Pattern Instructions Kansas (Civil) (Fourth) § 128.18 (2010).

17. *Jenkins*, 256 Kan. at 630, 886 P.2d at 886 (citation omitted).

18. *Delaney v. Deere & Co.*, 268 Kan. 769, 788, 999 P.2d 930, 944 (2000). *See* Pattern Instructions Kansas (Civil) (Fourth) § 128.17 (2010) (product considered unreasonably dangerous when, used in the way it is ordinarily used, it is more dangerous than the ordinary consumer who purchased it would expect, modifying the consumer expectation test adopted by *Lester v. Magic Chef, Inc.*, 230 Kan. 643, 653, 641 P.2d 353, 361 (1982), to conform with *Jenkins*, 256 Kan. at 635, 886 P.2d at 889); *see also McCroy v. Coastal Mart, Inc.*, 207 F. Supp. 2d 1265, 1273 (D. Kan. 2002).

19. *Jenkins*, 256 Kan. at 636, 886 P.2d at 890; *Gaumer*, 292 Kan. at 763-64, 257 P.3d at 302.

20. *Jenkins*, 256 Kan. at 636-37, 886 P.2d at 890.

21. *Jenkins*, 256 Kan. at 637, 886 P.2d at 890.

22. *Jenkins*, 256 Kan. at 637, 886 P.2d at 890.

23. *Samarah v. Danek Med., Inc.*, 70 F. Supp. 2d 1196, 1202 (D. Kan. 1999); *Jenkins*, 256 Kan. at 637, 886 P.2d at 890.

24. Pattern Instructions Kansas (Civil) (Fourth) § 128.17 (2010); *Brooks*, 218 Kan. at 704, 545 P.2d at 1109-10; *McCroy*, 207 F. Supp. 2d at 1271; *Vanderwerf v. SmithKline Beecham Corp.*, 414 F. Supp. 2d 1023, 1025 (D. Kan. 2006).

25. *Langehenning v. Sofamor, Inc.*, 1999 WL 1129683, at *8 (D. Kan. May 28, 1999); *Wilcheck v. Doonan Truck & Equip., Inc.*, 220 Kan. 230, Syl. 1, 552 P.2d 938, Syl. 1 (1976); *Miller v. Lee Apparel Co., Inc.*, 19 Kan. App. 2d 1015, 1031, 881 P.2d 576, 589 (1994).

26. *Jenkins*, 256 Kan. at 635, 886 P.2d at 889.

27. *Langehenning*, 1999 WL 1129683, at *8.

28. *Pekarek v. Sunbeam Prods., Inc.*, 672 F. Supp. 2d 1161, 1190 (D. Kan. 2008) (citing *Mays v. Ciba–Geigy Corp.*, 233 Kan. 38, 661 P.2d 348 (1983)).

29. *Edwards ex rel. Fryover v. Anderson Eng'g, Inc.*, 45 Kan. App. 2d 735, 743, 251 P.3d 660, 666 (2011) (affirming summary judgment for defendants because intervening negligent acts of general contractor broke any causal connection between the alleged negligence of pipe manufacturer and site designer, and the death of concrete worker).

30. Kan. Stat. Ann. § 60-258a.

31. *Pullen v. West*, 278 Kan. 183, 192, 92 P.3d 584, 592 (2004); *Tuley v. Kansas City Power & Light Co.*, 252 Kan. 205, 210-11, 843 P.2d 248, 252 (1992); *Smith v. Massey-Ferguson, Inc.*, 256 Kan. 90, 94-95, 883 P.2d 1120, 1125 (1994).

32. *Deines v. Vermeer Mfg. Co.*, 755 F. Supp. 350, 354 (D. Kan. 1990); *Kennedy v. City of Sawyer*, 228 Kan. 439, 449-51, 618 P.2d 788, 796-97 (1980); cf. *Haysville U.S.D. No. 2612 v. GAF Corp.*, 233 Kan. 635, Syl. 4, 666 P.2d 192, Syl. 4 (1983) (comparative negligence not applicable to breach of warranty cases where result of breach is simple economic loss).

33. Kan. Stat. Ann. § 60-258a; *Deines*, 755 F. Supp. at 354.

34. Kan. Stat. Ann. § 60-258a(b), (c).

35. Kan. Stat. Ann. § 60-258a(d).

36. *Hefley v. Textron, Inc.*, 713 F.2d 1487, 1496 (10th Cir. 1983); *Hardin v. Manitowoc-Forsythe Corp.*, 691 F.2d 449, 454 (10th Cir. 1982); *Cerretti v. Flint Hills Rural Elec. Co-op Ass'n*, 251 Kan. 347, 371, 837 P.2d 330, 347 (1992); *Brown v. Keill*, 224 Kan. 195, 206-07, 580 P.2d 867, 875-76 (1978). See also *Dodge City Implement, Inc. v. Bd. of Comm'rs of County of Barber*, 288 Kan. 619, 205 P.3d 1265 (2006) (discussing in detail the Kansas "one-action rule" and requirement that under section 60-258a, the fault of all tortfeasors must be decided in single action, thereby barring subsequent comparative implied indemnity action of tortfeasor).

37. *Lenherr v. NRM Corp.*, 504 F. Supp. 165, 168 (D. Kan. 1980); see also *Cooper v. Zimmer Holdings, Inc.*, 320 F. Supp. 2d 1154, 1157-62 (D. Kan. 2004) (discussing definition of "product seller"); *Golden v. Den-Mat Corp.*, 47 Kan. App. 2d 450, 497, 276 P.3d 773, 803 (2012) (definition of product seller under Kan. Stat. Ann. § 60-3302(a) expressly excludes "a health care provider . . . who utilizes a product in the course of rendering professional services.").

38. *Mid-America Sprayers, Inc. v. United States Fire Ins. Co.*, 8 Kan. App. 2d 451, 459, 660 P.2d 1380, 1387 (1983).

39. Kan. Stat. Ann. § 60-3306. *See, e.g., Wheeler v. FDL, Inc.*, 369 F. Supp. 2d 1271, 1275-77 (D. Kan. 2004) (summary judgment granted for seller under KPLA); *Jackson v. Thomas*, 28 Kan. App. 2d 734, 736-38, 21 P.3d 1007, 1009-10 (2001) (summary judgment granted for sellers under KPLA).

40. Kan. Stat. Ann. § 60-3306; *Netwig v. Georgia Pac. Corp.*, 2006 WL 2560277, at *7 (D. Kan. Mar. 8, 2006).

41. Kan. Stat. Ann. § 60-3306, amendment effective July 1, 2012, limits the liability of sellers of used products in most instances. This legislation was an apparent response to *Gaumer*, 292 Kan. 749, 257 P.3d 292 (Kansas Supreme Court provides detailed review of KPLA, legislative history, and sister states' decisions in permitting pursuit of product liability action against seller of used product).

42. *Stillie v. AM Intern. Inc.*, 850 F. Supp. 960, 962 (D. Kan. 1994).

43. *Stephenson v. Honeywell Int'l, Inc.*, 703 F. Supp. 2d 1250, 1261 (D. Kan. 2010).

44. *Savina v. Sterling Drug, Inc.*, 247 Kan. 105, 115, 121-22, 795 P.2d 915, 923-24, 927-28 (1990).

45. *Stratton v. Garvey Int'l Inc.*, 9 Kan. App. 2d 254, 258-59, 676 P.2d 1290, 1294-95 (1984).

46. *Kennedy*, 228 Kan. at 445-46, 618 P.2d at 794. *Cf. Koss Constr. v. Caterpillar, Inc.*, 25 Kan. App. 2d 200, Syl. 3, 208, 960 P.2d 255, Syl. 3, 260 (1998) (absent privity, corporate purchaser who has incurred only economic loss may not maintain cause of action for breach of implied warranty of merchantability).

47. Pattern Instructions Kansas (Civil) (Fourth) § 128.05 (2010); *Meyerhoff v. Michelin Tire Corp.*, 70 F.3d 1175, 1179 (10th Cir. 1995). The Tenth Circuit has declined to recognize a separate fraudulent concealment claim based upon failure to warn. *Burton v. R.J. Reynolds Tobacco Co.*, 397 F.3d 906, 913 (10th Cir. 2005).

48. *Am. Family Mut. Ins. Co. v. Techtronic Indus. N. Am., Inc.*, Civ. A. 12-2609-KHV, 2014 WL 2196416, at *3 (D. Kan. May 27, 2014) (citing *Wheeler*, 862 F.2d at 1413).

49. *Am. Family*, 2014 WL 2040158, at *9 (citing K.S.A. § 60-3305).

50. *Am. Family*, 2014 WL 2040158, at *9.

51. *Richter v. Limax Int'l, Inc.*, 45 F.3d 1464, 1470 (10th Cir. 1995).

52. *Arnold v. Riddell, Inc.*, 882 F. Supp. 979, 996 (D. Kan. 1995) (citing *Wooderson v. Ortho Pharm. Corp.*, 235 Kan. 387, 410, 681 P.2d 1038, 1057, *cert. denied*, 469 U.S. 965 (1984)); *Burton*, 397 F.3d at 918.

53. *Am. Family*, 2014 WL 2040158, at *9 (citing *Wooderson v. Ortho Pharm. Corp.*, 235 Kan. 387, 411 681 P.2d 1038, 1057 (1984)).

54. *Brand v. Mazda Motor Corp.*, 978 F. Supp. 1382, 1388-89 (D. Kan. 1997); *Wooderson*, 235 Kan. 387, Syl. 9, 681 P.2d 1038, Syl. 9; *Messer v. Amway Corp.*, 210 F. Supp. 2d 1217, 1229 (D. Kan. 2002); *Dockhorn v. Kitchens by Kleweno*, 2010 WL 1196425, at *20 (D. Kan. Mar. 23, 2010). *See also Deines*, 755 F. Supp. at 353 (inadequate warning is one that is unreasonable under the circumstances); *see also, e.g., Am. Family*, 2014 WL 2196416, at *3 ("Under Kansas law, whether a warning is adequate depends upon whether it is reasonable under the circumstances.") (citing *Ralston v. Smith & Nephew Richards, Inc.*, 275 F.3d 965, 975 (10th Cir. 2001)).

55. Kan. Stat. Ann. § 60-3305. *See Alvarado v. J.C. Penney Co., Inc.*, 735 F. Supp. 371, 374 (D. Kan. 1990) (plaintiff may attempt to demonstrate that standard does not meet necessary safety level).

56. *Am. Family*, 2014 WL 2196416, at *3 (citing *Graham v. Wyeth Labs., Div. of Am. Home Prod. Corp.*, 666 F. Supp. 1483, 1499 (D. Kan. 1987)).

57. Kan. Stat. Ann. § 60-3305; *Hiner v. Deere & Co., Inc.*, 340 F.3d 1190, 1193-94 (10th Cir. 2003); *Brand*, 978 F. Supp. at 1389; *Mays v. Ciba-Geigy Corp.*, 233 Kan. 38, 60, 661 P.2d 384, 364 (1983); *McCroy*, 207 F. Supp. 2d at 1275.

58. *Delaney*, 268 Kan. at 782-83, 999 P.2d at 940-41.

59. *Delaney*, 268 Kan. at 793, 999 P.2d at 946.

60. *Wooderson*, 235 Kan. 387, Syl. 4, 681 P.2d 1038, Syl. 4; *Neff v. Coleco Indus., Inc.*, 760 F. Supp. 864, 866-67 (D. Kan. 1991), *aff'd*, 961 F.2d 220 (10th Cir. 1992).

61. *Patton v. Hutchinson Wil-Rich Mfg. Co.*, 253 Kan. 741, 761-62, 861 P.2d 1299, 1314-15 (1993).

62. *Patton v. TIC United Corp.*, 77 F.3d 1235, 1240-41 (10th Cir.), *cert. denied*, 518 U.S. 1005 (1996).

63. *Kinser v. Gehl Co.*, 184 F.3d 1259, 1270 (10th Cir. 1999), *cert. denied*, 528 U.S. 1139 (2000), *abrogated on other grounds by Weisgram v. Marley Co.*, 528 U.S. 440 (2000); *Patton*, 253 Kan. 741, Syl. 1, 861 P.2d 1299, Syl. 1.

64. Kan. Stat. Ann. § 60-3307(b); *Blackburn, Inc. v. Harnischfeger Corp.*, 773 F. Supp. 296, 302 (D. Kan. 1991); *Griffin v. Suzuki Motor Corp.*, 280 Kan. 447, 463, 124 P.2d 57, 69 (2005) (evidence of wholly different design of manufacturer's

replacement model is inadmissible under Kan. Stat. Ann. § 60-3307); *Patton*, 253 Kan. at 751, 861 P.2d at 1308.

65. *Nichols v. Cent. Merch., Inc.*, 16 Kan. App. 2d 65, 67, 817 P.2d 1131, 1133 (1991) (citing *Wooderson v. Ortho Pharm. Corp.*, 235 Kan. 387, 409, 681 P.2d 1038, 1056, *cert. denied* 469 U.S. 965, 105 S. Ct. 365, 83 L. Ed. 2d 301 (1984)).

66. *Vanderwerf v. SmithKline Beecham Corp.*, 529 F. Supp. 2d 1294, 1309 (D. Kan. 2008); *Samarah*, 70 F. Supp. 2d at 1204; *Humes v. Clinton*, 246 Kan. 590, 603-05, 792 P.2d 1032, 1041-43 (1990); *Nichols v. Cent. Merch. Inc.*, 16 Kan. App. 2d 65, 67, 817 P.2d 1131, 1133 (1991).

67. Pattern Instructions Kansas (Civil) (Fourth) § 128.06 (2010).

68. Pattern Instructions Kansas (Civil) (Fourth) § 128.06 (2010).

69. *Mason v. E. L. Murphy Trucking Co., Inc.*, 769 F. Supp. 341, 345 (D. Kan. 1991).

70. Pattern Instructions Kansas (Civil) (Fourth) § 128.06 (2010). "[P]laintiff's fault must be compared with that of defendant whether it be characterized as contributory negligence, assumption of risk, product misuse, or unreasonable use. These defenses all depend on the reasonableness of plaintiff's conduct, a negligence concept." *Corr v. Terex USA, LLC*, 2011 WL 1097775, at *3 (D. Kan. Mar. 22, 2011) (citing *Hardin v. Manitowoc–Forsythe Corp.*, 691 F.2d 449, 455 (10th Cir. 1982) (in turn citing *Kennedy v. City of Sawyer*, 228 Kan. 439, 461 (1980))).

71. Kan. Stat. Ann. § 60-3307.

72. *Jenkins*, 256 Kan. at 635, 886 P.2d at 889.

73. Kan. Stat. Ann. § 60-3304.

74. Kan. Stat. Ann. § 60-3304(a) (2005). *See also O'Gilvie v. Int'l Playtex, Inc.*, 821 F.2d 1438, 1442-43 (10th Cir. 1987), *cert. denied*, 486 U.S. 1032 (1988); *Alvarado*, 735 F. Supp. at 374.

75. Kan. Stat. Ann. § 60-3304(b).

76. *Pfeiffer v. Eagle Mfg. Co.*, 771 F. Supp. 1141, 1143 (D. Kan. 1994); *cf. Rexrode v. American Laundry Press Co.*, 674 F.2d 826 (10th Cir.) ("[T]he issue of manufacturer compliance with industry standards is generally considered to be irrelevant in a strict liability case. Rather, it relates to the question of the manufacturer's duty of care under a negligence theory."), *cert. denied*, 459 U.S. 862 (1982).

77. *Kinser*, 184 F.3d at 1273; *Wheeler v. John Deere*, 862 F.2d 1404, 1407 (10th Cir. 1988); *King v. Emerson Elec. Co.*, 837 F. Supp. 1096, 1099 (D. Kan. 1993), *aff'd*,

69 F.3d 548 (10th Cir. 1995). *See Schaeffer v. Kansas Dep't of Transp.*, 227 Kan. 509, 517, 608 P.2d 1309, 1317 (1980).

78. *Wheeler*, 862 F.2d at 1407; *King*, 837 F. Supp. at 1099; *Schaeffer*, 227 Kan. at 517.

79. Kan. Stat. Ann. § 60-3302(c).

80. *Koplin v. Rosel Well Perforators, Inc.*, 241 Kan. 206, 215, 734 P.2d 1177, 1183 (1987) (refusing to recognize tort of intentional spoliation absent duty). *But see Foster v. Lawrence Mem'l Hosp.*, 809 F. Supp. 831, 838 (D. Kan. 1992) (predicting that Kansas Supreme Court would recognize tort of spoliation under some circumstances).

81. *Superior Boiler Works, Inc. v. Kimball*, 292 Kan. 885, 895-96, 259 P.3d 676, 683 (2011) (no duty to preserve evidence absent an agreement, a contract, a statute, or other special circumstance).

82. *103 Investors I, L.P. v. Square D Co.*, 470 F.3d 985, 988-89 (10th Cir. 2006) (affirming trial court's exclusion of fact witness based on plaintiff's spoliation of evidence even in absence of bad faith); *Workman v. AB Electrolux Corp.*, 2005 WL 1896246, at *7 (D. Kan. Aug. 8, 2005) ("The court also states that, because only the bad faith loss or destruction of a document will support an inference of consciousness of a weak case, no adverse inference should arise from spoliation that is merely negligent. The Tenth Circuit does not impose a similar requirement of bad faith when considering other sanctions for spoliation, however.") (citation, internal quotation marks, and footnotes omitted).

83. *Koss Constr. v. Caterpillar, Inc.*, 25 Kan. App. 2d 200, Syl. 2, 207, 960 P.2d 255, Syl. 2, 259 (1998); *see also Northwest Arkansas Masonry Inc. v. Summit Specialty Prods., Inc.*, 29 Kan. App. 2d 735, 741, 31 P.3d 982, 987 (2001); *David v. Hett*, 293 Kan. 679, 683, 270 P.3d 1102, 1105 (2011) (discussing development of the economic loss doctrine in Kansas); *Rinehart v. Morton Bldgs., Inc.*, 297 Kan. 926, 938, 305 P.3d 622, 631 (2013) (same; allowing recovery of economic damages for negligent misrepresentation claim).

84. *Koss Constr.*, 25 Kan. App. 2d at 207, 960 P.2d at 259; *Philippine Am. Life Ins. v. Raytheon Aircraft Co.*, 252 F. Supp. 2d 1138, 1143 (D. Kan. 2003).

85. *Nature's Share, Inc. v. Kutter Prods., Inc.*, 752 F. Supp. 371, 380 (D. Kan. 1990) (citing *Professional Lens Plan, Inc. v. Polaris Leasing Corp.*, 234 Kan. 742, 752-53, 675 P.2d 887, 897 (1984)).

86. *Koss Constr.*, 25 Kan. App. 2d at 207, 960 P.2d at 259-60.

87. *See Koss Constr.*, 25 Kan. App. 2d at 207, 960 P.2d at 259-60. (applying economic loss doctrine to commercial product setting); *Jordan v. Case Corp.*, 26 Kan. App. 2d 742, 744, 993 P.2d 650, 652 (1999) (applying doctrine to

consumer product setting); *see also David*, 293 Kan. at 700, 270 P.3d at 1114 (abrogating extension of economic loss doctrine to residential construction cases).

88. *See Albertson v. Volkswagenwerk Aktiengesellschaft*, 230 Kan. 368, 370, 634 P.2d 1127, 1130 (1981) (noting that court has not yet ruled on second collision doctrine and declining to do so here); *Young v. Deere & Co., Inc.*, 818 F. Supp. 1420, 1422 (D. Kan. 1992).

89. *See, e.g., Young v. Deere & Co., Inc.*, 818 F. Supp. 1420, 1422 (D. Kan. 1992); *Stueve v. American Honda Motors Co., Inc.*, 457 F. Supp. 740, 758-59 (D. Kan. 1978).

90. *Voelkel v. Gen. Motors Corp.*, 846 F. Supp. 1468, 1480 (D. Kan. 1994) (citing *Harvey v. Gen. Motors Corp.*, 873 F.2d 1343, 1349 (10th Cir. 1989)), *aff'd*, 43 F.3d 1484 (10th Cir. 1994).

91. *Miller v. Lee Apparel Co., Inc.*, 19 Kan. App. 2d 1015, 1023, 881 P.2d 576, 583 (1994).

92. *Kinser*, 184 F.3d at 1269; *Miller*, 19 Kan. App. 2d at 1032, 881 P.2d at 589.

93. *Kinser*, 184 F.3d at 1269.

94. *Gaumer v. Rossville Truck & Tractor Co., Inc.*, 41 Kan. App. 2d 405, 408, 202 P.3d 81, 84 (2009) (affirming summary judgment for plaintiff's failure to provide expert opinion on standard of care for used farm equipment dealer), *aff'd*, 257 P.3d 292 (Kansas Supreme Court, in limited review, was not asked to address this issue on transfer).

95. Pattern Instructions Kansas (Civil) (Fourth) § 128.02 (2010); *Garst v. Gen. Motors Corp.*, 207 Kan. 2, 19, 484 P.2d 47, 60 (1971).

96. Pattern Instructions Kansas (Civil) (Fourth) § 128.01 (2010); *Timsah v. Gen. Motors Corp.*, 225 Kan. 305, 313-14, 591 P.2d 154, 162 (1979).

97. Kan. Stat. Ann. § 60-3302(c). *See also, e.g., Hiner v. Deere & Co.*, 161 F. Supp. 2d 1279, 1282 (D. Kan. 2011) ("Under the Kansas Product Liability Act ("KPLA") . . . a plaintiff's various theories of recovery, i.e., negligence, strict liability, or breach of warranty, are melded into a single claim."), *reversed on other grounds by Hiner v. Deere & Co., Inc.*, 340 F.3d 1190 (10th Cir. 2003).

98. *Tetuan v. A. H. Robins Co.*, 241 Kan. 441, 481-82, 738 P.2d 1210, 1238-39 (1987); *Wooderson*, 235 Kan. at 415, 681 P.2d at 1061. *See* Pattern Instructions Kansas (Civil) (Fourth), § 171.44 (2010).

99. Kan. Stat. Ann. § 60-3702(a); *Hayes Sight & Sound, Inc. v. ONEOK, Inc.*, 136 P.3d 428, 451 (Kan. 2006) (affirming trial court's award of punitive damages).

But see Jones v. United Parcel Serv., Inc., 674 F.3d 1187, 1206 (10th Cir. 2012) (holding that Fed. R. Civ. P. 38, which preserves "the right to trial by jury as declared by the Seventh Amendment," requires that the jury determine the amount of punitive damage award in federal court, despite conflicting state law).

100. Kan. Stat. Ann. § 60-3702(e).

101. Kan. Stat. Ann. § 16-201 (1995); *Hamilton v. State Farm Fire & Cas. Co.*, 263 Kan. 875, Syl. 4, 953 P.2d 1027, Syl. 4 (1998); *In re Estate of Baum*, 279 P.3d 147 (Kan. Ct. App. 2012) (if claim is liquidated, pre-judgment interest award is mandatory under § 16-201).

102. Kan. Stat. Ann. § 16-201.

103. Kan. Stat. Ann. § 16-204 (unpublished).

104. Kan. Stat. Ann. § 44-501(b); *McGranahan v. McGough*, 249 Kan. 328, 337, 820 P.2d 403, 410 (1991).

105. Kan. Stat. Ann. § 60-513.

106. Kan. Stat. Ann. § 60-258a.

107. Kan. Stat. Ann. § 84-2-101 *et seq.*

108. Kan. Stat. Ann. § 60-3301 *et seq.*

109. Kan. Stat. Ann. §§ 60-3701, 60-3702, 60-19a01, 60-19a02.

110. Kan. Stat. Ann. § 44-501 *et seq.*

111. Kan. Stat. Ann. § 38-101 (note the exception for persons 16 years of age or over who are or have been married—such persons shall be considered of the age of majority in all matters relating to contracts, property rights, liabilities and the capacity to sue and be sued).

112. *Brown*, 224 Kan. at 204, 580 P.2d at 874. *See, e.g., Greenwood v. McDonough Power Equip., Inc.*, 437 F. Supp. 707, 710 (D. Kan. 1977) (defendant's liability limited by that defendant's share of total negligence).

Kentucky

A. CAUSES OF ACTION

Kentucky product liability law allows three causes of action: strict liability in tort, negligence, and breach of warranty.[1] Kentucky's Product Liability Act (KPLA) applies to all damage claims arising from the use of a product, regardless of the legal theory advanced.[2]

B. STATUTES OF LIMITATION

The statute of limitations for personal injury claims not based on warranty is one year after the cause of action accrues.[3] Generally, a cause of action accrues at the time of injury.[4] In actions involving a delayed appearance of the injury, the cause of action will not accrue until the plaintiff discovers or reasonably should have discovered the injury and its cause.[5] The limitations period is not tolled while the plaintiff seeks the identity of the person or entity causing the injury, unless there is fraudulent concealment or a misrepresentation by the defendant.[6] If there is fraudulent concealment or a misrepresentation by the defendant, the defendant may be estopped from asserting a statute of limitations defense if the plaintiff can show (1) a lack of knowledge or means to obtain knowledge of the true facts; (2) good faith reliance on the action or inaction of the defendant; and (3) that the plaintiff's reliance was detrimental.[7] For a cause of action to accrue, the plaintiff must suffer a present injury. The fear of future harm or fear of increased risk of harm does not constitute a present injury for which a cause of action accrues.[8]

Wrongful death and survival actions must be filed within one year from the date of appointment of the personal representative.[9] The personal representative must be appointed within one year of the date of death or the one-year anniversary of the date of death is considered the date of appointment.[10]

The statute of limitations for warranty actions is four years from the date of delivery.[11] That period may not be extended, but it may be reduced by the original agreement of the parties to not less than one year.[12] The cause of action for an express warranty extending to the future performance of a product accrues when the breach is or should have been discovered.[13]

An exception to these rules occurs when an injury arises out of a motor vehicle accident. For those actions, the limitations period is two years from the date of the injury.[14] The statute of limitations for personal property damage is two years.[15]

There is a statutory presumption, rebuttable by a preponderance of the evidence, that a product is not defective if the injury, death, or property damage occurred either more than five years after the date of the sale to the first consumer or more than eight years after the date of manufacture.[16]

C. STRICT LIABILITY

1. The Standard

Kentucky recognizes the theory of strict product liability as expressed in Section 402A of the Restatement (Second) of Torts.[17] Kentucky law provides for recovery when injury results from the use of a product that was "in a defective condition unreasonably dangerous," even though all due care was used in its manufacture and there was no privity of contract.[18]

Kentucky has not yet adopted the definition of "product defect" contained in the Restatement (Third) of Torts: Products Liability.[19] In a decision rendered in the context of vehicle "crashworthiness," a trial court may instruct the jury regarding evidence of a reasonable and safer alternative design, but it is "not required to do so."[20]

2. Definition of "Defect"

A product is defective if an ordinarily prudent seller, being fully aware of the risks, would not place the product on the market.[21] Expert testimony is generally required to meet the burden to show that a product is defective.[22] This general rule exists because the complex or technical matters in many product liability cases are outside the knowledge of ordinary lay people.[23] Expert testimony regarding the existence of a defect is subject to the factors for determining the admissibility of expert scientific testimony as set forth in *Daubert v. Merrell Dow Pharmaceuticals, Inc.*,[24] and adopted in *Goodyear Tire & Rubber Co. v. Thompson*.[25] An expert witness's personal assurance that a given theory is reliable is not itself a sufficient safeguard justifying the admission of expert testimony under *Daubert*.[26]

3. Causation

To establish liability for injury allegedly resulting from a product, whether on a theory of strict liability, negligence, or breach of warranty, the plaintiff must establish that the product was the legal cause of harm.[27] The measure of causation in a Kentucky design defect case is the substantial factor test: was defendant's conduct a substantial factor in bringing about plaintiff's harm?[28] In a product liability action, causation is an element that may be proved by either direct or circumstantial evidence; however, if the plaintiff seeks to establish causation by circumstantial evidence, the evidence must be sufficient to tilt the balance from possible cause to probable cause.[29]

4. Contributory Negligence/Assumption of Risk

Although KPLA provides that contributory negligence is a complete defense in all product liability actions,[30] Kentucky's highest court has ruled that Kentucky's comparative fault statute, enacted ten years after the KPLA, supersedes the contributory negligence provisions in the KPLA.[31] Pure comparative fault principles apply to products liability cases in Kentucky.[32] Comparative fault principles also apply to all other personal injury and property damage causes of action in Kentucky.[33]

The voluntary assumption of a known, unreasonable risk is a factor to be considered in assessing comparative fault; it is not a separate defense.[34]

5. Sale or Lease/Persons Liable

A plaintiff must prove that the defendant is a seller "engaged in the business of selling such a product."[35] An occasional seller is not subject to strict liability.[36] When a product is sold only on an occasion or incident to the business of the seller, the transaction does not come within the purview of the doctrine of strict liability.[37] One who employs a product for internal use does not incur the liability of a manufacturer and is not subject to strict liability.[38] Strict liability applies to each member of the product's chain of distribution, including manufacturers or others whose primary business may not be selling.[39] If a manufacturer is identified and subject to the court's jurisdiction, a wholesaler, distributor, or retailer who sells a product in its original manufactured condition or package is not liable absent special circumstances.[40] Kentucky courts have not decided whether strict product liability applies to lessors or bailors of products that prove defective.

A federal trial court has held electricity to be a product subject to strict liability.[41]

6. Inherently Dangerous Products

Kentucky follows the principle in comment k of Section 402A that an unavoidably unsafe product that is properly prepared and accompanied by proper directions and warnings is not defective or unreasonably dangerous.[42] An unavoidably unsafe product is one that, in the present state of human knowledge, is incapable of being made completely safe for its intended use. Because its benefit outweighs the risk of injury, marketing such a product is justified.[43]

Kentucky courts have not defined the scope of the "Unavoidably Unsafe Products Doctrine." U.S. District Courts in the Eastern and Western Districts of Kentucky predicted that Kentucky would follow the majority trend and apply comment k on a case-by-case basis—when the apparent benefits of the drug exceed the apparent risks.[44]

7. Successor Liability

A defendant that is a successor company to the seller will not be responsible for the seller's liability unless (1) the successor agreed to assume liabilities; (2) the companies merged; (3) the purchasing company is a continuation of the selling company; or (4) the transaction was entered into fraudulently to escape liability.[45]

8. **Enterprise Liability/Market Share Liability**

Kentucky recognizes concert of action principles, but it has not recognized enterprise liability and market share liability.[46]

9. **Privity**

No privity is required in strict liability actions; a plaintiff may sue even though she did not buy the product from the manufacturer.[47] The Sixth Circuit has predicted that Kentucky would also apply this rule in cases involving a commercial transaction in which the only damage was to the product.[48]

10. **Failure to Warn**

Kentucky law imposes a duty on manufacturers and suppliers of products to warn of known dangers or reasonably foreseeable misuse.[49] A manufacturer or supplier is not responsible, however, to warn of open and obvious dangers.[50] A plaintiff is adequately warned if given fair and adequate notice of the danger and possible consequences of using or even misusing the product.[51] There is a presumption that a proper warning will be read and heeded.[52]

A manufacturer has a nondelegable duty to warn the ultimate user of latent product dangers.[53] The duty is not abrogated by a warning to the immediate buyer unless the buyer takes responsibility for correcting the defect.[54] When an immediate buyer fails to advise the end consumer of a warning provided by the original product manufacturer, the buyer may be found strictly liable or negligent for failing to warn the end consumer.[55]

Product liability plaintiffs are entitled to a separate jury instruction on each theory of liability on which there is evidence to sustain it, including a theory of recovery based upon failure to warn.[56]

11. **Post-Sale Duty to Warn**

Kentucky has not decided whether to impose a continuing duty to warn after sale. The U.S. District Court for the Eastern District of Kentucky, however, predicted that Kentucky would not recognize a post-sale duty to warn claim.[57] A manufacturer who undertakes the duty to make a post-sale warning, however, must make the warning available to the end user.[58] A Kentucky federal court has held that a continuing duty to warn may arise if the manufacturer learns of significant product failures, unexpected or dangerous uses, or if a high accident rate demonstrates that a danger thought to be obvious was not recognized by users.[59]

When, after an event, measures are taken that if taken previously would have made an injury or harm allegedly caused by the event less likely to occur, evidence of the subsequent measures is not admissible to prove negligence in connection with the event.[60] In 2006, the Kentucky Supreme Court amended this rule to exclude evidence of subsequent remedial measures in products liability litigation.[61] The amendment of Kentucky's Rule 407 brings Kentucky law into conformity with prevailing federal law. Rule 407 does not require the exclusion of evidence of subsequent remedial measures when offered for another purpose.[62]

In Kentucky, a product manufacturer does not have an independent duty to retrofit a product that is not defective at the time of sale.[63] Kentucky declined to adopt Section 11 of the Restatement (Third) of Torts: Products Liability, holding that a manufacturer does not assume a duty by initiating a voluntary retrofit campaign.[64]

12. **Learned Intermediary Doctrine**

Kentucky recognizes the learned intermediary doctrine.[65] On a certified question from the United States Court of Appeals for the Sixth Circuit, the Supreme Court of Kentucky adopted Section 6(d) of the Restatement (Third) of Torts: Products Liability, which states that a product manufacturer has satisfied its duty to warn of possible side effects of a prescription drug if it provides adequate warnings to a patient's health care provider.[66] A product manufacturer may still be liable to the patient, however, if it fails to adequately warn the learned intermediary.[67]

13. **Substantial Change/Abnormal Use**

To establish liability, a product must reach the ultimate consumer without substantial change in the condition in which it was sold. "Substantial change" is any change that increases the likelihood of malfunction.[68] The KPLA provides that a manufacturer is liable only if the injury would have occurred if the product was used in its original, unaltered, and unmodified condition.[69] Product modification includes failure to observe routine maintenance and care, but not ordinary wear and tear, and applies to alterations made by any person or entity except those made in accordance with the manufacturer's specifications or instructions.[70] Given Kentucky's application of pure comparative fault in all tort actions, it is not clear that an unauthorized product modification can completely bar a product liability claim.[71]

Product alteration or modification includes the failure to follow a warning.[72] An unknowledgeable user, unaware of the danger, using the product for its intended purpose, is not necessarily negligent when using the product in a different manner from its intended use if such use is reasonably foreseeable.[73]

14. **State of the Art**

There is a presumption, rebuttable by a preponderance of the evidence, that a product is not defective if the design, methods of manufacture, and testing conform to the generally recognized and prevailing standards or the state of the art in existence at the time the design was prepared and the product was manufactured.[74] Proof that technology existed that, if implemented, could have feasibly avoided the dangerous condition does not alone establish a product's defectiveness.[75]

15. **Malfunction**

When an accident occurs that in common experience would not ordinarily occur without a defect in a product, the inference of a defect is permitted.[76] In an unpublished opinion, a panel of the Sixth Circuit Court of Appeals recently suggested that a plaintiff "can prove a product liability claim using the fact of the malfunction if [the plaintiff] eliminates those causes for which the manufacturer would not be liable."[77] In this panel's view, a plaintiff need not show whether the malfunction is attributable to a manufacturing or design defect but must show that it is the result of a defect that is attributable only to the defendant.[78]

16. **Standards**

Compliance and noncompliance with government or industry standards is admissible, but not determinative, on the issue of liability.[79]

17. **Other Accidents**

Evidence of similar product failures under similar conditions is relevant and admissible.[80] Evidence of lack of prior claims against a manufacturer is admissible to show lack of defective design and notice of defect.[81] Plaintiffs do not have to establish substantial similarity before discovery of other product failures.[82]

18. **Misrepresentation**

Kentucky has not expressly adopted Section 402B of the Restatement (Second) of Torts regarding innocent or strict liability misrepresentation.

A seller is liable for representing a product as safe or concealing known defects when injury occurs from the product's use.[83] An actionable misrepresentation is a representation of false, material fact that, at the time of its making, the seller knew was false or made recklessly, without knowledge of its truth.[84] The seller must have intended to induce the buyer to act, and the buyer must have, in fact, relied on its misrepresentation.[85] Kentucky has adopted Section 552 of the Restatement (Second) of Torts, but Kentucky courts have not applied it to a product liability action.[86]

Kentucky does not require privity between the parties in a misrepresentation claim; however, the party claiming fraud must prove a nexus between the injury and the misrepresentation by demonstrating that he or she relied on the misrepresentation.[87] In a federal district court case, the plaintiff's claim that the manufacturer misrepresented the misuse of the product in its application for approval from the Federal Food and Drug Administration was rejected as failing to demonstrate proximate causation between the alleged fraud and the resulting injury.[88]

19. **Destruction or Loss of Product**

    Kentucky does not recognize a separate tort for a claim of destroyed or missing evidence.[89] Under Kentucky law, the issue of missing or destroyed evidence is remedied through evidentiary rules and jury instructions.[90]

20. **Economic Loss**

    Damage to the product itself is recoverable under a warranty theory, but in an action based on tort, the plaintiff may need to prove that the damage to the product occurred as a result of a "damaging event."[91] In cases involving a commercial transaction in which the only damage is to the product, the Kentucky Supreme Court ruled in 2011 that the "economic loss rule" applies and precludes recovery in tort.[92] The relevant product for purposes of the rule is "[t]he entire item bargained for by the parties and placed in the stream of commerce by the manufacturer."[93]

    The Sixth Circuit has predicted that the Kentucky Supreme Court would also apply the economic loss rule to immunize potential defendants who are not in privity with a plaintiff.[94]

21. **Crashworthiness**

    Although Kentucky has not expressly adopted Section 2(b) of the Restatement (Third) of Torts: Product Liability,[95] Kentucky recognizes the traditional elements of a crashworthiness claim, including proof of a safer and feasible alternative design.[96] With respect to satisfying the alternative design prong in a crashworthiness claim, the mere mention that alternative possibilities exist is not sufficient. A plaintiff must show something more than that a different design is theoretically feasible.[97]

D. NEGLIGENCE

The negligence standard in Kentucky product liability law is whether a prudent seller by the exercise of ordinary care should have discovered and foreseen the condition and potential problems with the product when the seller put the product on the market.[98] Kentucky does not recognize an independent duty to test, but the KPLA suggests that testing is indicative of whether the manufacturer satisfied its more general duty to exercise ordinary care.[99]

Product liability plaintiffs are entitled to a separate jury instruction on a theory of negligence if there is evidence to sustain it.[100] However, the Sixth Circuit, interpreting Kentucky product liability law, decided that a negligence claim based on the failure to use ordinary care in design and manufacture required proof of a defect, and therefore a jury verdict for the defendant on the strict liability instruction and against the defendant on a negligence instruction was logically inconsistent.

E. **BREACH OF WARRANTY**

A warranty that goods are merchantable is implied in a contract for their sale.[101] Liability for breach of implied warranty of merchantability depends on the condition of the goods, not on misconduct or fault of the seller.[102]

Any affirmation of fact or promise made by the seller to the buyer that relates to the goods and becomes part of the basis of the bargain creates an express warranty that the goods shall conform to the affirmation or promise.[103] Although Kentucky courts have not defined "basis of the bargain," a federal court found in a pharmaceutical case involving package inserts that when the plaintiff did not see the package inserts any warranty included in them was not part of the basis of the bargain and no express warranty arose.[104]

Traditional horizontal privity is not required; however, actions on an express or implied warranty extend only to the buyer's family, household, or guests reasonably expected to use the goods.[105] Vertical privity is required in warranty actions; the plaintiff must be in privity with the seller-defendant.[106]

Kentucky also recognizes an implied warranty of fitness for a particular purpose. Liability attaches if the seller had reason to know of the purpose to which the goods were to be put and the buyer relied on the seller's skill or judgment in selecting the appropriate goods.[107]

There is no implied warranty of habitability imposed on a builder/seller of a home beyond the initial buyer.[108]

F. **DAMAGES**

Past and future medical expenses, lost wages, permanent impairment of the power to labor and earn money, and past and future physical and mental pain and suffering are recoverable damages in personal injury cases in Kentucky.[109] The increased likelihood of future complications, including mental distress created by the increased risk of future complications, may also be compensable.[110] However, a harmful change of some nature (present injury) must exist before a plaintiff can recover for enhanced risk of future complications and accompanying mental distress.[111] Under Kentucky law, mere increased risk or fear of future harm does not alone constitute a present physical injury for which a plaintiff may recover.[112] Kentucky does not recognize "medical monitoring" claims, absent a present injury.[113]

The Kentucky Supreme Court recently abrogated the "physical impact" rule in claims for emotional distress, allowing recovery irrespective of contact, provided that the plaintiff satisfies the elements of a negligence claim.[114] Previously, physical contact was a prerequisite to the recovery of damages for emotional distress.[115]

The spouse of an injured plaintiff may recover for loss of consortium and may recover those damages even after the death of the injured spouse.[116] Loss of consortium claims are derivative of the underlying tort claim.[117] Minor children have an independent claim for parental loss of consortium after the death of a parent.[118] Unadopted minor stepchildren, however, do not have a claim for and may not recover parental loss of consortium upon the death of a step-parent.[119] In determining the amount of damages recoverable by a minor child for loss of parental consortium, the court cannot consider other consortium-giving relationships that may be available to the child.[120]

Kentucky's version of the Uniform Commercial Code governs damages for breach of warranty and includes the difference between the value of the goods as warranted and the value of the goods accepted, and incidental or consequential damages if appropriate.[121]

Although one section of Kentucky's punitive damages statute, Ky. Rev. Stat. Ann. § 411.184(1)(c), was found unconstitutional,[122] punitive damages are generally recoverable upon clear and convincing evidence of oppression, fraud or malice.[123] The definition of malice under § 411.184(1)(c) was declared unconstitutional because it violated Kentucky's jural rights doctrine by requiring a defendant to be subjectively aware that his conduct would result in death or bodily harm.[124] The current standard for awarding punitive damages is common law gross negligence, defined as a failure to exercise reasonable care coupled with a "wanton or reckless disregard for the lives, safety or property of others."[125] A manufacturer's failure to test its product for defects posing a risk of serious injury may, if the product is readily testable, justify an award of punitive damages.[126] Punitive damages may not be recovered in breach of warranty actions, if the action is considered a breach of contract.[127]

G. GOVERNMENT CONTRACTOR DEFENSE

Manufacturers are not liable for product failures if (1) the government approves reasonably precise specifications, (2) the product conforms to the specifications, and (3) the supplier warns the government of the danger in using the product.[128]

H. EMPLOYER IMMUNITY FROM SUIT

Employers are protected from civil liability by the exclusive remedy provision of the Workers' Compensation Act, KRS § 342.690. In circumstances in which an employee is injured by the negligence of a third party, but where the employer is required to pay Workers' Compensation benefits, the employer is entitled to recover such sums from the party at fault. To facilitate recovery, KRS § 342.700 authorizes an employer to intervene in civil litigation brought by the employee against a negligent party and, if the third party's negligence is established, recover the Workers' Compensation benefits paid.

Under Kentucky's comparative fault law, courts allow an apportionment of liability instruction against a negligent employer in cases in which the employer has intervened into the civil action for recovery of Workers' Compensation benefits,[129] or in cases in which the defendant has brought the negligent employer into the action on a third-party complaint.[130]

I. STATUTES

Relevant statutes for product liability actions are the KPLA,[131] statutes of limitation, the commercial code sections when a breach of warranty is alleged, and, if capacity is at issue, the age of majority is eighteen.[132]

J. JOINT AND SEVERAL LIABILITY

Liability among tortfeasors is several, not joint and several, under Kentucky's pure comparative fault statutes.[133] All parties and released tortfeasors, whether or not the latter are named in the lawsuit, are included in the allocation of fault.[134] A court may provide an apportionment instruction against a dismissed defendant, provided that the defendant was not dismissed on the merits.[135] When a defendant tries to transfer responsibility to an empty-chair defendant, the burden of proof shifts to the active defendant to show that the empty-chair defendant legally caused the plaintiff's injuries.[136]

K. PREEMPTION

Kentucky state courts have twice found that a plaintiff's product liability claims are not preempted by the 1976 Amendments to the Federal Food, Drug and Cosmetic Act.[137] In the first case, the Supreme Court of Kentucky held that a plaintiff's claims involving a Class III medical device that had been marketed under an investigational device exemption (IDE) were not preempted by federal law because Kentucky did not impose any requirements which were different from or in addition to any federal requirements for the device.[138] Relying on this reasoning, the Court of Appeals similarly rejected a preemption claim involving a Class II medical device.[139]

A federal court in Kentucky held that medical device claims for design defect, manufacturing defect, failure to warn, negligence, and breach of express and implied warranties are preempted by the Food and Drug Administration pre-market approval application procedure for Class III medical devices, as provided for by the Medical Device Amendments.[140] The court held that an action is preempted if it imposes a state requirement that "differs from, adds to, or impedes the implementation and enforcement of the design, manufacturing process, or labeling" contained in the product's pre-market approval application.[141] Following this approach, the Western District of Kentucky held that the Medical Device Amendments to the Food Drug and Cosmetic Act preempted a plaintiff's claims alleging negligence, breach of implied warranty, strict liability, and misrepresentation associated with the replacement of allegedly defective breast implants.[142] Therefore, a court will analyze each state claim separately.[143]

With respect to pharmaceutical products, in January 2006, the Food and Drug Administration unveiled major revisions to the required content and format of prescription drug labeling and promulgated what has become known as the "Preemption Preamble."[144] The Preemption Preamble states that, "under existing preemption principles, FDA approval of labeling under the act, whether it be in the old or new format, preempts conflicting or contrary state law."[145] Notwithstanding the FDA's position on preemption of state law claims, a U.S. District Court opinion held that drugs approved and prescribed to a plaintiff prior to the FDA's adoption of the new regulations does not preempt state law failure-to-warn claims.[146] The court refused to defer to the FDA's position regarding preemption and stated that FDA regulations specifically provided avenues for pharmaceutical companies to strengthen label warnings.[147]

L. EX PARTE CONTACTS WITH TREATING PHYSICIANS

The physician-patient privilege does not exist under Kentucky common law or statute.[148] Kentucky courts historically allowed informal interviews with treating physicians before enactment of the Health Insurance Portability and Accountability Act (HIPAA).[149] A product manufacturer's counsel might be permitted to have *ex parte* contact with a plaintiff's treating physicians and to conduct *ex parte* interviews with these treating physicians if the treating physicians are willing to engage in such contacts.[150]

John L. Tate
J. Brittany Cross Carlson
Stites & Harbison, PLLC
400 West Market Street
Suite 1800
Louisville, Kentucky 40202
(502) 587-3400
(Fax) (502) 587-6391

ENDNOTES - KENTUCKY

1. *Williams v. Fulmer*, 695 S.W.2d 411, 413 (Ky. 1985); *Ostendorf v. Clark Equip. Co.*, 122 S.W.3d 530, 535 (Ky. 2003).

2. Ky. Rev. Stat. Ann. § 411.300 (Michie 2005) *et seq.*; *Monsanto Co. v. Reed*, 950 S.W.2d 811, 814 (Ky. 1997).

3. Ky. Rev. Stat. Ann. § 413.140(1)(a).

4. *Caudill v. Arnett*, 481 S.W.2d 668, 669 (Ky. 1972), *overruled in part by Louisville Trust Co. v. Johns-Manville Prods. Corp.*, 580 S.W.2d 497, 500 (Ky. 1979).

5. *Fluke Corp. v. LeMaster*, 306 S.W.3d 55, 60 (Ky. 2010); *Perkins v. Northeastern Log Homes*, 808 S.W.2d 809, 818-19 (Ky. 1991); *Drake v. B.F. Goodrich Co.*, 782 F.2d 638, 641 (6th Cir. 1986); *Louisville Trust Co.*, 580 S.W.2d at 501.

6. *Simmons v. South Cent. Skyworkers, Inc.*, 936 F.2d 268, 269 (6th Cir. 1991); *Combs v. Albert Kahn Assocs., Inc.*, 183 S.W.3d 190, 199 (Ky. Ct. App. 2006); *Reese v. Gen. Am. Door Co.*, 6 S.W.3d 380, 383 (Ky. Ct. App. 1998); *see also* Ky. Rev. Stat. Ann. § 413.190(2).

7. *Fluke*, 306 S.W.3d at 62.

8. *Capital Holding Corp. v. Bailey*, 873 S.W.2d 187, 192 (Ky. 1994); *Wood v. Wyeth-Ayerst Labs.*, 82 S.W.3d 849, 853-54 (Ky. 2002).

9. Ky. Rev. Stat. Ann. § 413.180(1).

10. Ky. Rev. Stat. Ann. § 413.180(2); *Conner v. George W. Whitesides Co.*, 834 S.W.2d 652, 654-55 (Ky. 1992).

11. Ky. Rev. Stat. Ann. § 355.2-725 (Michie 2008).

12. Ky. Rev. Stat. Ann. § 355.2-725(1).

13. Ky. Rev. Stat. Ann. § 355.2-725(2).

14. Ky. Rev. Stat. Ann. § 304.39-230(6) (Michie 2006); *Troxell v. Trammel*, 730 S.W.2d 525, 528 (Ky. 1987).

15. Ky. Rev. Stat. Ann. § 413.125.

16. Ky. Rev. Stat. Ann. § 411.310(1) (The presumption has not been interpreted by a Kentucky court).

17. *Dealers Transp. Co., Inc. v. Battery Distrib. Co., Inc.*, 402 S.W.2d 441, 446-47 (Ky. 1965); *Griffin Indus., Inc. v. Jones*, 975 S.W.2d 100, 102 (Ky. 1998); *Dalton v. Animas Corp.*, 913 F. Supp. 2d 370, 373 (W.D. Ky. 2012).

18. *Griffin Indus., Inc.*, 975 S.W.2d at 102.

19. *Toyota Motor Corp. v. Gregory*, 136 S.W.3d 35, 42 (Ky. 2004).

20. *Gregory*, 136 S.W.3d at 42 (citing Restatement (Third) of Torts: Products Liability § 2(b) (1998)); *see also Burke v. U-Haul Int'l Inc.*, 501 F. Supp. 2d 930, 933 (W.D. Ky. 2007).

21. *Tobin v. Astra Pharm. Prods., Inc.*, 993 F.2d 528, 536 (6th Cir. 1993), *cert. denied*, 510 U.S. 914 (1993); *Walker v. Phillip Morris U.S.A., Inc.*, 610 F. Supp. 2d 785, 787 (W.D. Ky. 2009); *Vaughn v. Alternative Design Mfg. & Supply, Inc.*, 2008 U.S. Dist. LEXIS 82325, at *18-19 (E.D. Ky. Oct. 16, 2008); *Nichols v. Union Underwear Co., Inc.*, 602 S.W.2d 429, 433 (Ky. 1980); *Boon Edam, Inc. v. Saunders*, 324 S.W.3d 422, 430 (Ky. App. 2010); *see also* Palmore & Cetrulo, Kentucky Jury Instructions § 49.02.

22. *Honaker v. Innova, Inc.*, 2007 U.S. Dist. LEXIS 30225, at *4 (W.D. Ky. Apr. 23, 2007); *Thomas v. Manchester Tank & Equip. Corp.*, 2005 U.S. Dist. LEXIS 9225, at *3 (W.D. Ky. May 13, 2005).

23. *Thomas*, U.S. Dist. LEXIS 9225, at *4; *see also Commonwealth, Dep't of Highways v. Robbins*, 421 S.W.2d 820, 824 (Ky. 1967) (holding that "for a proper understanding of that which requires scientific or specialized knowledge and which cannot be determined intelligently from testimony on the basis of ordinary knowledge gained in the ordinary affairs of life, expert testimony is needed").

24. 509 U.S. 579 (1993).

25. 11 S.W.3d 575, 578-79 (Ky. 2000); *Hyman & Armstrong, P.S.C. v. Gunderson*, 279 S.W.3d 93, 100-01 (Ky. 2008).

26. *Alfred v. Mentor Corp.*, 479 F. Supp. 2d 670 (W.D. Ky. 2007).

27. *Morales v. American Honda Motor Co.*, 151 F.3d 500, 507 (6th Cir. 1998); *Holbrook v. Rose*, 458 S.W.2d 155, 157 (Ky. 1970); *Wilson v. Wyeth, Inc.*, 2008 U.S. Dist. LEXIS 50328, at *4 (W.D. Ky. June 30, 2008) ("The identity of the product that caused a plaintiff's injury is the threshold requirement of a products liability claim."); *Morris v. Wyeth, Inc.*, 2008 U.S. Dist. LEXIS 50341, at *12 (W.D. Ky. June 30, 2008) (explaining that "in the generic drug context, Kentucky does not recognize[] a cause of action against a manufacturer for its representations concerning its own product, based on an injury caused from the use of another manufacturer's product").

28. *CertainTeed Corp. v. Dexter*, 330 S.W.3d 64, 77 (Ky. 2010); *Estate of Bigham v. DaimlerChrysler Corp.*, 462 F. Supp. 2d 766, 771-72 (E.D. Ky. 2006).

29. *Holbrook*, 458 S.W.2d at 158; *Calhoun v. Honda Motor Co.*, 738 F.2d 126, 130 (6th Cir. 1984); *Kentucky Farm Bureau Mut. Ins. Co. v. Deere & Co.*, 2008 U.S. Dist. LEXIS 8856, at *5-13 (W.D. Ky. Feb. 5, 2008); *Briner v. General Motors Corp.*, 461 S.W.2d 99 (Ky. 1971); *Ingersoll-Rand Co. v. Rice*, 775 S.W.2d 924 (Ky. App. 1988).

30. Ky. Rev. Stat. Ann. § 411.320 (Michie 2005).

31. *Caterpillar, Inc. v. Brock*, 915 S.W.2d 751, 753 (Ky. 1996) (holding comparative fault statute supersedes KRS § 411.320(1)), *rev'd on other grounds, Brock v. Caterpillar, Inc.*, 94 F.3d 220 (6th Cir. 1996); *Smith v. Louis Berkman Co.*, 894 F. Supp. 1084, 1090 (W.D. Ky. 1995) (holding comparative fault statute supersedes KRS § 411.320(2) and (3)).

32. Ky. Rev. Stat. Ann. § 411.182; *Caterpillar*, 915 S.W.2d at 753.

33. *Hilen v. Hays*, 673 S.W.2d 713 (Ky. 1984) (*superseded by statute*, Ky. Rev. Stat. Ann § 411.182); *but see* Ky. Rev. Stat. Ann. § 413.241 (Michie 2005) for dram shop actions.

34. *Parker v. Redden*, 421 S.W.2d 586, 590-93 (Ky. 1967).

35. *Dealers Transp. Co., Inc.*, 402 S.W.2d at 446.

36. *Griffin Indus., Inc.*, 975 S.W.2d at 103.

37. *Griffin Indus., Inc.*, 975 S.W.2d at 103.

38. *Griffin Indus., Inc.*, 975 S.W.2d at 102.

39. *Embs v. Pepsi-Cola Bottling Co. of Lexington, Ky., Inc.*, 528 S.W.2d 703, 705 (Ky. 1975).

40. Ky. Rev. Stat. Ann. § 411.340 (Michie 2005); *Parker v. Henry A. Petter Supply Co.*, 165 S.W.3d 474 (Ky. App. 2005); *Smith v. Wyeth Inc.*, 488 F. Supp. 2d 625, 628 (W.D. Ky. 2007).

41. *Bryant v. Tri-County Elec. Membership Corp.*, 844 F. Supp. 347, 352 (W.D. Ky. 1994).

42. *McMichael v. Am. Red Cross*, 532 S.W.2d 7, 9-11 (Ky. 1975).

43. *Larkin v. Pfizer, Inc.*, 153 S.W.3d 758, 761 (Ky. 2004); *McMichael*, 532 S.W.2d at 9 (blood used in transfusion is an unavoidably unsafe product); *Tobin*, 993 F.2d at 540; *McKee v. Cutter Labs., Inc.*, 866 F.2d 219, 221-22 (6th Cir. 1989)

(blood transfusion found to be a rendition of service, not a sale under the Kentucky Blood Shield Statute, strict product liability inapplicable).

44. *Weiss v. Fujisawa Pharm. Co.*, 2006 U.S. Dist. LEXIS 88737, at *4 (E.D. Ky. Dec. 7, 2006); *Prather v. Abbott Labs*, 2013 U.S. Dist. LEXIS 47511, at *14 (W.D. Ky. Apr. 1, 2013).

45. *Conn v. Fales Div. of Mathewson Corp.*, 835 F.2d 145, 146 (6th Cir. 1987) (applying Kentucky law); *Wallace v. Midwest Fin. & Mortgage Servs.*, 728 F. Supp. 2d 906 (E.D. Ky. 2010), *rev'd in part on other grounds, Wallace v. Midwest Fin. & Mortgage Servs.*, 714 F.3d 414 (6th Cir. 2013); *American Ry. Express Co. v. Commonwealth*, 190 Ky. 636, 228 S.W. 433, 441 (1920), *error dismissed*, 263 U.S. 674 (1923); *Pearson v. Nat'l Feeding Sys.*, 90 S.W.3d 46 (Ky. 2002).

46. *Dawson v. Bristol Labs.*, 658 F. Supp. 1036, 1038-41 (W.D. Ky. 1987); *Farmer v. City of Newport*, 748 S.W.2d 162, 164-65 (Ky. App. 1988).

47. *Dealers Transp. Co., Inc.*, 402 S.W.2d at 446.

48. *Mount Lebanon Pers. Care Home, Inc. v. Hoover Universal, Inc.*, 276 F.3d 845, 851 (6th Cir. 2002).

49. *Watters v. TSR, Inc.*, 904 F.2d 378, 381 (6th Cir. 1990); *Post v. Am. Cleaning Equip. Corp.*, 437 S.W.2d 516, 520 (Ky. 1968).

50. *McCabe Powers Body Co. v. Sharp*, 594 S.W.2d 592, 594-95 (Ky. 1980).

51. *Post*, 437 S.W.2d at 520.

52. *Bryant v. Hercules, Inc.*, 325 F. Supp. 241, 246-47 (W.D. Ky. 1970); *Sturm, Ruger & Co., Inc. v. Bloyd*, 586 S.W.2d 19 (Ky. 1979).

53. *Montgomery Elevator Co. v. McCullough*, 676 S.W.2d 776, 782 (Ky. 1984).

54. *Bohnert Equip. Co., Inc. v. Kendall*, 569 S.W.2d 161, 166 (Ky. 1978), *overruled and limited to cases in which purchaser assumed responsibility for correcting defect, Montgomery Elevator Co.*, 676 S.W.2d at 782.

55. *Edwards v. Hop Sin, Inc.*, 140 S.W.3d 13, 17 (Ky. App. 2003).

56. *Clark v. Hauck Mfg. Co.*, 910 S.W.2d 247, 250 (Ky. 1995), *overruled on other grounds, Martin v. Ohio Cnty. Hosp. Corp.*, 295 S.W.3d 104 (Ky. 2009).

57. *Cameron v. DaimlerChrysler, Corp.*, 2005 U.S. Dist. LEXIS 24361, at *17-20 (E.D. Ky. Oct. 20, 2005).

58. *Montgomery Elevator Co.*, 676 S.W.2d at 779, 782.

59. *Louis Berkman Co.*, 894 F. Supp. at 1092.

60. Ky. R. Evid. 407 (2007).

61. Ky. R. Evid. 407 (2007).

62. Ky. R. Evid. 407 (2007).

63. *Ostendorf*, 122 S.W.3d at 538-39.

64. *Ostendorf*, 122 S.W.3d at 539.

65. *Larkin v. Pfizer, Inc.*, 153 S.W.3d 758, 765 (Ky. 2004); *Hyman & Armstrong, P.S.C.*, 279 S.W.3d at 109-10.

66. *Larkin*, 153 S.W.3d at 770.

67. *Larkin*, 153 S.W.3d at 770.

68. *C&S Fuel, Inc. v. Clark Equip. Co.*, 552 F. Supp. 340, 345-46 (E.D. Ky. 1982).

69. Ky. Rev. Stat. Ann. § 411.320(1) (Michie 2005); *Monsanto Co. v. Reed*, 950 S.W.2d 811, 814 (Ky. 1997).

70. *Id.*; *Ingersoll-Rand Co. v. Rice*, 775 S.W.2d 924, 929 (Ky. App. 1988).

71. *Jarrett v. Duro-Med Indus.*, 2007 U.S. Dist. LEXIS 13163, at *10 (E.D. Ky. Feb. 26, 2007).

72. *Sturm, Ruger & Co., Inc. v. Bloyd*, 586 S.W.2d 19, 22 (Ky. 1979); *see also Hutt v. Gibson Fiber Glass Prods., Inc.*, 914 F.2d 790, 794 (6th Cir. 1990).

73. *Burke Enters., Inc. v. Mitchell*, 700 S.W.2d 789, 793 (Ky. 1985).

74. Ky. Rev. Stat. Ann. § 411.310(2) (Michie 2005); *Estate of Bigham*, 462 F. Supp. 2d at 772.

75. *Jones v. Hutchinson Mfg., Inc.*, 502 S.W.2d 66, 70-71 (Ky. 1973); *Brock v. Caterpillar, Inc.*, 94 F.3d 220, 224 (6th Cir. 1996).

76. *Embs*, 528 S.W.2d at 706; *Perkins v. Trailco Mfg. & Sales Co.*, 613 S.W.2d 855, 858 (Ky. 1981).

77. *Siegel v. Dynamic Cooking Sys., Inc.*, 2012 U.S. App. LEXIS 20416 (6th Cir. Sept. 26, 2012).

78. *Siegel*, 2012 U.S. App. LEXIS 20416; *Dalton v. Animas Corp.*, 2012 U.S. Dist. LEXIS 180741, at *6-8 (W.D. Ky. Dec. 20, 2012).

79. *Jones*, 502 S.W.2d at 70.

80. *Montgomery Elevator Co.*, 676 S.W.2d at 783.

81. *Hines v. Joy Mfg. Co.*, 850 F.2d 1146, 1153-54 (6th Cir. 1988).

82. *Volvo Car Corp. v. Hopkins*, 860 S.W.2d 777, 779 (Ky. 1993).

83. *Siler v. Morgan Motor Co.*, 15 F. Supp. 468, 471 (E.D. Ky. 1936); *Coca-Cola Bottling Works v. Shelton*, 282 S.W. 778, 779 (Ky. 1926).

84. *Keck v. Wacker*, 413 F. Supp. 1377, 1383 (E.D. Ky. 1976).

85. *Keck*, 413 F. Supp. at 1383; *Wahba v. Don Corlett Motors, Inc.*, 573 S.W.2d 357, 359 (Ky. App. 1978).

86. *Presnell Constr. Managers, Inc. v. EH Constr., LLC*, 134 S.W.3d 575, 580-82 (Ky. 2004); *Giddings & Lewis, Inc. v. Risk Insurers*, 348 S.W.3d 729, 743-46 (Ky. 2011).

87. *Clark v. Danek Med., Inc.*, 64 F. Supp. 2d 652, 655-56 (W.D. Ky. 1999).

88. *Clark*, 64 F. Supp. 2d at 656.

89. *Monsanto Co. v. Reed*, 950 S.W.2d 811, 815 (Ky. 1997).

90. *Reed*, 950 S.W.2d at 815; *see also Adams v. Lexington-Fayette Urban County Government*, 2009 Ky. App. LEXIS 27, at *29 (Ky. App. Feb. 13, 2009).

91. *Real Estate Mktg., Inc. v. Franz*, 885 S.W.2d 921, 926 (Ky. 1994).

92. *Giddings & Lewis*, 348 S.W.3d 729 (Ky. 2011); *Morris Aviation v. Diamond Aircraft Indus.*, 2011 U.S. Dist. LEXIS 135535 (W.D. Ky. Nov. 23, 2011).

93. *Giddings & Lewis*, 348 S.W.3d at 734.

94. *Mt. Lebanon Pers. Care Home, Inc. v. Hoover Universal, Inc.*, 276 F.3d 845, 852 (6th Cir. 2002).

95. *Toyota Motor Corp.*, 136 S.W.3d at 41.

96. *Toyota Motor Corp.*, 136 S.W.3d at 41; *see also McCoy v. Gen. Motors Corp.*, 47 F. Supp. 2d 838, 839 (E.D. Ky. 1998), *aff'd*, 179 F.3d 396 (6th Cir. 1999); *Gray v. Gen. Motors Corp.*, 133 F. Supp. 2d 530, 534-35 (E.D. Ky. 2001), *aff'd*, 312 F.3d 240 (6th Cir. 2002); *Estate of Bigham*, 462 F. Supp. 2d at 773.

97. *Estate of Bigham*, 462 F. Supp. 2d at 776.

98. *Ulrich v. Kasco Abrasives Co.*, 532 S.W.2d 197, 200 (Ky. 1976); *James v. Meow Media, Inc.*, 300 F.3d 683 (6th Cir. 2002), *cert. denied*, 537 U.S. 1159 (2003).

99. *Prather v. Abbott Lab.*, 2013 U.S. Dist. LEXIS 47511, at *33 (W.D. Ky. Apr. 2, 2013).

100. *Hauck Mfg.*, 910 S.W.2d at 250.

101. Ky. Rev. Stat. Ann. § 355.2-314(1) (Michie 2008).

102. *Belcher v. Hamilton*, 475 S.W.2d 483, 485 (Ky. 1971).

103. Ky. Rev. Stat. Ann. § 355.2-313(1)(a).

104. *Snawder v. Cohen*, 749 F. Supp. 1473, 1481 (W.D. Ky. 1990).

105. Ky. Rev. Stat. Ann. § 355.2-318; *Real Estate Mktg., Inc. v. Franz*, 885 S.W.2d 921, 926 (Ky. 1994).

106. *Munn v. Pfizer Hosp. Prods. Grp., Inc.*, 750 F. Supp. 244, 248 (W.D. Ky. 1990); *Roberts v. Solideal Tire, Inc.*, 2007 U.S. Dist. LEXIS 75512, at *7 (E.D. Ky. Oct. 10, 2007); *Pruitt v. Genie Indus.*, 2013 U.S. Dist. LEXIS 4035, *11-14 (E.D. Ky. Jan. 10, 2013); *Williams v. Fulmer*, 695 S.W.2d 411, 414 (Ky. 1985).

107. Ky. Rev. Stat. Ann. § 355.2-315.

108. *Real Estate Mktg., Inc.*, 885 S.W.2d at 926.

109. 2 Palmore and Cetrulo, *Kentucky Instructions to Juries*, Civil, §§ 39.02-39.08 (5th ed. 2006).

110. *Davis v. Graviss*, 672 S.W.2d 928, 932 (Ky. 1984), *overruled on other grounds*, *Morgan v. Scott*, 291 S.W.3d 622 (Ky. 2009).

111. *Bailey*, 873 S.W.2d at 193-94.

112. *Bailey*, 873 S.W.2d at 192.

113. *Wood v. Wyeth-Ayerst Lab.*, 82 S.W.3d 849 (Ky. 2002).

114. *Osborne v. Keeney*, 399 S.W.3d 1, 3 (Ky. 2012).

115. *Deutsch v. Shein*, 597 S.W.2d 141, 146 (Ky. 1980).

116. Ky. Rev. Stat. Ann. § 411.145 (Michie 2005); *Martin*, 295 S.W.3d at 109.

117. *Floyd v. Gray*, 657 S.W.2d 936 (Ky. 1983).

118. *Giuliani v. Guiler*, 951 S.W.2d 318, 323 (Ky. 1997).

119. *Davis v. Johnson*, 295 S.W.3d 841, 843-44 (Ky. App. 2009).

120. *Hyman & Armstrong, P.S.C.*, 279 S.W.3d at 116.

121. Ky. Rev. Stat. § 355.2-714(2)–(3) (Michie 2008).

122. *Williams v. Wilson*, 972 S.W.2d 260, 269 (Ky. 1998).

123. Ky. Rev. Stat. § 411.184(2);*Estate of Embry v. GEO Transp. of Indiana, Inc.*, 478 F. Supp. 2d 914 (E.D. Ky. 2007).

124. *Williams*, 972 S.W. 2d at 269.

125. *City of Middlesboro v. Brown*, 63 S.W.3d 179 (Ky. 2001); *Phelps v. Louisville Water Co.*, 103 S.W.3d 46, 52-53 (Ky. 2003); *see also Horton v. Union Light, Heat & Power Co.*, 690 S.W.2d 382, 389-90 (Ky. 1985).

126. *Sufix, U.S.A., Inc. v. Cook*, 128 S.W.3d 838, 842 (Ky. App. 2004).

127. Ky. Rev. Stat. Ann. § 411.184(4).

128. *Landgraf v. McDonnell Douglas Helicopter Co.*, 993 F.2d 558, 559-60 (6th Cir. 1993) (interpreting Kentucky law).

129. *Griffin Indus., Inc.*, 975 S.W.2d at 103.

130. *Dix & Assoc. Pipeline Contractors, Inc. v. Key*, 799 S.W.2d 24, 29 (Ky. 1990).

131. Ky. Rev. Stat. Ann. § 411.300 *et seq.*

132. Ky. Rev. Stat. Ann. § 2.015 (Michie 2008).

133. Ky. Rev. Stat. Ann. § 411.182; *Dix & Assoc.*, 799 S.W.2d at 29; *Degener v. Hall Contracting Corp.*, 27 S.W.3d 775, 779 (Ky. 2000).

134. *Bass v. Williams*, 839 S.W.2d 559, 564 (Ky. App. 1992); *Owens Corning Fiberglas Corp. v. Parrish*, 58 S.W.3d 467, 480 (Ky. 2000).

135. *Ky. Farm Bureau Mut. Ins. Co. v. Ryan*, 177 S.W.3d 797, 803-04 (Ky. 2005); *Barnes v. Owens-Corning Fiberglas Corp.*, 201 F.3d 815, 827 (6th Cir. 2000).

136. *Sadler I v. Adv. Bionics, Inc.*, 2013 U.S. Dist. LEXIS 54697, at *3 (W.D. Ky. Apr. 16, 2013).

137. *Niehoff v. Surgidev Corp.*, 950 S.W.2d 816 (Ky. 1997); *Leslie v. Cincinnati Sub-Zero Prods., Inc.*, 961 S.W.2d 799 (Ky. App. 1998).

138. *Niehoff*, 950 S.W.2d at 818-23.

139. *Leslie*, 961 S.W.2d at 801-05.

140. *Alfred v. Mentor Corp.*, 2007 U.S. Dist. LEXIS 15535, at *9 (W.D. Ky. Mar. 5, 2007).

141. *Alfred*, 2007 U.S. Dist. LEXIS 15535, at *9.

142. *Alfred*, 2007 U.S. Dist. LEXIS 15535, at *9; *see also Cottengim v. Mentor Corp.*, 2007 U.S. Dist. LEXIS 71731 (E.D. Ky. Sept. 24, 2007).

143. *Enlow v. St. Jude Med., Inc.*, 171 F. Supp. 2d 684, 688-89 (W.D. Ky. 2001); *see also Sadler II v. Adv. Bionics, Inc.*, 2013 U.S. Dist. LEXIS 32228 (W.D. Ky. Mar. 8, 2013) (discussing preemption of plaintiff's strict liability, negligence, and breach of warranty, and fraud claims related to a cochlear implant)..

144. Requirements on Content and Format of Labeling for Human Prescription Drug and Biological Products, 71 Fed. Reg. 3922-97 (Jan. 24, 2006).

145. 71 Fed. Reg. 3922, 3934.

146. *Weiss v. Fujisawa Pharm. Co.*, 464 F. Supp. 2d 666 (E.D. Ky. 2006).

147. *Weiss*, 464 F. Supp. 2d at 675.

148. *Weiss v. Astellas Pharma, US, Inc.*, 2007 U.S. Dist. LEXIS 53453, at *9 (E.D. Ky. July 23, 2007).

149. *See, e.g., Roberts v. Estep*, 845 S.W.2d 544, 547 (Ky. 1993) (there is no Kentucky statute that precludes *ex parte* contact with treating physicians); *Davenport v. Ephraim Mem'l Hosp., Inc.*, 769 S.W.2d 56, 62 (Ky. App. 1988).

150. *Weiss*, 2007 U.S. Dist. LEXIS 53453, at *15.

LOUISIANA

A. CAUSES OF ACTION

The Louisiana Products Liability Act (LPLA), has codified the law and established the exclusive theories of liability for manufacturers for damage caused by their products.[1] Under the LPLA, plaintiff has the burden of proving the following:

(1) the defendant was the manufacturer[2] of the product;[3]

> A person or entity who labels a product as his own or who otherwise holds himself out to be the manufacturer of the product.
>
> A seller of a product who exercises control over or influences a characteristic of the design, construction or quality of the product that causes damage.
>
> A manufacturer of a product who incorporates into the product a component or part manufactured by another manufacturer.
>
> A seller of a product of an alien manufacturer if the seller is in the business of importing or distributing the product for resale and the seller is the alter ego of the alien manufacturer. The court shall take into consideration the following in determining whether the seller is the alien manufacturer's alter ego: whether the seller is affiliated with the alien manufacturer by way of common ownership or control; whether the seller assumes or administers product warranty obligations of the alien manufacturer; whether the seller prepares or modifies the product for distribution; or any other relevant evidence. A "product of an alien manufacturer" is a product that is manufactured outside the United States by a manufacturer who is a citizen of another country or who is organized under the laws of another country. La. Rev. Stat. Ann. § 9:2800.53(1).

(2) the claimant's[4] damage[5] was proximately caused by a characteristic of the product;

(3) the characteristic made the product unreasonably dangerous in one or more of four ways (see discussion *infra* [6]); and

(4) the claimant's damage arose from a reasonably anticipated use[7] of the product by the claimant or someone else.

Louisiana also recognizes a cause of action against a manufacturer for breach of an implied warranty of fitness, *i.e.*, a redhibition claim.[8]

B. **STATUTE OF LIMITATION (PRESCRIPTION)**

Delictual actions are subject to a liberative prescription of one year. This prescription commences to run from the day injury or damage is sustained.[9]

C. **NEGLIGENCE**

1. **The Standard**

   When a plaintiff is alleging a product is unreasonably dangerous due to its construction or composition, design or lack of adequate warnings, the standard of liability is negligence.[10]

2. **Definition of "Defect" (Unreasonably Dangerous)**

   a. **Unreasonably Dangerous in Construction or Composition**

   A product is unreasonably dangerous in construction or composition if, at the time the product left is manufacturer's control, the product deviated in a material way from the manufacturer's specifications or performance standards for the product or from otherwise identical products manufactured by the same manufacturer.[11]

   b. **Unreasonably Dangerous in Design**

   A product is unreasonably dangerous in design if, at the time the product left its manufacturer's control (a) there existed an alternative design for the product that was capable of preventing the claimant's damage; and (b) the likelihood that the product's design would cause the claimant's damage and the gravity of the damage outweighed the burden on the manufacturer of adopting such alternative design and the adverse effect, if any, of such alternative design on the utility of the product.[12]

   An adequate warning about a product shall be considered in evaluating the likelihood of damage when the manufacturer has used reasonable care to provide the adequate warning to users and handlers of the product.[13]

   c. **Unreasonably Dangerous Because of Inadequate Warning**

   A product is unreasonably dangerous because of an adequate warning[14] about the product has not been provided if, at the time the product left its manufacturer's control, the product possessed a characteristic that might cause damage and the manufacturer failed to use reasonable care to provide an adequate warning of such characteristic and its danger to users and handlers of the product.[15]

   A manufacturer is not required to provide an adequate warning about his product when (a) the product is not dangerous to an extent beyond that which would be contemplated by the ordinary user or handler of the product, with the ordinary knowledge common to the community as to the product's characteristics; or (b) the user or handler of the product already knows or reasonably should be expected to know of the characteristic of the product that may cause damage and the danger of such characteristic.[16]

d. Unreasonable Dangerous Because of Nonconformity to an Express Warranty

A product is unreasonably dangerous when it does not conform to an express warranty[17] made at any time by the manufacturer about the product if the express warranty has induced the claimant or another person or entity to use the product and the claimant's damage was proximately caused because the express warranty was untrue.[18]

3. Causation

"Causation" under the LPLA and under prior law are identical. The LPLA does not change the duty/risk analysis of proximate cause or the notion of cause-in-fact as articulated in Louisiana case law.[19]

The principle of *res ipsa loquitur* may be utilized to prove causation under the LPLA.[20]

4. Contributory Negligence/Assumption of the Risk

The defenses of contributory negligence and assumption of the risk are not complete bars to recovery in product liability cases, but the doctrine of comparative fault does apply in reducing a plaintiff's recovery.[21]

5. Sale or Lease/Persons Liable

A non-manufacturer seller/lessor of a defective product is not responsible for damages in tort absent showing that he knew or should have known the product was defective and failed to declare it. A non-manufacturer seller/lessor is not required to inspect a product prior to sale to determine the possibility of inherent vices or defects.[22]

6. Inherently Dangerous Products

A product containing an inherent danger that is not obvious or exposed to the ordinary consumer who normally uses the product must also contain a warning that must be adequately worded and placed.[23]

7. Successor Liability

When a corporation sells all of its assets to another, the latter is not responsible for the seller's debts or liabilities, except where (1) the purchaser expressly or impliedly agrees to assume the obligations; (2) the purchaser is merely a continuation of the selling corporation; or (3) the transaction is entered into to escape liability.[24]

8. Market Share Liability/Enterprise Liability

Market share liability cannot serve as a liability theory to support proof of proximate cause under the LPLA.[25]

9. **Privity**

   There is no requirement that the claimant be in contractual *privity* with the manufacturer in order to recover or that the claimant be a product user.[26]

10. **Failure to Warn**

    See Section C.2.c, *supra*.

11. **Post-Sale Duty to Warn and Remedial Measures**

    A manufacturer of a product who, after the product has left his control, acquires knowledge of a characteristic of the product that may cause damage and the danger of such characteristic, or who would have acquired such knowledge had he acted as a reasonably prudent manufacturer, is liable for damage caused by his subsequent failure to use reasonable care to provide an adequate warning of such characteristic and its danger to users and handlers of the product.[27]

12. **Learned Intermediary Doctrine**

    Under Louisiana's "learned intermediary doctrine," a manufacturer has no duty to warn a patient but need only warn the patient's physician.[28]

    To recover for failure to warn under Louisiana's learned intermediary doctrine, plaintiff must show that (1) defendant failed to warn physician of risk associated with use of a product not otherwise known to the physician, and (2) failure to warn the physician was both the cause in fact and proximate cause of plaintiff's injury; as to the latter factor, plaintiff must show that a proper warning would have changed the decision of the treating physician, *i.e.*, "but for" the inadequate warning treating physician would not have used or prescribed the product.[29]

13. **Substantial Alteration/Abnormal Use**

    If plaintiff is urging a design defect, he must prove that the characteristic of the product that renders it unreasonably dangerous existed at the time the product left the control of its manufacturer, or resulted from a reasonably anticipated alteration or modification of the product.[30]

    A manufacturer can be liable only if the damage arose from a reasonably anticipated use of the product, and if not, then a court need not reach the issue of whether the product is unreasonably dangerous.[31]

14. **State of the Art**

    The LPLA recognizes the state of the art defense in design and warning cases.[32]

15. **Malfunction**

    See Section C.2, *supra*.

16. **Standards and Governmental Regulation**

    Compliance and non-compliance with governmental or industry standards are admissible, but not determinative on the issue of liability.[33]

17. **Other Accidents**

    Evidence of other accidents are admissible if they occurred substantially at the same place, and under substantially the same conditions and were caused by the same or similar defect, danger, act or omission as the accident at issue.[34]

18. **Misrepresentation**

    See Section C.2.d, *supra*.

19. **Destruction or Loss of Product (Spoliation of Evidence)**

    When a litigant fails to produce evidence available to it and gives no reasonable explanation, the evidentiary presumption is that the evidence would have been unfavorable to his cause.[35]

    Louisiana recognizes a cause of action for impairment of a civil claim when a product is intentionally or negligently spoliated.[36]

20. **Economic Loss**

    Damage to the product itself and economic loss arising from a deficiency in or loss of use of the product is recoverable.[37]

21. **Crashworthiness**

    The "crashworthiness" or "second collision" doctrine provides that the manufacturer/seller is liable when the defect increases the severity of an injury over that which would have occurred absent the design defect, even though the defect did not cause the accident or initial impact. The doctrine is now encompassed in the LPLA.[38]

D. **NEGLIGENCE**

See Sections C.1 and C.2, *supra*.

E. **BREACH OF WARRANTY**

See Sections C.2.d and C.20, *supra*.

F. **PUNITIVE DAMAGES**

Punitive damages are not recoverable.[39]

G. **PRE- AND POST-JUDGMENT INTEREST**

Legal interest shall attach from date of judicial demand, on all judgments, sounding in damages, "*ex delicto*," which may be rendered by any of the courts.[40]

H. EMPLOYER IMMUNITY FROM SUIT

The Louisiana Worker's Compensation Act's "exclusive remedy provision" exempts the plaintiff's employer from suit, with the exception of intentional acts.[41]

I. STATUTES

The LPLA has codified the law and established the exclusive theories of liability for manufacturers for damage caused by their products.[42]

J. JOINT AND SEVERAL LIABILITY

When a plaintiff settles with and releases one of several joint tortfeasors, he thereby deprives remaining obligors of the right to contribution against the released obligor. Accordingly, settlement with the one solitary obligor reduces his recovery against the remaining obligor by the percentage of the proportion at fault of the released obligor.[43]

Louisiana's legislature revoked solidary liability for non-conspiratorial acts and expresses defendants liability as a joint and divisible obligation. A joint tortfeasor shall not be liable for more than his degree of fault and shall not be solidarily liable with any other person.[44]

Darnell Bludworth
Sher Garner Cahill
Richter Klein & Hilbert
909 Poydras St. 28th Floor
New Orleans, Louisiana 70112
Telephone (504) 299-2114
dbludworth@shergarner.com

ENDNOTES - LOUISIANA

1. La. Rev. Stat. Ann. § 9:2800.51 *et seq.*; *Scianneaux v. St. Jude Med. S.C., Inc.*, 961 F. Supp. 808 (E.D. La. 2013) (claims for negligence, strict liability, and breach of warranty do not exist against a manufacturer independent of the LPLA).

2. "Manufacturer" means a person or entity who is in the business of manufacturing a product for placement into trade of commerce. "Manufacturing a product" means producing, making, fabricating, constructing, designing, remanufacturing, reconditioning or refurbishing a product. "Manufacturer" also means:

    (a) A person or entity who labels a product as his own or who otherwise holds himself out to be the manufacturer of the product.

    (b) A seller of a product who exercises control over or influences a characteristic of the design, construction or quality of the product that causes damage.

    (c) A manufacturer of a product who incorporates into the product a component or part manufactured by another manufacturer.

    (d) A seller of a product of an alien manufacturer if the seller is in the business of importing or distributing the product for resale and the seller is the alter ego of the alien manufacturer. The court shall take into consideration the following in determining whether the seller is the alien manufacturer's alter ego: whether the seller is affiliated with the alien manufacturer by way of common ownership or control; whether the seller assumes or administers product warranty obligations of the alien manufacturer; whether the seller prepares or modifies the product for distribution; or any other relevant evidence. A "product of an alien manufacturer" is a product that is manufactured outside the United States by a manufacturer who is a citizen of another country or who is organized under the laws of another country. La. Rev. Stat. Ann. § 9:2800.53(1).

3. A "product" means a corporeal movable that is manufactured for placement into trade or commerce, including a product that forms a component part of or that is subsequently incorporated into another product or an immovable. "Product" does not mean human blood, blood components, human organs, human tissue or approved animal tissue to the extent such are governed by Rev. Stat. 9:2797. La. Rev. Stat. Ann. § 9:2800.53(3).

4. The "claimant" is a person or entity who asserts a claim against the manufacturer of a product or his insurer for damage caused by the product. La. Rev. Stat. Ann. § 9:2800.53(4). A claimant who did not consume the manufacturer's product, but instead consumed a generic, has no claim

against the name brand manufacturer. *Johnson v. Teva Pharm. USA, Inc.*, 758 F.3d 605 (5th Cir. 2014).

5. "Damage" means all damage caused by a product, including survival and wrongful death damages, for which Civil Code Articles 2315, 2315.1, and 2315.2 allow recovery. "Damage" includes damage to the product itself and economic loss arising from a deficiency in or loss of use of the product only to the extent that Chapter 9 of Title VII of Book III of the Civil Code, entitled "Redhibition," does not allow recovery for such damage or economic loss. Attorneys' fees are not recoverable under this Chapter. La. Rev. Stat. Ann. § 9:2800.53(5). A defect is redhibitory when it renders the thing useless, or its use is so inconvenient that it must be presumed that a buyer would not have bought the thing had he known of the defect. The existence of such a defect gives a buyer the right to obtain recision of the sale. A manufacturer of a product with a redhibitory defect is liable for return of the purchase price with interest, reimbursement for reasonable expenses occasioned by the sale and for the preservation of the thing as well as damages and attorney's fees. La. Civ. Code art. 2545; *Live Oak Homes Corp. v. Carrier Sales & Dist., LLC*, 140 So. 3d 362 (La. App. 5th Cir. 2014).

A defect is redhibitory also when, without rendering the thing totally useless, it diminishes its usefulness or its value so that it must be presumed that a buyer will still have bought it but for a lesser price. The existence of such defect limits the right of a buyer to a reduction of the price. La. Civ. Code art. 2520 *et seq.; see also, e.g., Pratt v. Himel Marine, Inc.*, 823 So. 2d 394 (La. App. 1st Cir. 2002); *Safeco Ins. v. Pfizer Corp.*, 2002 WL 1772925 (La. App. 3d Cir. 7/31/02).

6. Defects are not presumed by the mere occurrence of an accident. *St. Pierre v. Maingot*, 2002 WL 31473850 (E.D. La. 2002); *Welch v. Technotrion, Inc.*, 778 So. 2d 728 (La. App. 2d Cir. 2001).

7. "Reasonably anticipated use" means a use or handling of a product that the product's manufacturer should reasonably expect of an ordinary person under the same or similar circumstances. La. Rev. Stat. Ann. § 9:2800.53(7). *See, e.g., Gladney v. Milam*, 911 So. 2d 366 (La. App. 2d Cir. 2005); *Schram v. Chaisson*, 888 So. 2d 247 (La. App. 1st Cir. 9/17/04); *Delphen v. Department of Transp. & Dev.*, 657 So. 2d 328 (La. App. 4th Cir. 1995), *writ denied*, 663 So. 2d 716 (La. 11/17/95).

8. La. Civ. Code Ann. art. 2520 *et seq.; Malmay v. Western Star Trucks*, 903 So. 2d 1208 (La. App. 3d Cir. 2003); *Draten v. Winn Dixie of Louisiana, Inc.*, 652 So. 2d 675 (La. App. 1st Cir. 1995); *Monk v. Scott Truck & Tractor*, 619 So. 2d 890 (La. App. 3d Cir. 1993).

9. La. Civ. Code art. 3492, 3595. *See also* La. Civ. Code art. 2534 concerning the prescriptive period for a redhibition claim.

10. Effective April 1996, the legislature repealed La. Civ. Code art. 2317, Louisiana's strict liability article and changed it to a negligence standard. Plaintiff's must now arguably prove that the manufacturer either knew or should have known of the manufacturing defect.

The standard of liability for defective design appears to be *negligence*, because the LPLA employs the "risk-utility balancing test" and requires proof of both manufacturer's knowledge of the purported design defect and the manufacturer's ability to prevent it as predicates to liability. La. Rev. Stat. Ann. § 9:2800.56 and 59. *Bernard v. Ferrellgas, Inc.*, 689 So. 2d 554 (La. App. 3d Cir. 1997).

The standard of liability in a warning case is negligence. Plaintiff must prove that the manufacturer failed to use reasonable care to provide an adequate warning of a dangerous characteristic of the product. Additionally, a manufacturer is not responsible for warning of a products dangerous characteristic that was either known or should have been known by a reasonable prudent person. La. Rev. Stat. Ann. § 9:2800.57(A).

11. La. Rev. Stat. Ann. § 9:2800.55. *See, e.g., Schram v. Chaisson*, 888 So. 2d 247 (La. App. 1st Cir. Sept. 17, 2004); *Welch v. Technotrion, Inc.*, 778 So. 2d 728 (La. App. 2d Cir. 2001).

12. This specific element codifies prior law and has come to be known as the "risk-utility balancing test" under pre-LPLA products jurisprudence. *See, e.g., Andrews v. Dufour*, 882 So. 2d 15 (La. App. 4th Cir. 2004); *Seither v. Winnebago Indus., Inc.*, 853 So. 2d 37 (La. App. 4th Cir. 2003); *Bernard v. Ferrellgas*, 689 So. 2d 554 (La. App. 3d Cir. 1997); *Halphen v. Johns-Manville Sales Corp.*, 484 So. 2d 110, 114 n.2, 115 (La. 1986); *Hunt v. City Stores, Inc.*, 387 So. 2d 585, 588 (La. 1980).

13. La. Rev. Stat. Ann. § 9:2800.56.

14. An "adequate warning" is a warning or instruction that would lead an ordinary reasonable user or handler of a product to contemplate the danger in using or handling the product and either to decline to use or handle the product or, if possible, to use or handle the product in such a manner as to avoid the damage for which the claim is made. La. Rev. Stat. Ann. § 9:2800.53(9). *State Farm Mut. Auto Ins. Co. v. Ford*, 925 So. 2d 1 (La. App. 1st Cir. 2005). The mere fact that revised warnings for subsequently manufactured products are instituted does not render the prior warnings defective. *Alexander v. Toyota Motor Sales, U.S.A.*, 123 So. 3d 712 (La. 2013).

15. Plaintiff has the burden of proving some reasonable connection between the omission of the manufacturer and the damages that the plaintiff has suffered. *Marks v. OHMEDA*, 871 So. 2d 1148 (La. App. 3d Cir. 2004); *Seither v. Winnebago Indus., Inc.*, 853 So. 2d 37 (La. App. 4th Cir. 2003); *Gray v. Cannon*, 807 So. 2d 924 (La. App. 5th Cir. 2002).

16. La. Rev. Stat. Ann. § 9:2800.57. *See Hines v. Remington Arms Co., Inc.*, 648 So. 2d 331 (La. 1994); *Davis v. Avondale Indus., Inc.*, 975 F.2d 169 (5th Cir. 1992) (when a manufacturer or distributor sells an industrial product to a sophisticated purchaser, and that purchaser then supplies that product to its employees for use, the manufacturer and distributor have no legal duty to provide any warnings to the employee/user concerning possible hazards or dangers associated with the product's use); *Fernandez v. Tamko Bldg. Prods., Inc.*, 2014 WL 905115 (M.D. La. Apr. 11, 2014) (employee of roofing contractor and roofing contractor were both sophisticated users and there was thus no duty to warn).

    A sophisticated purchaser is one who by experience and expertise is aware of the possible hazards and/or dangers associated with the use of the product and who has an obligation to inform its employees of such potential hazards. *See, e.g., Ross v. Porthau Indus.*, 2005 WL 1907528 (W.D. La. 2005).

17. An "express warranty" is a representation, statement of alleged fact, or promise about a product or its nature, material, or workmanship that represents, affirms, or promises that the product or its nature, material, or workmanship possesses specified characteristics or qualities or will meet a specified level of performance. Express warranty does not mean a general opinion about a general praise of a product. A sample or model of a product is an express warranty. La. Rev. Stat. Ann. § 9:2800.53(6). *See, e.g., Caboni v. Gen. Motors Corp.*, 398 F.3d 357 (5th Cir. 2005).

18. La. Rev. Stat. Ann. § 9:2800.58.

19. *Moody v. Blanchard Place Apartments*, 793 So. 2d 281 (La. App. 2d Cir. 2001); *Todd v. State, through Dep't of Soc. Servs.*, 699 So. 2d 35 (La. 1997); *Hill v. Ludin & Assocs., Inc.*, 256 So. 2d 620, 622-623 (La. 1972); *Dixie Drive-It-Yourself Sys. v. American Beverage Co.*, 137 So. 2d 298, 302-308 (La. 1962). An intermediary purchaser and seller of a used product who does not sell to the injured user owes that user no duty. *Alexander v. Toyota Motor Sales, U.S.A.*, 123 So. 3d 712 (La. 2013).

20. *Condiff v. R.D. Werner Co., Inc.*, 2003 WL 21977167 (E.D. La. 2003); *Batiste v. Gen. Motors Corp.*, 802 So. 2d 686 (La. App. 4th Cir. 2001), *writ denied*; *Williams v. Emerson Elec. Co.*, 909 F. Supp. 395 (M.D. La. 1995). *State Farm v. Wrap-On Co.*, 626 So. 2d 874 (La. App. 3d Cir. 1993).

21. La. Civ. Code Ann. art. 2323; *Kampen v. American Isuzu Motors, Inc.*, 157 F.3d 306 (5th Cir. 1998).

22. *Adams v. Owens-Corning Fiberglass Corp.*, 2005 WL 2320272 (La. App. 1st Cir. 2005); *Tantillo v. Cordis Corp.*, 2004 WL 2212113 (E.D. La. Sept. 28, 2004); *Matthews v. Wal-Mart Stores, Inc.*, 708 So. 2d 1248 (La. App. 4th Cir. 1998); *Wilson v. State Farm Fire & Cas. Ins. Co.*, 654 So. 2d 385 (La. App. 3d Cir. 1995),

writ denied, 661 So. 2d 476 (La. 1995); *Nelton v. Astron Lounger MFG. Co., Inc.*, 542 So. 2d 128 (La. App. 1st Cir. 1989).

23. La. Rev. Stat. Ann. § 9:2800.57; *Asbestos v. Bordelon, Inc.*, 726 So. 2d 926, 955 (La. App. 4th Cir. 1998).

24. *Allstate Ins. Co. v. Wal-Mart*, 2000 WL 388844 (E.D. La. 2000). *See also Hallowell v. Orleans Reg'l Hosp., LLC*, 217 F.3d 379 (5th Cir. 2000); *cf. Mozingo v. Correct Mfg. Corp.*, 752 F.2d 168 (5th Cir. 1985), which held that a successor corporation may have a duty to warn of discovered defects in its predecessor's products, but this duty does not arise unless there is some continuation of the relationship between the successor and the customers of the predecessor. Some of the factors to consider in determining whether there is a continuity of a relationship is whether the successor takes over the service contracts of the predecessor, the successor knows of defects in the equipment, and whether successor knows of the location of owners of the equipment.

25. *Cheeks v. Bayer Corp.*, 2003 U.S. Dist. LEXIS 5236 (E.D. La. Mar. 28, 2003); *Jefferson v. Lead Indus. Ass'n Inc.*, 930 F. Supp. 241 (E.D. La. 1996), *aff'd*, 106 F.3d 1245 (5th Cir. 1997).

26. *Touro Infirmary v. Sizeler Architect*, 900 So. 2d 200 (La. App. 4th Cir. 2005); *Media Prod. Consultants, Inc. v. Mercedes Benz of N. Am., Inc.*, 377 So. 2d 388 (La. 1972).

27. La. Rev. Stat. Ann. § 9:2800.57.C.

28. *Hall v. Elkins Sinn, Inc.*, 102 Fed. Appx. 846 (5th Cir. 2004); *Stahl v. Novartis Pharms. Corp.*, 283 F.3d 254 (5th Cir. 2002). *Willett v. Baxton Int'l, Inc.*, 929 F.2d 1094 (5th Cir. 1991).

29. *Willett v. Baxton Int'l, Inc.*, 929 F.2d 1094 (5th Cir. 1991); *Zachary v. Dow Corning Corp.*, 884 F. Supp. 1061 (M.D. La. 1995).

30. "Reasonably anticipated alteration or modification" means a change in a product that the product's manufacturer should reasonably expect to be made by an ordinary person in the same or similar circumstances, and also means a change arising from ordinary wear and tear. "Reasonably anticipated alteration or modification" does not mean the following:

    (e) Alteration, modification or removal of an otherwise adequate warning provided about a product.

    (f) The failure or a person or entity, other than the manufacturer of a product, reasonably to provide to the product user or handler an adequate warning the manufacturer provided about the product, when the manufacturer has satisfied his obligation to use reasonable care to provide the adequate warning by providing it to such person or entity rather than to the product user or handler.

(g) Changes to or in a product or its operation because a product does not receive reasonable care and maintenance." *Johnson v. Black & Decker U.S., Inc.*, 701 So. 2d 1360 (La. App. 2d Cir. 1997).

31. *Johnson v. Black & Decker U.S., Inc.*, 701 So. 2d 1360 (La. App. 2d Cir. 1997); *Daigle v. Audi of Am., Inc.*, 598 So. 2d 1304 (La. App. 3d Cir. 1992).

32. Notwithstanding Rev. Stat. § 9:2800.56, a manufacturer of a product shall not be liable for damage proximately caused by a characteristic of the product's design if the manufacturer proves that, at the time the product left his control:

    (1) He did not know and, in light of then-existing reasonably available scientific and technological knowledge, could not have known of the design characteristic that caused the damage or the danger of such characteristic; or

    (2) He did not know and, in light of then-existing reasonably available scientific and technological knowledge, could not have known of the alternative design identified by the claimant under Rev. Stat. § 9:2800.56(1); or

    (3) The alternative design identified by the claimant under Rev. Stat. § 9:2800.56(1) was not feasible, in light of then-existing reasonably available scientific and technological knowledge or then-existing economic practicality.

    Notwithstanding Rev. Stat. § 9:2800.57(A) or (B), a manufacturer of a product shall not be liable for damage proximately caused by the characteristic of the product if the manufacturer proves that at the time of the product left his control, he did not know and, in light of then-existing reasonably available scientific and technological knowledge, could not have known of the characteristic that caused the damage or the danger of such characteristic.

33. *Dunne v. Wal-Mart Stores, Inc.*, 679 So. 2d 1034 (La. Ct. App. 1st Cir. 1996); *Hopper v. Crown*, 646 So. 2d 933 (La. App. 1st Cir. 1994), *writ denied*.

34. *Brodtmann v. Duke*, 708 So. 2d 447 (La. App. 4th Cir. 1998); *Lee v. K-Mart Corp.*, 483 So. 2d 609, 613 (La. App. 1st Cir. 1985), *writ denied*, 484 So. 2d 661 (La. 1986).

35. *Moorehead v. Ford Motor Co.*, 694 So. 2d 650 (La. App. 2d Cir. 1997); *Randolph v. Gen. Motors Corp.*, 646 So. 2d 1019 (La. App. 1st Cir. 1994); *Kammerer v. Sewerage & Water Board*, 633 So. 2d 1357 (La. App. 4th Cir. 1994); *Boh Bros. Constr. v. Luberfiner, Inc.*, 612 So. 2d 270 (La. App. 4th Cir. 1992), *writ denied*, 614 So. 2d 1256 (La. 1993).

36. *Guillory v. Dillards Dep't Store, Inc.*, 777 So. 2d 1 (La. App. 3d Cir. 2000); *Bethea v. Modern Biomedical Servs.*, 704 So. 2d 1227 (La. App. 3d Cir. 1997), which recognizes such a cause of action even where no statutory or contractual duty is imposed on the alleged party at fault. *But see Carter v. Exide Corp.*, 661 So. 2d 698 (La. App. 2d Cir. 1995), which requires that a specific source of that duty be alleged. *See also Desselle v. Jefferson Hosp. Dist. No. 2*, 887 So. 2d 524 (La. App. 5th Cir. 2004); *Quinn v. RISO Invs., Inc.*, 869 So. 2d 922 (La. App. 4th Cir. 2004); *Catoire v. Caprock Telecomms. Corp.*, 2003 WL 21223258 (E.D. La. 2003); *Burge v. St. Tammany Parish Sheriff's Office*, 2000 WL 815879 (E.D. La. 2000); *Pham v. Contico Int'l, Inc.*, 759 So. 2d 880 (La. App. 5th Cir. 2000), which do not recognize a spoliation of evidence claim based on negligence; the evidence must have been intentionally destroyed. *See also Fischer v. Travelers Ins. Co.*, 429 So. 2d 538 (La. App. 4th Cir. 1983) and *Duhe v. Delta Airlines, Inc.*, 635 F. Supp. 1414 (E.D. La. 1986).

37. La. Rev. Stat. Ann. § 9:2800.53(5); La. Civ. Code Ann. Art. 2520 *et seq. See also Bearly v. Brunswick Mercury Marine Div.*, 888 So. 2d 309 (La. App. 2d Cir. 2004); *De Atley v. Victoria's Secret Catalogue, LLC*, 876 So. 2d 112 (La. App. 4th Cir. 2004).

38. La. Rev. Stat. Ann. § 9:2800.56 *Battistella v. Daimler Chrysler Motors, Inc., LLC*, 2004 WL 1336444 (E.D. La. 6/14/04); *see also Tolliver v. Naor*, 2001 WL 1356264 (E.D. La. 2002); *Batiste*, 802 So. 2d 686; *Jaeger v. Auto. Cas. Ins. Co.*, 682 So. 2d. 292 (La. App. 4th Cir. 1996); *Armstrong v. Lorino*, 580 So. 2d 528 (La. App. 4th Cir. 1991).

39. *International Harvester Credit v. Seale*, 518 So. 2d 1039 (La. 1988); *Ricard v. State*, 390 So. 2d 882 (La. 1980). La. Rev. Stat. Ann. § 9:2800.53 *et seq.*

40. La. Rev. Stat. Ann. § 13:4203. La. Rev. Stat. Ann. § 13:4202 sets the judicial interest rates. *See, e.g., Cooks v. Rental Serv. Corp.*, 900 So. 2d 1146 (La. App. 3d Cir. 2005).

41. La. Rev. Stat. Ann. § 23:1032; *Elmore v. Kelly*, 909 So. 2d 36 (La. App. 2d Cir. 2005); *Brown v. Diversified Hospitality Grp.*, 600 So. 2d 902 (La. App. 4th Cir. 1992); *White v. Monsanto Co.*, 585 So. 2d 1205 (La. 1991).

42. La. Rev. Stat. Ann. § 9:2800.51 *et seq.*

43. *Oxley v. Sabine River Auth.*, 663 So. 2d 497 (La. App. 3d Cir. 1995); *Buckbee v. AWECO, Inc.*, 614 So. 2d 1233 (La. App. 1993). *Faulkner v. State, DOTD*, 645 So. 2d 268 (La. App. 2d Cir. 1994); *Taylor v. USF&G*, 630 So. 2d 237 (La. 1993). La. Civ. Code Ann. arts. 1803, 1804.

44. La. Civ. Code Ann. arts. 1804, 2323, 2324. *Aucoin v. State, DOTD*, 712 So. 2d 62 (La. 1998).

MAINE

A. CAUSES OF ACTION

Product liability lawsuits include claims based on strict liability, negligence, and breach of warranty.

B. STATUTES OF LIMITATION

Claims based on strict liability, negligence, and breach of warranty where the injury is to the person must be brought within six years.[1] Claims based on breach of warranty where the injury is to property must be brought within four years.[2] There is a two-year statute of limitations for wrongful death actions[3] and lawsuits against ski areas.[4]

With regard to strict liability and negligence claims, the applicable limitations statute does not specify when a cause of action accrues.[5] "The general test for determining when a cause of action accrues is when a plaintiff 'received a judicially recognizable injury.'"[6] In a strict liability case in which the injury resulted from inhalation of asbestos dust, the Maine Law Court held that "a judicially recognizable claim does not arise until there has been a manifestation of physical injury to a person, sufficient to cause him actual loss, damage or suffering from a defective, unreasonably dangerous product."[7]

With regard to claims based on breach of warranty, where the injury is to the person, the period begins to run when the injury takes place; where the injury is to property, the period begins to run at the time of delivery of the goods.[8] The discovery rule is unavailable in cases involving damage to property absent some fiduciary relationship between the parties.[9]

C. STRICT LIABILITY

1. The Standard

Maine's strict liability statute is based on Section 402A of the Restatement (Second) of Torts and has been interpreted as closely resembling a negligence action.[10] In a defective manufacturing/design case, the defect must be *unreasonably* dangerous; in a failure to warn case, the product's danger must be foreseeable based on the "scientific, technological, and other information available when the product was distributed."[11] In both instances, plaintiff must prove that the defendant's conduct proximately caused her injuries.[12] In defective food product cases, the Maine Supreme Judicial Court has adopted the "reasonable expectation" test, consistent with the Restatement.[13]

When establishing the existence of an *unreasonably* dangerous defect, the plaintiff's proof will "involve the examination of the utility of its design, the risk of the design and the feasibility of safer alternatives."[14] The

Maine Law Court has never addressed whether proof of a feasible design alternative is a necessary element, or, rather, merely a factor to be considered by the fact finder in defective design claims.[15]

2. **Definition of "Defect"**

A product can be in a defective condition or unreasonably dangerous to the user or consumer, as a result of: (a) an error in the manufacturing or design process or (b) the failure to warn of a danger associated with a foreseeable use of the product.[16]

3. **Causation**

It is the plaintiff's burden in any products liability case to demonstrate that the injuries sustained were proximately caused by the fact that the product in question was defective and unreasonably dangerous.[17] A cause is proximate if "in natural and continuous sequence, unbroken by an efficient intervening cause, [it] produces the injury and without [it] the result would not have occurred."[18] The Maine Law Court recently adopted Section 3(b) of the Restatement (Third) of Torts, which provides that, even without proof of a specific defect, evidence that an injury was not solely the result of causes other than a product defect existing at the time of sale or distribution can lead to an inference that a product was defective.[19]

4. **Contributory Negligence/Assumption of Risk**

"It is clear that the doctrine of assumption of risk was abolished as an available defense to claims of negligence in Maine when the state legislature adopted comparative negligence principles."[20] It is "equally clear under Maine law that the doctrine of assumption of risk is an available legal defense to strict liability claims."[21] When a comparative negligence defense is asserted, there must be a comparison of a manufacturer's or seller's fault, if any, with a plaintiff's negligence, if any, in voluntarily and unreasonably proceeding to encounter a known danger.[22]

5. **Sale or Lease/Persons Liable**

Maine's strict liability statute imposes liability on sellers of defective products.[23] The Maine Law Court has not had the opportunity to directly address the question of whether a claim may be brought against a *lessor* of a defective product. However, in 1986 a Maine Superior Court expanded strict liability to apply to lessors in addition to sellers.[24] Recently, a Maine Superior Court was faced with the question of whether healthcare professionals are deemed sellers for purposes of strict liability product claims, and determined that a doctor retained for services involving medical treatment is not a seller of products.[25]

6. **Inherently Dangerous Products**

Maine follows the "danger utility test" in evaluating design defect cases.[26] Under that test, a supplier of products will not be held strictly liable simply because the product is inherently dangerous unless plaintiff proves the product was defectively manufactured or designed, or that the manufacturer failed to give adequate warning of the danger, thereby exposing the user to an unreasonable risk of harm.[27] Such proof will involve an examination of the utility of its design, the risks of the design, and the feasibility of safer alternatives.[28]

7. **Successor Liability**

Maine case law has been interpreted to preclude successor liability.[29]

8. **Market Share Liability/Enterprise Liability**

Market share liability and enterprise liability have not been adopted in Maine.[30]

9. **Privity**

Lack of privity is no defense to a claim based on strict liability.[31]

10. **Failure to Warn**

A product liability action for failure to warn requires a three-part analysis: (1) whether the defendant has a duty to warn the plaintiff; (2) whether the actual warning on the product, if any, was inadequate; and (3) whether the inadequate warning proximately caused the plaintiff's injury.[32] This analysis is substantially the same regardless of whether the failure-to-warn claim is phrased in terms of negligence or strict liability.[33] Sellers have a duty to warn only against dangers that are not obvious and apparent.[34] Moreover, sellers breach that duty only when they know or should know the product is dangerous and fail to exercise reasonable care to inform the user.[35]

11. **Post-Sale Duty to Warn and Remedial Measures**

Under limited circumstances, a manufacturer may have a post-sale duty to warn known indirect purchasers.[36] Further, based on Rule 407 of the Maine Rules of Evidence, evidence of any such post-sale warning is admissible against the defendant.[37] Note that the Maine Law Court has specifically declined to adopt the more expansive duty to warn as described in Section 10 of the Restatement (Third) of Torts: Product Liability.[38]

12. **Learned Intermediary Doctrine**

A manufacturer must provide expected users of its product with a warning of the risks and "specific directions for the product's safe use."[39] A manufacturer of a medical device has a duty to exercise reasonable care to inform users of facts that may make the device dangerous. Under the "learned intermediary" doctrine, a manufacturer of such a device may satisfy this duty by furnishing adequate warnings and instruction to the physician or surgeon, but is not required to give them directly to the patient.

The Maine Law Court has not had the opportunity to directly address the issue; however, in 2004 a Maine Superior Court adopted the doctrine.[40] Additionally, the United States Court of Appeals for the First Circuit, in applying Maine law, stated: "[w]hile the Supreme Judicial Court of Maine has not decided the matter, the general rule regarding medical devices (and, more frequently and by analogy, prescription drugs) is that the manufacturer must warn the physician—the so called 'learned intermediary'—and not the patient directly."[41] "The rationale of the doctrine is that the prescribing physician is in the best position to evaluate the potential risks and benefits of ingesting a certain drug."[42] Even where this doctrine is applied, showing that the manufacturer's duty to warn the physician was fulfilled is not necessarily an easy hurdle to surmount.[43]

13. **Substantial Change/Abnormal Use**

A manufacturer is not relieved of strict liability for injuries caused by substantive alterations in its product if the changes were, or should have been, foreseeable and were a contributing cause of the injury, enhanced the injury, or increased the likelihood of its occurrence.[44]

14. **State of the Art**

"State of the art" evidence is admissible in the context of a strict liability claim based on a failure to warn.[45]

15. **Malfunction**

Under the "malfunction theory" of products liability, proof of a malfunction may be used as evidence to establish a defect.[46] However, such evidence will not be determinative of causation. Under Maine law, evidence of malfunction notwithstanding, the plaintiff must still establish that the product was defective.[47] Thus, in Maine, the malfunction theory in no way relieves the plaintiff of its burden of proving a defect. Malfunction evidence simply allows the plaintiff to show that the defect is the most likely explanation for an accident by eliminating other reasonable explanations.[48]

16. **Standards and Governmental Regulations**

Although there are no Maine cases specifically holding that compliance or noncompliance with government or industry standards is admissible in a strict liability action,[49] a plaintiff may introduce government or industry standards in order to provide evidence of a defendant's standard of care as to an allegation of negligence in a products liability case.[50] As claims based on strict liability substantially overlap with negligence claims, such evidence is often admissible in cases involving overlapping claims.[51]

17. **Other Accidents**

Evidence of similar accidents or the absence thereof is admissible on issues of defective conditions, notice, or causation so long as the foundational requirement of substantial similarity of conditions or adequate number of situations is met.[52]

18. **Misrepresentation**

The Maine Law Court has held that in a malpractice action involving a physician's duty to warn in connection with defective medical device implants, the physician's fraudulent concealment tolls the statute of limitations in malpractice actions.[53]

19. **Destruction or Loss of Product from Spoliation**

Defendant must establish plaintiff's conscious wrongdoing and that the defendant has been prejudiced by the plaintiff's destruction of the evidence.[54] The spoliation doctrine is designed to rectify prejudice suffered by the non-offending party due to the loss of evidence and to deter future purposeful conduct having the tendency to result in the loss of evidence.[55] Potential sanctions include exclusion of evidence, a corrective jury instruction, and dismissal of the case.[56]

20. **Economic Loss**

Maine has expressly adopted the "economic loss" doctrine.[57] Maine courts will not permit tort recovery for a defective product's damage to itself.[58] Economic loss, as used in this context, has been defined as "damages for inadequate value, costs of repair and replacement of a defective product, or consequent loss of profits—without any claim of personal injury or damage to other property."[59] "The rationale underlying this rule is that damage to a product itself means simply that the product has not met the customer's expectations, or . . . that the customer has received an insufficient product value."[60] The maintenance of product value and quality is precisely the purpose of express and implied warranties, and subsequent claim for damages is more properly addressed under a warranty theory.[61]

The "integrated product rule" is used to determine whether a negligently designed product has injured only itself or caused injury to other property. In a claim based on defective components, the relevant "product" is the finished product into which the component is integrated.[62]

21. **Crashworthiness**

Courts applying Maine law, so far, have been unwilling to admit evidence of the "crashworthiness" of a vehicle by a plaintiff or a defendant, stating that such evidence is irrelevant unless there is a particular legal standard that a vehicle must meet with respect to crashworthiness and that the evidence sought to be admitted shows that the vehicle either meets or fails to meet such standard.[63]

D. **NEGLIGENCE**

Claims based on negligence and strict liability substantially overlap.[64]

Comparative negligence is a defense to product liability claims and precludes recovery when the plaintiff is 50 percent or more at fault.[65]

E. BREACH OF WARRANTY

Maine recognizes the implied warranties of merchantability and fitness for a particular purpose.[66] In order to recover under either of these theories, a product liability plaintiff must establish some defect in the product at the time it was sold.[67] The Maine legislature has removed claims for injuries to the person based on breach of warranty from the UCC's four-year limitations provision, placing them under the general six-year provision.[68]

F. PUNITIVE DAMAGES

Punitive damages are generally recoverable on proof of malice, actual or implied established by clear and convincing evidence.[69] However, the Maine Law Court has reserved ruling on the application of punitive damages in product liability cases.[70]

G. PRE- AND POST-JUDGMENT INTEREST

1. Pre-Judgment Interest

Pre-judgment interest is provided by statute.[71] In civil actions, pre-judgment interest begins to accrue from the time a notice of claim is served upon the defendant, or if no notice is given to the defendant, from the date the complaint is filed, and shall accrue until the date on which an order for judgment is entered.[72]

Pre-judgment interest is allowed at the one-year United States Treasury bill rate plus three percent.[73] Pre-judgment interest may not be added to the judgment amount in determining the sum upon which post-judgment interest accrues.[74]

2. Post-Judgment Interest

Post-judgment interest shall accrue from and after the date of entry of judgment, including the period of pendency of an appeal.[75] For civil actions, the interest rate shall be equal to the one-year United States Treasury bill rate plus six percent.[76] The applicable interest rate must be stated in the judgment except in the case of small claims judgments.[77]

H. EMPLOYER IMMUNITY FROM SUIT

The Maine Workers' Compensation Act provides the exclusive means for an employee to obtain compensation from an employer for injuries caused by that employer's negligence.[78] The exclusivity provision exempts plaintiff's employer from liability, and from being joined as a party to an action for an employee's injury.[79] Under Maine law, employers can contractually waive workers' compensation immunity provided that the waiver meets strict standards.[80] To constitute waiver of immunity, "a contractual indemnification provision must either specifically waive immunity or state that [indemnification] assumes potential liability for actions brought by its own employees."[81] Intentional torts fall within the exclusivity and immunity provisions of the Workers' Compensation Act.[82]

I. STATUTES

Statutes relevant to product liability actions are the strict liability statute,[83] statutes of limitations,[84] and the UCC sections involving warranties accompanying the sale of goods.[85] The age of majority in Maine is 18.[86]

J. JOINT AND SEVERAL LIABILITY

Under Maine law, defendants may be held jointly and severally liable to a plaintiff for the full amount of plaintiff's damages.[87] However, any defendant has a right to a determination by a jury of the percentage of fault attributable to each defendant, and a right to obtain contribution from any other parties at fault.[88] Maine's comparative fault statute applies to statutory strict products liability actions and in such cases, the defendant's strict liability constitutes "fault" for the purposes of comparing the responsibilities of the other parties.[89]

Bernard J. Kubetz
Jeremy S. Grant
Eaton Peabody
80 Exchange Street
P.O. Box 1210
Bangor, Maine 04402-1210
(207) 947-0111
(Fax) (207) 942-3040

Endnotes - Maine

1. 14 Me. Rev. Stat. Ann. § 752 (2013); 11 Me. Rev. Stat. Ann. § 2-725(2) (2013) ("A cause of action for personal injuries . . . for breach of warranty occurs when the injury takes place and is governed by the limitation of action period under Title 14, section 752.").

2. 11 Me. Rev. Stat. Ann. § 2-725(1) (2013).

3. 18-A Me. Rev. Stat. Ann. § 2-804(b) (2013).

4. 14 Me. Rev. Stat. Ann. § 752-B (2013).

5. 14 Me. Rev. Stat. Ann. § 752 (2013).

6. *Johnston v. Dow & Coulombe, Inc.*, 686 A.2d 1064, 1065-66 (Me. 1996) (citing *Bozzuto v. Ouellette*, 408 A.2d 697, 699 (Me. 1979)). See also *Descoteau v. Analogic Corp.*, 696 F. Supp. 2d 138, 141 (D. Me. 2010) (stating the general rule that a tort claim accrues when the defendant's wrongful act caused an injury for which the plaintiff is entitled to seek judicial vindication); *McLaughlin v. Superintending Sch. Comm. of Lincolnville*, 2003 ME 114, ¶22, 832 A.2d 782; *Maine Mun. Emps. Health Trust v. Maloney*, 2004 ME 51, ¶10, 846 A.2d 336.

7. *Bernier v. Raymark Indus., Inc.*, 516 A.2d 534, 543 (Me. 1986).

8. 11 Me. Rev. Stat. Ann. § 2-725(2) (2013); *Oceanside at Pine Point Condo. Owners Ass'n v. Peachtree Doors, Inc.*, 659 A.2d 267, 272 (Me. 1995).

9. *Dunelawn Owners' Ass'n v. Gendreau*, 2000 ME 94, ¶¶13-14, 750 A.2d 591 (explaining that "[t]he discovery rule is an exception to the general rule that accrual occurs at the time of a judicially cognizable injury."). The Law Court applies "the discovery rule in three limited areas: (1) legal malpractice; (2) foreign object and negligent diagnosis medical malpractice; and (3) asbestosis." *Descoteau v. Analogic Corp.*, 696 F. Supp. 2d 138, 142 (D. Me. 2010).

10. 14 Me. Rev. Stat. Ann. § 221 (2013); *Austin v. Raybestos-Manhattan, Inc.*, 471 A.2d 280, 286 (Me. 1984) ("Maine's section 221 derives almost verbatim from the black letter of section 402A of the *Restatement (Second) of Torts* (1965).").

11. 14 Me. Rev. Stat. Ann. § 221 (2013); *Bernier v. Raymark Indus., Inc.*, 516 A.2d 534, 538 (Me. 1986).

12. *Ames v. Dipietro-Kay Corp.*, 617 A.2d 559, 561 (Me. 1992) (citing *Marois v. Paper Converting Mach. Co.*, 539 A.2d 621, 623 (Me. 1988)).

13. *Estate of Pinkham v. Cargill, Inc.*, 2012 ME 85, ¶15, 55 A.3d 1 (stating that "the test considers the condition of the product as it compares to the ordinary consumer's reasonable expectation for that product.").

14. *Stanley v. Schiavi Mobile Homes, Inc.*, 462 A.2d 1144, 1148 (Me. 1983); *Canning v. Broan-Nutone, LLC*, 480 F. Supp. 2d 392, 403 (D. Me. 2007).

15. *Phillips v. Emerson Elec. Co.*, 2003 WL 21011349, at *3, n.1 (D. Me. May 5, 2003) (stating that although the Law Court has never clarified the design alternative analysis set forth in *Stanley*, the court interprets the *Stanley* decision as suggesting that the feasible design alternative is a prerequisite rather than a mere factor to be considered); *But see Reali v. Mazda Motor of Am., Inc.*, 106 F. Supp. 2d 75, 80 (D. Me. 2000) ("[I]n Maine, a plaintiff in a design defect case must prove that an alternative design is feasible and safer.").

16. *Moores v. Sunbeam Prods.*, 425 F. Supp. 2d 151, 156 (D. Me. 2006) (citing *Bernier v. Raymark Indus., Inc.*, 516 A.2d 534, 537 n.3 (Me. 1986)); *Ames v. Dipietro-Kay Corp.*, 617 A.2d 559, 561 (Me. 1992). *See also Pottle v. Up-Right, Inc.*, 628 A.2d 672, 674-75 (Me. 1993) (citing *Walker v. Gen. Elec. Co.*, 968 F.2d 116, 119 (1st Cir. 1992)).

17. *Austin v. Raybestos-Manhattan, Inc.*, 471 A.2d 280, 285 (Me. 1984); *Ames v. Dipietro-Kay Corp.*, 617 A.2d 599, 561 (Me. 1992); *Canning v. Broan-Nutone, LLC*, 480 F. Supp. 2d 392, 410 (D. Me. 2007).

18. *Ames v. Dipietro-Kay Corp.*, 617 A.2d 559, 561 (Me. 1992) (noting "an intervening cause does not automatically break the chain of causation stemming from the original actor's conduct. In order to break that chain, the intervening cause must also be a superseding cause, that is, neither anticipated nor reasonably foreseeable."); *Merriam v. Wagner*, 2000 ME 85, ¶19, 55 A.3d 1 (stating that proximate cause requires a showing that "the evidence and inferences that may reasonably be drawn from the evidence indicate that the negligence played a substantial part in bringing about or actually causing injury or damage and that the injury or damage was either a direct result or a reasonably foreseeable consequence of the negligence.").

19. *Estate of Pinkham v. Cargill, Inc.*, 2012 ME 85, ¶19, 55 A.3d 1.

20. *Johnson v. Chrysler Corp.*, 187 F.R.D. 440, 441-42 (D. Me. 1999) (citing *Wilson v. Gordon*, 354 A.2d 398, 401-03 (Me. 1976)); 14 Me. Rev. Stat. Ann. § 156 (2012).

21. *Johnson v. Chrysler Corp.*, 187 F.R.D. 440, 442 (D. Me. 1999) (citing *Austin v. Raybestos-Manhattan, Inc.*, 471 A.2d 280, 286 (Me. 1984)).

22. *See Austin v. Raybestos-Manhattan, Inc.*, 471 A.2d 280, 286 (Me. 1984); *Maietta v. Int'l Harvester Co.*, 496 A.2d 286, 291 n.4 (Me. 1985).

23. 14 Me. Rev. Stat. Ann. § 221 (2013).

24. *Turner v. Hudson*, 1986 Me. Super. LEXIS 278, at *4-8 (Dec. 12, 1986).

25. *Jordan v. Cap Quality Care, Inc.*, 2009 WL 1106423 (Me. Super. Mar. 16, 2009).

26. *Violette v. Smith & Nephew Dyonics, Inc.*, 62 F.3d 8, 12-13 (1st Cir. 1995); *Guiggey v. Bomberdier*, 615 A.2d 1169, 1172 (Me. 1992); *Porter v. Pfizer Hosp. Prod. Grp., Inc.*, 783 F. Supp. 1466, 1474 (D. Me. 1992) (holding that a plaintiff cannot prevail on a defective design claim where he introduced no evidence that the utility of the design was outweighed by the risks); *Hinton v. Outboard Marine Corp.*, 2012 WL 7638061, at *4 (D. Me. Jan. 20, 2012).

27. *St. Germain v. Husqvarna Corp.*, 544 A.2d 1283, 1285-86 (Me. 1988).

28. *Moores v. Sunbeam Prods., Inc.*, 425 F. Supp. 2d 151, 156 (D. Me. 2006) (quoting *St. Germain v. Husqvarna Corp.*, 544 A.2d 1283, 1285 (Me. 1988)).

29. *Jordan v. Hawker Dayton Corp.*, 62 F.3d 29, 31-32 (1st Cir. 1995) (citing *Dir. of Bureau of Labor Standards v. Diamond Brands, Inc.*, 588 A.2d 734, 736 (Me. 1991)).

30. *Dube v. Pittsburgh-Corning Corp.*, 1988 WL 64733, at *9, n.27 (D. Me. June 9, 1988), *rev'd on unrelated grounds*, 870 F.2d 790 (1st Cir. 1989).

31. *Doe v. Solvay Pharm., Inc.*, 350 F. Supp. 2d 257, 266 (D. Me. 2004); *Jordan v. Hawker Dayton Corp.*, 62 F.3d 29, 31-32 (1st Cir. 1995) (citing *Dir. of Bureau of Labor Standards v. Diamond Brands, Inc.*, 588 A.2d 734, 736 (Me. 1991)). *See also* 14 Me. Rev. Stat. Ann. § 221 (2013) (seller's liability extends to "a person whom the manufacturer, seller or supplier might reasonably have expected to use, consume or be affected by the goods, or to his property . . . [even if] the user or consumer has not bought the product from or entered into any contractual relation with the seller"); 14 Me. Rev. Stat. Ann. § 161 (2013) (lack of privity is no defense in an action against a manufacturer, seller, or supplier of goods if the plaintiff was a person reasonably expected to use or be affected by the goods).

32. *Koken v. Black & Veatch Constr., Inc.*, 426 F.3d 39, 45 (1st Cir. 2005) (quoting *Pottle v. Up-Right, Inc.*, 628 A.2d 672, 675 (Me. 1993)); *Bouchard v. Am. Orthodontics*, 661 A.2d 1143, 1145 (Me. 1995); *Burns v. Architectural Doors & Windows*, 2011 ME 61, ¶23, 19 A.3d 823.

33. *See Pottle v. Up-Right, Inc.*, 628 A.2d 672, 675 (Me. 1993).

34. *Lorfano v. Dura Stone Steps, Inc.*, 569 A.2d 195, 197 (Me. 1990) (the manufacturer of a mobile home is not required to warn users of staircase of the obvious danger presented by the absence of handrail); *Brawn v. Oral Surgery*

Assocs., 2003 ME 11, ¶29, 819 A.2d 1014 (plaintiffs no longer had viable claim against defendants for failing to advise them of known risks earlier because defendants' duty to warn expired when plaintiffs became aware of the problem); *Speed v. Giddings & Lewis, LLC*, 2007 WL 4245903, at * 10 (D. Me. Nov. 29, 2007).

35. *Varano v. Jabar*, 197 F.3d 1, 4 (1st Cir. 1999) (quoting *Pottle v. Up-Right, Inc.*, 628 A.2d 672, 675 (Me. 1993)).

36. *Brown v. Crown Equip. Corp.*, 2008 ME 186, ¶3, 960 A.2d 1188; *Maietta v. Int'l Harvester Co.*, 496 A.2d 286, 295 (Me. 1985) (holding that evidence of product recalls may be admissible).

37. M.R. Evid. 407(b).

38. *Brown v. Crown Equip. Corp.*, 2008 ME 186, ¶3, 960 A.2d 1188.

39. *Pottle v. Up-Right, Inc.*, 628 A.2d 672, 675 (Me. 1993) (citing *McNeal v. Hi-Lo Powered Scaffolding, Inc.*, 836 F.2d 637, 643 (D.C. Cir. 1988)); *see also Williams v. Inverness Corp.*, 664 A.2d 1244, 1249 (Me. 1995).

40. *Tardy v. Eli Lilly & Co.*, 2004 WL 1925536 (Me. Super. Aug. 3, 2004).

41. *Violette v. Smith & Nephew Dyonics, Inc*, 62 F.3d 8, 13 (1st Cir. 1995) (citing *Knowlton v. Deseret Med., Inc.*, 930 F.2d 116, 120 n.2 (1st Cir. 1991)) (in a failure to warn suit against a catheter manufacturer, the court noted that it "is generally accepted that in a case involving medical products prescribed or used by a physician or trained medical personnel, the warning runs to the physician, not to the patient"); *Doe v. Solvay Pharm., Inc.*, 153 Fed. Appx. 1, 3 (1st Cir. 2005); *see also Glenwood Farms, Inc. v. Ivey*, 2005 U.S. Dist. LEXIS 24403, at *43-44 (D. Me. Oct. 20, 2005).

42. *Glenwood Farms, Inc. v. Ivey*, 2005 U.S. Dist. LEXIS 24403, at *43-44 (D. Me. Oct. 20, 2005); *see also Doe v. Solvay Pharm., Inc.*, 350 F. Supp. 2d 257, 270-71 (D. Me. 2004).

43. *See Violette v. Smith & Nephew Dyonics, Inc*, 62 F.3d 8, 14 (1st Cir. 1995) (manufacturer found to have failed in its duty to warn physician of possible complications).

44. *Marois v. Paper Converting Mach. Co.*, 539 A.2d 621, 624 (Me. 1988) (stating that "even if a substantive change is made in a product, the manufacturer will not be relieved of liability unless the change was an unforeseen and intervening proximate cause of the injury.") .

45. *Bernier v. Raymark Indus., Inc.*, 516 A.2d 534, 540 (Me. 1986); *see also St. Germain v. Husqvarna Corp.*, 544 A.2d 1283, 1286, n.1 (Me. 1988).

46. *See Walker v. Gen. Elec. Co.*, 968 F.2d 116, 120 (1st Cir. 1992); *see also Pratt v. Freese's, Inc.*, 438 A.2d 901, 904 (Me. 1981) (suggesting that evidence establishing product malfunction will be sufficient to survive a directed verdict motion *only* where all reasonable alternative explanations have been disproved).

47. *Walker v. Gen. Elec. Co.*, 968 F.2d 116, 120 (1st Cir. 1992); *but see TNT Rd. Co. v. Sterling Truck Corp.*, 2004 U.S. Dist. LEXIS 13461, at *21-22 (D. Me. July 19, 2004).

48. *Walker v. Gen. Elec. Co.*, 968 F.2d 116, 120 (1st Cir. 1992).

49. *Libby v. Griffith Design & Equip. Co.*, 1991 WL 185178, at *3 (D. Me. June 19, 1990); *Brown v. Crown Equip. Corp.*, 445 F. Supp. 2d 59, (D. Me. 2006) (holding that American National Standards Institute standard relevant to lift trucks was admissible in action arising from workplace accident involving lift truck, where the parties agreed the standard applied); *but see Johnston v. Deere & Co.*, 967 F. Supp. 578, 579 (D. Me. 1997) (holding that Consumer Product Safety Commission activities are admissible as evidence pertinent to information available to manufacturers in determining whether they met a relevant standard of care).

50. *Libby v. Griffith Design & Equip. Co.*, 1991 WL 185178, at *3 (D. Me. June 19, 1990).

51. *Libby v. Griffith Design & Equip. Co.*, 1991 WL 185178, at *3 (D. Me. June 19, 1990).

52. *Moulton v. Rival Co.*, 116 F.3d 22, 26-27 (1st Cir. 1997); *Espeaignnette v. Gene Tierney Co.*, 43 F.3d 1, 9-10 (1st Cir. 1994); *Marois v. Paper Converting Mach. Co.*, 539 A.2d 621, 625 (Me. 1988); *Libby v. Griffith Design & Equip. Co.*, 1991 WL 185178, at *3 (D. Me. June 19, 1990); *Stanley v. Schiavi Mobile Homes, Inc.*, 462 A.2d 1144, 1149 (Me. 1983); *Simon v. Town of Kennebunkport*, 417 A.2d 982, 984-85 (Me. 1980).

53. *Brawn v. Oral Surgery Assocs.*, 2003 ME 11, ¶¶24-28, 819 A.2d 1014; 14 Me. Rev. Stat. Ann. § 859 (2013).

54. *McLaughlin v. Denharco, Inc.*, 129 F. Supp. 2d 32, 36 (D. Me. 2001).

55. *Driggin v. Am. Sec. Alarm Co.*, 141 F. Supp. 2d 113, 120 (D. Me. 2000) (quoting *Collazo-Santiago v. Toyota Motor Corp.*, 149 F.3d 23, 29 (1st Cir. 1998)).

56. *Driggin v. Am. Sec. Alarm Co.*, 141 F. Supp. 2d 113, 120 (D. Me. 2000).

57. *Driggin v. Am. Sec. Alarm Co.*, 141 F. Supp. 2d 113, 120 (D. Me. 2000); *Oceanside at Pine Point Condo. Owners Ass'n v. Peachtree Doors, Inc.*, 659 A.2d 267, 270-71 (Me. 1995).

58. *Oceanside, at Pine Point Condo. Owners Ass'n v. Peachtree Doors, Inc.*, 659 A.2d 267, 270 (Me. 1995); *see also Maine Rubber Int'l v. Env't Mgmt. Grp. Inc.*, 298 F. Supp. 2d 133, 135 (D. Me. 2004) (finding that "[a]lthough there is no guidance from the Law Court, I do agree with the Magistrate Judge that the Maine Law Court would probably apply the [economic loss] doctrine to service contracts.") *but see Fireman's Fund Ins. Co. v. Childs*, 52 F. Supp. 2d 139, 145 (D. Me. 1999) ("The Law Court may determine that the economic loss doctrine does not apply to bar a tort claim for the negligent rendering of services, as opposed to the negligent manufacturing or selling of a product.").

59. *Oceanside at Pine Point Condo. Owners Ass'n v. Peachtree Doors, Inc.*, 659 A.2d 267, 270 n.4 (Me. 1995) (citing *Moorman Mfg. Co. v. Nat'l Tank Co.*, 435 N.E.2d 443 (Ill. 1982)).

60. *Oceanside at Pine Point Condo. Owners Ass'n v. Peachtree Doors, Inc.*, 659 A.2d 267, 270-71 (Me. 1995).

61. *Oceanside at Pine Point Condo. Owners Ass'n v. Peachtree Doors, Inc.*, 659 A.2d 267, 270-71 (Me. 1995).

62. *Fireman's Fund Ins. Co. v. Childs*, 52 F. Supp. 2d 139, 142-43 (D. Me. 1999) (quoting *Sebago, Inc. v. Beazer East, Inc.*, 18 F. Supp. 2d 70, 90 (D. Mass. 1988)); *McLaughlin v. Denharco, Inc.*, 129 F. Supp.2d 32, 36 (D. Me. 2001).

63. *Brawn v. Fuji Heavy Indus. Ltd.*, 817 F. Supp. 184, 186 (D. Me. 1993); *but see Taylor v. Ford Motor Co.*, 2006 WL 2228973, at *2 (D. Me. Aug. 3, 2006) (noting that crashworthiness or enhanced injury doctrine is a type of defect and not a separate and distinct cause of action that extends a manufacturer's liability in cases where the plaintiff suffers separate or enhanced injuries in the course of an initial accident caused by his own vehicle).

64. *Espeaignnette v. Gene Tierney Co., Inc.*, 43 F.3d 1, 10 n.12 (1st Cir. 1994) (citing *Marois v. Paper Converting Mach. Co.*, 539 A.2d 621, 623 (Me. 1988); *Stanley v. Schiavi Mobile Homes, Inc.*, 462 A.2d 1144, 1148 (Me. 1983); *see also Ames v. Dipietro-Kay Corp.*, 617 A.2d 559, 561 (Me. 1992).

65. 14 Me. Rev. Stat. Ann. § 156 (2013); *see also Austin v. Raybestos-Manhattan, Inc.*, 471 A.2d 280, 284-85 (Me. 1984); *In re Game Tracker, Inc.*, 799 F. Supp. 2d 102, 106 (D. Me. 2011) (holding that defaulted defendants in products liability action could present evidence of plaintiff's comparative negligence at damages hearing).

66. 11 Me. Rev. Stat. Ann. §§ 2-314 & 2-315 (2013); *see also Porter v. Pfizer Hosp. Prods. Grp. Inc.*, 783 F. Supp. 1466, 1471, 1473-74 (D. Me. 1992).

67. *Walker v. Gen. Elec. Co.*, 968 F.2d 116, 119 (1st Cir. 1992); *Canning v. Broan-Nutone, LLC*, 480 F. Supp. 2d 392, 412-13 (D. Me. 2007).

68. 11 Me. Rev. Stat. Ann. § 2-725(2) (2013).

69. *Bratton v. McDonough*, 2014 ME 64, ¶25, 91 A.3d 1050; *Tuttle v. Raymond*, 494 A.2d 1353, 1361 (Me. 1985).

70. *Tuttle v. Raymond*, 494 A.2d 1353, 1360 n.20 (Me. 1985); *see Thorndike v. DaimlerChrysler Corp.*, 288 F. Supp. 2d 50, 54 n.1 (D. Me. 2003) (noting that a Maine Court is unlikely to adopt a "conscious disregard" punitive damages standard in product liability cases in place of *Tuttle*'s "implied malice" standard).

71. 14 Me. Rev. Stat. Ann. § 1602-B (2013).

72. 14 Me. Rev. Stat. Ann. § 1602-B(5) (2013).

73. 14 Me. Rev. Stat. Ann. § 1602-B(3)(2013).

74. 14 Me. Rev. Stat. Ann. § 1602-B(6) (2013).

75. 14 Me. Rev. Stat. Ann. § 1602-C(2) (2013).

76. 14 Me. Rev. Stat. Ann. § 1602-C(1)(B) (2013).

77. 14 Me. Rev. Stat. Ann. § 1602-C(1) (2013).

78. 39-A Me. Rev. Stat. Ann. § 104 (2013). *See also Fanion v. McNeal*, 577 A.2d 2, 4 (Me. 1990); *Samson v. DiConzo*, 669 A.2d 760, 762 (Me. 1996).

79. *Caldwell v. Fed. Exp. Corp.*, 908 F. Supp. 29, 32-33 (D. Me. 1995) ("The exclusivity provision of the [Maine Workers' Compensation] Act bars employees from bringing [a] civil action against insured employers for work-related injuries."); *See also Frank v. L.L. Bean, Inc.*, 352 F. Supp. 2d 8, 13 (D. Me. 2005).

80. *Int'l Paper Co. v. A & A Brochu*, 899 F. Supp. 715, 718 (D. Me. 1995) (citing *Roberts v. Am. Chain & Cable Co.*, 259 A.2d 43, 51 (Me. 1961)).

81. *Int'l Paper Co. v. A & A Brochu*, 899 F. Supp. 715, 718 (D. Me. 1995).

82. *Breton v. Travelers Ins. Co.*, 147 F.3d 58, 63-64 (1st Cir. 1998); *Searway v. Rainey*, 709 A.2d 735, 736 (Me. 1998).

83. 14 Me. Rev. Stat. Ann. § 221 (2013).

84. 14 Me. Rev. Stat. Ann. §§ 752 & 752-B (2013); 11 Me. Rev. Stat. Ann. § 2-725 (2013); 18-A Me. Rev. Stat. Ann. § 2-804 (2013); 14 Me. Rev. Stat. Ann. § 752 (2013).

85. 11 Me. Rev. Stat. Ann. §§ 2-314 & 2-318 (2013).

86. 1 Me. Rev. Stat. Ann. § 72(11) (2013).

87. 14 Me. Rev. Stat. Ann. § 156 (2013); *Baker v. Jandreau*, 642 A.2d 1354, 1355 (Me. 1994).

88. 14 Me. Rev. Stat. Ann. § 156 (2013); *Gagne v. Carl Bauer Schraubenfabrick*, 595 F. Supp. 1081, 1086 n.5 (D. Me. 1984); *Austin v. Raybestos-Manhattan, Inc.*, 471 A.2d 280, 282 (Me. 1984).

89. *Prentiss & Carlisle Co. v. Koehring-Waterous Div. of Timberjack, Inc.*, 972 F.2d 6, 10-11 (1st Cir. 1992); *Austin v. Raybestos-Manhattan, Inc.*, 471 A.2d 280, 284 (Me. 1984).

MARYLAND

A. CAUSES OF ACTION

Maryland recognizes causes of action in negligence, breach of warranty, and strict liability.[1] In any of these causes of action, the plaintiff must (1) prove that the product was defective or in a defective condition; (2) attribute that product to a "seller"; and (3) prove that the defect proximately caused plaintiff's injury.[2]

B. STATUTES OF LIMITATION

Maryland has a three-year statute of limitations for all negligence actions and tort-based claims.[3] Actions founded in strict liability must also be brought within three years of the time the cause of action accrues.[4] Under the Maryland "discovery rule," a cause of action in negligence or strict liability accrues once a plaintiff knows or should know he or she has been wronged.[5] In a product liability action, therefore, the discovery rule mandates that the statute of limitations should not begin to run until the plaintiff knows or, through the exercise of due diligence, should know of the injury, its probable cause, and either manufacturer wrongdoing or product defect.[6]

If a product liability case arose in another jurisdiction and is barred by the limitations statute of that state, it is also barred in Maryland, except as to a Maryland resident plaintiff.[7] This exception does not apply to cases arising prior to July 1, 1991, nor to cases involving wrongful death actions.[8]

In a death case, Maryland recognizes two separate causes of action: a survival claim brought by the estate of the decedent and a statutorily created wrongful death action.[9] The statute of limitations for a survival claim is treated like any other tort-based claim as outlined above. The statute of limitations for wrongful death claims, however, must be brought within three years of the date of death.[10] In the case of an occupational disease, however, an action must be filed within ten years of the date of death or within three years of the date when the cause of death was discovered, whichever is the shorter.[11] Maryland's intermediate appellate court has determined that the date when a cause of action is discovered by the decedent for purposes of the survival action is not necessarily the same date that the cause of action is discovered by the beneficiaries for purposes of a wrongful death claim, and the date the cause of action accrues for a wrongful death claim will depend on the date the beneficiaries had sufficient knowledge to know, or should know, that the cause of action had accrued.[12]

All actions based on a breach of warranty, whether express or implied, must be commenced within four years from the date of sale of the product, unless reduced by the original agreement of sale.[13] The limitations period may not be reduced to less than one year.[14]

C. STRICT LIABILITY

1. Standard

Maryland has adopted the standard laid out in Section 402A of the Restatement (Second) of Torts.[15] In order to recover under a theory of strict liability, the plaintiff need not prove any specific act of negligence, as strict liability permits the imposition of liability without fault.[16] Rather, the plaintiff must demonstrate that: (1) the product was in a defective condition at the time that it left the possession or control of the seller; (2) it was unreasonably dangerous to the user or consumer; (3) the defect was a cause of the injuries; and (4) the product was expected to and did reach the consumer without substantial change in its condition.[17]

2. "Defect"

A defect may arise from the manufacture or design of any product "which may reasonably be expected to be capable of inflicting substantial harm."[18] In addition, the failure to give adequate warning can constitute a defect for which recovery can be obtained.[19]

a. Manufacturing Defect

A plaintiff may prove a product has a manufacturing defect simply by showing that the product fails to conform to the manufacturer's specifications.[20] As one court has explained, in a case alleging a manufacturing defect, "the focus is on the conduct of the manufacturer."[21] By contrast, in a design defect case, "the inquiry focuses on the product itself."[22]

b. Design Defect

For a party to be liable for a design defect, the product must be both in a "defective condition" and "unreasonably dangerous."[23] These requirements are met if the condition causing the injury is not one that would be contemplated by an ordinary consumer, and is one which will be unreasonably dangerous to him (i.e., "dangerous to an extent beyond that which would be contemplated by the ordinary consumer and the ordinary knowledge . . . as to its characteristics").[24] When a product fails to meet the reasonable expectations of the user, "the inference is that there was some sort of a defect, the precise definition of which is unnecessary."[25] Maryland courts apply the consumer expectation test in strict liability design defect cases, unless the product malfunctions.[26] In these limited circumstances, the courts can apply a risk/utility test to determine whether a design defect exists.[27]

Courts have cited to the following factors in the application of the risk/utility test: (1) the usefulness and desirability of the product; (2) the safety aspects of the product; (3) the availability of a substitute product;

(4) the manufacturer's ability to eliminate the unsafe character of the product without impairing its usefulness or making it too expensive to maintain its utility; (5) the user's ability to avoid danger by the exercise of care; (6) the user's anticipated awareness of the dangers inherent in the product and their avoidability, whether based on general knowledge, the obvious condition of the product, or the existence of suitable warnings or instructions; and (7) the feasibility of the manufacturer's spreading the loss by setting the price of the product or carrying liability insurance.[28]

3. **Proof of Defect**

Proof of a defect "must arise above surmise, conjecture, or speculation," and a plaintiff may not base recovery solely on any presumption that might arise from the happening of an accident.[29] Rather, it is the plaintiff's burden to establish that it is more probable than not that the defect existed at the time of sale.[30]

It is not always necessary for the plaintiff to provide expert testimony to establish a defect.[31] Expert testimony is only required when the subject of the inference is so particularly related to a science or profession that it is beyond the ken of the average layman.[32]

4. **Proof of Causation**

Proximate cause is established if cause in fact and legally cognizable cause is proven.[33] To determine cause in fact, two tests have been recognized—the "but for" test and the "substantial factor" test.[34] Generally, the "substantial factor" test is used when two independent causes concur to bring about an injury and either one, standing alone, would cause identical harm, but the "substantial factor" test is also recognized in other circumstances.[35] If cause in fact exists, the plaintiff must still establish legally cognizable cause by demonstrating that, at the time of the negligence, the defendant should have foreseen the "general field of danger," but not necessarily the specific harm.[36]

5. **Defenses**

Contributory negligence is not a defense to a strict liability claim.[37] Defenses recognized in Maryland are as follows:

a. **Assumption of Risk**

Assumption of risk is an affirmative defense. The defendant must show "(1) that the plaintiff knew and appreciated the particular risk or danger created by the defect; (2) that the plaintiff voluntarily encountered the risk while realizing the danger; and (3) that the plaintiff's decision to encounter the known risk was unreasonable."[38]

One decision has addressed the problematic area of "voluntariness" as it relates to assumption of risk.[39] Although not specifically addressing the doctrine's applicability to the product liability arena, the court expressly held that conduct is to be regarded as "voluntary" "even though [a plaintiff] is acting under the compulsion of circumstances, not created by the tortious conduct of the defendant, which have left him no reasonable alternative."[40]

b. Misuse

Although not characterized as an affirmative defense in Maryland, misuse of a product can bar recovery where it is either the sole proximate cause of damage, or it is the intervening or superseding cause.[41] In one instance, the court held that the plaintiffs' conduct constituted misuse as a matter of law, when they stored a gasoline can in the basement of their home and allowed unsupervised children access to the can in spite of instructions on the can not to do either.[42] That misuse, according to the court, "negated" the element of defect and required dismissal of the plaintiffs' claims.[43]

c. Heeding Presumption

Maryland's Court of Appeals has held that when a manufacturer of a product provides adequate warnings, the failure to heed those warnings also provides an absolute defense to a strict liability claim; "it follows that misuse of a product and failure to read or follow a product's warnings and instructions exist as two distinct, though at times intertwined (as in the present case), defenses to strict products liability."[44] This "heeding presumption" defense would apply in the context of a warnings claim even where the "misuse" of the product, or failing to heed adequate warnings, was foreseeable.[45]

d. Sophisticated User/Bulk Supplier Defense

This defense has been recognized in Maryland, and focuses upon the conduct of the supplier in light of the circumstances. The circumstances a court should examine include: (1) the feasibility of giving direct warnings to all who are entitled to them; and (2) where that is not feasible, examining whether the supplier acted in a manner reasonably calculated to assure either that the necessary information would be passed on to the ultimate handlers of the product or that their safety would otherwise be addressed.[46]

e. State of the Art

Although not strictly speaking a "defense," the defendant may, in a design case, negate plaintiff's proof of the availability of a safer alternative design by showing that the technology did not exist to develop the design at the time of manufacture.[47] It should be noted, however, that in a negligence or strict liability case, the manufacturer of the product is responsible for knowing what was generally known in the scientific or expert community about a product's hazards; state of the art includes all available knowledge at a given time including scientific, medical, engineering, and any other available knowledge.[48]

f. **Product Alteration**

Alteration of a product after it leaves the manufacturer constitutes a defense to a strict liability claim.[49]

6. **Lease**

The liability of a lessor of a chattel, if it is to be imposed at all in Maryland, must be imposed in a tort action for negligence[50] or in an action for breach of warranty.[51]

7. **Inherently Dangerous Products**

Maryland courts have not had occasion to develop the doctrine of inherently dangerous products in any great detail. In one case, the Court of Special Appeals looked to other states to lay out the appropriate standard.[52] Under that standard the court explained that in order for a product to be deemed "inherently dangerous" it must be dangerous in its ordinary non-defective state.[53]

The question of whether a particular product is "inherently dangerous" has been subsequently determined to be a question for the court to determine prior to submission to the jury.[54] As the Court of Special Appeals has explained, judicial determination of whether a product creates an inherently unreasonable risk prevents strict liability from being imposed inconsistently.[55]

8. **Successor Liability**

The general rule of successor liability in Maryland, as in many other jurisdictions, is that

> a corporation which acquires all or part of the assets of another corporation does not acquire the liabilities and debts of the predecessor, unless: (1) there is an express or implied agreement to assume the liabilities; (2) the transaction amounts to a consolidation or merger; (3) the successor entity is a mere continuation or reincarnation of the predecessor entity; or (4) the transaction was fraudulent, not made in good faith, or made without sufficient consideration. Thus, the general rule is one of successor nonliability, subject to four 'traditional' exceptions. . . .[56]

Importantly, the Court of Appeals has declined to adopt continuity of the *enterprise* as the basis for imposing successor liability (as opposed to continuity of the *entity*, which permits a finding of successor liability).[57] That is, in order to justify imposition of successor liability, the plaintiff must demonstrate "continuation of directors and management, shareholder interest and, in some cases, inadequate consideration," establishing "a substantial continuity of pretransaction and posttransaction business activities resulting from the use of the acquired assets. . . ."[58]

In analyzing the continuation of the entity, the Court of Appeals found in *Nissen* that it was inconsistent to impose strict liability upon a successor corporation, in that inherent in the doctrine of strict liability was the premise that a seller placing a defective product in the stream of commerce is somehow at fault, and should be liable to those injured by that product.[59] The *Nissen* Court reasoned that the corporate successor is not the seller and "bears no blame in bringing the product and the user together," and that it would be unfair to "require such a party to bear the cost of unassumed and uncontemplated products liability claims primarily because it is still in business and is perceived as a 'deep pocket.' "[60]

9. **Market Share Liability**

Maryland courts have not been presented with the theory of market share liability to determine its applicability. Several federal courts, however, have determined that Maryland courts would not recognize this theory, as it represents a "radical departure from the traditional concepts of product liability law."[61]

10. **Subsequent Remedial Measures**

Evidence of subsequent remedial measures is not admissible to prove culpable conduct. It may, however, be admitted for other purposes (consistent with FRE 407) such as proving ownership; control; feasibility of precautionary measures, if controverted; or impeachment.[62]

11. **Indeterminate Defect/Malfunction**

Proof of a defect "must arise above surmise, conjecture, or speculation," and a plaintiff may not base recovery solely on any presumption that might arise from the happening of an accident.[63] An inference of a defect may be drawn from the happening of an accident where circumstantial evidence tends to eliminate other causes, such as product misuse or alteration. Factors to be considered when determining whether a product defect may be inferred include: (1) expert testimony as to possible causes; (2) the occurrence of an accident a short time after the sale; (3) same accidents in similar products; (4) the elimination of other causes of the accident; and (5) the type of accident that does not happen without a defect.[64]

12. **Standards and Governmental Regulations**

Industry safety standards promulgated by organizations such as ANSI may be admitted in negligence and product liability cases.[65] In a negligence case, safety and industry standards may be admitted to show an accepted standard of care, the violation of which may be regarded as evidence of negligence.[66]

13. **Other Accidents**

In Maryland, like most jurisdictions, evidence of prior accidents or defects is admissible, not only to show notice, but as bearing on the dangerous nature or tendency of the product involved in the current accident.[67] If the court believes, in its discretion, that evidence of prior accidents will cause unfair surprise or confusion by raising collateral issues, the court can exclude the evidence.[68] Evidence of other accidents will be admissible only if there is proof of a similarity of time, place, and circumstance.[69]

14. **Spoliation of Evidence/Destruction of Product**

In considering the issue of spoliation of evidence, the jurisdictions are split regarding whether spoliation is a substantive or procedural issue. Maryland courts have systematically treated spoliation questions as procedural, and have relied upon the Maryland discovery rules or the courts' inherent powers in order to impose sanctions or remedies for spoliation of evidence.[70] Accordingly, when reviewing a trial court's imposition of spoliation sanctions, the appellate court is bound to the trial court's factual findings unless they are "clearly erroneous." When considering the actual imposition of the discovery sanctions by the trial court, the review is narrower still: abuse of discretion.[71]

Prior to sanctioning a party for spoliation, a Maryland court must find the existence of the following four elements: "(1) an act of destruction; (2) discoverability of the evidence; (3) an intent to destroy the evidence; and (4) occurrence of the act at a time after suit has been filed, or if before, at a time when the filing is fairly perceived as imminent."[72] Generally, a product has not been spoliated if the opposing party has an opportunity to test the product, and/or the testing of the product has been sufficiently documented to allow that party's expert to draw independent conclusions.[73]

There are many different sanctions or remedies available once spoliation has occurred, including dismissal of the action,[74] exclusion of expert witness testimony or an instruction to the trier of fact allowing an adverse inference to be drawn against the spoliator.[75] In choosing a remedy, the court must look to the degree of fault of the spoliator, the prejudice caused by the spoliation of the evidence, the "effectiveness of less drastic sanctions," and the "need for deferring the particular type of non-compliance."[76] To justify the harsh sanction of dismissal, a court must consider both the spoliator's conduct and the prejudice caused and be able to conclude either that the spoliator's conduct was so egregious as to amount to a forfeiture of his claim, or that the effect of the conduct was so prejudicial that it substantially denied the defendant the ability to defend against the claim.[77]

The "mere failure, without more, to produce evidence that naturally would have elucidated a fact at issue permits an inference that 'the party fears [to produce the evidence].'"[78] Thus, bad faith is not a requirement for the imposition of a jury instruction stating that the spoliated evidence was contrary to the spoliating party's interests.[79] However, if a party can prove bad faith, the courts will impose harsher sanctions, such as an inference that the spoliator was conscious of the weakness in his case, or actual dismissal of the case.[80]

Although a party may obtain an adverse inference instruction in the face of spoliation of evidence, that inference does not rise to the level of substantive proof.[81] "The presumption that arises from a party's spoliation of evidence cannot be used by [a party] as a surrogate for presenting evidence of . . . negligence in a prima facie case."[82]

15. **Purely Economic Losses**

There is no recovery in tort for purely economic losses resulting from a defective product, unless the defect causes a dangerous condition creating risk of death or personal injury.[83] Under Maryland's two-part approach for determining the degree of risk required to circumvent the economic loss rule and allow recovery in tort for economic loss suffered when a product fails to meet the contractual expectations of the purchaser, both the nature of the damage threatened and the probability of the damage occurring are examined to determine whether the two, viewed together, exhibit clear, serious, and unreasonable risk of death or personal injury.[84] For example, where the possible injury is extraordinarily severe, such as multiple deaths, the probability of injury is not required to be as high as if the injury threatened were less severe.[85] The economic loss rule exception even applies to cases involving unmanifested product defects where the plaintiff has alleged that the potential failure presents an unreasonable risk of substantial harm.[86] In the absence of such a dangerous condition, a purchaser is normally limited to contract causes of action, including breach of implied and express warranties.[87]

16. **Crashworthiness**

Maryland courts recognize strict liability claims based upon allegations of defective design in "crashworthiness" cases.[88] The "crashworthiness" or "second collision" doctrine concerns the extent of a manufacturer's liability for a design defect resulting in enhanced injuries, where the defect did not cause the accident or initial impact.[89] In Maryland, a manufacturer is liable for a defect in design which the manufacturer could have reasonably foreseen would cause or enhance injuries or impact, which is not patent or obvious to the user, and which in fact leads to or enhances the injuries in an accident.[90] The courts have made clear, however, that a manufacturer is under no duty to design a "crash-proof" product; rather the manufacturer must use reasonable care in the design of a product to avoid subjecting the user to an unreasonable risk of injury in an accident.[91] In determining "reasonableness," there must be a "balancing of the likelihood of harm, and the gravity of harm if it happens against the burden of the precautions which would be effective to avoid the harm."[92] Finally, there can be no recovery if the danger inherent in the particular design was obvious or patent to the user of the vehicle.[93]

D. DUTY TO WARN

Maryland recognizes actions for failure to warn under negligence, breach of implied warranty and strict liability theories.[94] A failure to warn action arises when a manufacturer or seller either does not supply a warning, or supplies a warning that is inadequate.[95] The manufacturer has a duty to warn of latent dangers inherent in its product for all uses that are reasonably foreseeable.[96] However, this duty requires only that the manufacturer's warning is reasonable under the circumstances, and does not require a warning detailing every possible mishap or injury that may occur.[97] In Maryland, generally, manufacturers do not have a duty of care to "indeterminate classes of people."[98]

1. Elements

An action brought in negligence or strict liability for a failure to warn is based primarily on the Restatement (Second) of Torts, Section 388.[99] Under either theory, the plaintiff must show: "(1) that the defendant owed a duty to warn; (2) that the defendant breached that duty; (3) that there was a direct causal connection between the defendant's failure and the alleged injuries; and (4) that the plaintiff was harmed."[100] In addition, the plaintiff must show that the defendant knew or should have known[101] of a defect or defective condition inherent in the product, and that distribution of the product involved unreasonable risk of causing injury or harm.[102] The plaintiff also has the burden of proving any state-of-the-art evidence.[103]

2. Latent/Patent Rule

While the manufacturer has a duty to warn of the latent dangers inherent in the reasonably foreseeable uses of a product, there is no duty to warn of a danger that should be obvious to a user.[104]

3. Learned Intermediary Doctrine

A licensed health care professional stands between a manufacturer or supplier of prescription drugs or medical devices and a patient receiving treatment. Therefore, a manufacturer or supplier meets the duty to warn by adequately warning the health care professional rather than the patient.[105]

4. Post-Sale Duty to Warn

The duty to warn continues after the sale of a product when a latent defect becomes known by the manufacturer or seller shortly after the product is put on the market.[106] When a manufacturer discovers a product defect after a sale, the post-sale duty to warn "requires reasonable efforts to inform users of the hazard once the manufacturer is or should be aware of the need for a warning."[107] In addition, the " 'seller is not entitled to automatic relief from its continuing duty to warn because it no longer manufactures a defective product.' "[108]

5. **Defenses**

   a. **Contributory Negligence and Assumption of the Risk**

   Contributory negligence and assumption of the risk remain defenses to a failure to warn claim grounded in negligence.[109] However, contributory negligence is not a defense to a strict liability failure to warn claim.[110]

   b. **Misuse**

   Misuse of the product is a defense to a failure to warn claim under both negligence and strict liability theories.[111] The same evidence used to support a defense of contributory negligence may be admissible to show product misuse in strict liability cases.[112]

   c. **Sophisticated User**

   In Maryland, when a manufacturer sells its product to a "sophisticated user," there is no duty to warn.[113]

6. **Heeding Presumption**

   Maryland recognizes a heeding presumption.[114] Under the "heeding presumption," where a warning is given, the manufacturer or seller may reasonably presume that it will be read and heeded; and a product bearing such a warning, which is safe for use if the warning is followed, will not be deemed to be in a defective condition nor will it be found unreasonably dangerous.[115] Of course, "warnings on products that are vague or otherwise difficult to understand will not bar a product liability claim when those warnings go unheeded."[116] Importantly, "Maryland imposes no duty to predict that a consumer will violate clear, easily understandable safety warnings."[117] In short, Maryland courts attach no significance to whether the product misuse was foreseeable in holding that a failure to heed an adequate safety warning will bar a claim.[118] Accordingly, if there was no practical way or reason for a manufacturer or seller to design a danger away, a user's failure to read or heed adequate instructions for safe use, *i.e.*, misuse, bars recovery.

E. **NEGLIGENCE**

In addition to pursuing a product liability claim based on strict liability, a product liability plaintiff in Maryland may also pursue a claim grounded upon negligence.[119]

1. **Elements**

   A cause of action in negligence requires evidence of each of the following: (1) a duty owed by the defendant to the plaintiff; (2) a breach of that duty by the defendant; (3) an injury to the plaintiff; and (4) that the injury was proximately caused by the defendant's breach.[120]

2. **Theories of Recovery**

Actions under theories of negligence in product liability suits may include causes of action for negligent failure to warn of dangerous attributes of the product;[121] negligent failure to provide adequate instructions for safe use of the product;[122] and negligent design or manufacture[123] that results in an unreasonably dangerous product or which enhances injuries.[124]

3. **Purely Economic Losses**

As discussed more fully in the section entitled "Strict Liability," see Section C.15 *supra*, Maryland courts do not permit recovery under a negligence theory for purely economic losses resulting from a defective product, unless the defect causes a dangerous condition creating risk of death or personal injury.[125]

4. **Defenses**

   a. **Contributory Negligence**

   In a negligence action, contributory negligence will operate as a complete bar to plaintiff's claim.[126]

   b. **Assumption of Risk**

   Maryland recognizes assumption of risk as an affirmative defense to a negligence claim.[127]

   c. **Product Misuse or Abuse**

   Product misuse or abuse is also recognized as a defense to a negligence claim.[128]

   d. **Product Alteration**

   A material alteration of the product once it has left the hands of the manufacturer is a defense to a negligence claim.[129]

   e. **Statutory Compliance**

   Compliance with a statute does not necessarily preclude a finding of negligence or product defectiveness when a reasonable person would take precautions beyond the statutorily required measure, but where no special circumstances require extra caution, a court may find that conformity with a statutory standard amounts to due care as a matter of law.[130]

F. **BREACH OF WARRANTY**

Actions based on a breach of implied or express warranties are governed by Sections 2-313 through 2-318 of the Commercial Law Article, Annotated Code of Maryland.[131] These Statutes are based primarily on the Uniform Commercial Code.

1. **Breach of Express Warranty**

   An action will arise where a good does not conform to an affirmation of fact or promise made by the seller to the buyer that relates to the goods and becomes a basis of the bargain.[132] "A claim that there is a warranty by omission is at odds with the UCC definition of an express warranty."[133] Breach of an express warranty occurs when "a product fails to exhibit the properties, characteristics, or qualities specifically attributed to it by its warrantor, and therefore fails to conform to the warrantor's representations."[134] The Maryland Court of Appeals has ruled that an express warranty may arise after the contract of sale is consummated.[135] Specifically, the court held that a pharmacy package insert stating that the drug should be taken with food or milk constituted an express warranty that the drug was safe for consumption with dairy products.[136]

2. **Breach of Implied Warranty of Merchantability**

   An action arises where it is shown that a product is not fit for the ordinary purposes for which such a good is used.[137] An "ordinary purpose" for which a good is used encompasses the concept of merchantability and those uses that are customarily made of the good in question.[138] To establish a breach of warranty of merchantability, the seller must be a merchant with respect to goods of the kind.[139]

3. **Breach of Implied Warranty of Fitness for a Particular Purpose**

   An action arises where the seller at the time of contracting has reason to know of a particular purpose for which the goods are required, the buyer relies upon the seller's skill and judgment to select suitable goods, and the goods ultimately are not suitable for this purpose.[140] A "particular purpose" is a specific use by the buyer that is peculiar to the nature of his/her business.[141] To establish breach of warranty for a particular purpose, there is no requirement that the seller be a merchant with respect to goods of that kind.[142]

4. **Sale or Lease**

   Express and implied warranties have been extended to the lease of goods pursuant to Sections 2A-210, 2A-212 and 2A-213 of the Commercial Law Article of the Annotated Code of Maryland.[143]

5. **Exclusion or Modification of Warranties**

   a. **Non-Consumer Goods**

   A warrantor, under certain circumstances, may exclude or modify both express and implied warranties, as well as limit the remedies for such a breach.[144]

i. Implied Warranties

To exclude or modify an implied warranty of merchantability, the language must mention merchantability and be conspicuous.[145] To exclude an implied warranty of fitness, the exclusion must be in writing and be conspicuous.[146] All implied warranties can be excluded by language that alerts the buyer to the exclusion and makes plain that there is no implied warranty.[147]

b. Consumer Goods

The right to disclaim or limit warranties on consumer goods has been limited in Maryland.[148] Consumer goods are goods that are used or bought for use primarily for personal, family or household purposes.[149]

i. Express Warranties

A manufacturer of consumer goods cannot limit or modify a consumer's remedies for breach of the manufacturer's express warranties unless reasonable and expeditious means of performing the warranty obligations are provided by the manufacturer.[150]

ii. Implied Warranties

"Any oral or written language used by a seller of consumer goods and services [that] attempts to exclude or modify any implied warranties of merchantability and [the] fitness for a particular purpose," or a consumer's remedies for breach of those warranties, is unenforceable.[151]

a. Motor Vehicle Exception

Implied warranties can be excluded or modified for motor vehicles that are over six years old, and have over 60,000 miles. The exclusion or modification must be conspicuous, in writing, mention "merchantability," and be acknowledged separately in writing by the buyer.[152]

6. Privity

a. Actions Involving Personal Injury

The requirement of privity has been virtually eliminated by statute in actions for damages for personal injury grounded on breach of an express or implied warranty.[153]

b. Actions Not Involving Personal Injury

Privity is required in an action for breach of express warranty in which only economic loss is claimed.[154] By statute, Maryland has abolished the common law requirement of privity for all claims of breach of implied warranty of merchantability.[155] In an action for breach of an implied warranty of fitness for a particular purpose, a plaintiff only needs to prove that the buyer had a particular purpose known to seller, privity itself is not a required element that must be shown independently.[156]

7. Elements

A plaintiff must show that a warranty existed, that the product did not conform to the warranty, and that the breach of warranty was the proximate cause of the occurrence.[157] To succeed on a breach of express warranty claim, it must be proven that the product was defective.[158] "The test of defectiveness in a breach of express warranty action is whether the product performs in accordance with the express warranty given."[159] Similarly, in an implied warranty claim, the existence of a defect at the time that the product left the manufacturer must be proven.[160] In an action based on an implied warranty of fitness for a particular purpose, if a special or unusual purpose is intended, it must also be shown that the "seller had reason to know, at the time of sale, that the purchaser had that particular use of the good in mind and that the purchaser was relying on the seller's expertise to select an appropriate product for that purpose."[161]

8. Defenses

A plaintiff's use or misuse of a product can operate as a defense to a breach of warranty claim.[162] Knowledge by the purchaser of the breach or defect, prior to the injury, will bar recovery.[163] In certain circumstances, the purchaser's use of the product can break the chain of proximate causation, and also bar recovery.[164] Though reluctant to engage in the "semantics" of labeling this conduct, Maryland courts have recognized that such acts can be characterized as either contributory negligence or assumption of risk.[165]

9. Breach of Warranty Compared to Other Claims

Regardless of whether the claim is titled breach of warranty, negligence, or strict liability, there are three essential elements to a viable claim. These "products litigation basics" are: (1) a defect; (2) attributed to the seller; and (3) injury caused by the defect.[166] In Maryland, these "product litigation basics" also extend to limited warranty claims under the Magnuson-Mosso Warranty Act and to the Maryland Automotive Warranty Enforcement Act.[167]

G. DAMAGES

Under Maryland law, "compensatory damages are not to be awarded in negligence or strict liability actions absent evidence that the plaintiff suffered a loss or detriment."[168]

1. Damages Cap

Maryland has imposed a statutory cap on noneconomic damages in tort claims involving personal injury, including survival and wrongful death actions.[169] When first enacted in 1986 (and applicable only to causes of action arising on or after July 1, 1986), the cap imposed a limit on recovery of noneconomic damages of $350,000. The Maryland Court of Appeals held that the initial cap did not apply to wrongful death actions.[170] The legislature then modified the statute in 1994 to include wrongful death actions and to increase the cap to $500,000 for causes of action arising after October 1, 1994. By further legislation, the cap increases by an additional $15,000 for each year thereafter in which a cause of action arises.[171] There are separate caps for survival and wrongful death claims,[172] but the award for noneconomic damages to multiple wrongful death claimants cannot exceed 150 percent of the currently applicable cap for a single wrongful death claimant.[173] There is no separate cap, however, for a loss of consortium claim.[174]

In order to avoid imposition of the cap, the plaintiff bears the burden of demonstrating that the injury occurred before the cap applied.[175]

2. Joint and Several Liability

Maryland has adopted in its entirety the Uniform Contribution Among Tortfeasors Act.[176] Under Maryland law, defendants may be held jointly and severally liable, with no apportionment of damages based on degrees of negligence between or among those defendants.[177]

3. Punitive Damages

To be held liable for punitive damages, a defendant must be shown by clear and convincing evidence to have acted with "actual malice," which is defined as "evil motive, intent to injure, or fraud" in strict liability cases.[178] "Negligence alone, no matter how gross, wanton or outrageous, will not satisfy [the] standard [of actual malice]."[179] A two-part test to determine whether punitive damages should be awarded has evolved: the plaintiff must show actual knowledge of the defect and deliberate disregard of the consequences—both as of the time the product left the defendant's possession or control.[180] Among the factors the court will address in assessing excessiveness are: (1) "the degree of heinousness" of the defendant's conduct; (2) the need for deterrence based on the continuing nature of the defendant's malicious conduct; (3) a comparison of the punitive damages award (the "civil fine") with the maximum fine that could be imposed for comparable criminal conduct; (4) a comparison of the award with other final punitive damages awards in the jurisdiction; and (5) whether the punitive damages award bears a reasonable relationship to the compensatory damages awarded in the case.[181]

H. PRE- AND POST-JUDGMENT INTEREST

The general purpose of pre-judgment interest to "best afford full and fair compensation . . . to the injured party . . ." so as to place the injured party in the same position he or she would have occupied had the defaulting party performed as he or she was supposed to perform.[182]

As a general matter, the question of pre-judgment interest is left to the discretion of the fact finder, unless the contract is so clear as to allow calculation of pre-judgment as a matter of right.[183] "Pre-judgment interest is allowable as a matter of right when the obligation to pay and the amount due has become certain, definite, and liquidated by a specific date prior to judgment. . . ."[184] In cases involving personal injuries or other unliquidated damage, however, the courts have held that where recovery is for "intangible elements of damage" such as bodily harm, emotional distress, or similar items, the claim "is unliquidated and not reasonably ascertainable" until the amount of the award is fixed by the jury. Therefore, under such circumstances, pre-judgment interest is not recoverable.[185] The only exception to this rule occurs when the tortious conduct involves conversion of goods that have a readily ascertainable value.[186]

Post-judgment interest begins to run from the date judgment is entered by the court,[187] and is calculated at a rate of 10 percent per year.[188]

I. EMPLOYER IMMUNITY FROM SUIT

The Maryland Workers' Compensation Act provides the exclusive means for an employee to obtain compensation from an employer for injuries caused by that employer's alleged negligence.[189] This immunity accorded to employers extends to third parties absent contractual indemnity,[190] thus preventing manufacturers, for example, from impleading an employer in a suit brought against the manufacturer for an injury on the job.[191]

J. SEALED CONTAINER

By statute, nonmanufacturer sellers cannot be held liable under any theory for the defective design or manufacture of a product if: (1) the product was acquired and sold in a sealed container; (2) the seller had no knowledge of the defect; (3) in the exercise of reasonable care, the seller could not have discovered the defect; and (4) the seller did not design, manufacture, or alter the product in any way.[192] A seller or nonmanufacturer who is only a conduit ordinarily has no liability unless it had "reason to know" of the defect or danger inherent in the use of the product.[193] The defense is not available if: (1) the manufacturer is not subject to service of process; (2) the manufacturer is judicially insolvent; (3) the claimant would be unable to enforce a judgment against the manufacturer; (4) the claimant cannot identify the manufacturer; (5) the manufacturer is immune from suit; or (6) the seller made express warranties.[194]

K. OTHER ISSUES

1. Contributory/Comparative Negligence

Maryland has always adhered to the doctrine of contributory negligence, and the Maryland Court of Appeals has specifically declined to adopt the doctrine of comparative negligence.[195] Although outcry from the plaintiff's bar has threatened this well-established doctrine, as of this writing the legislature has similarly declined to adopt any form of comparative negligence by statute.

2. **Developments in Asbestos Cases**

One significant development is the application of the cap on noneconomic damages imposed by the legislature for actions "arising after" July 1, 1986. In one instance, the court held that in a strict liability asbestos case, the cause of action would not arise until a plaintiff suffered "functional impairment."[196] The Maryland Court of Appeals has held that "functional impairment" in the context of asbestos-related illness did not occur until the plaintiff began experiencing shortness of breath that curtailed his normal activities; because in that instance the functional impairment began in 1990, the court held that the cap on noneconomic damages applied to limit the plaintiff's claim.[197] The Maryland Court of Appeals decided two cases significantly affecting the applicability of the cap to asbestos cases. The Court of Appeals held that a cause of action arises in the context of asbestos cases when the plaintiff inhales a fiber that causes cellular changes leading to disease.[198] Thus, if the inhalation that is shown to cause cellular disease occurred before 1986, the cap does not apply.

In the context of plaintiff's burden of proving exposure, the Court of Special Appeals has overturned one of two multimillion dollar awards against Ford Motor Co., which at trial was found responsible for asbestos exposure from brake linings for the first time. The court held that the "evidence simply was too thin" to prove that the plaintiff, a mechanic, regularly and often worked where Ford brake and clutch products were used.[199] Subsequently, the Court of Appeals held that "substantial factor" causation applies to bystander asbestos exposure claims.[200]

Another recent development concerns the application of Maryland's wrongful death statute in the context of an asbestos-related occupational disease. Maryland's intermediate appellate court has held that the date that a cause of action accrues for purposes of determining the statute of limitations for a survival claim is not the same as the date that a cause of action accrues for the beneficiaries in a wrongful death claim.[201] The court held that, even though the decedent was on inquiry notice when he was diagnosed with mesothelioma and that he had been exposed to asbestos, the wrongful death action may not accrue until the beneficiaries acquire such knowledge.[202] The court also held that the knowledge of one beneficiary may not be imputed to another beneficiary.[203]

In *Dixon, et al. v. Ford Motor Co.*, the Maryland Court of Appeals recently reversed the Maryland Court of Special Appeals decision that had held, where multiple causal factors are at issue, a plaintiff in an asbestos case must prove each and every substantial contributing cause with quantitative epidemiological evidence such that the jury, not the expert, can determine whether a given exposure was a substantial cause.[204] Specifically, the Court of Appeals held, in proving substantial contributing causation, an expert may opine that each and "every exposure to asbestos is a substantial contributing cause."[205] Although the Court of Appeals raised questions as to whether the "every exposure to asbestos is a substantial contributing factor" testimony would be viable if the evidence did not establish the frequency, regularity, and proximity of the exposure, the court found that, in this case, such evidence had been presented.[206]

In another case argued the same day, the Maryland Court of Appeals held in a case involving exposure to a "bystander of a bystander," that there is no duty to warn when the exposure occurs before 1972 when OSHA published regulations regarding bringing asbestos dust into the home.[207]

3. Wrongful Death Claims

In 1997, Maryland made substantial changes in the area of wrongful death remedies. Under current law, beneficiaries can recover noneconomic damages for the wrongful death of an adult child or the parent of an adult child, regardless of the age, marital status, or dependency of the adult child.[208] The changes also establish two classes of beneficiaries in wrongful death actions: "primary" beneficiaries (spouse, parent, or child of the decedent) and "secondary" beneficiaries (any other person related to the decedent by blood or marriage). Under the new statute, if the decedent has no primary beneficiaries, secondary beneficiaries now are entitled to recover noneconomic damages for the wrongful death of the decedent if they can demonstrate that they were "substantially" dependent on the decedent.[209]

4. Handgun-related Litigation

In 1985, the Maryland Court of Appeals held that it was proper to impose strict liability on the manufacturer of a "Saturday Night Special" that was used during a robbery and caused injury to the plaintiff.[210] The court reasoned that the "Saturday Night Special" as a product line was "particularly problematic for law enforcement officials," and was so unreliable and unsafe—and used almost solely in the course of criminal activity—as to present no legitimate reason for its sale.[211] The court also applied this holding to anyone in the marketing chain including the retailer.[212]

The Court of Appeals has held that a gun retailer does not owe a duty to third persons to exercise reasonable care in the *display and sale* of handguns in order to prevent the theft and illegal use of the weapons by others against third parties.[213] The court premised its holding largely on the rationale that a retailer could not foresee the actions of third parties' criminal conduct, and to impose such an expectation was too big a burden on retailers.[214] The court was careful, however, to narrow its holding to the facts of the *Valentine* case.[215] Subsequently, the Court of

Appeals affirmed the trial court's granting of summary judgment in favor of a gun manufacturer where it was alleged the gun was defective because it did not have a trigger lock.[216] Significantly, the Court of Appeals held that Maryland's consumer expectation test applied and reasoned that, under that test, the gun functioned as intended and there could be no defect.[217]

Daniel R. Lanier
Michael J. Halaiko
Christopher R. Daily
Leianne S. McEvoy
Miles & Stockbridge
100 Light Street
Baltimore, Maryland 21202-1487
(410) 385-3651/(Fax) (410) 385-3700

ENDNOTES - MARYLAND

1. *Owens-Illinois v. Zenobia*, 325 Md. 420, 461, 601 A.2d 633, 653 (1992).

2. *Mohammad v. Toyota Motor Sales, U.S.A., Inc.*, 179 Md. App. 693, 706, 947 A.2d 598, 605-06 (2008); *Loh v. Safeway Stores, Inc.*, 47 Md. App. 110, 121, 422 A.2d 16, 23 (1980).

3. Md. Code Ann., Cts. & Jud. Proc. § 5-101 (2013 Repl. Vol.).

4. Md. Code Ann., Cts. & Jud. Proc. § 5-101 (2013 Repl. Vol.); *Phipps v. Gen. Motors Corp.*, 278 Md. 337, 350, 363 A.2d 955, 962 (1976).

5. *Poffenberger v. Risser*, 290 Md. 631, 634-35, 431 A.2d 677, 679 (1981).

6. *Pennwalt Corp. v. Nasios*, 314 Md. 433, 455-56, 550 A.2d 1155, 1167 (1988); *see also Helinski v. Appleton Papers*, 952 F. Supp. 266 (D. Md. 1997), *aff'd*, 139 F.3d 891 (4th Cir. 1998) (plaintiff's product liability action against manufacturer of carbonless copy paper (CCP) accrued when physicians first suggested to plaintiff that CCP could be causing some of her symptoms; the mere fact that plaintiff had earlier attempted to determine the genesis of her health problems, and even suspected CCP might be a factor, was not enough to commence limitations period).

7. Md. Code Ann., Cts. & Jud. Proc. § 5-115(b) (2013 Repl. Vol.).

8. Md. Code Ann., Cts. & Jud. Proc. § 5-115(c) (2013 Repl. Vol.).

9. *Globe Am. Cas. v. Chung*, 76 Md. App. 524, 526-27, 547 A.2d 654, 655 (1988), *vacated on other grounds*, 322 Md. 713, 589 A.2d 956 (1991).

10. Md. Code Ann., Cts. & Jud. Proc. § 3-904(g) (2013 Repl. Vol.).

11. Md. Code Ann., Cts. & Jud. Proc. § 3-904(g) (2013 Repl. Vol.).

12. *See Georgia-Pacific Corp. v. Benjamin*, 394 Md. 59, 94-96, 904 A.2d 511, 532-33 (2006).

13. Md. Code Ann., Com. Law I § 2-725 (2005 Repl. Vol.).

14. Md. Code Ann., Com. Law I § 2-725 (2005 Repl. Vol.).

15. *Phipps*, 278 Md. at 353, 363 A.2d at 963; *see also Binakonsky v. Ford Motor Co.*, 133 F.3d 281, 285 (4th Cir. 1998); *Hartford Cas. Ins. Co. v. Marpac Corp.*, 193 F. Supp. 2d 859, 862 (D. Md. 2002); *Shreve v. Sears, Roebuck & Co.*, 166 F. Supp.

2d 378, 406-07 (D. Md. 2001); *Ford Motor Co. v. Gen. Accident Ins. Co.*, 365 Md. 321, 334 n.13, 779 A.2d 362, 370 n.13 (2001).

16. *See Suburban Hosp., Inc. v. Kirson*, 128 Md. App. 533, 567, 739 A.2d 875, 893 (1999), *aff'd in part, rev. in part, vacated in part*, 362 Md. 140, 763 A.2d 185 (2000).

17. *Phipps*, 278 Md. at 344, 363 A.2d at 958; *Nissan Motor Co. Ltd. v. Nave*, 129 Md. App. 90, 118, 740 A.2d 102, 117 (1999); *see also Hartford Cas. Ins. Co.*, 193 F. Supp. 2d at 862; *Klein v. Sears, Roebuck & Co.*, 92 Md. App. 477, 484-85, 608 A.2d 1276, 1280 (1992).

18. *Lahocki v. Contee Sand & Gravel Co.*, 41 Md. App. 579, 583, 398 A.2d 490, 494 (1979), *rev'd on other grounds sub nom., Gen. Motors Corp. v. Lahocki*, 286 Md. 714, 410 A.2d 1039 (1980).

19. *Zenobia*, 325 Md. at 437, 601 A.2d at 641; *Shreve*, 166 F. Supp. 2d at 413-14.

20. *Singleton v. Int'l Harvester Co.*, 685 F.2d 112, 114-15 (4th Cir. 1981) (citing *Phipps*, 278 Md. at 344, 363 A.2d at 959); *see also Hood v. Ryobi N. Am., Inc.*, 17 F. Supp. 2d 448, 450 (D. Md. 1998), *aff'd*, 181 F.3d 608 (4th Cir. 1999).

21. *Klein*, 92 Md. App. at 485, 608 A.2d at 1280.

22. *Klein*, 92 Md. App. at 485, 608 A.2d at 1280; *Nave*, 129 Md. App. at 118, 740 A.2d at 117.

23. *Phipps*, 278 Md. at 344, 363 A.2d at 959.

24. *Phipps*, 278 Md. at 344, 363 A.2d at 959 (citing Restatement (Second) of Torts, § 402A, cmt. i).

25. *Virgil v. Kash N' Karry Serv. Corp.*, 61 Md. App. 23, 31, 484 A.2d 652, 656 (1984) (citing *Heaton v. Ford Motor Co.*, 248 Or. 467, 435 P.2d 806 (1967)); *see also Shreve*, 166 F. Supp. 2d at 407.

26. *Halliday v. Sturm, Ruger & Co.*, 368 Md. 186, 193-209, 792 A.2d 1145, 1149-59 (2002); *see Kelley v. R. G. Indus., Inc.*, 304 Md. 124, 138, 497 A.2d 1143, 1149 (1985); *but see Lloyd v. Gen. Motors Corp.*, 2011 WL 2433091 (D. Md. June 16, 2011) (noting the consumer expectation test should be applied unless the product malfunctions in handgun cases).

27. In several cases following *Kelley*, the Court of Special Appeals held that the risk/utility test also applies where the alleged defect is a failure to include a safety device. *See C&K Lord, Inc. v. Carter*, 74 Md. App. 68, 86, 536 A.2d 699, 707-08 (1988); *Ziegler v. Kawasaki Heavy Indus., Ltd.*, 74 Md. App. 613, 622-23, 539 A.2d 701, 706 (1988); *see also Klein*, 92 Md. App. at 486, 608 A.2d at 1280-81; *Nicholson v. Yamaha Motor Co.*, 80 Md. App. 695, 717-19, 566 A.2d

135, 146-47 (1989); *Valk Mfg. Co. v. Rangaswamy*, 74 Md. App. 304, 317, 537 A.2d 622, 628 (1988) (extending risk/utility test to product the design flaw of which was not the absence of a safety device but which had an "indirect . . . influence on safety . . . [by] making it less likely that the safety feature would be utilized"), *rev'd on other grounds sub nom. Montgomery County v. Valk Mfg. Co.*, 317 Md. 185, 562 A.2d 1246 (1989). However, the Court of Appeals has since cast doubt on these opinions: "In a string of . . . cases . . . the Court of Special Appeals continued to apply the risk/utility test in design defect cases involving the lack of a safety device, sometimes, unfortunately, by misconstruing, side-stepping, or ignoring what we said in *Kelley*. The holdings in *Kelley*, that the risk/utility test does not apply to a design defect unless the product malfunctions in some way and that a handgun does not malfunction when it shoots a bullet into a person in whose direction it is fired, remain the law in Maryland." *Halliday*, 368 Md. at 199-200, 792 A.2d at 1153-54 (citations omitted).

28. *Phipps*, 278 Md. at 346 n.4, 363 A.2d at 959 n.4; *Troja v. Black & Decker Mfg. Co.*, 62 Md. App. 101, 108, 488 A.2d 516, 519 (both citing Wade, *On the Nature of Strict Tort Liability for Products*, 44 Miss. L.J. 825, 837-38 (1973)).

29. *Jensen v. Am. Motors Corp.*, 50 Md. App. 226, 232, 437 A.2d 242, 245 (1981); *Int'l Motors, Inc. v. Ford Motor Co.*, 133 Md. App. 269, 275 n.7, 754 A.2d 1115, 1118 n.7 (2000), *rev'd on other grounds sub nom. Ford Motor Co. v. Gen. Accident Ins. Co.*, 365 Md. 321, 779 A.2d 362 (2001); *see also Maryland Cas. Co. v. Therm-O-Disc, Inc.*, 137 F.3d 780, 786 (4th Cir. 1998).

30. *Jensen*, 50 Md. App. at 232, 437 A.2d at 245.

31. *Virgil*, 61 Md. App. at 31, 484 A.2d at 656 (holding that it is not necessary to provide expert testimony to establish that a thermos bottle that explodes or implodes when liquids are poured into it is defective).

32. *Virgil*, 61 Md. App. at 31, 484 A.2d at 656.

33. *Yonce v. SmithKline Beecham Clinical Labs., Inc.*, 111 Md. App. 124, 137, 680 A.2d. 569, 575 (1996).

34. *See Peterson v. Underwood*, 258 Md. 9, 16, 264 A.2d. 851, 855 (1970); *Bartholomee v. Casey*, 103 Md. App. 34, 56-57, 651 A.2d. 908, 918-19 (1994), *cert. denied*, 338 Md. 557, 659 A.2d. 1293 (1995).

35. *See Yonce*, 111 Md. App. at 136, 680 A.2d. at 575; *see also Lohrmann v. Pittsburgh Corning Corp.*, 782 F.2d 1156, 1162 (4th Cir. 1986) (citing to *Robin Express Transfer, Inc. v. Canton R.R.*, 26 Md. App. 321, 338 A.2d 335, 343 (1975)).

36. *See Stone v. Chicago Title Ins. Co.*, 330 Md. 329, 337, 624 A.2d. 496, 500 (1993); *Yonce*, 111 Md. App. at 137-39, 680 A.2d. at 575-76.

37. *Zenobia*, 325 Md. at 435 n.7, 601 A.2d at 640 n.7; *Ellsworth v. Sherne Lingerie, Inc.*, 303 Md. 581, 597-98, 495 A.2d 348, 356 (1985).

38. *Crews v. Hollenbach*, 126 Md. App. 609, 628, 730 A.2d 742, 753 (1999), *aff'd*, 358 Md. 627, 751 A.2d 481 (2000); *Ellsworth*, 303 Md. at 597-98, 495 A.2d at 356 (quoting *Sheehan v. Anthony Pools*, 50 Md. App. 614, 626 n.11, 440 A.2d 1085, 1092 n.11 (1982), *aff'd*, 295 Md. 285, 455 A.2d 434 (1983)).

39. *Baltimore Gas & Elec. Co. v. Flippo*, 348 Md. 680, 705-06, 705 A.2d 1144, 1156 (1998).

40. *Baltimore Gas & Elec. Co.*, 348 Md. at 705-06, 705 A.2d at 1156; *see also ADM P'ship v. Martin*, 348 Md. 84, 92-93, 702 A.2d 730, 734-35 (1997); *Crews*, 126 Md. App. at 628, 730 A.2d at 753.

41. *Ellsworth*, 303 Md. at 596-97, 495 A.2d at 355-56.

42. *See Simpson v. Standard Container Co.*, 72 Md. App. 199, 206, 527 A.2d 1337, 1341 (1987).

43. *Simpson*, 72 Md. App. at 206-07, 527 A.2d at 1341.

44. *Lightolier v. Hoon*, 387 Md. 539, 556, 876 A.2d 100, 110 (2005). In *Lightolier*, a lighting manufacturer sold lights for installation into the ceiling of a house, and the lights contained an adequate warning advising not to install insulation within three inches of the lights. The insulation company installed the insulation within three inches of the light fixtures in contravention of the warnings. A fire ensued. The homeowners filed a lawsuit against the insulation company and the lighting manufacturer. The lighting manufacturer obtained summary judgment after the trial court found that the failure to follow the warnings was the proximate cause of the accident. Maryland's Court of Appeals upheld the summary judgment and reaffirmed the heeding presumption in Maryland. Notably, however, the court indicated that its decision was based, in part, on the fact that there was no evidence that there was a concurrent cause of the fire due to the defective design or manufacture of the light fixture. Thus, the Court of Appeals has left open the possible scenario in which a manufacturer could be held into a case under circumstances where an adequate warning that would have prevented the accident was not heeded, but the plaintiff's expert witness offers an alternative theory that, despite the warnings, the product was defectively designed and that the defect concurrently caused the alleged damage.

45. *Lightolier*, 387 Md. at 556-60, 876 A.2d at 110-12.

46. *Kennedy v. Mobay Corp.*, 84 Md. App. 397, 413, 579 A.2d 1191, 1199 (1990), *aff'd*, 325 Md. 385, 601 A.2d 123 (1992); *see also O'Neal v. Celanese Corp.*, 10 F.3d 249, 251-52 (4th Cir. 1993).

47. *Ragin v. Porter Hayden Co.*, 133 Md. App. 116, 122 n.3, 754 A.2d 503, 506 n.3, *cert. denied*, 361 Md. 232, 760 A.2d 1107 (2000); *Troja*, 62 Md. App. at 109, 488 A.2d at 519; *Ziegler*, 74 Md. App. at 625, 539 A.2d at 707.

48. *ACandS, Inc. v. Asner*, 344 Md. 155, 164, 686 A.2d 250, 254 (1996).

49. *Ellsworth*, 303 Md. at 591, 495 A.2d at 353; *Int'l Motors*, 133 Md. App. at 277-78, 754 A.2d at 1119, *rev'd on other grounds sum nom. Ford Motor Co. v. General Acc. Ins. Co.*, 365 Md. 321, 779 A.2d 362 (2001); *see Holman v. Mark Indus., Inc.*, 610 F. Supp. 1195, 1201-02 (D. Md. 1985), *aff'd*, 796 F.2d 473 (4th Cir. 1986).

50. *See Bona v. Graefe*, 264 Md. 69, 77-78, 285 A.2d 607, 611 (1972) (holding that Section 402A is not applicable to a lessor; a lessee's only right of action against a lessor is under Section 408).

51. Md. Code Ann., Com. Law §§ 2A-210, 212-13 (2008).

52. *See Bernstein v. Reforzo*, 37 Md. App. 724, 729-31, 379 A.2d 181, 184-86 (1977).

53. *Bernstein*, 37 Md. App. at 729-31, 379 A.2d at 184-86 (citing *Watts D. Bacon & Van Buskirk Glass Co.*, 18 Ill. 2d 226, 163 N.E.2d 425 (1959); *La Plant v. E.I. Du Pont de Nemours & Co.*, 346 S.W.2d 231 (Mo. App. 1961); *General Bronze Corp. v. Kostopulos*, 203 Va. 66, 122 S.E.2d 548 (1961)). In *Bernstein*, the court held that a pane of glass through which a child had fallen was not inherently dangerous, and it explained that there was no evidence that there was any "inherent danger in the use of plate glass such that special precautions . . . must be taken in order to prevent injury." 37 Md. App. at 730-31, 379 A.2d at 185.

54. *See Lundgren v. Ferno-Washington Co.*, 80 Md. App. 522, 565 A.2d 335 (1989). The court explained that if a product creates a risk that is inherently unreasonable, the plaintiff must only show that the seller is in the business of selling the product, and that it was expected and did reach the user without substantial change in the condition in which it was sold. If the court does not find so, the burden is then on the plaintiff to persuade the jury that the product is unreasonably dangerous as well. *See Lundgren*, 80 Md. App. at 528, 565 A.2d at 338.

55. *Lundgren*, 80 Md. App. at 528, 565 A.2d at 338.

56. *Nissen Corp. v. Miller*, 323 Md. 613, 617, 594 A.2d 564, 565-66 (1991) (quoting 1 American Law of Products Liability 3d § 7:1, at 10-12 (Travers, rev. ed. 1990)).

57. *Nissen*, 323 Md. at 620, 594 A.2d at 567 (quoting 1 L. Frumer & M. Friedman, Products Liability § 2.06[2][c] at 2-182-2-183 (1989)).

58. *Nissen Corp.*, 323 Md. at 620, 594 A.2d at 567 (quoting 1 L. Frumer & M. Friedman, Products Liability § 2.06[2][c] at 2-182-2-183 (1989)); *see also Academy of IRM v. LVI Envtl. Servs., Inc.*, 344 Md. 434, 451-52, 687 A.2d 669, 677-78 (1997).

59. *Nissen*, 323 Md. at 623-24, 594 A.2d at 568-69.

60. *Nissen*, 323 Md. at 624, 594 A.2d at 569.

61. *Tidler v. Eli Lilly & Co.*, 95 F.R.D. 332, 334 (D. D.C. 1982); *see also McClelland v. Goodyear Tire & Rubber Co.*, 735 F. Supp. 172, 174 (D. Md. 1990).

62. *Troja*, 62 Md. App. at 113-14, 488 A.2d at 522. For example, if feasibility is not being denied, then evidence of subsequent remedial measures is inadmissible. *Maryland v. Thurston*, 128 Md. App. 656, 667-68, 739 A.2d 940, 946-47 (1999).

63. *Int'l Motors, Inc. v. Ford Motor Co.*, 133 Md. App. 269, 275 n.7, 754 A.2d 1115, 1118 n.7 (2000), *rev'd on other grounds, Ford Motor Co. v. Gen. Accident Ins. Co.*, 365 Md. 321, 779 A.2d 362 (2001); *Jensen v. Am. Motors Corp.*, 50 Md. App. 226, 232, 437 A.2d 242, 245 (1981); *see also Md. Cas. Co. v. Therm-O-Disc, Inc.*, 137 F.3d 780, 786 (4th Cir. 1998), *cert. denied, Thermo-O-Disk, Inc. v. Md. Cas. Co.*, 525 U.S. 827, 119 S. Ct. 74 (1998).

64. *Ford Motor Co. v. Gen. Accident Ins. Co.*, 365 Md. 321, 338 n.16, 779 A.2d 362, 371 n.16 (2001); *Harrison v. Bill Cairns Pontiac of Marlow Heights, Inc.*, 77 Md. App. 41, 51, 549 A.2d 385, 390 (1988); *Gross v. Daimler Chrysler Corp.*, 2003 U.S. Dist. LEXIS 24673 (D. Md. Sept. 29, 2003) (unpublished); *Riley v. De'Longhi Corp.*, 238 F.3d 414, 417 (4th Cir. 1999) (unpublished decision); *Little v. United States*, 181 F.3d 89 (4th Cir. 1999) (unpublished decision).

65. *See Kent Village Assocs. Joint Venture v. Smith*, 104 Md. App. 507, 657 A.2d 330 (1995); *see also Kennedy v. Mobay Corp.*, 84 Md. App. 397, 579 A.2d 1191 (1990), *aff'd*, 325 Md. 385, 601 A.2d 123 (1992); *Troja v. Black & Decker Mfg. Co.*, 62 Md. App. 101, 488 A.2d 516, *cert. denied*, 303 Md. 471, 494 A.2d 939 (1985).

66. *See CSX Transp., Inc. v. Pitts*, 430 Md. 431, 463, 61 A.3d 767, 786 (2013); *Kent Village*, 104 Md. App. at 522, 657 A.2d at 337.

67. *See Locke, Inc. v. Sonnenleiter*, 208 Md. 443, 447-48, 451, 118 A.2d 509, 511-13 (1955); *Morris v. Wilson*, 74 Md. App. 663, 675, 539 A.2d 1151, 1157 (1988), *aff'd*, 317 Md. 284, 563 A.2d 392 (1989); *see also CSX Transp., Inc. v. Miller*, 159 Md. App. 123, 858 A.2d 1025 (2003); *Southern Mgmt. Corp. v. Mariner*, 144 Md. App. 188, 797 A.2d 110 (2002); *Halliday v. Sturm, Ruger & Co.*, 138 Md. App. 136, 770 A.2d 1072 (2001), *aff'd*, 368 Md. 186, 792 A.2d 1145 (2002).

68. *See Locke*, 208 Md. at 447-48, 451, 118 A.2d at 511-13; *CSX Transp.*, 159 Md. App. 123, 858 A.2d 1025; *Southern Mgmt.*, 144 Md. App. at 196, 797 A.2d at

116; *Halliday v. Sturm, Ruger & Co.*, 138 Md. App. at 154-55, 770 A.2d at 1083 (2001), *aff'd*, 368 Md. 186, 792 A.2d 1145 (2002).

69. *Locke*, 208 Md. at 447-48, 451, 118 A.2d at 511-13; *CSX Transp.*, 159 Md. App. at 858 A.2d at 1025; *Southern Mgmt.*, 144 Md. App. at 196, 797 A.2d at 116; *Halliday v. Sturm, Ruger & Co.*, 138 Md. App. at 154-55, 770 A.2d at 1083 (2001), *aff'd*, 368 Md. 186, 792 A.2d 1145 (2002).

70. *Klupt v. Krongard*, 126 Md. App. 179, 198-202, 728 A.2d 727, 736-38 (1999), *cert. denied*, 355 Md. 612, 735 A.2d 1107 (1999); *see also Hodge v. Wal-Mart Stores, Inc.*, 360 F.3d 446, 450 (4th Cir. 2004), *aff'd*, 360 F.3d 446 (4th Cir. 2004); *Vodusek v. Bayliner Marine Corp.*, 71 F.3d 148, 156 (4th Cir. 1995); *White v. Office of the Public Defender for the State of Md.*, 170 F.R.D. 138, 147 (D. Md. 1997).

71. *Klupt*, 126 Md. App. at 192-94, 728 A.2d 727, 733-34; *see also Bryte v. American Household, Inc.*, 2005 WL 1805603 *703 (4th Cir. Nov. 21, 2005).

72. *Klupt*, 126 Md. App. at 199, 728 A.2d 727, 737 (citing *White*, 170 F.R.D. at 147-48); *see also Hollingsworth & Vose Co. v. Connor*, 136 Md. App. 91, 137, 764 A.2d 318, 343 (2000).

73. *See Tucker v. Ohtsu Tire & Rubber Co., Ltd.*, 49 F. Supp.2d 456, 463-64 (D. Md. 1999).

74. *See Klupt*, 126 Md. App. at 211, 728 A.2d 727, 743 (dismissing action); *see also Silvestri v. Gen. Motors Corp.*, 271 F.3d 583, 595 (4th Cir. 2001) (affirming dismissal of action); *Cole v. Keller Indus., Inc.*, 132 F.3d 1044, 1048 (4th Cir. 1998) (applying Virginia law) (finding error for lower court to dismiss case where plaintiff, without bad faith, destroyed product in question); *cf. Ellicott Mach. Corp. Int'l v. Jesco Constr. Corp.*, 199 F. Supp. 2d 290, 296 (D. Md. 2002) (declining to grant summary judgment where no bad faith existed).

75. *Anderson v. Litzenberg*, 115 Md. App. 549, 561-62, 694 A.2d 150, 156 (1997) (adverse presumption may arise even if no fraudulent intent exists); *see also Vodusek*, 71 F.3d at 156 (holding that a showing of bad faith is not necessary to justify a trial court's instruction that it could draw an adverse inference from a party's destruction of evidence); *White*, 170 F.R.D. at 153 (dismissal of suit). *But see Hodge*, 360 F.3d at 455 (affirming lower court's decision not to permit adverse inference where retailer negligently lost witnesses' contact information, which led to destruction of evidence); *Potomac Elec. Power Co. v. Elec. Motor Supply, Inc.*, 192 F.R.D. 511, 515-16 (D. Md. 2000) (expert testimony not excluded), *rev'd on other grounds, Potomac Elec. Power Co. v. Elec. Motor Supply, Inc.*, 262 F.3d 260 (4th Cir. 2001); *Hollingsworth*, 136 Md. App. at 140, 764 A.2d 318, 344 (denying motion to dismiss because court found no deliberate spoliation).

76. *See White*, 170 F.R.D. at 152.

77. *Silvestri*, 271 F.3d at 593-94 (affirming dismissal where plaintiff's attorney allowed destruction of vehicle when he knew vehicle was central piece of evidence and had been reminded that it should be preserved or that the defendant should be notified).

78. *Vodusek*, 71 F.3d at 156 (quoting 2 Wigmore on Evidence), § 285, at 192 (Chadbourn rev. 1979).

79. *Vodusek*, 71 F.3d at 156 (quoting 2 Wigmore on Evidence), § 285, at 192; *Hartford Ins. Co. v. Am. Automatic Sprinkler Sys., Inc.*, 23 F. Supp. 2d 623, 627 (D. Md. 1998), *aff'd*, 201 F.3d 538 (4th Cir. 2000); *see also Potomac Elec. Power Co.*, 192 F.R.D. at 514-15.

80. *See Klupt*, 126 Md. App. at 202, 728 A.2d 727, 738; *Anderson*, 115 Md. App. at 561, 694 A.2d 150, 156; *see also White*, 170 F.R.D. at 152; *but see Elliott Mach. Corp.*, 199 F. Supp. 2d at 294 (finding it inappropriate to grant summary judgment where no bad faith or intentional destruction had occurred).

81. *Hartford Ins. Co.*, 23 F. Supp. 2d at 627; *DiLeo v. Nugent*, 88 Md. App. 59, 71, 592 A.2d 1126, 1132 (1991) (citing *Miller v. Montgomery Co.*, 64 Md. App. 202, 214, 494 A.2d 761, 761 (1985)).

82. *Anderson*, 115 Md. App. at 563, 694 A.2d 150, 157.

83. *Morris v. Osmose Wood Preserving*, 340 Md. 519, 535-36, 667 A.2d 624, 632-33 (1995) (homeowners failed to establish that defects in plywood used in construction of roofs in their homes had created serious and unreasonable risk of death or personal injury, and were barred from recovery in tort for economic loss rule, where there was no allegation that any injury had ever occurred since roofs were installed or that any roofs had collapsed because of weather conditions or alleged degradation of wood, even though homeowners contended that degradation caused risk of injury to occupants and persons with cause to be on the roof); *A. J. Decoster Co. v. Westinghouse Elec. Corp.*, 333 Md. 245, 250, 634 A.2d 1330, 1332 (1994); *Council of Co-Owners v. Whiting-Turner*, 308 Md. 18, 33-42, 517 A.2d 336, 344-48 (1986); *see also Nat'l Coach Works v. Detroit Diesel Corp.*, 128 F. Supp. 2d 821 (D. Md. 2001).

84. *Morris v. Osmose Wood Preserving*, 340 Md. 519, 535-36, 667 A.2d 624, 632-33 (1995) (homeowners failed to establish that defects in plywood used in construction of roofs in their homes had created serious and unreasonable risk of death or personal injury, and were barred from recovery in tort for economic loss rule, where there was no allegation that any injury had ever occurred since roofs were installed or that any roofs had collapsed because of weather conditions or alleged degradation of wood, even though homeowners contended that degradation caused risk of injury to occupants and persons with cause to be on the roof); *A. J. Decoster Co. v. Westinghouse Elec. Corp.*, 333 Md. 245, 250, 634 A.2d 1330, 1332 (1994); *Council of Co-Owners*

v. *Whiting-Turner*, 308 Md. 18, 33-42, 517 A.2d 336, 344-48 (1986); *see also Nat'l Coach Works v. Detroit Diesel Corp.*, 128 F. Supp. 2d 821 (D. Md. 2001).

85. *Morris v. Osmose Wood Preserving*, 340 Md. 519, 535-36, 667 A.2d 624, 632-33 (1995) (homeowners failed to establish that defects in plywood used in construction of roofs in their homes had created serious and unreasonable risk of death or personal injury, and were barred from recovery in tort for economic loss rule, where there was no allegation that any injury had ever occurred since roofs were installed or that any roofs had collapsed because of weather conditions or alleged degradation of wood, even though homeowners contended that degradation caused risk of injury to occupants and persons with cause to be on the roof); *A. J. Decoster Co. v. Westinghouse Elec. Corp.*, 333 Md. 245, 250, 634 A.2d 1330, 1332 (1994); *Council of Co-Owners v. Whiting-Turner*, 308 Md. 18, 33-42, 517 A.2d 336, 344-48 (1986); *see also Nat'l Coach Works v. Detroit Diesel Corp.*, 128 F. Supp. 2d 821 (D. Md. 2001).

86. *Lloyd v. Gen. Motors Corp.*, 397 Md. 108, 130, 916 A.2d 257, 270 (2007) (holding that plaintiffs had pleaded sufficient facts to withstand a motion to dismiss where they alleged that the seatbacks in their automobiles were defective even though the seatbacks had not yet failed or caused any personal injury; plaintiffs' complaint averred that numerous other individuals had been severely injured or killed when their identical seatbacks failed during collisions).

87. *U.S. Gypsum Co. v. Mayor & City Council of Baltimore*, 336 Md. 145, 156, 647 A.2d 405, 410 (1994); *A.J. Decoster Co.*, 333 Md. at 250, 634 A.2d. at 1332; *see also Ford Motor Co. v. Gen. Accident Ins. Co.*, 365 Md. 321, 779 A.2d 362 (2001) (discussing recovery under a breach of warranty theory).

88. *Binakonsky v. Ford Motor Co.*, 133 F.3d 281, 284 (4th Cir. 1998) (holding that fact that negligent driver may be initial cause of accident does not abrogate manufacturer's duty to use reasonable care in designing automobile to reduce risk of "secondary injuries"); *see Nissan Motor Co., Ltd. v. Nave*, 129 Md. App. 90, 120, 740 A.2d 102, 118 (1999), *cert. denied*, 357 Md. 482, 745 A.2d 437 (2000) (explaining that in crashworthiness cases, plaintiffs are claiming that after accident occurred, the design defect caused increased injuries to occupant when he or she collided with interior of vehicle); *see also Nicholson v. Yamaha Motor Co., Ltd.*, 80 Md. App. 695, 714, 566 A.2d 135, 145 (1989), *cert. denied*, 318 Md. 683, 569 A.2d 1242 (1990).

89. *Volkswagen of Am., Inc. v. Young*, 272 Md. 201, 206-07, 321 A.2d 737, 740 (1974) (adopting *Larsen v. Gen. Motors Corp.*, 391 F.2d 495 (8th Cir. 1968)).

90. *Volkswagen of Am.*, 272 Md. at 216, 321 A.2d at 745.

91. *Volkswagen of Am.*, 272 Md. at 218-19, 321 A.2d at 745-46.

92. *Volkswagen of Am.*, 272 Md. at 219, 321 A.2d at 746 (quoting *Larsen*, 391 F.2d at 502 n.3.).

93. *Volkswagen of Am.*, 272 Md. at 219-20, 321 A.2d at 747.

94. *See, e.g., Liesener v. Weslo, Inc.*, 775 F. Supp. 857 (D. Md. 1991); *Moran v. Faberge, Inc.*, 273 Md. 538, 332 A.2d 11 (1975); *Dechello v. Johnson Enters.*, 74 Md. App. 228, 536 A.2d 1203 (1988), *cert. denied, Albert E. Recora Importers v. Dechello*, 312 Md. 601, 541 A.2d 964 (1988); *Mayor & City Council of Balt. v. Utica Mut. Ins. Co.*, 145 Md. App. 256, 802 A.2d 1070 (2002).

95. *See, e.g., Liesener*, 775 F. Supp. at 857; *Ellsworth v. Sherne Lingerie, Inc.*, 303 Md. 581, 495 A.2d 348 (1985); *Am. Laundry Mach. Indus. v. Horan*, 45 Md. App. 97, 412 A.2d 407 (1980).

96. *Moran*, 273 Md. at 545, 332 A.2d 11, 15-16; *Ellsworth*, 303 Md. at 598 n.12, 495 A.2d 348, 356 n.12.

97. *Hood v. Ryobi*, 181 F.3d 608, 610-11 (4th Cir. 1999); *Shreve v. Sears, Roebuck & Co.*, 166 F. Supp. 2d 378, 415 (D. Md. 2001); *In re Bay Runner Rentals, Inc.*, 113 F. Supp. 2d 795, 803-04 (D. Md. 2000).

98. *Gourdine v. Crews*, 403 Md. 612, 943 A.2d 1244 (2008) (holding that drug manufacturer did not owe a duty of care to plaintiff whose car was hit by a driver that blacked out while taking manufacturer's medications).

99. *Dechello*, 74 Md. App. at 236, 536 A.2d 1203, 1207; *Kennedy v. Mobay Corp.*, 84 Md. App. 397, 411, 579 A.2d 1191, 1198 (1990), *aff'd*, 325 Md. 385, 601 A.2d 123 (1992).

100. *Higgens v. Diversey Corp.*, 998 F. Supp. 598, 604 (D. Md. 1997), *aff'd*, 135 F.3d 769 (4th Cir. 1998); *Christian v. Minnesota Min. & Mfg. Co.*, 126 F. Supp. 2d 951, 958 (D. Md. 2001); *Wells v. Ford Motor Co.*, 2001 WL 1262223, at *5 (D. Md. May 25, 2001) (unreported decision).

101. *Higgens*, 998 F. Supp. at 604-05.

102. *Higgens*, 998 F. Supp. at 604-05.

103. *Owens-Illinois, Inc. v. Zenobia*, 325 Md. 420, 438 n.8, 601 A.2d 633, 641 n.8 (1992) ("*Zenobia II*").

104. *Emory v. McDonnell Douglas Corp.*, 148 F.3d 347, 350 (4th Cir. 1998); *Moran*, 273 Md. at 545, 332 A.2d 11, 15-16; *Mazda Motor of Am., Inc. v. Rogowski*, 105 Md. App. 318, 325, 659 A.2d 391, 394 (1995); *Simpson v. Standard Container Co.*, 72 Md. App. 199, 207, 527 A.2d 1337, 1341 (1987), *cert. denied*, 311 Md. 286, 533 A.2d 1308 (1987); *Banks v. Iron Hustler Corp.*, 59 Md. App. 408, 423, 475 A.2d 1243, 1250 (1984).

105. *Miller v. Bristol-Meyers Squibb Co.*, 121 F. Supp. 2d 831, 838 (D. Md. 2000); *Doe v. American Nat'l Red Cross*, 866 F. Supp. 242, 248 (D. Md. 1994); *Lee v. Baxter Healthcare Corp.*, 721 F. Supp. 89, 95 (D. Md. 1989), *aff'd*, 898 F.2d 146 (4th Cir. 1990).

106. *Zenobia II*, 325 Md. at 446, 601 A.2d 633, 645; *U.S. Gypsum Co. v. Mayor & City Council of Balt.*, 336 Md. 145, 160, 647 A.2d 405, 412 (1994).

107. *Ragin v. Porter Hayden Co.*, 133 Md. App. 116, 140, 754 A.2d 503, 517 (2000), *cert. denied, Porter Hayden v. Ragen*, 361 Md. 323, 760 A.2d 1102 (2000) (citing *Zenobia II*, 325 Md. at 447-48); *Hollingsworth*, 136 Md. App. at 120, 764 A.2d 318, 333.

108. *Ragin*, 133 Md. App. at 140 754, A.2d 503, 517 (citing *Zenobia II*, 325 Md. at 448).

109. *See Mayor & City Council of Balt.*, 145 Md. App. at 288, 802 A.2d 1070, 1089; *Ellsworth*, 303 Md. at 597-98, 495 A.2d 348, 356; *see Simpson*, 72 Md. App. at 205-07, 527 A.2d 1337, 1340-41.

110. *See Mayor & City Council of Balt.*, 145 Md. App. at 288, 802 A.2d 1070, 1089; *Zenobia II*, 325 Md. at 435 n.7, 601 A.2d 633, 640 n.7; *Mazda*, 105 Md. App. at 326, 659 A.2d 391, 395.

111. *Kline v. ABCO Eng'g*, 991 F. Supp. 747, 750 (D. Md. 1997); *Lightolier*, 387 Md. at 552-53, 876 A.2d 100, 108-09; *Ellsworth*, 303 Md. at 596-98, 495 A.2d 348, 355-56; *Simpson*, 72 Md. App. at 204-05, 527 A.2d 1337, 1340; *see also Halliday*, 138 Md. App. at 150, 770 A.2d 1072, 1080, *aff'd*, 368 Md. 186, 792 A.2d 1145 (2002).

112. *Ellsworth*, 303 Md. at 596-98, 495 A.2d 348, 355-56.

113. *SaraLee Corp. v. Homasote Co.*, 719 F. Supp. 417, 420 (D. Md. 1989); *Higgins v. E.I. DuPont de Nemours & Co., Inc.*, 671 F. Supp. 1055, 1060 (D. Md. 1987); *Emory*, 148 F.3d at 352; *Eagle-Picher Indus., Inc. v. Balbos*, 326 Md. 179, 218, 604 A.2d 445, 464 (1992); *Kennedy v. Mobay Corp.*, 84 Md. App. 397, 413-14, 579 A.2d 1191, 1200 (1990), *aff'd*, 325 Md. 385, 601 A.2d 123 (1992).

114. *See, e.g., Higgins*, 671 F. Supp. 1063, 1066 (D. Md. 1987), *aff'd*, 863 F.2d 1162 (4th Cir. 1988); *Lightolier*, 387 Md. at 552-53, 876 A.2d 100, 108-09 (2005);

115. *See Zenobia II*, 325 Md. 420, 601 A.2d 633; *U.S. Gypsum* 336 Md. 145, 647 A.2d 405.

116. *Lightolier*, 387 Md. at 558, 876 A.2d 100, 111.

117. *Hood*, 181 F.3d at 611.

118. *Lightolier*, 387 Md. at 555-56, 876 A.2d 100, 110.

119. *See Banks v. Iron Hustler Corp.*, 59 Md. App. 408, 422, 475 A.2d 1243, 1250 (1984) (citations omitted); *see also Adams v. Owens-Illinois, Inc.*, 119 Md. App. 395, 409-10, 705 A.2d 58, 65-66 (1998) (holding that findings of "negligent but not strictly liable" and "not negligent but strictly liable" are not inconsistent findings warranting reversal).

120. *Pennwalt Corp. v. Nasios*, 314 Md. 433, 453, 550 A.2d 1155, 1165 (1988) (citations omitted); *see also Ford Motor Co. v. Gen. Accident Ins. Co.*, 365 Md. 321, 334-35, 779 A.2d 362, 369-70 (2001) (explaining the elements that must be proved by a plaintiff in a product liability action) (citations omitted).

121. *See Shreve v. Sears, Roebuck & Co.*, 166 F. Supp. 2d 378 (D. Md. 2001) (explaining that a general warning of danger generally suffices and the manufacturer need not warn of every possible mishap or source of injury) (citations omitted); *Moran v. Faberge, Inc.*, 273 Md. 538, 554, 332 A.2d 11, 21 (1975) (manufacturer may be held liable for injuries sustained when cologne was intentionally applied to lit candle to make it "scented," since manufacturer knew product was highly flammable and placed no warnings whatsoever on the product); *see also U.S. Gypsum Co. v. Mayor & City Council of Baltimore*, 336 Md. 145, 159-60, 647 A.2d 405, 412 (1994); *Ragin v. Porter Hayden Co.*, 133 Md. App. 116, 140-41, 754 A.2d 503, 516-17 (2000), *cert. denied*, 361 Md. 232, 760 A.2d 1107 (2000); *Mazda Motor of Am., Inc. v. Rogowski*, 105 Md. App. 318, 325-32, 659 A.2d 391, 394-97, *cert. denied*, 340 Md. 501, 667 A.2d 342 (1995). *But see Lightolier v. Hoon*, 387 Md. 539, 558, 876 A.2d 100, 111-12 (2005) (noting that "vague" or "generalized" warnings might not be sufficient under the circumstances).

122. *See Moran*, 273 Md. at 554, 332 A.2d at 21.

123. *See, e.g., Fredricks v. Gen. Motors Corp.*, 274 Md. 288, 336 A.2d 118 (1975); *Harley Davidson Motor Co. v. Wisniewski*, 50 Md. App. 339, 437 A.2d 700, *cert. denied*, 292 Md. 596 (1981); *Banks*, 59 Md. App. at 408, 475 A.2d at 1243.

124. *See, e.g., Volkswagen of Am., Inc. v. Young*, 272 Md. 201, 321 A.2d 737 (1974).

125. *Morris v. Osmose Wood Preserving*, 340 Md. 519, 531-36, 667 A.2d 624, 631-33 (1995); *A.J. Decoster Co. v. Westinghouse Elec. Corp.*, 333 Md. 245, 250, 634 A.2d 1330, 1332 (1994).

126. *Moran*, 273 Md. at 554, 332 A.2d at 21; *Figgie Int'l, Inc. v. Tognocchi*, 96 Md. App. 228, 239, 624 A.2d 1285, 1291 (1993), *cert. denied*, 332 Md. 381, 631 A.2d 451 (1993).

127. *Ellsworth v. Sherne Lingerie, Inc.*, 303 Md. 581, 597-99, 495 A.2d 348, 356-57 (1985).

128. *See Hood v. Ryobi Am. Corp.*, 181 F.3d 608, 611 (4th Cir. 1999); *see also Ellsworth*, 303 Md. at 597, 495 A.2d at 356 (explaining that misuse may bar recovery when it is the sole proximate cause of damage or intervening or superseding cause; also explains misuse is a defense only in the sense that proof of misuse negates one or more essential elements of plaintiff's case).

129. *Ellsworth*, 303 Md. at 591, 495 A.2d at 353; *Holman v. Mark Indus., Inc.*, 610 F. Supp. 1195, 1201-02 (D. Md. 1985), *aff'd*, 796 F.2d 473 (4th Cir. 1986).

130. *Beatty v. Trailmaster Prods., Inc.*, 330 Md. 726, 743-44, 625 A.2d 1005, 1014 (1993).

131. Md. Code Ann., Com. Law I §§ 2-313 to 2-318 (2013 Repl. Vol.).

132. *See* Md. Code Ann., Com. Law I § 2-313; *Pulte Home Corp. v. Parex, Inc.*, 174 Md. App. 681, 723, 923 A.2d 971, 994-95 (2007); *Rite Aid Corp. v. Levy-Gray*, 162 Md. App. 673, 692, 876 A.2d 115, 126 (2005); *Int'l Motors, Inc. v. Ford Motor Co., Inc.*, 133 Md. App. 269, 272 n.2, 754 A.2d 1115, 1116 n.2 (2000), *rev'd on other grounds, Ford Motor Co., Inc. v. Gen. Accident Ins. Co.*, 365 Md. 321, 779 A.2d 362 (2001).

133. *Rite Aid Corp.*, 162 Md. App. at 692, 876 A.2d at 126.

134. *Int'l Motors*, 133 Md. App. at 274, 754 A.2d at 1117 (quoting *McCarty v. E.J. Korvette, Inc.*, 28 Md. App. 421, 437, 347 A.2d 253 (1975)); *see also Joswick v. Chesapeake Mobile Homes, Inc.*, 362 Md. 261, 273, 765 A.2d 90, 96 (2001).

135. *Rite Aid Corp. v. Levy-Gray*, 391 Md. 608, 625, 894 A.2d 563, 573.

136. *Levy-Gray*, 391 Md. at 624, 894 A.2d at 572-73.

137. *See* Md. Code Ann., Com. Law I § 2-314; *Contract Materials Processing, Inc. v. Kata Levna GmbH*, 303 F. Supp. 2d 612, 653 n.13 (D. Md. 2003); *Shreve v. Sears, Roebuck & Co.*, 166 F. Supp. 2d 378, 422 (D. Md. 2001); *Ford Motor Co., Inc.*, 365 Md. at 327 n.7, 779 A.2d at 366 n.7; *Eaton Corp. v. Wright*, 281 Md. 80, 91, 375 A.2d 1122, 1128 (1977).

138. *Ford Motor Co.*, 365 Md. at 343, 779 A.2d at 375 (quoting § 2-315, cmt. 2).

139. *See* Md. Code Ann., Com. Law I § 2-314(1); *Shreve*, 166 F. Supp. 2d at 421; *Bond v. NIBCO, Inc.*, 96 Md. App. 127, 138, 623 A.2d 731, 736 (1993).

140. *See* Md. Code Ann., Com. Law I § 2-315; *Contract Materials Processing, Inc.*, 303 F. Supp. 2d at 653 n.14; *Ford Motor Co.*, 365 Md. at 343-44, 779 A.2d at 375; *Washington Freightliner, Inc. v. Shaneytown Pier, Inc.*, 351 Md. 616, 633 n.6, 719 A.2d 541, 549 n.6 (1998); *Pulte Home Corp. v. Parex, Inc.*, 174 Md. App. 681, 732, 923 A.2d 971, 1000 (2006).

141. *See Ford Motor Co.*, 365 Md. at 343, 779 A.2d at 375.

142. *See* Md. Code Ann., Com. Law I § 2-315; *Wood Prods., Inc. v. CMI Corp.*, 651 F. Supp. 641, 651, n.10 (D. Md. 1986).

143. Md. Code Ann., Com. Law I §§ 2A-210, 2A-212-213 (2013 Repl. Vol.). "All of the express and implied warranties of the Title on Sales (Title 2) are included in this Title, revised to reflect the differences between a sale of goods and a lease of goods." Md. Code Ann., Com. Law I § 2A-210, Official Comment.

144. *See* Md. Code Ann., Com. Law I § 2-316; *Dowty Commc'ns, Inc. v. Novatel Computer Sys. Corp.*, 817 F. Supp. 581, 584 (D. Md. 1992); *Boatel Indus. Inc. v. Hester*, 77 Md. App. 284, 300, 550 A.2d 389, 397 (1988).

145. *See* Md. Code Ann., Com. Law I § 2-316(2); *Boatel Indus.*, 77 Md. App. at 300, 550 A.2d at 397.

146. *See* Md. Code Ann., Com. Law I § 2-316(2); *Boatel Indus.*, 77 Md. App. at 300, 550 A.2d at 397.

147. *See* Md. Code Ann., Com. Law I § 2-316(3), *Boatel Indus.*, 77 Md. App. at 300, 550 A.2d at 397.

148. *See* Md. Code Ann., Com. Law I § 2-316.1; *Anthony Pools v. Sheehan*, 295 Md. 285, 289, 455 A.2d 434, 436-37 (1983); *Phipps v. Gen. Motors Corp.*, 278 Md. 337, 349, 363 A.2d 955, 961 (1976); *Boatel Indus.*, 77 Md. App. at 300-01, 550 A.2d at 397.

149. *See* Md. Code Ann., Com. Law I § 9-102(23); *Anthony Pools*, 295 Md. at 289, 455 A.2d at 437.

150. *See* Md. Code Ann., Com. Law I § 2-316.1(3); *Joswick v. Chesapeake Mobile Homes, Inc.*, 362 Md. 261, 266 n.1, 765 A.2d 90, 92 n.1 (2001).

151. *See* Md. Code Ann., Com. Law I § 2-316.1(2); *Anthony Pools*, 295 Md. at 289, 455 A.2d at 436-37; *Houck v. DeBonis*, 38 Md. App. 85, 97 n.10 379 A.2d 765, 772 n.10 (1977).

152. *See* Md. Code Ann., Com. Law I § 2-316.1(4).

153. *See* Md. Code Ann., Com. Law I § 2-318; *Copiers, Typewriters, Calculators, Inc. v. Toshiba Corp.*, 576 F. Supp. 312, 323 (D. Md. 1983); *Pulte Home Corp. v. Parex, Inc.*, 174 Md. App. 681, 724, 923 A.2d 971, 995 (2006).

154. *See Wood Products, Inc. v. CMI Corp.*, 651 F. Supp. 641, 649 (D. Md. 1986); *Copiers, Typewriters, Calculators, Inc.*, 576 F. Supp. at 322.

155. *See* Md. Code Ann., Com. Law I § 2-314(1)(b); *Copiers, Typewriters, Calculators, Inc.*, 576 F. Supp. at 323; *Pulte Home Corp.*, 174 Md. App. at 724, n.14, 923 A.2d at 995 n. 14 (2006).

156. *Ford Motor Co., Inc. v. Gen. Accident Ins., Co.*, 365 Md. 321, 344-45, 779 A.2d 362, 376 (2001). The requirement of specific knowledge on the part of the seller, however, "may create a near requirement of direct dealing, if not actual privity." *Ford Motor Co.*, 365 Md. at 343, 779 A.2d at 375.

157. *Ford Motor Co.*, 365 Md. at 343, 779 A.2d at 375; *Pinney v. Nokia, Inc.*, 402 F.3d 430, 444 (4th Cir. 2005); *Fischbach & Moore Int'l v. Crane-Barge R-14*, 632 F.2d 1123, 1125 (4th Cir. 1980); *SpinCycle, Inc. v. Kalender*, 186 F. Supp. 2d 585, 589 (D. Md. 2002); *Mattos Inc. v. Hash*, 279 Md. 371, 379, 368 A.2d 993, 997 (1977).

158. *Int'l Motors Inc. v. Ford Motor Co.*, 133 Md. App. 269, 274-75, 754 A.2d 1115, 1117-18 (2000) (citing *McCarty v. E.J. Korvette, Inc.*, 28 Md. App. 421, 437, 397 A.2d 253, 264 (1975)).

159. *Int'l Motors Inc.*, 133 Md. App. at 274-75, 754 A.2d at 1117-18 (internal quotations omitted).

160. *See Shreve v. Sears, Roebuck & Co.*, 166 F. Supp. 2d 378, 422 (D. Md. 2001); *Ford Motor Co.*, 365 Md. at 334, 779 A.2d at 369.

161. *Ford Motor Co.*, 365 Md. at 343, 779 A.2d at 375.

162. *See Erdman v. Johnson Bros. Radio & Television Co.*, 260 Md. 190, 196-97, 271 A.2d 744, 748 (1970).

163. *See Fischbach & Moore Int'l v. Crane-Barge R-14*, 632 F.2d 1123, 1125 (4th Cir. 1980); *Erdman*, 260 Md. at 198, 271 A.2d at 747.

164. *See Higgins v. E.I. Dupont de Nemours & Co.*, 671 F. Supp. 1063, 1066 (D. Md. 1987).

165. *See Mattos Inc. v. Itash*, 279 Md. 371, 382-83, 368 A.2d 993, 999 (1977); *Erdman*, 260 Md. at 197, 271 A.2d at 748.

166. *Laing v. Volkswagen, Inc.*, 180 Md. App. 136, 158, 949 A.2d 26, 39 (2008) (internal citations omitted).

167. *See Laing*, 180 Md. App. at 154-58, 949 A.2d at 36-39.

168. *Owens-Illinois v. Armstrong*, 87 Md. App. 699, 735, 591 A.2d 544, 561 (1991), *aff'd in part and rev'd in part on other grounds*, 326 Md. 107, 604 A.2d 47 (1992).

169. *See* Md. Code Ann., Cts. & Jud. Proc. § 11-108 (2006 Repl. Vol.); *see also Gooslin v. State*, 132 Md. App. 290, 752 A.2d 642 (2000) (holding cap does not

result in denial of equal protection), *cert. denied*, 359 Md. 334, 753 A.2d 1031 (2000); *Owens-Corning v. Walatka*, 125 Md. App. 313, 335-36, 725 A.2d 579, 592 (1999) (holding that cap does not violate the doctrine of separation of powers); *Edmonds v. Murphy*, 325 Md. 342, 601 A.2d 102 (1992) (holding cap on noneconomic damages constitutional); *Oaks v. Connors*, 339 Md. 24, 37-38, 660 A.2d 423, 430 (1995) (holding that a single cap applies to both the action of the injured spouse and the joint award for loss of consortium).

170. *United States v. Streidel*, 329 Md. 533, 620 A.2d 905 (1993).

171. Md. Code Ann., Cts. & Jud. Proc. § 11-108 (2006 Repl. Vol.)

172. *Goss v. Estate of Jennings*, 207 Md. App. 151, 172-74, 51 A.3d 761, 773-72 (2012).

173. Md. Code Ann., Cts. & Jud. Proc. § 11-108(b)(3)(ii) (2006 Repl. Vol.).

174. *See Oaks v. Connors*, 339 Md. 24, 660 A.2d 423 (1995); *see also Owens-Illinois, Inc. v. Cook*, 386 Md. 468, 872 A.2d 969 (2005).

175. *Porter Hayden Co. v. Wyche*, 128 Md. App. 381, 738 A.2d 326 (1999), *cert. denied*, 357 Md. 324, 743 A.2d 246 (2000).

176. *See* Md. Code Ann., Cts. & Jud. Proc. §§ 3-1401 through 1409 (2006 Repl. Vol.); *Rivera v. Prince George's County Health Dep't*, 102 Md. App. 456, 649 A.2d 1212 (1994), *cert. denied*, 338 Md. 117, 656 A.2d 772 (1995).

177. *See Orient Overseas Line v. Globemaster Baltimore, Inc.*, 33 Md. App. 372, 374, 365 A.2d 325, 330 (1976), *cert. denied*, 279 Md. 682 (1977).

178. *Zenobia*, 325 Md. 420, 601 A.2d 633 (1992).

179. *Zenobia*, 325 Md. at 463, 601 A.2d at 654.

180. *Zenobia*, 325 Md. at 463, 601 A.2d at 654; *see also Bowden v. Caldor, Inc.*, 350 Md. 4, 710 A.2d 267 (1998); *AC & S, Inc. v. Asner*, 344 Md. 155, 686 A.2d 250, 265 (1996); *Owens Corning v. Bauman*, 125 Md. App. 454, 533, 726 A.2d 745, 784, *cert. denied*, 354 Md. 572, 731 A.2d 970 (1999).

181. *See Darcars Motors of Silver Spring v. Borzym*, 150 Md. App. 18, 84-86, 818 A.2d 1159, 1196-97 (2003), *aff'd*, 379 Md. 249, 841 A.2d 828 (2004) (quoting *Bowden v. Caldor*, 350 Md. at 26-41, 710 A.2d at 278-85).

182. *Brethren Mut. Ins. v. Filsinger*, 54 Md. App. 357, 365, 458 A.2d 880, 885 (1983).

183. *See Affiliated Distillers Potents Corp. v. R.W.L. Wine & Liquor Co.*, 213 Md. 509, 516-17, 132 A.2d 582, 586 (1957). Maryland Rule of Procedure 2-604 does require, however, that any pre-judgment interest awarded by the jury (or the

court sitting without a jury) must be separately stated in the verdict or decision and included in the judgment. *See* Md. Rule 2-604(a).

184. *Buxton v. Buxton*, 363 Md. 634, 656, 770 A.2d 152, 165 (2001).

185. *Buxton v. Buxton*, 363 Md. 634, 656-57, 770 A.2d 152, 165 (2001); *Taylor v. Wahby*, 271 Md. 101, 113, 314 A.2d 100, 106 (1974); *Tricat Indus., Inc. v. Harper*, 131 Md. App. 89, 123, 748 A.2d 48, 66, *cert. denied*, 359 Md. 334, 753 A.2d 1032 (2000).

186. *See, e.g., Robert C. Herd & Co. v. Krawill Mach. Corp.*, 256 F.2d 946, 952 (D. Md. 1958) (involving tort claim but permitting pre-judgment interest because the case involved a chattel with readily ascertainable market value.), *aff'd*, 359 U.S. 297 (1959); *Wartzman v. Hightower Prods., Ltd.*, 53 Md. App. 656, 456 A.2d 82 (1983).

187. *Maxima Corp. v. 6933 Arlington Dev. Ltd. P'ship*, 100 Md. App. 441, 464, 641 A.2d 977, 988 (1994); *see also Brown v. Medical Mut. Liab. Ins. Soc. of Md.*, 90 Md. App. 18, 22, 599 A.2d 1201, 1203, *cert. denied*, 326 Md. 366, 605 A.2d 101 (1992).

188. Md. Code Ann., Cts. & Jud. Proc. § 11-107(a) (2006 Repl. Vol.).

189. *See* Md. Code Ann., Lab. & Emp. § 9-101*et seq.* (2008 Repl. Vol. & 2009 Supp.); *Athas v. Hill*, 300 Md. 133, 139, 476 A.2d 710, 713 (1984).

190. *American Radiator & Standard Sanitary Corp. v. Mark Eng. Co.*, 230 Md. 584, 589-90, 187 A.2d 864, 867 (1963).

191. *See American Radiator & Standard Sanitary Corp.*, 230 Md. at 590, 187 A.2d at 867.

192. Md. Code Ann., Cts. & Jud. Proc. § 5-405 (2006 Repl. Vol.).

193. *Eagle-Picher Indus., Inc. v. Balbos*, 326 Md. 179, 202-03, 604 A.2d 445, 456 (1992); *see also Reed v. Sears, Roebuck & Co.*, 934 F. Supp. 713 (1996) (holding that sealed container defense protected store from liability under theories of strict liability, implied warranty, or negligence, where purchaser of screen door whose young child was injured brought action against store from which door was purchased through catalog order and manufacturer of glass used in door).

194. Md. Code Ann., Cts. & Jud. Proc. § 5-405(c) (2006 Repl. Vol.).

195. *Coleman v. Soccer Ass'n of* Columbia, 9 SEPT. TERM 2012, 2013 WL 3449426 (Md. July 9, 2013); *Harrison v. Montgomery County Bd. of Educ.*, 295 Md. 442, 463, 456 A.2d 894, 905 (1983).

196. *Owens-Illinois, Inc. v. Armstrong*, 326 Md. 107, 121-22, 604 A.2d 47, 54, *cert. denied*, 113 S. Ct. 204 (1992).

197. *ACandS v. Abate*, 121 Md. App. 590, 693710 A.2d 1315, 1337-38 (1998).

198. *See John Crane, Inc. v. Scribner*, 369 Md. 369, 800 A.2d 727 (2002); *Georgia-Pacific Corp. v. Pransky*, 369 Md. 360, 800 A.2d 722 (2002).

199. *Wood v. Ford Motor Co.*, 119 Md. App. 1, 48, 703 A.2d 1315, 1337-38 (1998).

200. *See Pransky*, 369 Md. at 360, 800 A.2d at 722.

201. *See Benjamin v. Union Carbide Corp.*, 162 Md. App. 173, 205, 873 A.2d 463, 481-82 (2004).

202. *See Benjamin*, 162 Md. App. at 205, 873 A.2d at 481.

203. *Benjamin*, 162 Md. App. 206, 873 A.2d at 482.

204. *Dixon, et al. v. Ford Motor Co.*, 2013 WL 3821431 (Md. July 25, 2013).

205. *Dixon*, 2013 WL 3821431.

206. *Dixon*, 2013 WL 3821431.

207. *Georgia Pacific LLC v. Farrar*, 2013 WL 3456573 (Md. July 8, 2013).

208. Md. Code Ann., Cts. & Jud. Proc. § 3-904(e) (2006 Repl. Vol.).

209. Md. Code Ann., Cts. & Jud. Proc. § 3-904(b); *see Ditto v. Stoneberger*, 145 Md. App. 469, 805 A.2d 1148 (2002).

210. *Kelley v. R.G. Indus., Inc.*, 304 Md. 124, 162, 497 A.2d 1143, 1162 (1985). The case was on certification from the United States District Court for the District of Maryland.

211. *Kelley*, 304 Md. at 146-47, 497 A.2d at 1154.

212. *Kelley*, 304 Md. at 158, 497 A.2d at 1160.

213. *Valentine v. On Target, Inc.*, 353 Md. 544, 546-57, 727 A.2d 947, 948 (1999).

214. *Valentine*, 353 Md. at 552-53, 727 A.2d at 951.

215. The Court explained that "[i]f we would hold today that gun merchants owe an indefinite duty to the general public effectively we would be regulating

the merchants. This type of regulation is the realm of the legislature and is not appropriate as a judicial enactment." *Valentine*, 353 Md. at 556, 727 A.2d at 953.

216. *See Halliday v. Sturm, Ruger & Co.*, 368 Md. 186, 792 A.2d 1145 (2002).

217. *Halliday*, 368 Md. 186, 792 A.2d 1145.

MASSACHUSETTS

A. CAUSES OF ACTION

The causes of action most commonly asserted in product liability actions under Massachusetts law are for negligence, breach of the implied warranty of merchantability (the near-equivalent of strict liability), and unfair or deceptive acts or practices in violation of Chapter 93A of the Massachusetts General Laws. These claims are discussed in Sections C, D, and E, respectively, below. Other claims, such as for breach of an express warranty or the implied warranty of fitness for a particular purpose, discussed in Section F, below, are also sometimes asserted.

B. STATUTES OF LIMITATIONS AND REPOSE

1. General Limitations Periods

A plaintiff must commence a negligence action "within three years next after the cause of action accrues."[1] A three-year limitation period also applies to "tort-based" warranty actions, *i.e.*, express or implied warranty actions for personal injuries or property damage other than to the product itself.[2] Actions for wrongful death must be commenced three years from the date of decedent's death or three years from when the deceased's executor knew or should have known of the factual basis for the cause of action.[3]

Actions for unfair or deceptive acts or practices in violation of Chapter 93A must be brought within four years.[4] Actions in which plaintiff seeks "contract-based" damages—*i.e.*, economic damage such as the cost of repairs and lost profits—also must be brought within four years, whether plaintiff's claims are styled as being for breach of contract or for breach of warranty.[5]

2. General Accrual Rule

A cause of action ordinarily accrues on the occurrence of some appreciable injury, regardless of whether the full extent of the injury is known at that time.[6] Where a product is alleged to have caused "separate and distinct" diseases, the causes of action for each disease accrue separately.[7]

3. Exceptions to Limitations and Accrual Rules

a. Discovery Rule Exception

Where the injury is latent or "inherently unknowable," the discovery rule applies and the action does not accrue until plaintiff knows or reasonably should have known that he has been injured.[8] In such a case, plaintiff need not know with certainty that the injury was caused by defendant; knowledge that another party "may have caused" plaintiff's injuries, or of "a possible connection" between some other party and plaintiff's injury, suffices.[9]

b. **Fraudulent Concealment Exception**

If defendant—either through actual fraud or breach of a fiduciary duty of full disclosure—keeps from plaintiff knowledge of the facts giving rise to a cause of action and the means of acquiring such knowledge, the statute of limitations may be tolled until plaintiff actually learns of the cause of action.[10]

c. **Tolling for Minor's Claims**

The age of majority in Massachusetts is 18.[11] The statute of limitations on a claim by a minor is tolled until plaintiff reaches the age of majority.[12]

d. **Tolling for Mental Incapacity**

If a person is incapacitated by mental illness when her claim first accrues, the statute of limitations on that claim is tolled until the disability is removed.[13]

e. **Limitations Period After Death of Injured Party**

Where a decedent dies before the statute of limitations expires or within 30 days after such expiration, the executor of decedent's estate may file a survival action up to the later of (a) the last date decedent could have filed or (b) two years after the executor posts bond.[14]

f. **Medical Monitoring**

A claim for the costs of future medical monitoring following a claimant's exposure to allegedly hazardous substances that substantially increase the risk of serious disease accrues when the claimant has notice of: (1) a physiological change in the claimant resulting in a substantial increase in the risk of disease; and (2) that increase, under the standard of care, triggers the need for available diagnostic testing that has been accepted in the medical community as an efficacious method of screening for the disease.[15]

4. **Statute of Repose**

There is no Massachusetts statute of repose specifically applicable to product liability actions. The six-year statute of repose for tort actions arising out of improvements to real property may apply in some circumstances, in which case the cause of action begins to run when the improvement is opened for use or when the owner takes possession for occupancy after substantial completion.[16] In addition, other states' statutes of repose may apply to product liability actions in Massachusetts courts.[17]

C. NEGLIGENCE

1. General Standard

Massachusetts negligence law imposes a duty of reasonable care on persons such as manufacturers, "apparent manufacturers," distributors, and non-manufacturing sellers.[18] The standard for manufacturers—the most common defendants—is that of "the ordinary, reasonably prudent manufacturer in like circumstances."[19] A seller of a product manufactured by another is not liable for negligence unless it knew or had reason to know of a defect in the product that caused the accident.[20] In deciding negligence claims, the inquiry focuses on defendant's conduct, rather than on the product's characteristics.[21]

2. Types of Negligence

Generally, a defendant may be found liable in negligence with respect to a product upon proof of negligence in the (a) manufacture, (b) design, or (c) warning of a product's risks.[22]

3. Negligent Manufacturing

In a negligent manufacturing case, plaintiff must prove that "a particular product, rather than a line of products, is . . . defective because of negligence in the manufacturing process."[23] Under negligence law, a "manufacturer's duty is one of reasonable care, not perfection": a manufacturer is liable only for failing to exercise ordinary and reasonable care to ensure that its products do not expose consumers to unreasonable risks about which the manufacturer knew or should have known.[24]

4. Negligent Design

a. General Standard

In a negligent design case, the factfinder must engage in an analysis that weighs the gravity and likelihood of the danger posed by the challenged design against the feasibility, cost, and adverse consequences to the product's function of a safer alternative design.[25] Plaintiff must offer proof of the existence of a safer alternative design that defendant reasonably should have adopted,[26] but need not offer evidence on every factor of the analysis.[27] The defendant, of course, may also offer evidence on any factor.[28]

b. Foreseeable Uses, Misuses, and Alterations

The manufacturer "must anticipate the environment in which its product will be used" and "design against the reasonably foreseeable risks attending the product's use in that setting."[29] This includes reasonably foreseeable misuse or alteration of the product.[30] While the issue of reasonable foreseeability ordinarily is a jury question, the court may decide the issue as matter of law in certain circumstances, such as when plaintiff adduces no evidence that the risk which resulted in injury should reasonably have been anticipated by the defendant.[31]

c. Crashworthiness/Enhanced Injury Claims

Where it is reasonably foreseeable that particular products may be involved in collisions, the manufacturer has a duty to design the product "so that users are not subjected to unreasonable risks of injury" when such collisions take place.[32] Thus, even if the manufacturer's negligence does not cause the accident, a manufacturer nonetheless may be liable in negligence for foreseeably enhancing plaintiff's injuries in a reasonably foreseeable accident.[33]

5. Negligent Failure to Warn

a. General Standard

"A manufacturer has a duty to warn expected users of its product of latent dangers in its normal and intended use."[34] To be reasonably adequate, an instruction or warning must be "comprehensible to the average user," calculated to convey the material risks "to the mind of a reasonably prudent person," and of an intensity commensurate with the danger involved.[35] Under Massachusetts law, there is no duty to warn expected users of product-connected dangers that are obvious.[36] In addition, courts have stated that there is "no duty" to warn of a product-connected danger that a user already appreciates,[37] although analytically the lack of liability in such a circumstance is better viewed as flowing from a lack of proximate causation.[38]

b. Foreseeable Uses, Misuses, and Alterations

In addition to having a duty to warn expected users of latent dangers in the normal and intended use, a manufacturer may be liable if it fails to warn of the hazards of a foreseeable misuse of the product.[39] There is no Massachusetts authority explicitly requiring a manufacturer to warn of the hazards of foreseeable alterations to a product.[40]

c. Post-Sale Duty to Warn

Massachusetts' negligence law subjects manufacturers to "a continuing duty to warn (at least purchasers) of risks discovered following the sale of the product at issue."[41] That duty does not extend to "remote," second-hand purchasers of risks discovered, or that have become discoverable, after the product's sale.[42] In 2001, the Supreme Judicial Court expressly adopted the position of the Restatement (Third) of Torts: Product Liability (1998) (the "Third

Restatement") § 10, "which imposes a rule of reasonableness on a seller's post-sale duty to warn users of dangerous products," namely, a duty to warn of *substantial* risks of harm if (a) a reasonable person in the seller's position would provide a warning, (b) those to whom a warning might be provided can be identified, and (c) the warning can be "effectively communicated" to them.[43]

6. **Requirement of Injury to Person or Property; Economic Loss Rule**

Recovery for negligence requires a showing of personal injury or property damage. When only economic loss (such as lost profits or the cost of repairs) is claimed, without injury to persons or property other than the product itself, recovery in negligence ordinarily is not allowed.[44]

The personal injury requirement is satisfied, and supports an award of future medical monitoring costs, where: plaintiff's exposure to a hazardous substance produces subcellular changes that substantially increase the risk of a serious disease, illness or injury for which an effective medical test for reliable early detection exists; early detection of that disease, illness or injury combined with prompt and effective treatment would significantly decrease the risk of death or the severity of the disease, illness or injury; and such diagnostic medical examinations are reasonably and periodically necessary, conformably with the standard of care.[45]

D. IMPLIED WARRANTY OF MERCHANTABILITY (THE NEAR-EQUIVALENT OF STRICT LIABILITY)

1. General Standard

a. Massachusetts Uniform Commercial Code "Nearly" Congruent with Restatement (Second) § 402A

Massachusetts does not recognize the common law tort of strict liability as set forth in the Restatement (Second) of Torts § 402A ("§ 402A").[46] However, the Massachusetts version of the Uniform Commercial Code (UCC) establishes an implied warranty of merchantability that merchants cannot disclaim and abolishes any privity requirements for such warranty to arise.[47] Accordingly, the Massachusetts courts treat a personal injury or property damage claim for breach of the implied warranty as being "congruent in nearly all respects with the principles expressed in Restatement (Second) of Torts § 402A" and further look to "the strict liability cases of other jurisdictions [as] a useful supplement to [Massachusetts'] own warranty case law."[48] As Massachusetts courts have addressed specific issues, they have generally construed the statutory warranty remedy in conformity with the provisions of the Third Restatement.[49]

b. **Requirement of Injury to Person or Property; When Implied Warranty Arises**

   i. **Requirement of Sale or Lease**

   Because Massachusetts' strict liability-analogue claims are based on the UCC's implied warranty of merchantability, such claims must be grounded on a sale or lease of new or used goods by a merchant.[50] One who holds out as his own a product that is actually manufactured by another—including a trademark licensor who participates substantially in the design, manufacture, or distribution of a product that its licensee distributes under the licensor's trademark or logo—may be liable as an "apparent manufacturer," however, even if he is neither a seller nor manufacturer of that product.[51]

   ii. **No Requirement of Privity**

   In a "tort-based" warranty action (*i.e.*, for personal injuries or property damage other than to the product itself) plaintiff need not have bought or leased the product directly from defendant, so long as plaintiff is a person whom defendant "might reasonably have expected to use, consume or be affected by" the product.[52] But an actual purchase or lease by somebody is required.[53]

   iii. **Negation of Implied Warranty by Detailed Specifications**

   Where a manufacturer has followed "detailed, precise and complete" specifications supplied by the buyer, implied warranties of merchantability and fitness for a particular purpose may be negated unless those specifications are "so obviously bad that a competent [fabricator] would realize that there was a grave chance that his product would be dangerously unsafe."[54]

c. **General Standard for Breach of Implied Warranty**

   Under the Commonwealth's version of the Uniform Commercial Code, a seller or lessor impliedly warrants that its product is "fit for the ordinary purposes for which such goods are used."[55] A product is deemed to be unfit for its ordinary purposes if it is defective and "unreasonably dangerous."[56]

d. **Relationship to Negligence**

   Ostensibly, a claim of breach of the implied warranty of merchantability under Massachusetts law focuses on "whether the product was defective and unreasonably dangerous" without regard to the seller's exercise of due care, whereas a negligence claim focuses on the defendant's conduct.[57] As discussed below, that distinction remains important with respect to manufacturing defect claims, because Massachusetts warranty law essentially imposes true strict liability for such claims, without regard to the manufacturer's negligence.[58] Otherwise, Massachusetts courts apply "essentially the same analysis"—an evaluation of the reasonableness of defendant's actions—regardless of whether one proceeds under a negligence theory or a warranty theory.[59] However, Massachusetts has not yet adopted the position of the Third Restatement that only one tort theory should be submitted to the jury.

In addition, due to the theoretically stricter (or at least no less strict) standard posed by warranty law, a finding of negligence in a product liability case as a matter of law requires a finding that defendant also breached the implied warranty of merchantability, while the reverse is not true.[60] As discussed below in Section G, however, there remain differences with respect to the *affirmative defenses* available under negligence and implied warranty theories.

2. Types of Product "Defect"

Paralleling its negligence law, Massachusetts' implied warranty of merchantability law generally recognizes three types of product "defect" that may form a basis for liability: (a) a manufacturing defect, (b) a design defect, and (c) an inadequate warning.[61]

3. Manufacturing Defect

Under an implied warranty of merchantability theory, the manufacturer's conduct is immaterial to a manufacturing defect claim. Instead, the jury compares the characteristics of the product as sold with those of the product as designed; if a deviation from the design "rendered the product unreasonably dangerous and therefore unfit for its ordinary purposes," liability will attach without regard to the defendant's negligence.[62] Consistent with § 402A, however—which only imposes liability when a product is defective "at the time it leaves the seller's hands"—plaintiff must show that the defect existed at the time of sale.[63]

4. Design Defect

The standards and analysis applicable in a design defect claim brought under the implied warranty of merchantability are essentially identical to those brought under a negligence theory.[64] As in a negligence claim, the plaintiff must offer proof of the existence of a safer alternative design.[65] To determine whether a product is unreasonably dangerous in design, Massachusetts follows a "risk-utility" balancing standard drawing on both § 402A and § 2 of the Third Restatement.[66] Massachusetts has rejected the use of consumer expectations of a product's dangers as conclusive proof that the product is not unreasonably dangerous, as contemplated by § 402A, comment i, but such expectations remain an "important factor" in the balancing analysis.[67] As a matter of law, everyday items such as knives and razor blades, for example, are not unreasonably dangerous, in part because of the obviousness of the danger.[68] Additionally, Massachusetts courts have also favorably cited § 402A, comment k, whereby certain useful but unavoidably unsafe products such as pharmaceuticals are as a matter of law not defective or unreasonably dangerous in design; such products therefore, may not be the subject of an implied warranty of merchantability claim so long as there is no defect in their manufacture or warning.[69]

5. **Inadequate Warnings**

The standards applicable in a failure-to-warn claim brought under the implied warranty of merchantability are essentially identical to those brought under a negligence theory.[70]

6. **Requirement of Injury to Person or Property; Economic Loss Rule**

Massachusetts' expanded warranty remedy applies only to "tort-based" claims, *i.e.*, claims for personal injury or damage to property other than the product itself, and not to "contract-based" claims, *i.e.*, claims for purely "economic loss," such as lost profits or the cost of repair or replacement of the product itself.[71] A plaintiff meets the personal injury requirement where she alleges the elements described in Section C(6) above.[72] For "contract-based" claims, more limited warranty remedies and the ordinary commercial expectations of buyer and seller apply.[73]

E. **CHAPTER 93A: UNFAIR OR DECEPTIVE ACTS**

1. **General Statutory Provisions**

Section 2 of Chapter 93A of the Massachusetts General Laws prohibits "[u]nfair methods of competition and unfair or deceptive acts or practices in the conduct of any trade or commerce."[74] A successful plaintiff is entitled to recover reasonable attorneys' fees and costs.[75] Double and triple damages also are available against a party who commits a "willful or knowing" violation of Chapter 93A.[76]

2. **"Consumer" and "Business" Claims**

There are two different kinds of Chapter 93A claims available. So-called "business" claims under § 11 of the statute may be brought by any "person who engages in the conduct of any trade or commerce," which includes the sale and distribution of products.[77] A plaintiff in a § 11 case must be able to show an actual loss of money or property as a proximate result of an unfair or deceptive act or practice.[78]

Additionally, anyone *other* than a person entitled to bring an action under § 11 of the statute may bring an action under § 9. Although sometimes referred to as "consumer" actions, in fact the plaintiffs in such cases need not be consumers, nor need they be in privity with defendant in order to bring a claim under § 9.[79]

Actual economic loss to the plaintiff caused by the deceptive or unfair act is a necessary predicate for recovery.[80] Where defendant has caused actual damage but that damage is not quantifiable, plaintiff in a § 9 case may recover $25 per violation, subject to doubling or trebling, plus reasonable attorneys' fees and costs.[81] The typical product liability personal injury claim under Chapter 93A is brought under § 9.

3. **General Standard for "Unfair or Deceptive" Act**

In analyzing what constitutes unfair methods of competition and unfair or deceptive acts or practices, which are not defined in Chapter 93A, Massachusetts courts look to interpretations by the Federal Trade Commission and federal courts of § 5(a)(1) of the Federal Trade Commission Act, 15 U.S.C. § 45(a)(1), as well as regulations promulgated by the Massachusetts Attorney General under Chapter 93A itself.[82]

In a § 11 or "business" case, a practice may be considered "unfair" if it is "within . . . the penumbra of some common-law, statutory, or other established concept of unfairness; . . . is immoral, unethical, oppressive, or unscrupulous; [and] . . . causes substantial injury to [another business]."[83] Defendants generally are held to a higher standard of conduct in a § 9—or non-business plaintiff—case, although no hard and fast rules apply and the court will judge each case on its individual facts.[84]

4. **Relationship to Negligence and Warranty**

It is relatively common for plaintiff in a product liability action to contend that the same actions by defendant that constitute negligence and/or breach of the implied warranty of merchantability also amount to an unfair or deceptive act or practice in violation of Chapter 93A, § 9, thus necessitating payment of plaintiff's reasonable attorneys' fees and costs. Historically, and even recently, Massachusetts courts held that establishing a Chapter 93A violation requires something more than mere negligence or breach of contract.[85] Intervening case law, however, applies a Massachusetts Attorney General regulation defining any "fail[ure] to perform or fulfill any promises or obligations under a warranty" as a violation of Chapter 93A to conclude that any breach of the implied warranty of merchantability is a *per se* violation of Chapter 93A, Section 9.[86] This development appears subject to question, not only as a matter of regulatory construction but also on the grounds of its inconsistency with (1) the historical precedent, (2) warranty law's relative lack of focus on a defendant's conduct (especially in the case of manufacturing defect claims), in contrast to Chapter 93A's focus on a defendant's "acts" or "practices," and (3) the long-standing recognition that each Chapter 93A determination is highly fact-specific.[87]

5. **Procedural Aspects of Chapter 93A Claims**

Prior to bringing a § 9 claim, a would-be plaintiff must send a demand letter to the putative defendant "identifying the claimant and reasonably describing the unfair or deceptive act or practice relied upon and the injury suffered."[88] A party's failure to make a good faith settlement offer in response to the demand may make it liable for double or triple damages.[89] The demand requirements are inapplicable if the putative defendant has no assets or place of business within the Commonwealth.[90]

A plaintiff may bring a putative class action under § 9 on behalf of both himself and appropriate other persons "if the use or employment of the unfair or deceptive act or practice has caused similar injury to numerous other persons similarly situated and if the court finds in a preliminary hearing that he adequately and fairly represents such other persons . . . ."[91]

Although class certification under § 9 requires a plaintiff to satisfy the same elements of numerosity, commonality, typicality, and adequacy of representation that a plaintiff is required to satisfy in order to certify a class under Mass. R. Civ. P. 23(a), it does not expressly require that common issues predominate over individual ones or that a class action be superior to other methods of litigation. Thus, "a certification that fails under [Chapter] 93A would fail under the requirements of rule 23 as well."[92] Nonetheless, courts often apply the same functional requirements in considering class certification under § 9 as they do under Rule 23(a).[93] An agreement made in interstate commerce that requires individual arbitration is enforceable pursuant to the Federal Arbitration Act,[94] which preempts the Massachusetts public policy favoring class proceedings for the resolution of small-value consumer claims.[95]

Although there is no right to a jury trial of Chapter 93A claims,[96] the trial judge may, in his or her discretion, submit such claims to a jury.[97] But if the court reserves decision on a Chapter 93A claim, its findings of fact on that claim are independent of, and therefore may differ from, the jury's findings of fact on a parallel common law claim.[98]

F. OTHER THEORIES OF LIABILITY

1. Breach of Express Warranty

Under Massachusetts law, express warranties may arise from descriptions or samples of goods, as well as affirmations of fact or promises made to buyers or lessees relating to the seller's or lessor's goods and becoming part of "the basis of the bargain."[99]

2. Breach of Implied Warranty of Fitness for a Particular Purpose

An implied warranty of fitness for a particular purpose may arise where: (1) the seller has reason to know of the particular purpose for which the goods are provided; (2) the seller has reason to know that the buyer is relying on the seller's skill or judgment to furnish appropriate goods; and (3) the buyer in fact relies on the seller's skill or judgment.[100]

3. Misrepresentation

Massachusetts has not adopted § 402B of the Restatement (Second) of Torts, addressing liability for harm caused by a misrepresentation concerning a product, nor has it considered the equivalent provisions of § 9 of the Third Restatement.

G. DEFENSES

1. Defenses to Negligence Claims

a. Assumption of Risk

The Massachusetts legislature has abolished the defense of assumption of risk in negligence actions.[101] Accordingly, a plaintiff's knowing and unreasonable use of a product is not an automatic bar to recovery on a negligence claim.[102]

b. Comparative Negligence

Massachusetts follows a modified comparative negligence scheme, whereby a plaintiff's negligence will bar recovery only if it was greater than the total amount of negligence attributable to the parties against whom recovery is sought at the time of the verdict.[103] If plaintiff's negligence does not exceed 50 percent, plaintiff may recover damages in an amount reduced by the percentage of plaintiff's negligence.[104] Conduct that was formerly argued to constitute an assumption of the risk would now be argued as part of comparative negligence.[105]

2. Defenses to Warranty Claims

a. Assumption of Risk

Although the statute abolishing assumption of risk as a defense does so only in "negligence" actions, the Supreme Judicial Court has stated that the defense also does not apply in implied warranty claims.[106]

b. Knowing and Unreasonable Misuse

Massachusetts is among the small minority of states that do not allow a plaintiff's own negligence to decrease plaintiff's recovery in implied warranty cases.[107] In taking this position, the Supreme Judicial Court has relied on the fact that the Massachusetts comparative negligence statute specifically refers only to actions for "negligence" and not strict liability or warranty.[108] Notably, however, the statute was enacted prior to the UCC amendments that the court has found make Massachusetts' implied warranty of merchantability the "near equivalent" of strict liability.

In any event, the court has imposed an "all or nothing" rule which is a near equivalent of assumption of risk: plaintiff in an implied warranty action "may not recover if it is found that, after discovering the product's defect and being made aware of its danger, he nevertheless proceeded unreasonably to make use of the product and was injured by it."[109] The burden is on defendant to prove such knowing and unreasonable misuse as an affirmative defense.[110] It remains to be seen whether Massachusetts will revise this position to conform to the comparative fault approach set forth in § 17 of the Third Restatement and the Supreme Judicial Court's recent decisions recognizing the merger of warranty liability and negligence liability in design defect and failure-to-warn cases.[111]

c. **Lack of Reasonable Notice of Breach of Warranty**

Even if the statute of limitations has not run, plaintiff's claim for breach of the implied warranty of merchantability may be barred where plaintiff failed to give reasonable notice of the alleged breach and defendant proves that he was "prejudiced thereby,"[112] as by loss of evidence.[113] No prejudice need be shown if the parties are in privity and plaintiff brings a "contract-based" claim for damage to the product itself.[114]

d. **Attempted Disclaimer or Limitation of Warranty or Remedies**

In an action seeking to impose liability for personal injury, any attempt to modify or exclude an implied warranty of merchantability or fitness for a particular purpose, or to limit the consumer's remedies for a breach of those warranties, is unenforceable against the injured person.[115]

3. **Special Defenses to Failure-to-Warn Claims**

a. **Learned Intermediary Doctrine**

As a matter of both warranty and negligence law, a manufacturer in some circumstances may reasonably rely on a knowledgeable or "learned intermediary"—typically a physician prescribing medication—who has received an appropriate warning.[116]

b. **Bulk Supplier Doctrine**

Massachusetts generally follows comment n to § 388 of the Restatement (Second) of Torts, under which a bulk supplier generally may reasonably rely on an intermediate vendee to convey appropriate warnings to end users.[117] The relevant inquiry turns on the intermediary's knowledge of the product's hazard, its ability to pass on appropriate warnings to end users, the burdens this would entail, and whether defendant has reason to believe the intermediary will not convey the warnings.[118] However, a bulk supplier has no duty to "police" or monitor the adequacy of warnings actually given by the intermediary.[119]

c. **Sophisticated User Doctrine**

The sophisticated user defense "protects a supplier from liability for failure to warn when the end user knows or reasonably should know of a product's dangers."[120] The relevant inquiry turns on the end user's level of sophistication.[121] Because the doctrine's rationale is to relieve a supplier of the need to provide superfluous warnings to an end user who already appreciates the product's risks, where the relevant end user is an employer or other intermediary, the reasonableness of the supplier's reliance on the intermediary to transmit warnings to its employees does not affect application of the doctrine.[122]

4. Employer Immunity From Suit

The Massachusetts workers' compensation statute provides an exclusive remedy and, accordingly, employees ordinarily may not bring product liability actions against their employers for personal injuries incurred on the job.[123] For the same reason, a defendant manufacturer may not bring a third-party claim for contribution against plaintiff's employer.[124] However, an express or implied agreement by the employer to indemnify the manufacturer or seller or otherwise share risk with respect to claims for personal injuries may be enforceable.[125]

5. Spoliation of Evidence

Parties who are involved or are on notice that they are reasonably likely to become involved in a litigation, or persons such as experts who are affiliated with such parties, have a duty to preserve evidence that is relevant to such litigation.[126] Failure to do so may result in a number of sanctions, from adverse inferences concerning the missing evidence to preclusion of evidence addressing the issue to which the missing evidence relates, and even default judgment or dismissal.[127] The same rule may apply to parties that lose evidence (such as medical records) in violation of a statutory duty to maintain it, even if the loss occurs before they have reason to believe that litigation is likely.[128] Like most jurisdictions, however, Massachusetts does not recognize an independent cause of action in tort, or under the unfair or deceptive trade practices statute, for negligent or intentional spoliation of evidence.[129]

By contrast, persons not involved or likely to be involved as parties in litigation are under no obligation to preserve evidence until served with a subpoena, even if such non-parties are aware of pending or imminent litigation.[130]

Although an exclusionary sanction may not be applied against a party that is not responsible for the spoliation,[131] as noted earlier a claim for breach of warranty may be barred for lack of timely notice if the delay results in the loss of material evidence.[132]

H. CAUSATION

1. General Standard

To establish causation, a plaintiff must show that: (1) defendant's actions were a but-for cause of the loss; (2) defendant's actions were a substantial factor in bringing about the loss; and (3) the loss was a reasonably foreseeable consequence of defendant's actions.[133]

2. Exception to Requirement of "But For" Causation

Where two or more negligent defendants cause a single, indivisible harm, plaintiff need not prove "but for" causation as to each defendant; rather, plaintiff may make his case as against any defendant by showing that the conduct or product of the defendant in question, although not the only cause, was a "substantial factor" (as distinguished from a merely "negligible factor") which, along with other factors, produced the injury.[134]

3. Proximate and Superseding Causes

A defendant may be found to have proximately caused plaintiff's injuries where the intervening acts of a third party combine with defendant's actions to cause plaintiff's injury, so long as the third party's intervening actions were reasonably foreseeable.[135] However, the intervening act of a third party is a superseding cause which breaks the chain of causation when the original actor could not reasonably have foreseen the occurrence of such an act.[136] Thus, a manufacturer is not liable for a design defect where the buyer's subsequent modification of the product is found by the jury to be an unforeseeable superseding cause that broke the chain of causation between the design defect and plaintiff's injury.[137]

Logically, a defendant's showing that the "sole proximate cause" of plaintiff's injuries lies with someone other than the defendant may be thought of as a refutation of causation, rather than an affirmative defense.[138] For example, a plaintiff's knowing and unreasonable use of a defective product is an absolute bar to recovery under an implied warranty of merchantability theory, even if the misuse was foreseeable, because plaintiff's conduct "implies consent to the risk and thus is viewed as the sole proximate cause of the injury."[139] That said, however, Massachusetts courts treat plaintiff's knowing and unreasonable use as an affirmative defense to an implied warranty claim, as described above in Section G.[140]

I. DAMAGES

1. Punitive Damages

Punitive damages are only available in Massachusetts when specifically authorized by statute.[141] One such statute allows punitive damages in wrongful death actions in which death was caused by defendant's wanton or reckless conduct or gross negligence.[142] Applying federal due process standards, the Supreme Judicial Court has affirmed an award of punitive damages in a wrongful death action that totaled approximately seven times the compensatory damages award.[143] As noted earlier, if an unfair or deceptive act or practice is determined to be "willful or knowing," actual damages may be doubled or tripled under Chapter

93A, and a failure to tender a good faith settlement in response to a Chapter 93A, § 9 demand also may justify double or treble damages.[144]

2. **Pre-Judgment Interest**

By statute, successful plaintiffs in tort-based actions for property damage or personal injury are entitled to pre-judgment interest at the annual rate of 12 percent, running from the date of the action's commencement.[145] Pre-judgment interest accrues at the same annual rate of 12 percent for breach of contract claims, but interest in such cases accrues from the date of the breach or demand, rather than the date of the commencement of the action.[146] These statutory pre-judgment interest rates apply not only to state court actions, but also to actions brought in or removed to the federal district court, to the extent the underlying claims are based on Massachusetts law.[147]

3. **Post-Judgment Interest**

In Massachusetts state court, judgment on a product liability claim—whether "contract-based" or "tort-based"—bears post-judgment interest at the rate of 12 percent per annum from the date judgment enters.[148] Post-judgment interest accrues on the combined total of the underlying award and any pre-judgment interest.[149] Massachusetts federal court judgments bear post-judgment interest at a statutory rate based on the rate for United States Treasury bills at the time judgment enters.[150]

J. LIABLE PARTIES

1. **Joint and Several Liability**

In both negligence and "tort-based" warranty actions, liability of all tortfeasors is joint and several, subject to a statutory right of contribution.[151] Each tortfeasor is liable for contribution to the extent of its own "pro rata" share of the entire common liability, *i.e.*, in proportion to the total *number* of defendants rather than the tortfeasor's relative degree of fault.[152] Thus, in a two-defendant case, a defendant found 1 percent negligent can be compelled to contribute 50 percent of the judgment amount.[153]

If a joint tortfeasor enters into a good faith settlement, it is discharged from all liability for contribution to any other tortfeasor, and the plaintiff's claim is reduced by the amount of the settlement.[154] Discharging the entire common liability through settlement entitles the settling party to seek pro rata contribution from any non-settling joint tortfeasors.[155] A settling party who merely obtains a release of his own liability, however, is not entitled to contribution.[156]

2. **Market Share Liability/Enterprise Liability/Concert of Action Liability**

The Supreme Judicial Court has held that identifying the "party responsible for causing injury to another is a longstanding prerequisite to a successful negligence action" because it "separate[s] wrongdoers from innocent actors" and "ensure[s] that wrongdoers are held liable only for the harm that they have caused."[157] On that basis, Massachusetts courts have refused to find liability in circumstances where a plaintiff is unable to link a product to a specific manufacturer.[158] However, the Supreme Judicial Court has stated that it may recognize—although it has not yet done so—"some relaxation of the traditional identification requirement in appropriate circumstances" and permit plaintiffs to recover from negligent defendants based on a market share liability theory.[159] The Court has also not recognized the theory of alternative liability, which shifts the burden of disproving causation to defendants in circumstances where plaintiff cannot prove which one of several tortfeasors caused plaintiff's injury.[160]

Enterprise liability—under which an entire industry may be held jointly and severally liable for its collective wrongdoing—is "not a viable cause of action" in Massachusetts.[161] However, Massachusetts courts have cited with approval the "concert of action" approach of § 876 of the Restatement (Second) of Torts, pursuant to which a defendant who has an agreement with another to perform a tortious act, or who renders substantial assistance to another whom he knows to be performing a tortious act, may be liable to a plaintiff even if that defendant's own acts were not the cause-in-fact of plaintiff's injury.[162]

3. **Successor Liability**

Massachusetts law imposes liability for claims relating to products sold by a predecessor only "(1) where the purchaser impliedly or explicitly agrees to assume the liability of the seller, (2) where the transaction is entered into fraudulently to avoid liability, (3) where the transaction amounts to a de facto merger, or (4) where the purchasing corporation is 'merely a continuation' of the selling corporation" *and* the predecessor has ceased to exist.[163] In a merger, the surviving corporation is liable if the predecessor would have been.[164] Massachusetts courts do not recognize the "product line" theory of successor liability.[165]

4. **Component Parts Manufacturer**

The manufacturer of a component part that is not itself defective is not liable for injury resulting from the functioning of that component in a defectively integrated product.[166]

5. **Fabricator**

One who fabricates a product to the specifications of another will not be liable under an implied warranty of merchantability theory, unless the specified design or material was so obviously bad that a competent fabricator would have realized that there was a grave chance that the product would be dangerously unsafe.[167]

6. Apparent Manufacturer

One who holds out as his own a product that is actually manufactured by another may be liable on negligence and/or implied warranty of merchantability theories as the "apparent manufacturer" of that product.[168] "Apparent manufacturer" liability extends to a trademark licensor who participates substantially in the design, manufacture, or distribution of a product that its licensee distributes under the licensor's trademark or logo.[169]

K. COMMON EVIDENTIARY ISSUES

1. Necessity of and Standard for Expert Testimony

Proof of a product defect requires expert testimony if it is beyond the common knowledge of the fact finder.[170] Proof of causation also requires expert testimony if it is beyond the common knowledge of the fact finder, such as on issues of medical causation.[171]

Massachusetts state courts have followed the lead of the United States Supreme Court in recent years concerning the admissibility of expert testimony and the trial court's "gatekeeper" role. The Massachusetts courts require "demonstrated reliability" of proffered opinion testimony by considering factors such as whether the challenged theory or technique can be tested, whether it has been peer reviewed and published, and whether it is generally accepted in the scientific community.[172] These principles apply equally to purely "scientific" testimony and to expert testimony that is purportedly based on personal observations or clinical experience.[173] The trial court's decisions in this regard are reviewed under an abuse of discretion standard.[174]

2. Product Malfunction/Res Ipsa Loquitur

Ordinarily, the mere happening of an injury or accident is *not* proof of negligence or a breach of warranty.[175] However, a fact finder may infer that a product was defective when sold merely from the occurrence of a malfunction, injury or accident if the incident is one that lay jurors can conclude generally would not occur unless the product was defectively manufactured or designed.[176] The plaintiff who relies on such circumstantial evidence bears the burden of showing that a defect in the product was the probable cause of plaintiff's injury, and of eliminating other reasonably possible causes such as intermediate mishandling.[177] If determining the presence or absence of other causes is beyond the common knowledge of the fact finder, expert testimony may be required.[178]

3. Evidence of Government Regulations

While generally admissible to prove negligence or breach of warranty, evidence of a violation of a governmental safety regulation is not conclusive.[179] Similarly, evidence of compliance with a safety regulation is admissible to show the absence of negligence or breach of warranty, but it is not conclusive.[180]

4. **Evidence of Industry Standards/"State of the Art"**

Evidence of prevailing industry standards at the time of sale is also admissible, though not controlling, under both negligence and warranty theories.[181] Such standards may be admissible for a number of purposes, including to show negligence or breach of warranty, notice or knowledge of a defect, or the feasibility of a remedy.[182] "Evidence that all product designers in the industry balance the competing factors in a particular way clearly is relevant to the issue before the jury."[183] Likewise, evidence of "an industry-wide custom . . . influences, but does not conclusively determine, the applicable standard of care."[184]

5. **Evidence of Other Accidents**

Plaintiff may seek to introduce evidence of other accidents to prove notice or knowledge, the existence of a defect, or causation, but only if such accidents occurred under "substantially similar" circumstances.[185] Admissibility is left to the discretion of the trial judge, who must assess the dangers of unfairness, confusion and undue devotion of time to collateral matters.[186]

6. **Evidence of Subsequent Remedial Measures and Investigations**

Evidence of post-accident safety improvements generally is not admissible to prove negligence or breach of warranty.[187] In the judge's discretion and subject to limiting instructions, however, such evidence—including evidence of a recall—may be admissible for other purposes, such as to show the feasibility of technical improvements or knowledge of a defect.[188] Evidence of post-sale but pre-accident remedial measures also may be admissible, again subject to the judge's discretion and limiting instructions, for such purposes as feasibility, knowledge of defect or the existence of a defect at the time of sale.[189]

The Massachusetts state and federal courts are split on the issue of whether the results of a post-accident investigation are admissible. The Supreme Judicial Court does not allow the admission of such reports, on the theory that doing so "would discourage potential defendants from conducting such investigations, and so preclude safety improvements, and frustrate the salutary public policy underlying the rule [that post-accident improvements are not admissible]."[190] The United States Court of Appeals for the First Circuit, however, like the majority of circuits, does *not* exclude such reports, reasoning that "the fact that the analysis may often result in remedial measures being taken" does not mean that the analysis itself may not be admitted.[191]

7. **Evidence of Fair and Reasonable Charges for Medical Services**

Hospital and other medical bills are "admissible as evidence of the fair and reasonable charge" for medical and related services,[192] even where the amounts billed are significantly higher than the amounts actually paid to the hospital by a plaintiff's medical insurer.[193] Although the collateral source rule in such a circumstance bars a defendant from introducing evidence of the amounts actually paid, the defendant may elicit testimony from a representative of the hospital concerning "the range of payments that [the hospital] accepts for the particular type or types of services the plaintiff received."[194]

David R. Geiger
Jeffrey S. Follett
Matthew C. Baltay
Foley Hoag LLP
155 Seaport Boulevard
Boston, Massachusetts 02210
(617) 832-1000
(Fax) (617) 832-7000

ENDNOTES - MASSACHUSETTS

1. Mass. Gen. Laws ch. 260, § 2A.

2. Mass. Gen. Laws ch. 106, § 2-318 (abolishing lack of privity as defense for negligence, express warranty and implied warranty claims, and setting three-year limitations period for "actions of contract to recover for personal injuries"); *Bay State-Spray & Provincetown Steamship, Inc. v. Caterpillar Tractor Co.*, 404 Mass. 103, 107, 533 N.E.2d 1350, 1353 (1989).

3. Mass. Gen. Laws ch. 229, § 2 (three-year limitation period for wrongful death claims).

4. Mass. Gen. Laws ch. 260, § 5A.

5. Mass. Gen. Laws ch. 106, § 2-725; *see Rosario v. M.D. Knowlton Co.*, 54 Mass. App. Ct. 796, 803, 767 N.E.2d 1126, 1132 (2002); *Bay State-Spray*, 404 Mass. at 107, 533 N.E.2d at 1353.

6. *Gore v. Daniel O'Connell's Sons, Inc.*, 17 Mass. App. Ct. 645, 649, 461 N.E.2d 256, 259 (1984) ("When an injury or disease resulting from injury becomes manifest, the statute of limitations does not stay in suspense until the full extent, gravity, or permanence of that same injury or consequential disease is known."); *cf. Evans v. Lorillard Tobacco Co.*, 465 Mass. 411, 450, 990 N.E.2d 997, 1028 (2013) (stating in dicta that claim that product caused cancer accrues on diagnosis; "cancer does not lend itself to lay identification").

7. *Evans*, 465 Mass. at 449-50, 990 N.E.2d at 1028; *see also Donovan v. Philip Morris USA, Inc.*, 455 Mass. 215, 227, 914 N.E.2d 891, 902 (2009) (in medical monitoring context, cause of action relating to subsequent development of actual disease does not accrue until disease is manifested).

8. *McGuinness v. Cotter*, 412 Mass. 617, 627-29, 591 N.E.2d 659 (1992) (negligence); *Bowen v. Eli Lilly & Co.*, 408 Mass. 204, 208, 557 N.E.2d 739, 741 (1990) (negligence); *Fidler v. E. M. Parker Co., Inc.*, 394 Mass. 534, 545, 476 N.E.2d 595, 602 (1985) (warranty); *International Mobiles Corp. v. Corroon & Black/Fairfield & Ellis, Inc.*, 29 Mass. App. Ct. 215, 221, 560 N.E.2d 122, 126 (1990) (Ch. 93A).

9. *McGuinness*, 412 Mass. at 627-29, 591 N.E.2d at 665-66; *see also Bowen*, 408 Mass. at 208 (rejecting plaintiff's argument that claim accrues only when plaintiff has "probable cause" to believe that defendant caused her injury); *compare Genereux v. Am. Beryllia Corp.*, 577 F.3d 350, 360-61 (1st Cir. 2009) (citing *Bowen* for proposition that negligence, breach of warranty, and

failure-to-warn claims accrue when plaintiff has notice of "likely cause" of her injuries).

10. Mass. Gen. Laws ch. 260, § 12; *Puritan Med. Ctr., Inc. v. Cashman*, 413 Mass. 167, 177, 596 N.E.2d 1004, 1010 n.6 (1992).

11. Mass. Gen. Laws ch. 4, § 7, cl. 48-51.

12. Mass. Gen. Laws ch. 260, § 7. *See Harris v. Wilcox*, 384 Mass. 57, 424 N.E.2d 193 (1981).

13. Mass. Gen. Laws ch. 260, § 7;*McGuinness*, 412 Mass. at 624-25, 591 N.E.2d at 663-64.

14. Mass. Gen. Laws ch. 260, § 10.

15. *Donovan v. Philip Morris USA, Inc.*, 455 Mass. 215, 227-29, 914 N.E.2d 891, 902-04 (2009).

16. Mass. Gen. Laws ch. 260, § 2B; *Parent v. Stone & Webster Eng'g Corp.*, 408 Mass. 108, 111, 556 N.E.2d 1009, 1010 (1990) (electrical distribution panel); *McDonough v. Marr Scaffolding Co.*, 412 Mass. 636, 591 N.E.2d 1079 (1992) (ice rink bleachers); *Snow v. Harnischfeger Corp.*, 12 F.3d 1154 (1st Cir. 1993) (overhead cranes).

17. Applicability of the out-of-state statute of repose turns on whether Massachusetts or the other state has the "more significant relationship to the parties and the occurrence." *Cosme v. Whitin Mach. Works, Inc.*, 417 Mass. 643, 650, 632 N.E.2d 832, 836 (1994). *See also Romani v. Cramer, Inc.*, 992 F. Supp. 74 (D. Mass. 1998) (applying Connecticut statute of repose).

18. One who holds out as his own a product that is actually manufactured by another may be liable on a negligence theory as the "apparent manufacturer" of that product. *Fahey v. Rockwell Graphic Sys., Inc.*, 20 Mass. App. Ct. 642, 650, 482 N.E.2d 519, 525 (1985) (applying Restatement (Second) of Torts § 400, cmt. d, in claim alleging negligent design); *see* § J.5 *infra*.

19. *Back v. Wickes Corp.*, 375 Mass. 633, 643, 378 N.E.2d 964, 971 (1978).

20. *Enrich v. Windmere Corp.*, 416 Mass. 83, 86, 616 N.E.2d 1081, 1084 (1993).

21. *Correia v. Firestone Tire & Rubber Co.*, 388 Mass. 342, 355, 446 N.E.2d 1033, 1040 (1983). *But see* § D.1.d *infra* (discussing convergence of warranty liability and negligence liability in design and warning defect cases).

22. *Smith v. Ariens Co.*, 375 Mass. 620, 626, 377 N.E.2d 954, 958 (1978) (negligent manufacture); *Simmons v. Monarch Mach. Tool Co.*, 413 Mass. 205, 211, 596

N.E.2d 318, 322 (1992) (negligent design); *Carey v. Lynn Ladder & Scaffolding Co., Inc.*, 427 Mass. 1003, 691 N.E.2d 223 (1998) (negligent failure to warn).

23. *Smith*, 375 Mass. 620, 626, 377 N.E.2d 954, 958.

24. *Tibbetts v. Ford Motor Co.*, 4 Mass. App. Ct. 738, 740, 385 N.E.2d 460 (1976).

25. *See, e.g., Simmons v. Monarch Mach. Tool Co.*, 413 Mass. 205, 211, 596 N.E.2d 318, 322 (1992) (citing *Back v. Wickes*, 375 Mass. 633, 640-41, 378 N.E.2d 964, 969 (1978), a warranty case, for appropriate multi-factor analysis to use in a defective design claim based in negligence); *Ducharme v. Hyundai Motor Am.*, 45 Mass. App. Ct. 401, 404, 698 N.E.2d 412, 414 (1998) (same).

26. *Evans*, 465 Mass. at 443-44, 990 N.E.2d at 1024; *Kotler v. American Tobacco Co.*, 926 F.2d 1217, 1225 (1st Cir. 1990), *vacated*, 505 U.S. 1215, 112 S. Ct. 3019, *reaff'd*, 981 F.2d 7 (1st Cir. 1992); *Colter v. Barber-Greene Co.*, 403 Mass. 50, 57, 525 N.E.2d 1305, 1311 (1988); *see also Osorio v. One World Techs., Inc.*, 659 F.3d 81, 86-87 (1st Cir. 2011) (after holding that plaintiff presented adequate evidence of feasible alternative design, suggesting in dicta that plaintiffs need not present expert evidence of safer alternative design in all circumstances).

27. *Marchant v. Dayton Tire & Rubber Co.*, 836 F.2d 695, 699-700 (1st Cir. 1988); *Osorio*, 659 F.3d at 86.

28. *Marchant*, 836 F.2d at 700.

29. *Back*, 375 Mass. at 640-41, 378 N.E.2d at 970.

30. *Fahey v. Rockwell Graphic Sys., Inc.*, 20 Mass. App. Ct. 642, 652, 482 N.E.2d 519, 525-26 (1985); *Colter*, 403 Mass. 50, 57, 525 N.E.2d 1305, 1311.

31. *Bergendahl v. Massachusetts Elec. Co.*, 45 Mass. App. Ct. 715, 725, 701 N.E.2d 656, 663 (1998).

32. *Smith v. Ariens Co.*, 375 Mass. 620, 624, 377 N.E.2d 954, 957 (1978).

33. *Smith*, 375 Mass. at 624, 377 N.E.2d at 957 (holding that scope of intended use "should include foreseeable participation in collisions and that manufacturers have a duty to design products so that users are not subjected to unreasonable risks of injury in the event of a collision"); *Simmons v. Monarch Mach. Tool Co.*, 413 Mass. 205, 212, 596 N.E.2d 318, 322-23 (1992); *Lally v. Volkswagen Aktiengesellschaft*, 45 Mass. App. Ct. 317, 326-30, 698 N.E.2d 28, 37-39 (1998) (standard of proof).

34. *Carey v. Lynn Ladder & Scaffolding Co., Inc.*, 427 Mass. 1003, 691 N.E.2d 223 (1998).

35. *Wasylow v. Glock, Inc.*, 975 F. Supp. 370, 378 (D. Mass. 1996); *MacDonald v. Ortho Pharm. Corp.*, 394 Mass. 131, 139-41, 475 N.E.2d 65, 71 (1985).

36. *Carey*, 427 Mass. 1003, 691 N.E.2d 223; *Colter*, 403 Mass. 50, 59, 525 N.E.2d 1305, 1312; *see also Evans*, 465 Mass. at 439, 990 N.E.2d at 1021 (noting that Massachusetts law is consistent with Restatement (Third) of Torts: Products Liability § 2, cmt. j).

37. *Evans*, 465 Mass. at 442, 990 N.E. 2d at 1023; *Carey*, 427 Mass. at 1004, 691 N.E.2d at 224-25.

38. *Cf. Bell v. Wysong & Miles Co.*, 26 Mass. App. Ct. 1011, 1013-14, 531 N.E.2d 267, 269 (1988) (no liability where warning would not have "so alerted the plaintiff that the accident would not have occurred"); *Geshke v. Crocs, Inc.*, 889 F. Supp. 3d 253, 263-64 (D. Mass. 2012) (same).

39. *See Galvin v. Welsh Mfg. Co.*, 382 Mass. 340, 344, 416 N.E.2d 183, 186 (1981) (if trial judge had provided instruction concerning duty under implied warranty of merchantability to warn of dangers relating to reasonably foreseeable misuse of product, jury properly could have found manufacturer negligent for same failure to warn).

40. Other jurisdictions have split on this issue. *Compare Witthauer v. Burkhart Roentgen, Inc.*, 467 N.W.2d 439 (N.D. 1991) (duty to warn extends to foreseeable alterations) *with Hill v. Gen. Motors Corp.*, 637 S.W.2d 382, 384 (Mo. App. 1982) (no duty on the part of a manufacturer to anticipate and warn of dangerous alterations to its product).

41. *Vassallo v. Baxter Healthcare Corp.*, 428 Mass. 1, 23, 696 N.E.2d 909, 923 (1998) (adopting the Third Restatement's position with respect to post-sale duty to warn under warranty of merchantability theory, and affirming defense verdict on negligent failure-to-warn claim).

42. *Lewis v. Ariens Co.*, 434 Mass. 643, 751 N.E.2d 862 (2001) (no duty to warn second-hand purchaser of snowblower); *Hayes v. Ariens Co.*, 391 Mass. 407, 411, 462 N.E.2d 273, 276 (1984); *doCanto v. Ametek, Inc.*, 367 Mass. 776, 781, 328 N.E.2d 873, 876 (1975).

43. *Lewis*, 434 Mass. 643, 647-49, 751 N.E.2d 862, 866-67.

44. *Bay State-Spray & Provincetown S.S., Inc. v. Caterpillar Tractor Co.*, 404 Mass. 103, 107, 533 N.E.2d 1350, 1353 (1989); *see also Rule v. Fort Dodge Animal Health, Inc.*, 604 F. Supp. 2d 288, 292-93 (D. Mass. 2009), *aff'd*, 607 F.3d 250 (1st Cir. 2010) (observing that Massachusetts' economic loss rule is consistent with Restatement (Third) of Torts: Products Liability § 21 (1998)).

45. *Donovan v. Philip Morris USA, Inc.*, 455 Mass. 215, 226, 914 N.E.2d 891, 901-02 (2009); *see also Generaux v. Raytheon Co.*, --- F.3d ----, 2014 U.S. App. LEXIS

10718 at *8-13 (1st Cir. 2014) (affirming grant of summary judgment where plaintiffs offered no evidence of subcellular changes). The measure of damages for such an injury is the present value of the reasonable cost of such tests and care, as of the date the complaint was filed. *Donovan*, 455 Mass. at 226.

46. *Swartz v. Gen. Motors Corp.*, 375 Mass. 628, 631, 378 N.E.2d 61, 64 (1978).

47. Mass. Gen. Laws ch. 106, §§ 2-314 to 2-318 (sales), §§ 2A-212 to 2A-216 (leases); *Back v. Wickes Corp.*, 375 Mass. 633, 639, 378 N.E.2d 964, 968 (1978).

48. *Back*, 375 Mass. 633, 640, 378 N.E.2d 964, 969. *See also* Mass. Gen. Laws ch. 106, §§ 2-314 to 2-318 (sales), §§ 2A-212 to 2A-216 (leases).

49. *See e.g., Evans*, 465 Mass. at 423-28, 990 N.E.2d at 1011-14 (role of consumer expectations of product safety in determining unreasonable dangerousness of product design); *Vassallo v. Baxter Healthcare Corp.*, 428 Mass. 1, 20-23, 696 N.E.2d 909, 924 (1998) ("state of the art" standard in failure-to-warn cases); *Lewis v. Ariens Co.*, 434 Mass. 643, 751 N.E.2d 862 (2001) (post-sale duty to warn); *Lally v. Volkswagen Aktiengesellschaft*, 45 Mass. App. Ct. 317, 326-30, 698 N.E.2d 28, 37-39 (1998) (standard for proof of enhanced injuries).

50. *See* Mass. Gen. Laws ch. 106, §§ 2-102, 2-106, 2-313, 2-314, 2-318 (sales); *Fernandes v. Union Bookbinding Co., Inc.*, 400 Mass. 27, 34, 507 N.E.2d 728, 732 (1987) (sales of new or used goods); Mass. Gen. Laws ch. 106, §§ 2A-102, 2A-210, 2A-212, 2A-216, (leases); *Draleau v. Ctr. Capital Corp.*, 49 Mass. App. Ct. 783, 787, 732 N.E.2d 929, 933 n.8 (2000) (leases).

51. *Lou v. Otis Elevator Co.*, 77 Mass. App. Ct. 571, 581, 933 N.E.2d 140, 148 (2010); *see* § J.5 *infra*.

52. Mass. Gen. Laws ch. 106, §§ 2-318, 2A-216; *Theos & Sons, Inc. v. Mack Trucks, Inc.*, 431 Mass. 736, 740, 729 N.E.2d 1113, 1117 (2000) (noting that ch. 106, § 2-318 extends all warranties, express or implied, to third parties who may reasonably be expected to use the warranted product); *Draleau v. Ctr. Capital Corp.*, 49 Mass. App. Ct. 783, 785, 732 N.E.2d 929, 931 (2000) (noting the applicability of ch. 106, § 2-318 to leases); *cf. First Choice Armor & Equip., Inc. v. Toyobo Am., Inc.*, 839 F. Supp. 2d 407, 412-13 (D. Mass. 2012) (granting summary judgment against "commercial" breach of warranty claims where plaintiff lacks privity with defendant).

53. *Mason v. Gen. Motors Corp.*, 397 Mass. 183, 186-91, 490 N.E.2d 437, 439-42 (1986) (affirming dismissal on summary judgment of implied warranty claim against automobile dealer, where dealer had neither sold nor leased allegedly-warranted vehicle, but rather had allowed decedent to take it for a test drive).

54. *Hatch v. Trail King Indus., Inc.*, 656 F.3d 59, 67-68 (1st Cir. 2011) (quoting Restatement (Second) of Torts § 404, comment a, as an accurate statement of Massachusetts law); *Commonwealth v. Johnson Insulation*, 425 Mass. 650, 655-56, 682 N.E.2d 1323, 1327-28 (1997). Merely specifying a brand name or trade name will not negate an implied warranty of merchantability. 425 Mass. at 656, 682 N.E.2d at 1328.

55. *Hitchcock v. Emergency Lighting & Sys., Inc.*, 12 Mass. App. Ct. 930, 930-31, 425 N.E.2d 396, 397 (1981).

56. *Commonwealth v. Johnson Insulation*, 425 Mass. 650, 660, 682 N.E.2d 1323, 1330 (1997).

57. *Johnson Insulation*, 425 Mass. at 660, 682 N.E.2d at 1330; *Colter v. Barber-Greene Co.*, 403 Mass. 50, 61-62, 525 N.E.2d 1305, 1313 (1988); *Correia v. Firestone Tire & Rubber Co.*, 388 Mass. 342, 355, 446 N.E.2d 1033, 1040 (1983).

58. *Back*, 375 Mass. at 637, 378 N.E.2d at 948. *Compare Tibbetts v. Ford Motor Co.*, 4 Mass. App. Ct. 738, 740, 385 N.E.2d 460 (1976) (under negligence theory, a "manufacturer's duty is one of reasonable care, not perfection").

59. *Back*, 375 Mass. at 642, 378 N.E.2d at 971 (jury evaluating an implied warranty claim based on a theory of design defect must "weigh competing factors much as they would in determining the fault of the defendant in a negligence case"); *Hoffman v. Houghton Chem. Corp.*, 434 Mass. 624, 637, 751 N.E.2d 848, 859 (2001) (theories of negligent failure to warn and failure to warn as a breach of warranty "are to be judged by the same standard: the reasonableness of defendant's actions in the circumstances"); *cf. Evans*, 465 Mass. at 443-45, 990 N.E.2d at 1024-25 (affirming verdict on warranty but reversing verdict on negligence where court gave different instructions on design defect under the two theories).

60. *Hayes v. Ariens Co.*, 391 Mass. 407, 410, 462 N.E.2d 273, 275 (1984); *Caccavale v. Raymark Indus., Inc.*, 404 Mass. 93, 97, 533 N.E.2d 1345, 1348 (1989).

61. *Back v. Wickes*, 375 Mass. 633, 641, 378 N.E.2d 964, 970 (1978) (manufacturing defect and design defect); *Hoffman v. Houghton*, 434 Mass. 624, 637, 751 N.E.2d 848, 854 (2001) (failure to warn).

62. *Back*, 375 Mass. 633, 641, 378 N.E.2d 964, 970 (1978).

63. *Enrich v. Windmere Corp.*, 416 Mass. 83, 89, 616 N.E.2d 1081, 1085 (1993); *Fernandes v. Union Bookbinding Co.*, 400 Mass. 27, 37, 507 N.E.2d 728, 734 (1987).

64. *See Back*, 375 Mass. at 640-41, 378 N.E.2d at 969; *see also Cigna Ins. Co. v. Oy Saunatec, Ltd.*, 241 F.3d 1, 16 (1st Cir. 2001) (the "cornerstone" of negligence and warranty duties "is the anticipation of foreseeable uses. . . . A defendant

manufacturer may not escape liability solely by showing that the plaintiff has used the product in a way that was not intended by the manufacturer").

65. *Evans*, 465 Mass. at 428, 990 N.E.2d at 1014 (2013). The court in *Evans* also stated that to prove causation in a design defect claim brought under the implied warranty of merchantability, a plaintiff need not prove that he would have used the alternative design had it been available, but rather simply that the defective design caused his injury. *Evans*, 465 Mass. at 438, 990 N.E.2d at 1021-22. The court did not explain how the evidence in that case supported a finding that the plaintiff's decedent would not have suffered her harm if the defendant's cigarettes had not contained the defect, given the availability of numerous other cigarette brands that did.

66. *Back*, 375 Mass. at 642, 378 N.E.2d at 970 (relevant factors include the "gravity of the danger posed by the challenged design, the likelihood that such danger would occur, the mechanical feasibility of a safer alternative design, the financial cost of an improved design, and the adverse consequences to the product and to the consumer that would result from an alternative design"); *Evans*, 465 Mass. at 426-28, 990 N.E.2d at 1012-14 (citing *Back* and Third Restatement).

67. *Evans*, 465 Mass. at 426-28, 990 N.E.2d at 1013-14; *but cf. Johnson Insulation*, 425 Mass. at 660, 682 N.E.2d at 1330 (1997) (citing § 402A, comment i, with approval in failure-to-warn case); *Johnson v. Brown & Williamson Tobacco Corp.*, 345 F. Supp. 2d 16, 22 (D. Mass. 2004) (cigarettes not unreasonably dangerous in light of common knowledge of risks of smoking).

68. *Killeen v. Harmon Grain Prods., Inc.*, 11 Mass. App. 20, 23, 413 N.E.2d 767, 770 (1980); *Kearney v. Philip Morris, Inc.*, 916 F. Supp. 61, 72-73 (D. Mass. 1996).

69. *Payton v. Abbott Labs.*, 386 Mass. 540, 573, 437 N.E.2d 171, 189 (1982) (DES); *Lareau v. Page*, 840 F. Supp. 920, 933 (D. Mass. 1993), *aff'd*, 39 F.3d 384 (1st Cir. 1994) (use of contrast injection during brain surgery).

70. *Hoffman v. Houghton*, 434 Mass. 624, 637, 751 N.E.2d 848, 854 (2001) (recognizing convergence of warranty and negligence theories on failure-to-warn claims); *Vassallo v. Baxter Healthcare Corp.*, 428 Mass. 1, 21, 696 N.E.2d 909, 923 (1998) (liability attaches "when the foreseeable risks of harm posed by the product could have been reduced or avoided by the provision of reasonable instructions or warnings . . . and the omission of the instructions or warnings renders the product not reasonably safe") (quoting Restatement (Third) of Torts: Product Liability § 2(c)). The *Vassallo* court did remark in dicta that, in determining reasonable foreseeability of product dangers, "[a] manufacturer will be held to the standard of knowledge of an expert in the appropriate field." *Vassallo*, 428 Mass. 1, 21, 696 N.E.2d 909, 923. This dictum—which arguably imposes a higher standard on manufacturers—appears to be inconsistent with prior and subsequent case law. *See, e.g., Back*, 375 Mass. at 642, 378 N.E.2d at 971 (trial judge correctly

declined to instruct jurors on negligence claim that manufacturer could be held to "the knowledge and skill of some unspecified 'expert' rather than simply the knowledge and skill of a reasonable person in the same circumstances"); *Hoffman*, 434 Mass. at 637, 751 N.E.2d at 854 (recognizing convergence of warranty and negligence theories on failure-to-warn claims).

71. *Bay State-Spray & Provincetown S.S., Inc. v. Caterpillar Tractor Co.*, 404 Mass. 103, 107, 533 N.E.2d 1350, 1353 (1989).

72. *Donovan*, 455 Mass. at 226 & n.13.

73. *Marcil v. John Deere Indus. Equip. Co.*, 9 Mass. App. Ct. 625, 632, 403 N.E.2d 430, 434 (1980) (Sections 2-313 through 318 of the Massachusetts version of the Uniform Commercial Code govern the commercial expectations of buyer and seller; "We do not believe that entirely distinct principles of tort law should be permitted to frustrate those expectations.").

74. Mass. Gen. Laws ch. 93A, § 2.

75. Mass. Gen. Laws §§ 9(3a) & 11.

76. Mass. Gen. Laws §§ 9(3a) & 11.

77. Mass. Gen. Laws § 1(b) (definitions of "trade" and "commerce"); § 11 (providing cause of action for persons engaging in trade or commerce).

78. *Frank Cook, Inc. v. Hurwitz*, 10 Mass. App. Ct. 99, 111, 406 N.E.2d 678, 686 (1980).

79. *Maillet v. ATF-Davidson Co., Inc.*, 407 Mass. 185, 189, 522 N.E.2d 95, 98 (1990) (affirming printing press operator's Ch. 93A judgment against manufacturer of printing press on failure-to-warn theory).

80. *Compare Iannacchino v. Ford Motor Co.*, 451 Mass. 623, 629-31, N.E.2d 879, 885-87 (2008) (If defendant knowingly sold vehicles that did not comply with applicable federal safety regulations, "plaintiffs would have paid for more (viz., safety regulation-compliant vehicles) than they received. Such an overpayment would represent an economic loss—measurable by the cost to bring the vehicles into compliance—for which the plaintiffs could seek redress under G.L.ch. 93A, § 9."), *with Hershenow v. Enter. Rent-A-Car Co. of Boston, Inc.*, 445 Mass. 790, 840 N.E.2d 526 (2006) (holding that consumer suffered no injury actionable under ch. 93A, § 9, by paying extra for collision damage waiver containing terms contravening Massachusetts statute, absent defendant's invocation of invalid portion of waiver); *see also Rule v. Fort Dodge Animal Health, Inc.*, 607 F.3d 250, 253-55 (1st Cir. 2010) (under ch. 93A, plaintiff who fully consumed and received expected benefit of product that was allegedly deceptively marketed to conceal latent defect suffered no actionable injury). *See also Maillet*, 407 Mass. at 192, 552 N.E.2d at 99-100

(personal injury is actionable injury under ch. 93A, § 9); *Haddad v. Gonzalez*, 410 Mass. 855, 576 N.E.2d 658 (1991) (severe emotional distress is actionable injury under ch. 93A, § 9); *Donovan*, 455 Mass. at 226 & n.13 (plaintiff adequately claims an "injury" under ch. 93A where she alleges the elements described in Section C(6) above).

81. Mass. Gen. Laws ch. 93A, §§ 9(1), (3) and (4); *Lord v. Commercial Union Ins. Co.*, 60 Mass. App. Ct. 309, 321, 801 N.E.2d 303, 314 (2004); *Shapiro v. Pub. Serv. Mut. Ins. Co.*, 19 Mass. App. Ct. 648, 657, 477 N.E.2d 146, 153 (1985); *Aspinall v. Philip Morris Cos., Inc.*, 442 Mass. 381, 401, 813 N.E.2d 476, 491 (2004).

82. Mass. Gen. Laws ch. 93A, §§ 2(b)-(c); *see Ciardi v. F. Hoffmann-La Roche, Ltd.*, 436 Mass. 53, 59, 762 N.E.2d 303, 309 (2002).

83. *Linkage Corp. v. Trustees of Boston Univ.*, 425 Mass. 1, 27, 679 N.E.2d 191, 209 (1997).

84. *See Spence v. Boston Edison Co.*, 390 Mass. 604, 616, 459 N.E.2d 80, 87-88 (1983) ("One can easily imagine cases where an act might be unfair if practiced upon a commercial innocent yet would be common practice between two people engaged in business"); *Arthur D. Little, Inc. v. Dooyang Corp.*, 147 F.3d 47, 55 (1st Cir. 1998) (specific circumstances surrounding allegations under Chapter 93A must be considered on a case-by-case basis).

85. *See, e.g., Swanson v. Bankers Life Co.*, 389 Mass. 345, 349 (1983) (negligent act standing by itself does not give rise to claim under Chapter 93A); *Darviris v. Petros*, 442 Mass. 274, 278, 812 N.E.2d 1188, 1193 (2004) (same); *Whitinsville Plaza, Inc. v. Kotseas*, 378 Mass. 85, 100-01, 1390 N.E.2d 243 (1979) (mere breach of contract, without more, does not constitute violation of Chapter 93A).

86. *Maillet v. ATF-Davidson Co., Inc.*, 407 Mass. 185, 194, 552 N.E.2d 95, 98 (1990) (citing 940 CMR, § 3.08(2)); *Knapp Shoes, Inc. v. Sylvania Shoe Mfg. Corp.*, 418 Mass. 737, 745, 640 N.E.2d 1101, 1105 (1994) (holding that 940 CMR, § 3.08(2) applies only to section 9 claims).

87. The regulation in question does not proscribe a mere "breach of warranty" but rather only a "fail[ure] to perform or fulfill any promises or obligations *arising under* a warranty," which arguably may apply only to failure to provide a promised warranty remedy. 940 CMR, § 3.08(2) (emphasis added). Notably, however, the United States Court of Appeals for the First Circuit has suggested that a cause of action may lie under Chapter 93A even in the *absence* of a breach of warranty. *See Cummings v. HPG Int'l, Inc.*, 244 F.3d 16, 26 (1st Cir. 2001) (speculating that manufacturer with no common law post-sale duty to warn nonetheless may violate Ch. 93A by failing to provide warning in some circumstances).

88. Mass. Gen. Laws ch. 93A, § 9(3).

89. Mass. Gen. Laws ch. 93A, § 9(3).

90. Mass. Gen. Laws ch. 93A, § 9(3).

91. Mass. Gen. Laws ch. 93A, § 9(2).

92. *Kwaak v. Pfizer, Inc.*, 71 Mass. App. Ct. 293, 298, 881 N.E.2d 812, 816 (2008); *cf. Fletcher v. Cape Cod Gas Co.*, 394 Mass. 595, 605-06, 477 N.E.2d 116, 123 (1985) (affirming trial court's denial of class certification under § 9(2) where court previously had certified same class under Rule 23(a)).

93. *See Moelis v. Berkshire Life Ins. Co.*, 451 Mass. 483, 490, 887 N.E.2d 214, 220 (2008) (court has discretion to consider issues of predominance and superiority in determining whether members of the proposed class meet the "similar injury" and "similarly situated" requirements of § 9(2)).

94. *See Feeney v. Dell, Inc.*, 466 Mass. 1001, 993 N.E.2d 329 (2013); *AT&T Mobility LLC v. Concepcion*, ___ U.S. ___, 131 S. Ct. 1740 (2011).

95. *Feeney v. Dell, Inc.*, 454 Mass. 192, 201-02, 908 N.E.2d 753, 762-64 (2009).

96. *Nei v. Burley*, 388 Mass. 307, 314-15, 446 N.E.2d 674, 680 (1983).

97. *Service Pubs., Inc. v. Government*, 396 Mass. 567, 577-78, 487 N.E.2d 520, 527 (1986).

98. *Klairmont v. Gainsboro Rest., Inc.*, 465 Mass. 165, 186-88, 987 N.E.2d 1247, 1263-64 (2013).

99. Mass. Gen. Laws ch. 106, § 2-313.

100. Mass. Gen. Laws § 2-315; *Fernandes v. Union Bookbinding Co.*, 400 Mass. 27, 34, 507 N.E.2d 729, 732-33 (1987).

101. Mass. Gen. Laws ch. 231, § 85.

102. *Richard v. American Mfg. Co.*, 21 Mass. App. Ct. 967, 968, 489 N.E.2d 214, 215 (1986).

103. Mass. Gen. Laws ch. 231, § 85; *Colter v. Barber-Greene Co*, 403 Mass. 50, 62, 525 N.E.2d 1305, 1313-14 (1988); *see also Shantigar Found. v. Bear Mountain Builders*, 441 Mass. 131, 137-38, 804 N.E.2d 324, 329-30 (2004) (holding that the negligence of a settling defendant is not considered under the comparative negligence standard).

104. *Colter*, 403 Mass. at 62, 525 N.E.2d at 1313-14.

105. *Sultis v. Gen. Motors Corp.*, 690 F. Supp. 100, 104 (D. Mass. 1988).

106. *See Correia v. Firestone Tire & Rubber Co.*, 388 Mass. 342, 355, 356, 357, 446 N.E.2d 1033, 1040, 1041 (1983) (explaining that an affirmative defense in a strict liability scheme is available when "a user unreasonably proceeds to use a product which he knows to be defective and dangerous" and that "the user is denied recovery, not because of his . . . assumption of the risk but rather because his conduct is the proximate cause of his injuries." Further, the court explained that other than the above described defense, "[n]o recovery by the plaintiff shall be diminished on account of any other conduct which might be deemed contributorily negligent."). *See also Allen v. Chance Mfg. Co.*, 398 Mass. 32, 34, 494 N.E.2d 1324, 1326 (1986) (explaining that the defense described in *Correia* "differs from the traditional doctrine of assumption of the risk" because it combines a subjective with an objective element).

107. *Correia v. Firestone Tire & Rubber Co.*, 388 Mass. 342, 354-57, 446 N.E.2d 1033, 1039-41 (1983) (holding that comparative negligence statute, Mass. Gen. Laws. ch. 231, § 85, does not apply to warranty actions). *Compare* Third Restatement § 17, cmt. d. (noting majority rule that comparative negligence principles apply to implied warranty actions).

108. *Correia*, 388 Mass. at 354-55, 446 N.E.2d at 1039-40; *Fernandes v. Union Bookbinding Co.*, 400 Mass. 27, 37, 507 N.E.2d 728, 734 (1987).

109. *Correia*, 388 Mass. at 357, 446 N.E.2d at 1041 (adopting the reasoning of Restatement (Second) of Torts § 402A, cmt. n (1965)). *See Allen v. Chance Mfg. Co., Inc.*, 398 Mass. 32, 34, 494 N.E.2d 1324, 1326 (1986) (affirmative defense of unreasonable use differs from traditional doctrine of assumption of risk because it combines a subjective element, *i.e.*, plaintiff's actual knowledge and appreciation of the risk of using a product known to be defective and dangerous, with an objective standard, *i.e.*, the reasonableness—or lack thereof—of plaintiff's conduct in face of known danger). *But see Haglund v. Philip Morris, Inc.*, 446 Mass. 741, 743, 847 N.E.2d 315, 319-20 (2006) (unreasonable use defense not available to cigarette manufacturer unless smoker's use of product was "so overwhelmingly unreasonable as to make the imposition of warranty liability . . . fundamentally unfair").

110. *See Colter v. Barber-Greene Co.*, 403 Mass. 50, 64 n.14, 525 N.E.2d 1305, 1315 (1988).

111. When it declined to apply the comparative negligence statute to warranty claims in 1983, the Supreme Judicial Court noted that negligence liability and warranty liability each were "well defined" spheres, that the Legislature had shown no intent "to merge negligence liability with warranty liability" and that the court itself would leave any "restructuring" of the law of warranty to the Legislature. *Correia*, 388 Mass. at 357, 446 N.E.2d at 1041. More recently, however, the court has acknowledged the convergence of

negligence liability and warranty liability in the context of design defect and failure-to-warn cases. *See, e.g., Hoffman v. Houghton*, 434 Mass. 624, 637, 751 N.E.2d 848, 854 (2001) (recognizing convergence of warranty and negligence theories). *See also* David R. Geiger & Stephanie Copp Martinez, *Design and Warning Defect Claims Under Massachusetts Product Liability Law: Completing the Merger of Negligence and Warranty*, 43 Boston Bar Journal No. 2 (1999) (arguing that courts should follow comparative negligence statute by analogy in implied warranty claims).

112. Mass. Gen. Laws ch. 106, §§ 2-318, 2A-216.

113. *Sacramona v. Bridgestone/Firestone, Inc.*, 106 F.3d 444, 449 (1st Cir. 1997) (claim barred where delayed notice may have "deprived the defense of useful evidence"; "[n]o showing is required that lost evidence would inevitably have altered the outcome"); *Smith v. Robertshaw Controls Co.*, 410 F.3d 29, 36-37 (1st Cir. 2005); *Castro v. Stanley Works*, 864 F.2d 961, 964 (1st Cir. 1989).

114. *Atlantic Pipe Corp. v. R.J. Longo Constr. Co.*, 35 Mass. App. Ct. 459, 463, 622 N.E.2d 279, 281 (1993) (buyer of pipe was barred from recovery for any alleged breach of warranty due to its failure to provide adequate and timely notice to seller of breach).

115. Mass. Gen. Laws ch. 106, § 2-316A and 2-318.

116. *Cottam v. CVS Pharmacy*, 436 Mass. 316, 322, 764 N.E.2d 814, 821 (2002) (pharmacies); *MacDonald v. Ortho Pharm. Co.*, 394 Mass. 131, 136, 475 N.E.2d 65, 68 (1985), *cert. denied*, 474 U.S. 920 (1985) (prescription drugs).

117. *Hoffman v. Houghton Chem. Corp.*, 434 Mass. 624, 634, 751 N.E.2d 848, 857 (2001).

118. *Hoffman*, 434 Mass. at 634, 751 N.E.2d at 857; *see also Tilton v. Union Oil Co. of California*, 64 Mass. App. Ct. 115, 116-17, 831 N.E.2d 391, 394-95 (2005).

119. *Tilton*, 64 Mass. App. Ct. at 117 n.2, 831 N.E.2d at 395 n.2.

120. *Tilton*, 64 Mass. App. Ct. at 117 n.2, 831 N.E.2d at 395 n.2; *see also Carrel v. Nat'l Cord & Braid Corp.*, 447 Mass. 431, 441, 852 N.E.2d 100, 109 (2006) (expressly adopting sophisticated user defense); *Taylor v. Am. Chemistry Council*, 576 F.3d 16, 24 n.6 (1st Cir. 2009) (treating plaintiff's former employer, rather than plaintiff, as relevant end user of vinyl chloride used by plaintiff in manufacturing employer's products).

121. *Taylor*, 576 F.3d at 28-31 (affirming summary judgment for supplier where end user, claimant's employer, had direct contacts with researchers conducting relevant medical studies, was promptly apprised of those studies, maintained a library of medical literature on product's risks, and employed a staff of industrial hygienists, physicians, and toxicologists).

122. *Taylor*, 576 F.3d at 25-27.

123. Mass. Gen. Laws ch. 152, § 23 ("If an employee . . . accepts payment of [workers'] compensation on account of personal injury . . . such action shall constitute a release to the insurer of all claims or demands at common law, if any, arising from the injury."); *Larkin v. Ralph O. Porter, Inc.*, 405 Mass. 179, 181, 539 N.E.2d 529, 530 (1989). *But see Barrett v. Rodgers*, 408 Mass. 614, 617, 562 N.E.2d 480, 482 (1990) ("allud[ing] favorably" to, although not adopting, "dual capacity" doctrine, which provides that an employer may be regarded as a third party and thus be subject to suit, if the employer's liability to the injured employee derives from a "second persona so completely independent from and unrelated to his status as employer that by established standards the law recognizes it as a separate legal person") citing *Gurry v. Cumberland Farms, Inc.*, 406 Mass. 615, 620-21, 550 N.E.2d 127 (1990) (allowing action against employer where worker had been killed by a machine designed, built and sold by a corporation later acquired by the employer).

124. *Liberty Mut. Ins. Co. v. Westerlind*, 374 Mass. 524, 526, 373 N.E.2d 957, 959 (1978).

125. *See Decker v. Black & Decker Mfg. Co.*, 389 Mass. 35, 37, 449 N.E.2d 641 (1983) ("any right of a third-party tortfeasor to recover indemnity from an employer who paid workmen's compensation benefits to an injured employee, must stem, if at all, from an express or implied contract of indemnity or from an obligation implied from the relationship of the parties"); *City of Haverhill v. George Brox, Inc.*, 47 Mass. App. Ct. 717, 724-25, 716 N.E.2d 138, 144 (1999) (affirming summary judgment for contractor seeking indemnification from employer).

126. *Fletcher v. Dorchester Mut. Ins. Co.*, 437 Mass. 544, 549-50, 773 N.E.2d 420, 425 (2002) ("We have implicitly recognized that persons who are actually involved in litigation (or know that they will likely be involved) have a duty to preserve evidence for use by others who will also be involved in that litigation. Where evidence has been destroyed or altered by persons who are parties to the litigation, or by persons affiliated with a party (in particular, their expert witnesses), and another party's ability to prosecute or defend the claim has been prejudiced as a result, we have held that a judge may exclude evidence to remedy that unfairness."); *Kippenhan v. Chaulk Servs., Inc.*, 428 Mass. 124, 127, 697 N.E.2d 527, 530 (1998) ("The threat of a lawsuit must be sufficiently apparent . . . that a reasonable person in the spoliator's position would realize, at the time of spoliation, the possible importance of the evidence to the resolution of the potential dispute"); *cf. Hofer v. The Gap, Inc.*, 516 F. Supp. 2d 161, 170 n.10 (D. Mass. 2007) (federal law controls spoliation issues in product liability suit in federal court pursuant to diversity jurisdiction).

127. *Gath v. M/A-Com, Inc.*, 440 Mass. 482, 499, 802 N.E.2d 521, 534 (2003) (dismissing cause of action based on spoliation as non-cognizable and listing potential sanctions, including preclusion of testimony, dismissal, or judgment by default); *Keene v. Brigham & Women's Hosp., Inc.*, 439 Mass. 223, 236, 786 N.E.2d 824, 834 (2003) (default judgment); *Fletcher v. Dorchester Mut. Ins. Co.*, 437 Mass. 544, 550-51, 773 N.E.2d 420, 425-26 (2002) (dismissal); *Kippenham*, 428 Mass. at 127 (finding factual issue as to when the spoliator knew or should have known of the prospect of litigation and reversing lower court's exclusion of expert testimony on same grounds); *Nally v. Volkswagen of Am., Inc.*, 405 Mass. 191, 197-98, 539 N.E.2d 1017, 1021 (1989) (finding outstanding factual issues precluded exclusion of expert testimony); *Bolton v. Massachusetts Bay Transp. Auth.*, 32 Mass. App. Ct. 654, 657, 593 N.E.2d 248, 249 (1992) (exclusion of expert testimony); *Sacramona v. Bridgestone/Firestone, Inc.*, 106 F.3d 444, 445-47 (1st Cir. 1997) (exclusion of evidence leading to dismissal of claims); *Westover v. Leiserv, Inc.*, 64 Mass. App. Ct. 109, 114, 831 N.E.2d 400, 405 (2005) (preclusion of evidence resulting in dismissal was abuse of discretion where claim was that entire line of chairs was defective and despite destruction of chair involved in accident, other chairs were available for inspection).

128. *Keene*, 439 Mass. at 232, 786 N.E.2d at 832.

129. *Fletcher*, 437 Mass. at 547, 773 N.E.2d at 424 (no cause of action in tort); *Gath*, 440 Mass. at 498, 802 N.E.2d at 534 (no cause of action under the unfair or deceptive trade practices statute).

130. *Fletcher*, 437 Mass. at 549, 773 N.E.2d at 425.

131. *Kippenhan*, 428 Mass. at 128, 697 N.E.2d at 531.

132. *Sacramona v. Bridgestone/Firestone, Inc.*, 106 F.3d 444, 449 (1st Cir. 1997); *Castro v. Stanley Works*, 864 F.2d 961, 964 (1st Cir. 1989); *Smith v. Robertshaw Controls Co.*, 410 F.3d 29, 36-37 (1st Cir. 2005).

133. *Jorgensen v. Massachusetts Port Auth.*, 905 F.2d 515, 522-23 (1st Cir. 1990) (articulating standard in negligence case).

134. *O'Connor v. Raymark Indus.*, 401 Mass. 586, 591-92, 518 N.E.2d 510, 513 (1988).

135. *Correia v. Firestone Tire & Rubber Co.*, 388 Mass. 342, 352 n.10, 446 N.E.2d 1033, 1038 (1983).

136. *Roberts v. Southwick*, 415 Mass. 465, 481, 614 N.E.2d 659 (1993). In some circumstances, a court may find as a matter of law that a remote risk is not reasonably foreseeable. *See, e.g., Young v. Atlantic Richfield Co.*, 400 Mass. 837, 512 N.E.2d 272 (1987) (even assuming owner of gas station had duty to post an "attendant will pump gas" sign, and the failure to do so "increased the

likelihood that customers would leave their vehicles to pump gas, the risk that a customer who left his vehicle to pump gas would be injured by a negligently operated motor vehicle was not a reasonably foreseeable consequence of any negligent failure to post such a sign").

137. *Cocco v. Deluxe Sys., Inc.*, 25 Mass. App. 151, 155, 516 N.E.2d 1171, 1173 (1987).

138. *Lussier v. Louisville Ladder Co.*, 938 F.2d 299, 301-02 (1st Cir. 1991) (in failure-to-warn case based on negligence and implied warranty, where user appreciated danger "[t]he failure to warn was not the proximate cause of the knowledgeable user's injury"). *See also Allen v. Chance Mfg. Co.*, 873 F.2d 465, 467 (1st Cir. 1989); *Hoffman v. Houghton Chem. Corp.*, 434 Mass. 624, 640, 751 N.E.2d 848, 861 (2001); *Carey v. Lynn Ladder & Scaffolding Co.*, 427 Mass. 1003, 691 N.E.2d 223 (1998); *Correia v. Firestone Tire & Rubber Co.*, 388 Mass. 342, 346-52, 446 N.E.2d 1033, 1035-38 (1983).

139. *Colter v. Barber-Greene Co.*, 403 Mass. 50, 60, 525 N.E.2d 1305, 1314 (1988). *See also Lussier v. Louisville Ladder Co.*, 938 F.2d 299, 301 (1st Cir. 1991) ("failure to warn was not the proximate cause of injury" where plaintiff used product unreasonably and admittedly knew of danger that absent warning would have described).

140. *Colter*, 403 Mass. at 60, 525 N.E.2d at 1312.

141. *Santana v. Registrars of Voters of Worcester*, 398 Mass. 862, 867, 502 N.E.2d 132, 135 (1986).

142. Mass. Gen. Laws ch. 229, § 2.

143. *Aleo v. SLB Toys USA, Inc.*, 466 Mass. 398, 412-21, 995 N.E.2d 740, 754-59 (2013) (citing *BMW of N. Am., Inc. v. Gore*, 517 U.S. 559 (1996)).

144. Mass. Gen. Laws ch. 93A, §§ 9(3) & 9(11).

145. Mass. Gen. Laws ch. 231, § 6B. *See Commonwealth v. Johnson Insulation*, 425 Mass. 650, 664, 682 N.E.2d 1323, 1333 (1997).

146. Mass. Gen. Laws ch. 231, § 6C.

147. *Commercial Union Ins. Co. v. Walbrook Ins. Co.*, 41 F.3d 764, 774 (1st Cir. 1994); *Brayman v. 99 West, Inc.*, 116 F. Supp. 2d 225, 236 (D. Mass. 2000), *aff'd*, 2002 U.S. App. LEXIS 1227 (1st Cir. Jan. 10, 2002).

148. Mass. Gen. Laws ch. 235, § 8.

149. *City Coal Co. of Springfield, Inc. v. Noonan*, 424 Mass. 693, 695, 677 N.E.2d 1141, 1143 (1997).

150. 28 U.S.C. § 1961. *But see Budish v. Daniel*, 417 Mass. 574, 631 N.E.2d 1009 (1994) (plaintiff suing to enforce state court judgment entitled to post-judgment interest at state law rate).

151. Mass. Gen. Laws ch. 231B, §§ 1-4; *Flood v. Southland Corp.*, 33 Mass. App. Ct. 287, 301, 601 N.E.2d 23, 32 (1992), *vacated on other grounds*, 416 Mass. 62, 616 (1993); *Wolfe v. Ford Motor Co.*, 386 Mass. 95, 98, 434 N.E.2d 1008, 1010 (1982).

152. Mass. Gen. Laws ch. 231B, §§ 1-2; *Martignetti v. Haigh-Farr, Inc.*, 425 Mass. 294, 313, 680 N.E.2d 1131, 1144 (1997).

153. *But see Rathbun v. W. Massachusetts Elec. Co.*, 395 Mass. 361, 364-65, 479 N.E.2d 1383, 1385 (1985) (observing in dicta that one negligent actor may be entitled to *indemnification* from another where the indemnitee's negligence "has been insignificant in relation to that of the indemnitor").

154. Mass. Gen. Laws ch. 231B, § 4; *Chapman v. Bernard's, Inc.*, 198 F.R.D. 575, 577 (D. Mass. 2001); *Dorel Steel Erection Corp. v. Corbett*, 52 Mass. App. Ct. 1109, 1110, 753 N.E.2d 845 (Table) (2001); *Slocum v. Donahue*, 44 Mass. App. Ct. 937, 693 N.E.2d 179 (1998).

155. *Framingham Union Hosp., Inc. v. Travelers Ins. Co.*, 744 F. Supp. 29, 34 (D. Mass. 1990); *Hayon v. Coca Cola Bottling Co. of New England*, 375 Mass. 644, 648, 378 N.E.2d 442, 445 (1978) ("It is plain that the evil to be remedied [by statute] was the unfairness of allowing a disproportionate share of the plaintiff's recovery to be borne by one of several joint tortfeasors, and the object to be accomplished was a more equitable distribution of that burden among those liable in tort for the same injury.").

156. *Medical Prof'l Mut. Ins. Co. v. Breon Labs., Inc.*, 966 F. Supp. 120, 123-25 (D. Mass. 1997); *Robertson v. McCarte*, 13 Mass. App. Ct. 441, 443, 433 N.E.2d 1262, 1264 (1982); *Dorel Steel Erection Corp. v. Corbett*, 52 Mass. App. Ct. 1109, 1110, 753 N.E.2d 845 (Table) (2001).

157. *Payton v. Abbott Labs.*, 386 Mass. 540, 571, 437 N.E.2d 171, 188-89 (1982).

158. *See, e.g., Enrich v. Windmere Corp.*, 416 Mass. 83, 86, 616 N.E.2d 1081, 1083-84 (1993) (finding no liability because name on instruction booklet was insufficient to identify defendant as fan's manufacturer).

159. *Payton*, 386 Mass. at 574, 437 N.E.2d at 190-91. *See Mills v. Allegiance Healthcare Corp.*, 178 F. Supp. 2d 1, 8 (D. Mass. 2001) (reviewing Massachusetts market share liability cases and noting that, "[A]lthough the Supreme Judicial Court of Massachusetts has never categorically rejected the theory, neither has it clearly sanctioned its validity or used it, thus far, to uphold a remedy to injured plaintiffs.").

160. *See Spencer v. Baxter Int'l, Inc.*, 163 F. Supp. 2d 74, 78 (D. Mass. 2001) (noting confusion in lower courts as to the applicability of alternative liability in Massachusetts).

161. *Hoffman v. Houghton Chem. Corp.*, 434 Mass. 624, 630, 751 N.E.2d 848, 854 (2001); *Santiago v. Sherwin-Williams Co.*, 794 F. Supp. 29, 33 (D. Mass. 1992), *aff'd on other grounds*, 3 F.3d 546 (1st Cir. 1993).

162. *See Kyte v. Philip Morris Inc.*, 408 Mass. 162, 166-67, 556 N.E.2d 1025, 1027 (1990); *Payton v. Abbott Labs.*, 512 F. Supp. 1031, 1035 (D. Mass. 1981).

163. *Guzman v. MRM/Elgin*, 409 Mass. 563, 566, 567 N.E.2d 929, 931-32 (1991); *Cargill, Inc. v. Beaver Coal & Oil Co.*, 424 Mass. 356, 359, 676 N.E.2d 815, 818 (1997).

164. Mass. Gen. Laws ch. 156B, § 80(b); *Cargill*, 424 Mass. at 360, 676 N.E.2d at 819; *Gurry v. Cumberland Farms, Inc.*, 406 Mass. 615, 620, 550 N.E.2d 127, 130-31 (1990).

165. *Guzman v. MRM/Elgin*, 409 Mass. 563, 567 N.E.2d 929 (1991); *Garcia v. Kusan, Inc.*, 39 Mass. App. Ct. 322, 330, 655 N.E.2d 1290, 1295 (1995).

166. *Cipollone v. Yale Indus. Prods., Inc.*, 202 F.3d 376, 379 (1st Cir. 2000); *Mitchell v. Sky Climber, Inc.*, 396 Mass. 629, 631, 487 N.E.2d 1374 (1986) (supplier of component part with no latent defect had no duty to warn subsequent assembler or its customers of any danger that might arise after assembly of components); *Murray v. Goodrich Eng'g Corp., Inc.*, 30 Mass. App. Ct. 918, 566 N.E.2d 631 (1991); *Freitas v. Emhart Corp.*, 715 F. Supp. 1149, 1152 (D. Mass. 1989) ("Defendant, as a supplier of parts, cannot be held liable [under negligence or warranty theory] unless there was a defect in the parts it sold or it was responsible for designing the [assembled product] in question"). *Compare Schaeffer v. General Motors Corp.*, 372 Mass. 171, 174, 360 N.E.2d 1062, 1065 (1977) (automobile manual should have warned of a foreseeable risk in the use of a component part manufactured by the defendant).

167. *Hatch v. Trail King Indus., Inc.*, 656 F.3d 59, 67-68 (1st Cir. 2011) (quoting Restatement (Second) of Torts § 404, comment a).

168. *Fahey v. Rockwell Graphic Sys., Inc.*, 20 Mass. App. Ct. 642, 650, 482 N.E.2d 519, 525 (1985) (applying Restatement (Second) of Torts § 400, cmt. d, in claim alleging negligent design); *Lou v. Otis Elevator Co.*, 77 Mass. App. Ct. 571, 581, 933 N.E.2d 140, 148 (2010) (applying Restatement (Second) of Torts § 400 and Restatement (Third) of Torts: Products Liability § 14, cmt. d, in claim alleging breach of implied warranty of merchantability).

169. *Lou*, 77 Mass. App. Ct. at 581, 933 N.E.2d at 148.

170. *Goffredo v. Mercedes-Benz Truck Co.*, 402 Mass. 97, 104, 520 N.E.2d 1315, 1318 (1988) (whether vehicle door latch is defectively designed requires expert testimony); *Smith v. Ariens Co.*, 375 Mass. 620, 625, 377 N.E.2d 954, 957-58 (1978) (whether metal protrusion on snowmobile handle bar constitutes defective design is within knowledge of jury); *Esturban v. Mass. Bay Transp. Auth.*, 68 Mass. App. Ct. 911, 911-12, 865 N.E.2d 834, 835 (2007) (whether escalator is defectively designed requires expert testimony).

171. *Lally v. Volkswagen Aktiengesellschaft*, 45 Mass. App. Ct. 317, 324-35, 698 N.E.2d 28, 36 (1998); *Canavan's Case*, 432 Mass. 304, 316, 733 N.E.2d 1042, 1051 (2000) (proof of medical causation requires expert testimony). *But see Bailey v. Cataldo Ambulance Serv., Inc.*, 64 Mass. App. Ct. 228, 832 N.E.2d 16 (2005) (allowing medical causation opinion evidence to be given in paper medical records pursuant to Mass. Gen. Laws. ch. 233, § 79G; live testimony not required).

172. *Commonwealth v. Lanigan*, 419 Mass. 15, 641 N.E.2d 1342 (1994) (accepting the "basic reasoning" of *Daubert v. Merrell Dow Pharms., Inc.*, 509 U.S. 579, 113 S. Ct. 2786, 125 L. Ed. 2d 469 (1993)); *Federico v. Ford Motor Co.*, 67 Mass. App. Ct. 454, 457-58, 854 N.E.2d 448, 452 (2006) (affirming exclusion of expert testimony in absence of verification through actual testing or peer review).

173. *Canavan's Case*, 432 Mass. at 306-07, 733 N.E.2d at 1045 (adopting the reasoning of *Kumho Tire Co. v. Carmichael*, 526 U.S. 137 (1999)).

174. *Canavan's Case*, 432 Mass. at 312, 733 N.E.2d at 1049 (adopting the reasoning of *General Elec. Co. v. Joiner*, 522 U.S. 136 (1997)).

175. *Abrahams v. Rice*, 306 Mass. 24, 24, 27 N.E.2d 193, 193 (1940) ("[T]he mere happening of an accident is not proof of negligence"); *Makuc v. Am. Honda Motor Co., Inc.*, 835 F.2d 389, 393 (1st Cir. 1987) ("under Massachusetts law, a malfunction in itself is not sufficient to establish a breach of warranty").

176. *Benavides v. Stop & Shop, Inc.*, 346 Mass. 154, 157, 190 N.E.2d 894, 896 (1963); *McCabe v. L.K. Liggett Drug Co.*, 330 Mass. 177, 180, 112 N.E.2d 254, 257 (1953).

177. *White v. W. W. Grainger Co.*, CCH Prod. Liab. Rptr. 111, 695 (D. Mass. 1988); *Wilson v. Honeywell, Inc.*, 409 Mass. 803, 806-07, 569 N.E.2d 1011, 1013-14 (1991); *MacCuish v. Volkswagenwerk A.G.*, 22 Mass. App. Ct. 380, 396, 494 N.E.2d 390, 394 (1986), *aff'd*, 400 Mass. 1003, 508 N.E.2d 842 (1987); *Corsetti v. Stone Co.*, 396 Mass. 1, 24, 483 N.E.2d 793, 805-06 (1985); *Coyne v. John S. Tilley Co.*, 368 Mass. 230, 235, 331 N.E.2d 541, 545 (1975).

178. *Beauvais v. New England Dev., Inc.*, 51 Mass. App. Ct. 1110, 1110, 747 N.E.2d 758, 758 (2001); *Enrich v. Windmere Corp.*, 416 Mass. 83, 87, 616 N.E.2d 1081, 1084 (1993); *Kourouvacilis v. General Motors Corp.*, 410 Mass. 706, 717, 575

N.E.2d 734, 741 (1991); *Coyne v. John S. Tilley Co.*, 368 Mass. 230, 235, 331 N.E.2d 541, 545 (1975).

179. *Aleo*, 466 Mass. at 408-09, 995 N.E.2d at 750-51; *MacCuish v. Volkswagenwerk A.G.*, 22 Mass. App. Ct. 380, 389 n.12, 494 N.E.2d 390, 396 (1986), *aff'd*, 400 Mass. 1003, 508 N.E.2d 842 (1987); *Rochleau v. Town of Millbury*, 115 F. Supp. 2d 173, 179 (D. Mass. 2000).

180. *Rice v. James Hanrahan & Sons*, 20 Mass. App. Ct. 701, 707-08, 482 N.E.2d 833, 839 (1985); *McDonald v. Ortho Pharm. Corp.*, 394 Mass. 131, 139, 475 N.E.2d 65, 71 (1985). *But see Rice*, 20 Mass. App. Ct. at 712 n.8, 482 N.E.2d at 833 (excluding testimony concerning later-enacted UFFI regulations, but stating in dicta that "the fact that a determination of a product's unsafeness succeeds the sale of the product does not render it irrelevant" under implied warranty of merchantability theory "[b]ecause the inquiry in breach of warranty focuses on the defective and unreasonably dangerous nature of the product and not on the defendant's knowledge").

181. *Back*, 375 Mass. at 641-43, 378 N.E.2d at 970 (1978) (design and warning claims under warranty theory); *Fidalogo v. Columbus McKinnon Corp.*, 56 Mass. App. Ct. 176, 184, 775 N.E.2d 803, 809 (2002) (negligence).

182. *Johnson v. City of Boston*, 22 Mass. App. Ct. 24, 27, 490 N.E.2d 1204, 1206 (1986); *Torre v. Harris-Seybold Co.*, 9 Mass. App. Ct. 660, 671-72, 404 N.E.2d 96, 105 (1980); *McKinnon v. Skil Corp.*, 638 F.2d 270, 274-76 (1st Cir. 1981).

183. *Back*, 375 Mass. at 642-43, 378 N.E.2d at 970 (1978).

184. *Santiago v. Sherwin-Williams Co.*, 794 F. Supp. 29, 33 n.7 (1992). *See also supra*, note 70 (discussing dicta in *Vassallo* suggesting that manufacturer may be held to the standard of an "expert" under warranty claim).

185. *Santos v. Chrysler Corp.*, 430 Mass. 198, 202, 715 N.E.2d 47, 52 (1999).

186. *McKinnon v. Skil Corp.*, 638 F.2d 270, 277 (1st Cir. 1981); *Ducharme v. Hyundai Motor Am.*, 45 Mass. App. Ct. 401, 408, 698 N.E.2d 412, 417 (1998) (admissibility of demonstrations, tests and experiments).

187. *Martel v. Mass. Bay Transp. Auth.*, 403 Mass. 1, 4, 525 N.E.2d 662, 664 (1988). *See also Raymond v. Raymond Corp.*, 938 F.2d 1518, 1522 (1st Cir. 1991) (Fed. R. Evid. 407).

188. *doCanto v. Ametek, Inc.*, 367 Mass. 776, 780, 328 N.E.2d 873, 876 (1975) (summarizing law relating to post-accident design improvements); *Carey v. Gen. Motors Corp.*, 377 Mass. 736, 744, 387 N.E.2d 583, 587 (1979) (recall). The Massachusetts state and federal courts arguably take different approaches with respect to the admissibility of evidence of subsequent design improvements to prove feasibility. The Supreme Judicial Court has allowed such

evidence even where the defendant conceded "in a general way that the design improvements were practical." *doCanto*, 367 Mass. at 781, 328 N.E.2d at 876. The First Circuit, however, applies Federal Rule of Evidence 407 to preclude the introduction of such evidence where feasibility is not controverted. *Raymond v. Raymond Corp.*, 938 F.2d 1518, 1523 (1st Cir. 1991).

189. *doCanto*, 367 Mass. at 780, 328 N.E.2d at 876 (trial court properly admitted evidence of post-sale but pre-accident design improvements); *Raymond*, 938 F.2d at 1523 (Fed. R. Evid. 407 not applicable to pre-accident remedial measures but trial court properly excluded evidence pursuant to Fed. R. Evid. 403 as prejudicial and only marginally relevant).

190. *Martel v. Massachusetts Bay Transp. Auth.*, 403 Mass. 1, 4-5, 525 N.E.2d 662, 664 (1988).

191. *Prentiss & Carlisle Co., Inc. v. Koehring-Waterous Div. of Timberjack, Inc.*, 972 F.2d 6, 10 (1st Cir. 1992). *See, e.g., Hochen v. Bobst Grp., Inc.*, 193 F.R.D. 22, 24-25 (D. Mass. 2000) (evidence of post-accident investigations admissible).

192. *See* Mass. Gen. Laws ch. 233, § 79G.

193. *Law v. Griffith*, 457 Mass. 349, 352-53, 930 N.E.2d 126, 130 (2010).

194. *Law*, 457 Mass. at 352-53, 930 N.E.2d at 130.

Michigan

A. CAUSES OF ACTION

Product liability lawsuits commonly include causes of action for negligence[1] and breach of implied warranty.[2] There is no separate cause of action for strict liability;[3] however, the requisite elements for a cause of action based on strict liability in tort are essentially the same as those for breach of implied warranty.[4]

B. STATUTES OF LIMITATION

The period of limitations is three years for a product liability action. In a wrongful death action, the statute of limitations may be extended up to an additional three years. An extra-statutory, equity-based "discovery rule" is not normally available to extend the accrual of an action for purposes of applying the limitations period.[5] For latent disease claims such as asbestosis, however, Michigan does apply a discovery rule to determine when a claim accrues and the statute of limitations begins to run.[6]

C. BREACH OF IMPLIED WARRANTY

1. The Standard

A cause of action for breach of implied warranty in a product liability case is established by proof of injury caused by a defect in the product. The defect must be attributable to the manufacturer, and it must have made the product not reasonably fit for its intended, anticipated, or reasonably foreseeable use, including reasonably foreseeable misuse.[7] If the claimed defect is that the product did not perform according to, or meet, the manufacturer's specifications, negligence need not be shown. However, where the defect alleged is the adequacy of warnings, the issue is one of reasonable care, regardless of whether the theory pled is negligence or breach of implied warranty.[8]

2. Definition of "Defect"

In actions grounded on a breach of implied warranty, a product is deemed defective it if is "not reasonably fit" for its intended, anticipated, or reasonably foreseeable use, including reasonably foreseeable misuse.[9]

3. Defective Design

The focus of a design defect case is usually on the quality of the manufacturer's decisions: did the manufacturer properly weigh alternatives and evaluate trade-offs and thereby develop a reasonably safe product?[10] Michigan has specifically rejected the apparent manufacturer theory of liability, which holds retailers liable for design defects where the retailer's only conduct was the relabeling of the product with its identity.[11] In Michigan, there is no continuing duty for a manufacturer to repair or recall a product to bring it up to the current state of the art for safety features.[12]

Michigan applies the risk-utility test to determine whether a plaintiff has made out a case for a product liability claim for design defect. Under the risk-utility test, a plaintiff must show (1) that the severity of the injury was foreseeable by the manufacturer, (2) that the likelihood of occurrence of her injury was foreseeable by the manufacturer at the time of the distribution of the product, (3) that there was a reasonable alternative design available, (4) that the available alternative design was practicable, (5) that the available and practicable reasonable alternative design would have reduced the foreseeable risk of harm posed by defendant's product, and (6) that the omission of the available alternative design rendered defendant's product not reasonably safe.[13]

4. **Comparative Negligence**

Comparative negligence applies where plaintiff is injured as a result of a breach of implied warranty. Plaintiff's recovery is reduced to the extent of plaintiff's own negligence, and plaintiff is not entitled to recover the full amount of damages if he or she was also negligent.[14]

5. **Successor Liability**

As a general rule, a purchaser of all or substantially all of the assets of another corporation is not liable for injuries caused by products manufactured by the predecessor corporation before the sale so long as the successor corporation did not participate in the manufacture, sale, or installation of the product or assume liability either by contract or by law.[15] However, a successor corporation may be liable for a predecessor's injury-causing product where the totality of the acquisition demonstrates a basic continuity of enterprise between the seller and buyer.[16]

6. **Privity**

No privity is required; a plaintiff may sue even though he or she did not buy the product from the manufacturer.[17]

7. **Failure to Warn**

If a manufacturer or distributor of a product knows or ought to know of a danger inherent in the product or in the use for which the product is intended, it has a duty to give adequate warnings.[18] Whether a duty to warn exists depends on whether the consumer's use of the product and the injury sustained was foreseeable, not whether the use was intended.[19] The duty to warn has been relaxed for simple products where the danger is open and obvious to all.[20] The manufacturer of such a simple product (one whose essential characteristics are fully apparent) has no duty to warn of the product's potentially dangerous conditions or characteristics that are readily apparent or visible on casual inspection and reasonably expected to be recognized by the average user of ordinary intelligence.[21] The duty may also be relaxed where the product has been sold to a sophisticated user[22] or where the providing of an additional warning would have been futile.[23]

8. **Remedial Changes in Product**

   Evidence of any subsequent change with regard to the product is not admissible in a product liability action to prove liability, but it is admissible when offered for another purpose, such as proving ownership, control, feasibility of precautionary measures, if controverted, or impeachment.[24]

9. **Substantial Alteration/Abnormal Use**

   A plaintiff may not recover if the proximate cause of his or her injury is found to have stemmed from his or her own conduct, such as misuse of a product, and not from a product's lack of fitness.[25] However, the substantial change or misuse must be one that could not have been reasonably foreseen or anticipated.[26]

10. **Malfunction**

    A demonstrable malfunction of a product may create an inference that the defect is attributable to the manufacturer where failure is caused by a defect in a relatively inaccessible part integral to the structure of the product and not generally required to be repaired, replaced, or maintained.[27]

11. **Standards**

    Evidence that a product complied with governmental and industrial standards is admissible, but compliance is not conclusive as to whether the defendant was negligent or the product was defective.[28]

12. **Other Accidents**

    Evidence of other accidents is inadmissible unless plaintiff proves that the product is the same and there is substantial factual similarity in time, place, and circumstances.[29] Under these circumstances, such evidence is admissible on the issue of the manufacturer's knowledge and/or notice regarding the same.[30] The absence of prior accidents is admissible to show lack of knowledge or notice where these issues have been presented in the plaintiff's case.[31]

13. **Economic Loss Doctrine**

    Michigan has adopted the economic loss doctrine for disputes between commercial parties where the only damages alleged are economic, that is, lost profits or anticipated commercial benefits. The doctrine, as set forth by the Michigan Supreme Court, bars tort claims in such situations and provides that the UCC is the exclusive remedy in cases involving economic loss arising from the purchase of goods.[32]

14. Crashworthiness

Michigan has adopted the "crashworthiness" or "second collision" doctrine. The liability of a manufacturer in crashworthiness cases is limited to the portion of damage or injury caused by the defective design over and above the damage or injury that would have occurred as result of impact or collision absent the defective design.[33] Plaintiff has the burden of proving an enhanced injury.[34]

D. NEGLIGENCE

1. The Standard

The plaintiff in an action based on a negligence theory must make out a prima facie case establishing that the manufacturer breached its duty to use reasonable or ordinary care under the circumstances in planning or designing the product so that it is reasonably safe for the purposes for which it is intended.[35] The "unreasonably dangerous" standard is generally applied in product liability actions premised on negligence principles.[36] Thus, a product is deemed defective if it is unreasonably dangerous in light of the foreseeable risks of injury.[37]

2. Comparative Negligence and Assumption of Risk

In a product liability action brought to recover damages, the damages sustained by the plaintiff must be diminished in proportion to the amount of negligence attributed to him or her.[38] By statute, a manufacturer or seller is not liable in a product liability action "if the purchaser or user of the product was aware that use of the product created an unreasonable risk of personal injury and voluntarily exposed himself or herself to that risk and the risk that he or she exposed himself or herself to was the proximate cause of the injury."[39] This section of the statute does not, however, negate the duty of a manufacturer or seller to use reasonable care in the production of a product.[40] Several cases have examined the issue of usage of adult products by children, as well.[41]

E. PUNITIVE DAMAGES

Punitive damages are not recoverable in a product liability action, or otherwise under Michigan law. Exemplary damages may be awarded for mental suffering consisting of a sense of insult, indignity, humiliation, or injury to feelings.[42] However, courts generally only will award exemplary damages "where the defendant commits a voluntary act" or where conduct is "malicious or so willful and wanton as to demonstrate a reckless disregard of the plaintiff's rights."[43]

F. PRE- AND POST-JUDGMENT INTEREST

Pre- and post-judgment interest is provided by statute in Michigan.[44] The statute authorizes a party to collect interest on a money judgment recovered in a civil action until satisfaction of the judgment, with the interest calculated from the date of filing the complaint on the entire amount of the money judgment, including attorney fees and other costs.[45] The purpose of such interest is to compensate the prevailing party for expenses incurred in bringing an action for money damages and for any delay in receiving such damages.[46] The interest is calculated at six-month intervals at a rate of interest that is equal to one percent plus the average interest rate paid at auctions of five-year United States Treasury notes during the six months immediately preceding July 1 and January 1, compounded annually.[47]

Accrual of pre-judgment interest ceases after the date the defendant files a written offer of settlement that is not less than 90 percent of the amount actually received by the plaintiff in a judgment.[48] If a defendant rejects a written offer of settlement not more than 110 percent of the amount actually received by the plaintiff in a judgment, interest is calculated from the date the offer is rejected to the date of satisfaction of judgment at a rate of two percent plus the average interest rate paid at auctions of five-year United States Treasury notes.[49]

G. EMPLOYER IMMUNITY FROM SUIT

The Worker's Disability Compensation Act's[50] "exclusive remedy provision" exempts an employer from liability for an employee's personal injury or occupational disease except in instances of an intentional tort.[51] The Act, therefore, protects employers from negligence claims by an injured employee[52] and from contribution claims grounded in negligence.[53] However, fault can be "allocated" to employers by product liability defendants under tort reform legislation passed in the 1990s (discussed in Section J, *infra*). Employee actions for intentional torts against employers, however, are not barred. Michigan has statutorily adopted a certainty test[54] for these actions.[55]

H. STATUTES

Relevant statutes for product liability actions are the statutes of limitation for product liability actions,[56] the UCC section for breach of warranty,[57] and the statute governing product liability actions in general.[58]

I. JOINT AND SEVERAL LIABILITY

In 1995, Michigan enacted two tort reform laws (Public Acts 161 and 245 of 1995) with far-reaching implications in product liability actions filed in Michigan on or after March 28, 1996. As part of this legislation, Michigan abolished joint and several liability.[59] Under the tort reform laws, the trier of fact assesses liability against all parties to the action in direct proportion to their percentage of fault.[60] Moreover, Michigan has adopted an "empty chair" provision.[61] Pursuant to this provision, a party may file a motion within 91 days after identification of a non-party, seeking the addition of the non-party for the purposes of comparative fault.[62] A finding of fault against a non-party does not subject the non-party to liability in that action and may not be introduced as evidence of liability in another action.[63] However, at trial, remaining defendants may request the trier of fact to assess a percentage of fault to former parties with whom the plaintiff settled.[64]

In instances where a defendant is found liable for personal injury, property damage, or wrongful death due to criminal conduct that includes an element of gross negligence or is an alcohol or a controlled substance offense, and where the defendant is convicted of such a crime, joint and several liability still applies.[65]

J. TORT REFORM

Michigan's tort reform provisions (Public Acts 161 and 249 of 1995) have been in effect since 1996. The most significant changes that tort reform brought about include the following:

- Venue that previously had been established "where all or part of the cause of action arose," was recast as arising where "the original injury occurred."[66]

- Joint and several liability, which allowed an unfair shifting of responsibility for uncollectible defendants, was replaced by "several only and not joint" liability.[67] Exceptions still exist, however, for injuries suffered due to medical malpractice[68] or to criminal conduct involving gross negligence or the use of drugs or alcohol.[69]

- Fault can be allocated to non-parties (including an employer protected by the Worker's Disability Compensation Act).[70]

- Pure comparative negligence was replaced by modified comparative negligence. That is, where a plaintiff is found to be more than 50 percent liable, his or her economic damages will be reduced by that percentage and non-economic damages shall not be awarded.[71]

- An interesting and important effect of this "several only and not joint" liability is that, in actions based on tort or another legal theory seeking damages for personal injury, property damage, or wrongful death, as covered by the tort reform statutes, there is no basis for a claim of contribution under Michigan's Contribution Act under MCL 600.2925a.[72]

- An absolute defense exists where the plaintiff was impaired due to alcohol or controlled substances and, as a result of that impairment, the plaintiff was 50 percent or more at fault.[73]

- In an action for product liability, non-economic damages are capped, with higher caps for injuries where death or permanent loss of a vital bodily function occurred. The damage caps are adjusted yearly by the state treasurer based on variations in the consumer price index. For 2014, the caps, as adjusted, were $440,200 and $786,000, respectively.[74]

- No product liability action may lie against a manufacturer or seller of a drug where (1) the United States Federal Drug Administration approved the drug and its labeling; and (2) the drug complied with that approval at the time it left the manufacturer's or seller's control.[75]

- Manufacturers are not liable for alteration or misuse unless the alteration or misuse was reasonably foreseeable.[76]

- The duty to warn is relaxed for sophisticated users[77] or where such risks should be apparent to reasonably prudent users.[78]

- Non-manufacturing sellers are relieved of liability unless, under an implied warranty theory, they fail to exercise reasonable care or they breach an express warranty.[79]

- There is a rebuttable presumption of nonliability for compliance with governmental standards, with no inverse presumption for failure to comply.[80]

- Michigan codified *Daubert v. Merrell Dow*, 509 U.S. 579, 113 S. Ct. 2786 (1993), and the court's "gatekeeper" responsibility for expert witness testimony.[81] In fact, the Tort Reform Act may go farther than *Daubert*, as the Act sets forth seven factors which the trial court "shall" consider in determining whether expert testimony will be admissible. The Act also requires a specific determination by the court that the proffered opinion will be reliable and will assist the trier of fact.

- Michigan's seat belt statute provides that although the failure to wear a safety belt may be considered evidence of negligence and may reduce the recovery for damages arising out of the ownership, maintenance, or operation of a motor vehicle, evidence of such negligence shall not reduce the recovery for damages by more than 5 percent.[82] However, because the Michigan Supreme Court determined in *Klinke v. Mitsubishi Motors Corp.*, 458 Mich. 582, 581 N.W.2d 272 (1998), that the seat belt statute does not apply to product liability actions, there is no percentage cap on the amount of negligence that can be attributed to the plaintiff for failing to wear a safety belt in product liability actions.

James E. Wynne
Phillip C. Korovesis
Daniel R. Rustmann
John C. Valenti
William J. Kliffel
James F. Gehrke
Bernard J. Fuhs
Paul M. Mersino
Brian E. McGinty
Butzel Long
150 West Jefferson, Suite 100
Detroit, Michigan 48226-4430
(313) 225-7000
(Fax) 225-7080
http://www.butzel.com

Endnotes - Michigan

1. *See, e.g., Moning v. Alfono*, 400 Mich. 425, 254 N.W.2d 759 (1977); *Prentis v. Yale Mfg. Co.*, 421 Mich. 670, 365 N.W.2d 176 (1984); *Shipman v. Fontaine Truck Equip. Co.*, 184 Mich. App. 706, 459 N.W.2d 30 (1990).

2. *Lemire v. Garrard Drugs*, 95 Mich. App. 520, 291 N.W.2d 103 (1980); *Holdsworth v. Nash Mfg., Inc.*, 161 Mich. App. 139, 409 N.W.2d 764 (1987).

3. *Pelc v. Bendix Mach. Tool Corp.*, 111 Mich. App. 343, 314 N.W.2d 614 (1981); *Dooms v. Stewart Bolling & Co.*, 68 Mich. App. 5, 241 N.W.2d 738 (1976); *see also Parr v. Cent. Soya Co.*, 732 F. Supp. 738 (E.D. Mich. 1990).

4. *Trotter v. Hamill Mfg. Co.*, 143 Mich. App. 593, 372 N.W.2d 622 (1985); *Owens v. Allis-Chalmers Corp.*, 83 Mich. App. 74, 268 N.W.2d 291 (1978), *aff'd*, 414 Mich. 413, 326 N.W.2d 372 (1982).

5. *Trentadue v. Gorton*, 479 Mich. 378, 738 N.W.2d 664 (2007); *reh'g denied*, 739 N.W.2d 79 (Mich. 2007).

6. *Larson v. Johns-Manville Sales Corp.*, 427 Mich. 301, 399 N.W.2d 1 (1986); *Moll v. Abbott Lab.*, 444 Mich. 1, 506 N.W.2d 816 (1993).

7. *Vincent v. Allen Bradley Co.*, 95 Mich. App. 426, 291 N.W.2d 66 (1980); *Glavin v. Baker Material Handling Corp.*, 132 Mich. App. 318, 347 N.W.2d 222 (1984), *on remand*, 144 Mich. App. 147, 373 N.W.2d 272 (1985); *Nichani v. Schroeder Homes*, No. 267688, 2006 Mich. App. LEXIS 2280 (Mich. Ct. App. July 20, 2006).

8. *Manzoni v. Detroit Coca-Cola Bottling Co.*, 363 Mich. 235, 109 N.W.2d 918 (1961); *Smith v. E.R. Squibb & Sons, Inc.*, 69 Mich. App. 375, 381, 245 N.W.2d 52, 55 (1976), *aff'd*, 405 Mich. 79, 273 N.W.2d 476 (1979).

9. *Ghrist v. Chrysler Corp.*, 451 Mich. 242, 547 N.W.2d 272 (1996); *Hartford Fire Ins. Co. v. Walter Kidde & Co.*, 120 Mich. App. 283, 328 N.W.2d 29 (1982); *Villar v. E.W. Bliss Co.*, 134 Mich. App. 116, 350 N.W.2d 920 (1984).

10. *Prentis v. Yale Mfg. Co.*, 421 Mich. 670, 365 N.W.2d 176 (1984); *Hindelang v. R.D. Werner Co.*, 188 Mich. App. 122, 469 N.W.2d 2 (1991).

11. *Seasword v. Hilti, Inc.*, 207 Mich. App. 609, 525 N.W.2d 501 (1994), *aff'd*, 449 Mich. 542, 537 N.W.2d 221 (1995).

12. *Gregory v. Cincinnati, Inc.*, 450 Mich. 1, 538 N.W.2d 325 (1995).

13. *Peck v. Bridgeport Machs., Inc.*, 237 F.3d 614 (6th Cir. 2001).

14. Mich. Comp. Laws § 600.2959; *Young v. E.W. Bliss Co.*, 130 Mich. App. 363, 343 N.W.2d 553 (1983).

15. *Foster v. Cone-Blanchard Mach. Co.*, 460 Mich. 696, 597 N.W.2d 506 (1999); *Denolf v. Frank L. Jursik Co.*, 54 Mich. App. 584, 221 N.W.2d 458 (1974), *rev'd on other grounds*, 395 Mich. 661, 238 N.W.2d 1 (1976).

16. *Foster v. Cone-Blanchard Mach. Co.*, 460 Mich. 696, 597 N.W.2d 506 (1999); *Langley v. Harris Corp.*, 413 Mich. 592, 321 N.W.2d 662 (1982); *Fenton Area Pub. Sch. v. Sorensen-Gross Constr. Co.*, 124 Mich. App. 631, 335 N.W.2d 221 (1983).

17. *Gimino v. Sears, Roebuck & Co.*, 308 Mich. 666, 14 N.W.2d 536 (1944); *Gauthier v. Mayo*, 77 Mich. App. 513, 258 N.W.2d 748 (1977); *Pack v. Damon Corp.*, 434 F.3d 810 (6th Cir. 2006).

18. Mich. Comp. Laws § 600.2948(3); *Van Eizenga v. Straley*, 1998 Mich. App. LEXIS 1259 (Mich. Ct. App. Mar. 31, 1998); *Durkee v. Cooper of Canada, Ltd.*, 99 Mich. App. 693, 298 N.W.2d 620 (1980).

19. *Gutowski v. M & R Plastics & Coating, Inc.*, 60 Mich. App. 499, 231 N.W.2d 456 (1975); *Ferlito v. Johnson & Johnson Prods., Inc.*, 771 F. Supp. 196 (E.D. Mich. 1991), *aff'd*, 983 F.2d 1066 (6th Cir. 1992).

20. Mich. Comp. Laws § 600.2948(2); *Michal v. PDK Labs*, No. 234943, 2003 Mich. App. LEXIS 2357 (Mich. Ct. App. Sept. 18, 2003); *Wiegerink v. Mitts & Merrill*, 182 Mich. App. 546, 452 N.W.2d 872 (1990) (woodchipper); *Raines v. Colt Indus., Inc.*, 757 F. Supp. 819 (E.D. Mich. 1991) (guns and simple tools); *Resteiner v. Sturm, Ruger & Co.*, 223 Mich. App. 374, 566 N.W.2d 53 (1997) (firearms); *Kirk v. Hanes Corp.*, 16 F.3d 705 (6th Cir. 1994) (cigarette lighter).

21. Mich. Comp. Laws § 600.2948(2); *Glittenberg v. Doughboy Recreational Indus., (on reh'g)* 441 Mich. 379, 491 N.W.2d 208 (1992) (pool).

22. Mich. Comp. Laws § 600.2947(4); *David v. Mach. Distrib. Inc.*, No. 239231, 2003 Mich. App. LEXIS 1904 (Mich. Ct. App. Aug. 12, 2003); *Portelli v. I.R. Constr. Prods. Co.*, 218 Mich. App. 591, 554 N.W.2d 591 (1996); *Antcliff v. State Employees Credit Union*, 414 Mich. 624, 639, 327 N.W.2d 814 (1982); *Tasca v. GTE Prods. Corp.*, 175 Mich. App. 617, 438 N.W.2d 625 (1988); *Kudzia v. Carboloy Div. of Gen. Elec. Co.*, 190 Mich. App. 285, 475 N.W.2d 371 (1991), (cobalt to large-scale manufacturer); *Jodway v. Kennametal, Inc.*, 207 Mich. App. 622, 525 N.W.2d 883 (1994).

23. *Spencer v. Ford Motor Co.*, 141 Mich. App. 356, 367 N.W.2d 393 (1985).

24. Mich. Comp. Laws § 600.2946(3); *Smith v. E. R. Squibb & Sons, Inc.*, 405 Mich. 79, 273 N.W.2d 476 (1979); *Downie v. Kent Prods., Inc.*, 420 Mich. 197, 362 N.W.2d 605 (1984), *modified*, 421 Mich. 1202, 367 N.W.2d 831 (1985); Mich. Rule Evid. 407.

25. Mich. Comp. Laws § 600.2947(2); *Wells v. Coulter Sales, Inc.*, 105 Mich. App. 107, 306 N.W.2d 411 (1981); *Trotter v. Hamill Mfg. Co.*, 143 Mich. App. 593, 372 N.W.2d 622 (1985), *lv. denied*, 424 Mich. 882 (1986); *Wiegernik v. Mitts & Merrill*, 182 Mich. App. 546, 452 N.W.2d 872 (1990).

26. Mich. Comp. Laws § 600.2947(2); *Snider v. Bob Thibodeau Ford, Inc.*, 42 Mich. App. 708, 202 N.W.2d 727 (1972); *Shipman v. Fontaine Truck Equip. Co.*, 184 Mich. App. 706, 459 N.W.2d 30 (1990).

27. *Holloway v. Gen. Motors Corp.*, 403 Mich. 614, 271 N.W.2d 777 (1978); *Chambers v. Gen. Motors Corp.*, 123 Mich. App. 619, 333 N.W.2d 9 (1982); *Hastings Mut. Ins. v. Gen. Motors Corp.*, No. 252427, 2005 Mich. App. LEXIS 849 (Mich. Ct. App. Mar. 28, 2005).

28. Mich. Comp. Laws § 600.2946(1); *Granger v. Fruehauf Corp.*, 147 Mich. App. 190, 383 N.W.2d 162 (1985), *rev'd on other grounds*, 429 Mich. 1, 412 N.W.2d 199 (1987).

29. *Holbrook v. Koehring Co.*, 75 Mich. App. 592, 255 N.W.2d 698 (1977); *see also Croskey v. BMW of N. Am., Inc.*, 532 F.3d 511, 518 (6th Cir. 2008); *Anderson v. Whittaker Corp.*, 894 F.2d 804 (6th Cir. 1990); *Lohr v. Stanley-Bostitch, Inc.*, 135 F.R.D. 162 (W.D. Mich. 1991).

30. *Muilenberg v. Upjohn Co.*, 115 Mich. App. 316, 320 N.W.2d 358 (1982); *Dowood Co. v. Michigan Tool Co.*, 14 Mich. App. 158, 165 N.W.2d 450 (1968).

31. *Belfry v. Anthony Pools, Inc.*, 80 Mich. App. 118, 262 N.W.2d 909 (1977).

32. *Neibarger v. Universal Coops., Inc.*, 439 Mich. 512, 486 N.W.2d 612 (1992).

33. *Sumner v. Gen. Motors Corp.*, 212 Mich. App. 694, 699, 538 N.W.2d 112 (1995), *overruled on other grounds, Lopez v. Gen. Motors Co.*, 224 Mich. App. 618, 569 N.W.2d 861 (1997) ("A manufacturer's liability in crashworthiness cases is limited [in that the manufacturer will only] be liable for that portion of the damage or injury caused by the defective design over and above the damage or injury that probably would have occurred as a result of the impact or collision absent the defective design." (Internal quotation omitted.)).

34. *Sumner*, 212 Mich. App. at 699-700.

35. *Bullock v. Gulf & W. Mfg.*, 128 Mich. App. 316, 340 N.W.2d 294 (1983); *Shipman v. Fontaine Truck Equip. Co.*, 184 Mich. App. 706, 459 N.W.2d 30 (1990);

Nichani v. Schroeder Homes, No. 267688, 2006 Mich. App. LEXIS 2280 (Mich. Ct. App. July 20, 2006).

36. *Huff v. Ford Motor Co.*, 127 Mich. App. 287, 338 N.W.2d 387 (1983).

37. *Owens v. Allis-Chalmers Corp.*, 414 Mich. 413, 326 N.W.2d 372 (1982).

38. Mich. Comp. Laws § 600.2959.

39. Mich. Comp. Laws § 600.2947(3).

40. Mich. Comp. Laws § 600.2947(3).

41. *Kirk v. Hanes Corp.*, 16 F.3d 705 (6th Cir. 1994); *Moning v. Alfono*, 400 Mich. 425, 254 N.W.2d 759 (1977); *Stopczynski v. Woodcox*, 258 Mich. App. 226, 671 N.W.2d 119 (2003).

42. *Wise v. Daniel*, 221 Mich. 229, 190 N.W. 746 (1922); *Smith v. Jones*, 382 Mich. 176, 169 N.W.2d 308 (1969); *see also Law Offices of Lawrence J. Stockler, P.C. v. Rose*, 174 Mich. App. 14, 436 N.W.2d 70 (1989).

43. *See, e.g., Jackson Printing Co. v. Mitan*, 169 Mich. App. 334, 341 (1988).

44. Mich. Comp. Laws § 600.6013.

45. Mich. Comp. Laws § 600.6013(8); *Ballog v. Knight Newspapers, Inc.*, 381 Mich. 527, 164 N.W.2d 19 (1969); *Attard v. Citizens Ins. Co. of Am.*, 237 Mich. App. 311, 602 N.W.2d 633 (1999).

46. *Phinney v. Verbrugge*, 222 Mich. App. 513, 540-41, 564 N.W.2d 532 (1997); *McDaniel v. Macomb Cnty. Bd. of Rd. Comm'rs*, 169 Mich. App. 474, 426 N.W.2d 747 (1988).

47. Mich. Comp. Laws § 600.6013(8).

48. Mich. Comp. Laws §§ 600.6013(9), (15)(a)(i).

49. Mich. Comp. Laws §§ 600.6013(13), (15)(a)(ii).

50. Mich. Comp. Laws §§ 418.101*et seq.*

51. Mich. Comp. Laws § 418.131(1); *Hesse v. Ashland Oil, Inc.*, 466 Mich. 21, 642 N.W.2d 330 (2002); *Gray v. Morley*, 460 Mich. 738, 741, 596 N.W.2d 922, 924 (1999); *Stalzer v. Shape Corp.*, 177 Mich. App. 572, 442 N.W.2d 648 (1989).

52. Mich. Comp. Laws § 418.131.

53. *Prosky v. Nat'l Acme Co.*, 404 F. Supp. 852 (E.D. Mich. 1975); *Husted v. Consumers Power Co.*, 376 Mich. 41, 135 N.W.2d 370 (1965); *Nanasi v. Gen. Motors Corp.*, 56 Mich. App. 652, 224 N.W.2d 914 (1974).

54. Mich. Comp. Laws § 418.131(1).

55. *Arnold v. Nat'l Steel Corp.*, 95 F. Supp. 2d 685 (E.D. Mich. 2000); *Pawlak v. Redox Corp.*, 182 Mich. App. 758, 453 N.W.2d 304 (1990); *Schefsky v. Evening News Ass'n*, 169 Mich. App. 223, 425 N.W.2d 768 (1988); *McNees v. Cedar Springs Stamping Co.*, 184 Mich. App. 101, 457 N.W.2d 68 (1990); *Smith v. Gen. Motors Corp.*, 192 Mich. App. 652, 481 N.W.2d 819 (1992); *Adams v. Shepherd Prods., U.S., Inc.*, 187 Mich. App. 695, 468 N.W.2d 332 (1991).

56. Mich. Comp. Laws § 600.5805(13).

57. Mich. Comp. Laws § 440.2314.

58. Mich. Comp. Laws § 600.2945 *et seq.*

59. Mich. Comp. Laws § 600.2956 (In an action "seeking damages for personal injury, property damage, or wrongful death, the liability of each defendant for damages is several only and is not joint.").

60. Mich. Comp. Laws § 600.2957(1).

61. Mich. Comp. Laws § 600.2957(1).

62. Mich. Comp. Laws § 600.2957(2).

63. Mich. Comp. Laws § 600.2957(3).

64. *Smiley v. Corrigan*, 248 Mich. App. 51, 638 N.W.2d 151 (2001).

65. Mich. Comp. Laws § 600.6312.

66. Mich. Comp. Laws § 600.1629.

67. *Wall v. Cherrydale Farms, Inc.*, 9 F. Supp. 2d 784 (E.D. Mich. 1998).

68. Mich. Comp. Laws § 600.6304(6).

69. Mich. Comp. Laws § 600.6312.

70. Mich. Comp. Laws §§ 600.2956, 600.6304.

71. Mich. Comp. Laws §§ 600.2959, 600.6306(3).

72. *Kokx v. Bylenga*, 241 Mich. App. 655, 617 N.W.2d 368 (2000).

73. Mich. Comp. Laws § 600.2955a(1).

74. Mich. Comp. Laws § 600.2946a(1). The Michigan Department of Treasury's notice regarding the updated amounts can be found online at http://www.michigan.gov/documents/nonecolimit101_3658_7.pdf.

75. Mich. Comp. Laws § 600.2946(5).

76. Mich. Comp. Laws § 600.2947(1) & (2) (The issue of foreseeability is a legal question for the court.).

77. Mich. Comp. Laws §§ 600.2945(j) ("sophisticated user" defined), 600.2947(4).

78. Mich. Comp. Laws § 600.2948(2).

79. Mich. Comp. Laws § 600.2947(6); *Dreyer v. Exel Indus., S.A.*, 32 F. App'x 353, 368 (6th Cir. 2009).

80. Mich. Comp. Laws § 600.2946(4).

81. Mich. Comp. Laws § 600.2955; Mich. R. Evid. 702.

82. Mich. Comp. Laws § 257.710e(7).

MINNESOTA

A. CAUSES OF ACTION

Minnesota recognizes strict liability, negligence, and breach of warranty as theories of recovery in a product liability action.[1] In cases in which a design defect is alleged, the plaintiff must elect either strict liability or negligence, but not both.[2] Breach of implied warranty includes merchantability and fitness for a particular purpose.[3]

B. STATUTES OF LIMITATION

A cause of action for wrongful death must be brought within three years after the cause of action accrues.[4] A cause of action based on strict liability must be brought within four years after the cause of action accrues.[5] A cause of action for negligence resulting in personal injury or damage to property must be brought within six years after the cause of action accrues.[6] A cause of action for breach of warranty must be brought within four years after the cause of action accrues.[7] Except where the contract provides otherwise, breach of warranty occurs when tender of delivery is made.[8] Otherwise, a cause of action accrues when the breach occurs, regardless of whether the plaintiff is aware of the breach.[9] Claims "arising out of the defective and unsafe condition of an improvement to real property" may not be brought "more than two years after discovery of the injury," and no such claims can accrue "more than ten years after substantial completion of construction."[10] Minnesota has adopted a "borrowing statute," which applies the limitations period of the state in which the cause of action accrued.[11]

C. STRICT LIABILITY

1. The Standard

Although Minnesota originally adopted the definition of strict liability set forth in Section 402A of the Restatement (Second) of Torts,[12] the Minnesota Supreme Court has since held that the Restatement definition will not be used in all product defect cases.[13] To recover under strict liability, the claimant must show (1) the product was in a defective condition and unreasonably dangerous for its intended use; (2) such defect existed when the product left defendant's control; and (3) the defect was the proximate cause of the injury sustained.[14]

2. "Defect"

A product is defective in manufacture if the product is unreasonably dangerous. Minnesota follows the "consumer expectation" standard in determining whether a product is unreasonably dangerous in manufacture.[15] In design defect cases, the Minnesota Supreme Court has adopted a "reasonable care" balancing test.[16] What constitutes reasonable care will vary with the surrounding circumstances and will involve a balancing of the likelihood of harm, and the gravity of the harm if it happens, against the burden on the manufacturer of preventing the harm.[17]

The Minnesota Supreme Court has held that the "existence of a safer, practical alternative design is not an element of an alleged defective product design prima facie case."[18] However, "the existence or nonexistence of a feasible alternative design" is a factor bearing upon the issue of whether the product was unreasonably dangerous.[19] Thus, although not technically a required element in all cases, "[t]o establish a prima facie case that [the product] was unreasonably dangerous *normally* requires production of evidence of the existence of a feasible, alternative safer design."[20]

3. **Contributory Negligence/Assumption of Risk**

Minnesota has established a modified form of comparative fault as set forth in Minn. Stat. § 604.01. This statute reduces the recovery of an at-fault plaintiff, in both strict liability and negligence, according to plaintiff's percentage of fault and bars the claim completely if plaintiff's percentage of fault is more than that of a defendant.[21] The fault of defendants is not aggregated for comparison purposes.[22]

Minnesota may recognize primary assumption of the risk in a product liability case. Secondary assumption of the risk is treated as fault and compared under Minnesota's comparative fault statute.[23]

4. **Sale or Lease**

Strict liability can be imposed on manufacturers and all those within the chain of distribution.[24] Under certain circumstances, sellers may obtain indemnification from manufacturers.[25]

5. **Inherently Dangerous Products**

While Minnesota has not specifically adopted comment k to Section 402A of the Restatement (Second) of Torts, the reasonable care balancing test applied in strict liability cases permits the jury to consider, in assessing a manufacturer's conduct, the usefulness and desirability of the product and the possibility of eliminating the danger without impairing the usefulness of the product.[26]

6. **Successor Liability**

A corporation purchasing the assets of another corporation will not succeed to liabilities of the selling corporation for products manufactured by the seller unless: (1) the successor corporation expressly or impliedly agrees to assume such debts or liabilities; (2) the transaction amounts to a consolidation or merger of the predecessor; (3) the successor is merely a continuation of the predecessor corporation; (4) the transfer of assets was entered fraudulently to escape liability for debts; or (5) there is inadequate consideration for the sale or transfer of assets.[27] Minnesota courts have rejected the "product line" exception to the nonliability rule.[28]

7. **Privity**

   Lack of privity is not a defense in strict product liability actions.[29] A manufacturer's duty to warn extends to all reasonably foreseeable users.[30] A manufacturer may not delegate its duty to produce a reasonably safe product.[31]

8. **Failure to Warn**

   A manufacturer has a duty to provide instructions for safe use of a product and a duty to warn of foreseeable dangers inherent in the proper use or foreseeable improper use of a product.[32] A manufacturer has no duty to warn of dangers of unforeseeable improper use[33] or dangers that are obvious.[34] Nor do manufacturers or suppliers have a duty to train users in the safe use of their products.[35] Strict liability may be imposed on a nonmanufacturing seller of a product that is defective for failure to warn, regardless of the seller's negligence.[36]

9. **Post-Sale Duty to Warn**

   A post-sale duty to warn arises only in special cases, such as where the product has a long life span and is sold used to other consumers, where the manufacturer continues to advertise and sell components for the product, where the manufacturer is aware of the defect, where the product defect is hidden, where the manufacturer has previously warned of dangers, and where potential injuries are severe.[37]

10. **Learned Intermediary Doctrine**

    Minnesota recognizes the "learned intermediary" doctrine, under which a manufacturer of a prescription drug may satisfy its duty to warn by supplying the prescribing physician with adequate warnings or instructions.[38] This doctrine applies to contraceptives[39] and to medical devices.[40]

11. **Substantial Change/Abnormal Use**

    A manufacturer is not liable for defects that develop after the product leaves the manufacturer's control.[41] A manufacturer has a duty to warn against dangers inherent in improper uses of a product.[42]

12. **State of the Art**

    Evidence of industry custom and practice and state of the art is admissible.[43]

13. **Standards and Government Regulations**

    Evidence of industry standards and governmental regulations is admissible, although not conclusive, on the issue of whether the defendant exercised reasonable care.[44]

14. **Other Accidents**

    Evidence of accidents suffered by others under similar circumstances at times not too remote from the accident involved in the litigation is admissible to show notice or design defect.[45]

15. **Misrepresentation**

    There are eleven elements in a misrepresentation action: (1) there must be a representation; (2) the representation must be false; (3) the representation must deal with past or present fact; (4) the fact must be material; (5) the fact must be susceptible of knowledge; (6) the representer must know the fact is false or assert it as of his or her own knowledge without knowing whether it is true or false; (7) the representer must intend to have the other person be induced to act or be justified in acting on it; (8) the other person must be induced to act or be justified in acting; (9) that person's actions must be in reliance on the representation; (10) that person must suffer damages; and (11) the misrepresentation must be the proximate cause of injury.[46]

16. **Spoliation of Evidence**

    Trial courts have inherent power to impose sanctions for spoliation of evidence. When one party intentionally or negligently spoliates the alleged defective product, the trial court must determine whether the opposing party is prejudiced and what sanction, if any, is appropriate.[47]

17. **Seat Belt Evidence**

    Minnesota's seat belt evidence "gag rule" provides that proof of use or nonuse of seat belts or child restraint systems, or proof of installation or failure to install seat belts or child restraints, is not admissible "in any litigation involving personal injuries or property damage resulting from the use or operation of any motor vehicle."[48] This bar "does not affect the right of a person to bring an action for damages arising out of an incident that involves a defectively designed, manufactured, installed, or operating seat belt or child passenger restraint system," nor does it preclude the introduction of seat belt use in such a products liability lawsuit.[49]

18. **Crashworthiness**

    Minnesota has long recognized the crashworthiness doctrine, *i.e.*, when the defective design or manufacture of a vehicle does not actually cause a crash but instead increases the severity of injuries suffered by occupants, manufacturers may be liable for enhanced injuries over and above those which otherwise would have resulted.[50] The plaintiff has the burden of proving that the defect in question was a substantial factor in causing the plaintiff's enhanced injuries, but does not need to show specifically which injuries would have been received in the absence of the defect and which were enhanced.[51] The manufacturer does not have a duty to produce an "accident proof" vehicle.[52]

D. NEGLIGENCE

Minnesota's comparative fault statute diminishes the plaintiff's recovery in proportion to the plaintiff's negligence. The plaintiff may not recover against the defendant if the plaintiff's negligence is greater than that of the particular defendant.[53]

In design defect cases, strict liability and negligence theories of recovery are merged.[54] A failure-to-warn case is submitted to the jury under a negligence standard.[55] In manufacturing flaw cases, the court may instruct the jury on both strict liability and negligence.[56]

E. BREACH OF WARRANTY

Minnesota has adopted the provisions of the Uniform Commercial Code dealing with express warranty,[57] implied warranty of merchantability,[58] and implied warranty of fitness for a particular purpose.[59]

If supported by the evidence, the plaintiff may assert both breach of express warranty and strict liability.[60] The Minnesota Court of Appeals has concluded that a strict liability claim preempts a claim of implied warranty of merchantability.[61]

F. PUNITIVE DAMAGES

Punitive damages are available in a product liability action only where a plaintiff suffers personal injury.[62] However, a plaintiff may not seek punitive damages in the complaint. After filing suit, a party may move to amend the pleadings to assert punitive damages.[63] Punitive damages are thereafter recoverable if the plaintiff proves by clear and convincing evidence that the defendant's conduct showed "deliberate disregard for the rights or safety of others."[64] The trier of fact shall, if requested by any of the parties, first determine whether compensatory damages should be awarded. "After a determination has been made, the trier of fact shall, in a separate proceeding, determine whether and in what amount punitive damages will be awarded."[65]

G. STATUTES, INCLUDING APPLICABLE "TORT REFORM" STATUTES

The plaintiff may not seek punitive damages in the complaint. After filing the suit, a party may move to amend the pleadings to assert punitive damages.[66]

As to claims arising from events that occur on or after August 1, 2003, any person whose fault is 50 percent or less shall be liable only for the percentage of fault attributable to that person.[67] A person whose fault is greater than 50 percent will be jointly and severally liable for the whole award.[68] A person in the chain of manufacture or distribution must contribute toward any amount uncollectible from another person in the chain, but liability is limited to the person's fault if it is less than the claimant's fault.[69]

Minnesota's "economic loss" doctrine is codified in Minn. Stat. § 604.101.[70] Under § 604.101, a plaintiff cannot seek tort remedies in a product defect case that alleges damage only to the product itself, *i.e.*, where there is no damage to other tangible or real property, or personal injury.[71] If the product defect causes economic loss to other tangible or real property, Minn. Stat. § 604.101 limits the plaintiff's tort recovery to direct damages for the value of the other property damaged; business interruption losses; and other personal or household out-of-pocket expenses incurred during the period of restoring the damaged property.[72] Intentional or reckless misrepresentation claims are not barred by Minn. Stat. § 604.101.[73]

H. PRE- AND POST-JUDGMENT INTEREST

1. Pre-Judgment Interest

Minnesota Stat. § 549.09 provides, in part:

> Except as otherwise provided . . . preverdict . . . interest on pecuniary damages shall be computed as provided in paragraph (c) from the time of the commencement of the action . . . or the time of a written notice of claim, whichever occurs first, except as provided herein. The action must be commenced within two years of a written notice of claim for interest to begin to accrue from the time of the notice of claim.

For a judgment or award of $50,000 or less, the correct amount of interest is calculated by multiplying the defined annual interest rates (to the extent all or a portion of a year is implicated) by the amount of the judgment.[74] In 2014, the defined annual interest rate was 4 percent.[75] Effective August 1, 2009, the interest rate is 10 percent per year on judgments or awards of more than $50,000.[76] Pre-judgment interest may not be awarded on "judgments or awards for future damages," "punitive damages," or "that portion of any verdict . . . founded upon interest, or costs, disbursements, attorney fees, or other similar items added by the court[.]"[77]

2. Post-Judgment Interest

Pursuant to Minnesota Stat. § 549.09, post-judgment interest shall be calculated at the same annual rates as pre-judgment interest "from the time of the verdict . . . until judgment is finally entered. . . ." Post-judgment interest should be calculated on the verdict and pre-judgment interest. The applicable rate for 2014 is 4 percent. Effective August 1, 2009, the interest rate on judgments or awards of more than $50,000 is 10 percent per year.[78]

I. EMPLOYER SUIT FROM IMMUNITY

A third-party tortfeasor (such as a product manufacturer) may seek contribution from an injured plaintiff's employer in an amount proportional to the employer's percentage of negligence, but not to exceed its total workers' compensation liability to the plaintiff/employee.[79] The Minnesota Supreme Court has set forth a three-prong approach for allocating the damages in the employer liability context after a verdict has been reached.[80]

J. JOINT AND SEVERAL LIABILITY

As to claims arising from events that occur on or after August 1, 2003, any person whose fault is 50 percent or less shall be liable only for the percentage of fault attributable to that person.[81] As to claims arising from events that occurred prior to August 1, 2003, however, loss is allocated between co-tortfeasors in proportion to their relative fault, under Minnesota's Comparative Fault Statute; however, each tortfeasor remains jointly and severally liable for the whole award;[82] and a party whose fault is 15 percent or less is liable for a percentage of the whole award no greater than four times that party's percentage of fault.[83] Contribution is available pursuant to the Comparative Fault Statute. Any amount that is uncollectable from any person in the chain of manufacture and distribution "shall be reallocated among all other persons in the chain . . . but not among the claimant or others at fault who are not in the chain of manufacture or distribution of the product."[84] If a person's fault is less than the claimant's, however, then that person is only liable for the portion of the judgment which represents the percentage of fault attributable to that person.[85]

George W. Soule
Soule & Stull LLC
Eight West 43rd Street, Suite 200
Minneapolis, Minnesota 55409
(612) 353-6491
(Fax) (612) 573-6484
(E-mail) gsoule@soulestull.com

Endnotes - Minnesota

1. *Hapka v. Paquin Farms*, 458 N.W.2d 683 (Minn. 1990); *Bilotta v. Kelley Co.*, 346 N.W.2d 616 (Minn. 1984).

2. *Hauenstein v. Loctite Corp.*, 347 N.W.2d 272, 275 (Minn. 1984); *Bilotta*, 346 N.W.2d at 623; *see also Piotrowski v. Southworth Prods. Corp.*, 15 F.3d 748, 751 (8th Cir. 1994).

3. Minn. Stat. § 336.2-314, 315.

4. Minn. Stat. § 573.02, subd. 1.

5. Minn. Stat. § 541.05, subd. 2.

6. Minn. Stat. § 541.05, subd. 1.

7. Minn. Stat. § 336.2-725(1).

8. Minn. Stat. § 336.2-725(2).

9. *Leisure Dynamics, Inc. v. Falstaff Brewing Corp.*, 298 N.W.2d 33, 39 (Minn. 1980).

10. Minn. Stat. § 541.051, subd. 1.

11. Minn. Stat. § 541.30-.36. Lawsuits filed in Minnesota that arise from incidents occurring prior to August 1, 2004, however, will be governed by Minnesota's statutes of limitations, as Minnesota courts apply the law of the forum to procedural conflicts, and the Minnesota Supreme Court has "considered statutes of limitations to be procedural without exception." *Fleeger v. Wyeth*, 771 N.W.2d 524, 528-29 (Minn. 2009).

12. *Olson v. Babbitt*, 189 N.W.2d 701, 705 (Minn. 1971).

13. *Bilotta v. Kelley Co.*, 346 N.W.2d 616, 621 (Minn. 1984).

14. *Lee v. Crookston Coca-Cola Bottling Co.*, 188 N.W.2d 426, 432 (Minn. 1971); *see also Kallio v. Ford Motor Co.*, 407 N.W.2d 92 (Minn. 1987).

15. *Bilotta*, 346 N.W.2d at 621-22.

16. *Bilotta*, 346 N.W.2d at 621-22.

17. *Bilotta*, 346 N.W.2d at 621-22.

18. *Kallio*, 407 N.W.2d at 97.

19. *Kallio*, 407 N.W.2d at 96.

20. *Kallio*, 407 N.W.2d at 96 (emphasis added); *see also Wagner v. Hesston Corp.*, 450 F.3d 756, 760 (8th Cir. 2006).

21. Minn. Stat. § 604.01, subd. 1; *see also Omnetics, Inc. v. Radiant Tech. Corp.*, 440 N.W.2d 177, 182 (Minn. Ct. App. 1989).

22. *Cambern v. Sioux Tools, Inc.*, 323 N.W.2d 795, 798 (Minn. 1982).

23. *Andren v. White-Rogers Co.*, 465 N.W.2d 102, 104 (Minn. Ct. App.), *rev. denied* (Minn. 1991).

24. *Tolbert v. Gerber Indus., Inc.*, 255 N.W.2d 362, 364 (Minn. 1977).

25. *Jacobs v. Rosemount Dodge-Winnebago South*, 310 N.W.2d 71, 80 (Minn. 1981).

26. *Kociemba v. G.D. Searle & Co.*, 695 F. Supp. 432, 434 (D. Minn. 1988); *Bilotta*, 346 N.W.2d at 621; *Krein v. Raudabough*, 406 N.W.2d 315, 318 (Minn. Ct. App. 1987).

27. *Carstedt v. Grindeland*, 406 N.W.2d 39, 41 (Minn. Ct. App. 1987).

28. *Niccum v. Hydra Tool Corp.*, 438 N.W.2d 96, 100 (Minn. 1989).

29. *Milbank Mut. Ins. Co. v. Proksch*, 244 N.W.2d 105, 110 (Minn. 1976); *Farr v. Armstrong Rubber Co.*, 179 N.W.2d 64, 71 (Minn. 1970).

30. *Smits v. E-Z Por Corp.*, 365 N.W.2d 352, 355 (Minn. Ct. App. 1985).

31. *Bilotta*, 346 N.W.2d at 624.

32. *Kallio v. Ford Motor Co.*, 391 N.W.2d 860, 864 (Minn. Ct. App. 1986), *aff'd*, 407 N.W.2d 92 (Minn. 1987); *Germann v. F.L. Smithe Mach. Co.*, 381 N.W.2d 503, 507 (Minn. Ct. App. 1986), *aff'd*, 395 N.W.2d 922 (Minn. 1986).

33. *Huber v. Niagara Mach. & Tool Works*, 430 N.W.2d 465, 467 (Minn. 1988).

34. *Westerberg v. Sch. Dist. No. 792*, 148 N.W.2d 312, 317 (Minn. 1967); *Hart v. FMC Corp.*, 446 N.W.2d 194, 198 (Minn. Ct. App. 1989); *Mix v. MTD Prods., Inc.*, 393 N.W.2d 18, 19-20 (Minn. Ct. App. 1986).

35. *Glorvigen v. Cirrus Design Corp.*, 816 N.W.2d 572, 583 (Minn. 2012).

36. *Marcon v. Kmart Corp.*, 573 N.W.2d 728, 731 (Minn. Ct. App.), *rev. denied* (Minn. 1998).

37. *Hodder v. Goodyear Tire & Rubber Co.*, 426 N.W.2d 826, 833 (Minn. 1988), *cert. denied*, 492 U.S. 926 (1989); *see also Ramstad v. Lear Siegler Diversified Holdings Corp.*, 836 F. Supp. 1511, 1517 (D. Minn. 1993).

38. *Mulder v. Parke Davis & Co.*, 181 N.W.2d 882, 885 (Minn. 1970); *Todalen v. U.S. Chem. Co.*, 424 N.W.2d 73, 79 (Minn. Ct. App. 1988), *overruled on other grounds by Tyroll v. Private Label Chems., Inc.*, 505 N.W.2d 54, 62 (Minn. 1993).

39. *Kociemba v. G.D. Searle & Co.*, 680 F. Supp. 1293, 1305-06 (D. Minn. 1988).

40. *Mozes v. Medtronic, Inc.*, 14 F. Supp. 2d 1124, 1130 (D. Minn. 1998).

41. *W. Sur. & Cas. Co. v. Gen. Elec. Co.*, 433 N.W.2d 444, 447 (Minn. Ct. App. 1988).

42. *Huber v. Niagara Mach. & Tool Works*, 430 N.W.2d 465, 467 (Minn. 1988).

43. *See* Minnesota Dist. Judges Ass'n, Minnesota Jury Instruction Guides, JIG 75.35, 4A Minnesota Practice 172 (5th ed. 2006) ("[A manufacturer must keep up with scientific knowledge and advances in the field. You should judge whether the manufacturer used reasonable care in the light of that duty.]"); *see also Kallio v. Ford Motor Co.*, 407 N.W.2d 92, 96-97 (Minn. 1987) (upholding, without objection, instruction based on precursor to current JIG 75.20 and adding that the jury may consider state-of-the-art-evidence); *Schmidt v. Beninga*, 173 N.W.2d 401, 408 (Minn. 1970) (admitting evidence of industry custom on the issue of standard of care in negligence cases).

44. *Gryc v. Dayton-Hudson Corp.*, 297 N.W.2d 727, 734-35 (Minn. 1980), *cert. denied*, 449 U.S. 921 (1980).

45. *Hodder v. Goodyear Tire & Rubber Co.*, 426 N.W.2d 826, 834 (Minn. 1988), *cert. denied*, 492 U.S. 926 (1989); *Colby v. Gibbons*, 276 N.W.2d 170, 176 (Minn. 1979); *Buzzell v. Bliss*, 358 N.W.2d 695, 700 (Minn. Ct. App. 1984).

46. *Davis v. Re-Trac Mfg. Corp.*, 149 N.W.2d 37, 38-39 (Minn. 1967).

47. *Patton v. Newmar Corp.*, 538 N.W.2d 116, 118-19 (Minn. 1995); *see also Hoffman v. Ford Motor Co.*, 587 N.W.2d 66, 71-72 (Minn. Ct. App. 1998).

48. Minn. Stat. § 169.685, subd. 4.

49. Minn. Stat. § 169.685, subd. 4

50. *See Mitchell v. Volkswagenwerk, AG*, 669 F.2d 1199, 1203 (8th Cir. 1982) (applying Minnesota law).

51. *Mitchell*, 669 F.2d at 1206.

52. *Mitchell*, 669 F.2d at 1207.

53. Minn. Stat. § 604.01, subd. 1.

54. *Bilotta v. Kelley Co.*, 346 N.W.2d 616, 622 (Minn. 1984).

55. *Hauenstein v. Loctite Corp.*, 347 N.W.2d 272, 275 (Minn. 1984).

56. *Bilotta*, 346 N.W.2d at 622.

57. Minn. Stat. § 336.2-313.

58. Minn. Stat. § 336.2-314.

59. Minn. Stat. § 336.2-315.

60. *Bilotta*, 346 N.W.2d at 625.

61. *Cont'l Ins. Co. v. Loctite Corp.*, 352 N.W.2d 460, 463 (Minn. Ct. App. 1984).

62. *Indep. Sch. Dist. No. 622 v. Keene Corp.*, 511 N.W.2d 728, 732 (Minn. 1994), overruled on other grounds by *Jensen v. Walsh*, 623 N.W.2d 247, 250-52 (Minn. 2001); *Eisert v. Greenberg Roofing & Sheet Metal Co.*, 314 N.W.2d 226, 228 (Minn. 1982).

63. Minn. Stat. § 549.191.

64. Minn. Stat. § 549.20, subd. 1(a).

65. Minn. Stat. § 549.20, subd. 4.

66. Minn. Stat. § 549.191.

67. Minn. Stat. § 604.02, subd. 1; *Staab v. Diocese of St. Cloud*, 853 N.W.2d 713 (Minn. 2014).

68. Minn. Stat. § 604.02, subd. 1. Under Minn. Stat. § 604.02, for claims arising-from events that occurred prior to August 1, 2003, a person whose fault is 15 percent or less is liable for a percentage of the whole award no greater than four times the percentage of fault. Minn. Stat. § 604.02, subd. 1.

69. Minn. Stat. § 604.02, subd. 3.

70. Minn. Stat. § 604.101, subd. 3 (applicable to actions where the buyer and seller entered the relevant chain of distribution on or after August 1, 2000).

71. Minn. Stat. § 604.101, subd. 3.

72. Minn. Stat. § 604.101, subd. 3.

73. Minn. Stat. § 604.101, subd. 4.

74. *See* Minn. Stat. § 549.09, subd. 1(c)(1).

75. http://www.mncourts.gov/Documents/0/Public/administration/2014_Interest_Rates_on_State_Court_Judgements_-_12-10-13.pdf.

76. Minn. Stat. § 549.09, subd. 1(c)(2).

77. *See* Minn. Stat. § 549.09, subd. 1(b).

78. Minn. Stat. § 549.09, subd. 1(c)(2).

79. Minn. Stat. § 176.061, subd. 11; *Lambertson v. Cincinnati Corp.*, 257 N.W.2d 679, 689 (Minn. 1977).

80. *See Johnson v. Raske Bldg. Sys., Inc.*, 276 N.W.2d 79, 80-81 (Minn. 1979); *see also* Minn. Stat. § 176.061, subd. 6; *Folstad v. Eder*, 467 N.W.2d 608, 613-14 (Minn. 1991).

81. Minn. Stat. § 604.02, subd. 1.

82. *See* Minn. Stat. § 604.02, subd. 1.

83. Minn. Stat. § 604.02, subd. 1.

84. Minn. Stat. § 604.02, subd. 3.

85. Minn. Stat. § 604.02, subd. 3.

MISSISSIPPI

A. CAUSES OF ACTION

Product liability lawsuits commonly include causes of action for strict liability, negligence, and breach of warranty. The Mississippi Product Liability Act (MPLA) governs all product liability actions.[1]

B. STATUTES OF LIMITATION

1. Personal Injury and Property Damage

Causes of action for negligence and strict liability must be brought within three years of accrual.[2]

2. Breach of Warranty

Causes of action for personal injury and property damage resulting from breach of warranty must be brought within six years from tender of delivery of goods.[3]

3. Real Property

Causes of action for personal injury and injury to real and personal property from deficiencies in design and construction of improvements to real property must be brought within six years of written acceptance or actual occupancy, whichever occurs first.[4] Privity of contract is not required.[5]

4. Discovery Rule

In product liability actions involving latent injury or disease, the cause of action does not accrue until the plaintiff has discovered, or by reasonable diligence should have discovered, the injury.[6]

C. STRICT LIABILITY

1. The Standard

Product liability actions are governed by the MPLA.[7] A plaintiff must prove that the defective condition rendered the product unreasonably dangerous to the user or consumer.

2. "Defect"

A product is defective by design if, at the time the product left the control of the manufacturer or seller, (a) the manufacturer or seller knew, or in light of reasonably available knowledge or in the exercise of reasonable care should have known, about the danger that caused the damage for which recovery is sought; and (b) the product failed to function as expected and there existed a feasible design alternative that would have to a reasonable probability prevented the harm.[8] A product may also be defective if (a) it deviated in a material way from the manufacturer's specifications or from otherwise identical units manufactured to the same manufacturing specifications; or (b) it failed to contain adequate warnings or instructions; or (c) the product breached an express warranty.[9]

3. **Causation**

    The plaintiff must prove that the defective and unreasonably dangerous condition of the product proximately caused the damages for which recovery is sought.[10] In asbestos cases, the plaintiff must prove product identification and frequency, regularity, and proximity of exposure to establish proximate cause.[11]

4. **Contributory Negligence/Assumption of Risk**

    Contributory negligence and assumption of risk are defenses to causes of action for negligence and strict liability.[12] Mississippi is a pure comparative negligence state, and all questions of contributory negligence are for the jury to determine.[13] Assumption of risk operates as a bar to recovery.[14] The elements of assumption of risk are knowledge of the condition, appreciation of the danger of the condition, and a deliberate and voluntary choice to expose oneself to the danger.[15]

5. **Sellers**

    Tort reform legislation enacted in 2004 immunizes innocent sellers who are not actively negligent, but instead are mere conduits of a product, from liability.[16]

6. **Inherently Dangerous Products**

    A product is not defective if the harm was caused by an inherent characteristic of the product which is a generic aspect that cannot be eliminated without substantially compromising the product's usefulness or desirability and which is recognized by the ordinary person.[17]

7. **Successor Liability**

    As a general rule, when one corporation purchases or acquires manufacturing assets from another corporation, the successor does not become responsible for the debts and liabilities of the predecessor.[18]

8. **Market Share and Enterprise Liability**

    Market share and enterprise liability have not been recognized in Mississippi.

9. **Privity**

    Privity is not required to maintain any action for negligence, strict liability, or breach of warranty.[19]

10. **Failure to Warn**

    Under the MPLA, the plaintiff must prove that at the time the product left the control of the manufacturer or seller, the manufacturer or seller knew, or in light of reasonably available knowledge should have known, about the danger that caused the damage for which recovery is sought and that the ordinary user or consumer would not realize its dangerous condition.[20] An adequate product warning is one that a reasonably prudent person in the same or similar circumstances would have provided and that communicates sufficient information on the dangers and safe use of the product, taking into account the ordinary knowledge common to an ordinary consumer who purchases the product.[21] A manufacturer or seller shall not be liable if the danger posed by the product is, or should have been, known or open and obvious to the user or consumer of the product.[22] A manufacturer or seller is not liable in an inadequate warnings case unless the plaintiff read and relied upon the allegedly inadequate warning.[23]

11. **Post-Sale Duty to Warn**

    Mississippi law has not imposed a post-sale duty to warn on manufacturers.[24]

12. **Learned Intermediary Doctrine**

    A manufacturer's duty to warn is discharged by providing information to a third person upon whom it can reasonably rely to communicate the information to the ultimate users of the product.[25] The learned intermediary doctrine applies to a prescription drug or product used under the supervision of a physician or other licensed professional.[26] Legislation effective January 1, 2003 bars suits against prescribers of FDA-approved prescription drugs unless the plaintiff pleads specific facts which, if proven, amount to negligence on the part of the medical provider.[27]

13. **Substantial Change/Abnormal Use**

    The plaintiff must prove that the product reached the consumer without substantial change in its condition. A manufacturer is not liable for injuries resulting from abnormal or unintended use of the product if such use was not reasonably foreseeable.[28]

14. **State of the Art**

    "State-of-the-art" evidence is admissible.[29]

15. **Standards**

    Evidence that the product complied with customary or industry standards is admissible.[30]

16. **Other Accidents**

    Evidence of other accidents is inadmissible unless the plaintiff proves similarity of product and circumstances.[31]

17. **Misrepresentation**

    Mississippi follows the traditional common law elements of misrepresentation.[32]

18. **Spoliation of Evidence**

    A plaintiff's case may be dismissed where the product is unavailable or destroyed and there is no other evidence of defect.[33] There is no independent cause of action for spoliation of evidence.[34]

19. **Crashworthiness**

    Crashworthiness is a recognized theory of liability against motor vehicle manufacturers.[35]

20. **Economic Loss**

    There is no recovery solely for economic damage to the product in strict liability and negligence actions.[36]

21. **Medical Monitoring**

    No cause of action for medical monitoring is recognized under Mississippi law.[37]

D. **NEGLIGENCE**

A negligence cause of action is commonly asserted in product liability actions, but is no longer a separate cause of action.[38] Contributory negligence is a defense to negligence and strict liability causes of action. Mississippi is a pure comparative negligence state.

E. **BREACH OF WARRANTY**

Breach of express warranty is available in product liability lawsuits for personal injury.[39] The cause of action and proof required for breach of warranty are generally similar to the cause of action and proof required for strict liability.[40]

F. **CAPS ON NONECONOMIC DAMAGES**

Tort reform legislation enacted in 2004 places caps on the amount of recovery for noneconomic damages (death, pain, suffering, mental and emotional distress, disfigurement, hedonic damages, loss of consortium, bystander injury, etc.). The cap in medical negligence actions is $500,000. The cap in all other actions is $1 million.[41]

G. **PUNITIVE DAMAGES**

Punitive damages are recoverable in causes of action for negligence, strict liability, and breach of warranty. By statute, Mississippi law provides a procedure for a bifurcated trial to assess punitive damages.[42] Punitive damages may not be awarded unless the claimant proves by clear and convincing evidence that the defendant acted with actual malice or gross negligence that evinces a willful, wanton, or reckless disregard for the safety of others, or committed actual fraud.[43] Relevant factors for the jury to consider in assessing the amount of punitive damages to be awarded are (1) the amount necessary to punish and deter the defendant, (2) the amount necessary to make an example of the defendant to deter others, and (3) the pecuniary ability or financial net worth of the defendant.[44] In 2002, the Mississippi Legislature amended the punitive damages statute to bar recovery of punitive damages from a product seller under certain circumstances and to place caps on certain punitive damage awards. The caps are tied to the net worth of the defendant, which is determined in accordance with generally accepted accounting principles. The cap on punitive damages decreases with the net worth of the defendant: more than $1 billion net worth, $20 million cap; more than $750 million but less than $1 billion net worth, $15 million cap; more than $500 million but not more than $750 million net worth, 5 million cap more than $100 million but not more than $500 million net worth, $3,750,000 cap; more than $50 million but not more than $100 million net worth, $2,500,000 cap; $50 million or less net worth, cap is 2 percent of the defendant's net worth.[45]

H. PRE- AND POST-JUDGMENT INTEREST

Pre-judgment interest is not recoverable in personal injury actions. A plaintiff is entitled to interest on a judgment at a per annum rate set by the judge.[46] The interest rate is usually the statutory legal rate of interest, which is 8 percent.[47]

I. EMPLOYER IMMUNITY FROM SUIT

The Mississippi Workers' Compensation Act exempts the plaintiff's employer from liability and from being joined as a defendant in an action for injuries sustained by the employee.[48]

J. STATUTES

Relevant statutes for product liability actions are the MPLA (amended in 2004),[49] punitive damages statute (amended in 2004),[50] statutes of limitation,[51] venue statute (amended in 2004),[52] caps on noneconomic damages (enacted in 2004),[53] joint and several liability (amended in 2004),[54] and abolition of the privity requirement.[55]

K. JOINT AND SEVERAL LIABILITY

Liability is several only, except where two or more tortfeasors consciously and deliberately pursue a common plan or design to commit a tortious act, or actively take part in it.[56] Each defendant is liable only for the percentage of fault allocated to it by the jury, and one defendant cannot be forced to pay any damages caused by the conduct of another tortfeasor.

L. JOINDER OF PLAINTIFFS

In 2004, the Mississippi Supreme Court severely curtailed joinder of multiple plaintiffs in a single lawsuit by revising Mississippi Rule of Civil Procedure 20, Permissive Joinder of Parties,[57] and through a series of opinions addressing joinder of plaintiffs in a single lawsuit.[58]

Lewis W. Bell
Watkins & Eager, PLLC
The Emporium Building, Suite 300
400 East Capitol Street
Post Office Box 650
Jackson, Mississippi 39205
(601) 965-1977
(Fax) (601) 965-1901
Email: lbell@watkinseager.com

ENDNOTES - MISSISSIPPI

1. Miss. Code Ann. § 11-1-63 (1993).

2. Miss. Code Ann. § 15-1-49 (rev. 1995).

3. Miss. Code Ann. § 75-2-725 (1972).

4. Miss. Code Ann. § 15-1-41 (rev. 1995). *See generally Collins v. Trinity Indus., Inc.*, 861 F.2d 1364 (5th Cir. 1988); *Reich v. Jesco, Inc.*, 526 So. 2d 550 (Miss. 1988); *Smith v. Fluor Corp.*, 514 So. 2d 1227 (Miss. 1987).

5. Miss. Code Ann. § 11-7-20 (Supp. 1999); *Keyes v. Guy Bailey Homes, Inc.*, 439 So. 2d 670 (Miss. 1983).

6. Miss. Code Ann. § 15-1-49(2) (rev. 1995); *Owens-Illinois, Inc. v. Edwards*, 573 So. 2d 704 (Miss. 1990). While there is a specific statute of limitations rule for medical malpractice, the Mississippi Supreme Court in *Williams v. Kilgore*, 618 So. 2d 51 (Miss. 1992), discusses latent injury. The discussion may have relevance to a products case. In a tobacco case, *Schiro v. American Tobacco Co.*, 611 So. 2d 962 (Miss. 1992), the court discusses the discovery rule as announced in *Edwards*, and appears to add a doctor's diagnosis as a new requirement on the issue of plaintiff's reasonableness.

7. Miss. Code Ann. § 11-1-63 (1993).

8. Miss. Code Ann. § 11-1-63(f) (1993).

9. Miss. Code Ann. § 11-1-63(a)(i) (1993).

10. Miss. Code Ann. § 11-1-63(a)(iii) (1993).

11. *Monsanto Co. v. Hall*, No. 2004-IA-00918-SCT, slip op. at 5 (Oct. 6, 2005).

12. Miss. Code Ann. § 11-1-63(d) & (h) (1993); *Nichols v. Western Auto Supply Co., Inc.*, 477 So. 2d 261 (Miss. 1985).

13. Miss. Code Ann. §§ 11-7-15, 11-7-17 (1972).

14. Miss. Code Ann. § 11-1-63(d) (1993); *Nichols*, 477 So. 2d at 261; *Elias v. New Laurel Radio Station, Inc.*, 146 So. 2d 558 (Miss. 1962).

15. Miss. Code Ann. § 11-1-63(d) (1993); *Alley v. Praschak Mach. Co.*, 366 So. 2d 661 (Miss. 1979).

16. Miss. Code Ann. § 11-1-63(h) (2004).

17. Miss. Code Ann. § 11-1-63(b) (1993).

18. *Mozingo v. Correct Mfg. Corp.*, 752 F.2d 168 (5th Cir. 1985); *Johnston v. Pneumo Corp.*, 652 F. Supp. 1402 (S.D. Miss. 1987).

19. Miss. Code Ann. § 11-7-20 (Supp. 1999).

20. Miss. Code Ann. § 11-1-63(c)(i) (1993).

21. Miss. Code Ann. § 11-1-63(c)(ii) (1993).

22. Miss. Code Ann. § 11-1-63(e) (1993).

23. *Palmer v. Volkswagon of Am., Inc.*, 2001 CT-00875-SCT, 2005 WL 774917 (Miss. Apr. 7, 2005).

24. Courts have consistently held that a product manufacturer is liable only if the defect existed at the time the product left the control of the manufacturer. *See Ward v. Hobart Mfg. Co.*, 450 F.2d 1176, 1184 n.23 (5th Cir. 1971); *Coca-Cola Bottling Co., Inc. v. Reeves*, 486 So. 2d 374, 378 (Miss. 1986); *Early-Gary, Inc. v. Walters*, 294 So. 2d 181, 186 (Miss. 1974); *State Stove Mfg. Co. v. Hodges*, 189 So. 2d 113, 121 (Miss. 1966); *but see Ford Motor Co. v. Matthews*, 291 So. 2d 169, 176 (Miss. 1974). Product liability legislation codifies this principle and strengthens the argument that claims based on post-sale duties to warn, recall, or retrofit are not viable. *See* Miss. Code Ann. § 11-1-63(a) & (f) (Supp. 1999).

25. *Swan v. I.P., Inc.*, 613 So. 2d 846 (Miss. 1993); *Wyeth Labs., Inc. v. Fortenberry*, 530 So. 2d 688 (Miss. 1988).

26. Miss. Code Ann. § 11-1-63(c)(ii) (1993).

27. Miss. Code Ann. § 11-1-62 (2002).

28. Miss. Code Ann. § 11-1-63(a) (1993).

29. Miss. Code Ann. § 11-1-63(f)(ii) (1993); *Hall v. Mississippi Chem. Express, Inc.*, 528 So. 2d 796 (Miss. 1988); *Brown v. Williams*, 504 So. 2d 1188 (Miss. 1987); *Toliver v. Gen. Motors Corp.*, 482 So. 2d 213 (Miss. 1985).

30. *Ward*, 450 F.2d 1176; *Fincher v. Ford Motor Co.*, 399 F. Supp. 106 (S.D. Miss. 1975), *aff'd*, 535 F.2d 657 (5th Cir. 1976); *Hall*, 528 So. 2d 796; *Brown*, 504 So. 2d at 1188; *Toliver*, 482 So. 2d at 213.

31. *Johnson v. Ford Motor Co.*, 988 F.2d 573, 579 (5th Cir. 1993); *Hardy v. Chemetron Corp.*, 870 F.2d 1007 (5th Cir. 1989); *Shields v. Sturm, Ruger & Co.*, 864 F.2d 379 (5th Cir. 1989).

32. *Stonecipher v. Kornhaus*, 623 So. 2d 955 (Miss. 1993).

33. *Powe v. Wagner Elec. Sales Corp.*, 589 F. Supp. 657 (S.D. Miss. 1984).

34. *Richardson v. Sara Lee Corp.*, 847 So. 2d 821 (Miss. 2003).

35. *Tolliver v. Gen. Motors Corp.*, 482 So. 2d 213 (Miss. 1989).

36. Miss. Code Ann. § 11-1-63 (1993); *State Farm Mut. Auto. Ins. Co. v. Ford Motor Co.*, 1999 WL 119330 (Miss. App. 1999); *Lee v. Gen. Motors Corp.*, 950 F. Supp. 170 (S.D. Miss. 1996); *Mississippi Elec. Power Ass'n v. Porcelain Prod. Co.*, 729 F. Supp. 512 (S.D. Miss. 1990).

37. *Paz v. Brush Engineered Materials, Inc.*, 351 F. Supp. 2d 580 (S.D. Miss. 2005).

38. The Mississippi Supreme Court has stated that negligence is not a separate cause of action. *See Estate of Hunter v. Gen. Motors Corp.*, 729 So. 2d 1264, 1277-78 (Miss. 1999).

39. Miss. Code Ann. § 11-1-63(a)(i)(4) (1993).

40. Miss. Code Ann. § 11-1-63(a) (1993).

41. Miss. Code Ann. § 11-1-60(2) (2004).

42. Miss. Code Ann. § 11-1-65 (1993).

43. Miss. Code Ann. § 11-1-65(1)(a) (1993).

44. Miss. Code Ann. § 11-1-65(1)(e) (1993).

45. Miss. Code Ann. § 11-1-65(3)(a) (2004).

46. Miss. Code Ann. § 75-17-7 (rev. 1991).

47. Miss. Code Ann. § 75-17-1 (Supp. 1999).

48. Miss. Code Ann. § 71-3-9 (1972); *Stringfellow v. Reed*, 739 F. Supp. 324 (S.D. Miss. 1990).

49. Miss. Code Ann. § 11-1-63 (2004).

50. Miss. Code Ann. § 11-1-65 (2004).

51. Miss. Code Ann. § 15-1-49 (rev. 1995) (negligence and strict liability); § 75-2-725 (1972) (breach of warranty); § 15-1-41 (rev. 1995) (improvements to real property).

52. Miss. Code Ann. § 11-11-3 (2004).

53. Miss. Code Ann. § 11-1-60(2) (2004).

54. Miss. Code Ann. § 85-5-7 (2004).

55. Miss. Code Ann. § 11-7-20 (Supp. 1999).

56. Miss. Code Ann. § 85-5-7 (2004).

57. M.R.C.P. 20, cmt. (amended Feb. 20, 2004).

58. *See Janssen Pharmaceutica, Inc. v. Armond*, 866 So. 2d 1092 (Miss. 2004); *Janssen Pharmaceutica, Inc. v. Bailey*, 878 So. 2d 231 (Miss. 2004); *Janssen Pharmaceutica, Inc. v. Grant*, 873 So. 2d 100 (Miss. 2004); *Janssen Pharmaceutica, Inc. v. Scott*, 876 So. 2d 306 (Miss. 2004); *Harold's Auto Parts, Inc. v. Flower Mangialardi*, 889 So. 2d 493 (Miss. 2004); *Janssen Pharmaceutica, Inc. v. Culbert*, 883 So. 2d 550 (Miss. 2004).

MISSOURI

A. CAUSES OF ACTION

Product liability suits brought in Missouri commonly include causes of action for strict liability, negligence, and breach of express or implied warranty.[1]

B. STATUTES OF LIMITATION

A cause of action for personal injury or property damage must be brought within five years, whether brought in negligence, strict liability, or breach of warranty.[2]

A cause of action accrues when the resultant damage is sustained and capable of ascertainment, or in other words, when the injury is manifested.[3] If death results from use of the product, a cause of action under the wrongful death statute must be brought within three years from the death.[4]

If, at the time of the injury, the plaintiff is less than twenty-one years of age, he/she generally has five years from the date on which he turns twenty-one in which to bring the action.[5] The same is true for mentally incapacitated persons, who have five years from the time their disability is removed to bring a cause of action.

C. STRICT LIABILITY

1. The Standard

Missouri has adopted Section 402A of the Restatement (Second) of Torts.[6] This means that one who sells a product in a defective condition, unreasonably dangerous to the user or consumer, is subject to liability for any injury caused by the defect.[7] Unless the court can say, as a matter of law, that the product is not unreasonably dangerous, the question is one for the jury.[8] A plaintiff must prove that the product was defective and dangerous when put to a reasonably anticipated use, and that the plaintiff sustained damages as a direct result of the defect in order to prevail under this doctrine of strict liability.[9] However, Missouri courts have recognized that claims for strict product liability and for negligence may be preempted by federal law.[10]

2. Definition of "Defect"

The jury is instructed that the product is defective if the defendant sold the product in the course of defendant's business and the product was then in a defective condition unreasonably dangerous when put to a reasonably anticipated use.[11] The jury must also find that the product was used in a manner reasonably anticipated and that plaintiff was damaged as a direct result of such defective condition, which existed at the time the product was sold.[12]

An unreasonably dangerous product may result from a design defect, a manufacturing defect, or a failure to warn of the danger.[13] A manufacturer is not obligated to market only the one version of a product that is the very safest design possible.[14] Moreover, Missouri has, to date, rejected the alternative design/risk-utility theory utilized in the Restatement (Third) of Torts.[15] Consequently, a plaintiff is not required to present alternative design evidence to create a submissible case for design defect.[16]

3. **Contributory Negligence/Assumption of Risk/Comparative Fault**

Contributory fault was abolished in Missouri in 1987 and principles of pure comparative fault are now applied in both negligence and strict liability cases.[17]

The applicable statutes further allow the defendant to plead and prove the plaintiff's fault. "Fault" is defined as:

(a) failure to use the product as reasonably anticipated by the manufacturer;

(b) use of the product for a purpose not intended by the manufacturer;

(c) use of the product with knowledge of a danger involved in such use with reasonable appreciation of the consequences and the voluntary and unreasonable exposure to said danger;

(d) unreasonable failure to appreciate the danger involved in use of the product or the consequences thereof and the unreasonable exposure to said danger;

(e) failure to undertake the precautions a reasonably careful user of the product would take to protect himself against dangers that he would reasonably appreciate under the same or similar circumstances; or

(f) failure to mitigate damages.[18]

4. **Sale or Lease**

Strict liability applies to any entity or individual in the product's chain of distribution, including manufacturers, sellers, and wholesale distributors.[19] However, the seller must be in the business of selling the product, and the product must reach the user in substantially the same condition in which it was sold.[20] The word "sold" does not have a technical meaning but rather indicates the time at which defendant relinquishes control or possession of the product.[21] A seller or retailer has no duty to test or inspect the product, unless a reasonably prudent seller should have discovered the defect before selling.[22] In Missouri, strict liability applies to commercial lessors and bailors as well.[23]

For causes of action arising after July 1, 1987, a defendant in a strict product liability claim whose liability is based solely on its status as a seller in the stream of commerce may be dismissed if there is another defendant in the suit further "upstream" from which full recovery may be had.[24] The defendant seller should move for dismissal within the time for filing an answer or other responsive pleading but may file its motion later for good cause shown.[25] An affidavit should accompany the motion stating that the defendant seller knows of no reason why she should be liable other than her status as a seller in the stream of commerce.[26] However, this dismissal should only relate to claims for strict liability, and independent claims for negligence are not subject to dismissal.[27]

5. **Inherently Dangerous Products**

   A manufacturer has a duty to warn an ultimate user of an inherently dangerous product.[28] Liability is imposed where injury resulting from the use of the product is attributable to a breach of this duty to warn.[29]

6. **Successor Liability**

   A successor entity may be liable for injuries suffered by a plaintiff in a product liability action if certain conditions are met, including: whether the purchaser expressly or impliedly agrees to assume such debts; whether the purchasing entity is merely a continuation of the selling corporation; whether the transaction amounts to a consolidation or merger of the entities; or whether the transaction is fraudulently entered into in order to escape liability for debts.[30] Additionally, the "product line" rule of corporate successor liability is not applied in Missouri.[31]

7. **Market Share Liability/Enterprise Liability**

   Missouri currently rejects the theory of market share liability.[32] Instead, Missouri tort law continues to require that a plaintiff establish a direct causal relationship between the defendant(s) and the injury-producing agent as a prerequisite to maintaining his or her cause of action.[33] However, the plaintiff may do so with circumstantial evidence.[34] For circumstantial evidence to support a verdict in a product liability action, the evidence must not only lead to the conclusion without resort to conjecture and speculation, but the evidence must also tend to exclude any other reasonable conclusions. If an equally plausible alternative conclusion exists, the circumstantial evidence is insufficient to make a submissible case.[35]

8. **Privity**

   Strict privity is not required under Missouri product liability law.[36] Bystanders may recover under a theory of either strict product liability[37] or negligence.[38]

9. **Failure to Warn**

   A manufacturer or distributor can be held liable on a failure to warn theory of strict liability, if injury results from the failure to provide an adequate warning of danger inherent in the use of the product, but a plaintiff must prove a causal connection between lack of a warning and plaintiff's injuries.[39] However, the plaintiff does not have to prove with certainty that the warning would have been seen and heeded.[40] Additionally, a manufacturer has no duty to warn of those dangers that are open and obvious, or to warn someone or instruct someone of things they already know or reasonably may be expected to know.[41]

Even though a warning will not alter the inherently dangerous nature of a product, a manufacturer may be required to warn the public of the danger so that precautions can be taken to minimize the risk.[42]

10. **Learned Intermediary Doctrine**

Missouri courts have upheld the application of the learned intermediary doctrine as an affirmative defense to strict liability product defect claims based upon failure to warn.[43] This doctrine has traditionally been utilized in cases involving the manufacture of prescription medications.

Under this doctrine, a manufacturer has a duty to properly warn "learned intermediaries," such as physicians or other health care professionals, of the dangers involved with the consumption of the manufactured product.[44] The physicians act as a "learned intermediary" between the manufacturer and the patient/consumer, and any warnings given to the physician are deemed a warning to the patient.[45]

11. **Substantial Alteration/Abnormal Use**

A manufacturer will not be held liable under a theory of strict liability, if substantial change[46] or abnormal use[47] of the product has occurred, unless the change or use was foreseeable.[48] Generally, substantial change and abnormal use will also go to the issue of comparative fault.[49] The plaintiff has the burden of proving the product was not altered.[50]

12. **State of the Art**

Since July 1, 1987, Missouri has recognized the "state-of-the-art" defense only in strict liability failure to warn cases.[51] This defense does not affect a cause of action sounding in negligence or in other forms of strict liability. "State of the art" means that the dangerous nature of the product was not known and could not reasonably be discovered at the time the product was placed in the stream of commerce.[52] It is a complete defense and shall be pleaded affirmatively. The party asserting the defense has the burden of proof.

13. **Industry Standards**

Evidence of industry standards can be used in Missouri as evidence of whether the product presents an unreasonable risk of danger.[53]

14. **Other Accidents**

Other accidents involving the product at issue may be admissible if the facts are substantially similar.[54] In determining if other accidents are admissible, the degree of "substantial similarity" that must be shown depends upon the purpose for which they are offered.[55] A greater showing of similarity is necessary to demonstrate a "defect" than is required to show "notice" to the seller.[56]

15. Economic Loss

A purchaser of a defective product cannot recover in either strict liability or negligence for damage solely to the product itself, as that element of damage constitutes "economic loss."[57] Moreover, remedies for consequential or incidental losses purportedly sustained due to defects within a product sold, including losses such as lost profits, consumer good will, and/or business reputation are generally limited to recourse under warranty provisions set forth in the Missouri version of the Uniform Commercial Code.[58]

16. Second Collision Doctrine/"Crashworthiness"

Missouri recognizes the second-collision doctrine as a valid cause of action.[59] In doing so, Missouri has extended the manufacturer's scope of liability under the Restatement (Second) of Torts, Section 402A to situations where the design or manufacture of its products causes separate and/or enhanced injuries in the course of an initial independently-caused accident.[60]

To recover under the second-collision doctrine, the plaintiff must prove all of the necessary elements of any product defect claim.[61] In addition, the plaintiff must also prove that the manufacturer's defective product enhanced the injuries sustained in the original accident.[62] Although the Missouri Supreme Court has never addressed the issue, it appears that a plaintiff need not prove with specificity the exact injuries that were caused by the defect, as opposed to the initial accident.[63] Instead, a plaintiff need only demonstrate that the defective product was a "substantial factor" (rather than the "sole factor") in producing plaintiff's injuries.[64]

17. Subsequent Remedial Measures

In Missouri, evidence of post-sale remedial measures may be used for limited purposes in strict liability cases, such as to demonstrate whether or not there was a defect in the product or its warning label at the time the plaintiff was injured.[65]

D. NEGLIGENCE

In an action based upon a negligence theory, a plaintiff must prove (1) the existence of a duty; (2) breach of that duty; and (3) injury resulting from that breach.[66] In negligence, the duty owed is based on the foreseeability of the harm that is a likely result of the seller's acts or omissions.[67] Whereas strict liability focuses on the condition of the product, negligence focuses on the conduct of the seller/manufacturer.[68]

E. BREACH OF WARRANTY

In the context of personal injury, a breach of warranty claim is substantially similar to that of strict liability.[69]

F. PUNITIVE DAMAGES

In order to recover punitive damages in Missouri, the fact-finder must conclude that the defendant knew of the defect and danger in the product and that by selling the product with that knowledge, the defendant showed complete indifference to or conscious disregard for the safety of others.[70] Punitive damages may be awarded only if supported by clear and convincing evidence.[71]

Missouri does not permit submission of punitive damages on the theory of constructive knowledge. However, a plaintiff may recover such damages if there is evidence to show that the defendant had notice of information indicating that the product was actually known to constitute a health hazard to a given class of individuals and that the defendant chose to ignore this information.[72] However, the conduct must be sufficiently egregious that it is "tantamount to wrongdoing."[73] Generally, a party acting in good faith and with an honest belief that his/her conduct is lawful cannot be liable for punitive damages.[74] Accordingly, such a remedy must be, and is, applied sparingly.[75]

In accordance with newly enacted tort reform legislation that took effect on August 28, 2005, punitive damages are capped in Missouri to a maximum award of:

(1) $500,000, or

(2) five times the "net amount" of the judgment to the plaintiff against the defendant

whichever is greater.[76] However, this limitation does not apply if the State of Missouri is a plaintiff, if the defendant has pleaded guilty to or is convicted of a felony arising from the acts for which punitive damages were awarded, or if the action relates to certain civil rights actions involving discrimination in housing or real estate.[77] Additionally, this limitation may not apply to damages for "aggravating circumstances," which are available in statutory wrongful death actions.[78]

When punitive damages are sought in a particular case, the plaintiff may be entitled to discover information relating to the defendant's net worth.[79] Under the 2005 tort reform legislation, a defendant's assets are discoverable only after the trial court finds it is "more likely than not" that the plaintiff can make a submissible case for punitive damages.[80]

G. PRE-JUDGMENT INTEREST AND POST-JUDGMENT INTEREST

Until the Tort Reform Act of 1987, there were no provisions for pre-judgment interest on tort judgments. However, a claimant may now seek and recover pre-judgment interest on the judgment, provided the claimant follows certain procedures.[81] The current requirements are generally set forth below.

In order to seek and recover pre-judgment interest, a claimant must now submit a written demand for payment by certified mail that describes the general nature of the injury, the nature of the claim, the nature of the claimant's injuries, and a general computation of damages with supporting documentation.[82]

In cases involving wrongful death, personal injury, or bodily injury, the demand must be accompanied by a list of treating medical providers, all "reasonably available" medical bills, a list of employers (if the claimant is seeking damages for lost income), and written authorizations to obtain records for medical treatment and employment.[83]

No pre-judgment interest will be awarded if the claimant fails to file his or her action within 120 days after the demand was received.[84] Such demand must also be left open for 90 days.[85]

In addition, a plaintiff must technically plead all of the statutorily-required elements in order to recover these amounts.[86]

Post-judgment interest is governed by statute in Missouri. Post-judgment interest is now calculated from the date judgment is entered until the date of satisfaction, and such interest must be paid in accordance with the Federal Fund Rate established by the Federal Reserve Board plus five percent.[87]

H. EMPLOYER IMMUNITY FROM SUIT

In Missouri, compensation for injured workers is governed by a comprehensive statutory scheme.[88] Under these provisions, an employer is required to provide any employee that is injured while in the course and scope of his or her employment with such treatment "as may reasonably be required after the injury or disability, to cure and relieve from the effects of the injury."[89] In addition to the provision of necessary medical expenses, the statutory scheme also provides for various other remedies, including payment of lost wages and disability payments, where appropriate.[90]

In exchange for this obligation to provide treatment and compensation for employment-related injuries, the statutory scheme bestows complete immunity from civil suit upon the employer.[91] This immunity from suit applies not only to direct actions brought by the injured employee but also to related actions for indemnity or contribution.[92] It further prohibits the trier of fact from assessing the employer's alleged fault, regardless of whether the employer was named as a defendant to the action.[93]

Prior to August 28, 2005, this "exclusive remedy" defense was "liberally construed" and applied to co-employees of a plaintiff/claimant. While 2005 revisions to the statute, which were enacted as part of major "tort reform," modified the analysis and temporarily limited the defense only to the "employer,"[94] subsequent legislative changes, along with recent appellate decisions, have clarified that a co-employee has no legal duty, and thus no liability, to co-employees for an employer's non-delegable duty to provide a safe workplace.[95] Co-employees are generally not liable to fellow employees, unless they engage in "something more," which is now statutorily defined as an "affirmative negligent act that purposefully and dangerously caused or increased the risk of injury."[96]

I. STATUTES

In 1987, the Missouri legislature enacted legislation that expressly codified the elements of a product liability claim under Missouri law. Under these provisions, a valid product liability claim consisted of the following elements: (1) the defendant transferred a product in the course of its business; (2) the product was used in a reasonably anticipated manner; (3) the product contained an unreasonably dangerous and defective condition, which condition existed at the time of sale; and (4) the plaintiff was damaged as a direct result of either the defective condition or as a direct result of the product being sold without an adequate warning.[97]

In addition to codifying the elements of a valid product liability claim, the legislature expressly adopted affirmative defenses relating to product sellers in the stream of commerce[98] and to products complying with the "state of the art."[99] These provisions also expressly provided that the doctrine of comparative fault was to apply to product liability actions and prescribed that only certain types of "fault" were appropriate in such actions.[100]

The relevant statutes pertaining to product liability actions are the statutes of limitation, the Commercial Code, and Mo. Rev. Stat. §§ 537.760 to .765 (2005). The relevant verdict directors are Missouri Approved Instructions (M.A.I.) 25.04, 25.05, 25.06, 25.09.

J. JOINT AND SEVERAL LIABILITY

Although Missouri previously followed traditional joint and several liability principles, new tort reform legislation was enacted, effective August 28, 2005, which significantly modify these provisions. Under these new provisions, a defendant may be held jointly and severally liable only if his or her fault is found to be greater than or equal to 51 percent.[101] Defendants adjudged less than 51 percent at fault are only severally liable for their proportional share, unless the other defendant is an employee or the party's liability arises out of FELA.[102]

K. Christopher Jayaram
Robert A. Horn
Horn Aylward & Bandy, LLC
2600 Grand Boulevard, Suite 1100
Kansas City, Missouri 64108
(816) 421-0700
(Fax) (816) 421-0899
E-mail: cjayaram@hab-law.com
E-mail: rhorn@hab-law.com

ENDNOTES - MISSOURI

1. *Ragland Mills v. Gen. Motors*, 763 S.W.2d 357 (Mo. App. 1989).

2. Mo. Rev. Stat. § 516.120 (2008). Although, warranty claims under the Missouri version of the UCC must generally be brought within four years. *See* Mo. Rev. Stat. § 400.2-725 (2008).

3. Mo. Rev. Stat. § 516.100 (2010); *King v. Nashua Corp.* 763 F.2d 332 (8th Cir. 1985).

4. Mo. Rev. Stat. § 537.100 (2010).

5. Mo. Rev. Stat. § 516.170 (2010).

6. *Keener v. Dayton Elec. Mfg. Co.*, 445 S.W.2d 362, 364 (Mo. 1969); *Coulter v. Michelin Tire Corp.*, 622 S.W.2d 421 (Mo. App. 1981); *Bachtel v. Taser Int'l, Inc.*, 2013 WL 317538, at *6 (E.D. Mo. 2013); Missouri Approved Instructions (M.A.I.) 25.05.

7. *Welkener v. Kirkwood Drug Store*, 734 S.W.2d 233, 239 (Mo. App. 1987).

8. *Racer v. Utterman*, 629 S.W.2d 387, 394 (Mo. App. 1981); *Nesselrode v. Executive Beechcraft, Inc.*, 707 S.W.2d 371, 378 (Mo. banc 1986).

9. *Welkener*, 734 S.W.2d at 241.

10. *See, e.g., Mwesigwa v. Dap, Inc.*, 2010 WL 979697 (E.D. Mo. Mar. 12, 2010); *see also* 15 U.S.C. § 2075(a).

11. *Welkener*, 734 S.W.2d at 241; M.A.I. 25.04.

12. *Welkener*, 734 S.W.2d at 241; M.A.I. 25.04; *see also Bass v. Gen. Motors Corp.*, 150 F.3d 842, 847 (8th Cir. 1998).

13. *See Racer*, 629 S.W.2d at 392-93.

14. *Linegar v. Armour of Am., Inc.*, 909 F.2d 1150, 1154 (8th Cir. 1990).

15. *Rodriguez v. Suzuki Motor Corp.*, 996 S.W.2d 47, 65 (Mo. 1999).

16. *Thompson v. Brown & Williamson Tobacco Corp.*, 207 S.W.3d 76, 91 (Mo. Ct. App. 2006).

17. Mo. Rev. Stat. § 537.765 (2010).

18. Mo. Rev. Stat. § 537.765(3) (2010).

19. *Welkener*, 734 S.W.2d at 241.

20. *Winters v. Sears, Roebuck & Co.*, 554 S.W.2d 565, 569 (Mo. App. 1977).

21. *Winters*, 554 S.W.2d at 572.

22. *Welkener*, 734 S.W.2d at 241.

23. *Wright v. Newman*, 735 F.2d 1073, 1077 (8th Cir. 1984).

24. Mo. Rev. Stat. § 537.762(1), (2) (2010).

25. Mo. Rev. Stat. § 537.762(1), (2).

26. Mo. Rev. Stat. § 537.762(1), (2).

27. *See Malone v. Schapun*, 965 S.W.2d 177, 182 (Mo. App. 1997) (noting that "seller is still liable for its own negligence or other conduct other than its status as a seller in the stream of commerce").

28. *Duke v. Gulf & W. Mfg. Co.*, 660 S.W.2d 404, 418 (Mo. App. 1983).

29. *Duke*, 660 S.W.2d at 418; *see also Griggs v. Firestone Tire & Rubber Co.*, 513 F.2d 851, 856 (8th Cir. 1975).

30. *Young v. Fulton Ironworks Co.*, 709 S.W.2d 927 (Mo. App. 1986).

31. *Young*, 709 S.W.2d 927.

32. *Zafft v. Eli Lilly & Co.*, 676 S.W.2d 241, 247 (Mo. banc 1984); *City of St. Louis v. Benjamin Moore & Co.*, 226 S.W.3d 110 (Mo. 2007).

33. *Zafft*, 676 S.W.2d at 247; *City of St. Louis v. Benjamin Moore & Co.*, 226 S.W.3d 110.

34. *Foster v. Catalina Indus. Inc.*, 55 S.W.3d 385, 390 (Mo. App. 2001).

35. *Martin v. Survivair Respirators, Inc.*, 2009 WL 2366129, at *3 (Mo. App. Aug. 4 2009). However, a plaintiff need not exclude all other possible causes and need not produce undisputed evidence to make a submissible case. *Martin*, 2009 WL 2366129, at *4.

36. *Williams v. Ford Motor Co.*, 454 S.W.2d 611, 617 (Mo. App. 1970).

37. *Giberson v. Ford Motor Co.*, 504 S.W.2d 8 (Mo. 1974).

38. *Stevens v. Durbin-DurCo, Inc.*, 377 S.W.2d 343 (Mo. 1964).

39. *Tuttle v. Steris Corp.*, 2014 WL 1117582, at 6-7 (E.D. Mo. Mar. 20, 2014) (holding that a two-prong causation analysis is required: first, the product for which no adequate warning was given must have caused the plaintiff's injury; and second, a warning would likely have altered the plaintiff's behavior). *Grady v. Am. Optical Corp.*, 702 S.W.2d 911 (Mo. App. 1985); *Church v. Martin-Baker AirCraft Co., Ltd.*, 643 F. Supp. 499 (E.D. Mo. 1986).

40. *Hill v. Air Shields, Inc.*, 721 S.W.2d 112 (Mo. App. 1986). Indeed, Missouri law recognizes a presumption that a warning given would likely be heeded. *See Tuttle, supra; but see Moore v. Ford Motor Co.*, 2009 WL 4932736, at 2 (Mo. App. Dec. 22 2009) (holding that a "failure to warn claim must be supported by evidence that the plaintiff would have pursued an alternative course of action in heeding the warning").

41. *Grady*, 702 S.W.2d at 915.

42. *Heifner v. Synergy Gas Corp.*, 883 S.W.2d 29 (Mo. App. 1994).

43. *Doe v. Alpha Therapeutic Corp.*, 3 S.W.3d 404, 419-20 (Mo. App. 1999).

44. *Krug v. Sterling Drug, Inc.*, 416 S.W.2d 143, 146 (Mo. 1967).

45. *Johnston v. Upjohn Co.*, 442 S.W.2d 93, 95 (Mo. App. 1969), *Doe v. Alpha Therapeutic Corp.*, 3 S.W.3d 404, 420 (Mo. App. 1999).

46. *Williams v. Deere & Co.*, 598 S.W.2d 609 (Mo. App. 1980); *Glass v. Allis-Chalmers Corp.*, 789 F.2d 612 (8th Cir. 1986).

47. *See Nesselrode v. Executive Beechcraft, Inc.*, 707 S.W.2d 371, 381-82. (Mo. banc 1986).

48. *Higgins v. Paul Hardeman, Inc.*, 457 S.W.2d 943 (Mo. App. 1970); *Threats v. Gen. Motors Corp.*, 890 S.W.2d 327 (Mo. App. 1994).

49. Mo. Rev. Stat. § 537.765 (2010).

50. *Waggoner v. Mercedes Benz of N. Am., Inc.*, 879 S.W.2d 692 (Mo. App. 1994).

51. Mo. Rev. Stat. § 537.764 (2010).

52. Mo. Rev. Stat. § 537.764.

53. *Nesselrode*, 707 S.W.2d at 381; *Strong v. Am. Cyanamid Co.*, 2007 WL 2445938 (Mo. Dec. 18, 2007).

54. *Pierce v. Platte-Clay Elec. Coop., Inc.*, 769 S.W.2d 769 (Mo. banc 1989); *but see In re S.M.R. ex rel. Ryan*, 404 S.W.3d 369, 376-377 (Mo. App. 2013) (finding no error in denying admission of other "incidents").

55. *See, e.g., Eagleburger v. Emerson Elec. Co.*, 794 S.W.2d 210 (Mo. App. 1990).

56. *Eagleburger*, 794 S.W.2d 210.

57. *Sharp Bros. Contracting Co. v. American Hoist & Derrick Co.*, 703 S.W.2d 901 (Mo. 1986); *Pollard v. Remington Arms, LLC*, 2013 WL 3039797, at *2 (W.D. Mo. 2013).

58. *Wienberg v. Independence Lincoln Mercury, Inc.*, 948 S.W.2d 685 (Mo. App. 1997).

59. *Cryts v. Ford Motor Co.*, 571 S.W.2d 683 (Mo. App. 1978); *Richardson v. Volkswagenwerk, A.G.*, 552 F. Supp. 73 (W.D. Mo. 1982).

60. *Cryts*, 571 S.W.2d at 687.

61. *Cryts*, 571 S.W.2d at 688; *Keener v. Dayton Elec. Mfg. Co.*, 445 S.W.2d 362, 364 (Mo. 1969).

62. *Cryts*, 571 S.W.2d at 688.

63. *Richardson*, 552 F. Supp. at 81-84; *McDowell v. Kawasaki Motors Co., U.S.A.*, 799 S.W.2d 854, 867 (Mo. App. 1990).

64. *Richardson*, 552 F. Supp. at 81-84; *McDowell*, 799 S.W.2d at 867.

65. *Pollard v. Ashby*, 793 S.W.2d 394 (Mo. App. 1990); *Stinson v. E.I. DuPont De Nemours & Co.*, 904 S.W.2d 428 (Mo. App. 1995).

66. *Chubb Group of Ins. v. C.F. Murphy & Assoc.*, 656 S.W.2d 766, 774 (Mo. App. 1983).

67. *Blevins v. Cushman Motors*, 551 S.W.2d 602, 607 (Mo. banc 1977).

68. *Racer*, 629 S.W.2d at 395.

69. *Witherspoon v. Gen. Motors Corp.*, 535 F.2d 432 (W.D. Mo. 1982); *Matulunas v. Baker*, 569 S.W.2d 791, 794 (Mo. App. 1978).

70. *Rodriguez v. Suzuki Motor Corp.*, 936 S.W.2d 104, 110 (Mo. banc 1996).

71. *Rodriguez*, 936 S.W.2d at 110.

72. *Angotti v. Celotex Corp.*, 812 S.W.2d 742, 746 (Mo. App. 1981).

73. *Alcorn v. Union Pac. R.R. Co.*, 50 S.W.3d 226, 248 (Mo. banc 2001).

74. *City of Harrisonville v. McCall Serv. Station*, 2014 WL 705432, at 18 (Mo. App. Feb. 25, 2014).

75. *Alcorn*, 50 S.W.3d 226, 248.

76. Mo. Rev. Stat. § 510.265 (2010).

77. Mo. Rev. Stat. § 510.265.

78. *Mansfield v. Horner*, 2014 WL 2724854, at 11-12, 29-30 (holding that while "aggravating circumstances" damages are subject to constitutional due process limits, they are not subject to the limits in 510.265). This case is currently on appeal to the Missouri Supreme Court.

79. *State ex rel. Newman v. O'Malley*, 54 S.W.3d 695, 697 (Mo. App. 2001).

80. Mo. Rev. Stat. § 510.265 (2010).

81. Mo. Rev. Stat. § 408.040(2) (2010). Tort reform legislation, which became effective on August 28, 2005, modified these provisions. *See also Pilley v. K-Mart Co.*, 849 S.W.2d 293, 298-99 (1993).

82. Mo. Rev. Stat. § 408.040 (2010).

83. Mo. Rev. Stat. § 408.040.

84. Mo. Rev. Stat. § 408.040.

85. Mo. Rev. Stat. § 408.040.

86. Mo. Rev. Stat. § 408.040; *Pilley*, 849 S.W.2d at 298-99. Arguably, a plaintiff must also prove these elements at trial.

87. Mo. Rev. Stat. § 408.040 (2010).

88. *See* Mo. Rev. Stat. §§ 287.010 to .855 (2010).

89. Mo. Rev. Stat. § 287.140(1) (2010).

90. Mo. Rev. Stat. § 287.160 (2010) (wages); Mo. Rev. Stat. § 287.170 to .250 (2010) (disability and death benefits).

91. Mo. Rev. Stat. § 287.120 (2010).

92. *State ex rel. Maryland Heights Concrete Co., Inc. v. Ferriss*, 588 S.W.2d 489 (Mo. banc 1979).

93. *Ferriss*, 588 S.W.2d 489; *Sweet v. Herman Bros., Inc.*, 688 S.W.2d 31, 32 (Mo. App. 1985).

94. *Robinson v. Hooker*, 323 S.W. 3d 418 (Mo. App. 2010).

95. *Hansen v. Ritter*, 375 S.W.3d 201, 208 (Mo. App. 2012); *Garman v. Weiland*, 2013 WL 3667931, at *5-8 (Mo. App. 2013).

96. Mo. Rev. Stat. § 287.120 (2013); *Amesquita v. Gilster Mary Lee Corp.*, 2013 WL 4813996, at *3-7 (Mo. App. 2013).

97. Mo. Rev. Stat. § 537.760 (2010).

98. Mo. Rev. Stat. § 537.762 (2010).

99. Mo. Rev. Stat. § 537.764 (2010).

100. Mo. Rev. Stat. § 537.765 (2010).

101. Mo. Rev. Stat. § 537.067 (2010).

102. Mo. Rev. Stat. § 537.067.

MONTANA

A. CHOICE OF LAW

The initial question in product liability cases can be: which state law governs? Montana courts will apply the "most significant relationship" test of Section 145(1) of the Restatement (Second) of Conflict of Laws.[1] The central purpose of Montana product liability law is to protect its residents from injuries caused by defective products.[2] Therefore, Montana law governs an action brought by an injured Montanan, outweighing the usual presumption that the place of injury controls the choice of law.[3] In addition, Montana residence of the plaintiff outweighs both the place of manufacture and the place of sale in determining which state law applies.[4]

B. CAUSES OF ACTION

Product liability cases commonly include causes of action for strict liability, negligence, and breach of warranty.[5]

Claims based on strict liability have been categorized into manufacturing defects,[6] design defects,[7] and failure to warn.[8] The "failure to warn" theory is a type of "design defect" claim.[9] Design defect cases have been subcategorized into: inadvertent design error and conscious design choice.[10]

Breach of warranty claims are either express (any affirmation of fact or promise about a product) or implied (implied as a matter of law, most commonly, the implied warranties of merchantability or fitness for a particular purpose).[11]

C. STATUTES OF LIMITATION

Causes of action for personal injury, wrongful death, or property damage must be brought within three years after accrual if the claim is in strict liability.[12] For strict liability actions involving damage to property, the Montana Supreme Court has held that the limitation period is three years.[13] A Montana Federal District Court has held that for strict liability actions involving damage to property, the limitation period is two years.[14]

For negligence actions, the limitation period is three years if for personal injury or wrongful death and two years if for property damage.[15]

A breach of warranty claim based on a contractual theory (express warranty), when arising from a contract subject to the Uniform Commercial Code (UCC) is subject to a four-year statute of limitation.[16] The accrual of the claim depends on the type of warranty made. If the warranty relates to the quality or specification of the product, the warranty is breached when the product is delivered, unless there is an express extension of the warranty to a later date.[17] If the warranty relates instead to the performance of the product, the claim accrues when the breach is or should have been discovered.[18]

On the other hand, a breach of warranty claim based on an obligation imposed by law (implied warranty) has a three-year statute of limitation.[19]

The accrual of most claims in Montana, including product liability, is subject to a general discovery doctrine.[20] That doctrine allows a belated "discovery" of the *facts* constituting the claim, but only if such facts are, by their nature concealed or self-concealing, or the defendant took some action to prevent discovery of the injury or cause.[21] For example, a product liability case involving exposure to a chemical, which results in a latent disease or injury, involves facts which are, by their nature, self-concealing.[22] The "fraudulent concealment by the defendant" aspect of the doctrine requires some affirmative act, and mere failure to disclose is insufficient.[23] In product liability cases, the discovery doctrine has been extended also to cases in which a medical opinion was required to causally link injuries to the product in question.[24] However, this doctrine does not extend to the plaintiff's discovery of "legal" rights as contrasted with factual or causal matters.[25]

There is a ten-year statute of repose, accruing at the completion of a real estate project, which applies to damage caused by a defective product.[26]

The statute of limitations is tolled by the filing of a separate class action by other individuals.[27]

D. STRICT LIABILITY

1. The Standard

By 1973, the Montana Supreme Court had adopted Section 402A of the Restatement (Second) of Torts.[28] However, in 1987, Montana passed a statute that incorporated the language of Section 402A, clarifying that a manufacturer, wholesaler, or retailer may be held strictly liable in tort for products which cause injury or damage.[29] In addition, the statute made clear that contributory negligence, in general, was not a defense in a strict liability case.[30] However, the statute did provide two defenses which are specific types of contributory negligence, covered in Section D.4, below.[31] To the extent that both the 1987 and 1997 versions of the strict liability statute contain 402A's language, prior judicial interpretations of 402A appear to apply.[32] Because both the case law and the statute provide for recovery for loss of property as well as personal injury, the unreasonably dangerous standard of 402A is modified.[33]

2. Definition of "Defect"

A product is in a defective condition if it is unreasonably unsuitable or unreasonably dangerous for its intended or foreseeable purposes.[34] Although the unreasonably dangerous language is used in the statute, because damage to the user's property may give rise to a cause of action, it is assumed that this standard has not changed from the case law. It would appear that an adequate warning may overcome some defects.[35]

It is sufficient to establish that the product was in a "defective condition."[36]

To establish a manufacturing defect, the product user must present sufficient evidence that it existed at the time of sale.[37]

In defective design cases, evidence that a particular product complied with federal safety standards was irrelevant to the issue of liability.[38] In holding the "standards" evidence to be irrelevant, the Montana Supreme Court explicitly rejected adoption of Section 4, Restatement (Third) of Torts, Products Liability. A design defect is one which presents an unreasonable risk of harm, notwithstanding that it was meticulously made according to the detailed plan and specifications of the manufacturer.[39] A design is defective if, at the time of manufacture, an alternative designed product would have been safer than the original designed product, and was both technologically feasible and a marketable reality.[40] Further, a manufacturer's refusal or failure to use a feasible alternative could subject the manufacturer to punitive damages.[41]

3. Causation

A showing of proximate cause is necessary for recovery in strict liability cases.[42] A flexible standard of proof exists on causation which may be met by either circumstantial or direct evidence.[43] A prima facie case can be established with evidence of: (1) circumstances of the incident; (2) similar occurrences under similar circumstances; and (3) elimination of alternative causes.[44] The Montana Supreme Court has recognized that some factors exist which may break the causal chain and operate to shift the responsibility to prevent the accident from the manufacturer to the product user.[45]

4. Contributory Negligence/Assumption of Risk

The 1987 402A statute greatly reduced any significance of prior case law on the defenses of contributory negligence and assumption of risk in strict liability cases. As noted earlier, the statute made clear that contributory negligence, in general, was not a defense.[46] The statute recognizes only two defenses, both of which are a type of contributory negligence and both of which involve the assumption of risk. Product defendants may defeat liability in whole or in part if they can establish: (1) the product user discovered the defect or the defect was open and obvious and then unreasonably made use of the product and was injured by it; or (2) the product was unreasonably misused by the user and such misuse caused or contributed to the injury.[47]

In 1997, the legislature created a new statutory framework for comparative fault and joint and several liability, discussed at Section K below. As part of that effort, the legislature also amended the 402A statute, creating two versions: a temporary version and one effective upon the occurrence of a contingency: the Montana Supreme Court ruling the legislature's first choice of framework unconstitutional.[48]

The "temporary" version of the 402A statute remains in effect, and does not alter the law as set forth in 1987. The "contingent" version of the statute would permit "contributory fault" in strict liability cases, but would require it to be applied in accordance with the principles of "comparative fault" set forth in the contingent companion statutes enacted for all tort cases.[49]

In a case decided 23 years after enactment of the 1987 statute on contributory negligence (Mont. Code Ann. § 27-1-711), and 13 years after enactment of the 1997 statute on comparative negligence (Mont. Code Ann. § 27-1-703), the Montana Supreme Court determined that a manufacturer held liable under strict liability principles cannot use comparative negligence to reduce an award of damages.[50] In other words, when—after a trial—a jury has found the retailer to have been negligent and attributed 30 percent fault to that retailer, the manufacturer was not permitted to reduce the award by the 30 percent. In so holding, however, the Court also determined that although reducing the award under Mont. Code Ann. § 27-1-703 was improper, a reduction of the award by the amount (dollar and cents) paid in settlement by the retailer was proper.[51]

5. **Sale or Lease/Persons Liable**

The statute indicates that a "seller" is a manufacturer, wholesaler, or retailer.[52] Case law indicates that lessors can be held liable.[53] Although Montana law is somewhat confusing, it would appear that a wholesaler or retailer may obtain indemnity from a manufacturer of a defectively manufactured product.[54] However, indemnity may be barred if the manufacturer has settled.[55]

6. **Inherently Dangerous Products**

Montana recognizes that a product may be so dangerous that it is defective unless it contains an adequate warning of the danger.[56]

Montana has ruled on the "inherently dangerous product" doctrine by holding that certain tangible items which are alleged to cause injury are not products.[57]

Certain statutory protection is provided to product defendants when the product is either a firearm or ammunition.[58] Firearms and ammunitions are not to be considered defective in design on the basis that the benefits of the product do not outweigh the risk of injury posed by its potential to cause serious injury, damage, or death. The limited immunity does not extend to the improper selection of design alternatives.[59]

7. **Successor Liability**

The surviving corporation of a corporate merger acquires successor liability.[60]

8. **Market Share Liability/Enterprise Liability**

Two Montana cases, with similar facts, but reaching different results, shed some light on the market share/enterprise theory of liability, although not expressly referring to it as such.[61] The earlier case contains an express statement that the court was unwilling to adopt a standard imposing absolute liability on manufacturers solely on the basis of placing products into the stream of commerce.[62] The more recent case does not address the issue, but holds that the plaintiff established a prima facie case of product liability without identifying which product caused which injury.[63] Instead it was sufficient to establish the causal link between "many" of the defendants' products and the identifiable injuries.[64]

9. **Privity**

No privity is required in a product action.[65]

10. **Failure to Warn**

If the product does not contain a warning, or if the warning is such that the unguided user exposes himself or his property to risk or danger in using the product, then the product is "in a defective condition unreasonably dangerous to the user or his property."[66] There may be a duty to warn even if the risk is known[67] or if the danger is open and obvious.[68] In addition, a manufacturer is not relieved of the duty to warn because of any prior experience by the consumer with the product.[69] The plaintiff must prove that any warning would have caused him or her to avoid the injury.[70] In a case involving pesticides as the product, the "failure to warn claim" was not preempted by the Federal Insecticide, Fungicide and Rodenticide Act [FIFRA].[71]

11. **Post-Sale Duty to Warn and Remedial Measures**

While there appears to be no cases directly on point, a post-sale duty to warn does not appear to be precluded, and certainly if the newly discovered risk were substantial, Montana law would appear to require such a warning.[72] Evidence of subsequent design change is not admissible in a strict liability action under either design or manufacturing defect theories.[73] However, such evidence may be probative for other purposes such as technological feasibility or impeachment.[74]

12. **Learned Intermediary Doctrine**

The "Learned Intermediary Doctrine" is available as a defense to pharmaceutical manufacturers in "duty to warn" cases.[75] The scope of the doctrine was extensively discussed by the Montana Supreme Court.[76] In the seminal case on the doctrine, the manufacturer argued that the duty to warn applied to warning the prescribing physician.[77] While not specifically adopting the doctrine as stated in *Restatement (Third) of Torts: Products Liability* § 6(d)(1), the court looked at the "greater body of common law" and adopted the "fuller, more perspicacious perspective on the doctrine."[78] Accordingly, a manufacturer, to rely on the defense more fully needs to warn a broader class of health care providers, including the doctor responsible for making decisions related to the patient's care.[79]

13. **Substantial Change/Abnormal Use**

If the defect is a manufacturing defect, then changes in the product appear to be a defense.[80] However, if the alteration was foreseeable[81] or if the claimed defect is a design defect,[82] then subsequent changes may not be a defense. Abnormal use, if not foreseeable, appears to be a defense.[83]

14. **State of the Art**

The Montana Supreme Court has rejected the state-of-the-art defense as set forth in comment j of Section 402A.[84] In design cases, the knowledge that was available at the time that the product was manufactured is relevant to the issue of misdesign.[85]

15. **Malfunction**

The Montana Supreme Court has recognized that malfunction may be evidence of defect.[86]

16. **Standards and Government Regulation**

Government regulations are not admissible in strict liability cases.[87] However, in one case, a district court allowed testimony regarding industry standards, but it was not an issue on appeal.[88]

17. **Other Accidents**

In Montana, other accidents may be admitted as evidence of defect if the circumstances were substantially the same as or similar to those of the accident at issue.[89] Other accidents may also be used as the basis of an expert opinion under appropriate circumstances.[90]

18. **Misrepresentation**

Section 402B of the Restatement (Second) of Torts, dealing with misrepresentation, does not appear to have been adopted in Montana.

19. **Destruction or Loss of Product**

In a case of first impression, the Montana Supreme Court recognized the tort of negligent spoliation of evidence with respect to third persons who destroy evidence.[91] It further stated that it would also recognize the tort of intentional spoliation of evidence. The court stated that a duty to preserve can arise simply from a request to preserve the evidence.[92] However, the tort of spoliation applies only to third persons, not to litigants.[93] Litigants who destroy evidence may be subject to actual damages arising from such destruction.[94] A Montana Federal District

Court has admitted evidence that defendant auto manufacturer destroyed raw test data regarding the product in question, despite a finding that it was not destroyed in bad faith.[95] Moreover, because a product defect may be proved by circumstantial evidence, unavailability of particular evidence may not necessarily warrant dismissal of plaintiff's claim.[96]

20. Economic Loss

Strict liability is still a viable theory even though damages are limited to lost profits in a commercial setting.[97]

21. Crashworthiness

The Montana Supreme Court first recognized the "crashworthiness" or "second collision" cause of action in the same case in which it adopted the doctrine of strict liability.[98] The legal reasoning supporting a "second collision" cause of action is that it is foreseeable that (most often automobiles) will collide as an incident to the normal and expected use and therefore manufacturers have a duty to use reasonable care in design so as to minimize risk of injuries.[99] At the other end of the spectrum, the court has stated that manufacturers have no duty to manufacture a "crash proof" vehicle.[100] Proof of defect may be established by circumstantial as well as direct evidence.[101] A Montana Federal District Court has anticipated that the Montana Supreme Court would hold that in a "second collision" case a manufacturer may not bring a third-party claim for contribution against the original tortfeasor on the basis of the third-party's alleged negligence in causing the initial accident.[102]

E. NEGLIGENCE

1. Liability

Four elements comprise a negligence claim in Montana: (1) duty; (2) breach of duty; (3) causation; and (4) damages.[103] Duty is the first element of a negligence claim and is a question of law.[104] The existence of a duty is based on the relationship between the plaintiff and defendant.[105] It also depends on the foreseeability of the risk and upon the weighing of policy considerations for and against imposition of liability.[106] Everyone is responsible not only for willful acts but also for injury occasioned to another by the want of ordinary care in the management of his property or person.[107] Negligence is the breach of a legal duty and involves the failure of the actor to use reasonable care under the circumstances.[108]

In Montana, a manufacturer must use reasonable care to avoid creating an undue risk of harm to those who might be reasonably expected to use its design or product.[109] The duty to use reasonable care may include a duty to warn of potential danger unknown to users or consumers.[110] An action for negligence does not depend upon privity of contract between the manufacturer and user of the product.[111]

2. **Causation**

Montana follows the general rule that to establish a prima facie case in negligence, the plaintiff must demonstrate that the defendant's negligence was the proximate cause of the plaintiff's injury.[112] The applicable causation rule or test differs depending upon the circumstances of the case. In negligence cases which do not involve issues of intervening cause, proof of causation is satisfied by proof that a party's conduct was a cause-in-fact of an event, *i.e.*, if the event would not have occurred *but for* that conduct.[113] Conversely, a party's conduct is not the cause-in-fact of an event under the "but for" test if the event would have occurred without it.[114] The "substantial factor" test, rather than the "but for" test applies in cases in which the acts of more than one party combined to produce the result (e.g., plaintiff alleged to be contributorily negligent or multiple defendants).[115] Under the "substantial factor" or "legal cause" rule, a legal cause of damage is a cause which is a substantial factor in bringing about the damage.[116] In cases involving multiple causes or independent intervening cause, the relevant inquiry is whether and to what extent the defendant's conduct foreseeably and substantially caused the specific injury incurred by the plaintiff.[117]

3. **Contributory/Comparative Negligence**

Contributory negligence of the plaintiff does not bar recovery unless it is greater than the combined negligence of all defendants.[118] However, the plaintiff's damages must be diminished in proportion to the percentage of negligence attributable to the plaintiff.[119]

F. **BREACH OF WARRANTY**

A product liability cause of action for breach of warranty may arise under the warranty provisions contained in the Montana Uniform Commercial Code.[120] Contractual sale or lease warranties may include an implied warranty of merchantability[121] and other implied warranties arising from course of dealing or usage of trade,[122] an implied warranty of fitness for a particular purpose[123] and any express warranties made by the seller through promises, affirmations of fact, descriptions of the goods, or samples or models.[124] Express warranties can be created even though the formal words "warrant" or "guarantee" are not used by the seller.[125]

Privity of contract is not required to maintain a product liability action based upon breach of warranty.[126] The sale or lease warranties provided by the seller or lessor of goods extend to any natural person who is in the family or household of the buyer or who is a guest in the buyer's home if it is reasonable to expect that such person may use, consume or be affected by the goods and who is injured in person by breach of the warranty.[127] Subject to various restrictions and requirements, these warranties may be excluded or modified.[128]

In addition to contractual warranties, the law imposes warranties of fitness for a particular purpose, merchantability and performance in a workmanlike manner, regardless of contract.[129] A breach of these warranties implied by law sounds in tort rather than contract.[130]

Warranties with respect to automobiles are contained in separate statutes.[131]

G. PUNITIVE DAMAGES

Punitive damages are recoverable in product liability actions, including strict liability, negligence, and non-contract warranty actions.[132] If the conduct of the defendant is tortious, the fact that there is an underlying contract does not defeat an award of punitive damages.[133]

In addition to recovering punitive-type damages under the common law theories of product liability, Montana plaintiffs who are injured by products are entitled to a potential award of treble damages under the Montana Consumer Protection Act.[134] Such an award is discretionary and does not require intentional conduct on the part of the defendant.[135] The treble damage award under the Act is intended to be compensatory and not punitive; therefore such an award does not require the findings generally associated with punitive damages.[136]

Reasonable punitive damages may be awarded when the defendant has been found guilty of actual fraud or actual malice.[137] Punitive damages may be awarded where no monetary value has been assigned to the actual damages suffered.[138] The terms "actual fraud" and "actual malice" are separately and specifically defined for purposes of determining entitlement to punitive damages,[139] and the contract definitions of fraud[140] do not apply to proof of actual fraud for purposes of punitive damages.[141]

For purposes of punitive damages, a defendant is guilty of actual fraud if the defendant makes a representation with knowledge of its falsity, or conceals a material fact with the purpose of depriving the plaintiff of property or legal rights or otherwise causing injury.[142] Actual fraud exists only when the plaintiff has a right to rely upon the representation of the defendant and suffers injury as a result of that reliance.[143] A defendant is guilty of actual malice if the defendant has knowledge of facts or intentionally disregards facts that create a high probability of injury to the plaintiff and deliberately proceeds to act in conscious or intentional disregard of, or with indifference to, the high probability of injury to the plaintiff.[144] For example, showing that a defendant knew that it had a defective product and attempted to prevent public knowledge of that defect might prove malice and be the basis for punitive damages.[145]

Liability for punitive damages must be determined by the trier of fact, whether judge or jury.[146] All elements of the claim for punitive damages must be proved by clear and convincing evidence.[147] Evidence regarding a defendant's financial affairs, financial condition, and net worth is not admissible in a trial to determine whether a defendant is liable for punitive damages, but must be considered and determined in an immediate, separate proceeding following a determination of liability for punitive damages.[148]

A jury award of punitive damages must be reviewed by the judge.[149] When an award of punitive damages is made by the judge, or when the judge reviews a jury's award of punitive damages, the judge must consider each of nine factors specified in the punitive damages statute.[150] The judge may increase or decrease a jury award of punitive damages, and must clearly state the reasons for increasing, decreasing, or not increasing or decreasing the jury's punitive damage award.[151] In the 2003 legislative session, a cap was placed on such damages: They may not exceed $10 million, or 3 percent of a defendant's net worth, whichever is less.[152]

H. PRE- AND POST-JUDGMENT INTEREST

A prevailing claimant is entitled to pre-judgment interest at a rate of 10 percent on liquidated damages beginning 30 days after the claimant presented a written statement to the opposing party stating the claim and how the specific sum was calculated.[153] Notwithstanding the certainty requirement, a judge or jury may award pre-judgment interest as a purely discretionary decision.[154] Post-judgment interest is payable at the rate of 10 percent per annum.[155]

I. EMPLOYER IMMUNITY FROM SUIT

The Montana Workers' Compensation Act's "exclusive remedy provision" provides that an employer is "not subject to any liability whatever for the death of or personal injury to an employee covered by the [Act] or for any claims for contribution or indemnity asserted by a third person from whom damages are sought on account of [such] injuries or death."[156] Montana has not adopted the "dual capacity" doctrine which would permit an employee who has suffered a workplace injury to maintain an action against the employer as a manufacturer of a product in a products liability action. A Montana Federal District Court did note that a minority of other jurisdictions have recognized the doctrine as an exception to Workers' Compensation exclusivity.[157] The Federal District Court also noted that some support exists in Montana for the dual capacity doctrine.[158] However, the two Montana cases that have addressed the issue have held that the Workers' Compensation exclusivity provision bars negligence and strict liability actions against the employer arising out of a provision of a faulty product.[159]

J. STATUTES

Relevant Montana statutes for product liability actions are the various statutes of limitations and commercial code sections, as well as the express statutes relating to product liability and firearms.[160]

While a Montana statute (Mont. Code Ann. § 61-13-106) prohibits the use of seatbelt evidence (whether the injured person was wearing one) in a negligence case, it does not prevent the use of such evidence in a product liability case based on the design or condition of a particular seatbelt restraint system.[161]

K. JOINT AND SEVERAL LIABILITY

If the jury finds that the plaintiff–product user was more than 51 percent at fault for an accident leading to injuries, the jury need not apportion liability among the product sellers.[162]

Multiple tortfeasors who are parties to an action are jointly and severally liable for the amount that may be awarded to the claimant, but each has the right of contribution from any other person whose negligence may have contributed as a proximate cause to the injury.[163] This rule is subject to multiple exceptions.[164] A party to the action whose negligence is determined to be 50 percent or less of the combined negligence of all persons whose negligence may be considered[165] is severally liable only and is responsible only for the percentage of negligence attributable to that party.[166] However, a party may be jointly liable for all damages caused by the negligence of another if both acted in concert or if one acted as an agent of the other in causing the claimant's damages.[167]

On the motion of a party against whom a negligence claim is asserted, any other person whose negligence may have contributed as a proximate cause to the injury may be joined as a party to the action.[168] For purposes of determining the percentage of liability attributable to each party whose action contributed to the claimant's injury, the trier of fact must consider the negligence of and apportion the percentage of negligence among the claimant, injured person, defendants, third-party defendants, and, subject to certain conditions,[169] persons who have settled with or been released by the claimant.[170] In apportioning liability, the trier of fact may not consider the fault of any person who is immune from liability, who is not subject to the court's jurisdiction or who could have been but was not named as a third-party defendant.[171]

If for any reason all or part of the contribution from a party liable for contribution cannot be obtained, each of the other parties shall contribute a proportional part of the unpaid portion of the noncontributing party's share and may obtain a judgment against the noncontributing party in a pending or subsequent action.[172] However, a party found to be 50 percent or less negligent for the injury complained of is liable for contribution only to the extent negligence is attributed to that party.[173]

A release or covenant not to sue given to one of two or more persons liable in tort for the same injury does not discharge any other tortfeasor from liability for that tortfeasor's several pro rata share of liability for the injury unless the release or covenant not to sue provides otherwise.[174] The release or covenant not to sue reduces the aggregate claim against the other tortfeasors to the extent of any percentage of fault attributed by the trier of fact[175] to the tortfeasor to whom the release or covenant is given.[176] The release or covenant not to sue discharges the tortfeasor to whom it is given from all liability for contribution.[177] The Montana Supreme Court has held that in product liability cases, as in negligence cases, a joint tortfeasor who settles with the claimant is not subject to claims for contribution or indemnity from the nonsettling joint tortfeasors.[178]

While contribution is not available from a settling tortfeasor or releasee,[179] a defendant may assert as a defense that the claimant's damages were caused in full or in part by a settling tortfeasor or releasee [180] and the negligence of a settling tortfeasor or releasee may be considered in apportioning liability among the parties to the action.[181] The claimant is deemed to have assumed the liability apportioned to the settling tortfeasor or releasee, and the claimant's claim against other persons is reduced by the percentage of the setting tortfeasor's or releasee's "equitable share of the obligation."[182]

The defendant alleging that the claimant's damages were caused in full or in part by a settling tortfeasor or releasee must affirmatively plead the settlement or release as a defense in the answer or with reasonable promptness if the defendant gains actual knowledge of the settling tortfeasor or releasee after filing of the answer,[183] and bears the burden of proving negligence and causation with respect to apportionment of fault to a settling tortfeasor or releasee.[184] In addition, the defendant alleging that a settling tortfeasor or releasee is at fault must notify the settling tortfeasor or releasee[185] and the settled or released party must be provided an opportunity to intervene in the action and defend against the claims affirmatively asserted.[186] When a strict liability case brought against a manufacturer was resolved after a jury trial and the manufacturer was held responsible for damages, the percentage of fault attributable to the retailer based on negligence was not used to reduce the plaintiff's award; however, the amount paid in settlement (dollars and cents) by the retailer was subtracted from the amount to be paid plaintiff by the manufacturer.[187]

The current statutory provisions regarding apportionment of liability among multiple defendants were enacted[188] in response to a decision of the Montana Supreme Court which declared unconstitutional the previous version of the statute because, *inter alia*, it permitted apportionment of liability to a nonparty without providing an opportunity for the nonparty to defend, and because it required the plaintiff to act in a dual capacity by representing nonparties.[189]

While the Montana Supreme Court has not specifically ruled that the current version of Mont. Code Ann. § 27-1-703 is constitutional, sufficient cases have been decided, and enough time has passed, for practitioners to conclude that the statute represents the state of the law in Montana. If all or part[190] of the current statute should ever be invalidated or found unconstitutional, there are contingent statutory provisions which would become effective.[191] The contingent provisions would abolish joint and several liability and provide only several liability for most tort actions,[192] resurrect the nonparty or "empty chair" defense in its entirety,[193] implement the percentage credit rule contained in the current statute,[194] replace comparative negligence with comparative fault,[195] and allow comparison of the claimant's negligence with the combined fault of the defendants and nonparties.[196] Then, if history is any predictor, the Montana Supreme Court would find fault with that statutory scheme and liberalize the doctrine of comparative negligence, and then the Montana legislature would again create a new, more conservative scheme.

Kristi Blazer
Missouri River Law Office P.C.
145 Bridge Street, Suite B
Craig, Montana 59648
(406) 235-4000
(Fax) (406) 235-4082
www.missouririverlaw.com

ENDNOTES - MONTANA

1. *Phillips v. Gen. Motors Corp.*, 2000 MT 55, 298 Mont. 438, 995 P.2d 1002, Prod. Liab. Rep. (CCH) P 15,758. *Phillips* involved a product liability claim against General Motors. The plaintiffs were from Montana, the accident occurred in Kansas, the product (a pickup truck) was designed and manufactured in Michigan, the pickup was originally sold in North Carolina, and one of the plaintiffs purchased the pickup in North Carolina.

2. *Phillips*, 995 P.2d at 1012.

3. *Phillips*, 995 P.2d at 1012. *Phillips* held that Montana law applied even though the only surviving plaintiff had moved away from Montana after the injury.

4. *Phillips*, 995 P.2d at 1011, 1012.

5. Two law review articles summarize and analyze Montana product liability law up to 1987: Carl W. Tobias & William A. Rossbach, *A Framework for Analysis of Product Liability in Montana*, 38 Mont. L. Rev. 221 (1977); William O. Bronson, *Developments in Montana Products Liability Law, 1977-1987*, 48 Mont. L. Rev. 297 (1987). Montana cases indicate that items such as mechanical equipment affixed to a building (*Papp v. Rocky Mountain Oil & Minerals, Inc.*, 236 Mont. 330, 769 P.2d 1249 (1989)) and speedbumps (*Harrington v. Labelle's of Colo., Inc.*, 235 Mont. 80, 765 P.2d 732 (1988)) are not products. If a product, which is itself not defective, is applied in a defective manner, that does not per se render the product defective. *Sunset Point P'ship v. Stuc-O-Flex Int'l., Inc.*, 1998 MT 42, 287 Mont. 388, 396, 954 P.2d 1156, 1162. Procedurally, an attempted belated change in the theory of a product liability case, from negligence to warranty, was denied when it came shortly before trial. *McGuire v. Nelson*, 162 Mont. 37, 508 P.2d 558 (1973).

6. *Duncan v. Rockwell Mfg. Co.*, 173 Mont. 382, 567 P.2d 936 (1977).

7. *Rix v. Gen. Motors Corp.*, 222 Mont. 318, 723 P.2d 195 (1986).

8. *Brown v. North Am. Mfg. Co.*, 176 Mont. 98, 576 P.2d 711 (1978).

9. Bronson, *supra* note 5, at 305.

10. Bronson, *supra* note 5, at 302-03.

11. Bronson, *supra* note 5, at 314-15. *See, e.g., Whitaker v. Farmhand, Inc.*, 173 Mont. 345, 567 P.2d 916 (1977) (express warranty); *Streich v. Hilton-Davis*, 214 Mont. 44, 692 P.2d 440 (1984) (implied warranty).

12. *Thompson v. Nebraska Mobile Homes Corp.*, 198 Mont. 461, 647 P.2d 334 (1982); Mont. Code Ann. § 27-2-202.

13. *Thompson*, 198 Mont. 461, 647 P.2d 334.

14. *Montana Pole & Treating Plant v. I.F. Laucks & Co.*, 775 F. Supp. 1339 (D. Mont. 1991), *aff'd*, 993 F.2d 676 (9th Cir. 1993).

15. Mont. Code Ann. §§ 27-2-204, 207.

16. Mont. Code Ann. § 30-2-725.

17. *Iowa Mfg. Co. v. Joy Mfg. Co.*, 206 Mont. 26, 32, 669 P.2d 1057, 1060 (1983).

18. *Iowa Mfg. Co.*, 206 Mont. at 32, 669 P.2d at 1060.

19. *Bennett v. Dow Chem. Co.*, 220 Mont. 117, 713 P.2d 992 (1986).

20. Mont. Code Ann. § 27-2-102(3). The text accompanying this footnote includes the qualification of "most claims" due to special treatment accorded medical malpractice claims with respect to the discovery doctrine and a repose limitation period. *Major v. N. Valley Hosp.*, 233 Mont. 25, 759 P.2d 153 (1988), *overruled on other grounds by Blackburn v. Blue Mountain Women's Clinic*, 286 Mont. 60, 951 P.2d 1 (1997); *Bennett*, 220 Mont. 117, 713 P.2d 992. In medical products cases, the statute of limitations may be tolled during the time a related malpractice case is pending before the Montana Medical Legal Panel. *Eisenmenger by Eisenmenger v. Ethicon, Inc.*, 264 Mont. 393, 399, 871 P.2d 1313, 1317 (1994), *cert. denied, Ethicon, Inc. v. Eisenmenger by Eisenmenger*, 115 S. Ct. 298, 130 L. Ed. 2d 211 (1994). *Cf. Kaeding v. W.R. Grace & Co.*, 1998 MT 160, 289 Mont. 343, 961 P.2d 1256; *Blackburn v. Blue Mountain Women's Clinic*, 286 Mont. 60, 951 P.2d 1 (1997), *cert. denied*, 118 S. Ct. 2062141 L. Ed. 2d 139 (1998). The statute of limitations on claims against the State filed with the Risk Management Tort Defense (RMTD) Division of the Department of Administration prior to bringing suit is tolled for 120 days from the date the RMTD receives the claim. Mont. Code Ann. § 2-9-301(2); *Gomez v. State*, 1999 MT 67, 293 Mont. 531, 535, 975 P.2d 1258, 1260. Also, the statute of limitations is tolled when an injury is concealed or self-concealing, such as when exposure to substances results in a latent disease or injury. *Gomez*, 293 Mont. at 534, 975 P.2d at 1260.

21. Mont. Code Ann. § 27-2-102(3). *Major*, 233 Mont. 25, 759 P.2d 153, *overruled on other grounds by Blackburn*, 286 Mont. 60, 951 P.2d 1; *Bennett*, 220 Mont. 117, 713 P.2d 992. In medical products cases, the statute of limitations may be tolled during the time a related malpractice case is pending before the Montana Medical Legal Panel. *Eisenmenger by Eisenmenger*, 264 Mont. at 399, 871 P.2d at 1317, *cert. denied, Ethicon, Inc.*, 115 S. Ct. 298, 130 L. Ed. 2d 211 (1994). *Cf. Kaeding*, 1998 MT 160, 289 Mont. 343, 961 P.2d 1256; *Blackburn*, 286 Mont. 60, 951 P.2d 1, *cert. denied*, 118 S. Ct. 2062141 L. Ed. 2d 139 (1998). The

statute of limitations on claims against the State filed with the Risk Management Tort Defense Division of the Department of Administration prior to bringing suit is tolled for 120 days from the date the RMTD receives the claim. Mont. Code Ann. § 2-9-301(2); *Gomez*, 1999 MT 67, 293 Mont. at 535, 975 P.2d at 1260. Also, the statute of limitations is tolled when an injury is concealed or self-concealing, such as when exposure to substances results in a latent disease or injury. *Gomez*, 293 Mont. at 534, 975 P.2d at 1260.

22. *Kaeding*, 1998 MT 160, 289 Mont. 343, 961 P.2d 1256.

23. *Much v. Sturm, Ruger & Co., Inc.*, 502 F. Supp. 743 (D.C. Mont. 1980).

24. *Hando v. PPG Indus., Inc.*, 236 Mont. 493, 771 P.2d 956 (1989).

25. *Carl v. Chilcote*, 255 Mont. 526, 844 P.2d 79 (1992); *Gomez*, 1999 MT 67, 293 Mont. 531, 975 P.2d 1258.

26. Mont. Code Ann. § 27-2-208. If the "injury" to the real property occurs during the tenth year after completion, the action is still timely filed if brought within one year of the injury. Mont. Code Ann. § 27-2-208.

27. *Stevens v. Novartis Pharms. Corp.*, 2010 MT 282, 358 Mont. 474, 247 P.3d 244.

28. *Brandenburger v. Toyota Motor Sales, U.S.A., Inc.*, 162 Mont. 506, 513 P.2d 268 (1973).

29. Mont. Code Ann. § 27-1-719 (1987).

30. Mont. Code Ann. § 27-1-719 (1987). *See also Lutz v. National Crane Corp.*, 267 Mont. 368, 884 P.2d 455 (1994) (contributory negligence is not a defense in a strict liability action); *Bell v. Glock, Inc.*, 92 F. Supp. 2d 1067 (D. Mont. 2000) (defenses of intervening and superseding cause are not available in strict liability case).

31. Mont. Code Ann. § 27-1-719 (1987). *See also Lutz*, 267 Mont. 368, 884 P.2d 455 (contributory negligence is not a defense in a strict liability action); *Bell*, 92 F. Supp. 2d 1067 (defenses of intervening and superseding cause are not available in strict liability case).

32. *See, e.g., Wise v. Ford Motor Co.*, 284 Mont. 336, 943 P.2d 1310 (1997).

33. *McJunkin v. Kaufman & Broad Home Sys., Inc.*, 229 Mont. 432, 748 P.2d 910 (1987) (the lack of a dangerous aspect does not automatically preclude a finding that the product is defective); *Thompson*, 198 Mont. 461, 647 P.2d 334.

34. *McJunkin*, 229 Mont. 432, 748 P.2d 910. For there to be a cause of action, the defect in the product must have a causal relationship to the injury claimed. Any credible evidence of causation (or lack of causation) is sufficient to

submit the case to a jury. *Durden v. Hydro Flame Corp.*, 288 Mont. 1, 8-11, 955 P.2d 160, 165 (1998).

35. *Gauthier v. AMF, Inc.*, 788 F.2d 634, 636, *amended, reh'g denied*, 805 F.2d 337 (9th Cir. 1986).

36. *McAlpine v. Rhone-Poulenc Ag. Co.*, 2000 MT 383, 304 Mont. 31, 16 P.3d 1054. It was error to instruct the jury that it must find the product to be in a "defective condition unreasonably dangerous"; instead the jury should only have been instructed that the product was in a "defective condition."

37. *Baldauf v. Arrow Tank & Eng'g Co., Inc.*, 1999 MT 81, 294 Mont. 107, 979 P.2d 166.

38. *Malcolm v. Evenflo Co., Inc.*, 2009 MT 285, 352 Mont. 325, 217 P.3d 514.

39. *Rix*, 222 Mont. 318, 723 P.2d 195.

40. *Krueger v. Gen. Motors Corp.*, 240 Mont. 266, 783 P.3d 1340.

41. *Malcolm v. Evenflo Co.*, 2009 MT 285, 352 Mont. 325, 217 P.3d 514.

42. *Wood v. Old Trapper Taxi*, 286 Mont. 18, 30, 952 P.2d 1375, 1383 (1997); *Schelske v. Creative Nail Design, Inc.*, 280 Mont. 476, 933 P.2d 799 (1997).

43. *Wood*, 286 Mont. at 30, 952 P.2d at 1383.

44. *Hagen v. Dow Chem. Co.*, 261 Mont. 487, 863 P.2d 413 (1993).

45. In *Rost v. C.F. & I. Steel Corp.*, 189 Mont. 485, 490, 616 P.2d 383, 386 (1980), the court suggested that such factors include the owner's knowledge and ability to prevent the danger, the relative safety of the product in the condition which it was sold, or the lapse of time from the date of sale to the accident in question.

46. *Rost*, 189 Mont. at 490, 616 P.2d at 386. *See also Lutz*, 267 Mont. 368, 884 P.2d 455.

47. *Rost*, 189 Mont. at 490, 616 P.2d at 386; *Lutz*, 267 Mont. 368, 884 P.2d 455. *See also* Bronson, *supra* note 5, at 345.

48. Mont. Code Ann. § 27-1-719 (temporary) (1997); Mont. Code Ann. § 27-1-719 (effective on occurrence of contingency).

49. The Montana legislature created the "temporary" and "contingent" statutes as the result of several Montana Supreme Court cases invalidating the previous attempts to provide law in the area of comparative fault and joint and several liability. As a result, the legislature attempted to create a backup

system should the first "temporary" statute be again invalidated. The "temporary" and "contingent" statutes are found at Mont. Code Ann. § 27-1-719 (strict liability); § 27-1-702 (comparative negligence); and § 27-1-703 (joint and several liability). The "temporary" statutes employ the phrase "comparative negligence" while the "contingent" statutes use the term "comparative fault." One of the essential differences is that current law ("temporary") does not allow apportionment of fault to nonparties. Under the "contingent" law, the fault of all actors would be considered, but joint liability would be eliminated.

50. *Hulstine v. Lennox Indus.*, 2010 MT 180, 237 P.3d 1277.

51. *Hulstine*, 2010 MT 180, 237 P.3d 1277.

52. Mont. Code Ann. § 27-1-719(1) (temporary).

53. *Canada v. Blain's Helicopters, Inc.*, 831 F.2d 920 (9th Cir. 1987).

54. *Jones v. Aero-Chem Corp.*, 680 F. Supp. 338 (D. Mont. 1987).

55. *Durden v. Hydro Flame Corp.*, 295 Mont. 318, 327, 983 P.2d 943, 948 (1999). *Cf. State ex rel. Deere & Co. v. Dist. Court*, 224 Mont. 384, 730 P.2d 396 (1986); *modified by* Mont. Code Ann. § 27-1-703.

56. *Knudson v. Edgewater Auto. Div.*, 157 Mont. 400, 486 P.2d 596 (1971).

57. *Dayberry v. East Helena*, 2003 MT 321, 318 Mont. 301, 80 P.3d 1218 (swimming pool is not in the stream of commerce, nor is it mass-produced or prefabricated; therefore, it is not a product for purposes of imposing "strict liability."); *see also Papp v. Rocky Mountain Oil & Minerals*, 236 Mont. 330, 769 P.2d 1249 (1989) (speed bump is not a product); *Harrington v. LaBelle's of Colorado, Inc.*, 235 Mont. 80, 765 P.2d 732 (1988) (building is not a product).

58. Mont. Code Ann. § 27-1-720 (1987).

59. Mont. Code Ann. § 27-1-720 (1987).

60. *Travelers Ins. Co. v. Western Fire Ins. Co.*, 218 Mont. 452, 709 P.2d 639 (1985).

61. *Compare Schelske v. Creative Nail Design, Inc.*, 280 Mont. 476, 933 P.2d 799 (1997), *with Meyer v. Creative Nail Design, Inc.*, 1999 MT 74, 294 Mont. 46, 975 P.2d 1264.

62. *Schelske*, 280 Mont. at 487, 933 P.2d at 805.

63. *Meyer*, 294 Mont. at 57, 975 P.2d at 1269.

64. *Meyer*, 294 Mont. at 57, 975 P.2d at 1269.

65. *Streich v. Hilton-Davis, a Div. of Sterling Drug, Inc.*, 214 Mont. 44, 60, 692 P.2d 440, 448 (1984); *Brandenburger*, 162 Mont. 506. As to negligence actions, *see Singleton v. L.P. Anderson Supply Co.*, 284 Mont. 40, 943 P.2d 968 (1997).

66. *Streich*, 214 Mont. 44, 692 P.2d 440.

67. *Tacke v. Vermeer Mfg. Co.*, 220 Mont. 1, 713 P.2d 527 (1986).

68. *Stenberg v. Beatrice Foods Co.*, 176 Mont. 123, 576 P.2d 725 (1978); *see also Sleath v. West Mont Home Health Servs., Inc.*, 2000 MT 381, 304 Mont. 1, 16 P.3d 1042 (failure to warn claims pleaded in negligence, strict liability, and breach of express warranty were not preempted by Federal Insecticide, Fungicide and Rodenticide Act (FIFRA)), *overruling McAlpine v. Rhone-Poulenc Ag. Co.*, 285 Mont. 224, 947 P.2d 474 (1997).

69. *Rost*, 189 Mont. 485, 616 P.2d 383 (1980), *distinguished in Krueger v. General Motors Corp.*, 240 Mont. 266, 783 P.2d 1340 (1989).

70. The Montana Supreme Court has refused to create a presumption that a consumer would have read an adequate warning and acted to prevent the accident. *Riley v. American Honda Motor Co.*, 259 Mont. 128, 135, 856 P.2d 196, 200 (1993). *Cf. Wood v. Old Trapper Taxi*, 286 Mont. 18, 30, 952 P.2d 1375, 1383 (1997) (affidavit that conduct would have been altered by a warning held to be sufficient to overcome summary judgment).

71. *Sleath v. West Mont. Home Health Servs.*, 2000 MT 381, 304 Mont. 1, 16 P.3d 1042.

72. *See* cases cited under notes 58-62.

73. *Rix*, 222 Mont. at 329, 723 P.2d at 202.

74. *Rix*, 222 Mont. at 330, 723 P.2d at 203.

75. *Stevens v. Novartis Pharm. Corp.*, 2010 MT 282, 358 Mont. 474, 247 P.3d 244.

76. *Stevens*, [*P52] to [*P63]. 358 Mont. at 491-96, 247 P.3d at 257-60.

77. *Stevens*, [*P53]. 358 Mont. at 491, 247 P.3d at 257.

78. *Stevens*, [*P53] to [*54]. 358 Mont. 492, 247 P.3d at 257.

79. *Stevens*, [*P59]. 358 Mont. at 495, 247 P.3d at 259.

80. *Duncan v. Rockwell Mfg. Co.*, 173 Mont. 382, 567 P.2d 936 (1977); *Brothers v. Gen. Motors Corp.*, 202 Mont. 477, 658 P.2d 1108 (1983); *St. Paul Mercury Ins. Co. v. Jeep Corp.*, 175 Mont. 69, 572 P.2d 204 (1977).

81. *Kuiper v. District Ct. of the Judicial Dist. of State of Montana*, 193 Mont. 452, 632 P.2d 694 (Mont. 1981).

82. *Streich*, 214 Mont. 44, 692 P.2d 440.

83. *Kuiper*, 193 Mont. 452, 632 P.2d 694; *Lutz v. Nat'l Crane Corp.*, 267 Mont. 368, 373-77, 884 P.2d 455, 458-60 (1994). *See* Mont. Code Ann. § 27-1-719(5)(b).

84. *Sternhagen v. Dow Co.*, 282 Mont. 168, 935 P.2d 1139 (1997).

85. *Preston v. Montana Eighteenth Judicial Dist. Ct., Gallatin Cnty.*, 282 Mont. 200, 936 P.2d 814 (1997).

86. *Duncan v. Rockwell Mfg. Co.*, 173 Mont. 382, 567 P.2d 936 (1977).

87. *Lutz*, 267 Mont. at 385, 884 P.2d at 465 (holding that OSHA and ANSI standards are inadmissible in a strict liability case).

88. *Tacke v. Vermeer Mfg. Co.*, 220 Mont. 1, 713 P.2d 527 (1986).

89. *Kuiper*, 193 Mont. 452, 632 P.2d 694.

90. *Krueger v. Gen. Motors Corp.*, 240 Mont. 266, 783 P.2d 1340 (1989).

91. *Oliver v. Stimson Lumber Co.*, 1999 MT 328, 297 Mont. 336, 993 P.2d 11.

92. *Oliver*, 1999 MT 328, 297 Mont. 336, 993 P.2d 11.

93. *Oliver*, 1999 MT 328, 297 Mont. 336, 993 P.2d 11.

94. *Lawman v. Lee*, 192 Mont. 84, 89, 626 P.2d 830, 833 (1981).

95. *Livingston v. Isuzu Motors, Ltd.*, 910 F. Supp. 1473, 1494 (D. Mont. 1995).

96. *Wood v. Old Trapper Taxi*, 286 Mont. 18, 32, 952 P.2d 1375, 1384 (1997). *See also Wise v. Ford Motor Co.*, 284 Mont. 336, 943 P.2d 1310 (1997) (Ford Motor Company disposed of car door after testing it; not an issue due to relaxed standard of circumstantial evidence allowed in strict liability cases).

97. *Streich*, 214 Mont. at 53, 692 P.2d at 445.

98. *Brandenburger v. Toyota Motor Sales, U.S.A., Inc.*, 162 Mont. 506, 513 P.2d 268 (1973).

99. *Brandenburger*, 162 Mont. at 515, 513 P.2d at 274.

100. *Brandenburger*, 162 Mont. at 515, 513 P.2d at 274.

101. *Brandenburger*, 162 Mont. at 515, 513 P.2d at 274.

102. *Fredenberg v. Superior Bus Co., Div. of Sheller-Globe Corp.*, 631 F. Supp. 66, 70 (D. Mont. 1986).

103. *Jackson v. State*, 287 Mont. 473, 956 P.2d 35 (1998).

104. *Yager v. Deane*, 258 Mont. 453, 853 P.2d 1214 (1995).

105. *Krieg v. Massey*, 239 Mont. 469, 781 P.2d 277 (1989) (no duty to protect another from harm in absence of special relationship of custody or control).

106. *Maguire v. State*, 254 Mont. 178, 835 P.2d 755 (1992).

107. Mont. Code Ann. § 27-1-701. *See also* Mont. Code Ann. § 28-1-201 (general duty of care, even in absence of contract, to abstain from injuring the person or property of another of infringing upon his rights).

108. *Starkenburg v. State*, 282 Mont. 1, 934 P.2d 1018 (1997).

109. *Streich*, 214 Mont. 44, 692 P.2d 440.

110. *Streich*, 214 Mont. 44, 692 P.2d 440.

111. *Streich*, 214 Mont. 44, 60, 692 P.2d 440, 448-49.

112. *Knowlton v. Sandaker*, 150 Mont. 438, 436 P.2d 98 (1968).

113. *Busta v. Columbus Hosp. Corp.*, 276 Mont. 342, 371-73, 916 P.2d 122, 139-41 (1996).

114. *Busta*, 276 Mont. at 371-73, 916 P.2d at 139-41. *Busta* reversed *Kitchen Krafters v. Eastside Bank of Montana*, 242 Mont. 155, 789 P.2d 567 (1990), which had previously been the seminal case on causation in Montana. *Kitchen Krafters* used a two-tiered analysis of causation as it related to independent intervening causes. Under *Busta*, foreseeability is now a part of the duty analysis rather than proximate cause. *Lacock v. 4B's Restaurant, Inc.*, 277 Mont. 17, 919 P.2d 373 (1996), is another exception to the foreseeability analysis: the specific injury need not have been foreseen. *See also Estate of Strever v. Cline*, 278 Mont. 165, 924 P.2d 666 (1996) (owner who stored handgun and ammunition in unlocked vehicle breached duty to safely store his firearm. However, two intervening criminal acts and an intervening grossly negligent act were not reasonably foreseeable and cut off gun owner's liability).

115. *Young v. Flathead Cnty.*, 232 Mont. 274, 757 P.2d 772 (1988), *appeal after remand*, 241 Mont. 223, 786 P.2d 658 (1988).

116. *Rudeck v. Wright*, 218 Mont. 41, 709 P.2d 621 (1990).

117. *LaTray v. City of Havre*, 2000 MT 119, ¶28, 299 Mont. 449, 999 P.2d 1010. *See also Cusenbary v. Mortensen*, 1999 Mont. 221, ¶25, 296 Mont. 25, 987 P.2d 351; *Estate of Strever v. Cline*, 278 Mont. 165, 924 P.2d 666 (1996); *Goodnough v. State*, 199 Mont. 9, 16, 647 P.2d 364, 367-68 (1982); citing *Halsey v. Uithof*, 166 Mont. 319, 327-28, 532 P.2d 686, 690-91 (1975).

118. Mont. Code Ann. § 27-1-702 (temporary).

119. Mont. Code Ann. § 27-1-702 *(temporary)*.

120. Mont. Code Ann. §§ 30-2-313 through 318 and 30-2A-210 through 216. *See Streich*, 214 Mont. at 58-60, 692 P.2d at 447-48). *See also* Mont. Code Ann. §§ 30-11-212 through 217, providing warranties applicable to sales and exchanges which are not subject to the UCC.

121. Mont. Code Ann. § 30-2-314(1) (sales); § 30-2A-212 (leases).

122. Mont. Code Ann. § 30-2-314(3) (sales); § 30-2A-212(3) (leases).

123. Mont. Code Ann. § 30-2-315 (sales); § 30-2A-213 (leases).

124. Mont. Code Ann. § 30-2-313.

125. Mont. Code Ann. § 30-2-313(2) (sales); § 30-2A-210(2) (leases).

126. *Streich*, 214 Mont. at, 60, 692 P.2d at 448, citing *Whitaker v. Farmhand, Inc.*, 173 Mont. 345, 567 P.2d 916 (1977).

127. Mont. Code Ann. § 30-2-318 (sales); Mont. Code Ann. § 30-2A-216 (leases). *See also* Mont. Code Ann. § 30-2A-209 regarding extension to lessee of the benefit of supplier's promises to lessor.

128. Mont Code Ann. § 30-2-316 (sales); Mont Code Ann. § 30-2A-214 (leases).

129. *Bennett v. Dow Chem. Co.*, 220 Mont. 117, 122, 713 P.2d 992, 995 (1986).

130. *Bennett*, 220 Mont. at 122, 713 P.2d at 995. Because a breach of the warranties implied by law sounds in tort, the three-year tort statute of limitation applies, rather than the four-year breach of contract statute of limitation provided in the UCC sales article at Mont. Code Ann. § 30-2-725.

131. Mont. Code Ann. § 61-4-501 *et seq.*

132. Mont. Code Ann. § 27-1-220.

133. *Purcell v. Automatic Gas Distribs., Inc.*, 207 Mont. 223, 230, 673 P.2d 1246, 1250 (1983); *Lee v. Armstrong*, 244 Mont. 289, 296, 798 P.2d 84, 88 (1990).

134. *Plath v. Schonrock*, 2003 MT 21, 314 Mont. 101, 64 P.3d 984.

135. *Plath*, 2003 MT 21, 314 Mont. 101, 64 P.3d 984.

136. *Plath*, 2003 MT 21, 314 Mont. 101, 64 P.3d 984.

137. Mont. Code Ann. § 27-1-221(1).

138. *Weinberg v. Farmers St. Bank of Worden*, 231 Mont. 10, 31, 752 P.2d 719, 732-33 (1988).

139. Mont. Code Ann. § 27-1-221(2), (3).

140. Mont. Code Ann. tit. 28, ch. 2.

141. Mont. Code Ann. § 27-1-221(4).

142. Mont. Code Ann. § 27-1-221(3).

143. Mont. Code Ann. § 27-1-221(4).

144. Mont. Code Ann. § 27-1-221(2).

145. *Kuiper*, 193 Mont. at 468, 632 P.2d at 703.

146. Mont. Code Ann. § 27-1-221(6).

147. Mont. Code Ann. § 27-1-221(5).

148. Mont. Code Ann. § 27-1-221(7).

149. Mont. Code Ann. § 27-1-221(7).

150. Mont. Code Ann. § 27-1-221(7)(b) and (c).

151. Mont. Code Ann. § 27-1-221(7)(c). *See Dees v. Am. Nat'l Fire Ins. Co.*, 260 Mont. 431, 448-49, 861 P.2d 141, 151-52 (1993) (trial court's reduction of punitive damages award upheld where court performed its duty of reviewing the damages and reducing them when it found passion and prejudice).

152. Mont. Code Ann. § 27-1-220(3) (2003).

153. Mont. Code Ann. §§ 27-1-210 and 27-1-211.

154. Mont. Code Ann. § 27-1-212; *Semenza v. Bowman*, 268 Mont. 118, 127, 885 P.2d 451, 457 (1994).

155. Mont. Code Ann. § 25-9-205.

156. Mont. Code Ann. § 39-71-411.

157. *Mitchell v. Shell Oil Co.*, 579 F. Supp. 1326, 1329 (D. Mont. 1984).

158. *Mitchell*, 579 F. Supp. at 1330, citing *Vesel v. Jardine Mining Co.*, 110 Mont. 82, 100 P.2d 75 (1939) (injured employee may maintain common law action for negligence against his employer in the latter's capacity as the provider of medical care).

159. *Torres v. State of Montana*, 273 Mont. 83, 86-89, 902 P.2d 999, 1002 (1995); *Herron v. Pack & Co.*, 217 Mont. 429, 705 P.2d 587 (1985); *Papp v. Rocky Mountain Oil & Minerals, Inc.*, 236 Mont. 330, 769 P.2d 1249 (1989); *but see Sherner v. Conoco, Inc.*, 2000 MT 50, 298 Mont. 401, 995 P.2d 990 (employer may be liable to the employee for intentional or malicious act or omission based upon intentional disregard of or deliberate indifference to high probability of injury to employee), limited by Ch. 229, Mont. L. 2001 (amending Mont. Code Ann. § 39-71-413 to limit liability to deliberate and intentional acts specifically and actually intended to cause injury to the employee injured).

160. *See* statutes cited in other notes.

161. *Stokes v. Montana Thirteenth Judicial Dist. Ct.*, 2011 MT 182, 361 Mont. 279, 259 P.3d 754.

162. *Payne v. Knutson*, 2004 MT 271, 323 Mont. 165, 99 P.3d 200.

163. Mont. Code Ann. § 27-1-703(1) (temporary).

164. Mont. Code Ann. § 27-1-703(1) (temporary).

165. *See* Mont. Code Ann. § 27-1-703(4) (temporary).

166. Mont. Code Ann. § 27-1-703(2) (temporary).

167. Mont. Code Ann. § 27-1-703(3) (temporary).

168. Mont. Code Ann. § 27-1-703(4) (temporary).

169. Mont. Code Ann. § 27-1-703(6)(b) (temporary).

170. Mont. Code Ann. § 27-1-703(4) (temporary); *but see Plumb v. Dist. Court*, 279 Mont. 363, 371-380, 927 P.2d 1011, 1016-1021 (1996) (in absence of joinder of

settling tortfeasor, apportionment of percentage of negligence to settling tortfeasor violates substantive due process); *see also State ex rel. Maffei v. Second Judicial Dist. Ct.*, 282 Mont. 65, 67-68, 935 P.2d 266, 267 (1997) (absent joinder of a third party, admission of evidence of the third party's negligence may be otherwise admissible in the trial court's discretion for another purpose); *Weaselboy v. Ingersoll-Rand Co.*, No. CV 89-24-BLG-JFB (D. Mont. Apr. 10, 1991) (absent joinder of third party, evidence of the third party's negligence may be admissible for purpose of proving lack of causation).

171. Mont. Code Ann. § 27-1-703(6)(c).

172. Mont. Code Ann. § 27-1-703(5) (temporary).

173. Mont. Code Ann. § 27-1-703(5) (temporary).

174. Mont. Code Ann. § 27-1-704(1).

175. *See* Mont. Code Ann. § 27-1-703(4).

176. Mont. Code Ann. § 27-1-704(2).

177. Mont. Code Ann. § 27-1-704(3).

178. *Durden v. Hydroflame Corp.*, 1999 MT 186, 295 Mont. 318, 325-326, 983 P.2d 943, 947-48.

179. Mont. Code Ann. §§ 27-1-703, 27-1-704(3) (temporary).

180. Mont. Code Ann. § 27-1-703(6)(a) (temporary).

181. Mont. Code Ann. § 27-1-703(6)(b) (temporary).

182. The "equitable share of the obligation" appears to refer to the percentage of negligence apportioned by the trier of fact to the settling tortfeasor or releasee pursuant to Mont. Code Ann. § 27-1-703(4) (temporary).

183. Mont. Code Ann. § 27-1-703(6)(f) (temporary).

184. Mont. Code Ann. § 27-1-703(6)(e) (temporary).

185. Mont. Code Ann. § 27-1-703(6)(g) (temporary).

186. Mont. Code Ann. § 27-1-703(6)(f)(ii) (temporary).

187. *Hulstine*, 2010 MT 180, 237 P.3d 1277.

188. 1997 Mont. Laws, 293 and 429.

189. *Plumb v. Dist. Court*, 279 Mont. 363, 371-80, 927 P.2d 1011, 1016-21 (1996).

190. The bill enacting the current statutory provisions contains a nonseverability clause, so that if the Montana Supreme Court finds any part of the bill to be unconstitutional or invalid, the entire bill is invalid. *See* Section 5, ch. 293, L. 1997.

191. Mont. Code. Ann. § 27-1-703 (contingent).

192. Mont. Code Ann. § 27-1-705 (contingent).

193. Mont. Code Ann. § 27-1-703 (contingent).

194. Mont. Code Ann. § 27-1-705 (contingent).

195. Mont. Code Ann. §§ 27-1-702, 27-1-705 (contingent).

196. Mont. Code Ann. § 27-1-702 (1990) (contingent). For an in-depth discussion of the history and issues regarding multiple defendant liability and the "empty chair" defense in Montana, *see* Neuhardt, S., *Settlement or Release Under Montana's Multiple Defendant Statute*, 59 Mont. L. Rev. 113 (Winter 1998).

NEBRASKA

A. CAUSES OF ACTION

Negligence, breach of warranty, and strict liability are alternative theories of product liability.[1] The theories of strict liability in tort and implied warranty in contract have been merged under Nebraska law, although express warranty remains separate.[2]

Statutes modifying the common law define a "product liability action" to be "any action brought against a manufacturer, seller, or lessor of a product, regardless of the substantive legal theory or theories upon which the action is brought, for or on account of personal injury, death, or property damage caused by or resulting from the manufacture, construction, design, formulation, installation, preparation, assembly, testing, packaging, or labeling of any product, or the failure to warn or protect against a danger or hazard in the use, misuse, or intended use of any product, or the failure to provide proper instructions for the use of any product."[3]

B. STATUTES OF LIMITATION

The product liability statute of limitations bars actions not "commenced within four years next after the date on which the death, injury, or damage complained of occurs."[4] Notwithstanding the four-year limit, the product liability statute of repose bars actions not brought within ten years after the date a product manufactured in Nebraska "was first sold or leased for use of consumption," or, for products manufactured outside Nebraska, with the applicable repose period of the place of manufacture, limited to ten years, except that only the four-year limitation applies if the place of manufacture has no statute of repose.[5] The four-year limitation begins when the person bringing the cause of action discovers, or reasonably should have discovered, the existence of the injury or damage.[6] A defendant may be equitably estopped from asserting the statute because of wrongful concealment of a material fact necessary to accrual of a cause of action, but a plaintiff may not use estoppel to excuse failure to timely file suit if he or she had ample time to do so after the inducement for delay has ceased.[7] The statute is tolled by infancy (up to age 21), mental disorder, or imprisonment.[8] The ten-year period begins to run when the product is first released to a person for its ultimate consumption or use.[9] The repose period runs from the sale of a refurbished product if the refurbishing lengthened the product's useful life beyond that contemplated when the product first was sold, but only if the refurbishing itself was defective and proximately caused the injury.[10] The product liability limits do not apply to indemnity or contributions actions brought by a manufacturer or seller.[11] There is a separate discovery rule for asbestos cases.[12] The product liability statute, rather than contract or UCC statutes, limits actions for personal injury or property damage caused by negligence in the performance of a contract.[13]

When the four-year limitations period for breach of warranty applies, the cause of action accrues upon tender of delivery, except that "where a warranty explicitly extends to future performance of the goods and discovery of the breach must await the time of such performance the cause of action accrues when the breach is or should have been discovered."[14] The future performance exception does not apply to implied warranties[15] and does not include warranties to repair or replace goods.[16] Merger of the theories of strict tort liability and implied warranty in a demurrer context leaves open the question of whether the product liability statute of repose or the UCC limitation on warranty action will govern claims fitting the merged theory.[17]

C. STRICT LIABILITY

1. The Standard

With the exception of prescription drug cases,[18] Nebraska essentially follows Section 402A of the Restatement (Second) of Torts,[19] which embodies the user-contemplation test.[20] Under that test, a plaintiff is required to prove by a preponderance of evidence that (1) the defendant placed the product on the market for use and knew, or in the exercise of reasonable care should have known, that the product would be used without inspection for defects; (2) the product was in a defective condition when it was placed on the market and left the defendant's possession; (3) the defect was the proximate or a proximately contributing cause of plaintiff's injury sustained while the product was being used in the way and for the general purpose for which it was designed and intended; (4) the defect, if existent, rendered the product unreasonably dangerous and unsafe for its intended use; and (5) plaintiff's damages were a direct and proximate result of the alleged defect.[21] Whether a product is in a defective condition unreasonably dangerous to its user is, generally, a question of fact.[22] A product is unreasonably dangerous if it creates a risk of harm beyond that which would be contemplated by the ordinary user or consumer who purchases it, with ordinary knowledge common to the foreseeable class of users as to its characteristics.[23] In a case of strict liability for a design defect, Nebraska law does not require a plaintiff to prove an alternative, safer design.[24]

Nebraska applies a somewhat different standard in prescription drug cases. The court recently overruled a previous blanket immunity from strict liability for design defects in prescription drugs, which had been based on government approval for prescription drugs, and which represented a minority interpretation of Restatement (Second) of Torts § 402A, comment k (dealing with unavoidably unsafe products).[25] Instead, the court adopted the majority view of comment k, and ruled that comment k is to be applied on a case-by-case basis using a risk-utility analysis.[26] The result is that the plaintiff in a prescription drug design defect case is required to plead the consumer expectations test, as in any products liability case, and that the defendant may then raise the unavoidably unsafe product doctrine as an affirmative defense.[27]

2. **Definition of "Defect"**

In Nebraska, a product is defectively manufactured if it differs from the manufacturer's plan, specification,[28] or intended result[29] or if it differs from apparently identical products from that same manufacturer.[30] A product is defectively designed if it meets the manufacturer's specifications but nonetheless poses an unreasonable risk of danger[31] or fails to perform as safely as would be expected by an ordinary consumer when the product is used in a manner either intended or reasonably foreseeable by the manufacturer.[32] A manufacturer also may be liable for a product that is defective because of a lack of sufficient warnings.[33]

3. **Causation**

An essential element of the strict liability standard is that an unreasonably dangerous defect was the proximate cause or a proximately contributing cause of the plaintiff's injury and damages. To be recoverable, injury and damage must be a direct and proximate result of the defect.[34] Although a product may have an unreasonably dangerous defect, there is no liability if the proven defect played no part in causing the injury.[35] An injury is proximately caused by a defect if it is a substantial factor in bringing about the injury.[36] The fact that the active negligence of a third person also is a substantial factor in causation does not protect the defendant from liability, and each person whose actions combine in causing injury is responsible although one of them alone could not have caused the result.[37]

4. **Contributory Negligence/Assumption of Risk**

Assumption of the risk is a complete defense by statute (before 1992, by common law); the elements are that (1) the person knew of and understood the specific danger,[38] (2) the person voluntarily exposed himself or herself to the danger, and (3) the person's damages occurred as a result of his or her exposure to the danger.[39]

The status of comparative negligence as a defense to strict tort liability is in some doubt. From 1913 to 1978, Nebraska followed a statutory slight-gross standard that applied in "all actions brought to recover damages . . . caused by the negligence of another."[40] Because Nebraska did not adopt strict tort liability until 1971,[41] there was no opportunity for the court to consider contributory negligence as a defense to strict tort liability under the common law, but it held in 1973 that traditional contributory negligence is not a defense to a suit in strict tort, although assumption of the risk and misuse are.[42] However, in 1978, the statute was amended to expressly apply the slight-gross contributory negligence defense to "all actions brought to recover damages . . . caused by the negligence or act or omission giving rise to strict liability in tort of another."[43] In 1992, the foregoing statute, complete with its reference to strict liability, was amended to restrict it to actions accruing before February 8, 1992.[44] For actions accruing after that point, a whole new comparative fault scheme was enacted, complete with a bar on all recovery for a plaintiff whose negligence is at least equal to that of all persons against whom recovery is sought, an allocation of liability for noneconomic damages among defendants, and a reduction of the plaintiff's claim by the amount of a settling persons' share of the obligation.[45] The new comparative fault act makes no mention of strict liability (or, for that matter, negligence or any other specific form of action), but states that its provisions "apply to all civil actions to which contributory negligence may be, pursuant to law, a defense that accrue on or after February 8, 1992, for damages arising out of injury to or death of a person or harm to property regardless of the theory of liability."[46] The Nebraska Supreme Court however held that neither contributory nor comparative negligence is a defense to an action in strict liability.[47] Therefore, Nebraska's comparative negligence scheme, applying to actions on or after February 8, 1992, does not apply to causes of action in strict liability.[48]

5. **Sale or Lease/Persons Liable**

A plaintiff may bring a product liability action in strict liability only against the manufacturer of the product. Therefore, unless the seller or lessor of the product is also the manufacturer, no such action may be brought.[49] This rule is specifically applicable in asbestos strict liability actions.[50] A seller may be liable for negligence.[51]

6. **Inherently Dangerous Products**

Nebraska recognizes the unavoidably unsafe product exception to strict liability, but has recently modified the rule's application in prescription drug cases.[52] Once a plaintiff alleges the consumer expectation test in a strict-liability prescription drug case, the defendant manufacturer may assert as an affirmative defense that (1) the product was properly manufactured and contains adequate warnings, (2) its benefits justify its risks, and (3) the product was at the time of manufacture and distribution incapable of being made safer.[53]

7. **Successor Liability**

A successor corporation may be liable for the debts and liabilities of the predecessor corporation if any one of the four circumstances exist:

(1) the buyer corporation expressly or impliedly agrees to assume the selling corporation's liability;

(2) there is a consolidation or merger of the buyer and seller corporations;

(3) the buying corporation is a continuation of the seller corporation; or

(4) the parties entered into the transaction fraudulently to escape liability for their obligations.[54]

8. **Market Share Liability/Enterprise Liability**

Nebraska has not addressed the question of imposing liability against any or all manufacturers of products having similar defects without proof that injury was caused by the defect in a particular defendant's product. However, a federal court has predicted that Nebraska would adopt alternative liability and shift the burden of proving causation to each defendant to prove that it was not the cause of the plaintiff's injury, after the plaintiff proves that the product that caused the injury was made by one of the defendants or that each of the defendants' products contributed at least some harm, but that such liability would be joint or prorated rather than joint and several.[55]

9. **Privity**

No privity is required for strict liability in tort. A manufacturer will be held strictly liable when a defective product injures someone rightfully using the product,[56] unless the nature of the product or the conditions of the sale make it improbable that it will be resold or that the vendee will allow others to use it or to share its use, or unless the product is made to special order for the peculiar use of a particular person.[57]

10. **Failure to Warn**

A product is defective if lack of sufficient warnings renders it unreasonably dangerous.[58] To be sufficient, a warning must inform a product's user of any risk of harm that is not readily recognizable by an ordinary user while using the product in a manner reasonably foreseeable by the manufacturer.[59] Nebraska law holds that the duty to warn does not arise if the user knows or should know of the potential danger, especially when the user is a professional who should be aware of the characteristics of the product,[60] and that neither the supplier nor the manufacturer is under a duty to anticipate improper use and warn against all possible dangers.[61] However, the court more recently has reasoned that when product misuse and its attendant risks are reasonably foreseeable, the manufacturer is in the best position to avoid product-related injuries by giving an adequate warning, so it held that the duty to warn includes a duty to warn with respect to foreseeable misuse of a product.[62] A jury question about failure to warn about misuse may be based on expert testimony that lack of warning caused the accident, despite other evidence that the person misusing the product already knew how to properly use it.[63]

11. **Post-sale Duty to Warn and Remedial Measures**

The Eighth Circuit has predicted that Nebraska law would hold that a manufacturer does not have either a post-sale duty to warn of dangers or a post-sale duty to retrofit a product, but expressly did not address whether others in the chain of distribution might have such a duty.[64]

Evidence of subsequent measures is not admissible to prove negligence or culpable conduct. Such evidence is admissible to prove ownership, control, or feasibility of controverted precautionary measures or for purposes of impeachment, including impeachment of a defense witness who testifies that the product conformed to the state of the art.[65]

12. Learned Intermediary Doctrine

Nebraska has adopted the learned intermediary doctrine of Restatement (Third) of Torts: Product Liability § 6(d) (1997), in prescription drug cases.[66] Under that doctrine, a prescription drug or medical device is not reasonably safe due to inadequate instructions or warnings if reasonable instructions or warnings regarding foreseeable risks of harm are not provided to either prescribing doctors and other healthcare providers in a position to reduce risks of harm in accordance with the instructions or warnings, or to the patient when the manufacturer has reason to know that health-care providers will not be in a position to heed the warning and reduce risks.[67] Outside the prescription drugs area, it has held that there is no duty to warn an expert user about dangers already known, but that there is a duty to warn a user already knowledgeable about proper use of the danger of a foreseeable misuse.[68]

13. Substantial Change/Abnormal Use

Misuse is a separate and complete defense.[69] Misuse is use of a product in a way not reasonably foreseeable by the supplier or manufacturer.[70] Misuse includes failure to follow instructions and using the product in a way that is not reasonably foreseeable to the manufacturer or supplier.[71] A manufacturer is likewise not responsible when the product is altered after leaving the manufacturer's hands.[72] However, the defense is considerably weakened by the doctrine that a product is defective if failure to warn of a foreseeable misuse renders it unreasonably dangerous.[73] Nebraska has left open the question of recognizing an affirmative defense for third-party misuse.[74]

14. State of the Art

In Nebraska, the state-of-the-art defense is a complete defense to strict liability. The defendant must prove that the testing, design, or labeling of the product was in conformity with the generally recognized state of the art in the industry, which is defined as the best technology that was reasonably available at that time.[75] Accordingly, feasibility of a safer design is not an element of the plaintiff's case.[76] The manufacturer has the burden to demonstrate that an instruction on the state-of-the-art affirmative defense is warranted by the evidence.[77]

15. Malfunction

Evidence that an accident occurred is insufficient to establish a defect when the evidence does not establish why the accident happened.[78]

16. Standards and Governmental Regulations

FDA-approved drugs that are properly prepared, packaged, compounded, and distributed and that display approved warnings and direction are, as a matter of law, not defective.[79] However, evidence that a product satisfies the requirements of voluntary standards set by a private industry association is not sufficient to prove that the product was in conformity with the generally recognized and prevailing state of the art in the industry.[80]

If the FDA gives pre-market approval to a product, then the approval will preempt an action against a manufacturer that challenges the safety and effectiveness of the device.[81] However, a plaintiff is not precluded from claiming that the manufacturer made the product in a manner that failed to comply with the FDA's specifications as contained in the Premarket Approval assessment.[82] Furthermore, a plaintiff is not precluded from arguing that the manufacturer had breached a duty to warn.

17. Other Accidents

Evidence of other accidents will be admissible if sufficiently similar to be considered relevant and if the evidence does not present a disproportionate risk of prejudice.[83]

18. Destruction or Loss of Product

Strict liability extends to physical harm to property.[84] However, recovery in tort for damages to the product alone is disallowed. Even when the harm to the product itself occurs through an abrupt, accident-like event, the resulting loss due to repair costs, decreased value, and lost profits is essentially the failure of the purchaser to receive the benefit of the bargain, which is traditionally the core concern of contract law.[85]

19. Economic Loss

The economic loss doctrine precludes tort remedies *only* in cases where the damages were limited to commercial losses and either (1) the defective product caused the damage or (2) the duty that was allegedly breached arose solely from the contractual relationship between the parties.[86] The rule states that where a defective product causes harm only to itself, unaccompanied by either personal injury or damage to other property, contract law provides the exclusive remedy to the plaintiff, as opposed to tort law.[87] The rule also states that where the alleged breach is only of a contractual duty, and no independent tort duty is breached, a tort action will be barred.[88] Nebraska courts adopted this doctrine in order to maintain the "line of demarcation" between tort law and contract law.[89] However, Nebraska has qualified this doctrine and declared that tort theories *will not be barred* where (1) the damages alleged are not solely economic losses or (2) there existed an independent tort duty alleged to be breached, which was separate and distinct from the contractual duty.[90]

20. Crashworthiness

Nebraska has extended liability for defective design cases to encompass those based on the vehicle's crashworthiness.[91] Under this theory, the manufacturer is liable for only that portion of the damages caused by the defective design.[92] In cases involving an indivisible injury, the plaintiff must show that his injuries were enhanced by the defective vehicle design.[93] As is true in other design defect cases, the plaintiff need not prove an alternative design would have prevented the enhanced injuries.[94]

D. NEGLIGENCE

A plaintiff may assert a theory of negligence concerning a manufacturer's lack of reasonable care during any part of the process of creating and selling a product, in addition to or instead of any theories of strict liability for specific product defects.[95] In a prescription drug case, even if a strict liability claim fails because of a successful defense asserting that the benefits of a properly manufactured but unavoidably unsafe product justified its risks, the plaintiff is still free to attempt to show that the defendant acted negligently.[96] A supplier or manufacturer is liable under a negligence theory if the supplier or manufacturer fails to use reasonable care to ensure that the goods supplied or manufactured are carefully made so as not to present an unreasonable risk of causing physical harm when used for a purpose which the manufacturer should expect, in view of the foreseeable risk of injury.[97] The basic elements are duty, breach of duty, proximate causation, and damages; the plaintiff need not prove a feasible alternative design.[98] Proof of product defectiveness is evidence of the manufacturer's negligence.[99]

A supplier or manufacturer can also be held liable for negligence if the supplier or manufacturer failed to sufficiently warn foreseeable users of dangers associated with the product's use, and if there is reason to believe they would not realize the danger.[100] But a warning is unnecessary if the supplier has reason to believe the users will have such special experience as will enable them to perceive the danger.[101] Furthermore, a supplier of a product does not have a duty to inspect the product, and may rely on the tests performed by the manufacturer, unless the supplier has good cause to believe that another inspection should be made.[102]

A user of a product may be liable in negligence for a misuse of the product that harms a third party, a principal who employs and asserts sufficient control over an independent contractor whose product misuse harms a third party may have vicarious or imputed liability in negligence, and one in possession of land on which a third party is harmed by misuse of a product while the possessor an agent conducts activities on the land may be held accountable through premises liability.[103]

A seller of a refurbished product is not liable in negligence for harm caused by a defect existing from the original manufacturing process if the refurbishing did not contribute to causing the injury and if the preexisting defect was not known to the refurbisher or reasonably discoverable during the refurbishing process.[104] A "lemon law" creates additional remedies for failed attempts to fix defects in new motor vehicles.[105]

Contributory negligence and assumption of risk are separate defenses by statute.[106] For actions that accrued before February 8, 1992, a slight-gross standard applies; for later actions, a modified comparative fault standard applies.[107] Assumption of risk is a complete defense, not subject to comparison.[108] Misuse is part of the contributory negligence defense in a negligence action, although it is a separate affirmative defense in strict liability.[109]

Instructions on specific acts of negligence and contributory negligence, if pled and supported by evidence, must be submitted to the jury, rather than general instruction.

E. BREACH OF WARRANTY

With respect to product liability actions, Nebraska has merged the theory of breach of implied warranty with strict liability theories of design and manufacturing defects.[110] However, because express warranties arise from negotiated aspects of the individual bargain, the court retained a separate theory of breach of express warranty in product liability cases.[111] Notice of breach within a reasonable time is a condition to any remedy.[112] Nebraska extends warranties to injured persons not in privity with the seller if the person is in the buyer's family or household or is a guest in his or her home if it is reasonable to expect that such person may use, consume, or be affected by the goods.[113] An express warranty in a product brochure may not be limited by fine print provisions in the brochure.[114] A seller adopts a manufacturer's warranty by using it to induce a sale, but not by merely giving notice of it.[115] Damages for breach of warranty are measured from the date damages were or could have been discovered.[116] The UCC remedy for revocation of acceptance[117] (or similar "lemon law" remedy for replacement of a defective vehicle or repayment of the price plus attorney fees)[118] may be sought at the same time as the remedy for breach of warranty (including compensatory, incidental, and consequential damages),[119] and both may be presented to the jury, but if both are awarded the plaintiff must elect between the remedies.[120]

F. MISREPRESENTATION

One injured by a product may recover in tort for damages proximately caused by fraudulent misrepresentation with respect to the product by showing that: (1) a representation was made; (2) the representation was false; (3) when made, the representation was known to be false or was made recklessly without knowledge of its truth and as a positive assertion; (4) it was made with the intention that the plaintiff should rely upon it; (5) the plaintiff did so rely; and (6) the plaintiff suffered damage as a result.[121]

G. PUNITIVE DAMAGES

Punitive damages are not recoverable in Nebraska.[122]

H. STATUTES

Relevant statutes for product liability actions are the statute of limitations,[123] contributory negligence statutes,[124] the statute exempting the lessor or seller from strict liability in tort,[125] the state-of-the-art defense statute,[126] the statute defining "product liability action,"[127] evidence code provisions on subsequent remedial measures and relevancy,[128] the Uniform Commercial Code warranty sections,[129] and the motor vehicle "lemon law."[130]

I. PRE-AND POST-JUDGMENT INTEREST

Interest on judgments accrues from entry of the judgment at a rate dependent upon the U.S. Treasury bond equivalent yield.[131] Pre-judgment interest at the judgment interest rate accrues on the unpaid balance of liquidated claims from the date the cause of action arose.[132] Pre-judgment interest accrues on the unpaid balance of unliquidated claims from the date of the plaintiff's first offer of settlement which is exceeded by the judgment, if specified conditions are met.[133]

J. EMPLOYER IMMUNITY FROM SUIT

An employee injured in the course of employment has no right to compensation from the employer or its other employees and officers through any means other than workers compensation payments, except in the instance of willful and unprovoked physical aggression.[134] The employee retains rights to seek compensation from third parties responsible for the injuries, and the employer has a right of subrogation to the extent of workers compensation payments.[135] A suit by an employee against a third party for injuries compensated under the workers compensation laws must also name the employer as a party.[136]

K. JOINT AND SEVERAL LIABILITY

Generally, where two causes produce a single indivisible injury, joint and several liability attaches.[137] However, in multiple defendant cases in which the comparative negligence laws apply, the defendants are separately liable for noneconomic damages and jointly and severally liable for economic damages, except that when defendants, as part of a common enterprise or plan, act in concert and cause harm, their liability for all damages is joint and several.[138] A judgment arising from a single injury caused by breach of warranty by more than one defendant must be joint and several against the defendants, who can then seek indemnity or contribution from one another, but no allocation of damages can be made in the initial judgment.[139]

Anne Marie O'Brien
Sarah F. Macdissi
Lamson, Dugan and Murray, LLP
10306 Regency Parkway Drive
Omaha, Nebraska 68114-3743
(402) 397-7300
(Fax) (402) 397-7824

ENDNOTES - NEBRASKA

1. *Adams v. Am. Cyanamid Co.*, 498 N.W.2d 577 (Neb. App. 1992); *Hillcrest Country Club v. N. D. Judds Co.*, 236 Neb. 233, 461 N.W.2d 55 (1990); *Delgado v. Inryco, Inc.*, 230 Neb. 662, 433 N.W.2d 179 (1988); *Morris v. Chrysler Corp.*, 208 Neb. 341, 303 N.W.2d 500 (1981).

2. *Freeman v. Hoffman-La Roche, Inc.*, 260 Neb. 552, 618 N.W.2d 827 (2000). *Freeman* treated implied warranty allegations as falling under strict tort liability allegations regarding design and manufacturing defects in the context of a demurrer to a personal injury claim, so the court did not address whether the merged cause of action would be treated as one in tort or in contract for other purposes. As such, there should be no effect on implied warranty actions that do not involve personal injury, death, or property damage. *Freeman* also reaffirmed that a plaintiff may assert a negligence theory in addition to strict liability theories. *Freeman* refused to recognize a separate cause of action for "fear of future product failure," but noted that in *Hartwig v. Oregon Trail Eye Clinic*, 254 Neb. 777, 580 N.W.2d 86 (1998), it had allowed a plaintiff to prove as an element of damages the mental suffering and anxiety she suffered due to her fear of contracting AIDS after being stuck with a hypodermic needle. *See also Malena v. Marriott Int'l*, 264 Neb. 759, 651 N.W.2d 850 (2002).

3. Neb. Rev. Stat. § 25-21,180 (2012).

4. Neb. Rev. Stat. § 25-224(1) (2012).

5. Neb. Rev. Stat. § 25-224(2)(a) (2012).

6. *Thomas v. Countryside of Hastings, Inc.*, 246 Neb. 907, 524 N.W.2d 311 (1994); *Lindsay Mfg. Co. v. Universal Sur. Co.*, 246 Neb. 495, 519 N.W.2d 530 (1994); *Murphy v. Spelts-Schultz Lumber Co.*, 240 Neb. 275, 481 N.W.2d 422 (1992); *Condon v. A. H. Robins Co.*, 217 Neb. 60, 349 N.W.2d 622 (1984).

7. *Gillam v. Firestone Tire & Rubber Co.*, 241 Neb. 414, 489 N.W.2d 289 (1992); *MacMillen v. A. H. Robins Co.*, 217 Neb. 338, 348 N.W.2d 869 (1984).

8. Neb. Rev. Stat. § 25-213 (2012); *Lawson v. Ford Motor Co.*, 225 Neb. 725, 408 N.W.2d 256 (1987).

9. *Witherspoon v. Sides Constr. Co.*, 219 Neb. 117, 362 N.W.2d 35 (1985); *Spilker v. City of Lincoln*, 238 Neb. 188, 469 N.W.2d 546 (1991) (upholding constitutionality of statute of repose). *See Fritchie v. Alumax Inc.*, 931 F. Supp. 662 (D. Neb. 1996) (repose period ran from date entire scaffold deck was sold by distributor to equipment leasing company, not when later sold to contractor

and not when contractor installed replacement part, where the defect claim related to the design of the deck and the replacement part was the same as the original). The repose provision is constitutional. *Gillam v. Firestone Tire & Rubber Co.*, 241 Neb. 414, 489 N.W.2d 289 (1992); *Radke v. H. C. Davis Sons' Mfg. Co.*, 241 Neb. 21, 486 N.W.2d 204 (1992). Even if an injury occurs after the ten-year period, no cause of action ever accrues and the claim is barred. *Gillam*, 241 Neb. 414. *See also Farber v. Lok-N-Logs, Inc.*, 270 Neb. 356, 701 N.W.2d 368 (2005).

10. *Divis v. Clarklift of Nebraska, Inc.*, 256 Neb. 384, 590 N.W.2d 696 (1999) (because weld failure was caused by flaw in original manufacturing process, later modifications of product not related to weld held not to extend repose period); *Fritchie*, 931 F. Supp. 662.

11. Neb. Rev. Stat. § 25-224(3) (2012).

12. Neb. Rev. Stat. § 25-224(5) (2012); *see Givens v. Anchor Packing, Inc.*, 237 Neb. 565, 466 N.W.2d 771 (1991) (holding amendment of § 25-224(5) could not resurrect a cause of action that the prior version of the statute had extinguished). The 1981 amendment adding the asbestos exception does not apply retroactively to revive a cause of action already barred before the amendment. Neb. Rev. Stat. 25-225(5); *See also Norwest Bank v. W. R. Grace & Co.*, 960 F.2d 754 (8th Cir. 1992) (quoting *Givens*); *Farber v. Lok-N-Logs, Inc.*, 270 Neb. 356, 701 N.W.2d 368 (2005).

13. *Thomas v. Countryside*, 246 Neb. 907, 524 N.W.2d 311 (1994); (fire caused by negligent installation of furnace sold with new mobile home); *Fritchie*, 931 F. Supp. 662.

14. Neb. Rev. Stat. UCC § 2-725 (2012).

15. *Fritchie*, 931 F. Supp. 662; *Murphy*, 240 Neb. 275; *Grand Island School Dist. #2 v. Celotex Corp.*, 203 Neb. 559, 279 N.W.2d 603 (1979).

16. *Nebraska Popcorn, Inc. v. Wing*, 258 Neb. 60, 602 N.W.2d 18 (1999) (one-year repair-or-replace warranty did not extend four-year period running from date of delivery).

17. The four-year limit on bringing "[a]ll product liability actions," § 25-224(1), applies without regard to legal theory, § 25-21,180, but the ten-year repose limit (perhaps longer for products made outside of Nebraska) running from the first sale, § 25-224(2)(a), specifically excepts actions governed by UCC § 2-725. *Freeman v. Hoffman-La Roche, Inc.*, 260 Neb. 552, 618 N.W.2d 827 (2000) treated the implied warranty count as part of the strict tort liability count, but that case did not involve a limitations or repose defense. Still open is the question of whether the strict tort liability and implied warranty theories, though merged for pleading and proof purposes, will be treated as

separate for the purpose of the statute of repose because of the express exception in § 25-224(2)(a) for warranty actions.

18. *Freeman*, 260 Neb. 552.

19. *Rahmig v. Mosley Mach. Co.*, 226 Neb. 423, 412 N.W.2d 56 (1987); *Adams v. Am. Cyanamid Co.*, 498 N.W.2d 577 (Neb. App. 1992) (quoting *Rahmig*).

20. *Rahmig*, 226 Neb. 423 (expressly leaving adoption of the risk-utility test as "a matter for the future").

21. *Stahlecker v. Ford Motor Co.*, 266 Neb. 601, 667 N.W.2d 244 (2003); *Haag v. Bongers*, 256 Neb. 170, 589 N.W.2d 318 (1999); *Rahmig*, 226 Neb. 423.

22. *Haag*, 256 Neb. 170; *Rahmig*, 226 Neb. 423.

23. *Freeman*, 260 Neb. 552; *Haag*, 256 Neb. 170; *Rahmig*, 226 Neb. 423; Nebraska Jury Instructions 2d Civ. § 11.24 (2011-12). *See also Adams*, 498 N.W.2d 577. The question under the strict liability theory involves the quality of the product (that is, whether the product was unreasonably dangerous), rather than the reasonableness of the manufacturer's conduct in designing or making the product. *Freeman*, 260 Neb. 552. *Freeman* acknowledged that the court has applied the user-contemplation test from Restatement (Second) of Torts § 402A in cases not involving prescription drugs, but noted that it has not recently been presented with a case challenging that test for general purposes.

24. *Rahmig*, 223 Neb. 423 (overruling *Nerud v. Haybuster Mfg.*, 215 Neb. 604, 340 N.W.2d 369 (1983)) (noting an inconsistency with such a requirement and Nebraska Evidence Rule 407 regarding subsequent remedial measures). The Nebraska Supreme Court recognized the overruling of the alternative design requirement in *Kudlacek v. Fiat*, 244 Neb. 822, 509 N.W.2d 603 (1994).

25. *Freeman*, 260 Neb. 552 (partially overruling *McDaniel v. McNeil Labs., Inc.*, 196 Neb. 190, 241 N.W.2d 822 (1976)).

26. *Freeman*, 260 Neb. 552. *Freeman* considered and rejected the "reasonable physician test" of Restatement (Third) of Torts: Products Liability § 6(c) (1997) and declined to address whether to apply to prescription drugs, or to any product, the "reasonable alternative design test" of § 2(b) of the Third Restatement.

27. *Freeman*, 260 Neb. 552. *See infra* Section C.6.

28. *Freeman*, 260 Neb. 552 (holding that although the plaintiff alleged the drug was improperly and carelessly manufactured and inspected and that the manufacturer was aware the drug could cause injury if improperly made,

these were mere conclusions and the petition failed to allege facts sufficient to state a manufacturing defect theory).

29. *Kudlacek v. Fiat, S.p.A.*, 244 Neb. 822, 509 N.W.2d 603 (1994); *Nerud v. Haybuster Mfg.*, 215 Neb. 604, 340 N.W.2d 369 (1983), *overruled on other grounds; Rahmig*, 226 Neb. 423.

30. Nebraska Jury Instructions 2d Civ. § 11.21 (2011-12).

31. *Freeman*, 260 Neb. 552; *Jay v. Moog Auto., Inc.*, 264 Neb. 875, 652 N.W.2d 872 (2002).

32. *Peitzmeier v. Hennessy Indus., Inc.*, 97 F.3d 293 (8th Cir. 1996); *Meisner v. Patton Elec. Co.*, 781 F. Supp. 1432 (1990); *Kudlacek*, 244 Neb. 822.; *Erickson v. Monarch Indus., Inc.*, 216 Neb. 875, 347 N.W.2d 99 (1984); Nebraska Jury Instructions 2d Civ. § 11.22 (2011-12).

33. *Freeman*, 260 Neb. 552. *See infra* Section C.10.

34. *Haag v. Bongers*, 256 Neb. 170, 589 N.W.2d 318 (1999); *Rahmig*, 226 Neb. 423; Nebraska Jury Instructions § 11.24 (2011-12). *See also Adams*, 498 N.W.2d 577.

35. *Divis v. Clarklift of Nebraska, Inc.*, 256 Neb. 384, 590 N.W.2d 696 (1999) (defective weld not shown to be cause of accident); *Peitzmeier*, 97 F.3d 293 (If, despite deficient warnings by the manufacturer, a user fully aware of the danger which a warning would alert him or her of, then the lack of warning is not the proximate cause of the injury.").

36. *Kudlacek*, 244 Neb. 822.

37. *Kudlacek*, 244 Neb. 822.

38. Neb. Rev. Stat. § 25-21,185.12 (2012) *Krajewski v. Enderes Tool Co.*, 396 F. Supp. 2d 1045 (D. Neb. 2005). ("When an injury results from the commonly known characteristics of a product, then knowledge of those common characteristics is sufficient to establish...awareness of the "specific" harm required by Neb. Rev. Stat. § 25-21,185.12 (2012)." "It is only when injury results from latent defects or unusual or atypical characteristics that knowledge of the latent defect or unusual or atypical characteristic is required to establish assumption of the risk." *Krajewski*, 396 F. Supp. 2d 1045.

39. Neb. Rev. Stat. § 25-21,185.12 (2008); *Jameson v. Liquid Controls Corp.*, 260 Neb. 489, 618 N.W.2d 637 (2000); *Rahmig*, 226 Neb. 423. Nebraska Jury Instructions 2d Civ. § 11.26 (2011-12).

40. Neb. Rev. Stat. § 25-21.185 (1975) (superseded).

41. *Kohler v. Ford Motor Co.*, 187 Neb. 428, 191 N.W.2d 601 (1971).

42. *Hawkins Constr. Co. v. Matthews Co.*, 190 Neb. 546, 209 N.W.2d 643 (1973), overruled on other grounds, *Nat'l Crane Corp. v. Ohio Steel Tube Co.*, 213 Neb. 782, 332 N.W.2d 39 (1983). Accord *Melia v. Ford Motor Co.*, 534 F.2d 795 (8th Cir. 1976).

43. Neb. Rev. Stat. § 25-1151 (1979) (superseded). Nonetheless, dicta in a post-amendment case, *Rahmig v. Mosley Mach. Co.*, 226 Neb. 423, 412 N.W.2d 56 (1987), cited the amended statute, but then cited pre-amendment cases and stated that "contributory negligence, which consists merely of a plaintiff's failure to discover a defect or guard against the possibility of a defect's existence, is not a defense in an action based on strict liability." When presented with an argument that *Rahmig's* dicta and the amended statute (which specifically referred to strict liability) could be harmonized by finding that a failure to discover a defect is not a defense but that active contributory negligence is a defense in strict liability, a federal appeals court rejected the distinction and affirmed a defense verdict based on instructions allowing the jury to consider, under the 1978 version of the statute, a contributory negligence defense based on failure to guard against a possible defect. *Tillwick v. Sears, Roebuck & Co.*, 963 F.2d 1097 (1992).

44. Neb. Rev. Stat. § 25-21,185 (2012).

45. Neb. Rev. Stat. §§ 25-21,185.07 to .12 (2012).

46. Neb. Rev. Stat. §§ 25-21,185.07 to .12 (2012).

47. *Shipler v. Gen. Motors Corp.*, 271 Neb. 194, 212, 710 N.W.2d 807, 826 (2006); Nebraska Jury Instructions 2d Civ. § 11.20, comment II.B (2011-12).

48. Nebraska Jury Instructions 2d Civ. § 11.20, comment II.B (2011-12).

49. Neb. Rev. Stat. § 25-21,181 (2012). The Nebraska Supreme Court has left open whether the apparent manufacturer doctrine of the Restatement (Second) of Torts § 400 (1965) "is in conflict with the plain language of § 25-21,181." *Stones v. Sears, Roebuck & Co.*, 251 Neb. 560, 558 N.W.2d 540 (1997).

50. Neb. Rev. Stat. § 25-224(5) (2012).

51. Nebraska Jury Instructions 2d Civ. § 11.11 (2011-12).

52. *McDaniel v. McNeil Labs., Inc.*, 196 Neb. 190, 241 N.W.2d 822 (1976), partially overruled by *Freeman v. Hoffman-La Roche, Inc.*, 260 Neb. 552, 618 N.W.2d 827 (2000). Both *McDaniel* and *Freeman* apply comment k of the Second Restatement, but *Freeman* rejected *McDaniel's* "blanket immunity for prescription drugs" and instead held that a defendant may assert a risk-utility version of comment k's unavoidably unsafe product doctrine as an affirmative defense.

53. *Freeman*, 260 Neb. 552.

54. *Earl v. Priority Key Servs.*, 232 Neb. 584, 441 N.W.2d 610 (1989).

55. *Menne v. Celotex Corp.*, 861 F.2d 1453 (10th Cir. 1988) (applying Nebraska law). Despite its age, *Menne* has not been cited by any Nebraska court.

56. *Kohler v. Ford Motor Co.*, 187 Neb. 428, 191 N.W.2d 601 (1971). *But see Mann v. Weyerhaeuser Co.*, 703 F.2d 272 (8th Cir. 1983) (privity disfavored in Nebraska but not abolished).

57. *Morris v. Chrysler Corp.*, 208 Neb. 341, 303 N.W.2d 500 (1981).

58. *Freeman*, 260 Neb. 552 (noting that Restatement (Third) of Torts: Products Liability § 2(c) (1997) reflects the same failure-to-warn rule Nebraska cases have applied).

59. *Nebraska Jury Instructions 2d Civ.* § 11.23 (2011-12); *Haag v. Bongers*, 256 Neb. 170, 589 N.W.2d 318 (1999); *Erickson v. Monarch Indus., Inc.*, 216 Neb. 875, 347 N.W.2d 99 (1984); *Waegli v. Caterpillar Tractor Co.*, 197 Neb. 824, 251 N.W.2d 370 (1977); *Meisner v. Patton Elec. Co., Inc.*, 781 F. Supp. 1432 (D. Neb. 1990).

60. *Peitzmeier v. Hennessy Indus., Inc.*, 97 F.3d 293 (1996); *Strong v. E.I. DuPont de Nemours Co.*, 667 F.2d 682 (8th Cir. 1981); *Waegli*, 197 Neb. 824; *Tamayo v. CGS Tires US, Inc.*, 2012 WL 2129353, at *5 (D. Neb. June 12, 2012).

61. *Erickson*, 216 Neb. 875.

62. *Haag*, 256 Neb. 170 (finding jury question about foreseeability of misuses of trailer hitch ball and about duty to warn about such misuses).

63. *Haag*, 256 Neb. 170.

64. *Anderson v. Nissan Motor Co.*, 139 F.3d 599 (8th Cir. 1998).

65. Neb. Rev. Stat. § 27-407 (2012); *Rahmig v. Mosley Mach. Co.*, 226 Neb. 423, 412 N.W.2d 56 (1987).

66. *Freeman*, 260 Neb. 552.

67. *Freeman*, 260 Neb. 552 (adopting § 6(d) of the Third Restatement).

68. *Erickson*, 216 Neb. 875; *Haag*, 256 Neb. 170.

69. *Rahmig*, 226 Neb. 423; *Hawkins Constr. Co. v. Matthews Co., Inc.*, 190 Neb. 546, 209 N.W.2d 643 (1973), *overruled on other grounds, Nat'l Crane Corp. v. Ohio Steel Tube Co.*, 213 Neb. 782, 332 N.W.2d 39 (1983); *Hancock v. Paccar, Inc.*, 204

Neb. 468, 283 N.W.2d 25 (1979); *Meisner v. Patton Elec. Co., Inc.*, 781 F. Supp. 1432 (D. Neb. 1990). Nebraska Jury Instructions 2d Civ. § 11.25 (2011-12).

70. *Rahmig*, 226 Neb. 423.

71. *Jay v. Moog Auto.*, 264 Neb. 875, 652 N.W.2d 872 (2002); *Erickson*, 216 Neb. 875.; *Rahmig* 226 Neb. 423.; *Meisner*, 781 F. Supp. 1432.

72. *Erickson*, 216 Neb. 875.

73. *Haag v. Bongers*, 256 Neb. 170, 589 N.W.2d 872 (1999) (*see supra* Section C.10.).

74. *Jameson v. Liquid Controls Corp.*, 260 Neb. 489, 618 N.W.2d 637(2000) (holding that the defendant was not prejudiced by failure to instruct on a co-worker's misuse because the jury was instructed to deny recovery against the manufacturer if the injury was caused solely by the plaintiff's employer and its employees).

75. Neb. Rev. Stat. § 25-21,182 (2012); *Hancock*, 204 Neb. 468. Nebraska Jury Instructions 2d Civ. § 11.31 (2011-12).

76. *Rahmig*, 226 Neb. 423.

77. *Jameson*, 260 Neb. 489 (finding general expert testimony that the product was manufactured "under" the standards of the state of the art to be insufficient to warrant an instruction, in the absence of testimony that the specific challenged aspects of the product's design and manufacture, identification of a defect or hazard, or warnings related thereto were state of the art).

78. *Delgado v. Inryco, Inc.*, 230 Neb. 662, 433 N.W.2d 179 (1988).

79. *McDaniel v. McNeil Labs.*, 196 Neb. 190, 241 N.W.2d 822 (1976) *overruled in part by Freeman*, 260 Neb. 552, 618 N.W.3d 827, to extent *McDaniel* applies Section 402A, comment K of Restatement (Second) of Torts, which provides a blanket immunity from strict liability for prescription drugs.

80. *Meisner*, 781 F. Supp. 1432 (D. Neb. 1990) (citing Neb. Rev. Stat. § 25-21,182).

81. 21 U.S.C. § 360(k) (2012); *Tierney v. AGA Med. Corp.*, 2012 WL 395545, at *1 (D. Neb. Feb. 7, 2012).

82. *Tierney*, 2012 WL 395545, at *1.

83. Neb. Rev. Stat. §§ 27-401, 27-403 (2008); *Herman v. Midland AG Serv., Inc.*, 200 Neb. 356, 264 N.W.2d 161 (1978).

84. *Nat'l Crane Corp. v. Ohio Steel Tube Co.*, 213 Neb. 782, 332 N.W.2d 39 (1983).

85. *Dobrovolny v. Ford Motor Co.*, 281 Neb. 86, 793 N.W.2d 445 (2011).

86. *Lesiak v. Central Valley Ag Coop Inc.*, 283 Neb. 103, 120-21, 808 N.W.2d 67, 81-82 (2012); *Hilt Truck Line, Inc. v. Pullman, Inc.*, 222 Neb. 65 (Neb. 1986); *National Crane*, 213 Neb. 782; *Dobrovolny*, 281 Neb. 86.

87. *Lesiak*, 283 Neb. at 121.

88. *Lesiak*, 283 Neb. at 122.

89. *Lesiak*, 283 Neb. at 121.

90. *Lesiak*, 283 Neb. at 123.

91. *Kudlacek*, 244 Neb. 822; *Friedrich v. Anderson*, 191 Neb. 724, 217 N.W.2d 831 (1974).

92. *Peitzmeier v. Hennessy Indus., Inc.*, 97 F.3d 293 (1996); *Kudlacek*, 244 Neb. 822.

93. *Peitzmeier*, 97 F.3d 293; *Kudlacek*, 244 Neb. 822.

94. *Kudlacek*, 244 Neb. 822.

95. *Freeman v. Hoffman-La Roche*, 260 Neb. 552, 618 N.W.2d 827 (2000).

96. *Freeman*, 260 Neb. 552.

97. *Morris v. Chrysler Corp.*, 208 Neb. 341, 303 N.W.2d 500 (1981) (citing Restatement (Second) of Torts § 395 (1965)); *Rahmig*, 226 Neb. 423; Nebraska Jury Instructions 2d Civ. § 11.10 (2010-11). In contrast to the focus on product quality under a strict liability theory, the question in a negligence action involves the manufacturer's conduct, that is, whether the conduct was reasonable in view of the foreseeable risk of injury. *Freeman*, 260 Neb. 552.

98. *Rahmig*, 226 Neb. 423; Neb. Rev. Stat. § 25-21,181 (2012), protecting sellers and lessors of products, does not apply to negligence actions.

99. *Morris*, 208 Neb. 341.

100. Nebraska Jury Instructions 2d Civ. § 11.11 (2011-12).

101. *Erickson v. Monarch Indus., Inc.*, 216 Neb. 875, 347 N.W.2d 99 (1984) (citing Restatement (Second) of Torts § 388, comment k (1965)); *Tamayo v. CGS Tires US, Inc.*, 2012 WL 2129353, at *5 (D. Neb. June 12, 2012).

102. *Tamayo*, 2012 WL 2129353, at *5.

103. *Haag*, 256 Neb. 170 (estate and auctioneer liable for auctioneer's misuse of trailer hitch, even though manufacturer also was strictly liable for failure to warn of such a misuse).

104. *Divisv. Clarklift of Nebraska, Inc.*, 256 Neb. 384, 590 N.W.2d 696 (1999)..

105. Neb. Rev. Stat. § 60-2701. *See Genetti v. Caterpillar, Inc.*, 261 Neb. 98, 621 N.W.2d 529 (2001).

106. *Haag*, 256 Neb. 170. *See supra* discussion and notes in Section C.4.

107. *See supra* discussion and notes in Section C.4.

108. *See supra* discussion and notes in Section C.4. With respect to causes of action accruing before Feb. 8, 1992, *see Mandery v. Chronicle Broad. Co.*, 228 Neb. 391, 423 N.W.2d 115 (1988); *Makovicka v. Lukes*, 182 Neb. 168, 153 N.W.2d 733 (1967).

109. Nebraska Jury Instructions 2d Civ. § 11.12 comment (2011-12).

110. *Freeman v. Hoffman-La Roche*, 260 Neb. 552, 618 N.W.2d (2000). The scope of the merger was left in doubt by the court's description of Freeman's theory under challenge by the manufacturer's demurrer as "breach of implied warranty on the basis that [the drug] was not fit for its intended purpose." The court's reasoning was based in large part on authorities advocating merger of the implied warranty of merchantability into strict liability, including comment n to the Restatement (Third) of Torts: Products Liability § 2. However, comment n states that claims based on implied warranty of fitness for particular purpose are unaffected by the Restatement rule effecting merger of defect theories, as are other theories not premised on product defects existing at time of distribution. Therefore, it is not clear if the court read the petition to assert a claim for implied warranty of merchantability and intended to limit the merger to that theory, or instead read it as a claim for implied warranty of fitness for particular purpose and meant to broadly merge all implied warranties into strict liability.
Another instance of imprecise language in the implied warranty discussion in *Freeman* more clearly was not intended as a broad change in the law. After quoting from comment n to § 2 of the Third Restatement, the court wrote: "Commentators have generally recommended adoption of § 2(b) of the Third Restatement approach, which in effect merges warranty liability theories of recovery with design and warning defect theories. . . . We find this reasoning persuasive." Although this could be taken, in isolation, as a wholesale adoption of § 2(b), the court had already written: "we decline to address § 2(b) as the test for prescription drugs, or any product, at this time." As such, the court apparently intended only to endorse the aspect of § 2(b) that reflects a merger of defect theories, and not to adopt the rule generally.

111. *Freeman*, 260 Neb. 552. *See* Neb. UCC § 2-313 (2012); *Murphy v. Spelts-Schultz Lumber Co.*, 240 Neb. 275, 481 N.W.2d 422 (1992); *Hillcrest Country Club v. N.D. Judds Co.*, 236 Neb. 233, 461 N.W.2d 55 (1990); *Delgado v. Inryco, Inc.*, 230 Neb. 662, 433 N.W.2d 179 (1988).

112. Neb. Rev. Stat. UCC § 2-607(3)(a).

113. Neb. Rev. Stat. UCC § 2-318.

114. *Hillcrest Country Club v. N.D. Judds Co.*, 236 Neb. 233, 461 N.W.2d 55 (1990).

115. *Hillcrest Country Club*, 236 Neb. 233.

116. *Hillcrest Country Club*, 236 Neb. 233 (date when roof began to flake).

117. *Hillcrest Country Club*, 236 Neb. 233. Neb. Rev. Stat. UCC § 2-608.

118. Neb. Rev. Stat. §§ 60-2703, 60-2707 (2012).

119. Neb. Rev. Stat. UCC §§ 2-714, 2-715 (2012).

120. *Genetti v. Caterpillar, Inc.*, 261 Neb. 98, 621 N.W.2d 529 (2001).

121. *Freeman v. Hoffman-La Roche*, 260 Neb. 552, 618 N.W.2d (2000) (adapting for a product claim the elements of the cause of action set out in *Gibb v. Citicorp Mortgage, Inc.*, 246 Neb. 355, 518 N.W.2d 910 (1994)). *Freeman* declined to adopt § 9 of the Third Restatement, which would impose liability for harm caused by negligent and innocent misrepresentations of material fact concerning a product, as well as for harm caused by fraudulent misrepresentations.

122. *Distinctive Printing & Packaging Co. v. Cox*, 232 Neb. 846, 443 N.W.2d 566 (1989); *Miller v. Kingsley*, 194 Neb. 123, 230 N.W.2d 472 (1975).

123. Neb. Rev. Stat. § 25-224 (2012).

124. Neb. Rev. Stat. §§ 25-21,185 (2012), 25-21,185.07 to 25-21,185.12 (2012).

125. Neb. Rev. Stat. §§ 25-21,181, 25-284(5) (2012).

126. Neb. Rev. Stat. § 25-21,182 (2012).

127. Neb. Rev. Stat. § 25-21,180 (2012).

128. Neb. Rev. Stat. §§ 27-401, 27-403, 27-407 (2012).

129. Neb. Rev. Stat. UCC §§ 2-313, 2-314, 2-315, -318 (2001).

130. Neb. Rev. Stat. § 60-2701 *et seq.* (2012).

131. Neb. Rev. Stat. §§ 45-103, 45-103.01 (2012).

132. Neb. Rev. Stat. § 45-103.02(2) (2012).

133. Neb. Rev. Stat. § 45-103.02(1) (2012).

134. Neb. Rev. Stat. § 48-111 (2012); *Peterson v. Cisper*, 231 Neb. 450, 436 N.W.2d 533 (1989) (upholding constitutionality of co-employee immunity provision); *Pettigrew v. Home Ins. Co.*, 191 Neb. 312, 214 N.W.2d 920 (1974).

135. Neb. Rev. Stat. § 48-118 (2012).

136. *Oliver v. Nelson*, 128 Neb. 160, 258 N.W. 69 (1934).

137. *Kudlacek v. Fiat S.p.A.*, 244 Neb. 822, 509 N.W.2d 603 (1994).

138. Neb. Rev. Stat. § 25-21,185.10 (2008).

139. Neb. Rev. Stat. § 25-21,185.10 (2008).

NEVADA

A. **CAUSES OF ACTION**

Product liability suits commonly include causes of action for strict liability, negligence, and breach of warranty.[1] Since contributory negligence and comparative fault are not defenses to an action of strict liability, it is common for cases to be pled solely on the theory of strict liability when there is a possibility of contributory or comparative negligence.[2]

B. **STATUTES OF LIMITATION/REPOSE**

Causes of action for personal injuries must be brought within two years, irrespective of whether the theory is negligence or strict liability.[3] The statute of limitations for property damages, however, is three years, irrespective of the theory.[4]

A cause of action for personal injuries resulting from breach of warranty falls within the four- or six-year statute of limitations: a period of six years applies to actions for breach of an express promise in writing, and a period of four years applies to claims based upon an implied warranty.[5]

In Nevada, a statute of repose applies to protect owners, occupiers, or any person performing design, planning, supervision or observation of construction, or the construction or improvements to real property from actions for injuries or wrongful death resulting from deficiency of construction or improvements to real property. The statutes setting forth the limitations periods have been the subject of much dispute and they are somewhat ambiguous. The practitioner should carefully review the statutes and caselaw application of the statutes. The statute of repose is not a defense for damages for injury or wrongful death caused by deficiency in construction of improvements in lawsuits based upon liability for defect in product.[6] The statute of repose also does not run for damages or injuries that are caused by deficiencies that are fraudulently concealed; however, this section does not apply to actions against any person on account of a defect in product.[7]

With respect to damages that are the result of known construction or improvement deficiencies, that is, deficiencies that are known, or should have been known, by the owner, occupier, or person who is in possession of the land, such an action must be brought within ten years after substantial completion of the project.[8] However, in the event injury or death occurs in the tenth year, it must be brought within two years after the date of injury, irrespective of the date of death. In this specific case, the action cannot be commenced more than twelve years after substantial completion of the project.[9]

The statute of limitations for latent deficiencies is eight years after substantial completion; however, in the event there is an injury or death in the eighth year, the action must be prosecuted within two years.[10] No action can be commenced more than ten years after the substantial completion of the improvement.[11] A "latent deficiency" is a deficiency that is "not apparent by reasonable inspection."[12]

The statute of limitations for patent deficiencies is six years after substantial completion; however, in the event there is an injury or death in the sixth year, the action must be prosecuted within two years.[13] No action can be commenced more than eight years after the substantial completion of the improvement.[14] A "patent deficiency" is a deficiency that is "apparent by reasonable inspection."[15]

C. STRICT LIABILITY

1. The Standard

Nevada has applied Section 402A of the Restatement (Second) of Torts. A claim for strict products liability consists of the following elements: (1) the product had a defect which rendered it unreasonably dangerous; (2) the defect existed at the time the product left the manufacturer; and (3) the defect caused the plaintiff's injury.[16] The plaintiff carries both the burden of production and the burden of persuasion.[17] Nevada has yet to expressly adopt the Third Restatement, but it has followed a comment to the Third Restatement.[18]

2. Definition of "Defect"

A product is defective if it is dangerous because it fails to perform in a manner reasonably expected in light of its nature and intended function.[19]

Nevada has applied Restatement of Torts, Section 402A, paragraph (h). Where the defendant has reason to anticipate that danger may result from particular use of his product and fails to give adequate warning of such danger, a product sold without such a warning is in a defective condition.[20]

In cases involving design defects, courts have been divided as to whether proof of an alternative safer design must be presented to establish a prima facie case.[21] In Nevada, the existence of an alternative safer design is one factor that the finder of fact may consider to determine whether a product is defective.[22]

Expert testimony is not always necessary to establish that a manufacturing defect exists.[23] Evidence of an unexpected, dangerous malfunction gives rise to an inference of the manufacturing defect.[24] In that context, circumstantial evidence can prove the manufacturing defect, and direct proof is unnecessary.[25]

3. **Causation**

Plaintiff has the burden to prove that the product defect was a substantial factor in causing injury. Where the injury is identical to that which would have been received absent the claimed defect, the defendant may be absolved of liability.[26]

An intentional intervening act by a third party that is both unforeseeable and the proximate cause of the injury may insulate the manufacturer of a defective product from liability.[27]

To present a prima facie case for strict liability in tort, plaintiff must establish that plaintiff's injuries were caused by a defect in the product, and that the defect existed when the product left the defendant's control.[28]

To demonstrate actual cause of injury with respect to a product, a products liability plaintiff must prove that, but for the allegedly defective product, the injury would not have occurred.[29]

4. **Contributory/Comparative Negligence, Assumption of Risk, and Misuse**

Contributory or comparative negligence is not a defense to a strict product liability claim, but assumption of risk and misuse are defenses.[30] The misuse that constitutes a defense is that use which the designer or manufacturer could not reasonably foresee.[31]

5. **Sale or Lease/Persons Liable**

While Nevada has not specifically ruled on whether a lessor may be held strictly liable in a product liability action, the *Burns*[32] decision suggests that a lessor may be a proper defendant to such an action. However, a contractor has been found not to be strictly liable based upon the fact that the contractor was not a "manufacturer" nor in the business of selling a product.[33]

6. **Inherently Dangerous Products**

The Nevada Supreme Court has questioned Restatement (Second) of Torts, Section 402A, comment k, as it applies to drugs that are incapable of being made safe for their intended and ordinary use. The Court suggests that a manufacturer may avoid strict liability for injuries caused by unavoidably unsafe products only where ample warning that the product is unsafe has been given.[34]

7. **Occasional Seller**

Strict liability applies only to one who sells a product in the regular course of business. It is generally not applicable to the occasional seller of a product.[35]

8. **Market Share Liability/Enterprise Liability**

Under the theory of market share liability, when it is impossible for a plaintiff alleging injury to prove which of the numerous manufacturers produced the offending product, each manufacturer is responsible for a percentage of the plaintiff's recovery corresponding to its share of the market for the drug.[36]

Under the theory of enterprise liability, if the plaintiff can prove that an entire industry was negligent, the burden shifts to the members of the industry to prove that they did not supply the specific product that caused the injury.[37]

While other states have applied these theories to permit the plaintiff to bring a lawsuit when the plaintiff does not know the identity of the actual tortfeasor, the Nevada Supreme Court has not addressed these theories.

9. **Privity**

Vertical privity (i.e., when a buyer or one in the buyer's place is attempting to take advantage of warranties made by those who did not sell to the buyer) is not required in strict liability lawsuits brought for personal or property injuries resulting from defective products.[38] Horizontal privity (i.e. when the injured party is trying to place himself or herself in the position of the buyer and take advantage of warranties made to the buyer) is required unless the injured party is a member of the buyer's family or a guest in the buyer's home.[39]

10. **Failure to Warn**

Where defendant has reason to anticipate that danger may result from a particular use of his product, and he fails to warn adequately of such a danger, the product sold without a warning is in a defective condition.[40]

Nevada law requires that warnings adequately communicate any dangers that may flow from the use or foreseeable misuse of the product.[41] A manufacturer is not required to warn against dangers that are generally known.[42]

In Nevada, the plaintiff carries the burden of proving, among other things, that the inadequate warning caused the plaintiff's injuries.[43] As a result, Nevada courts will not presume that a person injured by a product would have heeded an adequate warning if one had been given.[44]

11. **Post-Accident Remedial Measures**

Evidence of post-accident warnings is admissible to prove the existence of a defect in the product, but not to prove negligence or culpable conduct. The court has discretion to exclude evidence of such warnings if the evidence would prove to be more prejudicial than probative.[45]

Where appropriate, evidence of post-accident remedial measures may be admitted for the jury to decide if the manufacturer should have known how to correct the defect at the time it built the product.[46]

12. **Learned Intermediary Doctrine/Bulk Supplier Doctrine**

    Under the learned intermediary doctrine, manufacturers are generally immune from strict liability where they have provided physicians with adequate warnings of the risk from use of the product.[47] The Nevada Supreme Court has only applied the learned intermediary defense in favor of pharmacists and held that they have no duty to warn of the generalized risks of prescription medications unless the pharmacist has knowledge of a risk specific to a certain customer.[48]

    The United States District Court of Nevada has opined that the Nevada Supreme Court would adopt some form of the "bulk supplier doctrine." Under this defense, a bulk supplier who supplies a dangerous product to a sophisticated purchaser cannot be held liable for not warning the ultimate users of the product of its dangers.[49]

13. **Product Alteration**

    Generally, a substantial alteration will shield a manufacturer from liability from injury that results from that alteration.[50] The defendant has the burden to prove the product was altered.[51]

14. **State of the Art**

    Manufacturers are required to make their products as safe as commercial feasibility and the state of the art will allow. If the technology is available, the cost is not prohibitive, and the product remains efficient, then a potentially dangerous product which lacks a safety device is in a defective condition.[52]

    Evidence of safety devices installed on analogous machines in existence is admissible to show that the machine could have been made without the defect and to dispute the claim of the manufacturer's expert that the design was reasonably safe and was state of the art when the machine was built.[53]

15. **Malfunction**

    It is not always necessary to prove a specific defect in the product. Rather, it is sufficient to show an unexpected, dangerous malfunction with no other identifiable cause of the malfunction. Such a showing is sufficient to establish a prima facie case for the existence of a product defect.[54]

16. **Standards and Governmental Regulations**

    Legislative or administrative regulatory standards are admissible as evidence of a product's safety. In addition, post-manufacturer industry standards are circumstantial evidence that alternate courses of conduct may have been available to an entire industry.[55]

17. **Other Accidents**

In strict tort liability cases, evidence of prior or subsequent mishaps similar to the one in issue, involving the same product, is admissible to show faulty design or manufacture or other elements of the strict liability cause of action.[56]

Plaintiff has the right in strict liability to introduce evidence of a substantially similar accident to prove that the design of the product involved in the accident is defective.[57]

18. **Misrepresentation**

Nevada case law suggests that misrepresentation concerning a product may be a proper basis for a strict liability action against the manufacturer.[58]

19. **Economic Loss**

When injury to life or other property results from the use of a defective product, the law of strict products liability provides a basis for recovery. When a product "injures itself," protection derived from the interplay of manufacturer's warranties and insurance supplies an adequate basis for consumer redress. The manufacturer is not generally liable on tort theories of negligence and strict liability when a defective product damages only itself, even when it crashes calamitously or exposes persons to an unreasonable risk of harm.[59] Purely economic losses usually are not recoverable under tort theories of negligence and strict liability.[60] An action based on purely economic damages cannot be maintained under theories of strict liability or negligence.[61] However, a negligence claim can be alleged in a construction defects action initiated under Chapter 40 of the Nevada Revised Statutes.[62]

20. **Crashworthiness**

The doctrine of crashworthiness extends liability of the manufacturer to situations in which the defect did not cause the accident or initial impact, but rather increased the severity of the injury over that which would have occurred absent the defective design.[63]

A manufacturer has a duty to design a reasonably crashworthy vehicle. In regard to the crashworthiness of a vehicle, once a court or jury determines that a design defect exists misuse precludes recovery only when the plaintiff misuses the product in a manner in which the defendant could not reasonably foresee.[64]

D. **NEGLIGENCE/ASSUMPTION OF THE RISK**

If liability is to be placed on a retailer or manufacturer of goods, it must rest on negligence or a declared public policy, that is, strict liability.[65]

The defense of assumption of the risk applies to strict product liability claims.[66] Express assumption of the risk is also a defense to a negligence claim, although primary implied assumption of the risk is not addressed as a separate defense but is part of the court's duty analysis.[67]

E. BREACH OF WARRANTY

Nevada has adopted the Uniform Commercial Code with regard to breach of warranty.[68] Vertical privity is not required to bring a breach of warranty action.[69] The defendant must be engaged in the business of selling or supplying the goods that are the subject of the suit in the defendant's regular course of business.[70] Purely economic loss may be recovered under a breach of warranty theory.[71]

F. PUNITIVE DAMAGES

Nevada's punitive damages statute, Nev. Rev. Stat. § 42.005, allows for an award of punitive damages where it is proven by clear and convincing evidence that the defendant has acted with oppression, fraud or malice, express or implied. Although formerly confined to malice in fact, the Nevada Supreme Court has held that malice can be either express or implied.[72] Malice is defined as conduct which is intended to injure a person or despicable conduct which is engaged in with a conscious disregard of the rights or safety of others.[73] Prior to the enactment of Section 42.005, the Nevada Supreme Court held that, in the context of product liability, malice in fact may be established by a showing that the defendant consciously and deliberately disregarded known safety measures in reckless disregard of the possible results.[74] The amount of a punitive damages award is not statutorily limited in a strict product liability action brought against the manufacturer, distributor, or seller of a defective product.[75]

To warrant punitive damages, a defendant's conduct must exceed mere recklessness or gross negligence.[76]

G. PRE- AND POST-JUDGMENT INTEREST

When no rate of interest is provided by contract or otherwise by law, or specified in the judgment, the judgment draws interest from the time of service of the summons and complaint until satisfied, except for any amount representing future damages, which draws interest only from the time of the entry of the judgment until satisfied, at a rate equal to the prime rate at the largest bank in Nevada as ascertained by the Commissioner of Financial Institutions on January 1 or July 1, as the case may be, immediately preceding the date of judgment, plus two percent. The rate must be adjusted accordingly on each January 1 and July 1 thereafter until the judgment is satisfied.[77]

In a civil action, the plaintiff is not entitled to receive pre-judgment interest pursuant to Nev. Rev. Stat. § 17.130 on an award of punitive damages because pre-judgment interest is viewed as compensation for the use by defendant of money to which plaintiff is entitled from the time the cause of action accrues until the time of judgment, and plaintiff is not entitled to punitive damages unless they are awarded by the trier of fact.[78] Plaintiff is entitled to post-judgment interest on an award of punitive damages.[79]

H. EMPLOYER IMMUNITY FROM SUIT

The rights and remedies provided in Chapters 616A and 616D, inclusively, of NRS for an employee on account of an injury by accident sustained arising out of and in the course of employment shall be exclusive, except as otherwise provided in those chapters, of all other rights and remedies of the employee, his personal or legal representatives, dependents or next of kin, at common law or otherwise, on account of such injury.[80]

The terms, conditions and provisions of Chapters 616A to 616D, inclusive, of NRS for the payment of compensation and the amount thereof for injuries sustained or death resulting from such injuries shall be conclusive, compulsory and obligatory upon both employers and employees coming within the provisions of those chapters.[81]

If an employee receives any compensation or accident benefits under Chapters 616A to 616D, inclusive, of NRS, the acceptance of such compensation or benefits shall be in lieu of any other compensation, award or recovery against his employer under the laws of any other state or jurisdiction and such employee is barred from commencing any action of proceeding for the enforcement or collection of any benefits or awards under the laws of any other state of jurisdiction.[82]

Employers who accept the Industrial Insurance Act and provide and secure compensation for injuries by accidents sustained by an employee arising out of and in the course of employment are relieved from other liability for recovery of damages or other compensation for such personal injuries; the exclusive remedy provision of the Act is exclusive in the sense that no other common law or statutory remedy under local law is possessed by an employee against his employer.[83]

The exclusivity provision of the Industrial Insurance Act not only insulates an employer from liability to employees, but also from liability by way of indemnity to a third party who supplied the defective product found to have caused injury to employees.[84]

I. MISCELLANEOUS STATUTES

A state law tort claim based upon a failure to properly label a pesticide is preempted by FIFRA (Federal Insecticide, Fungicide, and Rodenticide Act, 7 U.S.C. § 136 *et seq.*).[85]

The manufacturer or distributor of firearms or ammunition is not subject to suit merely because its product is capable of causing serious injury, damage, or death, nor is the product defective in design simply because such results may occur. This statute does not extinguish a cause of action against such a manufacturer or distributor based on defect in design or production.[86]

The lender of money that is used to finance the design, manufacture, construction, repair, modification or improvement of real or personal property is not liable to the borrower or third persons injured by a defect therein, unless the loss or damage is the result of activity by the lender other than the loan transaction.[87]

J. JOINT AND SEVERAL LIABILITY

1. The Rule

Where two or more causes proximately contribute to the injuries complained of, recovery may be had against either one or both of the joint tortfeasors.[88]

2. Effect of Settlement

When a release or covenant not to sue or not to enforce a judgment is given in good faith to one of two or more persons liable in tort for the same injury or the same wrongful death, the following applies:

1) It does not discharge any of the other tortfeasors from liability for the injury or wrongful death unless its terms so provide, but it reduces the claim against the others to the extent of any amount stipulated by the release, or in the amount of the consideration paid for it, whichever is greater and

2) It discharges the tortfeasor to whom it is given from all liability for contribution and for equitable indemnity to any other tortfeasor.[89]

Where the plaintiff settles with one of several defendants, the jury must not be informed as to either the fact of the settlement or the amount paid.[90]

3. Contribution

Where two or more persons become jointly or severally liable in tort for the same injury to person or property or for the same wrongful death, there is a right of contribution among them even though the judgment has not been recovered against all or any of them.[91]

The right of contribution exists only in favor of a tortfeasor who has paid more than his equitable share of the common liability, and his total recovery is limited to the amount paid by him in excess of his equitable share. No tortfeasor is compelled to make contribution beyond his own equitable share of the entire liability.[92]

A tortfeasor who enters into a settlement with a claimant is not entitled to recover contribution from another tortfeasor whose liability for the injury or wrongful death is not extinguished by the settlement nor in respect to any amount paid in a settlement which is in excess of what was reasonable.[93]

4. Comparative Fault Statute

In any action to recover damages for death or injury to persons or for injury to property in which comparative negligence is asserted as a defense, the comparative negligence of the plaintiff or his decedent does not bar a recovery if the negligence was not greater than the negligence of the parties to the action against whom recovery is sought. Where recovery is allowed against more than one defendant in such an action, each defendant is severally liable to the plaintiff only for that portion of the judgment which represents the percentage of negligence attributable to him. This statutory section does not affect joint and several liability of the defendants in actions based upon (a) strict liability; (b) an intentional tort; (c) the emission, disposal or spillage of a toxic or hazardous substance; (d) the concerted acts of the defendants; or (e) an injury to any person or property resulting from a product which is manufactured, distributed, sold or used in this state.[94]

It is currently a disputed issue on appeal before the Nevada Supreme Court whether, in an action where the plaintiff is not negligent, NRS 41.141 would not apply and the defendants would remain jointly and severally liable.[95]

Wayne Shaffer
Holly Parker

(Albert F. Pagni and Wayne O. Klomp of Reno authored the earlier version of this chapter.)

ENDNOTES - NEVADA

1. *Shoshone Coca Cola v. Dolinsky*, 82 Nev. 439, 420 P.2d 855 (1966); *Ginnis v. Mapes*, 86 Nev. 408, 470 P.2d 135 (1970).

2. Young's Mach. Co. v. Long, 100 Nev. 692, 694, 692 P.2d 24, 25 (1984); *Jeep Corp. v. Murray*, 101 Nev. 640, 645, *708 P.2d 297*, 301 (1985) (superseded by statute on other grounds).

3. Nev. Rev. Stat. § 11.190(4)(e).

4. Nev. Rev. Stat. § 11.190(3)(c); Hartford Ins. Grp. v. Statewide Appliances, Inc., 87 Nev. 195, 197-98, 484 P.2d 569, 570-71 (1971).

5. Nev. Rev. Stat. § 11.190(1)(b); Nev. Rev. Stat. § 11.190(2)(c).

6. Nev. Rev. Stat. § 11.206(2).

7. Nev. Rev. Stat. § 11.202(1).

8. Nev. Rev. Stat. § 11.203.

9. Nev. Rev. Stat. § 11.203.

10. Nev. Rev. Stat. § 11.204.

11. Nev. Rev. Stat. § 11.204.

12. Nev. Rev. Stat. § 11.204(4).

13. Nev. Rev. Stat. § 11.205.

14. Nev. Rev. Stat. § 11.205(2).

15. Nev. Rev. Stat. § 11.205(4).

16. *Fyssakis v. Knight Equip. Corp.*, 108 Nev. 212, 214, 826 P.2d 570, 571 (1992). See also Ward v. Ford Motor Co., 99 Nev. 47, 657 P.2d 95 (1983).

17. *Rivera v. Philip Morris, Inc.*, 125 Nev. 185, 191, 209 P.3d 271, 275 (2009).

18. *Rivera v. Philip Morris, Inc.*, 125 Nev. 185, 195-96, 209 P.3d 271, 277 (2009).

19. *Ginnis v. Mapes*, 86 Nev. 408, 413, 470 P.2d 135, 138 (1970); *Allison v. Merck & Co. Inc.*, 110 Nev. 762, 767, 878 P.2d 948, 952 (1994).

20. *Outboard Marine Corp. v. Schupbach*, 93 Nev. 158, 162-63, 561 P.2d 450, 453 (1977).

21. *Compare Potter v. Chicago Pneumatic Tool Co.*, 694 A.2d 1319, 1334 (Conn. 1997) ("The availability of a feasible alternative design is a factor that the plaintiff may, rather than must, prove in order to establish that a product's risks outweigh its utility."), *with Timpte Indus., Inc. v. Gish*, 286 S.W.3d 306, 311 (Tex. 2009) (To recover on a design defect claim, the plaintiff must prove, among other things, that a "safer alternative design existed.")

22. *Robinson v. G.G.C., Inc.*, 107 Nev. 135, 140, 808 P.2d 522, 525 (1991); *McCourt v. J.C. Penney Co., Inc.*, 103 Nev. 101, 104, 734 P.2d 696, 698 (1987).

23. *Krause, Inc. v. Little*, 117 Nev. 929, 937, 34 P.3d 566, 571 (2001).

24. *Krause, Inc. v. Little*, 117 Nev. 929, 937-38, 34 P.3d 566, 571-72 (2001).

25. *Krause, Inc. v. Little*, 117 Nev. 929, 938, 34 P.3d 566, 572 (2001).

26. *Price v. Blain Kern Artista, Inc.*, 111 Nev. 515, 520, 893 P.2d 367, 370 (1995).

27. *Price v. Blain Kern Artista, Inc.*, 111 Nev. 515, 520, 893 P.2d 367, 371 (1995).

28. *Maduike v. Agency Rent-A-Car*, 114 Nev. 1, 6, 953 P.2d 24, 27 (1998) (abrogated in part on other grounds).

29. *Dow Chem. Co. v. Mahlum*, 114 Nev. 1468, 1481, 970 P.2d 98, 107 (1998) (disfavored on other grounds by *GES, Inc. v. Corbitt*, 21 P.3d 11 (Nev. 2001)).

30. *Young's Mach. Co. v. Long*, 100 Nev. 692, 694, 692 P.2d 24, 25 (1984); *Jeep Corp. v. Murray*, 101 Nev. 640, 645, *708 P.2d 297,* 301 (1985) (superseded by statute on other grounds).

31. *Crown Controls Corp. v. Corella*, 98 Nev. 35, 639 P.2d 555 (1982). *See also Asay v. Kolberg-Pioneer*, 2010 U.S. Dist. LEXIS 83105 (D. Nev. Aug. 13, 2010); *Rowell v. Powerscreen Int'l, Ltd.*, 808 F. Supp. 1459 (D. Nev. 1992).

32. *Burns v. District Ct.*, 97 Nev. 237, 627 P.2d 403 (1981).

33. *Calloway v. City of Reno*, 116 Nev. 250, 270-71, 993 P.2d 1259, 1272 (2000) (overruled on other grounds by *Olson v. Richard*, 120 Nev. 240, 89 P.3d 31 (2004)).

34. *Allison v. Merck & Co. Inc.*, 110 Nev. 762, 774, 878 P.2d 948, 956 (1994).

35. *Elley v. Stephens*, 104 Nev. 413, 418, 760 P.2d 768, 771 (1988).

36. *Doe v. Cutter Biological, Inc.*, 971 F.2d 375, 379 (9th Cir. 1992).

37. *Doe v. Cutter Biological, Inc.*, 971 F.2d 375, 379 (9th Cir. 1992).

38. *Hiles Co. v. Johnston Pump Co.*, 93 Nev. 73, 78, 560 P.2d 154, 157 (1977).

39. *Hiles Co. v. Johnston Pump Co.*, 93 Nev. 73, 78, 560 P.2d 154, 157 (1977); Nev. Rev. Stat. § 104.2318; *Zaika v. Del E. Webb Corp.*, 508 F. Supp. 1005, 1012 (D. Nev. 1981).

40. *General Elec. Co. v. Bush*, 88 Nev. 360, 364-65, 498 P.2d 366, 369 (1972); *Outboard Marine Corp. v. Schupbach*, 93 Nev. 158, 162, 561 P.2d 450, 453 (1977). See also *Fyssakis v. Knight Equip. Corp.*, 108 Nev. 212, 214, 826 P.2d 570, 571-72 (1992).

41. *Yamaha Motor Co. v. Arnoult*, 114 Nev. 233, 238-39, 955 P.2d 661, 665 (1998).

42. *Yamaha Motor Co. v. Arnoult*, 114 Nev. 233, 241, 955 P.2d 661, 666 (1998).

43. *Rivera v. Philip Morris, Inc.*, 125 Nev. 185, 190, 209 P.3d 271, 274 (2009).

44. *Rivera v. Philip Morris, Inc.*, 125 Nev. 185, 195, 209 P.3d 271, 277 (2009).

45. *Jeep Corp. v. Murray*, 101 Nev. 640, 646-47, 708 P.2d 297, 302 (1985) (superseded by statute on other grounds as stated in *Countrywide Home Loans v. Thitchener*, 124 Nev. 725, 192 P.3d 243 (2008)). See also Nev. Rev. Stat. § 48.095.

46. *Robinson v. G.G.C., Inc.*, 107 Nev. 135, 141, 808 P.2d 522, 526 (1991).

47. *Moses v. Danek Med., Inc.*, 1998 U.S. Dist. LEXIS 21110 (D. Nev. Nov. 18, 1998).

48. *Klasch v. Walgreen Co.*, 264 P.3d 1155, 1157-158 (Nev. 2011).

49. *Forest v. E.I. DuPont*, 791 F. Supp. 1460, 1465 (D. Nev. 1992).

50. *Robinson v. G.G.C., Inc.*, 107 Nev. 135, 140, 808 P.2d 522, 525 (1991).

51. Andrews v. Harley Davidson, Inc., 106 Nev. 533, 539-40, 796 P.2d 1092, 1097 (1990).

52. *Robinson v. G.G.C., Inc.*, 107 Nev. 135, 139, 808 P.2d 522, 525 (1991).

53. *Robinson v. G.G.C., Inc.*, 107 Nev. 135, 140-41, 808 P.2d 522, 525-26 (1991).

54. *Stackiewicz v. Nissan Motor Corp.*, 100 Nev. 443, 448-49, 686 P.2d 925, 928 (1984).

55. *Robinson v. G.G.C., Inc.*, 107 Nev. 135, 142, 808 P.2d 522, 526-27 (1991).

56. *Ginnis v. Mapes*, 86 Nev. 408, 415-16, 470 P.2d 135, 139-40 (1970); *Beattie v. Thomas*, 99 Nev. 579, 585, 668 P.2d 268, 272 (1983); *Robinson v. G.G.C., Inc.*, 107 Nev. 135, 140, 808 P.2d 522, 525 (1991).

57. *Andrews v. Harley Davison, Inc.*, 106 Nev. 533, 538, 796 P.2d 1092, 1096 (1990).

58. *See Jeep Corp. v. Murray*, 101 Nev. 640, 643, 708 P.2d 297, 299 (1985) (superseded by statute on other grounds).

59. *National Union Fire Ins. Co. v. Pratt & Whitney Canada, Inc.*, 107 Nev. 535, 541, 815 P.2d 601, 604-05 (1991).

60. *National Union Fire Ins. Co. v. Pratt & Whitney Canada, Inc.*, 107 Nev. 535, 538, 815 P.2d 601, 603 (1991).

61. *Arco Prods. Co. v. D. May*, 113 Nev. 1295, 1299, 948 P.2d 263, 266 (1997).

62. *Olson v. Richard*, 120 Nev. 240, 243-44, 89 P.3d 31, 33 (2004).

63. *Roe v. Deere & Co.*, 855 F.2d 151, 153 (3d Cir. 1988) (questioned on other grounds).

64. *Andrews v. Harley Davison, Inc.*, 106 Nev. 533, 537, 796 P.2d 1092, 1095 (1990).

65. *Long v. Flanigan Whse. Co.*, 79 Nev. 241, 247, 382 P.2d 399, 403 (1963).

66. *Central Tel. Co. v. Fixtures Mfg.*, 103 Nev. 298, 300, 738 P.2d 510, 512 (1987).

67. *Turner v. Mandalay Sports Entm't, LLC*, 124 Nev. 213, 220-221, 180 P.3d 1172, 1177 (2008).

68. *Long v. Flanigan Whse. Co.*, 79 Nev. 241, 245, 382 P.2d 399, 402 (1963). *See also* Nev. Rev. Stat. § 104.2312; Nev. Rev. Stat. § 104.2313; Nev. Rev. Stat. § 104.2314; Nev. Rev. Stat. § 104.2315; Nev. Rev. Stat. § 104.2316; Nev. Rev. Stat. § 104.2317; Nev. Rev. Stat. § 104.2318.

69. Hiles Co. v. Johnston Pump Co., 93 Nev. 73, 78, 560 P.2d 154, 157 (1977); Nev. Rev. Stat. 104.2318; *Zaika v. Del E. Webb Corp.*, 508 F. Supp. 1005, 1012 (D. Nev. 1981).

70. *Elley v. Stephens*, 104 Nev. 413, 418, 760 P.2d 768, 771 (1988).

71. *Central Bit Supply v. Waldrop Drilling*, 102 Nev. 139, 140-41, 717 P.2d 35, 36-37 (1986).

72. *Countrywide Home Loans v. Thitchener*, 124 Nev. 725, 742-43, 192 P.3d 243, 254-55 (2008).

73. Nev. Rev. Stat. § 42.001(3).

74. *Jeep Corp. v. Murray*, 101 Nev. 640, 650, *708 P.2d 297*, 304 (1985) (superseded by statute); *Leslie v. Jones Chem. Co.*, 92 Nev. 391, 393, 551 P.2d 234, 235 (1976) (superseded by statute)..

75. Nev. Rev. Stat. § 42.005(2)(a).

76. NRS 42.001(1); *Wyeth v. Rowatt*, 244 P.3d 765, 783 (Nev. 2010); *Countrywide Home Loans, Inc. v. Thitchener*, 124 Nev. 725, 742-743, 192 P.3d 243, 254-255 (Nev. 2008).

77. Nev. Rev. Stat. § 17.130(2).

78. *Ramada Inns, Inc. v. Sharp*, 101 Nev. 824, 826, 711 P.2d 1, 2 (1985).

79. *Evans v. Dean Wittier Reynolds, Inc.*, 116 Nev. 598, 615, 5 P.3d 1043, 1054 (2000).

80. Nev. Rev. Stat. § 616A.020(1).

81. Nev. Rev. Stat. § 616A.020(2).

82. Nev. Rev. Stat. § 616A.020(6).

83. *Outboard Motor Corp*, 93 Nev. 158, 164, 561 P.2d 450, 454 (1977).

84. *Outboard Motor Corp*, 93 Nev. 158, 164, 561 P.2d 450, 454 (1977).

85. *Davidson v. Velsicol Chem. Corp.*, 108 Nev. 591, 600, 834 P.2d 931, 936 (1992).

86. Nev. Rev. Stat. § 41.131.

87. Nev. Rev. Stat. § 41.590.

88. *L.W. Mahan v. Hafen*, 76 Nev. 220, 225, 351 P.2d 617, 620 (1960).

89. Nev. Rev. Stat. § 17.245(1). *See also Doctors Co. v. Vincent*, 120 Nev. 644, 98 P.3d 681 (2004); *Evans v. Dean Wittier Reynolds, Inc.*, 116 Nev. 598, 610, 5 P.3d 1043, 1050-51 (2000).

90. *Moore v. Bannen*, 106 Nev. 679, 680-81, 799 P.2d 564, 565 (1990); *Evans v. Dean Wittier Reynolds, Inc.*, 116 Nev. 598, 608, 5 P.3d 1043, 1049-50 (2000).

91. Nev. Rev. Stat. § 17.225(1).

92. Nev. Rev. Stat. § 17.225(2).

93. Nev. Rev. Stat. § 17.225(3); *Doctors Co. v. Vincent*, 120 Nev. 644, 652-53, 98 P.3d 681, 687 (2004).

94. Nev. Rev. Stat. § 41.141(1); Nev. Rev. Stat. § 41.141(4); Nev. Rev. Stat. § 41.141(5).

95. See appeal before the Nevada Supreme Court in *Donahue Chriber Realty Grp., LP & Malco Nevada, Inc., Appellants, v. Tyrin Salinas, Respondent*, Appeal from the Eighth Judicial District Court Case No. A547417, Appeal No. 59071.

NEW HAMPSHIRE

A. CAUSES OF ACTION

Claims for injury arising out of a product liability setting may be pursued in negligence, strict liability in tort, and warranty.

B. STATUTES OF LIMITATION

Claims in negligence and strict liability in tort are generally subject to a three-year statute of limitations.[1] In some instances, however, a plaintiff's claim may be barred by New Hampshire's statute of repose.[2]

New Hampshire applies a "discovery" rule.[3]

Causes of action for breach of warranty, express or implied, must be brought within four years of the date of sale.[4]

C. NEGLIGENCE

Standard common law negligence duties apply to claims of damage arising from product losses.

If a claim is made for economic or commercial losses, the plaintiff must rely on negligence or warranty principles.[5]

Comparative negligence principles apply to claims of negligence. A plaintiff's award will be reduced based on percentage of comparative negligence. A plaintiff's claim is barred if plaintiff is more than 50 percent at fault.[6]

The New Hampshire Supreme Court has adopted the Restatement (Second) of Torts Section 389 as a proper statement of the law of supplier negligence.[7]

The New Hampshire Supreme Court also recognizes the right of a bystander, within the scope of foreseeability of risk, to recover for injuries caused by a supplier's provision of a product known by the supplier to be dangerous.[8]

New Hampshire seems to recognize the "sophisticated user" defense in negligence product liability actions. However, it is likely the New Hampshire Supreme Court would limit its application to negligence claims in light of the fact that the defense is a negligence theory derived from the Restatement (Second) of Torts.[9]

D. STRICT LIABILITY

New Hampshire has adopted Restatement (Second) of Torts Section 402A.[10]

The New Hampshire Supreme Court cites extensively from comments to Section 402A in its decisions. However, the court has made it clear that it does not adopt the comments in their entirety and has specifically rejected "risk-spreading" analysis.[11]

Although strict liability in tort has been adopted in New Hampshire, the New Hampshire Supreme Court has made it clear that this does not establish absolute liability, and issues of product defect, causation, and foreseeability are important elements for a jury.[12]

The occurrence of an injury from a product is not sufficient evidence to prove either that it is "defective" or that it is "unreasonably dangerous." These are questions of fact for determination by a jury, which will normally require expert testimony.[13]

In order to maintain a claim for products liability based upon the negligent actions of a defendant, the plaintiff must demonstrate everything necessary to prove the underlying negligence action.[14]

Strict liability will not apply to providers of services,[15] nor will it apply to non-manufacturers and non-sellers.[16] The New Hampshire Supreme Court has also refused to apply strict liability to a health care provider who supplies a defective prosthesis.[17] The rationale behind this decision is that the health care provider primarily renders a service, and the provision of any prosthetic device is merely incidental to that service.[18]

Under New Hampshire's strict liability law, manufacturer liability may still attach even if the danger is obvious to a reasonable consumer or if the user employs the product in an unintended but foreseeable manner, depending on the cost and efficiency of reducing the danger of the product.[19]

A hybrid sales-service transaction can give rise to a cause of action for strict liability if the sales aspect of the transaction predominates and the service aspect is incidental.[20]

Pursuant to the Restatement (Second) of Torts Section 402A, to set forth a viable claim of strict liability against a manufacturer, New Hampshire law requires a plaintiff to plead separately a product's defective condition and a product's unreasonably dangerous condition.[21]

Manufacturing defect, design defect, and warning defect are not merely factors bearing on a single theory of strict liability but are separate theories of liability.[22] In design defect claims, "the plaintiff is not required to present evidence of a safer alternative design."[23] This is due to the fact that under New Hampshire law, "[p]roof of an alternative design is neither a controlling factor nor an essential element that must be proved in every case."[24] In addition to factors listed in Restatement (Second) of Torts, Section 402A, New Hampshire law may require a plaintiff to show that the product was expected to and does reach the consumer without substantial change in the condition in which it was sold to make out a viable design defect case.[25]

E. **DEFENSES**

Plaintiff misconduct is a defense analogous to comparative negligence. Plaintiff's misconduct, including product misuse, abnormal use, assumption of the risk, and so on, will result in a proportionate reduction in award to a plaintiff. If plaintiff's misconduct is more than 50 percent of the cause of the accident, then plaintiff will be barred from recovery.[26]

A third party's misconduct acts as a defense only if it is the sole proximate cause of the plaintiff's injuries, and provided such misconduct was not foreseeable to a manufacturer such that the misconduct should be accounted for in the design.[27]

Non-use of safety devices such as kill-switch lanyards or life vests is not admissible to show comparative fault or failure to mitigate damages.[28]

New Hampshire does not yet recognize a "private contractor" defense.[29]

New Hampshire does not recognize the component-part defense allowing a finding of no-liability where defendant's component was an innocent component in an otherwise defective product.[30]

F. LEASING AGREEMENTS

Strict liability is likely to apply to a lessor of a product if that lessor is in the business of routinely leasing a product, but it will not apply to lessor-lessee arrangements that appear to be nothing more than financing arrangements.[31]

G. INHERENTLY DANGEROUS PRODUCTS

A supplier of products will not be held strictly liable simply because a product is inherently dangerous, unless the product is deemed otherwise defective for failure to give adequate warnings.[32]

H. WARNINGS

A failure to warn of dangers not otherwise obvious to a user can constitute a design defect giving rise to strict liability if the product was used in a fashion that would foreseeably incur an injury and the failure to properly warn was causal.[33]

The product manufacturer or seller has no duty to warn of obvious risks.[34] However, liability may attach even though the danger was obvious or there was adequate warning when an unreasonable danger could have been eliminated without excessive cost or loss of product efficiency.[35] Whether the risk is obvious is a question of fact to be decided by a jury.[36]

There is no duty to warn on the basis of speculation that a product might be dangerous.[37] A manufacturer has no duty to warn of all potential dangers associated with a product.

The New Hampshire Supreme Court has not addressed the sophisticated user defense as it might apply to warnings. However, knowledge and experience of a product's user are relevant to a defendant's negligence in failing to warn of a product's dangers.[38]

The New Hampshire Supreme Court has suggested in dicta that imposing a duty to warn of risks unknowable at the time of sale is unreasonable and amounts to absolute liability.[39] However, the New Hampshire Supreme Court has not directly addressed the issue of whether a duty to warn exists where a manufacturer or seller becomes aware of widespread buyer alterations, misuse, or increased hazards with a product.

In *Beaudette v. Louisville Ladder, Inc.*,[40] the United States District Court for the District of New Hampshire held that expert testimony was required to support a claim for inadequate warning where a ladder collapsed while it was being used as part of a scaffolding assembly. The Court held that expert testimony was required because "[a]lthough the average juror may have experience with ladders, the average juror will not have knowledge as to the use of a ladder jack, the construction of scaffolding out of ladders, and the contribution of factors that would make such a situation safe or unsafe."

I. PRIVITY

Privity is not required.[41]

J. SUBSTANTIAL CHANGE

A manufacturer or seller is not liable for injuries or damages caused by a product that has been substantially changed or that has been subject to abnormal use, provided the change or abnormal use is not that which could be reasonably foreseen or expected by the manufacturer and/or seller.[42]

K. STATE OF THE ART

While state of the art is available as a defense, post-manufacture evidence can be introduced to rebut defense claims of infeasibility.[43]

L. STANDARDS

Evidence that a product complies with state or federal standards does not require a finding that the product is not defective.[44]

M. LIABILITY AMONG MULTIPLE DEFENDANTS

New Hampshire has recognized the right of indemnification by non-negligent sellers against upstream sellers and manufacturers.[45] New Hampshire law allows for contribution among joint tortfeasors.[46] The contribution statute does not refer specifically to negligence claims, but rather applies to parties liable for the same indivisible claim or same injury. For purposes of determining contribution under New Hampshire Revised Statute Annotated § 507-d, where the jury has apportioned fault to a party not named as a defendant in the litigation, the trial court must consider the "aggregated fault" of both the named defendant and the unnamed party to whom the jury has apportioned fault.[47] It is likely that this statute will apply to claims of strict liability and tort.

Where there are multiple tortfeasors, New Hampshire's apportionment statute, New Hampshire Revised Statute Annotated § 507:7-e ("RSA 507:7-e"), applies in all actions, not only those involving comparatively negligent plaintiffs.[48] In *DeBenedetto v. CLD Consulting Engineers, Inc.*, the New Hampshire Supreme Court held that for purposes of apportionment under RSA 507:7-e, the term "party" includes not only the parties to the action and settling parties but also "all parties contributing to the occurrence giving rise to an action, including those immune from liability or otherwise not before the court."[49] A defendant seeking to apportion fault to a non-litigant must present "adequate evidence" of the non-litigant's alleged fault before the trier of fact will be permitted to consider the alleged fault for apportionment purposes.[50] Under *Nilsson* or *DeBenedetto*, two controlling cases on the application of the apportionment statute, a defendant is not permitted to bring a settling tortfeasor into the case as an active litigant. The purpose of the apportionment statute "is to protect minimally liable defendants."[51]

In *Tierghein v. B.R. Jones Roofing Co.*,[52] the New Hampshire Supreme Court held that RSA 507:7-h entitles "a non-settling tortfeasor to a dollar-for-dollar reduction in the amount of the judgment equal to the consideration the plaintiff received from a good faith settlement with one of two or more tortfeasors" even with respect to arbitration awards because the language of the statute is not limited to court proceedings.

N. RELATED THEORIES OF LIABILITY

1. Successor Liability

Under some circumstances, a successor corporation may be held liable for a product manufactured or sold by a predecessor.[53] New Hampshire courts will impose liability upon a successor corporation in any one of the following circumstances: "(1) when the purchasing corporation expressly or impliedly agrees to assume the obligations of the selling corporation; (2) when the asset transfer amounts to a *de facto* merger of the two corporations; (3) when the purchasing corporation becomes a 'mere continuation' of the selling corporation; and (4) when the transaction is fraudulent because its only purpose is to evade corporate liability."[54] The New Hampshire Supreme Court has rejected "risk spreading" as a theory for imposing successor liablity.[55] The court has also rejected the "product line" theory as a basis for imposing successor liability.[56]

2. Market Share Liability

The New Hampshire Supreme Court has not specifically addressed this concept. It is likely that the New Hampshire Supreme Court would reject this theory because it is reliant upon a risk-spreading analysis.[57]

3. Enterprise Liability

The New Hampshire Supreme Court has held that it does not recognize the expanded "continuity of the enterprise" test for successor liability in products liability, but it does recognize the traditional "mere continuation" exception to the prohibition against successor liability.[58]

O. BREACH OF WARRANTY

While a breach of warranty claim is available in a product liability setting, this claim is virtually identical to the strict liability and tort theory.

In *Ace American Insurance Co. v. Fountain*,[59] the United States District Court for the District of New Hampshire held that in consumer transactions "the New

Hampshire Supreme Court would likely hold that the notice requirements of RSA 382-A:2-207 require a buyer to notify only his immediate seller of potential U.C.C. warranty claims; the buyer need not provide such notice directly to remote sellers."

P. **PUNITIVE DAMAGES**

Punitive damages are not recoverable in tort actions in New Hampshire.[60]

Q. **NON-ECONOMIC DAMAGES**

A statute limiting recovery for damages for non-economic loss, such as pain and suffering, to $875,000 has been declared unconstitutional by the New Hampshire Supreme Court.[61]

R. **JOINT AND SEVERAL LIABILITY**

In all cases where parties are found to have knowingly pursued or to have taken an active part in a common plan or design resulting in the harm complained of, judgment shall be granted against the parties on the basis of joint and several liability.[62] If, however, the fault of any party shall be less than 50 percent, that party's liability shall be several, not joint, and he shall be liable only for the damages attributable to him.[63]

S. **PRE- AND POST-JUDGMENT INTERESTS**

In all civil actions at law or in equity, other than actions on a debt or where liquidated damages are sought, interest shall be added to any verdict rendered or to any finding for pecuniary damages.[64] The interest begins to accrue "from the date of the writ or the filing of the petition to the date of judgment even though such interest brings the amount of the judgment beyond the maximum liability imposed by law."[65]

The rate of interest on judgments, including pre-judgment interest, shall be the prime interest rate on a 26-week United States Treasury Bill plus two percent, not compounded.[66]

T. **EMPLOYER IMMUNITY FROM SUIT**

New Hampshire's Workers' Compensation Statute provides a no fault system under which limited compensation is available to an injured employee as a substitute for common law remedies in tort.[67]

Under the statute's exclusivity provision, employers are immune from their injured employee's tort claims and are also immune from the third party tortfeasor's claim for contribution.[68]

New Hampshire does recognize, however, the Dual Capacity Doctrine as an exception to the employer immunity otherwise granted under its workers' compensation law.[69] This Dual Capacity Doctrine permits an employer, normally shielded from tort liability by the exclusive remedy principle, to become liable in tort to his employee if he acts, not only as an employer, but in a second capacity which confers upon him obligations independent of those imposed upon him as an employer.[70]

U. CRASHWORTHINESS

Under the Crashworthiness Doctrine, a supplier of products is liable for injuries sustained in a vehicular accident because of a defect that, while not the cause of the accident, caused or enhanced the degree of injuries suffered. The Crashworthiness Doctrine has been held to overrule the position previously held by some courts that a driver's negligence will bar a plaintiff's right to recover against a manufacturer. The doctrine is founded on the premise that accidents caused by driver negligence are foreseeable and that, therefore, manufacturers should design their vehicles to be reasonably safe in light of such foreseeable negligent use. The Crashworthiness Doctrine does not, however, foreclose proof of plaintiff's negligence in assessing comparative fault.[71]

Principles of contribution and apportionment between joint tortfeasors apply in crashworthiness cases involving indivisible injury.[72]

In a crashworthiness case involving indivisible injuries, the plaintiff must make a prima facie showing that the defendants' conduct contributed as a proximate cause to his or her injuries. The burden then shifts to the defendants to apportion their respective liability.[73]

V. DESIGN DEFECT CLAIMS

In the case of *Davis S. Vautour v. Body Masters Sports Industries, Inc.*,[74] the New Hampshire Supreme Court rejected the Restatement (Third) of Torts, Section 2(b) (1998), which requires a plaintiff in a product design defect case to prove that the risk of harm posed by the product could have been reduced or avoided by a reasonable alternative design. The lower court ruled that it was an essential element of the plaintiff's case to prove a reasonable alternative design at trial. However, the Supreme Court in *Vautour* held this was an error.

Relying upon the prior New Hampshire Supreme Court's decision in *Thibeault v. Sears Roebuck Co.*,[75] the Court noted that to prevail in a defective product liability claim, a plaintiff must prove the following four elements: (1) the design of the product created a defective condition unreasonably dangerous to the user; (2) the condition existed when the product was sold by a seller in the business of selling such product; (3) the use of the product was reasonably foreseeable by the manufacturer; and (4) the condition caused injury to the user or to the user's property.[76] The Court went on to note that while proof of an alternative design is relevant in a design defect case, it should neither be a controlling factor nor an essential element that must be proved in every case.

Fred J. Desmarais, Jr.
Desmarais, Ewing & Johnston, P.L.L.C.
175 Canal Street
Manchester, New Hampshire 03101
(Fax) (603) 623-6383/(Phone) (603) 623-5524
E-mail: desmaraisf@dejlawfirm.com
http://www.dejlawfirm.com

ENDNOTES - NEW HAMPSHIRE

1. N.H. Rev. Stat. Ann. § 508:4, I; *see Chesley v. Harvey Indus., Inc.*, 157 N.H. 211, 214 (2008) (ruling that "the day upon which the incident occurred . . . is excluded from the [three-year] time limit" set forth in N.H. Rev. Stat. Ann. (sometimes "RSA") 508:4 due to the operation of RSA 21:35).

2. *See, e.g., Bourget d/b/a Bourget Amusement Co.*, Dkt. No. 11-cv-88-SM (D.N.H. Sept. 9, 2013) (unpublished decision) (ruling that New Hampshire's statute of repose, codified at RSA 508:4-b, I, barred plaintiff's claims for negligence and breach of warranty against a manufacturer and distributor relating to the collapse of a pre-fabricated steel building because the plaintiff failed to bring his claims within eight years from the date of the improvement to the real property—*i.e.*, the building—had been "substantially complete[d]" for the purpose for which the plaintiff had been using the building).

3. *Perez v. Pike Indus. Inc.*, 153 N.H. 158 (2005); *but see Thomas v. King Ridge, Inc.*, 771 F. Supp. 478, 482 (D.N.H. 1991) (explaining that under RSA 382-A:2-725 the limitations period in warranty actions "normally commences . . . upon tender of delivery, and . . . runs even though the buyer does not know the good are defective"); *see also Phaneuf Funeral Home v. Little Giant Pump Co.*, 163 N.H. 727, 734-35 (2012) (suggesting that in limited circumstances, such as perhaps where a product is designed to be or become an "improvement" to real property, a products liability action may be time-barred under the statute of repose codified at RSA 508:4-b, I); *see* RSA 508:4-b, I (providing: "Except as otherwise provided in this section, all actions to recover damages for injury to property, injury to the person, wrongful death or economic loss arising out of any deficiency in the creation of an improvement to real property, including without limitation the design, labor, materials, engineering, planning, surveying, construction, observation, supervision or inspection of that improvement, shall be brought within 8 years from the date of substantial completion of the improvement, and not thereafter").

4. N.H. Rev. Stat. Ann. § 382-A:2-725.

5. *Pub. Serv. Co. of N.H. v. Westinghouse Elec. Corp.*, 685 F. Supp. 1281 (D.N.H. 1988).

6. N.H. Rev. Stat. Ann. § 507:7-d.

7. *Buckingham v. R.J. Reynolds Tobacco Co.*, 142 N.H. 822 (1998).

8. *Buckingham*, 142 N.H. 822.

9. *Bernier v. Simon-Telelect, Inc. & James A. Kiley Co.*, Dkt. No. CV-96-009-M (D.N.H. June 2, 1998).

10. *Buttrick v. Lessard*, 110 N.H. 36 (1969); *Thibault v. Sears, Roebuck & Co.*, 118 N.H. 802 (1978); *Precourt v. Fairbank Reconstruction Corp.*, 856 F. Supp. 2d 327, 334 (D.N.H. 2012).

11. *Simoneau v. South Bend Lathe, Inc.*, 130 N.H. 466 (1988).

12. *Thibault*, 118 N.H. 802; *McLaughlin v. Sears, Roebuck & Co.*, 111 N.H. 265 (1971).

13. *Vantour v. Body Master Sports Indus.*, 147 N.H. 150 (2001); *Price v. BIS Corp.*, 142 N.H. 386 (1997).

14. *Georgia Palmer v. Nan King Rest., Inc.*, 147 N.H. 681 (2002).

15. *Siciliano v. Capitol City Shows, Inc.*, 124 N.H. 719 (1984).

16. *Moulton v. Groveton Paper Co.*, 112 N.H. 50 (1972); *see also Bruzga v. PMR Architects*, 141 N.H. 756 (1997).

17. *See Royer v. Catholic Med. Ctr.*, 144 N.H. 330 (1999).

18. *Royer*, 144 N.H. 330.

19. *Price v. BIC Corp.*, 142 N.H. 386 (1997).

20. *Eaton v. Wal-Mart Stores, Inc.*, Dkt. No. CV-97-245-SD (D.N.H. July 23, 1998).

21. *Buckingham*, 142 N.H. 822.

22. *Cheshire Med. Ctr. v. W.R. Grace & Co.*, 49 F.3d 26 (1st Cir. 1995).

23. *Kelleher v. Marvin Lumber & Cedar Co.*, 152 N.H. 813, 831 (2005) (quotation and citation omitted).

24. *Kelleher*, 152 N.H. 831 (quotation and citation omitted).

25. *Isabelle v. Nissan Motor Acceptance Corp.*, Dkt. No. CV-96-490-JD (D.N.H. May 28, 1998).

26. *Thibault v. Sears*, 118 N.H. 802 (1978); *Union Mut. Fire Ins. v. Hamilton Beach Proctor-Silex, Inc.*, No. 0S-CV-170-JD, 2006 U.S. Dist. LEXIS 92829 (D.N.H. 2006) (unpublished decision).

27. *Reid v. Spadone Mach. Co.*, 119 N.H. 457 (1979); *Murray v. Bullard Co.*, 110 N.H. 220 (1970).

28. *Warren v. Am. Marine Holdings*, 2002 U.S. Dist. LEXIS 7930 (D.N.H. Apr. 30, 2002).

29. *Bernier v. Simon-Telelect, Inc. & James A. Kiley Co.*, Dkt. No. CV-96-009-M (D.N.H. June 2, 1998).

30. *Bernier*, Dkt. No. CV-96-009-M.

31. *Brescia v. Great Road Realty Trust*, 117 N.H. 154 (1977).

32. *Thibault*, 118 N.H. 802.

33. *Thibault*, 118 N.H. 802; *Reid v. Spadone Mach. Co.*, 119 N.H. 457 (1979).

34. *Thibault*, 118 N.H. 802; *Plante v. Hobart Corp.*, 771 F.2d 617 (1st Cir. 1985).

35. *LeBlanc v. American Honda Motor Co.*, 141 N.H. 579 (1997); *Price v. BIC Corp.*, 142 N.H. 386 (1997).

36. *Collins v. Tool Exch., LLC*, 2002 U.S. Dist. LEXIS 20729 (D.N.H. Oct. 16, 2002).

37. *Cheshire Med. Ctr. v. W.R. Grace & Co.*, 49 F.3d 26 (1st Cir. 1995).

38. *Laramie v. Sears, Roebuck & Co.*, 142 N.H. 653 (1998); *but see* Section C, Negligence, *supra*.

39. *Heather v. Sears, Roebuck & Co.*, 123 N.H. 512 (1983).

40. 462 F.3d 22, 27 (1st Cir. 2006).

41. N.H. Rev. Stat. Ann. § 382-A:2-318.

42. *Reid*, 119 N.H. 457.

43. *Estate of Spinosa*, 621 F.2d 1154 (1st Cir. 1980).

44. *Raymond v. Riegel Textile Corp.*, 484 F.2d 1025 (1st Cir. 1973).

45. *Consolidated Util. Equip. Servs., Inc. v. Emhart Mfg. Corp.*, 123 N.H. 258 (1983).

46. N.H. Rev. Stat. Ann. § 507:7-f.

47. *Ocasio v. Fed. Express Corp.*, 162 N.H. 436, 450-52 (2011).

48. *Nilsson v. Bierman*, 150 N.H. 393 (2003).

49. *DeBenedetto v. CLD Consulting Eng'rs, Inc.*, 153 N.H. 793 (2006).

50. *Goudreault v. Kleeman*, 158 N.H. 236, 255-57 (2009) (citing *DeBenedetto v. CLD Consulting Eng'rs, Inc.*, 153 N.H. 793 (2006)).

51. *Ocasio*, 162 N.H. at 446 (quoting *Rodgers v. Colby's Ol' Place*, 148 N.H. 41, 44 (2002)).

52. 156 N.H. 110 (2007).

53. *Bielagus v. EMRE of New Hampshire Corp.*, 149 N.H. 635 (2003).

54. *Bielagus*, 149 N.H. 635 (emphasis added).

55. *Simoneau*, 130 N.H. 466.

56. *Bielagus*, 149 N.H. 635.

57. *Simoneau*, 130 N.H. 466.

58. *Bielagus*, 149 N.H. 635.

59. No. 06-CV-66-SM, 2007 U.S. Dist. LEXIS 62818, *12 (D.N.H. 2007).

60. N.H. Rev. Stat. Ann. § 507:16.

61. *Brannigan v. Usitalo*, 134 N.H. 50 (1991); *West v. Bell Helicopter Textron, Inc.*, Dkt. No. 10-cv-214-JL (D.N.H. Sept. 9, 2013) (ruling that a plaintiff could not recover damages for "shortened life expectancy" because New Hampshire does not recognize that type of damages).

62. N.H. Rev. Stat. Ann. § 507:7-e, I(b); § 507:7-e, I(c); *Energy North Gas, Inc. v. Century Indem. Co.*, No. 99-CV-049-JD, 2007 U.S. Dist. LEXIS 19445, *4-5 (D.N.H. 2007) (explaining that "[j]oint and several liability means that one defendant is liable for the entire judgment despite the existence of others who might also be liable, and the burden of recovering from those others is on that defendant"); *Tiberghein v. B.R. Jones Roofing Co.*, 156 N.H. 110 (2007) (holding that "a defendant is jointly and severally liable and entitled to a credit for the settlement received unless there is a finding of minimal fault").

63. N.H. Rev. Stat. Ann. § 507:7-e, I(b).

64. N.H. Rev. Stat. Ann. § 524:1-a.

65. N.H. Rev. Stat. Ann. § 524:1-b.

66. N.H. Rev. Stat. Ann. § 336:1; *see also Metro. Prop. & Liab. Ins. Co. v. Ralph*, 138 N.H. 378 (1994).

67. N.H. Rev. Stat. Ann. Chapter § 281-A.

68. N.H. Rev. Stat. Ann. § 281-A:8, I(a); *Thompson v. Forest*, 136 N.H. 215 (1992); *William H. Field Co. v. Nuroco Woodwork*, 115 N.H. 632 (1975).

69. *Ryan v. Hiller*, 138 N.H. 348 (1994).

70. *Quinn v. National Gypsum Co.*, 124 N.H. 418 (1983).

71. *Ritch v. AM Gen. Corp.*, Dkt. No. 93-451-SD (D.N.H. Nov. 17, 1997); *McNeil v. Nissan Motor Co., Ltd.*, 365 F. Supp. 2d 206 (D.N.H. 2005).

72. *McNeil*, 365 F. Supp. 2d 206.

73. *McNeil*, 365 F. Supp. 2d 206.

74. 147 N.H. 150 (2001).

75. 118 N.H. 802 (1978).

76. *See also Bartlett v. Mutual Pharm. Co., Inc.*, Civil No. 08-CV-00358-JL, 2010 U.S. Dist. LEXIS 84924, *3-4 (D.N.H. Aug. 12, 2010) (explaining that under New Hampshire law "a plaintiff may prove a defect by showing that the product's risks outweigh its benefits, making it unreasonably dangerous to consumers"), overruled on other grounds by *Mutual Pharm. Co. v. Bartlett*, 133 S. Ct. 2466 (2013).

NEW JERSEY

A. CAUSES OF ACTION

The Products Liability Act (the Act) subsumes common law claims and basically is the sole basis of relief for harm caused by defective products.[1] The Act was not, however, intended to codify all issues of product liability law. For example, the Act does not address certain defenses such as product misuse.[2] Product liability lawsuits include claims based on strict liability, negligence, and breach of warranty. A state cause of action is commenced in a manner consistent with federal practice, except a response is required within 35 days after service of the summons and complaint.[3]

B. STATUTES OF LIMITATION

A cause of action for personal injuries must be brought within two years after the cause of action accrues, regardless of whether the claim is based on strict liability, negligence, or warranty, except for actions by or on behalf of a minor for medical malpractice where an injury is sustained at birth[4] and in certain wrongful death actions.[5]

Although strict liability and negligence claims generally accrue at the time of injury, New Jersey courts apply a rather liberal "discovery rule." The discovery rule tolls the limitations period where a plaintiff was not, and reasonably could not have been, aware of the underlying factual basis for a cause of action.[6] The trial judge determines the applicability of the discovery rule at a pretrial hearing.[7] The limitations period is also tolled for minors.[8]

A cause of action for property damage must be brought within six years, unless it is a warranty claim, which must be brought within four years from the time the product is delivered.[9] However, if a warranty explicitly extends to future performance then the cause of action accrues when the breach of duty to perform is or should have been discovered.[10] Claims for injuries arising from improvements to real property have a ten-year statute of repose, running from the date of the improvement.[11] The statute of repose has limited application to manufacturers.[12]

New Jersey's courts have liberally applied the doctrine of equitable tolling based on a defendant's conduct, such as trickery,[13] concealing or withholding information,[14] or intentionally protracting settlement negotiations,[15] or based on the doctrine of substantial compliance, *i.e.* when the defendant had notice of the suit prior to the expiration of the statute[16] or when plaintiff timely filed the complaint in another forum.[17]

C. STRICT LIABILITY

1. The Standard

Under New Jersey law, manufacturers and sellers are strictly liable for damages resulting from the use of their products if they fail to produce and distribute products that are reasonably fit, suitable, and safe when used for their intended or reasonably foreseeable purposes.[18] Although the Act is intended to clarify certain issues related to product liability claims, it does not purport to be a comprehensive codification of all matters.[19] It applies to all actions for harm caused by products except actions based on breach of express warranties[20] and environmental tort actions.[21]

2. Definition of "Defect"

A plaintiff may show a "defect" by establishing: (1) a manufacturing defect; (2) a design defect; and/or (3) an inadequate warning. With respect to a manufacturing defect, the product is measured against the same product made in accordance with the manufacturer's standards.[22]

In a design defect case, the trier of fact engages in a "risk-utility" analysis weighing the following factors: (1) usefulness and desirability of product aspects; (2) the safety aspects of the product; (3) availability of substitutes; (4) ability to eliminate its unsafe characteristics without great expense or impairing usefulness; (5) user's ability to avoid danger; (6) user's anticipated awareness of inherent dangers and their avoidability; and (7) feasibility of spreading loss. For a plaintiff to succeed on a design defect claim, the plaintiff must show either that the product's risks outweighed its utility or that a practical and feasible, safer, alternative design existed that would have reduced or prevented the harm.[23] The Act converted three elements into absolute affirmative defenses: state of the art; obvious-danger/consumer expectations; and unavoidably unsafe products. The question in a strict liability design defect case is whether, assuming that the manufacturer knew of the defect in the product, he acted in a reasonably prudent manner in marketing the product or in providing the warnings given.[24]

In an inadequate warnings case, the Act defines an adequate warning[25] and knowledge of the defect is imputed to the manufacturer.[26]

3. Causation

A plaintiff must prove that the product was defective, that the defect existed when the product left the manufacturer's control, and that the defect proximately caused injuries to the plaintiff, who was a reasonably foreseeable or intended user.[27] New Jersey has relaxed the standard for determining medical causation in several tort litigation fields.[28]

4. Contributory Negligence/Assumption of Risk

Plaintiff's assumption of risk type negligence is a comparative defense, *i.e.*, plaintiff's conduct amounts to voluntarily and unreasonably proceeding to encounter a known danger, which is the specific risk alleged to have existed in the product. Plaintiff's negligence is not a defense if it consists of a mere failure to discover a defect in the product or to guard against the possibility of its existence.[29] However, plaintiff's conduct may be admissible if it relates to the issue of causation.[30] An employee engaged in an assigned task cannot be held comparatively negligent, because the employee has no meaningful choice.[31]

5. **Obvious Danger/Consumer Expectation**

An open and obvious danger/consumer expectations defense is an absolute defense to products liability claims under the Act. This absolute defense is not available to the defendant in two circumstances: if the product is workplace equipment or if the danger can "feasibly be eliminated without impairing the usefulness of the product."[32]

6. **Entities Liable**

The Act defines a manufacturer as anyone who designs, formulates, produces, creates, makes, packages, labels or constructs a product.[33] Under New Jersey law, strict liability extends not only to those who manufacture a defective product, but also to any party in the chain of distribution, including distributors, retailers,[34] and lessors.[35] However, these entities can relieve themselves of liability by filing an affidavit correctly identifying a solvent manufacturer of the product that can be served in the United States.[36] A party in the chain of distribution that files such an affidavit can still be held liable if it has exercised significant control over the design, manufacture, packaging, or labeling of the product; knew or should have known of the defect; or created the defect in the product.[37]

Neither the Act nor common law strict liability extends to an occasional seller who is not in the business of supplying such products.[38] Strict liability may apply in hybrid transactions involving the provision of a product with services.[39] A component part manufacturer can be held strictly liable for injuries caused by a defect in that part, provided that the part did not undergo a substantial change after leaving its maker's control.[40] Manufacturers will not be held liable for defects created or caused by someone further down the distribution line.[41]

7. **Inherently Dangerous/Unavoidably Unsafe Products**

According to the Act, a manufacturer or seller will not be held liable under a design defect theory if the harm was caused by an unsafe aspect of the product that is an inherent characteristic of the product and if the harm would be recognized by the ordinary person.[42] A manufacturer will also not be held liable for an unavoidably unsafe aspect of a product that is accompanied by adequate warnings.[43]

8. **Successor Liability**

   If the successor corporation acquires all or substantially all of the manufacturing assets of the predecessor corporation and continues to manufacture essentially the same product line, it may be subject to strict liability for injuries caused by defects in the product. This is so even if the product was manufactured and sold by the predecessor, especially if the predecessor is no longer financially viable and where the successor corporation benefits from trading its product line on the name of the predecessor, taking advantage of its goodwill, business reputation, and established customers.[44]

9. **Market Share Liability**

   New Jersey has refused to apply market share liability in product liability cases against manufacturers of vaccines, pharmaceuticals and asbestos,[45] but has commented that it may not be inhospitable to market share liability in an appropriate context.[46]

10. **Privity**

    Privity is not required for recovery under strict products liability.[47]

11. **Failure to Warn/Inadequate Warning**

    In a failure to warn case, the alleged product defect is the absence of a warning or an adequate warning to unsuspecting users that the product can potentially cause injury.[48] When a manufacturer requires the use of a component part, the manufacturer has a duty to warn of reasonably anticipated dangers posed by that component even as to replacement parts manufactured by others.[49] Plaintiff is required to prove that the absence of a warning was a proximate cause of his harm and there is a rebuttable presumption that plaintiff would have heeded the warning.[50] An "adequate product warning or instruction" is defined by the Act and is evaluated in terms of what the manufacturer knew at the time it produced the product and what it should have known based on reasonably available information, taking into account the ordinary knowledge common to anticipated users of the product.[51] Ordinarily, the question of whether a warning is adequate is one for a jury to resolve but in some situations may be determined as a matter of law.[52] A product seller or manufacturer may nullify an otherwise suitable warning by promoting, advertising, or encouraging a specific use of a product that it simultaneously warns against.[53]

    The Act creates a rebuttable presumption of an adequate warning in the case of a drug, device, or food product approved or prescribed by the Food and Drug Administration (FDA).[54] In pharmaceutical litigation, absent "deliberate concealment or nondisclosure of after-acquired knowledge of harmful effects" compliance with FDA standards is virtually dispositive.[55] An additional exception to the presumption may apply where there is substantial evidence of economically driven manipulation of the post-market regulatory process.[56]

New Jersey's intermediate appellate court has rejected the Third Circuit's conclusion that where the FDA publicly rejects the need for a warning with regard to an FDA-approved pharmaceutical label, a failure to warn claim is preempted, but accepts that the Act's punitive damages provision is preempted by federal law.[57]

12. **Post-Sale Duty to Warn**

When a manufacturer fails to include a warning on a product, but subsequently learns, or should have learned, of the dangers associated with the product (or if the product contains an inadequate warning to address the later-discovered danger), the manufacturer owes a duty to warn of the dangers as soon as reasonably feasible.[58]

13. **Learned Intermediary Doctrine**

A pharmaceutical manufacturer generally discharges its duty to warn the ultimate user of prescription drugs or devices by supplying physicians with information about the dangerous propensities of the drug.[59] This rule, known as the learned intermediary doctrine, does not apply where the manufacturer directly markets the prescription drug or device to consumers, or in cases involving mass inoculation or oral contraceptives.[60]

14. **Substantial Alteration/Misuse**

A manufacturer will not be held strictly liable if there were substantial alterations of the product that caused injury, and if those alterations were not reasonably foreseeable.[61] Plaintiff has the burden of proving there was no misuse of the product or that the misuse was objectively foreseeable.[62] Accordingly, misuse of a product is not an affirmative defense in a products liability case.

15. **State of the Art**

Under the Act, "state-of-the-art" is an absolute defense to claims based on design defects.[63] A defendant asserting this defense must prove only the technological state-of-the-art at the time the product left its control, *i.e.*, there was no practical or technologically feasible alternative design that both would have prevented the harm and not substantially impaired the function of the product. It remains plaintiff's burden to prove non-conformity to the feasible technology.[64] A defendant challenging only the practicality of the alternative device, and not its technological feasibility, has not asserted the state-of-the-art defense and bears no burden.[65]

16. **Malfunction/Indeterminate Product Defect Test**

Malfunctioning of a product in the absence of abnormal use or a reasonable secondary cause is evidence of a defect.[66] New Jersey has adopted the indeterminate product defect test of the Restatement (Third) of Torts. Plaintiff need not prove a specific defect if the incident is of the kind that ordinarily occurs as a result of a product defect, and if the incident was not solely the result of causes other than a defect existing when the product left the defendant's control.[67]

17. Standards and Governmental Regulations

Although a defendant's compliance with legislative enactments, administrative regulations, or industry safety codes is admissible, it is not conclusive as to absence of defect or negligence.[68]

18. Other Accidents

Evidence of prior substantially similar accidents or occurrences is admissible in product liability actions to prove a defect.[69]

19. Misrepresentation/Fraud

The Act subsumes Consumer Fraud Act claims based on harm caused by a product.[70] Some courts have concluded that the Act also subsumes common law fraud and misrepresentation claims.[71]

20. Destruction or Loss of a Product

Traditional remedies such as an adverse inference and discovery sanctions, including counsel fees and dismissal of the action as a last resort, may be available against a party to an action who intentionally destroys or conceals evidence.[72] Negligent spoliation may result in sanctions, but the spoilator's state of mind has a bearing on the remedy to be applied,[73] as may the timing of a request for production.[74]

New Jersey has not recognized a separate tort action for intentional or negligent spoliation; however, intentional spoliation may give rise to a cause of action for fraudulent concealment.[75] In order to support such a claim, the plaintiff must establish: (1) a legal obligation to disclose evidence in connection with an existing or pending litigation; (2) that the evidence was material to the litigation; (3) that plaintiff could not reasonably have obtained access to the evidence from another source; (4) that defendant intentionally withheld, altered or destroyed the evidence with purpose to disrupt the litigation; and (5) damages in the underlying action proximately caused by defendant's acts.[76]

New Jersey appellate courts have suggested that a remedy for negligent spoliation may be available by applying traditional negligence concepts if a defendant in the underlying case, or a third party, owed a duty to preserve the evidence.[77] Such a duty can be established if: (1) defendant had knowledge of a potential lawsuit and accepted responsibility for preserving the evidence; (2) defendant voluntarily undertook to preserve the evidence and plaintiff reasonably and detrimentally relied thereon; (3) defendant agreed with plaintiff to preserve the evidence; or (4) plaintiff made a specific request to defendant to preserve a particular item.[78]

Causes of action for concealment or negligence are inapplicable where the spoliation is by a plaintiff or his agent in the context of a defendant's ability to defend a lawsuit;[79] instead, the traditional remedies discussed will apply.[80]

21. Economic Loss

The Act embodies the economic loss doctrine by limiting recovery to "physical damage to property, other than the product itself."[81] A consumer cannot maintain a cause of action sounding in strict products liability or negligence to recover damages solely for the economic loss resulting from a defect in the product.[82]

22. Crashworthiness

The crashworthiness doctrine imposes strict liability on a manufacturer for injuries sustained in an accident involving a design or manufacturing defect that enhanced injuries but did not cause the accident. Plaintiff bears the burden of proving that the alleged defect was a substantial factor increasing the harm beyond that which would have resulted absent the defect. The burden then shifts to the defendant to prove apportionment. An indivisible harm such as death may be apportioned between two or more causes.[83]

D. NEGLIGENCE

Contributory negligence is a defense; however, the doctrine of comparative negligence is applied unless the plaintiff is more than 50 percent at fault. If plaintiff is found to be 51 percent or more at fault, recovery is barred.[84]

E. BREACH OF WARRANTY

The principles underlying strict liability and implied warranty are identical in New Jersey.[85] Strict liability theories impose warranty obligations without the need for contractual privity.[86] The value of the damages in a non-personal injury warranty claim is determined by prorating the amount of damages claimed over the life of the warranty.[87]

F. DAMAGES

1. Limitations on Compensatory Damages

A plaintiff may present to the jury the total amount of medical expenses required for his examination, treatment and care, but may only recover the fair and reasonable value of such medical expenses.[88] However, the collateral source rule[89] bars health carriers[90] that expend funds on behalf of covered persons from recouping such payments through subrogation or contract reimbursement.[91] Accordingly, the trial judge will reduce the verdict by the amount paid by sources other than joint tortfeasors, workers' compensation carriers, or the proceeds from life insurance policies.[92] An exception to the collateral source rule is employer self-funded ERISA health plans.[93]

2. Punitive Damages

Punitive damages must be specifically pled in the complaint.[94] A defendant shall not be liable for more than five times the amount of compensatory damages or $350,000, whichever is greater.[95] In order to recover punitive damages, the plaintiff must prove, by clear and convincing evidence, actual malice or a wanton and willful disregard of persons who foreseeably might be harmed.[96] A case involving punitive damages must be bifurcated, with compensatory damages being determined in the first stage and punitive damages, if warranted, determined in the second stage.[97]

Punitive damages are not permissible for products that have been licensed or approved by the Food and Drug Administration, except where the manufacturer knowingly withheld or misrepresented material, relevant information required to be submitted under the agency's regulations.[98]

G. PRE- AND POST-JUDGMENT INTEREST

In tort actions, including products liability actions, the court shall include in the judgment simple interest from the date of the institution of the action or from a date six months after the date the cause of action arises, whichever is later, provided that in exceptional cases the court may suspend the running of such pre-judgment interest.[99] Pre-judgment interest may not be awarded on a punitive damages verdict.[100] Post-judgment interest shall apply to judgments, awards and orders for the payment of money, taxed costs and counsel fees. The annual rate of interest varies and is published in the Court Rules.[101] Post-judgment interest may be included in the calculation of an attorney's contingent fee.[102]

H. EMPLOYER IMMUNITY FROM SUIT

By statute, employers are generally immune from suit by an injured employee.[103] However, an employer may be liable under the "intentional wrong" exception to the workers' compensation exclusivity rule, if the employer objectively knew that his actions were substantially certain to result in injury or death to the employee and the resulting injury and circumstances of its infliction are more than a fact of life of industrial employment.[104]

The dual capacity doctrine has not found favor in New Jersey.[105] The statute does not preclude an employer from assuming a contractual duty to indemnify a third party through an express agreement. To be entitled to indemnification, the third party must be without fault.[106]

I. **JOINT AND SEVERAL LIABILITY**

1. **The Rule**

    Under the New Jersey Comparative Negligence Act, the percentage of liability is apportioned by the factfinder as to all named parties who have been found negligent or strictly liable based on each party's contribution to causation of the event that produced the injury.[107] The plaintiff's negligence, unless assumption of risk type negligence,[108] can be compared only to that of the negligent defendants, and does not reduce the comparative fault of strictly liable defendants, who may be responsible for plaintiff's share.[109] In some circumstances, the burden of allocating fault will shift to the defendant.[110]

    A party may seek recovery of the entire verdict from any party found to be 60 percent or more responsible for the total damages. A party may recover only the percentage of damages directly attributable to that party's negligence or fault from any other party determined to be less than 60 percent responsible for the total damages.[111]

2. **Contribution**

    A joint tortfeasor who is compelled to pay more than his percentage share may seek contribution from other tortfeasors who are liable for plaintiff's injuries.[112]

3. **Effect of Settlement**

    Under New Jersey law, a nonsettling defendant does not have a viable crossclaim for contribution against a settling defendant, however, claims for indemnification against a settling defendant survive.

    Even though a nonsettling defendant's crossclaim for contribution against the settling tortfeasor will be dismissed as a matter of law, the nonsettling defendant is entitled to a credit reflecting the settlor's fair share of the amount of the verdict.[113]

J. **FICTITIOUS PARTY PRACTICE**

   A plaintiff may name a defendant in the complaint under a fictitious name if, despite diligent efforts, the defendant's true name and identity is unknown, as long as plaintiff includes an appropriate description sufficient for identification.[114] Failure to use the fictitious pleading device may result in the action being time-barred, if suit is instituted against a party after the statute of limitations has run.[115] To be entitled to the benefit of the rule, a plaintiff must also act with diligence to determine an unknown defendant's identity and to amend the complaint to correctly identify that defendant.[116]

K. **STATUTES**

   Relevant statutes for product liability actions include the Products Liability Act,[117] Punitive Damages Act,[118] Workers' Compensation Act,[119] Comparative Negligence Act,[120] Joint Tortfeasors Contribution Law,[121] collateral source rule,[122] statutes of limitations,[123] and the commercial code section when a breach of warranty is alleged.[124] Jurisdiction in New Jersey is governed by Court rule rather than statute.[125]

New Jersey state courts generally follow *Model Civil Jury Charges*.[126]

Gerhard P. Dietrich
Amy L. Hansell
Ward Greenberg Heller & Reidy LLP
701 East Gate Drive, Suite 220
Mt. Laurel, New Jersey 08054
(856) 866-8920
(Fax) (856) 866-8761
E-mail: gdietrich@wardgreenberg.com
Web site: www.wardgreenberg.com

ENDNOTES - NEW JERSEY

1. N.J. Stat. Ann. § 2A:58C-1 through 58C-11; *Dewey v. R.J. Reynolds Tobacco Co.*, 121 N.J. 69, 577 A.2d 1239 (1990); *Sinclair v. Merck*, 195 N.J. 51, 948 A.2d 587 (2008); *In re Lead Paint Litig.*, 191 N.J. 405, 924 A.2d 484 (2007); *Gupta v. Asha Enters., L.L.C.*, 422 N.J. Super. 136, 27 A.3d 953 (App. Div. 2011); *Ramos v. Silent Hoist & Crane Co.*, 256 N.J. Super. 467, 607 A.2d 667 (App. Div. July 18, 1992); *Tirrell v. Navistar Int'l, Inc.*, 248 N.J. Super. 390, 591 A.2d 643 (App. Div. 1991); *Canty v. Ever-Last Supply Co.*, 296 N.J. Super. 68, 685 A.2d 1365 (Law Div. 1996). *See also Port Auth. of N.Y. & N.J. v. Arcadian Corp.*, 189 F.3d 305 (3d Cir. 1999); *Worrell v. Elliott & Frantz*, 799 F. Supp. 2d 343 (D.N.J. 2011). Express warranty claims are preserved by the Act. N.J. Stat. Ann. § 2A:58C-1b(3).

2. *Jurado v. W. Gear Works*, 131 N.J. 375, 619 A.2d 1312 (1993).

3. N.J. Court Rules 4:2-2, 4:6-1.

4. N.J. Stat. Ann. § 2A:14-2 (exception is applicable to cases accruing on or after June 7, 2004).

5. The Wrongful Death Act requires that such an action "shall be commenced within 2 years after the death of the decedent, and not thereafter," except in limited circumstances where death resulted from murder or manslaughter. N.J. Stat. Ann. 2A:31-3 (exceptions applicable to cases accruing on or after November 17, 2000). *See Lafage v. Jani*, 166 N.J. 412, 420, 766 A.2d 1066, 1070 (2001).

6. *See, e.g., Kendall v. Hoffman-La Roche, Inc.*, 209 N.J. 173, 36 A.3d 541 (2012); *Graves v. Church & Dwight Co.*, 225 N.J. Super. 49, 541 A.2d 725 (App. Div. 1988), *aff'd*, 115 N.J. 256, 558 A.2d 463 (1989) (per curiam); *Vispisiano v. Ashland Chem. Co.*, 107 N.J. 416, 527 A.2d 66 (1987); *Tevis v. Tevis*, 79 N.J. 422, 400 A.2d 1189 (1979). *See also Cipollone v. Liggett Group, Inc.*, 893 F.2d 541 (3d Cir. 1990), *cert. granted*, 499 U.S. 935, 111 S. Ct. 1386 (1991), *aff'd in part, rev'd in part*, 505 U.S. 504, 112 S. Ct. 2608 (1992).

7. *Lopez v. Swyer*, 62 N.J. 267, 275-76, 300 A.2d 563 (1973).

8. *Lafage v. Jani*, 166 N.J. 412, 420, 766 A.2d 1066, 1070 (2001); *Mansour v. Leviton Mfg. Co., Inc.*, 382 N.J. Super. 594, 890 A.2d 336 (App. Div. 2006).

9. N.J. Stat. Ann. § 2A:14-1; N.J. Stat. Ann. § 12A:2-725; *Yttro Corp. v. X-Ray Marketing, Ass'n*, 233 N.J. Super. 347, 559 A.2d 3 (App. Div. 1989); *Biocraft Lab., Inc. v. USM Corp.*, 163 N.J. Super. 570, 395 A.2d 521 (App. Div. 1978); *Raskin v. Shulton, Inc.*, 92 N.J. Super. 315, 223 A.2d 284 (App. Div. 1966).

10. N.J. Stat. Ann. § 12A:2-725(2); *Poli v. DaimlerChrysler Corp.*, 349 N.J. Super. 169, 793 A.2d 104 (App. Div. 2002).

11. N.J. Stat. Ann. § 2A:14-1.1. This limitation applies to injuries to real or personal property, injuries to the person, and bodily injuries or wrongful death. It preserves causes of action against those in possession or control.

12. *Dziewiecki v. Bakula*, 180 N.J. 528, 853 A.2d 234 (2004); *Cherilus v. Fed. Express*, 435 N.J. Super. 172, 87 A.3d 269 (App. Div. 2013); *State v. Perini Corp.*, 425 N.J. Super. 62, 39 A.3d 918 (App. Div. 2012), *appeal granted*, 210 N.J. 476, 45 A.3d 981 (2012).

13. *Villalobos v. Fava*, 342 N.J. Super. 38, 775 A.2d 700 (App. Div. 2001).

14. *Bernoskie v. Zarinsky*, 383 N.J. Super. 127, 890 A.2d 1013 (App. Div. 2006).

15. *Friedman v. Friendly Ice Cream Co.*, 133 N.J. Super. 333, 336 A.2d 493 (App. Div. 1975).

16. *Zaccardi v. Becker*, 88 N.J. 245, 440 A.2d 1329 (1982); *Estate of Vida v. City of Garfield*, 330 N.J. Super. 225, 749 A.2d 391 (App. Div. 2000). *But see Troum v. Newark Beth Israel Med. Ctr.*, 338 N.J. Super. 1, 768 A.2d 177 (App. Div. 2001) (the doctrine did not apply when prior suit alerted defendant only in the most ephemeral sense and was voluntarily dismissed before discovery proceedings completed).

17. *Galligan v. Estfield Ctr. Serv., Inc.*, 82 N.J. 188, 412 A.2d 122 (1990); *Negron v. Llarena*, 156 N.J. 296, 716 A.2d 1158 (1998); *Mitzner v. W. Ridgelawn Cemetery*, 311 N.J. Super. 233, 709 A.2d 825 (App. Div. 1998); *Bernstein v. Bd. of Trustees of Teachers' Pension & Annuity Fund*, 151 N.J. Super. 71, 376 A.2d 563 (App. Div. 1977).

18. N.J. Stat. Ann. § 2A:58C-2; *Zaza v. Marquess & Nell, Inc.*, 144 N.J. 34, 675 A.2d 620 (1996); *Feldman v. Lederle Lab.*, 125 N.J. 117, 592 A.2d 1176 (1991); *Soler v. Castmaster, Div. of H.P.M. Corp.*, 98 N.J. 137, 484 A.2d 1225 (1984); *Navarro v. George Koch & Sons, Inc.*, 211 N.J. Super. 558, 512 A.2d 507 (App. Div. 1986); *Molino v. B.F. Goodrich Co.*, 261 N.J. Super. 85, 617 A.2d 1235 (App. Div. 1992).

19. N.J. Stat. Ann. § 2A:58C-1 through 58C-8; *Zaza v. Marquess & Nell, Inc.*, 144 N.J. 34, 675 A.2d 620 (1996); *Fabian v. Minster Mach. Co.*, 258 N.J. Super. 261, 609 A.2d 487 (App. Div. 1992).

20. N.J. Stat. Ann. § 2A:58C-1b(3).

21. N.J. Stat. Ann. §§ 2A:58C-1b(3), 2A:58C-1(4), and 58C-6; *James v. Bessemer Processing Co.*, 155 N.J. 279, 714 A.2d 898 (1998).

22. N.J. Stat. Ann. § 2A:58C-2.

23. *Lewis v. Am. Cyanamid Co.*, 155 N.J. 544, 715 A.2d 967 (1998), citing *Dewey v. R.J. Reynolds Tobacco Co.*, 121 N.J. 69, 74, 577 A.2d 1239 (1990), *Smith v. Keller Ladder Co.*, 275 N.J. Super. 280, 284-85, 645 A.2d 1269 (App. Div. 1994), and Restatement (Third) of Torts: Product Liability § 2 cmt. f; *Cavanaugh v. Skil Corp.*, 331 N.J. Super. 134, 751 A.2d 564 (App. Div. 1999).

24. *Lewis v. Am. Cyanamid Co.*, 155 N.J. 544, 715 A.2d 967 (1998); *Zaza v. Marquess & Nell, Inc.*, 144 N.J. 34, 675 A.2d 620 (1996); *Roberts v. Rich Foods, Inc.*, 139 N.J. 365, 654 A.2d 1365 (1995); *Johansen v. Makita U.S.A., Inc.*, 128 N.J. 86, 607 A.2d 637 (1992); *McGarvey v. G.I. Joe Septic Serv., Inc.*, 293 N.J. Super. 129, 679 A.2d 733 (App. Div. 1996); *Adelman v. Lupo*, 291 N.J. Super. 207, 677 A.2d 230 (App. Div. 1996); *Fabian v. Minster Mach. Co.*, 258 N.J. Super. 261, 609 A.2d 487 (App. Div. 1992).

25. "An adequate product warning or instruction is one that a reasonably prudent person in the same or similar circumstances would have provided with respect to the danger and that communicates adequate information on the dangers and safe use of the product, taking into account the characteristics of, and the ordinary knowledge common to, the persons by whom the product is intended to be used . . ." N.J. Stat. Ann. § 2A:58C-4; *Zaza v. Marquess & Nell, Inc.*, 144 N.J. 34, 675 A.2d 620 (1996); *Feldman v. Lederle Lab.*, 97 N.J. 429, 479 A.2d 374 (1984).

26. *Zaza v. Marquess & Nell, Inc.*, 144 N.J. 34, 675 A.2d 620 (1996); *Malin v. Union Carbide Corp.*, 219 N.J. Super. 428, 530 A.2d 794 (App. Div. 1987).

27. N.J. Stat. Ann. § 2A:58C-2; *Fedorczyk v. Caribbean Cruise Lines, Ltd.*, 82 F.3d 69 (3d Cir. 1996); *Myrlak v. Port Auth. of New York & New Jersey*, 157 N.J. 84, 723 A.2d 45 (1999); *Grassis v. Johns-Manville Corp.*, 248 N.J. Super. 446, 591 A.2d 671 (App. Div. 1991); *O'Brien v. Muskin Corp.*, 94 N.J. 169, 463 A.2d 298 (1983). See also *Reiff v. Convergent Techs.*, 957 F. Supp. 573 (D.N.J. 1997); *Brown v. United States Stove Co.*, 98 N.J. 155, 171-75, 484 A.2d 1234 (1984) (manufacturer relieved of liability if superseding intervening cause); *Coffman v. Keene Corp.*, 133 N.J. 581, 608-09, 628 A.2d 710 (1993) (employer's negligent maintenance of an industrial machine may constitute superseding cause).

28. *Kemp v. State*, 174 N.J. 412, 809 A.2d 77 (2002) (rubella vaccination); *James v. Bessemer Processing Co.*, 155 N.J. 279, 297-98, 714 A.2d 898 (1998) (petroleum products); *Landrigan v. Celotex Corp.*, 127 N.J. 404, 413, 605 A.2d 1079 (1992) (asbestos); *Rubanick v. Witco Chem. Corp.*, 125 N.J. 421, 434, 593 A.2d 733 (1991) (polychlorinated biphenyls). In *Rubanick* and *Kemp*, the courts held that a theory of causation that had not yet reached general acceptance in the scientific community may be found to be sufficiently reliable if based on a sound, adequately-founded scientific methodology, involving data and information of the type reasonably relied on by experts in the scientific field. *Rubanick*, 125 N.J. 449; 174 N.J. 430.

29. *Lewis v. American Cyanamid*, 155 N.J. 544, 715 A.2d 967 (1988). *See also Coffman v. Keene Corp.*, 133 N.J. 581, 628 A.2d 710 (1993); *Cartel Capital Corp. v. Fireco of N.J.*, 81 N.J. 548, 410 A.2d 674 (1980); *Fabian v. Minster Mach. Co.*, 258 N.J. Super. 261, 609 A.2d 487 (App. Div. 1992); *Ramos v. Silent Hoist & Crane Co.*, 256 N.J. Super. 467, 607 A.2d 667 (App. Div. 1992).

30. *Wallace v. Ford Motor Co.*, 318 N.J. Super. 427, 723 A.2d 1226 (App. Div. 1999); *Jurado v. Western Gear Works*, 131 N.J. 375, 619 A.2d 1312 (1993).

31. *Suter v. San Angelo Foundry & Mach. Co.*, 81 N.J. 150, 406 A.2d 140 (1979). In *Suter*, the court held that in "workplace accidents" defendants may not introduce evidence of plaintiff's comparative negligence. *See also Grier v. Cochran W. Corp.*, 308 N.J. Super. 308, 324, 705 A.2d 1262 (App. Div. 1998); *Johansen v. Makita U.S.A., Inc.*, 128 N.J. 86, 607 A.2d 637 (1992) (plaintiff's conduct not defense to strict liability or relevant to issue of injury avoidance but introduction permitted if specific manner of operation alleged sole cause of accident); *Cavanaugh v. Skil Corp.*, 164 N.J. 1, 751 A.2d 518 (2000) (noting that *Suter* is not limited to factory settings). *But see Butler v. PPG Indus., Inc.*, 201 N.J. Super. 558 (App. Div. 1985); New Jersey Civil Jury Charge 5.40J.

32. N.J. Stat. Ann. § 2A:58C-3a(2); *Roberts v. Rich Foods, Inc.*, 139 N.J. 365, 375, 654 A.2d 1365 (1995). In *Roberts*, the New Jersey Supreme Court held that in order to preclude the defendant from using the 3a(2) absolute defense, the plaintiff must prove that the product is workplace equipment or that the danger of the product could feasibly be eliminated without impairing the usefulness of the product. *See also McWilliams v. Yamaha Motor Corp., USA*, 987 F.2d 200 (3d Cir. 1993); *Dewey v. R.J. Reynolds Tobacco Co.*, 121 N.J. 69, 577 A.2d 1239 (1990); *Mercer Mut. Ins. Co. v. Proudman*, 396 N.J. Super. 309, 933 A.2d 967 (App. Div. 2007); *Mathews v. Univ. Loft Co.*, 387 N.J. Super. 349, 903 A.2d 1120 (App. Div. 2006); *Fabian v. Minster Mach. Co.*, 258 N.J. Super. 261, 609 A.2d 487 (App. Div. 1992).

33. N.J. Stat. Ann. § 2A:58C-8; *Smith v. Alza Corp.*, 400 N.J. Super. 529, 948 A.2d 686 (App. Div. 2008); *Hinojo v. New Jersey Mfr. Ins. Co.*, 353 N.J. Super. 261, 802 A.2d 551 (App. Div. 2002).

34. *Promaulayko v. Johns Manville Sales Corp.*, 116 N.J. 505, 562 A.2d 202 (1989); *Michalko v. Cooke Color & Chem. Corp.*, 91 N.J. 386, 451 A.2d 179 (1982); *Smith v. Alza Corp.*, 948 N.J. Super. 529, 948 A.2d 686 (App. Div. 2008); *Ramos v. Silent Hoist & Crane Co.*, 256 N.J. Super. 467, 607 A.2d 667 (App. Div. 1992).

35. *Cintrone v. Hertz Truck Leasing & Rental Servs.*, 45 N.J. 434, 212 A.2d 769 (1965); *Santiago v. E.W. Bliss Div., Gulf & W. Mfg. Co.*, 201 N.J. Super. 205, 492 A.2d 1089 (App. Div. 1985).

36. N.J. Stat. Ann. § 2A:58C-9 (L. 1995, c. 141) (effective June 29, 1995). *Claypotch v. Heller, Inc.* 360 N.J. Super. 472, 823 A.2d 844 (App. Div. 2003). *See Hinojo v.*

New Jersey Mfr. Ins. Co., 353 N.J. Super. 261, 269 n.1, 802 A.2d 551, 555 n.1 (App. Div. 2002).

37. N.J. Stat. Ann. § 2A:58C-9; *Smith v. Alza Corp.*, 948 N.J. Super. 529, 948 A.2d 686 (App. Div. 2008).

38. *Agurto v. Guhr*, 381 N.J. Super. 519, 526-27, 887 A.2d 159, 163 (App. Div. 2005) (quoting *Santiago v. E.W. Bliss Div., Gulf & W. Mfg. Co.*, 201 N.J. Super. 205, 216, 492 A.2d 1089, 1095 (App. Div. 1985)). *See also* N.J. Stat. Ann. § 2A:58C-8; *Allen v. Nicole, Inc.*, 172 N.J. Super. 442, 445-46, 412 A.2d 824, 826 (Law Div. 1980). Note that an occasional seller may still be liable under traditional negligence theories. *See Santiago*, 201 N.J. Super. at 223, 492 A.2d at 1099.

39. *Michalko v. Cooke Color & Chem. Corp.*, 91 N.J. 386, 451 A.2d 179 (1982); *Newmark v. Gimbel's Inc.*, 54 N.J. 585, 258 A.2d 697 (1969).

40. *Zaza v. Marquess & Nell, Inc.*, 144 N.J. 34, 675 A.2d 620 (1996); *McGarvey v. G.I. Joe Septic Service, Inc.*, 293 N.J. Super. 129, 679 A.2d 733 (App. Div. 1996); *Michalko v. Cooke Color & Chem. Corp.*, 91 N.J. 386, 451 A.2d 179 (1982); *Boyle v. Ford Motor Co.*, 399 N.J. Super. 18, 942 A.2d 850 (App. Div. 2008); *Seeley v. Cincinnati Shaper Co., Ltd.*, 256 N.J. Super. 1, 606 A.2d 378 (App. Div. 1992); *Ramos v. Silent Hoist & Crane Co.*, 256 N.J. Super. 467, 607 A.2d 667 (App. Div. 1992).

41. *Miltz v. Borroughs-Shelving, a Div. of Lear Siegler, Inc.*, 203 N.J. Super. 451, 497 A.2d 516 (App. Div. 1985).

42. N.J. Stat. Ann. § 2A:58C-3a(2); *Roberts v. Rich Foods, Inc.*, 139 N.J. 365, 654 A.2d 1365 (1995); *Dewey v. R.J. Reynolds Tobacco Co.*, 121 N.J. 69, 577 A.2d 1239 (1990); *Fabian v. Minster Mach. Co.*, 258 N.J. Super. 261, 609 A.2d 487 (1992).

43. N.J. Stat. Ann. § 2A:58C-3a(3). This section is not intended to apply to machinery or other equipment encountered in the workplace for which dangers can feasibly be eliminated. *See Fabian v. Minster Mach. Co.*, 258 N.J. Super. 261, 609 A.2d 487 (App. Div. 1992). *See also Snyder v. Mekhjian*, 244 N.J. Super. 281, 582 A.2d 307 (App. Div. 1990), *aff'd*, 125 N.J. 328, 593 A.2d 318 (1991).

44. *Lefever v. K.P. Hovnanian Enters., Inc.*, 160 N.J. 307, 734 A.3d 290 (1999); *Mettinger v. Globe Slicing Mach. Co.*, 153 N.J. 371, 709 A.2d 779 (1998); *Ramirez v. Amsted Indus., Inc.*, 86 N.J. 332, 431 A.2d 811 (1981); *Potwora ex rel. Gray v. Grip*, 319 N.J. Super. 386, 725 A.3d 697 (App. Div. 1999); *Saez v. S&S Corrugated Paper Mach. Co.*, 302 N.J. Super. 545, 695 A.2d 740 (App. Div. 1997); *Bussell v. DeWalt Prod. Corp.*, 259 N.J. Super. 499, 614 A.2d 622 (App. Div. 1992); *Class v. Am. Roller Die Corp.*, 294 N.J. Super. 407, 683 A.2d 595 (Law Div. 1996), *aff'd in part, rev'd in part*, 308 N.J. Super. 47, 705 A.2d 390 (App. Div. 1998). *See also Leo v. Kerr-McGee Chem. Corp.*, 37 F.3d 96 (3d Cir.

1994); *Ramos v. Silent Hoist & Crane Co.*, 256 N.J. Super. 467, 607 A.2d 667 (App. Div. 1992); *Brotherton v. Celotex Corp.*, 202 N.J. Super. 148, 493 A.2d 1337 (Law Div. 1985). *But see Nieves v. Bruno Sherman Corp.*, 86 N.J. 361, 431 A.2d 826 (1981) (doctrine extended to intermediate successor where it sold purchased assets to subsequent successor that discontinued product line). *See also Emoral, Inc. v. Diacetyl*, 740 F.3d 875 (3d Cir. 2014) (holding that persons who claimed to have been injured by a product manufactured by a bankrupt company could not maintain action against successor corporation because their claims were property of bankruptcy estate.)

45. *Shackil v. Lederle Lab., a Div. of Am. Cyanamid Co.*, 116 N.J. 155, 561 A.2d 511 (1989) (DPT vaccine). *See Namm v. Charles E. Frosst & Co.*, 178 N.J. Super. 19, 427 A.2d 1121 (App. Div. 1981) (manufacturers and distributors of prescription drug DES); *Sholtis v. Am. Cyanamid Co.*, 238 N.J. Super. 8, 568 A.2d 1196 (App. Div. 1989) (asbestos).

46. *Shackil v. Lederle Lab., a Div. of Am. Cyanamid Co.*, 116 N.J. 155, 561 A.2d 511 (1989). *See Lewis v. Am. Cyanamid Co.*, 155 N.J. 544, 715 A.2d 967 (1998) (noting opinion is "confined solely to the context of vaccines" and should not be considered *per se* to bar the imposition of market share liability in appropriate context).

47. *Dewey v. R.J. Reynolds Tobacco Co.*, 121 N.J. 69, 577 A.2d 1239 (1990); *Spring Motor Distrib., Inc. v. Ford Motor Co.*, 98 N.J. 555, 489 A.2d 660 (1985); *H. Rosenblum, Inc. v. Adler*, 93 N.J. 324, 461 A.2d 138 (1983).

48. N.J. Stat. Ann. § 2A:58C-4; *Taylor by Wurgaft v. General Elec. Co.*, 208 N.J. Super. 207, 505 A.2d 190 (App. Div. 1986); *Coffman v. Keene Corp.*, 257 N.J. Super. 279, 608 A.2d 416, *aff'd*, 133 N.J. 581, 628 A.2d 710 (1993) (*cited with approval in Clark v. Safety-Kleen Corp.*, 179 N.J. 318, 845 A.2d 857 (2004)).

49. *Hughes v. A.W. Chesterton Co.*, 435 N.J. Super. 326, 89 A.3d 179 (App. Div. 2014).

50. *Sharpe v. Bestop Inc.*, 314 N.J. Super. 54, 713 A.2d 1079 (App. Div. 1998), *aff'd*, 158 N.J. 329, 730 A.2d 285 (1999); *Theer v. Philip Carey Co.*, 133 N.J. 610, 628 A.2d 724 (1993); *Campos v. Firestone Tire & Rubber Co.*, 98 N.J. 198, 485 A.2d 305 (1984); *Coffman v. Keene Corp.*, 257 N.J. Super. 279, 608 A.2d 416, *aff'd*, 133 N.J. 581, 628 A.2d 710 (1993); *Graves v. Church & Dwight Co.*, 267 N.J. Super. 445, 631 A.2d 1248 (App. Div. 1993). *See also Reiff v. Convergent Techs.*, 957 F. Supp. 573 (D.N.J. 1997).

51. N.J. Stat. Ann. § 2A:58C-4; *Canty v. Ever-Last Supply Co.*, 296 N.J. Super. 68, 685 A.2d 1365 (Law Div. 1996); *Butler v. PPG Indus., Inc.*, 201 N.J. Super. 558, 493 A.2d 619 (App. Div. 1985).

52. *Rowe v. Hoffman-La Roche, Inc.*, 189 N.J. 615, 917 A.2d 767 (2007); *Banner v. Hoffman-La Roche Inc.*, 383 N.J. Super. 364, 891 A.2d 1229 (App. Div. 2006).

53. *Koruba v. Am. Honda Motor Co., Inc.*, 396 N.J. Super. 517, 528, 935 A.2d 787, 793 (App. Div. 2007).

54. N.J. Stat. Ann. § 2A:58C-4.

55. *Kendall v. Hoffman-La Roche, Inc.*, 209 N.J. 173, 36 A.3d 541 (2012) (acknowledging "super-presumption" of adequacy); *Perez v. Wyeth Lab., Inc.*, 161 N.J. 1, 734 A.2d 1245 (1999); *Bailey v. Wyeth*, 424 N.J. Super. 278, 37 A.3d 549 (Law Div. 2008), *aff'd, DeBoard v. Wyeth*, 422 N.J. Super. 360, 28 A.3d 1245 (App. Div. 2011).

56. *McDarby v. Merck*, 401 N.J. Super. 10, 949 A.2d 223 (App. Div., 2008), *cert. denied as improvidently granted*, 200 N.J. 267, 979 A.2d 766 (2009), citing *Wyeth v. Levine*, 555 U.S. 555, 129 S. Ct. 1187 (2009).

57. *McDarby*, 401 N.J. Super. 10, 949 A.2d 223.

58. N.J. Stat. Ann. § 2A:58C-4; *Dixon v. Jacobsen*, 270 N.J. Super. 569, 637 A.2d 915 (App. Div. 1994); *Molino v. B.F. Goodrich Co.*, 261 N.J. Super. 85, 617 A.2d 1235 (App. Div. 1992); *Seeley v. Cincinnati Shaper Co., Ltd.*, 256 N.J. Super. 1, 606 A.2d 378 (App. Div. 1992); *Lally v. Printing Mach. Sales & Serv. Co.*, 240 N.J. Super. 181, 572 A.2d 1187 (App. Div. 1990).

59. *Perez v. Wyeth Lab., Inc.*, 161 N.J. 1, 734 A.2d 1245 (1999). See also N.J. Stat. Ann.. § 2A:58C-4; *Spychala v. G.D. Searle & Co.*, 705 F. Supp. 1024 (D.N.J. 1988); *Niemiera by Niemiera v. Schneider*, 114 N.J. 550, 555 A.2d 1112 (1989); *London v. Lederle Lab., Div. of Am. Cyanamid Co.*, 290 N.J. Super. 318, 675 A.2d 1133 (App. Div. 1996), *aff'd, Batson v. Lederle Lab.*, 152 N.J. 14, 702 A.2d 471 (1997).

60. *Perez v. Wyeth Lab., Inc.*, 161 N.J. 1, 734 A.2d 1245 (1999); *Banner v. Hoffman-La Roche Inc.*, 383 N.J. Super. 364, 376, 891 A.2d 1229 (App. Div. 2006) (holding that the placement of informational brochures in a physician's office is not deemed to be direct-to-consumer advertising so as to remove the predicates of the learned intermediary doctrine).

61. *Rivera v. Westinghouse Elevator Co.*, 107 N.J. 256, 526 A.2d 705 (1987); *Brown v. United States Stove Co.*, 98 N.J. 155, 484 A.2d 1234 (1984).

62. *Lewis v. Am. Cyanamid Co.*, 155 N.J. 544, 715 A.2d 967 (1998); *Jurado v. W. Gear Works*, 131 N.J. 375, 619 A.2d 1312 (1993); *Johansen v. Makita U.S.A., Inc.*, 128 N.J. 86, 607 A.2d 637 (1992); *Brown v. United States Stove Co.*, 98 N.J. 155, 484 A.2d 1234 (1984); *Ridenour v. Bat Em Out*, 309 N.J. Super. 634, 707 A.2d 1093 (App. Div. 1998); *London v. Lederle Lab., Div. of Am. Cyanamid Co.*, 290 N.J. Super. 318, 675 A.2d 1133 (App. Div. 1996), *aff'd, Batson v. Lederle Lab.*, 152 N.J. 14, 702 A.2d 471 (1997).

63. N.J. Stat. Ann. § 2A:58C-3a(1). N.J. Stat. Ann. § 2A:58C-3(b) recognizes an exception with certain egregiously unsafe or ultrahazardous products that have hidden risks or could seriously injure third persons and have little or no usefulness. *See also Lewis v. Am. Cyanamid Co.*, 155 N.J. 544, 715 A.2d 967 (1998); *Roberts v. Rich Foods, Inc.*, 139 N.J. 365, 654 A.2d 1365 (1995); *Fabian v. Minster Mach. Co.*, 258 N.J. Super. 261, 609 A.2d 487 (App. Div. 1992).

64. N.J. Stat. Ann. § 2A:58C-3a(1), 3b; *Cavanaugh v. Skil Corp.*, 164 N.J. 1, 751 A.2d 518 (2000); *Lewis v. Am. Cyanamid Co.*, 155 N.J. 544, 715 A.2d 967 (1998); *Seeley v. Cincinnati Shaper Co., Ltd.*, 256 N.J. Super. 1, 606 A.2d 378 (App. Div. 1992); *Fabian v. Minster Mach. Co.*, 258 N.J. Super. 261, 609 A.2d 487 (App. Div. 1992).

65. *Cavanaugh v. Skil Corp.*, 164 N.J. 1, 751 A.2d 518 (2000).

66. *Scanlon v. Gen. Motors Corp., Chevrolet Motors Div.*, 65 N.J. 582, 326 A.2d 673 (1974) (*cited with approval in Myrlak v. Port Auth. of New York & New Jersey*, 157 N.J. 84, 723 A.2d 45 (1999) and *Lauder v. Teaneck Volunteer Ambulance Corps.*, 368 N.J. Super. 320, 845 A.2d 1271 (App. Div. 2004)).

67. *Myrlak v. Port Auth. of New York & New Jersey*, 157 N.J. 84, 723 A.2d 45 (1999).

68. *Mettinger v. W.W. Lowensten, Inc.*, 292 N.J. Super. 293, 678 A.2d 1115 (App. Div. 1996); *Smith v. Kris-Bal Realty, Inc.*, 242 N.J. Super. 346, 576 A.2d 934 (App. Div. 1990); *Sanna v. National Sponge Co.*, 209 N.J. Super. 60, 506 A.2d 1258 (App. Div. 1986).

69. *Ryan v. KDI Sylvan Pools, Inc.*, 121 N.J. 276, 579 A.2d 1241 (1990). *See also Wolf by Wolf v. Proctor & Gamble Co.*, 555 F. Supp. 613 (D.N.J. 1982).

70. *Sinclair v. Merck*, 195 N.J. 51, 948 A.2d 587 (2008); *McDarby v. Merck*, 401 N.J. Super. 10, 949 A.2d 223 (App. Div., 2008), *cert. denied as improvidently granted*, 200 N.J. 267, 979 A.2d 766 (2009). *See also Arlandson v. Hartz Mtn. Corp.*, 792 F. Supp. 2d 691 (D.N.J. 2011).

71. *Bailey v. Wyeth*, 424 N.J. Super. 278, 334, 37 A.3d 549, 584 (Law Div. 2008), *aff'd*, *DeBoard v. Wyeth*, 422 N.J. Super. 360, 28 A.3d 1245 (App. Div. 2011); *Indian Brand Farms v. Novartis Crop Prot., Inc.*, 890 F. Supp. 2d 534 (D.N.J. 2012); *Brown v. Philip Morris Inc.*, 228 F. Supp. 2d 506, 515-17 (D.N.J. 2002). As one commentator has stated, while it is open to question whether New Jersey's Supreme Court would preclude common law fraud claims, the court has, in other areas, held that it will not force manufacturers to serve two inconsistent masters. William A. Dreier, *Liability for Drug Advertising, Warnings, and Frauds*, 58 Rutgers L. Rev. 615 (Spring 2006).

72. *Rosenblit v. Zimmerman*, 166 N.J. 391, 766 A.2d 749 (2001); *Hewitt v. Allen Canning Co.*, 321 N.J. Super. 178, 728 A.2d 31 (App. Div. 1999); *Aetna Life &*

Cas. Co. v. Imet Mason Contractors, 309 N.J. Super. 358, 707 A.2d 180 (App. Div. 1998); N.J. Court Rule 4:23-4.

73. *Hewitt v. Allen Canning Co.*, 321 N.J. Super. 178, 728 A.2d 31 (App. Div. 1999); *Aetna Life & Cas. Co. v. Imet Mason Contractors*, 309 N.J. Super. 358, 707 A.2d 180; *Hirsch v. Gen. Motors Corp.*, 266 N.J. Super. 222, 628 A.2d 1108 (Law Div. 1993).

74. *Barbera v. DiMartino*, 305 N.J. Super. 617, 702 A.2d 1370 (App. Div. 1997) (refusing to require an adverse inference spoliation charge absent a showing of willful destruction of evidence and where plaintiff's discovery requests were not prompt).

75. *Rosenblit v. Zimmerman*, 166 N.J. 391, 766 A.2d 749 (2001); *Gilleski v. Cmty. Med. Ctr.*, 336 N.J. Super. 646, 765 A.2d 1103 (App. Div. 2001).

76. *Rosenblit v. Zimmerman*, 166 N.J. 391, 766 A.2d 749 (2001); *Viviano v. CBS, Inc.*, 251 N.J. Super. 113, 597 A.2d 543 (App. Div. 1991).

77. *Swick v. The New York Times Co.*, 357 N.J. Super. 371, 815 A.2d 508 (App. Div. 2003); *Gilleski v. Community Med. Ctr.*, 336 N.J. Super. 646, 765 A.2d 1103 (App. Div. 2001).

78. *Swick v. The New York Times Co.*, 357 N.J. Super. 371, 815 A.2d 508 (App. Div. 2003); *Gilleski v. Cmty. Med. Ctr.*, 336 N.J. Super. 646, 765 A.2d 1103 (App. Div. 2001).

79. *Hewitt v. Allen Canning Co.*, 321 N.J. Super. 178, 728 A.2d 31 (App. Div. 1999).

80. *Aetna Life & Cas. Co. v. Imet Mason Contractors*, 309 N.J. Super. 358, 707 A.2d 180 (App. Div. 1998); *Hewitt v. Allen Canning Co.*, 321 N.J. Super. 178, 728 A.2d 31 (App. Div. 1999); N.J. Court Rule 4:23-4.

81. N.J. Stat. Ann. § 2A:58c-1b(2); *Dean v. Barrett Homes, Inc.*, 204 N.J. 286, 8 A.3d 766 (2010). *See also Montich v. Miele USA, Inc.*, 849 F. Supp. 2d 439 (D.N.J. 2012).

82. *Easling v. Glen-Gery Corp.*, 804 F. Supp. 585 (D.N.J. 1992); *Alloway v. Gen. Marine Indus., L.P.*, 149 N.J. 620, 695 A.2d 264 (1997); *Spring Motors Distrib., Inc. v. Ford Motor Co.*, 98 N.J. 555, 498 A.2d 660 (1985); *Goldson v. Carver Boat Corp.*, 309 N.J. Super. 384, 707 A.2d 193 (App. Div. 1998).

83. *Poliseno v. Gen. Motors Corp.*, 328 N.J. Super. 41, 744 A.2d 679 (App. Div. 2000). *See also Green v. Gen. Motors Corp.*, 310 N.J. Super. 507, 709 A.2d 205 (App. Div. 1998).

84. N.J. Stat. Ann. § 2A:15-5.1-5.3; *Suter v. San Angelo Foundry & Mach. Co.*, 81 N.J. 150, 406 A.2d 140 (1979); *see also Ryan v. KDI Sylvan Pools, Inc.*, 121 N.J. 276, 579 A.2d 1241 (1990) (establishing formula for calculating damages

where plaintiff contributorily negligent, one defendant negligent, and other defendant strictly liable).

85. *Realmuto v. Straub Motors, Inc.*, 65 N.J. 336, 322 A.2d 440 (1974). *See also Dawson v. Chrysler Corp.*, 630 F.2d 950 (3d Cir. 1980).

86. *Huddell v. Levin*, 537 F.2d 726 (3d Cir. 1976) (called into question by *Crispin v. Volkswagenwerk AG*, 248 N.J. Super. 540, 591 A.2d 966 (App. Div. 1991)).

87. *525 Main Street Corp. v. Eagle Roofing Co.*, 34 N.J. 251, 168 A.2d 33 (1961).

88. *Ayers v. Jackson Tp.*, 106 N.J. 557, 603525 A.2d 287, 311 (1987); *Schroeder v. Perkel*, 87 N.J. 53, 69432 A.2d 834, 842 (1981). *See also* New Jersey Civil Jury Charge 8.11A.

89. N.J. Stat. Ann. § 2A:15-97.

90. Health carriers include health insurance companies, health maintenance organizations, health service corporations, hospital service corporations, and medical service corporations. New Jersey Insurance Bulletins 2001-11 (July 5, 2001).

91. *Perreira v. Rediger*, 169 N.J. 399, 778 A.2d 429 (2001); *White Consolidated Indus. v. Lin*, 372 N.J. Super. 480, 859 A.2d 729 (App. Div. 2004).

92. N.J. Stat. Ann. § 2A:15-97. *Thomas v. Toys 'R' Us, Inc.*, 282 N.J. Super. 569, 660 A.2d 1236 (App. Div. 1995).

93. Self-insured ERISA plans are not deemed an insurance company and are thus exempt from state laws regulating insurance. *FMC Corp. v. Holliday*, 498 U.S. 52 (1990). *See also Levine v. United Health Care*, 402 F.3d 166 (3d Cir. 2005).

94. N.J. Stat. Ann. § 2A:15-5.11.

95. N.J. Stat. Ann. § 2A:15-5.14.

96. N.J. Stat. Ann. § 2A:15-5.12; *Herman v. Sunshine Chem. Specialties, Inc.*, 133 N.J. 329, 627 A.2d 1081 (1993). In determining whether punitive damages are to be awarded, the trier of fact must consider all the relevant evidence, including the following: (1) the likelihood, at the relevant time, that serious harm would arise from the defendant's action; (2) the defendant's awareness of reckless disregard of the likelihood that serious harm would arise from his conduct; (3) the conduct of the defendant upon learning that its initial conduct would likely cause harm; and (4) the duration of the conduct or any concealment of it by the defendant. N.J. Stat. Ann. § 2A:15-5.12.

97. N.J. Stat. Ann. § 2A:15-5.13; Civil Model Jury Charge 8.62.

98. N.J. Stat. Ann. § 2A:58C-5c; *Rowe v. Hoffman-La Roche, Inc.*, 189 N.J. 615, 917 A.2d 767 (2007).

99. N.J. Court Rule 4:42-11.

100. *Potente v. Cnty. of Hudson*, 187 N.J. 103, 900 A.2d 787 (2006); *Ward v. Zelikovsky*, 263 N.J. Super. 497, 623 A.2d 285 (App. Div. 1993), *rev'd on other grounds*, 136 N.J. 516, 643 A.2d 972 (1994); *Belinski v. Goodman*, 139 N.J. Super. 351, 354 A.2d 92 (App. Div. 1976).

101. N.J. Court Rule 4:42-11 and Publisher's Note. The rate has varied from 8.5% to 0.25% in recent years. The annual rate of interest commencing January 1, 2014 and for the remainder of that calendar year was 0.25% pursuant to Supreme Court Order relaxing the rule. By rule amendment effective September 2014, the annual rate of interest commencing January 1, 2015 and for the remainder of that calendar year is expected to be 0.25%.

102. N.J. Court Rule 4:42-11(b).

103. N.J. Stat. Ann. § 34:15-1.

104. N.J. Stat. Ann. § 34:15-8; *Van Dunk v. Reckson Assocs. Realty Corp.*, 210 N.J. 449, 45 A.3d 965 (2012) (exception did not apply because court could not determine whether OSHA violation was an intentional disregard or plain indifference, there was no history of prior violations, and employer's poor decision did not satisfy substantial-certainty standard); *Tomeo v. Thomas Whitesell Constr. Co.*, 176 N.J. 366, 823 A.2d 769 (2003) (exception did not apply because intentionally disabling a safety device is not a per se intentional wrong); *Mull v. Zeta Consumer Prods.*, 176 N.J. 385, 823 A.2d 782 (2003) (exception applied despite lack of deception of OSHA officials because under the totality of the circumstances both conduct and context prongs were satisfied); *Crippen v. Cent. Jersey Concrete Pipe Co.*, 176 N.J. 397, 823 A.2d 789 (2003) (exception applied where employer deliberately failed to correct OSHA violations, admitted that there was a substantial certainty of death, and deceived OSHA regarding compliance); *Laidlow v. Hariton Mach. Co.*, 170 N.J. 602, 790 A.2d 884 (2002) (exception applied when employer removed safety guard, deceived OSHA officials, and ignored complaints by plaintiff and prior near accidents); *Millison v. E.I. DuPont de Nemours & Co.*, 101 N.J. 161, 501 A.2d 505 (1985) (exception did not apply to initial exposure to asbestos but did apply to company's fraudulent concealment of illness already in progress); *Kaczorowska v. Nat'l Envelope Corp.*, 342 N.J. Super. 580, 770 A.2d 941 (App. Div. 2001) (exception did not apply because neither gross negligence nor an excessive lack of concern will be sufficient to satisfy the "conduct prong"). *See also Torres v. Lucca's Bakery*, 487 F. Supp. 2d 507 (D.N.J. 2007) (exception did not apply when there was insufficient evidence to establish requisite level of knowledge that the employer was substantially certain that plaintiff would be injured).

105. *DeFigueiredo v. U.S. Metals Refining Co.*, 235 N.J. Super. 407, 563 A.2d 50 (App. Div. 1989); *Doe v. Saint Michael's Med. Ctr.*, 184 N.J. Super. 1, 445 A.2d 40 (App. Div. 1982).

106. *Ramos v. Browning Ferris Indus. of South Jersey, Inc.*, 103 N.J. 177, 510 A.2d 1152 (1986); *Kane v. Hartz Mountain Indus., Inc.*, 278 N.J. Super. 129, 650 A.2d 808 (App. Div. 1994), *aff'd*, 143 N.J. 141, 669 A.2d 816 (1994).

107. N.J. Stat. Ann. § 2A:15-5.3; *Sholtis v. Am. Cyanamid Co.*, 238 N.J. Super. 8, 568 A.2d 1196 (App. Div. 1989); *James v. Chevron U.S.A., Inc.*, 301 N.J. Super. 512, 694 N.J. 270 (App. Div. 1997); *Higgins v. Owens-Corning Fiberlas*, 282 N.J. Super. 600 (App. Div. 1995).

108. See Section C.4, Contributory Negligence/Assumption of Risk, *supra*.

109. *Ryan v. KDI Sylvan Pools, Inc.*, 121 N.J. 276, 579 A.2d 1241 (1990).

110. *James v. Bessemer Processing Co.*, 155 N.J. 279, 714 A.2d 898 (1998) (holding that in a case of cumulative injury, such as environmental tort actions, the burden of apportioning responsibility is shifted to defendants whose products were substantial factors in causing the injury). *See also Chin v. St. Barnabus Med. Ctr.*, 160 N.J. 454, 734 A.2d 778 (1999). In *Chin*, the Court held that in order to shift the burden of proof to defendants, plaintiff must show three things: (1) the plaintiff must be entirely blameless, (2) the injury must be one which bespeaks negligence on the part of one or more defendants, and (3) all of those defendants who participated in the chain of events must be before the court. *See also Anderson v. Picciotti*, 144 N.J. 195, 676 A.2d 127 (1996); *Shackil v. Lederle Lab.*, 116 N.J. 155, 561 A.2d 511 (1989).

111. N.J. Stat. Ann. § 2A:15-5.3.

112. N.J. Stat. Ann. § 2A:15-5.3(e); *Ripa v. Owens-Corning Fiberglas Corp.*, 282 N.J. Super. 373, 660 A.2d 521 (App. Div. 1995); *Promaulayko v. Johns Manville Sales Corp.*, 116 N.J. 505, 562 A.2d 202 (1989).

113. N.J. Stat. Ann. § 2A:53A-1*et seq.*; *Mort v. Besser Co.*, 287 N.J. Super. 423, 671 A.2d 189 (App. Div. 1996); *Tefft v. Tefft*, 192 N.J. Super. 561, 471 A.2d 790 (App. Div. 1983); *Young v. Latta*, 123 N.J. 584, 589 A.2d 1020 (1991); *Ripa v. Owens-Corning Fiberglas Corp.*, 282 N.J. Super. 373, 660 A.2d 521 (App. Div. 1995).

114. N.J. Court Rule 4:26-4.

115. *Dunn v. Borough of Mountainside*, 301 N.J. Super. 262, 693 A.2d 1248 (App. Div. 1997).

116. *Farrell v. Votator Div. of Chemetron Corp.*, 62 N.J. 111, 120-23 (1973); *Matynska v. Fried*, 175 N.J. 51 (2002); *Claypotch v. Heller, Inc.*, 360 N.J. Super. 472 (App.

Div. 2003); *Johnston v. Muhlenberg Reg'l Med. Ctr.*, 326 N.J. Super. 203 (App. Div. 1999); *Mears v. Sandoz Pharms., Inc.*, 300 N.J. Super. 622 (App. Div. 1997).

117. N.J. Stat. Ann. § 2A:58C-1*et seq.*

118. N.J. Stat. Ann. § 2A:15-5.9*et seq.*

119. N.J. Stat. Ann. § 34:15-1*et seq.*

120. N.J. Stat. Ann. § 2A:15-5.1*et seq.*

121. N.J. Stat. Ann. § 2A:53A-1*et seq.*

122. N.J. Stat. Ann. § 2A:15-97.

123. N.J. Stat. Ann. § 2A:14-2*et seq.*

124. N.J. Stat. Ann. § 12A:2-313 through 2-318.

125. N.J. Court Rule 4:4-4(b)(1).

126. http://www.judiciary.state.nj.us/civil/civindx.htm.

NEW MEXICO

A. CAUSES OF ACTION

Generally, product liability lawsuits include causes of action for strict liability, negligence, and breach of warranty.[1]

B. STATUTES OF LIMITATION

1. Personal Injury and Wrongful Death

Causes of action for personal injury must be filed within three years.[2] New Mexico has adopted the "discovery" rule, under which the statute of limitations runs from when the plaintiff knew, or by the exercise of reasonable diligence should have discovered, that he or she had been injured, as well as the cause of the injury.[3] However, the discovery rule is not applicable to wrongful death claims, which simply accrue at the time of death.[4]

2. Property Damage

Causes of action must be filed within four years for property damage,[5] whether brought in negligence or strict liability.

3. Breach of Warranty

Generally, causes of action based on breach of warranty must be brought within four years of the tender of delivery of the goods.[6] The four-year Uniform Commercial Code statute of limitations applies in an action for personal injury that is predicated on breach of an implied warranty.[7]

4. Statute of Repose

A 10-year statute of repose presumptively bars actions involving improvements to real property.[8]

C. STRICT LIABILITY

1. The Standard

New Mexico has adopted Section 402A of the Restatement (Second) of Torts.[9] The New Mexico Court of Appeals has relied upon the Restatement (Third) of Torts: Product Liability (Tentative Draft No. 2, 1995) as stating the basic rule of strict product liability.[10]

2. Definition of "Defect"

A product is considered defective if an unreasonable risk of injury proximately results from a condition of the product or from the manner of its use.[11] An unreasonable risk of injury is one that a reasonably prudent person having full knowledge of the risk would find unacceptable.[12] A product does not present an unreasonable risk of harm simply because it is possible to be harmed by it.[13] In a design defect case, the product's design need not necessarily adopt features that represent the ultimate in safety; the jury should consider the ability to eliminate the risk without seriously impairing the usefulness of the product or making it unduly expensive.[14]

3. **Causation**

   a. **Proximate Cause**

   A products liability plaintiff must prove not only that the product was defective in order to prevail, but also that such defect was a proximate cause of the injuries alleged.[15] Unless all facts regarding causation are undisputed or, as a matter of law, there is an independent intervening cause, the issue of causation is a question of fact.[16]

   b. **Independent Intervening Cause**

   An independent intervening cause will prevent recovery for the act or omission of a wrongdoer. An independent intervening cause "interrupts the natural sequence of events, turns aside their cause, prevents the natural and probable results of the original act or omission, and produces a different result, that could not have been reasonably foreseen."[17] For example, in the case of prescription drugs, a physician's negligence may constitute an independent intervening cause sufficient to prevent recovery against a pharmaceutical company, but where such negligence was reasonably foreseeable, the pharmaceutical company may not escape liability for failure to adequately warn.[18] Suicide was found to be an independent intervening cause breaking the chain of causation in a negligence case against a gun owner.[19] As an affirmative defense against a plaintiff, the doctrine is rather limited and does not apply to the negligent actions of a plaintiff. However, the New Mexico Court of Appeals recently held that an independent intervening cause instruction should have been given in a wrongful death case where there was evidence that the plaintiff committed suicide, reasoning that the jury should have been allowed to resolve the conflict between this defense evidence, and the plaintiffs' evidence that Ms. Silva's suicide was a foreseeable result of defendant's alleged negligence.[20]

   c. **Causation in Warning Cases**

   In products liability cases dealing with the adequacy of warnings, a product with inadequate warnings will be found to be the proximate cause of the injury if an adequate warning would have been noticed and acted upon to guard against the danger.[21] A supplier will not be held liable for failure to warn of risks which can reasonably be expected to be known or obvious to foreseeable users of the product.[22]

4. **Contributory Negligence/Assumption Risk**

Comparative fault is a defense in a product liability case, whether brought in strict liability, negligence, or breach of warranty.[23] The plaintiff's negligence, whether consisting of what is conventionally known as contributory negligence or assumption of risk, reduces the amount of damages the plaintiff may recover by the percentage of fault assessed against him.[24]

Likewise, the jury can apportion damages among the defendants based on each defendant's individual percentage of fault.[25] Fault may also be assessed against nonparties,[26] even if such nonparties are immune from suit.[27] Comparative fault is applicable to intentional conduct.[28]

5. **Sale or Lease/Persons Liable**

A plaintiff must allege that the defendant sold, leased, or otherwise placed the product into the stream of commerce.[29] Strict liability extends to any "supplier" in the chain of distribution of the product, including manufacturers, retailers, distributors, and lessors.[30] The "supplier" must be in the business of putting this product on the market.[31] For public policy reasons, the New Mexico courts have declined to extend strict liability to hospitals and doctors for the distribution or supply of medical products designed and manufactured by others.[32] A supplier of a component part or raw material that is not inherently defective or dangerous at the time it leaves the manufacturer's control, and which part or material is used in the manufacture or making of another product, does not owe a duty to warn the ultimate consumer concerning the suitability or safety of the finished product; in such situation any duty to warn the ultimate consumer rests on the manufacturer of the finished product.[33] A bulk supplier is required to warn its immediate purchaser of any known dangers, with the intent that its warning be passed on to the ultimate consumer.[34]

6. **Inherently Dangerous Products**

A supplier of a product that is unavoidably unsafe (that is, one that cannot be made safe for its intended and ordinary use even when properly prepared and accompanied by proper directions and warnings) will not be held liable unless the product unreasonably exposes users to risk of injury.[35] Determining whether users are unreasonably exposed to risk of injury requires a balancing of the dangers and benefits resulting from the product's use.[36]

7. **Successor Liability**

A corporation that purchases the assets of another corporation does not automatically acquire its liabilities except: "(1) where there is an agreement to assume those obligations; (2) where the transfer results in a consolidation or merger; (3) where there is a continuation of the transferor corporation; or (4) where the transfer is for the purpose of fraudulently avoiding liability."[37] However, New Mexico has adopted the product line exception.[38] A successor, who continues to produce and market the same product, using the same designs, equipment, and name, may be responsible for design defects in its predecessor's product.[39] Such a successor may also have an independent duty to warn of defects in its predecessor's product, depending on whether there is a nexus between the successor, its predecessor's customers, and the product sufficient to warrant an inference that the successor had actual or constructive notice of the alleged defect.[40]

8. **Market-Share Liability**

There are no New Mexico state court decisions on the issue of market share or enterprise liability.

9. **Privity**

A "supplier" is directly liable for its active conduct causing injury to a consumer, despite the presence of an intermediate seller.[41]

10. **Failure to Warn**

A product presents an unreasonable risk of injury if put on the market without warning of a risk that could be avoided by the giving of an adequate warning.[42] The warning must be communicated by a means that can reasonably be expected to reach the user and persons in the vicinity during the use of the product.[43] Also, the warning must: (1) be in a form that can reasonably be expected to catch the attention of the reasonably foreseeable user; (2) be understandable to the reasonably foreseeable user; and (3) disclose the nature and extent of the danger. The warning must specify any harmful consequences that a reasonably foreseeable user would not understand from a general warning of the product's danger or from a simple directive to use or not to use the product for a certain purpose or in a certain way.[44]

11. **Post-sale Duty to Warn and Remedial Measures**

A supplier's duty to use ordinary care continues after the product has left its possession. A supplier who later learns, or in the exercise of ordinary care should know, of a risk of injury caused by a condition of the product or a manner in which it could be used, must then use ordinary care to avoid the risk.[45] A post-sale duty can be created by a post-sale relationship between the supplier and the product owner under which the supplier voluntarily undertakes a post-sale relationship.[46] New Mexico has not decided whether a manufacturer has a post-sale duty to take steps to address risks that become evident only as a result of technological developments occurring after a product leaves the manufacturer's control.[47]

12. **Learned Intermediary Doctrine**

    Under this doctrine, a manufacturer or seller of prescription pharmaceuticals is under no duty to warn the ultimate user where the product has been supplied with adequate warnings to the prescribing physician who acts as a "learned intermediary" between the supplier and the consumer.[48] The New Mexico Court of Appeals has adopted the rule that a drug manufacturer has a duty to warn the medical profession and is liable to the ultimate user of the drug for failure to do so, without specifically referring to this rule as the "learned intermediary doctrine."[49] In a diversity case in United States District Court, one District Judge predicted that the New Mexico Supreme Court, if presented with the issue, would decline to follow the decisions of the New Mexico Court of Appeals and would reject the learned intermediary doctrine.[50] More recently, however, another District Judge without hesitation predicted that New Mexico law was as stated in the multiple Court of Appeals decisions.[51]

13. **Substantial Change/Abnormal Use**

    In order for a supplier to be liable, the injury must have been proximately caused by a condition of the product that was not substantially changed from the condition in which the supplier placed the product on the market or in which the supplier could have reasonably expected it to be used. For a substantial change in the product to relieve a supplier of liability, the change itself must be a cause of the harm done.[52] Incorporation of a component into a final product may not necessarily be a "substantial change" of the component.[53]

    The supplier's duty is limited to use of the product for a purpose or in a manner that could reasonably be foreseen, including foreseeable misuses.[54] Where an injury is caused by a risk or misuse of the product that was not reasonably foreseeable to the supplier, he is not liable.[55]

14. **State of the Art**

    The New Mexico Supreme Court has not expressly approved of the state-of-the-art defense. However, it has indicated that in appropriate cases, state-of-the-art evidence and the state-of-the-art defense may be utilized.[56]

15. **Malfunction**

    A product that malfunctions by not performing as intended may be unreasonably dangerous.[57] However, no New Mexico authority expressly establishes malfunction as evidence of a defect.

16. **Standards and Governmental Regulation**

    Proof that a product complies with industry standards or custom is evidence of whether a risk of injury would be acceptable to a reasonably prudent person[58] and in a negligence case, is evidence of ordinary care.[59] However, industry standards or custom and usage are not dispositive of whether a manufacturer was negligent or whether a product was defective.[60] It has been held that admission into evidence of OSHA standards is not reversible error even though such standards are directed toward employers rather than manufacturers.[61]

17. Other Accidents

The New Mexico Court of Appeals has held that the exclusion of evidence of four prior lawsuits claiming that defendant's seatbelt buckle inadvertently released was not an abuse of discretion, noting that the lawsuits never went to trial and the claims were never proved.[62] Similarly, the court held that the exclusion of evidence of verbal claims made by consumer call-ins to a National Highway Transportation Safety Administration "hotline" about buckle release in vehicles with defendant's seat belts was not an abuse of discretion, noting that no evidence indicated that any complaint was confirmed or investigated.[63] The Court also explained that plaintiffs' briefs had not detailed any specifics to show how these claims were substantially similar,[64] and cited federal cases giving an extremely deferential standard of review under Rule of Evidence 403 to the trial judge's evidentiary ruling on these matters.[65]

Guidance can also be found in several reported New Mexico cases addressing the admissibility of other accidents in negligence actions.[66] In general, other accidents are not admissible.[67] However, other accidents may be admissible, in limited circumstances, if they are probative of a relevant fact.[68] Even if other accidents are relevant, a court may choose to exclude them under New Mexico Rule of Evidence 403 if their admission would cause unfair prejudice, confusion of the issues, mislead the jury, cause undue delay, waste time, or if such admission constitutes the needless presentation of cumulative evidence.[69]

Federal courts applying New Mexico law have also addressed these issues in product liability cases.[70] These courts have held that other accidents are admissible to show notice, demonstrate the existence of a defect, or refute the testimony of a defense witness if they are substantially similar.[71] The precise degree of similarity depends on the theory of defect underlying the case.[72] A high degree of similarity is required when plaintiff offers the other accidents to prove causation in his case but a lesser degree of similarity is required when offered to show the defendant had notice of potential defects in the product.[73] To be admissible on the theory of notice, the other accidents must be similar enough to the event in question that they would have alerted the defendant to the problem or danger at issue.

Subsequent accidents are not admissible to show notice.[74] However, the federal court held that subsequent accidents may be admissible to prove a product is defective,[75] or to prove the defendant had the culpable mental state necessary to award punitive damages.[76]

The federal court also held that the requirement of substantial similarity does not require identical products. It requires substantial similarity among the variables relevant to the plaintiff's theory of defect.[77] Similarity of circumstances surrounding the other accidents is also dependent on the plaintiff's theory of defect.[78]

18. **Misrepresentation**

New Mexico has neither adopted nor rejected Section 402B of the Restatement (Second) of Torts, or Section 9 of the Restatement (Third) of Torts; Product Liability, dealing with the product liability theory of misrepresentation.[79]

19. **Destruction or Loss of Product**

New Mexico recognizes the intentional spoliation of evidence as a distinct category of tort liability and defines it as "the intentional destruction, mutilation, or significant alteration of potential evidence for the purpose of defeating another person's recovery in a civil action."[80] In order to prevail on a claim for intentional spoliation of evidence, a plaintiff must prove each of the following elements: (1) the existence of a potential lawsuit; (2) the defendant's knowledge of the potential lawsuit; (3) the destruction, mutilation, or significant alteration of potential evidence; (4) intent on the part of the defendant to disrupt or defeat the lawsuit; (5) a causal relationship between the act of spoliation and the inability to prove the lawsuit; and (6) damages.[81]

It is not necessary that a complaint be filed at the time of the spoliation or that express notice has been given that a complaint is about to be filed. All that is required is that the defendant knew of the probability of a future lawsuit. The standard applied is one of reasonableness.[82] The element of intent to disrupt or defeat the lawsuit requires a malicious intent to harm; this means that the defendant not only intended to do the act which is ascertained to be wrongful, but also knew it was wrong at the time he committed the act.[83] Furthermore, the malicious intent to disrupt or defeat the lawsuit must be the sole motivation for the destruction, alteration, or mutilation of the evidence.[84]

The spoliation claim should be tried in conjunction with the underlying claim, rather than in a bifurcated or separate trial.[85] At the directed verdict stage of such a concurrent proceeding, a plaintiff can satisfy the requirements of causation and damages by presenting evidence from which a reasonable jury, upon finding in favor of the defendant on the underlying claim, could conclude that the intentional spoliation of evidence caused the plaintiff's failure to satisfy the burden of proof in the underlying claim.[86]

New Mexico has declined to recognize a distinct category of tort liability for the negligent destruction of potential evidence.[87] However, traditional negligence principles apply and could support the finding of a duty to preserve potential evidence based on an agreement or contract between the parties, on applicable state statutes and regulations, or on other special circumstances.[88] New Mexico courts may also use their inherent equitable powers to impose sanctions based on a party's spoliation of evidence. Sanctions include an adverse evidentiary inference instruction, exclusion of certain of the spoliator's evidence, outright dismissal of a spoliator's case, and/or sanctions similar to those provided in Rule 1-037(B).[89]

Where the elements of the tort of intentional spoliation of evidence are not met, it may be appropriate to instruct the jury on a permissible adverse evidentiary inference. The jury may be instructed that it is permissible to infer that evidence which was intentionally destroyed, concealed, mutilated, or altered by a party without reasonable explanation would have been unfavorable to the spoliator.[90] In deciding whether to give such instruction, the trial court should consider whether the spoliation was intentional, whether the spoliator knew of the reasonable possibility of a lawsuit involving the spoliated object, whether the party requesting the instruction acted with due diligence with respect to the spoliated evidence, and whether the evidence would have been relevant to a material issue in the case. It is not necessary that the spoliator act with malice or bad faith.[91]

20. **Economic Loss**

In the context of commercial transactions when there is no great disparity of bargaining power between the parties, economic losses from injury of a product to itself are not recoverable in tort actions.[92] Such losses are exclusively recoverable in contract actions as parties may allocate the risk of such losses by warranties and/or insurance.[93] New Mexico has not determined whether this rule should apply to noncommercial consumers who suffer economic losses.[94]

21. **Crashworthiness**

New Mexico recognizes the "crashworthiness," "second collision," or "enhanced injury" doctrine which provides that a manufacturer can be liable where a defect in the design or manufacture of a product does not cause the original accident and resulting injury but causes an additional injury or enhances the original injury.[95] Strict liability, as well as negligence, is applicable in crashworthiness cases in New Mexico.[96] While the original tortfeasor is liable for all foreseeable injuries (including the enhanced injury), a crashworthiness defendant is only liable for the enhanced injury.[97]

New Mexico has adopted the reasoning of *Huddell v. Levin*, 537 F.2d 726, 737 (3d Cir. 1976), that plaintiff must prove (1) that the party responsible for the "second collision" proximately caused an injury separate from and in addition to the injuries which otherwise would have been caused by the "first collision," and (2) the degree of enhancement caused by the "second collision" by proving what injuries would have occurred absent the second collision.[98]

Uniform Jury Instructions 13-1802(C) through (E) and 13-2222 (Successive tortfeasors; sample verdict form; divisible injuries) provide that the first inquiry is whether the plaintiff's injuries are divisible or not (*i.e.*, whether the original tortfeasor caused an injury that is separate in nature or extent from the injury caused by the successive tortfeasor, or, as far as the successive tortfeasor is concerned, whether the successive tortfeasor caused a separate injury or made the original injury measurably worse).[99] If the injuries are not divisible, then the fault of all responsible persons (including plaintiff) is compared. If the injuries are divisible, then the jury determines the amount of damages caused by each injury and compares the fault of all persons (including plaintiff) responsible for each injury. The fault of those persons who contributed to the original injury is compared, and the fault of those persons who contributed to the second injury is compared, but the fault of those responsible for the first injury is not compared with the fault of those responsible for the second injury.[100] UJI 13-1802(E) is drafted on the assumption that the trial court will place the burden of proving divisible injuries on the party asserting divisibility, rather than placing the burden on the plaintiff to prove an enhanced injury. However, the UJI Committee has noted that the law is not perfectly clear.[101] Indeed the New Mexico Supreme Court seems to have decided that the burden of proof is on plaintiff to prove both an enhanced injury and the degree of enhancement.[102]

22. Reasonable Alternative Designs

The New Mexico Court of Appeals has held that presently, unlike the Restatement (Third) of Torts, New Mexico courts do not require, as an element of tort, a specific showing of a reasonable alternative design in strict products liability design defect cases.[103] Under New Mexico law, the existence of a reasonable alternative design is a relevant consideration by a jury, but a specific finding on this issue is not required.[104] Thus, while a jury is required to make risk-benefit calculations, consideration of alternative designs is but one of several risk-benefit considerations that a jury may balance in determining whether a product created an unreasonable risk of injury.[105]

D. NEGLIGENCE

Manufacturers and suppliers have a duty to use ordinary care to avoid foreseeable risks of injury caused by the condition of a product or the manner in which it is used.[106] This duty is owed to all persons who can reasonably be expected to use the product or be in the vicinity during use.[107] The duty continues after the product has left the supplier's hands. *See* Section C.11, *supra*. To recover, a plaintiff must show that the injury resulted from a reasonably foreseeable use of the product.[108]

New Mexico has adopted the doctrine of pure comparative negligence. *See* Section C.4, *supra*.

E. **BREACH OF WARRANTY**

The creation and exclusion of warranties, both expressed and implied, are governed by the Uniform Commercial Code.[109] Implied warranty theories do not differ significantly from strict liability claims.[110] Plaintiffs may proceed under both tort and contract theories. No election is required,[111] though double recovery is not allowed.[112]

F. **PUNITIVE DAMAGES**

Punitive damages are not available for mere negligence, but they are available in both tort and contract actions[113] (including breach of warranty),[114] where the defendant has a culpable mental state, indivisible from the conduct constituting liability, and its conduct is willful, wanton, malicious, oppressive, fraudulent, or reckless.[115] Gross negligence is not sufficient.[116] Punitive damages are intended to punish the defendant and to deter future wrongdoing,[117] and cannot be recovered without a recovery of compensatory or nominal damages.[118] Punitive damages generally must be separately determined when assessed against two or more defendants.[119]

Punitive damages do not have to be in reasonable proportion to actual damages, but they must not be so unrelated to the injury as to plainly manifest passion and prejudice rather than reason and justice.[120] New Mexico courts use the following factors when determining whether an award of punitive damages is excessive: (1) the degree of reprehensibility of the defendant's misconduct; (2) the disparity between the harm (or potential harm) suffered by the plaintiff and the punitive damages award; and (3) the difference between the punitive damages awarded by the jury and the civil penalties authorized or imposed in comparable cases.[121] Punitive damage awards are not subject to pre-judgment interest.[122]

G. **PRE- AND POST-JUDGMENT INTEREST**

1. **Pre-judgment Interest**

    Pre-judgment interest is available in a variety of situations pursuant to NMSA 1978, Sections 56-8-3 and 56-8-4. Section 56-8-3 allows pre-judgment interest as a remedy for lost opportunity of money, usually in cases involving money due by contract, conversion, or money due on the settlement of matured accounts.[123] Section 56-8-4(B) allows pre-judgment interest in the discretion of the court after the court considers, among other things, whether the plaintiff caused unreasonable delay in the adjudication of his or her claims and whether the defendant made a reasonable and timely offer of settlement.[124] A political subdivision, such as a city, is exempt from pre-judgment interest under Section 56-8-4, but not under Section 56-8-3.[125]

    In some cases, pre-judgment interest can be awarded as a matter of right, but "only when a party has breached a duty to pay a definite sum of money or 'the amount due under the contract can be ascertained with reasonable certainty by a mathematical standard fixed in the contract or by established market prices.'"[126] When a plaintiff is entitled to pre-judgment interest as a matter of right, the absence of any findings by the trial court to justify its denial of pre-judgment interest is an abuse of discretion.[127] In cases falling under Section 56-8-3, where the amount owed is not fixed or readily ascertainable, as in tort cases, the trial court has discretion to award pre-judgment interest at a rate of up to 15 percent.[128]

Awards of pre-judgment interest are available at the court's discretion in products liability and other tort cases.[129] Notably, pre-judgment interest is not available as a matter of right in tort cases.[130] The court is not limited to any specific factors when deciding whether to award pre-judgment interest; rather, it should consider all relevant equitable considerations, as well as the factors set forth under Section 56-8-4(B).[131] When a court decides to award or deny pre-judgment interest in products liability cases, it does not need to make specific factual findings supporting its decision.[132] Rather, the reasons for denying pre-judgment interest need only be ascertainable from the record and not contrary to logic or reason.[133]

The New Mexico Supreme Court has ruled that it is not an abuse of discretion to deny a request for pre-judgment interest on an award of punitive damages.[134] The court ruled that "pre-judgment interest serves two purposes, promoting early settlements and compensating persons; however, it was never intended to encompass an award of punitives."[135] Thus, while the court recognized that pre-judgment interest was available on awards of compensatory damages to make a plaintiff whole, it held that pre-judgment interest should not be added to punitive damages.[136]

2. **Post-judgment Interest**

Like pre-judgment interest, post-judgment interest is available in New Mexico. "Generally, post-judgment interest is intended to prevent the inequity of denying the prevailing party the cost of the lost opportunity of using the money that the judgment debtor had use of during the pendency of the appeal."[137] Post-judgment interest "compensates a plaintiff for being deprived of compensation from the time of judgment until payment of the judgment debt" and "'serves a salutary housekeeping purpose . . . by creating an incentive for unsuccessful defendants to avoid frivolous appeals and by minimizing the necessity for court-supervised execution upon judgments.'"[138]

Post-judgment interest on judgments and decrees for payment of money is mandatory and accrues at the statutory rate from the date of entry of judgment.[139] Post-judgment interest on an award of punitive damages is likewise mandatory.[140] A higher post-judgment interest will apply where a defendant is found to have acted willfully.[141]

Absent express authority, Section 56-8-4(D) prohibits post-judgment interest against the state.[142]

H. EMPLOYER IMMUNITY

The New Mexico Workers' Compensation Act protects employers from being joined in suits arising out of an employee's injuries.[143] However, when an employer knows that its conduct is substantially certain to result in the worker's serious injury or death, the employer's behavior does not fall within the Act's exclusivity provisions.[144] Willfulness renders a worker's injury non-accidental, and therefore outside the scope of the Workers' Compensation Act, when: (1) the employer engages in an intentional act or omission, without just cause or excuse, that is reasonably expected to result in the injury suffered by the worker; (2) the employer expects the intentional act or omission to result in the injury, or has utterly disregarded the consequences; and (3) the intentional act or omission proximately causes the injury.[145] This three-part test is referred to as the *Delgado* test. Under the *Delgado* test, the critical measure is whether the employer has, in a specific dangerous circumstance, required the employee to perform a task where the employer is or should clearly be aware that there is a substantial likelihood the employee will suffer injury or death by performing the task.[146] The *Delgado* test applies retroactively.[147] The only reported case in which an appellate court has found that the employer's conduct was egregious enough to permit a tort action despite the exclusive remedy provisions of the Workers' Compensation was *Delgado*.[148]

Statutory employers, as defined by NMSA 1978, Section 52-1-22 (1989) of the Workers' Compensation Act, fall within the general definition of employers who are subject to the Act's terms, and who, in return, are immune from tort liability under the Act's exclusivity provisions, set forth in NMSA 1978, Section 52-1-6(E), NMSA 1978, Section 52-1-8, and NMSA 1978, Section 52-1-9.[149] One requirement that New Mexico courts have stressed is that employers must maintain the mandated workers' compensation insurance, or lose their immunity.[150]

Some contractors may qualify as "statutory employers" in New Mexico. With regard to general contractors, "when the subcontractor is determined not to be an independent contractor, immunity is extended to the general contractor if workers' compensation coverage is provided by either the general contractor or the subcontractor."[151] Even though plaintiff's employer may be immune from suit, a product manufacturer may still use the employer's negligence as comparative fault to reduce its share of liability.[152]

When a general employer supplies labor, not work, to a third party, the special employment test applies.[153] The three-part test for special employment is whether "(1) the employee has made a contract of hire, express or implied, with the special employer; (2) the work being done is essentially that of the special employer; and (3) the special employer has the right to control the details of the work."[154] Like statutory employers, special employers can also acquire immunity if they comply with the Workers' Compensation Act.[155]

I. STATUTES

Relevant statutes in product liability actions are the statutes of limitation,[156] the commercial code sections dealing with warranties,[157] and the statute dealing with joint and several liability.[158] A person reaches the age of majority on his or her 18th birthday.[159]

J. JOINT AND SEVERAL LIABILITY

1. The Rule

New Mexico defines joint tortfeasors as "two or more persons jointly or severally liable in tort for the same injury to person or property, whether or not judgment has been recovered against all or some of them."[160]

There is generally no joint and several liability for the acts of concurrent tortfeasors.[161] Where there are successive tortfeasors causing separate and causally-distinct injuries, joint and several liability exists.[162] For example, the initial tortfeasor who causes an injury that is enhanced by subsequent medical malpractice is jointly and severally liable for the entire harm.[163] Participants in a chain reaction automobile accident which did not result in a distinct original injury followed by a second distinct injury or enhancement are not successive tortfeasors; the lapse of time between the various chain reaction impacts is not enough to render the participants successive tortfeasors.[164]

Joint and several liability exists for intentional acts, persons vicariously liable, persons strictly liable for the manufacture and sale of a defective product (but only to that portion of the total liability attributed to those persons), and in other situations "having a sound basis in public policy."[165] It is unclear whether joint and several liability would be extended to the initial tortfeasor in a product liability crashworthiness case.[166]

Joint and several liability may be imposed on the employer of an independent contractor for failure to take precautions reasonably necessary to prevent injuries caused by an inherently dangerous activity.[167] For an activity to be "inherently dangerous," it must: (1) involve an "unusual or peculiar" risk of harm that is not a normal routine matter of customary human activity (this "addresses the relative rarity of the activity and the concomitant lack of contact or experience with the activity and its dangers by the general public"); (2) the activity must be "likely to cause a high probability of harm" in the absence of reasonable precautions; and (3) the danger or probability of harm "must flow from the activity itself when carried out in its ordinary, expected way" such that reasonable precautions aimed at lessening the risk can be expected to have an effect.[168] This doctrine does not apply to injuries to the employees of the independent contractor.[169] Whether the work the employer engaged the independent contractor to perform was inherently dangerous is a question of law for the trial court.[170]

This theory has been extended to impose joint and several liability on the national Boy Scouts Association for injuries caused by an employee of the local council while engaged in the inherently dangerous activity of felling large dead trees, under circumstances where the national organization retained sufficient control over the local activities to impose a duty of care on it with regard to safety issues.[171] However, our courts have held the following not to be inherently dangerous: the operation of a swimming pool;[172] the operation of a wave pool;[173] and the operation of an 18-wheeled truck to deliver water.[174]

2. **Effect of Settlement**

A release of liability executed in favor of one defendant does not operate to extinguish liability of all joint tortfeasors unless the release specifically so provides.[175] A general release raises a rebuttable presumption that only those persons specifically designated by name or by some other specific identifying terminology are discharged.[176] Release language must be read in the context of the entire instrument, the intent of the parties cannot be construed by relying only on excerpts.[177]

With regard to punitive damages, the release of one tortfeasor has no effect on a plaintiff's ability to recover full punitive damages from the other joint tortfeasors.[178]

3. **Contribution**

New Mexico has adopted the Uniform Contribution Among Tortfeasors Act, but does not apply it to concurrent tortfeasors.[179] Where joint and several liability is applicable, a release by the injured party of a joint tortfeasor does not relieve the released tortfeasor of the obligation to make contribution to fellow tortfeasors unless the release is given before the right to seek contribution has accrued and provides for a reduction of the pro rata share of the released tortfeasor's liability from the amount recoverable from other tortfeasors.[180] A settlement with one tortfeasor for the full amount of damages or more does not preclude the injured party from seeking recovery from each severally liable tortfeasor without reduction.[181]

4. **Indemnification**

New Mexico applies traditional indemnification principles in negligence, breach of warranty, and strict liability cases in which the indemnitee is in the chain of supply of a product.[182] Under traditional indemnification, a party who has been held liable for a wrong, but whose conduct in causing the harm was "passive," can recover from a party who was "actively" at fault in causing the harm.[183] Active conduct occurs when the indemnitee personally participated in an affirmative act of negligence, was connected with negligent acts or omissions by knowledge or acquiescence, or has failed to perform a precise duty, which the indemnitee had agreed to perform. Passive conduct occurs when the party seeking indemnification fails to discover and remedy a dangerous situation created by the negligence or wrongdoing of another, or when a party is only the retailer in the chain of distribution of a defective product. As a result, the party seeking indemnification may recover for damages due to a defective product from an active wrongdoer if that party's conduct was passive.

Alex C. Walker
Modrall, Sperling, Roehl, Harris & Sisk
500 Fourth Street, N.W., Suite 1000
P.O. Box 2168
Albuquerque, New Mexico 87103-2168
www.modrall.com
(505) 848-1800
(Fax) (505) 848-1882

ENDNOTES - NEW MEXICO

1. *See Brooks v. Beech Aircraft Corp.*, 120 N.M. 372, 373, 383, 902 P.2d 54, 55, 65 (1995), *overruling Duran v. Gen. Motors Corp.*, 101 N.M. 742, 688 P.2d 779 (Ct. App. 1983).

2. *See* NMSA 1978, § 37-1-8 (1976).

3. *See Martinez v. Showa Denko, K.K.*, 1998-NMCA-111, ¶19, 125 N.M. 615, 964 P.2d 176; *see also Sawtell v. E.I. DuPont de Nemours & Co.*, 22 F.3d 248, 251-52 (10th Cir. 1994).

4. *Clark v. Lovelace Health Sys., Inc.*, 2004-NMCA-119, ¶20 136 N.M. 411, 416, 99 P.3d 232, 237.

5. *See* NMSA 1978, § 37-1-4.

6. *See* NMSA 1978, § 55-2-725(1).

7. *See Fernandez v. Char-Li-Jon, Inc.*, 119 N.M. 25, 28, 888 P.2d 471, 474 (Ct. App. 1994), *overruled on other grounds by Romero v. Bachica*, 2001-NMCA-048, ¶16, 130 N.M. 610, 614-15, 28 P.3d 1151, 1155-56.

8. NMSA 1978, § 37-1-27.

9. *See Stang v. Hertz Corp.*, 83 N.M. 730, 734-35, 497 P.2d 732, 736-37 (1972); *see also Aalco Mfg. Co. v. City of Espanola*, 95 N.M. 66, 67, 618 P.2d 1230, 1231 (1980).

10. *See Spectron Dev. Lab. v. Am. Hollow Boring Co.*, 1997-NMCA-025, ¶13, 123 N.M. 170, 174, 936 P.2d 852, 856.

11. *See* UJI 13-1406 NMRA (New Mexico Rules Annotated); *Spectron Dev. Lab.*, 1997-NMCA-025, ¶13, 123 N.M. at 174, 936 P.2d at 856 ("A product is defective if, at the time of sale or distribution, it contains a manufacturing defect, is defective in design or is defective because of inadequate instruction or warnings.").

12. *See* UJI 13-1407 NMRA; *see also Fernandez v. Ford Motor Co.*, 118 N.M. 100, 112, 879 P.2d 101, 113 (Ct. App. 1994).

13. UJI 13-1407 NMRA. Note—In 2009, the New Mexico Supreme Court adopted a revision to UJI 13-1407's companion instruction, UJI 13-1406 NMRA (2009), and in doing so reaffirmed in a use note that "UJI 13-1407[] must be used in every strict products liability case based upon Restatement

(Second) of Torts § 402A." UJI 13-1406 (use note); *see* Supreme Court Order No. 09-8300-011, effective May 15, 2009.

14. *See Brooks v. Beech Aircraft Corp.*, 120 N.M. 372, 379-81, 902 P.2d 54, 61-63 (1995).

15. *See Tenney v. Seven-Up Co.*, 92 N.M. 158, 159, 584 P.2d 205, 206 (Ct. App. 1978); *Bendorf v. Volkswagenwerk Aktiengeselischaft II*, 90 N.M. 414, 416, 564 P.2d 619, 621 (Ct. App. 1977); *Bendorf v. Volkswagenwerk Aktiengeselischaft, I*, 88 N.M. 355, 540 P.2d 835 (Ct. App. 1975).

16. *See Couch v. Astec Indus., Inc.*, 2002-NMCA-084, ¶43, 132 N.M. 631, 640-41, 53 P.3d 398, 407-08; *see also Pollock v. State Highway & Transp. Dep't*, 1999-NMCA-083, ¶6, 127 N.M. 521, 523-24, 984 P.2d 768, 770-71; *Richards v. Upjohn*, 95 N.M. 675, 678, 625 P.2d 1192, 1195 (Ct. App. 1980) (citing *Harless v. Ewing*, 80 N.M. 149, 150, 452 P.2d 483, 484 (Ct. App. 1969)).

17. *Torres v. El Paso Elec. Co.*, 1999-NMSC-029, ¶12, 127 N.M. 729, 734, 987 P.2d 386, 391 (citing *Thompson v. Anderman*, 59 N.M. 400, 411-12, 285 P.2d 507, 514 (1955)), *overruled on other grounds by Herrera v. Quality Pontiac*, 2003-NMSC-018, ¶23, 134 N.M. 43, 53-54, 73 P.3d 181, 191-92.

18. *See Richards*, 95 N.M. at 679, 625 P.2d at 1196 ("A doctor's negligence is not, as a matter of law, an intervening cause exonerating the drug company, if the doctor's act is reasonably foreseeable.").

19. *Johnstone v. City of Albuquerque*, 2006-NMCA-119, ¶22, 140 N.M. 596, 603, 145 P.3d 76, 83.

20. *Silva v. Lovelace Health Sys.*, 2014 N.M. App. LEXIS 49 (May 6, 2014).

21. UJI 13-1425 NMRA.

22. *See* UJI 13-1415 NMRA; *see also Torres v. El Paso Elec. Co.*, 1999-NMSC-029, ¶29, 127 N.M. 729, 740, 741; 987 P.2d 386, 397, 398 (*overruled on other grounds by Herrera v. Quality Pontiac*, 2003-NMSC-018, 134 N.M. 43, 73 P.3d 181); *Jones v. Minn. Mining & Mfg. Co.*, 100 N.M. 268, 273, 669 P.2d 744, 749 (Ct. App. 1983).

23. *See* UJI 13-1427 NMRA and Committee Comment.

24. *See* UJI 13-1427 NMRA and Committee Comment; *see, e.g., Crespin v. Albuquerque Baseball Club, LLC*, 2009-NMCA-105, 2009 N.M. App. LEXIS 123, 216 P.3d 827, *overruled on other grounds by Edward v. City of Albuquerque*, 2010-NMSC-043, 148 N.M. 646, 241 P.3d 1086; *Lewis v. Samson*, 1999-NMCA-145, 128 N.M. 269, 992 P.2d 282, *rev'd on other grounds*, 2001-NMSC-035, 131 N.M. 317, 35 P.3d 972 (2001); *Norwest Bank N.M., N.A. v. Chrysler Corp.*, 1999-NMCA-070, 127 N.M. 397, 981 P.2d 1215; *Torres*, 1999-NMSC-029, ¶16;

Baer v. Regents of the Univ. of Cal., 1999-NMCA-005, ¶18 126 N.M. 508, 972 P.2d 9; *Jaramillo v. Kellogg*, 1998-NMCA-142, 126 N.M. 84, 966 P.2d 792; *Lopez v. Ski Apache Resort*, 114 N.M. 202, 836 P.2d 648 (Ct. App. 1992); *Reichert v. Atler*, 117 N.M. 623, 875 P.2d 379 (1994); *Baxter v. Noce*, 107 N.M. 48, 752 P.2d 240 (1988); *Jaramillo v. Fisher Controls Co.*, 102 N.M. 614, 698 P.2d 887 (Ct. App. 1985); *Marchese v. Warner Commc'n, Inc.*, 100 N.M. 313, 317, 670 P.2d 113, 117 (Ct. App. 1983); *Bartlett v. N.M. Welding Supply, Inc.*, 98 N.M. 152, 646 P.2d 579 (Ct. App. 1982); *Scott v. Rizzo*, 96 N.M. 682, 634 P.2d 1234 (1981); *Williamson v. Smith*, 83 N.M. 336, 491 P.2d 1147 (1971).

25. *See* UJI 13-2219 NMRA.

26. *See Sena v. N.M. State Police*, 119 N.M. 471, 474, 892 P.2d 604, 607 (Ct. App. 1995); *Lamkin v. Garcia*, 106 N.M. 60, 62, 738 P.2d 932, 934 (Ct. App. 1987); *Bartlett*, 98 N.M. 152, 646 P.2d 579.

27. *See Taylor v. Delgarno Transp., Inc.*, 100 N.M. 138, 667 P.2d 445 (1983).

28. *See Barth v. Coleman*, 118 N.M. 1, 2-3, 878 P.2d 319, 320-21 (1994); *Reichert*, 117 N.M. at 623, 875 P.2d at 379; *Garcia v. Gordon*, 2004-NMCA-114, ¶¶9-10, 136 N.M. 394, 98 P.3d 1044.

29. *See Aalco Mktg. Co. v. City of Espanola*, 95 N.M. 66, 68, 618 P.2d 1230, 1232 (1980); *Stang v. Hertz*, 83 N.M. 730, 732, 497 P.2d 732, 734 (1972); *Fernandez v. Ford Motor Co.*, 118 N.M. 100, 108, 879 P.2d 101, 109 (Ct. App. 1994).

30. *See Livingston v. Begay*, 98 N.M. 712, 716, 652 P.2d 734, 738 (1982); *Stang*, 83 N.M. at 734, 497 P.2d at 736.

31. *See Arenivas v. Cont'l Oil Co.*, 102 N.M. 106, 108, 692 P.2d 31, 33 (Ct. App. 1983), *cert. quashed*, 102 N.M. 88, 691 P.2d 881 (1984).

32. *See Parker v. St. Vincent Hosp.*, 1996-NMCA-070, ¶26, 122 N.M. 39, 919 P.2d 1104; *Tanuz v. Carlberg*, 1996-NMCA-076, ¶11, 122 N.M. 113, 116, 921 P.2d 309, 312.

33. *See Parker v. E.I. Du Pont de Nemours & Co.*, 121 N.M. 120, 126, 909 P.2d 1, 7 (Ct. App. 1995).

34. *See Parker*, 121 N.M. at 128-29, 909 P.2d at 9-10.

35. *See* UJI 13-1419 NMRA and Committee Comment; *Davila v. Bodelson*, 103 N.M. 243, 251, 704 P.2d 1119, 1127 (Ct. App. 1985); *Perfetti v. McGhan Med.*, 99 N.M. 645, 648-49, 662 P.2d 646, 649-50 (Ct. App. 1983).

36. *See* UJI 13-1419 NMRA.

37. *Garcia v. Coe Mfg. Co.*, 1997-NMSC-013, ¶12, 123 N.M. 34, 933 P.2d 243 (quoting *Sw. Dist. Co. v. Olympia Brewing Co.*, 90 N.M. 502, 505, 565 P.2d 1019, 1022 (1977)).

38. *See Garcia*, 1997-NMSC-013, ¶21.

39. *See Garcia*, 1997-NMSC-013, ¶17.

40. *See Garcia*, 1997-NMSC-013, ¶24.

41. *See Budget Rent-A-Car Sys. v. Bridgestone Firestone N. Am. Tire, LLC*, 2009-NMCA-013, ¶19, 145 N.M. 623, 203 P.3d 154; *Aalco Mfg. Co. v. City of Espanola*, 95 N.M. 66, 68, 618 P.2d 1230, 1232 (1980); *Stang v. Hertz*, 83 N.M. 730, 735, 497 P.2d 732, 737 (1972).

42. *See* UJI 13-1415 NMRA.

43. *See* UJI 13-1417 NMRA.

44. *See* UJI 13-1417 NMRA, UJI 13-1418 NMRA.

45. *See* UJI 13-1418 NMRA; UJI 13-1402 NMRA; *see also Couch*, 2002-NMCA-084, ¶¶45-46, 132 N.M. at 641-42, 53 P.3d at 408-09.

46. *See Couch*, 2002-NMCA-084, ¶¶50-52, 132 N.M. at 642-43, 53 P.3d at 409-10.

47. *Couch*, 2002-NMCA-084, ¶52, 132 N.M. at 643, 53 P.3d at 410.

48. *Serna v. Roche Labs.*, 101 N.M. 522, 524, 684 P.2d 1187, 1189 (Ct. App. 1984); *Jones*, 100 N.M. at 284-85, 669 P.2d at 760-61 (Lopez, J., specially concurring) (citing *Reyes v. Wyeth Labs.*, 498 F.2d 1264, 1276 (5th Cir. 1974)); *Perfetti v. McGhan Med.*, 99 N.M. 645, 650, 662 P.2d 646, 651 (Ct. App. 1983); *Hines v. St. Joseph's Hosp.*, 86 N.M. 763, 764, 527 P.2d 1075, 1076 (Ct. App. 1974).

49. *Serna*, 101 N.M. at 524, 684 P.2d at 1189; *Jones*, 100 N.M. at 284, 669 P.2d at 760; *Richards*, 95 N.M. at 678-79, 625 P.2d at 1195-96.

50. *Rimbert v. Eli Lilly & Co.*, 577 F. Supp. 2d 1174, 1214-24 (D.N.M. 2008).

51. *In re Trasylol Prods. Liab. Litig.*, No. 08-cv-80399, slip op. at 8-9 & n. 11 (S.D. Fla. June 23, 2011).

52. *See* UJI 13-1422 NMRA; *see also Tenney*, 92 N.M. at 159, 584 P.2d at 206.

53. *See First Nat'l Bank v. Nor-Am Agric. Prods.*, 88 N.M. 74, 86, 537 P.2d 682, 694 (Ct. App. 1975) (explaining that a manufacturer of a component part is still strictly liable "where there is no change in the component part itself, but it is merely incorporated into something larger, the strict liability will be found

to carry through to the ultimate user," quoting Restatement (Second) of Torts § 402(A) cmt. q).

54. UJI 13-1403 NMRA; *see also Smith v. Bryco Arms*, 2001-NMCA-090, ¶17, 131 N.M. 87, 94, 33 P.3d 638, 645.

55. *See* UJI 13-1403 NMRA; *see also Van de Valde v. Volvo of Am. Corp.*, 106 N.M. 457, 459, 744 P.2d 930, 932 (Ct. App. 1987) (foreseeability is limited to that which is objectively reasonable to expect, not merely what might conceivably occur); *Chairez v. James Hamilton Constr. Co.*, 2009-NMCA-93, 146 N.M. 794, 215 P.3d 732 (holding that whether a modification consisting of removal of guard sometime during the 22 years after delivery of rock crusher was foreseeable to manufacturer was question of fact for jury).

56. *See Brooks*, 120 N.M. at 381, 902 P.2d at 63; *Saiz v. Belen Sch. Dist.*, 113 N.M. 387, 402, 827 P.2d 102, 117 (1992).

57. *See Fernandez*, 118 N.M. at 108, 879 P.2d at 109; *Armijo v. Ed Black's Chevrolet Ctr., Inc.*, 105 N.M. 422, 424, 733 P.2d 870, 872 (Ct. App. 1987); *Carter Farms Co. v. Hoffman-Laroche, Inc.*, 83 N.M. 383, 385, 492 P.2d 1000, 1002 (Ct. App. 1971) (finding that product defect can be shown by circumstantial evidence).

58. *See* UJI 13-1408 NMRA.

59. *See* UJI 13-1405 NMRA; *Brooks*, 120 N.M. at 382, 902 P.2d at 64.

60. *See* UJI 13-1405, 13-1408 NMRA; *see also Brooks*, 120 N.M. at 382, 902 P.2d at 64.

61. *Couch*, 2002-NMCA-084, ¶¶21-22, 132 N.M. at 636, 53 P.3d at 403.

62. *Kilgore v. Fuji Heavy Indus. Ltd.*, 2009-NMCA-078, ¶¶40-43, 146 N.M. 698, 710-11, 213 P.3d 1127, 1139-40.

63. *Kilgore*, 2009-NMCA-078, ¶¶44-46.

64. *Kilgore*, 2009-NMCA-078, ¶¶41, 45.

65. *Kilgore*, 2009-NMCA-078, ¶46.

66. *See Ohlson v. Kent Nowlin Constr. Co.*, 99 N.M. 539, 544, 660 P.2d 1021, 1026 (Ct. App. 1983); *Ruiz v. S. Pac. Transp. Co.*, 97 N.M. 194, 202, 638 P.2d 406, 414 (Ct. App. 1981); *cf. Kirk Co. v. Ashcraft*, 101 N.M. 462, 469, 684 P.2d 1127, 1134 (1984) (where evidence of prior claims related to the quality of the goods was admissible in a contract dispute).

67. *See Ruiz*, 97 N.M. at 202, 638 P.2d at 414.

68. *See Ruiz*, 97 N.M. at 202, 638 P.2d at 414; *Ohlson*, 99 N.M. at 543, 660 P.2d at 1025; *Enriquez v. Cochran*, 1998-NMCA-157, ¶¶74-75, 126 N.M. 196, 217-18, 967 P.2d 1136, 1157-58.

69. *See* Rule 11-403 NMRA; *Ohlson*, 99 N.M. at 543, 660 P.2d at 1025.

70. *Smith v. Ingersoll-Rand Co.*, 214 F.3d 1235, 1246-50 (10th Cir. 2000); *Morales v. E.D. Etnyre & Co.*, 382 F. Supp. 2d 1252, 1265 (D.N.M. 2005).

71. *See Smith*, 214 F.3d at 1246; *Morales*, 382 F. Supp. 2d at 1265.

72. *Smith*, 214 F.3d at 1246.

73. *See Smith*, 214 F.3d at 1246-47.

74. *See Smith*, 214 F.3d at 1247-48.

75. *See Smith*, 214 F.3d at 1248.

76. *See Smith*, 214 F.3d at 1249.

77. *See Smith*, 214 F.3d at 1248.

78. *See Smith*, 214 F.3d at 1249.

79. *See* UJI 13-1409, UJI 13-1426 NMRA, and Committee Comments; *Rudisaile v. Hawk Aviation, Inc.*, 92 N.M. 778, 790, 595 P.2d 751, 763 (Ct. App. 1978) (Appendix 'A'), *rev'd on other grounds*, 92 N.M. 575, 592 P.2d 175 (1979).

80. *Coleman v. Eddy Potash, Inc.*, 120 N.M. 645, 649, 905 P.2d 185, 189 (1995), *overruled on other grounds by Delgado v. Phelps Dodge Chino, Inc.*, 2001-NMSC-034, 131 N.M. 272, 34 P.3d 1148 (2001).

81. *Id.*

82. *Torres v. El Paso Elec. Co.*, 1999-NMSC-029, ¶44, 127 N.M. 729, 746, 987 P.2d 386, 403, *overruled on other grounds by Herrera v. Quality Pontiac*, 2003-NMSC-018, 134 N.M. 43, 73 P.3d 181 (2001).

83. *Torres*, 1999-NMSC-029, ¶48, 127 N.M. at 748, 987 P.2d at 405 (quoting *Kitchell v. Public Serv. Co.*, 1998-NMSC-51, ¶17, 126 N.M. 525, 972 P.2d 344).

84. *Torres*, 1999-NMSC-029, ¶50, 127 N.M. at 748, 987 P.2d at 405.

85. *Torres*, 1999-NMSC-029, ¶46, 127 N.M. at 747, 987 P.2d at 404.

86. *Torres*, 1999-NMSC-029, ¶46, 127 N.M. at 747, 987 P.2d at 404.

87. *Coleman v. Eddy Potash, Inc.*, 120 N.M. 645, 650, 905 P.2d 185, 190 (1995), *overruled on other grounds by Delgado v. Phelps Dodge, Chino, Inc.*, 2001-NMSC-034, 131 N.M. 272, 34 P.3d 1148 (2001).

88. *See Coleman*, 120 N.M. at 650-51, 905 P.2d at 190-91.

89. *See Restaurant Mgmt. Co. v. Kidde-Fenwal, Inc.*, 1999-NMCA-101, ¶¶11-21, 127 N.M. 708, 711-14, 986 P.2d 504, 507-10 (recognizing a court's inherent power to sanction for spoliation of evidence but directing trial courts to consider the degree of fault, the degree of prejudice, and the availability of lesser sanctions); *Segura v. K-Mart Corp.*, 2003-NMCA-013, ¶¶10-13, 133 N.M. 192, 195-96, 62 P.3d 283, 286-87 (upholding a jury instruction that "K-Mart was negligent and that its negligence was a proximate cause of Segura's fall" as a sanction for spoliation of evidence).

90. *Torres v. El Paso Elec. Co.*, 1999-NMSC-029, ¶53, 127 N.M. 729, 749, 987 P.2d 386, 406, *overruled on other grounds by Herrera v. Quality Pontiac*, 2003-NMSC-018, 134 N.M. 43, 173 P.3d 181 (2001).

91. *Torres*, 1999-NMSC-029, ¶53, 127 N.M. 729, 749, 987 P.2d 386, 406, *overruled on other grounds by Herrera*, 2003-NMSC-018, 134 N.M. 43, 173 P.3d 181.

92. *Utah Int'l, Inc. v. Caterpillar Tractor Co.*, 108 N.M. 539, 542, 775 P.2d 741, 744 (Ct. App. 1989), *cert. denied*, 108 N.M. 354, 772 P.2d 884 (1989) (denying claims for economic loss from a product injuring itself due to negligent failure to warn); *see also AMREP Sw. Inc. v. Shollenbarger Wood Treating, Inc.*, 119 N.M. 542, 551, 893 P.2d 438, 447 (1995) (declining to overrule *Utah International* and holding that the economic loss rule does not bar a claim for indemnification); *Spectron Dev. Lab. v. Am. Hollow Boring Co.*, 1997-NMCA-25, ¶20, 123 N.M. 170, 175, 936 P.2d 852, 857 (reaffirming *Utah International*).

93. *Utah Int'l, Inc.*, 108 N.M. at 542, 772 P.2d at 744.

94. *Utah Int'l, Inc.*, 108 N.M. at 542, 772 P.2d at 744.

95. *See Duran v. Gen. Motors Corp.*, 101 N.M. 742, 745, 688 P.2d 779, 783 (Ct. App. 1983), *overruled in part by Brooks v. Beech Aircraft Corp.*, 120 N.M. 372, 902 P.2d 54 (1995); *Brooks v. Beech Aircraft*, 120 N.M. 372, 902 P.2d 54 (1995).

96. *Brooks v. Beech Aircraft*, 120 N.M. 372, 902 P.2d 54 (1995).

97. *Duran*, 101 N.M. at 750, 688 P.2d at 787.

98. *Duran*, 101 N.M. at 750, 688 P.2d at 787; *Lewis v. Samson*, 2001-NMSC-035, ¶34, 131 N.M. 317, 330, 35 P.3d 972.

99. UJI 13-1802 E.

100. UJI 13-1802 E; *see* Use Notes to UJI 13-1802 E NMRA; UJI 13-2222 NMRA.

101. *See* Committee Comment to UJI 13-1802 E NMRA.

102. *Lewis v. Samson*, 2001-NMSC-035, ¶¶33-43, 131 N.M. 317, 330-33, 35 P.3d 972.

103. *Bustos v. Hyundai Motor Co.*, 2010-NMCA-90, ¶50, 149 N.M. 1, 243 P.3d 440.

104. *See Bustos*, 2010-NMCA-90, ¶54.

105. *See Bustos*, 2010-NMCA-90, ¶54 (citing Committee Comment for UJI 13-1407).

106. UJI 13-1402, NMRA.

107. *See* UJI 13-1402, NMRA.

108. *See* UJI 13-1403, NMRA.

109. *See* NMSA 1978, §§ 55-2-313 to -318; *see also* UJI 13-1428 to 1433 NMRA.

110. *See* UJI 13-1430 NMRA, Committee Comment; *see also Perfetti v. McGhan Med.*, 99 N.M. 645, 653, 662 P.2d 646, 654 (Ct. App. 1983), *cert. denied*, 99 N.M. 644, 662 P.2d 645 (1983) (noting comparable standards of product liability claim and claim for breach of implied warranty of merchantability).

111. *Perfetti v. McGhan Med.*, 99 N.M. 645, 653, 662 P.2d 646, 654 (Ct. App. 1983), *cert. denied*, 99 N.M. 644, 662 P.2d 645 (1983).

112. *Chavarria v. Fleetwood Retail Corp.*, 2005-NMCA-082, ¶17, 137 N.M. 783, 115 P.3d 799, *rev'd on other grounds*, 2006-NMSC-46, 140 N.M. 478, 143 P.3d 717; *Hale v. Basin Motor Co.*, 110 N.M. 314, 320, 795 P.2d 1006, 1012 (1990); *Hood v. Falkerson*, 102 N.M. 677, 699 P.2d 608, 611 (1985).

113. UJI 13-861 NMRA and UJI 13-1827 NMRA; *Robison v. Katz*, 94 N.M. 314, 321, 610 P.2d 201, 208 (Ct. App. 1980).

114. *See Hood v. Fulkerson*, 102 N.M. 677, 680, 699 P.2d 608, 611 (1985); *Grandi v. LeSage*, 74 N.M. 799, 810-11, 399 P.2d 285, 293 (1965).

115. *See* UJI 13-861 NMRA; UJI 13-1827 NMRA; *Weststar Mortgage Corp. v. Jackson*, 131 N.M. 493, 507, 39 P.3d 710, 724 (Ct. App. 2001), *rev'd on other grounds*, 2003-NMSC-2, 133 N.M. 114, 61 P.3d 823; *Torres v. El Paso Elec. Co.*, 1999-NMSC-029, ¶27, 127 N.M. 729, 740, 987 P.2d 386, 397, *overruled on other grounds, Herrera v. Quality Pontiac*, 2003-NMSC-18, 134 N.M. 43, 73 P.3d 181; *Allsup's Convenience Stores, Inc. v. North River Ins. Co.*, 1999-NMSC-6, ¶53, 127 N.M. 1, 976 P.2d 1; *Enriquez v. Cochran*, 1998-NMCA-157 ¶121, 126 N.M. 196, 967 P.2d 1136, 1167, *cert. denied*, 126 N.M. 532, 972 P.2d 351 (1998); *Clay*

v. *Ferrellgas, Inc.*, 118 N.M. 266, 269, 881 P.2d 11, 14 (1994); *Green Tree Acceptance, Inc. v. Layton*, 108 N.M. 171, 174, 769 P.2d 84, 87 (1989).

116. *Paiz v. State Farm Fire & Cas. Co.*, 118 N.M. 203, 211-13, 880 P.2d 300, 308-10 (1994) (rejecting gross negligence as basis for punitive damages in contract action); UJI 13-1827 NMRA; *but see Smith v. Ingersoll-Rand Co.*, 214 F.3d 1235, 1250-51 (10th Cir. 2000) (federal court applying New Mexico law affirmed jury instruction that punitive damages may be awarded for gross negligence so long as gross negligence is defined as an act or omission done with conscious indifference to harmful consequences); *Torres v. El Paso Elec. Co.*, 1999-NMSC-029, ¶27, 127 N.M. 729, 987 P.2d 986 (although gross negligence is not a basis for punitive damages in a contract action, Supreme Court has declined to reach the issue in the context of a negligence action), *overruled on other grounds*, *Herrera v. Quality Pontiac*, 2003-NMSC-18, 134 N.M. at 43, 73 P.3d at 181.

117. *Bogle v. Summit Inv. Co., L.L.C.*, 2005-NMCA-024, ¶34, 137 N.M. 80, 107 P.3d 520; UJI 13-1827 NMRA.

118. *Sanchez v. Clayton*, 117 N.M. 761, 767, 877 P.2d 567, 573 (1994).

119. *Robertson v. Carmel Builders Real Estate*, 2004-NMCA-056, ¶39, 135 N.M. 641, 92 P.3d 653; *Vickrey v. Dunivan*, 59 N.M. 90, 94, 279 P.2d 853, 856 (1955).

120. *Allsup's Convenience Stores v. North River Ins. Co.*, 1999-NMSC-006, ¶51, 127 N.M. 1, 976 P.2d 1 (1998); *Green Tree Acceptance, Inc. v. Layton*, 108 N.M. 171, 174, 769 P.2d 84, 87 (1989).

121. *Chavarria v. Fleetwood Retail Corp.*, 2006-NMSC-046, ¶37-39, 140 N.M. 478, 143 P.3d 717; *Atler v. Murphy Enters.*, 2005-NMCA-006, ¶23, 136 N.M. 701, 104 P.3d 1092; *Aken v. Plains Elec. Gen. & Transp. Corp., Inc.*, 2002-NMSC-021, ¶20, 132 N.M. 401, 49 P.3d 662.

122. *Kaveny v. MDA Enters.*, 2005-NMCA-118, ¶29, 138 N.M. 432, 120 P.3d 854.

123. *Sunwest Bank, N.A. v. Colucci*, 117 N.M. 373, 377-78, 872 P.2d 346, 350-51 (1994); *see also State Farm Mut. v. Barker*, 2004-NMCA-105, ¶18, 136 N.M. 211, 96 P.3d 336 (finding that the "certainty of damages does not provide the basis for an award of prejudgment interest under Section 56-8-3").

124. *State Farm Fire & Cas. Co. v. Farmers Alliance Mut. Ins. Co.*, 2004-NMCA-101, ¶17, 136 N.M. 259, 265, 96 P.3d 1179, 1185; *Sunwest Bank*, 117 N.M. at 378, 872 P.2d at 351.

125. *See City of Carlsbad v. Grace*, 1998-NMCA-144 ¶32, 126 N.M. 95, 104-05, 966 P.2d 1178, 1187-88.

126. *Sunwest Bank*, 117 N.M. at 377-78, 872 P.2d at 350-51 (quoting *Smith v. McKee*, 116 N.M. 34, 36, 859 P.2d 1061, 1063 (1993); *Kueffer v. Kueffer*, 110 N.M. 10, 12, 791 P.2d 461, 463 (1990)). *See also State Farm Mut. Auto Ins. Co. v. Barker*, 2004-NMCA-105, ¶21, 136 N.M. 211, 216, 96 P.3d 336, 341 (upholding trial court's decision to deny pre-judgment interest because there was no breach of contract).

127. *Sunwest Bank*, 117 N.M. at 379, 872 P.2d at 352.

128. *Sunwest Bank*, 117 N.M. at 378, 872 P.2d at 351 (citing *Aztec Well Servicing Co. v. Prop. & Cas. Ins. Guar. Ass'n*, 115 N.M. 475, 486, 853 P.2d 726, 737 (1993)); *see also Smith*, 116 N.M. at 36, 859 P.2d at 1063.

129. NMSA 1978, § 56-8-4 (B); *Gonzales v. Surgidev Corp.*, 120 N.M. 133, 150, 899 P.2d 576, 593 (1995).

130. *See Gonzales*, 120 N.M. at 150, 899 P.2d at 593.

131. *Gonzales*, 120 N.M. at 150, 899 P.2d at 593.

132. *Gonzales*, 120 N.M. at 150, 899 P.2d at 593.

133. *Gonzales*, 120 N.M. at 150, 899 P.2d at 593.

134. *Coates v. Wal-Mart Stores, Inc.*, 1999-NMSC-013, ¶56, 127 N.M. 47, 59, 976 P.2d 999, 1011.

135. *Coates*, 1999-NMSC-013, at ¶55, 127 N.M. at 59, 976 P.2d at 1011.

136. *Coates*, 1999-NMSC-013, at ¶55, 127 N.M. at 59, 976 P.2d at 1011; *see also Kaveny v. MDA Enters., Inc.*, 2005-NMCA-118, ¶29, 138 N.M. 432, 438, 120 P.3d 854, 860.

137. *Folz v. New Mexico*, 115 N.M. 639, 642, 857 P.2d 39, 42 (Ct. App. 1993) (citing *Ulibarri v. Gee*, 107 N.M. 768, 769, 764 P.2d 1326, 1327 (1988)); *see also Yardman v. San Juan Downs*, 120 N.M. 751, 762, 906 P.2d 742, 753 (Ct. App. 1995) (while post-judgment interest is authorized generally, it is not available for claims against a governmental agency).

138. *Public Serv. Co. v. Diamond D Constr. Co. Inc.*, 2001-NMCA-082, ¶51, 131 N.M. 100, 115, 33 P.3d 651, 666 (quoting *Bailey v. Chattem, Inc.*, 838 F.2d 149, 152 (6th Cir. 1988)).

139. NMSA 1978, § 56-8-4(A); *see also Sunwest Bank*, 117 N.M. at 379, 872 P.2d at 352.

140. *Weststar Mortgage Corp. v. Jackson*, 2002-NMCA-9, ¶¶54-55, 131 N.M. 493, 508-09, 39 P.3d 710, 725-26 (Ct. App. 2001), *overruled on other grounds by* 2003-NMSC-2, 61 P.3d 823.

141. *Public Serv. Co.*, 2001-NMCA-082, ¶59, 131 N.M. at 117, 33 P.3d at 668 (citing Section 56-8-4(A) and *Teague-Strebeck Motors, Inc.*, 1999-NMCA-109, ¶61, 127 N.M. 603, 985 P.2d 1183, *overruled in irrelevant part by Sloan v. State Farm Mut. Auto Ins. Co.*, 360 F.3d 1220, 1224-25 (10th Cir. 2004)).

142. *Nava v. City of Santa Fe*, 2004-NMSC-39, ¶23, 136 N.M. 647, 654, 103 P.3d 571, 578 (New Mexico Human Rights Act does not explicitly waive state's immunity from post-judgment interest); *see Franco v. Carlsbad Mun. Schs.*, 2001-NMCA-042, ¶25, 130 N.M. 543, 550, 28 P.3d 531, 538; *Trujillo v. City of Albuquerque*, 1998-NMSC-031, ¶46, 125 N.M. 721, 733, 965 P.2d 305, 317 (1998) (New Mexico Tort Claims Act does not provide for post-judgment interest against state entity when read with § 56-8-4(D)).

143. *See* NMSA 1978, §§ 52-1-6(E) (1990), 52-1-9 (1973).

144. *Delgado v. Phelps Dodge Chino, Inc.*, 2001-NMSC034, ¶24, 131 N.M. 272, 279-80, 34 P.3d 1148, 1155. In *Delgado*, the decedent died following an explosion that occurred at a smelting plant after a supervisor ordered him to perform a task that, according to his widow, was virtually certain to kill or cause him serious bodily injury. *Delgado*, 2001-NMSC034, at ¶1, 131 N.M. at 274, ¶1, 34 P.3d at 1150. The court rejected the application of the actual intent test because that test impermissibly favored employers. *Delgado*, 2001-NMSC034, at ¶23, 131 N.M. at 279, 34 P.3d at 1155.

145. *Delgado*, 2001-NMSC034, at ¶26-7, 131 N.M. at 280, 34 P.3d at 1156. The new test lifted the bar of exclusivity when an employer knew that its conduct was substantially certain to result in the worker's serious injury or death. *Delgado*, 2001-NMSC034, at ¶26-7, 131 N.M. at 280, 34 P.3d at 1156. All case law that required allegation or proof of an employer's actual intent to injure a worker as a precondition to a worker's tort recovery was overruled. *Delgado*, 2001-NMSC034, ¶23, 131 N.M. at 279, 34 P.3d at 1155.

146. *Dominguez v. Perovich Props.*, 2005-NMCA-50, ¶22, 137 N.M. 401, 407, 111 P.3d 721, 727. The court stated that the employee had to "plead or present evidence that the employer met each of the three *Delgado* elements in order to survive a pre-trial dispositive motion." *Dominguez*, 2005-NMCA-50, at ¶16, 137 N.M. at 405, 111 P.3d at 725 (quoting *Morales v. Reynolds*, 2004-NMCA-98, ¶14, 136 N.M. 200, 285, 97 P.3d 612, 617). The court noted that having the employee perform the routine task he was asked to perform, a task with which he was familiar and which he had performed in the past, was hardly the equivalent of sending the employee into certain injury. *Dominguez*, 2005-NMCA-50, at ¶16, 137 N.M. at 405, 111 P.3d at 725. The possibility that an accident could occur because of an unexpected careless

act of a co-employee does not meet the *Delgado* standard. *Dominguez*, 2005-NMCA-50, at ¶21, 137 N.M. at 407, 111 P.3d at 725.

147. *Padilla v. Wall Colmonoy Corp.*, 2006-NMCA-137, ¶6, 140 N.M. 630, 631, 145 P.3d 110, 111.

148. *See Chairez, supra* at ¶30 (*Delgado* is "a very, very narrow exception" and "worker must establish that the employer's conduct was unconscionable . . . and that it 'exemplif[ied] a comparable degree of egregiousness' as that in *Delgado*.").

149. *Harger v. Structural Servs., Inc.*, 1996-NMSC-018, ¶5, 121 N.M. 657, 661, 916 P.2d 1324, 1328 (1996).

150. *See Peterson v. Wells Fargo Armored Serv. Corp.*, 2000-NMCA-043, ¶10, 129 N.M. 158, 161, 3 P.3d 135, 138; *Matkins v. Zero Refrigerated Lines*, 93 N.M. 511, 517, 602 P.2d 195, 201 (Ct. App. 1979).

151. *Chavez v. Sundt Corp.*, 1996-NMSC-046, ¶14, 122 N.M. 78, 83, 920 P.2d 1032, 1037.

152. *See Tipton v. Texaco, Inc.*, 103 N.M. 689, 697, 712 P.2d 1351, 1359 (1985); *Taylor v. Delgarno Trans.*, 100 N.M. 138, 667 P.2d 445 (1983).

153. *Hamberg v. Sandia Corp.*, 2008-NMSC-15, ¶10, 143 N.M. 601, 604, 179 P.3d 1209, 1212.

154. *Hamberg*, 2008-NMSC-15, at ¶¶11-13, 143 N.M. at 604, 179 P.3d at 1212 (citing *Rivera v. Sagebrush Sales, Inc.*, 118 N.M. 676, 678-79, 884 P.2d 832, 834-35 (Ct. App. 1994)).

155. *Hamberg*, 2008-NMSC-15, at ¶18, 143 N.M. at 604, 179 P.3d at 1213 (holding immune from tort liability a special employer complying with the Workers' Compensation Act by requiring the general employer to carry workers' compensation insurance and also paying as part of its contract with the general employer an amount sufficient to cover the premiums).

156. *See* NMSA 1978, §§ 37-1-4, 37-1-7, 37-1-8, § 55-2-725.

157. NMSA 1978, §§ 55-2-313 to -318, 55-2-725.

158. *See* NMSA 1978, § 41-3A-1.

159. NMSA 1978, § 28-6-1.

160. NMSA 1978, § 41-3-1 (1947).

161. *See* NMSA 1978, § 41-3A-1;*Torres v. El Paso Elec. Co.*, 1999-NMSC-029, ¶13, 127 N.M. 729, 734-35, 987 P.2d 386, 391-92 (*overruled on other grounds by Herrera v. Quality Pontiac*, 2003-NMSC-018, ¶23, 134 N.M. 43, 54, 73 P.3d 181, 192); *Reichert v. Atler*, 117 N.M. 623, 625, 875 P.2d 379, 381 (1994); *Saiz v. Belen Sch. Dist.*, 113 N.M. 387, 400, 827 P.2d 102, 115 (1992); *Gulf Ins. Co. v. Cottone*, 2006-NMCA-150, ¶12, 140 N.M. 728, 732-33, 148 P.3d 814, 818-19; *Bartlett v. N.M. Welding Supply, Inc.*, 98 N.M. 152, 159, 646 P.2d 579, 586 (Ct. App. 1982).

162. *Payne v. Hall*, 2006-NMSC-029, ¶¶11-14, 139 N.M. 659, 664, 137 P.3d 599, 604.

163. *Payne*, 2006-NMSC-029 at ¶13, 139 N.M. at 664, 137 P.3d at 604; *Lewis v. Samson*, 2001-NMSC-035, ¶33, 131 N.M. 317, 330, 35 P.3d 972, 985; Megan P. Duffy, *Multiple Tortfeasors Defined by the Injury: Successive Tortfeasor Liab. After Payne v. Hall*, 37 N.M. L. Rev. 603, 618-19 (2007).

164. *Gulf Ins. Co. v. Cottone*, 2006-NMCA-150, ¶22, 140 N.M. 728, 734-35, 148 P.3d 814, 820-21.

165. NMSA 1978, § 41-3A-1; *see also Saiz*, 113 N.M. at 400, 827 P.2d at 115; M. E. Occhialino, *Bartlett Revisited New Mexico Tort Law Twenty Years After the Abolition of Joint and Several Liability—Part One*, 33 N.M. L. Rev. 1, 3-14 (2003). When joint and several liability applies, *see* Uniform Contribution Among Tortfeasors Act, NMSA 1978, § 41-3-1 to -8 (1947, as amended through 1987).

166. *See supra* discussion at Section C.21.

167. *See Saiz*, 113 N.M. at 400, 827 P.2d at 115; *see also Hinger v. Parker & Parsley Petro. Co.*, 120 N.M. 430, 436, 902 P.2d 1033, 1039 (Ct. App. 1995); UJI 13-1634 NMRA.

168. *Gabaldon v. ERISA Mortgage Co.*, 1999-NMSC-039, ¶¶13, 17, 19, 128 N.M. 84, 87-89, 990 P.2d 197, 200-02.

169. *N.M. Elec. Serv. Co. v. Montanez*, 89 N.M. 278, 281-82, 551 P.2d 634, 637-38 (1976); *see Saiz*, 113 N.M. at 398 n.10, 827 P.2d at 113 n.10; *Enriquez v. Cochran*, 1998-NMCA-157, ¶112, 126 N.M. 196, 225, 967 P.2d 1136, 1165, *cert. denied*, Sup. Ct. No. 25, 365, 126 N.M. 532, 972 P.2d 351.

170. *Saiz*, 113 N.M. at 395-96, 827 P.2d at 110-11.

171. *Enriquez v. Cochran*, 1998-NMCA-157, ¶85, 126 N.M. 196, 967 P.2d 113.

172. *Seal v. Carlsbad Indep. Sch. Dist.*, 116 N.M. 101, 105-06, 860 P.2d 743, 747-48 (1993).

173. *Gabaldon v. Erisa Mortgage Co.*, 1999-NMSC-039, ¶13, 21, 128 N.M. 84, 87, 89, 990 P.2d 197, 200, 202.

174. *Valdez v. Yates Petroleum Co.*, 2007-NMCA-38, ¶10, 141 N.M. 381, 384, 155 P.3d 786, 789.

175. *See* NMSA 1978, § 41-3-4; *Martinez v. Albuquerque Collection Servs., Inc.*, 867 F. Supp. 1495, 1501 (D.N.M. 1994); *Johnson v. City of Las Cruces*, 86 N.M. 196, 197, 521 P.2d 1037, 1038 (Ct. App. 1974).

176. *Hansen v. Ford Motor Co.*, 120 N.M. 203, 212, 900 P.2d 952, 961 (1995); *Gulf Ins. Co. v. Cottone*, 2006-NMCA-150, ¶27, 140 N.M. 728, 736, 148 P.3d 814, 822.

177. *Garrison v. Navajo Freight Lines*, 74 N.M. 238, 241, 392 P.2d 580, 582 (1964).

178. *Sierra Blanca Sales Co. v. Newco Indus., Inc.*, 88 N.M. 472, 475, 542 P.2d 52, 55 (Ct. App. 1975), *rev'd on other grounds, Fortuna Corp. v. Sierra Blanca Sales Co.*, 89 N.M. 187, 548 P.2d 865 (1976).

179. *Wilson v. Galt*, 100 N.M. 227, 231, 668 P.2d 1104, 1108 (Ct. App. 1983), *cert. quashed*, 100 N.M. 192, 668 P.2d 308; *see* NMSA 1978, §§ 41-3-1 to -8 (1947, as amended through 1987).

180. NMSA 1978, § 41-3-5.

181. *Wilson*, 100 N.M. at 232, 668 P.2d at 1109.

182. *Budget Rent-A-Car Sys. v. Bridgestone Firestone N. Am. Tire, LLC*, 2009-NMCA-013, ¶¶8-12, 145 N.M. 623, 203 P.3d 154 (Ct. App. 2008).

183. *See In re Consol. Vista Hills Retaining Wall Litig. (Amrep)*, 119 N.M. 542, 545, 893 P.2d 438, 441 (1995).

NEW YORK

A. CAUSES OF ACTION

A plaintiff in New York may assert four separate causes of action for injuries resulting from allegedly defective products: strict product liability, negligence, breach of express warranty, and breach of implied warranty.[1]

B. STATUTES OF LIMITATION

1. Strict Product Liability and Negligence

A claim sounding in strict product liability or negligence for personal injury or property damage is governed by a three-year limitations period.[2] A cause of action accrues when injury occurs, unless provided otherwise by statute.[3]

2. Warranty Theories

A claim based on breach of warranty is governed by a four-year statute of limitations.[4] The limitations period is measured from the tender of delivery by the defendant to defendant's purchaser, regardless of when the plaintiff may have acquired or come into contact with the product.[5] Thus, the time of accrual may differ for each entity in the product's chain of distribution.[6]

3. Wrongful Death

A wrongful death action must be commenced within two years of the decedent's death.[7]

4. The Discovery Rule

In 1986, the New York Legislature modified the three-year statute of limitations period for actions to recover for personal injury or property damage "caused by the latent effects of exposure to any substance or combination of substances, in any form, upon or within the body or upon or within the property. . . ."[8] The Court of Appeals recently made clear that the "discovery rule" only applies to latent injuries caused by exposure to a "toxic substance."[9] The three-year statute of limitations period for these latent injuries begins to run from the earlier of the date of discovery of the injury by the plaintiff or the date when, through the exercise of "reasonable diligence," the plaintiff should have discovered the injury.[10] The date on which a plaintiff discovered or should have discovered an injury has been treated as a mixed question of law and fact.[11] The Court of Appeals recently clarified what constitutes discovery of an "injury" within the meaning of CPLR § 214-c. The Court ruled that a plaintiff will be deemed to have discovered an "injury" when he becomes aware of the primary medical condition underlying his claim.[12] The Court rejected decisions by several federal and state courts that held that a plaintiff will not be deemed to have discovered an "injury" until he becomes aware of both the medical condition at issue and facts demonstrating that the condition is attributable to an injury inflicted upon the plaintiff by a third party.[13]

There is no continuing-wrong exception to the discovery rule;[14] nor may a plaintiff extend the statute of limitations by alleging breach of a continuing duty to warn.[15] In addition, the rule has been held inapplicable to a cause of action for personal injuries based on breach of implied warranty.[16] Although a claim for breach of express warranty of future performance accrues with discovery of the breach (rather than delivery of the offending product), the limitations period will not be extended based on continuing breaches of the same warranty of future performance.[17]

There also is authority holding that the "discovery rule" supplied by CPLR § 214-c does not apply to wrongful death actions because its express language limits it to actions to recover for personal injuries or property damage.[18]

The discovery statute permits an action for injury caused by the latent effects of exposure to be commenced more than three years after the discovery of the injury where the cause of the injury is unknown at the time of injury. Under this rule, if the cause is discovered within five years of the injury or when, with reasonable diligence, the injury should have been discovered, the plaintiff has an additional one-year period from that date to commence an action.[19] The Court of Appeals has held that even effects concealed for a time period as brief as a few hours may be "latent" within the meaning of the discovery statute, and, thus, may qualify for this extension if the cause of the injury is unknown at the time the injury is discovered or should have been discovered.[20] The plaintiff has the burden of alleging and proving that "technical, scientific or medical knowledge and information sufficient to ascertain the cause of his injury had not been discovered, identified or determined within three years of discovery of the injury."[21] This requires proof that during that timeframe there was not information sufficient for the technical, scientific, or medical community to ascertain the probable causal relationship between the substance and injury.[22]

One appellate case has held that a plaintiff can only have the benefit of the one-year extension provided by CPLR § 214-c(4) if he or she has, in fact, discovered the cause of the injury.[23] In other words, a plaintiff otherwise time-barred, because he sued more than three years after discovery of the injury, cannot maintain that he sued within a year of discovery of the cause if he has not actually discovered it; otherwise, he could indefinitely extend the statute of limitations (up to five years from discovery of the injury) while he searches for the cause.[24]

Another issue under § 214-c concerns the so-called "two-injury" rule. Some cases have held that, even if suit is barred as to one injury, because it is discovered more than three years before suit is filed, it may be timely as to "separate and distinct" injuries caused by the defective product if they are discovered within the three years before suit is commenced.[25] It has been held, moreover, that the two-injury rule applies even if the exposure and discovery of the first injury pre-date the effective date of CPLR § 214-c.[26]

The discovery rule of CPLR § 214-c is not applicable to actions which satisfy the following three criteria: (a) the action is based on acts or omissions that occurred prior to July 1, 1986, (b) the action is based on acts or omissions that caused or contributed to an injury that either was discovered or, through the exercise of reasonable diligence, should have been discovered prior to July 1, 1986, *and* (c) such action was or would have been barred due to the expiration of the applicable limitations period prior to July 1, 1986.[27]

C. STRICT LIABILITY

1. The Standard

Strict product liability is imposed upon a manufacturer or nonmanufacturing entity in a product's chain of distribution for personal injury or property damage caused by a defect in the product.[28] In order to establish liability, the plaintiff must prove that the defect was a substantial factor in bringing about the injury and that: at the time of the occurrence, the product was being used by the injured person, or a third person, for the purpose and in the manner normally intended; if the injured person was the user of the product, that he could not, by the exercise of reasonable care, have discovered the defect and perceived its danger; and by the exercise of reasonable care, the injured person could not have avoided the injury.[29] A prospective purchaser injured by a product held out for sale may recover under a strict products theory.[30]

2. Definition of "Defect"

Strict product liability claims may take one of three forms: manufacturing mistake or defect, defective or improper design, or failure to provide adequate warning.[31]

In a manufacturing defect case, the plaintiff claims that the product as manufactured deviated from the defendant's design or internal quality standards.[32]

A plaintiff alleging a design defect must show that the manufacturer "marketed a product designed so that it was not reasonably safe and that the defective design was a substantial factor in causing plaintiff's injury."[33] A product is defectively designed if its utility does not outweigh the danger inherent in its introduction into the stream of commerce.[34] Whether a product is defectively designed turns on an analysis of the following utility/risk factors: (a) the utility of the product to the public as a whole and to the individual user; (b) the nature of the product and the likelihood of its causing injury; (c) the availability of a safer design; (d) the potential for designing and manufacturing the product so that it is safer but remains functional and reasonably priced; (e) the ability of the plaintiff to have avoided injury by careful use of the product; (f) the degree of awareness of the potential danger of the product reasonably attributable to the plaintiff; and (g) the manufacturer's ability to spread any cost related to improving the safety of the design.[35]

In order to succeed on a design defect claim, the plaintiff must establish the existence of a feasible design alternative that would make the product safer.[36] The alternative design will not support liability if it would fail to retain the inherent usefulness the product offers when manufactured according to the design that was actually used.[37] A failure to plead or prove a safer design alternative will result in the dismissal of the claim.[38]

Where a product is manufactured in accordance with plans and specifications provided by the purchaser, an injured party has no design defect claim against the manufacturer unless the specifications are so patently defective that a manufacturer of ordinary prudence would recognize that the product is defective and likely to cause injury.[39] A product offered without an optional safety feature is not considered defectively designed where the evidence shows: (1) the buyer is thoroughly knowledgeable about the product and is actually aware that the safety feature is available; (2) there are normal circumstances under which the product is not unreasonably dangerous without the optional safety feature; and (3) the buyer is in a position to balance the benefits and risks of not having the safety feature in the specifically contemplated circumstances of the buyer's use of the product.[40]

3. **Causation**

The plaintiff has the burden of proving that the defect in defendant's product was a substantial factor in the cause of plaintiff's injury.[41] Where the plaintiff alleges injuries as a result of exposure to a toxic substance, the plaintiff must establish the levels of exposure that are hazardous to humans generally, and that the plaintiff's level of exposure to defendant's product exceeded that threshold, before the plaintiff may recover.[42] Where a "signature disease" is present, minimal evidence of exposure to the toxic substance responsible for the disease coupled with proof that plaintiff has developed the signature disease is sufficient to prove a prima facie case for strict products liability in New York.[43] To prove causation in a failure to warn case, plaintiff must show that adequate warnings would have prevented the use or misuse of the product that allegedly caused the injury.[44] Some courts have held that a plaintiff's failure to read the warning accompanying a product does not necessarily preclude a failure to warn claim based on the allegation that plaintiff would have read and heeded the warning if an adequate warning had been effectively communicated.[45]

4. **Contributory Negligence/Assumption of Risk**

Plaintiff's own negligence or assumption of risk will not bar his or her recovery; however, the amount of the plaintiff's recovery will be reduced in proportion to the culpable conduct attributable to plaintiff.[46] Plaintiff's negligence, culpable conduct and assumption of the risk are affirmative defenses which the defendant must assert in its answer and prove at trial.[47]

5. **Persons Liable/Sale or Lease**

In addition to manufacturers,[48] strict product liability may be imposed upon those who are regularly engaged in the sale of products, such as wholesalers, retailers and distributors.[49] A seller or distributor of a defective product has an implied right of indemnification against the manufacturer of the defective product.[50] An agreement to indemnify a party for damages or defense costs arising from product liability claims is enforceable, regardless of the actual fault of either of the parties to the agreement, so long as the parties' intent is clear in the contract.[51]

Strict product liability does not apply to the casual or occasional seller or manufacturer of an allegedly defective product.[52] However, a manufacturer may be held strictly liable for defects in one-time, custom-made products if such products are produced in the regular course of the manufacturer's business activities.[53] Also, the occasional seller or manufacturer may be held liable for negligent failure to warn where he has actual knowledge of "known defects that are not obvious or readily discernible."[54]

Recent cases have rejected plaintiffs' efforts to hold parent corporations liable for their subsidiaries' products, where the parent corporations had no meaningful role in the development, design, manufacture, or distribution of the products. In these cases, the courts rejected attempts to impose liability on the parent corporations under one or more of the following theories: alter ego,[55] agency,[56] apparent manufacture,[57] and concerted action.[58] A state court has held that a parent corporation is not liable, on a theory of "negligent undertaking," for its testing of component materials, which it substantially relied upon to make an allegedly defective product. The court found that the parent owed no duty to unknown, future purchasers of the finished goods made by the subsidiary.[59] A federal court recently has refused to dismiss a cause of action against a manufacturer for conspiracy to market defective products.[60]

6. **Inherently Dangerous Products**

These are products which cannot be made entirely safe for their intended purpose despite proper design and manufacture. Such products are not deemed defective or unreasonably dangerous if they are accompanied by proper direction and adequate warnings.[61]

7. **Successor Liability**

Although a successor corporation is generally not liable for torts committed by its predecessor, including product liability,[62] there are four exceptions to the general rule. A successor corporation will be liable in a product liability action for a defective product manufactured by the predecessor corporation if: (a) the successor expressly or impliedly agreed to assume liability; (b) the transfer of assets was a consolidation or merger; (c) the successor was a continuation of the predecessor corporation; or (d) the transfer of assets was entered into fraudulently to escape liabilities.[63] In addition, a successor corporation also may be liable based on its own conduct subsequent to the corporate change. New York's highest court recently rejected both the "continuity of the enterprise" and the "product line" exceptions to the general rule that successor corporations are not liable for their predecessor's torts.[64]

8. **Market Share Liability/Enterprise Liability**

New York first recognized market share liability in the context of the DES litigation.[65] The relevant factors for application of the doctrine are (a) a great number of possible wrongdoers, some of whom no longer exist; (b) defendants are in no better position than plaintiff to identify the manufacturer; and (c) all of the defendants are not before the court.[66] Under a market share theory, liability is premised on a defendant's participatory activities in the industry that produced the defective product, not on causation in any individual case.

Since the decision in *Hymowitz*, the courts in New York have refused to apply the market share theory beyond cases involving DES.[67] An intermediate appeals court has recently refused to apply the doctrine in an infant lead poisoning case based upon the plaintiff's failure to satisfy the *Hymowitz* factors.[68]

9. **Privity**

Privity is not a requirement for recovery under strict product liability.[69]

10. **Failure to Warn**

A defendant is liable for the absence or inadequacy of a warning of "latent dangers resulting from foreseeable uses of its products of which it knew or should have known."[70] The nature of the required warning and to whom it should be given depend on a number of factors including the harm that may result from the use of the product without the warning, the reliability and adverse interest of the person to whom the warning is given, the type of product involved, and the burden of disseminating the warning.[71] A manufacturer's duty to warn applies not only to intended uses of its product, but also to unintended but reasonably foreseeable uses.[72]

To be adequate, a warning must be commensurate with the risk involved in the ordinary use of a product.[73] Relevant considerations include the location and conspicuousness of the warning as well as the method of communication of the warning.[74] The adequacy of a given warning is typically a question of fact for the jury.[75]

11. **Post-Sale Duty to Warn**

The duty to issue warnings can extend past the delivery of the product. Even though a product may "be reasonably safe when manufactured and sold and involve no then-known risks of which warning need be given, risks thereafter revealed by user operation and brought to the attention of the manufacturer or vendor may impose upon one or both a duty to warn."[76] The question of what triggers the post-delivery duty to warn is a function of the degree of danger that the product presents and the number of instances reported.[77] A manufacturer also must keep abreast of the state of the art and may be liable for failing to warn of dangers that come to light after initial distribution of the product.[78] New York courts have declined to impose a post-sale duty to recall or retrofit a product, and instead, have limited post-sale obligations to the duty to warn.[79]

12. **Learned Intermediary Doctrine/Bulk Supplier Doctrine**

In certain failure to warn cases, manufacturers or sellers who supply products to sophisticated or knowledgeable purchasers or intermediaries are not liable for a failure to warn the ultimate users of product-related hazards. The learned intermediary or responsible intermediary doctrine typically is applied to cases involving prescription drugs and medical devices.[80] In order to invoke the doctrine, the warning supplied to the physician "must be correct, fully descriptive, and complete and it must convey updated information as to known side effects."[81] The bulk supplier doctrine is related in that it imposes practical limitations on a manufacturer's duty to warn the ultimate user of the product where the manufacturer sells the product in bulk with the contemplation that it will be repackaged and resold by the manufacturer's distributee. Under such circumstances, the manufacturer's duty to warn is satisfied by providing the distributee with an adequate warning.[82] Similarly, under certain circumstances, an employer's failure to provide warnings or instruction to its employees about the hazards associated with a manufacturer's product may constitute an intervening and superseding cause that relieves the manufacturer of liability.[83]

The learned intermediary doctrine cannot be used as an exception to the hearsay rule to admit evidence of warnings given by drug manufacturers.[84]

13. **Substantial Change/Abnormal Use**

The manufacturer of a product that is reasonably safe for its intended use at the time the product is manufactured and sold cannot be held liable for personal injury under strict liability (or negligence) based upon a product defect if, after the product leaves the possession and control of the manufacturer, there is a substantial modification that renders the product unsafe and proximately causes the plaintiff's injuries.[85] This subsequent modification defense does not apply to a design defect claim where the product is designed to permit the removal of a safety feature even when the product's safety device is deliberately bypassed by a third party.[86] Likewise, this defense does not apply where the plaintiff demonstrates that a safety device itself was defective.[87] It is usually for the jury to determine the scope of the product's intended purposes and whether the product was reasonably safe when sold.[88] Liability can exist under a failure to warn theory even in cases in which the subsequent modification defense bars a design defect claim.[89]

14. **State-of-the-Art**

A defendant may seek to avoid liability based on a claim that it complied with the then-applicable state-of-the-art. While this is often termed a defense to a product claim, in reality it is less a defense and more a measure of whether the defendant has met its obligation of due care.[90] In fulfilling its duty, a manufacturer may not rest content with industry practice because the industry may be lagging behind in its knowledge about a product, or in what is reasonably knowable about a product.[91]

15. **Malfunction/Inference of Defect**

A plaintiff is not required to prove a specific defect in the defendant's product as part of his prima facie case. A jury may infer that a defect existed if plaintiff has proven that (1) the product has not performed as intended and (2) plaintiff has excluded all reasonable causes of the accident not attributable to a product defect.[92]

16. **Standards and Regulations**

Evidence of industry standards and procedures and governmental regulations are admissible to prove or refute a claim that a product is defective.[93]

17. **Other Accidents**

Evidence of other, similar accidents may be introduced to establish a dangerous condition.[94] Evidence of prior accidents may not be offered, however, to establish the existence of a dangerous condition or to prove notice unless the requisite substantial similarity of circumstances is demonstrated.[95]

18. **Misrepresentation**

Restatement (Second) of Torts Section 402B has questionable viability in New York. Plaintiffs have pleaded fraud claims in a product liability context as a means of extending the typical statute of limitations applicable to product liability actions.[96]

19. **Destruction or Loss of Product**

Generally, a party has no duty to save an item unless litigation has commenced or it has received actual notice of a claim.[97] New York courts will impose sanctions on a litigant who alters, destroys or loses a product which has been identified as relevant evidence in an ongoing litigation. In addition, a prospective plaintiff who examines an item in anticipation of bringing a lawsuit must retain the item for inspection by the defendant.[98] The applicable sanction can range from dismissal of plaintiff's action or the striking of defendant's answer to less drastic remedies, such as an adverse jury instruction or inference, and/or preclusion of evidence.[99]

20. **Economic Loss/Damages Recoverable**

New York's highest court has held that tort recovery in strict product liability (and negligence) for economic loss flowing from damage to the product is not available to a downstream purchaser of the product.[100] The relevant factors in determining whether or not tort liability will attach are: (a) the nature of the defect; (b) the injury; (c) the manner in which the injury occurred; and (d) the damages sought. The focus is whether or not the plaintiff is merely seeking the benefit of the bargain, which sounds in contract, or for injury to person or property, which, in appropriate circumstances, may be recoverable in tort.[101] Thus, tort damages are not generally recoverable where the product fails to meet the expectations of a customer and where the claimed injury is solely to the product itself. The "economic loss" doctrine also bars recovery for consequential damages resulting from the defect.[102]

21. **Crashworthiness/Second Collision Doctrine**

New York recognizes the "second collision doctrine," which provides that a product manufacturer/seller can be held liable when a defect in its product enhances the plaintiff's injuries, even where the product did not cause the initial accident.[103] The three-prong test requires plaintiff to prove (a) a defective design; (b) an alternative safer design, practicable under the circumstances; and (c) the extent of enhanced injuries attributable to the defective design.[104]

22. **Commonly Known Dangers**

It has long been the law in New York that a manufacturer or seller of a product will not be held liable for failure to warn against known or obvious risks or dangers.[105] However, the Second Circuit Court of Appeals (interpreting New York law) recently ruled that a manufacturer may have a duty to provide a warning even where a danger is obvious as a matter of law.[106] The "obviousness" of the risk or danger is usually a question of fact for the jury.[107]

23. Admissibility of Subsequent Remedial Measures

Evidence of post-accident repairs or improvements is generally not admissible in negligence claims or in strict product liability claims based on design defect or failure to warn.[108] Evidence of subsequent remedial measures is admissible in a strict product liability claim based on a manufacturing defect[109] to establish feasibility of design, to prove defendant's control of the premises or instrumentality at the time of the accident, or for impeachment purposes.[110] However, if the defendant concedes feasibility, such evidence will not be admitted.[111]

D. NEGLIGENCE

1. The Standard

In order to establish a prima facie case of negligence, a plaintiff must prove: (a) that defendant owed a duty to the plaintiff; (b) that the duty was breached; and (c) that the breach of the duty caused the injury.[112]

2. Breach of Duty

A manufacturer may breach its duty by, for example, inadequate testing,[113] inadequate design,[114] or failure to reasonably inspect the product.[115]

New York's Court of Appeals recently concluded that handgun manufacturers do not owe a legal duty to persons injured or killed through the use of illegally obtained handguns.[116]

3. Component Part Manufacturer/Final Assembler

A manufacturer who incorporates a component produced by another into its product has a duty to inspect the component in a reasonably prudent fashion to achieve a finished product that is reasonably safe for its intended use. The failure to do so is negligence.[117] The manufacturer of a component or the processor of materials that are part of a finished product created by another may be held liable for defects in the component caused by its negligence, even though the assembler tests the component, or fails to do so.[118] Where a component part manufacturer produces a product in accordance with the buyer's designs, plans, or specifications, which do not reveal any inherent danger in the component or assembled unit, the component part manufacturer will not be liable.[119]

4. Privity

A plaintiff need not establish privity to recover on a negligence claim.[120]

E. BREACH OF WARRANTY

A breach of warranty action is based on contract (*i.e.*, the express or implied contract of sale); therefore, it is independent of negligence and obviates some of the proof problems arising in negligence cases. In order to prove a breach of warranty claim, the plaintiff must demonstrate that: (a) he has been injured by a product; (b) the injury occurred because the product was defective and unfit for its intended purpose; and (c) the defect existed when the product left the control of the manufacturer.[121] New York's highest court recently clarified that the definition of "defective" product design differs considerably as between strict liability and breach of warranty. Under a breach of warranty theory, a product is defective if it is not safe for the ordinary purpose for which it is sold. However, under a strict liability design defect theory, a product is defective if it fails the risk/utility test, which focuses on whether the benefits of the product outweigh the dangers of its design. A jury may properly reach different conclusions under these two theories.[122]

The Uniform Commercial Code recognizes both express warranties[123] and implied warranties.[124] Express warranties are created where a manufacturer, in advertising or labeling its product, represents its quality so that the public is induced to purchase the product. If the product does not conform to the express warranty created, that warranty is breached.[125] The implied warranty of merchantability is breached where the product was not "fit for the ordinary purposes for which such goods are used."[126] A breach of the implied warranty of merchantability may be established based solely upon circumstantial evidence.[127]

A seller's express or implied warranty extends to any person who may reasonably be expected to use, consume, or be affected by the goods.[128]

A breach of warranty claim requires a sale. A defendant retained primarily for servicing a product is liable only for negligence unless a contract establishes a higher duty.[129]

With few exceptions, lack of privity generally bars recovery for breach of warranty under either express or implied warranty theories.[130] If privity of contract exists, a plaintiff may recover direct and consequential damages resulting from the product's failure under both an express or implied warranty theory.[131] Even without privity, a plaintiff may recover under breach of warranty theories where plaintiff sustains a physical injury.[132] Privity also is not required where the plaintiff purchased a defective product based on the manufacturer's express representations in trade publications, direct mailings, or on product labels.[133]

F. PUNITIVE DAMAGES

Punitive damages may be recovered in tort actions, including product liability suits, where a plaintiff proves exceptional misconduct that surpasses negligence—such as where the evidence shows the defendant acted "maliciously, wantonly, or with a recklessness suggesting an improper motive or vindictiveness."[134] The evidentiary standard for proving punitive damages in New York appears to be "preponderance of the evidence."[135] Punitive damages are recoverable in a wrongful death action.[136] Recent decisions by the United States Supreme Court establish constitutional limitations on punitive damage awards.[137]

A corporate defendant cannot be held liable for punitive damages unless it can be shown that a "superior officer" of the corporation in the course of employment ordered, participated in, or ratified the conduct.[138] Similarly, officers and directors are liable for punitive damages only if plaintiff proves complicity in the oppressive conduct—*i.e.*, the officer or director authorized, participated in, or ratified the conduct giving rise to the punitive damages.[139]

G. PRE- AND POST-JUDGMENT INTEREST

Pre-judgment interest is not recoverable in a personal injury action, but is recoverable in a wrongful death action.[140] Every judgment, including those based on personal injury, bears interest at nine percent per annum from the date of entry of judgment.[141]

H. EMPLOYER IMMUNITY FROM SUIT

On September 10, 1996, the "Omnibus Workers' Compensation Reform Act of 1996" ("the Act") took effect, radically changing the previous rule, which had allowed manufacturers and sellers freely to implead employers for contribution or indemnity.[142] The Act amended the Workers' Compensation law to prohibit third-party actions against employers except in cases in which a plaintiff has suffered a "grave injury," which is statutorily defined to include a list of specific injuries such as death, amputation, paraplegia and others.[143] Impleader remains available against the employer in the absence of grave injury, where the basis for indemnity or contribution is a written contract entered into prior to the accident that caused the plaintiff's injury.[144] The Act also amended CPLR §§ 1401 and 1601, to prohibit juries from apportioning fault to non-party employers in cases where the plaintiff did not sustain grave injury.[145] New York's highest court has ruled that the Act applies prospectively only.[146]

I. MEDICAL MONITORING

The New York Court of Appeals recently refused to recognize a judicially created, independent cause of action for medical monitoring, but the Court noted that plaintiffs who have established an actionable tort can still obtain the remedy of medical monitoring.[147]

J. STATUTES

Many of the New York statutes relevant to product liability and negligence actions are discussed herein. The age of majority in New York is 18.[148]

K. JOINT AND SEVERAL LIABILITY

1. The Rule

With some exceptions provided by statute, the general rule in New York is that defendants are jointly and severally liable.[149] However, in a product liability case involving multiple tortfeasors where the manufacturer of the product is joined or subject to jurisdiction, a tortfeasor found to be 50 percent or less liable will not be required to pay more than his equitable share for noneconomic loss sustained by the plaintiff.[150] An appellate court has held that plaintiff is required to plead and prove by a preponderance of the evidence the specific statutory exception that applies to the action.[151] The same appellate court concluded that a defendant is entitled to the protections of the statute in actions where fault is attributed to a non-party, bankrupt tortfeasor.[152] The New York courts are currently divided as to whether a defendant bears the burden of pleading and proving that it is 50 percent or less at fault and, thus, subject only to several liability.[153]

2. Contribution and Indemnification

A joint tortfeasor may seek contribution from other tortfeasors who are liable for plaintiff's injuries.[154] The joint tortfeasor may seek contribution for any excess that it paid over its equitable share (its percentage of fault).[155] A party from whom contribution is sought, however, cannot be forced to pay more than its equitable share.[156]

3. Effect of Settlement

New York has codified its rules pertaining to the release of tortfeasors.[157] Under the statute, a release reduces the claim of the releasor against the other tortfeasors by the *greatest* of: the amount stipulated in the release, the amount actually paid for the release, or the amount of the released tortfeasor's equitable share of the damages.[158]

In multidefendant situations, the "aggregate" approach to offsetting the settling defendants' share of liability is to be used.[159] Under this approach, the *total* amounts paid in settlement by all settling defendants is compared to the *total* amount of apportioned liability. The greater amount represents the set-off. In addition, New York's highest court recently adopted the "settlement first" method, which requires the court to reduce a verdict by the amount of the plaintiff's settlement with another defendant before reducing the verdict for the plaintiff's comparative fault.[160]

A release further acts to relieve the settling party from liability for any claims for contribution; it similarly precludes the settling party from bringing any claim for contribution against any other person.[161]

L. OTHER ASPECTS OF NEW YORK LAW

1. Surveillance

In New York, a defendant's ability to surprise plaintiff at trial with secret surveillance tapes was virtually eliminated by a recent amendment to New York's disclosure rules. The amendment provides that "there shall be full disclosure of any films, photographs, video tapes or audio tapes, including transcripts or memoranda thereof" involving a party, including out-takes and *regardless* of whether a defendant intends to use the materials at trial.[162]

All surveillance materials must be disclosed on demand and may not be withheld until after the investigated party has been deposed.[163]

2. **Ultrahazardous Activity Doctrine**

Courts applying New York law have stated that this doctrine primarily applies to activities conducted on lands. In general, courts have refused to extend the doctrine to include manufacturers of allegedly defective products.[164]

Thomas E. Reidy
Tony R. Sears
Ward Greenberg Heller & Reidy LLP
300 State Street
Rochester, New York 14614
(585) 454-0700
(Fax) (585) 423-5910

ENDNOTES - NEW YORK

1. *Heller v. U.S. Suzuki Motor Corp.*, 64 N.Y.2d 407, 412, 477 N.E.2d 434, 437 (1985); *Victorson v. Bock Laundry Mach. Co.*, 37 N.Y.2d 395, 400, 335 N.E.2d 275, 277 (1975).

2. N.Y. C.P.L.R. 214 (McKinney 1990). *See generally Snyder v. Town Insulation, Inc.*, 81 N.Y.2d 429, 432, 615 N.E.2d 999, 1000 (1993).

3. *Snyder*, 81 N.Y.2d at 436, 615 N.E.2d at 1003 (holding accrual of cause of action against insulation manufacturer occurred at time of installation, *i.e.*, when all elements of tort could be truthfully alleged in complaint); *but see Blanco v. AT&T Co.*, 90 N.Y.2d 757, 767-68, 689 N.E.2d 506, 510 (1997) (action for repetitive stress injury sustained from keyboard use accrues on date of injury or date of last use of keyboard, whichever is earlier); *see also Consorti v. Owens-Corning Fiberglas Corp.*, 86 N.Y.2d 449, 657 N.E.2d 1301 (1995) (rejecting wife's loss of consortium claim when husband's exposure to harmful substance and his injury occurred prior to date of marriage).

4. N.Y. U.C.C. § 2-725 (McKinney 1993).

5. *Heller*, 64 N.Y.2d at 411, 477 N.E.2d at 436.

6. *Heller*, 64 N.Y.2d at 411, 477 N.E.2d at 436.

7. N.Y. Est. Powers & Trusts Law § 5-4.1 (McKinney 1999).

8. N.Y. C.P.L.R. 214-c(2) (McKinney 1990).

9. *Blanco v. AT&T*, 90 N.Y.2d 757, 767, 689 N.E.2d 506, 509 (1997) (CPLR 214-c does not apply to a claim alleging latent musculoskeletal injuries allegedly caused by use of keyboard, because "a keyboard is not a toxic substance . . ."). *See* McLaughlin, Practice Commentaries (McKinney's Cons. Laws of NY, Book 7B, C.P.L.R. C214-c:1, p. 631 (1990)). *See also Parajecki v. Int'l Bus. Mach. Corp.*, 899 F. Supp. 1050, 1053-1054 (E.D.N.Y. 1995) (holding New York's discovery rule under C.P.L.R. 214-c inapplicable to plaintiffs claiming latent "repetitive stress injuries" from keyboard use); Joseph J. Ortego & Kevin McElroy, *Latent Injuries and Statute of Limitations*, N.Y.L.J., Dec. 1, 1994, at 1 (discussing two recent trial level decisions refusing application of the discovery rule to plaintiffs claiming latent "repetitive stress injuries" from typing on a keyboard).

10. N.Y. C.P.L.R. § 214-c(2) (McKinney 1990).

11. *See Bimbo v. Chromalloy Am. Corp.*, 226 A.D.2d 812, 815-16, 640 N.Y.S.2d 623, 625-26 (3d Dep't 1996); *see also Bano v. Union Carbide Corp.*, 361 F.3d 696, 712 (2d Cir. 2004) (applying Section 214-c(2)).

12. *Wetherill v. Eli Lilly & Co.*, 89 N.Y.2d 506, 678 N.E.2d 474 (1997).

13. *Wetherill*, 89 N.Y.2d at 511-13, 678 N.E.2d at 476-78.

14. *Jensen v. Gen. Elec. Co.*, 82 N.Y.2d 77, 88, 623 N.E.2d 547, 552 (1993).

15. *Blanco v. AT&T*, 90 N.Y.2d 757, 767, 689 N.E.2d 506, 509-10 (1997) ("the mere continuation of [the duty to warn] into the limitations period is not enough to resurrect a cause of action premised upon an injury occurring earlier").

16. *Rothstein v. Tennessee Gas Pipeline Co.*, 204 A.D.2d 39, 45, 616 N.Y.S.2d 902, 905-06 (2d Dep't 1994), *aff'd on other grounds*, 87 N.Y.2d 90, 661 N.E.2d 146 (1995). *See also* Alexander, Supplementary Practice Commentaries (McKinney's Cons. Law of NY, Book 7B, C.P.L.R. C213-c2, p. 136 (1996)).

17. *See Sackman v. Liggett Group, Inc.*, 167 F.R.D. 6, 15-16 (E.D.N.Y. 1996) (claim that cigarette maker breached express warranty that cigarettes would be safe was untimely when brought more than four years after plaintiff discovered injury was caused by cigarettes).

18. *Annunziato v. City of New York*, 224 A.D.2d 31, 37, 647 N.Y.S.2d 850, 854 (2d Dep't 1996).

19. N.Y. C.P.L.R. § 214-c(4) (McKinney 1990).

20. *Giordano v. Market Am., Inc.*, 15 N.Y.3d 590, 597-600, 941 N.E.2d 727, 730-32 (2010) (reasoning that the effects of a dietary supplement that were concealed for a few hours after its consumption could make it difficult to discover the causal connection between the supplement and effects).

21. N.Y. C.P.L.R. § 214-c(4) (McKinney 1990); *see Whitney v. Agway, Inc.*, 238 A.D.2d 782, 785, 656 N.Y.S.2d 455, 457-58 (3d Dep't 1997).

22. *Giordano*, 15 N.Y.2d at 600-02, 941 N.E.2d 732-33 (holding that the extension runs until scientific experts could ascertain the cause as opposed to when laypersons or lawyers could do so, and further holding that the probable causal relationship test is one of general acceptance of that relationship in the relevant technical, scientific, or medical community).

23. *Annunziato*, 224 A.D. at 38-39, 647 N.Y.S.2d at 855.

24. *Annunziato* actually involved a suit against the City of New York, which was governed by a one-year, 90-day limitations period supplied by General Municipal Law §§ 50-e and 50-i. The "discovery rule" created by C.P.L.R.

§ 214-c, however, applied the same way it would have applied had the limitations period been supplied by C.P.L.R. § 214(3). *See Annunziato*, 224 A.D. at 38-39, 647 N.Y.S.2d at 855.

25. *See, e.g., Sackman*, 167 F.R.D. at 13.

26. *See Sackman*, 167 F.R.D. at 14.

27. N.Y. C.P.L.R. § 214-c(6) (McKinney 1990). *See also Rothstein v. Tennessee Gas Pipeline Co.*, 87 N.Y.2d 90, 661 N.E.2d 46 (1995).

28. *Amatulli v. Delhi Constr. Corp.*, 77 N.Y.2d 525, 532, 571 N.E.2d 645, 648 (1991); *Codling v. Paglia*, 32 N.Y.2d 330, 342, 298 N.E.2d 622, 628 (1973).

29. *Codling*, 32 N.Y.2d at 342, 298 N.E.2d at 628-29.

30. *Rivera-Emerling v. M. Fortunoff of Westbury Corp.*, 281 A.D.2d 215, 721 N.Y.S.2d 653 (1st Dep't 2001).

31. *Momen v. United States*, 946 F. Supp. 196, 207 (N.D.N.Y. 1996); *Sage v. Fairchild-Swearingen Corp.*, 70 N.Y.2d 579, 585, 517 N.E.2d 1304, 1306 (1987); *Sukljian v. Charles Ross & Son Co.*, 69 N.Y.2d 89, 94, 503 N.E.2d 1358, 1360 (1986).

32. *Caprara v. Chrysler Corp.*, 52 N.Y.2d 114, 417 N.E.2d 545, *rearg. denied*, 52 N.Y.2d 1073, 420 N.E.2d 413 (1981); *Rainbow v. Albert Elia Bldg. Co.*, 79 A.D.2d 287, 294, 436 N.Y.S.2d 480, 484, *aff'd*, 56 N.Y.2d 550, 434 N.E.2d 1345 (1982).

33. *Voss v. Black & Decker Mfg. Co.*, 59 N.Y.2d 102, 107, 450 N.E.2d 204, 208 (1983); *see Doomes v. Best Transit Corp.*, 17 N.Y.3d 594, 608, 958 N.E.2d 1183, 1191 (2011).

34. *Yung Tung Chow v. Reckitt & Colman, Inc.*, 17 N.Y.3d 29, 33, 950 N.E.2d 113, 116 (2011) (citing *Voss*, 59 N.Y.2d 102, 450 N.E.2d 204).

35. *Voss*, 59 N.Y.2d at 109, 450 N.E.2d at 208-09. *See also Tomasino v. Am. Tobacco Co.*, 23 A.D.3d 546, 548-49, 807 N.Y.S.2d 603, 605-06 (2d Dep't 2005) (explaining that consumer expectations are relevant but do not provide an independent standard for determining whether a product is defectively designed); *cf. McCarthy v. Olin Corp.*, 119 F.3d 148, 155 (2d Cir. 1997) (risk/utility analysis not relevant to case involving inherently dangerous product, such as gun or knife because "the risks arise from the function of the product, not any defect in the product").

36. *Voss*, 59 N.Y.2d at 108, 450 N.E.2d at 208; *see, e.g., Adams v. Genie Indus., Inc.*, 14 N.Y.3d 535, 542-44, 929 N.E.2d 380, 383-85 (2010) (existence of reasonable

alternative design was established via testimony regarding a competitor's product that had included safety outriggers during the relevant time period).

37. *Voss*, 59 N.Y.2d at 108, 450 N.E.2d at 208. Where a product's only function is satisfying the consumer, a plaintiff alleging a design defect must establish that the safer design is as acceptable to consumers as the product the defendant sold. *Adamo v. Brown & Williamson Tobacco Corp.*, 11 N.Y.3d 545, 549-51, 900 N.E.2d 966 (2008) (holding that plaintiffs had failed to make out prima facie case that "light" cigarettes were feasible alternative design without presenting evidence that consumers would accept the "light" cigarettes in place of regular cigarettes).

38. *Sabater v. Lead Indus. Ass'n, Inc.*, 183 Misc. 2d 759, 764-66, 704 N.Y.S.2d 800, 803-05 (Sup. Ct. Bronx County 2000) (granting defendant's motion to dismiss plaintiff's claim for design defect for failure to allege a safer alternative design).

39. *Houlihan v. Morrison Knudsen Corp.*, 2 A.D.3d 493, 494, 768 N.Y.S.2d 495, 496 (2d Dep't 2003).

40. *Scarangella v. Thomas Built Buses, Inc.*, 93 N.Y.2d 655, 661, 717 N.E.2d 679, 681, 683 (1999) (lack of optional back-up alarm on bus was not a design defect); *Warlikowski v. Burger King Corp.*, 9 A.D.3d 360, 780 N.Y.S.2d 608 (2d Dep't 2004) (lack of optional hot-shortening disposal equipment was not a design defect); *see Passante v. Agway Consumer Prods., Inc.*, 12 N.Y.3d 372, 381-82, 909 N.E.2d 563, 568 (2009) (finding issue of fact as to whether normal circumstances exist under which mechanical dock leveler could be safely used without optional locking device); *Campbell v. Int'l Truck & Engine Corp.*, 32 A.D.3d 1184, 1185, 822 N.Y.S.2d 188, 189-90 (4th Dep't 2006) (holding that absent actual awareness by injured party that the optional safety feature was available, the lack of the safety feature may still constitute a defect under *Scarangella*).

41. *Codling v. Paglia*, 32 N.Y.2d 330, 342, 298 N.E.2d 622, 628 (1973); *Amatulli v. Delhi Constr. Corp.*, 77 N.Y.2d 525, 532, 571 N.E.2d 645, 648 (1991).

42. *Parker v. Mobil Oil Corp.*, 7 N.Y.3d 434, 448, 857 N.E.2d 1114, 1121 (2006) (holding that "it is not always necessary for a plaintiff to quantify exposure levels precisely"); *see Cornell v. 360 W. 51st St. Realty, LLC*, 2014 NY Slip Op. 2096 (2014) (noting that while *Parker* held that a "precise quantification" is not required it "by no means ... dispensed with a plaintiff's burden to establish sufficient exposure to a substance to cause the claimed adverse health defect"). Prior to *Parker* some courts required plaintiffs to quantify their actual level of exposure. *See Ruffing v. Union Carbide Corp.*, 193 Misc. 2d 350, 746 N.Y.S.2d 798 (Sup. Ct. Westchester Co. Jan. 16, 2001).

43. *Lloyd v. W.R. Grace & Co.*, 215 A.D.2d 177, 626 N.Y.S.2d 147 (1st Dep't 1995) (plaintiff's evidence sufficient to establish plaintiff's exposure to defendant's asbestos products); *Dollas v. W.R. Grace & Co.*, 225 A.D.2d 319, 320, 639 N.Y.S.2d 323 (1st Dep't 1996).

44. *Banks v. Makita, USA, Inc.*, 226 A.D.2d 659, 641 N.Y.S.2d 875 (2d Dep't 1996).

45. *See Sosna v. Am. Home Prods.*, 298 A.D.2d 158, 748 N.Y.S.2d 548 (1st Dep't 2002) (explaining that a plaintiff's failure to read a warning bars a claim that the warning was "substantively inadequate" but does not necessarily bar a claim that the warning was "insufficiently conspicuous or prominent"); *see also Johnson v. Johnson Chem. Co.*, 183 A.D.2d 64, 588 N.Y.S.2d 607 (2d Dep't 1992) (plaintiff's admitted failure to read warnings concerning use of product did not necessarily sever the causal connection between the alleged inadequacy of the communication of those warnings and her accident). Cf. *Reis v. Volvo Cars of N. Am., Inc.*, 73 A.D.3d 420, 423-24, 901 N.Y.S.2d 10, 13-14 (1st Dep't 2010) (holding that it was immaterial how prominent or conspicuous any warnings in an owner's manual or inside the vehicle could have been where the user did not read the manual and where the accident occurred while the user started the vehicle from outside); *Guadalupe v. Drackett Prods. Co.*, 253 A.D.2d 378, 676 N.Y.S.2d 177 (1st Dep't 1998) (affirming dismissal where plaintiff testified that she made no attempt to read the warnings accompanying the product and that it was her custom not to do so).

46. N.Y. C.P.L.R. § 1411 (McKinney 1997); *Voss v. Black & Decker Mfg. Co.*, 59 N.Y.2d 102, 450 N.E.2d 204 (1983); *but see Ruffing v. Union Carbide Corp.*, 186 Misc. 2d 679, 720 N.Y.S.2d 328 (Sup. Ct. Westchester County 2000) (striking defendants' defenses of contributory negligence, comparative fault and assumption of risk after concluding that parents' allegedly negligent conduct could not be imputed to infant plaintiff).

47. N.Y. C.P.L.R. § 1412 (McKinney 1997).

48. The plaintiff bears the burden to prove the manufacturer's identity, but may do so with circumstantial proof if the product is no longer available. *See Healey v. Firestone Tire Co.*, 87 N.Y.2d 596, 601, 663 N.E.2d 901, 903 (1996).

49. *See Sukljian*, 69 N.Y.2d 89, 503 N.E.2d 1358 (1986); *see also In re New York State Silicone Breast Implant Litig.*, 227 A.D.2d 310, 311, 642 N.Y.S.2d 681, 682 (1st Dep't 1996) (a party who gives advice to a manufacturer of consumer goods does not owe a duty to then-unknown individual purchasers of the finished goods).

50. *German v. Morales*, 24 A.D.3d 246, 247, 806 N.Y.S.2d 493, 494 (1st Dep't 2005) (citing *Godoy v. Abamaster of Miami, Inc.*, 302 A.D.2d 57, 62, 754 N.Y.S.2d 301, 306 (2d Dep't 2003)); *see also McDermott v. City of New York*, 50 N.Y.2d 211, 406 N.E.2d 460 (1980) (discussing underlying principles of indemnification

claims in the context of city's indemnification claim against manufacturer of product that caused injury to sanitation worker).

51. *Bradley v. Earl B. Feiden, Inc.*, 8 N.Y.3d 265, 274-75, 863 N.E.2d 600, 605-06 (2007).

52. *Jaramillo v. Weyerhaeuser Co.*, 12 N.Y.3d 181, 192, 906 N.E.2d 387, 394 (2009) (holding that third-hand seller of machinery sold in "as is" condition and that had been repaired and reassembled was not subject to strict product liability for injuries caused by machinery); *Gebo v. Black Clawson Co.*, 92 N.Y.2d 387, 393, 703 N.E.2d 1234, 1238 (1998); *Stiles v. Batavia Atomic Horseshoes, Inc.*, 81 N.Y.2d 950, 951, 613 N.E.2d 572, 573, *rearg. denied*, 81 N.Y.2d 1068, 619 N.E.2d 664 (1993); *Sukljian*, 69 N.Y.2d at 95-96, 511 N.Y.S.2d at 823-24.

53. *Sprung v. MTR Ravensburg, Inc.*, 99 N.Y.2d 468, 474, 788 N.E.2d 620, 623-24 (2003).

54. *Sukljian*, 69 N.Y.2d at 97, 511 N.Y.S.2d at 824-25; *Gebo v. Black Clawson Co.*, 92 N.Y.2d 387, 703 N.E.2d 1234 (1998) (casual manufacturer not liable in negligence or strict liability; sole duty is to warn of known risks).

55. *Fletcher v. Atex, Inc.*, 68 F.3d 1451, 1458 (2d Cir. 1995) (applying law of Delaware, as state of subsidiary's incorporation, to issue of alter ego liability). *See also King v. Eastman Kodak Co.*, 219 A.D.2d 550, 551, 631 N.Y.S.2d 832, 833 (1st Dep't 1995) (applying Delaware law to issue of alter ego liability).

56. *Fletcher*, 68 F.3d at 1461 (applying New York law and holding that parent corporation did not authorize subsidiary to act on its behalf); *see King*, 219 A.D.2d at 552, 631 N.Y.S.2d at 833 (holding that parent corporation never authorized actions of subsidiary); *Porter v. LSB Indus., Inc.*, 192 A.D.2d 205, 215, 600 N.Y.S.2d 867, 874 (4th Dep't 1993) (finding no evidence to support imposition of liability on parent corporation as principal of its subsidiary).

57. *Fletcher*, 68 F.3d at 1462 (applying New York law and holding apparent manufacturer theory inapplicable where parent corporation not involved in the chain of distribution, where parent corporation never held itself out as manufacturer of product, and where parent corporation's name never appeared on product); *see King*, 219 A.D.2d at 551-52, 631 N.Y.S.2d at 833 (apparent manufacturer liability inapplicable where parent corporation not involved in manufacture, sale, or distribution of product and where parent corporation's name never appeared on product): *Pangallo v. Mitsubishi Int'l Corp.*, 220 A.D.2d 650, 651, 632 N.Y.S.2d 647, 648 (2d Dep't 1995) (parent corporation not liable where product itself identified product's manufacturer as subsidiary of parent).

58. *Fletcher*, 68 F.3d at 1464-66 (applying New York law and holding that parent corporation did not engage in concerted action with subsidiary because parent not involved in decisions regarding manufacture, marketing, or warnings); *see King*, 219 A.D.2d at 552, 631 N.Y.S.2d at 833 (parent corporation not liable under concerted action theory where parent never agreed to pursue a tortious plan with subsidiary).

59. *In re New York State Silicone Breast Implant Litig.*, 227 A.D.2d 310, 642 N.Y.S.2d 681 (1st Dep't 1996).

60. *Sackman v. Liggett Grp., Inc.*, 965 F. Supp. 391 (E.D.N.Y. 1997) (court also held that concert of action claim may be maintained based on allegations that manufacturer conspired with other manufacturers to conceal health risks associated with product use).

61. *Bravman v. Baxter Healthcare Corp.*, 984 F.2d 71, 75-76 (2d Cir. 1993); *Lindsay v. Ortho Pharm. Corp.*, 637 F.2d 87, 90 (2d Cir. 1980).

62. *Schumacher v. Richards Shear Co.*, 59 N.Y.2d 239, 244, 451 N.E.2d 195, 198 (1983).

63. *Schumacher*, 59 N.Y.2d at 245, 451 N.E.2d at 198; *Hartford Accident & Indem. Co. v. Canron, Inc.*, 43 N.Y.2d 823, 825, 373 N.E.2d 364, 365 (1977).

64. *Semenetz v. Sherling & Walden, Inc.*, 7 N.Y.3d 194, 851 N.E.2d 1170 (2006); *see Ortiz v. Green Bull, Inc.*, No. 10-CV-3747, 2011 WL 5554522, at *5-*13 (E.D.N.Y. Nov. 14, 2011).

65. *Hymowitz v. Eli Lilly & Co.*, 73 N.Y.2d 487, 539 N.E.2d 1069 (1989).

66. *Hymowitz*, 73 N.Y.2d at 506, 539 N.E.2d at 1074.

67. *See, e.g., Brenner v. Am. Cyanamid Co.*, 263 A.D.2d 165, 170, 699 N.Y.S.2d 848, 851 (4th Dep't 1999) (setting forth cases in which the New York courts have refused to apply the doctrine of market share liability).

68. *Brenner*, 263 A.D.2d at 171-73, 699 N.Y.S.2d at 170-74.

69. *Heller v. U.S. Suzuki Motor Corp.*, 64 N.Y.2d 407, 411, 477 N.E.2d 434, 436 (1985); *Giuffrida v. Panasonic Indus. Co.*, 200 A.D.2d 713, 607 N.Y.S.2d 72 (2d Dep't 1994).

70. *Rastelli v. Goodyear Tire Co.*, 79 N.Y.2d 289, 297, 591 N.E.2d 222, 225 (1992); *Robinson v. Reed-Prentice*, 49 N.Y.2d 471, 478-79, 403 N.E.2d 440, 442-43 (1980).

71. *Repka v. Arctic Cat, Inc.*, 20 A.D.3d 916, 918, 798 N.Y.S.2d 629, 631 (4th Dep't 2005).

72. *Lugo v. LJN Toys Ltd.*, 75 N.Y.2d 850, 852, 552 N.E.2d 162, 163 (1990); *see also Estrada v. Berkel Inc.*, 14 A.D.3d 529, 531, 789 N.Y.S.2d 172, 174 (2d Dep't 2005) (holding that a two-year-old child was not a foreseeable user of a meat grinder).

73. *Cooley v. Carter-Wallace Inc.*, 102 A.D.2d 642, 645, 478 N.Y.S.2d 375, 377-78 (4th Dep't 1984) (citing *McLaughlin v. Mine Safety Appliance Co.*, 11 N.Y.2d 62, 69, 181 N.E.2d 430 (1962)).

74. *Cooley*, 102 A.D.2d at 645-46, 478 N.Y.S.2d at 378.

75. *Cooley*, 102 A.D.2d at 647, 478 N.Y.S.2d at 378.

76. *Cover v. Cohen*, 61 N.Y.2d 261, 275, 461 N.E.2d 864, 871 (1984).

77. *Cover*, 61 N.Y.2d at 275, 461 N.E.2d at 871.

78. *Cover*, 61 N.Y.2d at 274-75, 461 N.E.2d at 871; *see Lindsay v. Ortho Pharm. Corp.*, 637 F.2d 87, 91 (2d Cir. 1980).

79. *Adams v. Genie Indus., Inc.*, 14 N.Y.3d 535, 544-45, 929 N.E.2d 380, 385 (2010).

80. *Martin v. Hacker*, 83 N.Y.2d 1, 9, 628 N.E.2d 1308, 1311 (1993); *Wolfgruber v. Upjohn*, 72 A.D.2d 59, 61, 423 N.Y.S.2d 95, 96 (4th Dep't 1979), *aff'd*, 52 N.Y.2d 768, 417 N.E.2d 1002 (1980); *Polimeni v. Minolta Corp.*, 227 A.D.2d 64, 67, 653 N.Y.S.2d 429, 431 (3d Dep't 1997).

81. *Martin*, 83 N.Y.2d at 11, 628 N.E.2d at 1313. *See, e.g., Fane v. Zimmer*, 927 F.2d 124, 130 (2d Cir. 1991) (where manufacturer of internal fixation device warned physician but not patient of risks, no liability imposed on manufacturer); *see also, e.g., Rivers v. AT&T Techs., Inc.*, 147 Misc. 2d 366, 372, 554 N.Y.S.2d 401, 405 (Sup. Ct. N.Y. County 1990) (same result in case involving purchase and use of bulk chemicals).

82. *Polimeni v. Minolta Corp.*, 227 A.D.2d 64, 67, 653 N.Y.S.2d 429, 431 (3d Dep't 1997).

83. *Billsborrow v. Dow Chem.*, 177 A.D.2d 7, 16-19, 579 N.Y.S.2d 728, 733-36 (2d Dep't 1992); *In re Brooklyn Navy Yard Asbestos Litig.*, 971 F.2d 831, 838-39 (2d Cir. 1992).

84. *Spensieri v. Lasky*, 94 N.Y.2d 231, 723 N.E.2d 544 (1999) (holding that the doctrine does not permit a party to introduce the Physician's Desk Reference into evidence to establish the standard of care in medical malpractice actions).

85. *Amatulli v. Delhi Constr. Corp.*, 77 N.Y.2d 525, 532, 571 N.E.2d 645, 649 (1991); *Robinson v. Reed-Prentice Div. of Package Mach. Co.*, 49 N.Y.2d 471, 479, 403

N.E.2d 440, 443 (1980); *Wyda v. Makita Elec. Works, Ltd.*, 232 A.D.2d 407, 648 N.Y.S.2d 154 (2d Dep't 1996); *Paul v. Ford Motor Co.*, 200 A.D.2d 724, 725-26, 607 N.Y.S.2d 90, 92 (2d Dep't 1994).

86. *Lopez v. Precision Papers, Inc.*, 107 A.D.2d 667, 669, 484 N.Y.S.2d 585, 587-88 (2d Dep't 1985), *aff'd*, 67 N.Y.2d 871, 492 N.E.2d 1214 (1986) (forklift manufactured and marketed with an attached but removable overhead safety guard).

87. *Hoover v. New Holland N. Am., Inc.*, 2014 N.Y. Slip Op. 2215 (2014) (holding that plaintiff raised triable issues of fact as to whether safety shield, which had been removed after it was damaged while the product was in use, was itself defective).

88. *Lopez*, 107 A.D.2d at 669, 484 N.Y.S.2d at 587-88. *See LaPaglia v. Sears Roebuck & Co.*, 143 A.D.2d 173, 177, 531 N.Y.S.2d 623, 627 (2d Dep't 1988) (jury was warranted in refusing to absolve manufacturer from liability for design defect where lawn mower was manufactured with purpose of permitting, if not requiring, the facile removal of a chute deflector for purposes of installing a grass catcher).

89. *Liriano v. Hobart Corp.*, 92 N.Y.2d 232, 241, 700 N.E.2d 303, 309 (1998).

90. *George v. Celotex Corp.*, 914 F.2d 26, 28 (2d Cir. 1990) (applying New York and federal law in holding that a manufacturer is held to the knowledge of an expert in its field and has a duty "'to keep abreast of scientific knowledge, discoveries, and advances and is presumed to know what is imparted thereby'").

91. *George*, 914 F.2d at 28.

92. *Ramos v. Howard Indus., Inc.*, 10 N.Y.3d 218, 223-24, 885 N.E.2d 176, 178-79 (2008); *Speller v. Sears, Roebuck & Co.*, 100 N.Y.2d 38, 41, 790 N.E.2d 252, 254-55 (2003); *Halloran v. Virginia Chems., Inc.*, 41 N.Y.2d 386, 388, 361 N.E.2d 991, 993 (1977).

93. *See Voss v. Black & Decker Mfg. Co.*, 59 N.Y.2d 102, 450 N.E.2d 204 (1983); *Vannucci v. Raymond Corp.*, 258 A.D.2d 198, 200, 693 N.Y.S.2d 347, 349 (3d Dep't 1999); *Jemmott v. Rockwell Mfg. Co.*, 216 A.D.2d 444, 628 N.Y.S.2d 184 (2d Dep't 1995).

94. *Sawyer v. Dreis & Krump Mfg. Co.*, 67 N.Y.2d 328, 336, 493 N.E.2d 920, 925 (1986); *Bolm v. Triumph Corp.*, 71 A.D.2d 429, 438, 422 N.Y.S.2d 969, 975 (4th Dep't 1979).

95. *Sawyer*, 67 N.Y.2d at 336; *Hyde v. County of Rensselaer*, 51 N.Y.2d 927, 929, 415 N.E.2d 972, 973 (1980); *White v. Timberjack, Inc.*, 209 A.D.2d 968, 630 N.Y.S.2d 1005 (4th Dep't 1994).

96. *See City of New York v. Lead Indus. Assoc.*, 190 A.D.2d 173, 597 N.Y.S.2d 698 (1st Dep't 1993).

97. *Conderman v. Rochester Gas & Elec. Corp.*, 262 A.D.2d 1068, 693 N.Y.S.2d 787 (4th Dep't 1999).

98. *Kirkland v. NYCHA*, 236 A.D.2d, 170, 666 N.Y.S.2d 609 (1st Dep't 1997); *Squitieri v. City*, 248 A.D.2d 201, 669 N.Y.S.2d 589 (1st Dep't 1998); *Strelov v. Hertz Corp.*, 171 A.D.2d 420, 566 N.Y.S.2d 646 (1st Dep't 1991).

99. *Kirkland*, 236 A.D.2d at 174, 666 N.Y.S.2d at 611-12; *West v. Goodyear Tire & Rubber Co.*, 167 F.3d 776 (2d Cir. 1999); New York Pattern Jury Instructions § 1:77.1 (3d ed. West 2006).

100. *Bocre Leasing Corp. v. Gen. Motors Corp.*, 84 N.Y.2d 685, 694, 645 N.E.2d 1195, 1199 (1995); *Bellevue South Assoc. v. HRH Constr. Corp.*, 78 N.Y.2d 282, 293-95, 579 N.E.2d 195, 199 (1991); *Schiavone Constr. Co. v. Elgood Mayo Corp.*, 56 N.Y.2d 667, 668, 436 N.E.2d 1322, 1322 (1982), *rev'g on dissent*, 81 A.D.2d 221, 439 N.Y.S.2d 933 (1981).

101. *See Village of Groton v. Tokheim Corp.*, 202 A.D.2d 728, 608 N.Y.S.2d 565 (3d Dep't 1994).

102. *See, e.g., Weiss v. Polymer Plastics Corp.*, 21 A.D.3d 1095, 1096, 802 N.Y.S.2d 174, 175-76 (2d Dep't 2005) (ultimate purchaser could not recover from manufacturer for damages to siding itself or consequential damages to plywood substrate).

103. *Garcia v. Rivera*, 160 A.D.2d 274, 553 N.Y.S.2d 378 (1st Dep't 1990); *Cornier v. Spagna*, 101 A.D.2d 141, 146, 475 N.Y.S.2d 7, 11-12 (1st Dep't 1984).

104. *Caiazzo v. Volkswagenwerk A.G.*, 647 F.2d 241, 250 (2d Cir. 1981).

105. *See Smith v. Stark*, 67 N.Y.2d 693, 694, 490 N.E.2d 841, 842 (1986); *see Banks v. Makita USA, Inc.*, 226 A.D.2d 659, 660, 641 N.Y.S.2d 875, 877; *Wood v. Peabody*, 187 A.D.2d 824, 826, 589 N.Y.S.2d 960, 962 (3d Dep't 1992); *Belling v. Haugh's Pools Ltd.*, 126 A.D.2d 958, 959, 511 N.Y.S.2d 732, 733 (4th Dep't 1987), *appeal denied*, 70 N.Y.2d 602, 512 N.E.2d 550,*recons. dismissed*, 70 N.Y.2d 748, 514 N.E.2d 393 (1987).

106. *Liriano v. Hobart Corp.*, 170 F.3d 264 (2d Cir. 1999).

107. *Frederick v. Niagara Mach. & Tool Works*, 107 A.D.2d 1063, 1064, 486 N.Y.S.2d 564, 565 (4th Dep't 1985). *But see Bazerman v. Gardall Safe Corp.*, 203 A.D.2d 56, 609 N.Y.S.2d 610 (1st Dep't 1994) (holding that danger from turning over a heavy safe was obvious as a matter of law).

108. *Cover*, 61 N.Y.2d at 270, 461 N.E.2d at 868; *Caprara v. Chrysler Corp.*, 52 N.Y.2d 114, 126, 417 N.E.2d 545, 551 (1981).

109. *Cover*, 61 N.Y.2d at 270, 461 N.E.2d at 868.

110. *Ramundo v. Town of Guilderland*, 142 A.D.2d 50, 54, 534 N.Y.S.2d 543, 545-46 (3d Dep't 1988), *appeal after remand*, 163 A.D.2d 712, 558 N.Y.S.2d 310 (3d Dep't 1990); *Bolm v. Triumph Corp.*, 71 A.D.2d 429, 436, 422 N.Y.S.2d 969, 974 (4th Dep't 1979), *appeal dismissed*, 50 N.Y.2d 801, 407 N.E.2d 1353 (1980).

111. *Cover*, 61 N.Y.2d at 270, 461 N.E.2d at 868; *Demirovski v. Skil Corp.*, 203 A.D.2d 319, 610 N.Y.S.2d 551 (2d Dep't 1994).

112. *Solomon v. City of New York*, 66 N.Y.2d 1026, 1027, 489 N.E.2d 1294, 1295 (1985).

113. *Bichler v. Eli Lilly & Co.*, 55 N.Y.2d 571, 436 N.E.2d 182 (1982).

114. *Micallef v. Miehle Co.*, 39 N.Y.2d 376, 348 N.E.2d 571 (1976); *Kriz v. Schum*, 75 N.Y.2d 25, 549 N.E.2d 1155 (1989).

115. *Markel v. Spencer*, 5 A.D.2d 400, 171 N.Y.S.2d 770 (4th Dep't 1958), *aff'd without opinion*, 5 N.Y.2d 958, 157 N.E.2d 713 (1959).

116. *Hamilton v. Beretta U.S.A. Corp.*, 96 N.Y.2d 222, 750 N.E.2d 1055 (2001).

117. *Mueller v. Teichner*, 6 N.Y.2d 903, 161 N.E.2d 14 (1959).

118. *Smith v. Peerless Glass Co.*, 259 N.Y. 292, 181 N.E. 576, *reh'g denied*, 259 N.Y. 664, 182 N.E. 225 (1932); *Mueller*, 6 N.Y.2d 903, 161 N.E.2d 14; *see Feuerverger v. Hobart Corp.*, 738 F. Supp. 76 (E.D.N.Y. 1990) (applying New York law). Cf. *Bellantoni v. Gen. Motors Corp.*, No. 08 Civ. 2407, 2012 WL 1948779, at *5-*6 (S.D.N.Y. May 3, 2012) (company that modified truck so that it could be used as tow-truck owed no duty with respect to mirror assembly unit that it did not manufacture, design or integrate into the finished truck).

119. *Gray v. R.L. Best Co.*, 78 A.D.3d 1346, 1349, 910 N.Y.S.2d 307, 309 (2010).

120. *Heller v. U.S. Suzuki Motor Corp.*, 64 N.Y.2d 407, 411, 477 N.E.2d 434, 436 (1985); *Giuffrida v. Panasonic Indus. Co.*, 200 A.D.2d 713, 715, 607 N.Y.S.2d 72, 74 (2d Dep't 1994).

121. *Codling v. Paglia*, 38 A.D.2d 154, 327 N.Y.S.2d 978 (3d Dep't 1972), *aff'd in part and rev'd in part on other grounds*, 32 N.Y.2d 330, 298 N.E.2d 622 (1973).

122. *Denny v. Ford Motor Co.*, 87 N.Y.2d 248, 662 N.E.2d 730 (1995) (refusing to overturn verdict that found manufacturer liable for a defect under breach of implied warranty, but not liable for any defect under strict product liability);

Castro v. QVC Network, Inc., 139 F.3d 114 (2d Cir. 1998) (plaintiff is entitled to separate jury charges on strict liability and warranty claims).

123. N.Y. U.C.C. § 2-313 (McKinney 1993); *Cornier v. Spagna*, 101 A.D.2d 141, 475 N.Y.S.2d 7 (1st Dep't 1984).

124. N.Y. U.C.C. § 2-314 (McKinney 1993) (implied warranty of merchantability); *Di Prospero v. R. Brown & Sons*, 110 A.D.2d 250, 494 N.Y.S.2d 181 (3d Dep't 1985).

125. N.Y. U.C.C. § 2-313(1)(a) (McKinney 1993). *See also Randy Knitwear v. Am. Cyanamid Co.*, 11 N.Y.2d 5, 181 N.E.2d 399 (1962).

126. N.Y. U.C.C. § 2-314(2)(c) (McKinney 1993). *See also Denny*, 87 N.Y.2d at 258-59, 662 N.E.2d at 736.

127. *Bradley v. Earl B. Feiden, Inc.*, 8 N.Y.3d 265, 273, 863 N.E.2d 600, 604 (2007).

128. N.Y. U.C.C. § 2-318 (McKinney 1993).

129. *Milau Assocs. v. North Ave. Dev. Corp.*, 42 N.Y.2d 482, 368 N.E.2d 1247 (1977).

130. *Martin v. Julius Dierck Equip. Co.*, 43 N.Y.2d 583, 589-90, 374 N.E.2d 97, 100 (1978); *Mfrs. & Traders Trust Co. v. Stone Conveyor, Inc.*, 91 A.D.2d 849, 850, 458 N.Y.S.2d 116, 117 (4th Dep't 1982); *Fargo Equip. Co., Inc. v. Carborundum Co.*, 103 A.D.2d 1002, 1003, 478 N.Y.S.2d 382, 384 (4th Dep't 1984).

131. *All-O-Matic Indus., Inc. v. S. Specialty Paper Co., Inc.*, 49 A.D.2d 935, 374 N.Y.S.2d 331 (2d Dep't 1975).

132. N.Y. U.C.C. § 2-318 (McKinney 1993); *Hole v. Gen. Motors Corp.*, 83 A.D.2d 715, 716, 442 N.Y.S.2d 638, 640 (3d Dep't 1981).

133. *Randy Knitwear*, 11 N.Y.2d 5, 14-15, 181 N.E.2d 399, 402-04 (allowing express warranty claim).

134. *Home Ins. Co. v. Am. Home Prods.*, 75 N.Y.2d 196, 203-04, 550 N.E.2d 930, 934-35 (1990); *Camillo v. Geer*, 185 A.D.2d 192, 194, 587 N.Y.S.2d 306, 307 (1st Dep't 1992); *see O'Neill v. Yield House, Inc.*, 892 F. Supp. 76 (S.D.N.Y. 1995) (upholding jury's award of punitive damages where manufacturer of stepstool made no meaningful efforts to ensure the safety of its product).

135. *In re Seventh Judicial Dist. Asbestos Litig.*, 190 A.D.2d 1068, 1069, 593 N.Y.S.2d 685, 686-87 (4th Dep't 1993) (citing *Corrigan v. Bobbs-Merrill Co.*, 228 N.Y. 58, 126 N.E. 260 (1920)); *see Simpson v. Pittsburgh Corning Corp.*, 901 F.2d 277, 282-83 (2d Cir. 1990) (applying New York preponderance standard while noting possibility that due process may require higher standard). *But see*

Camillo, 185 A.D.2d at 194, 587 N.Y.S.2d at 309 (applying clear and convincing standard).

136. N.Y. Est. Powers and Trust Law § 5-4.3(b) (McKinney Supp. 1995).

137. *See State Farm Mut. Auto. Ins. Co. v. Campbell*, 538 U.S. 408 (2003); *Cooper Indus., Inc. v. Leatherman Tool Grp., Inc.*, 532 U.S. 424 (2001); *BMW of N. Am., Inc. v. Gore*, 517 U.S. 559 (1996).

138. *Camillo*, 185 A.D.2d at 195-96, 587 N.Y.S.2d at 310 (citing *Loughry v. Lincoln First Bank*, 67 N.Y.2d 369, 494 N.E.2d 70 (1986)).

139. *Roginsky v. Richardson-Merrell, Inc.*, 378 F.2d 832, 842 (2d Cir. 1967) (applying New York law).

140. N.Y. C.P.L.R. § 5004 (McKinney 1992), New York Est. Powers and Trusts Law § 5-4.3(a) (McKinney Supp. 1995).

141. N.Y. C.P.L.R. §§ 5003, 5004 (McKinney 1992).

142. *Dole v. Dow Chem. Co.*, 30 N.Y.2d 143, 152-53, 282 N.E.2d 288, 294 (1972).

143. N.Y. Workers' Comp. Law § 11 (McKinney Supp. 1996).

144. N.Y. Workers' Comp. Law § 11 (McKinney Supp. 1996).

145. N.Y. C.P.L.R. §§ 1401, 1601(1) (McKinney 1997).

146. *Majewski v. Broadalbin-Perch Cent. Sch. Dist.*, 91 N.Y.2d 577, 696 N.E.2d 978 (1998).

147. *Caronia v. Philip Morris USA, Inc.*, 22 N.Y.3d 439, 5 N.E.3d 11 (2013) (noting that physical injury or property damage must be proven to establish an existing tort).

148. N.Y. C.P.L.R. § 105(j) (McKinney 1990) and § 1201 (McKinney 1997).

149. N.Y. C.P.L.R. §§ 1601-1603 (McKinney 1997); *see Ravo v. Rogatnick*, 70 N.Y.2d 305, 309-10, 514 N.E.2d 1104, 1106 (1987).

150. N.Y. C.P.L.R. § 1602(10) (McKinney 1997).

151. *Roseboro v. New York City Transit Auth.*, 286 A.D.2d 222, 729 N.Y.S.2d 472 (1st Dep't 2001) (allegation that "one or more of the exceptions set forth in C.P.L.R. Article 16" is insufficient notice to defendant).

152. *Kharmah v. Metropolitan Chiropractic Ctr.*, 288 A.D.2d 94, 733 N.Y.S.2d 165 (1st Dep't 2001).

153. *Compare Marsala v. Weintraub*, 208 A.D.2d 689, 690, 617 N.Y.S.2d 809, 810-11 (2d Dep't 1994) (holding that defendants do not have to plead statutory scheme as an affirmative defense) *with Ryan v. Beavers*, 170 A.D.2d 1045, 566 N.Y.S.2d 112 (4th Dep't 1991) (holding that defendants must plead and particularize entitlement to avoid joint liability pursuant to CPLR Article 16).

154. N.Y. C.P.L.R. § 1401 (McKinney 1997).

155. N.Y. C.P.L.R. § 1402 (McKinney 1997).

156. N.Y. C.P.L.R. § 1402 (McKinney 1997).

157. N.Y. Gen. Oblig. Law § 15-108 (McKinney 1989).

158. N.Y. Gen. Oblig. Law § 15-108(a) (McKinney 1989).

159. *In re New York City Asbestos Litig.*, 82 N.Y.2d 342, 353, 624 N.E.2d 979, 985 (1993).

160. *Whalen v. Kawasaki Motors Corp.*, 92 N.Y.2d 288, 703 N.E.2d 246 (1998).

161. N.Y. Gen. Oblig. Law § 15-108(b), (c) (McKinney 1989).

162. N.Y. C.P.L.R. § 3101(i) (McKinney 1991 & Supp. 1996).

163. *Rotundi v. Massachusetts Mut. Life Ins. Co.*, 263 A.D.2d 84, 702 N.Y.S.2d 150 (3d Dep't 2000); *DiNardo v. Koronowski*, 252 A.D.2d 69, 684 N.Y.S.2d 736 (4th Dep't 1998); *Lindsey v. Cnty. of Erie*, 188 Misc. 2d 97, 727 N.Y.S.2d 596 (Sup. Ct. Erie Co. 2001) (ruling that insurer must produce surveillance tapes of plaintiff prior to proceedings before Workers' Compensation Board); *but see DeMarco v. Millbrook Equestrian Ctr.*, 287 A.D.2d 916, 732 N.Y.S.2d 121 (3d Dep't 2001) (affirming Workers' Compensation Board's decision that carrier was obligated to disclose the existence of any surveillance materials, but that it was not obligated to turn over a copy of the surveillance videotape until the carrier had the opportunity to cross-examine the claimant).

164. *Hamilton v. Accu-tek*, 935 F. Supp. 1307 (E.D.N.Y. 1996) (court distinguishes between injuries caused by abnormally dangerous activities, for which strict liability applies, and injuries caused by the use of a dangerous instrumentality, such as refrigerant, poison, pesticide or firearm).

NORTH CAROLINA

A. CAUSES OF ACTION

Product liability lawsuits are governed by a general products liability statute.[1] Causes of action commonly include negligence and breach of warranty.

B. STATUTES OF LIMITATION AND REPOSE

Causes of action for personal injury or property damage (beyond damage to the product), whether brought as claims for negligence or breach of warranty, must be commenced within three years of the date that damage or injury "becomes apparent or ought reasonably to have become apparent to the claimant"[2]—the date when the cause of action accrues. When the injury is disease, a cause of action grounded in negligence accrues when the disease is diagnosed.[3] Any general negligence action accrues no "more than 10 years from the last act or omission of the defendant."[4] Contract or breach of warranty actions based on the sale of goods, in which damages are limited to the product itself, are subject to the four-year UCC statute of limitations.[5] The statute runs from the date of sale or delivery, unless the date of accrual is altered by contract.[6] The statute of limitations for wrongful death suits is limited to two years from the date of death.[7]

The statute of limitation for malpractice in the performance of professional services (e.g., medicine,[8] law,[9] accounting[10]), except for those professional services involving improvements to real property (e.g., architecture and engineering in some cases), is three years from the "last act of the defendant giving rise to the cause of action."[11] A one-year extension from the date of discovery is available for losses "not readily apparent to the claimant," and a four-year repose provision runs "from the last act of the defendant giving rise to the cause of action."[12] The statute of limitations for constructive fraud in breach of a fiduciary duty is ten years.[13]

Statutes of repose have a substantial practical effect on litigation. For causes of action that accrued on or before September 30, 2009, a product liability cause of action on any theory is barred more than six years after the date of "initial purchase for use or consumption."[14] For causes of action accruing on or after October 1, 2009, the period of repose for product liability claims is 12 years.[15] The plaintiff bears the burden to prove jurisdiction, including satisfaction of the statute of repose. Sale to an intermediary or distributor is not a sale for initial use or consumption for purposes of the repose period.[16] However, if the defendant presents evidence showing that the product was manufactured before the date of sale needed to satisfy the statute of repose, the plaintiff must counter with some evidence that the product was sold after that date in order to meet the burden.[17] Suits involving improvements to real property are limited by a six-year statute of repose, with the triggering event the later of the "specific last act or omission of the defendant" or "substantial completion of the improvement."[18] The limitation and repose periods are tolled by statute for minors and others with disabilities whose claims accrue before expiration of the repose period.[19] Further, no statute of repose may be asserted as a defense to a claim of willful and wanton misconduct if the product is an improvement to property.[20]

C. STRICT LIABILITY

By statute, North Carolina does not recognize strict liability in product liability actions.[21] Evidence of negligence is required, except in cases of breach of warranty (see E., *infra*). [Sub-headings appearing for other states under "Strict Liability" are listed below, under "Negligence" (D.) and/or "Breach of Warranty" (E.).]

D. NEGLIGENCE

A products liability claim grounded in negligence requires the plaintiff to prove (1) the product was defective at the time it left control of the defendant, (2) the defect was the result of defendant's negligence, and (3) the defect proximately caused plaintiff damage.[22] There must be evidence that the defect resulted from negligent design, selection of materials, assembly, inspection by the manufacturer,[23] or evidence of failure to adequately warn or instruct about unreasonably dangerous conditions which the manufacturer or seller knew, or should have known, posed substantial risk of harm and were not open, obvious risks.[24] Inferences that are admissible in evidence may not be "stacked" to prove negligence. For example, a manufacturer's negligence normally may be inferred if a product is defective; however, this is impermissible when the defect itself is inferred from evidence that the product malfunctions when put to ordinary use.[25]

As to qualifications of experts, North Carolina rejected *Daubert* in 2004 and adopted a three-part test that requires the trial court to determine: (1) whether the expert's method of proof is sufficiently reliable, (2) whether the witness is actually qualified in that field, and (3) whether the expert's testimony is relevant.[26] Scientific theories, not previously accepted as reliable by North Carolina courts, are to be examined for indices of reliability, some of which are listed to be considered by the court.[27]

Expert qualification was changed by statute in 2011. For all actions arising on and after October 1, 2011, a *Daubert* standard for the admissibility of expert opinion testimony applies.[28] Under North Carolina's revised Rule 702(a), which now follows Rule 702 of the Federal Rules of Evidence, an expert only may testify in the form of an opinion, or otherwise, if: "(1) [t]he testimony is based upon sufficient facts or data[;] (2) [t]he testimony is the product of reliable principles and methods[;] [and] (3) [t]he witness has applied the principles and methods reliably to the facts of the case."[29]

1. **Standard of Care**

    The jury is instructed that the standard of care is that of a reasonably prudent person.[30] The degree of care required of the "reasonably prudent man . . . varies with the exigencies of the occasion."[31]

2. **Definition of Defect**

    A product is defective if its proper use would involve an unreasonable risk of harm to those using it for the purpose for which it was manufactured.[32] If there is evidence that the product malfunctions when it is put to ordinary use, then a defect may be inferred.[33] Defect in design or formulation is determined by a statutory risk-utility analysis as of the time of manufacture,[34] except in the case of firearms, defective design of which must cause them not to operate as reasonably expected.[35] A product is also defective if it is not accompanied by adequate warnings and instructions about unreasonably dangerous conditions which the manufacturer or seller knows, or should know, pose substantial risks of harm and which are not open, obvious risks.[36] (See D.10, "Failure to Warn.")

3. **Causation**

    The plaintiff must present evidence showing that the product was defective when it left the manufacturer's control and that the chain of causation has not been significantly interrupted by the intervention of third parties.[37] A manufacturer may not be held liable for injury, death, or damage caused by misuse or modification of the product done without instruction or express consent of the manufacturer.[38] In 2012, the North Carolina Supreme Court reversed a contrary interpretation of the law by the Court of Appeals, and held that the modification defense applies, regardless of whether the modifying "party" is a party to the litigation.[39]

    Neither negligence[40] nor proximate cause[41] may be presumed by the mere fact of accident or injury while using a product. *Res ipsa loquitur* may apply only in those cases in which the instrumentality is shown to be under the exclusive control of the defendant and the incident or event is one that does not occur in the ordinary course of events under proper care.[42]

    Allowable evidence of causation is specifically limited in some instances. In civil suits involving weight gain or obesity, or any health problems that "result from long-term consumption of food," the liability of food manufacturers, advertisers, sellers, and others in the industry is limited.[43]

4. **Contributory Negligence/Assumption of Risk**

    Contributory negligence[44] and assumption of risk[45] are complete defenses to claims of negligence or breach of implied warranty.[46] Contributory negligence does not, however, bar damages based on an action for breach of contract alone.[47] In 2009 and 2010, renewed legislative efforts to modify North Carolina law to drop "contributory negligence" as a complete defense and to adopt some variation of "comparative negligence" failed to be adopted.[48]

5. **Sale or Lease/Persons Liable**

Negligence does not attach to a seller, lessor, or bailor in the chain of a product's distribution if that product was acquired and sold in a sealed container, or if the product was acquired and sold under circumstances that afforded no reasonable opportunity to inspect the product for the alleged defect.[49] However, a breach of express warranty claim may survive (see E., *infra*).

6. **Inherently Dangerous Products**

North Carolina recognizes that control of "dangerous instrumentalities" requires a high degree of care[50] that, in very limited circumstances, may approach strict liability.[51]

7. **Successor Liability**

North Carolina follows the general rule that "a corporation which purchases all, or substantially all, of the assets of another corporation is generally not liable for the old corporation's debts or liabilities."[52] The four exceptions recognized are: (a) an express or implied agreement by the purchasing corporation to assume the debts or liabilities of the original corporation; (b) a transfer which amounts to a *de facto* merger of the two corporations; (c) a fraudulent transfer; and (d) a situation where the purchasing corporation is a "mere continuation" of the selling corporation.[53] The elements of the "mere continuation" test in this jurisdiction include continuity of ownership, inadequacy of consideration, and lack of some elements of a good-faith purchase for value.[54]

8. **Market-Share Liability/Enterprise Liability**

There are no North Carolina state court decisions on the issue of "market share" or "enterprise liability." In 1986, a federal district court predicted that North Carolina would *not* adopt such theories of liability at any point in the near future.[55]

9. **Privity**

A negligence cause of action requires no privity of contract.[56] The privity of contract requirement under the North Carolina Uniform Commercial Code has been statutorily eliminated for many categories of plaintiffs.[57] However, significant privity restrictions remain (see E., *infra*).

10. **Failure to Warn**

Failure to warn is based upon the reasonable person standard.[58] Where plaintiff knew of the danger,[59] the danger was obvious or a matter of common knowledge,[60] or where warnings were ignored,[61] no cause of action for failure to warn may be sustained. To prove a claim for failure to warn, a plaintiff must show that, at the time the product left defendant's control, it lacked adequate warning or instruction and created an unreasonably dangerous condition that the defendant knew or should have known would pose a substantial risk of harm to foreseeable plaintiffs.[62] These warnings must be "sufficiently intelligible and prominent to reach and protect all those who may reasonably be expected to come into contact with" the product.[63] Usage of warnings as directed by the responsible governmental agency may preempt claims for negligent failure to warn.[64]

11. **Post-Sale Duty to Warn and Remedial Measures**

Failure of a manufacturer or seller to give adequate warning or instruction is a basis for a statutory cause of action if, *after* the product left defendant's control, defendant became aware that the product posed a substantial risk of harm to foreseeable users and yet did not take reasonable steps to warn or instruct.[65] The cases defining a post-sale duty to warn before the enactment of the statute in 1995 concern situations in which the knowledge of the alleged danger related to: (1) an omitted safety feature known and available prior to the date of manufacture,[66] and (2) a chemical whose alleged dangerous propensity was known at time of manufacture.[67] Evidence of subsequent remedial measures is not admissible to prove negligence but may be used for impeachment purposes.[68] The court may exclude evidence when the probative value of the evidence is substantially outweighed by the danger of unfair prejudice, confusion of the issues, or misleading the jury.[69]

12. **Learned Intermediary Doctrine**

The manufacturer of a prescription drug or medical device is not required to warn or instruct individual patients, if the manufacturer has adequately warned or instructed the relevant physician or other legally authorized person prescribing or dispensing the drug (unless the FDA requires such direct warning or instruction to the patient in the particular instance).[70]

13. **Substantial Alteration/Abnormal Use**

A manufacturer is not responsible for injuries caused by an alteration or modification to the product unless the alteration was made in accordance with product instructions or with the express consent of the manufacturer or seller.[71] A manufacturer is similarly not responsible for misuse of the product.[72] In negligence actions, plaintiffs must also be able to prove that the chain of causation was not broken by a third party.[73]

14. **State-of-the-Art Evidence**

    State-of-the-art evidence is admissible in determining the applicable standard of care[74] and is implicit in the statutory risk-utility analysis of an alleged defect in design or formulation.[75]

15. **Malfunction**

    No North Carolina authority expressly distinguishes "malfunction" from other latent or patent defects. (See D.2, "Definition of Defect.")

16. **Standards and Governmental Regulation**

    Violation of a regulatory or statutory safety standard is generally held to be negligence *per se* if the purpose of the standard is (1) to protect the persons and interests harmed (2) against the harm alleged, and (3) from injuries caused by the particular hazard addressed by the standard.[76] Nonstatutory safety codes are generally inadmissible,[77] but this is not an inflexible rule.[78] Such non-statutory standards may be admissible when they are published by a source that is considered reliable by persons involved in the subject matter area, when they are adopted by the defendant,[79] or when they have become a standard in the industry manufacturing the product.[80] Compliance with governmental standards is evidence of reasonableness of design.[81]

17. **Other Accidents**

    Evidence of substantially similar events or conditions, when shown to be relevant in terms of time and circumstances, may be admissible on the issues of causation, defect, or knowledge,[82] unless the probative value is substantially outweighed by the danger of unfair prejudice, confusion of the issues, or misleading the jury.[83]

18. **Misrepresentation**

    No North Carolina cases have discussed or adopted Section 402B of the Restatement (Second) of Torts.[84] However, see D.10, "Failure to Warn."

19. **Destruction or Loss of Product**

    The remedy for spoliation of evidence, whether in bad faith or not, is a jury instruction permitting, but not requiring, the jury to infer that the spoiled evidence would probably be harmful to the spoiler's case.[85] The inference the jury is permitted to make does not take "the place of evidence of material facts and does not shift the burden of proof so as to relieve the party upon whom it rests of the necessity of establishing a prima facie case, although it may turn the scale when the evidence is closely balanced."[86] The inference the jury may draw is permissive, not mandatory. If the jury believes the evidence was destroyed for an innocent reason, the jury is free to reject the inference.[87] Importantly, the spoliation rule that applies to physical evidence also applies to documentary evidence, including critical e-mail correspondence.[88]

The North Carolina Rules of Professional Conduct prohibit destruction of evidence.[89] Absent exceptional circumstances, however, courts are not permitted to impose sanctions for the failure to produce electronically stored evidence when it is destroyed as a result of the routine, good-faith operation of an electronic business system.[90] The Fourth Circuit, in which the North Carolina federal district courts reside, has required a showing of prejudice and bad faith in destruction of evidence to warrant dismissal of a pleading based on Virginia law.[91]

20. **Economic Loss**

North Carolina has adopted the "economic loss rule," which states that purely economic loss from damage to the product itself is not recoverable in a product liability negligence action.[92] Recovery for solely economic loss can be pursued only in a contract/UCC claim.[93]

21. **Crashworthiness**

Federal courts, predicting in 1987 the future actions of the state courts, generally anticipated rejection of crashworthiness in North Carolina.[94] However, the associated doctrine of "enhanced injury" was endorsed in a 1989 Court of Appeals decision,[95] and a later North Carolina Supreme Court case discussed the Court of Appeals opinion without rejecting it.[96] Thus, crashworthiness is likely to be applied in North Carolina, although the question is far from settled.

22. **Seat Belt Use**

By statute, evidence relating to the use or non-use of seat belts is generally inadmissible in any action.[97] However, if misuse of a seatbelt causes injury, the misuse may be found to have been an alteration or modification of the product for which the manufacturer is not liable.[98]

23. **No Liability for Inherent Characteristics**

A manufacturer cannot be held liable for a design defect claim that is grounded on an inherent product characteristic, when such characteristic is recognized by an ordinary person with knowledge common to the community and when such characteristic cannot be eliminated without substantially compromising the product's usefulness or desirability.[99]

E. **BREACH OF WARRANTY**

1. **Causes of Action and General Defenses**

Under North Carolina's adoption of the UCC, a warranty that goods are merchantable is implied in a contract of sale.[100] A product defect may be inferred from a malfunction, if there is evidence the product had been put to its ordinary use.[101] Plaintiff has the burden of proof, and the defect must exist at the time of the sale.[102] The seller's liability arises out of contract and does not depend upon proof of his negligence.[103] To be merchantable, goods must be fit for the ordinary purposes for which they are used.[104] Failure to warn of a product's dangerous propensity may give rise to an action for breach of the implied warranty of merchantability.[105] Implied warranty claims are subject to the defenses found in North Carolina's Product Liability Act.[106] Evidence of compliance with governmental standards is admissible.[107] When the buyer, before entering into a contract, has examined the goods or sample as fully as desired, or has refused to do so, there is no implied warranty with regard to defects that such examination ought to have revealed.[108]

A claim for breach of implied warranty of fitness for a particular purpose requires proof that the seller had reason to know of the particular purpose for which the buyer wanted the goods and that the buyer relied on the seller's judgment or skill.[109] When the buyer provides the specifications for the goods, there may be no reliance on the seller's skill.[110]

A claim for breach of express warranty is founded upon an affirmation of fact or promise made by the seller to the buyer that relates to the goods and becomes part of the basis for the bargain.[111] A statement purporting to be merely the seller's opinion or "puffing" of the goods does not create an express warranty.[112] The "sealed container" defense is not available in an express warranty claim.[113]

Warranties may be expressly excluded, modified, or subjected to liquidated damages provisions, as allowed by statute.[114]

2. **Privity**

Actions against a manufacturer or seller for breach of express warranty are limited to buyer, buyer's family, and "guests in his home."[115] Breach of implied warranty actions against a manufacturer are limited to buyer, member or guest of buyer's family, guest of buyer, and buyer's employee.[116]

Where there is no privity, a plaintiff may neither revoke acceptance of a product[117] nor recover for damages or injury under an express or an implied warranty theory.[118]

F. **PUNITIVE DAMAGES**

Punitive damages are subject of a comprehensive 1995 statute.[119] They are recoverable in negligence actions only when plaintiff recovers compensatory damages and where there is clear and convincing evidence of actual fraud, malice, or willful or wanton conduct related to the injury.[120] The conduct must be more than gross negligence.[121] Specificity is required in pleading,[122] and only nine categories of evidence may be considered by the jury.[123] Vicarious liability cannot be the basis for punitive damages.[124]

Generally, the amount of punitive damages awarded is limited to the greater of three times compensatory damages, or $250,000.[125] However, the jury is not thus instructed.[126] A separate trial is required if such motion is made by defendant.[127] Attorney's fees shall be awarded for frivolous pleading regarding punitive damages.[128] Punitive damages are not recoverable under breach of warranty or breach of contract.[129]

G. PRE- AND POST-JUDGMENT INTEREST

Interest in all actions other than contract actions is awarded at the legal rate of eight percent, calculated in tort actions from the date an action is instituted until the time the judgment is satisfied.[130] In breach of contract actions, interest is calculated from the date of the breach.[131] This interest calculation applies only to compensatory damage awards.[132] Settlements must be taken into account in calculating pre-judgment interest.[133] No interest is available on an award of attorney's fees.[134] Interest is also not available on any award against the State, unless specifically required by contract or by statute.[135]

H. EMPLOYER IMMUNITY FROM SUIT

By statute, the rights and remedies afforded an employee by the Workers' Compensation Act are exclusive, and those rights preclude any other remedy against an employer covered by the Act, regardless of negligence on the part of the employer.[136] The North Carolina Supreme Court has created a narrow exception to the exclusive remedy provision where an employer's conduct is intentional and substantially certain to cause the injury or death (a "Woodson" claim).[137] An employee, or the employee's estate, may then pursue *both* a worker's compensation claim and a civil action against the employer, though there can be only one remedy.[138] An employer's subrogated claim against a third party for injury to an employee may not be recovered if the employer's negligence concurred in causing the injury, and the amount of any verdict against the third party is offset by the amount paid by the employer.[139] The third party defending must plead the negligence of the employer and serve the pleading on the employer, though the latter is *not* a party, and the employer has a right to appear and participate in trial.[140]

I. STATUTES

Relevant statutes for product liability actions are the product liability chapter (see A. and D., *supra*), various statutes of limitation and repose (see B., *supra*), the UCC when a breach of warranty is alleged (see E., *supra*), the punitive damages chapter (see F., *supra*), and the Workers' Compensation Act (see H., *supra*). Rule 414 of the North Carolina Rules of Evidence was enacted in 2011 and limits medical expense evidence to evidence of the amounts actually paid to satisfy the bills, or actually necessary to satisfy unpaid bills.[141]

J. JOINT AND SEVERAL LIABILITY

Common law provides joint and several liability among tortfeasors for resulting injury.[142] There is no apportionment of fault.[143] The Uniform Contribution Among Tort-Feasors Act applies.[144] In 2009 and 2010, renewed legislative efforts to modify North Carolina law to adopt some variation of "comparative negligence" which would do away with joint and several liability among tortfeasors failed to be adopted. *See* Endnote 47, *supra*.

K. PSYCHOLOGICAL DAMAGES

North Carolina generally follows a conservative approach toward damages for alleged psychological harm. Recent cases have stated that claims in which plaintiffs did not personally witness the accident, and were not in close proximity to the event, should ordinarily be rejected unless the plaintiff can produce evidence that the defendant had *actual knowledge* before the accident of plaintiff's particular susceptibility to emotional distress.[145] Furthermore, where plaintiff alleges emotional distress, a strong showing of "severe emotional distress" must be made.[146] While the testimony of friends, family, and pastors can be sufficient proof of severe emotional distress, proper medical documentation is highly persuasive, such as a record of diagnosis of the alleged emotional or mental condition.[147]

William F. Womble, Jr.
Womble Carlyle Sandridge & Rice, L.L.P.
One West Fourth Street
Winston-Salem, North Carolina 27101
(336) 721-3600
(Fax) (336) 721-3660
Frederick W. Rom
Womble Carlyle Sandridge & Rice, L.L.P.
150 Fayetteville Street, Suite 2100
Raleigh, North Carolina 27601
(919) 755-2100
(Fax) (919) 755-2150

ENDNOTES - NORTH CAROLINA

1. N.C. Gen. Stat. § 99B *et seq.* (amendments effective January 1, 1996, apply to claims for relief arising on or after that date; claims for injury from silicone gel breast implants implanted after January 1, 1996, are excluded (Session Laws 1995, c. 522, s. 3)). *See particularly* N.C. Gen. Stat. § 99B-1(3); *Driver v. Burlington Aviation, Inc.*, 110 N.C. App. 519, 527, 430 S.E.2d 476, 482 (1993).

2. N.C. Gen. Stat. § 1-52(16) ("[u]nless otherwise provided by law, (an action) for personal injury or physical damages to claimant's property . . ." is subject to three-year limitation); *Hanover Ins. Co. v. Amana Refrigeration, Inc.*, 106 N.C. App. 79, 82, 415 S.E.2d 99, 101, *rev. denied*, 332 N.C. 344, 421 S.E.2d 147 (1992) (property damage); *Bernick v. Jurden*, 306 N.C. 435, 447, 293 S.E.2d 405, 413 (1982) (personal injury, non-privity); *Smith v. Cessna Aircraft Co.*, 571 F. Supp. 433, 435-36 (M.D.N.C. 1983) (personal injury).

3. *Dunn v. Pac. Employers Ins. Co.*, 332 N.C. 129, 132, 418 S.E.2d 645, 647 (1992); *Wilder v. Amatex Corp.*, 314 N.C. 550, 560-61, 336 S.E.2d 66, 72 (1985).

4. N.C. Gen. Stat. § 1-52(16); *Doe v. Doe*, 973 F.2d 237, 239 (4th Cir. 1992).

5. N.C. Gen. Stat. § 25-2-725(1); *Reece v. Homette Corp.*, 110 N.C. App. 462, 467, 429 S.E.2d 768, 771 (1993) (product liability remedies not available for damage to product; UCC limitation period ran from date of sale); *Smith v. Cessna Aircraft*, 571 F. Supp. 433 (M.D.N.C. 1983); *Bobbitt v. Tannewitz*, 538 F. Supp. 654, 656-57 (M.D.N.C. 1982).

6. *See* N.C. Gen. Stat. § 25-2-725(2); *Reece*, 110 N.C. App. at 467, 429 S.E.2d at 770-71; *Bobbitt*, 538 F. Supp. at 656-67.

7. N.C. Gen. Stat. § 1-53(4).

8. *Nelson v. Patrick*, 58 N.C. App. 546, 548-49, 293 S.E.2d 829, 831 (1982).

9. *Clodfelter v. Bates*, 44 N.C. App. 107, 111-12, 260 S.E.2d 672, 675-76 (1979), *rev. denied*, 299 N.C. 329, 265 S.E.2d 394 (1980).

10. *Barger v. McCoy Hilliard & Parks*, 120 N.C. App. 326, 335, 462 S.E.2d 252, 259 (1995), *aff'd in part, rev'd in part*, 346 N.C. 650, 488 S.E.2d 215 (1997).

11. N.C. Gen. Stat. § 1-15(c).

12. N.C. Gen. Stat. § 1-15(c).

13. N.C. Gen. Stat. § 1-56; *Barger*, 120 N.C. App. at 335-36, 462 S.E.2d at 259; *NationsBank of N.C., N.A. v. Parker*, 140 N.C. App. 106, 113, 535 S.E.2d 597, 602 (2000).

14. N.C. Gen. Stat. § 1-50(a)(6), *as amended*, N.C. Gen. Stat. § 1-46.1(a)(1); *Vogl v. LVD Corp.*, 132 N.C. App. 797, 810, 514 S.E.2d 113, 115 (1999) (evidence of subsequent purchase of replacement parts insufficient to overcome six-year bar); *but see Hyer v. Pittsburg Corning Corp.*, 790 F.2d 30, 34 (4th Cir. 1986) (predicting that the Supreme Court of North Carolina would hold that N.C. Gen. Stat. § 1-50(6) would not bar plaintiff's claim for damages for asbestosis even though the product was purchased more than six years prior to the alleged onset of the disease); *contra Klein v. Depuy*, 506 F.3d 553 (7th Cir. 2007) (*Hyer* and its progeny have yet to be cited in a North Carolina state court decision.).

15. N.C. Gen. Stat. § 1-46.1 (2010) ("Within 12 years an action—(1) No action for the recovery of damages for personal injury, death, or damage to property based upon or arising out of any alleged defect or any failure in relation to a product shall be brought more than 12 years after the date of initial purchase for use or consumption."). The amendment adopted on August 5, 2009, changing the period of repose from six years to 12 years states that nothing in the Act "is intended to change existing law relating to product liability actions based upon disease."

16. *Chicopee, Inc. v. Sims Metal Works, Inc.*, 98 N.C. App. 423, 427, 391 S.E.2d 211, 214, *rev. denied*, 327 N.C. 426, 395 S.E.2d 674 (1990).

17. *Robinson v. Bridgestone/Firestone N. Am. Tire, L.L.C.*, 209 N.C. App. 310, 315-16, 703 S.E.2d 883, 887 (2011).

18. N.C. Gen. Stat. § 1-50(a)(5)a; *Monson v. Paramount Homes, Inc.*, 133 N.C. App. 235, 242, 515 S.E.2d 445, 450 (1999) (repairs "did not reset the running of the statute of repose"); *Forsyth Mem'l Hosp., Inc. v. Armstrong World Indus., Inc.*, 336 N.C. 438, 443, 444 S.E.2d 423, 426 (1994).

19. N.C. Gen. Stat. § 1-17; *Bryant v. Adams*, 116 N.C. App. 448, 458, 448 S.E.2d 832, 837 (1994), *rev. denied*, 339 N.C. 736, 454 S.E.2d 647 (1995).

20. *Forsyth Mem'l Hosp.*, 336 N.C. at 446, 444 S.E.2d at 423.

21. N.C. Gen. Stat. § 99B-1.1; *Smith v. Fiber Controls Corp.*, 300 N.C. 669, 678, 268 S.E.2d 504, 509-10 (1980); *Warren v. Colombo*, 93 N.C. App. 92, 102, 377 S.E.2d 249, 255 (1989).

22. *Red Hill Hosiery Mill, Inc. v. MagneTek, Inc.*, 138 N.C. App. 70, 75, 530 S.E.2d 321, 326, *rev. denied*, 353 N.C. 268, 546 S.E.2d 112 (2000); *Jolley v. Gen. Motors Corp.*, 55 N.C. App. 383, 385-86, 285 S.E.2d 301, 303-04 (1982).

23. *Jolley*, 55 N.C. App. at 385, 285 S.E.2d at 303-04; *Cockerham v. Ward*, 44 N.C. App. 615, 620-22, 262 S.E.2d 651, 655-56, *cert. denied*, 300 N.C. 195, 269 S.E.2d 622 (1980).

24. N.C. Gen. Stat. § 99B-5(a), (b); *Ziglar v. E.I. Du Pont De Nemours & Co.*, 53 N.C. App. 147, 153-55, 280 S.E.2d 510, 515-16, *rev. denied*, 304 N.C. 393, 285 S.E.2d 838 (1981) (sufficiency of warnings on "inherently dangerous" insecticide in a jug).

25. *Red Hill Hosiery*, 138 N.C. App. at 77 n.7, 79, 530 S.E.2d at 326 n.7, 328.

26. *Howerton v. Arai Helmet, Ltd.*, 358 N.C. 440, 457-59, 597 S.E.2d 674, 686 (2004); *Miller v. Forsyth Mem'l Hosp., Inc.*, 173 N.C. App. 385, 390-91, 618 S.E.2d 838, 842-43 (2005) (partial exclusion of proffered expert's testimony).

27. *Howerton*, 358 N.C. at 459, 597 S.E.2d at 686.

28. N.C.R. Evid. 702(a); *see also* S.L. 2011-283 (H.B. 542) § 4.2, 2011-2012 Gen. Assem., (N.C. 2011) (as amended by S.L. 2011-317, § 1.1) (setting forth the effective date).

29. N.C.R. Evid. 702(a).

30. *Bolkhir v. N.C. State Univ.*, 321 N.C. 706, 709, 365 S.E.2d 898, 900 (1988); *City of Thomasville v. Lease-Afex, Inc.*, 300 N.C. 651, 656, 268 S.E.2d 190, 194 (1980); *see also* N.C. Pattern Jury Instructions—Civil 102.11.

31. *Greene v. Meredith*, 264 N.C. 178, 183, 141 S.E.2d 287, 291 (1965); *Ziglar*, 53 N.C. App. at 154-55, 280 S.E.2d at 515-16.

32. *Cockerham v. Ward*, 44 N.C. App. 615, 620-22, 262 S.E.2d 651, 655-56, *cert. denied*, 300 N.C. 195, 269 S.E.2d 622 (1980); *DeWitt v. Eveready Battery Co., Inc.*, 144 N.C. App. 143, 150, 550 S.E.2d 511, 516 (2001).

33. *Red Hill Hosiery Mill, Inc. v. Magnetek, Inc.*, 138 N.C. App. 70, 76, 530 S.E.2d 321, 326-27, *disc. rev. denied*, 353 N.C. 268, 546 S.E.2d 112 (2000).

34. N.C. Gen. Stat. § 99B-6(a), (b).

35. N.C. Gen. Stat. § 99B-11.

36. N.C. Gen. Stat. § 99B-5(a), (b); *Ziglar*, 53 N.C. App. at 155, 280 S.E.2d at 516.

37. *Goodman v. Wenco Foods, Inc.*, 333 N.C. 1, 26-27, 423 S.E.2d 444, 457 (1992).

38. N.C. Gen. Stat. § 99B-3(a); *Rich v. Shaw*, 98 N.C. App. 489, 492, 391 S.E.2d 220, 223, *rev. denied*, 327 N.C. 432, 395 S.E.2d 689 (1990); *Leinhart v. Dryvit Sys., Inc.*, 255 F.3d 138, 148 (4th Cir. 2001).

39. *Stark ex rel. Jacobsen v. Ford Motor Co.*, 365 N.C. 468, 723 S.E.2d 753 (2012).

40. *Kekelis v. Whitin Mach. Works*, 273 N.C. 439, 442-43, 160 S.E.2d 320, 322 (1968).

41. *Pack v. Auman*, 220 N.C. 704, 18 S.E.2d 247, 248-49 (1942).

42. *Madden v. Carolina Door Controls*, 117 N.C. App. 56, 59, 449 S.E.2d 769, 771 (1994); *Schaffner v. Cumberland Cnty. Hosp. Sys., Inc.*, 77 N.C. App. 689, 694-95, 336 S.E.2d 116, 119-20 (1985), *rev. denied*, 316 N.C. 195, 341 S.E.2d 578 (1986).

43. N.C. Gen. Stat. § 99E-42, the "Commonsense Consumption Act" (2013).

44. N.C. Gen. Stat. § 99B-4(3); *Smith v. Fiber Controls Corp.*, 300 N.C. 669, 672, 268 S.E.2d 504, 506 (1980); *Nicholson v. Am. Safety Util. Corp.*, 346 N.C. 767, 773, 488 S.E.2d 240, 244 (1997), *aff'd as modified*, 346 N.C. 767, 488 S.E.2d 240 (1997); *see also* N.C. Pattern Jury Instructions—Civil 744.10 (contributory negligence may apply to claims of failure to warn, defective design, and defective manufacture); *Leinhart*, 255 F.3d at 148.

45. N.C. Gen. Stat. § 99B-4(2); *Alston v. Monk*, 92 N.C. App. 59, 62-63, 373 S.E.2d 463, 465-66 (1988), *rev. denied*, 324 N.C. 246, 378 S.E.2d 420 (1989).

46. *Nicholson*, 346 N.C. at 772-73, 488 S.E.2d at 244 (citing cases); *see also Champs Convenience Stores, Inc. v. United Chem. Co.*, 329 N.C. 446, 406 S.E.2d 856 (1991) (defense applies to all product liability actions).

47. *Steelcase, Inc. v. Lilly Co., Inc.*, 93 N.C. App. 697, 701, 379 S.E.2d 40, 43, *rev. denied*, 325 N.C. 276, 384 S.E.2d 530 (1989).

48. In 2010, the North Carolina legislature explored compromises to a 2009 comparative fault bill based heavily upon the Uniform Apportionment of Tort Responsibility Act ("UATRA"). The compromises included providing pure several liability among tortfeasors. No bill was passed and the common law is unchanged.

49. N.C. Gen. Stat. § 99B-2(a) (applies to implied warranty claims); *Davis v. Siloo Inc.*, 47 N.C. App. 237, 247-48, 267 S.E.2d 354, 360, *rev. denied*, 301 N.C. 234, 283 S.E.2d 131 (1980); *Jones v. GMRI Inc.*, 144 N.C. App. 558, 561-62, 551 S.E.2d 867, 870 (2001); *see* N.C. Pattern Jury Instructions—Civil 744.05 and 744.06; *Morrison v. Sears, Roebuck & Co.*, 319 N.C. 298, 302-03, 354 S.E.2d 495, 498 (1987) (identified manufacturer of component part may be liable); *Haymore v. Thew Shovel Co.*, 116 N.C. App. 40, 44-45, 446 S.E.2d 865, 868 (1994).

50. *McCollum v. Grove Mfg. Co.*, 58 N.C. App. 283, 287, 293 S.E.2d 632, 635 (1982), *aff'd*, 307 N.C. 695, 300 S.E.2d 374 (1983); *Haymore*, 116 N.C. App. at 45, 446 S.E.2d at 869; *see also* N.C. Pattern Jury Instructions—Civil 744.16.

51. *Maybank v. S. S. Kresge Co.*, 46 N.C. App. 687, 689-90, 266 S.E.2d 409, 411 (1980), *aff'd in part, rev'd in part on other grounds*, 302 N.C. 129, 273 S.E.2d 681 (1981); *Jones v. Willamette Indus., Inc.*, 120 N.C. App. 591, 596, 463 S.E.2d 294, 298 (1995), *rev. denied*, 342 N.C. 656, 467 S.E.2d 714 (1996).

52. *Budd Tire Corp. v. Pierce Tire Co., Inc.*, 90 N.C. App. 684, 687, 370 S.E.2d 267, 269 (1988) (emphasis added).

53. *G.P. Publ'ns, Inc. v. Quebecor Printing—St. Paul, Inc.*, 125 N.C. App. 424, 432-33, 481 S.E.2d 674, 679, *rev. denied*, 346 N.C. 546, 488 S.E.2d 800 (1997).

54. *G.P. Publ'ns*, 125 N.C. App. at 439, 481 S.E.2d at 683.

55. *Griffin v. Tenneco Resins, Inc.*, 648 F. Supp. 964, 967 (W.D.N.C. 1986) (plaintiffs alleged exposure to chemical dyes manufactured by some or all of the named defendants, but could not identify which specific defendant or defendants manufactured the dye that caused the injury) (citing *Elledge v. Pepsi Cola Bottling Co.*, 252 N.C. 337, 113 S.E.2d 435 (1960)); *Wilder v. Amatex Corp.*, 314 N.C. 550, 336 S.E.2d 66 (1985)).

56. *Wyatt v. N.C. Equip. Co.*, 253 N.C. 355, 359, 117 S.E.2d 21, 24 (1960).

57. N.C. Gen. Stat. § 99B-2(b); *Bernick v. Jurden*, 306 N.C. 435, 449-50, 293 S.E.2d 405, 414 (1982).

58. *Buck v. Tweetsie R.R., Inc.*, 44 N.C. App. 588, 591, 261 S.E.2d 517, 519, *rev. denied*, 299 N.C. 735, 267 S.E.2d 660 (1980); *see also Crews v. W.A. Brown & Son, Inc.*, 106 N.C. App. 324, 329-30, 416 S.E.2d 924, 929 (1992) (holding that assembler of a product has a duty to warn).

59. *Strickland v. Dri-Spray Div. Equip. Dev.*, 51 N.C. App. 57, 62, 275 S.E.2d 503, 506 (1981).

60. N.C. Gen. Stat. § 99B-5(b); *Ashe v. Acme Builders, Inc.*, 267 N.C. 384, 386-87, 148 S.E.2d 244, 246 (1966); *Britt v. Mallard-Griffin, Inc.*, 1 N.C. App. 252, 253, 161 S.E.2d 155, 156 (1968); *Simpson v. Hurst Performance, Inc.*, 437 F. Supp. 445, 447 (M.D.N.C. 1977), *aff'd*, 588 F.2d 1351 (4th Cir. 1978); *see also* N.C. Pattern Jury Instructions—Civil 744.12.

61. N.C. Gen. Stat. § 99B-4(1); *Jenkins v. Helgren*, 26 N.C. App. 653, 660-61, 217 S.E.2d 120, 124 (1975); *Edwards v. ATRO SpA*, 891 F. Supp. 1074, 1077-78, *order supplemented*, 891 F. Supp. 1085 (E.D.N.C. 1995).

62. N.C. Gen. Stat. § 99B-5(a)(1), § 99B-5(c) (duty to warn for prescription drugs).

63. *Ziglar v. E.I. DuPont De Nemours and Co.*, 53 N.C. App. 147, 155-56, 280 S.E.2d 510, 516 (1981).

64. *Helms v. Sporicidin Int'l*, 871 F. Supp. 837, 839 (E.D.N.C. 1994).

65. N.C. Gen. Stat. § 99B-5(a)(2).

66. *Smith v. Selco Prods., Inc.*, 96 N.C. App. 151, 158, 385 S.E.2d 173, 176-77, (1989), *rev. denied*, 326 N.C. 598, 393 S.E.2d 883 (1990); *see also ATRO SpA*, 891 F. Supp. at 1085.

67. *Davis v. Siloo, Inc.*, 47 N.C. App. 237, 245-46, 267 S.E.2d 354, 359 (1980).

68. N.C.R. Evid. 407; *Benton v. Hillcrest Foods, Inc.*, 136 N.C. App. 42, 52-53, 524 S.E.2d 53, 60-61 (1999).

69. N.C.R. Evid. 403.

70. N.C. Gen. Stat. § 99B-5(c); *see* N.C. Pattern Jury Instructions—Civil 744.17; *see also Foyle v. Lederle Labs.*, 674 F. Supp. 530, 535-36, (E.D.N.C. 1987); *Padgett v. Synthes, Ltd. (U.S.A.)*, 677 F. Supp. 1329, 1335 (W.D.N.C. 1988), *aff'd*, 872 F.2d 418 (4th Cir. 1989).

71. N.C. Gen. Stat. § 99B-3(a); *Rich v. Shaw*, 98 N.C. App. 489, 492, 391 S.E.2d 220, 223 (1990); *Phillips v. Rest. Mgmt. of Carolina, L.P.*, 146 N.C. App. 203, 218-19, 552 S.E.2d 686, 696 (2001), *cert. denied*, 355 N.C. 214, 560 S.E.2d 132 (2002); *see also Stark, ex rel. Jacobsen v. Ford Motor Co.*, 365 N.C. 468, 723 S.E.2d 753 (2012); *and see* N.C. Pattern Jury Instructions—Civil 744.07.

72. N.C. Gen. Stat. § 99B-4; *see also* N.C. Pattern Jury Instructions—Civil 744.08 and 744.09.

73. *Goodman v. Wenco Foods, Inc.*, 333 N.C. 1, 26-27, 423 S.E.2d 444, 457 (1992).

74. *Horne v. Owens-Corning Fiberglas Corp.*, 4 F.3d 276, 280 (4th Cir. 1993).

75. N.C. Gen. Stat. § 99B-6(a), (b) and (c).

76. *Williams v. City of Durham*, 123 N.C. App. 595, 598, 473 S.E.2d 665, 667 (1996); *Baldwin v. GTE South, Inc.*, 110 N.C. App. 54, 57-58, 428 S.E.2d 857, 859-60, *cert. denied*, 334 N.C. 619, 435 S.E.2d 331 (1993), *rev'd on other grounds*, 335 N.C. 544, 439 S.E.2d 108 (1994).

77. *Sloan v. Carolina Power & Light Co.*, 248 N.C. 125, 130, 102 S.E.2d 822, 826 (1958).

78. *Slade v. New Hanover Cnty. Bd. of Educ.*, 10 N.C. App. 287, 296-97, 178 S.E.2d 316, 322, *cert. denied*, 278 N.C. 104, 179 S.E.2d 453 (1971); *Manganello v. Permastone, Inc.*, 291 N.C. 666, 673, 231 S.E.2d 678, 682 (1977).

79. *Stone v. Proctor*, 259 N.C. 633, 636-37, 131 S.E.2d 297, 299 (1963); *Bucham v. King*, 182 N.C. 171, 108 S.E. 635, 636 (1921); *see also Horne*, 4 F.3d at 280 (industry standards and state of the art evidence); *Edwards v. ATRO SpA*, 891 F. Supp. 1074, 1082 (E.D.N.C. 1995).

80. *Beck v. Carolina Power & Light Co.*, 57 N.C. App. 373, 379-80, 291 S.E.2d 897, 901, *aff'd*, 307 N.C. 267, 297 S.E.2d 397 (1982).

81. N.C. Gen. Stat. § 99B-6(b)(3).

82. N.C.R. Evid. 401 is identical to the federal rule. *Murrow v. Daniels*, 321 N.C. 494, 501, 364 S.E.2d 392, 397 (1988); *see also State v. Frazier*, 344 N.C. 611, 614-16, 476 S.E.2d 297, 299-300 (1996); *Purvis v. Bryson's Jewelers, Inc.*, 115 N.C. App. 146, 147-48, 443 S.E.2d 768, 769-70, *cert. denied*, 338 N.C. 520, 452 S.E.2d 816 (1994); *Smith v. Pass*, 95 N.C. App. 243, 250, 382 S.E.2d 781, 786 (1989); *Sass v. Thomas*, 90 N.C. App. 719, 721, 370 S.E.2d 73, 74-75 (1988); *Enloe v. Charlotte Coca-Cola Bottling Co.*, 208 N.C. 305, 180 S.E. 582, 584 (1935); *Etheridge v. Atl. Coast Line R. Co.*, 206 N.C. 657, 175 S.E. 124, 125-26 (1934).

83. N.C.R. Evid. 403; *Benton v. Hillcrest Foods, Inc.*, 136 N.C. App. 42, 53, 524 S.E.2d 53, 61 (1999).

84. Negligent misrepresentation under § 552 of the Restatement (Second) of Torts has been allowed where pecuniary loss results from supplying false information to others as guidance in business transactions, but not as a basis for personal injury claims. *See Driver v. Burlington Aviation, Inc.*, 110 N.C. App. 519, 525, 430 S.E.2d 476, 480-81 (1993).

85. *McLain v. Taco Bell Corp.*, 137 N.C. App. 179, 184, 527 S.E.2d 712, 716-17, *rev. denied*, 352 N.C. 357, 544 S.E.2d 563 (2000); and *Red Hill Hosiery Mill, Inc. v. MagneTek, Inc.*, 138 N.C. App. 70, 78, 530 S.E.2d 321, 328, *disc. rev. denied*, 353 N.C. 268, 546 S.E.2d 112 (2000); *see also* N.C. Pattern Jury Instructions-Civil 101.39.

86. *McLain*, 137 N.C. App. at 184, 527 S.E.2d at 716.

87. *McLain*, 137 N.C. App. at 184, 527 S.E.2d at 716.

88. *Arndt v. First Union Nat'l Bank*, 170 N.C. App. 518, 527-31, 613 S.E.2d 274, 281-83 (2005).

89. N.C.R. Prof'l Conduct 3.4(a).

90. N.C.R. Civ. P. 37(b1).

91. *Cole v. Keller Indus., Inc.*, 132 F.3d 1044, 1047 (4th Cir. 1998) (applying Virginia law); *but see King v. Am. Power Conversion Corp.*, 181 Fed. Appx. 373, 376 (4th Cir. 2006) (unpublished) (stating that courts should not generally dismiss a

case based on spoliation without bad faith, but dismissing complaint because the spoliation effectively rendered the defendant unable to defend its case).

92. *Chicopee, Inc. v. Sims Metal Works, Inc.*, 98 N.C. App. 423, 432, 391 S.E.2d 211, 217, *rev. denied*, 327 N.C. 426, 395 S.E.2d 674 (1990); *AT&T Corp. v. Med. Review of N.C., Inc.*, 876 F. Supp. 91, 95 (E.D.N.C. 1995).

93. *See AT&T Corp.*, 876 F. Supp. at 94.

94. *See, e.g., Erwin v. Jeep Corp.*, 812 F.2d 172, 173 (4th Cir. 1987); *Martin v. Volkswagen of Am., Inc.*, 707 F.2d 823, 824 (4th Cir. 1983).

95. *Warren v. Colombo*, 93 N.C. App. 92, 95-96, 377 S.E.2d 249, 251-52 (1989).

96. *Murphey v. Ga. Pac. Corp.*, 331 N.C. 702, 707, 417 S.E.2d 460, 464 (1992); *see generally* Kerry A. Shad, *Warren v. Colombo: North Carolina Recognizes Claim for Enhanced Injury*, 68 N.C.L. Rev. 1330 (1990), and N.C. Pattern Jury Instructions—Civil 102.19 ("Multiple Causes") and 102.20 ("Peculiar Susceptibility").

97. N.C. Gen. Stat. § 20-135.2A(d); *Chaney v. Young*, 122 N.C. App. 260, 264, 468 S.E.2d 837, 840 (1996); *Hagwood v. Odom*, 88 N.C. App. 513, 516-17, 364 S.E.2d 190, 192 (1988); *Miller v. Miller*, 273 N.C. 228, 231, 160 S.E.2d 65, 68 (1968).

98. *Stark, ex rel. Jacobsen v. Ford Motor Co.*, 365 N.C. 468, 723 S.E.2d 753 (2012).

99. N.C. Gen. Stat. § 99B-6(c); *see* N.C. Pattern Jury Instructions—Civil 744.16.

100. N.C. Gen. Stat. § 25-2-314; *see* N.C. Pattern Jury Instructions—Civil 744.05 *et seq.*

101. *Red Hill Hosiery Mill, Inc. v. MagneTek, Inc.*, 138 N.C. App. 70, 76, 530 S.E.2d 321, 326-27, *disc. rev. denied*, 353 N.C. 268, 546 S.E.2d 112 (2000).

102. *Morrison v. Sears, Roebuck & Co.*, 319 N.C. 298, 301, 354 S.E.2d 495, 497 (1987).

103. *Veach v. Bacon Am. Corp.*, 266 N.C. 542, 550, 146 S.E.2d 793, 799 (1966).

104. N.C. Gen. Stat. § 25-2-314(2); *Goodman v. Wenco Foods, Inc.*, 333 N.C. 1, 10, 423 S.E.2d 444, 447 (1992).

105. *Reid v. Eckerd Drugs*, 40 N.C. App. 476, 482, 253 S.E.2d 344, 348-49, *rev. denied*, 297 N.C. 612, 257 S.E.2d 219 (1979) (involving an aerosol can); *Bryant v. Adams*, 116 N.C. App. 448, 469-70, 448 S.E.2d 832, 843-44 (1994), *rev. denied*, 339 N.C. 736, 454 S.E.2d 647 (1995) (involving a trampoline).

106. *Morrison*, 319 N.C. at 303, 354 S.E.2d at 499; *see* N.C. Gen. Stat. § 99B-1 *et seq.*

107. *Goodman*, 333 N.C. at 17, 423 S.E.2d at 452; N.C. Gen. Stat. § 99B-6(b)(3).

108. N.C. Gen. Stat. § 25-2-316(3)(b).

109. N.C. Gen. Stat. § 25-2-315; *Angola Farm Supply & Equip. Co. v. FMC Corp.*, 59 N.C. App. 272, 277-78, 296 S.E.2d 503, 507 (1982).

110. *Southeastern Adhesives Co. v. Funder Am., Inc.*, 89 N.C. App. 438, 443-44, 366 S.E.2d 505, 508 (1988); *Hobson Constr. Co., Inc. v. Hajoca Corp.*, 28 N.C. App. 684, 688-89, 222 S.E.2d 709, 712-13 (1976).

111. N.C. Gen. Stat. § 25-2-313.

112. N.C. Gen. Stat. § 25-2-313(2); *Performance Motors, Inc. v. Allen*, 280 N.C. 385, 393-94, 186 S.E.2d 161, 166 (1972); *Warzynski v. Empire Comfort Sys., Inc.*, 102 N.C. App. 222, 226, 401 S.E.2d 801, 803-04 (1991).

113. N.C. Gen. Stat. § 99B-2(a).

114. N.C. Gen. Stat. § 25-2-316, § 25-2-718, § 25-2-719.

115. N.C. Gen. Stat. § 25-2-318 (a seller's express or implied warranty extends to any "natural person who is in the family or household of his buyer or who is a guest in his home if it is reasonable to expect that such person may use, consume or be affected by the goods and who is injured in person by breach of the warranty").

116. N.C. Gen. Stat. § 99B-2(b) (plaintiff cannot sue a manufacturer on an implied warranty if plaintiff is not "a buyer ... or ... a member or a guest of a member of the family of the buyer, a guest of the buyer, or an employee of the buyer"); *see also Crews v. W.A. Brown & Sons, Inc.*, 106 N.C. App. 324, 332-33, 416 S.E.2d 924, 930-31 (1992); *Nicholson v. Am. Safety Util. Corp.*, 124 N.C. App. 59, 68, 476 S.E.2d 672, 678 (1996), *aff'd as modified*, 346 N.C. 767, 488 S.E.2d 240 (1997) (holding that buyer's employee has action against manufacturer, not seller, of safety gloves).

117. *Alberti v. Manufactured Homes, Inc.*, 329 N.C. 727, 735, 407 S.E.2d 819, 824 (1991).

118. *Gregory v. Atrium Door & Window Co.*, 106 N.C. App. 142, 144, 415 S.E.2d 574, 575 (1992); *Crews*, 106 N.C. App. at 331-34, 416 S.E.2d at 929-31.

119. N.C. Gen. Stat. § 1D-1 *et seq.* (applies to claims arising on or after January 1, 1996).

120. N.C. Gen. Stat. § 1D-15(a), (b); § 1D-5(4) (defining fraud).

121. N.C. Gen. Stat. § 1D-15(a); § 1D-5(7).

122. N.C.R. Civ. P. 9(k).

123. N.C. Gen. Stat. § 1D-35(2).

124. N.C. Gen. Stat. § 1D-15(c).

125. N.C. Gen. Stat. § 1D-25(b) and (c) (cap on punitive damages and jury instructions); § 1D-26 (exception for driving while impaired cases); *see* N.C. Pattern Jury Instructions—Civil 810.90 *et seq.*; *Hutelmyer v. Cox*, 133 N.C. App. 364, 375, 514 S.E.2d 554, 562 (1999) (alienation of affections).

126. N.C. Gen. Stat. § 10-25(c).

127. N.C. Gen. Stat. § 1D-30.

128. N.C. Gen. Stat. § 1D-45.

129. *Stanback v. Stanback*, 297 N.C. 181, 196, 254 S.E.2d 611, 621 (1979) (disapproved of on other grounds by *Dickens v. Puryear*, 302 N.C. 437, 276 S.E.2d 325 (1981)); *Newton v. Standard Fire Ins. Co.*, 291 N.C. 105, 111, 229 S.E.2d 297, 301 (1976); *Miller v. Nationwide Mut. Ins. Co.*, 112 N.C. App. 295, 305, 435 S.E.2d 537, 544 (1993), *rev. denied*, 335 N.C. 770, 442 S.E.2d 519 (1994).

130. N.C. Gen. Stat. § 24-5(b), § 24-1 (legal rate of interest); *see also Baxley v. Nationwide Mut. Ins. Co.*, 334 N.C. 1, 8, 430 S.E.2d 895, 900 (1993) (holding that interest paid to plaintiff for loss-of-use of money during pendency of lawsuit is element of plaintiff's damages).

131. N.C. Gen. Stat. § 24-5(a).

132. N.C. Gen. Stat. § 24-5(a).

133. *Brown v. Flowe*, 349 N.C. 520, 526-27, 507 S.E.2d 894, 898 (1998) (adopting scheme for determining pre-judgment interest against non-settling tortfeasors, and fairly offsetting interest attributable to earlier settlement received by plaintiff).

134. *Washington v. Horton*, 132 N.C. App. 347, 352, 513 S.E.2d 331, 335 (1999).

135. *Faulkenbury v. Teachers' & State Emps.' Ret. Sys. of N.C.*, 132 N.C. App. 137, 149, 510 S.E.2d 675, 683, *rev. denied*, 350 N.C. 379, 536 S.E.2d 620 (1999).

136. N.C. Gen. Stat. § 97-10.1; *Brown v. Motor Inns of N.C.*, 47 N.C. App. 115, 117-18, 266 S.E.2d 848, 849, *rev. denied*, 301 N.C. 86 (1980).

137. *Woodson v. Rowland*, 329 N.C. 330, 340-41, 407 S.E.2d 222, 228 (1992).

138. *Woodson*, 329 N.C. at 340-41, 407 S.E.2d at 228.

139. N.C. Gen. Stat. § 97-10.2(e).

140. N.C. Gen. Stat. § 97-10.2(e).

141. N.C.R. Evid. 414; S.L. 2011-283, § 1.1, eff. Oct. 1, 2011.

142. *Young v. Baltimore & Ohio R.R. Co.*, 266 N.C. 458, 465, 146 S.E.2d 441, 445 (1966).

143. *Hall v. Carroll*, 253 N.C. 220, 222, 116 S.E.2d 459, 461 (1960); *Jefferson Pilot Fin. Ins. Co. v. Marsh USA Inc.*, 159 N.C. App. 43, 52, 582 S.E.2d 701, 706 (2003); N.C. Gen. Stat. § 1B-2(1) (relative degree of fault not considered).

144. N.C. Gen. Stat. § 1B-1 *et seq.*

145. *E.g., Hickman ex rel. Womble v. McKoin*, 337 N.C. 460, 464, 446 S.E.2d 80, 83 (1994) (parent-child relation alone insufficient to show foreseeable distress); *Andersen v. Baccus*, 335 N.C. 526, 531-32, 439 S.E.2d 136, 139-40 (1994); *Sorrells v. M.Y.B. Hospitality Ventures of Asheville*, 334 N.C. 669, 674, 435 S.E.2d 320, 323 (1993); *Gardner v. Gardner*, 334 N.C. 662, 667-68, 435 S.E.2d 324, 328 (1993).

146. *E.g., Waddle v. Sparks*, 331 N.C. 73, 83-84, 414 S.E.2d 22, 27-28 (1992); *Pardasani v. Rack Room Shoes Inc.*, 912 F. Supp. 187, 192 (M.D.N.C. 1996).

147. *Williams v. HomEq Servicing Corp.*, 184 N.C. App. 413, 419, 646 S.E.2d 381, 385 (2007); *Kaplan v. Prolife Action League*, 111 N.C. App. 1, 17-18, 431 S.E.2d 828, 836, *rev. denied*, 335 N.C. 175, 436 S.E.2d 379 (1993), *cert. denied*, 512 U.S. 1253 (1994); *Clark v. Perry*, 114 N.C. App. 297, 316-17, 442 S.E.2d 57, 68 (1994); *Bryant v. Thalhimer Bros., Inc.*, 113 N.C. App. 1, 12, 437 S.E.2d 519, 525 (1993), *rev. denied*, 336 N.C. 71, 445 S.E.2d 29 (1994).

NORTH DAKOTA

A. CAUSES OF ACTION

Product liability lawsuits commonly include causes of action for strict liability, negligence, and breach of warranty.

B. STATUTES OF LIMITATION

The statute of limitations for strict product liability and negligence claims is six years.[1] When a case involves a latent injury, a discovery rule may apply.[2] The statute of limitations for wrongful death claims is two years from the date of death.[3] The six-year statute of limitations governs survival claims,[4] but there is a one-year extension from the date of death if the death occurs in the sixth year.[5] The statute of limitations for an action to recover for damages resulting from asbestos exposure is the earlier of three years from being informed of the discovery of the injury and its cause by a competent medical authority, or three years from discovery of facts that would lead to the discovery.[6] The time for bringing a claim, including a wrongful death claim, is tolled while the claimant is under the age of 18.[7] A limitation exists, however, on the total time allowed after the claimant reaches majority.[8] The claimant gets the longer of the limitation period measured from the date of accrual, or one year measured from the date of reaching majority, to start the lawsuit.[9] The statute of limitations for breach of warranty claims is four years from the date of delivery of the goods, unless the warranty explicitly extends to future performance of the goods.[10] There is a ten-year statute of repose for improvements to real property, but it does not apply to manufacturers or suppliers of products used in an improvement.[11]

C. STRICT LIABILITY

1. The Standard

The North Dakota Supreme Court has adopted the elements of Section 402A of the Restatement (Second) of Torts.[12]

2. Definition of "Defect"

A product is defective if "there was a defect or defective condition in the product which made the product unreasonably dangerous."[13] A product is unreasonably dangerous if it is dangerous to an extent beyond which would be contemplated by the ordinary buyer, consumer, or user, "considering the product's characteristics, propensities, risks, dangers, and uses, together with any actual knowledge, training, or experience possessed by that particular buyer, user, or consumer."[14] The North Dakota Supreme Court has not decided whether a plaintiff, to succeed with a design defect claim, must show there is a practical and feasible safer alternative.

3. **Causation**

   The plaintiff must prove that the defect was a proximate cause of the plaintiff's injuries, but may do so with circumstantial evidence.[15]

4. **Contributory Negligence/Assumption of Risk**

   Comparative negligence and assumption of risk are defenses on a modified comparative fault basis.[16] The plaintiff cannot recover if the plaintiff's fault is as great as or exceeds the combined fault of all other persons who contributed to the injury.[17]

5. **Sale or Lease/Persons Liable**

   To be liable for strict product liability, the defendant must have sold the product and be in the business of selling that type of product.[18] Strict product liability does not apply to those who provide services, or who do not standardize or mass market the particular good.[19] If a nonmanufacturing seller identifies the manufacturer, the court must dismiss all product liability claims against the nonmanufacturing seller regardless of the substantive legal theory, unless certain exceptions exist.[20]

   The North Dakota Supreme Court has declined to adopt the apparent manufacturer rule.[21] A manufacturer must assume the cost of defense and any liability that may be imposed on a nonmanufacturing seller when the nonmanufacturing seller did not substantially alter the product and the alleged defect existed when the product left the control of the manufacturer.[22]

6. **Inherently Dangerous Products**

   There are no statutes or case law on inherently dangerous products.

7. **Successor Liability**

   The North Dakota Supreme Court has rejected the continuity of enterprise and product line theories of successor liability.[23] The North Dakota Supreme Court has held that "a successor corporation may acquire an independent duty to warn where defects in its predecessor's products come to its attention."[24]

8. **Market Share Liability/Enterprise Liability**

   The North Dakota Supreme Court has held in an asbestos case that, assuming market share liability were recognized, the plaintiff had failed to present admissible evidence that the "friction products" the defendants manufactured carried equivalent risks of harm and were fungible.[25] It also held that since all possible manufacturers of asbestos-containing brake and clutch "friction products" were not before the court, alternative liability, assuming it were recognized, would not apply.[26]

9. **Privity**

   Privity is not required.[27]

10. **Failure to Warn**

When no warning has been given, there is a presumption that if an adequate warning had been given, the plaintiff would have read and heeded it.[28] The obviousness of danger does not automatically preclude liability in a failure-to-warn case, but is only one factor to be considered in determining whether the product is unreasonably dangerous.[29] The North Dakota Supreme Court held in a negligence case that it is a question of fact whether communicating a warning to an employer satisfies the duty to warn an employee.[30]

11. **Post-Sale Duty to Warn and Subsequent Remedial Measures**

A manufacturer that learns about dangers associated with its products after they are sold has a post-sale duty under negligence principles to take reasonable steps to warn foreseeable users about those dangers.[31] A North Dakota federal district court has predicted that the North Dakota Supreme Court would reject a duty to recall or retrofit.[32] Subsequent remedial measures are not admissible to prove "fault, culpable conduct, a defect in a product, a defect in a product's design, or a need for a warning or instruction."[33]

12. **Learned Intermediary Doctrine**

The United States Court of Appeals for the Eighth Circuit has predicted that the North Dakota Supreme Court would adopt the learned intermediary doctrine.[34]

13. **Substantial Alteration/Abnormal Use**

By statute, no manufacturer or seller is liable when an alteration or modification of the product was a substantial contributing cause of the accident.[35] The North Dakota Supreme Court has held that the statute does not absolve a defendant from liability unless the alteration or modification was unforeseeable.[36] Unforeseeable product misuse is a defense on a modified comparative basis.[37]

14. **State of the Art**

The North Dakota Supreme Court has held that a trial court did not err in excluding state-of-the-art evidence.[38]

15. **Standards and Governmental Regulation**

There is a rebuttable presumption that a product is free from defect if it complied with applicable government or industry standards.[39]

16. **Malfunction**

Under some circumstances, a defect may be inferred from proof that the product did not perform as intended by the manufacturer.[40]

17. **Other Accidents**

   Evidence of another accident is not admissible unless the proponent shows that the circumstances of the accident are substantially similar to the circumstances of the accident in the pending lawsuit.[41]

18. **Misrepresentation**

   The North Dakota Supreme Court has held that the substance of the representations, directions, and warnings on a product container provided minimal support for an instruction on Section 402B of the Restatement (Second) of Torts.[42]

19. **Destruction or Loss of Product**

   The North Dakota Supreme Court has affirmed dismissal of cases in which a plaintiff failed to preserve the evidence, and a defendant submitted an expert's affidavit explaining why the product had to be inspected to determine causation.[43] A North Dakota federal district court has predicted that the North Dakota Supreme Court would not recognize a first-party tort claim for spoliation of evidence.[44]

20. **Economic Loss**

   A manufacturer of a product cannot be held liable in tort for damage to the product itself, even though the event may have created a risk of harm.[45] This doctrine applies to products purchased in consumer as well as commercial transactions.[46] A North Dakota federal district court has predicted that the North Dakota Supreme Court would apply the economic loss doctrine to component-to-component damage when the consumer bought the components, made by the same manufacturer, from the manufacturer's dealer, at the same time.[47]

21. **Crashworthiness**

   A manufacturer whose product did not cause the accident may be held liable for a defect that enhanced the injuries.[48] The accident-producing fault of the plaintiff and others should be considered with the injury-enhancing fault of the manufacturer.[49]

D. **NEGLIGENCE**

1. **Separate Theories**

   The court must instruct the jury on both strict product liability and negligence and require the jury to assess fault separately for each theory.[50] The plaintiff is entitled to judgment on the theory that allows the greater recovery.[51]

2. **Defenses**

   Comparative negligence, assumption of risk, and unforeseeable product misuse are defenses on a modified comparative fault basis.[52]

E. **BREACH OF WARRANTY**

1. **Disclaimers and Limitations of Remedy**

   To be effective, a disclaimer or limitation of remedy provision must be part of the "basis of the bargain."[53] The North Dakota Supreme Court has held a limitation of remedy provision unconscionable in a commercial transaction.[54]

2. **Defenses**

   Comparative negligence, assumption of risk, and unforeseeable product misuse are defenses on a modified comparative fault basis.[55] Comparative fault does not apply when the economic loss rule limits the plaintiff to a claim for breach of implied warranty, except perhaps to the extent the plaintiff seeks recovery for consequential economic losses.[56]

F. **PUNITIVE DAMAGES**

1. **Availability**

   Punitive damages are available "[i]n any action for the breach of an obligation not arising from contract, when the defendant has been guilty by clear and convincing evidence of oppression, fraud, or actual malice."[57] Punitive damages are not available if the product complied with federal statutes or regulations, or if an agency of the federal government gave pre-market approval or certification of the product.[58] This exception does not apply if the defendant withheld or misrepresented material information to the federal agency or bribed it.[59]

   The amount of punitive damages awarded in a case may not exceed the greater of twice the amount of compensatory damages or $250,000.[60] Upon election of either party, the court must try the issue of punitive damages separately from the issues of liability and compensatory damages.[61] Evidence of a defendant's financial condition is not admissible in the proceeding on punitive damages.[62]

2. **Procedure**

   A party must offer affidavits showing the factual basis for the claim and obtain a court order to assert a claim for punitive damages.[63]

G. **DAMAGES**

A statutory cap exists for noneconomic damages in a healthcare malpractice case.[64] The cap applies to the healthcare provider and all others joined in the action, regardless of the theory of liability asserted.[65] The amount of the cap is $500,000.[66]

H. **PRE- AND POST-JUDGMENT INTEREST**

Pre-judgment interest, at the rate of six percent, is allowed in tort actions in the discretion of the factfinder.[67] Post-judgment interest accrues at the rate of three percentage points above the prime rate determined annually.[68]

I. EMPLOYER IMMUNITY FROM SUIT

Employers who have obtained workers compensation coverage are immune from suit.[69] A few categories of employers, most notably farmers, are not covered under the workers compensation act, and remain subject to liability.[70] North Dakota has neither adopted nor rejected the dual capacities doctrine.[71] A third-party tortfeasor may recover from an employer under contractual indemnity.[72] Fault may be assigned to an employer, whether or not a party.[73] Because North Dakota has abolished joint and several liability, the plaintiff does not recover for fault assigned to an employer who is not a party.[74]

J. STATUTES

Relevant statutes for product liability actions are the chapter on time for commencing actions, the chapter on products liability, the chapter on comparative fault, damages, collateral source payments and periodic payments, and, when a breach of warranty is alleged, the chapter on sales.[75]

K. JOINT AND SEVERAL LIABILITY

North Dakota has abolished joint and several liability.[76] The fact finder must apportion the fault of all persons, whether or not a party, and liability is several only.[77] Because a party is responsible only for its own share of fault, it may not seek contribution from others.[78]

Patrick W. Durick
Larry L. Boschee
Zachary E. Pelham
Pearce & Durick
314 East Thayer Avenue
P.O. Box 400
Bismarck, North Dakota 58502
(701) 223-2890
(Fax) (701) 223-7865
E-mail: pwd@pearce-durick.com
llb@pearce-durick.com
zep@pearce-durick.com

ENDNOTES - NORTH DAKOTA

1. N.D. Cent. Code § 28-01-16(5) (2006); *Erickson v. Scotsman, Inc.*, 456 N.W.2d 535, 537 (N.D. 1990).

2. *BASF Corp. v. Symington*, 512 N.W.2d 692, 695 (N.D. 1994).

3. N.D. Cent. Code § 28-01-18(4) (2006).

4. *Hulne v. Int'l Harvester Co.*, 322 N.W.2d 474, 477 (N.D. 1982).

5. N.D. Cent. Code § 28-01-26 (2006).

6. N.D. Cent. Code § 28-01.3-08(4) (2006). The North Dakota Supreme Court has found an unrelated portion of this statute to be unconstitutional. *Dickie v. Farmers Union Oil Co. of LaMoure*, 611 N.W.2d 168, 173 (N.D. 2000). However, when part of a statute is found unconstitutional, unrelated portions remain in effect. N.D. Cent. Code § 1-02-20 (2008); *Tooz v. State*, 38 N.W.2d 285, 291 (N.D. 1949).

7. N.D. Cent. Code § 28-01-25 (2006); *Sprecher v. Magstadt*, 213 N.W.2d 881, 885 (N.D. 1973).

8. N.D. Cent. Code § 28-01-25 (2006).

9. *BASF Corp.*, 512 N.W.2d at 697.

10. N.D. Cent. Code § 41-02-104(1) (2010); *Superior, Inc. v. Behlen Mfg. Co.*, 738 N.W.2d 19, 27 (N.D. 2007).

11. N.D. Cent. Code § 28-01-44 (2006); *Blikre v. ACandS, Inc.*, 593 N.W.2d 775, 780 (N.D. 1999).

12. *Johnson v. Am. Motors Corp.*, 225 N.W.2d 57, 66 (N.D. 1974).

13. N.D. Cent. Code § 28-01.3-06 (2006).

14. N.D. Cent. Code § 28-01.3-01(4) (2006).

15. *Endresen v. Scheels Hardware & Sports Shop, Inc.*, 560 N.W.2d 225, 229 (N.D. 1997).

16. N.D. Cent. Code § 32-03.2-02 (2010).

17. N.D. Cent. Code § 32-03.2-02 (2010).

18. *Johnson*, 225 N.W.2d at 66.

19. *Sime v. Tvenge Assocs. Architects & Planners, P.C.*, 488 N.W.2d 606, 611-12 (N.D. 1992).

20. N.D. Cent. Code § 28-01.3-04 (2006); *see Dakota, Missouri Valley & W. R.R., Inc. v. JMA Rail Prods. Co.*, No. 1:06-CV-02, 2006 WL 2349976, *3 (D.N.D. Aug. 9, 2006) (product liability action under the statute includes breach of warranty claim).

21. *Bornsen v. Pragotrade, LLC*, 804 N.W.2d 55, 61 (N.D. 2011).

22. N.D. Cent. Code § 28-01.3-05 (2006).

23. *Downtowner, Inc. v. Acrometal Prods., Inc.*, 347 N.W.2d 118, 124-25 (N.D. 1984).

24. *Downtowner, Inc.*, 347 N.W.2d at 125.

25. *Black v. Abex Corp.*, 603 N.W.2d 182, 189, 191 (N.D. 1999).

26. *Black*, 603 N.W.2d at 191-92.

27. *Johnson*, 225 N.W.2d at 62.

28. *Butz v. Werner*, 438 N.W.2d 509, 517 (N.D. 1989).

29. *Olson v. A. W. Chesterton Co.*, 256 N.W.2d 530, 537 (N.D. 1977).

30. *Seibel v. Symons Corp.*, 221 N.W.2d 50, 57 (N.D. 1974).

31. *Crowston v. Goodyear Tire & Rubber Co.*, 521 N.W.2d 401, 409 (N.D. 1994).

32. *Eberts v. Kawasaki Motors Corp.*, No. A1-02-43, 2004 WL 224683, at *3 (D.N.D. Feb. 2, 2004).

33. N.D. R. Evid. 407.

34. *Ehlis v. Shire Richwood, Inc.*, 367 F.3d 1013, 1017 (8th Cir. 2004).

35. N.D. Cent. Code § 28-01.3-03 (2006).

36. *Oanes v. Westgo, Inc.*, 476 N.W.2d 248, 252 (N.D. 1991).

37. N.D. Cent. Code § 32-03.2-02 (N.D. 2010).

38. *Olson*, 256 N.W.2d at 540.

39. N.D. Cent. Code § 28-01.3-09 (2006).

40. *Herman v. Gen. Irrigation Co.*, 247 N.W.2d 472, 478 (N.D. 1976).

41. *Crowston*, 521 N.W.2d at 411; *Olson v. Ford Motor Co.*, 410 F. Supp. 2d 855, 866 (D.N.D. 2006).

42. *Olson*, 256 N.W.2d at 541.

43. *Fines v. Ressler Enters., Inc.*, 820 N.W.2d 688, 693 (N.D. 2012); *Bachmeier v. Wallwork Truck Ctrs.*, 544 N.W.2d 122, 123-25, 127 (N.D. 1996).

44. *Schueller v. Remington Arms Co.*, No. 2:11-cv-108, 2012 U.S. Dist. LEXIS 86768, at *7 (D.N.D. June 6, 2012).

45. *Coop. Power Ass'n v. Westinghouse Elec. Corp.*, 493 N.W.2d 661, 665-66 (N.D. 1992).

46. *Clarys v. Ford Motor Co.*, 592 N.W.2d 573, 578 (N.D. 1999).

47. *Albers v. Deere & Co.*, 599 F. Supp. 2d 1142, 1161-62 (D.N.D. 2008).

48. *Day v. Gen. Motors Corp.*, 345 N.W.2d 349, 358 (N.D. 1984).

49. N.D. Cent. Code § 32-03.2-02 (2010). *See Haff v. Hettich*, 593 N.W.2d 383, 389 (N.D. 1999) (comparative fault statute requires apportionment of damages between original tortfeasor and medical care providers who negligently treat injury).

50. *Butz*, 438 N.W.2d at 515-16.

51. *Butz*, 438 N.W.2d at 516.

52. N.D. Cent. Code § 32-03.2-02 (2010).

53. *Fleck v. Jacques Seed Co.*, 445 N.W.2d 649, 654 (N.D. 1989).

54. *Construction Assocs., Inc. v. Fargo Water Equip. Co.*, 446 N.W.2d 237, 242-44 (N.D. 1989).

55. N.D. Cent. Code § 32-03.2-02 (2010).

56. *Leno v. K & L Homes, Inc.*, 803 N.W.2d 543, 550-51 (N.D. 2011).

57. N.D. Cent. Code § 32-03.2-11(1) (2010).

58. N.D. Cent. Code § 32-03.2-11(6); *see Poitra v. DaimlerChrysler Corp.*, No. 4:04-CV-58, 2006 WL 2349981, *3 (D.N.D. Aug. 10, 2006) (punitive damages not available when vehicle complied with NHTSA regulations).

59. N.D. Cent. Code § 32-03.2-11(7).

60. N.D. Cent. Code § 32-03.2-11(4).

61. N.D. Cent. Code § 32-03.2-11(2).

62. N.D. Cent. Code § 32-03.2-11(3).

63. N.D. Cent. Code § 32-03.2-11(1).

64. N.D. Cent. Code § 32-42-02 (2010).

65. N.D. Cent. Code § 32-42-02(03).

66. N.D. Cent. Code § 32-42-02.

67. N.D. Cent. Code § 32-03-05 (2010); *Bismarck Realty Co. v. Folden*, 354 N.W.2d 636, 642 (N.D. 1984) (at legal rate); N.D. Cent. Code § 47-14-05 (1999 & Supp. 2013) (legal rate is six percent).

68. N.D. Cent. Code § 28-20-34 (2006).

69. N.D. Cent. Code § 65-01-08(1) (2010).

70. N.D. Cent. Code § 65-01-17.

71. *Latendresse v. Preskey*, 290 N.W.2d 267, 272 (N.D. 1980).

72. *Barsness v. Gen. Diesel & Equip. Co., Inc.*, 422 N.W.2d 819, 825 (N.D. 1988).

73. N.D. Cent. Code § 32-03.2-02 (2010).

74. N.D. Cent. Code § 32-03.2-02 (2010).

75. N.D. Cent. Code ch. 28-01 (2006 & Supp. 2013) (time for commencing actions); ch. 28-01.3 (2006) (products liability); ch. 32-03.2 (2010) (comparative fault, damages, collateral source payments, and periodic payments); ch. 41-02 (2010 & Supp. 2013) (sales).

76. N.D. Cent. Code § 32-03.2-02 (2010).

77. N.D. Cent. Code § 32-03.2-02 (2010).

78. *Target Stores, a Div. of Dayton Hudson Corp. v. Automated Maint. Servs., Inc.*, 492 N.W.2d 899, 904 (N.D. 1992).

OHIO

A. CAUSES OF ACTION

1. Product Liability Claims

The Ohio Product Liability Act (OPLA)[1] took effect in 1988, and amendments to the OPLA took effect in 1997, 2001, 2005, and 2007.[2] The OPLA provides for the recovery of compensatory damages, as well as punitive or exemplary damages, for "product liability claims."[3] With respect to "product liability claims" arising on or after April 7, 2005, the OPLA abrogates all common law causes of action.[4] Specific subjects addressed in the OPLA are discussed below in Part C, along with other closely related topics.

Generally, the OPLA defines a "product liability claim" as an action seeking compensatory damages from the manufacturer or supplier of a product "for death, physical injury to person, emotional distress, or physical damage to property other than the product in question."[5] The damages must have arisen from (1) the product's defective manufacture or construction; (2) the product's defective design or formulation; (3) inadequate warning or instruction associated with the product; or (4) the product's failure to conform to a representation or warranty.[6] The Ohio General Assembly amended the OPLA in 2007 to clarify that "product liability claims" include "any public nuisance claim or cause of action at common law in which it is alleged that the design, manufacture, supply, marketing, distribution, promotion, advertising, labeling, or sale of a product unreasonably interferes with a right common to the general public."[7] A claim seeking recovery for only economic loss typically is not a "product liability claim" and, thus, does not state a cause of action under the OPLA.[8]

2. Asbestos and Silicosis Claims

In 2004, the Ohio General Assembly enacted House Bill 292,[9] which extensively revised state laws governing asbestos and silicosis litigation in response to the legislative finding that "[t]he current asbestos personal injury litigation system is unfair and inefficient, imposing a severe burden on litigants and taxpayers alike."[10] As a result, asbestos, silicosis, and mixed dust disease claims are treated separately from other product liability claims.[11] The Supreme Court of Ohio has held that these provisions may apply retroactively.[12]

Among other topics, these provisions address tolling of the statute of limitations[13] and the "substantial factor" test in multiple defendant cases.[14] Moreover, they establish certain threshold requirements for bringing claims. For example, a plaintiff may not bring or maintain asbestos or silicosis claims alleging a nonmalignant condition without first filing with the court certain qualifying medical evidence of physical impairment, which must be supported by the written opinion of a competent medical authority stating that the claimant's exposure to asbestos or silica was a substantial contributing factor to his or her medical condition.[15] The claim of any plaintiff who does not file the required preliminary medical evidence and physician's statement is to be administratively dismissed without prejudice with the court retaining jurisdiction, meaning that a plaintiff cannot be barred from reinstating the claim in the future when and if the plaintiff can meet the threshold evidentiary requirements.[16] "[W]hen a tort action includes an asbestos claim that is administratively dismissed, non-asbestos claims can be severed from the asbestos claim and proceed to trial."[17]

B. **STATUTES OF LIMITATIONS AND REPOSE**

The statute of limitations for an action based on a "product liability claim" and for actions for "bodily injury or injuring personal property" is two years.[18] A product-related action for damage to real property would be governed by a four-year or ten-year statute of limitations.[19] The cause of action generally accrues when the loss to person or property occurs.[20] The Ohio General Assembly has expressly provided for a discovery rule in circumstances involving exposure to (1) hazardous or toxic chemicals, ethical drugs, or ethical medical devices; (2) chromium; (3) chemical defoliants, herbicides, or other causative agents; (4) DES or similar compounds; and (5) asbestos.[21]

Ohio has a statute of repose under which a "product liability claim" may not accrue against the manufacturer or supplier of the product "later than ten years from the date that the product was delivered to its first purchaser or first lessee who was not engaged in a business in which the product was used as a component in the production, construction, creation, assembly, or rebuilding of another product."[22] There are limited exceptions to the statute of repose, including exceptions for circumstances when (1) the manufacturer or supplier engaged in fraud with regard to information about the product and the fraud contributed to the harm, (2) the manufacturer or supplier made an express, written warranty as to the safety of the product that was for a period of over ten years and that warranty had not expired at the time the cause of action accrued, and (3) the discovery rule applies and the exposure to the substance or device causing the injury occurred during the ten-year period.[23]

If the injured person is deceased, the personal representative of the decedent's estate may, under Ohio's survival statute,[24] pursue the decedent's product liability claims for the benefit of the estate subject to the statute of limitations, statute of repose, and accrual rules that would have applied had the decedent survived.[25] In addition, the personal representative may pursue a wrongful death claim on behalf of the statutory wrongful death beneficiaries.[26] Wrongful death claims are subject to a two-year statute of limitations running from the date of death.[27] Wrongful death product liability claims are subject to a discovery rule[28] and a statute of repose analogous to those governing other product liability claims.[29]

The pendency of a putative class action, either in Ohio or in the federal system, tolls the statute of limitations for all members of the class "who would have been parties had the suit been permitted to continue as a class action."[30]

C. OHIO PRODUCT LIABILITY ACT ACTIONS

1. The Standard for Liability

A "manufacturer" is subject to liability for compensatory damages based on a product liability claim brought under the OPLA only if the claimant establishes that the product in question is "defective" and that the defective aspect of the product proximately caused the claimant harm.[31] A claimant may prove that a product is defective by showing (a) defective manufacture or construction,[32] (b) defective design or formulation,[33] (c) inadequate warning or instruction,[34] or (d) failure to conform to a representation made about the product.[35] When bringing claims under the OPLA, claimants should specify which OPLA provision governs the claims in their complaint.[36]

A "supplier,"[37] as distinguished from a manufacturer, generally is subject to liability for compensatory damages based on a product liability claim brought under the OPLA only if the claimant establishes that (a) the supplier was negligent and the negligence proximately caused the claimant harm or (b) the product in question, when it left the supplier's control, did not conform to a representation made by the supplier and that representation and failure to conform proximately caused the claimant harm.[38] Some form of express conduct by the seller is required to maintain a cause of action based on the seller's misrepresentation.[39] Although the statutory definition of "supplier" excludes manufacturers,[40] a supplier may be held liable as if it were a manufacturer under certain specified conditions.[41] For example, a supplier can be held liable as a manufacturer if the supplier marketed the defective product under its own label or if the supplier modified the product and those modifications rendered the product defective.[42]

2. Definition of "Product"

The OPLA defines the term "product" as tangible personal property that is (a) delivered by itself, as a component, or as an ingredient; (b) made for introduction into trade or commerce; and (c) intended for sale or lease in commercial or personal use.[43] Human tissue, blood, and organs are not "products" under the OPLA.[44] Custom-designed products that are not for resale also may not be "products" under the OPLA.[45] While component parts are expressly included in the OPLA's definition of a "product," "a manufacturer of a component part is not liable for a defect in a completed product unless: (1) the component itself is defective or dangerous, or (2) the component manufacturer constructs or assembles the completed product or substantially participated in the design of the final completed product."[46]

3. **Defective Manufacture or Construction**

Claimants may establish defective manufacture or construction under the OPLA by showing that, when a product left the manufacturer's control, it deviated in a material way from (a) "design specifications, formula, or performance standards of the manufacturer; or (b) otherwise identical units manufactured to the same design specifications."[47] A manufacturer's exercise of "all possible care in [a product's] manufacture or construction" does not preclude a conclusion that the product is defective.[48]

4. **Defective Design or Formulation**

Claimants may establish defective design or formulation under the OPLA by showing that the foreseeable risks associated with a product's design or formulation exceeded the benefits.[49] The legislature has identified the following non-exhaustive list of factors to consider when determining the foreseeable risks and benefits associated with a product: (a) "[t]he nature and magnitude of the risks of harm associated with that design or formulation in light of the intended and reasonably foreseeable uses, modifications, or alterations of the product"; (b) "[t]he likely awareness of product users, whether based on warnings, general knowledge, or otherwise, of those risks of harm"; (c) "[t]he likelihood that that design or formulation would cause harm in light of the intended and reasonably foreseeable uses, modifications, or alterations of the product"; (d) "[t]he extent to which that design or formulation conformed to any applicable public or private product standard that was in effect when the product left the control of its manufacturer"; (e) "[t]he extent to which that design or formulation is more dangerous than a re[a]sonably prudent consumer would expect when used in an intended or reasonably foreseeable manner"; (f) "[t]he intended or actual utility of the product, including any performance or safety advantages associated with that design or formulation"; (g) "[t]he technical and economic feasibility, when the product left the control of its manufacturer, of using an alternative design or formulation"; and (h) "[t]he nature and magnitude of any foreseeable risks associated with an alternative design or formulation."[50]

An ethical drug or medical device is not considered defective in design or formulation simply because an aspect of the drug or device is unavoidably unsafe if the manufacturer provides adequate warning and instruction as provided in the OPLA's warnings provision.[51] Effectively then, the OPLA makes design defect claims relating to "unavoidably unsafe" aspects of prescription drugs and medical devices turn on the adequacy of the warnings rather than on the adequacy of the manufacturer's design.[52]

A product is not defective in design or formulation if the claimant's injury was caused by "an inherent characteristic of the product which is a generic aspect of the product that cannot be eliminated without substantially compromising the product's usefulness or desirability and which is recognized by the ordinary person with the ordinary knowledge common to the community."[53] Likewise, a product is not defective in design or formulation if, when the product left the manufacturer's control, "a practical and technically feasible alternative design or formulation was not available that would have prevented the harm for which the claimant seeks to recover compensatory damages without substantially impairing the usefulness or intended purpose of the product."[54]

5. **Inadequate Warning or Instruction**

Claimants may establish that a product is defective due to inadequate warning or instruction under the OPLA by showing that the manufacturer knew or should have known of the relevant risk at the time of marketing the product, where the warning or instruction was required "in light of the likelihood that the product would cause harm of the type for which the claimant seeks to recover . . . and in light of the likely seriousness of that harm."[55] Claimants may establish a post-marketing warnings defect by showing that the manufacturer knew or should have known of the relevant risk "at a relevant time after [the product] left the control of its manufacturer" and the "manufacturer failed to provide the post-marketing warning or instruction that a manufacturer exercising reasonable care would have provided . . . in light of the likelihood that the product would cause harm of the type" at issue and "in light of the likely seriousness of that harm."[56]

A product is not defective due to inadequate warning or instruction where the manufacturer fails "to warn or instruct about an open and obvious risk or a risk that is a matter of common knowledge."[57]

"A component manufacturer's duty to warn the end user of the final product does not extend 'to the speculative anticipation of how manufactured components . . . can become potentially dangerous dependent upon their integration into a unit designed and assembled by another.'"[58]

The OPLA incorporates the learned intermediary doctrine and provides that a prescription drug prescribed or dispensed by a physician or other person legally authorized to do so is not defective due to inadequate warning or instruction "if its manufacturer provides otherwise adequate warning and instruction to the physician or other legally authorized person who prescribes or dispenses [it] . . . and if the federal food and drug administration has not provided that warning or instruction relative to that ethical drug is to be given directly to the ultimate user of it."[59] The Ohio Supreme Court has applied the learned intermediary doctrine to prescription medical devices.[60]

6. **Conformance to Representation**

   Under the OPLA, claimants may establish that a product is defective due to its failure to conform to a representation made by the manufacturer or supplier by showing that the product did not so conform, even where the manufacturer or supplier did not act "fraudulently, recklessly, or negligently in making the representation."[61]

7. **Causation**

   Consistent with Ohio's common law rule,[62] a plaintiff proceeding with an OPLA claim has the burden to prove, by a preponderance of the evidence, that the defective aspect of the product was the proximate cause of the harm for which the plaintiff seeks to recover compensatory damages.[63]

8. **Assumption of Risk & Comparative Fault**

   Assumption of risk may be asserted as an affirmative defense in product liability actions and, whether express or implied, generally serves as a complete bar to recovery.[64] Contributory negligence and other contributory tortious conduct may also be asserted as affirmative defenses to a product liability action.[65] A claimant's contributory tortious conduct does not bar the recovery of damages where it is no greater than the combined tortious conduct of other persons, whether or not they are parties to the action.[66] When contributory fault is asserted as an affirmative defense, the court shall make findings of fact or the jury shall return a general verdict accompanied by interrogatories that provide the "percentage of tortious conduct attributable to all persons."[67] The compensatory damages award is then reduced by the percentage of tortious conduct attributed to plaintiff.[68]

9. **Retailer, Distributor, and Lessor Liability**

   Liability under the OPLA extends to "manufacturers" and "suppliers" although their liabilities under the OPLA for compensatory damages typically differ.[69] A "manufacturer" is defined as a person or entity "engaged in a business to design, formulate, produce, create, make, construct, assemble, or rebuild a product or a component of a product."[70] A "supplier" is a person or entity that, in the course of business conducted for that purpose, either (a) "sells, distributes, leases, prepares, blends, packages, labels, or otherwise participates in the placing of a product in the stream of commerce;" or (b) "installs, repairs, or maintains any aspect of a product that allegedly causes harm."[71] In general, liability under the OPLA is imposed on manufacturers rather than suppliers.[72] A supplier is liable in its own right, however, if the plaintiff establishes that (a) the supplier's negligence was a proximate cause of the harm for which the plaintiff seeks compensatory damages or (b) the product failed to conform to the supplier's representation and the failure to conform to that representation was a proximate cause of the harm for which the plaintiff seeks recovery.[73] A supplier also may be liable if the manufacturer would be liable under the OPLA and (a) the manufacturer is not subject to judicial process in Ohio, (b) the claimant will be unable to enforce a judgment against the manufacturer due to actual or asserted insolvency, (c) the supplier owns or owned the manufacturer, (d) the manufacturer owns or owned the supplier, (e) the supplier furnished the manufacturer with the design or formulation used for the product, (f) an alteration by the supplier rendered the product defective, (g) the supplier marketed the product under its own label or trade name, or (h) the supplier failed to respond timely to a request by the claimant to disclose the manufacturer.[74]

10. **Inherently Dangerous Products**

A product is not defectively designed if "the harm for which the claimant seeks to recover compensatory damages was caused by an inherent characteristic of the product which is a generic aspect of the product that cannot be eliminated without substantially compromising the product's usefulness or desirability and which is recognized by the ordinary person with the ordinary knowledge common to the community."[75]

11. **Nontraditional Theories of Liability**

Under the OPLA, "[a] manufacturer may not be held liable in a product liability action based on market share, enterprise, or industrywide liability."[76] Alternative liability, which shifts the burden to defendants to show that they did not cause the harm at issue where one of several defendants caused the harm, but there is uncertainty as to which one,[77] has been applied in non-OPLA actions when all possible tortfeasors were named and subject to the court's jurisdiction, the plaintiff showed that all of the defendants acted tortiously, and the tortfeasors' products created a substantially similar risk of harm.[78]

12. **Privity**

Privity is not required to state a "product liability claim" under the OPLA.

13. **Substantial Alteration/Abnormal Use**

A manufacturer is not responsible for harm caused by a product if the product was substantially altered in a manner that was not reasonably foreseeable after it left the manufacturer's control.[79]

14. **State of the Art**

"A product is not defective in design or formulation if, at the time the product left the control of its manufacturer, a practical and technically feasible alternative design or formulation was not available that would have prevented the harm for which the claimant seeks to recover compensatory damages without substantially impairing the usefulness or intended purpose of the product."[80] Similarly, a manufacturer's liability for failures to warn is limited to what the "manufacturer knew, or in the exercise of reasonable care, should have known about" the relevant risk.[81]

15. **Compliance with Safety Standards**

Generally, and apart from the circumstances outlined in the following two paragraphs, a manufacturer's compliance or noncompliance with government safety standards is not necessarily a complete defense to a strict liability claim.[82] Similarly, compliance or noncompliance with industrial or professional safety standards does not constitute either a complete defense to or proof of a strict liability claim.[83]

With respect to product liability claims for harm caused by a drug or device, a manufacturer is not liable for punitive damages if the drug or device in question was manufactured and labeled in accordance with federal law.[84] Under the terms of the OPLA, this bar on punitive damages does not apply if plaintiff can prove that the manufacturer fraudulently withheld from the government agency or misrepresented to the government agency material information known to be relevant to the harm suffered by the plaintiff.[85] The Sixth Circuit found that a similar "fraud-on-the-FDA" exception in a Michigan product liability statute was preempted based on *Buckman Co. v. Plaintiffs' Legal Committee*[86] and then applied the statutory bar.[87]

For "product liability claims" relating to products other than drugs or devices, manufacturers and suppliers are not liable for punitive or exemplary damages if they "fully complied with all applicable government safety and performance standards . . . when the product left the[ir] control . . . and the claimant's injury result[ed] from an alleged defect . . . for which there [wa]s an applicable government safety or performance standard."[88] This bar on punitive damages does not apply if the claimant establishes that the manufacturer or supplier "fraudulently and in violation of applicable government safety and performance standards . . . withheld . . . information known to be material and relevant to the harm that the claimant allegedly suffered or misrepresented to an applicable government agency information of that type."[89]

16. **Prior Accidents and Occurrences**

The Supreme Court of Ohio has held that evidence of prior accidents and occurrences may be admissible in product liability cases where the accidents or occurrences transpire under circumstances that are substantially similar to those in the case at hand.[90] Evidence of prior accidents and occurrences therefore may be admitted to establish the "nature and magnitude of the risks of harm associated with [a] design" under the OPLA provided that the party offering the evidence establishes that the prior accidents or occurrences are sufficiently similar.[91] Evidence showing the absence of prior accidents or injuries may also be admitted to prove "whether the product caused the injury at issue."[92] However, such evidence is not admissible to show that a manufacturer knew or should have known of an injury-causing defect because proof of fault is not necessary to prevail on a product liability claim.[93]

17. Subsequent Remedial Measures

Ohio Rule of Evidence 407 prohibits the admission of evidence of subsequent remedial measures "to prove negligence or culpable conduct," but evidence of subsequent remedial measures is admissible for any relevant purpose in product liability actions based on strict liability in tort.[94] Under Federal Rule of Evidence 407, which applies in diversity actions pending in federal court,[95] evidence of subsequent measures is not admissible to prove "negligence; culpable conduct; a defect in a product or its design; or a need for a warning or instruction."

18. Destruction or Loss of Product

A plaintiff may use circumstantial evidence to prove that a product is defective if the product that allegedly caused the harm was destroyed.[96]

19. Economic Loss

A plaintiff pursuing a "product liability claim" must be entitled to compensatory damages for harm before recovery for economic loss will be awarded.[97]

20. Crashworthiness

Ohio courts have recognized the principle of crashworthiness.[98] The plaintiff must prove, by a preponderance of the evidence, that the defect proximately caused or enhanced plaintiff's injuries.[99] Asserting a crashworthiness claim may render admissible otherwise inadmissible evidence relating to seatbelt use.[100]

D. COMMON LAW ACTIONS

For injuries from "product liability claims" arising on or after April 7, 2005, the OPLA abrogates all common law causes of action,[101] including nuisance actions.[102] Courts also have held that the OPLA abrogates claims brought under the Ohio Consumer Sales Practice Act, Ohio Rev. Code §§ 1345.01 *et seq.*,[103] and abrogates claims for certain types of common law fraud.[104] For injuries from "product liability claims" arising before April 7, 2005, as well as for claims that seek recovery for injuries outside the purview of "product liability claims" under the OPLA, common law and other statutory causes of action may remain.[105]

E. BREACH OF WARRANTY

The OPLA abrogates common law claims for breach of implied warranty relating to injuries from "product liability claims" although § 2307.77 provides an analogous claim under the OPLA when products do not conform to representations made by manufacturers and suppliers.[106] Several courts have found that the OPLA does not abrogate UCC-based warranty claims.[107]

F. SUCCESSOR LIABILITY

"Ohio does not follow the . . . product-line successor liability theory" and "has adopted the general rule of successor liability, which provides that the purchaser of a corporation's assets is not liable for the debts and obligations, including liability for tortious conduct, of the seller corporation" unless one of four exceptions applies.[108] Those exceptions are that (1) liability has been assumed, (2) the sale amounted to a *de facto* merger or consolidation, (3) the buyer corporation was merely a continuation of the seller corporation, or (4) the transaction was entered into fraudulently for the purpose of avoiding liability.[109]

G. DAMAGES

Compensatory damages for the economic loss of the plaintiff are not capped under the OPLA.[110] Damages for noneconomic loss "shall not exceed the greater of two hundred fifty thousand dollars or an amount that is equal to three times the economic loss, as determined by the trier of fact, of the plaintiff in that tort action to a maximum of three hundred fifty thousand dollars for each plaintiff in that tort action or a maximum of five hundred thousand dollars for each occurrence that is the basis of that tort action."[111] The cap on damages for noneconomic loss does not apply if the plaintiff suffered "[p]ermanent and substantial physical deformity, loss of use of a limb, or loss of a bodily organ system" or "[p]ermanent physical functional injury that permanently prevents the injured person from being able to independently care for self and perform life-sustaining activities."[112]

Upon motion of any party, the trial shall be bifurcated so that claims for compensatory damages and punitive damages occur in separate stages.[113] Punitive and exemplary damages are permitted only once compensatory damages are awarded, and punitive and exemplary damages are not recoverable unless plaintiff proves that defendant's actions or omissions "demonstrate malice or aggravated or egregious fraud"[114] or "manifested a flagrant disregard of the safety of persons who might be harmed by the product in question."[115] An award for punitive and exemplary damages cannot exceed two times the amount of the compensatory damages awarded.[116] If the defendant is a small employer, an award for punitive and exemplary damages cannot exceed the lesser of "two times the amount of the compensatory damages awarded to the plaintiff from the defendant or ten percent of the employer's or individual's net worth when the tort was committed up to a maximum of three hundred fifty thousand dollars."[117]

In addition to caps on noneconomic loss and punitive and exemplary damages, the OPLA also seeks to avoid multiple punitive and exemplary damages awards for the same conduct. Punitive or exemplary damages shall not be awarded if the defendant "files with the court a certified judgment, judgment entries, or other evidence showing that punitive or exemplary damages have already been awarded and have been collected, in any state or federal court, against that defendant based on the same act or course of conduct that is alleged to have caused the injury or loss to person or property for which the plaintiff seeks compensatory damages and that the aggregate of those previous punitive or exemplary damage awards exceeds the maximum amount of punitive or exemplary damages that may be awarded."[118]

Wrongful death claimants may recover compensatory damages as provided in the wrongful death statute.[119] The wrongful death statute makes no provision for punitive damages, and for that reason, punitive damages may not be recovered based on wrongful death claims.[120]

H. PRE- AND POST-JUDGMENT INTEREST

Interest on a judgment or settlement decree for the payment of money rendered in a civil action based on tortious conduct is computed by taking the federal short-term interest rate plus three percent from the date of judgment or settlement until the date the money is paid.[121] A party seeking pre-judgment interest must show both its own good faith efforts to settle the case and that the opposing party failed "to make a good faith effort to settle."[122] Pre-judgment interest begins to run on the date the cause of action accrued.[123]

I. EMPLOYER IMMUNITY FROM SUIT

Putting aside intentional tort claims,[124] employers that participate in Ohio's workers' compensation system are immune from liability for an employee's injuries "arising out of his employment."[125] If an employer is a manufacturer or supplier of a product that injures an employee, that employee cannot sue under the OPLA if he or she was injured while using the product within the scope of his or her employment.[126]

J. COLLATERAL BENEFITS

By statute, evidence relating to collateral benefits for which the provider of the collateral benefits has no statutory or contractual subrogation rights may be considered when awarding damages in "a civil action for damages for injury, death, or loss to person or property," including in "a civil action upon a product liability claim and an asbestos claim."[127] If a defendant introduces evidence of collateral benefits, "the plaintiff may introduce evidence of any amount that the plaintiff has paid or contributed to secure the plaintiff's right to receive the benefits of which the defendant has introduced evidence."[128] Further, when evidence of collateral benefits is introduced under the statute, that fact cuts off the rights of the source of those collateral benefits to recover against the plaintiff, as well as its right to be subrogated to the rights of the plaintiff against the defendant.[129]

K. JOINT AND SEVERAL LIABILITY

When two or more persons proximately caused the injury, the defendant to whom the jury attributes over 50 percent of the tortious conduct is jointly and severally liable for all compensatory damages that represent economic loss.[130] Any defendant responsible for less than 50 percent of the tortious conduct is liable for only his or her proportionate share of the compensatory damages that represent economic loss.[131] There is no joint and several liability for compensatory damages that represent noneconomic loss.[132]

L. PREEMPTION

Federal preemption is an inherently federal doctrine based on the U.S. Constitution's Supremacy Clause.[133] Ohio courts, of course, follow controlling federal authority interpreting whether particular types of product liability claims are preempted.[134] In the last two decades, the United States Supreme Court has addressed the preemptive effect of federal law on state-law tort claims in, among others, the contexts of (1) cigarettes,[135] (2) automobiles,[136] (3) prescription medical devices,[137] (4) prescription drugs and vaccines,[138] (5) boat propellers,[139] and (6) pesticides.[140] Very generally, the extent to which federal law preempts state law will depend on whether (1) federal law expressly preempts particular state laws, (2) federal law completely occupies a particular field, or (3) the nature, scope, and extent of any conflict between the respective federal and state laws.[141]

David B. Alden
Katrina L. S. Caseldine
Jones Day
North Point
901 Lakeside Avenue
Cleveland, Ohio 44114
(216) 586-3939
(Fax) (216) 579-0212

ENDNOTES - OHIO

1. Ohio Rev. Code Ann. §§ 2307.71-2307.80 (LexisNexis 2010 & 2014 Supp.).

2. **1988:** Amended Substitute H.B. 1, 117th Gen. Assem., 142 Ohio Laws 1661 (1987-88) (eff. Jan. 5, 1988) (enacting Ohio Rev. Code Ann. §§ 2307.71-2307.80); **1997:** Amended Substitute H.B. 350, 121st Gen. Assem., 146 Ohio Laws 3867 (1995-96) (eff. Jan. 27, 1997) (repealed) (amending Ohio Rev. Code Ann. §§ 2307.71, 2307.72, 2307.73, 2307.75, 2307.78, 2307.80 and enacting Ohio Rev. Code Ann. §§ 2307.791, 2307.792, 2307.801); **2001:** Substitute S.B. 108, 124th Gen. Assem., 149 Ohio Laws 382 (2001-02) (eff. July 6, 2001) (repealing 1997 amendments and reenacting pre-1997 versions of Ohio Rev. Code Ann. §§ 2307.71, 2307.72, 2307.73, 2307.75, 2307.78, 2307.80); **2005:** Amended Substitute S.B. 80, 125th Gen. Assem., 150 Ohio Laws 7915 (2003-04) (eff. Apr. 7, 2005) (amending Ohio Rev. Code Ann. §§ 2307.71, 2307.75, 2307.80 and enacting Ohio Rev. Code Ann. § 2307.711); **2007:** Amended Substitute S.B. 117, 126th Gen. Assem., 151 Ohio Laws 2274 (2005-06) (eff. Oct. 31, 2007) (amending Ohio Rev. Code Ann. §§ 2307.71, 2307.73). The 1997 OPLA amendments were found to violate the Ohio constitutional doctrine of separation of powers and to be unconstitutional *in toto* based on the one-subject rule in § 15(D) of Article II of the Ohio Constitution in *Ohio ex rel. Ohio Academy of Trial Lawyers v. Sheward*, 86 Ohio St. 3d 451, 494, 514, 715 N.E.2d 1062, 1097, 1111 (1999). The 2001 amendments (1) repealed the 1997 amendments "in conformity with" *Sheward*; (2) "clarif[ied] the status of the law"; and (3) "revive[d] the law as it existed prior to" the 1997 amendments. Substitute S.B. 108, § 1, 124th Gen. Assem., 149 Ohio Laws 382, 384 (2001-02) (eff. July 6, 2001).

3. Ohio Rev. Code Ann. § 2307.72(A), (B).

4. Ohio Rev. Code Ann. § 2307.71(B); Amended Substitute S.B. 80, § 3(D), 125th Gen. Assem., 150 Ohio Laws 7915, 8031 (2003-04) (eff. Apr. 7, 2005) ("The General Assembly declares its intent that the amendment made by this Act to section 2307.71 of the Revised Code is intended to supersede . . . *Carrel v. Allied Products Corp.* (1997), 78 Ohio St. 3d 284, that the common law product liability cause of action of negligent design survives the enactment of the Ohio Product Liability Act . . . and to abrogate all common law product liability causes of action."); *see, e.g., Evans v. Hanger Prosthetics & Orthotics, Inc.*, 735 F. Supp. 2d 785, 796-97 (N.D. Ohio 2010) (granting motion to dismiss common law claims in action subject to OPLA); *Crisp v. Stryker Corp.*, No. 5:09-cv-02212, 2010 U.S. Dist. LEXIS 51390, at *10 (N.D. Ohio May 21, 2010) (same); *Miles v. Raymond Corp.*, 612 F. Supp. 2d 913, 922 (N.D. Ohio 2009) (OPLA abrogated common law negligence and common law breach of warranty claims in action relating to October 2006 injury); *Rose v. Truck Ctrs., Inc.*, 611 F. Supp. 2d 745, 748 (N.D. Ohio 2009) (OPLA abrogated common

law product liability claims in action relating to May 2006 injury), *aff'd*, 388 F. App'x 528 (6th Cir. 2010). Common law claims that accrued before the effective date of the 2005 OPLA amendments, however, are not abrogated. *See Wimbush v. Wyeth*, 619 F.3d 632, 639 (6th Cir. 2010) (2005 OPLA amendments applied prospectively and did not abrogate common law claims relating to 2003 injury); *Doty v. Fellhauer Elec., Inc.*, 175 Ohio App. 3d 681, 686-87, 2008-Ohio-1294, ¶36, 888 N.E.2d 1138, 1142 (6th Dist.) (2005 OPLA amendments applied prospectively and did not abrogate common law claims that arose from 2003 event), *review denied*, 119 Ohio St. 3d 145, 2008-Ohio-4487, 893 N.E.2d 516 (2008); *Carrel v. Allied Prod. Corp.*, 78 Ohio St. 3d 284, 287-89, 677 N.E.2d 795, 798-800 (1997) (OPLA as it existed before the 2005 amendments did not abrogate common law claims).

5. Ohio Rev. Code Ann. § 2307.71(A)(13).

6. Ohio Rev. Code Ann. § 2307.71(A)(13)(a)-(c).

7. Ohio Rev. Code Ann. § 2307.71(A)(13); *see* Amended Substitute S.B. 117, § 3, 126th Gen. Assem., 151 Ohio Laws 2274, 2291 (2005-06) (eff. Aug. 1, 2007) (the 2006 amendments to Ohio Rev. Code § 2307.71 "are not intended to be substantive but are intended to clarify the General Assembly's original intent . . . as initially expressed in Section 3 of Am. Sub. S.B. 80 of the 125th General Assembly").

8. Ohio Rev. Code Ann. § 2307.72(C); *see also* Ohio Rev. Code Ann. §§ 2307.71(A)(2), (A)(7), (A)(13); 2307.79; *Holbrook v. La.-Pac. Corp.*, No. 12-4166, 2013 U.S. App. LEXIS 14170, at *10 (6th Cir. July 12, 2013); *Kuns v. Ford Motor Co.*, 926 F. Supp. 2d 976, 987 (N.D. Ohio), *aff'd*, 543 F. App'x 572 (6th Cir. 2013); *LaPuma v. Collinwood Concrete*, 75 Ohio St. 3d 64, 66, 661 N.E.2d 714, 716 (1996).

9. Amended Substitute H.B. 292, 125th Gen. Assem., 150 Ohio Laws 3946 (2003-04) (eff. Sept. 2, 2004).

10. Amended Substitute H.B. 292, § 3(A)(2), 125th Gen. Assem., 150 Ohio Laws 3946, 3988 (2003-04) (eff. Sept. 2, 2004).

11. *See* Ohio Rev. Code Ann. §§ 2307.84-2307.902; 2307.91-2307.98.

12. *Ackison v. Anchor Packing Co.*, 120 Ohio St. 3d 228, 239, 2008-Ohio-5243, ¶62, 897 N.E.2d 1118, 1130 (2008).

13. Ohio Rev. Code Ann. §§ 2307.88, 2307.94.

14. Ohio Rev. Code Ann. §§ 2307.901, 2307.96.

15. Ohio Rev. Code Ann. §§ 2307.85, 2307.92.

16. Ohio Rev. Code Ann. §§ 2307.93(C), 2307.87(C).

17. *Riedel v. Consol. Rail Corp.*, 125 Ohio St. 3d 358, 360, 2010-Ohio-1926, ¶11, 928 N.E.2d 448, 451 (2010).

18. Ohio Rev. Code Ann. § 2305.10(A).

19. *Taylor v. Multi-Flo, Inc.*, 69 Ohio App. 2d 19, 22-23, 429 N.E.2d 1086, 1089 (1st Dist. 1980) (the statute of limitations applied in a product-related action for injury to real property is found in either § 2305.09(D) (four-year time limit) or § 2305.14 (ten-year time limit)).

20. Ohio Rev. Code Ann. § 2305.10(A) ("a cause of action accrues under this division when the injury or loss to person or property occurs").

21. Ohio Rev. Code Ann. § 2305.10(B)(1)-(5). Under these provisions, the cause of action "accrues upon the date on which the plaintiff is informed by competent medical authority that the plaintiff has an injury that is related to the exposure or upon the date on which by the exercise of reasonable diligence the plaintiff should have known that the plaintiff has an injury that is related to the exposure, whichever date occurs first." Ohio Rev. Code Ann. § 2305.10(B)(1)-(5); *see also Dunn v. Ethicon, Inc.*, 168 F. App'x 539, 541 (6th Cir. 2006).

22. Ohio Rev. Code Ann. § 2305.10(C)(1). The statute of repose applies to cases filed on or after April 7, 2005, regardless of when the cause of action accrued. Ohio Rev. Code Ann. § 2305.10(G). In *Groch v. Gen. Motors Corp.*, the Supreme Court of Ohio rejected facial constitutional challenges to the statute of repose in Ohio Rev. Code Ann. § 2305.10(C) and former § 2305.10(F), which now is § 2305.10(G). 117 Ohio St. 3d 192, 230, 2008-Ohio-546, ¶213, 883 N.E.2d 377, 413 (2008).

23. Ohio Rev. Code Ann. § 2305.10(C)(2)-(7).

24. Ohio Rev. Code Ann. § 2305.21.

25. *See Ball v. Victor K. Browning & Co.*, 21 Ohio App. 3d 175, 177, 487 N.E.2d 329, 329 (11th Dist. 1984) ("As the survival action in the present appeal stems from a cause of action for personal injury, R.C. 2305.10 governs. A two year statute of limitations was properly enforced.").

26. Ohio Rev. Code Ann. § 2125.02(A).

27. Ohio Rev. Code Ann. § 2125.02(D)(1) ("Except as provided in division (D)(2) of this section, a civil action for wrongful death shall be commenced within two years after the decedent's death.").

28. Ohio Rev. Code Ann. § 2125.02(D)(2)(f)(i)-(ii); *see also Collins v. Sotka*, 81 Ohio St. 3d 506, 506, 692 N.E.2d 581, 581 (1998) (Syllabus ¶1) ("The discovery rule applies to toll R.C. 2125.02(D), the two-year statute of limitations for a wrongful death claim.").

29. The statute of repose is set forth in Ohio Rev. Code Ann. § 2125.02(D)(2)(a), and the exceptions are in Ohio Rev. Code Ann. § 2125.02(D)(2)(b)-(f).

30. *Vaccariello v. Smith & Nephew Richards, Inc.*, 94 Ohio St. 3d 380, 382-83, 763 N.E.2d 160, 163 (2002).

31. Ohio Rev. Code Ann. § 2307.73(A); *see also* Ohio Rev. Code Ann. § 2307.71(A)(9) (defining a "manufacturer" as "a person engaged in a business to design, formulate, produce, create, make, construct, assemble, or rebuild a product or a component of a product").

32. Ohio Rev. Code Ann. §§ 2307.73(A)(1), 2307.74.

33. Ohio Rev. Code Ann. §§ 2307.73(A)(1), 2307.75.

34. Ohio Rev. Code Ann. §§ 2307.73(A)(1), 2307.76.

35. Ohio Rev. Code Ann. §§ 2307.73(A)(1), 2307.77.

36. *Tolliver v. Bristol-Myers Squibb Co.*, No. 1:12-cv-00745, 2012 U.S. Dist. LEXIS 105518, at *7 (N.D. Ohio July 30, 2012); *Delahunt v. Cytodyne Techs.*, 241 F. Supp. 2d 827, 843 n.6 (S.D. Ohio 2003).

37. A "supplier" means either "[a] person that, in the course of a business conducted for the purpose, sells, distributes, leases, prepares, blends, packages, labels, or otherwise participates in the placing of a product in the stream of commerce; [or] [a] person that, in the course of a business conducted for the purpose, installs, repairs, or maintains any aspect of a product that allegedly causes harm." Ohio Rev. Code Ann. § 2307.71(A)(15)(a). Manufacturers, sellers of real property, those engaged primarily in providing professional services, and those primarily acting in a financial capacity with respect to the sale of a product are excluded from the definition of a "supplier." Ohio Rev. Code Ann. § 2307.71(A)(15)(b)(i)-(iv).

38. Ohio Rev. Code Ann. § 2307.78(A); *Chase v. Brooklyn City Sch. Dist.*, 141 Ohio App. 3d 9, 18, 749 N.E.2d 798, 805 (8th Dist. 2001) (affirming summary judgment for a supplier where plaintiffs failed to show that the supplier acted negligently in selling a product and presented no evidence that the supplier made any misrepresentations about the product).

39. *See Tekavec v. Van Waters & Rogers, Inc.*, 12 F. Supp. 2d 672, 680-81 (N.D. Ohio 1998); Ohio Rev. Code Ann. § 2307.71(A)(14) (representation "means an express representation").

40. Ohio Rev. Code Ann. § 2307.71(A)(15)(b)(i).

41. Ohio Rev. Code Ann. § 2307.78(B); *Convention Ctr. Inn, Ltd. v. Dow Chem. Co.*, 70 Ohio App. 3d 243, 248, 590 N.E.2d 898, 900 (8th Dist. 1990) (under § 2307.78(B), even "a non-negligent supplier of a defective product can be liable to an injured consumer as if it were the manufacturer").

42. Ohio Rev. Code Ann. § 2307.78(B)(6)-(7).

43. Ohio Rev. Code Ann. § 2307.71(A)(12)(a).

44. Ohio Rev. Code Ann. § 2307.71(A)(12)(b).

45. *Estep v. Rieter Auto. N. Am., Inc.*, 148 Ohio App. 3d 546, 553-54, 2002-Ohio-3411, ¶44, 774 N.E.2d 323, 329 (6th Dist. 2002) (entities that designed and built pinch roller/shear press machine for use in manufacturing plant were neither manufacturers nor suppliers under the OPLA), *appeal denied*, 97 Ohio St. 3d 1424, 2002-Ohio-5820, 777 N.E.2d 277 (2002).

46. *Romans v. Texas Instruments, Inc.*, No. CA2013-04-012, 2013-Ohio-5089, ¶28 (12th Dist. 2013) (citations omitted), *appeal denied*, 138 Ohio St. 3d 1451, 2014-Ohio-1182, 5 N.E.3d 668 (2014); *see also Mohney v. USA Hockey, Inc.*, 138 F. App'x 804, 814 (6th Cir. 2005) (applying Ohio law; "A manufacturer who markets a product in an unassembled state and is not involved in the design or assembly or the integrated product or system cannot be liable for a defect introduced by a third party.") (citations omitted), *cert. denied*, 547 U.S. 1020 (2006); *Wells v. Komatsu Am. Int'l Co.*, 162 Ohio App. 3d 827, 832, 2005-Ohio-4415, ¶12, 835 N.E.2d 771, 775 (1st Dist. 2005) ("under Ohio law, component-parts manufacturers are only subject to strict liability for defects in a completed product when they either construct or assemble the completed product or significantly participate in its design") (footnote omitted); *U.S. Aviation Underwriters, Inc. v. B.F. Goodrich Co.*, 149 Ohio App. 3d 569, 2002-Ohio-5429 , 778 N.E.2d 122 (9th Dist. 2002) (affirming directed verdict entered for component part manufacturer).

47. Ohio Rev. Code Ann. § 2307.74. *Compare Kerg v. Atl. Tool & Die Co.*, 176 Ohio App. 3d 437, 447, 2008-Ohio-2364, ¶¶37-38, 892 N.E.2d 481, 489 (8th Dist. 2008) (affirming summary judgment for product manufacturer on manufacturing defect claim where plaintiff failed to submit evidence of defect), *with Eastman v. Stanley Works*, 180 Ohio App. 3d 844, 858-59, 2009-Ohio-634, ¶¶37-38, 907 N.E.2d 768, 779 (10th Dist. 2009) (affirming denial of motion for directed verdict because there was sufficient evidence of manufacturing defect).

48. Ohio Rev. Code Ann. § 2307.74.

49. Ohio Rev. Code Ann. § 2307.75(A). Before the OPLA amendments that took effect in 2007, § 2307.75(A) provided that "a product is defective in design

or formulation if either of the following applies: (1) When it left the control of the manufacturer, the foreseeable risks associated with its design or formulation... exceeded the benefits associated with that design or formulation...; (2) It is more dangerous than an ordinary consumer would expect when used in an intended or reasonably foreseeable manner." *See Newell Rubbermaid, Inc. v. Raymond Corp.*, 676 F.3d 521, 529 (6th Cir. 2012) (applying pre-2007 version of Ohio Rev. Code Ann. § 2307.75(A); "This statute offers two alternative approaches for demonstrating a design defect: a risk-benefit test in subsection (A)(1), and a consumer-expectations test in subsection (A)(2). A jury may consider either or both theories of liability.") (citations omitted). After the 2007 OPLA amendments, a consumer expectations test no longer is an independent standard for evaluating a product's design or formulation; instead, it is the fifth non-exclusive factor for judging a product's foreseeable risks and is set forth in Ohio Rev. Code Ann. § 2307.75(B)(5).

50. Ohio Rev. Code Ann. § 2307.75(B)(1)-(5), (C)(1)-(3).

51. Ohio Rev. Code Ann. § 2307.75(D).

52. *See Wimbush v. Wyeth*, 619 F.3d 632, 638-39 (6th Cir. 2010) (affirming summary judgment dismissing design defect claim against prescription drug manufacturer relating to prescription drug based on Ohio Rev. Code Ann. § 2307.75(D) because the plaintiff "failed to point to any evidence creating a factual dispute as to the adequacy of warning"); *In re Meridia Prods. Liab. Litig.*, 328 F. Supp. 2d 791, 815-17 (N.D. Ohio 2004) (applying multiple states' laws, including OPLA, and granting summary judgment dismissing design defect claims for prescription drug), *aff'd*, 447 F.3d 861 (6th Cir. 2006); *Kennedy v. Merck & Co.*, No. 19591, 2003-Ohio-3774, ¶36 (2d Dist. 2003) (affirming summary judgment dismissing design defect claim against prescription drug manufacturer based on Ohio Rev. Code Ann. § 2307.75(D) because it was "undisputed that [the manufacturer] did provide [an] adequate warning to" the prescribing physician), *review denied*, 100 Ohio St. 3d 1485, 2003-Ohio-5992, 798 N.E.2d 1093 (2003); *cf. Miller v. ALZA Corp.*, 759 F. Supp. 2d 929, 940 (S.D. Ohio 2010) (denying motion for summary judgment on design defect claim against prescription drug patch manufacturer relating to prescription fentanyl patch under Ohio Rev. Code Ann. § 2307.75(D) because patch was not "unavoidably unsafe").

53. Ohio Rev. Code Ann. § 2307.75(E); *Glassner v. R.J. Reynolds Tobacco Co.*, 223 F.3d 343, 349, 352 (6th Cir. 2000) (affirming dismissal of OPLA claims when "there existed a widespread public awareness of the health risks associated with smoking such that [the Court] must impute this 'common knowledge' to [decedent] and presume that she was aware of and assumed those risks"); *Vermett v. Fred Christen & Sons Co.*, 138 Ohio App. 3d 586, 607-08, 741 N.E.2d 954, 969-70 (6th Dist. 2000) (affirming summary judgment for manufacturer on OPLA design defect claim because injury was caused by inherent product characteristic).

54. Ohio Rev. Code Ann. § 2307.75(F); *Nationwide Mut. Ins. Co. v. ICON Health & Fitness, Inc.*, No. 04AP855, 2005-Ohio-2638, ¶15 (10th Dist. 2005) (reversing trial court's denial of summary judgment on design defect claim where plaintiff failed to produce evidence of a technically feasible alternative design); *see also Jacobs v. E.I. DuPont de Nemours & Co.*, 67 F.3d 1219, 1242 (6th Cir. 1995) (exempting a manufacturer from liability where the claimant failed to identify a safe and efficacious alternative design).

55. Ohio Rev. Code Ann. § 2307.76(A)(1). A manufacturer has no duty to warn of a risk that is unknown and unknowable. *Bartel v. John Crane, Inc.*, 316 F. Supp. 2d 603, 611-12 (N.D. Ohio 2004).

56. Ohio Rev. Code Ann. § 2307.76(A)(2).

57. Ohio Rev. Code Ann. § 2307.76(B); *see Bouher v. Aramark Servs., Inc.*, 181 Ohio App. 3d 599, 604-05, 2009-Ohio-1597, ¶¶20-22, 910 N.E.2d 40, 45 (1st Dist. 2009) (affirming summary judgment for manufacturer of coffee maker because dangers of hot water were open and obvious); *Hanlon v. Lane*, 98 Ohio App. 3d 148, 154, 648 N.E.2d 26, 29-30 (9th Dist. 1994) (natural gas manufacturer had no duty to warn of the danger of carbon monoxide poisoning where danger was open and obvious).

58. *Romans v. Texas Instruments, Inc.*, No. CA2013-04-012, 2013-Ohio-5089, ¶46 (12th Dist. 2013) (*quoting Temple v. Wean United, Inc.*, 50 Ohio St. 2d 317, 364 N.E.2d 267 (1977) (syllabus ¶4)), *appeal denied*, 138 Ohio St. 3d 1451, 2014-Ohio-1182, 5 N.E.3d 668 (2014); *see also Aldridge v. Reckart Equip. Co.*, No. 04CA17, 2006-Ohio-4964, ¶69 (4th Dist. 2006) (same), *appeal denied*, 114 Ohio St. 3d 1479, 2007-Ohio-3699, 870 N.E.2d 731 (2007); *Schaffer v. A.O. Smith Harvestore Prods., Inc.*, 74 F.3d 722, 729 (6th Cir. 1996) ("Under Ohio law a manufacturer of a non-defective component part has no duty to warn about dangers that may result when the part is integrated into another product or system, *where the component manufacturer was not involved in the design or assembly of the integrated product or system.*") (citation omitted) (italics in original); *Jacobs v. E.I. du Pont de Nemours & Co.*, 67 F.3d 1219, 1236 (6th Cir. 1995) ("Ohio law is settled that a component part manufacturer has no duty to warn end-users of the finished product of the potentially dangerous nature of its parts in that product.") (citations omitted).

59. Ohio Rev. Code Ann. § 2307.76(C); *see Wimbush v. Wyeth*, 619 F.3d 632, 637 (6th Cir. 2010) ("the common law 'learned intermediary doctrine' is codified in the" OPLA); *Miller v. ALZA Corp.*, 759 F. Supp. 2d 929, 934 (S.D. Ohio 2010) ("With regard to prescription drugs, a manufacturer's duty is discharged 'if the manufacturer warns the patient's doctor of those risks' ") (citing Ohio Rev. Code Ann. § 2307.76(C) and quoting *Graham v. Am. Cyanamid Co.*, 350 F.3d 496, 514 (6th Cir. 2003)); *Lorenzi v. Pfizer Inc.*, 519 F. Supp. 2d 742, 749-50 (N.D. Ohio 2007) (observing that the "OPLA . . . makes clear that a manufacturer's duty to warn a consumer regarding the dangers of a drug that requires a prescription is discharged where the physician

receives adequate warning" and entering summary judgment for prescription drug manufacturer on failure-to-warn claim); *Reece v. AstraZeneca Pharms., LP*, 500 F. Supp. 2d 736, 748-51 (S.D. Ohio 2007) (entering summary judgment for prescription drug manufacturer because the plaintiff failed to raise genuine issue of fact with respect to the adequacy of the warnings provided to prescribing physician).

60. *Vaccariello v. Smith & Nephew Richards, Inc.*, 94 Ohio St. 3d 380, 384-85, 763 N.E.2d 160, 164-65 (2002). A federal court has held that the learned intermediary doctrine also applies in favor of parties other than pharmaceutical manufacturers. *See Midwest Specialties, Inc. v. Crown Indus. Prods. Co.*, 940 F. Supp. 1160, 1167 (N.D. Ohio 1996) (recognizing the sophisticated-user doctrine in non-pharmaceutical cases), *aff'd*, 142 F.3d 435 (6th Cir. 1998).

61. Ohio Rev. Code Ann. §§ 2307.77, 2307.78(A)(2); *see Jordan v. Paccar, Inc.*, 37 F.3d 1181, 1185 (6th Cir. 1994) (trial court did not err in refusing to instruct the jury based on Ohio Rev. Code Ann. § 2307.77 because statements about truck's roof were "enthusiastic subjective claims . . . made in the commercial marketplace" that were "part of the commercial puffery to which ordinary consumers are inured"); *Gawloski v. Miller Brewing Co.*, 96 Ohio App. 3d 160, 164-65, 168, 644 N.E.2d 731, 734, 736 (9th Dist. 1994) (affirming trial court's grant of motion to dismiss misrepresentation claim based on brewer's advertising claims that allegedly showed that beer enhanced the "quality of life" because they were subjective claims that "failed to allege an essential element of their claim: an actionable representation"), *review denied*, 71 Ohio St. 3d 1411, 641 N.E.2d 1110 (1994).

62. *See, e.g., State Auto Mut. Ins. Co. v. Chrysler Corp.*, 36 Ohio St. 2d 151, 156, 304 N.E.2d 891, 894-95 (1973); *Lonzrick v. Republic Steel Corp.*, 6 Ohio St. 2d 227, 230, 218 N.E.2d 185, 188 (1966).

63. Ohio Rev. Code Ann. § 2307.73(A)(2).

64. Ohio Rev. Code Ann. § 2307.711(B); *see Broyles v. Kasper Mach. Co.*, 517 F. App'x 345, 352 (6th Cir. 2013) (applying Ohio law and affirming summary judgment for product manufacturer; "where the plaintiff's actions are wholly voluntary, or even contrary to his employer's instruction, training, and notice, or common sense of the risks involved with his actions, the action should be barred" by assumption of risk); *Carnes v. Gordon Food Serv.*, No. 06-CA-86, 2007-Ohio-2350, ¶84 (2d Dist. 2007) (affirming entry of summary judgment for product manufacturer based on implied assumption of risk under former Ohio Rev. Code § 2315.20(A), which has been repealed but was, in relevant part, identical to Ohio Rev. Code § 2307.711(B)(2)). The assumption of risk defense is not available when an employee "is required to encounter the risk while performing normal job duties." *Hubbard v. PPG Indus., Inc.*, No. 5:12-cv-1124, 2014 U.S. Dist. LEXIS 86405, at *14 (N.D. Ohio June 25, 2014) (citation omitted).

65. Ohio Rev. Code Ann. §§ 2307.711(A), 2315.32-2315.36.

66. Ohio Rev. Code Ann. § 2315.33; *see also* Ohio Rev. Code Ann. §§ 2307.23, 2315.34; *see, e.g., Delta Fuels, Inc. v. Consol. Envtl. Servs.*, No. L-11-1054, 2012-Ohio-2227, ¶23 (6th Dist. 2012) ("A defendant is not liable if a plaintiff's degree of fault is 50 percent or more."); *Byrne v. CSX Transp., Inc.*, No. 3:09-CV-919, 2012 U.S. Dist. LEXIS 75409, at *8-9 (N.D. Ohio May 31, 2012) ("Under Ohio's comparative negligence statute, a defendant is not liable if a plaintiff's negligence is fifty percent or more responsible for the plaintiff's damages.") (citations omitted).

67. Ohio Rev. Code Ann. § 2315.34; *see also* Ohio Rev. Code Ann. § 2307.23.

68. Ohio Rev. Code Ann. § 2315.33; *see, e.g., Delta Fuels, Inc. v. Consol. Envtl. Servs.*, No. L-11-1054, 2012-Ohio-2227, ¶23 (6th Dist. 2012) ("Ohio is a comparative negligence state. Under the doctrine of comparative negligence, if a plaintiff's own negligence contributed to his or her injuries, a defendant's liability for those injuries is reduced in an amount commensurate with the plaintiff's degree of fault.") (citation omitted) *Shepherd v. Ohio Dep't of Rehab. & Corr.*, No. 2007-06446, 2009-Ohio-2354, ¶12 (Ct. Cl. 2009) (action by inmate against correctional facility; finding degree of fault attributable to plaintiff was 40% and reducing award by that amount).

69. Ohio Rev. Code Ann. § 2307.73 (manufacturer's liability for compensatory damages), § 2307.78 (supplier's liability for compensatory damages).

70. Ohio Rev. Code Ann. § 2307.71(A)(9).

71. Ohio Rev. Code Ann. § 2307.71(A)(15)(a).

72. *See* Ohio Rev. Code Ann. § 2307.73(A) (creating "product liability claim" against "[a] manufacturer" and not addressing suppliers).

73. Ohio Rev. Code Ann. § 2307.78(A)(1), (2).

74. Ohio Rev. Code Ann. § 2307.78(B)(1)-(7).

75. Ohio Rev. Code Ann. § 2307.75(E); *see Thompson v. Sunbeam Prods.*, No. 2:10-cv-98, 2011 U.S. Dist. LEXIS 110677, at *24-25 (S.D. Ohio Sept. 28, 2011) (entering summary judgment on OPLA design defect claim because injury to plaintiff's fingers caused by hand mixer was caused by inherent characteristic of product), *aff'd*, 503 F. App'x 366 (6th Cir. 2012); *Vermett v. Fred Christen & Sons Co.*, 138 Ohio App. 3d 586, 607-08, 741 N.E.2d 954, 969-70 (6th Dist. 2000) (affirming summary judgment for manufacturer on OPLA design defect claim because injury was caused by inherent product characteristic); *Glassner v. R.J. Reynolds Tobacco Co.*, 223 F.3d 343, 349, 352 (6th Cir. 2000) (affirming dismissal of OPLA claims when "there existed a widespread public awareness of the health risks associated with smoking

such that [the Court] must impute this 'common knowledge' to [decedent] and presume that she was aware of and assumed those risks").

76. Ohio Rev. Code Ann. § 2307.73(C). This language in Ohio Rev. Code Ann. § 2307.73(C) was added to the OPLA in 2006. Amended Substitute S.B. 117, 125th Gen. Assem., 151 Ohio Laws 2274 (2005-06) (eff. Oct. 31, 2007) (amending Ohio Rev. Code Ann. § 2307.73 to add paragraph (C)). Even before this amendment, the Supreme Court of Ohio had found that neither the OPLA nor Ohio's common law provided for market-share liability. *Sutowski v. Eli Lilly & Co.*, 82 Ohio St. 3d 347, 355, 696 N.E.2d 187, 192-93 (1998) ("The Ohio Products Liability Act does not provide for market-share liability. Furthermore, . . . the market-share theory is not a part of Ohio common law that could be deemed . . . to survive the enactment of" the OPLA.).

77. *See* Restatement (Second) of Torts § 433B(3) (1965) ("Where the conduct of two or more actors is tortious, and it is proved that harm has been caused to the plaintiff by only one of them, but there is uncertainty as to which one has caused it, the burden is upon each such actor to prove that he has not caused the harm."); *see also Summers v. Tice*, 33 Cal. 2d 80, 199 P.2d 1 (1948).

78. *See Minnich v. Ashland Oil Co.*, 15 Ohio St. 3d 396, 397-98, 473 N.E.2d 1199, 1201 (1984) (adopting the doctrine of alternative liability and reversing summary judgment in favor of two defendant ethyl acetate suppliers where plaintiff was unable to identify which defendant supplied the ethyl acetate that exploded and caused the injury); *see also Horton v. Harwick Chem. Corp.*, 73 Ohio St. 3d 679, 688, 653 N.E.2d 1196, 1203 (1995) (rejecting application of alternative liability in action involving asbestos products and observing that alternative liability "is a unique theory to be employed in unique situations" and "cannot apply if the defendants' products do not create a substantially similar risk of harm"); *Goldman v. Johns-Manville Sales Corp.*, 33 Ohio St. 3d 40, 46, 514 N.E.2d 691, 696 (1987) (affirming summary judgment for asbestos manufacturing defendants and observing that "[a]lternative liability does not do away entirely with the burden of showing proximate causation; rather, this theory relaxes only the traditional requirement that the plaintiff demonstrate that a specific defendant (or defendants) caused the injury. But the relaxation is only warranted where plaintiff shows that all defendants acted tortiously."). The 1997 OPLA amendments adopted alternative liability in Ohio Rev. Code Ann. § 2307.791(B), which allowed alternative liability "when all possible tortfeasors are named and subject to the jurisdiction of the court," but the 2001 OPLA amendments repealed § 2307.791. Amended Substitute H.B. 350, 121st Gen. Assem., 146 Ohio Laws 3867 (1995-96) (eff. Jan. 27, 1997) (enacting Ohio Rev. Code Ann. § 2307.791(B)); Substitute S.B. 108, 124th Gen. Assem., 149 Ohio Laws 382 (2001-02) (eff. July 6, 2001) (repealing 1997 amendments).

79. *Temple v. Wean United, Inc.*, 50 Ohio St. 2d 317, 323, 364 N.E.2d 267, 271 (1977); *see also* Ohio Rev. Code Ann. §§ 2307.74-2307.75 (manufacturer is not

liable for a product defect in manufacture, construction, design or formulation if such defect did not exist when it left the manufacturer's control).

80. Ohio Rev. Code Ann. § 2307.75(F); *see Nationwide Mut. Ins. Co. v. ICON Health & Fitness, Inc.*, No. 04AP855, 2005-Ohio-2638, ¶15 (10th Dist. 2005) (reversing trial court's denial of summary judgment on design defect claim where plaintiff failed to produce evidence of a technically feasible alternative design); *Jacobs v. E.I. DuPont de Nemours & Co.*, 67 F.3d 1219, 1242 (6th Cir. 1995) (affirming summary judgment for manufacturer because § 2307.75 "exempt[ed] [the manufacturer] from liability" for the alleged design defects where the plaintiff failed to identify a safe and efficacious alternative design).

81. Ohio Rev. Code Ann. § 2307.76(A)(1)(a), (A)(2)(a).

82. *See Knitz v. Minster Mach. Co.*, 69 Ohio St. 2d 460, 464, 432 N.E.2d 814, 817 (1982) (statutory regulations act only as "guide[s]" in determining the reasonableness of a manufacturer's design choice); *see, e.g., Gable v. Vill. of Gates Mills*, 151 Ohio App. 3d 480, 491-92, 2003-Ohio-399, ¶¶56-58, 784 N.E.2d 739, 747-48 (8th Dist. 2003) (compliance with federal regulations on air bags is relevant evidence but "not conclusive of non-liability"), *rev'd on other grounds*, 103 Ohio St. 3d 449, 2004-Ohio-571, 816 N.E.2d 1049 (2004); *Hardiman v. Zep Mfg. Co.*, 14 Ohio App. 3d 222, 226, 470 N.E.2d 941, 946 (8th Dist. 1984) (compliance with Ohio "safe-place-to-work" statutes does not insulate a manufacturer from liability in strict liability cases).

83. *Welch Sand & Gravel, Inc. v. O & K Trojan, Inc.*, 107 Ohio App. 3d 218, 225, 668 N.E.2d 529, 534 (1st Dist. 1995) (compliance with professional engineering standard can be evidence in support of the safety of a design, but does not conclusively defeat a design defect claim); *Evanoff v. Grove Mfg. Co.*, 99 Ohio App. 3d 339, 346, 650 N.E.2d 914, 919 (11th Dist. 1994) (noncompliance with industrial safety guidelines does not necessarily establish strict liability).

84. Ohio Rev. Code Ann. § 2307.80(C)(1)(a) (prescription drugs and devices), § 2307.80(C)(1)(b) (over-the-counter drugs).

85. Ohio Rev. Code Ann. § 2307.80(C)(2); *see also Monroe v. Novartis Pharms. Corp.*, No. 1:12-cv-00746, 2014 U.S. Dist. LEXIS 93777, at *35 (S.D. Ohio July 10, 2014) ("Because there is no finding of fraud by the FDA here, no punitive damages claim is permissible" under Ohio law); *In re Gadolinium-Based Contrast Agents Prods. Liab. Litig.*, Nos. 1:08 GD 5000, 2013 U.S. Dist. LEXIS 20887, at *61 (N.D. Ohio Feb. 13, 2013) ("a punitive-damages claim for an FDA-approved drug is allowed under Ohio law only if the FDA has made a finding of either fraud or misrepresentation").

86. 531 U.S. 341 (2001).

87. *Garcia v. Wyeth-Ayerst Labs.*, 385 F.3d 961, 966 (6th Cir. 2004). *But see Desiano v. Warner-Lambert & Co.*, 467 F.3d 85 (2d Cir. 2006) (finding that the same provision of the Michigan statute was not preempted), *aff'd by an equally divided court sub nom., Warner-Lambert & Co. v. Kent*, 552 U.S. 440 (2008).

88. Ohio Rev. Code Ann. § 2307.80(D)(1).

89. Ohio Rev. Code Ann. § 2307.80(D)(2).

90. *Renfro v. Black*, 52 Ohio St. 3d 27, 31-32, 556 N.E.2d 150, 154-55 (1990).

91. *Ogden v. Raymond Corp.*, No. 95CA0001, 1995 Ohio App. LEXIS 5796, at *7-8 (9th Dist. Dec. 27, 1995) (quoting § 2307.75(B)(1)), *review denied*, 76 Ohio St. 3d 1404, 666 N.E.2d 565 (1996).

92. *Blanton v. Int'l Minerals & Chem. Corp.*, 125 Ohio App. 3d 22, 30, 707 N.E.2d 960, 965-66 (1st Dist. 1997).

93. *Onderko v. Richmond Mfg. Co.*, 31 Ohio St. 3d 296, 301, 511 N.E.2d 388, 392 (1987); *Mulloy v. Longaberger, Inc.*, 47 Ohio App. 3d 77, 81, 547 N.E.2d 411, 415-16 (10th Dist. 1989).

94. *McFarland v. Bruno Mach. Corp.*, 68 Ohio St. 3d 305, 308, 312, 626 N.E.2d 659, 661 (1994) (reversing jury verdict for defendant because trial court improperly excluded evidence of post-accident design changes based on Ohio R. Evid. 407; "[i]n a products case based on strict liability, the focus is solely on the defective condition of the product and not, as in an action premised on negligence, on what the defendant knew or should have known of the defect which caused the injury") (citation omitted); *see also Minton v. Honda of Am. Mfg., Inc.*, 80 Ohio St. 3d 62, 79-81, 684 N.E.2d 648, 661-62 (1997) (following *McFarland v. Bruno Mach. Corp.* in case involving alleged design defect and finding that trial court erred in excluding evidence of addition of air bags to automobile two years after the model that was at issue). Ohio courts have not directly addressed whether, given that the OPLA applies negligence-like standards to claims based on alleged failures to warn, *McFarland v. Bruno Machine Corp.*'s interpretation of Ohio Rule of Evidence 407 applies to OPLA failure-to-warn claims. *See Wagner v. Roche Labs.*, 77 Ohio St. 3d 116, 124, 671 N.E.2d 252, 258 (1996) (noting that, in action relating to alleged failure to warn of the dangers of the prescription drug Accutane, the trial court excluded warnings for the drug after the injury at issue); *Immormino v. J&M Powers, Inc.*, 91 Ohio Misc. 2d 198, 698 N.E.2d 516 (Cuyahoga Cty. Com. Pl. 1998) (questioning whether *McFarland v. Bruno Mach. Corp.*'s approach to Ohio R. Evid. 407 applies to OPLA failure-to-warn claims, but resolving case on other grounds). Indeed, *McFarland v. Bruno Mach. Corp.*'s premise that the manufacturer's conduct is not at issue in design defect claims is subject to legitimate question given the balancing that Ohio Rev. Code Ann. § 2307.75 requires in evaluating a product's design. In the 2000 amendments to Ohio Rule of Evidence 407, however, the drafters expressly declined to adopt the

1997 change to Federal Rule of Evidence 407, which clarified that the federal rule applied to strict liability claims.

95. *See Bryan v. Emerson Elec. Co.*, 856 F.2d 192 (6th Cir. 1988) (table) (applying Fed. R. Evid. 407 in diversity action); *Bush v. Michelin Tire Corp.*, 963 F. Supp. 1436, 1448 (W.D. Ky. 1996) ("While [the plaintiff's] argument that FRE 407 is substantive in nature has strong appeal, the fact that the rule has substantive implications is not reason enough to apply the state rule in this case."); *accord Kelly v. Crown Equip. Co.*, 970 F.2d 1273, 1277-78 (3d Cir. 1992) (Fed. R. Evid. 407 applies in diversity actions); *Flaminio v. Honda Motor Co.*, 733 F.2d 463, 472 (7th Cir. 1984) (same). *See generally Sims v. Great Am. Life Ins. Co.*, 469 F.3d 870, 877-83 (10th Cir. 2006) (discussing applicability of Federal Rules of Evidence in diversity actions under *Erie* and Rules Enabling Act).

96. Ohio Rev. Code Ann. § 2307.73(B).

97. Ohio Rev. Code Ann. § 2307.79.

98. *Leichtamer v. Am. Motors Corp.*, 67 Ohio St. 2d 456, 467, 424 N.E.2d 568, 577 (1981) (roll-bar design defect).

99. *Leichtamer*, 67 Ohio St. 2d at 467, 424 N.E.2d at 577.

100. Ohio Rev. Code Ann. § 4513.263(F)(2); *see Gable v. Vill. of Gates Mills*, 103 Ohio St. 3d 449, 2004-Ohio-5719, 816 N.E.2d 1049 (2004) (applying Ohio Rev. Code Ann. § 4513.263(F)(2)).

101. A "product liability claim" is defined in Ohio Rev. Code Ann. § 2307.71(A)(13) as: "[A] claim or cause of action that is asserted in a civil action pursuant to sections 2307.71 to 2307.80 of the [Ohio] Revised Code and that seeks to recover compensatory damages from a manufacturer or supplier for death, physical injury to person, emotional distress, or physical damage to property other than the product in question, that allegedly arose from any of the following: (a) The design, formulation, production, construction, creation, assembly, rebuilding, testing, or marketing of that product; (b) Any warning or instruction, or lack of warning or instruction, associated with that product; (c) Any failure of that product to conform to any relevant representation or warranty. 'Product liability claim' also includes any public nuisance claim or cause of action at common law in which it is alleged that the design, manufacture, supply, marketing, distribution, promotion, advertising, labeling, or sale of a product unreasonably interferes with a right common to the general public."

102. Ohio Rev. Code Ann. § 2307.71(A)(13), (B); *see, e.g., Evans v. Hanger Prosthetics & Orthotics, Inc.*, 735 F. Supp. 2d 785, 796-97 (N.D. Ohio 2010) (granting motion to dismiss common-law claims in action subject to OPLA); *Crisp v. Stryker Corp.*, No. 5:09-cv-02212, 2010 U.S. Dist. LEXIS 51390, at *10 (N.D. Ohio May 21, 2010) (same). Common law claims that accrued before the

amendments to the OPLA that became effective on April 7, 2005, however, are not abrogated. *See Wimbush v. Wyeth*, 619 F.3d 632, 639 (6th Cir. 2010) (2005 OPLA amendments applied prospectively and did not abrogate common law claims relating to 2003 injury); *Doty v. Fellhauer Elec., Inc.*, 175 Ohio App. 3d 681, 686-87, 2008-Ohio-1294, ¶36, 888 N.E.2d 1138, 1142 (6th Dist. 2008) (2005 OPLA amendments applied prospectively and did not abrogate common law claims that arose from 2003 event), *review denied*, 119 Ohio St. 3d 145, 2008-Ohio-4487, 893 N.E.2d 516 (2008); *Carrel v. Allied Prod. Corp.*, 78 Ohio St. 3d 284, 287-89, 677 N.E.2d 795, 798-800 (1997) (pre-2005 version of OPLA did not abrogate common law claims).

103. *S.S. v. Leatt Corp.*, No. 1:12-cv-483, 2013 U.S. Dist. LEXIS 99814, at *6 (N.D. Ohio July 17, 2013) (granting summary judgment on plaintiff's claims under the OCSPA because "those claims are abrogated by the OPLA"); *Fulgenzi v. PLIVA, Inc.*, 867 F. Supp. 2d 966, 972 (N.D. Ohio 2012), *rev'd on other grounds*, 711 F.3d 578 (6th Cir. 2013); *Mitchell v. Procter & Gamble Co.*, No. 2:09-cv-426, 2010 U.S. Dist. LEXIS 17956, at *11-13 (S.D. Ohio Mar. 1, 2010).

104. *See generally Hogue v. Pfizer, Inc.*, 893 F. Supp. 2d 914, 918 (S.D. Ohio 2012) (collecting cases discussing whether the OPLA abrogates common law fraud claims, noting that "courts have reached differing conclusions as to whether the OPLA abrogates claims sounding in fraud and misrepresentation, often with little analysis," and finding fraud claims premised on "omission and concealment" abrogated); *Hendricks v. Pharmacia Corp.*, No. 2:12-cv-613, 2014 U.S. Dist. LEXIS 76125, at *9-12 (S.D. Ohio June 4, 2014) (plaintiff's allegations of "deceit," including claims based on alleged "active[] misrepresent[ations]," were abrogated by the OPLA).

105. *See* Ohio Rev. Code Ann. § 2307.72(C) ("Any recovery of compensatory damages for economic loss based on a claim that is asserted in a civil action, other than a product liability claim, is not subject to [the OPLA], but may occur under the common law of this state or other applicable sections of the [Ohio] Revised Code."); *CCB Ohio LLC v. Chemque, Inc.*, 649 F. Supp. 2d 757, 763 (S.D. Ohio 2009) ("Ohio Revised Code § 2307.72(C) makes it clear that a claim for compensatory damages for economic damages, other than a product liability claim, is not subject to the OPLA, but may occur under the common law of Ohio or other applicable sections of the Revised Code."); *see also Musgrave v. Breg, Inc.*, No. 2:09-cv-01029, 2011 U.S. Dist. LEXIS 99491, at *21 (S.D. Ohio Sept. 2, 2011).

106. *See* Ohio Rev. Code Ann. §§ 2307.71(B), 2307.77, 2307.78(A)(2).

107. *See Miller v. ALZA Corp.*, 759 F. Supp. 2d 929, 943 (S.D. Ohio 2010) ("Courts in this District have . . . determined that UCC warranty claims are not abrogated by virtue of" the OPLA) (citation omitted); *Miles v. Raymond Corp.*, 612 F. Supp. 2d 913, 924-25 (N.D. Ohio 2009) (permitting UCC-based claims to proceed notwithstanding fact that plaintiff was asserting claims under the OPLA); *CCB Ohio LLC v. Chemque, Inc.*, 649 F. Supp. 2d 757, 763

(S.D. Ohio 2009) ("Plaintiffs' warranty claims can find a basis grounded in the Uniform Commercial Code and therefore are not claims abrogated by the OPLA.").

108. *Pilkington N. Am., Inc. v. Travelers Cas. & Sur. Co.*, 112 Ohio St. 3d 482, 491, 2006-Ohio-6551, ¶48, 861 N.E.2d 121, 130 (2006) (answering certified questions relating to insurance anti-assignment clause).

109. *Flaugher v. Cone Automatic Mach. Co.*, 30 Ohio St. 3d 60, 62, 507 N.E.2d 331, 334 (1987) (affirming summary judgment for defendant that purchased assets; "[w]here there is merely a sale of a corporation's assets, the buyer corporation is not liable for the seller corporation's tortious conduct unless one of the following four exceptions applies: (1) the buyer expressly or impliedly agrees to assume such liability; (2) the transaction amounts to a de facto consolidation or merger; (3) the buyer corporation is merely a continuation of the seller corporation; or (4) the transaction is entered into fraudulently for the purpose of escaping liability") (citing 1 Furmer & Friedman, *Products Liability* § 70.58(3) (1983)).

110. Ohio Rev. Code Ann. § 2315.18(B)(1); *see also Holbrook v. Louisiana-Pacific Corp.*, 533 F. App'x 493, 497 (6th Cir. 2013) (affirming dismissal of OPLA claims because the "complaint alleged only economic damages").

111. Ohio Rev. Code Ann. § 2315.18(B)(2); *see Williams v. Bausch & Lomb Co.*, No. 2:08-cv-910, 2010 U.S. Dist. LEXIS 62018 (S.D. Ohio June 22, 2010) (granting partial summary judgment based on Ohio Rev. Code Ann. § 2315.18(B)(2)). The Ohio Supreme Court has upheld the facial constitutionality of the OPLA's cap on noneconomic damages. *See Arbino v. Johnson & Johnson*, 116 Ohio St. 3d 468, 492, 2007-Ohio-6948, ¶114, 880 N.E.2d 420, 445 (2007).

112. Ohio Rev. Code Ann. § 2315.18(B)(3)(a)-(b).

113. Ohio Rev. Code Ann. § 2315.21(B).

114. Ohio Rev. Code Ann. § 2315.21(C)(1).

115. Ohio Rev. Code Ann. § 2307.80. This statute, however, excludes punitive damages liability for drugs that have received FDA approval unless the manufacturer fraudulently withheld from the FDA material and relevant information or the manufacturer misrepresented such information to the FDA. Ohio Rev. Code Ann. § 2307.80; *see also supra* nn. 82-85 & accompanying text.

116. Ohio Rev. Code Ann. § 2315.21(D)(2)(a).

117. Ohio Rev. Code Ann. § 2315.21(D)(2)(b). A "small employer" is defined as an employer who employs not more than 100 persons on a full-time permanent basis, or, if the employer is classified as being in the manufacturing sector by

the North American industrial classification system, an employer who employs not more than 500 persons on a full-time permanent basis. Ohio Rev. Code Ann. § 2315.21(A)(5).

118. Ohio Rev. Code Ann. § 2315.21(D)(5)(a). This limit on multiple punitive and exemplary damage awards does not apply if the court determines by clear and convincing evidence that "plaintiff will offer new and substantial evidence of previously undiscovered, additional behavior" that would justify punitive and exemplary damages or if the court determines that the prior punitive and exemplary damages award was insufficient to punish the defendant and deter future behavior. Ohio Rev. Code Ann. § 2315.21(D)(5)(b).

119. Ohio Rev. Code Ann. § 2125.02(D).

120. *Rubeck v. Huffman*, 54 Ohio St. 2d 20, 23, 374 N.E.2d 411, 413 (1978) ("Damages in wrongful-death actions are limited to those for 'the pecuniary injury resulting from such death.' That is, they are limited to damages for 'loss of money, or something by which money or something of money value may be acquired' and 'which have been cut off by the premature death of the person from whom they would have proceeded.' Since punitive damages are 'assessed over and above that amount adequate to compensate an injured party,' they are, by definition, not available in a wrongful-death action."); *Estate of Beavers*, 175 Ohio App. 3d 758, 768, 2008-Ohio-2023, ¶15, 889 N.E.2d 181, 188 (10th Dist. 2008) ("punitive damages . . . are . . . not available in a wrongful-death action"); *see also Freudeman v. The Landing of Canton*, 702 F.3d 318, 332 (6th Cir. 2012) (applying Ohio law; "[p]unitive damages are not available for a wrongful death claim") (citations omitted); *Miller v. ALZA Corp.*, 759 F. Supp. 2d 929, 945 (S.D. Ohio 2010) (same).

121. Ohio Rev. Code Ann. § 1343.03(A)-(B). The tax commissioner sets the interest rate in effect each year. Ohio Rev. Code Ann. § 5703.47.

122. Ohio Rev. Code Ann. § 1343.03(C)(1); *see also Moskovitz v. Mt. Sinai Med. Ctr.*, 69 Ohio St. 3d 638, 659, 635 N.E.2d 331, 348 (1994) (party seeking pre-judgment interest has burden).

123. Ohio Rev. Code Ann. § 1343.03(C); *Musisca v. Massillon Cmty. Hosp.*, 69 Ohio St. 3d 673, 676, 635 N.E.2d 358, 360 (1994) (trial court cannot alter the date on which pre-judgment interest began to run for equitable reasons).

124. Intentional tort claims by employees against employers now are governed by Ohio Rev. Code Ann. § 2745.01. *See Kaminski v. Metal Wire & Prods. Co.*, 125 Ohio St. 3d 250, 2010-Ohio-1027, 927 N.E.2d 1066 (2010) (rejecting challenges to Ohio Rev. Code Ann. § 2745.01 based on §§ 34 and 35 of Article II of the Ohio Constitution); *Stetter v. R.J. Corman Derailment Servs., L.L.C.*, 125 Ohio St. 3d 280, 2010-Ohio-1029, 927 N.E.2d 1092 (2010) (rejecting challenges to Ohio Rev. Code Ann. § 2745.01 based on §§ 5 and 16 of Article

I and § 2 of Article I of the Ohio Constitution, as well as a challenge based on the separation-of-powers doctrine).

125. Ohio Rev. Code Ann. § 4123.74.

126. *Schump v. Firestone Tire & Rubber Co.*, 44 Ohio St. 3d 148, 152-53, 541 N.E.2d 1040, 1045 (1989) (Ohio does not recognize the dual-capacity doctrine).

127. Ohio Rev. Code Ann. § 2315.20(A), (D)(1). Collateral benefits are excluded from this rule "if the source of collateral benefits has a mandatory self-effectuating federal right of subrogation, a contractual right of subrogation, or a statutory right of subrogation or if the source pays the plaintiff a benefit that is in the form of a life insurance payment or a disability payment." Ohio Rev. Code Ann. § 2315.20(A); *see Jaques v. Manton*, 125 Ohio St. 3d 342, 344, 2010–Ohio-1838, ¶10, 928 N.E.2d 434, 437 (2010) ("The subrogation exception [in § 2315.20] will generally prevent defendants from offering evidence of insurance coverage for a plaintiff's injury, because insurance agreements generally include a right of subrogation."); *Schlegel v. Song*, 547 F. Supp. 2d 792, 799 (N.D. Ohio 2008) (evidence relating to Bureau of Workers Compensation benefits paid to plaintiff's medical providers was not admissible under Ohio Rev. Code Ann. § 2315.20(A) because there was a statutory right of subrogation). Section 2315.20, which is not analogous to earlier code sections bearing the same numbering, became effective in 2005. Amended Substitute S.B. 80, § 1, 125th Gen. Assem., 150 Ohio Laws 7915 (2003-04) (eff. Apr. 7, 2005). Previously, Ohio had applied "the collateral-source rule," and "the plaintiff's receipt of benefits from sources other than the wrongdoer [wa]s deemed irrelevant and immaterial on the issue of damages." *Robinson v. Bates*, 112 Ohio St. 3d 17, 21, 2006-Ohio-6362, ¶11, 857 N.E.2d 1195, 1199 (2006) (citing *Pryor v. Webber*, 23 Ohio St. 2d 104, 109, 263 N.E.2d 235, 239 (1970)).

128. Ohio Rev. Code Ann. § 2315.20(B).

129. Ohio Rev. Code Ann. § 2315.20(C) ("A source of collateral benefits of which evidence is introduced [under Ohio Rev. Code. Ann. § 2315.20(A)] shall not recover any amount against the plaintiff nor shall it be subrogated to the rights of the plaintiff against a defendant.").

130. Ohio Rev. Code Ann. § 2307.22(A)(1).

131. Ohio Rev. Code Ann. § 2307.22(A)(2). A defendant liable for an intentional tort is jointly and severally liable for the compensatory damages that represent economic loss regardless of the percentage of tortious conduct attributed to that defendant. Ohio Rev. Code Ann. § 2307.22(A)(1), (A)(3).

132. Ohio Rev. Code Ann. § 2307.22(C).

133. U.S. Const. art. VI, cl. 2.

134. *See, e.g., Nelson v. Ford Motor Co.*, 145 Ohio App. 3d 58, 62-63, 761 N.E.2d 1099, 1103 (11th Dist. 2001) (reversing prior ruling and finding that "no-airbag" claims were preempted under *Geier v. Am. Honda Motor Co.*, 529 U.S. 861 (2000)).

135. *Altria Grp., Inc. v. Good*, 555 U.S. 70 (2008); *Cipollone v. Liggett Grp., Inc.*, 505 U.S. 504 (1992).

136. *Williamson v. Mazda Motor*, 131 S. Ct. 1131 (2011); *Geier v. Am. Honda Motor Co.*, 529 U.S. 861 (2000).

137. *Riegel v. Medtronic, Inc.*, 552 U.S. 312 (2008); *Medtronic, Inc. v. Lohr*, 518 U.S. 470 (1996).

138. *PLIVA, Inc. v. Mensing*, 131 S. Ct. 2567 (2011) (generic prescription drug); *Bruesewitz v. Wyeth LLC*, 131 S. Ct. 1068 (2011) (vaccine); *Wyeth v. Levine*, 555 U.S. 555 (2009) (branded or innovator prescription drug).

139. *Sprietsma v. Mercury Marine*, 537 U.S. 51 (2002).

140. *Bates v. Dow Agrosciences LLC*, 544 U.S. 431 (2005).

141. *See Hillsborough Cnty. v. Automated Med. Labs., Inc.*, 471 U.S. 707, 712-13 (1985).

OKLAHOMA

A. INTRODUCTION

Products liability law in Oklahoma underwent significant changes over the past few years. The legislature passed the "Comprehensive Lawsuit Reform Act of 2009" (CLRA) that altered law and procedure related to products liability cases. However, the Supreme Court of Oklahoma found the CLRA, unconstitutional in 2013 primarily because the CLRA violated the Oklahoma Constitution's single-subject rule.[1] In the face of the Court's rebuke, the legislature reconsidered separately many of the individual parts of what comprised the CLRA. Therefore, what the Supreme Court struck from the law for 2013 has been revived or amended by the legislature for 2014.

B. CAUSES OF ACTION

Product liability lawsuits in Oklahoma commonly include causes of action for negligence, manufacturers' products liability,[2] and breach of express and implied warranty as provided by the Oklahoma Uniform Commercial Code.[3]

Recovery under a theory of manufacturers' products liability is allowed for bodily injury and for damage to property under some circumstances.[4] Recovery of purely economic damages to the product itself must be based on the parties' contractual relationship and specifically the Uniform Commercial Code warranty provisions.[5] However, recovery for damage to the property itself has been allowed, where there is both personal injury and property damage.[6]

C. STATUTES OF LIMITATION

The limitations period for a cause of action in tort alleging personal injury or damage to property is two years from the date of injury.[7] Similarly, the statutory period to be applied in product liability actions is two years from the date of injury.[8] However, Oklahoma applies the "discovery rule," so that the two-year period in a product liability case does not commence until plaintiff actually knows or should have known that he has been injured and defendant's product caused such injury.[9]

A cause of action seeking recovery for damages under the Uniform Commercial Code resulting from breach of warranty must be brought within five years from when the cause of action accrues. The cause of action accrues when the breach occurs, regardless of the lack of knowledge by the party of the breach.[10] Oklahoma has not adopted a statute of repose or a useful-life defense, for products liability *per se*.

While Oklahoma has not adopted a specific statute of repose for products, the State does allow for repose in tort actions for injury arising from "the design, planning, supervision or observation of construction or construction of an improvement to real property."[11] The statute does not bar claims for "failure to warn."[12] The "discovery rule" is applicable to an action sounding in tort against engineers and architects; but the statute of repose prohibits its use to extend the time period for bringing an action beyond the ten-year statute of repose.[13] The argument has been raised that certain products may be considered an "improvement to real property," and, as such, subject to repose after the passage of ten years.[14] The Oklahoma Supreme Court has announced that in deciding whether a particular product constitutes an "improvement to real property" the determinative factor will be the state scheme of taxation.[15] The Oklahoma Supreme Court has upheld as constitutional the barring of a manufacturers' products liability action to recover for wrongful death.[16] The statute of repose was not intended to cover "prefabricated" products produced in mass quantities to be used in construction, but will protect a manufacturer if the suit is based on the performance of one of the activities set out in the statute.[17]

D. STRICT LIABILITY—MANUFACTURERS' PRODUCTS LIABILITY

1. The Standard

Oklahoma is considered a "pure Restatement jurisdiction."[18] In the seminal case of *Kirkland v. General Motors Corp.*,[19] Oklahoma embraced the doctrine of strict product liability in tort as described in Restatement (Second) of Torts, Section 402A. In *Kirkland*, in addition to adopting 402A, the Oklahoma Supreme Court accepted the Restatement definition of "unreasonably dangerous" found in comment g of that provision.[20]

In order to prevail in an action for manufacturers' products liability in Oklahoma, the plaintiff must establish that:

(1) the product in question was the cause of the injury;

(2) the product was defective when it left the hands of the manufacturer; and

(3) the defect made the product unreasonably dangerous to an extent beyond that which would be contemplated by the ordinary consumer.[21]

In a case involving an allegation of a design defect, Oklahoma law, unlike the laws of some other states, does not require proof of a feasible alternative design in order to make a case.[22]

2. Definition of "Defect"

Oklahoma defines "defect" under the "consumer expectation test" found in comment i of Restatement (Second) of Torts, Section 402A.[23] Generally, a product is considered defective if it is more dangerous than the ordinary user or consumer would expect.[24] Thus, Oklahoma applies an "objective" standard in determining defectiveness.

However, Oklahoma has also endorsed the "knowledgeable user" test. A consumer may have specialized knowledge, and her expectations may be tempered by this greater knowledge of the product.[25]

Under the consumer expectation test, a product cannot be defective where it contains an open and obvious danger, because it is, by definition, not more dangerous than expected.[26] Additionally, where the danger of using a product is obvious to the general community, plaintiffs may be automatically barred from recovery.[27] In Oklahoma, the "inherently unsafe defense is an affirmative defense, which must be pled and proved (also see section D.6 below). The elements are:

(1) The product was a common consumer product intended for personal consumption;

(2) The product's utility outweighs the risk created by its use;

(3) The risk posed by the product was one known by the ordinary consumer who consumes the product with the ordinary knowledge common to the community;

(4) The product was properly prepared and reached the consumer without substantial changes in its condition; and

(5) Adequate warning of the risk posed by the product was given by the manufacturer or seller.

The defense of "inherently unsafe" does not apply to claims of manufacturing defect or breach of warranty.[28]

The plaintiff need not identify the exact defect. Circumstantial evidence may be used to support the probability of a defect.[29]

3. Causation

Proof of causation is required. The Oklahoma Supreme Court has specifically applied the "significant probability test" requiring plaintiff to identify the product which allegedly caused his injury. However, that test has been held inapplicable to a case involving a design defect, where plaintiff's expert testified that two products, manufactured by the same defendant, were identical and it would make no difference which one was actually used.[30] As noted previously, the defect involved in plaintiff's claim of manufacturers' products liability must be a direct cause of plaintiff's injury.

Additionally, Oklahoma has specifically rejected the "market share" theory of liability.[31]

4. Contributory Negligence/Assumption of Risk

In addition to the potential defenses arising from the absence of proof of the basic elements of the "prima facie" case, Oklahoma now recognizes two affirmative defenses to the cause of action of manufacturers' products liability: (1) abnormal use, sometimes called "misuse," and (2) assumption of the risk.

With respect to the issue of assumption of risk as a defense in products liability, the Oklahoma Supreme Court has recognized the difficulties inherent in the use of the phrase, "assumption of risk," because of confusion with its common law counterpart. The court in *Kirkland* expressly stated that the term should be narrowly defined as a voluntary assumption of the risk of a known defect. Using the Restatement (Second) of Torts, the court held that assumption of risk is the defense which consists of voluntarily and unreasonably encountering a known danger.

The Supreme Court, in *Kirkland,* specifically stated that Oklahoma's statutorily imposed comparative negligence doctrine has no application to products liability. The theory is that unless a plaintiff's negligence is sufficient to negate causation, it is irrelevant to the issues of liability. That decision remains valid after recent amendments to the comparative negligence statute and the statutory abolishment of joint and several liability.[32]

5. **Sale or Lease/Persons Liable**

Oklahoma assigns liability in a product liability action to sellers of products. However, occasional sellers of products are not liable under that theory.[33] Although Oklahoma has named the cause of action "manufacturers' products liability," retailers and wholesalers are also liable.[34] Similarly, lessors of products are considered "suppliers" of defective products and are liable under Oklahoma law.[35] Oklahoma has held that a seller of a used product is not liable under products liability theory unless the defect was created by the seller.[36]

The Oklahoma Supreme Court has not specifically ruled on the question of whether successor corporations retain liability under a product liability theory. However, the general standard for successor liability was set forth in *Pulis v. United States Elect. Tool Co.,*[37] which has been applied by the Oklahoma Court of Civil Appeals to a product liability case.[38]

Oklahoma extends liability under a theory of manufacturers' products liability not only to manufacturers and sellers but to "suppliers" as well.[39] A "supplier" is defined under Oklahoma law according to the Restatement (Second) of Torts as "one who injects a product into the stream of commerce 'whether through a sale or other means' and regardless of whether title to the product is retained by the supplier."[40] The Oklahoma Supreme Court has yet to address the question of whether liability under a theory of manufacturers' products liability is extended to a bailor, although it recognized that one Oklahoma court had done so.[41]

6. Inherently Dangerous Products

Pursuant to the "inherently unsafe product" defense (also see section D.2 above), a product manufacturer or seller is not liable if the product is inherently unsafe and known to be unsafe by the ordinary consumer with the ordinary knowledge common to the community. The defense must be properly pled pursuant to the Code of Civil Procedure, and the defendant must show:

(1) The product was a common consumer product intended for personal consumption;

(2) The product's utility outweighs the risk created by its use;

(3) The risk posed by the product was one known by the ordinary consumer who consumes the product with ordinary knowledge common to the community;

(4) The product was properly prepared and reached the consumer without substantial change in its condition; and

(5) Adequate warning of the risk posed by the product was given by the manufacturer or seller.

The defense does not apply to actions based on manufacturing defects or breach of warranty.[42]

Oklahoma courts had previously recognized the doctrine of "unavoidable unsafe product," following comment (k) of the Restatement (Second) of Torts, §402A, as applied to pharmaceutical products. When the product is incapable of being made safe under present technology but the social need for the product warrants it production, an affirmative defense is raised.[43] Because the recently adopted statute is addressed to "common consumer products," it is anticipated that the common law affirmative defense recognized for pharmaceutical products will continue to be applied.

The defense does not provide blanket protection for all medical devices. Rather, it applies as an affirmative defense only when the following criteria are met:

(1) the product is properly manufactured and contains adequate warnings;

(2) its benefits justify its risks; and

(3) the product was, at the time of manufacture and distribution, incapable of being made more safe.

The comment (k) defense does not apply when the product is defective due to faulty manufacturing or inadequate warnings.[44]

Oklahoma has adopted a statute which provides a qualified immunity for "transactions" related to the provision of blood, blood products, and human tissues.[45]

7. **Successor Liability**

The court in *Pulis v. United States Elect. Tool Co.* determined successor liabilities when it found that where one company sells or otherwise transfers all its assets to another company, the latter is not liable for the debts and liabilities of the transferor.[46] The rule is subject to the following exceptions: first, where there is an agreement to assume such debts or liabilities; second, where the circumstances surrounding the transaction warrant a finding that there was a consolidation or merger of the corporations; third, where there is a finding that the transaction was fraudulent in fact or that the purchasing corporation was a mere continuation of the selling company.[47]

Oklahoma has specifically rejected the so-called product line test of successor liability.[48]

8. **Market Share Liability/Enterprise Liability**

Whether Oklahoma law recognizes a theory of collective (commonly called "market share") liability as an alternative theory of relief in a products liability action remains unclear. While the Oklahoma Supreme Court has answered a certified question from the Tenth Circuit Court of Appeals in the negative, it has left room to embrace under certain circumstances.[49] The court distinguished the asbestos case with which it was dealing from *Sindell v. Abbott Laboratories*,[50] the California DES case which is typically advanced to support the theory.

The court stated that it was of major importance that *Sindell* was decided in the context of a product that was truly fungible. It remains to be seen, when the issue again arises, whether the Supreme Court will adopt the theory in a case involving truly fungible products.[51]

9. **Privity**

Section 402A of the Restatement (Second) of Torts provides that "users or consumers" of products may bring product liability actions. Oklahoma has expanded the class of those protected under product liability to include bystanders.[52] No privity of contract is required to sue in strict liability for a defective product.[53]

10. **Failure to Warn**

Plaintiff may rely on failure to warn as a theory of recovery in product liability. However, in order to prevail on this cause of action, plaintiff must show that the failure to warn actually caused his injury.[54] The duty to warn extends only to ordinary consumers and users of the product. An "ordinary consumer" is defined as one who is "foreseeably expected to purchase the product involved."[55] Similarly, there is no duty to warn of a product-connected danger that is obvious or generally known. There is no duty to warn a knowledgeable user of the product of the dangers associated with the product's use.[56]

11. Post-Sale Duty to Warn and Remedial Measures

In Oklahoma, the issue of whether a manufacturer has a "post-sale duty to warn" remains unclear. In a case involving a drug manufacturer, the Oklahoma Supreme Court has made it clear that there exists a continuing duty to warn of all potential danger of which the manufacturer knew, or should have known, in the exercise of reasonable care. This duty requires the manufacturer to maintain current information gleaned from research, adverse reaction reports, scientific literature, and other available methods. However, on at least two occasions, the Federal District Court for the Western District of Oklahoma found that the rule is inapplicable in a typical product liability case.[57]

Evidence of remedial measures, such as post-sale warnings, may not be used to prove negligence or otherwise evidence culpable conduct. The Oklahoma legislature has recently made this evidentiary prohibition explicitly apply to products liability cases. The currently existing evidentiary rule in subsequent remedial measures remains in the Oklahoma Evidence Code.[58]

12. Learned Intermediary Doctrine

A drug manufacturer, like any other manufacturer, may be held liable for a defective product under the doctrine of strict liability. Within the purview of manufacturers' products liability, those drugs which are described as "unavoidably unsafe products" are not deemed defective or unreasonably dangerous if they are accompanied by proper directions for use and adequate warnings concerning potential side effects. A plaintiff seeking recovery for an injurious side effect from a properly manufactured prescription drug must prove that the drug caused the injury and that the manufacturer breached a duty to warn of possible detrimental reactions. The manufacturer has a continuing duty to warn of all potential danger, which it knew or should have known, in the exercise of reasonable care, to exist. This duty requires the manufacturer to maintain current information gleaned from research, adverse reaction reports, scientific literature, and other available methods.

However, Oklahoma adopted the learned intermediary doctrine with respect to prescription drugs.[59] As such, and in the absence of FDA regulations to the contrary, the manufacturer has no obligation to warn a consumer if the prescribing physician has been adequately warned of any adverse side effects. The manufacturer's duty is to warn the physician, who acts as a learned intermediary between the manufacturer and the consumer, because he is in the best position to evaluate the patient's needs, assess the benefits and risks of a particular therapy, and to supervise its use. Therefore, if the product is properly labeled and carries the necessary instructions and warnings to fully apprise the physician of the proper procedures for use and the dangers involved, the manufacturer may reasonably assume that the physician will exercise an informed judgment in the best interest of the patient. Once the physician is warned, the choice of treatment and the duty to explain the risk is incumbent on the physician. Oklahoma also recognizes the exception to the general rule, which occurs if the FDA has mandated that warnings be given to the patient as well as to the physician.[60]

13. **Substantial Alteration/Abnormal Use**

Abnormal use, or "misuse," has been defined under a common sense definition: use of a product for a purpose not intended, or use of a product in an unforeseeable way. Although a consumer's failure to follow instructions or heed warnings does not constitute misuse, such conduct still may preclude recovery if it constitutes the sole proximate cause of the injuries.[61]

Assumption of the risk requires showing that (1) the danger was known; (2) the risk was appreciated or understood; and (3) the taking of the risk was unreasonable.[62] The Oklahoma definition of assumption of the risk parallels comment n of Restatement, Section 402A.[63] A consumer can assume the risk of a known defect without specific technical knowledge of the cause of the product's dangerous, defective condition.[64] The subsequent material alteration of a product precludes recovery under products liability because the product cannot be said to have been defective when it left the manufacturer's control.[65]

14. **State of the Art**

Oklahoma recognizes the "state of the art" doctrine, which provides that liability is only imposed if a product was defective when first distributed, not at the time plaintiff was injured.[66] "State-of-the-art" evidence is admissible to establish the feasibility of safer design alternatives,[67] the reasonable expectations of the consumer,[68] and whether the defect existed when the product left the defendant-seller's control.[69]

15. **Malfunction**

While Oklahoma cases have sometimes used the term "malfunction" in discussing products cases, there is no body of law which distinguishes malfunction and defect.[70]

16. **Standards and Governmental Regulation**

Evidence of compliance or noncompliance with relevant government regulations is admissible, but it is not necessarily dispositive.[71]

17. **Other Accidents**

Evidence of other accidents may be admissible provided such information is relevant and its probative value is not outweighed by its tendency to prejudice the outcome.[72] The other accidents must have happened at the same place while the product was in the same condition, and under similar circumstances.[73]

18. **Misrepresentation**

   Oklahoma has not adopted the Restatement (Second) of Torts, Section 402B, concerning misrepresentation. However, there are several cases in which misrepresentation has been pled as an alternative theory of recovery.[74] Recently, an opinion from the District Court for the Western District of Oklahoma dealt with allegations of misrepresentation in the context of an allegedly defective product. In discussing a hip implant, the physician allegedly stated that the hip was a "30 year hip." In overruling a motion for summary judgment, the court opined that sufficient factual issues existed to preclude summary judgment.[75]

19. **Destruction or Loss of Product**

   Spoliation is defined as the destruction of evidence or the significant and meaningful alteration of a document or instrument. Spoliation occurs when evidence relevant to prospective civil litigation is destroyed, adversely affecting the ability of a litigant to prove his or her claim.

   Oklahoma has not recognized a separate legal theory, which would impose damages for spoliation of evidence. Although discussing the various remedies for such conduct in the context of the pending litigation, the Oklahoma Supreme Court, in *Patel v. OMH Medical Center*, "explicitly decline[d] . . . to provide redress for that civil harm through the adoption of a new tort." The refusal to decide the issue was grounded in part on the lack of allegations of conduct which would constitute spoliation.[76] The court had previously held, in *Cooper v. Parker-Hughey*,[77] that no civil action may be maintained for damages caused by perjury, whether denominated "perjury" or "fraud or deceit," because perjurious testimony is an offense against the finders of fact and the judicial system as a whole, rather than an individual litigant. The Tenth Circuit distinguished *Cooper* in *Advantor Capital Corp. v. Yeary*,[78] allowing a fraud claim where defendant's counsel misrepresented facts both to the court and in a letter to plaintiff's counsel.

   In *Patel*, the allegedly wrongful conduct consisted of defendants' failure to respond fully in the course of discovery and of the oral misrepresentation at trial by defendant's attorney as to the existence of a document. The court held that adequate remedies for this conduct exist, which would include vacation of a prior judgment, discovery, or other sanctions. However, destruction or spoliation of evidence has long been held to create an adverse presumption.[79]

20. **Economic Loss**

   No action may be premised on manufacturers' products liability when injury occurs solely to the product itself.[80] Such claims must be grounded on claims of breach of warranty or negligence.[81]

21. Crashworthiness

Oklahoma adopted the products liability theory based on "crashworthiness," also called the "second impact" theory. The landmark case in Oklahoma is *Lee v. Volkswagen*.[82]

Products are involved in "second impact injuries" when they operate as a causative agent after the original impact. As such, the manufacturer's liability for injuries proximately caused by latent defects is not limited to collisions in which the defect caused the accident, but extends to situations in which the defect caused injuries over and above that which would have occurred from the accident, but for the defective design.

Plaintiff has the same burden as in other products cases to prove the product was in a defective condition that was unreasonably dangerous, as defined by ordinary consumer expectations, when it left the control of the manufacturer. However, second impact cases require a slightly different perspective when discussing the plaintiff's causation burden. The manufacturer's liability in second impact cases is thought of in terms of "enhancement" or "aggravation" of injuries. The manufacturer is liable for damages only if the plaintiff can prove that he suffered injuries as a result of the latent defect or "second impact" in addition to those suffered as a result of the accident or "first impact." Further, the manufacturer is liable for damages only for enhanced injuries attributable to the second impact. This "aggravation" or "enhancement" can occur in two ways: an increase in the severity of the injury as a result of the "second impact," or an entirely new injury.

In either situation, the causation burden is the same as in all products cases. Plaintiff must offer sufficient proof to convince the jury that the defect was responsible for a new injury or enhancement of an injury sustained as a result of the first impact. Thus "aggravation" or "enhancement" are labels applied to second impact injuries to avoid confusion with injuries caused by the first impact. The court applies the same preponderance of evidence test in second impact cases that it did in *Kirkland*. The plaintiff must prove by a preponderance of the evidence: (1) that the product was in a defective condition that was unreasonably dangerous (as defined by ordinary consumer expectations) when it left the control of the manufacturer; (2) that after the original impact, such defect caused or enhanced his injuries; and (3) the extent of the enhanced injuries resulting from the defect. The manufacturer will only be liable for the injuries resulting from the latent defect, which was caused or enhanced by such defect.

However, where the injury is catastrophic, such as resulting in death or quadriplegia, it is considered "indivisible" and therefore incapable of apportionment. There can be no "enhancement" and the plaintiff's burden is to present sufficient evidence to prove to the jury that the alleged tortfeasor's acts were contributing factors in producing the injury.[83]

E. NEGLIGENCE

A plaintiff who brings an action under the theory of manufacturers' products liability is not precluded from bringing a cause of action for negligence.[84] The elements of a negligence action in Oklahoma are similar to those of other states: (1) duty; (2) breach of duty; (3) proximate (or "direct") cause; and (4) resulting injuries.

Pursuant to statute, Oklahoma recognizes "comparative negligence" in the context of negligence based claims.[85] It does not do so under theories of products liability. Thus, in an action sounding in negligence for a defect in a product, the plaintiff's comparative negligence may be considered,[86] but in an action sounding in products liability only, in order to prevail, the defendant must establish that the plaintiff's negligence was the *sole proximate cause* of the injury and damages.

F. BREACH OF WARRANTY

Any recovery under a warranty theory is restricted to the terms of Article 2 of the Oklahoma Uniform Commercial Code.[87]

The Oklahoma Uniform Commercial Code authorizes recovery under theories of breach of the implied warranty of merchantability,[88] breach of the implied warranty of fitness for a particular purpose,[89] and breach of express warranty.[90]

Recovery for purely economic damages to the product itself must be based on the parties' contractual relationship, specifically, the warranty provisions, express or implied.[91] Horizontal privity of contract, as extended by the legislature to members of the household, is required. Vertical privity is not required for claims under the U.C.C.[92]

G. PUNITIVE DAMAGES

In Oklahoma, punitive damages may be assessed under theories of negligence[93] or products liability[94] but not under the contractually based theories of breach of warranty.[95] Oklahoma's punitive damage scenario is governed by statute.[96] An award of punitive damages must be based on the following factors: (1) the seriousness of the hazard to the public arising from the defendant's misconduct; (2) the profitability of the misconduct to the defendant; (3) the duration of the misconduct and any concealment of it; (4) the degree of the defendant's awareness of the hazard and of its excessiveness; (5) the attitude and conduct of the defendant upon discovery of the misconduct or hazard; (6) in the case of a defendant which is a corporation or other entity, the number and level of employees involved in causing or concealing the misconduct; and (7) the financial condition of the defendant.

The burden of proof to establish an award of punitive damages is "clear and convincing evidence," and there are "categories" of conduct, each of which mandates a different permissible ceiling on the damages awarded. Where the jury finds the defendant has been guilty of reckless disregard for the rights of others, the jury may, in a bifurcated proceeding, after actual damages have been assessed, award exemplary damages in an amount not to exceed the greater of $100,000 or the amount of the actual damages awarded. If the jury finds intentional or malicious conduct, the jury, in the same type of bifurcated proceeding, may award exemplary damages in an amount not to exceed the greatest of $500,000, twice the amount of actual damages awarded, or the increased financial benefit derived by the defendant as a direct result of the conduct causing the injury to the plaintiff and other persons or entities.

The statute provides that the trial court shall reduce any award for damages awarded under the last category by the amount it finds the defendant has previously paid as a result of all punitive damage verdicts entered in any court of the State of Oklahoma for the same conduct by the defendant.

If the jury finds the defendant has acted intentionally and with malice towards others; and the court finds, on the record and out of the presence of the jury, that there is evidence beyond a reasonable doubt that the defendant, intentionally and with malice engaged in conduct life-threatening to humans, the jury, in a separate proceeding conducted after the jury has made such finding and awarded actual damages, may award exemplary damages in any amount the jury deems appropriate, without limitations.[97]

H. PRE- AND POST-JUDGMENT INTEREST

Pre-judgment interest accrues on actions for damages by reason of personal injuries or injury to personal rights including, but not limited to, injury resulting from bodily restraint, personal insult, defamation, invasion of privacy, injury to personal relations, or detriment due to an act or omission of another. The interest is included in the amount of the judgment and runs from 24 months after the date the suit commenced to the date of the verdict. The interest rate for computation of pre-judgment interest begins with the rate in effect for that calendar year, but changes from year to year, based upon the rate in effect for that calendar year, until the date judgment is rendered. The total amount of pre-judgment interest is then added to the amount of the judgment rendered, and that becomes the amount upon which post-judgment interest is computed.[98] There is no authority in Oklahoma by which the running of pre-judgment interest may be suspended during the pendency of an action.[99]

All judgments of courts of record in Oklahoma bear interest post-judgment. Post-judgment interest accrues from the earlier of the date the judgment is rendered, if expressly stated in the judgment, or the date the judgment or order is filed with the court clerk. It accrues at the rate in effect for the calendar year during which the judgment is rendered, and fluctuates from year to year, until paid.[100]

If exemplary or punitive damages are awarded in an action for personal injury or injury to personal rights including, but not limited to, injury resulting from bodily restraint, personal insult, defamation, invasion of privacy, injury to personal relations, or detriment due to an act or omission of another, the interest on such an award begins to accrue as of the date the judgment is rendered by the trial court as stated in its judgment or the date the judgment is filed with the court clerk, whichever comes first.[101]

The interest rate is different for pre- and post-judgment interest. Pre-judgment interest is a rate equal to the average United States Treasury Bill rate of the preceding calendar year. That figure is determined and published by the Court Administrator each year. Post-judgment interest is the prime rate plus 2 percent (2%).[102]

I. EMPLOYER IMMUNITY FROM SUIT

Since Oklahoma has adopted the exclusivity doctrine of workers' compensation, employees may not bring actions against their employers for work related injuries, even where the employer is the manufacturer of the defective product that injured the employee. As relates to manufacturers products liability, the so-called dual capacity doctrine as applied to products theories has been expressly rejected in Oklahoma.[103] The doctrine of *dual persona* however, has met with limited acceptance. Thus, where an employer acts in a capacity so far removed from his capacity as employer as to be acting in another *persona*, the immunity of workers' compensation may not apply.[104] Since Oklahoma's theory of products liability has no system of comparative responsibility, a manufacturer will remain fully liable for all injuries suffered as a result of a defective product despite fault of the employer that contributed to the injury.[105]

The sovereign immunity of a political subdivision is waived only in accordance with the strictures of the Oklahoma Governmental Tort Claims Act.[106] Pursuant to the Act, the state or a political subdivision is not liable under a theory of manufacturer's products liability or breach of warranty, either express or implied.[107] However, a 1992 Oklahoma Court of Appeals decision would allow the state or a political subdivision to remain liable for breach of express or implied warranties in contract.[108] The Appeals Court reasoned that the provisions of the Governmental Tort Claims Act apply only to "tort based" claims, and thus did not apply to contractual warranties.[109]

J. STATUTES

The theory of products liability, based initially upon judicial pronouncements, has been somewhat refined by statute. However, several statutes have potential impact on the application of products liability law. Oklahoma has codified its prior case law dealing with indemnification of sellers by manufacturers under products liability theories.[110] The legislature has codified the "inherently unsafe" defense, making it an affirmative defense.[111] The doctrine of "joint and several liability" has been, with some exceptions, abolished in Oklahoma.[112]

In 2011, the Oklahoma Legislature set the limit to the amount of recovery for non-economic damages at $350,000.00. Most of the prior exceptions to the cap have been eliminated, leaving only an exception for wrongful death actions, cases brought under the Governmental Tort Claims Act and cases in which the jury finds the defendant's conduct amounted to the same conduct which would support a claim for punitive damages.[113]

Several other significant statutory changes were adopted during the 2011 legislative session. Provisions curtail the amount of medical expenses recoverable under certain circumstances. Where medical bills have not been paid, recovery is limited to the amount of the Medicare reimbursement rates in effect when the injury occurred. Where bills have only been partially paid, only the actual amount paid is recoverable.[114] An award of "future damages" exceeding $100,000.00 may be ordered paid in periodic payments for a period no longer than seven years.[115] Finally, where the plaintiff in a personal injury action involving a motor vehicle is uninsured, with certain exceptions, the plaintiff's damages will exclude any award for pain and suffering.[116]

The legislature adopted a new law in 2013, known as the Asbestos and Silica Claims Priorities Act.[117] The Act is designed to provide a new procedural remedy allowing for increased judicial supervision and control of asbestos and silica litigation. It prioritized cases for claimants with demonstrable physical impairments while preserving the rights of claimants without such impairments. Before a case is set on the trial docket, a claimant must establish a prima facie showing of asbestos- or silica-related malignancy or impairment.[118] For currently pending actions, the claimant must produce a report to each defendant served, and for newly filed cases, there must be a report filed with the initial pleading.[119] Where a prima facie showing is made, the claimant may request an expedited trial setting, not less than one hundred twenty (120) days from the order granting such motion and six months after the initial filing.[120]

As previously discussed, the statute of limitations in Oklahoma is two years for injuries to person and property, not arising from contract.[121] However, the period of limitations applicable to a claim accruing outside the state is the longer of the limitations period of that state or of Oklahoma's statute of limitations.[122]

Other statutory provisions related to the limitations of actions include the tolling of limitations where a minor (or other person under disability) is involved. The statute of limitations is tolled until the expiration of one year from the time the disability is removed.[123] Additionally, Oklahoma has adopted a statute of repose that deals with the liability of architects and builders with respect to improvements to real property.[124]

Oklahoma has a "savings statute." Under the savings statute, if an action is filed timely, but fails "otherwise than upon the merits" (which includes a voluntary dismissal without prejudice) a new action may be commenced within one year, even though the time limit for commencing an action may have expired before the new action is filed.[125]

Also significant to defendants is the effect of the exclusive remedy of the Workers' Compensation Act, which protects employers from the possibility of becoming liable under either products or negligence theories as a result of injuries to their workers. A similar exclusion for liability under the Governmental Tort Claims Act may shield political subdivisions from liability.

Finally, evidence of the use or non-use of seat belts in civil actions is admissible in any civil suit, unless the plaintiff in the action is under 16 years of age.[126]

K. JOINT AND SEVERAL LIABILITY

Joint and several liability has been abolished in Oklahoma in cases that accrue on or after November 1, 2011. The statue applies to cases in which there are multiple defendants, and are based on "fault" and not arising out of contract.[127]

Because this statute is at odds with prior Oklahoma Supreme Court cases relating to the "faultless plaintiff," it is questionable whether the current Oklahoma law making multiple tortfeasors each responsible for the entire result if the plaintiff is free from negligence continues to be effective.[128] When an injury is the result of a defect in a product as well as the conduct of others, both the defect and the conduct of the others are direct causes of the injury regardless of the extent to which each contributed to the injury. How the court will reconcile the statute with its holding in *Kirkland v. General Motors* also remains to be seen.

The right of contribution among tortfeasors remains unchanged by the new statute. Thus, when two persons are jointly or severally liable for the same injury, there is a right of contribution among them. This is true, even though judgment has not been recovered against all or any of them.[129]

However, the right of contribution exists only in favor of a tortfeasor who has paid more than his pro rata share of the common liability, and the total recovery is limited to the amount paid by the tortfeasor in excess of his pro rata share. There is no right of contribution in favor of any tortfeasor who has intentionally caused or contributed to the injury. [Where a tortfeasor enters into a settlement which does not extinguish the liability of another tortfeasor, that tortfeasor is not entitled to recover contribution from the tortfeasor whose liability is not extinguished by the settlement.] Further, a tortfeasor is not entitled to contribution for any amount paid in a settlement which is unreasonable.

A release, covenant not to sue, or a similar agreement, given in good faith to one of two or more persons liable in tort for the same injury discharges tortfeasor specifically named. Parties that are only vicariously liable are also discharged. Claims against others are reduced by the amount of consideration for the release.[130] Further, such a release discharges the tortfeasor to whom it is given from all liability for contribution to any other tortfeasor.[131]

John C. Niemeyer
Linda G. Alexander
Niemeyer, Alexander & Phillips, P.C.
Three Hundred North Walker
Oklahoma City, Oklahoma 73102-1822
(405) 232-2725
(Fax) (405) 239-7185

ENDNOTES - OKLAHOMA

1. *Wall v. Marouk*, 2013 OK 36 (Okla. 2013) (found section 2 of the CLRA, codified as 12 O.S. 2011 § 19, an unconstitutional special law and an unconstitutional financial burden on access to the courts); *Douglas v. Cox Ret. Props., Inc.*, 2013 OK 37 (Okla. 2013) (found the CLRA as a whole unconstitutional for violating the single subject rule pronounced in Article 5, § 57 of the Oklahoma Constitution).

2. Although Oklahoma has adopted strict liability in tort under Restatement (Second) of Torts, Section 402A, the Oklahoma Supreme Court has designated this cause of action as "Manufacturers' Products Liability." *See Kirkland v. Gen. Motors Corp.*, 1974 OK 52, ¶21, 521 P.2d 1353, 1361.

3. Okla. Stat. tit. 12A, § 1-101 *et seq.*; *United Gen. Ins. Co. v. Crane Carrier*, 1984 OK 47, 695 P.2d 1334.

4. *Dutsch v. Sea Ray Boats, Inc.*, 1992 OK 155, 845 P.2d 187, discussing *Waggoner v. Town & Country Mobile Homes*, 1990 OK 139, 808 P.2d 649.

5. *Waggoner*, 1990 OK 139, ¶14, 808 P.2d at 653.

6. *Dutsch*, 1992 OK 155, ¶31, 845 P.2d at 193; *see also Okla. Gas & Elec. v. McGraw-Edison*, 1992 OK 108, 834 P.2d 980.

7. Okla. Stat. tit. 12, § 95.

8. *Kirkland*, 1974 OK 52, ¶24, 521 P.2d at 1361.

9. *Daugherty v. Farmers Coop. Ass'n*, 1984 OK 72, 689 P.2d 947.

10. Okla. Stat. tit. 12A, § 2-725.

11. Okla. Stat. tit. 12, § 109, which provides:
No action in tort to recover damages

    (i) for any deficiency in the design, planning, supervision or observation of construction or construction of an improvement to real property,

    (ii) for injury to property, real or personal, arising out of any such deficiency, or

    (iii) for injury to the person or for wrongful death arising out of any such deficiency, shall be brought against any person owning, leasing, or in possession of such an improvement or performing or furnishing the design, planning, supervision or observation of construction or construction of such an improvement more than ten (10) years after substantial completion of such an improvement.

12. *Abott v. Wells*, 2000 OK 75, 11 P.3d 1247.

13. *Samuel Roberts Noble Found., Inc. v. Vick*, 1992 OK 140, 840 P.2d 619; *Lincoln Bank & Trust Co. v. Neustadt*, 1996 OK CIV APP 10, 917 P.2d 1005.

14. *Smith v. Westinghouse Elec. Corp.*, 1987 OK 3, 732 P.2d 466 (where the issue considered was whether transformers were an "improvement to real property" and, as such, subject to the ten-year statute of repose at Okla. Stat. tit. 12, § 109). *See also O'Dell v. Lamb-Grays Harbor Co.*, 911 F. Supp. 490 (W.D. Okla. 1995) (distinguishing *Smith* on the basis that the "product" was a "fixture").

15. *Smith*, 1987 OK 3, ¶9, 732 P.2d at 470. *See also Goad v. Bushman*, 2008 WL 906173 (N.D. Okla. 2008); *Durham v. Herbert Olbrich GMBH & Co.*, 404 F.3d 1249 (10th Cir. 2005).

16. *Riley v. Brown & Root, Inc.*, 1992 OK 114, 836 P.2d 1298. *See also Morin v. Coral Swimming Pool Supply Co.*, 1993 OK CIV APP 197, 867 P.2d 494.

17. *Ball v. Harhischfeger Corp.*, 1994 OK 65, 877 P.2d 45.

18. V. Lawrence-MacDougall, *Products Liability Law in Oklahoma* 12 (1990). Oklahoma has yet to adopt the Restatement (Third) of Torts in product liability cases.

19. *Kirkland*, 1974 OK 52, 521 P.2d 1353.

20. *Kirkland*, 1974 OK 52, ¶26, 521 P.2d 1363.

21. *Kirkland*, 1974 OK 52, ¶¶29-31, 521 P.2d at 1362-63.

22. *Graves v. Mazda Motor Corp.*, 405 F. Appx. 296, 2010 WL 5094286 (10th Cir. 2010) (not selected for publication in the Federal Reporter); *Karns v. Emerson Elec. Co.*, 817 F.2d 1452 (10th Cir. 1987); *Smith v. Minster Mach. Co.*, 669 F.2d 628 (10th Cir. 1982).

23. *Woods v. Fruehauff Trailer Corp.*, 1988 OK 105, ¶¶11-17, 765 P.2d 770, 774-76 (citing Restatement (Second) of Torts § 402k).

24. *Kirkland*, 521 P.2d at 1362-63.

25. *Woods v. Fruehauff Trailer Corp.*, 1988 OK 105, ¶¶12-17, 765 P.2d 770, 774-76.

26. *Lamke v. Futorian Corp.*, 1985 OK 47 ¶17, 709 P.2d 684, 686; *Woods v. Fruehauf Corp.*, 1988 OK 105, 765 P.2d 770, 774.

27. *Lamke*, 1985 OK 47, ¶11, 709 P.2d 684, 686.

28. Okla. Stat. tit. 76 § 57.1.

29. *Dutsch*, 1992 OK 155, ¶14, 845 P.2d 187, 189.

30. *Case v. Fibreboard*, 1987 OK 79, 743 P.2d 1062; cf. *Basford v. Gray Mfg. Co.*, 2000 OK CIV APP 106, 11 P.3d 1281 *(reversing a grant of summary judgment)*.

31. *Case*, 1987 OK 79, ¶10, 743 P.2d at 1067.

32. Okla. Stat. tit. 23, §§ 13, 14, and 15.

33. *Spence v. Brown-Minneapolis Tank Co.*, 2008 OK CIV APP 90, 198 P.3d 395.

34. *Moss v. Polyco, Inc.*, 1974 OK 53, ¶13, 522 P.2d 622, 626-27.

35. *Dewberry v. LaFollette*, 1979 OK 113, ¶4, 598 P.2d 241, 243.

36. *Allenberg v. Bentley Hedges*, 2001 OK 22, 22 P.3d 223.

37. *Pulis v. United States Elec. Tool Co.*, 1977 OK 36, 561 P.2d 68.

38. *Goucher v. Parmac, Inc.*, 1984 OK CIV APP 46, 694 P.2d 953. In a subsequent case, *Crutchfield v. Marine Power Engine Co.*, 2009 OK 27, 209 P.3d 295, the Oklahoma Supreme Court recognized the persuasive authority of the case.

39. *Dewberry v. LaFollette*, 1979 OK 113, ¶¶4-7 598 P.2d at 242.

40. *Dewberry*, 1979 OK 113, ¶4, 598 P.2d 242 (citing *Allison Steel Mfg. Co. v. Superior Court of Maricopa Cnty.*, 20 Ariz. App. 185, 511 P.2d 198 (1973)) and Restatement (Second) of Torts § 402A, cmts. c and f (1965).

41. *Allenberg v. Bentley Hedges Travel Serv. Inc.*, 2001 OK 22, 22 P.3d 223 at n.13. See also *Coleman v. Hertz Corp.*, 1975 OK CIV APP 5, 534 P.2d 940.

42. Okla. Stat. tit. 76, § 57.1.

43. *McKee v. Moore*, 1982 OK 71, 648 P.2d 21.

44. *Tansy v. Dacomed Corp.*, 1994 OK 146, 890 P.2d 881.

45. Okla. Stat. tit. 63, § 2151.

46. *Pulis*, 1977 OK 36, 561 P.2d at 68.

47. *Pulis*, 1977 OK 36, 561 P.2d at 68.

48. *Goucher v. Parmac, Inc.*, 1984 OK CIV APP 46, 694 P.2d 953.

49. *Case v. Fibreboard Corp.*, 1987 OK 79, 743 P.2d 1062; *Basford v. Gray Mfg. Co.*, 2000 OK CIV APP 106, 11 P.3d 1281.

50. 607 P.2d 924 (Cal. 1980).

51. *Case v. Fibreboard Corp.*, 1987 OK 79, 743 P.2d 1062.

52. *Moss*, 1974 OK 53, ¶12, 522 P.2d 622, 626.

53. *Waggoner v. Town & Country*, 1990 OK 139, ¶21, 808 P.2d 649, 652.

54. *Duane v. Okla. Gas & Elec. Co.*, 1992 OK 97, ¶3, 833 P.2d 284, 286.

55. *Rohrbaugh v. Owens-Corning Fiberglass Corp.*, 965 F.2d 844, 846 (10th Cir. 1992), citing *Woods v. Fruehauff Trailer Corp.*, 1988 OK 105, ¶11, 765 P.2d 770, 774; *Bohnstedt v. Robscon Leasing*, 1999 OK CIV APP 115, 993 P.2d 135.

56. *See Duane*, 1992 OK 97, ¶¶3-6 (manufacturer had no duty to warn plaintiff that a power surge could transform dielectric oil into a volatile substance); *Hutchins v. Silicone Specialties, Inc.*, 1993 OK 70, 881 P.2d 64 (manufacturer that markets its product solely to professional consumers with specialized training is entitled to expect its instructions to be followed and has no duty additionally to warn of dangers associated with product's use).

57. *McKee v. Moore*, 1982 OK 71, 648 P.2d 21. *See also Shuman v. Laverne Farmers Co-op.*, 1991 OK CIV APP 2, 809 P.2d 76, in which the Court of Appeals seems to accept, without analysis, the proposition that every manufacturer has a continuing duty to warn. *But see Wicker v. Ford*, 393 F. Supp. 2d 1229 (W.D. Okla. 2005) (no duty to retrofit or warn post-sale); *Smith v. Sears Roebuck & Co.*, 2006 WL 687151 (W. D. Okla. Jan. 9, 2006), *aff'd*, 232 F. Appx. 780, 73 Fed. R. Evid. Serv. 415, Prod. Liab. Rep. (CCH) P 17,736 (10th Cir. 2007).

58. Okla. Stat. tit. 76, § 58.1 (the language mirrors the current Federal Rule of Evidence); Okla Stat. tit. 12, § 2407.

59. *Cunningham v. Charles Pfizer & Co., Inc.*, 1974 OK 146, 532 P.2d 1377 (announcing the general rule and the exception for mass immunizations).

60. *Edwards v. Basel Pharms.*, 1997 OK 22, 933 P.2d 298.

61. *Treadway v. Uniroyal Tire Co.*, 1988 OK 37, 766 P.2d 938. *See also Hutchins v. Silicone Specialties, Inc.*, 1993 OK 70, 881 P.2d 64.

62. *Kirkland*, 1974 OK 52, ¶46, 521 P.2d at 1366.

63. *Kirkland*, 1974 OK 52, ¶46, 521 P.2d at 1366.

64. *Holt v. Deere & Co.*, 24 F.3d 1289, 1293 (10th Cir. 1994); citing *Jordan v. Gen. Motors Corp.*, 1979 OK 10, 590 P.2d 193; *Alleman v. Delta Int'l Mach. Corp.*, 89 F.3d 849 (10th Cir. 1996).

65. *Dutsch v. Sea Ray Boats, Inc.*, 1992 OK 155, ¶18, 845 P.2d 187 (subsequent modifications of boat caused injuries); *Stuckey v. Young Exploration Co.*, 1978 OK 128, ¶22, 586 P.2d 726 (cab and chassis of truck had undergone two modifications); *Prince v. B.G. Ascher Co., Inc*, 2004 OK CIV APP 39 (inhaler disassembled and active ingredient removed).

66. *See, e.g., Smith v. Minster Mach. Co.*, 669 F.2d 628 (10th Cir. 1982); *Lamke v. Futorian Corp.*, 1985 OK 47, 709 P.2d 684, dissent by Doolin, J. *See also O'Banion v. Owens-Corning Fiberglas Corp.*, 968 F.2d 1011 (10th Cir. 1992).

67. *Karns v. Emerson Elec. Co.*, 817 F.2d 1452, 1457 (10th Cir. 1987).

68. *Robinson v. Audi NSU Auto Union*, 739 F.2d 1481, 1486 (10th Cir. 1984).

69. *Kirkland*, 1974 OK 52, ¶30, 521 P.2d at 1360.

70. *But see Holt v. Deere & Co.*, 24 F.3d 1289 (10th Cir. 1994), Holloway, J., concurring and dissenting (implying a distinction in relation to the affirmative defense of voluntary assumption of the risk of a known defect).

71. *Edwards v. Basel Pharms.*, 1997 OK 22, 933 P.2d 298.

72. Okla. Stat. tit. 12, §§ 2402, 2403 (2001). *See, e.g., Barringer v. Wal-Mart Stores, Inc.*, 699 F. Supp. 1496, 1498 n.2 (N.D. Okla. 1988); *see also Roper v. Mercy Health Ctr.*, 1995 OK 82, 903 P.2d 314 (dicta dealing with admissibility of evidence of prior accidents in a premises liability case); *Moore v. Albertson's, Inc.*, 2000 OK CIV APP 58, 7 P.3d 506.

73. See the general discussion in *St. Louis-San Francisco Ry. Co. v. Powell*, 1963 OK 465, 385 P.2d 465.

74. *See Ysbrand v. DaimlerChrysler Corp.*, 2003 OK 17, 81 P.3d 618.

75. *Shelton v. Apex Surgical, LLC*, 2009 WL 3837411 (W.D. Okla. Nov. 13, 2009).

76. *Patel v. OMH Med. Ctr.*, 1999 OK 33, 987 P.2d 1185 (*cert. denied*, 528 U.S. 1188. See also *Estate of Trentadue ex rel. Aguilar v. United States*, 397 F.3d 840 (10th Cir. 2005).

77. *Cooper v. Parker-Hughey*, 1995 OK 35, 894 P.2d 1096.

78. *Advantor Capital Corp. v. Yeary*, 136 F.3d 1259 (10th Cir. 1998).

79. *Beverly v. Wal-Mart*, 2000 OK CIV APP 45, 3 P.3d 163. *See also Barnett v. Simmons*, 2008 OK 100, 197 P.3d 12 (willfulness is not required for imposition of sanctions for spoliation of evidence). The case is an interesting discussion of spoliation in the context of electronic discovery.

80. *Okla. Gas & Elec. Co. v. McGraw-Edison Co.*, 1992 OK 108, 834 P.2d 980; *Waggoner*, 1990 OK 139, ¶14, 808 P.2d at 653.

81. *Waggoner v. Town & Country Mobile Homes, Inc.*, 1990 OK 139, 808 P.2d 649.

82. *Lee v. Volkswagen of Am., Inc.*, 1984 OK 48, 688 P.2d 1283.

83. *Johnson v. Ford Motor Co.*, 2002 OK 24, 45 P.3d. 86.

84. *Kirkland*, 1974 OK 52, ¶14, 521 P.2d at 1359.

85. Okla. Stat. tit. 23, §§ 13, 14.

86. *Kirkland*, 1974 OK 52, ¶47, 521 P.2d at 1364.

87. Okla. Stat. tit. 12A, §§ 2-101 *et seq.*

88. Okla. Stat. tit. 12A, § 2-314.

89. Okla. Stat. tit. 12A, § 2-315.

90. Okla. Stat. tit. 12A, § 2-313.

91. *Waggoner*, 1990 OK 139, ¶19, 808 P.2d at 653.

92. *Elden v. Simmons*, 1981 OK 81, 631 P.2d 739; *Old Albany Estates v. Highland Carpet Mills*, 1979 OK 144, 604 P.2d 849.

93. Okla. Stat. tit. 23, § 9.1.

94. *Thiry v. Armstrong World Indus.*, 1983 OK 28, 661 P.2d 515.

95. *Waggoner*, 1990 OK 139, 808 P.2d 649.

96. Okla. Stat. tit. 23, § 9.1.

97. Okla. Stat. tit. 23, § 9.1.

98. Okla. Stat. tit. 12, § 727.1(E).

99. *Compare Parker v. O'Rion Indus., Inc.*, 767 F.2d 647 (10th Cir. 1985), *with Johnson v. Ford Motor Co.*, 2002 OK 24, 45 P.3d 86.

100. Okla. Stat. tit. 12, § 727.1 (A-C).

101. 12 O.S. § 727.1(G).

102. Okla. Stat. tit. 12, § 727.1(l).

103. Okla. Const. Art. XXIII, § 7; Okla. Stat. tit. 85, § 12 (2002); *Rios v. Nicor Drilling Co.*, 1983 OK 74, 665 P.2d 1183.

104. *Dyke v. St. Francis Hosp., Inc.*, 1993 OK 114, 861 P.2d 295 (dealing with *dual persona* in a medical negligence case).

105. *Harter Concrete Prods., Inc. v. Harris*, 1979 OK 38, 592 P.2d 526. Exception to this immunity exists only in the case of intentional tort; defined as willful, deliberate, specific intents of the employer to cause such injury. Okla. Stat. tit. 85, § 302.

106. Okla. Stat. tit. 51, § 151*et seq.*

107. Okla. Stat. tit. 51, § 155(26).

108. *Lucas v. Canadian Valley Area Vo-Tech Sch.*, 1992 OK CIV APP 1, 824 P.2d 1140.

109. *Lucas*, 1992 OK CIV APP 1, ¶¶6-11, 824 P.2d at 1141-42.

110. Okla. Stat. tit. 12, § 832.1.

111. Okla. Stat. tit. 76, § 57.1.

112. Okla. Stat. tit. 23, § 15.

113. Okla. Stat. tit. 23, § 61.2. The cap is lifted where defendant's acts were in reckless disregard for the rights of others, grossly negligent, fraudulent or intentional or with malice.

114. Okla. Stat. tit. 12, § 3009.1.

115. Okla. Stat. tit. 23, § 9.3.

116. Okla. Stat. tit. 47, § 7-116. Excluded from the statute are situations in which the defendant was operating the vehicle under the influence of drugs or alcohol, or intentionally caused the accident, left the scene, or was acting in furtherance of commission of a felony. The statute does not apply to wrongful death claims.

117. Okla. Stat. tit. 76, § 90.1 *et seq.*

118. Okla. Stat. tit. 76, §§ 90.2-90.5.

119. Okla. Stat. tit. 76, § 90.8.

120. Okla. Stat. tit. 76, § 90.8.

121. Okla. Stat. tit. 12, § 95(3).

122. Okla. Stat. tit. 12, § 105.

123. Okla. Stat. tit. 12, § 96.

124. Okla. Stat. tit. 12, § 109

125. Okla. Stat. tit. 12, § 100.

126. Okla. Stat. tit. 47, § 12-420.

127. Okla. Stat. tit. 23, § 15.

128. *See Boyles v. Okla. Natural Gas Co.*, 1980 OK 163, ¶10, 619 P.2d 613, 617; *All Am. Bus Lines v. Saxon*, 1946 OK 199, ¶33, 172 P.2d 424, 429.

129. Okla. Stat. tit. 12, § 832.

130. *Burke v. Webb Boats, Inc.*, 2001 OK 83, 37 P.3d 811.

131. Okla. Stat. tit. 12, § 832(H)(2).

OREGON

A. CAUSES OF ACTION

Oregon defines a product liability action to mean a cause of action against a manufacturer, distributor, seller or lessor for personal injury, death or property damage arising from the (1) design, inspection, testing, manufacturing or other defect in a product; (2) failure to warn; or (3) failure to properly instruct in the use of a product.[1] Oregon's product liability law embraces all theories in an action based on a product defect.[2]

A physician who provides a product as part of a medical procedure is not subject to a products liability action.[3]

B. STATUTES OF LIMITATION AND REPOSE

1. Statutes of Limitations

A product liability lawsuit for personal injury or property damage must be commenced no later than two years after the plaintiff discovered, or reasonably should have discovered, the injury and the causal relationship between the injury and the product at issue or between the injury and the conduct of the manufacturer.[4]

A product liability action alleging wrongful death must be commenced not later than three years after the causal relationship between the death and the product was discovered, or reasonably should have been discovered, or between the death and the conduct of the manufacturer.[5]

Product liability civil actions based upon death, injury, or damage caused by asbestos, sidesaddle gas tanks, COX-2 inhibitors, metal halide or mercury vapor light bulbs, or silicone-based breast implants are subject to separate limitations periods, specific to each type of claim.[6]

If, prior to the expiration of the applicable limitation period, a claimant dies for reasons unrelated to the claim, the deceased claimant's personal representative may commence a lawsuit after the expiration of the statute of limitations if the suit is commenced within one year of the claimant's death.[7] If the claim is for personal injury caused by a defective product, the personal representative has three years from the date of the claimant's death in which to commence the lawsuit.[8] If the claim is for injury to the deceased claimant's *property*, however, the shorter limitations period applies.[9]

2. Statute of Repose

Product liability actions, except those alleging wrongful death, must be commenced before the later of: (1) ten years after the date on which the product was first purchased; or (2) the expiration of a statute of repose for an equivalent civil action in the state in which the product was manufactured, or if the product was manufactured in a foreign country, the expiration of the statute of repose in the state into which the product was imported.[10]

Product liability actions alleging wrongful death must be commenced before the earlier of: (1) three years after the death; (2) ten years after the date on which the product was first purchased; or (3) the expiration of any statute of repose for an equivalent civil action in the state in which the product was manufactured, or if the product was manufactured in a foreign country, the expiration of the statute of repose in the state into which the product was imported.[11]

C. STRICT LIABILITY

1. The Standard

Any party that sells or leases a product in a defective condition unreasonably dangerous to the user or consumer is liable for personal injury or property damage caused by the dangerous condition.[12]

To establish a strict product liability claim, a plaintiff must prove the following:

(1) The seller or lessor is engaged in the business of selling or leasing the product;[13]

(2) The product was defective;[14]

(3) The defect rendered the product unreasonably dangerous;[15]

(4) The product is expected to and does reach the user or consumer without substantial change in the condition in which it is sold or leased;[16]

(5) Injury to the user or consumer, or damage to his or her property;[17] and

(6) The product's defective condition caused the injury or damage.[18]

The Oregon Legislature directed that Oregon's product liability statute be construed in accordance with Section 402A of the Restatement (Second) of Torts, comments a through m.[19]

2. Definition of "Defect" and "Unreasonably Dangerous"

A product liability plaintiff must prove both that (1) the product was defective, and that (2) the defect rendered the product "unreasonably dangerous."[20]

The terms "defective" and "unreasonably dangerous" are defined by the comments to Section 402A of the Restatement (Second) of Torts.[21] A product is defective if, at the time it leaves the seller's hands, the product is "in a condition not contemplated by the ultimate consumer, which will be unreasonably dangerous to him."[22] A product is unreasonably dangerous when it poses a risk beyond that which "an ordinary consumer would contemplate when purchasing a product with the knowledge of its characteristics common to the relevant community."[23]

Whether a product was in a "defective condition unreasonably dangerous to the user or consumer"[24] is determined exclusively according to the "consumer expectations test."[25] This test requires the product be evaluated in terms of the reasonable expectations of the ordinary consumer.[26]

While consumer expectation is generally a factual question, the court must ensure that the plaintiff has produced sufficient evidence "for the jury to make an informed decision about what ordinary consumers expect."[27]

a. **Risk-Utility Evidence**

Oregon courts recognize that in some design defect cases, consumer expectations about how a product should perform may not be within the realm of a juror's common experience.[28] Additional evidence about the ordinary consumer's expectations is necessary when a jury is "unequipped," either by general background or facts in the record, to determine whether a product failed to perform as safely as an ordinary consumer would expect. The additional evidence may relate to "consumer risk-utility" balancing,[29] intended to show that the magnitude of the product's risk outweighs its utility.[30] Such proof often takes the form of evidence that a safer alternative design was both practicable and feasible.[31] However, proof of a practical and feasible design alternative is not always necessary to prove that a product design is defective and unreasonably dangerous.[32] The Oregon Supreme Court has left open the question under what circumstances evidence related to risk-utility balancing is required to support a design defect claim.[33]

b. **Failure to Warn**

Where a manufacturer "has reason to anticipate that danger may result from a particular use," the product is defective if the manufacturer fails to give an adequate warning of the danger.[34] A drug manufacturer is under a continuous duty to keep abreast of scientific developments associated with the manufacturer's drug and to notify physicians of any additional side effects it discovers.[35] A product is not in a defective condition due to a lack of warning, however, where the danger is generally known and recognized.[36] The plaintiff should be prepared to prove that an adequate warning would have made the product safe for use.[37] The duty to warn extends to foreseeable users and purchasers and those who are likely to come in contact with the product.[38]

c. **Condition of Product at Time of Sale**

Under Oregon law, a plaintiff must establish, as part of her prima facie case, that the product "reach[ed] the user or consumer without substantial change in the condition in which it [was] sold...."[39] Once a plaintiff has shown that the product was defective at the time it left the manufacturer's hands, the burden shifts to the defendant to show, as an affirmative defense, that a post-sale modification precludes liability.[40]

d. **Indeterminate Defect**

Inability to specify a defect is not necessarily fatal to a claim if the plaintiff can show that the product failed under circumstances that reasonably tend to indicate that the defect existed at the time of the sale and that a defect is the only reasonable explanation for the accident.[41] However, in cases alleging a specific defect where there is no indication of an undiscoverable defect, the plaintiff is not entitled to recover simply because the product failed to perform as reasonably expected.[42]

3. **Causation**

The mere existence of a defect is not enough to establish liability. The plaintiff must also prove that the alleged defect caused plaintiff's injury.[43] In design defect cases, the jury may infer causation from sufficient evidence that the injury would not have occurred with an alternative design under the same conditions as the plaintiff's accident.[44] In cases based on inadequate warnings, causation may be established by evidence from which the jury can infer that a warning is generally effective in preventing the kind of injury suffered by the plaintiff.[45]

Generally, Oregon employs the substantial factor test to assess whether a defendant's conduct caused the plaintiff's injury.[46] Whether a particular defendant's conduct is a substantial factor in causing a particular result depends on the "totality of potentially causative circumstances."[47]

4. **Contributory Negligence/Assumption of Risk**

Oregon's legislature abolished both contributory negligence and implied assumption of the risk as defenses and replaced them with comparative fault.[48] Oregon's comparative fault statutes apply to strict liability claims.[49] Negligent conduct, such as misuse of the product, is a defense to a strict liability claim.[50] However, incidental carelessness or negligent failure to discover or guard against a latent product defect is not a defense.[51]

A plaintiff may not recover if the percentage of fault attributable to the plaintiff is greater than the combined fault of the defendant(s), third-party defendant(s), and any person with whom the plaintiff has settled.[52] If the percentage of fault attributed to the plaintiff is less than the combined fault of these others, the trial judge simply reduces plaintiff's recovery by that proportionate share.[53]

5. **Sale or Lease/Persons Liable**

In a strict liability claim, the plaintiff must allege a sale or lease of a product by defendant.[54] Sellers of used goods are generally not subject to strict liability as long as they are not the manufacturer. If, however, the nature of the sale implies a representation as to safety, a seller of used goods may be liable.[55] Similarly, a defendant who modifies a product as part of his business, may be held strictly liable.[56]

6. **Inherently Dangerous Products**

A supplier of products will not be held strictly liable simply because it supplies a product that is inherently dangerous unless it also fails to adequately warn of the danger.[57] A seller may reasonably assume that a warning that is actually given will be read and heeded.[58] Comment k of Restatement (Second) of Torts, Section 402A will apply.[59]

7. **Successor Liability**

Under Oregon law, in an asset purchase, the purchasing corporation does not become liable for the debts and liability of the selling corporation.[60] There are four exceptions: (1) where the purchaser expressly or impliedly agrees to assume the debts; (2) where the transaction amounts to a consolidation or merger of the corporations; (3) where the purchasing corporation is merely a continuation of the selling corporation; and (4) where the transaction is entered into fraudulently in order to escape liability for such debts.[61]

8. **Privity**

No privity is required in a strict products liability claim; a plaintiff may file suit even if she did not buy the product from the manufacturer.[62] A plaintiff may be a user, consumer, or other injured party.[63]

9. **Post-Sale Duty to Warn and Remedial Measures**

Oregon courts have not squarely articulated the circumstances in which sellers may have a continuing duty to warn. However, a post-sale duty to warn may exist in a proper case.[64]

A post-sale negligent act, such as a failure to warn of a latent product defect that the defendant learned about after the sale, may give rise to a negligence claim even where the statute of repose on a product liability claim has run. Such a claim is subject to the statute of limitations applicable to ordinary negligence, namely, two years from the date the plaintiff discovers or reasonably should have discovered the negligence and its causal connection to the claimed injury.[65]

10. **Learned Intermediary Doctrine**

   Under the learned intermediary doctrine, a prescription drug manufacturer has a "duty to warn the medical profession of untoward effects of which the manufacturer knows, or has reason to know."[66] While the duty is to warn the doctor, rather than the patient, the manufacturer is directly liable to the patient for breaching the duty.[67] The manufacturer's duty includes the duty to protect the doctor against foreseeable harms, including harm to the doctor's reputation.[68] Oregon has recognized aspects of the learned intermediary doctrine in the context of common-law negligence claims.[69] However, the Oregon Supreme Court has held that the learned intermediary doctrine is not a defense to strict liability claims.[70] Oregon courts have not yet determined whether the learned intermediary defense applies to negligence-based product claims.

11. **Abnormal Use**

   A product must be safe for normal handling and consumption.[71] Misuse may bar recovery where the use is so unusual that the average consumer could not reasonably expect the product to withstand it.[72] Otherwise, the seller must provide an adequate warning for reasonably foreseeable uses of a product.[73] A plaintiff who has knowledge of the product's dangerous and defective condition may not recover for unreasonably using the product.[74]

12. **Alteration or Modification**

   Unauthorized modification or alteration to a product that substantially contributed to the plaintiff's injury is a defense in a product liability action.[75] However, a seller must provide an adequate warning if the alteration or modification was reasonably foreseeable.[76]

13. **State of the Art**

   Oregon's appellate courts have not settled the question of whether evidence of the state of the art is admissible. However, comment j of Section 402A of the Restatement (Second) of Torts would seem to require that a state-of-the-art analysis should apply to a failure-to-warn claim.[77]

14. **Malfunction**

   Strict liability may not be imposed by merely proving a product malfunction. Rather, the malfunction must have proximately caused the accident.[78] Whether a malfunction caused the accident is a jury question.[79] See "Indeterminate Defect" section, above.

15. **Standards and Governmental Regulations**

   The jury may consider relevant governmental safety rules[80] and non-binding advisory standards[81] adopted by non-governmental entities to determine whether a manufacturer met the applicable standard of care. In deciding whether a rule is relevant, the trial court must examine the purpose, nature and circumstances of the risk the rule addresses.[82] The meaning of any relevant rule is for the court to decide and communicate to the jury.[83] Lack of compliance does not entitle the plaintiff to prevail on any element of its products liability claim; rather, it is only evidence the jury can consider in determining whether the defendant met the standard of care.[84]

16. **Other Accidents**

Evidence of other accidents is not admissible unless the accidents occurred under substantially similar circumstances and conditions as the plaintiff's accident.[85]

17. **Destruction or Loss of Product**

Damages to a product caused by a defective part thereof may be recoverable in a claim for strict liability.[86]

18. **Economic Loss**

A plaintiff may recover economic damages to the extent they are (1) traceable to the defendant's negligence; (2) foreseeable; and (3) a consequence of the kind of danger, and occurred under the circumstances, that gave rise to the products liability claim.[87] Economic losses resulting from poor performance or the reduced resale value of a defective product are not recoverable.[88]

D. NEGLIGENCE

A defendant is liable for conduct that "unreasonably created a foreseeable risk to the protected interest of the kind of harm that befell the plaintiff" unless a special status, relationship or specific standard otherwise defines the duty or standard of care.[89]

In a negligence action, the duty owed by a supplier of products is defined by Section 388 of the Restatement of (Second) Torts and includes the duty to warn the user of a product's dangerous propensities that it knows or reasonably should know.[90] By contrast, the elements of a strict liability action are governed by statute and construed in accordance with Section 402A of the Restatement (Second) of Torts.[91]

E. BREACH OF WARRANTY

An action for breach of warranty may be based on an express warranty,[92] the implied warranty of merchantability,[93] or the implied warranty of fitness for a particular purpose.[94] A breach of express warranty claim requires (1) an affirmation of fact or description of the goods by the seller; and (2) that factual affirmation or description must be the "basis of the bargain."[95] Privity of contract is not necessary to recover for economic loss arising from an express warranty.[96] Implied warranty claims, on the other hand, typically require privity.[97]

In the product liability setting, a cause of action for breach of warranty is similar to strict liability. However, privity between the plaintiff and defendant must exist to recover for personal injuries based on breach of warranty,[98] unless the product is a consumer good within the meaning of Or. Rev. Stat. § 72.8010(1).[99] Further, a member of a buyer's family or a guest in her home may recover for personal injuries if it was reasonable to assume the family member or guest would consume or be affected by the product.[100] A consumer plaintiff asserting a breach of warranty claim may also be entitled to attorneys' fees under the federal Magnuson-Moss Act.

F. PUNITIVE DAMAGES

Oregon permits recovery of punitive damages in a product liability case based upon specific criteria and in accordance with a specified procedure.[101] There is a limited safe harbor for drug manufacturers.[102]

In state court actions, a party's initial pleading may not contain a claim for punitive damages.[103] Rather, the party must move to amend the pleading to add a claim for punitive damages.[104] A party's motion to amend to add a claim for punitive damages may be denied if the court determines that the affidavits and supporting documentation fail to set forth specific facts supported by admissible evidence adequate to withstand a motion for a directed verdict.[105] The court must also deny the motion to amend if the opposing party establishes that the timing of such motion is prejudicial to that party.[106] Absent prejudice to the defendant, the court may deny the motion to amend only if there is *no* evidence from which a jury could find the facts necessary to support a claim for punitive damages.[107] One means of establishing that the jury could not award punitive damages is for the party opposing the motion to amend to establish that it is immune or enjoys some other exemption or complete defense to a punitive damages award.[108]

To recover punitive damages, a party must present "clear and convincing" evidence that the defendant acted with malice or showed a reckless and outrageous indifference to a highly unreasonable risk of harm and acted with a conscious indifference to the health, safety, and welfare of others.[109] In product liability actions, punitive damages are determined and awarded according to a list of statutory criteria.[110] However, a special exception from punitive damages exists for drug manufacturers falling within a specific statutory safe-harbor provision.[111]

In Oregon, it is the function of the jury to calculate punitive damages.[112] However, a "grossly excessive" punitive damage award that violates the Due Process Clause is grounds for a new trial or may alternatively be subject to remittitur.[113] Punitive damages may not be awarded to punish a defendant for the impact of the defendant's conduct on individuals in other states.[114]

Any punitive damage award is subject to mandatory post-verdict review by the trial judge.[115] In post-verdict review it may be necessary for the trial judge to consider *potential* damages (as opposed to the *actual* damages awarded by the jury) in determining whether the ratio of punitive to compensatory damages violated the Due Process Clause.[116]

G. PRE- AND POST-JUDGMENT INTEREST

1. Pre-judgment Interest

The general rule is that pre-judgment interest is not available in most tort actions, because the damages are usually not ascertainable until judgment is entered.[117] However, "the character of the damages, not the cause of action, is the determining factor."[118] Pre-judgment interest may be recovered "when the exact amount owing is ascertained or easily ascertainable by simple computation or by reference to generally recognized standards and where the time from which interest must run can be ascertained."[119] Thus, pre-judgment interest in a product liability action may not be proper where the amount of damages is contested and cannot be ascertained before the jury renders its verdict.[120]

2. Post-judgment Interest

The rate of post-judgment interest is to be fixed at the rate in effect on the date the judgment is entered, unless the judgment specifies another date.[121] Judgment on a contract bearing more than the statutory interest rate bears the contract rate.[122] Post-judgment interest also accrues on pre-judgment interest,[123] as well as on attorneys' fees and costs.[124]

If a plaintiff makes a *prima facie* showing of the existence of a service charge, the defendant may not challenge the court's award of pre- and post-judgment interest at that rate for the first time by objecting to the form of the judgment, or by requesting the trial court to modify the judgment within a reasonable time.[125]

H. JOINT AND SEVERAL LIABILITY

Under Oregon law, in "any civil action arising out of bodily injury, death or property damage . . . the liability of each defendant for damages awarded to plaintiff shall be several only and shall not be joint."[126] A retailer who is found strictly liable to a purchaser of a product may be entitled to indemnity from the manufacturer of that product if the retailer sold the product without alterations.[127] A finding that the tortfeasor was at fault to some degree is not fatal to the indemnity claim.[128]

I. EMPLOYER IMMUNITY FROM SUIT

Under Oregon's Workers' Compensation Laws, workers injured in the course and scope of employment may receive certain benefits from their employers, and with some notable exceptions, such benefits are exclusive of other remedies the worker could pursue.[129] Statutory exceptions to the general exclusive remedy rule allow an injured worker to bring a separate action for intentional and deliberate conduct.[130] The exclusive remedy rule is also subject to constitutional exceptions.[131]

J. **STATUTES**

Relevant statutes for product liability actions are Or. Rev. Stat. § 30.900 *et seq.*, and Or. Rev. Stat. Chapter 72 when breach of warranty is alleged.

The age of majority in Oregon is 18.[132]

Elizabeth A. Schleuning
Andrew J. Lee
Schwabe Williamson & Wyatt, P.C.
Pacwest Center
1211 S.W. Fifth Avenue
Suite 1900
Portland, Oregon 97204-3795
(503) 222-9981
(Fax) (503) 796-2900

ENDNOTES - OREGON

1. Or. Rev. Stat. § 30.900.

2. *See Brokenshire v. Rivas & Rivas, Ltd.*, 142 Or. App. 555, 562 n.3, 922 P.2d 696, 699 n.3 (1996); *Marinelli v. Ford Motor Co.*, 72 Or. App. 268, 273, 696 P.2d 1, 3-4, *rev. denied*, 299 Or. 251, 701 P.2d 784 (1985); *see also Jamison v. Spencer R.V. Center*, 98 Or. App. 529, 531-32, 779 P.2d 1091, 1092 (1989).

3. Or. Rev. Stat. § 30.902.

4. Or. Rev. Stat. § 30.905(1).

5. Or. Rev. Stat. §§ 30.905(3) and 30.020(1).

6. Or. Rev. Stat. § 30.907 (asbestos), § 30.908 (breast implants), § 12.278 (side-saddle gas tanks), § 30.928 (R type metal halide or mercury vapor light bulbs); Or. Laws 2007, ch. 536, § 1 (COX-2 inhibitors).

7. Or. Rev. Stat. § 12.190(1).

8. Or. Rev. Stat. § 30.075; *Giulietti v. Oncology Assocs. of Oregon, P.C.*, 178 Or. App. 260, 265-66, 36 P.3d 510, 513 (2001).

9. Or. Rev. Stat. § 30.075.

10. Or. Rev. Stat. § 30.905(2).

11. Or. Rev. Stat. § 30.905(4).

12. Or. Rev. Stat. § 30.920(1).

13. Or. Rev. Stat. § 30.920(1)(a).

14. Or. Rev. Stat. § 30.920(1).

15. Or. Rev. Stat. § 30.920(1).

16. Or. Rev. Stat. § 30.920(1)(b).

17. Or. Rev. Stat. § 30.920(1); *McCathern v. Toyota Motor Corp.*, 332 Or. 59, 77 n.15, 23 P.3d 320, 331 n.15 (2001) (*McCathern II*).

18. Or. Rev. Stat § 30.920(1)(b).

19. Or. Rev. Stat. § 30.920(3). The Legislative Assembly also directed that all of the references to sales and sellers in comments a to m be construed to apply to leases and lessors. Or. Rev. Stat. § 30.920(3).

20. Or. Rev. Stat. § 30.920(1); Restatement (Second) of Torts, § 402A, cmt. g (1965); *McCathern II*, 332 Or. at 77, 23 P.3d at 331.

21. Restatement (Second) of Torts, § 402A, cmts. g and i; *McCathern II*, 332 Or. at 77, 23 P.3d at 331.

22. Or. Rev. Stat. § 30.920(1); Restatement (Second) of Torts, § 402A, cmt. g (defining "defective"); *McCathern II*, 332 Or. at 77, 23 P.3d at 331.

23. *Ewen v. McLean Trucking Co.*, 300 Or. 24, 32, 706 P.2d 929 (1985); Or. Rev. Stat. § 30.920(1); Restatement (Second) of Torts, § 402A, cmt. i (defining "unreasonably dangerous"); *McCathern II*, 332 Or. at 77, 23 P.3d at 331.

24. Or. Rev. Stat. § 30.920(1).

25. *McCathern II*, 332 Or. at 76-77, 23 P.3d at 330. Prior to 1979, product liability claims were common-law claims. *McCathern II*, 332 Or. at 72, 23 P.3d at 328. In 1967, Oregon's Supreme Court expressly adopted the consumer expectations test contained in Section 402A of the Restatement (Second) of Torts (1965), as the standard in design defect cases. *McCathern II*, 332 Or. at 72, 23 P.3d at 328; *Heaton v. Ford Motor Co.*, 248 Or. 467, 470, 435 P.2d 806 (1967) (adopting Section 402A). However, the court later deviated from the "pure" Section 402A approach by announcing what became known as the reasonable manufacturer test in *Phillips v. Kimwood Mach. Co.*, 269 Or. 485, 525 P.2d 1033 (1974). *McCathern II*, 332 Or. at 72, 23 P.3d at 328. The *McCathern II* court concluded that the legislature intended to abrogate the reasonable manufacturer test when it enacted Or. Rev. Stat. § 30.900 *et seq. McCathern II*, 332 Or. at 76, 23 P.2d at 330. Thus, the *McCathern* court finally put the reasonable manufacturer test to rest, directing that "Oregon trial courts no longer may instruct juries according to the reasonable manufacturer test instruction approved in *Phillips*." *McCathern II*, 332 Or. at 76, 23 P.2d at 330.

26. *McCathern II*, 332 Or. at 76-77, 23 P.3d at 330 (concluding that "the consumer expectations test is the only theory of liability that ORS 30.920 expressly mandates").

27. *McCathern II*, 332 Or. at 77-78, 23 P.3d at 331; *see also Hoyt v. Vitek, Inc.*, 134 Or. App. 271, 281, 894 P.2d 1225 (1995) (stating "whether a product is defectively designed for some applications is first a question for the court to consider by balancing the product's utility against the magnitude of the risk associated with its use"); *Znaor v. Ford Motor Co.*, 213 Or. App. 191, 197, 159 P.3d 1252, 1255 (2007) (failing to identify particular design specifications to which a product failed to conform, *i.e.*, a specific manufacturing defect, is not fatal to a manufacturing defect claim. The claim may still go to the jury

if some manufacturing defect can be reasonably inferred from observations relating to the age and condition of the product, and comparison to properly manufactured examples).

28. *McCathern II*, 332 Or. at 78, 23 P.3d at 331; *Heaton*, 248 Or. at 472-74, 435 P.2d at 808-09.

29. Oregon's Court of Appeals had held that the consumer expectation test may be established under either the "representational" or "consumer risk utility" theories in *McCathern v. Toyota Motor Corp.*, 160 Or. App. 201, 218, 985 P.2d 804 (1999) ("*McCathern I*"). On appeal, Oregon's Supreme Court disagreed, concluding that "contrary to the Court of Appeals' opinion," neither the "consumer risk-utility" approach, nor the "representational" approach, are separate "theories of liability" under the consumer expectations test. *McCathern II*, 332 Or. at 79, 23 P.3d at 332.

30. *McCathern II*, 332 Or. at 78, 23 P.3d at 331.

31. *McCathern II*, 332 Or. at 79, 23 P.3d at 332. In *McCathern I*, the Court of Appeals determined that the "risk-utility" approach requires consideration of the following factors: (1) the relative cost of the product; (2) the gravity of the potential harm from the claimed defect; (3) the cost and feasibility of eliminating or minimizing the risk; and (4) other factors depending on the nature of the product or the defect. *McCathern I*, 160 Or. App. at 210 (citing *Seattle-First Nat'l Bank v. Tabert*, 86 Wash. 2d 145, 542 P.2d 774, 779 (1975) as exemplifying the consumer risk-utility analysis). Further, the *McCathern I* court determined the plaintiff must prove that a safer practicable alternative design existed. *Seattle-First Nat'l Bank*, 86 Wash. 2d at 221, 542 P.2d at 816.

32. *McCathern II*, 332 Or. at 78, 23 P.3d at 332.

33. *MaCathern II*, 332 Or. at 79, 23 P.3d at 331.

34. *See Anderson v. Klix Chem. Co.*, 256 Or. 199, 202, 472 P.2d 806, 808 (1970); Restatement (Second) of Torts, § 402A, cmts. h and j.

35. *McEwen v. Ortho Pharm. Corp.*, 270 Or. 375, 338, 528 P.2d 522, 528 (1974).

36. *Gunstone v. Blum*, 111 Or. App. 332, 335-37, 825 P.2d 1389, *rev. denied*, 313 Or. 354, 833 P.2d 1283 (1992) (finding trial court did not err in instructing jury that "a manufacturer or seller is not required to warn or instruct with regard to a danger which is generally known and recognized").

37. *Waddill v. Anchor Hocking*, 149 Or. App. 464, 473-74, 944 P.2d 957 (1997), *rev'd on other grounds by*, 330 Or. 376, 8 P.3d 200 (2000).

38. *Brizendine v. Visador Co.*, 437 F.2d 822, 826 (9th Cir. 1970).

39. Or. Rev. Stat. § 30.920; *see also Ensley v. Strato-Life, Inc.*, 116 F. Supp. 2d 1175, 2000 (D. Or. 2000) (stating that before a plaintiff is entitled to a jury determination in a products case, there must be evidence from which the jury could find that there has been no change in the condition of the product from the time of its purchase).

40. *Ensley*, 116 F. Supp. 2d at 1181.

41. *Brownell v. White Motor Corp.*, 260 Or. 251, 258, 490 P.2d 184 (1971).

42. *Gunstone*, 111 Or. App. at 337, 825 P.2d at 1393; *Helms v. Halton Tractor Co.*, 66 Or. App. 890, 893, 676 P.2d 347, 348, *rev. denied*, 297 Or. 82 (1980).

43. *Gilmour v. Norris Paint & Varnish Co., Inc.*, 52 Or. App. 179, 181, 184-85, 627 P.2d 1288 (1981).

44. *McCathern II*, 332 Or. at 81, 23 P.2d at 333 ("There was evidence from which the jury could have found that the 1996 4Runner, instead of rolling over [like the 1994 4Runner in which plaintiff was riding], would have skidded to a stop.").

45. *Baccelleri v. Hyster Co.*, 287 Or. 3, 7, 597 P.2d 351 (1979).

46. *Lyons v. Walsh & Sons Trucking Co., Ltd.*, 183 Or. App. 76, 83, 51 P.3d 625, 629 (2002); *McEwen v. Ortho Pharm. Corp.*, 270 Or. 375, 385, 528 P.2d 522, 528 (1974).

47. *Lyons*, 183 Or. App. at 83.

48. *See* Or. Rev. Stat. § 31.600 (abolishing contributory negligence standard and replacing it with comparative fault); Or. Rev. Stat. § 31.620, (abolishing doctrine of implied assumption of the risk); *Fulmer v. Timber Inn Rest. & Lounge, Inc.*, 330 Or. 413, 426, 9 P.3d 710, 717 (2000) (refusing to revive contributory negligence and assumption of the risk defenses for cases involving alcohol consumption).

49. *See* Or. Rev. Stat. § 31.600; *Hernandez v. Barbo Mach. Co.*, 327 Or. 99, 109, 957 P.2d 147 (1998); *Sandford v. Chevrolet Div. of Gen. Motors*, 292 Or. 590, 610, 642 P.2d 624 (1982).

50. *Jett v. Ford*, 192 Or. App. 113, 119, 84 P.3d 219 (2004), *on remand from* 335 Or. 493, 72 P.3d 71 (2003).

51. *Jett*, 192 Or. App. at 119, 84 P.3d 219.

52. Or. Rev. Stat. § 31.600(1)-(2).

53. Or. Rev. Stat. § 31.610(2).

54. Or. Rev. Stat. § 30.920.

55. *Tillman v. Vance Equip.*, 286 Or. 747, 596 P.2d 1299 (1979).

56. *Myers v. Cessna Aircraft Corp.*, 275 Or. 501, 553 P.2d 355 (1976).

57. *See Burkett v. Freedom Arms, Inc.*, 299 Or. 551, 556, 704 P.2d 118 (1985).

58. *Schmeiser v. Trus Joist Corp.*, 273 Or. 120, 133, 540 P.2d 998 (1975).

59. Or. Rev. State. § 30.920(3).

60. *Tyree Oil, Inc. v. Bureau of Labor & Indus.*, 168 Or. App. 278, 282, 7 P.3d 571, 573 (2000) (citing *Erickson v. Grande Ronde Lumber Co.*, 162 Or. 556, 568, 92 P.2d 170, *reh'g denied*, 162 Or. 579, 94 P.2d 139 (1939)).

61. *Tyree Oil, Inc.*, 168 Or. App. at 283.

62. Or. Rev. Stat. § 30.920(2)(b).

63. Or. Rev. Stat. § 30.920(2)(b).

64. *See, e.g., Sealey v. Hicks*, 309 Or. 387, 399, 788 P.2d 435, 441 (1990), *overruled in part on unrelated grounds by Smothers*, 332 Or. at 123; *Erickson Air-Crane v. United Tech. Corp.*, 79 Or. App. 659, 720 P.2d 389 (1986), *rev'd on other grounds*, 303 Or. 281, 735 P.2d 614 (1987).

65. *Simonsen v. Ford*, 196 Or. App. 460, 102 P.3d 710 (2004), *rev. denied*, 338 Or. 681, 115 P.3d 246 (2005).

66. *McEwen*, 270 Or. at 386-87, 528 P.2d at 529.

67. *McEwen*, 270 Or. at 386-87, 528 P.2d at 529.

68. *Oksenholt v. Lederle Lab.*, 51 Or. App. 419, 425-26, 625 P.2d 1357 (1981), *aff'd as modified*, 294 Or. 213, 656 P.2d 293 (1982).

69. *Oksenholt*, 51 Or. App. at, 425-26, 625 P.2d 1357; *McEwen*, 270 Or. at 387.

70. *Griffith v. Blatt*, 334 Or. 456, 51 P.3d 1256 (2002).

71. *Findlay v. Copeland Lumber Co.*, 265 Or. 300, 306, 509 P.2d 28, 31 (1973).

72. *Findlay*, 265 Or. at 306, 509 P.2d at 31.

73. *Findlay*, 265 Or. at 306, 509 P.2d at 31.

74. *Burkett v. Freedom Arms, Inc.*, 299 Or. at 558, 704 P.2d at 122; *Findlay v. Copeland Lumber*, 265 Or. 300, 509 P.2d 28 (1973).

75. Or. Rev. Stat. § 30.915.

76. Or. Rev. Stat. § 30.915(3). *See also Lavoie v. Power Auto, Inc.*, 259 Or. App. 90, 101-03, 312 P.3d 601, 607-08 (2013) (holding that under the modification defense, foreseeability of consumer utilizing aftermarket floor mats and dangers posed by same was jury question).

77. *See Hoyt v. Vitek, Inc.*, 134 Or. App. 271, 282, 894 P.2d 1225, 1231 (1995) (recognizing that comment j "requires that the seller give warning if the seller 'has knowledge, or by the application of reasonably developed human skill and foresight should have knowledge,' of the danger").

78. *O'Lander v. Int'l Harvester Co.*, 260 Or. 383, 390, 490 P.2d 1002, 1005 (1971).

79. *Cole v. Ford Motor Co.*, 136 Or. App. 45, 52-53, 900 P.2d 1059 (1995).

80. *Hagan v. Gemstate Mfg., Inc.*, 328 Or. 535, 542-43, 982 P.2d 1108, 1112-13 (1999).

81. *Hansen v. Abrasive Eng'g & Mfg., Inc.*, 317 Or. 378, 384, 856 P.2d 625, 628 (1993).

82. *Hagan*, 328 Or. at 542, 982 P.2d at 1112.

83. *Hagan*, 328 Or. at 542-43, 982 P.2d at 1112-13.

84. *Hagan*, at 543, 982 P.2d at 1113.

85. *Davis v. Homasote Co.*, 281 Or. 383, 387, 574 P.2d 1116, 1118 (1978). *But see Oberg v. Honda Motor Co. Ltd.*, 316 Or. 263, 851 P.2d 1084 (1993), *rev'd, remanded on other grounds*, 512 U.S. 415 (1994) (treating "substantial similarity" broadly and approving trial court's admission of Consumer Product Safety Commission records associated with accidents of other-but-similar products and accidents where alleged design defect was common to all such products and allegedly demonstrated by the records).

86. *Russell v. Ford Motor Co.*, 281 Or. 587, 595-96, 575 P.2d. 1383, 1387 (1978); *see also Bancorp Leasing & Fin. Corp. v. Agusta Aviation Corp.*, 813 F.2d 272, 277 (9th Cir. 1987) (finding that, under Oregon law, a claim remains a products liability claim even though the only property damage is to the product itself). *Compare City of Medford v. Budge-Hugh Supply Co.*, 91 Or. App. 213, 221, 754 P.2d 607, 610, *rev. denied*, 306 Or. 661, 763 P.2d 152 (1988) (defect in pipe that caused it to fail did not threaten personal safety, and plaintiff could not recover in strict liability to repair or replace it), *with Gladhart v. Oregon Vineyard Supply Co.*, 164 Or. App. 438, 453-54, 994 P.2d 134 (1999), *rev'd on other grounds*, 332 Or. 226, 26 P.3d 817 (2001) (distinguishing *Budge-Hugh*,

and finding that damages arising from defect in grape plants that allegedly caused damage to other plants in the vineyard gave rise to a cognizable product liability claim).

87. *Russell*, 281 Or. at 593-95, 575 P.2d at 1386-87.

88. *See Russell*, 281 Or. at 593-95, 575 P.2d at 1386-87; *Budge-Hugh*, 91 Or. App. at 220-21, 754 P.2d at 610-11.

89. *Hoyt v. Vitek*, 134 Or. App. 271, 287, 894 P.2d 1225 (1995) (quoting *Fazzolari v. Portland Sch. Dist. No. 1J*, 303 Or. 1, 17, 734 P.2d 1326 (1987)).

90. *Hoyt*, 134 Or. App. at 287, 894 P.2d at 1225.

91. Or. Rev. Stat. § 30.920(1)-(3).

92. Or. Rev. Stat. § 72.3130.

93. *B. W. Feed Co. Inc. v. Gen. Equip. Co.*, 44 Or. App. 285, 605 P.2d 1205 (1980); Or. Rev. Stat. §§ 72.1040(1) and 72.3140.

94. *Swan Island Sheet Metal Works v. Troy's Custom Smoking Co.*, 49 Or. App. 469, 619 P.2d 1326 (1980); Or. Rev. Stat. § 72.3150.

95. *Larrison v. Moving Floors, Inc.*, 127 Or. App. 720, 724, 873 P.2d 1092, 1094 (1994).

96. *Larrison*, 127 Or. App. at 724, 873 P.2d at 1094.

97. *Dravo Equip. Co. v. German*, 73 Or. App. 165, 169-70, 698 P.2d 63, 65 (1984).

98. *Colvin v. FMC Corp.*, 43 Or. App. 709, 716, 604 P.2d 157, 160 (1979).

99. *See* Or. Rev. Stat. §§ 72.8020, 72.8030.

100. Or. Rev. Stat. § 72.3180.

101. Or. Rev. Stat. § 30.925.

102. Or. Rev. Stat. § 30.927.

103. Or. Rev. Stat. § 31.725(1) and (2).

104. Or. Rev. Stat. § 31.725(2).

105. Or. Rev. Stat. § 31.725(2).

106. Or. Rev. Stat. § 31.725(3)(b) applies to lawsuits commenced on or after January 1, 2004.

107. *Bolt v. Influence, Inc.*, 333 Or. 572, 580, 43 P.3d 425, 429 (2002).

108. *Bolt*, 333 Or. at 582.

109. Or. Rev. Stat. § 31.730(1).

110. Or. Rev. Stat. § 30.925(2)(a)-(g). The criteria are: (a) the likelihood at the time that serious harm would arise from the defendant's misconduct; (b) the degree of the defendant's awareness of that likelihood; (c) the profitability of the defendant's misconduct; (d) the duration of the misconduct and any concealment of it; (e) the attitude and conduct of the defendant upon discovery of the misconduct; (f) the financial condition of the defendant; and (g) the total deterrent effect of other punishment imposed upon the defendant as a result of the misconduct, including, but not limited to, punitive damage awards to persons in situations similar to the claimant's which the defendant has been or may be subjected.

111. Or. Rev. Stat. § 30.927.

112. *Parrott v. Carr Chevrolet, Inc.*, 331 Or. 537, 555, 17 P.3d 473 (2001).

113. *Bocci v. Key Pharms., Inc.*, 189 Or. App. 349, 352, 76 P.3d 669, 671 (2003).

114. *Schwarz v. Philip Morris, Inc.*, 206 Or. App. 20, 49, 135 P.3d 409, 429 (2006).

115. Or. Rev. Stat. § 31.730(2).

116. *Vasquez-Lopez v. Beneficial Or. Inc.*, 210 Or. App. 553, 588, 152 P.3d 553, 558 (2007).

117. *Erickson Air-Crane Co. v. United Techs. Corp.*, 87 Or. App. 577, 582, 743 P.2d 747 (1987), *rev. denied*, 304 Or. 680, 748 P.2d 142 (1987).

118. *Smith v. Williams*, 98 Or. App. 258, 263, 779 P.2d 1057 (1989).

119. *Smith*, 98 Or. App. at 263, 779 P.2d 1057; *Tift v. Stevens*, 162 Or. App. 62, 82, 987 P.2d 1, 12 (1999) (following *Smith v. Williams*); *Robertson v. Jessup*, 117 Or. App. 460, 466, 845 P.2d 926, 930 (1992) (same); *see also Monte Carpenter v. Land O' Lakes, Inc.*, 985 F. Supp. 1249 (D.C. Or. 1997) (citing *Klokke Corp. v. Classic Exposition, Inc.*, 139 Or. App. 399, 410, 912 P.2d 929, *rev. denied*, 323 Or. 690, 920 P.2d 549 (1996); Or. Rev. Stat. § 82.010(1)(a)).

120. *See, e.g., Erickson Air-Crane Co.*, 87 Or. App. at 582.

121. Or. Rev. Stat. § 82.010(2)(a); *Butler v. Oregon Dep't of Corrections*, 138 Or. App. 190, 206-07, 909 P.2d 163, 173-74 (1995).

122. Or. Rev. Stat. § 82.010(2)(e).

123. Or. Rev. Stat. § 82.010(2)(c); *see also State Hwy. Comm'n*, 275 Or. 351, 357, 551 P.2d 102 (1976).

124. Or. Rev. Stat. § 82.020(2)(d).

125. *Morse Bros., Inc. v. Kemp Constr., Inc.*, 147 Or. App. 217, 223-24, 935 P.2d 464 (1997).

126. Or. Rev. Stat. § 31.610(1).

127. *Irwin Yacht Sales, Inc. v. Carver Boat Corp.*, 98 Or. App. 195, 198, 778 P.2d 982 (1989).

128. *Irwin Yacht Sales, Inc.*, 98 Or. App. at 198, 778 P.2d 982.

129. Or. Rev. Stat. § 656.018; *Hanson v. Versarail Sys., Inc.*, 175 Or. App. 92, 96, 28 P.3d 626, 627 (2001).

130. Or. Rev. Stat. §§ 656.156(2); 656.018(3)(a); *Hanson v. Versarail Sys., Inc.*, 175 Or. App. at 96, 28 P.3d at 628.

131. *See Smothers v. Gresham Transfer, Inc.*, 332 Or. 83, 23 P.3d 333 (2001); *Storm v. McClung*, 334 Or. 210, 47 P.3d 476 (2002).

132. Or. Rev. Stat. § 109.510.

PENNSYLVANIA

A. CAUSES OF ACTION

Product liability lawsuits commonly include causes of action for strict liability, negligence, and breach of warranty.[1]

B. STATUTES OF LIMITATION

Causes of action brought in negligence or strict liability for personal injuries[2] or property damage[3] must be brought within two years. An equitable "discovery rule" applies.[4] A cause of action seeking personal injuries or property damage resulting from a breach of warranty must be brought within four years of the date of sale.[5] The discovery rule does not apply to breach of warranty claims.[6]

A 12-year statute of repose is applicable to claims involving improvements to real property.[7] Generally, manufacturers are not a part of the class intended to be protected by the statute of repose in actions for personal injuries.[8] However, manufacturers are protected by the statute of repose when they supply "individual expertise" to the design of an improvement to real property.[9]

C. STRICT LIABILITY

1. The Standard

In November 2014, the Pennsylvania Supreme Court affirmed in *Tincher v. Omega Flex, Inc.* that Pennsylvania will continue to follow Section 402A of the Restatement (Second) of Torts.[10] That opinion also overruled its 1978 opinion in *Azzarello*.[11] *Azzarello*, along with its progeny, removed negligence concepts from strict liability cases to an unusual degree which proved difficult in practice, and had removed from the jury the determination of whether the product was "unreasonably dangerous."[12] The *Tincher* opinion explicitly rejected adoption of the Restatement (Third) of Torts: Products Liability as problematic.[13]

A product seller "has a duty to make and/or market the product—which 'is expected to and does reach the user or consumer without substantial change in the condition in which it is sold'—free from 'a defective condition unreasonably dangerous to the consumer or [the consumer's] property.'"[14]

Tincher recognizes that it left open many questions related to strict liability law.[15] Based on judicial modesty, the *Tincher* court was content to permit the common law to develop incrementally.[16]

Strict liability claims have been disallowed in cases involving prescription drugs and prescription medical devices.[17] This preclusion has been applied to bar all strict liability claims, including design defect, manufacturing defect, and failure to warn claims.[18] In cases involving prescription drugs and prescription medical devices, however, claims sounding in negligence have been permitted.[19] For practical purposes in these cases, there is no distinction between the negligent failure to warn and a failure to warn theory grounded on principles of strict liability.

In some circumstances the doctrine of *res ipsa loquitur* may allow a jury to infer the existence of a manufacturing defect or negligence where injury would not have otherwise ordinarily occurred.[20] Reminiscent of *res ipsa loquitur*, the malfunction theory can be used to establish a defect from merely circumstantial evidence that the product had a defect, even though the defect cannot be identified.[21]

2. **Definition of Defect**

In *Tincher*, the Pennsylvania Supreme Court adopted a composite consumer expectation/risk-utility approach largely based on California case law.[22] In a design defect case, a plaintiff may prove a product is in a "defective condition" by showing that the danger is unknowable and unacceptable to the ordinary consumer or proving that a reasonable person would conclude that the probability and seriousness of harm caused by the product outweigh the burden or costs of taking precautions.[23]

The Court recognized its decision to overrule *Azzarello* and articulate a composite consumer expectation/risk-utility approach may have an impact on manufacturing and failure to warn claims, but left this analysis to another day.[24]

3. **Alternative Safer Design**

Evidence related to an alternative design is relevant and probative to prove disputed issues such as technological feasibility, cost, etc., but plaintiff's failure to produce such evidence is not necessarily dispositive.[25] Prior to *Tincher*, evidence of a feasible alternative safer design was required in crashworthiness cases and occasionally in other cases.[26]

4. **Causation**

It is the plaintiff's burden in any product liability case to demonstrate that the injuries sustained were substantially caused by the product's defect.[27] However, assumption of the risk, product misuse, and highly reckless conduct do not merely negate causation, but have been held to be affirmative defenses.[28] In a failure to warn case, the undisclosed risk must manifest itself into actual injury in order to establish proximate causation.[29]

5. **Contributory Negligence/Assumption of Risk**

    Contributory negligence and comparative negligence are not defenses to a strict liability claim,[30] but assumption of risk is an available affirmative defense.[31] Similar to the defense of assumption of risk are the affirmative defenses of product misuse and highly reckless conduct.[32] Evidence of contributory negligence would probably not be admitted in strict liability cases, even as it relates to causation, unless the plaintiff's act initiated the accident.[33] The form of assumption of risk adopted is that the plaintiff knew and understood the specific danger and potential for serious injury and yet voluntarily chose to encounter it.[34] Where an employee is required to use a product furnished by his employer to perform his job, the defense of assumption of risk is unavailable[35] unless the employee misused the allegedly defective product in a manner contrary to training and instructions from the employer.[36]

6. **Sale or Lease/Persons Liable**

    The plaintiff must allege a sale or other commercial transaction of the product by the defendant.[37] Possible defendants that could be held liable are those who market products by sale, lease, or bailment.[38] Strict liability applies to any seller in the chain of a product's distribution.[39] However, the supplier must be in the business of supplying such products.[40] Under some circumstances, a distributor may obtain indemnity from the manufacturer.[41]

    Generally, strict liability applies to lessors who are in the business of supplying products.[42] The occasional seller of a product may avoid liability under Section 402A of the Restatement (Second) of Torts.[43]

7. **Inherently Dangerous Products**

    A supplier of inherently dangerous products will not be held strictly liable simply because the product is inherently dangerous, unless it fails to give adequate warning of the danger.[44]

8. **Successor Liability**

    A successor corporation acquiring all or substantially all of the manufacturing assets of another corporation and continuing the same product line may be liable for injuries caused by products made by the predecessor corporation.[45] Lack of a remedy against the predecessor corporation is a prerequisite to an action against the successor.[46]

9. **Market Share Liability/Enterprise Liability**

    Market share liability and enterprise liability have been rejected in the Commonwealth of Pennsylvania.[47]

10. **Privity**

No privity is required; plaintiffs may sue even though they did not buy the product from the manufacturer.[48]

11. **Failure to Warn**

Whether a warning is adequate and whether a product is defective due to inadequate warnings are questions of law for the trial judge.[49] If the plaintiffs rely on a theory of failure to warn, they must prove that the absence of the warning was a cause of the loss.[50]

If an adequate warning is provided, it can be presumed that the end user would have read and heeded the adequate warning.[51] In Pennsylvania, the corollary is sometimes followed, so if no warning or an inadequate warning is provided, it may be presumed that the end-user would have read and heeded an adequate warning had one been given by the manufacturer.[52] To rebut the presumption in Pennsylvania, the defendant should produce evidence that the plaintiff fully understood the risks, so that a warning would be futile because the plaintiff would already know, or that the plaintiff ignored an adequate warning given later.[53]

12. **Post-Sale Duty to Warn and Remedial Measures**

Generally, a manufacturer does not have a post-sale duty to recall or to warn about technological advances when a defect did not exist in the product at the time of sale.[54] Under limited circumstances, a manufacturer may have a post-sale duty to warn, such as when a component manufacturer advises of a defect and a manufacturer fails to pass such information along to the customer.[55] A manufacturer or supplier has a duty to stop distribution of a product once it knows or should know that it is too dangerous to be used.[56] Normally, post-manufacture remedial measures by the defendant are not admissible.[57] Subsequent design changes may be admissible to prove the feasibility of an alternate design or for impeachment.[58]

13. **Learned Intermediary Doctrine/Sophisticated User Defense**

A seller of prescription drug products and vaccines has a duty to exercise reasonable care to inform users of the facts that make a product dangerous.[59] A seller of such products may satisfy its duty to warn by furnishing adequate warnings and instructions to the prescribing physician, but is not required to give them directly to the patient.[60]

Pennsylvania law recognizes that a supplier of raw materials for a medical device may reasonably rely on a sophisticated intermediary to warn users about the dangers of its product.[61]

14. **Substantial Alteration/Abnormal Use**

    A manufacturer is not responsible for injuries caused by a substantial change in the product that occurs after initial sale.[62] But the substantial change must have caused the injury and be one that could not reasonably be foreseen or expected.[63]

    Assumption of the risk, product misuse, abnormal use, and highly reckless conduct are available affirmative defenses.[64]

15. **State of the Art**

    "State-of-the-art" evidence is generally not available as a defense to strict liability claims.[65]

16. **Malfunction**

    A malfunction of a product in the absence of evidence of abnormal use or reasonable secondary causes is evidence of a defect.[66]

17. **Standards and Governmental Regulations**

    Evidence that the product complied with customary standards or industry standards is usually inadmissible in a strict liability action with respect to the issue of defect.[67] However, evidence of industry standards or regulations is admissible in an action grounded in negligence,[68] or in a strict liability action in which negligence is also alleged.[69]

18. **Other Accidents**

    Evidence of other accidents is inadmissible unless plaintiff proves that the product is the same and there is substantial factual similarity in time, place, and circumstance. Evidence of lack of prior claims or accidents may be admissible to rebut causation.[70]

19. **Misrepresentation**

    Section 402B of the Restatement (Second) of Torts has been adopted in Pennsylvania.[71] That section imposes strict liability on a manufacturer for physical harm to a consumer caused by justifiable reliance on a misrepresentation of a material fact as to the character or quality of a product.

20. **Destruction or Loss of Product**

    Pennsylvania courts often impose sanctions against parties when the product at issue has been altered, lost or destroyed. Whether sanctions are appropriate and the level of sanctions warranted is determined by: (1) the degree of fault of the party who altered or destroyed the evidence; (2) the degree of prejudice suffered by the opposing party; and (3) the degree of sanction necessary to avoid substantial unfairness to the opposing party and, if the opposing party is seriously at fault, to deter such conduct by others in the future.[72] When they have found spoliation, courts have disposed of cases on summary judgment when the plaintiff is relying on a manufacturing defect[73] and have imposed less severe sanctions depending upon the facts and circumstances of each particular case.[74] Where plaintiff is relying on a design defect, however, the case will likely proceed if defendant is able to inspect a product identical to the one no longer available.[75]

There is not an independent cause of action for negligent spoliation, nor negligence based on spoliation.[76]

21. Economic Loss

The economic loss rule maintains the distinction between tort and contract actions and its application depends on whether the source of the duty owed to a plaintiff arises from tort or contract.[77] Under this rule, no cause of action exists for negligence that results solely in economic damages unaccompanied by physical injury or property damage.[78]

22. Crashworthiness/Enhanced Injuries

The "crashworthiness" or "second collision" doctrine, which is a subset of a cause of action for products liability under Section 402A, provides that the manufacturer/seller is liable when the defect increases the severity of an injury over that which would have occurred absent the design defect, even though the defect did not cause the accident or initial impact.[79] To prevail, a plaintiff must demonstrate (1) proof of an alternative safer design that is practicable under the circumstances, (2) the resulting injuries if the safer design had been used, and (3) the extent of the enhanced injuries attributable to the defective design.[80] Thus, a manufacturer has to include accidents among the intended uses of its product and has a legal duty to design and manufacture its product to be reasonably safe in a crash.[81]

If both the initial accident and the defect are found to be substantial factors in the resulting harm, both tortfeasors can be held jointly and severally liable.[82]

D. NEGLIGENCE

Unlike strict liability, there are few unique aspects of Pennsylvania product liability cases based on negligence.[83] A cause of action based on negligence may well be broader in scope than one based on strict liability. Thus, a manufacturer may be responsible in negligence for a foreseeable injury to an unintended user even though the product is found not to be defective under a strict liability theory.[84] A plaintiff can maintain a claim for negligent design and negligent marketing of a prescription drug even though the drug could not be deemed defective to support a strict liability claim.[85]

Comparative negligence applies unless the plaintiff is more than 50 percent at fault, in which event recovery is barred.[86]

E. BREACH OF WARRANTY

A cause of action for breach of warranty is generally quite similar to a strict liability cause of action.[87] However, with respect to the statute of limitations, the "discovery rule" does not apply to warranty actions.[88]

F. PUNITIVE DAMAGES

Punitive damages are recoverable in actions in strict liability[89] and negligence,[90] but not in lawsuits sounding only in breach of warranty.[91]

G. PRE- AND POST-JUDGMENT INTEREST

Pre-judgment interest is provided by rule of court and is characterized as delay damages.[92] In actions for personal injury and property damage, delay damages begin to accrue one year after service of original process on the original defendant and continue until verdict.[93] Delay damages are calculated using the prime interest rate listed in the first *Wall Street Journal* of each calendar year, plus 1 percent, not compounded.[94] Given the backlog in some Pennsylvania trial courts, delay damages can constitute a significant element of damages.

Accrual of delay damages ceases for periods in which the plaintiff has caused delay of trial or after the defendant makes a settlement offer amounting to at least 80 percent of the eventual verdict.[95] Joint and several tortfeasors are jointly and severally liable for delay damages.[96] However, amounts paid by settling joint tortfeasors are deducted from the verdict prior to calculation of delay damages.[97]

Plaintiff is entitled to interest on a judgment from the date of the verdict.[98] Post-judgment interest is calculated at the statutory rate of six percent.[99]

H. EMPLOYEE IMMUNITY

The Pennsylvania Workers' Compensation Act's "exclusive remedy provision" exempts the plaintiff's employer from liability and from being joined as a party to an action for an employee's injuries.[100] If, however, the employer deals with the employee in "dual capacities," the employee may be able to sue the employer for tortious conduct arising from the non-employer capacity, unless the employee's compensable injury occurs while he is actually engaged in the performance of his job.[101] Additionally, an employer may contractually obligate itself to defend and indemnify a product manufacturer, provided that the employer expressly agrees to be liable for indemnification and contribution in a written contract prior to the injury.[102] Although there generally is immunity from liability for the intentional torts of the employer,[103] where an employee is claiming that his or her injuries were aggravated by the employer's intentional conduct, the employee can maintain a common law cause of action against the employer.[104]

I. **STATUTES**

Relevant statutes for product liability actions include the statutes of limitation and the commercial code sections when a breach of warranty is alleged.[105]

J. **JOINT AND SEVERAL LIABILITY**

1. **The Rule**

   a. **Claims Accruing On or After June 28, 2011**

   For claims that accrued on or after June 28, 2011,[106] each defendant is only liable for the proportion of the total dollar amount awarded as damages for which that defendant has been apportioned liability.[107] However, joint and several liability still applies to a defendant if, inter alia, that defendant is found liable for intentional misrepresentation, an intentional tort, or that defendant has been held liable for 60 percent or more of the total liability apportioned to all parties.[108] A defendant held jointly and severally liable can seek contribution from other defendants.[109]

   b. **Claims That Accrued Before June 28, 2011**

   Under the prior Comparative Negligence Act, multiple defendants may be found jointly and severally liable for claims that accrued before June 28, 2011.[110] On such claims, tortfeasors are considered joint if they acted together or separately to cause a single, indivisible harm[111] and each joint tortfeasor is individually responsible for all harm brought about by the joint tortfeasors, regardless of comparative fault.[112] Joint tortfeasor status is a question of law to be determined by the court.[113]

2. **Effect of Settlement**

   In a simple case in which a manufacturer settles a strict liability defective product claim with a plaintiff, the settlement discharges the plaintiff's same claim against a distributor of that product when a distributor is only a conduit.[114]

   Pennsylvania has adopted the Uniform Contribution Among Tortfeasors Act (UCATA).[115] UCATA applies only to joint tortfeasors; it allows for the following three types of releases:

   A "general" release discharges the liability of the settling joint tortfeasor and all others even though the others have made no payment in settlement for the release.[116] In "subsequent medical malpractice" cases, a general release of the original tortfeasor can bar a claim against the subsequent health care provider even though the original tortfeasor and the health care provider are not considered joint tortfeasors.[117]

   A "pro tanto" release, or "dollar-for-dollar" release, discharges only the settling joint tortfeasor; it does, however, reduce the liability of the non-settling joint tortfeasors by the amount the settling joint tortfeasor paid to be released.[118]

A "pro rata" release also discharges only the settling joint tortfeasor; it then reduces the liability of the non-settling tortfeasors by the settling joint tortfeasor's proportionate share of liability.[119] In cases based solely on strict liability, the joint tortfeasors' *pro rata* shares of liability are allocated on a *per capita* basis.[120] In cases involving negligent tortfeasors and strictly liable tortfeasors, the *pro rata* shares of liability of each tortfeasor, negligent and strictly liable alike, are exactly the same as their proportionate shares of liability.[121] But in cases involving both negligent tortfeasors and strictly liable tortfeasors in which the plaintiff is found comparatively negligent, the strictly liable tortfeasor is responsible for its own proportionate share of the liability as well as the liability share assigned to the comparatively negligent plaintiff.[122]

3. **Contribution**

A joint tortfeasor compelled to pay more than its percentage share of liability may seek contribution from the other joint tortfeasors.[123]

Apportionment of liability between defendant tortfeasors who are only found strictly liable and not negligent is on a *pro rata* basis (*i.e.*, the total liability divided by the number of defendants).[124] Where defendants are only found strictly liable, the comparative negligence of the plaintiff is irrelevant and may not be used to reduce the responsibility of the strictly liable defendant for the entire damages award.[125]

On the other hand, Pennsylvania allows apportionment of damages based on causal fault among defendants who are found jointly and severally liable based on negligence.[126]

Apportionment is also possible where liability is based on both negligence and strict liability.[127] Where there is at least one negligent defendant and one strictly liable defendant, apportionment is determined by the percentage of fault of each defendant.[128] Thus, a strictly liable defendant is liable to the plaintiff for the entire verdict, without reducing the amount to account for any comparative fault of the plaintiff, but may seek contribution from the negligent defendant in the amount of the negligent defendant's percentage share of fault (*i.e.*, the strictly liable defendant ultimately pays its percentage share of fault and the plaintiff's share of fault).[129]

A settling joint tortfeasor who receives a "general" release specifically discharging its own liability and the liability of all others has a right of contribution against other joint tortfeasors.[130]

A settling joint tortfeasor who receives a *pro tanto* release has no right of contribution against others.[131] In the event the amount paid by the settling joint tortfeasor is less than its proportionate share of the liability, however, the non-settling joint tortfeasor has a claim for contribution against the settling joint tortfeasor for the difference between what the settling joint tortfeasor actually paid and what its proportionate liability would have required it to pay.[132]

Under a *pro rata* release, neither the settling joint tortfeasor nor the non-settling joint tortfeasors has a right of contribution against the other.[133]

Morton F. Daller
Cell Phone: (215) 738-3800
Mort.Daller@gmail.com

Gerhard P. Dietrich
Paul D. Lux
Ward Greenberg Heller & Reidy LLP
1835 Market Street, Suite 650
Philadelphia, PA 19103
(215) 836-1100/(215) 836-2845 (Fax)
gdietrich@wardgreenberg.com
plux@wardgreenberg.com

ENDNOTES - PENNSYLVANIA

1. *See Knipe v. SmithKline Beecham*, 583 F. Supp. 2d 602, 614 (E.D. Pa. 2008) ("Pennsylvania courts allow claims of negligence and breach of implied warranty to be brought in conjunction with a products [strict] liability claim."); *Lance v. Wyeth*, 85 A.3d 434, 461 (Pa. 2014) ("[N]egligent design defect claims long have been recognized against product manufacturers generally in this Commonwealth."); *Phillips v. Cricket Lighters*, 883 A.2d 439, 445 n.6 (Pa. 2005) ("[W]e reject Appellants' invitation that we hold that strict liability and implied breach of warranty claims are coterminous.").

2. 42 Pa. Cons. Stat. Ann. § 5524(2).

3. 42 Pa. Cons. Stat. Ann. § 5524(3).

4. *Moyer v. United Dominion Indus., Inc.*, 473 F.3d 532, 547-48 (3d Cir. 2007); *Vitalo v. Cabot Corp.*, 399 F.3d 536, 542-45 (3d Cir. 2005); *Debiec v. Cabot Corp.*, 352 F.3d 117, 129 (3d Cir. 2003); *Gleason v. Borough of Moosic*, 15 A.3d 479, 484-88 (Pa. 2011); *Cochran v. GAF Corp.*, 666 A.2d 245, 248-49 (Pa. 1995); *Romah v. Hygienic Sanitation Co.*, 705 A.2d 841, 858 (Pa. Super. 1997), *aff'd*, 737 A.2d 249 (Pa. 1999).

5. 42 Pa. Cons. Stat. Ann. § 5525; 13 Pa. Cons. Stat. Ann. § 2725; *Floyd v. Brown & Williamson Tobacco Corp.*, 159 F. Supp. 2d 823 (E.D. Pa. 2001); *Cucchi v. Rollins Protective Servs. Co.*, 574 A.2d 565 (Pa. 1990); *Williams v. W. Penn. Power Co.*, 467 A.2d 811 (Pa. 1983); *Patton v. Mack Trucks, Inc.*, 519 A.2d 959 (Pa. Super. 1986).

6. *McCracken v. Ford Motor Co.*, 588 F. Supp. 2d 635, 642 (E.D. Pa. 2008) (citing *Nationwide Ins. Co. v. Gen. Motors Corp.*, 625 A.2d 1172, 1174 (Pa. 1993)).

7. 42 Pa. Cons. Stat. Ann. § 5536; *Freeman v. Paco Corp.*, 2000 WL 709481, at *2 (E.D. Pa. June 1, 2000); *Vargo v. Koppers Co., Inc., Eng'g & Constr. Div.*, 715 A.2d 423, 425-26 (Pa. 1998); *Noll v. Harrisburg Area YMCA*, 643 A.2d 81, 84 (Pa. 1994); *McCormick v. Columbus Conveyor Co.*, 564 A.2d 907, 908-09 (Pa. 1989).

8. *Noll v. Harrisburg Area YMCA*, 643 A.2d 81, 85 (Pa. 1994).

9. *Noll v. Harrisburg Area YMCA*, 643 A.2d 81, 86 (Pa. 1994).

10. *Tincher v. Omega Flex, Inc.*, 2014 Pa. LEXIS 3031 (Pa. Nov. 19, 2014). The majority opinion is available at http://www.pacourts.us/assets/opinions/Supreme/out/J-80-2013mo%20-%201020173292832303.pdf.

11. *Tincher v. Omega Flex, Inc.*, Slip Op. at 1, 75 (overruling *Azzarello v. Black Bros. Co.*, 391 A.2d 1020 (Pa. 1978)).

12. *Tincher v. Omega Flex, Inc.*, Slip Op. at 1, 75 (discussing *Azzarello v. Black Bros. Co.*, 391 A.2d 1020 (Pa. 1978)).

13. *Tincher v. Omega Flex, Inc.*, Slip Op. at 2, 109-10.

14. *Tincher v. Omega Flex, Inc.*, Slip Op. at 88 (citing Restatement (Second) of Torts § 402A(1)).

15. *Tincher v. Omega Flex, Inc.*, Slip Op. at 129, 134-36.

16. *Tincher v. Omega Flex, Inc.*, Slip Op. at 129, 134-36.

17. *See Lance v. Wyeth*, 85 A.3d 434, 453 (Pa. 2014) ("[F]or policy reasons this Court has declined to extend strict liability into the prescription drug arena . . . ."); *Hahn v. Richter*, 673 A.2d 888, 889-90 (Pa. 1996) ("Comment k [to section 402A], titled 'Unavoidably unsafe products,' denies application of strict liability to products such as prescription drugs. . . ."); *Terrell v. Davol, Inc.*, 2014 U.S. Dist. LEXIS 103695, at *14 (E.D. Pa. July 30, 2014) ("In accordance with Pennsylvania law, federal district courts have held that in the case of prescription drugs and devices, strict liability claims based on all three defective conditions, including manufacturing defects, are barred in Pennsylvania.").

18. *See Terrell v. Davol, Inc.*, 2014 U.S. Dist. LEXIS 103695, at *18 (E.D. Pa. July 30, 2014).

19. *See Lance v. Wyeth*, 85 A.3d 434, 458 (Pa. 2014); *Terrell v. Davol, Inc.*, 2014 U.S. Dist. LEXIS 103695, at *24-33 (E.D. Pa. July 30, 2014).

20. *Bearfield v. Hauch*, 595 A.2d 1320 (Pa. Super. 1991); *Pullicino v. Perdue Farms Inc.*, 16 Pa. D. & C.4th 469, 473 (Pa. Com. Pl. 1993).

21. *Barnish v. KWI Bldg. Co.*, 980 A.2d 535, 541-42 (Pa. 2009); *Ellis v. Beemiller, Inc.*, 910 F. Supp. 2d 768, 778-79 (W.D. Pa. 2012).

22. *Tincher v. Omega Flex, Inc.*, Slip Op. at 2, 122-33 (citing *Barker v. Lull Engineering Co.*, 573 P.2d 443 (Cal. 1978) and *Soule v. Gen. Motors Corp.*, 882 P.2d 298 (Cal. 1994). The *Tincher* court declined to adopt the burden shifting of *Barker* and *Soule* when risk-utility is at issue.

23. *Tincher v. Omega Flex, Inc.*, Slip Op. at 2, 130.

24. *Tincher v. Omega Flex, Inc.*, Slip Op. at 135.

25. *Tincher v. Omega Flex, Inc.*, Slip Op. at 113, 115.

26. *See Duchess v. Langston Corp.*, 769 A.2d 1131, 1149 n.24 (Pa. 2001) (citing 63A Am. Jur. 2d *Products Liability* § 1095 (1997) (explaining that "[t]he reasonableness of choosing from among various alternative product designs and adopting the safest one if it is feasible is not only relevant in a design defect action, but is at the very heart of the case")); *United States v. Union Corp.*, 277 F. Supp. 2d 478, 492 (E.D. Pa. 2003) ("Liability for a design defect attaches where there is a discrepancy between the design of a product causing injury and an alternative specification that would have avoided the injury."); *Martinez v. Triad Controls, Inc.*, 593 F. Supp. 2d 741, 756 n.12 (E.D. Pa. 2009) ("While appropriate in a crashworthiness case, the 'feasible alternative design' standard has no place in a standard design defect case, in which 'the focus must remain . . . on whether the product at issue contains all of the elements necessary to make it safe for its intended use.'").

27. *Parks v. Allied Signal, Inc.*, 113 F.3d 1327, 1331 (3d Cir. 1997); *Blancha v. Raymark Indus.*, 972 F.2d 507, 513 (3d Cir. 1992); *Jacobini v. V&O Press Co.*, 588 A.2d 476, 479 (Pa. 1991); *Sherk v. Daisy-Heddon*, 450 A.2d 615, 617 (Pa. 1982).

28. *See Reott v. Asia Trend, Inc.*, 55 A.3d 1088, 1097 n.10, 1101 (Pa. 2012).

29. *Cochran v. Wyeth, Inc.*, 3 A.3d 673, 680 (Pa. Super. 2010), *appeal denied*, 20 A.3d 1209 (Pa. 2011).

30. *Parks v. Allied Signal, Inc.*, 113 F.3d 1327, 1334 (3d Cir. 1997); *Dillinger v. Caterpillar, Inc.*, 959 F.2d 430, 437 (3d Cir. 1992); *Davis v. R.H. Dwyer Indus., Inc.*, 548 F. Supp. 667, 670 (E.D. Pa. 1982); *Gaudio v. Ford Motor Co.*, 976 A.2d 524, 540 (Pa. Super. 2009), *appeal denied*, 989 A.2d 917 (Pa. 2010); *Frey v. Harley Davidson Motor Co.*, 734 A.2d 1, 10 (Pa. Super. 1999), *appeal denied*, 751 A.2d 191 (Pa. 2000).

31. *Wagner v. Firestone Tire & Rubber Co.*, 890 F.2d 652, 657 (3d Cir. 1989); *Frey v. Harley Davidson Motor Co.*, 734 A.2d 1, 6 (Pa. Super. 1999), *appeal denied*, 751 A.2d 191 (Pa. 2000); *Lonon v. Pep Boys, Manny, Moe & Jack*, 538 A.2d 22, 25 (Pa. Super. 1988); *see also Reott v. Asia Trend, Inc.*, 55 A.3d 1088, 1096 (Pa. 2012) ("Thus, we have no hesitation in initially concluding that assumption of the risk is an affirmative defense available to defendants in a products liability action.").

32. *See Reott v. Asia Trend, Inc.*, 55 A.3d 1088, 1100 (Pa. 2012).

33. *Dillinger v. Caterpillar, Inc.*, 959 F.2d 430, 442 (3d Cir. 1992); *Kern v. Nissan Indus. Equip. Co.*, 801 F. Supp. 1438, 1445 (M.D. Pa. 1992); *Gaudio v. Ford Motor Co.*, 976 A.2d 524, 540 (Pa. Super. 2009), *appeal denied*, 989 A.2d 917 (Pa. 2010); *Clark v. Bil-Jax, Inc.*, 763 A.2d 920, 923 (Pa. Super. 2000); *see also Reott v. Asia Trend, Inc.*, 55 A.3d 1088, 1101 (Pa. 2012).

34. *Reott v. Asia Trend, Inc.*, 55 A.3d 1088, 1096 (Pa. 2012); *Mackowick v. Westinghouse Elec. Corp.*, 575 A.2d 100, 102 (Pa. 1990); *Frey v. Harley Davidson*

Motor Co., Inc., 734 A.2d 1, 6 (Pa. Super. 1999), *appeal denied*, 751 A.2d 191 (Pa. 2000); *Mucowski v. Clark*, 590 A.2d 348, 350 (Pa. Super. 1991); *Staymates v. ITT Holub Indus.*, 527 A.2d 140, 146 (Pa. Super. 1987); *Walasavage v. Marinelli*, 483 A.2d 509, 516 (Pa. Super. 1984).

35. *Clark v. Bil-Jax, Inc.*, 763 A.2d 920, 924-25 (Pa. Super. 2000); *Jara v. Rex Works*, 718 A.2d 788, 795 (Pa. Super. 1998); *Sansom v. Crown Equip. Corp.*, 880 F. Supp. 2d 648, 666 (W.D. Pa. 2012).

36. *D'Angelo v. ADS Mach. Corp.*, 128 F. App'x 253, 256 (3d Cir. 2005); *Martinez v. Triad Controls, Inc.*, 593 F. Supp. 2d 741, 765 (E.D. Pa. 2009); *Nesbitt v. Sears, Roebuck & Co.*, 415 F. Supp. 2d 530, 545 (E.D. Pa. 2005).

37. *Greenwood v. Busch Entm't Corp.*, 101 F. Supp. 2d 292, 295-96 (E.D. Pa. 2000); *Klein v. Council of Chem. Assocs.*, 587 F. Supp. 213, 222 (E.D. Pa. 1984); *Cafazzo v. Cent. Med. Health Servs., Inc.*, 668 A.2d 521, 525 (Pa. 1994); *Musser v. Vilsmeier Auction Co.*, 562 A.2d 279, 283 (Pa. 1989); *Francioni v. Gibsonia Truck Corp.*, 372 A.2d 736, 739 (Pa. 1977); *Romeo v. Pittsburgh Assocs.*, 787 A.2d 1027, 1032 (Pa. Super. 2001).

38. *Musser v. Vilsmeier Auction Co.*, 562 A.2d 279, 281 (Pa. 1989); *Francioni v. Gibsonia Truck Corp.*, 372 A.2d 736, 739-40 (Pa. 1977).

39. *Meadows v. Anchor Longwall & Rebuild, Inc.*, 306 F. App'x 781, 785 (3d Cir. 2009); *Malloy v. Doty Conveyor*, 820 F. Supp. 217, 219-20 (E.D. Pa. 1993); *cf. Goodman v. PPG Indus.*, 849 A.2d 1239, 1244 (Pa. Super. 2004).

40. *Webb v. Zern*, 220 A.2d 853, 854 (Pa. 1966); *Pennsylvania Nat'l Mut. Ins. Co. v. Kaminski Lumber*, 580 A.2d 401, 404 (Pa. Super. 1990); *McKenna v. Art Pearl Works, Inc.*, 310 A.2d 677, 679 n.2 (Pa. Super. 1973); *J.P. Donmoyer, Inc. v. Util. Trailer Mfg. Co.*, 733 F. Supp. 2d 576, 582 (M.D. Pa. 2010); Restatement (Second) of Torts § 402A(1)(a).

41. *Walasavage v. Marinelli*, 483 A.2d 509, 518 (Pa. Super. 1984); *Burch v. Sears, Roebuck & Co.*, 467 A.2d 615 (Pa. Super. 1983).

42. *Francioni v. Gibsonia Truck Corp.*, 372 A.2d 736, 736 (Pa. 1977).

43. *Acevedo v. Start Plastics, Inc.*, 834 F. Supp. 808, 812 (E.D. Pa. 1993); *Jones v. SEPTA*, 834 F. Supp. 766, 769 (E.D. Pa. 1993); *Berkebile v. Brantly Helicopter Corp.*, 337 A.2d 893, 898 n.3 (Pa. 1975) (plurality).

44. *Mazur v. Merck & Co., Inc.*, 964 F.2d 1348, 1353-54 (3d Cir. 1992); *Greiner v. Volkswagenwerk Aktiengesellschaft*, 540 F.2d 85, 91 (3d Cir. 1976); *Martinez v. Triad Controls, Inc.*, 593 F. Supp. 2d 741, 763 (E.D. Pa. 2009); *Davis v. Berwind Corp.*, 690 A.2d 186, 190 (Pa. 1997); *Hahn v. Richter*, 673 A.2d 888 (Pa. 1996); *Incollingo v. Ewing*, 282 A.2d 206 (Pa. 1971); Restatement (Second) of Torts § 402A, cmt. k (1965).

45. *Kradel v. Fox River Tractor Co.*, 308 F.3d 328, 331-32 (3d Cir. 2002); *Conway v. White Trucks, A Div. of White Motor Corp.*, 885 F.2d 90, 93-94 (3d Cir. 1989); *Van Doren v. Coe Press Equip. Corp.*, 592 F. Supp. 2d 776, 787 (E.D. Pa. 2008); *Schmidt v. Boardman Co.*, 958 A.2d 498, 505 (Pa. Super. 2008), *aff'd*, 11 A.3d 924 (Pa. 2011); *Keselyak v. Reach All, Inc.*, 660 A.2d 1350, 1353 (Pa. Super. 1995); *Dawejko v. Jorgensen Steel Co.*, 434 A.2d 106, 110-12 (Pa. Super. 1981).

46. *Kradel v. Fox River Tractor Co.*, 308 F.3d 328, 332 (3d Cir. 2002); *Conway v. White Trucks, A Div. of White Motor Corp.*, 885 F.2d 90, 97 (3d Cir. 1989); *LaFountain v. Webb Indus. Corp.*, 951 F.2d 544, 548 (3d Cir. 1991); *Keselyak v. Reach All, Inc.*, 660 A.2d 1350, 1354 (Pa. Super. 1995).

47. *Skipworth v. Lead Indus.*, 690 A.2d 169, 172-73 (Pa. 1997); *Cummins v. Firestone Tire & Rubber Co.*, 495 A.2d 963, 971-72 (Pa. Super. 1985); *Warnick v. NMC-Wollard, Inc.*, 512 F. Supp. 2d 318, 334 (W.D. Pa. 2007).

48. *Mannsz v. MacWhyte*, 155 F.2d 445, 449-50 (3d Cir. 1946); *Phillips v. Cricket Lighters*, 841 A.2d 1000, 1005 (Pa. 2003) (plurality); *Moscatiello v. Pittsburgh Contractors*, 595 A.2d 1198, 1203-04 (Pa. Super. 1991).

49. *Mazur v. Merck & Co., Inc.*, 964 F.2d 1348, 1366 (3d Cir. 1992); *Nilson ex rel. Nilson v. Hershey Entm't & Resorts Co.*, 649 F. Supp. 2d 378, 387 (M.D. Pa. 2009); *Mackowick v. Westinghouse Elec. Corp.*, 575 A.2d 100, 102 (Pa. 1990); *French v. Commonwealth Assocs., Inc.*, 980 A.2d 623, 632-33 (Pa. Super. 2009); *Dauphin Deposit Bank & Tr. Co. v. Toyota Motor Corp.*, 596 A.2d 845 (Pa. Super. 1991). *But see Bruesewitz v. Wyeth, Inc.*, 508 F. Supp. 2d 430, 448 (E.D. Pa. 2007) ("Under Pennsylvania law, whether warning labels on prescription drugs are adequate is a matter for the jury to decide." (citing *Incollingo v. Ewing*, 282 A.2d 206 (Pa. 1971)).

50. *Philips v. A-Best Prods. Co.*, 665 A.2d 1167, 1171 (Pa. 1995); *Pavlik v. Lane Ltd./Tobacco Exporters Int'l*, 135 F.3d 876, 881 (3d Cir. 1998); *Coward v. Owens-Corning Fiberglass Corp.*, 729 A.2d 614, 618 (Pa. Super. 1999).

51. *Gigus v. Giles & Ransome, Inc.*, 868 A.2d 459, 462-63 (Pa. Super. 2005); Restatement (Second) of Torts § 402A, cmt. j ("Where a warning is given the seller may reasonably assume that it will be read and heeded.").

52. *Pavlik v. Lane Ltd./Tobacco Exporters Int'l*, 135 F.3d 876, 883-84 (3d Cir. 1998); *Coward v. Owens-Corning Fiberglass Corp.*, 729 A.2d 614, 618, 621 (Pa. Super. 1999) (citing *Coffman v. Keene Corp.*, 628 A.2d 710, 721 (N.J. 1993) and *Pavlik*). *But cf. Viguers v. Philip Morris USA, Inc.*, 837 A.2d 534 (Pa. Super. 2003) (refusing to apply heeding presumption outside employment/asbestos context, and, even if applicable, finding presumption rebutted as a matter of law where adequate warning given later was ignored), *aff'd*, 881 A.2d 1262 (Pa. 2005).

53. *Maya v. Johnson & Johnson & McNeil-Ppc*, 2014 PA Super 152 (Pa. Super. 2014); *Coward v. Owens-Corning Fiberglas Corp.*, 729 A.2d 614, 621-22 (Pa. Super. 1999).

54. *DeSantis v. Frick*, 745 A.2d 624, 630-31 (Pa. Super. 1999); *Lynch v. McStome & Lincoln Plaza Assocs.*, 548 A.2d 1276, 1281 (Pa. Super. 1988).

55. *Walton v. Avco Corp.*, 610 A.2d 454, 459 (Pa. 1992).

56. *Lance v. Wyeth*, 85 A.3d 434, 460 (Pa. 2014).

57. *Diehl v. Blaw-Knox*, 360 F.3d 426, 429 (3d Cir. 2004); *Stecyk v. Bell Helicopter Textron, Inc.*, 295 F.3d 408, 416 (3d Cir. 2002); *Kelly v. Crown Equip. Co.*, 970 F.2d 1273, 1275-76 (3d Cir. 1992); *Duchess v. Langston Corp.*, 769 A.2d 1131, 1137 (Pa. 2001).

58. *Duchess v. Langston Corp.*, 769 A.2d 1131, 1146 (Pa. 2001).

59. *Mazur v. Merck & Co., Inc.*, 964 F.2d 1348 (3d Cir. 1992); *Hahn v. Richter*, 673 A.2d 888 (Pa. 1996); *Incollingo v. Ewing*, 282 A.2d 206 (Pa. 1971), *abrogated on other grounds by Kaczkowski v. Bolubasz*, 421 A.2d 1027 (Pa. 1980).

60. *Mazur v. Merck & Co., Inc.*, 964 F.2d 1348 (3d Cir. 1992); *Cochran v. Wyeth, Inc.*, 3 A.3d 673, 676 (Pa. Super. 2010); *Taurino v. Ellen*, 579 A.2d 925 (Pa. Super. 1990).

61. *See, e.g., Kalinowski v. E.I. DuPont de Nemours & Co.*, 851 F. Supp. 149 (E.D. Pa. 1994) (applying sophisticated user defense to bulk supplier of raw material incorporated into medical devices).

62. *Davis v. Berwind Corp.*, 690 A.2d 186 (Pa. 1997), *called into doubt by Phillips v. Cricket Lighters*, 841 A.2d 1000 (Pa. 2003) (plurality opinion); *Sweitzer v. Dempster Sys.*, 539 A.2d 880 (Pa. Super. 1988); *see also Pa. Dep't of Gen. Servs. v. U.S. Mineral Prods. Co.*, 898 A.2d 590 (Pa. 2006); *Morris v. Phoenix Installation & Mgmt. Co.*, 2013 U.S. Dist. LEXIS 181018, at *13-14 (W.D. Pa. Dec. 30, 2013); *Kinsey v. Louisville Ladder, Inc.*, 2011 U.S. Dist. LEXIS 93272, at *15-16 (E.D. Pa. Aug. 19, 2011).

63. *Burch v. Sears, Roebuck & Co.*, 467 A.2d 615, 619 (Pa. Super. 1983); *Morris v. Phoenix Installation & Mgmt. Co.*, 2013 U.S. Dist. LEXIS 181018, at *13-14 (W.D. Pa. Dec. 30, 2013); *Kinsey v. Louisville Ladder, Inc.*, 2011 U.S. Dist. LEXIS 93272, at *15-16 (E.D. Pa. Aug. 19, 2011).

64. *See Reott v. Asia Trend, Inc.*, 55 A.3d 1088, 1097 n.10, 1101 (Pa. 2012).

65. *Santiago v. Johnson Mach. & Press Corp.*, 834 F.2d 84 (3d Cir. 1987); *Lewis v. Coffing Hoist Div.*, 528 A.2d 590 (Pa. 1987).

66. *Altronics of Bethlehem, Inc. v. Repco, Inc.*, 957 F.2d 1102 (3d Cir. 1992); *Walters ex rel. Walters v. Gen. Motors Corp.*, 209 F. Supp. 2d 481 (W.D. Pa. 2002); *Gordner v. Dynetics Corp.*, 862 F. Supp. 1303 (M.D. Pa. 1994); *Barnish v. KWI Bldg. Co.*, 980 A.2d 535, 541-42 (Pa. 2009); *Rogers v. Johnson & Johnson Prods.*, 565 A.2d 751 (Pa. 1989); *Dansak v. Cameron Coca-Cola Bottling Co., Inc.*, 703 A.2d 489 (Pa. Super. 1997).

67. *Nesbitt v. Sears, Roebuck & Co.*, 415 F. Supp. 2d 530 (E.D. Pa. 2005); *Hoffman v. Niagra Mach. & Tool Works Co.*, 683 F. Supp. 489 (E.D. Pa. 1988); *Lewis v. Coffing Hoist Div.*, 528 A.2d 590 (Pa. 1987); *Leaphart v. Whiting Corp.*, 564 A.2d 165 (Pa. Super. 1989).

68. *Birt v. Firstenergy Corp.*, 891 A.2d 1281, 1290 (Pa. Super. 2006).

69. *Arnoldy v. Forklift L.P.*, 927 A.2d 257, 263 (Pa. Super. 2007), *overruled on other grounds by Kiak v. Crown Equip. Corp.*, 989 A.2d 385, 388 (Pa. Super. 2010); *Martinez v. Triad Controls, Inc.*, 593 F. Supp. 2d 741, 762 n.21 (E.D. Pa. 2009).

70. *Tait v. Armor Elevator Co.*, 958 F.2d 563 (3d Cir. 1992); *Gumbs v. Int'l Harvester, Inc.*, 718 F.2d 88 (3d Cir. 1983); *Nesbitt v. Sears, Roebuck & Co.*, 415 F. Supp. 2d 530 (E.D. Pa. 2005); *Harley v. Makita USA, Inc.*, 1998 WL 156973 (E.D. Pa. July 14, 1998); *Spino v. John S. Tilley Ladder Co.*, 696 A.2d 1169 (Pa. 1997); *DiFrancesco v. Excam, Inc.*, 642 A.2d 529 (Pa. Super. 1994); *Madjic v. Cincinnati Mach. Co.*, 537 A.2d 334 (Pa. Super. 1988).

71. *Wolfe v. McNeil-PPC, Inc.*, 773 F. Supp. 2d 561, 573 (E.D. Pa. 2011); *Gower v. Savage Arms, Inc.*, 166 F. Supp. 2d 240, 253 (E.D. Pa. 2001); *Klages v. Gen. Ordnance Equip. Corp.*, 367 A.2d 304 (Pa. Super. 1976).

72. *Schmid v. Milwaukee Elec. Tool Co.*, 13 F.3d 76 (3d Cir. 1994); *Schroeder v. Dept. of Transp.*, 710 A.2d 23 (Pa. 1998); *Tenaglia v. Procter & Gamble, Inc.*, 737 A.2d 306 (Pa. Super. 1999); *Dansak v. Cameron Coca-Cola Bottling Co., Inc.*, 703 A.2d 489 (Pa. Super. 1997).

73. *Schwartz v. Subaru of Am., Inc.*, 851 F. Supp. 191 (E.D. Pa. 1994); *Smith v. Am. Honda Motor Co., Inc.*, 846 F. Supp. 1217 (M.D. Pa. 1994); *Sipe v. Ford Motor Co.*, 837 F. Supp. 660 (M.D. Pa. 1993); *Martin & Greenspan v. Volkswagen of Am.*, 1989 WL 81296 (E.D. Pa. July 13, 1989); *Tenaglia v. Procter & Gamble, Inc.*, 737 A.2d 306 (Pa. Super. 1999); *Roselli v. Gen. Elec. Co.*, 599 A.2d 685 (Pa. Super. 1991).

74. *Baliotis v. McNeill*, 870 F. Supp. 1285 (M.D. Pa. 1994); *Mensch v. Bic Corp.*, 1992 WL 236965 (E.D. Pa. Sept. 17, 1992).

75. *Schroeder v. Dep't of Transp.*, 710 A.2d 23 (Pa. 1998); *Troup v. Tri-County Confinement Sys., Inc.*, 708 A.2d 825 (Pa. Super. 1998); *Sebelin v. Yamaha Motor Corp.*, 705 A.2d 904 (Pa. Super. 1998); *O'Donnell v. Big Yank, Inc.*, 696 A.2d 846 (Pa. Super. 1997).

76. *Pyeritz v. Commonwealth*, 32 A.3d 687, 695 (Pa. 2011); *Hogan v. Raymond Corp.*, 536 F. App'x 207, 210 n.2 (3d Cir. 2013).

77. *Bilt-Rite Contractors, Inc. v. Architectural Studio*, 866 A.2d 270 (Pa. 2005).

78. *Knight v. Springfield Hyundai*, 81 A.3d 940, 952 (Pa. Super. 2013); *Azur v. Chase Bank, USA*, 601 F.3d 212, 222 (3d Cir. 2010).

79. *Roe v. Deere & Co.*, 855 F.2d 151, 153 (3d Cir. 1988); *Kupetz v. Deere & Co.*, 644 A.2d 1213, 1218 (Pa. Super. 1994), *appeal denied*, 653 A.2d 1232 (Pa. 1994).

80. *Roe v. Deere & Co.*, 855 F.2d 151, 153 (3d Cir. 1988); *Gaudio v. Ford Motor Co.*, 976 A.2d 524, 532 (Pa. Super. 2009), *appeal denied*, 989 A.2d 917 (Pa. 2010); *Kupetz v. Deere & Co.*, 644 A.2d 1213, 1218 (Pa. Super. 1994).

81. *Gaudio v. Ford Motor Co.*, 976 A.2d 524, 532 (Pa. Super. 2009); *Kupetz v. Deere & Co.*, 644 A.2d 1213, 1218 (Pa. Super. 1994).

82. *Harsh v. Petroll*, 887 A.2d 209 (Pa. 2005).

83. *Thompson v. Pennsylvania Power Co.*, 402 F.2d 88 (3d Cir. 1968); *Rosa v. United States*, 613 F. Supp. 469 (M.D. Pa. 1985) (in negligence actions generally, contributory negligence is a defense except where the defendant is wanton or willfully negligent).

84. *Surace v. Caterpillar, Inc.*, 111 F.3d 1039 (3d Cir. 1997); *Griggs v. BIC Corp.*, 981 F.2d 1429 (3d Cir. 1992); *Phillips v. Cricket Lighters*, 841 A.2d 100 (Pa. 2003) (plurality opinion); *Moroney v. Gen. Motors Corp.*, 850 A.2d 629 (Pa. Super. 2004); *compare with Riley v. Warren Mfg., Inc.*, 688 A.2d 221 (Pa. Super. 1997), and *Dambacher v. Mallis*, 485 A.2d 408 (Pa. Super. 1984).

85. *Lance v. Wyeth*, 85 A.3d 434, 458 (Pa. 2014).

86. 42 Pa. Cons. Stat. Ann. § 7102; *Williams v. United States*, 507 F. Supp. 121 (E.D. Pa. 1981); *Elder v. Orluck*, 515 A.2d 517 (Pa. 1986) (per curiam); *Christiansen v. Silfies*, 667 A.2d 396 (Pa. Super. 1995).

87. 13 Pa. Cons. Stat. Ann. § 2314; *Bogacki v. Am. Mach. & Foundry Co.*, 417 F.2d 400 (3d Cir. 1969); *Berkebile v. Brantly Helicopter Corp.*, 337 A.2d 893 (Pa. 1975). *But see Phillips v. Cricket Lighters*, 883 A.2d 439 (Pa. 2005) (noting that strict liability and breach of warranty claims are "not coterminous," so that a determination that a plaintiff's strict liability claim fails does not lead to a *de facto* finding that the breach of implied warranty claim is precluded).

88. *McCracken v. Ford Motor Co.*, 588 F. Supp. 2d 635, 642 (E.D. Pa. 2008) (citing *Nationwide Ins. Co. v. Gen. Motors Corp.*, 625 A.2d 1172, 1174 (Pa. 1993)).

89. *Neal v. Carey Canadian Mines, Ltd.*, 548 F. Supp. 357 (E.D. Pa. 1982), *aff'd sub nom. Van Buskirk v. Carey Canadian Mines, Ltd.*, 760 F.2d 481 (3d Cir. 1985)

90. *Phillips v. Cricket Lighters*, 883 A.2d 439 (Pa. 2005).

91. 13 Pa. Cons. Stat. Ann. § 2714; *Rose v. A&L Motor Sales*, 699 F. Supp. 75 (W.D. Pa. 1988); *Johnson v. Hyundai Motor Am.*, 698 A.2d 631 (Pa. Super. 1997); *Thorsen v. Iron & Glass Bank*, 476 A.2d 928 (Pa. Super. 1984).

92. Pa. R. Civ. P. 238; *LaBarre v. Werner Enters., Inc.*, 420 F. App'x 169, 170 (3d Cir. 2011); *Kirk v. Raymark Indus., Inc.*, 61 F.3d 147 (3d Cir. 1995); *Willet v. Pennsylvania Med. Catastrophe Loss Fund*, 702 A.2d 850 (Pa. 1997); *Costa v. Lauderdale Beach Hotel*, 626 A.2d 566 (Pa. 1993); *Schrock v. Albert Einstein Med. Ctr.*, 589 A.2d 1103 (Pa. 1991); *Krebs v. United Refining Co. of Pa.*, 893 A.2d 776 (Pa. Super. 2006); *Sun Pipe Line Co. v. Tri-State Telecomms., Inc.*, 655 A.2d 112 (Pa. Super. 1994).

93. Pa. R. Civ. P. 238.

94. Pa. R. Civ. P. 238.

95. Pa. R. Civ. P. 238; *Schrock v. Albert Einstein Med. Ctr.*, 589 A.2d 1103 (Pa. 1991). *But compare Sun Pipe Line Co. v. Tri-State Telecomms., Inc.*, 655 A.2d 112 (Pa. Super. 1994) (no delay damages after defendant's full liability policy limits are tendered and no money obtainable from defendant personally); *Krysmalaski v. Tarasovich*, 622 A.2d 298 (Pa. Super. 1993) (when defendant offers full amount available to it, no delay damages following offer regardless of verdict).

96. *Sun Pipe Line Co. v. Tri-State Telecomms., Inc.*, 655 A.2d 112 (Pa. Super. 1994).

97. *Wirth v. Miller*, 580 A.2d 1154 (Pa. Super. 1990).

98. 42 Pa. Cons. Stat. Ann. § 8101; *Incollingo v. Ewing*, 379 A.2d 79 (Pa. 1977); *Brown v. Nationwide Mut. Ins. Co.*, 713 A.2d 663 (Pa. Super. 1998); *Johnson v. Singleton*, 658 A.2d 1372 (Pa. Super. 1995).

99. *Sun Pipe Line Co. v. Tri-State Telecomms., Inc.*, 655 A.2d 112 (Pa. Super. 1994).

100. 77 Pa. Cons. Stat. Ann. § 481; *Heath v. Church's Fried Chicken, Inc.*, 546 A.2d 1120 (Pa. 1988); *Callender v. Goodyear Tire & Rubber Co.*, 564 A.2d 180 (Pa. Super. 1989) (products liability claim cannot be asserted against an employer who is also the manufacturer of the equipment that caused the employee's injury), *appeal denied*, 575 A.2d 560 (Pa. 1990).

101. *Thomeier v. Rhone-Poulenc, Inc.*, 928 F. Supp. 548 (W.D. Pa. 1996); *Snyder v. Pocono Med. Ctr.*, 690 A.2d 1152 (Pa. 1997) (affirming, by an evenly divided court, superior court's holding of employer immunity because injuries were

related to plaintiff's employment); *Lewis v. Sch. Dist. of Philadelphia*, 538 A.2d 862, 869 (Pa. 1988).

102. 77 Pa. Cons. Stat. Ann. § 481(b); *Thomeier v. Rhone-Poulenc, Inc.*, 928 F. Supp. 548 (W.D. Pa. 1996); *Pittsburgh Steel Co. v. Patterson-Emerson-Comstock, Inc.*, 171 A.2d 185 (Pa. 1961); *Bethlehem Steel Corp. v. MATX, Inc.*, 703 A.2d 39 (Pa. Super. 1997); *Snare v. Ebensburg Power Co.*, 637 A.2d 296 (Pa. Super. 1993), *appeal denied*, 646 A.2d 1181 (Pa. 1994); *Bester v. Essex Crane Rental Corp.*, 619 A.2d 304 (Pa. Super. 1993), *appeal denied*, 651 A.2d 530 (Pa. 1994).

103. *Barber v. Pitt. Corning Co.*, 555 A.2d 766 (Pa. 1989); *Poyser v. Newman & Co., Inc.*, 522 A.2d 548 (Pa. 1987); *Snyder v. Specialty Glass Prods., Inc.*, 658 A.2d 366 (Pa. Super. 1995).

104. *Martin v. Lancaster Battery Co., Inc.*, 606 A.2d 444 (Pa. 1992).

105. 42 Pa. Cons. Stat. Ann. §§ 5524, 5525, 5536; 13 Pa. Cons. Stat. Ann. §§ 2313, 2314, 2315.

106. 2011 Pa. Legis. Serv. Act 2011-17 (S.B. 1131) § 3. Legislation limiting joint and several liability was previously passed in 2002, but the bill was found to violate the Pennsylvania Constitution because the bill contained more than one subject. *See DeWeese v. Weaver*, 880 A.2d 54 (Pa. Commw. 2005) (holding that the 2002 amendments to the Comparative Negligence Act, which sought to abolish joint liability in many instances, were unconstitutional), *aff'd*, 906 A.2d 1193 (Pa. 2006).

107. 42 Pa. Cons. Stat. Ann. § 7102(a.1).

108. 42 Pa. Cons. Stat. Ann. § 7102(a.1)(3). The other exceptions triggering joint and several liability listed in this subsection are liability for a release or threatened release of a hazardous substance under the Hazardous Sites Cleanup Act and liability of licensees in dram shop actions.

109. 42 Pa. Cons. Stat. Ann. § 7102(a.1)(4).

110. 42 Pa. Cons. Stat. Ann. § 7102 (version prior to amendment on June 28, 2011). The amendment deleted the following paragraph that still applies to claims that accrued before the amendment:

> (b) Recovery against joint defendant; contribution.—Where recovery is allowed against more than one defendant, each defendant shall be liable for that proportion of the total dollar amount awarded as damages in the ratio of the amount of his causal negligence to the amount of causal negligence attributed to all defendants against whom recovery is allowed. The plaintiff may recover the full amount of the allowed recovery from any defendant against whom the plaintiff is not barred from recovery. Any defendant

who is so compelled to pay more than his percentage share may seek contribution.

2011 Pa. Legis. Serv. Act 2011-17 (S.B. 1131).

111. *Foflygen v. Zemel*, 615 A.2d 1345 (Pa. Super. 1992); *Farnell v. Winterloch Corp.*, 527 A.2d 204 (Pa. Commw. 1987).

112. *Glomb v. Glomb*, 530 A.2d 1362 (Pa. Super. 1987); *Riff v. Morgan Pharmacy*, 508 A.2d 1247 (Pa. Super. 1986); *Wade v. S. J. Groves & Sons Co.*, 424 A.2d 902 (Pa. Super. 1981); *see also Harsh v. Petroll*, 887 A.2d 209 (Pa. 2005) (permitting joint and several liability against negligent and strictly liable defendants).

113. *Martin v. Owens-Corning Fiberglas Corp.*, 528 A.2d 947 (Pa. 1987); *Brown v. Philadelphia College*, 449 Pa. Super. 667, 674 A.2d 1130 (1996).

114. *See Sochanski v. Sears, Roebuck & Co.*, 689 F.2d 45, 50 (3d Cir. 1982) (Pennsylvania law) ("Goodyear, because it manufactured the defective tire, is primarily liable. Sears acted only as a conduit between Goodyear and the purchaser of the cart and for that reason is only secondarily liable. . . . Consequently, Sears' liability for any misfeasance on Goodyear's part is discharged by the release in favor of Goodyear."); *Feeney v. Authentic Fitness Co.*, 54 Pa. D. & C. 4th 196, 201 (Pa. Com. Pl. Phila. 2001), *aff'd*, 792 A.2d 622 (Pa. Super. 2001), *appeal denied*, 798 A.2d 1290 (Pa. 2002).

115. 42 Pa. Cons. Stat. Ann. §§ 8321 *et seq.*

116. *Taylor v. Solberg*, 778 A.2d 664, 667 (Pa. 2001); *Buttermore v. Aliquippa Hosp.*, 561 A.2d 733 (Pa. 1989); *Wolbach v. Fay*, 412 A.2d 487 (Pa. 1980). *But see Nationwide Ins. Co. v. Schneider*, 906 A.2d 586, 596 (Pa. Super. 2006) (holding that a "general release" did not discharge an insurer), *aff'd*, 960 A.2d 442 (Pa. 2008); *Vaughn v. Didizian*, 648 A.2d 38, 41 (Pa. Super. 1994) (holding that claims of negligent medical treatment were not released when the claims accrued after signing of release); *Sparler v. Fireman's Ins. Co.*, 521 A.2d 433 (Pa. Super. 1987) ("Although the phrase 'and all other persons, firms and corporations' appeared in boilerplate print following Garber's name, the release did not otherwise suggest or identify Fireman's as a party being released or discharged. The only reasonable interpretation of the release, when it is considered in light of the circumstances surrounding its execution, is that Sparler did not intend to release Fireman's from its contractual obligation.").

117. *Brown v. Herman*, 665 A.2d 504 (Pa. Super. 1995), *aff'd*, 690 A.2d 232 (Pa. 1997); *Holmes v. Lankenau Hosp.*, 627 A.2d 763 (Pa. Super. 1993).

118. *Wirth v. Miller*, 580 A.2d 1154 (Pa. Super. 1990); *Capone v. Donovan*, 480 A.2d 1249 (Pa. Super. 1984).

119. *Walton v. Avco Corp.*, 610 A.2d 454, 460-62 (Pa. 1992); *Baker v. AC&S, Inc.*, 729 A.2d 1140, 1147 (Pa. Super. 1999), *aff'd*, 755 A.2d 664 (Pa. 2000).

120. *Walton v. Avco Corp.*, 610 A.2d 454, 462 (Pa. 1992); *Baker v. AC&S, Inc.*, 729 A.2d 1140, 1148 (Pa. Super. 1999).

121. *Smith v. Weissenfels, Inc.*, 657 A.2d 949, 955 (Pa. Super. 1995); *Ball v. Johns-Manville Corp.*, 625 A.2d 650 (Pa. Super. 1993); *McMeekin v. Harry M. Stevens, Inc.*, 530 A.2d 462, 469 (Pa. Super. 1987).

122. *Smith v. Weissenfels, Inc.*, 657 A.2d 949, 954 (Pa. Super. 1995).

123. 42 Pa. Cons. Stat. Ann. § 8324; 42 Pa. Cons. Stat. Ann. § 7102.

124. *Baker v. AC & S*, 755 A.2d 664 (Pa. 2000); *Walton v. Avco*, 610 A.2d 454 (Pa. 1992).

125. *Smith v. Weissenfels, Inc.*, 657 A.2d 949, 949 (Pa. Super. 1995).

126. *See Embrey v. Borough of West Mifflin*, 390 A.2d 765 (Pa. Super. 1978).

127. *McMeekin v. Harry M. Stevens, Inc.*, 530 A.2d 462 (Pa. Super. 1987); *see also Smith v. Weissenfels, Inc.*, 657 A.2d 949, 949 (Pa. Super. 1995).

128. *Smith v. Weissenfels, Inc.*, 657 A.2d 949, 949 (Pa. Super. 1995); *McMeekin v. Harry M. Stevens, Inc.*, 530 A.2d 462 (Pa. Super. 1987); *Svetz for Svetz v. Land Tool Co.*, 513 A.2d 403 (Pa. Super. 1986).

129. *Smith v. Weissenfels, Inc.*, 657 A.2d 949, 953 (Pa. Super. 1995).

130. *Buttermore v. Aliquippa Hosp.*, 561 A.2d 733 (Pa. 1989).

131. 42 Pa. Cons. Stat. Ann. § 8324.

132. *Wirth v. Miller*, 580 A.2d 1154 (Pa. Super. 1990).

133. *Walton v. Avco Corp.*, 610 A.2d 454 (Pa. 1992); *Charles v. Giant Eagle Markets*, 522 A.2d 1 (Pa. 1987).

RHODE ISLAND

A. CAUSES OF ACTION

Rhode Island recognizes product liability suits premised on strict liability, negligence, and breach of UCC warranties of merchantability and fitness.[1]

B. STATUTES OF LIMITATION

Claims for personal injuries or wrongful death sounding in strict liability, negligence, or breach of warranty must be brought within three years of the date of injury. The UCC four-year statute of limitations for breach of warranty applies only where there is a direct buyer-seller relationship between the parties.[2] A discovery rule has been applied in pharmaceutical and cigarette cases.[3]

Claims for property damage must be brought within ten years of the date of damage.[4]

A ten-year statute of repose is limited to improvements to real property and material suppliers who furnished materials for the construction of improvements.[5] A general ten-year statute of repose limiting product liability actions to ten years following purchase was held to violate the Rhode Island State Constitution.[6]

As to an infant or child, the statutes of limitation are tolled until age 18, the age of majority.

C. STRICT LIABILITY

1. The Standard

Rhode Island has adopted Section 402A of the Restatement (Second) of Torts.[7] There must be proof of a defect in the design or manufacture of a product when it leaves the manufacturer's hands that makes it unreasonably dangerous for its intended use.[8] Unreasonably dangerous means a strong likelihood of injury to a party unaware of the danger of using the product in a normal manner.[9] The scope of strict liability has been extended to cover a seller's or manufacturer's failure to warn of the product's dangerous propensity.[10]

Generally, all elements, including the "unreasonably dangerous" requirement, are reserved for jury determination. However, where a prescription drug is defended as "unavoidably unsafe" under Restatement (Second) of Torts Section 402A, comment k, the court must be satisfied that reasonable minds could differ in deciding whether a drug's risks outweigh its benefits before submitting the issue to the jury.[11]

In defective design cases, Rhode Island has neither adopted Restatement (Third) of Torts Section 2, requiring proof of an alternate, safer design, nor given any indication it would do so if confronted with the issue. In Rhode Island, the test of defect is the consumer expectation test. In establishing a defect, a party may offer evidence of an alternate, safer design, but a party is not required to produce evidence of an alternate, safer design.[12]

Strict liability arising from a defectively designed product cannot be disclaimed by one who places the product on the market, knowing that it is to be used without inspection for defects.[13]

2. **Definition of "Defect"**

Rhode Island uses a consumer expectation test, in that "unreasonably dangerous" means that the defect creates a "strong likelihood of injury" not contemplated by the user or consumer.[14] Plaintiff need not establish a specific defect as long as there is evidence of some unspecified dangerous condition. The jury may rely on circumstantial evidence to find the dangerous condition, and where the allegedly defective product is destroyed in the mishap, evidence of malfunction may be sufficient evidence of defect.[15] Common knowledge in the community of a product's dangers may be a defense to the product being unreasonably dangerous.[16]

3. **Causation**

A plaintiff who asserts a product liability claim against a manufacturer is required to prove that the defect attributed to the manufacturer's product was the proximate cause of the plaintiff's injury.[17] A jury finding of no proximate cause makes product defects, however well-proved, entirely immaterial.[18]

4. **Contributory Negligence/Assumption of Risk**

Assumption of the risk is a complete defense to a product liability action, whether in strict liability or breach of warranty.[19] The standard for assumption of the risk is entirely subjective—plaintiff must personally have assumed an encounter with a perceived danger—and is ordinarily a question for the fact-finder. Where the facts "suggest only one reasonable inference," assumption of the risk becomes a question of law for the court.[20] Rhode Island's comparative negligence statute, which reduces damages by the percent plaintiff was contributorily negligent (even as much as 99 percent), applies in product liability cases in strict liability, negligence, and warranty.[21]

5. **Sale or Lease/Persons Liable**

A seller or commercial lessor is liable to the same extent as the manufacturer, as long as the defect existed as of the time of sale or lease.[22] A seller or distributor of product components is subject to liability when the seller or distributor substantially participates in the integration of the component into the design or construction of the end product. A manufacturer of a component part who remains uninvolved in design or construction of the end product has no liability, even where injury might be less likely were the component accompanied by a warning or designed differently.[23]

6. **Inherently Dangerous Products**

The mere fact that an activity involves an ultra-hazardous or abnormally dangerous substance is not, by itself, sufficient to trigger strict liability. Strict liability is imposed only where the substance is used in a way that is inherently dangerous or creates an unreasonable risk of harm. Rhode Island recognizes strict liability for ultra-hazardous activity under Restatement (Second) of Torts Section 520. Restatement (Second) of Torts Section 402A, comment k, respecting unavoidably unsafe products, is applicable to drug product claims, including breach of warranty.[24] See Section C.1, *supra*, respecting the risk-benefit test applicable to drug products.

7. **Successor Liability**

A successor corporation that absorbs the predecessor's business and property by purchase or merger, and continues the predecessor's management personnel and policies, may be liable for injuries caused by the predecessor's products.[25]

8. **Market-Share Liability/Enterprise Liability**

Rhode Island refused to adopt the market-share doctrine California adopted in *Sindell v. Abbott Labs., Inc.*[26] Under Rhode Island law, the imposition of liability requires the identification of the specific defendant responsible for the injury.[27]

9. **Privity**

Privity is not required.

10. **Failure to Warn**

A manufacturer or seller has a duty to warn of dangers that are not open and obvious.[28] Moreover, incident to the duty to warn is the duty to acquire knowledge about products through reasonably adequate inspections and tests.[29] A product is defective if the seller does not warn of the product's danger, but only if such danger is reasonably foreseeable and knowable at the time of marketing.[30]

11. **Post-Sale Duty to Warn and Remedial Measures**

The Rhode Island Supreme Court has not formally imposed a post-sale duty to warn on product manufacturers. Defect, even defect by failure to warn, must be proved to have existed as of the time the product left the seller.[31] In contrast, under the Rhode Island Rules of Evidence, evidence of subsequent remedial measures is admissible if the subsequent measures would have made the injury less likely.[32]

12. **Learned Intermediary Doctrine**

Rhode Island is one of the few jurisdictions not to have ruled on acceptance or application of the learned intermediary doctrine. The learned intermediary doctrine is still considered a disputed area of Rhode Island law.[33]

13. **Substantial Alteration/Abnormal Use**

By statute, a product manufacturer or seller is not liable for personal injuries, death, or property damage where a substantial cause of the injury or damage is post-sale product alteration or modification.[34] The failure to follow routine maintenance requirements can be found an alteration or modification covered by the statute.[35]

14. **State of the Art**

State-of-the-art evidence is generally not admissible. Evidence in the nature of state of the art evidence is admissible in failure to warn cases, because the duty to warn extends only to dangers reasonably foreseeable and knowable at the time of marketing.[36]

15. **Malfunction**

Product malfunction, by itself, is ordinarily not sufficient evidence of defect, but may be deemed prima facie proof where the product itself is destroyed in the event causing injury.[37]

16. **Standards and Governmental Regulation**

Industry standards and government regulations are generally admissible where their violation is offered as evidence of defect or fault.[38] Compliance with standards or regulations is ordinarily ruled not probative.

17. **Other Accidents**

Evidence of other accidents or consumer complaints may be admissible as tending to show that the injury to plaintiff was probably caused by a product defect, as opposed to plaintiff's particular susceptibility, or as tending to show the dangerous character of the product and defendant's knowledge and duty to warn of that character. Such evidence, by itself, however, is not sufficient to establish defect, or causation as to a particular plaintiff.[39]

18. **Misrepresentation**

Rhode Island has not adopted Section 402B of the Restatement (Second) of Torts, dealing with misrepresentation.

19. **Destruction or Loss of Product**

Under the doctrine of spoliation of evidence, the deliberate or negligent destruction of relevant evidence by a party to litigation may give rise to an inference that the destroyed evidence would have been unfavorable to the spoliating party. Bad faith in the spoliator is not necessary to permit the inference, but it may be taken by the fact-finder to strengthen the inference.[40] Where an allegedly defective product is lost or destroyed before trial, depriving defendant of some means or the most direct means of countering the allegation of defect, evidence may be barred at trial, or the action may be dismissed involuntarily.[41]

20. **Economic Loss**

The economic loss doctrine has been applied in actions between commercial entities, having comparable bargaining power. However, the economic loss doctrine is not applicable to tort actions arising from consumer transactions.[42]

21. **Crashworthiness**

Crashworthiness, as a measure of product safety and a class of potential product liability, has been acknowledged in dicta but not adopted as Rhode Island law.[43]

D. NEGLIGENCE

Rhode Island negligence law contains no aspects unique to claims for defective products.[44] Most negligence defenses—such as comparative negligence and assumption of the risk—can also be asserted in strict liability cases.

Rhode Island has a so-called pure comparative negligence statute. Plaintiff may recover even if plaintiff's comparative fault is more than 50 percent. As a matter of law, manufacturers, sellers or lessors who enter a defective product into the stream of commerce cannot disclaim liability for personal injuries arising out of their own negligence.[45]

E. BREACH OF WARRANTY

In the products setting, a breach of warranty claim is substantively similar to a strict liability claim.[46] Differences in the statute of limitations do exist, as noted in Section B, *supra*.

Under the Rhode Island version of the UCC, merchantability and fitness warranties extend to any person who may reasonably be expected to use, consume, or be affected by the goods and who is injured by the breach of the warranty. This extension cannot be limited or excluded.[47] A disclaimer for personal injuries arising from the use of a consumer product introduced into the stream of commerce is unconscionable.[48]

F. PUNITIVE DAMAGES

Punitive damages are recoverable in negligence or strict liability, but not in breach of warranty. Punitive damages are awarded where the defendant acted maliciously, intending to harm plaintiff.[49]

G. **PRE- AND POST-JUDGMENT INTEREST**

Pre-judgment interest, at the rate of 12 percent per annum is provided by statute and runs from the date the cause of action accrues (typically, the injury date) to the date of final judgment. Pre-judgment interest does not violate the due process clause by infringing on a defendant's fundamental right to a jury trial.[50] Ordinarily, a judgment is not final until the appeal period expires, or an appeal is dismissed or decided by the Supreme Court. Once final, a judgment draws simple interest at the rate of 12 percent per annum to the time of its discharge.[51]

At the trial level, the judgment is entered for the amount resulting from addition of the verdict plus pre-judgment interest calculated to the trial judgment entry date.[52] If a judgment debtor appeals and is unsuccessful, interest is calculated at 12 percent per annum on the total trial judgment, from the trial court entry date, and added to the judgment following remand from the Supreme Court.[53]

A judgment debtor whose appeal is ultimately unavailing may avoid appeal period interest by paying the trial judgment amount into the registry of the court, or directly to the judgment creditor.[54]

A judgment debtor is liable for appeal period interest, even where the appeal is brought by a judgment creditor who retains the trial court award but seeks a greater award by appeal (for example, contending that comparative negligence was wrongly found or fixed).[55] In such circumstances, the judgment debtor may avoid appeal period interest only by making an offer to pay the trial judgment. However, the offer may not be conditioned on the opponent foregoing an appeal.[56]

In Rhode Island, pre-judgment interest is not awarded as delay damages, but as a matter of public policy encouraging early settlement.[57]

H. **EMPLOYER IMMUNITY FROM SUIT**

Under the provisions of the Rhode Island workers compensation statute, a plaintiff's employer cannot be held liable in contribution for a workplace injury, nor does an employer's fault reduce the plaintiff's recovery.[58] Similarly, equitable indemnity against the employer is not permitted, but express or implied contractual indemnity is actionable by a third-party against an employer.[59] Immunity is also available by statute to a "special employer," one who engages a "borrowed" or "loaned" employee injured in the course of work.[60]

I. **STATUTES**

Sections B. and C.13 discuss statutes directly pertinent to product liability issues and actions.

J. JOINT AND SEVERAL LIABILITY

1. Contribution and Indemnity

Rhode Island has adopted, in large part, the 1939 version of the Uniform Contribution Among Joint Tortfeasors Act.[61] Rhode Island's Contribution Act expressly provides that the right of contribution exists among joint tortfeasors; "provided that when there is a disproportion of fault among joint tortfeasors, the relative degree of fault" of each is used to determine pro rata shares of the damages.[62]

The pro rata share determination applies only to contribution rights. Each joint tortfeasor is jointly and severally liable for the entire amount of an injured party's damages, and the injured party may choose to pursue and recover from just one, some or all the joint tortfeasors.[63]

The Contribution Among Joint Tortfeasors Act preserves but does not define rights of indemnity between multiple actors liable for another's personal injuries.[64] Under Rhode Island law, a party may sue for indemnification based on either an express contractual provision, or equitable principles.[65] Contractual indemnity provisions are valid if sufficiently specific, but are strictly construed against the party alleging a contractual right of indemnification.[66] In contrast to proportionate recovery in contribution, equitable indemnity allows complete and full reimbursement to a party personally faultless, but legally compelled to pay damages occasioned by another who is the "active and primary cause" of an injury.[67]

2. Settlement

The Contribution Among Joint Tortfeasors Act governs the effect of a release of one joint tortfeasor on the liability of the rest. Unless the release discharges the other tortfeasors they remain liable, but their liability is reduced by the amount paid as consideration, or by a proportionate reduction as provided by the release. Assuming a settlement and release complying with the Contribution Act, failure to instruct the jury about the reduction of liability due the non-settling tortfeasors is reversible error.[68]

A Contribution Act release protects a settling party from contribution claims brought by non-settling joint tortfeasors but does not extinguish equitable indemnity rights. Thus, a settlement under the Contribution Act leaves the settling party still vulnerable to indemnity claims. Stated another way, where there are cross-claims or third-party claims for indemnity, absent severance, a joint tortfeasor release does not necessarily relieve the settling party from attendance at the trial between plaintiff and the non-settling joint tortfeasors.[69]

Causes of action for both contribution and indemnity accrue not on the date of the primary injury, but on the date of payment of more than a party's rightful share of the plaintiff's damages. Thus, a joint tortfeasor who secures the release of another joint tortfeasor has one year from the date of the payment to the claimant to bring a contribution action. A secondarily liable party, who pays the claimant for the damages actively and primarily caused by a third party, has ten years to institute an action for equitable indemnity and complete recoupment.[70]

Gordon P. Cleary
Vetter & White
Center Place
50 Park Row West—Suite 109
Providence, Rhode Island 02903
(401) 421-3060
(Fax) (401) 272-6803

ENDNOTES - RHODE ISLAND

1. *State v. Lead Indus. Ass'n*, 951 A.2d 428, 457 (R.I. 2008) (product liability and public nuisance separate and distinct causes of action). *But see Fry v. Allergan Med. Optics*, 695 A.2d 501 (R.I. 1997), *cert. denied*, 118 S. Ct. 374 (1997) (holding federal law preempts claims involving Class III medical devices).

2. *Nappi v. John Deere & Co.*, 717 A.2d 650 (R.I. 1998); *Kelley v. Ford Motor Co.*, 290 A.2d 607 (R.I. 1972); *Plouffe v. Goodyear Tire & Rubber Co.*, 373 A.2d 492 (R.I. 1977).

3. *Nicolo v. Phillip Morris, Inc.*, 201 F.3d 29 (1st Cir. 2000); *Anthony v. Abbott Labs.*, 490 A.2d 43 (R.I. 1985); *Renaud v. Sigma-Aldrich Corp.*, 662 A.2d 711 (R.I. 1995).

4. *Romano v. Westinghouse Elec. Co.*, 336 A.2d 555 (R.I. 1975).

5. R.I. Gen. Laws § 9-1-29.

6. *Kennedy v. Cumberland Eng'g Co.*, 471 A.2d 195 (R.I. 1984).

7. *Ritter v. Narragansett Elec. Co.*, 283 A.2d 255 (R.I. 1971).

8. *Olshansky v. Rehrig Int'l*, 872 A.2d 282, 287 (R.I. 2005); *Clift v. Vose Hardware, Inc.*, 848 A.2d 1130 (R.I. 2004); *Raimbeault v. Takeuchi Mfg. (U.S.) Ltd.*, 772 A.2d 1056 (R.I. 2001); *Simmons v. Lincoln Elec. Co.*, 696 A.2d 273 (R.I. 1997); *Peters v. Jim Walter Door Sales of Tampa, Inc.*, 525 A.2d 46 (R.I. 1987).

9. *Sheehan v. N. Am. Mktg. Corp.*, 2008 U.S. Dist. LEXIS 26882 (D.R.I. Apr. 2, 2008).

10. *Gray v. Derderian*, 365 F. Supp. 2d 218, 222 (D.R.I. 2005); *Thomas v. Amway Corp.*, 488 A.2d 716 (R.I. 1985).

11. *Gray v. Derderian*, 472 F. Supp. 2d 172, 178 (D.R.I. 2007); *Castrignano v. E.R. Squibb & Sons, Inc.*, 546 A.2d 775 (R.I. 1988).

12. *Buonanno v. Colmer Beltings Co., Inc.*, 733 A.2d 712 (R.I. 1999); *Austin v. Lincoln Equip. Assoc., Inc.*, 888 F.2d 934 (1st Cir. 1989); *Guilbeault v. R. J. Reynolds Tobacco Co.*, 84 F. Supp. 2d 263 (D.R.I. 2000).

13. *Ruzzo v. LaRose Enters.*, 748 A.2d 261, 268 (R.I. 2000).

14. *Castrignano*, 546 A.2d 779.

15. *Scittarelli v. Providence Gas Co.*, 415 A.2d 1040 (R.I. 1980).

16. *Guilbeault v. R.J. Reynolds Tobacco Co.*, 84 F. Supp. 2d 263 (D.R.I. 2000).

17. *Simmons v. Lincoln Elec. Co.*, 696 A.2d 273; *Castrignano*, 546 A.2d 783.

18. *Hodges v. Brannon*, 707 A.2d 1225 (R.I. 1998).

19. *Fiske v. MacGregor, Div. of Brunswick*, 464 A.2d 719 (R.I. 1983).

20. *Sheehan v. The N. Am. Mktg. Corp.*, 610 F.3d 144 (1st Cir. 2010).

21. *Sheehan*, 610 F.3d 144.

22. *Brimbau v. Ausdale Equip. Rental Corp.*, 440 A.2d 1292 (R.I. 1982).

23. *Buonanno v. Colmar Belting Co., Inc.*, 733 A.2d 712 (R.I. 1999).

24. *New England Gas Co., Inc. v. S. Union Co.*, 460 F. Supp. 2d 314, 321-22 (D.R.I. 2006); *Splendorio v. Bilray Demolition Co., Inc.*, 682 A.2d 461, 465-66 (R.I. 1996); *Selwyn v. Ward*, 879 A.2d 882, 889-90 (R.I. 2005); *Castrignano*, 546 A.2d 783.

25. *Casey v. San-Lee Realty, Inc.*, 623 A.2d 16 (R.I. 1993).

26. 163 Cal. Rptr. 132 (1980).

27. *Gorman v. Abbott Labs., Inc.*, 599 A.2d 1364 (1991).

28. *Kuras v. International Harvester Co.*, 820 F.2d 15 (1st Cir. 1987).

29. *Scittarelli*, 415 A.2d 1043.

30. *Crawford v. Cooper/T. Smith Stevedoring Co., Inc.*, 14 F. Supp. 2d 202 (D.R.I. 1998).

31. *Buonanno*, 733 A.2d 712; *Sweredoski v. Alfa Laval, Inc.*, 2013 R.I. Super LEXIS 30, at *2 (R.I. Super. 2013).

32. R.I. R. Evid., 407.

33. *Ellington v. Davol, Inc.*, 2012 U.S. Dist. LEXIS 77692, at *12 n.4 (D.R.I. 2012); *Koch v. I-Flow Corp.*, 715 F. Supp. 2d 297 (D.R.I. 2010).

34. R.I. Gen. Laws § 9-1-32.

35. *LaPlante v. Am. Honda Motor Co.*, 27 F.3d 731 (1st Cir. 1994); *Pietrafesa v. Board of Governors for Higher Educ.*, 846 F. Supp. 1066 (D.R.I. 1994).

36. *Gray v. Derderian*, 365 F. Supp. 2d 218, 228 (D.R.I. 2005); *Roy v. Star Chopper Co., Inc.*, 442 F. Supp. 1010 (D.R.I. 1977), *aff'd*, 584 F.2d 1124 (1st Cir. 1978); *Austin v. Lincoln Equip. Assocs., Inc.*, 888 F.2d 934 (1st Cir. 1989).

37. *Plouffe*, 373 A.2d 492; *Scittarelli*, 415 A.2d 1043.

38. *Crawford v. Cooper/T. Smith Stevedoring Co., Inc.*, 14 F. Supp. 2d 202 (D.R.I. 1998).

39. *Thomas*, 488 A.2d 722; *Castrignano*, 546 A.2d 782 (prescription drugs).

40. *Cahill v. Gagnon*, 794 A.2d 451 (R.I. 2002); *Rhode Island Hosp. Trust Nat'l Bank v. Eastern Gen. Contractors, Inc.*, 674 A.2d 1227 (R.I. 1996).

41. *Farrell v. Connetti Trailer Sales, Inc.*, 727 A.2d 183 (R.I. 1999).

42. *Franklin Grove Corp. v. Drexel*, 936 A.2d 1272, 1275-77 (R.I. 2007); *Robertson Stephens, Inc. v. Chubb Corp.*, 473 F. Supp. 2d 265, 278-79 (D.R.I. 2007); *Rosseau v. K.N. Constr., Inc.*, 727 A.2d 190 (1999).

43. *Swajian v. Gen. Motors Corp.*, 559 A.2d 1041 (R.I. 1989).

44. *See, e.g., Botelho v. Caster's, Inc.*, 970 A.2d 541 (R.I. 2009).

45. *Ruzzo*, 748 A.2d 269.

46. *Castrignano*, 546 A.2d 783.

47. R.I. Gen. Laws § 6A-2-318.

48. *Ruzzo*, 748 A.2d 269.

49. *Zarella v. Minnesota Mut. Life Ins. Co.*, 824 A.2d 1249, 1262 (R.I. 2003); *Bourque v. Stop & Shop Co., Inc.*, 814 A.2d 320, 326 (R.I. 2003).

50. R.I. Gen. Laws § 9-21-10; *Oden v. Schwartz*, 2013 R.I. LEXIS 80, at *49-50 (R.I. 2013).

51. *Imperial Cas. & Indem. Co. v. Bellini*, 947 A.2d 886, 894 (R.I. 2008); *Kurczy v. St. Joseph Veterans Ass'n, Inc.*, 820 A.2d 929 (R.I. 2003); *Cardi Corp. v. State*, 561 A.2d 384 (R.I. 1989).

52. R.I. Gen. Laws § 9-21-10(a).

53. *Catanzaro v. Cent. Congregational Church*, 723 A.2d 774 (R.I. 1999).

54. *Wayne Distrib. Co. v. Piti Bldg. Co.*, 512 A.2d 870 (R.I. 1986); *Paola v. Commercial Union Assurance Cos.*, 490 A.2d 498 (R.I. 1985).

55. *Cardi*, 561 A.2d 387.

56. *Catanzaro*, 723 A.2d 776-77.

57. *DiMeo v. Philbin*, 502 A.2d 825 (R.I. 1986).

58. R.I. Gen. Laws § 28-29-20.

59. *Sansone v. Morton Mach. Works, Inc.*, 957 A.2d 386 (R.I. 2008); *Roy*, 442 F. Supp. 1021-22.

60. *Campbell v. Ne. Beverage Corp.*, 714 A.2d 612 (R.I. 1998).

61. R.I. Gen. Laws § 10-6-1 *et seq.*

62. R.I. Gen. Laws § 10-6-3.

63. *Wilson v. Krasnoff*, 560 A.2d 335, 340 (R.I. 1989).

64. R.I. Gen. Laws § 10-6-9.

65. *Ciampi v. Zuczek*, 598 F. Supp. 2d 257 (D.R.I. 2009).

66. *Sansone v. Morton Mach. Works, Inc.*, 957 A.2d 386 (R.I. 2008).

67. *Hawkins v. Gadoury*, 713 A.2d 799 (R.I. 1998).

68. *Shephardson v. Consolidated Med. Equip., Inc.*, 714 A.2d 1181 (R.I. 1998).

69. *Wilson*, 560 A.2d 341.

70. *Hawkins*, 713 A.2d 805 n.8.

SOUTH CAROLINA

A. **THEORIES OF LIABILITY**

In South Carolina, a product liability claim may be brought under three theories: strict liability in tort,[1] negligence, or breach of warranty.[2] None are exclusive remedies; a plaintiff may bring claims under more than one theory simultaneously.[3] In a product liability case, the plaintiff must establish three elements, regardless of the theory of recovery: (1) the product injured the plaintiff; (2) the product, at the time of the accident, was in essentially the same condition as when it left the hands of the defendant; and (3) the injury occurred because the product was in a defective condition unreasonably dangerous to the user.[4] In addition to these three elements, in a product liability claim under a negligence theory, the plaintiff must also prove that the manufacturer breached its duty to exercise reasonable care to adopt a safe design.[5] In 2010, the South Carolina Supreme Court clarified that, even though negligence and strict liability are not mutually exclusive theories of recovery, a failure to prove any one of the elements common to all causes of action is fatal to all claims.[6] "If one claim is dismissed and the basis of the dismissal rests on a common element shared by the companion claim, the companion claim must also be dismissed."[7]

B. **STRICT LIABILITY**

1. **Standard of Liability**

South Carolina has adopted legislatively Section 402A of the Restatement (Second) of Torts (1965).[8] The comments to Section 402A have been incorporated by reference as the intent of the South Carolina General Assembly.[9] In addition, the South Carolina Supreme Court has recently looked to the Restatement (Third) of Torts: Products Liability for guidance.[10]

South Carolina's Defective Products Act does not apply to establish liability when the essence of the transaction is the provision of a service.[11]

2. **"Defective and Unreasonably Dangerous Condition"**

A plaintiff must prove both that the product was defective and that the defect was "unreasonably dangerous" to the user or consumer or her property.[12]

> Two tests have evolved to determine whether a product is in a defective condition unreasonably dangerous for its intended use. The first test is whether the product is unreasonably dangerous to the ordinary consumer or user given the conditions and circumstances that foreseeably attend the use of the product. Under the second test, a

product is unreasonably dangerous and defective if the danger associated with the use of the product outweighs the utility of the product.

* * *

[O]ur Supreme Court has held that while any product can be made safer, the fact that it is not does not automatically mean the product is unreasonably dangerous. Strict liability is not equivalent either to absolute liability or to insurance of the safety of the product's user. Likewise, the mere fact that a product malfunctions does not demonstrate the manufacturer's negligence nor does it establish that the product was defective. Rather, "[i]n the final analysis, we have another of the law's balancing acts and numerous factors must be considered, including the usefulness and desirability of the product, the cost involved for added safety, the likelihood and potential seriousness of injury, and the obviousness of danger." Thus, in South Carolina we balance the utility of the risk inherent in the design of the product with the magnitude of the risk to determine the reasonableness of the manufacturer's action in designing the product. This "balancing act" is also relevant to the determination that the product, as designed, is unreasonably dangerous in its failure to conform to the ordinary user's expectations.[13]

In 2010, the South Carolina Supreme Court clarified that the applicable test for determining whether a product is unreasonably dangerous is different for alleged design defects than for manufacturing defects. The court explained that "the exclusive test in a products liability design case is the risk-utility test with its requirement of showing a feasible alternative design," reserving the "consumer expectation" test only for manufacturing defect cases.[14] This rule applies retroactively to all pending design defect cases.[15]

When the consumer expectation test is applied, whether a product is unreasonably dangerous is an objective determination "measured by the 'ordinary consumer' for whom the product is designed."[16] A specific plaintiff's unique characteristics have "no place in the purely objective determination of whether the product itself is unreasonably dangerous to an ordinary consumer."[17]

Courts applying South Carolina law have suggested that a product is not defective or unreasonably dangerous if the hazard associated with the product's use is one that is generally known.[18] This principle is often referred to as the "open and obvious" defense.

Courts have also held that "[a] product bearing a warning that the product is safe for use if the user follows the warning is neither defective nor unreasonably dangerous; therefore, the seller is not liable for any injuries caused by the use of the product if the user ignores the warning."[19]

3. **Plaintiff's Conduct as a Bar to Recovery in Strict Liability Claims**

   While a plaintiff's general negligence is not a defense to a strict liability claim and does not allow for apportionment of liability, a plaintiff's continued use of a product after discovering a defect and becoming aware of the danger ("assumption of the risk") will bar recovery if the plaintiff's continued use of the product was unreasonable.[20] Ordinarily, the question of reasonableness is one for the jury,[21] but courts have recognized that certain conduct can be unreasonable as a matter of law.[22] This defense is generally referred to as assumption of the risk, but it may also implicate the "open and obvious" doctrine.[23]

4. **Sale or Lease/Persons Liable**

   Strict liability may be applied even though no sale has occurred.[24] The product must only be injected into the stream of commerce.

5. **Inherently Dangerous Products**

   South Carolina recognizes that a legitimate market exists for certain products even though, by reason of their nature or use, they cannot be made completely safe for use.[25] As long as these products "are properly prepared, manufactured, packaged and accompanied with adequate warnings and instructions, they cannot be said to be defective. To hold otherwise would discourage the marketing of many products because some danger attends their use."[26] The adequacy of the warning is generally a question for the jury once the plaintiff has presented evidence that the warning was inadequate.[27]

6. **Safety Features**

   A manufacturer's failure to install a safety feature or device does not necessarily render a product defective and unreasonably dangerous.[28] The manufacturer will be liable only if the product is unreasonably dangerous to the user or consumer or to his property absent such feature or device.[29]

7. **Failure to Warn**

   A sufficient warning must specify the danger or cause of danger, and if challenging the sufficiency of a warning, the plaintiff must show a proposed warning that would have changed his or her behavior.[30] A product is not unreasonably dangerous if accompanied by adequate warnings that, if followed, make the product safe for use.[31]

   A manufacturer of a product is responsible for failing to warn if it knows or has reason to know the product is or is likely to be dangerous for its intended use, the manufacturer has no reason to believe that the user will realize the potential danger, and the manufacturer fails to utilize reasonable care to inform of the product's dangerous condition or of the facts that make it likely to be dangerous.[32]

The seller of a product is not required to warn of dangers or potential dangers that are generally known and recognized or "open and obvious," and thus a product cannot be deemed defective or unreasonably dangerous if the danger associated with the product is one that the product's users generally recognize.[33]

a. No Post-Sale Duty to Warn or Retrofit

A manufacturer "has no duty to notify previous purchasers of its products about later developed safety devices or to retrofit those products if the products were nondefective under standards existing at the time of manufacture or sale."[34]

b. Sophisticated User or Learned Intermediary

A seller may fulfill its duty to warn end users of dangers associated with a product by warning the intermediate purchaser if the intermediary is a sophisticated user who is in a position to understand and assess the risks involved and has the ability to effectively communicate those dangers to the end user.[35] However, a seller may rely on the intermediary to provide warnings to the end user only if that reliance is reasonable under the circumstances. In determining whether a seller acted with reasonable care in fulfilling its duty to warn of potential risks or dangers inherent in a product, the jury must consider (1) what the purchaser already knew about the dangers associated with the product, and (2) whether under that circumstance, the seller can reasonably rely on the purchaser to warn others who might come into contact with the product.

At least one South Carolina case has used the phrase "sophisticated user defense" to refer to a learned intermediary under Restatement (Second) of Torts Section 388.[36] South Carolina courts appear to treat subparts (a)-(c) of Section 388 as an affirmative defense in typical products liability claims, *i.e.*, where the duty arises from the defendant's role in manufacturing or selling the product. However, to the extent a party relies on Section 388 as the *basis for imposing a duty of care,* that party has the burden of proving that all elements are satisfied.[37]

C. NEGLIGENCE

1. Standard

South Carolina follows the general negligence doctrine of reasonable care with regard to product liability.[38] In addition to a failure to exercise reasonable care, a plaintiff must prove: (1) the product injured the plaintiff; (2) the product, at the time of the accident, was in essentially the same condition as when it left the hands of the defendant; and (3) the injury occurred because the product was in a defective condition unreasonably dangerous to the user.[39] A manufacturer or seller is expected to anticipate both the environment that is normal for the use of the product and the reasonably foreseeable risks of the use of the product in such an environment.[40] South Carolina courts have explained that: "'[t]he distinction between strict liability and negligence in design-defect and failure-to-warn cases is that in strict liability, knowledge of the condition of the product and the risks involved in that condition will be imputed to the manufacturer, whereas in negligence these elements must be proven.'"[41]

To establish negligence, the plaintiff must prove that the defendant seller or manufacturer "failed to exercise due care in some respect, and, unlike strict liability, the focus is on the conduct of the defendant, and liability is determined according to fault."[42] "[T]he judgment and ultimate decision of the manufacturer must be evaluated based on what was known or 'reasonably attainable' at the time of manufacture."[43]

A negligent design claim "may be established by circumstantial evidence showing that, through the exercise of reasonable diligence, [the manufacturer] should have known" of the alleged design defect. As the South Carolina Supreme Court recently reiterated, the absence of direct evidence that the manufacturer knew of the alleged design defect does not, in itself, defeat a negligent design claim.[44]

The defendant designer or manufacturer will be held to the standard of an expert in the field.[45] The mere fact that a product malfunctions does not demonstrate the manufacturer's negligence nor tend to establish the product was defective.[46] Industry standards, customs and practices are relevant to defining the standard of care in negligence cases, even if the defendant has not adopted the standards.[47]

2. **Contributory/Comparative Negligence**

The defense of contributory negligence has been judicially repealed in South Carolina for all causes of action arising after July 1, 1991.[48] For all causes of action arising after that date, South Carolina applies the "not greater than" version of comparative negligence. Specifically, the South Carolina Supreme Court has explained:

> [A] plaintiff in a negligence action may recover damages if his or her negligence is not greater than that of the defendant. The amount of the plaintiff's recovery shall be reduced in proportion to the amount of his or her negligence. If there is more than one defendant, the plaintiff's negligence shall be compared to the combined negligence of all defendants.[49]

The burden of proof shifts to the defendant to prove comparative negligence.[50] Ordinarily, the comparison of the plaintiff's negligence with that of the defendant is a question of fact for the jury.[51] However, a court may "determine judgment as a matter of law if the sole reasonable inference drawn from the evidence is that the plaintiff's negligence exceeded fifty percent."[52]

The defendant's fault may be compared to and offset by the plaintiff's degree of fault regardless of whether each party's fault constitutes ordinary negligence, gross negligence, or recklessness.[53] "[A] jury may compare all forms of negligence as part of its assessment of fault."[54]

3. Damage

Under a negligence theory, an injury may be either physical or economic.[55] However, for a plaintiff to recover an economic loss, the defendant must violate a legal duty arising under contract or pursuant to a special relationship with the injured party.[56] Otherwise, the action is barred by the Economic Loss Rule. See Section G.3, *infra*.

4. Assumption of Risk

The defense of assumption of the risk is no longer an absolute bar to recovery under a negligence theory, but is included as part of the comparative negligence analysis.[57] However, a plaintiff's knowledge of the risk may render a product not unreasonably dangerous or defective as a matter of law, in which case a product liability action based on a negligence theory would fail. See Section B.2, *supra*. A defendant must still plead assumption of the risk as an affirmative defense.[58]

D. BREACH OF WARRANTY

In South Carolina, three warranties are potentially applicable to product liability cases: (1) express warranty,[59] (2) implied warranty of merchantability,[60] and (3) implied warranty of fitness for a particular purpose.[61] To recover under a breach of warranty theory, a plaintiff must prove that the product failed to conform to the warranty and that: (1) the product injured the plaintiff; (2) the product, at the time of the accident, was in essentially the same condition as when it left the hands of the defendant; and (3) the injury occurred because the product was in a defective condition unreasonably dangerous to the user.[62]

Section 36-2-313 of the South Carolina Uniform Commercial Code provides, in pertinent part:

> (1) Express warranties by the seller are created as follows:
>
> (a) Any affirmation of fact or promise, including those on containers or labels, made by the seller to the buyer, whether directly or indirectly, which relates to the goods and becomes part of the basis of the bargain creates an express warranty that the goods conform to the affirmation or promise.
>
> (b) Any description of the goods which is made part of the basis of the bargain creates an express warranty that the goods shall conform to the description.
>
> (c) Any sample or model which is made part of the basis of the bargain creates an express warranty that the whole of the goods shall conform to the sample or model.[63]

Pursuant to Section 36-2-314(2), for goods to be merchantable, they must be at least as such as:

(a) pass without objection in the trade under the contract description; and

(b) in the case of fungible goods, are of fair average quality within the description; and

(c) are fit for the ordinary purposes for which such goods are used; and

(d) run, within the variations permitted by the agreement, of even kind, quality and quantity within each unit and among all units involved; and

(e) are adequately contained, packaged, and labeled as the agreement may require.[64]

Section 36-2-315 provides:

Where the seller at the time of contracting has reason to know any particular purpose for which the goods are required and that the buyer is relying on the seller's skill or judgment to select or furnish suitable goods, there is unless excluded or modified under [S.C. Code Ann. § 36-2-316] an implied warranty that the goods shall be fit for such purpose.[65]

To evaluate whether a product or service is involved, South Carolina looks to the predominant factor of the transaction.[66] A sale of goods must occur before a warranty applies.[67] Physical injury to person or property (other than the product itself) must be alleged in order to pursue a breach of warranty claim under a product liability theory.[68]

The Code also provides that a seller and purchaser may contractually agree to limit the purchaser's remedies or exclude consequential damages.

An exclusive limited remedy is enforceable unless circumstances cause it "to fail of its essential purpose."[69] An exclusive limited remedy of repair or replacement fails of its essential purpose where the seller's repair or replacement of the defective product is unsuccessful.[70] In addition, "[t]he limited remedy of repair or replacement fails of its essential purpose if the seller will not or cannot repair or replace the defective product with a conforming product or there is unreasonable delay in repair or replacement."[71] The factors considered in determining whether a limited remedy fails of its essential purpose are: "(1) the facts and circumstances surrounding the contract; (2) the nature of the basic obligations of the party; (3) the nature of the goods involved; (4) the uniqueness or experimental nature of the items; (5) the general availability of the items; and (6) the good faith and reasonableness of the provision."[72] "[T]he court must determine whether the limited remedy as provided for by the parties fails of its purpose, rather than whether the limited remedy constituted appropriate relief or, with hindsight, objectively served the purpose of contract law."[73]

An exclusion of consequential damages is enforceable unless it is unconscionable.[74] The factors considered in determining unconscionability are: "(1) the nature of the injuries suffered by the plaintiff; (2) whether the plaintiff is a substantial business concern; (3) disparity in the parties' bargaining power; (4) the parties' relative sophistication; (5) whether there is an element of surprise in the exclusion; and (6) the conspicuousness of the clause."[75]

E. PRINCIPLES APPLICABLE TO ALL THEORIES OF LIABILITY

1. Feasible Alternative Design

In a case alleging a defective design, to recover under any theory of liability, a plaintiff must prove that a feasible alternative design for the product that caused his injury existed at the time the product was manufactured.[76] The alternative design must be one that is feasible for actual use, not just for demonstration purposes.[77] A "conceptual design" is insufficient to establish a reasonable alternative design.[78] A plaintiff is "required to set forth some evidence of an 'alternative design,' which necessarily include[s] the 'consideration of costs, safety, and functionality associated with the alternative design.'"[79]

2. "Essentially the Same Condition"

The plaintiff has the burden of proving the product that caused the injury was, at the time of the accident, in essentially the same condition as when it left the hands of the defendant.[80] The defendant is not required to prove the product's condition has changed.[81] Courts have granted summary judgment to defendants when the plaintiff "failed to offer any evidence establishing the history of the machine from the time it left Defendant's hands until Plaintiff's injury."[82] Such evidence can come from "records of the owner of the machine" or from expert testimony.[83] The passage of a substantial length of time between when the product leaves the defendant's hands and when the plaintiff is injured can be a factor in determining whether the product is in essentially the same condition.[84]

3. Venue

While venue is generally a procedural matter, it merits discussion here both because "[t]he right of a defendant in a civil action to a trial in the county of his residence is a substantial one"[85] and because South Carolina's venue provisions are somewhat unique.

a. Causes of Action Arising Prior to July 1, 2005

For causes of action arising prior to July 1, 2005, the applicable venue statute provided that a personal injury cause of action "shall be tried in the county in which the defendant resides at the time of the commencement of the action."[86] When there are multiple defendants, venue is proper in any county in which one or more of the defendants reside.[87] The plaintiff may designate a county other than the county in which one or more defendants reside only if none of the parties resides in South Carolina.[88]

"[F]or purposes of venue, a defendant corporation resides in any county where it (1) maintains its principal place of business or (2) maintains an office and agent for the transaction of business."[89]

In addition, for causes of action arising prior to July 1, 2005, venue is proper against a defendant motor carrier in any county through which the defendant operated.[90]

b. **Causes of Action Arising On or After July 1, 2005**

For causes of action arising on or after July 1, 2005, the determination of proper venue turns on whether the defendant is: (1) a resident individual; (2) a nonresident individual; (3) a domestic corporation, partnership, or LLC; (4) a foreign corporation, partnership, or LLC with a certificate of authority to transact business in South Carolina; or (5) some other foreign corporation, partnership or LLC.[91]

If the defendant is a resident individual, venue is proper in any county where the defendant resides or where the "most substantial part of the alleged act or omission giving rise to the cause of action occurred."[92]

If the defendant is a nonresident individual, venue is proper in any county where the "most substantial part of the alleged act or omission giving rise to the cause of action occurred," where the plaintiff resides, or if the plaintiff is a corporation, partnership, or LLC, at the plaintiff's principal place of business.[93]

If the defendant is a domestic corporation, partnership, or LLC, venue is proper in any county where the defendant had its principal place of business at the time the cause of action arose or where the "most substantial part of the alleged act or omission giving rise to the cause of action occurred."[94]

If the defendant is a foreign corporation, partnership, or LLC with a certificate of authority to transact business in South Carolina, venue is proper in any county where the "most substantial part of the alleged act or omission giving rise to the cause of action occurred" or where the defendant maintained its principal place of business at the time the cause of action arose.[95]

If the defendant is some other foreign corporation, partnership or LLC, venue is proper in any county where: (a) the "most substantial part of the alleged act or omission giving rise to the cause of action occurred;" (b) the plaintiff resides at the time the cause of action arose, or if the plaintiff is a corporation, partnership, or LLC, at the plaintiff's principal place of business; or (c) the defendant has its principal place of business at the time the cause of action arose.[96]

c. **Principal Place of Business**

For causes of action arising on or after July 1, 2005, "principal place of business" means either: (1) a business's home office location within South Carolina; or (2) if the business does not have a home office within South Carolina, "the location of the business's manufacturing, sales, or purchasing facility" within South Carolina. If the business has multiple facilities but no home office in South Carolina, the principle place of business is the location at which the majority of the business's activity takes place.[97]

d. **Multiple Defendants**

If there is more than one defendant, venue is proper "in any county where the action properly may be maintained against one of the defendants."[98]

e. **Change of Venue**

The court may change venue when: (1) the initial venue chosen by the plaintiff is improper; (2) a fair and impartial trial is unattainable in the initial venue; or (3) such a change would promote "the convenience of witnesses and the ends of justice."[99]

4. **Causation**

Under any of the product liability theories, a plaintiff must prove the product defect was the proximate cause of the injury sustained.[100] The connection between defect and injury must be established as a matter of probability, not mere possibility.[101]

Proximate cause requires proof of both causation in fact and legal cause.[102] Causation in fact is proved by establishing the injury would not have occurred "but for" the defendant's conduct or product defect.[103] Legal cause is proved by establishing foreseeability.[104] The test of foreseeability is whether some injury to another is the natural and probable consequence of the complained-of act.[105] While it is not necessary that the actor must have contemplated the particular event that occurred, the actor cannot be charged with that which is unpredictable or could not be expected to happen.[106] "[T]he actor's conduct must be viewed in light of the attendant circumstances."[107]

Proximate cause is the efficient or direct cause of injury,[108] but it does not mean the sole cause.[109] The defendant's conduct can be a proximate cause if it was at least one of the direct, concurring causes of the injury.[110] "A plaintiff suing under a products liability cause of action can recover all damages that were proximately caused by the defendant's placing an unreasonably dangerous product into the stream of commerce."[111] Similarly, under a breach of warranty theory, liability is imposed when an injury is proximately caused by a breach of warranty.[112]

Causation can be proven by circumstantial evidence.[113] However, in a products liability case where causation is based solely on circumstantial evidence, a plaintiff cannot recover if "the cause of [the plaintiff's] injuries may be as reasonably attributable to an act for which [a defendant] is not liable as to one for which it is liable."[114]

The test for whether a subsequent negligent act by a third party breaks the chain of causation to insulate a prior tortfeasor from liability is whether the subsequent actor's negligence was reasonably foreseeable.[115] "For an intervening act to break the causal link and insulate the tortfeasor from further liability, the intervening act must be unforeseeable."[116]

While a plaintiff may use circumstantial evidence to show a design defect, "[i]t is well-established that one cannot draw an inference of a defect from the mere fact a product failed."[117] Accordingly, "the plaintiff must offer some evidence beyond the product's failure itself to prove that it is unreasonably dangerous."[118] In design defect cases involving complex claims, expert testimony is required to make this showing.[119]

5. **"Post-Distribution Evidence"**

In a design defect case, the determination of the manufacturer's liability may be evaluated based only on information that "was known or 'reasonably attainable' at the time of manufacture. The use of post-distribution evidence to evaluate a product's design through the lens of hindsight is improper."[120]

6. **Successor Liability**

In the absence of a statute, a plaintiff may maintain a state-law based product liability claim against a successor company only where "(a) there was an agreement to assume such debts; (b) the circumstances surrounding the transaction indicate a consolidation of the two corporations; (c) the successor company was a mere continuation of the predecessor company; or (d) the transaction was fraudulently entered into for the purpose of wrongfully denying creditor claims."[121] The plaintiff may maintain a product liability claim under a successor liability theory when there are one or more other viable product liability defendants.[122]

7. **Market Share Liability/Enterprise Liability**

The doctrine of joint enterprise provides a means of imputing the wrongdoing of one entity to another. If two parties are engaged in a joint enterprise, "each is the agent of the other, and each the principal of the other, so as to bring into force the fixed precepts of the law of agency."[123] Generally, a joint enterprise exists where there are two or more persons united in the joint prosecution of a common purpose under such circumstances that each has authority, express or implied, to act for all in respect to the control of the means and the agencies employed to execute such common purpose. Further, in order to constitute a joint enterprise, there must be a common purpose and community of interest in the object of the enterprise and an equal right to direct and control the conduct of each other with respect thereto.[124]

With respect to tort liability, the joint enterprise theory is almost exclusively applied by South Carolina courts in cases involving automobile accidents with the driver's negligence being imputed to a passenger.[125] However, the South Carolina courts have not expressly limited the joint enterprise theory to that context.

8. **Substantial Alteration/Abnormal Use**

Liability may be imposed upon a manufacturer or seller notwithstanding the plaintiff's alteration of the product when the alteration could have been anticipated by the manufacturer or seller and was the proximate cause of the damages or injuries.[126] When an alteration to a product is shown, the foreseeability of the alteration must be examined.[127] The issue of foreseeability is normally a question of fact for the jury.

A defendant is liable for reasonably foreseeable misuses of the product.[128] A manufacturer must be able to anticipate the environment that is normal for the use of his product and must anticipate the reasonably foreseeable use of the product in such an environment.[129] However, the defendant is under no duty to prevent the product from deteriorating because of use (absent an original defect in the product).[130]

9. **Allegedly Similar Accidents**

"Evidence of similar accidents, transactions, or happenings is admissible in South Carolina where there is some special relation between the accidents tending to prove or disprove some fact in dispute."[131] A court should consider the following factors in determining whether to admit evidence of other incidents "to support a claim that the present accident was caused by the same defect: (1) the products are similar; (2) the alleged defect is similar; (3) causation related to the defect in the other incidents; and (4) exclusion of all reasonable secondary explanations for the cause of the other incidents."[132]

"[I]f the cause of an accident is known and the cause is not substantially similar to the accident at issue, evidence of the other accident should be excluded."[133] However, where the precise cause of an accident is not known, the South Carolina Supreme Court has allowed statistical accident-rate data of a particular model automobile as compared to other vehicles in its class, finding that such data was relevant to whether the automobile model in question was unreasonably dangerous.[134]

10. **Destruction or Loss of Evidence**

"[W]hen a party loses or destroys evidence, an inference may be drawn that the destroyed or lost evidence would have been adverse to that party."[135] The court also retains the inherent power to impose spoliation sanctions.[136]

11. **Crashworthiness**

In product liability cases involving motor vehicles such as automobiles, motorcycles, airplanes, snowmobiles, helicopters and recreational motorboats, the doctrine of "crashworthiness" applies.[137] South Carolina first adopted the crashworthiness doctrine in *Mickle v. Blackmon*.[138]

The concept focuses on the vehicle's capacity to withstand the physical stresses of a collision and its ability to minimize the additional or enhanced injuries that passengers may sustain as a result of the "second collision" between the occupants and the interior of the vehicle. The cause of the accident is largely irrelevant to the crashworthiness issue, and specifically, prior decisions suggested that the accident need not have been caused by a design or construction defect in the motor vehicle.[139] The South Carolina federal district court held in 2013 that evidence of accident causation or fault is admissible in crashworthiness cases.[140] However, South Carolina law is unsettled on this issue.[141]

The plaintiff has three elements of proof in crashworthiness cases. First, there must be "proof of an alternative, safer design, practicable under the circumstances."[142] Second, the plaintiff must prove the defective design enhanced the injuries. In other words, the injuries were over and above the injuries that probably would have occurred in the collision absent the defective design.[143] Moreover, the injuries must have occurred in the second collision.[144] Finally, the plaintiff must offer some method of establishing the extent of enhanced injuries attributable to the defective design.[145]

As noted above, South Carolina courts have not directly addressed whether comparative fault concepts apply in strict liability crashworthiness analysis,[146] and the Fourth Circuit has concluded that South Carolina law is unsettled and unpredictable in this area.[147]

12. **Offers of Judgment**

Any party may issue a written "offer of judgment" for a specified judgment by stipulation by filing it with the court and serving it on the opposing party. If the offer is accepted, the clerk of court enters a judgment accordingly. If the offer is not accepted within twenty days or prior to the tenth day before trial (whichever occurs first), it is deemed rejected. No evidence of a rejected offer of judgment is admissible except in a post-trial proceeding on costs and fees. An offer of judgment may be withdrawn at any time prior to acceptance.[148]

> If an offer of judgment is not accepted and the offeror obtains a verdict or determination at least as favorable as the rejected offer, the offeror shall be allowed to recover from the offeree: (1) any administrative, filing, or other court costs from the date of the offer until judgment; (2) if the offeror is a plaintiff, eight percent interest computed on the amount of the verdict or award from the date of the offer; or (3) if the offeror is a defendant, a reduction from the judgment or award of eight

percent interest computed on the amount of the verdict or award from the date of the offer.[149]

13. South Carolina Unfair Trade Practices Act

The South Carolina Unfair Trade Practices Act provides that "[u]nfair methods of competition and unfair or deceptive acts or practices in the conduct of any trade or commerce are hereby declared unlawful."[150]

To prevail on a claim under the South Carolina Unfair Trade Practices Act, a plaintiff must show: (1) an unfair or deceptive act or practice, (2) in the conduct of trade or commerce, (3) having an adverse impact on the public interest, (4) proximate cause, and (5) damage.[151] The South Carolina Supreme Court has further limited recovery under the Act to "immediate purchasers," disallowing recovery to remote buyers who could not have relied on any alleged misrepresentations or deceptive acts of the defendant.[152]

The Act allows for recovery of attorneys' fees and costs.[153] If the court finds that the defendant knew or should have known his conduct was an unfair method of competition or an unfair or deceptive act, the plaintiff may recover three times its actual damages.[154]

14. Expert Witnesses

The South Carolina Rules of Evidence provide that an expert witness may testify in the form of an opinion or otherwise if "scientific, technical, or other specialized knowledge will assist the trier of fact to understand the evidence or to determine a fact in issue."[155] South Carolina has not adopted the *Daubert v. Merrell Dow Pharmaceuticals* standard for qualification of expert witnesses or the corresponding amendments that were made to Federal Rule of Evidence 702 in 2000. Instead, South Carolina courts employ a more liberal approach to admitting expert testimony than federal courts.[156]

The court makes a gatekeeping determination of admissibility based on the expert's qualifications and the reliability of the testimony.[157] "[T]he trial judge must find the evidence will assist the trier of fact, the expert witness is qualified, and the underlying science is reliable."[158] South Carolina courts apply the following factors to determine reliability of scientific expert testimony: "(1) the publications and peer review of the technique; (2) prior application of the method to the type of evidence involved in the case; (3) the quality control procedures used to ensure reliability; and (4) the consistency of the method with recognized scientific laws and procedures."[159] Even if expert testimony "is admissible under Rule 702, SCRE, the trial judge should determine if its probative value is outweighed by its prejudicial effect."[160]

Whether an expert is qualified and will assist the trier of fact "is a matter largely within the trial court's discretion and will not be reversed absent an abuse of that discretion."[161] As the South Carolina Court of Appeals has held, a qualified expert needs to acquire "by study or practical experience such knowledge ... as would enable him to give guidance and assistance to the jury in resolving a factual issue which is beyond the scope of the jury's ... common knowledge."[162] Accordingly, trial courts may consider a number of factors in determining an expert's qualification, including whether the expert is licensed in his field, considerations outlined in the rules of evidence, statutory law, and "any other sources of authority that may be relevant to a purported expert witness's level of skill or knowledge."[163] However, a witness who has "no knowledge, skill, experience, training or education specifically related" to the specific product at issue in the case may not be allowed to offer expert testimony.[164]

In 2009, the South Carolina Supreme Court declared that the court's gatekeeping role applies to both scientific and "nonscientific" expert testimony, eliminating any distinction in the court's role for different types of expert testimony.[165] Unlike scientific testimony, however, the South Carolina Supreme Court has declined to set a general test for reliability of nonscientific testimony due to the multitude of Rule 702 qualification and reliability challenges which may arise with respect to nonscientific expert evidence.[166] Thus, reliability of nonscientific testimony "must be evaluated on an ad hoc basis."[167]

Assessing the reliability of an expert opinion rendered using the "reasoning to the best inference" methodology, the South Carolina Supreme Court stated that while an expert need not categorically exclude alternative causes, "when an expert cannot offer an explanation for the rejection of a possible alternative cause, the expert's testimony is not sufficiently reliable."[168] Whether testimony of an expert is deemed scientific or nonscientific, an expert does not assist the trier of fact in determining whether a product failed if he starts his analysis based upon the assumption that the product failed, and fails "to provide objective criteria for eliminating [alternative causes]."[169]

Unlike the Federal Rules, South Carolina's Rules of Civil Procedure and Rules of Evidence do not require an expert to issue a written report regarding his or her findings.[170]

15. Arbitration Provisions

South Carolina has adopted a version of the Uniform Arbitration Act.[171] In cases involving maritime transactions or transactions involving interstate commerce, however, the Federal Arbitration Act governs contractual arbitration provisions.[172]

For transactions not involving maritime transactions or interstate commerce, the South Carolina Uniform Arbitration Act (SCUAA) provides:

> A written agreement to submit any existing controversy to arbitration or a provision in a written contract to submit to arbitration any controversy thereafter arising between the parties is valid, enforceable and irrevocable, save upon such grounds as exist at law or in equity for

the revocation of any contract. Notice that a contract is subject to arbitration pursuant to this chapter shall be typed in underlined capital letters, or rubber-stamped prominently, on the first page of the contract and unless such notice is displayed thereon the contract shall not be subject to arbitration.[173]

Both federal and state policies favor arbitration of disputes.[174] Any doubts concerning the scope of an arbitration clause are resolved in favor of arbitration.[175] Nevertheless, the trial court determines whether a dispute is subject to arbitration,[176] and South Carolina courts strictly construe the technical requirements of the SCUAA.[177]

"[U]nless a court can say with positive assurance that the arbitration clause is not susceptible to any interpretation that covers the dispute, arbitration should generally be ordered."[178] "Arbitration will be denied if a court determines no agreement to arbitrate existed,"[179] however, and the court may not require a party to submit any matter to arbitration that is outside the scope of the arbitration provision.[180]

a. Enforceability of "Broadly Worded" Arbitration Provisions

A South Carolina court will characterize an arbitration provision as broadly worded if it purports to govern disputes "arising out of or related to" the underlying contract between the parties.[181] A court will enforce a broadly worded arbitration provision only in "disputes in which a 'significant relationship' exists between the asserted claims and the contract in which the arbitration clause is contained."[182] The Supreme Court recently limited the criteria for a significant relationship:

> "[W]e pronounce a more definitive rule for determining whether a significant relationship exists between a dispute between parties to a contract and the underlying contract, thereby implicating an arbitration agreement in the contract. Because even the most broadly-worded arbitration agreements still have limits founded in general principles of contract law, this Court will refuse to interpret any arbitration agreement as applying to outrageous torts that are unforeseeable to a reasonable consumer in the context of normal business dealings."[183]

b. Waiver

A party may waive its right to enforce an arbitration provision.[184]

> In order to establish waiver, a party must show prejudice through an undue burden caused by delay in demanding arbitration. There is no set rule as to what constitutes a waiver of the right to arbitrate; the question depends on the facts of each case.
>
> Generally, the factors our courts consider to determine if a party waived its right to compel arbitration are: (1) whether a substantial length of time transpired between the commencement of the action

and the commencement of the motion to compel arbitration; (2) whether the party requesting arbitration engaged in extensive discovery before moving to compel arbitration; and (3) whether the non-moving party was prejudiced by the delay in seeking arbitration. These factors, of course, are not mutually exclusive, as one factor may be inextricably connected to, and influenced by, the others.[185]

c. Unconscionable Arbitration Provisions

An unconscionable arbitration provision is not enforceable. "[U]nconscionability is defined as the absence of meaningful choice on the part of one party due to one-sided contract provisions, together with terms that are so oppressive that no reasonable person would make them and no fair and honest person would accept them."[186] A court may refuse to enforce all or part of an arbitration provision that offers no meaningful choice to one party and has oppressive terms.[187] The court must conduct its analysis for unconscionability on a case-by-case basis. "[T]here is no specific set of factual circumstances establishing the line which must be crossed when evaluating an arbitration clause for unconscionability."[188]

16. Trade Secrets

The balancing test associated with the discovery of trade secret information under South Carolina Rule of Civil Procedure 26(c) governs the discovery of trade secret information in a product liability action.[189] To be discoverable, trade secret information must meet the "relevant and necessary" standard of Rule 26(c).[190] The South Carolina Supreme Court has held:

> Regarding the requirement that the trade secret information must be "relevant," we hold that the information must be relevant not only to the general subject matter of the litigation, but also relevant specifically to the issues involved in the litigation. For the trade secret information to be deemed "necessary," we hold that the party seeking the information "cannot merely assert unfairness but must demonstrate with specificity exactly how the lack of the information will impair the presentation of the case on the merits to the point that an unjust result is a real, rather than a merely possible, threat." "Implicit in this is the notion that suitable substitutes must be completely lacking." In other words, the trial court must evaluate whether there are reasonable alternatives available to the party seeking the discovery of the information, and ultimately, the trial court must require the discovery of a trade secret only when "the issues cannot be fairly adjudicated unless the information is available."[191]

F. **ADDITIONAL DEFENSES**

1. **Statutes of Limitation and Repose**

    Because no "product liability" statute of limitations exists, the applicable statute of limitations is the equivalent of any personal injury, wrongful death, or property damage statute. For such actions, the limitations period is six years for causes of action accruing prior to April 5, 1988, and three years for causes of action arising on or after April 5, 1988.[192] For breach of warranty actions, the statute of limitations is six years.[193] The date of discovery is significant in determining the date to commence the running of the statute.[194] South Carolina also imposes an eight-year statute of repose on improvements to real property,[195] but there is no statute of repose for products other than improvement to real property.

2. **Privity**

    No privity of contract is required.[196]

3. **State of the Art**

    The state of the art and industry standards are relevant to show both the reasonableness of the design and that the product is dangerous beyond the expectations of the ordinary consumer.[197] Industry standards are also relevant in failure-to-warn claims.[198] Evidence of design customs and trade practices at the time of manufacture is admissible on the issue of design defects.[199]

4. **Standards and Governmental Regulation**

    A product must be measured against the standard existing at the time of sale or against reasonable customer expectations held at the time of sale. Hindsight opinions by experts suggesting that more should have been done are insufficient to discredit the conclusion that the manufacturer met the standard of care.[200]

    A product is not per se "defective" merely because safer equipment could be installed.[201] However, the defendant has the duty to keep abreast of current standards.[202]

    The South Carolina Court of Appeals recently held that when an automobile manufacturer chooses a passenger restraint system that complies with requirements under federal regulations, a plaintiff may not challenge that choice in a state law tort action.[203] However, this does not preempt a plaintiff "from asserting a defect in the design or implementation of a chosen passive restraint system."[204]

5. **Employer Immunity from Suit**

    Workers' compensation is the exclusive remedy against employers for personal injury to an employee arising out of and in the course of employment.[205] Accordingly, the South Carolina Workers' Compensation Commission generally has exclusive jurisdiction over tort actions brought by employees against their employer or against a co-employee.[206]

6. **Door Closing Statute**

A plaintiff who is not a resident of South Carolina may bring an action against a corporation created by or under the laws of another state only when the cause of action arose within South Carolina or the subject of the action is situated within South Carolina.[207] An out-of-state plaintiff may bring an action under the door closing statute if the plaintiff was exposed to a harmful product within South Carolina, even if the plaintiff was no longer in South Carolina when the resulting injury was first diagnosed.[208]

G. DAMAGES

1. **Punitive Damages**

"A plaintiff suing under a products liability cause of action can recover all damages that were proximately caused by the defendant's placing an unreasonably dangerous product into the stream of commerce."[209]

Punitive damages may be awarded against the tortfeasor who acted willfully, wantonly, or in reckless disregard for a plaintiff's rights.[210] A tort meets this standard if it was committed in "conscious disregard" of the rights of others.[211] Plaintiffs must be able to establish by clear and convincing evidence a consciousness of wrongdoing at the time of the tortious conduct at issue.[212]

Effective January 1, 2012, the South Carolina Fairness in Civil Justice Act of 2011 introduced a cap on punitive damages at $500,000 or three times the compensatory damages award, whichever is greater.[213] However, the award can be increased to the greater of $2 million or four times compensatory damages should the jury find that the defendant's wrongful conduct was motivated primarily by financial gain, or the defendant's actions rise to the level of felony charges.[214] This cap on punitive damages does not apply if the plaintiff proves that the defendant intended to harm the claimant, was convicted of a felony arising out of the same act or acted under the influence of drugs or alcohol.[215] If requested by a defendant, claims for punitive damages can be tried in a bifurcated proceeding, separate from compensatory or nominal damages, before the same jury.[216]

South Carolina follows the United States Supreme Court's precedent in *BMW of North America v. Gore*[217] in determining whether a punitive damages award comports with due process by analyzing the following factors: the reprehensibility of the defendant's conduct, the disparity or ratio between the actual or potential harm suffered by the plaintiff and the amount of the punitive damages award, and the difference between the punitive damages awarded and the civil penalties authorized or imposed in comparable cases.[218] The unique application of the ratio to the plaintiff's "potential" harm was set forth in a 2009 South Carolina Supreme Court case.[219] The plaintiff's actual damages were $186,000, and the plaintiff introduced expert testimony that his future potential damages were $1,081,189.40 for future medical treatment and costs.[220] The South Carolina Supreme Court remitted punitive damages to $10 million, stating that this resulted in a ratio of 9.2 to 1 when compared with the plaintiff's potential damages.[221] With the passage of the Fairness in Civil Justice Act of 2011, this "potential" harm principle is still applicable within the statutory caps on punitive damages.

The South Carolina Supreme Court has also developed eight factors relevant to the post-verdict due process review.[222] The factors are: (1) defendant's degree of culpability; (2) duration of the conduct; (3) defendant's awareness or concealment; (4) the existence of similar past conduct; (5) likelihood the award will deter the defendant or others from like conduct; (6) whether the award is reasonably related to the harm likely to result from such conduct; (7) defendant's ability to pay; and (8) "other factors deemed appropriate."[223] These factors are relevant to the post-judgment due process analysis only insofar as they add substance to the *Gore* guideposts.[224]

Evidence of a defendant's net worth is "a proper guide in assessing the 'ability to pay' factor."[225] However, the South Carolina Supreme Court has cautioned against use of evidence of the defendant's financial condition other than net worth.[226]

"[N]egligence per se is evidence of recklessness requiring the trial court to submit the issue of punitive damages to the jury."[227] "'It is always for the jury to determine whether a party has been reckless, willful, and wanton.'"[228]

Punitive damages may not be awarded in cases based solely on strict liability in tort or on a warranty theory.[229] Punitive damages are not reduced by the proportion of plaintiff's negligence under comparative negligence.[230]

2. **Accumulated Interest**

   a. **Pre-Judgment Interest**

   South Carolina common law permits the recovery of pre-judgment interest under certain circumstances. Generally, courts permit recovery of pre-judgment interest on obligations to pay money from the time when payment is demandable, either by agreement of the parties or by operation of law, if the sum is certain or capable of being reduced to certainty.[231] "The proper test for determining whether prejudgment interest may be awarded is whether or not the measure of recovery, not necessarily the amount of damages, is fixed by conditions existing at the time the claim arose."[232] In the absence of an agreement or statute, interest is not recoverable on an unliquidated claim.[233] Pursuant to these basic rules, interest is not generally recoverable for bodily injury, emotional distress, lost profits, or similar consequential loss,[234] but is recoverable for property loss or damage.[235]

When pre-judgment interest is recoverable, South Carolina Code Section 34-31-20(A) provides that the rate of interest will be eight (8) percent per annum.[236] Further, the Restatement indicates that compound interest is not permitted in actions at law, but may be granted in equity in appropriate cases.[237]

b. Post-Judgment Interest

South Carolina provides for post-judgment interest by statute:

> All money decrees and judgments of courts enrolled or entered shall draw interest according to law. For all judgments entered on or after July 1, 2005, the legal rate of interest is equal to the prime rate as listed in the first edition of the Wall Street Journal published for each calendar year for which damages are awarded, plus four percentage points, compounded annually.[238]

To stop the accrual of post-judgment interest, the judgment debtor may deposit the funds with the court pursuant to Rule 67 of the South Carolina Rules of Civil Procedure.[239] The South Carolina Supreme Court has overruled prior case law to find that when payment is delayed because the judgment creditor has appealed, interest continues to accrue whether "it has been modified upward or downward or remains the same."[240]

3. Economic Loss

The Defective Products Act allows recovery of tort damages when the defective product causes the user "physical harm."[241] Under the economic loss rule, South Carolina law does not provide for "liability for a product defect if the damage suffered by the plaintiff is only to the product itself."[242] The South Carolina economic loss rule has undergone multiple significant changes since 2007. In 2009, the South Carolina Supreme Court brought the rule into line with the majority of U.S. jurisdictions:

> In the context of products liability law, when a defective product only damages itself, the only concrete and measurable damages are the diminution in the value of the product, cost of repair, and consequential damages resulting from the product's failure. Stated differently, the consumer has only suffered an economic loss. The consumer has

purchased an inferior product, his expectations have not been met, and he has lost the benefit of the bargain. In this instance, however, the risk of product failure has already been allocated pursuant to the terms of the agreement between the parties. On the other hand, the parties have not bargained for the situation in which a defective product creates an unreasonable risk of harm and causes personal injury or property damage. Accordingly, where a product damages only itself, tort law provides no remedy and the action lies in contract; but when personal injury or other property damage occurs, a tort remedy may be appropriate.[243]

South Carolina recognizes a narrow exception to the economic loss rule in the residential home-buying context.[244] "[T]he economic loss rule does not preclude a homebuyer from recovering in tort against the developer or builder where the builder violates an applicable building code, deviates from industry standards, or constructs a house that he knows or should know will pose a serious risk of physical harm."[245]

There are exceptions under which a plaintiff may recover in tort for breach of a duty that arises under contract. First, a breach of a duty that arises under contract may support a tort action if "there is a special relationship between the alleged tortfeasor and the injured party not arising in contract."[246] "Whether such a duty exists will depend on the facts and circumstances of each case,"[247] and at least one court has held that the relationship between a buyer and seller, without more, does not constitute a "special relationship" that will support tort liability.[248]

4. **Joint and Several Liability**

For causes of action arising prior to July 1, 2005, each joint tortfeasor was individually liable for the full amount of the plaintiff's loss.[249] For causes of action arising on or after July 1, 2005, joint and several liability applies to any defendant whose conduct is 50 percent or more of the total fault.[250] Any other defendant is responsible only for its own percentage of the total fault.[251] South Carolina apportions the percentage of fault among defendants by either the jury, or the court if there is no jury, specifying the amount of damages and determining the percentage of fault of the plaintiff and the amount of recoverable damages under applicable rules concerning "comparative negligence."[252] Upon the motion of at least one defendant, the jury, or court, will determine the percentage of liability that is attributable to each defendant.[253] The total of the percentage of fault to be attributed to plaintiff and defendants must be 100 percent.[254] The statutory provisions on joint and several liability do not apply, however, to a defendant whose actions are willful, wanton, reckless, grossly negligent, or intentional.[255]

The plaintiff may elect to sue one, some, or all of the joint tortfeasors[256] and may sue them jointly in one suit or individually in separate suits.[257]

5. **Contribution**

South Carolina has adopted a version of the Uniform Contribution Among Tortfeasors Act.[258] The Act provides for a right of pro rata contribution among persons jointly and severally liable in tort except for cases involving an intentional tort or breach of trust. The Act applies to settlement but does not affect rights of indemnity.[259]

James T. Irvin, III
Jay T. Thompson
Jessica Peters Goodfellow
Nelson Mullins Riley & Scarborough, LLP
Meridian, Suite 1700
1320 Main Street
Columbia, South Carolina 29201
(803) 799-2000
(Fax) (803) 256-7500

ENDNOTES - SOUTH CAROLINA

1. South Carolina adopted Restatement (Second) of Torts § 402A (1965) in S.C. Code Ann. §§ 15-73-10 to -30, thereby establishing strict liability in tort in South Carolina. The South Carolina Court of Appeals declined to adopt Restatement (Third) of Products Liability. *Curcio v. Caterpillar, Inc.*, 543 S.E.2d 264, 268-69 (S.C. Ct. App. 2001), *rev'd on other grounds*, 585 S.E.2d 272 (S.C. 2003).

2. S.C. Code Ann. §§ 36-1-101 *et seq.*, 36-2-313, -314, -315, -318 (2003) (adopting UCC warranties with modified language).

3. *Branham v. Ford Motor Co.*, 701 S.E.2d 5, 9 (S.C. 2010); *Talkington v. Atria ReclamelucifersFabrieken BV*, 152 F.3d 254, 263 (4th Cir. 1998); *Bragg v. Hi-Ranger, Inc.*, 462 S.E.2d 321, 326 (S.C. Ct. App. 1995).

4. *Branham*, 701 S.E.2d at 8; *Rife v. Hitachi Constr. Mach. Co., Ltd.*, 609 S.E.2d 565, 568 (S.C. Ct. App. 2005); *Bragg*, 462 S.E.2d at 326. Interestingly, emotional injury to the operator of a product is sufficient to satisfy the first element in a South Carolina product liability action under any theory. *Bray v. Marathon Corp.*, 588 S.E.2d 93, 95 (S.C. 2003).

5. *Branham v. Ford Motor Co.*, 701 S.E.2d 5, 9 (S.C. 2010); *Rife*, 609 S.E.2d at 569; *Bragg*, 462 S.E.2d at 326.

6. *Branham v. Ford Motor Co.*, 701 S.E.2d 5, 9 (S.C. 2010).

7. *Branham v. Ford Motor Co.*, 701 S.E.2d 5, 9 (S.C. 2010).

8. S.C. Code Ann. § 15-73-10 (2005). Title 15, Chapter 73 of the South Carolina Code is known as the "Defective Products Act."

9. S.C. Code Ann. § 15-73-30 (2005).

10. *Branham v. Ford Motor Co.*, 701 S.E.2d 5, 14.

11. *In re Breast Implant Prod. Liab. Litig.*, 503 S.E.2d 445, 448 (S.C. 1998); *Duncan v. CRS SirrineEng'rs, Inc.*, 524 S.E.2d 115, 118 n.3 (S.C. Ct. App. 1999). *See also Madison v. Am. Home Prods. Corp.*, 595 S.E.2d 493, 496 (S.C. 2004) (finding a pharmacy provides "a service, rather than selling a product, and therefore, may not be held strictly liable for properly filling a prescription in accordance with a physician's orders").

12. S.C. Code Ann. § 15-73-10 (2005); *Bragg*, 462 S.E.2d at 328; *Allen v. Long Mfg. NC, Inc.*, 505 S.E.2d 354, 357 (S.C. Ct. App. 1998).

13. *Bragg*, 462 S.E.2d at 328. *See also* F. Patrick Hubbard & Robert L. Felix, The South Carolina Law of Torts 283 (3d ed. 2004).

14. *Branham*, 701 S.E.2d at 14.

15. *Miranda C. v. Nissan Motor Co., Ltd.*, 741 S.E.2d 34, 39-40 (S.C. Ct. App. 2013).

16. *Vaughn v. Nissan Motor Corp.*, 77 F.3d 736, 738 (4th Cir. 1996) (applying South Carolina law). *See also Young v. Tide Craft, Inc.*, 242 S.E.2d 671, 680 (S.C. 1978) (quoting cmt. i to Section 402A); Hubbard & Felix, *supra* note 13, at 302-03.

17. *Vaughn*, 77 F.3d at 739.

18. *Anderson v. Green Bull, Inc.*, 471 S.E.2d 708, 710-11 (S.C. Ct. App. 1996) (holding that danger of electrical conductivity of aluminum ladders is generally known); *Moore v. Barony House Rest., LLC*, 674 S.E.2d 500, 504 (S.C. Ct. App. 2009).

19. *Anderson*, 471 S.E.2d at 710.

20. S.C. Code Ann. §§ 15-73-20, -30 (2005); Restatement (Second) of Torts § 402A.

21. *Fleming v. Borden, Inc.*, 450 S.E.2d 589, 593-94 (S.C. 1994).

22. *See, e.g., Hilliard v. Manitowoc Co.*, 61 F.3d 900, No. 94-2430, 1995 WL 434828, at *4 (4th Cir. July 25, 1995) (affirming judgment of South Carolina district court finding that "[w]hen there is no question that the plaintiff was aware of the particular risk *and* of the fact that no safety device was present, there is no strict liability for failure to provide the device as a matter of law").

23. *See, e.g., Barony House Rest.*, 674 S.E.2d at 504 (operating unlighted golf cart at night was unreasonable risk that barred recovery as a matter of law).

24. *Priest v. Brown*, 396 S.E.2d 638, 641 (S.C. Ct. App. 1990); *Henderson v. Gould, Inc.*, 341 S.E.2d 806, 810 (S.C. Ct. App. 1986).

25. S.C. Code Ann. § 15-73-30 (2005) (adopting the Restatement (Second) of Torts § 402A, cmt. i); *Claytor v. General Motors Corp.*, 277 S.C. 259, 265, 286 S.E.2d 129, 132 (1982).

26. *Claytor*, 286 S.E.2d at 132.

27. *Allen*, 505 S.E.2d at 357.

28. *Rife*, 609 S.E.2d at 570-71 (affirming no liability for failure to install a seat belt on an excavator because the plaintiff failed to demonstrate the product was unreasonably dangerous without the seat belt).

29. *Young*, 242 S.E.2d at 679 (finding failure to install a "kill switch" in a boat was not a breach of warranty, did not constitute an unreasonably dangerous defect, and did not indicate a lack of due care).

30. *Gardner v. Q.H.S., Inc.*, 448 F.2d 238, 243 (4th Cir. 1971).

31. *Anderson*, 471 S.E.2d at 710.

32. *Bragg*, 462 S.E.2d at 331.

33. *Anderson*, 471 S.E.2d at 710-11 (holding that danger of electrical conductivity of aluminum ladders is generally known); *Barony House Rest.*, 674 S.E.2d at 504.

34. *Bragg*, 462 S.E.2d at 331; *but cf. Carolina Home Builders, Inc. v. Armstrong Furnace Co.*, 191 S.E.2d 774, 780 (S.C. 1972) (suggesting a post sale duty to warn may exist when product user would have altered behavior if notified of the negligent manufacture and installation); Hubbard & Felix, *supra* note 13, at 306-07 ("*Bragg* does not appear to be applicable to situations where a seller discovers dangers or defects after the sale. In this situation, the weight or authority clearly imposes a duty of due care on the seller.").

35. *Lawing v. Trinity Mfg. Inc.*, 749 S.E.2d 126, 132-33 (S.C. Ct. App. 2013) ("the sophisticated user doctrine applies when there is evidence the seller of a product was aware that an intermediate purchaser understood the dangers associated with the product and had the ability to effectively communicate those dangers to the end user.").

36. *Bragg*, 462 S.E.2d at 331-32.

37. *Stuart v. Springs Indus., Inc.*, 957 F. Supp. 2d 644, 653 (D.S.C. 2013) ("*Bragg* and the cases it cites involved typical products liability claims, with the duty arising from the defendants' role in manufacturing or selling the product. Under these circumstances, treating the listed criteria as a defense (that is, as if preceded by the word 'unless') is a logical adaptation of Section 388 because the duty does not arise from Section 388.").

38. *Carolina Home Builders, Inc.*, 191 S.E.2d at 778.

39. *Rife*, 609 S.E.2d at 568; *Bragg*, 462 S.E.2d at 326.

40. *Mickle v. Blackmon*, 166 S.E.2d 173, 187 (S.C. 1969) (quoting *Spruill v. Boyle-Midway, Inc.*, 308 F.2d 79, 83-84 (4th Cir. 1962)).

41. *Bragg*, 462 S.E.2d at 326 (quoting *Bilotta v. Kelley Co.*, 346 N.W.2d 616, 622 (Minn. 1984)).

42. *Bragg*, 462 S.E.2d at 326 (citing *Madden v. Cox*, 328 S.E.2d 108, 112 (S.C. Ct. App. 1985)).

43. *5 Star, Inc. v. Ford Motor Co.*, 759 S.E.2d 139, 143 (S.C. 2014).

44. *5 Star, Inc.*, 759 S.E.2d at 143 ("We hold that the absence of direct evidence that Ford knew of the design defect in the deactivation is not dispositive of a negligence claim.").

45. *Carolina Home Builders, Inc.*, 191 S.E.2d at 779.

46. *Sunvillas Homeowners Ass'n v. Square D Co.*, 391 S.E.2d 868, 870 (S.C. Ct. App. 1990).

47. *Elledge v. Richland/Lexington Sch. Dist. Five*, 573 S.E.2d 789, 793-94 (S.C. 2002).

48. *Nelson v. Concrete Supply Co.*, 399 S.E.2d 783, 784 (S.C. 1991).

49. *Nelson*, 399 S.E.2d at 784.

50. *Ross v. Paddy*, 532 S.E.2d 612, 616-17 (S.C. Ct. App. 2000) (per curiam).

51. *Creech v. S.C. Wildlife & Marine Res. Dep't*, 491 S.E.2d 571, 575 (S.C. 1997).

52. *Bloom v. Ravoira*, 529 S.E.2d 710, 713 (S.C. 2000).

53. *Berberich v. Jack*, 709 S.E.2d 607, 615-16 (S.C. 2011).

54. *Berberich*, 709 S.E.2d at 616.

55. *Beachwalk Villas Condo. Assoc., Inc. v. Martin*, 406 S.E.2d 372, 374 (S.C. 1991); *Kinard v. Augusta Sash & Door Co.*, 336 S.E.2d 465, 465-67 (S.C. 1985) (stating that in a bystander action, plaintiff may recover for physical injury resulting from emotional trauma even in the absence of physical impact if the bystander is related to the user/consumer).

56. *Beachwalk Villas Condo. Assoc., Inc.*, 406 S.E.2d at 374 n.1; *Tommy L. Griffin Plumbing & Heating Co. v. Jordon, Jones, & Goulding, Inc.*, 463 S.E. 2d 85, 88 (S.C. 1995).

57. *Davenport v. Cotton Hope Plantation Horizontal Prop. Regime*, 508 S.E.2d 565, 573-74 (S.C. 1998).

58. *Howard v. South Carolina Dep't of Highways*, 538 S.E.2d 291, 294 (S.C. Ct. App. 2000) (per curiam).

59. S.C. Code Ann. § 36-2-313 (2003).

60. S.C. Code Ann. § 36-2-314.

61. S.C. Code Ann. § 36-2-315.

62. *Rife*, 609 S.E.2d at 568; *Bragg*, 462 S.E.2d at 326.

63. S.C. Code Ann. § 36-2-313.

64. S.C. Code Ann. § 36-2-314(2).

65. S.C. Code Ann. § 36-2-315.

66. *Plantation Shutter Co., Inc. v. Ezell*, 492 S.E.2d 404, 406 (S.C. Ct. App. 1997).

67. *In re Breast Implant*, 503 S.E.2d at 452.

68. *Wilson v. Style Crest Prod.*, 627 S.E.2d 733, 737 (S.C. 2006).

69. S.C. Code Ann. § 36-2-719(2) (2003).

70. *Figgie Intern., Inc. v. DestileriaSerrales, Inc.*, 190 F.3d 252 (4th Cir. 1999).

71. *Myrtle Beach Pipeline Corp. v. Emerson Elec. Co.*, 843 F. Supp. 1027, 1043 (D.S.C. 1993); *Herring v. Home Depot, Inc.*, 565 S.E.2d 773, 776 (S.C. Ct. App. 2002).

72. *Myrtle Beach Pipeline*, 843 F. Supp. at 1044 (internal quotation marks omitted).

73. *Myrtle Beach Pipeline*, 843 F. Supp. at 1042.

74. S.C. Code Ann. § 36-2-719(3) (2003).

75. *Myrtle Beach Pipeline*, 843 F. Supp. at 1046 (internal quotation marks omitted); *Laidlaw Envt'lServs. (TOC), Inc. v. Honeywell, Inc.*, 966 F. Supp. 1401, 1413 (D.S.C. 1996).

76. *Bragg*, 462 S.E.2d at 543, 546; *Branham*, 701 S.E.2d at 14-16; *see also Miranda C. v. Nissan Motor Co., Ltd.*, 402 S.C. 577, 741 S.E.2d 34 (S.C. Ct. App. 2013) (citing *Branham* and holding that in a product liability design defect action, the plaintiff must present evidence of a reasonable alternative design and will be required to point to a design flaw in the product and show how his alternative design would have prevented the product from being unreasonably dangerous).

77. *Bragg*, 462 S.E.2d at 546.

78. *Holland ex rel. Knox v. Morbark, Inc.*, 754 S.E.2d 714, 720 (S.C. Ct. App. 2014), (finding the circuit court properly granted summary judgment when the

plaintiff failed to present evidence of a feasible alternative design or that a risk-utility analysis was conducted); Bragg, 462 S.E.2d at 330 (finding the circuit court properly granted a directed verdict and holding the plaintiff must introduce evidence that an alternative design is feasible and cannot rely upon mere conceptual design theories).

79. *Holland ex rel. Knox*, 754 S.E.2d at 720 (finding plaintiff failed to show a reasonable alternative design because (1) plaintiff's expert was unaware of anyone in the industry, including himself, who had performed a feasibility analysis for the alternative design, and (2) plaintiff's expert's alternative design was only "conceptual," and he had not prepared an "actual design.").

80. *Rife*, 609 S.E.2d at 568; *Bragg*, 462 S.E.2d at 326.

81. *Rife*, 609 S.E.2d at 568; *Bragg*, 462 S.E.2d at 326; *Ellison v. Rehab. Servs. of Columbus*, No. 3:06-1053-CMC, 2007 WL 486398, at *2 (D.S.C. Feb. 12, 2007).

82. *Ellison*, 2007 WL 486398, at *2; *Fernandez v. Spar Tek Indus., Inc.*, No. 0:06-3253-CMC, 2008 WL 2403647, at *7 (D.S.C. June 10, 2008).

83. *Ellison*, 2007 WL 486398, at *2; *Fernandez*, No. 0:06-3253-CMC, 2008 WL 2403647, at *7.

84. *Fernandez*, 2008 WL 2403647, at *7 (23 years from the time the product left the defendant's hands until the plaintiff's injury).

85. *Carroll v. Guess*, 394 S.E.2d 707, 708 (S.C. 1990).

86. S.C. Code Ann. § 15-7-30 (2005).

87. S.C. Code Ann. § 15-7-30 (2005).

88. S.C. Code Ann. § 15-7-30 (2005).

89. *Whaley v. CSX Transp., Inc.*, 609 S.E.2d 286, 296 (S.C. 2005).

90. S.C. Code Ann. § 58-23-90 (1977).

91. S.C. Code Ann. § 15-7-30 (2005).

92. S.C. Code Ann. § 15-7-30(C).

93. S.C. Code Ann. § 15-7-30(D).

94. S.C. Code Ann. § 15-7-30(E).

95. S.C. Code Ann. § 15-7-30(F).

96. S.C. Code Ann. § 15-7-30(G).

97. S.C. Code Ann. § 15-7-30(A)(10).

98. S.C. Code Ann. § 15-7-30(B).

99. S.C. Code Ann. § 15-7-100(A).

100. *Rife*, 609 S.E.2d at 569; *Small v. Pioneer Mach., Inc.*, 494 S.E.2d 835, 843 (S.C. Ct. App. 1997); *Livingston v. Noland Corp.*, 362 S.E.2d 16, 18 (S.C. 1987); *Young*, 242 S.E.2d at 677.

101. *See, e.g., Anderson*, 471 S.E.2d at 711 (mere possibility that electrocution was result of arcing); *Harris v. Rose's Stores*, 433 S.E.2d 905, 907 (S.C. Ct. App. 1993) (mere possibility that fire was caused by defect in fan which was destroyed by fire).

102. *Jamison v. Ford Motor Co.*, 644 S.E.2d 755, 765 (S.C. Ct. App. 2007); *Rife*, 609 S.E.2d at 569; *Bailey v. Segars*, 550 S.E.2d 910, 914 (S.C. Ct. App. 2001); *Hubbard v. Taylor*, 529 S.E.2d 549, 552 (S.C. Ct. App. 2000); *Vinson v. Hartley*, 477 S.E.2d 715, 721 (S.C. Ct. App. 1996); *Rush v. Blanchard*, 426 S.E.2d 802, 804 (S.C. 1993); *Oliver v. S.C. Dep't of Highways & Pub. Transp.*, 422 S.E.2d 128, 130 (S.C. 1992).

103. *Jamison*, 644 S.E.2d at 765; *Rife*, 609 S.E.2d at 569; *Bailey*, 550 S.E.2d at 914; *Hubbard*, 529 S.E.2d at 552; *Thomas v. S.C. Dep't of Highways & Pub. Transp.*, 465 S.E.2d 578, 580 (S.C. Ct. App. 1995); *Rush*, 426 S.E.2d at 804; *Oliver*, 422 S.E.2d at 131; *Bramlette v. Charter-Medical-Columbia*, 393 S.E.2d 914, 916 (S.C. 1990).

104. *Jamison*, 644 S.E.2d at 765; *Rife*, 609 S.E.2d at 569; *Bailey*, 550 S.E.2d at 914; *Hubbard*, 529 S.E.2d at 552; *Bramlette*, 393 S.E.2d at 916; *Young*, 242 S.E.2d at 675.

105. *Rife*, 609 S.E.2d at 569; *Jeffords v. Lesesne*, 541 S.E.2d 847, 851 (S.C. Ct. App. 2000); *Koester v. Carolina Rental Ctr., Inc.*, 443 S.E.2d 392, 394 (S.C. 1994); *Young*, 242 S.E.2d at 675.

106. *Rife*, 609 S.E.2d at 569; *Olson v. Faculty House of Carolina, Inc.*, 544 S.E.2d 38, 46-47 (S.C. Ct. App. 2001); *Young*, 242 S.E.2d at 675-76.

107. *Young*, 242 S.E.2d at 676 (internal quotes omitted).

108. *Willis v. Floyd Brace Co., Inc.*, 309 S.E.2d 295, 297 (S.C. Ct. App. 1983).

109. *Wallace v. Owens-Illinois, Inc.*, 389 S.E.2d 155, 156 (S.C. Ct. App. 1989).

110. *Wallace*, 389 S.E.2d at 156.

111. *Rife*, 609 S.E.2d at 569; *Parr v. Gaines*, 424 S.E.2d 515, 520 (S.C. Ct. App. 1992).

112. *Rife*, 609 S.E.2d at 569.

113. *Graves v. CAS Med. Sys., Inc.*, 735 S.E.2d 650, 658 (S.C. Aug. 29, 2012) ("Thus, the general rule is any fact can be shown through circumstantial evidence, and it is up to the trier of fact to determine whether it alone is worth as much merit as direct evidence.")

114. *Harris v. Rose's Stores, Inc.*, 433 S.E.2d 905, 907 (S.C. Ct. App. 1993). *See also Anderson*, 471 S.E.2d 708 (holding the trial court erred in refusing to grant the defendant's directed verdict and JNOV motions because the record contained "no evidence from which the jury could reasonably conclude that arcing most probably took place. At most, the evidence shows it was 'possible' that arcing occurred."); *Nguyen v. Uniflex Corp.*, 440 S.E.2d 887, 889 (S.C. Ct. App. 1994) (holding the plaintiff could not recover because South Carolina does not recognize *res ipsa loquitur* and the plaintiff "presented no evidence . . . that [the alleged event] most probably caused the fire.").

115. *Keeter v. Alpine Towers Int'l Inc.*, 730 S.E.2d 890, 897 (S.C. Ct. App. 2012).

116. *Keeter*, 730 S.E.2d at 897 (quoting *McKnight v. S.C. Dep't of Corr.*, 684 S.E.2d 566, 569 (S.C. Ct. App. 2009)).

117. *Graves*, 735 S.E.2d at 658. The *Graves* court noted that evidence of "other similar incidents" is a "classic" example of circumstantial evidence that can be used to show a design defect. *Graves*, 735 S.E.2d at 658.

118. *Graves*, 735 S.E.2d at 658.

119. *Graves*, 735 S.E.2d at 658.

120. *Branham*, 701 S.E.2d at 17-18. "[P]ost-distribution evidence is evidence of facts neither known nor available at the time of distribution." *Branham*, 701 S.E.2d at 17. When the claim is against the manufacturer, "the 'time of distribution' is the time of manufacture." *Branham*, 701 S.E.2d at 17.

121. *Simmons v. Mark Lift Indus., Inc.*, 622 S.E.2d 213, 215 (S.C. 2005); *Walton v. Mazda of Rock Hill*, 657 S.E.2d 67, 69 (S.C. Ct. App. 2008). *See also* Tim Orr, *Successor Liability: Not Just for Contracts Anymore*, 17 S.C. Law. 33 (Mar. 2006).

122. *Simmons*, 622 S.E.2d at 215.

123. *Tucker v. Albert Rice Furniture Sales, Inc.*, 367 S.E.2d 427, 429 (S.C. Ct. App. 1988).

124. *Peoples Fed. Savs. & Loan Assoc. v. Myrtle Beach Golf & Yacht Club*, 425 S.E.2d 764, 774 (S.C. Ct. App. 1992) (citations omitted).

125. *See, e.g., Gray v. Barnes*, 137 S.E.2d 594 (S.C. 1964) (finding no joint enterprise because automobile passenger had no "right or control over the car or to direct its movements").

126. *Fleming*, 450 S.E.2d at 592-93.

127. *Fleming*, 450 S.E.2d at 593.

128. *Gardner*, 448 F.2d at 243.

129. *Mickle*, 166 S.E.2d at 187.

130. *Mickle*, 166 S.E.2d at 189.

131. *Watson v. Ford Motor Co.*, 699 S.E.2d 169, 179 (S.C. 2010), *Whaley v. CSX Transp., Inc.*, 609 S.E.2d 286, 300 (S.C. 2005).

132. *Branham*, 701 S.E.2d at 20; *Watson*, 699 S.E.2d at 179.

133. *Branham*, 701 S.E.2d at 21.

134. *Branham*, 701 S.E.2d at 21.

135. *Gathers ex rel. Hutchinson v. S.C. Elec. & Gas Co.*, 427 S.E.2d 687, 689 (S.C. Ct. App. 1993). *See also Kershaw Cnty. Bd. of Educ. v. U.S. Gypsum Co.*, 396 S.E.2d 369, 372 (S.C. 1990) (holding that the trial court followed the appropriate procedure in giving jury instruction on spoliation of evidence rather than dismissing case).

136. *See generally Silvestri v. Gen. Motors Corp.*, 271 F.3d 583 (4th Cir. 2001) (affirming dismissal of case when defendant becomes highly prejudiced by spoliation).

137. Crashworthiness is defined in the Motor Vehicle Information and Costs Savings Act as "the protection a passenger motor vehicle gives its passengers against personal injury or death from a motor vehicle accident." 49 U.S.C.A. § 32301(1) (West 2006).

138. 166 S.E.2d 173, 186 (S.C. 1969) (approving the reasoning of the landmark crashworthiness case *Larsen v. General Motors Corp.*, 391 F.2d 495 (8th Cir. 1968)).

139. *See* David G. Owen et al., *Products Liability and Safety* 803 (5th ed. 2007).

140. *Quinton v. Toyota Motor Corp.*, No. 1:10-CV-2187, 2013 WL 2470083 (D.S.C. June 7, 2013).

141. *Quinton*, 2013 WL 2470083, at *2.

142. *Huddell v. Levin*, 537 F.2d 726, 737 (3d Cir. 1976).

143. *Larsen v. Gen. Motors Corp.*, 391 F.2d 495, 503 (8th Cir. 1968).

144. *Larsen*, 391 F.2d at 502.

145. *Huddell*, 537 F.2d at 738.

146. *See* Robert H. Brunson, *Comparing First Collision "Fault" with Second Collision "Defect,"* 11 S.C. Law. 38 (July/Aug. 1999) (arguing that "South Carolina courts should apply comparative negligence principles to crashworthiness cases and assign liability according to fault").

147. *Jimenez v. Daimler Chrysler Corp.*, 269 F.3d 439, 453 (4th Cir. 2001). Interestingly, the *Jimenez* court did rule that evidence of seatbelt nonuse should be admissible on the limited issues of enhanced injury and vehicle crashworthiness. *See Jimenez*, 269 F.3d at 458-59.

148. S.C. Code Ann. § 15-35-400 (Supp. 2008).

149. S.C. Code Ann. § 15-35-400 (Supp. 2008).

150. S.C. Code Ann. § 39-5-20 (1985); *see* S.C. Code Ann. §§ 39-5-10 through -170 (Supp. 2006).

151. *See Charleston Lumber Co. v. Miller Housing Corp.*, 458 S.E.2d 431, 438 (S.C. Ct. App. 1995); *Noack Enter., Inc. v. Country Corner Interiors*, 351 S.E.2d 347, 350 (S.C. Ct. App. 1986).

152. *See Reynolds v. Ryland Group, Inc.*, 531 S.E.2d 917, 919 (S.C. 2000).

153. S.C. Code Ann. § 39-5-140 (1985).

154. S.C. Code Ann. § 39-5-140 (1985).

155. Rule 702, SCRE.

156. *See State v. Council*, 515 S.E.2d 508, 517 (S.C. 1999) ("This standard is more liberal. . . ."); *State v. Morgan*, 485 S.E.2d 112, 115 n.2 (S.C. Ct. App. 1997) (referencing South Carolina's "more liberal approach"), *overruled in part on other grounds by State v. White*, 676 S.E.2d 684, 688 (S.C. 2009).

157. *State v. White*, 676 S.E.2d 684, 689 (S.C. 2009).

158. *State v. Council*, 515 S.E.2d 508, 518 (S.C. 1999); *Watson*, 699 S.E.2d at 179.

159. *Council*, 515 S.E.2d at 517.

160. *Council*, 515 S.E.2d at 517 (citing Rule 403, SCRE).

161. *Fields v. J. Haynes Waters Builders, Inc.*, 658 S.E.2d 80, 85 (S.C. 2008).

162. *State v. Henry*, 495 S.E.2d 463, 466 (S.C. Ct. App. 1997).

163. *Fields*, 658 S.E.2d at 86.

164. *Watson*, 699 S.E.2d at 176.

165. *White*, 676 S.E.2d at 689.

166. *Graves*, 735 S.E.2d at 656.

167. *Graves*, 735 S.E.2d at 656.

168. *Graves*, 735 S.E.2d at 656 (citing *Westberry v. Gislaved Gummi AB*, 178 F.3d 257, 265 (4th Cir.1999)).

169. *Graves*, 735 S.E.2d at 656.

170. *See State v. Northcutt*, 641 S.E.2d 873, 878 (S.C. 2007) (holding that trial judge abused his discretion by requiring an expert to submit a written report).

171. S.C. Code Ann. §§ 15-48-10 *et seq.* (2005).

172. 9 U.S.C.A. § 1 (West 1999); *Simpson v. MSA of Myrtle Beach, Inc.*, 644 S.E.2d 663, 667 n.1 (S.C. 2007).

173. S.C. Code Ann. § 15-48-10(a) (2005).

174. *Partain v. Upstate Auto. Grp.*, 689 S.E.2d 602, 603 (S.C. 2009); *Aiken v. World Fin. Corp. of S.C.*, 644 S.E.2d 705, 708 (S.C. 2007); *Chassereau v. Global Sun Pools, Inc.*, 644 S.E.2d 718, 720 (S.C. 2007); *Simpson*, 644 S.E.2d at 668; *Zabinski v. Bright Acres Assocs.*, 553 S.E.2d 110, 118 (S.C. 2001); *Gissel v. Hart*, 676 S.E.2d 320, 323 (S.C. 2009).

175. *S.C. Pub. Serv. Auth. v. Great W. Coal (Kentucky), Inc.*, 437 S.E.2d 22, 25 (S.C. 1993).

176. *Partain*, 689 S.E.2d at 604; *Chassereau*, 644 S.E.2d at 720; *Simpson*, 644 S.E.2d at 667.

177. *Zabinski*, 553 S.E.2d at 114. *See also Soil Remediation Co. v. Nu-Way Envtl., Inc.*, 476 S.E.2d 149 (S.C. 1996) (declining to enforce an arbitration clause that was printed on the first page of the contract in capital letters but not underlined).

178. *Partain*, 689 S.E.2d at 603-04; *Aiken*, 644 S.E.2d at 708; *Chassereau*, 644 S.E.2d at 720 (citations omitted); *Simpson*, 644 S.E.2d at 668; *Zabinski*, 553 S.E.2d at 118.

179. *Simpson*, 644 S.E.2d at 668 (citing S.C. Code Ann. § 15-48-20(a)).

180. *Aiken*, 644 S.E.2d at 708.

181. *Aiken*, 644 S.E.2d at 708 n.2.

182. *Aiken*, 644 S.E.2d at 708.

183. *Aiken*, 644 S.E.2d at 709; *Chassereau*, 644 S.E.2d at 720-21 (declining to enforce an arbitration provision in a dispute involving theft of plaintiffs' personal information by employees of defendant).

184. *Rhodes v. Benson Chrysler-Plymouth, Inc.*, 647 S.E.2d 249, 251 (S.C. Ct. App. 2007) (internal quotes and citations omitted).

185. *Rhodes*, 647 S.E.2d at 251.

186. *Simpson*, 644 S.E.2d at 668.

187. *Simpson*, 644 S.E.2d at 668 (citing S.C. Code Ann. § 36-2-302(1)).

188. *Simpson*, 644 S.E.2d at 674.

189. *Laffitte v. Bridgestone Corp.*, 674 S.E.2d 154, 162-63 (S.C. 2009).

190. *Laffitte*, 674 S.E.2d at 162-63.

191. *Laffitte*, 674 S.E.2d at 162-63.

192. S.C. Code Ann. §§ 15-3-530, -535, -545 (2005).

193. S.C. Code Ann. § 36-2-725 (2003); *Atlas Food Sys. & Serv., Inc. v. Crane Nat'l Vendors Div. of Unidynamics Corp.*, 462 S.E.2d 858, 860 (S.C. 1995) (actions arising under Article 2 of the UCC governed by six-year statute of limitations).

194. S.C. Code Ann. § 15-3-535 (2005).

195. S.C. Code Ann. § 15-3-640 (2005).

196. *Salladin v. Tellis*, 146 S.E.2d 875, 877 (S.C. 1966); *see also* S.C. Code Ann. § 36-2-318 (2003) (extending warranties to any foreseeable user, regardless of privity).

197. *Reed v. Tiffin Motor Homes, Inc.*, 697 F.2d 1192, 1196 (4th Cir. 1982), *Bragg*, 462 S.E.2d at 331.

198. *See Bragg*, 462 S.E.2d at 330 (allowing evidence that an aerial "bucket truck" device "met all appropriate standards regarding warnings at the time of its manufacture and sale").

199. *Bragg*, 462 S.E.2d at 329.

200. *See Bragg*, 462 S.E.2d at 331 (citing evidence that no manufacturer at the time the device in question was manufactured nor at the time of trial used a similar device).

201. *Marchant v. Mitchell Distrib. Co.*, 240 S.E.2d 511, 513 (S.C. 1977).

202. *Carolina Home Builders, Inc.*, 191 S.E.2d at 779.

203. *Jamison*, 644 S.E.2d at 764.

204. *Jamison*, 644 S.E.2d at 764.

205. S.C. Code § 42-1-540 (1985).

206. Hubbard & Felix, *supra* note 13, at 212.

207. S.C. Code Ann. § 15-5-150 (2005) (Door Closing Statute).

208. *Henderson v. Allied Signal, Inc.*, 644 S.E.2d 724, 727 (S.C. 2007) (finding no liability because the out-of-state plaintiff failed to show he was exposed to asbestos in South Carolina).

209. *Rife*, 609 S.E.2d at 569.

210. *McCourt v. Abernathy*, 457 S.E.2d 603, 607 (S.C. 1995).

211. *Willis*, 309 S.E.2d at 298.

212. S.C. Code Ann. § 15-33-135 (2005); *Jimenez*, 269 F.3d at 450; *Duncan v. Ford Motor Co.*, 682 S.E.2d 877, 886 (S.C. Ct. App. 2009).

213. S.C. Code Ann. § 15-32-530.

214. S.C. Code Ann. § 15-32-530.

215. S.C. Code Ann. § 15-32-530.

216. S.C. Code Ann. § 15-32-520.

217. 517 U.S. 559 (1996).

218. *Mitchell v. Fortis Ins. Co.*, 686 S.E.2d 176, 184-86 (S.C. 2009).

219. *Mitchell*, 686 S.E.2d at 184-86.

220. *Mitchell*, 686 S.E.2d at 182.

221. *Mitchell*, 686 S.E.2d at 188.

222. *Gamble v. Stevenson*, 406 S.E.2d 350, 354 (S.C. 1991).

223. *Gamble*, 406 S.E.2d 350; *Mitchell*, 686 S.E.2d at 184-85.

224. *Mitchell*, 686 S.E.2d at 185.

225. *Branham*, 701 S.E.2d at 24 (citing *Hicks v. Herring*, 144 S.E.2d 151, 154 (S.C. 1965)).

226. *Branham*, 701 S.E.2d at 25-25.

227. *Fairchild v. S.C. Dep't of Transp.*, 683 S.E.2d 818, 823 (S.C. Ct. App. 2009) (internal citation omitted).

228. *Fairchild*, 683 S.E.2d at 823 (internal citation omitted).

229. *Barnwell v. Barber-Colman Co.*, 393 S.E.2d 162, 163 (S.C. 1989) (strict liability); *Pinckney v. Orkin Exterminating Co.*, 234 S.E.2d 654, 655 (S.C. 1977) (warranty).

230. *Clark v. Cantrell*, 529 S.E.2d 528, 535 (S.C. 2000).

231. *Smith-Hunter Constr. Co. v. Hopson*, 616 S.E.2d 419, 421 (S.C. 2005); *Future Grp., II v. NationsBank*, 478 S.E.2d 45, 51 (S.C. 1996).

232. *Smith-Hunter*, 616 S.E.2d at 421.

233. *Republic Textile Equip. Co. of S.C., Inc. v. Aetna Ins. Co.*, 360 S.E.2d 540, 545 (S.C. Ct. App. 1987).

234. *Republic Textile Equip.*, 360 S.E.2d at 545; Hubbard & Felix, *supra* note 13, at 567.

235. Hubbard & Felix, *supra* note 13, at 567. *See also* 22 Am. Jur. 2d Damages §§ 462-79 (2003); Restatement (Second) of Torts § 913.

236. S.C. Code Ann. § 34-31-20(A) (Supp. 2006).

237. Restatement (Second) of Torts § 913, cmt. b; Hubbard & Felix, *supra* note 13, at 568.

238. S.C. Code Ann. § 34-31-20 (Supp. 2006).

239. *Russo v. Sutton*, 454 S.E.2d 895, 896-97 (S.C. 1995).

240. *Calhoun v. Calhoun*, 529 S.E.2d 14, 19 (S.C. 2000).

241. S.C. Code Ann. § 15-73-10 (2005); *Bray*, 588 S.E.2d at 95 n.5 (referring to Title 15, Chapter 73 of the South Carolina Code as the "Defective Products Act").

242. *Sapp v. Ford Motor Co.*, 687 S.E.2d 47, 49 (S.C. 2009); *Kennedy v. Columbia Lumber & Mfg. Co.*, 384 S.E.2d 730, 734 (S.C. 1989).

243. *Sapp*, 687 S.E.2d at 49.

244. *Kennedy v. Columbia Lumber & Mfg. Co.*, 384 S.E.2d 730 (S.C. 1989).

245. *Sapp*, 687 S.E.2d at 49; *Kennedy*, 384 S.E.2d at 737.

246. *Tommy L. Griffin Plumbing & Heating Co. v. Jordon, Jones & Goulding, Inc.*, 463 S.E.2d 85, 88 (S.C. 1995).

247. *Tommy L. Griffin Plumbing & Heating*, 463 S.E.2d at 89.

248. *See, e.g., Laidlaw Envtl. Servs. (TOC), Inc. v. Honeywell Inc.*, 966 F. Supp. 1401, 1414 (D.S.C. 1996) ("[a] buyer-seller relationship does not constitute a 'special relationship' precluding operation of the [economic loss] rule").

249. *See, e.g., American Fid. Fire Ins. Co. v. Hartford Accident & Indem. Co.*, 163 S.E.2d 926, 927 (S.C. 1968). *See also* Hubbard & Felix, *supra* note 13, at 650.

250. S.C. Code Ann. § 15-38-15 (Supp. 2006).

251. S.C. Code Ann. § 15-38-15 (Supp. 2006).

252. S.C. Code Ann. § 15-38-15 (Supp. 2006).

253. S.C. Code Ann. § 15-38-15 (Supp. 2006).

254. S.C. Code Ann. § 15-38-15 (Supp. 2006).

255. S.C. Code Ann. § 15-38-15 (Supp. 2006).

256. *See, e.g., Knight v. Autumn Co., Inc.*, 245 S.E.2d 602, 603-04 (S.C. 1978); *Conyers v. Stewart*, 147 S.E.2d 640, 641 (S.C. 1966); *Johns v. Castles*, 91 S.E.2d 721,

721-22 (S.C. 1956); *Simon v. Strock*, 39 S.E.2d 209, 211 (S.C. 1946). *See also* Hubbard & Felix, *supra* note 13, at 649.

257. *Christiansen v. Campbell*, 328 S.E.2d 351, 353 (S.C. Ct. App. 1985), *overruled in part on other grounds by Tobias v. Sports Club, Inc.*, 504 S.E.2d 318, 319 (S.C. 1998).

258. S.C. Code Ann. §§ 15-38-10 to 15-38-70 (Supp. 2008). *See also Scott v. Fruehauf Corp.*, 396 S.E.2d 354, 357-58 (S.C. 1990) (South Carolina common law indemnification does not apply among joint tortfeasors); Hubbard & Felix, *supra* note 13, at 649-50; James T. Irvin III, *Easing a Client's Pain After the Game Is Over: Contribution, Indemnification, and Set Off*, 13 S.C. Law. 28, 28 (Sept./Oct. 2001).

259. S.C. Code Ann. § 15-38-20 (2005).

SOUTH DAKOTA

A. CAUSES OF ACTION

Product liability lawsuits include causes of action for strict liability, negligence, and breach of warranty.

B. STATUTES OF LIMITATION

An action against a manufacturer, lessor, or seller of a product, regardless of the substantive legal theory upon which the action is brought, must be commenced within three years of the date when the damage occurred, became known, or should have become known to the injured party.[1] An action for personal injury must be brought within three years of its accrual.[2] A breach of warranty action must be brought within four years after the cause of action accrued, which occurs when tender of delivery is made.[3]

C. STRICT LIABILITY

1. The Standard

For strict liability cases, South Dakota has adopted Section 402A of the Restatement (Second) of Torts.[4] Ordinarily, an expert is required to testify that the product is unreasonably dangerous and the defect was a proximate cause of the injury in order to present a jury question.[5] For a strict liability defective design or manufacture claim, the jury must then find that: (1) the product was in a defective condition; (2) the condition made it unreasonably dangerous; (3) the defect existed at the time it left the control of the defendant; (4) the product was expected to and did reach the plaintiff without any substantial unforeseeable change in condition; and (5) the defective condition was a legal cause of the injuries.[6]

2. Definition of "Defect"

A product is defective when it fails to perform reasonably and safely the function for which it was intended; alternatively, a product is defective if it could have been designed to prevent a foreseeable harm without significantly hindering its function or increasing its price.[7] Three types of defects are actionable under strict liability: manufacturing defects, design defects, and defects due to failure to warn.[8] Because South Dakota recognizes both the consumer expectation and risk/benefit definitions of defect, evidence of an alternative design has not been required in design defect cases.[9]

3. Causation

Although South Dakota has adopted strict liability under Section 402A of the Restatement (Second) of Torts, the South Dakota Supreme Court has cautioned that strict liability is not to be equated with absolute liability.[10] Issues of product defect, adequate warnings, causation, and foreseeability remain important issues for the jury's determination.[11] The Court has also made clear that it is the unreasonable condition of the product, not the defendant's conduct, that creates liability.[12]

Whether an intervening act will constitute an independent intervening cause presents a question of foreseeability for the jury.[13] It is sufficient if what occurred was one of the kind of consequences which might reasonably be foreseen.[14]

4. **Contributory Negligence/Assumption of Risk**

Contributory negligence is not a defense in strict liability cases.[15] Assumption of the risk is a defense.[16] Misuse is a defense in strict liability cases,[17] and the Eighth Circuit Court of Appeals has held that misuse is also a defense in a breach of warranty case relevant to proximate cause.[18] The Eighth Circuit has further held that assumption of the risk and misuse defenses require proof that the consumer or user is aware of the defect and nevertheless proceeds to use the product.[19] The fact that the product was misused, however, does not necessarily bar recovery if the defendant did not warn of dangers involved in a use that could reasonably be anticipated.[20]

5. **Sale or Lease/Persons Liable**

The doctrine of strict liability applies to both sale and lease transactions.[21]

In accordance with Section 402A of the Restatement (Second) of Torts, anyone engaged in the business of selling products for use or consumption may be subject to the doctrine of strict liability.[22] This rule applies to manufacturers, wholesalers, dealers, and distributors, but not to occasional sellers.[23]

The South Dakota Supreme Court has stated, in dicta, that there is no strict liability for products sold on the broad, commercial used-product market.[24] The Court has subjected used-product merchants who rebuild or recondition goods to strict liability, however.[25]

By statute, no cause of action for strict liability may be asserted against any distributor, wholesaler, dealer, or retail seller of a product that contains a latent defect, unless the defendant is also the manufacturer or assembler of the product or a maker of a component part of the product, or unless the defendant knew, or in the exercise of ordinary care should have known, of the defective condition of the final product.[26]

6. **Inherently Dangerous Products**

South Dakota has not addressed this issue through statute. The South Dakota Supreme Court has stated that where a manufacturer or seller has reason to anticipate that danger may result from a particular use of a product, and fails to give adequate warnings of such danger, a product sold without such warnings is defective within the meaning of the strict liability doctrine.[27]

7. **Successor Liability**

A corporation that purchases the assets of another corporation does not succeed to the liabilities of the selling corporation, unless one of four exceptions is met: (1) the purchasing corporation expressly or implicitly agrees to assume the selling corporation's liability; (2) the transaction amounts to a consolidation or merger of the purchaser and seller corporations; (3) the purchaser corporation is merely a continuation of the seller corporation; or (4) the transaction is fraudulently entered into to escape liability for such obligations.[28] South Dakota courts have rejected the "product line" exception to the nonliability rule.[29] By statute, special rules apply to asbestos claims against successors that, in many instances, limit the successor's cumulative liability to the fair market value of the assets it purchased.[30]

8. **Market Share Liability/Enterprise Liability**

South Dakota has not addressed this issue through statute or case law.

9. **Privity**

No privity of contract is required to sustain an action for strict liability.[31]

10. **Failure to Warn**

When a manufacturer or seller has reason to anticipate that danger may result from a particular use of a product, the manufacturer or seller must warn of that danger. Failure to provide adequate warnings may render the product defective for purposes of the strict liability doctrine.[32] "The essential elements of a strict liability failure to warn claim are: (1) a danger existed associated with a foreseeable use of the product; (2) an inadequate warning was given regarding the danger; (3) as a result of the inadequate warning, the product was rendered defective and unreasonably dangerous; (4) the defective and unreasonably dangerous condition existed at the time it left the control of the manufacturer; (5) the product was expected and did reach the user without a substantial unforeseeable change in the condition that it was in when it left the manufacturer's control; and (6) the defective condition was the legal cause of [her] injuries."[33] Establishing a strict liability failure to warn claim ordinarily requires expert testimony.[34]

11. **Post-sale Duty to Warn and Remedial Measures**

The Eighth Circuit Court of Appeals has held that the duty to warn includes a post-sale duty to warn of defects existing at the time of sale, but discovered after the sale.[35] Evidence of subsequent remedial measures to prove product defect is inadmissible.[36] Evidence of recalls is admissible.[37]

12. **Learned Intermediary Doctrine**

South Dakota has not addressed this issue through statute or case law.

13. **Substantial Alteration/Abnormal Use**

Alteration and modification are legal defenses to strict liability.[38] A manufacturer, assembler, or seller will escape strict liability if the alteration or modification is a proximate cause of the injury, death, or damage, and: (1) the alteration or modification was made subsequent to the manufacture, assembly, or sale of the product; and (2) the alteration or modification changed the purpose, use, function, design, or manner of use of the product from that originally designed, tested, or intended by the manufacturer; and (3) neither the alteration or modification, nor the subsequent rendering of the product unsafe, was foreseeable by the manufacturer, assembler or seller.[39] Even when alteration and/or modification do not constitute a complete defense, they may require the plaintiff to obtain expert testimony in order to survive summary judgment.[40]

14. **State of the Art**

South Dakota has codified a state-of-the-art defense.[41] The statute provides that in any product liability action based upon negligence or strict liability, the issue of whether the design, manufacture, inspection, testing, packaging, warning, or labeling was in conformity with the generally recognized state of the art existing at the time the product was first sold to any person not engaged in the business of selling such products, may be considered in determining: (1) the standard of care; (2) whether that standard was breached; and (3) whether the product was defective or unreasonably dangerous to the user.[42]

15. **Malfunction**

A product is defective when it fails to perform reasonably and safely the function for which it was intended.[43] No specific defect need be shown if the evidence permits the inference that the accident was caused by a defect.[44]

16. **Standards and Governmental Regulation**

A defendant's conformity with industry standards and government regulations is allowed as evidence of reasonable care.[45]

17. **Other Accidents**

It appears South Dakota follows the general rule that evidence of substantially similar prior accidents is admissible.[46]

18. **Misrepresentation**

A seller's misrepresentation may give rise to a cause of action for breach of implied or express warranty.[47]

19. Destruction or Loss of Product

South Dakota has not addressed this issue through statute or case law.

20. Economic Loss

South Dakota follows the general rule that economic losses are not recoverable under tort theories.[48] The recovery of economic loss is therefore limited to the theories found in the Uniform Commercial Code.[49] Two exceptions to the rule are personal injury and damage to other property.[50] "Other property" is defined as damage to property collateral to the product itself.[51]

21. Crashworthiness

The South Dakota Supreme Court has recognized a cause of action for strict liability based on the theory known as "crashworthiness liability," the "second collision doctrine," or the "enhanced injury doctrine." The Court refused to limit strict liability actions to those situations where the defective product caused the accident, thereby extending strict liability to those instances where the defective product merely enhanced the injuries.[52]

D. NEGLIGENCE

For those product liability actions based on negligence, South Dakota's comparative fault statute reduces the plaintiff's recovery in proportion to the plaintiff's negligence.[53] The plaintiff's recovery is barred if the plaintiff's negligence, as compared to the defendant's negligence, is more than slight.[54] If the plaintiff's negligence is less than slight, his damages are reduced in proportion to the amount of his contributory negligence.

The plaintiff is relieved of the burden of proving negligence by the manufacturer in a product liability action based on strict liability.[55] The doctrines of comparative and contributory negligence are, therefore, inapplicable to actions for strict liability.[56]

Negligence theories include design, manufacture, and failure to warn.[57] To establish negligent design or manufacture, a plaintiff "must show that the defendant failed to use the amount of care in designing or manufacturing the product that a reasonably careful designer or manufacturer would use in exposing others to a foreseeable risk of harm."[58] "To determine whether the designer or manufacturer used reasonable care, one must balance what the designer or manufacturer knew or should have known about the likelihood and severity of potential harm from the product against the burden of taking safety measures to reduce or avoid the harm."[59]

The elements of a negligent failure to warn claim are: "(1) the manufacturer knew or reasonably should have known that the product was dangerous or was likely to be dangerous when used in a reasonably foreseeable manner; (2) the manufacturer knew or reasonably should have known that users would not realize the danger; (3) that the manufacturer failed to exercise reasonable care and adequately warn of the danger or instruct on the safe use of the product; (4) that a reasonable manufacturer under the same or similar circumstances would have warned of the danger or instructed on the use of the product; (5) that the claimant was harmed; (6) that the manufacturer's failure to warn or instruct was a proximate or legal cause of the claimant's injury."[60]

Expert testimony is ordinarily required to prove a product liability claim based on negligence.[61]

E. BREACH OF WARRANTY

The Uniform Commercial Code has been adopted.[62] Breach of warranty requires proof that a product did not conform to expectations or that the product was either nonmerchantable or unfit for an ordinary purpose.[63] The South Dakota Supreme Court has noted that once it is established that a product defect exists, there is little difference between the liability theories of breach of warranty and strict liability in tort apart from the availability of the defenses of lack of notice and disclaimer.[64]

F. EXPERT TESTIMONY

Product liability theories generally require expert testimony. South Dakota interprets *Daubert v. Merrell Dow Pharmaceuticals, Inc.*, 509 U.S. 579 (1993) to require a potential expert's testimony to be evaluated for: (1) qualification; (2) relevance; and (3) reliability.[65] The party offering the testimony bears the burden of demonstrating these elements by a preponderance of the evidence.[66] In order to be qualified, an expert must have "sufficient specialized knowledge to assist jurors in deciding the specific issues in the case."[67] Relevance "embraces 'evidence having any tendency to make the existence of any fact that is of consequence to the determination of the action more or less probable than it would be without the evidence.'"[68] A court has considerable leeway in deciding whether expert testimony is reliable.[69] *Daubert*'s criteria are flexible and no one factor is inherently dispositive.[70] All that must be shown is that the "expert's testimony rests upon good grounds, based on what is known."[71]

G. PUNITIVE DAMAGES

Punitive damages are permissible in actions not arising out of contract for injury to person or property through oppression, fraud, malice, or reckless disregard of plaintiff's rights.[72]

H. PRE- AND POST-JUDGMENT INTEREST

Pre-judgment interest is provided for by statute.[73] For actions based in tort or contract, interest begins to accrue at the time of the tortious conduct or the breach of contract, and ends on the date of the verdict. It may be recovered on items awarded as damages in product liability suits, except "future damages, punitive damages, or intangible damages such as pain and suffering, emotional distress, loss of consortium, injury to credit, reputation, or financial standing, loss of enjoyment of life, or loss of society and companionship."[74] Interest is calculated at the contract rate or as provided by statute. Interest must be calculated at a simple rate and cannot be compounded.[75]

Post-judgment interest is also provided for by statute.[76] The plaintiff is entitled to interest from and after the date of judgment. Post-judgment interest is to be calculated at the appropriate statutory rate.[77] The rate in effect is the statutory rate at the time of the outstanding judgment amount as adjusted over time for any change in the rate, not a fixed rate that attaches at the time of the judgment as applied over the life of the unpaid judgment.[78]

I. EMPLOYER IMMUNITY FROM SUIT

South Dakota's Workers' Compensation Act preempts common law causes of action against employers carrying workers' compensation insurance, except actions based on intentional torts.[79] As against employers failing to carry workers' compensation insurance, employees may elect to proceed under the workers' compensation laws or under common law theories of liability.[80]

J. STATUTES

Relevant statutes in product liability actions include the: (1) statutes of limitation;[81] (2) commercial code sections dealing with warranties;[82] (3) statutes dealing with joint and several liability;[83] (4) state of the art defense statute;[84] (5) latent defect statute;[85] (6) statute dealing with evidence of use or non-use of a seat belt;[86] and (7) statute setting the age of majority at 18.[87]

K. JOINT AND SEVERAL LIABILITY

A joint tortfeasor is without personal fault when he has not participated in the commission of the tort and his liability arises by operation of law.[88] Indemnification of those held jointly or severally liable is controlled by statute.[89] Indemnification is not available to a joint tortfeasor if he is contributorily negligent.[90]

The right of contribution exists among joint tortfeasors.[91] No right to contribution accrues among the tortfeasors until the common liability is discharged by payment to the plaintiff.[92] If a joint tortfeasor pays more than his pro rata share, he may seek contribution from the other tortfeasors.[93]

James E. Moore
James A. Power
Woods, Fuller, Shultz & Smith, P.C.
300 South Phillips Avenue, Suite 300
Sioux Falls, South Dakota 57117-5027
(605) 336-3890
(Fax) (605) 339-3357

Endnotes - South Dakota

1. S.D. Codified Laws § 15-2-12.2 Under South Dakota law, an action is commenced based on service, not filing. S.D. Codified Laws § 15-2-30.

2. S.D. Codified Laws § 15-2-14.

3. S.D. Codified Laws § 57A-2-725.

4. *Engberg v. Ford Motor Co.*, 205 N.W.2d 104, 109 (S.D. 1973).

5. *Burley v. Kytec Innovative Sports Equip., Inc.*, 737 N.W.2d 397, 408-09 (S.D. 2007) (granting summary judgment on strict liability design and manufacturing claims because plaintiff did not present expert testimony that alleged defect caused the injury).

6. South Dakota Civil Pattern Jury Instruction 150-01. *Engberg*, 205 N.W.2d at 109; *Smith v. Smith*, 278 N.W.2d 155, 158-59 n.2 (S.D. 1979); *Jahnig v. Coisman*, 283 N.W.2d 557, 560 (S.D. 1979).

7. *Shaffer v. Honeywell, Inc.*, 249 N.W.2d 251, 256 (S.D. 1976); *First Premier Bank v. Kolcraft Enters.*, 686 N.W.2d 430, 445 (S.D. 2004).

8. *Peterson v. Safway Steel Scaffolds Co.*, 400 N.W.2d 909, 912 (S.D. 1987); *Rynders v. E.I. DuPont, De Nemours & Co.*, 21 F.3d 835, 842 (8th Cir. 1994).

9. *Kolcraft Enters.*, 686 N.W.2d at 445 (plaintiff may rely on either definition of defect).

10. *Engberg*, 205 N.W.2d at 109.

11. *Peterson*, 400 N.W.2d at 912.

12. *Peterson*, 400 N.W.2d at 912.

13. *Zacher v. Budd Co.*, 396 N.W.2d 122, 135-36 (S.D. 1986).

14. *Zacher*, 396 N.W.2d at 135-36; Restatement (Second) of Torts § 447(b).

15. *Smith*, 278 N.W.2d at 161; *Berg v. Sukup Mfg. Co.*, 355 N.W.2d 833, 835 (S.D. 1984).

16. *Smith*, 278 N.W.2d at 161; *Berg*, 355 N.W.2d at 835.

17. *Smith*, 278 N.W.2d at 161; *Berg*, 355 N.W.2d at 835.

18. *Herrick v. Monsanto Co.*, 874 F.2d 594, 598-99 (8th Cir. 1989).

19. *Novak v. Navistar Int'l Transp. Corp.*, 46 F.3d 844, 849 (8th Cir. 1995).

20. *Peterson*, 400 N.W.2d at 913.

21. *Peterson*, 400 N.W.2d at 915.

22. *Peterson*, 400 N.W.2d at 914.

23. *Peterson*, 400 N.W.2d at 914.

24. *Crandell v. Larkin & Jones Appliance Co., Inc.*, 334 N.W.2d 31, 33-34 (S.D. 1983).

25. *Crandell*, 334 N.W.2d at 33-34. *See also Wynia v. Richard-Ewing Equip. Co.*, 17 F.3d 1084, 1087-89 (8th Cir. 1994).

26. S.D. Codified Laws § 20-9-9.

27. *Jahnig*, 283 N.W.2d at 560 (citing Section 402A of the Restatement (Second) of Torts, cmt. h).

28. *Hamaker v. Kenwel-Jackson Mach., Inc.*, 387 N.W.2d 515, 518 (S.D. 1986).

29. *Hamaker*, 387 N.W.2d at 520-21.

30. S.D. Codified Laws §§ 20-9-36 to -43.

31. *Engberg*, 205 N.W.2d at 109.

32. *Jahnig*, 283 N.W.2d at 560.

33. *Burley*, 737 N.W.2d at 409.

34. *Burley*, 737 N.W.2d at 410-11 (unless trial court found on remand that plaintiff had reliable expert testimony concerning her failure to warn claim, that claim should not be presented to the jury).

35. *Novak*, 46 F.3d at 850.

36. *Farner v. Paccar, Inc.*, 562 F.2d 518, 525-26 (8th Cir. 1977); *Kolcraft Enters.*, 686 N.W.2d at 452 (overruling in part, *Shaffer*, 249 N.W.2d at 257 n.7).

37. *Farner*, 562 F.2d at 526-27.

38. S.D. Codified Laws § 20-9-10; *Peterson*, 400 N.W.2d at 913-14; *Zacher*, 396 N.W.2d at 134.

39. S.D. Codified Laws § 20-9-10.

40. *Burley*, 737 N.W.2d at 411 (since product had been altered, plaintiff could not reach jury on failure to warn claims unless trial court found on remand that she had reliable expert testimony).

41. S.D. Codified Laws § 20-9-10.1.

42. S.D. Codified Laws § 20-9-10.1.

43. *Shaffer*, 249 N.W.2d at 256.

44. *Shaffer*, 249 N.W.2d at 256; *Crandell*, 334 N.W.2d at 34-35.

45. *Zacher*, 396 N.W.2d at 133-34; *Hofer v. Mack Trucks*, 981 F.2d 377, 383 (8th Cir. 1992); South Dakota Civil Pattern Jury Instruction 150-12.

46. *Novak*, 46 F.3d at 851; *see generally Durham v. Ciba-Geigy Corp.*, 315 N.W.2d 696, 699 (S.D. 1982); *Mattis v. Carlon Elec. Prod.*, 295 F.3d 856, 863 (8th Cir. 2002).

47. S.D. Codified Laws §§ 57A-2-313; 57A-2-315.

48. *Diamond Surface, Inc. v. State Cement Plant Comm'n*, 583 N.W.2d 155, 161 (S.D. 1998); *City of Lennox v. Mitek Indus., Inc.*, 519 N.W.2d 330, 334 (S.D. 1994). *Northwestern Pub. Serv. v. Union Carbide Corp.*, 115 F. Supp. 1164, 1167 (D.S.D. 2000); *Corsica Coop. Ass'n v. Behlen Mfg. Co., Inc.*, 967 F. Supp. 382, 395 (D.S.D. 1997).

49. *City of Lennox*, 519 N.W.2d at 333; *Agristor Leasing v. Spindler*, 656 F. Supp. 653, 655 (D.S.D. 1987).

50. *City of Lennox*, 519 N.W.2d at 333.

51. *City of Lennox*, 519 N.W.2d at 333.

52. *Engberg*, 205 N.W.2d at 108.

53. S.D. Codified Laws § 20-9-2.

54. S.D. Codified Laws § 20-9-2.

55. *Peterson*, 400 N.W.2d at 909, 912.

56. *Smith*, 278 N.W.2d at 161; *Klug v. Keller Indus. Inc.*, 328 N.W.2d 847, 852 (S.D. 1982).

57. *Burley*, 737 N.W.2d at 406-07 (design and manufacture), 410 (failure to warn).

58. *Burley*, 737 N.W.2d at 407.

59. *Burley*, 737 N.W.2d at 407.

60. *Burley*, 737 N.W.2d at 410.

61. *Burley*, 737 N.W.2d at 407-08 (ordinarily required for negligent design or manufacture), 410-11 (requiring plaintiff to show she had reliable expert testimony on remand in order to survive summary judgment on negligent failure to warn).

62. S.D. Codified Laws Ch. 57A.

63. *Zacher*, 396 N.W.2d at 140; *James River Equip. Co. v. Beadle Cnty. Equip., Inc.*, 646 N.W.2d 265, 271 (S.D. 2002).

64. *Zacher*, 396 N.W.2d at 140; S.D. Codified Laws § 57A-2-318.

65. *Burley*, 737 N.W.2d at 402-03.

66. *Burley*, 737 N.W.2d at 403.

67. *Burley*, 737 N.W.2d at 404 (quoting *Wheeling Pittsburgh Steel Cor. v. Beelman River Terminals, Inc.*, 254 F.3d 706, 715 (8th Cir. 2001)).

68. *Burley*, 737 N.W.2d at 403 (quoting *State v. Guthrie*, 627 N.W.2d 401, 415 (S.D. 2001)).

69. *Burley*, 737 N.W.2d at 406.

70. *Burley*, 737 N.W.2d at 406.

71. *Burley*, 737 N.W.2d at 406 (quoting *Daubert*, 509 U.S. 579, 590 (1993)).

72. S.D. Codified Laws § 21-3-2; *Holmes v. Wegman Oil Co.*, 492 N.W.2d 107, 113 (S.D. 1992); *Hofer*, 981 F.2d at 382-83.

73. S.D. Codified Laws § 21-1-13.1.

74. S.D. Codified Laws § 21-1-13.1.

75. *Tri-State Refining & Inv. Co., Inc. v. Appaloosa Co.*, 431 N.W.2d 311, 316-17 (S.D. 1988).

76. S.D. Codified Laws § 54-3-5.1.

77. S.D. Codified Laws § 54-3-16(2).

78. *Scotland Vet Supply v. ABA Recovery Serv., Inc.*, 583 N.W.2d 834, 838 (S.D. 1998).

79. S.D. Codified Laws § 62-3-2.

80. S.D. Codified Laws § 62-3-11.

81. S.D. Codified Laws §§ 15-2-12.2; 15-2-14; 57A-2-725.

82. S.D. Codified Laws § 57A-2-725.

83. S.D. Codified Laws Ch. 15-8.

84. S.D. Codified Laws § 20-9-10.1.

85. S.D. Codified Laws § 20-9-9.

86. S.D. Codified Laws § 32-38-4.

87. S.D. Codified Laws § 26-1-1.

88. *Degen v. Bayman*, 200 N.W.2d 134, 137 (S.D. 1972).

89. S.D. Codified Laws § 56-3-6.

90. *Degen*, 200 N.W.2d at 137; S.D. Codified Laws § 15-8-15.

91. S.D. Codified Laws § 15-8-12.

92. S.D. Codified Laws § 15-8-13.

93. S.D. Codified Laws § 15-8-13.

TENNESSEE

A. CAUSES OF ACTION

In the State of Tennessee, a "product liability action" is defined by statute to include, but not be limited to, all actions based on the following theories: strict liability in tort; negligence; breach of warranty, express or implied; breach of or failure to discharge a duty to warn or instruct, whether negligent or innocent; misrepresentation, concealment, or nondisclosure, whether negligent or innocent; or any other substantive legal theory in tort or contract whatsoever.[1] Any complaint filed in a product liability action is required to state the amount of damages sought to be recovered from any defendant.[2]

B. STATUTES OF LIMITATION

Any action against a manufacturer or seller of a product for injury to the personal property which is caused by its defective or unreasonably dangerous condition must be brought within the periods set forth as follows:

A cause of action for personal injury accrues from the date of the personal injury, not the date of the negligence or the sale of the product, and the person may maintain the cause of action until one year from the date of injury.[3]

For tort actions resulting in injuries to personal or real property, the action must be commenced within three years from the accrual of the cause of action.[4]

Actions to recover damages for any deficiency in the design, planning, supervision, observation of construction, or construction of an improvement to real property for injury to property, real or personal, that arises out of that deficiency, or for injury to the person or for wrongful death arising out of any deficiency, shall be brought within four years after substantial completion of such an improvement.[5]

Additionally, any action for breach of any contract for sale must be commenced within four years after the cause of action has accrued, unless the parties by original agreement reduce the period of limitation to not less than one year.[6] A cause of action accrues when the breach occurs, and a breach of warranty occurs when tender of delivery is made, except that where a warranty explicitly extends to future performance of the goods and discovery of the breach must await the time of such performance, the cause of action accrues when the breach is or should have been discovered.[7]

Notwithstanding these limitations of actions provisions, the action must be brought within six years of the date of the injury, and in any event the action must be brought within ten years from the date on which the product was first purchased for use or consumption, or within one year after the expiration of the anticipated life of the product, whichever is shorter.[8] An exception to this provision involves injury to minors, in which case the action must be brought within the limitations period as stated above or a period of one year after attaining the age of majority.[9]

Furthermore, note that the language requiring that in any event the action must be brought within the shorter of ten years from the date when the product was first purchased or within one year after the expiration of the anticipated life of the product does not apply to actions resulting from exposure to asbestos.[10] However, the asbestos exception cannot be applied retroactively to revive a plaintiff's cause of action which was already barred as of the enactment of the 1979 asbestos exception by the Tennessee legislature.[11]

The limitation of actions for the human implantation of silicone gel breast implants that are not pending or decided on or before May 26, 1993, provides that any action against a manufacturer or seller for injury to a person caused by a silicone gel breast implant must be brought within a period not to exceed 25 years from the date such product was implanted; however, such action must be brought within four years from the date the plaintiff knew or should have known of the injury.[12] In defining the statute of limitations for silicone gel breast implants, "seller" does not include a hospital or other medical care facility where the procedure took place, nor shall it include the physician or other medical personnel involved in the procedure.[13]

Under Tennessee law, a cause of action accrues when the injury occurs or is discovered, or when in the exercise of reasonable care and diligence it should have been discovered.[14]

Tennessee has recognized specific time and filing requirements for the joinder of additional defendants in civil actions where comparative fault is or becomes an issue and a defendant alleges in an answer or amended answer that a person not a party to the suit caused or contributed to the injury or damage for which the plaintiff seeks to recover.[15]

C. STRICT LIABILITY

1. The Standard

A manufacturer or seller of a product shall not be liable for any injury to person or property caused by the product unless the product is determined to be in a defective condition or unreasonably dangerous at the time it left the control of the manufacturer or seller.[16] Regardless of the legal theory, plaintiff must prove the product was defective.[17] However, there are no Tennessee cases which require that in order for a plaintiff to prove a design defect claim, the plaintiff must show a practical and feasible, safer alternative.

"Unreasonably dangerous" means a product is dangerous to an extent beyond that which would be contemplated by the ordinary consumer who purchases it, with the ordinary knowledge common to the community as to its characteristics, or that the product because of its dangerous condition would not be put on the market by a reasonable product manufacturer or seller assuming that he knew of its dangerous condition.[18]

Tennessee law imposes liability when a component manufacturer substantially participates in the integration of the non-defective component into the design of final product, if the integration of the component causes the final product to be defective and if the resulting defect causes the harm.[19]

2. **"Defective Condition"**

"Defective condition" means a condition of a product that renders it unsafe for normal or anticipatable handling and consumption.[20]

3. **Causation**

It is the plaintiff's burden in a product liability case to prove that the unreasonably dangerous or defective condition was the proximate cause of the plaintiff's injury.[21] To prove proximate cause, the plaintiff must show (1) that the conduct complained of was a substantial factor in bringing about the harm; (2) no rule or policy exists to relieve the wrongdoer from liability because of the manner in which the negligence resulted in the harm; and (3) the harm could have been foreseen or anticipated by a person of ordinary intelligence and prudence.[22]

4. **Contributory Negligence/Assumption of Risk**

Tennessee has rejected the doctrine of contributory negligence in favor of a modified comparative fault doctrine.[23] Tennessee courts have ruled that the modified comparative fault doctrine applies to strict liability cases.[24] Tennessee courts now differentiate between express and implied assumption of risk, having abolished the latter doctrine.[25]

5. **Sale or Lease/Persons Liable**

Under Tennessee law, "manufacturer" is defined as a designer, fabricator, producer, compounder, processor, or assembler of any product or its component parts.[26]

"Seller" includes a retailer, wholesaler, or distributor and any individual or entity engaged in the business of selling a product, whether such sale is for resale or for use or consumption. "Seller" also includes a lessor or bailor engaged in the business of leasing or bailment of a product.[27] The seller's liability is set forth by statute and provides that a seller is not liable when the product is acquired and sold by the seller in a sealed container and/or when the product is acquired and sold by the seller under circumstances in which the seller is afforded no reasonable opportunity to inspect the product in such a manner that would or should, in the exercise of reasonable care, reveal the existence of the defective condition.[28] This provision does not apply to actions based on breach of warranty, express or implied, to actions where the manufacturer of the product or part in question should not be subject to service of process in the State of Tennessee or by long-arm statutes of Tennessee, or in actions where the manufacturer has been judicially declared insolvent.[29]

A product liability action that is based on the doctrine of strict liability in tort shall not be commenced or maintained against any seller of a product that is alleged to contain or possess a defective condition unreasonably dangerous to the buyer, user, or consumer unless said seller is also the manufacturer of said product or the manufacturer of the part thereof claimed to be defective, or unless the manufacturer of the product or part in question shall not be subject to service of process in the State of Tennessee or service cannot be secured by the long-arm statutes of Tennessee or unless such manufacturer has been judicially declared insolvent.[30]

If the action is not a product liability action for personal injury or property damage, then provisions of the Uniform Commercial Code would control, and an actual sale would be required.[31]

6. **Inherently Dangerous Products**

A person who deals with inherently dangerous instrumentalities is recognized as having a duty to exercise caution commensurate with the danger or peril involved.[32] The basis of liability is negligence and not absolute liability.[33]

7. **Successor Liability**

There are no reported cases on this issue in Tennessee. However, the U.S District Court for the Eastern District of Tennessee anticipated how Tennessee would handle this issue by applying the traditional corporate test that a corporate acquisition structured as a purchase of assets for cash does not give rise to liability on the part of the successor corporation for injuries caused by a defective product manufactured and sold by the predecessor and for which the successor assumed no liability.[34]

8. **Market Share Liability/Enterprise Liability**

Market share liability and enterprise liability have been rejected in Tennessee.[35]

9. **Privity**

Privity is not a requirement for maintaining an action for personal injury or property damage brought on account of negligence, strict liability, or breach of warranty, including actions brought under the provisions of the Uniform Commercial Code.[36]

10. **Failure to Warn**

A plaintiff who relies on the theory of failure to warn must prove that the product was in a defective condition or unreasonably dangerous at the time it left the control of the manufacturer or seller.[37] A product is not recognized as being unreasonably dangerous because of failure to adequately warn of a danger or hazard that is apparent to the ordinary user.[38]

11. **Post-Sale Duty to Warn and Remedial Measures**

   There are no reported decisions by Tennessee courts regarding a post-sale duty to warn. The courts may, however, base a future decision concerning a post-sale duty to warn on the statute that provides that regardless of the theory of recovery, a manufacturer or seller is not liable in a product liability action unless the product is determined to be in a defective condition or unreasonably dangerous at the time it left the control of the manufacturer or seller.[39]

12. **Learned Intermediary Doctrine**

   Under the learned intermediary doctrine, makers of unavoidably unsafe products who have a duty to give warnings may reasonably rely on intermediaries to transmit their warnings and instructions.[40] The manufacturer of an unavoidably unsafe prescription drug can discharge its duty to warn by providing the physician with adequate warnings of the risks associated with the use of its drug.[41] The adequacy of a drug manufacturer's warnings is normally a question of fact, but becomes a question of law only when the instructions are accurate and unambiguous.[42]

13. **Substantial Change/Abnormal Use**

   If a product is not unreasonably dangerous at the time it leaves the control of the manufacturer or seller but was made unreasonably dangerous by subsequent unforeseeable alteration, change, improper maintenance, or abnormal use, the manufacturer or seller is not liable.[43]

14. **State of the Art**

   In determining whether a product is in a defective condition or unreasonably dangerous at the time it left the control of the manufacturer or seller, the state of scientific and technological knowledge available to the manufacturer or seller at the time the product was placed on the market, rather than at the time of injury, is applicable.[44] Consideration is given also to the customary designs, methods, standards, and techniques of manufacturing, inspecting, and testing by other manufacturers or sellers of similar products.[45]

15. **Malfunction**

   In a product liability action in which recovery is based on the theory of strict liability, the plaintiff must establish the existence of a defect in the product.[46]

16. **Standards and Government Regulations**

A manufacturer's or seller's compliance with any federal or state statute or administrative regulation existing at the time a product was manufactured and prescribing standards for design, inspection, testing, manufacture, labeling, warning, or instructions for use of a product raises a rebuttable presumption that the product is not in an unreasonably dangerous condition with regard to matters covered by these standards.[47]

17. **Other Accidents**

Tennessee law does not require proof of the exact identity of conditions in order to render evidence of prior accidents admissible, but does require conditions to be substantially the same.[48]

18. **Misrepresentation**

Tennessee recognizes a product liability action based on misrepresentation, concealment, or nondisclosure, whether negligent or innocent.[49] Section 402B of the Restatement (Second) of Torts has been adopted by Tennessee.[50] Tennessee no longer recognizes Restatement of Torts, Section 552(D) as giving rise to a product liability cause of action for pecuniary loss based on innocent misrepresentation.[51]

19. **Destruction or Loss of Product**

Rule 34A of the Tennessee Rules of Civil Procedure provides that "[b]efore a party or an agent of a party, including experts hired by a party or counsel, conducts a test materially altering the condition of tangible things that relate to a claim or defense in a civil action, or destroys or otherwise disposes of such tangible things, the party shall move the court for an order so permitting and specifying the conditions. Rule 37 sanctions may be imposed on an offending party."[52]

20. **Economic Loss**

Damages in product liability actions are limited to personal injury and property damage.[53] A consumer does not have an action in tort for the recovery of economic damages based upon strict liability.[54]

21. **Crashworthiness**

Tennessee has adopted the crashworthiness doctrine, holding that car collisions are foreseeable and that the manufacturer has a duty to minimize the harm of inevitable accidents by utilizing a reasonably safe design.[55]

D. **NEGLIGENCE**

In product liability cases based on negligence, the plaintiff must establish the existence of a defect in the product and has the additional burden of proving that the defective condition of the product was a result of negligence in the manufacturing process or that the manufacturer or seller knew or should have known of the defective condition.[56] The negligence standard is the failure to do what a reasonable and prudent person would ordinarily do under the circumstances.[57]

Tennessee has adopted a modified comparative fault system that entitles the plaintiff to recover so long as the plaintiff's negligence remains less than that of the defendant(s).[58] The comparative fault principles are to be applied to all cases tried or retried after May 4, 1992, and to all cases on appeal in which the application of comparative fault had been requested or asserted in the trial court and in which the request or assertion was preserved as a ground for appeal.[59] The doctrines of remote contributory negligence, last clear chance, and joint and several liability are now obsolete.[60] Furthermore, the allegation that a nonparty caused or contributed to the injury or damage for which recovery is sought is an affirmative defense.[61] A jury may generally apportion fault to immune non-parties, with the exception of an employer's liability, which is governed exclusively by the Tennessee Workers' Compensation Law.[62]

E. BREACH OF WARRANTY

Tennessee recognizes a product liability action based on the theories of breach of warranty, express or implied.[63]

The statute requiring that a manufacturer or seller of a product is not liable for any injury to person or property caused by the product unless the product is in a defective condition or is unreasonably dangerous at the time it left the control of the manufacturer or seller does not apply to an action based on express warranty.[64]

As in the case of negligence and strict liability, causes of action for personal injury or property damage brought on account of breach of warranty, including actions brought under the provisions of the Uniform Commercial Code, do not require privity in order for the plaintiff to maintain an action.[65]

F. PUNITIVE DAMAGES

Punitive damages are recoverable in product liability actions,[66] however, punitive damages are not recoverable as a matter of right, but rest within the sound discretion of the trier of fact.[67] To recover punitive damages, actual damages must be shown.[68] Punitive damages are awarded only in cases in which the court finds that the defendant acted intentionally, fraudulently, maliciously, or recklessly.[69] The plaintiff must prove defendant's conduct by clear and convincing evidence.[70] On motion of defendant, the court shall bifurcate the trial with the fact finder determining liability for and the amount of compensatory damages, as well as liability for punitive damages, in the first phase; the amount of punitive damages shall be determined in the second phase pursuant to the factors listed in the *Hodges* opinion.[71]

G. PRE- AND POST-JUDGMENT INTEREST

Tennessee law provides that pre-judgment interest cannot be awarded for personal injury claims.[72] However, the trier of fact may, in its discretion, award pre-judgment interest on a claim for loss or injury to property even where the claim is not certain or unliquidated.[73] Pre-judgment interest may be awarded by courts or juries in accordance with the principles of equity at any rate not in excess of a maximum effective rate of ten percent (10%) per annum.[74]

Plaintiff is entitled to interest on a judgment from the day on which the jury or the court returns a verdict without regard to a motion for a new trial.[75] Post-judgment interest is calculated at a statutory rate of ten percent per annum.[76]

H. EMPLOYER IMMUNITY FROM SUIT

The Tennessee Workers' Compensation Law provides for the exclusive remedy for an employee to recover for an injury by accident arising out of and in the course of employment that causes either the disablement or death of the employee.[77] The courts have carved out an exception to the exclusivity of Tennessee workers compensation laws for intentional acts committed by the employer against the employee.[78] In a product liability action arising out of an on-the-job injury, a defendant cannot plead or ask the fact finder to attribute fault to the plaintiff/employee's employer.[79]

I. STATUTES

The Tennessee Products Liability Act of 1978 provides the framework of law governing product liability actions.[80] The age of majority in Tennessee is 18 years of age or older.[81] Additionally, limitation of action statutes,[82] as well as particular Uniform Commercial Code sections governing breach of warranty actions, are applicable.[83]

J. JOINT AND SEVERAL LIABILITY

Upon the adoption of a modified form of comparative fault, *i.e.*, as long as plaintiff's fault is less than 50 percent of the total fault the plaintiff may recover, the Tennessee Supreme Court announced that the doctrine of joint and several liability was obsolete.[84] Therefore, a defendant is only responsible for liability arising from that defendant's own negligent acts. Currently, the Court has recognized exceptions to this finding and have recognized that joint and several liability still exists (1) in some circumstances where the tortfeasors knowingly act in concert;[85] (2) where the actors fail to perform a common duty owed to the plaintiff;[86] and (3) where there is a special relationship between the parties such as under the family purpose doctrine or where there is a master/servant relationship.[87]

The doctrine of contribution may still be viable in the following limited circumstances: (1) cases in which prior to *McIntyre* the cause of action arose, the suit was filed and the parties had made irrevocable litigation decisions based upon pre-*McIntyre* law; (2) cases in which joint and several liability continues to apply under doctrines such as the family purpose doctrine, cases in which tortfeasors act in concert or collectively with one another, cases in which the doctrine of respondeat superior permits vicarious liability due to an agency-type relationship, or in the appropriate products liability case; or (3) in the appropriate case in which fairness demands.[88]

Reported cases as of July 30, 2014.

W. Kyle Carpenter
J. Ford Little
Woolf, McClane, Bright, Allen & Carpenter, PLLC
Suite 900, Riverview Tower
P.O. Box 900
Knoxville, Tennessee 37901
(865) 215-1000
(Fax) (865) 215-1001
kcarpenter@wmbac.com
flittle@wmbac.com

Endnotes - Tennessee

1. Tenn. Code Ann. § 29-28-102(6) (2012).

2. Tenn. Code Ann. § 29-28-107 (2012).

3. Tenn. Code Ann. § 28-3-104(b) (2000).

4. Tenn. Code Ann. § 28-3-105 (2000).

5. Tenn. Code Ann. § 28-3-202 (2000).

6. Tenn. Code Ann. § 47-2-725(1) (2001).

7. Tenn. Code Ann. § 47-2-725(2) (2001).

8. Tenn. Code Ann. § 29-28-103(a) (2012).

9. Tenn. Code Ann. § 29-28-103(a) (2012); *e.g., Holt v. Hypro, a Div. of Lear Siegler, Inc.*, 746 F.2d 353 (6th Cir. 1984).

10. Tenn. Code Ann. § 29-28-103(b) (2012).

11. *Wyatt v. A-Best Prods. Co., Inc.*, 924 S.W.2d 98 (Tenn. Ct. App. 1995).

12. Tenn. Code Ann. § 29-28-103(c) (2012).

13. Tenn. Code Ann. § 29-28-103(c) (2012).

14. *Buckner v. GAF Corp.*, 495 F. Supp. 351 (E.D. Tenn. 1979); *see also McCroskey v. Bryant Air Conditioning Co.*, 524 S.W.2d 487 (Tenn. 1975); *Wyatt v. A-Best Co., Inc.*, 910 S.W.2d 851 (Tenn. 1995).

15. Tenn. Code Ann. § 20-1-119 (2009).

16. Tenn. Code Ann. § 29-28-105(a) (2012); *e.g., Smith v. Detroit Marine Eng. Corp.*, 712 S.W.2d 472 (Tenn. Ct. App. 1985).

17. *Fulton v. Pfizer Hosp. Prods. Grp., Inc.*, 872 S.W.2d 908 (Tenn. Ct. App. 1993).

18. Tenn. Code Ann. § 29-28-102(8) (2000); *e.g., Holman v. BIC Corp.*, 925 S.W.2d 527 (Tenn. 1996).

19. *Davis v. Komatsu Am. Indus. Corp.*, 42 S.W.3d 34 (Tenn. 2001).

20. Tenn. Code Ann. § 29-28-102(2) (2012).

21. *Davis v. Komatsu Am. Indus. Corp.*, 46 F. Supp. 2d 745, 751 (W.D. Tenn. 1999), *rev'd in part on other grounds*, 2001 WL 1042229 (6th Cir. Aug. 29, 2001).

22. *Davis v. Komatsu Am. Indus. Corp.*, 46 F. Supp. 2d 745, 751 (W.D. Tenn. 1999)

23. *McIntyre v. Balentine*, 833 S.W.2d 52 (Tenn. 1992).

24. *Whitehead v. Toyota Motor Corp.*, 897 S.W.2d 684 (Tenn. 1995); *see also McKinnie v. Lundell Mfg. Co., Inc.*, 825 F. Supp. 834 (W.D. Tenn. 1993).

25. *Perez v. McConkey*, 872 S.W.2d 897 (Tenn. 1994).

26. Tenn. Code Ann. § 29-28-102(4) (2012).

27. Tenn. Code Ann. § 29-28-102(7) (2012).

28. Tenn. Code Ann. § 29-28-106 (Supp. 2013).

29. Tenn. Code Ann. § 29-28-106 (Supp. 2013).

30. Tenn. Code Ann. § 29-28-106 (Supp. 2013).

31. *Baker v. Promark Prods. West, Inc.*, 692 S.W.2d 844 (Tenn. 1985).

32. *International Harvester Co. v. Sartain*, 222 S.W.2d 854 (Tenn. Ct. App. 1948), *superseded by statute on other grounds*, Tenn. Code Ann. §§ 20-10-101 and -102; *Messer Griesheim Indus. v. Cryotech of Kingsport, Inc.*, 45 S.W.3d 588 (Tenn. Ct. App. 2001).

33. *Messer Griesheim Indus. v. Cryotech of Kingsport, Inc.*, 45 S.W.3d 588 (Tenn. Ct. App. 2001). *See also Pierce v. United States*, 142 F. Supp. 721 (E.D. Tenn. 1955), *aff'd*, *United States v. Pierce*, 235 F.2d 466 (6th Cir. 1956); *see also Wilson v. Electric Power Bd. of Chattanooga*, 544 S.W.2d 92 (Tenn. 1976).

34. *Poole v. Amstead Indus., Inc.*, No. CIV-1-76-75 (E.D. Tenn. Oct. 5, 1976), 575 F.2d 1338 (6th Cir. 1978) (TABLE No. 76-2652). *See generally Woody v. Combustion Eng'g, Inc.*, 463 F. Supp. 817 (E.D. Tenn. 1978).

35. *Davis v. Yearwood*, 612 S.W.2d 917 (Tenn. Ct. App. 1980).

36. Tenn. Code Ann. § 29-34-104 (2012); *e.g., Commercial Truck & Trailer Sales v. McCampbell*, 580 S.W.2d 765 (Tenn. 1979).

37. *Pemberton v. American Distilled Spirits Co.*, 664 S.W.2d 690 (Tenn. 1984); *Smith v. Detroit Marine Eng'g Corp.*, 712 S.W.2d 472 (Tenn. Ct. App. 1985).

38. Tenn. Code Ann. § 29-28-105(d) (2012).

39. Tenn. Code Ann. § 29-28-105(a) (2012).

40. *Pittman v. Upjohn Co.*, 890 S.W.2d 425, 429 (Tenn. 1994).

41. *Pittman v. Upjohn Co.*, 890 S.W.2d 425, 429 (Tenn. 1994).

42. *Pittman v. Upjohn Co.*, 890 S.W.2d 425, 429 (Tenn. 1994).

43. Tenn. Code Ann. § 29-28-108 (2012).

44. Tenn. Code Ann. § 29-28-105(b) (2012).

45. Tenn. Code Ann. § 29-28-105(b) (2012).

46. *Browder v. Pettigrew*, 541 S.W.2d 402 (Tenn. 1976); *Whaley v. Rheem Mfg. Co.*, 900 S.W.2d 296 (Tenn. Ct. App. 1995).

47. Tenn. Code Ann. § 29-28-104 (Supp. 2013).

48. *Powers v. J. B. Michael & Co.*, 329 F.2d 674 (6th Cir. 1964), *cert. denied*, 377 U.S. 980 (1964); *see also Sweeney v. State*, 768 S.W.2d 253 (Tenn. 1989); *Graham v. Cloar*, 205 S.W.2d 764 (Tenn. Ct. App. 1947); *Winfree v. Coca-Cola Bottling Works of Lebanon*, 83 S.W.2d 903 (Tenn. Ct. App. 1935).

49. Tenn. Code Ann. § 29-28-102(6) (2012).

50. *Ford Motor Co. v. Lonon*, 398 S.W.2d 240 (Tenn. 1966), *overruled on other grounds by First Nat'l Bank of Louisville v. Brooks Farms*, 821 S.W.2d 925 (Tenn. 1991).

51. *First Nat'l Bank of Louisville v. Brooks Farms*, 821 S.W.2d 925 (Tenn. 1991).

52. Tenn. R. Civ. P. 34A.

53. *First Nat'l Bank of Louisville v. Brooks Farms*, 821 S.W.2d 925 (Tenn. 1991); *see also Ritter v. Custom Chemicides, Inc.*, 912 S.W.2d 128 (Tenn. 1995).

54. *Ritter v. Custom Chemicides, Inc.*, 912 S.W.2d 128 (Tenn. 1995).

55. *Ellithorpe v. Ford Motor Co.*, 503 S.W.2d 516, 519 (Tenn. 1973), *overruled in part by McIntyre v. Balentine*, 833 S.W.2d 52 (Tenn. 1992); *see also MacDonald v. Gen. Motors Corp.*, 784 F. Supp. 486, 496 (M.D. Tenn. 1992), *superseded by statute on other grounds*, Tenn. Code Ann. § 55-9-604.

56. *Browder*, 541 S.W.2d at 404.

57. *Groce Provision Co. v. Dortch*, 350 S.W.2d 409 (Tenn. Ct. App. 1961).

58. *McIntyre v. Balentine*, 833 S.W.2d 52 (Tenn. 1992).

59. *Cook v. Spinnaker's of Rivergate, Inc.*, 846 S.W.2d 810 (Tenn. 1993), *rev'd on other grounds*, 878 S.W.2d 934 (Tenn. 1994).

60. *McIntyre*, 833 S.W.2d at 57-58.

61. *McIntyre v. Balentine*, 833 S.W.2d 52, 58.

62. *Carroll v. Whitney*, 29 S.W.3d 14 (Tenn. 2000); *Dotson v. Blake*, 29 S.W.3d 26 (Tenn. 2000); *Ridings v. Ralph M. Parsons Co.*, 914 S.W.2d 79 (Tenn. 1996).

63. Tenn. Code Ann. § 29-28-102(6) (2012).

64. Tenn. Code Ann. § 29-28-105(c) (2012).

65. Tenn. Code Ann. § 29-34-104 (2012).

66. *Cathey v. Johns-Manville Sales Corp.*, 776 F.2d 1565 (6th Cir. 1985), *cert. denied*, 478 U.S. 1021 (1986).

67. *Huckeby v. Spangler*, 563 S.W.2d 555 (Tenn. 1978); *B. F. Myers & Son of Goodlettsville, Inc. v. Evans*, 612 S.W.2d 912 (Tenn. Ct. App. 1980).

68. *Solomon v. First Am. Nat'l Bank of Nashville*, 774 S.W.2d 935 (Tenn. Ct. App. 1989).

69. *Hodges v. S. C. Toof & Co.*, 833 S.W.2d 896 (Tenn. 1992).

70. *Hodges v. S. C. Toof & Co.*, 833 S.W.2d 896, 901 (Tenn. 1992).

71. *Hodges v. S. C. Toof & Co.*, 833 S.W.2d 896, 901-02 (Tenn. 1992).

72. *Sterling v. Velsicol Chem. Corp.*, 855 F.2d 1188, 1214 (6th Cir. 1988).

73. *Sterling v. Velsicol Chem. Corp.*, 855 F.2d 1188, 1213 (6th Cir. 1988).

74. Tenn. Code Ann. § 47-14-123 (2013).

75. Tenn. Code Ann. § 47-14-122 (2013).

76. Tenn. Code Ann. § 47-14-121 (2013); *see Vooys v. Turner*, 49 S.W.3d 318 (Tenn. Ct. App. 2001).

77. Tenn. Code Ann. § 50-6-108 (2008 & Supp. 2013).

78. *Coffey v. Foamex L.P.*, 2 F.3d 157 (6th Cir. 1993).

79. *See Ridings v. Ralph M. Parsons Co.*, 914 S.W.2d 79 (Tenn. 1996).

80. Tenn. Code Ann. § 29-28-101 *et seq.* (2012 & Supp. 2013).

81. Tenn. Code Ann. § 1-3-105(1) (Supp. 2013).

82. *See* Tenn. Code Ann. §§ 28-3-104, 28-3-105, 28-3-202 (2000); Tenn. Code Ann. § 47-2-725 (2001).

83. *See* Tenn. Code Ann. § 47-1-101 *et seq.* (2001 & Supp. 2013).

84. *McIntyre v. Balentine*, 833 S.W.2d 52, 58 (Tenn. 1992); *see also Bervoets v. Harde Ralls Pontiac-Olds, Inc.*, 891 S.W.2d 905, 907 (Tenn. 1994).

85. *Resolution Trust Corp. v. Block*, 924 S.W.2d 354 (Tenn. 1996).

86. *Owens v. Truckstops of Am.*, 915 S.W.2d 420 (Tenn. 1996).

87. *See Camper v. Minor*, 915 S.W.2d 437 (Tenn. 1996).

88. *Gen. Elec. Co. v. Process Control Co.*, 969 S.W.2d 914, 916 (Tenn. 1998).

Texas

A. CAUSES OF ACTION

A products liability lawsuit commonly means any action against a manufacturer or seller for recovery of damages arising out of personal injury, death, or property damage allegedly caused by a defective product whether the action is based in strict tort liability, strict products liability, negligence, misrepresentation, breach of warranty, or any other theory or combination of theories.[1] Product liability lawsuits can also include a violation of the Texas Deceptive Trade Practices Act (DTPA).[2] The DTPA, however, does not apply to suits for personal injury, death, or infliction of mental anguish.[3]

B. STATUTES OF LIMITATIONS

Almost all wrongful death, personal injury, or property damage causes of action, whether brought in strict liability or in negligence, must be brought within two years.[4] Causes of action for wrongful death accrue on the death of the injured person.[5] Most other causes of action accrue at the time of the injury.[6] A cause of action under the DTPA must be brought within two years,[7] but a liberal "discovery" rule applies.[8] A cause of action for breach of warranty under the Texas Uniform Commercial Code must be brought within four years of the date of delivery of the product.[9] With respect to minors, except in cases of wrongful death, the statute of limitations begins to run on the minor's 18th birthday.[10]

A 15-year statute of repose, amended on September 1, 2003, now protects all manufacturers or sellers of products, except where the manufacturer expressly represents that the product has a useful, safe life of longer than 15 years.[11]

C. STRICT LIABILITY

1. The Standard

Texas has adopted Section 402A of the Restatement (Second) of Torts.[12]

2. Definition of "Defect"

A "defect" is defined as a condition of the product that renders it "unreasonably dangerous,"[13] or dangerous to an extent beyond that which would be contemplated by the ordinary user of the product, in light of the ordinary knowledge common to the community as to the product's characteristics.[14]

3. Alternative Design

To recover for a strict products liability claim based on design defect, the plaintiff must prove that there was a "safer alternative design" that would have prevented or significantly reduced the risk of injury.[15] The alternative design must be both "reasonable" as well as economically and technologically feasible at the time the product left the seller's or manufacturer's control by the application of existing or reasonably achievable scientific knowledge.[16] Such "alternative design" evidence generally can only be provided by a qualified expert witness.[17]

4. **Causation**

Producing cause is required in strict liability cases.[18] A "producing cause" means that cause which, in a natural sequence, was a substantial factor in bringing about an injury, and without which the injury would not have occurred.[19]

There may be more than one producing cause.[20] A defendant cannot be found liable for an injury unless the preponderance of the evidence supports cause in fact.[21] If there are other plausible causes of the injury or condition that could be negated, the plaintiff must offer evidence excluding those causes with reasonable certainty.[22]

The defense of "sole cause" applies to product liability cases. If the conduct of a nonparty was the sole cause of the injury, then no other person or product could be a producing cause.[23] The conduct of a plaintiff's employer can constitute the sole cause of injury.[24] Even where the plaintiff's employer subscribes to workers' compensation, a defendant is entitled to submit evidence concerning the negligence of the subscribing employer, and is also entitled to a jury question that asks whether the subscribing employer's conduct caused the accident.[25]

Causation in the context of certain toxic tort inadequate-warning claims has two components: general causation and specific causation.[26] General causation is whether a product is capable of causing a particular injury or condition in the general population, while specific causation is whether a product caused a particular individual's injury.[27]

To prove general causation in certain toxic tort cases in which the nature of the injury-causing activities would pose an unreasonable risk of injury to test subjects, a plaintiff may rely on at least two properly designed and executed epidemiological studies showing more than a "doubling of the risk" of the particular injury after exposure to the particular product.[28] Courts may consider the Bradford Hill criteria to determine whether the studies were properly designed and executed.[29]

Chapter 90 of the Texas Civil Practice and Remedies Code outlines specific requirements for claims involving asbestos and silica-related injury, including pulmonary function testing and physician reports stating that, to a reasonable degree of medical probability, exposure to asbestos or silica was a cause of the diagnosed mesothelioma or cancer in the exposed person.[30]

5. **Contributory Negligence/Assumption of Risk**

Comparative responsibility is a defense. A claimant may not recover damages if his percentage of responsibility is greater than 50 percent.[31]

Texas law provides certain mechanisms for allocating responsibility to settling parties and responsible third parties.[32] A party can designate any person "alleged to have caused or contributed to causing in any way the harm for which recovery of damages is sought."[33] Once properly designated, a responsible third party can be considered by the trier of fact in determining the percentage of responsibility for the alleged harm caused by each claimant, each defendant, each settling party, or each responsible third party.[34] Responsible third parties can include bankrupt parties, employers, and unknown parties ("John Doe" and "Jane Doe" defendants).[35] If the claimant's percentage of responsibility is 50 percent or less, the court must reduce the amount of damages to be recovered by the claimant by a percentage equal to the claimant's percentage of responsibility.[36] Similarly, if a claimant has settled with one or more persons, the court shall further reduce the amount of damages to be recovered by the claimant with respect to a cause of action by the sum of the dollar amounts of all settlements.[37]

Effective September 1, 2011, if the applicable statute of limitations has run on the plaintiff's cause of action against a third party, that third party may not be designated as a responsible third party, unless the movant timely disclosed the third party as a potentially responsible party.[38]

A consumer has no duty to discover or guard against a product defect, but a consumer's conduct other than mere failure to discover or guard against a product defect is subject to comparative responsibility.[39] A consumer is not relieved of the responsibility to act reasonably, nor may a consumer fail to take reasonable precautions, regardless of a known or unknown product defect.[40]

Assumption of the risk and misuse are not separate defenses, but are subsumed in the contributory negligence question.[41] Under the rule in place at the time Texas adopted the comparative responsibility system, a plaintiff's actions amount to an assumption of the risk if he or she actually knew of the condition that caused the injury, fully appreciated the nature and extent of the danger involved, and voluntarily encountered the danger.[42]

6. **Sale or Lease/Persons Liable**

Strict liability applies to any person in the chain of a product's distribution.[43] Consequently, strict liability does not apply to a product that never actually entered the course of commerce.[44] The defendant must, as a part of its business, be involved in selling, leasing, or otherwise placing into the course of commerce, products involved in the suit by means of transactions that are essentially commercial in character.[45] For example, manufacturers of innovative products, such as brand-name prescription drugs, are not liable for harms caused by a generic equivalent.[46]

A party who merely sells a product that it did not design, manufacture, alter, or install is not liable for harm caused by the product, except under limited circumstances. A seller may be liable if (1) it exercised control over a product warning that was inadequate and caused harm; (2) it made an express factual misrepresentation about an aspect of a product and that misrepresentation was relied on and caused harm; (3) it knew of the defect at the time the seller supplied the product; or (4) the product manufacturer is insolvent or outside of the court's jurisdiction.[47] A non-manufacturing seller is also entitled to indemnity from the manufacturer so long as the seller did not negligently alter or modify the product or engage in some other act or omission for which the seller is independently liable.[48] This is so even if the seller also engaged in installation of the product[49] or if the seller is not in the manufacturer's "chain of distribution" and did not sell the particular product claimed to have harmed the plaintiff.[50]

7. **Inherently Dangerous Products**

A manufacturer or seller is not liable if a product is inherently unsafe and is known to be unsafe by the ordinary consumer or the product is a common consumer product intended for personal consumption, such as sugar, castor oil, alcohol, tobacco, and butter, as identified in comment (i) to Section 402A of the Restatement (Second) of Torts.[51]

8. **Unavoidably Unsafe Products**

Texas also has adopted comment (k) of Section 402A, which provides that a seller who provides an adequate warning cannot be held liable for the sale of products which "in the present state of human knowledge, are quite incapable of being made safe for their intended and ordinary use."[52]

9. **Successor Liability**

A successor corporation acquiring all or substantially all of the manufacturing assets of another corporation is not liable for injuries caused by products made by the predecessor corporation in the absence of an agreement to assume such liabilities or proof of actual fraud.[53]

10. **Market Share Liability/Enterprise Liability**

The Texas Supreme Court has rejected theories of collective liability in products liability cases and instead applies the "substantial factor" causation standard, which requires the defendant's product to be a substantial factor in bringing about the plaintiff's injury.[54] The Texas Supreme Court has rejected conspiracy as a products liability cause of action by holding that civil conspiracy is an intentional tort requiring a specific intent and thus it cannot be based on negligence.[55]

11. **Privity**

    Privity of contract is not required in strict product liability cases.[56]

12. **Failure to Warn**

    A strict liability action for failure to warn requires that the lack of an adequate warning renders the product unreasonably dangerous.[57] Such a product is said to have a "marketing defect."[58] A seller is liable if it fails to give adequate warnings of the product's dangers which were known or which should have been known, or if a seller fails to give adequate instructions to avoid such dangers, thereby rendering the product unreasonably dangerous.[59] The "consumer expectation" test applies.[60] A manufacturer does not have a duty to warn or instruct about another manufacturer's products, even though those products might be used in connection with the manufacturer's own product.[61] There is a rebuttable presumption that, if given, an adequate warning would have been read and heeded.[62] The existence of a duty to warn of the dangers of an alleged defective product is a question of law.[63]

    "Adequate" warnings and instructions are defined as warnings and instructions in a form that could reasonably be expected to catch the attention of a reasonably prudent person in the circumstances of a product's use; their content must be comprehensible to the average user and must convey a fair indication of the nature and extent of the danger and how to avoid it.[64] In the case of warning labels for prescription drugs, a rebuttable presumption exists that the warnings are adequate if approved by the United States Food and Drug Administration.[65]

    Moreover, a general rebuttable presumption exists that a manufacturer is not liable for any injury caused by some aspect of a product's formula, labeling, or design if the product's formula, labeling, or design complied with mandatory safety standards or regulations adopted and enforced by the federal government.[66]

    The extent of a manufacturer's duty to warn of a product's hazards depends on the purchaser's expertise and knowledge.[67] This is known as the "sophisticated user" doctrine. A product supplier has no duty to warn of a danger in using a product when the ultimate user possesses special knowledge, sophistication, or expertise.[68]

    A manufacturer or distributor is not required to warn of obvious risks.[69] The obviousness of a risk is determined from the perspective of the average user of the product rather than from the perspective of the average person.[70]

13. **Post-Sale Duty to Warn and Remedial Measures**

There is no post-sale duty to warn or to recall a product.[71] If a manufacturer regains control of a used product and resells it, however, the product may be judged by the technology available at the time of resale.[72]

Formerly, the Texas Rule of Evidence on subsequent remedial measures differed from the Federal Rule in that it did not "preclude admissibility of subsequent remedial measures in products liability cases based on strict liability."[73] However, the Texas Supreme Court later conformed Rule 407 to its federal counterpart. Now, both Texas Rule of Evidence 407 and Federal Rule 407 provide that evidence of subsequent remedial measures is not admissible to prove "negligence, culpable conduct, a defect in a product, a defect in a product's design, or a need for a warning or instruction."[74] The evidence can be admitted to prove "ownership, control, or feasibility of precautionary measures, if controverted," or for impeachment.[75]

14. **Learned Intermediary Doctrine**

As the Texas Supreme Court has made clear, in the case of prescription drugs and certain medical devices, a seller can fulfill its duty to warn end users of its products by furnishing adequate warnings and instructions to the prescribing physician, who is considered a "learned intermediary."[76] Once fulfilled, the manufacturer has no further duty to warn end users directly and may not be held liable for any causes of action that turn on a failure to warn theory, including in some instances, the manufacturer's direct-to-consumer advertising.[77] The learned intermediary doctrine is a common law doctrine, not an affirmative defense. Thus, the plaintiff bears the burden to prove the inadequacy of the warning to the prescribing doctor.[78]

15. **Substantial Alteration/Abnormal Use**

A manufacturer is not responsible for injuries caused by a substantial change to or alteration of the product, but the change or alteration must be one that could not be reasonably foreseen or expected.[79] Similarly, an original designer of a product cannot be held strictly liable when he licenses the design to another party who modifies the design and manufactures and markets a defective product based on the modified design.[80]

16. **State of the Art**

Whether a product is defectively designed is judged in the context of the state of technical knowledge existing at the time the product was manufactured.[81]

17. **Malfunction**

Evidence of a product's malfunction may be offered as circumstantial proof of the product's design, manufacturing, or marketing defect.[82]

18. **Standards and Governmental Regulation**

    A rebuttable presumption is established that a manufacturer or seller is not liable if (1) the product's formula, labeling, or design complied with mandatory federal standards or regulations existing at the time of manufacture; or (2) the product was subject to federal licensing or pre-marketing approval and the manufacturer complied with federal procedures or requirements so that the product was federally approved or licensed for sale.[83] In federal courts, compliance with government safety standards is considered "strong and substantial evidence that a product is not defective."[84]

    In pharmaceutical cases, a rebuttable presumption that the defendant is not liable is established if the warning or information distributed with the product was approved by the FDA or stated in FDA monographs with respect to products not requiring approval.[85] The claimant may rebut the presumption by establishing that (1) the defendant withheld or misrepresented required information from the FDA; (2) the defendant sold or prescribed the pharmaceutical product in the United States after the FDA ordered it removed from the market or withdrew its approval of the product; (3) the defendant promoted or prescribed the product in a manner not approved by the FDA; or (4) the defendant's bribery or improper influence of public officials in violation of 18 U.S.C. § 201 caused the FDA warnings or instructions to be inadequate.[86] However, courts have ruled that the first exception is preempted by federal law, unless the FDA itself has found fraud, because the presumption invalidates the FDA's own determination of what information is material and relevant.[87]

19. **Other Accidents**

    Evidence of other accidents is admissible if there is proof that the other accidents involved the same product and occurred under reasonably similar circumstances.[88]

20. **Misrepresentation**

    Section 402B of the Restatement (Second) of Torts has been adopted in Texas.[89]

21. **Destruction or Loss of Product**

    Methods used by Texas courts to discourage and remedy spoliation of evidence have included sanctions for discovery abuse under Texas Rule of Civil Procedure 215 and an instruction that the jury must presume that the destroyed evidence would not have been favorable to its destroyer.[90] Spoliation is not a separate tort.[91]

22. **Economic Loss**

    There can be no recovery in strict liability for purely economic loss,[92] which includes damage to the product itself.[93]

23. Crashworthiness

Strict liability applies to design defect cases in Texas where the defect does not cause the accident, but causes or aggravates the injuries sustained in the accident.[94]

D. NEGLIGENCE

Negligence is a well-established products liability cause of action in Texas. Unlike strict liability, which focuses on the product itself, negligence focuses on the conduct of the product manufacturer.[95] A claimant can bring concurrent claims for strict liability and negligence. However, to the extent the strict liability and negligence claims are based on the same underlying conduct, the claimant may only be entitled to submit one liability question to the jury.[96]

1. Causation

Proximate cause is required in negligence cases. Proximate cause means a cause that was a substantial factor in bringing about an event, and without which such event would not have occurred.[97] In negligence cases, the element of foreseeability is added to the definition of proximate cause. Thus, in order to be a proximate cause, the act or omission complained of must be such that a person using ordinary care would have foreseen that the event, or some similar event, might reasonably result therefrom.[98]

2. Claimant's Negligence/Comparative Responsibility

In negligence actions, a claimant's recovery against a negligent defendant is barred if the claimant is more than 50 percent responsible for the occurrence or injury.[99] As stated above, the trier of fact determines the percentage of responsibility for the alleged harm caused by each claimant, each defendant, each settling party, or each responsible third party.[100] If a claimant's responsibility is 50 percent or less, the claimant's damages are reduced by the percentage of the claimant's responsibility.[101]

3. Subsequent Remedial Measures

Subsequent remedial measures are inadmissible unless the subsequent remedial measure is offered to prove ownership; control or feasibility of precautionary measures, if controverted; or for impeachment.[102]

E. BREACH OF WARRANTY

1. Warranties Recognized

Texas has adopted the Uniform Commercial Code, including its definitions of express and implied warranties.[103]

2. Causation

Proximate cause, including foreseeability, is required in warranty cases.[104] Proximate cause means a cause that was a substantial factor in bringing about an event, and without which such event would not have occurred.[105]

3. **Used Products**

The resale of a used good does not automatically terminate remaining implied warranty obligations.[106]

4. **Sample Products**

There is no implied warranty when a product is provided to a plaintiff as a sample, or the manufacturer otherwise does not "sell" or "lease" the product to the plaintiff.[107]

5. **Claimant's Negligence/Comparative Responsibility**

In a breach of warranty case, a plaintiff's recovery is reduced to the extent (percentage) his actions were a concurring proximate cause of the damages. In contrast to the comparative responsibility system that applies to causes of action in tort, however, the aggrieved plaintiff may recover the damages that were proximately caused by the breach even where the plaintiff's fault constitutes a greater cause of the damages.[108]

6. **Community Knowledge**

Community knowledge must be considered in determining whether an implied warranty exists, and an implied warranty cannot contradict the community's common knowledge.[109]

7. **Reliance**

Express warranty claims require a showing of reliance on the part of the plaintiff.[110]

8. **Deceptive Trade Practices Act Remedies**

Breaches of express and implied warranty are included among the violations of the Texas DTPA,[111] which allows recovery of statutory penalties and up to three times the amount of "economic" damages.[112]

F. PUNITIVE DAMAGES

1. **The Standard**

Punitive damages may be awarded only if the plaintiff proves by clear and convincing evidence that the harm resulted from fraud, malice, or gross negligence.[113] Malice is defined as "a specific intent by the defendant to cause substantial injury or harm"[114] while fraud is defined as any fraud other than "constructive fraud."[115] Gross negligence is an act or omission which "when viewed objectively from the standpoint of the actor at the time of its occurrence involves an extreme degree of risk" and which "the actor has actual, subjective awareness of the risk involved, but nevertheless proceeds with conscious indifference to the rights, safety, or welfare of others."[116] Additionally, a jury finding must be unanimous on both the defendant's liability and the amount of punitive damages.[117]

2. Actual Damages Required

Punitive damages may not be awarded in the absence of actual damages.[118]

3. Limits on Punitive Damages

Punitive damages are limited to the greater of (a) two times "economic damages" plus noneconomic damages up to $750,000 or (b) $200,000.[119] "Economic damages" means compensatory damages for actual or pecuniary loss.[120] The only exception to these damages limits arises if the defendant's conduct on which the request for punitive damages is based arises from the knowing or intentional commission of certain felony conduct.[121] The applicability of this exception to product liability actions is currently unknown.

Evidence about the profitability of a defendant's misconduct and about any settlement amounts for punitive damages or prior punitive damages awards that the defendant has actually paid for the same course of conduct is admissible when the defendant offers it in mitigation of punitive damages.[122] However, the defendant's unlawful conduct in other states in inadmissible and lawful out-of-state conduct only is admissible if that conduct has a nexus to the plaintiff's specific harm.[123]

G. PRE- AND POST-JUDGMENT INTEREST

Statutory pre-judgment interest is awarded in wrongful death, personal injury, and property damage cases.[124] Both pre-judgment and post-judgment interest are equal to the Federal Reserve Bank's prime rate, with a floor of 5 percent and a ceiling of 15 percent.[125] The rate is calculated on the fifteenth of each month by the consumer credit commissioner for the succeeding calendar month.[126] No pre-judgment interest is to be awarded on future damages.[127] There is no interest on a punitive damages recovery.[128]

H. EMPLOYER IMMUNITY FROM SUIT

The Texas Workers' Compensation Act provides that a subscribing employer is exempt from common-law liability for injuries arising from the course of employment, except for certain exemplary damages in death cases specifically provided for in the Act.[129] This exemption has been held to extend to strict liability.[130] Texas courts have not adopted the "dual capacity" doctrine.[131] Under this doctrine, an employer may be liable to its employee if it occupies, in addition to its capacity as employer, a second capacity that confers on it obligations independent of those imposed on it as an employer.[132]

I. STATUTES

The age of majority under Texas law is 18 years.[133]

Other relevant statutes include the statutes of limitations,[134] comparative responsibility,[135] damage limitations,[136] Chapter 2 of the Uniform Commercial Code,[137] the Deceptive Trade Practices Act,[138] and the Products Liability Act.[139]

Texas state courts generally follow the *Texas Pattern Jury Charge*. The *Malpractice, Premises & Products* volume addresses product liability cases. The *Business, Consumer & Employment* volume addresses the Deceptive Trade Practices Act.[140]

TEXAS DECEPTIVE TRADE PRACTICES-CONSUMER PROTECTION ACT (DTPA):

Under the DTPA, a consumer may recover "economic" or "mental anguish" damages for certain acts defined as deceptive trade practices. Additional damages of up to two times the plaintiff's economic damages may be awarded if the defendant's conduct was committed knowingly. If the defendant's conduct was committed intentionally, the trier of fact may award additional damages of up to two times the plaintiff's economic *and* mental anguish damages.[141]

1. Who Can Sue

The plaintiff must be a statutorily defined "consumer." A business consumer with assets of $25 million or more (or controlled by an entity with assets of $25 million or more) has no standing to bring suit under the DTPA.[142] The DTPA does not apply to a claim for damages based on the rendering of a professional service, the essence of which is the providing of advice, judgment, opinion, or a professional skill, unless the claim involves:

(1) an express misrepresentation of a material fact that cannot be characterized as advice, judgment, or opinion;

(2) a failure to disclose information in order to fraudulently induce a consumer into a transaction;

(3) an unconscionable action that cannot be characterized as advice, judgment, or opinion;

(4) a breach of an express warranty that cannot be characterized as advice, judgment, or opinion; or

(5) an illegal promotion of an annuity contract subject to a salary reduction agreement.[143]

The DTPA also does not apply to:

(1) a claim for bodily injury, death, or the infliction of mental anguish, except to the extent that mental anguish damages would otherwise be properly recoverable under the DTPA or to the extent another statute permits recovery of DTPA damages;

(2) a claim arising out of a written contract if the transaction at issue involves consideration by a consumer of more than $100,000, the consumer is represented by counsel of his own choice while negotiating the contract, and the contract does not involve the consumer's residence; or

(3) a claim arising out of a transaction which involves consideration by the consumer of more than $500,000 and which does not involve the consumer's residence.[144]

2. **Deceptive Practices and Misrepresentations**

The DTPA penalizes a "laundry list" of 27 specific activities.[145] A breach of warranty is also a DTPA violation.[146] However, the DTPA does not create any new warranties or extend existing warranties.[147]

3. **In Connection with a Sale or Lease**

The DTPA protects consumers from "deceptive trade practices made in connection with the purchase or lease of any goods or services."[148] The Texas Supreme Court characterized this scope as a limitation on the liability of parties along the distribution or production chain of a product and determined that the DTPA was not intended "to reach upstream manufacturers and suppliers when their misrepresentations are not communicated to the consumer."[149] Nevertheless, the downstream seller found directly liable to the consumer may seek contribution if "the seller's DTPA liability is caused or contributed to by the otherwise actionable misconduct of upstream manufacturers or suppliers."[150]

4. **Causation**

Producing cause is required in a DTPA action.[151] Producing cause means that cause which, in a natural sequence, was a substantial factor in bringing about an injury, and without which the injury would not have occurred.[152]

5. **Damages**

For claims accruing on or after September 1, 1995, or suits filed on or after September 1, 1996, "economic" damages are recoverable. "Economic" damages are "compensatory damages for pecuniary loss." "Economic" damages do not include exemplary damages or damages for physical pain and mental anguish, loss of consortium, disfigurement, physical impairment, or loss of companionship or society.[153] Mental anguish damages are allowed only if the defendant acted intentionally or knowingly.[154] Pre-judgment interest awards are limited.[155]

Additional damages may also be available to a prevailing DTPA plaintiff. Under the current statute, if the defendant acted knowingly, the trier of fact may award an additional amount of up to two times the plaintiff's economic damages.[156] If the defendant acted intentionally, the trier of fact may award an additional amount of up to two times the sum of the plaintiff's economic and mental anguish damages.[157]

A plaintiff may not recover both punitive damages and additional DTPA damages.[158] Additional DTPA damages and attorneys' fees require an award of actual or economic damages.[159] In computing additional DTPA damages, attorneys' fees, costs, and pre-judgment interest may not be considered.[160]

6. Attorneys' Fees

An award of court costs and attorneys' fees is mandatory for prevailing DTPA plaintiffs.[161] Attorneys' fees and court costs may also be awarded against a party whose DTPA claim is groundless, brought in bad faith, or brought for the purpose of harassment.[162] However, attorneys' fees under the DTPA must be awarded as a specific dollar amount and not as a percentage of the judgment.[163]

7. Comparative Responsibility

The comparative responsibility statute applies to DTPA suits. The DTPA provides for contribution and indemnity rights to the extent provided by common law or statute.[164]

J. JOINT AND SEVERAL LIABILITY

A defendant is always liable for the percentage of actual damages equal to its own percentage of responsibility.[165]

A defendant is only jointly and severally liable if its share of responsibility is greater than 50 percent or it is responsible for certain criminal acts.[166]

Walter Lynch
Paige S. Goodwin
Baker Botts, L.L.P.
One Shell Plaza
910 Louisiana
Houston, Texas 77002-4995
(713) 229-1234
(Fax) (713) 229-1522

Endnotes - Texas

1. Tex. Civ. Prac. & Rem. Code Ann. § 82.001 (West Supp. 2014).

2. Tex. Bus. & Com. Code Ann. § 17.46-17.63 (West 2011).

3. Tex. Bus. & Com. Code Ann. § 17.49(e) (West 2011).

4. Tex. Civ. Prac. & Rem. Code Ann. § 16.003 (West 2002).

5. Tex. Civ. Prac. & Rem. Code Ann. § 16.003(b) (West 2002).

6. *Moreno v. Sterling Drug, Inc.*, 787 S.W.2d 348, 351 (Tex. 1990).

7. Tex. Bus. & Com. Code Ann. § 17.565 (West 2011).

8. Tex. Bus. & Com. Code Ann. § 17.565; *see also Burns v. Thomas*, 786 S.W.2d 266, 267-68 (Tex. 1990).

9. Tex. Bus. & Com. Code Ann. § 2.725 (Tex. U.C.C.) (West 2009); *see also Weeks v. J.I. Case Co.*, 694 S.W.2d 634, 636 (Tex. App.—Texarkana 1985, writ ref'd n.r.e.).

10. Tex. Civ. Prac. & Rem. Code Ann. § 16.001 (West 2002).

11. Tex. Civ. Prac. & Rem. Code Ann. § 16.012 (West 2002). *But see Vaughn v. Fedders Corp.*, 239 F. App'x 27, 30-32 (5th Cir. 2007) (explaining that application of statute of repose was unconstitutional to claims other than those where the statute could have run before it was even enacted on September 1, 2003).

12. *Firestone Steel Prods. Co. v. Barajas*, 927 S.W.2d 608, 613 (Tex. 1996); *Caterpillar, Inc. v. Shears*, 911 S.W.2d 379, 381 (Tex. 1995); *McKisson v. Sales Affiliates, Inc.*, 416 S.W.2d 787, 788-89 (Tex. 1967).

13. *Caterpillar, Inc. v. Shears*, 911 S.W.2d 379, 381-82 (Tex. 1995) (regarding marketing defect); *Lucas v. Tex. Indus., Inc.*, 696 S.W.2d 372, 377-78 (Tex. 1984) (regarding manufacturing defect); *see also Goodner v. Hyundai Motor Co.*, 650 F.3d 1034, 1040 (5th Cir. 2011) (providing five factors to be considered in determining whether a product is "unreasonably dangerous": the cost-benefit analysis of the utility of the design, available alternatives, the manufacturer's ability to eliminate the defect without impairing usefulness or increasing costs, consumer expectations, and the appropriateness of the warnings).

14. Restatement (Second) of Torts § 402A, cmt. i (1965); State Bar of Texas, Texas Pattern Jury Charges—Malpractice, Premises & Products PJC 71.3, 71.5 (2012); *Caterpillar, Inc.*, 911 S.W.2d at 383 (regarding marketing defect).

15. Tex. Civ. Prac. & Rem. Code Ann. § 82.005(a) (West 2011) (not applying to a drug or device as those terms are defined by the Federal Food, Drug, and Cosmetic Act (21 U.S.C. § 321) or to a toxic or environmental tort as defined by Tex. Civ. Prac. & Rem. Code Ann. § 33.013(c)(2) and (3) (Section 33.013(c) was repealed by Acts 2003, 18th Leg., ch. 204, § 4.10(5))); *see Hernandez v. Tokai Corp.*, 2 S.W.3d 251, 256 (Tex. 1999) (noting that the availability of a safer alternative design is elevated from a factor to be considered in risk-utility analysis to a requisite element of a cause of action for defective design); *see also Caterpillar, Inc.*, 911 S.W.2d at 384.

16. *Gen. Motors Co. v. Saenz*, 873 S.W.2d 353, 360-61 (Tex. 1993) ("Plaintiffs' argument that the warning could have been more prominent does not prove that it was not prominent enough. Every warning can always be made bigger, brighter, and more obvious."); *see also Uniroyal Goodrich Tire Co. v. Martinez*, 977 S.W.2d 328, 335 (Tex. 1998) (noting that the safer alternative design must be "reasonable," *i.e.*, capable of being implemented without destroying the utility of the product).

17. *Goodyear Tire & Rubber Co. v. Rios*, 143 S.W.3d 107, 117-18 (Tex. App.—San Antonio 2004, pet. denied).

18. Tex. Civ. Prac. & Rem. Code Ann. § 82.005(a)(2) (West 2011); *Technical Chem. Co. v. Jacobs*, 480 S.W.2d 602, 603-04 (Tex. 1972); *In re Mohawk Rubber Co.*, 982 S.W.2d 494, 497 (Tex. App.—Texarkana 1998, no pet.); *see also BIC Pen Corp. v. Carter*, 346 S.W.3d 533, 541-42 (Tex. 2011).

19. *See Ford Motor Co. v. Ledesma*, 242 S.W.3d 32, 46 (Tex. 2007).

20. *Ledesma*, 242 S.W.3d at 46.

21. *Merrell Dow Pharms., Inc. v. Havner*, 953 S.W.2d 706, 718 (Tex. 1997).

22. *Havner*, 953 S.W.2d at 720.

23. State Bar of Texas, Texas Pattern Jury Charges—Malpractice, Premises & Products PJC 70.4 (2012); *Ahlschlager v. Remington Arms Co.*, 750 S.W.2d 832, 833-35 (Tex. App.—Houston [14th Dist.] 1988, writ denied).

24. *Dresser Indus., Inc. v. Lee*, 880 S.W.2d 750, 753-54 (Tex. 1993); *Rankin v. Atwood Vacuum Mach. Co.*, 831 S.W.2d 463, 465 (Tex. App.—Houston [14th Dist.]), *writ denied*, 841 S.W.2d 856 (Tex. 1992) (per curiam).

25. *Dresser Indus., Inc.*, 880 S.W.2d at 754-55; *see also Lozano v. H.D. Indus., Inc.*, 953 S.W.2d 304, 317-18 (Tex. App.—El Paso 1997, no writ).

26. *Havner*, 953 S.W.2d at 718; *see also Merck & Co., Inc. v. Garza*, 347 S.W.3d 256, 261-62 (Tex. 2011).

27. *Havner*, 953 S.W.2d at 718; *see also Garza*, 347 S.W.3d at 261-62.

28. *Havner*, 953 S.W.2d at 716-17; *Garza*, 347 S.W.3d at 262-68 (discussing the requirements for epidemiological studies showing a "doubling of the risk"); *see also Bostic v. Ga.-Pac. Corp.*, No. 10-0775, 2013 WL 8808088 (Tex. July 11, 2014) (holding that, in cases involving multiple defendants, causation for asbestos-related illness requires substantial factor test and could be established by scientifically reliable epidemiological studies showing that worker's exposure to compound more than doubled his risk of contracting mesothelioma and that his exposure was similar to that of subjects of studies); *Borg-Warner Corp. v. Flores*, 232 S.W.3d 765, 770 (Tex. 2007) (requiring dose evidence in toxic exposure cases). *But see BIC Pen Corp.*, 346 S.W.3d at 545 (declining to permit plaintiff to use studies showing a "doubling of the risk" in a non-toxic tort case).

29. *See Garza*, 347 S.W.3d at 266-67 & n.41.

30. *See* Tex. Civ. Prac. & Rem. Code §§ 90.001, *et seq.*; *Union Carbide Corp. v. Synatzske*, No. 12-0617, 2014 WL 2994437 (Tex. July 3, 2014).

31. Tex. Civ. Prac. & Rem. Code Ann. § 33.001 (West 2008).

32. Tex. Civ. Prac. & Rem. Code Ann. § 33.003 (West 2008).

33. Tex. Civ. Prac. & Rem. Code § 33.011(6) (West 2008). To designate a responsible third party, the movant must file a motion for leave to designate on or before the 60th day before trial. Tex. Civ. Prac. & Rem. Code § 33.004(a). In its motion, the movant should plead sufficient facts concerning the responsible third party's proportionate responsibility to satisfy the pleading requirements of the Texas Rules of Civil Procedure. Tex. Civ. Prac. & Rem. Code § 33.011(6); *see also* Tex. Civ. Prac. & Rem. Code § 33.004(g). Unless another party files an objection to the motion within 15 days after the movant serves its motion, the court must grant leave to designate the responsible third parties. Tex. Civ. Prac. & Rem. Code § 33.004(f). Even with a timely objection, the court must grant leave to designate unless the objecting party establishes that the movant did not plead sufficient facts and, if given leave to replead, the movant failed to properly plead sufficient facts concerning the responsible third party's alleged responsibility. Tex. Civ. Prac. & Rem. Code § 33.004(g).

34. Tex. Civ. Prac. & Rem. Code § 33.011(6); *see also* Tex. Civ. Prac. & Rem. Code § 33.004(h).

35. Tex. Civ. Prac. & Rem. Code § 33.004.

36. Tex. Civ. Prac. & Rem. Code § 33.012 (West 2008).

37. Tex. Civ. Prac. & Rem. Code § 33.012(b).

38. H.B. 274 § 5.02 (Tex. 82d Leg.) (repealing Tex. Civ. Prac. & Rem. Code § 33.004(e)).

39. *Gen. Motors Corp. v. Sanchez*, 997 S.W.2d 584, 594 (Tex. 1999).

40. *Sanchez*, 997 S.W.2d at 594.

41. *Duncan v. Cessna Aircraft Co.*, 665 S.W.2d 414, 428 (Tex 1984).

42. *Henderson v. Ford Motor Co.*, 519 S.W.2d 87, 90-91 (Tex. 1974) (rejecting the definition of assumption of risk found in § 402A, comment n, of the Restatement (Second) of Torts). *But see* dissent in *Caterpillar, Inc. v. Shears*, 911 S.W.2d 379, 386 (Tex. 1995).

43. Restatement (Second) of Torts § 402A, cmt. f (1965); Tex. Civ. Prac. & Rem. Code Ann. § 82.001 (West Supp. 2014).

44. *Armstrong Rubber Co. v. Urquidez*, 570 S.W.2d 374, 376 (Tex. 1978).

45. Restatement (Second) of Torts § 402A, cmt. f (1965); Tex. Civ. Prac. & Rem. Code Ann. § 82.001 (West 2010) (defining "seller" and "manufacturer"); *Firestone Steel Prods. Co. v. Barajas*, 927 S.W.2d 608, 613 (Tex. 1996); *Armstrong Rubber*, 570 S.W.2d at 375; *McKisson v. Sales Affiliates, Inc.*, 416 S.W.2d 787, 788 (Tex. 1967) (holding that a distributor that handed out free samples could be held strictly liable where it did so with "the expectation of profiting therefrom through future sales").

46. *Eckhardt v. Qualitest Pharms. Inc.*, 858 F. Supp. 2d 792 (S.D. Tex. 2012); *Finnicum v. Wyeth, Inc.*, 708 F. Supp. 2d 616, 620-22 (E.D. Tex. 2010); *Burke v. Wyeth, Inc.*, No. G-09-82, 2009 WL 3698480, at *3 (S.D. Tex. Oct. 29, 2009); *Cousins v. Wyeth Pharm., Inc.*, No. 3:08-CV-0310-N, 2009 WL 648703, at *2 (N.D. Tex. Mar. 10, 2009); *Pustejovsky v. Wyeth, Inc.*, No. 4:07-CV-103-Y, 2008 WL 1314902, at *2 (N.D. Tex. Apr. 3, 2008); *Block v. Wyeth, Inc.*, No. 3:02-CV-1077-N, 2003 WL 203067, at *1 (N.D. Tex. Jan. 28, 2003).

47. Tex. Civ. Prac. & Rem. Code Ann. § 82.003 (West 2011).

48. Tex. Civ. Prac. & Rem. Code Ann. § 82.002 (West 2011); *see also Fresh Coat, Inc. v. K-2, Inc.*, 318 S.W.3d 893, 901-02 (Tex. 2010) (a manufacturer may be liable for a contractor's settlement payments to homebuilder, which the contractor incurred under its contractual indemnity obligations with homebuilder, where contractor also was a "seller"); *Bostrom Seating, Inc. v. Crane Carrier Co.*, 140 S.W.3d 681, 683 (Tex. 2004) (holding that a component-part manufacturer who does not participate in the integration of a component

into a finished product is not liable for defects in the final product if the component itself is not defective); *Owens & Minor, Inc. v. Ansell Healthcare Prods., Inc.*, 251 S.W.3d 481, 489 (Tex. 2008) (product manufacturers satisfy their statutory duty [under section 82.002] to the seller by offering to indemnify and defend it only for any costs associated with their own products).

49. *Fresh Coat*, 318 S.W.3d at 899.

50. *Fitzgerald v. Advanced Spine Fixation Sys., Inc.*, 996 S.W.2d 864, 865-68 (Tex. 1999).

51. Tex. Civ. Prac. & Rem. Code Ann. § 82.004 (West 2010); Restatement (Second) of Torts § 402A, cmt. i (1965).

52. Restatement (Second) of Torts § 402A, cmt. k; *Humble Sand & Gravel, Inc. v. Gomez*, 146 S.W.3d 170, 171 n.1 (Tex. 2004); *Centocor, Inc. v. Hamilton*, 310 S.W.3d 476, 515-16 (Tex. App.—Corpus Christi 2010, pet. granted) (*rev'd in part on other grounds*, 372 S.W.3d 140 (Tex. 2012)) ("Comment k to section 402A may provide a defense to a design defect claim, but it certainly does not absolve a manufacturer of its liability for completely failing to warn of a dangerous side effect.").

53. Tex. Bus. Org. Code Ann. § 10.254 (West 2012); *Celotex Corp. v. Tate*, 797 S.W.2d 197, 206 (Tex. App.—Corpus Christi 1990, writ dism'd).

54. *Borg-Warner Corp. v. Flores*, 232 S.W.3d 765, 770 (Tex. 2007); *Gaulding v. Celotex Corp.*, 772 S.W.2d 66, 68 (Tex. 1987).

55. *Triplex Commc'ns, Inc. v. Riley*, 900 S.W.2d 716, 720 & n.2 (Tex. 1995); *see Firestone Steel Prods. Co. v. Barajas*, 927 S.W.2d 608, 614 (Tex. 1996).

56. *Bernard Johnson, Inc. v. Cont'l Constructors, Inc.*, 630 S.W.2d 365, 370 n.4 (Tex. App.—Austin 1982, writ ref'd n.r.e.); *Milt Ferguson Motor Co. v. Zeretzke*, 827 S.W.2d 349, 354 (Tex. App.—San Antonio 1991, no writ); *Tex. Processed Plastics, Inc. v. Gray Enters., Inc.*, 592 S.W.2d 412, 415 (Tex. Civ. App.—Tyler 1979, no writ).

57. Restatement (Second) of Torts § 402A, cmt. i (1965).

58. *Caterpillar, Inc. v. Shears*, 911 S.W.2d 379, 382 (Tex. 1995).

59. Restatement (Second) of Torts § 402A, cmt. j (1965); *Caterpillar, Inc.*, 911 S.W.2d at 381-82.

60. Restatement (Second) of Torts § 402A, cmt. i (1965); State Bar of Texas, Texas Pattern Jury Charges—Malpractice, Premises & Products PJC 71.5 (2012); *see also Caterpillar, Inc.*, 911 S.W.2d at 381-82; *Joseph E. Seagram & Sons, Inc. v.*

McGuire, 814 S.W.2d 385, 388 (Tex. 1991). *But cf. Turner v. Gen. Motors Corp.*, 584 S.W.2d 844, 850-51 (Tex. 1979) (rejecting consumer expectation test for conscious design defect cases).

61. *Firestone Steel Prods. Co. v. Barajas*, 927 S.W.2d 608, 614 (Tex. 1996); *Wood v. Phillips Petroleum Co.*, 119 S.W.3d 870, 874-75 (Tex. App.—Houston [14th Dist.] 2003, pet. denied); *see also Finnicum v. Wyeth Inc.*, 708 F. Supp. 2d 616, 621-22 (E.D. Tex. 2010); *Burke v. Wyeth, Inc.*, No. G-09-82, 2009 WL 3698480, at *3 (S.D. Tex. Oct. 29, 2009); *Cousins v. Wyeth Pharm., Inc.*, No. 3:08-CV-0310-N, 2009 WL 648703, at *2 (N.D. Tex. Mar. 10, 2009); *Pustejovsky v. Wyeth, Inc.*, No. 4:07-CV-103-Y, 2008 WL 1314902, at *2 (N.D. Tex. Apr. 30, 2008); *Block v. Wyeth, Inc.*, No. 3:02- CV-1077-N, 2003 WL 203067, at *1 (N.D. Tex. Jan. 28, 2003).

62. *Gen. Motors Corp. v. Saenz*, 873 S.W.2d 353, 358-59 (Tex. 1993); *Magro v. Ragsdale Bros., Inc.*, 721 S.W.2d 832, 834 (Tex. 1986).

63. *Barajas*, 927 S.W.2d at 613.

64. *Shop Rite Foods, Inc. v. Upjohn Co.*, 619 S.W.2d 574, 578 (Tex. Civ. App.—Amarillo 1981, writ ref'd n.r.e.); *Lopez v. ARO Corp.*, 584 S.W.2d 333, 336 (Tex. Civ. App.—San Antonio 1979, writ ref'd n.r.e.); *Bituminous Cas. Corp. v. Black & Decker Mfg. Co.*, 518 S.W.2d 868, 872-73 (Tex. Civ. App.—Dallas 1974, writ ref'd n.r.e.).

65. Tex. Civ. Prac. & Rem. Code Ann. § 82.007 (West 2011); *see also Holland v. Hoffman-La Roche, Inc.*, NO. 3-06-CV-1298-BD, 2007 WL 4042757, at *2 (N.D. Tex. Nov. 15, 2007).

66. Tex. Civ. Prac. & Rem. Code Ann. § 82.008 (West 2011).

67. *Pavlides v. Galveston Yacht Basin, Inc.*, 727 F.2d 330, 338 (5th Cir. 1984) (applying Texas law).

68. *See Munoz v. Gulf Oil Co.*, 732 S.W.2d 62, 66 (Tex. App.—Houston [14th Dist.] 1987, writ ref'd n.r.e.) (holding that a warning is required only in order to impart special knowledge, and if that special knowledge already exists, further information is not necessary); *Koonce v. Quaker Safety Prods. & Mfg. Co.*, 798 F.2d 700, 716 (5th Cir. 1986) (applying Texas law); *Palvides*, 727 F.2d at 338-39 (the supplier may rely on the professional expertise of the user); *see also* Restatement (Second) of Torts § 388 (1965) (stating that warning of a product's defects is unnecessary where the supplier of the product has reason to believe that those who will use it will have such special experience as will enable them to perceive the danger).

69. *Caterpillar, Inc.*, 911 S.W.2d at 382.

70. *Sauder Custom Fabrication, Inc. v. Boyd*, 967 S.W.2d 349, 351 (Tex. 1998).

71. *Dion v. Ford Motor Co.*, 804 S.W.2d 302, 311 (Tex. App.—Eastland 1991, writ denied); *Arkwright-Boston Mfrs. Mut. Ins. Co. v. Westinghouse Elec. Corp.*, 844 F.2d 1174, 1185 (5th Cir. 1988); *Syrie v. Knoll Int'l*, 748 F.2d 304, 311-12 (5th Cir. 1984). *But cf. Bell Helicopter Co. v. Bradshaw*, 594 S.W.2d 519, 531-32 (Tex. Civ. App.—Corpus Christi 1979, writ ref'd n.r.e.), *overruled in part on other grounds by Torrington Co. v. Stutzman*, 46 S.W.3d 829 (Tex. 2001). *See Am. Tobacco Co., Inc. v. Grinnell*, 951 S.W.2d 420, 438 (Tex. 1997) (observing that Texas courts do not impose a post-sale duty to take remedial measures).

72. *Bell Helicopter Co.*, 594 S.W.2d at 530-32; *see also Torres v. Caterpillar, Inc.*, 928 S.W.2d 233, 240-41 (Tex. App.—San Antonio 1996, writ denied) (holding that manufacturer may become subject to post-sale strict liability if it regains control over the product and the product becomes defective during the period of control).

73. Tex. R. Evid. 407(a) (West 2003).

74. Tex. R. Evid. 407(a) (West Supp. 2007) (effective in all cases filed on or after July 1, 2003); Fed. R. Evid. 407.

75. Tex. R. Evid. 407(a) (West Supp. 2007) (effective in all cases filed on or after July 1, 2003); Fed. R. Evid. 407.

76. *Centocor, Inc. v. Hamilton*, 372 S.W.3d 140, 157-58 (Tex. 2012); *see also Alm v. Aluminum Co. of Am.*, 717 S.W.2d 588, 591-92 (Tex. 1986); *Reyes v. Wyeth Labs.*, 498 F.2d 1264, 1276 (5th Cir. 1974); *Rolen v. Burroughs Wellcome Co.*, 856 S.W.2d 607, 609 (Tex. App.—Waco 1993, writ denied); *Gravis v. Parke-Davis & Co.*, 502 S.W.2d 863, 870 (Tex. Civ. App.—Corpus Christi 1973, writ ref'd n.r.e.).

77. *Centocor*, 372 S.W.3d 140, 168-69. Although the patient in *Centocor* had viewed some direct-to-consumer advertising prior to requesting the prescription drug from her physician, the court refused to apply the direct-to-consumer advertising exception to the learned intermediary doctrine where plaintiff's claim rested on a video she had viewed after her doctor had already prescribed the prescription drug. *See Centocor*, 372 S.W.3d at 162-63.

78. *Centocor*, 372 S.W.3d 140, 164-65.

79. State Bar of Texas, Texas Pattern Jury Charges—Malpractice, Premises & Products PJC 70.6 (2012); *Woods v. Crane Carrier Co.*, 693 S.W.2d 377, 379-80 (Tex. 1985) (affirming the use of a definition regarding substantial change or alteration); *Miller v. Bock Laundry Mach. Co.*, 568 S.W.2d 648, 650 (Tex. 1977) (holding that the product must be defective at the time it is sold); *see also Feldman v. Kohler Co.*, 918 S.W.2d 615, 631 (Tex. App.—El Paso 1996, writ denied) (finding that the reasonably foreseeable use or alteration of a product imposed strict liability on the manufacturer).

80. *Firestone Steel Prods. Co. v. Barajas*, 927 S.W.2d 608, 616 (Tex. 1996).

81. Tex. Civ. Prac. & Rem. Code Ann. § 82.005(b)(2) (West 2011); *Boatland of Houston, Inc. v. Bailey*, 609 S.W.2d 743, 746 (Tex. 1980); *see also Am. Tobacco Co., Inc. v. Grinnell*, 951 S.W.2d 420, 438 (Tex. 1997) (observing that whether a product is dangerous is determined when it leaves the manufacturer's hands and enters the stream of commerce).

82. *Gen. Motors Corp. v. Hopkins*, 548 S.W.2d 344, 349-50 (Tex. 1977), *overruled in part on other grounds by Turner v. Gen. Motors*, 584 S.W.2d 844 (Tex. 1979); *Sipes v. Gen. Motors Corp.*, 946 S.W.2d 143, 155 (Tex. App.—Texarkana 1997, writ denied); *Temple EasTex, Inc. v. Old Orchard Creek Partners, Ltd.*, 848 S.W.2d 724, 732 (Tex. App.—Dallas 1992, writ denied); *cf. Plas-Tex, Inc. v. U.S. Steel Corp.*, 772 S.W.2d 442, 444-45 (Tex. 1989) (holding that in a breach of implied warranty of merchantability case, *prima facie* showing of defect can be made by proof of malfunction along with evidence of proper use of goods by plaintiff).

83. Tex. Civ. Prac. & Rem. Code § 82.008 (West 2011).

84. *Lorenz v. Celotex Corp.*, 896 F.2d 148, 150 (5th Cir. 1990).

85. Tex. Civ. Prac. & Rem. Code § 82.007 (West 2010).

86. Tex. Civ. Prac. & Rem. Code § 82.007 (West 2010); *see also Ackermann v. Wyeth Pharms.*, 471 F. Supp. 2d 739, 749 (E.D. Tex. 2006); *Holland v. Hoffman-La Roche, Inc.*, No. 3-06-CV-1298-BD, 2007 WL 4042757, at *2 (N.D. Tex. Nov. 15, 2007).

87. *Lofton v. McNeil Consumer & Specialty Pharms.*, 672 F.3d 372, 380 (5th Cir. 2012) (citing *Buckman Co. v. Pls.' Legal Commission*, 531 U.S. 341 (2001) (holding that plaintiffs' state tort causes of action for fraud-on-the FDA were impliedly preempted because they impermissibly imposed state law into the purely federal regulation of the approval process for prescription drugs)); *see also Murthy v. Abbott Labs.*, 847 F. Supp. 2d 958, 976 (S.D. Tex. 2012) (citing *Lofton*, 672 F.3d at 381 and holding that federal law preempted the exception at Tex. Civ. Prac. & Rem. Code § 82.007(b)(1)).

88. *Uniroyal Goodrich Tire Co. v. Martinez*, 977 S.W.2d 328, 341 (Tex. 1998); *McInnes v. Yamaha Motor Corp., U.S.A.*, 659 S.W.2d 704, 710 (Tex. App.—Corpus Christi 1983), *aff'd*, 673 S.W.2d 185 (Tex. 1984), *cert. denied*, 469 U.S. 1107 (1985); *Rush v. Bucyrus-Erie Co.*, 646 S.W.2d 298, 301 (Tex. App.—Tyler 1983, writ ref'd n.r.e.).

89. *Am. Tobacco Co., Inc. v. Grinnell*, 951 S.W.2d 420, 429-30 (Tex. 1997); *Crocker v. Winthrop Labs., Div. of Sterling Drug, Inc.*, 514 S.W.2d 429, 431 (Tex. 1974).

90. *Kang v. Hyundai Corp. (U.S.A.)*, 992 S.W.2d 499, 502 (Tex. App.—Dallas 1999, no pet.); *see also Offshore Pipelines, Inc. v. Schooley*, 984 S.W.2d 654, 667 (Tex. App.—Houston [1st Dist.] 1998, no pet.) (explaining that a trial court has broad discretion in instructing juries about the spoliation presumption).

91. *Trevino v. Ortega*, 969 S.W.2d 950, 953 (Tex. 1998).

92. *Nobility Homes of Tex., Inc. v. Shivers*, 557 S.W.2d 77, 79-80 (Tex. 1977); *Purina Mills, Inc. v. Odell*, 948 S.W.2d 927, 940 n.12 (Tex. App.—Texarkana 1997, writ denied); *see Brewer v. Gen. Motors Corp.*, 926 S.W.2d 774, 780 (Tex. App.—Texarkana 1996), *judgm't modified by Gen. Motors Corp. v. Brewer*, 966 S.W.2d 56 (Tex. 1998).

93. *Mid Continent Aircraft Corp. v. Curry Cnty. Spraying Serv., Inc.*, 572 S.W.2d 308, 312-13 (Tex. 1978); *see also Signal Oil & Gas Co. v. Universal Oil Prods.*, 572 S.W.2d 320, 325 (Tex. 1978) (allowing recovery for damage to product itself if collateral property damage has also occurred).

94. *Turner v. Gen. Motors Corp.*, 584 S.W.2d 844, 848 (Tex. 1979); *see Gen. Motors Corp. v. Castaneda*, 980 S.W.2d 777, 780 (Tex. App.—San Antonio 1998, pet. denied); *see also Hyundai Motor Co. v. Rodriguez*, 995 S.W.2d 661, 665 (Tex. 1999) (noting that in a crashworthiness case, strict liability's and breach-of-warranty's concepts of "defect" are functionally identical: an uncrashworthy vehicle cannot be unfit for ordinary use but not unreasonably dangerous, nor can it be unreasonably dangerous but fit for ordinary use; it must be both or neither).

95. *Gonzales v. Caterpillar Tractor Co.*, 571 S.W.2d 867, 871 (Tex. 1978); *Lozano v. H.D. Indus., Inc.*, 953 S.W.2d 304, 314 (Tex. App.—El Paso 1997, no writ); *Syrie v. Knoll Int'l*, 748 F.2d 304, 307 (5th Cir. 1984).

96. *Ford Motor Co. v. Miles*, 141 S.W.3d 309, 318-19 (Tex. App.—Dallas 2004, pet. denied).

97. *Rudes v. Gottschalk*, 324 S.W.2d 201, 203-04 (Tex. 1959); *Doe v. Boys Club of Greater Dallas, Inc.*, 907 S.W.2d 472, 477 (Tex. 1995); *Dico Tire, Inc. v. Cisneros*, 953 S.W.2d 776, 782-83 (Tex. App.—Corpus Christi 1997, writ denied).

98. *Transcontinental Ins. Co. v. Crump*, 330 S.W.3d 211, 221 n.7 (Tex. 2010); *see also* State Bar of Texas, Texas Pattern Jury Charges—General Negligence & Intentional Personal Torts PJC 2.4 (2012).

99. Tex. Civ. Prac. & Rem. Code Ann. § 33.001 (West 2008) (applying to actions that accrue on or after September 1, 1995, or suits filed on or after September 1, 1996).

100. Tex. Civ. Prac. & Rem. Code Ann. § 33.003 (West 2008).

101. Tex. Civ. Prac. & Rem. Code Ann. § 33.012(a) (West 2008).

102. Tex. R. Evid. 407(a) (West Supp. 2007).

103. Tex. Bus. & Com. Code Ann. (Tex. U.C.C.) §§ 2.313-2.315 (West Supp. 2008).

104. *Signal Oil & Gas Co. v. Universal Oil Prods.* 572 S.W.2d 320, 329 (Tex. 1978); *Stewart v. Transit Mix Concrete & Materials Co.*, 988 S.W.2d 252, 255 (Tex. App.—Texarkana 1998, pet. denied).

105. *See* discussion *supra* note 94.

106. *See MAN Engines & Components, Inc. v. Shows*, No. 12-0490, 2014 WL 2535963 (Tex. June 6, 2014) (holding that disclaimer of the implied warranty of merchantability is an affirmative defense that must be pleaded and that a subsequent buyer of used goods may sue the manufacturer of the goods for a breach of the implied warranty of merchantability).

107. *Woodhouse v. Sanofi-Aventis U.S. LLC.*, No. EP-11-CV-113-PRM, 2011 WL 3666595, at *4 (W.D. Tex. June 23, 2011).

108. *Signal Oil & Gas Co.*, 572 S.W.2d at 328-29.

109. *Am. Tobacco Co., Inc. v. Grinnell*, 951 S.W.2d 420, 435 (Tex. 1997).

110. *Am. Tobacco Co., Inc. v. Grinnell*, 951 S.W.2d 420, 436.

111. Tex. Bus. & Com. Code Ann. § 17.50(a)(2) (West 2011).

112. Tex. Bus. & Com. Code Ann. § 17.50(b)(1) (West 2002) (applying to causes of action that accrue on or after September 1, 1995, or suits filed on or after September 1, 1996).

113. Tex. Civ. Prac. & Rem. Code § 41.003 (West 2008).

114. Tex. Civ. Prac. & Rem. Code § 41.001 (West 2008).

115. Tex. Civ. Prac. & Rem. Code § 41.001(6).

116. Tex. Civ. Prac. & Rem. Code § 41.001(11).

117. Tex. Civ. Prac. & Rem. Code § 41.003(e).

118. Tex. Civ. Prac. & Rem. Code § 41.004(a) (West 2008).

119. Tex. Civ. Prac. & Rem. Code § 41.008(b) (West 2008).

120. Tex. Civ. Prac. & Rem. Code § 41.001(4).

121. Tex. Civ. Prac. & Rem. Code § 41.008(c).

122. *Owens-Corning Fiberglas Corp. v. Malone*, 972 S.W.2d 35, 40 (Tex. 1998).

123. *State Farm Mut. Auto. Ins. Co. v. Campbell*, 538 U.S. 408, 422 (2003).

124. Tex. Fin. Code Ann. § 304.102 (West 2006); *see Johnson & Higgins of Tex., Inc. v. Kenneco Energy, Inc.*, 962 S.W.2d 507, 530-31 (Tex. 1998), and *Concord Oil Co. v. Pennzoil Exploration & Prod. Co.*, 966 S.W.2d 451, 462 (Tex. 1998).

125. *See* Tex. Fin. Code Ann. § 304.103 and § 304.003 *et seq.* (West 2006).

126. Tex. Fin. Code Ann. § 304.103 and § 304.003 *et seq.* (West 2006). The secretary of state publishes the interest rate in the Texas Register. Tex. Fin. Code Ann. § 304.004.

127. Tex. Fin. Code Ann. § 304.1045 (West 2006).

128. *Ellis Cnty. State Bank v. Keever*, 888 S.W.2d 790, 798 (Tex. 1994).

129. *Davis v. Sinclair Ref. Co.*, 704 S.W.2d 413, 415 (Tex. App.—Houston [14th Dist.] 1985, writ ref'd n.r.e.).

130. *Davis*, 704 S.W.2d at 415; *see Cohn v. Spinks Indus., Inc.*, 602 S.W.2d 102 (Tex. Civ. App.—Dallas 1980, writ ref'd n.r.e.).

131. *Darensburg v. Tobey*, 887 S.W.2d 84, 88 n.3 (Tex. App.—Dallas 1994, writ denied); *Ramirez v. Pecan Deluxe Candy Co.*, 839 S.W.2d 101, 108 (Tex. App.—Dallas 1992, writ denied).

132. *Ramirez*, 839 S.W.2d at 107.

133. Tex. Civ. Prac. & Rem. Code Ann. § 129.001 (West 2011).

134. Tex. Civ. Prac. & Rem. Code Ann. ch. 16 (West 2008).

135. Tex. Civ. Prac. & Rem. Code Ann. ch. 33.

136. Tex. Civ. Prac. & Rem. Code Ann. ch. 41.

137. Tex. Bus. & Com. Code Ann. ch. 2 (West 1994).

138. Tex. Bus. & Com. Code Ann. §§ 17.41-17.63 (West 2002 and Supp. 2008).

139. Tex. Civ. Prac. & Rem. Code Ann. §§ 82.001-82.008 (West 2010).

140. State Bar of Texas, Texas Pattern Jury Charges (2012).

141. Tex. Bus. & Com. Code Ann. § 17.50 (West 2011).

142. Tex. Bus. & Com. Code Ann. § 17.45(4).

143. Tex. Bus. & Com. Code Ann. § 17.49(c) (West 2011).

144. Tex. Bus. & Com. Code Ann. § 17.49(e)-(g).

145. Tex. Bus. & Com. Code Ann. § 17.46(b) (West 2011).

146. Tex. Bus. & Com. Code Ann. § 17.50(a)(2).

147. *Parkway Co. v. Woodruff*, 901 S.W.2d 434, 438 (Tex. 1995); *La Sara Grain Co. v. First Nat'l Bank of Mercedes*, 673 S.W.2d 558, 565 (Tex. 1984).

148. *Cameron v. Terrell & Garrett, Inc.*, 618 S.W.2d 535, 541 (Tex. 1981).

149. *Amstadt v. U.S. Brass Corp.*, 919 S.W.2d 644, 649 (Tex. 1996).

150. *Amstadt*, 919 S.W.2d at 652.

151. Tex. Bus. & Com. Code Ann. § 17.50(a).

152. *Ford Motor Co. v. Ledesma*, 242 S.W.3d 32, 45-46 (Tex. 2007).

153. Tex. Bus. & Com. Code Ann. § 17.45(11).

154. Tex. Bus. & Com. Code Ann. § 17.50(b)(1).

155. Tex. Bus. & Com. Code Ann. § 17.50(f).

156. Tex. Bus. & Com. Code Ann. § 17.50(b)(1).

157. Tex. Bus. & Com. Code Ann. § 17.50(b)(1).

158. Tex. Civ. Prac. & Rem. Code Ann. § 41.004(b) (West 2008).

159. *Wheelways Ins. Co. v. Hodges*, 872 S.W.2d 776, 783 (Tex. App.—Texarkana 1994, no writ); Tex. Bus. & Com. Code Ann. § 17.50(b)(1).

160. Tex. Bus. & Com. Code Ann. § 17.50(e).

161. Tex. Bus. & Com. Code Ann. § 17.50(b)(1),§ 17.50(d).

162. Tex. Bus. & Com. Code Ann. § 17.50(b)(1),§ 17.50(c).

163. *Arthur Andersen & Co. v. Perry Equip. Corp.*, 945 S.W.2d 812, 818-19 (Tex. 1997).

164. Tex. Bus. & Com. Code Ann. § 17.555 (West 2011); *Plas-Tex, Inc. v. U.S. Steel Corp.*, 772 S.W.2d 442, 446 (Tex. 1989).

165. Tex. Civ. Prac. & Rem. Code Ann. § 33.013(a) (West 2008).

166. Tex. Civ. Prac. & Rem. Code Ann. § 33.013.

Utah

A. CAUSES OF ACTION

The Utah Products Liability Act[1] applies. Product liability lawsuits may include claims based on strict liability, negligence, tortious misrepresentation, and breach of warranty.[2]

B. STATUTES OF LIMITATION

1. Negligence

Claims for negligence resulting in personal injury, excluding wrongful death, must be brought within four years.[3] Claims for wrongful death must be brought within two years.[4] Claims for injury to personal or real property must be brought within three years.[5]

The discovery rule may toll the limitations period if the plaintiff makes an initial showing that he did not know and could not reasonably have known of the facts giving rise to the cause of action in time to file a timely claim and either (a) the defendant concealed the facts or misled the plaintiff or (b) exceptional circumstances exist that would make barring the claim irrational or unjust, where the hardship to the plaintiff, by applying the statute of limitations, outweighs the prejudice to the defendant from the passage of time.[6] The discovery rule, however, does not apply to a plaintiff who becomes aware of his injuries or damages and a possible cause of action before the limitations period expires.[7]

2. Strict Liability

All claims under Utah Products Liability Act, whether for personal injury, death, or property damage, must be brought within two years of the time the claimant discovered or should have discovered both the harm and the cause.[8] The UPLA statute begins to run when the plaintiff discovers or should have discovered: (1) that she has been injured; (2) the identity of the maker of the allegedly defective product; and (3) that the product has a possible causal relation to her injury.[9]

3. Construction Claims

Injuries due to defective design or construction of improvements to real property must be brought within two years of the earlier of when the claim was discovered or should have been discovered through reasonable diligence.[10] Breach of warranty claims must be brought within six years of completion of the improvement, unless an express contract or warranty provides otherwise.[11] In the absence of fraud, express warranty, or intentional wrongdoing, no claims may be commenced more than nine years after the improvement is completed.[12] Claims discovered in the eighth or ninth year of the nine-year period may be brought within two years of the discovery date.[13]

4. **Joint Claims**

Utah courts have determined that a plaintiff is not statutorily precluded from bringing a common law negligence and strict liability claim.[14]

5. **Breach of Warranty**

Utah has adopted the Uniform Commercial Code, and warranty claims must be brought within four years of the tender of delivery,[15] unless the warranty explicitly extends to future performance. Discovery of breach of warranty for future performance can only occur after the materials are used in construction.[16] However, claims for breach of warranty seeking damages for personal injury or tortious injury to personal property are treated as tort claims and are subject to the applicable tort limitations period.[17]

C. **STRICT LIABILITY**

1. **The Standard**

Utah has adopted Section 402A of the Restatement (Second) of Torts.[18] In Utah, a product liability action "encompasses all actions seeking money damages for injury to people or property resulting from defective products."[19] Under Utah law, to prove a case of strict products liability against a manufacturer, a plaintiff must establish: "(1) that the product was unreasonably dangerous due to a defect or defective condition, (2) that the defect existed at the time the product was sold, and (3) that the defective condition was a cause of the plaintiff's injuries."[20]

2. **Definition of "Defect"**

Utah recognizes only three types of product defects: design, manufacturing, and inadequate warning regarding use.[21] A product is in a defective condition if it is unreasonably dangerous to the user or consumer or to his property.[22] The defective condition must exist at the time of the sale, and must be a cause of the plaintiff's injuries.[23] " '[U]nreasonably dangerous' means that the product was dangerous to an extent beyond which would be contemplated by the ordinary and prudent buyer, consumer, or user of that product in that community considering the product's characteristics, propensities, risks, dangers, and uses together with any actual knowledge, training, or experience possessed by that particular buyer, user, or consumer."[24] In order to prevail on a design defect claim, the plaintiff must show that there is a feasible, safer alternative design available.[25]

3. **Causation**

   A plaintiff claiming strict liability must prove that a specific defect or defective condition proximately caused his or her injuries.[26] Proving that a defect existed and that an accident occurred is not enough to prove a proximate relationship between the defect and the plaintiff's injuries.[27] Proximate cause has been defined as "that cause, which in natural and continuous sequence (unbroken by an efficient intervening cause), produces the injury, and without which the result would not have occurred."[28] Utah recognizes the "enhanced injury" theory of liability outlined in Section 16(a) of the Restatement (Third) of Torts: Products Liability.[29]

4. **Contributory Negligence/Assumption of Risk**

   Utah applies a statutory comparative fault scheme to all product liability claims, including strict liability.[30] Fault by the plaintiff does not alone bar recovery; a plaintiff may recover the proportion of damages attributable to the product defect if the fault attributable to the plaintiff is less than fifty percent.[31] The fact finder may allocate fault to each person seeking recovery, to each defendant, and to any other person whether immune from suit or joined as a party to the suit.[32]

   Assumption of risk, meaning knowledge of the defect and awareness of the danger by the user or consumer who unreasonably proceeds to make use of the product, may be considered as fault by the plaintiff under the comparative fault scheme.[33]

5. **Sale or Lease/Persons Liable**

   Plaintiff must allege a sale or other commercial transaction of the product by the defendant, but strict liability applies to anyone in the chain of distribution, as long as that person or entity is engaged in the business of selling the product.[34] The District Court for the District of Utah has held that Utah courts will apply strict liability to lessors of products, in addition to sellers, at least in some circumstances.[35]

   A passive retailer, however, does not owe a duty to warn customers of a manufacturing defect that it does not know of itself, and Utah's Liability Reform Act precludes a strict liability claim against a passive retailer when the manufacturer is named in the lawsuit and the passive retailer does not know of or contribute to the defective condition of the product.[36]

   Utah limits products liability claims against component part manufacturers.[37] A component part manufacturer will only be liable under a products liability theory in two instances: (1) the component part is defective itself and the defect causes the harm; or (2) the seller or distributor of the component part "substantially participates" in the integration of the component part into the design of the product and the integration of the component part causes the product to be defective.[38]

6. **Inherently Dangerous Products**

    The "basic policy" of comment k of Section 402A has been adopted in Utah. All FDA-approved prescription drugs are exempt from design defect claims.[39]

7. **Successor Liability**

    The rule of successor liability in Utah is "where one company sells or otherwise transfers all its assets to another company the latter is not liable for the debts and liabilities of the transferor, except where: (1) the purchaser expressly or impliedly agrees to assume such debts; (2) the transaction amounts to a consolidation or merger of the seller and purchaser; (3) the purchasing corporation is merely a continuation of the selling corporation; or (4) the transaction is entered into fraudulently in order to escape liability for such debts."[40] Utah law further imposes a duty to warn on a successor corporation in accordance with Section 13 of the Restatement (Third) of Torts.[41] Utah has expressly rejected the continuity of enterprise theory and the product line exception with respect to successor corporation liability.[42]

8. **Market Share Liability/Enterprise Liability**

    The Utah Supreme Court has declined to adopt the "product" line or "continuity of enterprise" exceptions to successor non-liability.[43] No Utah authority addresses market share liability, and no authority addresses enterprise liability in a product liability setting.

9. **Privity**

    Privity is not required in Utah product liability actions based in negligence or strict product liability; the ultimate user may sue any seller.[44]

10. **Failure to Warn**

    To recover for a claimed failure to warn, the plaintiff must establish causation. An inadequate warning may make a product unreasonably dangerous.[45] An adequate warning must be designed to reasonably catch the attention of the consumer, be comprehensible and give a fair indication of the specific risks involved, and be of an intensity justified by the magnitude of the risk.[46] Whether a "sophisticated user" standard changes the duty to warn has been found to be a fact question for the jury to decide.[47] Utah has adopted a rebuttable "heeding presumption" that an adequate warning would have been followed.[48]

11. **Post-Sale Duty to Warn and Remedial Measures**

    Drug manufacturers have a continuous duty to warn the medical profession regarding additional side effects.[49] Under Utah law, a successor corporation has a post-sale duty to independently warn customers of defects in products manufactured and sold by the predecessor corporation, where successor undertakes to provide service or maintenance, or successor knows the product poses a substantial risk of harm and consumers to be warned can be identified and a warning effectively communicated to them.[50]

Utah adopted Rule 407 of the Federal Rules of Evidence pertaining to subsequent remedial measures. Rule 407 generally excludes evidence of steps taken after an injury that would have made an injury less likely, if the action had been undertaken earlier.[51] If the feasibility of alternative designs is contested, however, courts will normally admit subsequent remedial measures. The issue of "feasibility of particular precautionary measure clearly includes an analysis of its cost, as well as its physical possibility."[52] If the plaintiff's *prima facie* case depends upon cost feasibility, Rule 407 will be trumped with respect to rebutting testimony on that issue.[53]

12. **Learned Intermediary Doctrine**

The manufacturer of a prescription drug has a duty to warn the prescribing physician, but not the patient.[54] Utah law also extends the learned intermediary rule to exempt pharmacists from strict products liability under a failure-to-warn theory.[55]

13. **Substantial Alteration/Abnormal Use**

Under Utah's comparative fault scheme, "fault" includes "an alteration or modification of the product, which occurred subsequent to the sale by the manufacturer or seller to the initial user or consumer, and which changed the purpose, use, function, design, or intended use or manner of use of the product from that which the product was originally designed, tested, or intended."[56]

Misuse of the product by the user or consumer is not a complete bar to any recovery under strict liability, but is considered and applied according to statutory comparative fault principles.[57] If the fact finder determines the misuse is foreseeable, a defendant cannot use this defense.[58]

14. **State of the Art**

The Tenth Circuit has ruled that Utah law requires a plaintiff to show that an alternative safer design, practicable under the circumstances, was available at the time of sale of the product.[59] An open and obvious danger does not operate as a complete bar to recovery.[60]

15. **Malfunction**

A product liability claim requires proof of a specific defect, which in turn causes the plaintiff's injury. Testimony that a product "malfunctioned," or agreement that the product had a "problem," or an admission that an accident was the product's "fault," is not sufficient to establish the existence of a causal defect.[61]

16. **Standards and Governmental Regulation**

There is a rebuttable presumption that a product that fully complies with the applicable government standards at the time of marketing is not defective.[62] A preponderance of the evidence is sufficient to rebut the presumption.[63] A product liability defendant may rely upon legislative enactments or administrative regulations even if the enactment or regulation does not purport to establish a standard of conduct.[64]

17. **Other Accidents**

For evidence of a prior accident to be admissible in evidence, the prior accident must be substantially similar to the accident causing the plaintiff's injury.[65]

18. **Misrepresentation**

No Utah authorities address misrepresentation in the context of a strict product liability claim.

An independent claim of negligent misrepresentation exists if a plaintiff is injured by reasonable reliance upon a defendant's careless or negligent misrepresentation of a material fact, when the defendant had a pecuniary interest in the transaction, was in a superior position to know the material facts, and should have reasonably foreseen that the injured party was likely to rely upon the fact.[66]

"The elements of an action based on fraudulent misrepresentation are: '(1) a representation; (2) concerning a presently existing material fact; (3) which was false; (4) which the representor either (a) knew to be false, or (b) made recklessly, knowing that he had insufficient knowledge upon which to base such representation; (5) for the purpose of inducing the other party to act upon it; (6) that the other party, acting reasonably and in ignorance of its falsity; (7) did in fact rely upon it; (8) and was thereby induced to act; (9) to his injury and damage.'"[67]

19. **Destruction or Loss of Product**

Utah courts have discussed, but have not explicitly adopted, the doctrine of spoliation of evidence in the context of product liability actions.[68] The doctrine operates to provide the plaintiff an inference of a product defect "where one party wrongfully denies another the evidence necessary to establish a fact in dispute."[69] However, the doctrine will only apply in those circumstances in which the defendant destroys or discards the product after the plaintiff brings suit for his injuries or otherwise notifies the defendant that he or she is considering such an action.[70]

20. **Economic Loss**

Utah courts have recognized the economic loss doctrine and the Utah Supreme Court has adopted the following formulation: "[A] party suffering only economic loss from the breach of an express or implied contractual duty may not assert a tort claim for such a breach *absent an independent duty of care* under tort law."[71] The rule serves two purposes: "[f]irst, it bars recovery of economic losses in negligence actions unless the plaintiff can show physical damage to other property or bodily injury. Second, the economic loss rule prevents parties who have contracted with each other from recovering beyond the bargained-for risks."[72] In 2008, the Utah Legislature codified the economic loss rule.[73] Economic loss is defined as "[d]amages for inadequate value, costs of repair and replacement of the defective product, or consequent loss of profits—without any claim of personal injury or damage to other property . . . as well as the diminution in the value of the product because it is inferior in quality and does not work for the general purposes for which it was manufactured and sold."[74] The Utah Supreme Court has also strictly limited the reach of *W.R.H. Inc. v. Economy Builders Supply* to its facts, and declined to extend its rule to govern transactions between sophisticated commercial entities.[75]

21. **Crashworthiness**

The criteria for establishing the admissibility of crash test films are that "the data be relevant, that the tests be conducted under conditions substantially similar to those of the actual occurrence, and that its presentation not consume undue amounts of time, not confuse the issues, and not mislead the jury."[76] "The requirement of substantial similarity of conditions does not require absolute identity," but must "be so nearly the same in substantial particulars as to afford a fair comparison in respect to the particular *issue* to which the test is directed."[77]

D. **NEGLIGENCE**

In order to prevail on a negligence claim related to an allegedly defective product, there must be proof of a duty on the part of the manufacturer, breach of that duty, and resulting damages.[78] Utah applies the traditional standards of reasonableness for negligence cases.[79] Negligence cases apply modified comparative negligence principles, which limit each defendant to liability related to that defendant's proportion of fault.[80] Additionally, a plaintiff's claim is barred if her percentage of fault exceeds the defendant's.[81] The proportion of fault of immune nonparties, such as the plaintiff's employer or dismissed parties, should be determined by the finder of fact.[82]

E. **BREACH OF WARRANTY**

In a product setting, a cause of action for breach of warranty is generally quite similar to a strict liability cause of action.[83]

F. **PUNITIVE DAMAGES**

Punitive damages are recoverable in actions of strict liability and negligence, but not in actions sounding only in breach of warranty. The standard for imposing punitive damage awards is laid out by statute in Section 78B-8-201 of the Utah Code, which states:

Except as otherwise provided by statute, punitive damages may be awarded only if compensatory or general damages are awarded and it is established by clear and convincing evidence that the acts or omissions of the tortfeasor are the result of willful and malicious or intentionally fraudulent conduct, or conduct that manifests a knowing and reckless indifference toward, and a disregard of, the rights of others.[84]

Although "simple negligence will not support punitive damages, negligence manifesting a knowing and reckless indifference toward the rights of others will."[85] When evidence has been presented of such indifference or disregard, the question of punitive damages may be submitted to the jury.[86]

Punitive damages may not be awarded for injuries caused by drugs that receive premarket approval or licensing by the FDA, and are generally recognized as safe and effective, unless the drug manufacturer is shown by clear and convincing evidence to have knowingly withheld or misrepresented information submitted to the FDA that is relevant to the claimant's harm.[87] The District Court for the District of Utah has held that, to the extent this law "allows for an exception in cases where a plaintiff puts on his or her own independent evidence of information being withheld from the FDA," it is preempted by federal law, but there is no preemption where a plaintiff invokes this law "to seek punitive damages in cases where the FDA itself has found that there was fraud in the application process."[88]

G. PRE- AND POST-JUDGMENT INTEREST

In all tort actions, the plaintiff may claim pre-judgment interest on the special damages actually incurred from the date of the occurrence of the act giving rise to the cause of action.[89] Pre-judgment interest is calculated by the court from the amount of special damages assessed by the jury, using the rate of 7.5% simple interest per annum.[90] Special damages actually incurred do not include damages for future medical expenses, loss of future wages, or loss of future earning capacity.[91]

H. EMPLOYER IMMUNITY FROM SUIT

The right of an employee to recover under the Utah Workers' Compensation Act or Utah Occupational Disease Act is the exclusive remedy of the employee against the employer and against any officer, agent, or employee of the employer.[92]

I. STATUTES

Relevant statutes for product liability actions are the statutes of limitation, the Utah Products Liability Act, the Punitive Damages Act regarding drug claims mentioned, the comparative negligence statute, and commercial code sections regarding breaches of warranty.[93] The age of majority in the state of Utah is eighteen.[94]

J. JOINT AND SEVERAL LIABILITY

Under Utah's statutory comparative fault scheme, which applies in product liability actions, joint and several liability is effectively abolished. The maximum amount for which a defendant may be liable is the percentage of the total damages equivalent to the percentage of fault attributed to that defendant,[95] after any reallocation of fault that may be applicable if some fault is attributed to persons immune from suit in a combined amount of less than forty percent.[96] No defendant may seek contribution from any other person.[97]

Rick L. Rose
Kristine M. Larsen
Ray, Quinney & Nebeker
36 South State Street
Suite 1400
P.O. Box 45385
Salt Lake City, Utah 84145-0385
(801) 532-1500
(Fax) (801) 532-7543

Endnotes - Utah

1. Utah Code Ann. §§ 78B-6-701 to 78B-6-707 (2008).

2. Utah Code Ann. §§ 78B-6-701 to 78B-6-707.

3. Utah Code Ann. § 78B-2-307(3).

4. Utah Code Ann. § 78B-2-304(2).

5. Utah Code Ann. § 78B-2-305.

6. *Sevy v. Sec. Title Co.*, 902 P.2d 629, 634-36 (Utah 1995).

7. *Jensen v. Young*, 2010 UT 67, ¶18, 245 P.3d 731.

8. Utah Code Ann. § 78B-6-706.

9. *McCollin v. Synthes, Inc.*, 50 F. Supp. 2d 1119, 1122 (D. Utah 1999); *McKinnon v. Tambrands, Inc.*, 815 F. Supp. 415, 420 (D. Utah 1993); *Aragon v. Clover Club Foods Co.*, 857 P.2d 250, 253 (Utah Ct. App. 1993).

10. Utah Code Ann. § 78B-2-225(3)(b).

11. Utah Code Ann. § 78B-2-225(3)(a).

12. Utah Code Ann. § 78B-2-225(4).

13. Utah Code Ann. § 78B-2-225(4).

14. *Slisze v. Stanley-Bostitch*, 1999 UT 20, ¶8, 979 P.2d 317; *Barson v. E. R. Squibb & Sons, Inc.*, 682 P.2d 832, 834 (Utah 1984).

15. Utah Code Ann. § 70A-2-725(1) (2009).

16. *Salt Lake City Corp. v. Kasler Corp.*, 855 F. Supp. 1560, 1568 (D. Utah 1994).

17. *McCollin*, 50 F. Supp. 2d at 1122; *Davidson Lumber Sales, Inc. v. Bonneville Inv., Inc.*, 794 P.2d 11, 14 (Utah 1990).

18. *Schaerrer v. Stewart's Plaza Pharmacy, Inc.*, 2003 UT 43, ¶16, 79 P.3d 922; *Interwest Constr. v. Palmer*, 923 P.2d 1350, 1356 (Utah 1996); *Ernest W. Hahn, Inc. v. Armco Steel Co.*, 601 P.2d 152, 158 (Utah 1979).

19. *Utah Local Gov't Trust v. Wheeler Mach. Co.*, 2008 UT 84, ¶10, 199 P.3d 949.

20. *Lamb v. B & B Amusements Corp.*, 869 P.2d 926, 929 (Utah 1993).

21. *Grundberg v. Upjohn Co.*, 813 P.2d 89, 92 (Utah 1991).

22. Restatement (Second) of Torts § 402A(1) (1965); *Interwest Constr.*, 923 P.2d at 1356; *Ernest W. Hahn*, 601 P.2d at 156.

23. Utah Code Ann. § 78B-6-703(1) (2008); *Lamb v. B & B Amusements Corp.*, 869 P.2d 926, 929 (Utah 1993).

24. Utah Code Ann. § 78B-6-702; *Brown v. Sears, Roebuck & Co.*, 328 F.3d 1274, 1278-79 (10th Cir. 2003).

25. *Allen v. Minnstar, Inc.*, 8 F.3d 1470, 1479 (10th Cir. 1993).

26. *Interwest Constr.*, 923 P.2d at 1356.

27. *Burns v. Cannondale Bicycle Co.*, 876 P.2d 415, 418 (Utah Ct. App. 1994).

28. *Interwest Constr.*, 923 P.2d at 1356-57 (alteration in original) (citation and internal quotation marks omitted).

29. *Egbert v. Nissan N. Am., Inc.*, 2007 UT 64, ¶18, 167 P.3d 1058.

30. *Mulherin v. Ingersoll-Rand Co.*, 628 P.2d 1301, 1303-04 (Utah 1981); Utah Code Ann. § 78B-5-817(2).

31. Utah Code Ann. § 78B-5-818; *Mulherin*, 628 P.2d at 1304.

32. Utah Code Ann. § 78B-5-818(4)(a).

33. Utah Code Ann. § 78B-5-817(2); *Jacobsen Constr. Co. v. Structo-Lite Eng'g, Inc.*, 619 P.2d 306, 312 (Utah 1980); *Ernest W. Hahn, Inc.*, 601 P.2d at 158; Restatement (Second) of Torts § 402A (1965).

34. *Ernest W. Hahn, Inc.*, 601 P.2d at 156; Restatement (Second) of Torts § 402A(1).

35. *Ghionis v. Deer Valley Resort Co.*, 839 F. Supp. 789, 794 (D. Utah 1993).

36. *Sanns v. Butterfield Ford*, 2004 UT App 203, ¶¶15, 21, 94 P.3d 301.

37. *Gudmundson v. Delozone*, 2010 UT 33, ¶¶54, 55, 232 P.3d 1059.

38. *Gudmundson*, 2010 UT ¶¶54, 55, 232 P.3d at 1059.

39. *Grundberg v. Upjohn Co.*, 813 P.2d at 95; *see also Unthank v. United States*, 732 F.2d 1517, 1523 (10th Cir. 1984) (applying Utah law).

40. *Macris & Assocs., Inc. v. Neways, Inc.*, 1999 UT App 230, ¶15, 986 P.2d 748 (quoting *Florom v. Elliot*, 867 F.2d 570, 575 n.2 (10th Cir. 1989)).

41. *Tabor v. Metal Ware Corp.*, 2007 UT 71, ¶12, 168 P.3d 814.

42. *Tabor*, 2007 UT 71, ¶13.

43. *Tabor*, 2007 UT 71, ¶13.

44. *Ernest W. Hahn, Inc.*, 601 P.2d at 156; Restatement (Second) of Torts § 402A(1) (1965).

45. *Unthank*, 732 F.2d at 1521.

46. *House v. Armour of Am., Inc.*, 886 P.2d 542, 551 (Utah Ct. App. 1994), *aff'd*, 929 P.2d 340 (Utah 1996).

47. *House*, 886 P.2d at 550.

48. *House*, 886 P.2d at 553.

49. *Barson v. E. R. Squibb & Sons, Inc.*, 682 P.2d 832, 835-36 (Utah 1984).

50. *Tabor*, 2007 UT 71, ¶12.

51. Utah R. Evid. 407.

52. *Schreiter v. Wasatch Manor, Inc.*, 871 P.2d 570, 573 (Utah Ct. App. 1994) (citations omitted).

53. *Schreiter*, 871 P.2d at 573.

54. *Schaerrer v. Stewart's Plaza Pharmacy, Inc.*, 2003 UT 43, ¶¶21-22, 79 P.3d 922.

55. *Schaerrer*, 2003 UT 43, ¶¶21-22, 79 P.3d 922.

56. Utah Code Ann. § 78B-6-705.

57. Utah Code Ann. § 78B-5-817(2); *Mulherin*, 628 P.2d at 1303; *Ernest W. Hahn, Inc.*, 601 P.2d at 158.

58. *Allen v. Minnstar, Inc.*, 97 F.3d 1365, 1368-69 (10th Cir. 1996) (applying Utah law).

59. *Allen*, 8 F.3d 1470, 1479.

60. *House*, 886 P.2d at 548.

61. *Burns v. Cannondale Bicycle Co.*, 876 P.2d 415, 420 (Utah Ct. App. 1994).

62. Utah Code Ann. § 78B-6-703(2); *Egbert v. Nissan N. Am., Inc.*, 2007 UT 64, ¶9, 167 P.3d 1058; *Grundberg v. Upjohn Co.*, 813 P.2d 89, 97 (Utah 1991).

63. *Egbert*, 2007 UT 64, ¶14.

64. *Slisze v. Stanley-Bostitch*, 1999 UT 20, ¶18, 979 P.2d 317 ("Thus, despite UOSHA's provision prohibiting its use to affect the common law rights, duties, or liabilities of employers, this court can look to UOSHA and OSHA for evidence of industry standards in certain circumstances.").

65. *Braithwaite v. West Valley City Corp.*, 921 P.2d 997, 1002 (Utah 1996).

66. *Hermansen v. Tasulis*, 2002 UT 52, ¶22, 48 P.3d 235; *Maack v. Res. Design & Constr., Inc.*, 875 P.2d 570, 576 (Utah Ct. App. 1994), *abrogated by Davencourt at Pilgrims Landing Homeowners Ass'n v. Davencourt at Pilgrims Landing, LC*, 2009 UT 65, 221 P.3d 234.

67. *Maack*, 875 P.2d at 584 (quoting *Dugan v. Jones*, 615 P.2d 1239, 1246 (Utah 1980)).

68. *Cook Assocs., Inc. v. PCS Sales (USA) Inc.*, 271 F. Supp. 2d 1343, 1357 (D. Utah 2003); *Burns v. Cannondale Bicycle Co.*, 876 P.2d 415, 419 (Utah Ct. App. 1994).

69. *Burns*, 876 P.2d at 419 (citation and internal quotation marks omitted).

70. *Burns*, 876 P.2d at 419.

71. *Hermansen*, 2002 UT 52, ¶16 (citation and internal quotation marks omitted).

72. *Sunridge Dev. Corp. v. RB & G Eng'g, Inc.*, 2010 UT 6, ¶25, 230 P.3d 1000 (citations omitted).

73. Utah Code Ann. § 78B-4-513.

74. *Davencourt at Pilgrims Landing Homeowners Ass'n v. Davencourt at Pilgrims Landing, LC*, 2009 UT 65, ¶18, 221 P.3d 234 (quoting *Am. Towers Owners Ass'n, Inc. v. CCI Mech., Inc.*, 930 P.2d 1182, 1189 (Utah 1996)).

75. *Paul Mueller Co. v. Cache Valley Dairy Ass'n*, 657 P.2d 1279, 1286 (Utah 1982); *Salt Lake City Corp. v. Kasler Corp.*, 855 F. Supp. 1560, 1570 (D. Utah 1994).

76. *Whitehead v. Am. Motors Sales Corp.*, 801 P.2d 920, 923 (Utah 1990).

77. *Whitehead*, 801 P.2d at 923 (citation and internal quotation marks omitted).

78. *Slisze v. Stanley-Bostitch*, 1999 UT 20, ¶10, 979 P.2d 317, 319 (Utah 1999).

79. *Koer v. Mayfair Mkts.*, 431 P.2d 566, 569 (Utah 1967).

80. Utah Code Ann. § 78B-5-818.

81. Utah Code Ann. § 78B-5-818.

82. Utah Code Ann. § 78B-5-818(4)(a); *Bishop v. GenTec, Inc.*, 2002 UT 36, ¶12, 48 P.3d 218.

83. *Ernest W. Hahn, Inc.*, 601 P.2d at 159.

84. Utah Code Ann. § 78B-8-201(1)(a); *see also Smith v. Fairfax Realty, Inc.*, 2003 UT 41, ¶27, 82 P.3d 1064.

85. *Smith*, 2003 UT 41, ¶27.

86. *Smith*, 2003 UT 41, ¶27.

87. Utah Code Ann. § 78B-8-203. Applies only to causes of action accruing after July 1, 1989.

88. *Grange v. Mylan Labs., Inc.*, No. 1: 7-CV-107 TC, 2008 U.S. Dist. LEXIS 92460, at *18-19 (D. Utah Oct. 31, 2008).

89. Utah Code Ann. § 78B-5-824(1) (2009 Supp.).

90. Utah Code Ann. § 78B-5-824(2).

91. Utah Code Ann. § 78B-5-824(3).

92. Utah Code Ann. §§ 34A-2-105(1) (2005 & 2009 Supp.); 34A-3-102.

93. Utah Code Ann. §§ 70A-2-725 (2009), 78B-2-305, 78B-2-307, 78B-5-817, 78B-6-701 to 78B-6-707, 78B-8-203.

94. Utah Code Ann. § 15-2-1 (2009).

95. Utah Code Ann. § 78B-5-820(1).

96. Utah Code Ann. § 78B-5-819(2).

97. Utah Code Ann. § 78B-5-820(2).

VERMONT

A. CAUSES OF ACTION

Product liability lawsuits in the State of Vermont have been brought under theories of strict product liability, negligence, breach of implied warranty of merchantability, and breach of suitability for a particular purpose.[1] In many instances, all four causes of action may be alleged in the complaint. Vermont courts have treated claims based on implied warranty and strict liability as analytically the same.[2]

B. STATUTES OF LIMITATION

The statute of limitations applicable to a strict product liability or negligence action depends upon the nature of the harm suffered by the plaintiff.[3] Actions for "injury to the person suffered by the act or default of another" or for "[d]amage to personal property" must be brought within three years after the cause of action accrues.[4] A six-year statute of limitations applies in most other situations.[5] "[T]he cause of action shall be deemed to accrue as of the date of the discovery of the injury."[6] While the "discovery rule" has not been explicitly added to a section of the Vermont Code that creates a cause of action for damage occurring to personal property,[7] the Vermont Supreme Court has held that the "discovery rule" applies even in instances where the statute of limitations is silent.[8]

With respect to injuries suffered as a result of "noxious agents medically recognized as having prolonged latent development," Vermont law imposes a 20-year statute of repose running from the "date of the last occurrence to which the injury is attributed."[9]

The State of Vermont has adopted the provisions of the Uniform Commercial Code concerning the express and implied warranties that arise in contracts for the sale of goods.[10] A four-year statute of limitations governs causes of action brought for any breach of a contract for the sale of goods.

C. STRICT LIABILITY

1. The Standard

In 1975, the Supreme Court of Vermont explicitly adopted the provisions of § 402A of the Restatement (Second) of Torts (1965).[11] "To establish strict liability in a products liability action, a plaintiff must show that the defendant's product (1) is defective; (2) is unreasonably dangerous to the consumer in normal use; (3) reached the consumer without undergoing any substantial change in condition; and (4) caused injury to the consumer because of its defective design."[12]

2. **Definition of "Defect"**

   It is the plaintiff's burden to show a defective condition.[13] A product is defective if it is not "safe for normal handling and consumption."[14]

3. **Definition of "Unreasonably Dangerous"**

   Under current Vermont law, a product is unreasonably dangerous when it is "dangerous to an extent beyond that which would be contemplated by the ordinary consumer who purchases it, with the ordinary knowledge common to the community as to its characteristics."[15] It does not appear that the Vermont Supreme Court requires a showing by the plaintiff in a design defect claim that there are safer practical and feasible alternatives, although one trial court recently held that the provisions of the Restatement (Third) of Torts: Products Liability, which requires proof of a superior alternative design in place of the more subjective "consumer expectations" standard, applied to design defect claims against a component manufacturer.[16]

4. **Causation**

   Proximate cause, or proof that a product's defect legally caused the injury, is a prerequisite for recovery in a claim of strict liability in tort.[17] The Vermont Supreme Court has held that causation in a product liability case can be proved through circumstantial evidence.[18]

5. **Contributory Negligence/Assumption of the Risk**

   The defenses usually raised in a product liability action include contributory negligence, assumption of risk, and misuse of the product. However, there are no Vermont cases specifically discussing the application of those defenses to product liability litigation. Vermont has adopted a "modified" comparative negligence statute, in which a plaintiff's award for damages is reduced by the percentage of the plaintiff's own negligence up to 50 percent of the total liability. If the plaintiff is more than 50 percent liable, however, all recovery is barred.[19] In a multiple-defendant lawsuit, a finding by the jury that the plaintiff was more negligent than some of the defendants will not bar recovery as long as the plaintiff's negligence was not greater than that of all the defendants put together.[20] Where more than one defendant is found liable, each defendant is responsible for its proportionate share of the defendants' collective liability. Thus, in a case in which the jury finds a plaintiff 40 percent negligent, defendant A 30 percent negligent, and defendant B 30 percent negligent, the plaintiff will be able to recover 60 percent of the total damages, with each defendant contributing one-half of the award.

   However, in a 1996 product liability action, the Vermont Supreme Court could not agree on the role of comparative fault in product liability cases.[21] The case produced four separate opinions. Three of the five Justices agreed that "principles of comparative causation apply in this products liability action," but the three did not agree to a general rule on when comparative principles apply in strict product liability actions, or on how to implement those principles when they do apply.[22] The remaining two Justices dissented, arguing that comparative principles are not applicable in product liability actions.

Vermont has adopted a "safety belt statute," which imposes a fine on the operator of a motor vehicle if anyone occupying a seat with a federally approved safety belt system is not restrained by the belt while the vehicle is in motion on a public highway.[23] The statute also contains evidentiary components, and the Vermont Supreme Court has held that the statute prohibits the introduction of evidence of a failure to wear a safety belt in a civil proceeding irrespective of the legal theory advanced.[24]

6. Sale or Lease/Persons Liable

Vermont law requires "seller" status as an essential component of a strict product liability or breach of implied warranty claim.[25] The United States District Court for the District of Vermont has thus held that a company hired to refurbish an allegedly defective propane tank (which included replacement of several components) was hired to provide a service and was therefore not a "seller" for purposes of strict product liability.[26]

The Vermont Supreme Court has adopted the approach embodied in the Restatement (Second) of Torts § 402A (1965).[27] Under Vermont law, a seller may seek common-law indemnification from the manufacturer of a product in a strict liability case if the seller is found liable to the consumer, but is not independently culpable.[28]

7. Inherently Dangerous Products

It has been held, since 1959, that one who distributes an inherently dangerous substance or product owes a degree of protection to the public proportionate to and commensurate with the dangers involved.[29] If the distributor or producer fails to exercise such care and injury results therefrom, it is liable in negligence.[30]

In Vermont, a product may be so dangerous that it is defective absent a failure to warn.[31]

8. Successor Liability

The Vermont Supreme Court has adopted a general rule that "the liabilities of a predecessor corporation will pass to the successor only when the change is occasioned by statutory merger or consolidation."[32] Thus, a company that takes over ownership of another corporation by purchasing all of its stock will be liable for the torts committed by the purchased corporation.

However, if change is accomplished through sale of physical assets only, the purchasing corporation assumes no liability unless one of the following exceptions applies:

1. the buyer expressly or impliedly agrees to assume the liabilities;

2. the transaction amounts to a de facto merger or consolidation;

3. the purchasing corporation is merely a continuation of the selling corporation;

4. the sale is a fraudulent transaction intended to avoid debts and liabilities; or

5. inadequate consideration was given for the sale.[33]

The Vermont Supreme Court has previously rejected the "product-line theory" of liability, in which a successor corporation that continues to manufacture a product of the business it acquires, regardless of the method of acquisition or any possible attribution of fault, assumes strict liability for products manufactured and sold before the change of corporate ownership.[34]

9. **Market Share Liability/Enterprise Liability**

There are no reported Vermont cases dealing with or addressing this issue.[35]

10. **Privity**

The privity requirement was abolished in 1965 in Vermont.[36]

11. **Failure to Warn**

To prevail in a failure to warn case, the plaintiff must produce evidence from which a reasonable jury could find that: (1) the defendant owed a duty to warn the plaintiff; (2) lack of warning made the product unreasonably dangerous, hence defective; and (3) the defendant's failure to warn was the proximate cause of the plaintiff's injury.[37] Although strict liability and negligence are analytically distinct claims, Vermont courts treat them as one where liability rests on a failure to warn.[38]

A manufacturer has a duty to warn purchasers when the manufacturer has knowledge of a product defect that makes the product "dangerous to an extent beyond that which would be contemplated by the ordinary purchaser, i.e., a consumer possessing the ordinary and common knowledge of the community as to the product's characteristics."[39] A manufacturer's duty to warn also extends to employees of purchasers.[40]

A manufacturer generally does not have a duty to warn in instances where the product at issue is neither designed nor manufactured defectively. For instance, a properly made BB gun "is not dangerous beyond that [danger] which would be contemplated by the ordinary consumer with the ordinary knowledge common to the community."[41] However, it has been held that a cotton turtleneck that ignited without warning when its wearer was standing three feet from a wood stove could be found to be a latent danger beyond the knowledge of an ordinary consumer, thus requiring a warning by the manufacturer.[42]

Applying Vermont law, the United States Court of Appeals for the Second Circuit has held that a designer-manufacturer could not reasonably have foreseen the dangers that gave rise to the plaintiff's injuries when such dangers did not relate to the independent operability of the designer-manufacturer's product, but instead related solely to the dangerous way in which the plaintiff's employer used that product in its proprietary methods.[43] The plaintiff has the burden of showing that the lack of warning was a proximate cause of the injury.[44] Assuming the defendant manufacturer had a duty to warn and did not do so, a presumption of causation is created, one which suggests that had a warning been present, the plaintiff would have read it and heeded it.[45] A defendant may overcome this presumption, however, if it is shown that the plaintiff ignored other similar warnings with respect to the product.[46]

The Vermont Supreme Court has also indicated that a plaintiff could recover for a defendant's inadequate warnings, despite the plaintiff's failure to read existing warnings, if it could be shown that those warnings "were not properly designed to draw the attention of a reasonably prudent person."[47]

12. Post-Sale Duty to Warn and Remedial Measure

One case, in finding that a manufacturer had a duty to warn *employees* of a product purchaser about the dangers of the product, arguably acknowledged a post-sale duty to warn.[48] In another case, however, evidence of a post-injury warning to other persons was ruled inadmissible under Rule of Evidence 407.[49]

13. Learned Intermediary Doctrine

The Vermont Supreme Court has not addressed the "learned intermediary doctrine" in the context of a product liability claim.[50] However, one Vermont trial court has relied upon the doctrine to hold that a pharmacist owed no duty of care to a patient for the pharmacist's alleged negligence in filling a prescription given directly to the prescribing doctor.[51]

14. Substantial Alteration/Abnormal Use

Although the Vermont Supreme Court has not outlined the requirements for "substantial alteration," in general, to prove strict product liability it must be shown that the product reached the consumer without undergoing any substantial change in condition.[52] Product misuse also generally bars recovery.[53] In one case involving an allegedly defective snowmobile, the Vermont Supreme Court held that there was insufficient evidence of a defect, tacitly agreeing with the trial court that normal use did not include travel at speeds in excess of 60 m.p.h.[54]

15. **State of the Art**

    No reported Vermont products liability case has addressed a "state of the art" defense, so the availability of the defense presents an open issue. In one non-products-liability case, however, the "state of the art" concept was used to erode a traditional assumption-of-the-risk defense.[55]

16. **Malfunction**

    There are no reported Vermont cases dealing with or addressing this issue; however, the United States Court of Appeals for the Second Circuit has predicted that the Vermont Supreme Court would probably adopt the "malfunction" theory.[56]

17. **Standards and Governmental Regulation**

    Evidence of compliance with governmental regulations is admissible to show whether a defendant satisfied the applicable standard of care in negligence actions, and is apparently admissible in strict liability actions as well.[57]

18. **Other Accidents**

    In a product liability action brought by a vehicle passenger, the Vermont Supreme Court determined that internal documents obtained from the motor vehicle manufacturer that referenced seven incidents of steering system failure were relevant and admissible as business records, where the incidents involved steering systems identical to that of the vehicle in which the passenger was traveling, and the passenger alleged that the faulty steering system caused the accident that injured him.[58] The court also allowed the documents to be introduced to impeach the manufacturer's expert where the documents were relevant to bolster the passenger's theory of liability.[59]

19. **Misrepresentation**

    Whether the doctrine of strict liability misrepresentation as set forth in Section 402B of the Restatement (Second) of Torts (1965) is the law of Vermont remains an open question.[60]

20. **Destruction or Loss of Product**

    (See Economic Loss discussion below.)

21. **Economic Loss**

    In 1998, the Vermont Supreme Court adopted the economic loss rule, holding that where a plaintiff suffers a purely economic loss, that is to say, a diminution of the value of the product bought as the result of a product defect, he or she must seek recovery under a breach of warranty claim and not a product liability claim.[61] The court left open the question of whether the economic loss rule would apply where physical damage to the product was caused by the product's defective performance.

The Vermont Supreme Court has recognized potential exceptions to the economic loss rule.[62] For example, there may be recovery for purely economic losses where the tortfeasor violates a professional duty of care.[63] "To fit within this exception, the parties must have 'a special relationship, which creates a duty of care independent of contract obligations. . . . [T]he key is not whether one is licensed in a particular field . . . rather, the determining factor is the type of relationship created between the parties.'"[64] However, the Vermont Supreme Court has rejected an exception based on the threat of imminent harm, stating that if recovery were allowed based on this theory, "warranty law would, in effect, be subsumed into tort law."[65]

22. Crashworthiness

No reported Vermont case has addressed or recognized the "crashworthiness" or "second collision" doctrine.

D. NEGLIGENCE

1. General Principles

In the view of Vermont courts, it makes little difference whether a cause of action for product liability arises under a theory of negligence or implied warranty. The seller's responsibility to the consumer is the same under either theory.[66] Moreover, once causation is established, lack of privity will not relieve any legal obligation for injuries inflicted by the sale of a defective product.[67]

2. Vicarious Liability

Under the doctrine of vicarious liability recognized by the Vermont Supreme Court, an assembler-manufacturer may be held liable for the negligence of the makers of components used by the assembler-manufacturer in the final product.[68] While application of this doctrine does not require that the plaintiff demonstrate that the assembler-manufacturer itself was negligent, the plaintiff still bears the burden of showing that some negligence took place, at least on the part of the component maker.[69] To that extent, vicarious liability differs from strict liability in tort, under which an assembler-manufacturer may be held liable regardless of the negligent or non-negligent source of the defect.[70]

3. Comparative Negligence

Vermont has adopted a "modified" comparative negligence statute, in which a plaintiff's award for damages may be reduced by the percentage of plaintiff's own negligence up to 50 percent of the total liability. If the plaintiff is more than 50 percent liable, however, all recovery is barred.[71]

In a multiple-defendant lawsuit, a finding by the jury that the plaintiff was more negligent than some of the defendants will not bar recovery as long as the plaintiff's negligence was not greater than that of all the defendants put together.[72] Where more than one defendant is found liable, each defendant is responsible for its proportionate share of the defendants' collective liability; thus, in a case in which the jury finds a plaintiff 40 percent negligent, defendant A 30 percent negligent, and defendant B 30 percent negligent, the plaintiff will be able to recover 60 percent of the total damages, with each defendant contributing one-half of the award.

E. BREACH OF WARRANTY

The implied warranties of merchantability and fitness for a particular purpose are closely linked under Vermont law. The difference appears to lie in the scope of the seller's promise: an implied warranty of merchantability reflects the promise that the product is good for the purpose inherent in its nature, while that of fitness for a particular purpose is a promise that the product is good for a particular purpose specified by the buyer.[73]

1. Elements

Regardless of which particular implied warranty is at issue, the injured party must be able to show (a) that the product allegedly causing the injury was harmful or deleterious in some way; and (b) that the defect existed as of the time that the product was in the possession of or under the control of the seller.[74]

2. Time at Which Cause of Action Accrues

A cause of action for breach of warranties accrues upon tender of delivery of the goods, regardless of whether the plaintiff lacked knowledge of the breach of the warranty at that time.[75]

F. PUNITIVE DAMAGES

Although there are no Vermont cases explicitly discussing the application of punitive damages to the product liability field, there is no reason to think that such damages would not be awarded in an appropriate case.[76] The Vermont Supreme Court has recently clarified that an award of punitive damages requires a showing of two elements. "The first is wrongful conduct that is outrageously reprehensible."[77] "The second is malice, defined variously as bad motive, ill will, personal spite or hatred, reckless disregard, and the like."[78] In other words, it is not enough to show that the defendant's acts are wrongful or unlawful—there must be proof of the defendant's bad spirit and wrong intention to warrant an award of punitive damages.[79]

G. PRE- AND POST-JUDGMENT INTEREST

Pre-judgment interest may be awarded as damages for delay (*i.e.*, detention of money due for breach or default). This interest is awarded as of right when the principal sum recovered is liquidated or capable of ready ascertainment and may be awarded in the court's discretion for other forms of damage.[80]

Such interest may not be calculated on "soft" damages such as pain and suffering.[81] Interest ordinarily runs from the time of maturity or demand for payment or the time of default, which may be the date when the action is commenced.[82]

Plaintiff is entitled to interest on a judgment from the date of the verdict. By statute, interest on a judgment lien, or post-judgment interest, accrues at the rate of 12 percent per year.[83]

H. EMPLOYER IMMUNITY FROM SUIT

Under the statutory provisions for workers' compensation, employers are immune from tort liability.[84] A "statutory employer" may be "one who, although not the direct employer, is nevertheless the 'virtual proprietor or operator of the business there carried on.'"[85] It has also been held that the exclusivity of the workers' compensation bars contribution by the employer (although Vermont generally does not recognize contribution among joint tortfeasors).[86] With respect to the "dual capacity" situation, whether or not the challenged negligence occurred in the performance of a nondelegable duty of the employer as opposed to arising out of an obligation owed by the employer to the injured employee requires a determination "that there was a personal duty owed the plaintiff apart from the nondelegable duties of the employer."[87] Where a plaintiff attempts to bring suit against an employer, despite the prohibition against such suit by workers' compensation law, a plaintiff must therefore allege circumstances that reveal a duty that is "additional to and different from" the general nondelegable duty of the employer.[88] To be considered "other than the employer" the individual must not be involved in performing a nondelegable duty of the employer and "must not be exercising the managerial prerogatives—because both of these activities indicate that the individual is acting as employer."[89]

I. STATUTES

The relevant statutes for product liability actions are the various statutes of limitation and the commercial code sections when a breach of warranty is alleged.[90] The age of majority in Vermont is 18.[91]

J. JOINT AND SEVERAL LIABILITY

There is no right of contribution among joint tortfeasors in Vermont. Each defendant is responsible for its proportionate share of the defendants' collective liability, as long as the total combined liability of the defendants exceeds the plaintiff's negligence.[92] The Vermont Supreme Court has held that joint and several liability allows apportionment only as between tortfeasors joined in the same action and only when there is an allegation of negligence on the part of the plaintiff.[93] Thus, apportionment was denied in a case where one of the alleged joint tortfeasors settled with the plaintiff before trial, and the plaintiff was not alleged to have been negligent.[94]

Karen McAndrew
Wm. Andrew MacIlwaine
N. Joseph Wonderly
Dinse, Knapp & McAndrew, P.C.
209 Battery Street
P.O. Box 988
Burlington, Vermont 05402-0988
(802) 864-5751
(Fax) (802) 862-6409

ENDNOTES - VERMONT

1. *See Paquette v. Deere & Co.*, 168 Vt. 258, 259, 719 A.2d 410, 411 (1998) (plaintiffs asserted all four theories in complaint).

2. *Betz v. Highlands Fuel Delivery, LLC*, 5:10-CV-102, 2013 WL 392480, at *10 (D. Vt. Jan. 31, 2013) ("A claim of breach of an implied warranty of merchantability or fitness for a particular purpose shares this same analytical framework.").

3. *Kinney v. Goodyear Tire & Rubber Co.*, 134 Vt. 571, 574, 367 A.2d 677, 679-80 (1976).

4. Vt. Stat. Ann. tit. 12, § 512(4), (5) (2002).

5. Vt. Stat. Ann. tit. 12, § 511 (2002); *see Univ. of Vt. v. W.R. Grace & Co.*, 152 Vt. 287, 289, 565 A.2d 1354, 1356 (1989).

6. Vt. Stat. Ann. tit. 12, § 512(4) (2002).

7. Vt. Stat. Ann. tit. 12, § 512(5) (2002).

8. *Univ. of Vt. v. W.R. Grace & Co.*, 152 Vt. 287, 290, 565 A.2d 1354, 1357 (1989); *Cavanaugh v. Abbott Labs.*, 145 Vt. 516, 526, 496 A.2d 154, 160-61 (1985); *but see Leo v. Hillman*, 164 Vt. 94, 98-99, 665 A.2d 572, 575-76 (1995) (stating that neither *W.R. Grace* nor *Cavanaugh* requires that every limitation statute be construed in terms of when a statute "accrues," but rather that accrual be given uniform meaning where the date of accrual is a determinable fact, and courts should avoid determining the date of accrual by reference to extrinsic facts).

9. Vt. Stat. Ann. tit. 12, § 518(a) (2002); *see Cavanaugh v. Abbott Labs.*, 145 Vt. 516, 528, 496 A.2d 154, 161-62 (1985) (interpreting statute of repose).

10. Vt. Stat. Ann. tit. 9A, §§ 2-312–2-315 (1994); *see also Paquette v. Deere & Co.*, 168 Vt. 258, 265, 719 A.2d 410, 415 (1998).

11. *Zaleskie v. Joyce*, 133 Vt. 150, 155, 333 A.2d 110, 113-14 (1975); *see Farnham v. Bombardier, Inc.*, 161 Vt. 619, 620, 640 A.2d 47, 48 (1994) (stating elements of strict liability cause of action); *Paquette v. Deere & Co.*, 168 Vt. 258, 260, 719 A.2d 410, 412 (1998); *see* Moffitt v. Icynene, Inc., 407 F. Supp. 2d 591, 602 (D. Vt. 2005) (holding that component-part manufacturer may be strictly liable for defective product "only if the defect existed in the manufacturer's component itself") (citation omitted).

12. *Farnham v. Bombardier, Inc.*, 161 Vt. 619, 620, 640 A.2d 47, 48 (1994).

13. *Farnham v. Bombardier, Inc.*, 161 Vt. 619, 620, 640 A.2d 47, 48 (1994).

14. *Farnham v. Bombardier, Inc.*, 161 Vt. 619, 620, 640 A.2d 47, 48 (1994) (quoting Restatement (Second) of Torts § 402A, cmt. h).

15. *Farnham v. Bombardier, Inc.*, 161 Vt. 619, 620, 640 A.2d 47, 48 (1994).

16. *Heco v. Johnson Controls, Inc.*, No. S08692010, 2013 WL 6978667, at *2 (Vt. Super. Ct. Nov. 1, 2013) (Crawford, J.). It should be noted that at the time of this chapter update, *Heco* is pending appeal before the Vermont Supreme Court.

17. *Gilman v. Towmotor Corp.*, 160 Vt. 116, 120, 621 A.2d 1260, 1262 (1992); *see Ulm v. Ford Motor Co.*, 170 Vt. 281, 286, 750 A.2d 981, 987-88 (2000); *Allstate Ins. Co. v. Hamilton Beach/Proctor Silex, Inc.*, 473 F.3d 450, 456 (2d Cir. 2007) (stating that Vermont requires two elements be met to establish causation with respect to strict products liability actions: (1) "proof of a product defect"; and (2) "proof that a defect existed in the product at the time that it left the possession and control of the defendant").

18. *Travelers Ins. Cos. v. Demarle, Inc.*, USA, 2005 VT 53, ¶13, 178 Vt. 570, 574, 878 A.2d 267, 272 (citing *Hall v. Miller*, 143 Vt. 135, 140-41, 465 A.2d 222, 225 (1983)).

19. Vt. Stat. Ann. tit. 12, § 1036 (2002).

20. Vt. Stat. Ann. tit. 12, § 1036 (2002).

21. *Webb v. Navistar Int'l Transp. Corp.*, 166 Vt. 119, 121-22, 692 A.2d 343, 343-44 (1996).

22. *Webb v. Navistar Int'l Transp. Corp.*, 166 Vt. 119, 122, 692 A.2d 343, 343 (1996).

23. Vt. Stat. Ann. tit. 23, § 1259 (1999 and 2004 Supp.).

24. *Ulm v. Ford Motor Co.*, 170 Vt. 281, 288, 750 A.2d 981, 987-88 (2000).

25. *Betz v. Highlands Fuel Delivery, LLC*, 5:10-CV-102, 2013 WL 392480, at *10 (D. Vt. Jan. 31, 2013); *see also Darling v. Cent. Vermont Pub. Serv. Corp.*, 171 Vt. 565, 568, 762 A.2d 826, 829 (2000) (acknowledging that to the extent electricity may constitute a "product," the stray current, which allegedly damaged plaintiffs' property, was not "sold" to them whether considered in the context of the "meter test" or the "stream-of-commerce test").

26. *Betz v. Highlands Fuel Delivery, LLC*, 5:10-CV-102, 2013 WL 392480, at *10 (D. Vt. Jan. 31, 2013).

27. *Zaleskie v. Joyce*, 133 Vt. 150, 155, 333 A.2d 110, 114 (1975).

28. *Windsor Sch. Dist. v. State*, 2008 VT 27, ¶18, 183 Vt. 452, 464, 956 A.2d 528, 537 (citing Restatement (Third) of Torts: Apportionment of Liability § 22(a)(2)(ii) (2000)).

29. *Lewis v. Vt. Gas Corp.*, 121 Vt. 168, 182, 151 A.2d 297, 306 (1959).

30. *Lewis v. Vt. Gas Corp.*, 121 Vt. 168, 182, 151 A.2d 297, 306 (1959).

31. *McCullock v. H.B. Fuller Co.*, 61 F.3d 1038, 1044 (2d Cir. 1995).

32. *Ostrowski v. Hydra-Tool Corp.*, 144 Vt. 305, 307, 479 A.2d 126, 127 (1984); *see also Gladstone v. Stuart Cinemas, Inc.*, 178 Vt. 104, 110-11, 878 A.2d 214, 220 (2005).

33. *Ostrowski v. Hydra-Tool Corp.*, 144 Vt. 305, 307, 479 A.2d 126, 127 (1984); *Cab-Tek, Inc. v. E.B.M., Inc.*, 153 Vt. 432, 433, 571 A.2d 671, 671 (1990) (upholding a lower court's determination that a de facto merger occurred, creating successor liability for defendant corporation); *Gladstone v. Stuart Cinemas, Inc.*, 178 Vt. 104, 110-17, 878 A.2d 214, 219-24 (2005) (setting forth the factors whereby one corporation may be deemed the "mere continuation" of another, and thus not able to avoid its predecessor's liabilities).

34. *Ostrowski v. Hydra-Tool Corp.*, 144 Vt. 305, 307-08, 479 A.2d 126, 127 (1984).

35. *But see In re Methyl Tertiary Butyl Ether (MTBE) Prods. Liab. Litig.*, 379 F. Supp. 2d 348, 440 (S.D.N.Y. 2005) (predicting that Vermont Supreme Court would apply market-share liability theory in similar products liability action).

36. *O'Brien v. Comstock Foods, Inc.*, 125 Vt. 158, 162, 212 A.2d 69, 72 (1965); *see also Webb v. Navistar Int'l Transp. Corp.*, 166 Vt. 119, 126, 692 A.2d 343, 346 (1996).

37. *Blanchard v. Eli Lilly & Co.*, 207 F. Supp. 2d 308, 321 (D. Vt. 2002).

38. *McCullock v. H.B. Fuller Co.*, 61 F.3d 1038, 1044 (2d Cir. 1995). (citing *Ostrowski v. Hydra-Tool Corp.*, 144 Vt. 305, 308, 479 A.2d 126, 127 (1984)); *see also Moffitt v. Icynene, Inc.*, 407 F. Supp. 2d 591, 599 (D. Vt. 2005) ("The warranty of merchantability under the [Vermont] UCC is equivalent to strict product liability.").

39. *Town of Bridport v. Sterling Clark Lurton Corp.*, 166 Vt. 304, 307-08, 693 A.2d 701, 704 (1997); *Menard v. Newhall*, 135 Vt. 53, 55, 373 A.2d 505, 507 (1977).

40. *Ostrowski v. Hydra-Tool Corp.*, 144 Vt. 305, 308, 479 A.2d 126, 128 (1984).

41. *Menard v. Newhall*, 135 Vt. 53, 55-56, 373 A.2d 505, 507 (1977).

42. *Needham v. Coordinated Apparel Group, Inc.*, 174 Vt. 263, 268, 811 A.2d 124, 129 (2002).

43. *Wilson v. Glenro, Inc.*, 524 Fed. Appx. 739 (2d Cir. 2013).

44. *Menard v. Newhall*, 135 Vt. 53, 54, 373 A.2d 505, 506 (1977).

45. *Menard v. Newhall*, 135 Vt. 53, 54, 373 A.2d 505, 506 (1977).

46. *Town of Bridport v. Sterling Clark Lurton Corp.*, 166 Vt. 304, 308, 693 A.2d 701, 704 (1997)) (citing *Menard v. Newhall*, 135 Vt. 53, 55, 373 A.2d 505, 506-07 (1977) (stating that where child ignored instructions given by father, presumption that warning would have been read and heeded disappeared)).

47. *Town of Bridport v. Sterling Clark Lurton Corp.*, 166 Vt. 304, 309, 693 A.2d 701, 704-05 (1997).

48. *McCullock v. H.B. Fuller Co.*, 981 F.2d 656, 658 (2d Cir. 1992) (noting that a warning given to purchaser, that did not reach employee was an implicit acknowledgment of post-sale duty to warn).

49. *Fish v. Ga. Pac. Corp.*, 779 F.2d 836, 839 (2d Cir. 1985) (stating that post-injury warnings are not admissible).

50. *See Kellogg v. Wyeth*, 762 F. Supp. 2d 694, 700 (D. Vt. 2010) ("Vermont has neither adopted nor rejected the learned intermediary doctrine.").

51. *Estate of Baker v. Univ. of Vt.*, No. 233-10-03 Oscv, at 8-9 (Vt. Super. Ct. May 5, 2005) (Morris, J.) ("The learned intermediary doctrine, first recognized in 1966, initially stood for the proposition that a prescription drug manufacturer had a duty to warn of possible side effects in some patients only to a purchasing doctor, the learned intermediary between the manufacturer and patient, and not directly to the patient. The majority of jurisdictions have expanded this approach to cover pharmacists as well." (citations omitted)).

52. *Farnham v. Bombardier, Inc.*, 161 Vt. 619, 620, 640 A.2d 47, 48 (1994).

53. *Webb v. Navistar Int'l Transp. Corp.*, 166 Vt. 119, 127, 692 A.2d 343, 347 (1996).

54. *Farnham v. Bombardier, Inc.*, 161 Vt. 619, 620, 640 A.2d 47, 49 (1994).

55. *See Estate of Frant v. Haystack Grp., Inc.*, 162 Vt. 11, 20-21, 641 A.2d 765, 770 (1994) (observing that endemic hazards of skiing, whose risk is assumed by skiers, are reduced as result of advances in "state of the art" slope grooming techniques).

56. *Allstate Ins. Co. v. Hamilton Beach/Proctor Silex, Inc.*, 473 F.3d 450, 456 n.3 (2d Cir. 2007) ("It seems likely that the Vermont Supreme Court would adopt the malfunction theory in light of the fact that: (1) circumstantial evidence is treated similarly under both that theory and Vermont's breach of warranty law; (2) the Vermont Supreme Court has suggested that a plaintiff may rely on circumstantial evidence to establish causation in products liability actions in the same way he or she may in a breach of warranty action . . . and (3) the malfunction theory is consistent with the policy considerations that motivated Vermont to adopt strict products liability.").

57. *McCullock v. H.B. Fuller Co.*, 981 F.2d 656, 658 (2d Cir. 1992) (noting that compliance with OSHA labeling regulations was admissible, but did not *per se* insulate manufacturer from failure to warn purchaser's employee of dangers); *Ball v. Melsur Corp.*, 161 Vt. 35, 43, 633 A.2d 705, 712 (1993) (remarking that in negligence action, compliance with OSHA regulations admissible on standard-of-care issue once a duty had been shown to independently exist; court deliberately refrained from addressing whether OSHA regulations could create a duty in the first place).

58. *Ulm v. Ford Motor Co.*, 170 Vt. 281, 288-89, 750 A.2d 981, 988 (2000).

59. *Ulm v. Ford Motor Co.*, 170 Vt. 281, 290, 750 A.2d 981, 989 (2000).

60. *Brennen v. Mogul Corp.*, 151 Vt. 91, 94, 557 A.2d 870, 871 (1988).

61. *Paquette v. Deere & Co.*, 168 Vt. 258, 719 A.2d 410 (1998).

62. *Long Trail House Condo. Ass'n v. Engelberth Constr., Inc.*, 2012 VT 80, ¶13, 192 Vt. 322, 329, 59 A.3d 752, 756-57; *see Betz v. Highlands Fuel Delivery, LLC*, 5:10-CV-102, 2013 WL 392480, at *11 n.12 (D. Vt. Jan. 31, 2013) (declining to analyze application of the economic loss rule and "professional services" exception because not briefed by parties).

63. *Long Trail House Condo. Ass'n v. Engelberth Constr., Inc.*, 2012 VT 80, ¶13, 192 Vt. 322, 329, 59 A.3d 752, 756-57.

64. *Long Trail House Condo. Ass'n v. Engelberth Constr., Inc.*, 2012 VT 80, ¶13, 192 Vt. 322, 329, 59 A.3d 752, 756-57 (citation omitted).

65. *Paquette v. Deere & Co.*, 168 Vt. 258, 264, 719 A.2d 410, 414 (1998).

66. *O'Brien v. Comstock Foods, Inc.*, 125 Vt. 158, 161-62, 212 A.2d 69, 71-72 (1965); *see also DiGregorio v. Champlain Valley Fruit Co.*, 127 Vt. 562, 565, 255 A.2d 183, 185 (1969) (stating that duty of wholesaler to indemnify retailer for injuries caused by a banana containing a thermometer inside is not affected by whether the consumer's action was brought under negligence or breach of implied warranty).

67. *O'Brien v. Comstock Foods, Inc.*, 125 Vt. 158, 162, 212 A.2d 69, 72 (1965).

68. *Morris v. Am. Motors Corp.*, 142 Vt. 566, 573, 459 A.2d 968, 972 (1982).

69. *Morris v. Am. Motors Corp.*, 142 Vt. 566, 573, 459 A.2d 968, 972 (1982).

70. *Morris v. Am. Motors Corp.*, 142 Vt. 566, 573, 459 A.2d 968, 972 (1982).

71. Vt. Stat. Ann. tit. 12, § 1036 (2002).

72. Vt. Stat. Ann. tit. 12, § 1036 (2002).

73. *Rogers v. W.T. Grant Co.*, 132 Vt. 485, 487, 321 A.2d 54, 56-57 (1974); *see also Green Mountain Mushroom Co. v. Brown*, 117 Vt. 509, 513-14, 95 A.2d 679, 681-82 (1952).

74. *Rogers v. W.T. Grant Co.*, 132 Vt. 485, 487, 321 A.2d 54, 56-57 (1974).

75. *Gus' Catering, Inc. v. Menusoft Sys.*, 171 Vt. 556, 557, 762 A.2d 804, 806 (2000); Vt. Stat. Ann. tit. 9A, § 2-725(1) (1994).

76. *See Sweet v. Roy*, 173 Vt. 418, 440, 801 A.2d 694, 711 (2002) (citing decision by the United States Court of Appeals for the Tenth Circuit for proposition that in products liability action, plaintiff could show that allegedly defective milling machine had injured others as bearing on punitive damages).

77. *Fly Fish Vt., Inc. v. Chapin Hill Estates, Inc.*, 2010 VT 33, ¶18, 187 Vt. 541, 548-49, 996 A.2d 1167, 1173 (citations omitted).

78. *Fly Fish Vt., Inc. v. Chapin Hill Estates, Inc.*, 2010 VT 33, ¶18, 187 Vt. 541, 548-49, 996 A.2d 1167, 1173.

79. *Fly Fish Vt., Inc. v. Chapin Hill Estates, Inc.*, 2010 VT 33, ¶¶18-25, 187 Vt. 541, 548-54, 996 A.2d 1167, 1173-77; *see also Brueckner v. Norwich Univ.*, 169 Vt. 118, 129-30, 730 A.2d 1086, 1095 (1999); *Cooper v. Cooper*, 173 Vt. 1, 14, 783 A.2d 430, 441 (2001); *Monahan v. GMAC Mortgage* Corp., 179 Vt. 167, 171, 893 A.2d 298, 304 (2005).

80. *Newport Sand & Gravel Co. v. Miller Concrete Constr. Inc.*, 159 Vt. 66, 71, 614 A.2d 395, 398 (1992); *see also* Reporter's Notes to 1981 Amendment to V.R.C.P. 54(a).

81. *Gilman v. Towmotor Corp.*, 160 Vt. 116, 121, 621 A.2d 1260, 1263 (1992).

82. *Newport Sand & Gravel Co. v. Miller Concrete Constr. Inc.*, 159 Vt. 66, 72, 614 A.2d 395, 398-99 (1992).

83. Vt. Stat. Ann. tit. 12, § 2903(c) (2002); Vt. Stat. Ann. tit. 9, § 41a(a) (1993 and 2004 Supp.).

84. Vt. Stat. Ann. tit. 21, § 622 (1987 and 2004 Supp.) (employee's exclusive remedy against employer is under provisions of workers' compensation).

85. *Arnold v. Palmer*, 2011 VT 8, ¶9, 189 Vt. 608, 609-10, 19 A.3d 592, 594, *reargument denied* (Feb. 28, 2011) (citation omitted).

86. *Hiltz v. John Deere Indus. Equip. Co.*, 146 Vt. 12, 16, 497 A.2d 748, 752 (1985).

87. *Gerrish v. Savard*, 169 Vt. 468, 472, 739 A.2d 1195, 1198-99 (1999).

88. *Gerrish v. Savard*, 169 Vt. 468, 474, 739 A.2d 1195, 1200 (1999).

89. *Gerrish v. Savard*, 169 Vt. 468, 474, 739 A.2d 1195, 1200 (1999).

90. *See* Vt. Stat. Ann. tit. 12, §§ 511, 512(4)-(5), 518(a) (2002); Vt. Stat. Ann. tit. 9A, §§ 2-312 to 2-315, 2-725(1) (1994).

91. Vt. Stat. Ann. tit. 1, § 173 (1995).

92. *Howard v. Spafford*, 132 Vt. 434, 435, 321 A.2d 74, 74-75 (1974); *Levine v. Wyeth*, 2006 VT 107, ¶36, 183 Vt. 76, 99, 944 A.2d 179, 194 *aff'd*, 555 U.S. 555 (2009) ("Our traditional rule is that multiple tortfeasors are jointly and severally liable" (citing *Zaleskie v. Joyce*, 133 Vt. 150, 158, 333 A.2d 110, 115 (1975))); Vt. Stat. Ann. tit. 12, § 1036 (2002).

93. *Levine v. Wyeth*, 2006 VT 107, ¶37, 183 Vt. 76, 101, 944 A.2d 179, 195.

94. *Levine v. Wyeth*, 2006 VT 107, ¶38, 183 Vt. 76, 101, 944 A.2d 179, 195.

VIRGINIA

A. CAUSES OF ACTION

Product liability lawsuits in Virginia most often involve causes of action for negligence and breach of warranty.

B. STATUTES OF LIMITATION AND REPOSE

Actions for personal injuries must be brought within two years, whether founded in negligence or in breach of warranty.[1] An action for property damage must be brought within five years, except that if property subject to contract has been damaged, the statute of limitations is four years.[2]

A cause of action for personal injury accrues on the date the injury is sustained and not when the resulting damage is discovered, except where injury is due to asbestos exposure or breast implants.[3]

There is a five-year statute of repose applicable to claims that arise out of defective or unsafe improvements to real property.[4] However, the statute perpetuates a distinction between those who furnish ordinary building materials, which are incorporated into construction work outside the control of their manufacturers or suppliers, at the direction of architects, designers, and contractors, and those who furnish machinery or equipment. The latter group does not enjoy the protections of the five-year statute.[5] A further distinction is drawn in favor of mere installers of equipment, who are protected by the five-year statute of repose; manufacturers and suppliers of equipment and machinery, on the other hand, are not protected by the statute but can protect themselves by using close quality controls and warranties that are voidable if the equipment is not installed or used correctly.[6]

C. STRICT LIABILITY

Virginia has not adopted Section 402A of the Restatement (Second) of Torts and does not permit tort recovery on a strict-liability theory in product liability cases.[7] In fact, several federal courts sitting in Virginia have remarked that the assertion of strict liability in tort is, *per se*, sufficient grounds for the imposition of Rule 11 sanctions.[8] However, federal courts interpreting Virginia law have also opined that Virginia's warranty theory is the "functional equivalent" of strict tort.[9]

D. NEGLIGENCE

1. The Standard

The standard of safety of goods imposed on the seller or manufacturer of a product is essentially the same whether the theory of liability is labeled warranty or negligence. Under either theory, the plaintiff must show: (1) that the goods were unreasonably dangerous either for the use to which they would ordinarily be put or for some other reasonably foreseeable purpose, and (2) that the unreasonably dangerous condition existed when the goods left the defendant's hands.[10] A product is unreasonably dangerous if it is defective in assembly or manufacture, unreasonably dangerous in design, or unaccompanied by adequate warnings concerning its hazardous properties.[11]

The duty to provide a product that is reasonably safe includes a duty to warn. Virginia has adopted the test formulated by Section 388 of the Restatement (Second) of Torts, under which a manufacturer is liable for a failure to warn if it (1) knows or has reason to know that the chattel is or is likely to be dangerous for the use for which it is supplied; (2) has no reason to believe that those for whose use the chattel is supplied will realize its dangerous condition; and (3) fails to exercise reasonable care to inform users of the chattel's dangerous condition or of the facts that make it likely to be dangerous.[12]

Causation is another indispensable element of any products liability claim in Virginia. Whether the case is premised on a warranty theory or a negligence theory, the plaintiff must draw a causal connection between the defendant's conduct and the plaintiff's injury.[13] To prove causation, a plaintiff must introduce evidence sufficient to establish that the resulting injury was a probability, rather than a mere possibility.[14] Where the plaintiff only shows that the injury might be due to one of several causes, this is not sufficient to support a recovery.[15] Although it is not necessary to establish causation with such certainty as to exclude every other possible cause, where there is more than one possible cause of an injury, the plaintiff must show with "reasonable certainty" that the defendant caused the injury.[16] In a product liability action, proof of causation must ordinarily be supported by expert testimony given the complexity of the causation facts.[17]

2. **"Reasonably Safe"**

To support a recovery, the plaintiff's evidence must establish that the manufacturer failed to use "ordinary care" to provide a product that was reasonably safe for the purpose for which it was intended.[18] The product does not need to be completely "accident-proof"; nor must it incorporate only those features that represent the "ultimate in safety."[19] To satisfy his burden in a product defect case, a plaintiff must do more than merely demonstrate that a proposed alternative design would make the product "safer" than it currently is.[20] In light of the inherent limitations on access to relevant data, Virginia law does not require a plaintiff to establish with particularity the risks and benefits associated with adoption of the suggested alternative design; however, if the defendant argues that the alternative design poses safety risks of its own, a plaintiff must produce some affirmative evidence that, from a risk-benefit standpoint, the alternative design "will help more than it hurts."[21] When evaluating the reasonableness of a design alternative, the overall safety of the product must be considered; it is not sufficient that the alternative design would have reduced or prevented the harm suffered by the plaintiff if it would have introduced into the product other dangers of equal or greater magnitude.[22] A user's sophistication and knowledge, while relevant as to a claim of failure to warn, is not relevant as to a claim of manufacture of an unreasonably dangerous product.[23]

3. **Contributory Negligence/Assumption of Risk**

   In Virginia, contributory negligence is a complete bar to recovery on a negligence claim.[24] Virginia law does not compare the negligence of the parties.[25] The test is an objective one and looks to whether the plaintiff acted for his own safety as a reasonable person would have acted under similar circumstances.[26]

   Assumption of risk is also a defense. However, it is often a difficult defense to prove, as the law requires that the nature and extent of the risk must have been fully appreciated, and the risk was voluntarily incurred, by the plaintiff.[27] Unlike contributory negligence, assumption of the risk is determined using a subjective standard that looks to evidence of, *i.e.*, what the particular plaintiff actually saw, knew, understood, and appreciated.[28]

4. **Sale**

   Negligence applies to any seller in the chain of a product's distribution if the seller sells the product as its own.[29]

5. **Inherently Dangerous Products**

   A supplier of products will not be held liable simply because the product is inherently dangerous, unless the supplier fails to give adequate warning of the danger.[30]

6. **Successor Liability**

   If a corporation acquires all or substantially all of the assets of another corporation and continues the same manufacturing process, the successor is not liable for injuries caused by products made by the predecessor corporation unless (1) the purchasing corporation expressly or impliedly agreed to assume such liabilities, (2) the circumstances surrounding the transaction warrant a finding that there was a consolidation or de facto merger of the two corporations, (3) the purchasing corporation is merely a continuation of the selling corporation, or (4) the transaction is fraudulent in fact.[31]

7. **Privity**

   No privity is required. A plaintiff may sue for negligence even though he did not buy the product from the defendant, so long as the plaintiff is someone the defendant might reasonably have expected to use or be affected by the product.[32] However, where a plaintiff seeks economic loss damages, privity of contract is required, whether the theory of recovery sounds in negligence or warranty.[33]

8. **Failure to Warn**

The Supreme Court of Virginia has adopted Restatement (Second) of Torts Section 388, which governs a manufacturer's duty to warn about dangers associated with a product's use.[34] Courts must balance the following factors to determine what precautions the manufacturer or supplier of a product must take to satisfy the requirement of reasonable care found in Restatement (Second) of Torts Section 388: (1) the dangerous condition of the product; (2) the purpose for which the product is used; (3) the form of any warnings given; (4) the reliability of the third party as a conduit of necessary information about the product; (5) the magnitude of the risk involved; and (6) the burdens imposed upon the supplier by requiring that he directly warn all users.[35]

The duty to warn is only to give a reasonable warning, not the best possible one.[36] A warning is not insufficient because a plaintiff was not told exactly how a danger might operate.[37]

There is no liability for failure to warn of an open and obvious danger.[38] Similarly, a plaintiff's failure to read posted warnings or warnings printed in manuals precludes recovery for failure to warn.[39]

Virginia recognizes the "sophisticated user" defense, which relieves the manufacturer of liability if the employer-purchaser is aware of the dangers of the product that it purchases for its business, placing upon the employer the duty to warn its employees of those dangers.[40]

Likewise, there is no liability for failure to warn where the product has been manufactured in accordance with the plans and specifications of the purchaser, except when such plans are so obviously dangerous that they should not reasonably be followed.[41]

9. **Post-Sale Duty to Warn**

The Supreme Court of Virginia has not yet affirmatively recognized a post-sale duty to warn on the part of a manufacturer.[42]

A persuasive federal district court decision suggests that Virginia does not recognize a duty on the part of a manufacturer to warn its consumers of dangerous defects discovered by the manufacturer after the sale of its product.[43] However, contrary authority asserts that, under a theory of negligence, the duty to warn is continuous and is not interrupted by manufacture or sale of the product, although no duty to warn extends beyond the sale or manufacture of a product when the theory is breach of warranty.[44]

10. **Learned Intermediary Doctrine**

In the case of prescription drugs, the general rule is that the duty of the drug manufacturer is to warn the physician who prescribes the drug in question.[45] In circumstances where (1) drugs or medical devices that can be prescribed or installed only by a physician are involved and (2) a physician prescribes the drug or installs the medical device after having evaluated the patient, the manufacturer of the drug or device owes the patient only the duty to warn the physician and to provide the physician with adequate product instructions.[46] In order for the doctrine to apply, the physician must be an intervening and independent party between patient and manufacturer.[47]

11. **Substantial Change/Abnormal Use**

    A manufacturer may be responsible for injuries caused by a substantial change in the product occurring after initial sale or due to abnormal use, if such change or use is one that could have been reasonably foreseen or expected.[48]

    Common knowledge of a danger from the foreseeable misuse of a product does not alone give rise to a duty to safeguard against the danger of that misuse.[49] Instead, the purpose of making the finding of a legal duty a prerequisite to a finding of negligence or breach of implied warranty is to avoid the extension of liability for every conceivably foreseeable accident, without regard to common sense or good policy.[50]

12. **State of the Art**

    "State-of-the-art" or "custom in the industry" evidence is admissible.[51] See Section 14, Standards, *infra*.

13. **Malfunction**

    The mere fact that a product malfunctioned is not sufficient to establish the existence of a defect.[52]

14. **Standards**

    Evidence that the product complied with customary or industry standards is admissible, although such evidence does not establish conclusively that due care was exercised.[53]

    Manufacturers are required to design products that meet prevailing safety standards at the time the product is made.[54] When deciding whether a product's design meets those standards, a court should consider whether the product fails to satisfy applicable industry standards, applicable government standards, or reasonable consumer expectations.[55]

    Consumer expectations, which may differ from government or industry standards, can be established through evidence of actual industry practices, published literature, and from direct evidence of what reasonable purchasers consider defective.[56] In other words, determining the reasonable expectation of purchasers requires a factual examination of what society demanded or expected from a product; this may be proven using evidence of actual industry practices, knowledge at the time of other injuries, knowledge of dangers, the existence of published literature, and direct evidence of what reasonable purchasers considered defective at the time.[57]

An employer's failure to comply with mandatory safety regulations may be an independent, intervening, and superseding act shielding a manufacturer from liability for its original negligence.[58]

15. Other Accidents

Evidence of similar accidents, when relevant, is admissible to establish that defendant had notice and actual knowledge of a defective condition, provided the prior incident occurred under substantially the same circumstances and was caused by the same or similar defects and dangers as those at issue.[59] The criterion for admissibility is "substantial similarity."[60] Recognizing that a "failure to warn" claim may be brought even where the specific nature of the defect is not known, the Supreme Court of Virginia has recently affirmed that "substantial similarity" may be established in one of two ways: "(1) through identification of the accident's cause, which must be attributable to the manufacturer, or (2) through the elimination of other potential causes that are not attributable to the manufacturer."[61]

16. Crashworthiness

The Virginia Supreme Court has indicated that it finds no reason to confuse well-settled jurisprudence governing whether a manufacturer of a product owes a duty to a person injured by that product, and therefore continues to reject the doctrine of "crashworthiness."[62]

E. BREACH OF WARRANTY

1. The Standard

The standard of safety of goods imposed on the seller or manufacturer of a product is essentially the same whether the theory of liability is labeled warranty or negligence: the product must be fit for the ordinary purposes for which it is to be used.[63] Under either the warranty theory or the negligence theory the plaintiff must show (1) that the goods were unreasonably dangerous either for the use to which they would ordinarily be put or for some other reasonably foreseeable purpose, and (2) that the unreasonably dangerous condition existed when the goods left the defendant's hands.[64]

As previously discussed in the context of negligence actions, under any theory of tortious injury, one requisite element of a claim is a causal connection between the defendant's conduct and the plaintiff's injury.[65] In order to establish causation, a plaintiff must introduce evidence sufficient to establish that the resulting injury was a probability, rather than a mere possibility, and where the plaintiff only shows that the injury might be due to one of several causes, this is not sufficient to support a recovery.[66] However, it is not necessary to establish causation with such certainty as to exclude every other possible cause.[67] In a product liability action, proof of causation must ordinarily be supported by expert testimony given the complexity of the causation facts.[68]

A somewhat recent, albeit unpublished, decision from the Fourth Circuit notes that "with regard to a cause of action asserting that a product is unreasonably dangerous because of its defective design, a theory of breach of implied warranty of merchantability focuses on the product and its attributes, while a negligence theory focuses on the defendant's conduct."[69]

The same unpublished decision also observes that,

> with regard to a cause of action asserting that a product is unreasonably dangerous because it is accompanied by inadequate warnings, the most notable differences between a theory of breach of implied warranty and a negligence theory are that (1) a theory of implied warranty focuses on whether the inadequate warnings render the product unreasonably dangerous while a negligence theory looks at whether the manufacturer's conduct is unreasonable; and (2) under a negligence theory, the duty to warn is continuous and is not interrupted by manufacture or sale of the product.[70]

2. Defenses

Various defenses not available in negligence apply, namely, disclaimer,[71] failure to provide timely notice of breach,[72] and limitation through inconsistencies with express warranties.[73]

Warranty disclaimers and limitations can be enforced against third-party beneficiaries despite lack of privity.[74] However, warranties created through specific and express representations between parties outside the chain of distribution, such as representations by the manufacturer directly to the consumer, must be disclaimed between those parties themselves, and not through an intermediate distributor.[75]

Contributory negligence is not a defense to a warranty action.[76] However, the action can be barred by the similar defense that a manufacturer is not liable for danger that is known, visible, or obvious to the plaintiff.[77] Likewise, there cannot be a recovery against a manufacturer in a product liability case for breach of an implied warranty when there has been an unforeseen misuse of the article.[78] Assumption of risk is not a defense in an action for breach of implied warranty.[79]

F. PUNITIVE DAMAGES

In Virginia, an award of punitive damages cannot exceed $350,000, total, regardless of how many defendants are found to be liable.[80]

Punitive damages are recoverable in actions for negligence if the plaintiff proves a conscious disregard of the rights of others or wanton, willful, or malicious conduct by the defendant, but the plaintiff must prove more than simple negligence.[81]

In order to receive an award of punitive damages in a warranty action, a plaintiff must show that the alleged breach of the warranty amounts to an independent, willful tort.[82]

G. PRE- AND POST-JUDGMENT INTEREST

The award of pre-judgment interest is designed to compensate the plaintiff who has been without relief for an extended period of time.[83] Statutory law provides that the award of pre-judgment interest by the trier of fact is discretionary, and "may provide for" such interest and fix the time of its commencement.[84]

The award of post-judgment interest is mandatory. Statutory law provides that the entire amount of a judgment or decree "shall bear interest" from its date of entry.[85]

The judgment rate, where no rate is fixed by contract, applicable to both pre-judgment interest and post-judgment interest is calculated at the statutory rate of six percent.[86] An insurer has no duty to pay pre-judgment interest in excess of policy limits, absent a contractual provision to the contrary.[87]

H. EMPLOYER IMMUNITY FROM SUIT

When an employee in Virginia is injured in the performance of his or her duties of employment, the Virginia Workers' Compensation Act provides that employee's sole and exclusive remedy against the employer.[88] In return, the employee is assured of recovery without having to defend against allegations of contributory negligence, assumption of risk, or causation by fellow servants.[89]

The exclusive nature of the Act, however, does not bar a suit for negligence in all circumstances. When the negligence causing the injury is that of a "stranger to the business," the employee is not deprived of his common law right of action against such stranger.[90] A manufacturer of a product used on the job may be such a "stranger" subject to suit.[91]

I. STATUTES

Relevant statutes for product liability actions are the statutes of limitation and repose, as well as the commercial code sections when a breach of warranty is alleged.[92] The statutory age of majority in Virginia is eighteen years.[93]

J. JOINT AND SEVERAL LIABILITY

1. The Rule

At common law, a plaintiff's release of one tortfeasor released all joint tortfeasors.[94] A Virginia statute amended that common law rule by giving a plaintiff a right, under prescribed conditions, to settle selectively with some tortfeasors without forfeiting remedies against others.[95]

By statute, a release or covenant not to sue given in good faith shall discharge the tortfeasor to whom it is given from all liability for contribution to all other tortfeasors.[96] It does not discharge any of the other tortfeasors from liability unless its terms so provide.[97] The application of this statutory law is not limited to "joint tortfeasors," as that term is narrowly defined, but also applies to those vicariously liable as employers, masters, and principals.[98]

A release or covenant not to sue need not be in writing where parties to a pending action state in open court that they have agreed to enter into such release or covenant not to sue and have agreed further to subsequently memorialize the same in writing.[99] However, where a settlement agreement is expressly made "subject to" the execution of a formal agreement, the execution of a formal agreement is a condition precedent to the existence of a binding contract.[100]

2. **Effect of Settlement**

Any amount recovered against any or all of the other tortfeasors is reduced by the amount stipulated by the covenant or the release or the amount of the consideration paid, whichever is the greater.[101] A release or covenant not to sue is not admitted into evidence in the trial of the matter but is considered by the court in determining the amount for which judgment shall be entered.[102]

3. **Contribution**

The right to contribution is based upon the equitable principle that where two or more persons are subject to a common burden it shall be borne equally.[103] Contribution among wrongdoers may be enforced when the wrong results from negligence and involves no moral turpitude.[104] However, before contribution may be had, it is essential that a cause of action by the person injured lie against the alleged wrongdoer from whom contribution is sought.[105]

A tortfeasor who enters into a release or covenant not to sue with a claimant is not entitled to recover contribution from another tortfeasor whose liability for the injury, property damage or wrongful death is not extinguished by the release or covenant not to sue.[106] Also, the settling tortfeasor cannot recover any amount paid by him that is in excess of what was reasonable.[107]

Michael W. Smith
R. Braxton Hill, IV
S. Perry Coburn
Christian & Barton, LLP
909 East Main Street, Suite 1200
Richmond, Virginia 23219-3095
(804) 697-4100
(Fax) (804) 697-4112

ENDNOTES - VIRGINIA

1. Va. Code §§ 8.01-243, 8.01-246; *Friedman v. Peoples Serv. Drug Stores, Inc.*, 208 Va. 700, 704, 160 S.E.2d 563, 565 (1968).

2. Va. Code §§ 8.01-243, 8.01-246, 8.2-725.

3. Va. Code §§ 8.01-230, 8.01-243, 8.01-246, 8.01-249 8.2-725; *Hawks v. DeHart*, 206 Va. 810, 813-14, 146 S.E.2d 187, 189-90 (1966).

4. Va. Code § 8.01-250.

5. Va. Code § 8.01-250; *Cooper Indus., Inc. v. Melendez*, 260 Va. 578, 592-93, 537 S.E.2d 580, 588-89 (2000).

6. *Royal Indem. Co. v. Tyco Fire Prods., LP*, 281 Va. 157, 168, 704 S.E.2d 91, 97 (2011).

7. *Sensenbrenner v. Rust, Orling & Neale*, 236 Va. 419, 424 n.4, 374 S.E.2d 55, 57 (1988); *Sykes v. Bayer Pharm. Corp.*, 548 F. Supp. 2d 208, 214 (E.D. Va. 2008) (applying Virginia law).

8. *Cross v. S.V.H.H. Cable Acquisition L.P.*, 1995 U.S. Dist. LEXIS 18659, at *8-9 (W.D. Va. Nov. 2, 1995) (citing *St. Jarre v. Heidelberger Druckmaschinen A.G.*, 816 F. Supp. 424, 427 (E.D. Va. 1994), *aff'd*, 19 F.3d 1430 (4th Cir. 1994)).

9. *Bly v. Otis Elevator Co.*, 713 F.2d 1040, 1045 n.6 (4th Cir. 1983); *see also Abbott v. American Cyanamid Co.*, 844 F.2d 1108, 1114 (4th Cir. 1988).

10. *Garrett v. I.R. Witzer Co.*, 258 Va. 264, 267-68, 518 S.E.2d 635, 637 (1999); *Logan v. Montgomery Ward & Co.*, 216 Va. 425, 428, 219 S.E.2d 685, 687 (1975).

11. *Morgen Indus., Inc. v. Vaughan*, 252 Va. 60, 65-66, 471 S.E.2d 489, 492 (1996) (citing *Austin v. Clark Equip. Co.*, 48 F.3d 833, 836 (4th Cir. 1995) and *Bly v. Otis Elevator Co.*, 713 F.2d 1040, 1043 (4th Cir. 1983)). A federal district court in Virginia has observed that although the Virginia Supreme Court has decided at least three cases that involved a "failure to test" or "failure to inspect" claim, it has never explicitly recognized either of those claims. *Sykes v. Bayer Pharms. Corp.*, 548 F. Supp. 2d 208, 215 n.4 (E.D. Va. 2008) (citing *Jones v. Ford Motor Co.*, 263 Va. 237, 559 S.E.2d 592, 604, 606 (2002), *Locke v. Johns-Manville Corp.*, 221 Va. 951, 275 S.E.2d 900, 903-04 (1981) and *Robey v. Richmond Coca-Cola Bottling Works*, 192 Va. 192, 64 S.E.2d 723, 727 (1951)).

12. *Slone v. Gen. Motors Corp.*, 249 Va. 520, 527, 457 S.E.2d 51, 54 (1995); *Owens-Corning Fiberglas Corp. v. Watson*, 243 Va. 128, 134-35, 413 S.E.2d 630,

634 (1992); *Besser v. Hansen*, 243 Va. 267, 276-77, 415 S.E.2d 138, 144 (1992); *Featherall v. Firestone Tire & Rubber Co.*, 219 Va. 949, 962, 252 S.E.2d 358, 366 (1979); Restatement (Second) of Torts § 388.

13. *Logan v. Montgomery Ward & Co.*, 216 Va. 425, 427-28, 219 S.E.2d 685, 687-88; *Weinstein v. PVA I, L.P.*, 2005 U.S. Dist. LEXIS 8001, at *9-10 (E.D. Va. May 4, 2005) (quoting *Hartwell v. Danek Med., Inc.*, 47 F. Supp. 2d 703, 707 (W.D. Va. 1999)).

14. *McGuire v. Hodges*, 273 Va. 199, 208 (2007).

15. *Pepsi-Cola Bottling Co. v. Yeatts*, 207 Va. 534, 537, 151 S.E.2d 400, 403 (1966).

16. *Stokes v. Geismar*, 815 F. Supp. 904, 908 (E.D. Va. 1993), *aff'd*, 16 F.3d 411 (4th Cir. 1994) (citing *Boyle v. United Techs. Corp.*, 792 F.2d 413, 416 (4th Cir. 1986)), *vacated on other grounds*, 487 U.S. 500 (1988)). In a recent mesothelioma case in which the disease was found to have resulted from exposure to multiple asbestos products—only one of them the defendant's—the Virginia Supreme Court adopted the Restatement (Third) of Torts' "sufficient-to-have-caused" standard of causation, under which the plaintiff must prove that exposure to *the defendant's* product, without more, would have been sufficient to cause the mesothelioma. *Ford Motor Co. v. Boomer*, 285 Va. 141, 158-59, 736 S.E.2d 724, 732 (2013).

17. Charles E. Friend, Personal Injury Law in Virginia § 19.3(C) (3d ed. 2003) ("Only rarely is lay testimony alone sufficient. . . .") (citing *Logan v. Montgomery Ward & Co.*, 216 Va. 425). *See also Horton v. W.T. Grant Co.*, 537 F.2d 1215, 1219 (4th Cir. 1976) ("At a minimum, plaintiffs were required to show that the [television] set was defective when it left the factory, and that the defect caused the fire. Such proof was lacking because of the exclusion of testimony by plaintiffs' expert. . . ."); *McCauley v. Purdue Pharms. L.P.*, 331 F. Supp. 2d 449, 464 (W.D. Va. 2004) ("in a products liability action, proof of causation must ordinarily be supported by expert testimony because of the complexity of the causation facts") (citing *Rohrbbough v. Wyeth Labs., Inc.*, 916 F.2d 970, 972 (4th Cir. 1990) and *Hortwell v. Danek Med., Inc.*, 47 F. Supp. 2d 703, 707 (W.D. Va. 1999)).

18. *Turner v. Manning, Maxwell & Moore, Inc.*, 216 Va. 245, 251, 217 S.E.2d 863, 868 (1975).

19. *Jeld-Wen, Inc. v. Gamble*, 256 Va. 144, 148, 501 S.E.2d 393, 396 (1998); *Slone v. Gen. Motors Corp.*, 249 Va. 520, 526, 457 S.E.2d 51, 54; *Alevromagiros v. Hechinger Co.*, 993 F.2d 417, 420 (4th Cir. 1993); *Marshall v. H. K. Ferguson Co.*, 623 F.2d 882, 885 (4th Cir. 1980).

20. *Tunnell v. Ford Motor Co.*, 385 F. Supp. 2d 582, 583 (W.D. Va. 2005) (citing *Sexton v. Bell Helmets*, 926 F.2d 331, 336 (4th Cir. 1991)).

21. *Tunnell v. Ford*, 385 F. Supp. 2d 582, 586.

22. *Tunnell v. Ford*, 385 F. Supp. 2d 582, 584-85 (quoting Restatement (Third) of Torts: Products Liability § 2, cmt. f (1997)).

23. *Morgen Indus., Inc. v. Vaughan*, 252 Va. 60, 66-67, 471 S.E.2d 489, 493; *Oman v. Johns-Manville Corp.*, 764 F.2d 224, 233 (4th Cir. 1985), *cert. denied sub nom. Oman v. H. K. Porter*, 474 U.S. 973 (1985).

24. *Smith v. Va. Elec. & Power Co.*, 204 Va. 128, 133, 129 S.E.2d 655, 659 (1963); *Ford Motor Co. v. Bartholomew*, 224 Va. 421, 432, 297 S.E.2d 675, 680-81 (1982).

25. *Litchford v. Hancock*, 232 Va. 496, 499, 352 S.E.2d 335, 337 (1987).

26. *Hoar v. Great E. Resort Mgmt.*, 256 Va. 374, 390, 506 S.E.2d 777, 787 (1998).

27. *Lust v. Clark Equip. Co.*, 792 F.2d 436, 440 (4th Cir. 1986) (quoting *VanCollom v. Johnson*, 228 Va. 103, 106, 319 S.E.2d 745, 746 (1984)).

28. *Hoar v. Great E. Resort Mgmt.*, 256 Va. 374, 390, 506 S.E.2d 777, 787.

29. *Carney v. Sears, Roebuck & Co.*, 309 F.2d 300, 304 (4th Cir. 1962).

30. *Spruill v. Boyle-Midway, Inc.*, 308 F.2d 79 (4th Cir. 1962).

31. *See Harris v. T.I., Inc.*, 243 Va. 63, 70, 413 S.E.2d 605, 609 (1992) (citing *Pepper v. Dixie Splint Coal Co.*, 165 Va. 179, 191, 181 S.E. 406, 410 (1935); *Peoples Nat'l Bank v. Morris*, 152 Va. 814, 819, 148 S.E. 828, 829 (1929)).

32. Va. Code § 8.2-318.

33. Va. Code § 8.2-715; *Pulte Home Corp. v. Parex, Inc.*, 265 Va. 518, 525, 579 S.E.2d 188, 191 (2003); *Beard Plumbing & Heating, Inc. v. Thompson Plastics, Inc.*, 254 Va. 240, 491 S.E.2d 731 (1997); *Ward v. Ernst & Young*, 246 Va. 317, 326 n.3, 435 S.E.2d 628, 632 (1993); *cf. Gerald M. Moore & Son, Inc. v. Drewry*, 251 Va. 277, 467 S.E.2d 811 (1996).

34. *Featherall v. Firestone*, 219 Va. 949, 962, 252 S.E.2d 358, 366.

35. *Oman v. Johns-Manville Corp.*, 764 F.2d 224, 233.

36. *Pfizer, Inc. v. Jones*, 221 Va. 681, 684, 272 S.E.2d 43, 45 (1980) (quoting *Nolan v. Dillon*, 261 Md. 516, 523, 276 A.2d 36, 40 (1971)).

37. *Sadler v. Lynch*, 192 Va. 344, 64 S.E.2d 664 (1951).

38. *Austin v. Clark Equip. Co.*, 48 F.3d 833, 836 (4th Cir. 1995).

39. *Begley v. Gehl Co.*, 1996 U.S. Dist. LEXIS 8198 (W.D. Va. Apr. 2, 1996), *aff'd*, 1997 U.S. App. LEXIS 12182 (4th Cir. May 27, 1997).

40. *Willis v. Raymark Indus., Inc.*, 905 F.2d 793, 796 (4th Cir. 1990); *Beale v. Hardy*, 769 F.2d 213, 215 (4th Cir. 1985); *Featherall*, 219 Va. 949, 252 S.E.2d 358; *cf. Greater Richmond Civic Recreation, Inc. v. A.H. Ewing's Sons, Inc.*, 200 Va. 593, 106 S.E.2d 595, 597 (1959).

41. *Spangler v. Kranco, Inc.*, 481 F.2d 373 (4th Cir. 1973).

42. *Harris*, 243 Va. 63, 413 S.E.2d 605 (assuming, without deciding, that in a proper case the Supreme Court of Virginia would recognize a successor corporation's post-sale duty to warn, but holding that no such duty could arise under the facts alleged); *Hart v. Savage*, 72 Va. Cir. 41, 45-46 (2006) ("declin[ing] to adopt a post-sale duty to warn" and noting that "the Supreme Court of Virginia has not ruled on the existence of such a duty").

43. *Ambrose v. Southworth Prods. Corp.*, 953 F. Supp. 728, 734 (W.D. Va. 1997).

44. *McAlpin v. Leeds & Northrop Co.*, 912 F. Supp. 207, 211-12 (W.D. Va. 1996); *see also King v. Flinn & Dreffein Eng'g Co.*, 2012 U.S. Dist. LEXIS 68133, at *19 (W.D. Va. May 16, 2012) (reading dicta in *Featherall*, 219 Va. 949, 252 S.E.2d 358, to suggest "that the Virginia Supreme Court has at least contemplated a post-sale duty to warn, if not explicitly adopted one"). *Accord Rash v. Stryker Corp.*, 589 F. Supp. 2d 733, 735-36 (W.D. Va. 2008) ("predict[ing]" that the "Supreme Court of Virginia *would* allow a cause of action based on a negligent breach of a post-sale duty to warn to proceed. The Restatement (Third) of Torts: Products Liability § 10 (1998), the view of other states, and dicta from the Fourth Circuit's opinion in *Bly v. Otis Elevator Co.*, 713 F.2d 1040 (4th Cir. 1983), support this determination. . . .") (emphasis added).

45. *Pfizer v. Jones*, 221 Va. 681, 684, 272 S.E.2d 43, 44 (quoting 2 R. Hursh & H. Bailey, American Law of Products Liability § 8:11, 173 (2d ed. 1974)).

46. *Talley v. Danek Med., Inc.*, 179 F.3d 154 (4th Cir. 1999).

47. *Talley*, 179 F.3d 154.

48. *Featherall*, 219 Va. 949, 962, 252 S.E.2d 358, 366.

49. *Jeld-Wen, Inc.*, 256 Va. 144, 501 S.E.2d 393.

50. *Jeld-Wen, Inc.*, 256 Va. 144, 501 S.E.2d 393.

51. *Turner*, 216 Va. 245, 217 S.E.2d 863.

52. *Alevromagiros*, 993 F.2d 417; *White Consol. Indus. v. Swiney*, 237 Va. 23, 376 S.E.2d 283 (1989); *Logan v. Montgomery Ward*, 216 Va. 425, 219 S.E.2d 685.

53. *Turner*, 216 Va. 245, 217 S.E.2d 863; *Alevromagiros*, 993 F.2d 417.

54. *Redman v. John D. Brush & Co.*, 111 F.3d 1174, 1181 (4th Cir. 1997).

55. *Redman*, 111 F.3d 1174, 1181.

56. *Alevromagiros*, 993 F.2d 417, 420-21.

57. *Sutton v. Roth, LLC*, 361 F. App'x 543, 547 (4th Cir. 2010) (quoting *Sexton v. Bell Helmets, Inc.*, 926 F.2d 331, 337 (4th Cir. 1991)).

58. *Cooper v. Ingersoll Rand Co.*, 628 F. Supp. 1488 (W.D. Va. 1986).

59. *Jones v. Ford Motor Co.*, 263 Va. 237, 255, 559 S.E.2d 592, 601 (2002) (quoting *Ford Motor Co. v. Phelps*, 239 Va. 272, 276-77, 389 S.E.2d 454, 457 (1990)); *see also Jones v. Ford Motor Co.*, 320 F. Supp. 2d 440, 448-49 (E.D. Va. 2004); *Owens-Corning Fiberglas Corp. v. Watson*, 243 Va. 128, 137, 413 S.E.2d 630, 635-36.

60. *Roll 'R' Way Rinks v. Smith*, 218 Va. 321, 325, 237 S.E.2d 157, 160 (1977).

61. *Funkhouser v. Ford Motor Co.*, 285 Va. 272, 283-84 (2013) (citing *Jones v. Ford Motor Co.*, 263 Va. at 256-57) (emphasis added).

62. *Slone*, 249 Va. at 525, 457 S.E.2d at 53; *Mativity v. MTD Prods.*, 714 F. Supp. 2d 577, 582 (W.D. Va. 2010).

63. *Garrett v. I.R. Witzer Co.*, 258 Va. 264, 267, 518 S.E.2d 635, 637.

64. *Garrett*, 258 Va. 264, 267-68, 518 S.E.2d 635, 637.

65. *Weinstein*, 2005 U.S. Dist. LEXIS 8001, at *9-10.

66. *Wright v. Eli Lilly & Co.*, 66 Va. Cir. 195, 221 (2004) (citing *White Consol. Indus. v. Swiney*, 237 Va. 23, 28, 376 S.E.2d 283, 285-86 (1989) and *Pepsi-Cola Bottling Co. v. Yeatts*, 207 Va. 534, 537, 151 S.E.2d 400, 403 (1966)).

67. *Wright v. Eli Lilly*, 66 Va. Cir. 195, 221 and *Yeatts*, 207 Va. 534, 537, 151 S.E.2d 400, 403.

68. *McCauley v. Purdue Pharms.*, 331 F. Supp. 2d 449, 464; *see also Wright v. Eli Lilly*, 66 Va. Cir. 195, 222 (quoting *Logan v. Montgomery Ward & Co.*, 216 Va. 425, 430-32, 219 S.E.2d 685, 689 (1975)). *See also* authorities cited *supra* note 17.

69. *Moyers ex rel. Moyers v. Corometrics Med. Sys., Inc.*, 2000 U.S. App. LEXIS 6177, at *15 n.6 (4th Cir. Apr. 4, 2000) (citing *Abbot v. Am. Cyanamid Co.*, 844 F.2d 1108, 1115-16 (4th Cir. 1988)).

70. *Moyers ex rel. Moyers*, 2000 U.S. App. LEXIS 6177, at *15 n.6 (citing *Bly v. Otis Elevator Co.*, 713 F.2d 1040, 1045-46 (4th Cir. 1983)); *but see Ambrose v. Southworth Prod. Corp.*, 953 F. Supp. 728, 734 (W.D. Va. 1997), *supra* note 43.

71. *Williams v. Gradall Co.*, 990 F. Supp. 442 (E.D. Va. 1998).

72. Va. Code § 8.2-607(3); *Aqualon Co. v. MAC Equip., Inc.*, 149 F.3d 262 (4th Cir. 1998).

73. *Chestnut v. Ford Motor Co.*, 445 F.2d 967 (4th Cir. 1971).

74. *Va. Transformer Corp. v. P.D. George Co.*, 932 F. Supp. 156 (W.D. Va. 1996).

75. *Va. Transformer Corp.*, 932 F. Supp. 156.

76. *Brockett v. Harrell Bros., Inc.*, 206 Va. 457, 143 S.E.2d 897 (1965).

77. *Freeman v. Case Corp.*, 118 F.3d 1011 (4th Cir. 1997), *cert. denied*, 118 S. Ct. 739, 139 L. Ed. 2d 676 (1997); *Lust*, 792 F.2d 436; *Wood v. Bass Pro Shops, Inc.*, 250 Va. 297, 462 S.E.2d 101 (1995); *Besser*, 243 Va. 267, 415 S.E.2d 138; *Turner*, 216 Va. 245, 217 S.E.2d 863.

78. *Cooper Indus., Inc. v. Melendez*, 260 Va. 578, 537 S.E.2d 580 (2000).

79. *Wood v. Bass Pro Shops, Inc.*, 250 Va. 297, 462 S.E.2d 101 (1995).

80. Va. Code § 8.01-38.1.

81. *Wallen v. Allen*, 231 Va. 289, 343 S.E.2d 73 (1986); *Bartholomew*, 224 Va. 421, 297 S.E.2d 675.

82. *See Dudley v. Bungee Int'l Mfg. Corp.*, 1996 U.S. App. LEXIS 1267, at *15 n.11 (4th Cir. Jan. 31, 1996) (citing *Kamlar Corp. v. Haley*, 224 Va. 699, 299 S.E.2d 514 (1983)).

83. Va. Code § 8.01-382; *Gill v. Rollins Protective Servs. Co.*, 836 F.2d 194 (4th Cir. 1987).

84. Va. Code § 8.01-382; *Dairyland Ins. Co. v. Douthat*, 248 Va. 627, 631, 449 S.E.2d 799, 801 (1994).

85. Va. Code § 8.01-382; *Dairyland v. Douthat*, 248 Va. 627, 631, 449 S.E.2d 799, 801.

86. Va. Code §§ 8.01-382, 6.2-302.

87. *Dairyland*, 248 Va. 627, 632, 449 S.E.2d 799, 802.

88. Va. Code § 65.2-307; *McCotter v. Smithfield Packing Co.*, 849 F. Supp. 443 (E.D. Va. 1994).

89. *Rasnick v. Pittston Co.*, 237 Va. 658, 660, 379 S.E.2d 353, 354 (1989).

90. *Rasnick v. Pittston*, 237 Va. 658, 660, 379 S.E.2d 353, 354.

91. *See Austin v. Consolidation Coal Co.*, 256 Va. 78, 501 S.E.2d 161 (1998).

92. Va. Code §§ 8.01-243, 8.01-246, 8.01-249, 8.01-250, 8.2-607, 8.2-715, 8.2-725.

93. Va. Code § 1-204.

94. *Fairfax Hosp. Sys. v. Nevitt*, 249 Va. 591, 594, 457 S.E.2d 10, 12 (1995) (quoting *Wright v. Orlowski*, 218 Va. 115, 120, 235 S.E.2d 349, 352 (1977)).

95. Va. Code § 8.01-35.1; *Fairfax Hosp.*, 249 Va. 591, 457 S.E.2d 10.

96. Va. Code § 8.01-35.1.

97. Va. Code § 8.01-35.1.

98. *Thurston Metals & Supply Co. v. Taylor*, 230 Va. 475, 339 S.E.2d 538 (1986).

99. *Snyder-Falkinham v. Stockburger*, 249 Va. 376, 385, 457 S.E.2d 36, 41(1995) (citing *N. Am. Managers, Inc. v. Reinach*, 177 Va. 116, 121, 12 S.E.2d 806, 808 (1941) and *Boisseau v. Fuller*, 96 Va. 45, 46, 30 S.E. 457, 457 (1898)).

100. *Golding v. Floyd*, 261 Va. 190, 193, 539 S.E.2d 735, 737 (2001).

101. Va. Code § 8.01-35.1(A)(1).

102. Va. Code § 8.01-35.1(A)(1).

103. *Nationwide Mut. Ins. Co. v. Jewel Tea Co.*, 202 Va. 527, 118 S.E.2d 646 (1961).

104. Va. Code § 8.01-34.

105. *Va. Elec. & Power Co. v. Wilson*, 221 Va. 979, 981, 277 S.E.2d 149, 150 (1981) (quoting *Bartlett v. Roberts Recapping, Inc.*, 207 Va. 789, 792-93, 153 S.E.2d 193, 196 (1967)).

106. Va. Code § 8.01-35.1(B).

107. Va. Code § 8.01-35.1(B).

WASHINGTON

A. CAUSES OF ACTION

1. "Product Liability Claim"

The Washington legislature passed the Washington Product Liability Act (WPLA) in 1981.[1] The WPLA applies to all product liability claims arising on or after July 26, 1981.[2] The WPLA creates a single product liability cause of action, called a "product liability claim," that consolidates most of the common law theories of liability, including "[s]trict liability in tort; negligence; breach of express or implied warranty; breach of, or failure to, discharge a duty to warn or instruct . . . ; misrepresentation, concealment, or nondisclosure . . . ; or other claim or action previously based on any other substantive legal theory."[3]

2. Other Causes of Action

Although the WPLA does not contain an express preemption clause, and notwithstanding the WPLA's reservation clause,[4] the Washington Supreme Court has determined that the "product liability claim" preempts the enumerated common law remedies.[5] The WPLA specifically excepts from this preemptive definition "fraud, intentionally caused harm or a claim or action under the [Washington] consumer protection act."[6]

B. STATUTES OF LIMITATION

1. Three-Year Statute of Limitation

A product liability claim must be brought within three years from the time the claimant discovers "the harm and its cause."[7] The Washington Supreme Court has held the discovery rule satisfied when the claimant "discovered, or . . . should have discovered, a factual causal relationship of the product to the harm."[8] Where a claimant has sustained "separate and distinct" injuries, as distinguished from a progressive injury or disease, the discovery rule may apply separately as to each injury.[9]

2. Statute of Repose

The WPLA protects product sellers (including manufacturers) from liability for harm caused after "expir[ation]" of the product's "useful safe life."[10] The defendant must prove expiration by a preponderance of the evidence, but the WPLA provides a rebuttable presumption that a product's useful safe life expires 12 years from the date of delivery.[11] Although Washington imposes an absolute six-year repose period on causes of action based on real estate improvements,[12] a 2004 amendment to this statute excludes manufacturers from its coverage.[13]

C. LIABILITY UNDER THE WPLA

1. The Standard

a. Categories of Potential Liability for Manufacturers

The WPLA defines five categories of potential liability for product manufacturers:[14] construction defects, breach of warranty, design defects, failure to warn, and post-sale duty to warn.

i. *Construction Defects*

The WPLA uses the term "strict liability" to describe a manufacturer's responsibility for products that materially deviate from the manufacturer's design specifications or performance standards or materially deviate from otherwise identical units of the same product line.[15] If the deviation proximately causes the claimant's harm, the product is "not reasonably safe in construction" and the manufacturer is strictly liable.[16]

ii. *Breach of Warranty*

The manufacturer is also strictly liable for any breach of express warranty,[17] or breach of implied warranty,[18] as to any nonconformity rendering the product "not reasonably safe."[19]

iii. *Design Defects*

Although the WPLA uses the term "negligence" to describe a manufacturer's liability for claims based on design defects,[20] the Washington Supreme Court equates this statutory negligence with the strict liability standard as defined in the pre-WPLA Washington cases.[21]

A claimant can establish a design defect under either the risk-utility test or the consumer expectations test.[22] The risk-utility test requires a showing that, at time of manufacture, the likelihood that the product would cause the plaintiff's harm or similar harms, and the seriousness of those harms, outweighed the manufacturer's burden to design a product that would have prevented those harms and any adverse effect a practical, feasible alternative would have on the product's usefulness.[23] Alternatively, a claimant may employ the consumer expectations test, which requires the plaintiff to show that the product was unsafe to an extent beyond that which would be contemplated by the ordinary consumer.[24]

The existence of a feasible alternative design is a required element of a design defect claim under the risk-utility test.[25] The existence or non-existence of a feasible alternative design also may be relevant evidence under the consumer expectations test,[26] but is not required.[27] "[T]he alternative design or product must be technologically achievable and economically viable."[28] Feasibility of the alternative design is assessed at the time of manufacture.[29]

iv. *Failure to Warn*

The WPLA also adopts a risk-utility balancing test for determining when inadequate warnings or instructions render a product "not reasonably safe":

> A product is not reasonably safe because adequate warnings or instructions were not provided with the product, if, at the time of manufacture, the likelihood that the product would cause the claimant's harm or similar harms, and the seriousness of those harms, rendered the warnings or instructions of the manufacturer inadequate and the manufacturer could have provided the warnings or instructions which the claimant alleges would have been adequate.[30]

As with design defects, strict liability is the standard for inadequate warnings,[31] notwithstanding that the WPLA purports to impose liability only where "the claimant's harm was proximately caused by the negligence of the manufacturer."[32] Consequently, "foreseeability" is not an element of a strict liability claim based on failure to warn.[33]

v. *Post-Sale Duty to Warn*

The WPLA adopts a common law negligence standard for providing warnings or instructions where the manufacturer learned or should have learned about a danger after the product was manufactured. "The general rule is that a post-sale duty to warn arises after a manufacturer has sufficient notice about a specific danger associated with the product."[34] The manufacturer must act as a "reasonably prudent manufacturer" and "exercise[] reasonable care to inform product users."[35]

b. Consumer Expectations Test

In addition to the five specific categories of liability discussed above, the WPLA provides: "In determining whether a product was not reasonably safe . . . , the trier of fact shall consider whether the product was unsafe to an extent beyond that which would be contemplated by the ordinary consumer."[36] The Washington Supreme Court has determined that "consumer expectations" are not merely a factor to consider under risk-utility balancing; instead, consumer expectations provide an alternative test for manufacturer liability.[37]

2. **Definition of "Defect"**

The WPLA avoids the term "defect." Instead, the statute imposes liability for harm proximately caused by a product[38] that is "not reasonably safe" in its construction, its design, or its nonconformity with express or implied warranties.[39]

3. **Causation**

Recovery under the WPLA requires proof that the unsafe product was the proximate cause of the claimant's injuries.[40]

4. **Damages**

The WPLA permits recovery for emotional distress in the absence of physical injury "if the emotional distress is a reasonable response and manifest by objective symptomatology."[41]

5. **Contributory Negligence/Assumption of Risk**

The WPLA does not preempt existing common law defenses,[42] including obvious danger,[43] assumption of the risk,[44] and product alteration or modification.[45] Although assumption of risk is a damage-reducing factor in strict liability cases,[46] certain classifications of the defense (i.e., express assumption of risk and implied primary assumption of risk) may provide a complete defense in other contexts.[47] Under Washington's system of "pure" comparative fault, the remaining defenses do not bar recovery, but instead merely reduce the claimant's recoverable damages.[48]

6. **Sale or Lease/Persons Liable**

The WPLA subjects manufacturers and "product seller[s] other than manufacturer[s]" to different levels of liability.[49] Generally, if a solvent manufacturer is subject to the jurisdiction of the court,[50] the WPLA limits the liability of product sellers other than manufacturers to harm proximately caused by (1) common law negligence,[51] (2) breach of express warranty,[52] or (3) intentional misrepresentation or concealment.[53] There are, however, five circumstances under which a product seller "shall have the liability of a manufacturer."[54]

"Product seller" includes manufacturers, wholesalers, distributors and retailers, as well as parties engaged in leasing and bailing.[55] However, a product lessor's liability is limited to "cases where the lessor's leasing activities are sufficiently great to justify holding it accountable for the acts of the manufacturer."[56]

7. **Inherently Dangerous Products**

Washington has adopted comment k to the Restatement (Second) of Torts Section 402A, which precludes liability for certain "unavoidably unsafe products."[57] Moreover, a defendant will not be held strictly liable merely because a product is potentially unsafe, unless it also fails to provide adequate warnings.[58] The Washington Supreme Court has explained that many products, including knives, hatchets, planers, guns, and baseball bats, "may be capable of causing injury, but that alone does not mean they should be removed from the market."[59]

8. **Successor Liability**

In addition to the traditional bases of successor liability (agreement to assume liability, de facto merger, mere continuation, fraud),[60] Washington recognizes product line liability where the successor acquires substantially all of the predecessor's assets, holds itself out as a continuation, and benefits from the predecessor's good will.[61]

9. **Market-Share Liability/Enterprise Liability**

The Washington Supreme Court has adopted a somewhat unique rule of market-share alternate liability in DES cases.[62] To date, the Court has refused to extend this theory into other contexts.[63]

10. **Privity**

The WPLA broadly defines "claimant" as including "any person or entity that suffers harm."[64] The statute specifically abolishes any privity requirement.[65]

11. **Remedial Measures**

Evidence of subsequent remedial changes is generally inadmissible.[66]

12. **Learned Intermediary Doctrine**

Manufacturers of prescription drugs and certain medical devices fulfill their duty to warn by providing adequate warnings to the prescribing physicians; manufacturers are not required to warn individual patients of dangers associated with the product.[67]

13. **Substantial Alteration/Abnormal Use**

A claimant's damages will be reduced if the product underwent substantial change in its condition after leaving the manufacturer,[68] or if the claimant misused the product.[69]

14. **State of the Art**

The WPLA explicitly permits the trier of fact to consider evidence of industry custom and technological feasibility (*i.e.*, "state of the art").[70]

15. **Malfunction**

Circumstantial evidence may be used to infer that a product was not reasonably safe in construction or design.[71] The mere fact of a malfunction is generally insufficient to prove that a product was unsafe, unless "common experience" dictates that a particular accident would not occur absent a defect in the product.[72]

16. **Standards and Governmental Regulation**

The trier of fact may consider compliance with private, legislative, or administrative standards.[73] Washington recognizes compliance with a "specific mandatory government contract specification" as an "absolute defense" to a design defect claim.[74] Noncompliance with a "specific mandatory government specification" (the word "contract" is not included here) gives rise to an automatic finding that the product is "not reasonably safe."[75]

17. **Other Accidents**

Admissibility of "prior accident" evidence is left to trial court discretion.[76]

18. **Misrepresentation**

The WPLA preempts common law claims for "misrepresentation, concealment, or nondisclosure, whether negligent or innocent."[77] A claimant may, however, pursue a common law claim for fraud or "intentionally caused harm."[78]

19. **Destruction or Loss of Evidence**

To date, an independent civil cause of action for the tort of spoliation of evidence (*i.e.*, "[t]he intentional destruction of evidence")[79] has not been recognized in Washington.[80] However, courts may remedy spoliation with a rebuttable evidentiary presumption: "[W]here relevant evidence which would properly be a part of a case is within the control of a party whose interests it would naturally be to produce it and he fails to do so, without satisfactory explanation, the only inference which the finder of fact may draw is that such evidence would be unfavorable to him."[81] In determining whether to apply the presumption, courts evaluate two factors: "(1) the potential importance or relevance of the missing evidence; and (2) the culpability or fault of the adverse party."[82] In extreme cases, the court may enter default judgment against the spoliating party after considering whether a lesser sanction would suffice.[83]

20. **Economic Loss**

The WPLA restricts recovery for direct or consequential economic loss to the law of sales.[84] In drawing this line between contract and tort remedies, Washington has adopted a "risk of harm" analysis for defining "economic loss."[85]

21. **Crashworthiness**

The Washington Supreme Court has recognized a cause of action "premised upon an allegation that the claimed defect did not cause or contribute to the original collision, but caused enhanced injuries."[86] Under this theory, the manufacturer is liable for the claimant's injuries to the extent they exceed the harm that would have occurred had the product been reasonably safe.[87]

Crashworthiness is a relative concept that reflects the reasonable expectations of the ordinary consumer:

> [E]valuation of the product in terms of the reasonable expectations of the ordinary consumer allows the trier of the fact to take into account the intrinsic nature of the product. The purchaser of a Volkswagen cannot reasonably expect the same degree of safety as would the buyer of the much more expensive Cadillac. It must be borne in mind that we are dealing with a relative, not an absolute concept.[88]

D. NEGLIGENCE

Most traditional common law claims against manufacturers for product-related harm, including claims for negligence, are preempted by the WPLA.[89] Nonetheless, a negligence standard governs post-sale failure to warn claims,[90] and the WPLA permits common law negligence claims against a "product seller other than a manufacturer."[91]

E. BREACH OF WARRANTY

A product liability claim based on breach of an express or an implied warranty can be raised in tort under the WPLA or in contract under the Uniform Commercial Code.[92] Claims for personal injury or property damage are governed by the WPLA; claims for economic loss are governed by the UCC.[93]

F. PUNITIVE DAMAGES

Punitive damages are generally disfavored in Washington[94] and are not available in a product liability action.[95]

G. PRE- AND POST-JUDGMENT INTEREST

Pre-judgment interest is permitted "when a party to the litigation retains funds rightfully belonging to another and the amount of the funds at issue is liquidated, that is, the amount at issue can be calculated with precision and without reliance on opinion or discretion."[96] Because the touchstone of a pre-judgment interest award is the "nature of the claim" (*i.e.*, liquidated or readily determinable as opposed to unliquidated), not the underlying legal theory, certain tort claims may warrant an award of pre-judgment interest.[97] Pre-judgment interest accrues from the date the claim arose to the date of judgment.[98]

A claimant is entitled by statute to post-judgment interest, which generally accrues from the date of entry of judgment.[99]

Both pre-judgment and post-judgment interest are calculated at a rate of

> two percentage points above the prime rate, as published by the board of governors of the federal reserve system on the first business day of the calendar month immediately preceding the date of entry.[100]

H. EMPLOYER IMMUNITY FROM SUIT

As a general rule, Washington's Industrial Insurance Act (IIA) provides the exclusive remedy for personal injuries suffered by employees in the workplace.[101] However, injuries resulting from an employer's "deliberate intention" (*i.e.*, where "the employer had actual knowledge that an injury was certain to occur and willfully disregarded that knowledge")[102] fall outside the ambit of the IIA.[103] An employee also may circumvent the IIA's exclusive remedy provision under the "dual persona" doctrine, which provides that "[a]n employer may become a third person, vulnerable to tort suit by an employee, if—and only if—he possesses a second persona so completely independent from and unrelated to his status as employer that by established standards the law recognizes it as a separate legal person."[104]

An employer may waive its immunity through an indemnification agreement, provided that the agreement "clearly and specifically contains a waiver of the immunity of the workers' compensation act, either by so stating or by specifically stating that the indemnitor assumes potential liability for actions brought by its own employees."[105]

I. STATUTES

The WPLA provides the primary legal framework governing product liability actions. Other relevant statutes include the statutes of limitation,[106] the Consumer Protection Act,[107] the Uniform Commercial Code,[108] and the statutes governing contribution, contributory fault, and joint and several liability.[109] The age of majority in Washington is 18 years.[110] Statutes of limitation generally are tolled for causes of action that accrue during a plaintiff's minority.[111]

J. JOINT AND SEVERAL LIABILITY

1. General Rule: Several Liability

Tort reform in 1986 abolished joint and several liability of defendants in cases where the plaintiff carries a share of the fault.[112] Even if the plaintiff is blameless, the defendants against whom judgment is entered are only jointly and severally liable "for the sum of their proportionate shares of the claimant[']s total damages."[113] Since shares of fault are allocated to all responsible entities, the named defendants may be jointly responsible for only a portion of the plaintiff's total damages, and cannot be held jointly and severally liable for damages allocated to nonparties.[114]

2. Contribution

In general, "[a] right of contribution exists between or among two or more persons who are jointly and severally liable upon the same indivisible claim for the same injury, death or harm" and "may be enforced either in the original action or by a separate action brought for that purpose."[115] However, "[b]y restricting the applicability of joint and several liability, the [Washington] Legislature limited the instances in which contribution is needed or available."[116] For example, a 1993 Washington Supreme Court decision emphasizes that one tortfeasor may not seek contribution "from another tortfeasor who has prevailed on summary judgment with dismissal of the plaintiff's tort claim."[117]

K. APPORTIONMENT OF FAULT

Under Washington's general tort contributory fault rules, modified in 1993, fault is apportioned as follows:

> [T]he trier of fact shall determine the percentage of the total fault which is attributable to every entity which caused the claimant's damages except entities immune from liability to the claimant under Title 51 RCW. The sum of the percentages of the total fault attributed to at-fault entities shall equal one hundred percent. The entities whose fault shall be determined include the claimant or person suffering personal injury or incurring property damage, defendants, third-party defendants, entities released by the claimant, entities with any other individual defense against the claimant, and entities immune from liability to the claimant, but shall not include those entities immune from liability to the claimant under Title 51 RCW.[118]

Fault, which is statutorily defined in terms of "reckless[ness]" and "negligen[ce],"[119] may be apportioned to parties who are neither manufacturers nor product sellers.[120] However, fault may not be apportioned to an intentional tortfeasor.[121]

L. CHOICE OF LAW

Washington has adopted the "most significant relationship" rule for choice of law problems, as developed in the Restatement (Second) of Conflict of Laws.[122]

John D. Dillow
Kate Reddy
Perkins Coie, LLP
1201 Third Avenue, Suite 4900
Seattle, Washington 98101-3099
(206) 359-8000
(Fax) (206) 359-9000
JDillow@perkinscoie.com
KReddy@perkinscoie.com

ENDNOTES - WASHINGTON

1. Laws of 1981, ch. 27, §§ 1-7, Wash. Rev. Code §§ 7.72.010-.060. Based in large part on the Model Uniform Product Liability Act, the WPLA, on its face, substantially changed Washington's product liability law. However, subsequent interpretations of the WPLA by the Washington Supreme Court make the substance of the WPLA more consistent with prior common law than at first it might appear.

2. Wash. Rev. Code § 4.22.920(1); *see also Viereck v. Fibreboard Corp.*, 81 Wash. App. 579, 585, 915 P.2d 581, 584 (1996) (stating relevant inquiry is whether "substantially all the events producing the injury . . . occurred before [or after] 1981"). Strict liability claims arising before the WPLA's effective date are governed by Restatement (Second) of Torts § 402A (1965). *Lunsford v. Saberhagen Holdings, Inc.*, 166 Wash. 2d 264, 284-86, 208 P.2d 1092, 1102-04 (2009).

3. Wash. Rev. Code § 7.72.010(4); *Hue v. Farmboy Spray Co.*, 127 Wash. 2d 67, 75 n.10, 896 P.2d 682, 687 n.10 (1995) (WPLA "creates a single cause of action for product-related harm with specified statutory requirements for proof.").

4. "The previous existing applicable law of this state on product liability is modified only to the extent set forth in this chapter." Wash. Rev. Code § 7.72.020(1).

5. *Washington Water Power Co. v. Graybar Elec. Co.*, 112 Wash. 2d 847, 851-56, 774 P.2d 1199, 1202-05, *amended*, 779 P.2d 697 (Wash. 1989).

6. Wash. Rev. Code § 7.72.010(4).

7. Wash. Rev. Code § 7.72.060(3).

8. *N. Coast Air Servs., Ltd. v. Grumman Corp.*, 111 Wash. 2d 315, 319, 759 P.2d 405, 406 (1988). Washington Revised Code section 7.72.060(3) modifies and narrows the liberal common law discovery rule stated in *Ohler v. Tacoma Gen. Hosp.*, 92 Wash. 2d 507, 510-11, 598 P.2d 1358, 1360 (1979).

9. *Green v. A.P.C.*, 136 Wash. 2d 87, 95-96, 960 P.2d 912, 915-16 (1998) (suggesting that such a rule may apply, but declining to apply it in the absence of expert testimony establishing "truly separate and distinct" injuries).

10. Wash. Rev. Code § 7.72.060(1); *see Rice v. Dow Chem. Co.*, 124 Wash. 2d 205, 212, 875 P.2d 1213, 1217 (1994).

11. Wash. Rev. Code § 7.72.060(2); *see Rice*, 124 Wash. 2d at 212, 875 P.2d at 1217.

12. Wash. Rev. Code § 4.16.310.

13. Wash. Rev. Code § 4.16.300. The 2004 amendment limits the application of the repose period for real estate improvements to those "required to be . . . registered or licensed" as architects, contractors, engineers, land surveyors, landscape architects, or electrical contractors. Wash. Rev. Code § 4.16.300; Wash. Rev. Code §§ 18.08.310, 18.27.020, 18.43.040, 18.96.020, 19.28.041.

14. Wash. Rev. Code § 7.72.010(2) (broadly defining "manufacturer").

15. Wash. Rev. Code §§ 7.72.030(2), (2)(a).

16. Wash. Rev. Code § 7.72.030(2).

17. Wash. Rev. Code § 7.72.030(2)(b). The warranty must be "part of the basis of the bargain." Wash. Rev. Code § 7.72.030(2)(b).

18. Wash. Rev. Code § 7.72.030(2)(c) (incorporating Title 62A (the UCC)).

19. Wash. Rev. Code § 7.72.030(2).

20. Wash. Rev. Code § 7.72.030(1)(a).

21. *Falk v. Keene Corp.*, 113 Wash. 2d 645, 651-53, 782 P.2d 974, 978-79 (1989) (WPLA sets forth same "strict liability" design defect standard adopted in *Seattle-First Nat'l Bank v. Tabert*, 86 Wash. 2d 145, 542 P.2d 774 (1975)); *see also Macias v. Saberhagen Holdings, Inc.*, 175 Wash. 2d 402, 410, 282 P.3d 1069, 1074 (2012) (describing standards under RCW 7.72.030 as "the strict liability principles that were defined by this court under the common law prior to the WPLA.").

22. *Soproni v. Polygon Apartment Partners*, 137 Wash. 2d 319, 326-27, 971 P.2d 500, 504-05 (1999).

23. *Soproni*, 137 Wash. 2d at 326-27, 971 P.2d at 504-05; Wash. Rev. Code § 7.72.030(1)(a).

24. *Soproni*, 137 Wash. 2d at 326-27, 971 P.2d at 505.

25. *Ruiz-Guzman v. Amvac Chem. Corp.*, 141 Wash. 2d 493, 503, 7 P.3d 795, 800 (2000); *see also* Wash. Rev. Code § 7.72.030(1)(a).

26. *See Soproni*, 137 Wash. 2d at 326-27, 971 P.2d at 504-05; *Lamon v. McDonnell Douglas Corp.*, 91 Wash. 2d 345, 351-52, 588 P.2d 1346, 1350 (1979); *Seattle-First Nat. Bank v. Tabert*, 86 Wash. 2d 145, 154, 542 P.2d 774, 779 (1975).

27. *Couch v. Mine Safety Appliances Co.*, 107 Wash. 2d 232, 237, 241, 728 P.2d 585, 588, 590 (1986).

28. *Ruiz-Guzman*, 141 Wash. 2d at 505, n.8, 7 P.3d at 801, n.8 (internal quotation omitted).

29. Wash. Rev. Code § 7.72.030(1)(a); *see also Hyjek v. Anthony Indus.*, 133 Wash. 2d 414, 427-28, 944 P.2d 1036, 1042-43 (1997).

30. Wash. Rev. Code § 7.72.030(1)(b).

31. *Ayers v. Johnson & Johnson Baby Prods. Co.*, 117 Wash. 2d 747, 762-63, 818 P.2d 1337, 1345 (1991). However, in *Estate of LaMontagne v. Bristol-Myers Squibb*, 127 Wash. App. 335, 111 P.3d 857 (2005), the Court of Appeals stated that "[w]hether a prescription drug manufacturer provides adequate warnings to physicians is governed by the negligence standard under the Restatement (Second) of Torts § 402A, cmt. k (1965)," thereby distinguishing prescription drug products from the consumer products examined in *Ayers*. *LaMontagne*, 127 Wash. App. at 343, 111 P.3d at 861.

32. Wash. Rev. Code § 7.72.030(1).

33. *Ayers*, 117 Wash. 2d at 762-63, 765, 818 P.2d at 1345-46.

34. *Esparza v. Skyreach Equip., Inc.*, 103 Wash. App. 916, 935, 15 P.3d 188, 198 (2000).

35. Wash. Rev. Code § 7.72.030(1)(c).

36. Wash. Rev. Code § 7.72.030(3).

37. *Falk*, 113 Wash. 2d at 654-55, 782 P.2d at 980 (design defect); *Ayers*, 117 Wash. 2d at 765, 818 P.2d at 1346 (failure to warn).

38. The term "product" includes "any object possessing intrinsic value, capable of delivery either as an assembled whole or as a component part or parts, and produced for introduction into trade or commerce. Human tissue and organs, including human blood and its components, are excluded from this term." Wash. Rev. Code § 7.72.010(3); *accord Graham v. Concord Constr., Inc.*, 100 Wash. App. 851, 856, 999 P.2d 1264, 1267 (2000).

39. Wash. Rev. Code § 7.72.030.

40. Wash. Rev. Code §§ 7.72.030(1), .030(2), .040(1); *see also Soproni*, 137 Wash. 2d at 325, 971 P.2d at 504.

41. *Bylsma v. Burger King Corp.*, 176 Wash. 2d 555, 562, 293 P.3d 1168, 1171 (2013).

42. Wash. Rev. Code § 7.72.020(1).

43. *Baughn v. Honda Motor Co.*, 107 Wash. 2d 127, 138-39, 727 P.2d 655, 662 (1986) (en banc) (assessing pre-WPLA failure to warn claim); *Haysom v. Coleman Lantern Co.*, 89 Wash. 2d 474, 479, 573 P.2d 785, 789 (1978); *see also Little v. PPG Indus., Inc.*, 92 Wash. 2d 118, 123 & n.1, 594 P.2d 911, 914 & n.1 (1979).

44. *Campbell v. ITE Imperial Corp.*, 107 Wash. 2d 807, 819-20, 733 P.2d 969, 976 (1987).

45. *Parkins v. Van Doren Sales, Inc.*, 45 Wash. App. 19, 28, 724 P.2d 389, 395 (1986); *Bich v. Gen. Elec. Co.*, 27 Wash. App. 25, 29, 614 P.2d 1323, 1326 (1980).

46. *Campbell*, 107 Wash. 2d at 819-20, 733 P.2d at 976.

47. *Scott v. Pac. W. Mountain Resort*, 119 Wash. 2d 484, 496-98, 834 P.2d 6, 13 (1992).

48. Wash. Rev. Code § 4.22.005.

49. Wash. Rev. Code § 7.72.040.

50. Wash. Rev. Code §§ 7.72.040(1), .040(2).

51. Wash. Rev. Code § 7.72.040(1)(a); *see Martin v. Schoonover*, 13 Wash. App. 48, 54, 533 P.2d 438, 442 (1975).

52. Wash. Rev. Code § 7.72.040(1)(b). Although Washington Revised Code section 7.72.030(2) makes a manufacturer potentially liable for breach of UCC implied warranties, section 7.72.040(1) extinguishes a seller's liability for breach of those warranties except for economic loss that is pursued as a UCC claim. *See* Wash. Rev. Code § 7.72.010(6).

53. Wash. Rev. Code § 7.72.040(1)(c).

54. Wash. Rev. Code § 7.72.040(2) (no solvent manufacturer subject to court's jurisdiction; judgment-proof manufacturer; parent-controlled subsidiary relationship; seller provided plans or specifications; product marketed under seller's brand or trade name). Note that where a seller is sued as a manufacturer with respect to products marketed under the seller's brand or trade name, the seller may not allocate fault to the product manufacturer. *Johnson v. Recreational Equip., Inc.*, 159 Wash. App. 939, 948-51, 247 P.3d 18, 22-24 (2011).

55. Wash. Rev. Code § 7.72.010(1). A hospital providing a surgical device is a "provider of professional services" specifically excluded under Washington Revised Code section 7.72.010(1)(b) from the definition of "product seller." *McKenna v. Harrison Mem'l Hosp.*, 92 Wash. App. 119, 121-22, 960 P.2d 486,

487 (1998). The WPLA also provides that "[a] product seller acting primarily as a wholesaler, distributor, or retailer of a product may be a 'manufacturer' but only to the extent that it designs, produces, makes, fabricates, constructs, or remanufactures the product for its sale." Wash. Rev. Code § 7.72.010(2).

56. *Buttelo v. S.A. Woods-Yates Am. Mach. Co.*, 72 Wash. App. 397, 404, 864 P.2d 948, 952 (1993); *see also Bostwick v. Ballard Marine, Inc.*, 127 Wash. App. 762, 765, 112 P.3d 571, 574 (2005) (applying *Buttelo* test).

57. *Ruiz-Guzman*, 141 Wash. 2d at 505-11, 7 P.3d at 801-04 (citing, *inter alia*, *Terhune v. A. H. Robins Co.*, 90 Wash. 2d 9, 577 P.2d 975 (1978) (en banc)).

58. *Baughn*, 107 Wash. 2d at 137, 727 P.2d at 661 (interpreting pre-WPLA standard for strict liability).

59. *Baughn*, 107 Wash. 2d at 147, 727 P.2d at 667; *see also Baughn*, 107 Wash. 2d at 140-41, 727 P.2d at 663.

60. *Martin v. Abbott Labs.*, 102 Wash. 2d 581, 609, 689 P.2d 368, 384-85 (1984).

61. *Abbott Labs.*, 102 Wash. 2d at 614-15, 689 P.2d at 387-88 (adopting "product line" successor liability in product liability action as defined in *Ray v. Alad Corp.*, 19 Cal. 3d 22, 560 P.2d 3, 136 Cal. Rptr. 574 (1977)). *But see Hall v. Armstrong Cork, Inc.*, 103 Wash. 2d 258, 267, 692 P.2d 787, 793 (1984) (product line exception unavailable where plaintiff can pursue claim against predecessor corporation).

62. *Abbott Labs.*, 102 Wash. 2d at 602-07, 689 P.2d at 381-83 (creating right of defendant DES manufacturer to implead other drug manufacturers as third-party defendants solely for purpose of reducing presumptive or actual market share); *see also George v. Parke-Davis*, 107 Wash. 2d 584, 588-90, 601, 733 P.2d 507, 510-11, 517 (1987) (elaborating on *Abbott Labs.*).

63. *See, e.g., Lockwood v. AC & S, Inc.*, 109 Wash. 2d 235, 245-46 n.6, 744 P.2d 605, 612 n.6 (1987) (en banc) (declining to apply market-share alternate liability in asbestos case).

64. Wash. Rev. Code § 7.72.010(5). Rejecting the argument that the rescue doctrine is "nothing more than a common law remedy," and thus preempted by the WPLA, the Washington Supreme Court held that an injured rescuer may invoke the doctrine and bring a WPLA cause of action against the party causing the danger requiring the rescue. *McCoy v. Am. Suzuki Motor Corp.*, 136 Wash. 2d 350, 355-56, 961 P.2d 952, 955-56 (1998). The court emphasized that it could "conceive of no reason why th[e rescue] doctrine"—which it described as "shorthand for the idea that rescuers are to be anticipated and . . . a reflection of a societal value judgment that rescuers should not be barred from bringing suit for knowingly placing themselves

in danger to undertake a rescue"—"should not apply . . . when a product manufacturer causes the danger." *McCoy*, 136 Wash. 2d at 356, 961 P.2d at 956.

65. Wash. Rev. Code § 7.72.010(5). The WPLA's exclusion of recovery for economic loss, however, effectively imposes a privity requirement for such claims, reversing Washington's common law rule that allowed tort-based actions for economic loss. *See Washington Water Power Co.*, 112 Wash. 2d at 852, 857-58 & n.7, 774 P.2d at 1203, 1205-06 & n.7.

66. *Hyjek*, 133 Wash. 2d at 428, 944 P.2d at 1043 ("[E]vidence of subsequent remedial measures should not be admitted in a strict products liability action absent an exception under ER 407.").

67. *Terhune v. A. H. Robins Co.*, 90 Wash. 2d 9, 17, 577 P.2d 975, 979 (1978) (applying doctrine to case involving Dalkon Shield); *see also Washington State Physicians Ins. Exch. & Ass'n v. Fisons Corp.*, 122 Wash. 2d 299, 313, 858 P.2d 1054, 1061 (1993) (articulating doctrine). *But see May v. Dafoe*, 25 Wash. App. 575, 578-79, 611 P.2d 1275, 1277-78 (1980) (refusing to extend doctrine to case involving a medical incubator).

68. *Parkins*, 45 Wash. App. at 28, 724 P.2d at 395; *Bich*, 27 Wash. App. at 29, 614 P.2d at 1326.

69. Wash. Rev. Code § 4.22.015 (Contributory "fault" means "acts or omissions, *including misuse of a product*, that are in any measure negligent or reckless toward the person or property of the actor or others, or that subject a person to strict tort liability or liability on a product liability claim." (emphasis added)).

70. Wash. Rev. Code § 7.72.050(1); *cf. Lenhardt v. Ford Motor Co.*, 102 Wash. 2d 208, 210-11, 683 P.2d 1097, 1099 (1984) (distinguishing "state of the art" from "industry custom" evidence and concluding both types evidence inapplicable to pre-WPLA cause of action). Neither type of evidence was relevant under prior case law, and thus in this context at least the WPLA significantly changes Washington common law. *See also Crittenden v. Fibreboard Corp.*, 58 Wash. App. 649, 658, 794 P.2d 554, 559 (1990), *amended*, 803 P.2d 1329 (Wash. Ct. App. 1991); *Falk*, 113 Wash. 2d at 654, 782 P.2d at 979-80.

71. *Bich*, 27 Wash. App. at 30-31, 614 P.2d at 1327.

72. *Bombardi v. Pochel's Appliance & TV Co.*, 9 Wash. App. 797, 515 P.2d 540, *modified*, 10 Wash. App. 243, 246, 518 P.2d 202, 204 (1973); *see also Bich*, 27 Wash. App. at 31, 614 P.2d at 1327 (explaining that "mere fact of an accident alone does not establish that a product was defective").

73. Wash. Rev. Code § 7.72.050(1). Note, however, that "compliance with code requirements does not mandate a finding that a product is reasonably safe as designed." *Soproni*, 137 Wash. 2d at 329, 971 P.2d at 506.

74. Wash. Rev. Code § 7.72.050(2); *see Graham*, 100 Wash. App. at 856, 999 P.2d at 1267; *Koehler v. Fibreboard Corp. (In re Estate of Foster)*, 55 Wash. App. 545, 551-52, 779 P.2d 272, 275-76 (1989). The Washington Supreme Court has held, however, that "compliance with specific mandatory government contract specifications *relating to design* does not give rise to the absolute defense in [§] 7.72.050(2) to a postmanufacture *failure-to-warn* claim." *Timberline Air Serv., Inc. v. Bell Helicopter-Textron, Inc.*, 125 Wash. 2d 305, 318, 884 P.2d 920, 927 (1994) (emphasis added).

75. Wash. Rev. Code § 7.72.050(2).

76. *Seay v. Chrysler Corp.*, 93 Wash. 2d 319, 324, 609 P.2d 1382, 1385 (1980).

77. Wash. Rev. Code § 7.72.010(4).

78. Wash. Rev. Code § 7.72.010(4).

79. *Henderson v. Tyrrell*, 80 Wash. App. 592, 605, 910 P.2d 522, 531 (1996) (quoting *Black's Law Dictionary* 1401 (6th ed. 1990)).

80. *Unigard Sec. Ins. Co. v. Lakewood Eng'g & Mfg. Corp.*, 982 F.2d 363, 371 (9th Cir. 1992) (declining to reach the question of whether Washington would recognize a tort claim for spoliation of evidence).

81. *Henderson*, 80 Wash. App. at 606, 910 P.2d at 532 (quoting *Pier 67, Inc. v. King County*, 89 Wash. 2d 379, 385-86, 573 P.2d 2, 6 (1977)); *see also Lynott v. Nat'l Union Fire Ins. Co.*, 123 Wash. 2d 678, 689, 871 P.2d 146, 151-52 (1994) (en banc) (articulating presumption).

82. *Henderson*, 80 Wash. App. at 607, 910 P.2d at 532; *see also Homeworks Constr., Inc. v. Wells*, 133 Wash. App. 892, 900-01, 138 P.3d 654, 658 (2006) (acknowledging that a "party may be responsible for spoliation without a finding of bad faith"; but that "a party's actions are [only] 'improper' and constitute spoliation where the party has a duty to preserve the evidence"; rejecting the notion that a "potential litigant owes a general duty to preserve evidence"); *Marshall v. Bally's Pacwest, Inc.*, 94 Wash. App. 372, 381, 972 P.2d 475, 480 (1999) (applying *Henderson*).

83. *Magaña v. Hyundai Motor Am., et al.*, 167 Wash. 2d 570, 220 P.3d 191 (2010) (entering default judgment against manufacturer who spoliated evidence and obstructed discovery of other similar events).

84. *Washington Water Power Co.*, 112 Wash. 2d at 856-59, 774 P.2d at 1205-07 (discussing Wash. Rev. Code § 7.72.010(6)); *see also Berschauer/Phillips Constr.*

Co. v. Seattle Sch. Dist. No. 1, 124 Wash. 2d 816, 822-23, 881 P.2d 986, 990 (1994) (en banc).

85. *Washington Water Power Co.*, 112 Wash. 2d at 860-67, 774 P.2d at 1207-11 (discussing "sudden and dangerous" and "evaluative" risk of harm formulas, without choosing between them); *see also Touchet Valley Grain Growers, Inc. v. Opp & Seibold Gen. Constr., Inc.*, 119 Wash. 2d 334, 350-55, 831 P.2d 724, 732-35 (1992) (same). Note, however, that where a claim arises under admiralty jurisdiction, federal admiralty rules preclude application of the analysis in *Washington Water Power Co. See Stanton v. Bayliner Marine Corp.*, 123 Wash. 2d 64, 87-88, 866 P.2d 15, 28 (1993) ("[S]ubstantive admiralty law precludes recovery for economic loss"; only remedy, if any, is under the Uniform Commercial Code.).

86. *Seattle-First Nat'l Bank*, 86 Wash. 2d at 150, 542 P.2d at 776-77 (citing *Baumgardner v. Am. Motors Corp.*, 83 Wash. 2d 751, 522 P.2d 829 (1974) (en banc)); *see also Couch*, 107 Wash. 2d at 241-43, 728 P.2d at 590-91.

87. *Couch*, 107 Wash. 2d at 242-43, 728 P.2d at 591.

88. *Seattle-First Nat'l Bank*, 86 Wash. 2d at 154, 542 P.2d at 779; *see also Couch*, 107 Wash. 2d at 238, 728 P.2d at 588.

89. *Hue*, 127 Wash. 2d at 87, 896 P.2d at 693; *Fisons*, 122 Wash. 2d at 322-23, 858 P.2d at 1066; *Washington Water Power Co.*, 112 Wash. 2d at 853-57, 774 P.2d at 1203-05.

90. Wash. Rev. Code § 7.72.030(1)(c); *see Couch*, 107 Wash. 2d at 239 n.5, 728 P.2d at 589 n.5.

91. Wash. Rev. Code. § 7.72.040(1), (1)(a).

92. *Touchet Valley Grain Growers*, 119 Wash. 2d at 343, 831 P.2d at 729.

93. *Washington Water Power Co.*, 112 Wash. 2d at 856-59, 774 P.2d at 1205-07 (discussing Wash. Rev. Code § 7.72.010(6)); *see also Berschauer/Phillips Constr. Co.*, 124 Wash. 2d at 822, 881 P.2d at 990 (describing "economic loss" rule).

94. *Barr v. Interbay Citizens Bank*, 96 Wash. 2d 692, 697-700, 635 P.2d 441, 444 (1981), *amended*, 649 P.2d 827 (Wash. 1982) (describing Washington's 100-year history disfavoring punitive damages); *see also Winchester v. Stein*, 135 Wash. 2d 835, 858, 959 P.2d 1077, 1088 (1998) ("Punitive damages allowed only when expressly authorized by Legislature"); *Dailey v. N. Coast Life Ins. Co.*, 129 Wash. 2d 572, 574, 919 P.2d 589, 590 (1996) (en banc) (reiterating policy against punitives).

95. *See Sofie v. Fibreboard Corp.*, 112 Wash. 2d 636, 665-66, 771 P.2d 711, 726 (en banc), *amended*, 780 P.2d 260 (Wash. 1989). Note that neither the WPLA nor

Washington common law provides for recovery of attorneys' fees in product liability cases.

96. *Mahler v. Szucs*, 135 Wash. 2d 398, 429, 957 P.2d 632, 649, *amended*, 966 P.2d 305 (Wash. 1998); *see also Hansen v. Rothaus*, 107 Wash. 2d 468, 472-75, 730 P.2d 662, 664-66 (1986) (stating and applying pre-judgment interest rule).

97. *Hansen*, 107 Wash. 2d at 472-75, 730 P.2d at 664-66.

98. *See Hansen*, 107 Wash. 2d at 473, 730 P.2d at 665 ("[P]laintiff should be compensated for the 'use value' of the money representing [the] damages for the period of time from [the] loss to the date of judgment").

99. Wash. Rev. Code § 4.56.110(3)(b). However, "in any case where a judgment entered on a verdict is wholly or partly affirmed on review, interest on the judgment or on that portion of the judgment affirmed shall date back to and shall accrue from the date the verdict was rendered." Wash. Rev. Code § 4.56.110(3)(b); *see also Rufer v. Abbott Labs.*, 154 Wash. 2d 530, 552, 114 P.3d 1182, 1193-94 (2005) (reversing lower court decision relieving defendant from post-judgment interest obligation accrued during appeal delay; explaining that the post-judgment interest statute provides "no exception for delays, unreasonable or otherwise").

100. Wash. Rev. Code § 4.56.110(3)(b).

101. Wash. Rev. Code §§ 51.04.010, .32.010.

102. *Birklid v. Boeing Co.*, 127 Wash. 2d 853, 865, 904 P.2d 278, 285 (1995); *see also Vallandigham v. Clover Park Sch. Dist. No. 400*, 154 Wash. 2d 16, 35, 109 P.3d 805, 815 (2005) (holding employees' claims barred even though they were injured numerous times by disabled student because the student's behavior was too unpredictable for knowledge of injury to be certain); *Brame v. W. State Hosp.*, 136 Wash. App. 740, 749-51, 150 P.3d 637, 642 (2007) (holding employer immune where risk of harm "far from predictable" and employer took to steps to alleviate risk); *French v. Uribe*, 132 Wash. App. 1, 11-12, 130 P.3d 370, 374-75 (2006) (stating that "a showing of a pattern of injuries is required . . . to establish actual knowledge that injury is certain to occur" and that "mere presence of a dangerous situation is not sufficient to establish deliberate intent"); *Crow v. Boeing Co.*, 129 Wash. App. 318, 329, 118 P.3d 894, 900 (2005) (holding that "a prior complaint [of injury] does not meet the actual knowledge of certain injury requirement of the *Birklid* test"); *Shellenbarger v. Longview Fibre Co.*, 125 Wash. App. 41, 49, 103 P.3d 807, 811-12 (2004) (holding that employee's asbestos exposure claim was barred under the Industrial Insurance Act).

103. Wash. Rev. Code § 51.24.020.

104. *Folsom v. Burger King*, 135 Wash. 2d 658, 668, 958 P.2d 301, 307 (1998) (quoting 2A Arthur Larson, *The Law of Workmen's Compensation* § 72.81 (1984)). Note, however, that the Washington Supreme Court rejected the "dual capacity" doctrine, *see Spencer v. City of Seattle*, 104 Wash. 2d 30, 32-34, 700 P.2d 742, 743 (1985) (en banc), under which "an employer who normally enjoys immunity from common-law and statutory liability under the exclusive remedy provision of workers' compensation law may become liable to an employee when acting in a capacity outside the employer-employee relationship, which capacity may impose obligations apart from those imposed as an employer." *Corr v. Willamette Indus., Inc.*, 105 Wash. 2d 217, 219-20, 713 P.2d 92, 94 (1986) (quoting R. Carol Terry, Annotation, *Workmen's Compensation Act as Furnishing Exclusive Remedy for Employee Injured by Product Manufactured, Sold, or Distributed by Employer*, 9 A.L.R.4th 873, 875 n.2 (1981)).

105. *Brown v. Prime Constr. Co.*, 102 Wash. 2d 235, 239-40, 684 P.2d 73, 75 (1984) (en banc); *accord Waters v. Puget Sound Power & Light Co.*, 83 Wash. App. 407, 408-09, 924 P.2d 925, 926 (1996).

106. Wash. Rev. Code § 7.72.060.

107. Wash. Rev. Code §§ 19.86.010-.920.

108. Wash. Rev. Code §§ 62A.1-101 to .11-113.

109. Wash. Rev. Code §§ 4.22.005-.925.

110. Wash. Rev. Code § 4.16.190.

111. Wash. Rev. Code § 4.16.190.

112. Wash. Rev. Code § 4.22.070. An exception to the general rule of several liability only, Washington Revised Code § 4.22.070(1)(a) provides that "[a] party shall be responsible for the fault of another person or for payment of the proportionate share of another party where both were acting in concert or when a person was acting as an agent or servant of the party."

113. Wash. Rev. Code § 4.22.070(1)(b); *see Washburn v. Beatt Equip. Co.*, 120 Wash. 2d 246, 293-99, 840 P.2d 860, 886-89 (1992) (stating that from the statute "[i]t is clear that several liability is now intended to be the general rule").

114. *Washburn*, 120 Wash. 2d at 296-97, 840 P.2d at 887-88; *see also Washburn*, 120 Wash. 2d at 294, 840 P.2d at 886 ("*only* defendants against whom judgment is entered are jointly and severally liable and only for the sum of *their* proportionate shares of the total damages") (emphasis in original); *Kottler v. State*, 136 Wash. 2d 437, 446, 963 P.2d 834, 840 (1998) (same).

115. Wash. Rev. Code § 4.22.040(1).

116. *Kottler*, 136 Wash. 2d at 448, 963 P.2d at 840.

117. *Gerrard v. Craig*, 122 Wash. 2d 288, 298, 857 P.2d 1033, 1038-39 (1993). Gerrard does not explicitly overrule a prior Washington Supreme Court decision, *Smith v. Jackson*, 106 Wash. 2d 298, 721 P.2d 508 (1986) (en banc), but there is tension between the two cases. In *Smith*, the named defendant was allowed to bring a contribution action against certain third parties even though the statute of limitation would have precluded a direct action between the plaintiff and the third parties. *Smith*, 106 Wash. 2d at 304, 721 P.2d at 511. *Gerrard*, following *Washburn*, 120 Wash. 2d at 294, 840 P.2d at 886-87, holds that "only those defendants against whom a claimant has obtained a judgment can be jointly and severally liable" and thus susceptible to a contribution action. *Gerrard*, 122 Wash. 2d at 298, 857 P.2d at 1039; *see also* Wash. Rev. Code § 4.22.070(1).

118. Wash. Rev. Code § 4.22.070(1); *see also* Wash. Rev. Code § 4.22.060; *Schmidt v. Cornerstone Invs., Inc.*, 115 Wash. 2d 148, 157-59, 795 P.2d 1143, 1147 (1990) (recovery reduced by amount paid in settlement or reasonable amount). A decision offsetting an amount paid rather than the much higher reasonable settlement amount is of interest in the structured settlement context. *See Brewer v. Fibreboard Corp.*, 127 Wash. 2d 512, 532, 901 P.2d 297, 307-08 (1995).

119. Wash. Rev. Code § 4.22.015.

120. *Hiner v. Bridgestone/Firestone, Inc.*, 138 Wash. 2d 248, 260, 978 P.2d 505, 511 (1999).

121. *Welch v. Southland Corp.*, 134 Wash. 2d 629, 634-37, 952 P.2d 162, 165-66 (1998).

122. *See Rice*, 124 Wash. 2d at 213, 875 P.2d at 1217; *Barr*, 96 Wash. 2d at 697, 635 P.2d at 443; *Johnson v. Spider Staging Corp.*, 87 Wash. 2d 577, 580, 555 P.2d 997, 1000 (1976).

WEST VIRGINIA

A. CAUSES OF ACTION

Under West Virginia law, product liability lawsuits commonly include causes of action for strict liability, negligence, breach of warranty, and medical monitoring.

B. STATUTES OF LIMITATION

A cause of action for personal injury or personal property damages must be filed within two years, whether brought in negligence, strict liability, breach of warranty, or seeking medical monitoring damages.[1] West Virginia has adopted a discovery rule that is applicable in products liability cases, tolling the statute of limitations "until the individual discovers or could have discovered the alleged defect with reasonable diligence."[2] Under West Virginia law, "[a] five-step analysis should be applied to determine whether a cause of action is time-barred. First, the court should identify the applicable statute of limitation for each cause of action."[3] "Second, the court (or, if questions of material fact exist, the jury) should identify when the requisite elements of the cause of action occurred."[4] "Third, the discovery rule should be applied to determine when the statute of limitation began to run by determining when the plaintiff knew, or by the exercise of reasonable diligence should have known, of the elements of a possible cause of action. . . ."[5,6,7] "Fourth, if the plaintiff is not entitled to the benefit of the discovery rule, then determine whether the defendant fraudulently concealed facts that prevented the plaintiff from discovering or pursuing the cause of action. Whenever a plaintiff is able to show that the defendant fraudulently concealed facts which prevented the plaintiff from discovering or pursuing the potential cause of action, the statute of limitation is tolled."[8] For the fifth and final element of this analysis, "the court or the jury should determine if the statute of limitation period was arrested by some other tolling doctrine. Only the first step is purely a question of law; the resolution of steps two through five will generally involve questions of material fact that will need to be resolved by the trier of fact."[9]

A cause of action for economic or contractual damages resulting from a breach of warranty must be filed within four years, but by original agreement the parties may reduce the filing deadline to not less than one year; however, the parties may not extend it.[10] A cause of action for breach of warranty accrues when the breach occurs, regardless of the aggrieved party's lack of knowledge of the breach.[11] A breach of warranty occurs when tender of delivery is made; however, where a warranty explicitly extends to future performance of the goods and discovery of the breach must await the time of such performance, the cause of action accrues when the breach is or should have been discovered.[12]

The above statutes of limitations may be extended under West Virginia's general savings statute,[13] which tolls the statute of limitations for those who are under the age of majority[14] or mentally incapacitated; once the impediment is removed, the cause of action may be filed within the like number of years as is allowed to a person having no such impediment, but "in no case shall such action be brought after twenty years from the time that the right accrues." Additionally, the above statutes of limitations may be extended under another savings statute, which provides in part that a timely filed action that is involuntarily dismissed for reasons other than on the merits, may be refiled within one year of the dismissal, even if such filing is beyond the otherwise applicable limitations period.[15]

When a claim's characterization as a tort or contract is ambiguous, "a complaint that could be construed as being either in tort or on contract will be presumed to be on contract whenever the action would be barred by the statute of limitation if construed as being in tort."[16]

C. STRICT LIABILITY

1. The Standard

West Virginia has not adopted Section 402A of the Restatement (Second) of Torts and thus does not require that the defective condition be "unreasonably dangerous."[17] Nonetheless, the general test for establishing strict liability in tort in West Virginia is "not substantially different" from 402A.[18] The plaintiff must prove that "a product was defective when it left the manufacturer and the defective product was the proximate cause of the plaintiff's injuries."[19] The involved product is "defective" in the sense that it is not reasonably safe for its intended use as determined by what a reasonably prudent manufacturer's standards should have been at the time the product was made.[20]

A product defect may be inferred where there is sufficient evidence for a jury to conclude that the accident would not have occurred unless the product was defective.[21] In most instances, a plaintiff produces direct evidence of a product's defective condition. Nevertheless, in some instances, a plaintiff may not be able to prove the precise nature of the defect. In that case, a plaintiff may rely on the "malfunction" theory of product liability.[22] The malfunction theory is nothing more than circumstantial evidence of product malfunction that permits a plaintiff to prove a product defect with "evidence of a malfunction and with evidence eliminating abnormal or reasonable, secondary causes for the malfunction," thereby relieving a plaintiff from demonstrating the precise defect while still permitting the trier-of-fact to infer the defect from evidence of the malfunction, absence of abnormal use, and absence of reasonable, secondary causes.[23]

The theory of strict liability in tort does not apply to an independent contractor who assembles a product unless it can be shown that the condition complained of was so obvious and egregious that no reasonably competent assembler would have left the product in that condition.[24]

Strict liability in tort may be used to recover for property damage when the defective product damages property only.[25] Property damage to defective products that results from a sudden calamitous event, such as a fire, is recoverable under a strict liability cause of action.[26] Damages that result merely because of a "bad bargain," such as deterioration, internal breakage, or depreciation are outside the scope of strict liability.[27] In addition, the theory of strict liability cannot be used to recover loss of profits. That type of damages must be pursued under a warranty or contract theory.[28]

2. "Defect"

The product is to be tested by what a reasonably prudent manufacturer would accomplish with regard to the safety of the product, having in mind the general state of the art of the manufacturing process, including design,[29] labels, and warnings, as it relates to economic costs, at the time the product was made.[30]

Direct evidence of a defect is not required. Circumstantial evidence may be sufficient to make a *prima facie* case in a strict liability action, provided the evidence shows that a malfunction in the product occurred that would not ordinarily happen in the absence of a defect. In addition, the plaintiff must show that there was neither abnormal use nor a reasonable secondary cause for the malfunction.[31]

3. Contributory Negligence/Assumption of Risk

The defense of comparative negligence is available against the plaintiff in a product liability action, but the plaintiff's negligence must be something more than failing to discover a defect or to guard against it.[32] The defense of comparative assumption of the risk is available against the plaintiff in a product liability action when it is shown that, with full appreciation of the defective condition (actual knowledge on the part of the plaintiff), the plaintiff continued to use the product.[33]

4. Sale

The seller of a product may be entitled to implied indemnity from the manufacturer, but the party seeking implied indemnity must be without fault.[34] Settlement bars any action for contribution by the non-settling party, but settlement does not bar implied indemnity actions when liability is not predicated on independent fault or negligence of the non-settling party, but on a theory of strict liability.[35]

5. Inherently Dangerous Products

West Virginia has declined to adopt the doctrine of *Rylands v. Fletcher* into its tort product liability law.[36]

6. **Privity**

   Privity is not required. A plaintiff may sue even though the plaintiff did not buy the product from the manufacturer.[37] The plaintiff must, however, show that the defendant manufactured, distributed, or sold the product that injured her.[38]

7. **Failure to Warn**

   In failure-to-warn cases, "the focus is not so much on a flawed physical condition of the product, as on its unsafeness arising out of the failure to adequately label, instruct, or warn."[39] The elements of a failure-to-warn claim are: (1) use of the product must be foreseeable, (2) the product was defective due to a failure to warn, and (3) the failure to warn proximately caused the injury.[40] The duty to warn exists when the use made of the product is foreseeable to the manufacturer or seller.[41] The basic inquiry in this regard is whether it was "reasonably foreseeable to the manufacturer that the product would be unreasonably dangerous if distributed without a warning."[42] "Product unsafeness arising from failure to warn 'is to be tested by what the reasonably prudent manufacturer would accomplish in regard to the safety of the product, having in mind the general state of the art of the manufacturing process, including design, labels and warnings, as it relates to the economic costs, at the time the product was made.' "[43]

   The Supreme Court of Appeals specifically holds that West Virginia products liability law requires that manufacturers of prescription drugs be subject to the same duty to warn consumers about the risks of their products as other manufacturers.[44] The court declined to adopt the learned intermediary exception to that general rule.[45]

8. **Post-Sale Duty to Warn and Remedial Measures**

   The Supreme Court of Appeals has indicated, in dicta, that while there is no strict liability post-sale duty to warn (because product unsafeness, arising from failure to warn, is to be tested, for purposes of strict liability, by what a reasonably prudent manufacturer would have done at the time the product was made) there may be a post-sale duty to warn under a negligence theory.[46]

9. **Substantial Change/Abnormal Use**

   The defense of abnormal use is available against the plaintiff in a product liability action.[47] Plaintiff must show that there was neither "abnormal use nor a reasonable secondary cause for the malfunction."[48]

10. **State of the Art**

    "State-of-the-art" evidence is admissible.[49]

11. Standards and Government Regulations

Although there is a "general bias" against preemption of state common law causes of action in West Virginia, federal regulations may explicitly or implicitly preempt such actions.[50]

Failure to comply with a statute or regulation constitutes *prima facie* negligence if an injury proximately results from the noncompliance and is of the type the statute or regulation was intended to prevent. Conversely, compliance with the appropriate statute or regulation may serve as competent evidence of due care, but it does not constitute due care *per se*, nor does it create a presumption of due care.[51]

A statute or regulation sets a floor for due care, but greater care may be required where the risk is known or should have been known even when that risk was not contemplated by the regulation.[52]

12. Unavoidably Unsafe Products

Comment k to Section 402A, which defines an exception to the doctrine of strict liability for "unavoidably unsafe" products, has not been explicitly adopted by the Supreme Court of Appeals of West Virginia. However, a federal district court sitting in West Virginia has predicted that "[i]t seems likely . . . the West Virginia courts would also apply the comment k exception where a product is proven to be unavoidably unsafe."[53]

13. Crashworthiness

West Virginia has adopted the "crashworthiness" theory.[54] To recover on a theory of crashworthiness against the manufacturer of a motor vehicle, the plaintiff only has to show that a defect in the vehicle's design was "a factor in causing some aspect of the plaintiff's harm."[55]

The manufacturer may then limit its liability by showing that the plaintiff's "injuries are capable of apportionment between the first and second collisions."[56] In wrongful death crashworthiness causes of action, a defendant manufacturer, seeking to apportion liability for the indivisible injury of death, must prove, by a preponderance of the evidence, that the defective product was not a factor in causing the decedent's death.[57] Absent such a showing, the defendant manufacturer is jointly and severally liable for all of the harm.[58] The issue of whether the death can be apportioned among multiple collisions is a question of law to be decided by the trial judge.[59] If the trial judge concludes the fatal injury can be apportioned, the jury may then determine the apportionment of the defendant's liability and the consequent damages for which it is liable.[60]

In a crashworthiness or enhanced injury case involving a motor vehicle, the express provisions of West Virginia Code § 17C-15-49(d) limit the introduction of evidence of safety belt use in any civil action or proceeding for damages when, upon motion of the defendant, the trial court determines that failure to wear a safety belt was a proximate cause of the injuries sustained, and the trier of fact determines through use of a special interrogatory that (1) the injured party failed to wear a safety belt and (2) such omission constituted a failure to mitigate damages. Upon such findings, the trier of fact may reduce the injured party's recovery for medical damages in an amount not to exceed five percent. The statute further provides that introduction of safety belt use evidence is precluded when an injured party stipulates to a five percent reduction of medical damages. *Estep v. Mike Ferrell Ford Lincoln-Mercury, Inc.*, 672 S.E.2d 345, 353-54 (W. Va. 2008).

14. Destruction or Loss of Product

West Virginia recognizes intentional spoliation of evidence as a stand-alone tort when the spoliation is the result of the negligence of a third party who has a special duty to preserve the evidence, or when done by either a party to a civil action or a third party.[61] The tort consists of the following elements:

> (1) a pending or potential civil action; (2) knowledge of the spoliator of the pending or potential civil action; (3) willful destruction of evidence; (4) the spoliated evidence was vital to a party's ability to prevail in the pending or potential civil action; (5) the intent of the spoliator to defeat a party's ability to prevail in the pending or potential civil action; (6) the party's inability to prevail in the civil action; and (7) damages.[62]

The West Virginia Supreme Court has opined that the key factor in the spoliation test is the intent to defeat a person's ability to prevail in a civil action, so there must be evidence of the specific intent of the spoliator.[63] Also, such argument must be made in a timely manner.[64]

D. NEGLIGENCE

Unlike strict liability, there are few unique aspects of West Virginia product liability cases based on negligence.

1. Comparative Negligence

West Virginia has adopted the doctrine of comparative negligence. Under the West Virginia approach, which is known as modified comparative negligence, if the negligence of the plaintiff equals or exceeds the combined negligence of *all* of the parties involved in the accident, and not just the alleged negligence or fault of the defendant, the plaintiff is barred from recovery.[65]

2. Comparative Assumption of Risk

West Virginia has also adopted the doctrine of comparative assumption of the risk. Under that doctrine, a plaintiff is not barred from recovery by the doctrine of assumption of risk unless his degree of fault arising therefrom equals or exceeds the combined fault or negligence of the other parties to the accident.[66]

3. **Reasonable Care**

The duty of reasonable care owed by the assembler of a product is to recognize an unreasonable risk of harm to those who use the product as assembled unless the assembler "has a specialized skill or competence, or has represented that he has such a skill, to modify the product to enhance its safety."[67]

E. **BREACH OF WARRANTY**

In years past, there has been no requirement of privity of contract to maintain an action for breach of an express or implied warranty in West Virginia.[68] However, *Affholder Inc. v. N. Am. Drillers, Inc.* questions the strength of that declaration and indicates that the court may be retreating from the rule.[69] It appears that the court may, instead, begin to require privity of contract in cases where there is only economic injury.[70]

Lack of notice of the breach is not a defense in a product liability action for personal injuries.[71]

F. **MEDICAL MONITORING**

Under West Virginia law, a plaintiff may maintain a cause of action "for the recovery of medical monitoring costs, where it can be proven that such expenses are necessary and reasonably certain to be incurred as a proximate result of a defendant's tortious conduct."[72] The elements for this cause of action are as follows: "(1) [the plaintiff] has been significantly exposed; (2) to a proven hazardous substance; (3) through the tortious conduct of the defendant; (4) as a proximate result of the exposure, plaintiff has suffered an increased risk of contracting a serious latent disease relative to the general population; (5) the increased risk of disease makes it reasonably necessary for the plaintiff to undergo periodic diagnostic medical examinations different from what would be prescribed in the absence of the exposure; and (6) monitoring procedures exist that make the early detection of a disease possible."[73]

G. **PUNITIVE DAMAGES**

Punitive damages are recoverable in product liability actions.[74] Under West Virginia law, with respect to punitive damages, "there must be: (1) a reasonable constraint on jury discretion; (2) a meaningful and adequate review by the trial court using well-established principles; and (3) a meaningful and adequate appellate review, which may occur when an application is made for an appeal."[75] A jury may award punitive or exemplary damages against a defendant to punish willful, wanton, or malicious behavior toward a plaintiff.[76] When instructing a jury on punitive damages, West Virginia trial courts must explain the following factors:

(1) "Punitive damages should bear a reasonable relationship to the harm that is likely to occur from the defendant's conduct as well as to the harm that actually has occurred. If the defendant's actions caused or

would likely cause in a similar situation only slight harm, the damages should be relatively small. If the harm is grievous, the damages should be greater.

(2) The jury may consider (although the court need not specifically instruct on each element if doing so would be unfairly prejudicial to the defendant), the reprehensibility of the defendant's conduct. The jury should take into account how long the defendant continued in his actions, whether he was aware his actions were causing or were likely to cause harm, whether he attempted to conceal or cover up his actions or the harm caused by them, whether/how often the defendant engaged in similar conduct in the past, and whether the defendant made reasonable efforts to make amends by offering a fair and prompt settlement for the actual harm caused once his liability became clear to him.

(3) If the defendant profited from his wrongful conduct, the punitive damages should remove the profit and should be in excess of the profit, so that the award discourages future bad acts by the defendant.

(4) As a matter of fundamental fairness, punitive damages should bear a reasonable relationship to compensatory damages.

(5) The financial position of the defendant is relevant."[77]

If a jury awards punitive damages, the trial court must then review such award and should consider the following additional factors:

(1) "The costs of the litigation;

(2) Any criminal sanctions imposed on the defendant for his conduct;

(3) Any other civil actions against the same defendant, based on the same conduct; and

(4) The appropriateness of punitive damages to encourage fair and reasonable settlements when a clear wrong has been committed. A factor that may justify punitive damages is the cost of litigation to the plaintiff."[78]

Finally, "[u]pon petition, [the Supreme Court of Appeals of West Virginia] will review all punitive damages awards."[79,80]

H. PRE- AND POST-JUDGMENT INTEREST

Except where otherwise noted, every judgment or decree in West Virginia shall bear interest from the date thereof. Special or liquidated damages shall bear interest from the date the right to bring the action arose.[81]

I. EMPLOYER IMMUNITY FROM SUIT

In *Belcher v. J.H. Fletcher & Co.*,[82] the court held that a manufacturer of an allegedly defective product was barred from recovery against a deceased miner's employer by the immunity provisions of the West Virginia Worker's Compensation Act.

However, in *Sydenstricker v. Unipunch Products, Inc.*,[83] the court ruled an employer under the West Virginia Worker's Compensation Act may be held liable as a third-party defendant to such defendant manufacturers as third party plaintiffs, upon the theory of contribution and/or implied indemnity based upon allegations in the third party complaint that such employer was guilty of willful, wanton, and reckless misconduct or an intentional tort toward the plaintiff employee resulting in the plaintiff employee's personal injuries.

J. HEALTH CARE RELATED PRODUCT LIABILITY SUIT REQUIREMENTS

The Supreme Court of Appeals holds that the West Virginia Medical Professional Liability Act (MPLA) applies to any liability for damages based on health care services rendered.[84] The fact that patients' claims may be labeled as "products" liability claims does not change the basis for the tort action.[85] Accordingly, any product liability action relating to health care services rendered must be asserted under the MPLA and in conformity with its requirements.[86]

K. SUCCESSOR LIABILITY

The West Virginia Supreme Court of Appeals has concluded that a successor corporation can be held liable for the debts and obligations of a predecessor corporation if there was an express or implied assumption of liability, if the transaction was fraudulent, or if some element of the transaction was not made in good faith.[87] Such liability may also be imposed if the successor corporation is a mere continuation or reincarnation of its predecessor.[88] Additionally, liability will attach, statutorily, in the case of a consolidation or merger. Finally, a successor corporation may be found liable for punitive damages for liabilities incurred by its predecessor if the successor acquires or merges with a company manufacturing a product that is known to create serious health hazards, and the successor corporation continues to produce the same product in the same manner.[89]

L. STATUTES, INCLUDING APPLICABLE "TORT REFORM" STATUTES

Relevant statutes for product liability actions are the statutes of limitation, the lemon law, which establishes a manufacturer's duty to repair or replace a new motor vehicle,[90] and, when a breach of warranty is alleged, the commercial code sections.

Under West Virginia's Governmental Tort Claims and Insurance Reform Act,[91] a political subdivision is immune from liability if a loss or claim results from "any claim or action based on the theory of manufacturer West Virginia's products liability or breach of warranty or merchantability or fitness for a specific purpose, either express or implied."[92]

M. JOINT AND SEVERAL LIABILITY

When the concurrent negligence of two or more persons combined results in an injury to a third person, recovery may be had as to either one or all such wrongdoers. Each joint tortfeasor is liable for the entire damages without regard to the comparative degrees of negligence, though only one recovery may be had.[93]

When a plaintiff elects to sue fewer than all of the joint tortfeasors, the named defendants have the right to bring in the other joint tortfeasors based on a right of inchoate contribution.[94] The defendant's right of contribution against a joint tortfeasor "is derivative in the sense that it may be brought by a joint tortfeasor on any theory of liability that could have been asserted by the injured plaintiff."[95]

N. EFFECT OF SETTLEMENT ON CONTRIBUTION

A party in a civil action who has made a good faith settlement with the plaintiff prior to a judicial determination of liability is relieved from any liability for contribution.[96]

However, the defendants in a civil action against whom the verdict is rendered are entitled to have the verdict reduced by the amount of any good faith settlements previously made by plaintiffs with other jointly liable parties.[97]

Settlements are presumptively made in good faith, and a defendant seeking to establish that the settlement made by the plaintiff and joint tortfeasor lacks good faith has the burden of doing so by clear and convincing evidence.[98]

O. EXPERT WITNESSES

Fact evidence outside the knowledge and experience of the average person generally must be established by expert witness testimony.[99]

West Virginia has adopted the *Daubert* test for admission of expert scientific testimony.[100] The West Virginia Supreme Court of Appeals specifically declined to adopt the United States Supreme Court's analysis in *Kumho Tire Company, Ltd. v. Carmichael*,[101] wherein the Supreme Court held that a trial court's obligation under *Daubert*, to ensure that expert testimony is both relevant and reliable, extends to all expert testimony.[102] This issue was addressed again in a later case, and although the majority declined to express whether the *Kumho* analysis would be adopted, Justice Davis wrote that, "the author of this opinion, separate from the majority, does not believe that *Kumho* would be the death knell of the admission of non-scientific expert testimony."[103] Currently, under West Virginia law, in cases of nonscientific expert testimony, "[t]he question is not one for analysis under peer review, rate of error and publication and general acceptance but whether, based upon the witnesses's experience, his opinion will assist the trier of fact."[104]

The determination of who is an expert is a two-step inquiry. First, the court must determine whether the proposed expert (a) meets the minimal educational or experiential qualifications; (b) in a field relevant to the subject at issue; (c) which will assist the trier of fact. Second, the court must determine whether the expert's area of expertise covers the particular opinion as to which the expert seeks to testify.[105] The West Virginia Supreme Court of

Appeals has endorsed a very liberal stance in determining who is an expert, "reject[ing] any notion of imposing overly rigorous requirements of expertise"[106] and stating that "a broad range of knowledge, skills, and training qualify an expert as such[.]"[107] Further, according to the Court, West Virginia Rule of Evidence 702 "cannot be interpreted to require . . . that the experience, education, or training of the individual be in complete congruence with the nature of the issue sought to be proven."[108] Finally:

> In deciding the "reliability" prong of admissibility the focus of the trial court's inquiry is limited to determining whether the expert employed a methodology that is recognized in the scientific community for rendering an opinion on the subject under consideration. If the methodology is recognized in the scientific community, the court should then determine whether the expert correctly applied the methodology to render his or her opinion. If these two factors are satisfied, and the testimony has been found to be relevant, and the expert is qualified, the expert may testify at trial.[109]

P. VENUE

Plaintiffs are not required to establish venue for each named defendant in a products liability action.[110] Although a plaintiff's preference of West Virginia as a forum is entitled to "great deference," "this preference may be diminished when the plaintiff is a nonresident and the cause of action did not arise in this State."[111] However, products liability suits typically allege that a manufacturer put a product into the stream of commerce and that the product was unsafe or flawed so as to give rise to liability for resulting injuries. By putting a product into the stream of interstate commerce, manufacturers should expect that they may be liable for products in other states "even though no 'culpable' conduct by the manufacturer relating to the design or manufacture of the product occurred in the jurisdiction in which the claim against the manufacturer is brought."[112] A second fundamental venue principle in products liability cases is the "venue giving defendant principle whereby once venue is proper for one defendant, it is proper for all other defendants subject to process."[113]

J. David Bolen
Alexis B. Mattingly
Huddleston Bolen, LLP
611 Third Avenue
P.O. Box 2185
Huntington, West Virginia 25722-2185
(304) 529-6181
(Fax) (304) 522-4312

ENDNOTES - WEST VIRGINIA

1. W. Va. Code § 55-2-12 (2013); *Taylor v. Ford Motor Corp.*, 408 S.E.2d 270, 274 (W. Va. 1991).

2. *Beattie v. Skyline Corp.*, 906 F. Supp. 2d 528, 540 (S.D. W. Va. 2012) (applying West Virginia law).

3. As noted above, for causes of action alleging personal injury or tortious injury to personal property, whether founded in negligence, strict liability, or breach of warranty, the applicable statute of limitation is two years. *See* note 1, *supra. Dunn v. Rockwell*, 689 S.E.2d 255, at Syl. Pt. 5 (W. Va. 2009).

4. *Dunn*, 689 S.E.2d 255 at Syl. Pt. 5.

5. Specifically, a cause of action in negligence, strict liability, or breach of warranty accrues when the plaintiff knows, or by the exercise of reasonable diligence should know (1) that there has been an injury, (2) the identity of the maker of the product, and (3) that the product had a causal relation to the injury, which is a question of fact. *See Rucker v. Deere & Co. (In re Hearing Losses I)*, 539 S.E.2d 112 (W. Va. 2000); *Cecil v. Airco, Inc.*, 416 S.E.2d 728, 730-31 (W. Va. 1992); *Taylor*, 408 S.E.2d at 274; *Hickman v. Grover*, 358 S.E.2d 810, 813 (W. Va. 1987); *Goodwin v. Bayer Corp.; et al.*, 624 S.E.2d 562 (W. Va. 2005).

6. "A medical monitoring cause of action accrues when a plaintiff knows, or by the exercise of reasonable diligence should know, that he or she has a significantly increased risk of contracting a particular disease due to significant exposure to a proven hazardous substance and the identity of the party that caused or contributed to the plaintiff's exposure to the hazardous substance." *State ex rel. Chemtall, Inc. v. Madden*, 607 S.E.2d 772 at Pt. 10 (W. Va. 2004).

7. *Madden*, 607 S.E.2d 772 at Syl. Pt. 10.

8. *Madden*, 607 S.E.2d 772 at Syl. Pt. 10.

9. *Madden*, 607 S.E.2d 772 at Syl. Pt. 10.

10. W. Va. Code § 46-2-725(1) (2013).

11. W. Va. Code § 46-2-725(2) (2013); *see Roxalana Hills, Ltd. v. Masonite Corp.*, 627 F. Supp. 1194, 1199-1201 (S.D. W. Va. 1986), *aff'd*, 813 F.2d 1228 (4th Cir. 1987); *Basham v. Gen. Shale*, 377 S.E.2d 830, 835 (W. Va. 1988).

12. W. Va. Code § 46-2-725(2) (2013); *Roxalana Hills, Ltd.*, 627 F. Supp. at 1199; *Basham*, 377 S.E.2d at 835.

13. *See* W. Va. Code § 55-2-15 (2013); *Whitlow v. Board of Educ.*, 438 S.E.2d 15 (W. Va. 1993).

14. The age of majority in West Virginia is 18. *See* W. Va. Code § 2-3-1 (2013).

15. W. Va. Code § 55-2-18 (2013).

16. *Smith v. Stacy*, 482 S.E.2d 115, 120 (1996) (*quoting* Syl. Pt. 1, *Cochran v. Appalachian Power Co.*, 246 S.E.2d 624 (1978)); *see also Beattie v. Skyline Corp.*, 906 F. Supp. 2d 528, 539 (S.D. W. Va. 2012) (applying West Virginia law).

17. *Morningstar v. Black & Decker Mfg. Co.*, 253 S.E.2d 666, 684 (W. Va. 1979).

18. *Morningstar*, 253 S.E.2d 680 at Syl. Pt. 4.

19. *Dunn v. Kanawha Cnty. Bd. of Educ.*, 459 S.E.2d 151, 157 (1995) (citing *Morningstar v. Black & Decker Mfg. Co.*, 253 S.E.2d 666, 677 (1979)).

20. *Beatty v. Ford Motor Co.*, 574 S.E.2d 803 at Syl. Pt. 2 (W. Va. 2002) (quoting *Morningstar*, 253 S.E.2d 666 at Syl. Pt. 4); *Adkins v. K-Mart Corp.*, 511 S.E.2d 840 at Syl. Pt. 8 (W. Va. 1998); *see also Estep v. Mike Ferrell Ford Lincoln-Mercury, Inc.*, 672 S.E.2d 345, 355 (W. Va. 2008).

21. *Bennett v. ASCO Servs., Inc.*, 621 S.E.2d 710, 717 (W. Va. 2005); *see also Cmty. Antenna Serv., Inc. v. Charter Commc'ns VI, LLC*, 712 S.E.2d 504, 516-17 (W. Va. 2011) (holding that "[t]he defect need not be the only cause of the incident; if the plaintiff can prove that the most likely explanation of the harm involves the causal contribution of a product defect, the fact that there may be other concurrent causes of the harm does not preclude liability.").

22. *Bennett*, 621 S.E.2d at 717.

23. *Bennett*, 621 S.E.2d at 717.

24. *Yost v. Fuscaldo*, 408 S.E.2d 72, 77 (W. Va. 1991).

25. *Star Furniture Co. v. Pulaski Furniture Co.*, 297 S.E.2d 854, 857 (W. Va. 1982); *Basham*, 377 S.E.2d at 834.

26. *Star Furniture Co.*, 297 S.E.2d at 857; *Basham*, 377 S.E.2d at 834.

27. *Roxalana Hills, Ltd.*, 627 F. Supp. at 1195-99; *Taylor*, 408 S.E.2d at 273; *Basham*, 377 S.E.2d at 834; *Star Furniture Co.*, 297 S.E.2d at 859.

28. *Star Furniture Co.*, 297 S.E.2d at 859-60.

29. West Virginia's highest court has not addressed the issue of "whether a design defect claim requires proof of a safer alternative design of the allegedly defective product." *Hines v. Wyeth Pharms., Inc.*, 2011 U.S. Dist. LEXIS 55419, at *23 (S.D.W. Va. May 23, 2011). However, evidence of a safer alternative design may serve as evidence that the "product is 'not reasonably safe for its intended use' for the purposes of a design defect claim." *Hines*, 2011 U.S. Dist. LEXIS 55419, at *23

30. *Morningstar*, 253 S.E.2d at 682-83; *Beatty*, 574 S.E.2d at 806-07; *Bennett*, 621 S.E.2d at 717.

31. *Beatty*, 574 S.E.2d 803 at Syl. Pt. 3; *Adkins*, 511 S.E.2d 840 at Syl. Pt. 9; *Anderson v. Chrysler Corp.*, 403 S.E.2d 189, 193-94 (W. Va. 1991); *Bennett*, 621 S.E.2d at 717.

32. *Star Furniture Co.*, 297 S.E.2d at 862-63; *see also Morningstar*, 253 S.E.2d at 683.

33. *In re State Public Bldg. Asbestos Litig.*, 454 S.E.2d 413, 424 (W. Va. 1994); *King v. Kayak Mfg. Corp.*, 387 S.E.2d 511, 518 (W. Va. 1989); *see also Star Furniture Co.*, 297 S.E.2d at 863 n.5; *Morningstar*, 253 S.E.2d at 683-84.

34. *Hill v. Joseph T. Ryerson & Son, Inc.*, 268 S.E.2d 296, 301 (W. Va. 1980).

35. *Dunn v. Kanawha County Bd. of Educ.*, 459 S.E.2d 151, 156-58 (W. Va. 1995).

36. *Morningstar*, 253 S.E.2d at 684.

37. *Kaiser Aluminum & Chem. Corp. v. Westinghouse Elec. Corp.*, 981 F.2d 136, 143 (Fed. Cir. 1992); *Morningstar*, 253 S.E.2d at 680.

38. *Meade v. Parsley*, CIV. A. 2:09-CV-00388, 2009 WL 3806716 (S.D. W. Va. Nov. 13, 2009) (slip opinion) (applying West Virginia law) (rejecting the claim that a manufacturer of a brand name drug is responsible for misrepresentations when a generic manufacturer's product caused the plaintiff's injury: "a brand name manufacturer is not responsible for the damage resulting from a product that they did not manufacture, distribute or sell.").

39. *Ilosky v. Michelin Tire Corp.*, 307 S.E.2d 603, 609 (W. Va. 1983).

40. *Ilosky v. Michelin Tire Corp.*, 307 S.E.2d 603, 609 (W. Va. 1983).

41. *Ilosky*, 307 S.E.2d at 609.

42. *Church v. Wesson*, 385 S.E.2d 393, 396 (W. Va. 1989).

43. *Illosky*, 307 S.E.2d at 611 (quoting *Morningstar*, 253 S.E.2d at 682-83).

44. Syl. Pt. 3, *State ex rel. Johnson & Johnson Corp. v. Karl*, 647 S.E.2d 899, 917 (W. Va. 2007).

45. *Karl*, 647 S.E.2d at 917.

46. *See Johnson by Johnson v. Gen. Motors Corp.*, 438 S.E.2d 28, 36-40 (W. Va. 1993) (citing Robert A. Royal, *Post Sale Warnings: A Review and Analysis Seeking Fair Compensation Under Uniform Law*, 33 Drake L. Rev. 817, 831-32 (1983-84), for the proposition that "most courts have held that a seller has a post-sale duty to warn." *Johnson*, 438 S.E.2d at 37).

47. *Star Furniture Co.*, 297 S.E.2d at 862-63; *Morningstar*, 253 S.E.2d at 683.

48. *Anderson*, 403 S.E.2d at 193-94.

49. *Church*, 385 S.E.2d at 396; *Morningstar*, 253 S.E.2d at 666.

50. *See Morgan v. Ford Motor Co.*, 680 S.E.2d 77 (W. Va. 2009) (wherein the Supreme Court of Appeals of West Virginia held that a plaintiff's automobile side-window glass defect claims were implicitly preempted by the National Traffic and Motor Vehicle Safety Act, 49 U.S.C. § 30101, et seq.); *In re West Virginia Asbestos Litig.*, 592 S.E.2d 818 at Syl. Pt. 3 (W. Va. 2003) (wherein the Supreme Court of Appeals of West Virginia held that "[s]tate tort law claims against manufacturers of parts or components of railroad locomotives are preempted by federal law under the Locomotive Boiler Inspection Act."). *But see Davis v. Eagle Coal & Dock Co.*, 640 S.E.2d 81 at Syl. Pt. 2 (W. Va. 2006) (wherein the Supreme Court of Appeals of West Virginia held that "[s]tate tort law, product liability, breach of warranty, and failure to warn claims against manufacturers of roof bolter dust collection systems are not preempted by the Federal Mine Safety and Health Act."); *Harrison v. Skyline Corp.*, 686 S.E.2d 735 at Syl. Pts. 3 and 4 (W. Va. 2009) (wherein the Supreme Court of Appeals of West Virginia held that "[c]ommon law negligence claims based on formaldehyde exposure in manufactured homes which seek to establish a standard of performance not covered by the federal Manufactured Home Construction and Safety Standards Act, 42 U.S.C. §§ 5401-5426, or regulations promulgated thereunder and which pose no challenge to the federally established formaldehyde emission standards, 24 C.F.R. §§ 3280.308 and 3280.309, are not subject to preemption;" but "[a]mbient air testing for the presence of formaldehyde in wood products used in the construction of a manufactured home built in accordance with the provisions of the federal Manufactured Home Construction and Safety Standards Act, 42 U.S.C. §§ 5401-5426, is admissible as evidence in a common law negligence action seeking to establish a standard of performance not covered by the Act or associated regulations as long as the tests are not used to challenge to the formaldehyde emission levels established under the Act.").

51. *Miller v. Warren*, 390 S.E.2d 207 at Syl. Pt. 1 (W. Va. 1990); *In re Flood Litig.*, 607 S.E.2d 863, 877 (W. Va. 2004); *see also Estep v. Mike Ferrell Ford Lincoln-Mercury, Inc.*, 672 S.E.2d 345, 353-54 (W. Va. 2008) ("Pickup truck manufacture's alleged compliance with relevant motor vehicle safety standards . . . was merely a factor for jury to consider when determining the issue of product defect.").

52. *In re Flood Litig.*, 607 S.E.2d at 877 (quoting *Miller*, 390 S.E.2d at Syl. Pt. 1) (internal citations omitted).

53. Restatement (Second) of Torts § 402A, cmt. k (1965). *See Rohrbough v. Wyeth Labs., Inc.*, 719 F. Supp. 470 n.1 (N.D. W. Va. 1989), *aff'd*, 916 F.2d 970 (4th Cir. 1990) (citation omitted).

54. *Tracy v. Cottrell*, 524 S.E.2d 879 (W. Va. 1999); *Johnson by Johnson v. General Motors Corp.*, 438 S.E.2d 28, at 33 (W. Va. 1993); *Blankenship v. General Motors Corp.*, 406 S.E.2d 781, 786 (W. Va. 1991).

55. *Blankenship v. Gen. Motors Corp.*, 406 S.E.2d 781, 786. Further, "[a] complaint against the seller of a motor vehicle states a cause of action under West Virginia law if the complaint does not allege that a vehicle defect caused a collision, but alleges only that the injuries sustained by the occupant as a result of the collision were enhanced by a design defect in the vehicle." *Estep v. Mike Ferrell Ford Lincoln-Mercury, Inc.*, 672 S.E.2d 345.

56. *Blankenship v. Gen. Motors Corp.*, 406 S.E.2d 781, 786.

57. *Tracy v. Cottrell*, 524 S.E.2d 879, 897.

58. *Tracy v. Cottrell*, 524 S.E.2d 879, 897.

59. *Tracy v. Cottrell*, 524 S.E.2d 879, 897.

60. *Tracy v. Cottrell*, 524 S.E.2d 879, 897.

61. *Hannah v. Heeter*, 584 S.E.2d 560, 574 (W. Va. 2003).

62. *Hannah v. Heeter*, 584 S.E.2d 560, 573.

63. *Hannah v. Heeter*, 584 S.E.2d 560, 573.

64. *State ex rel. v. Zakaib*, 618 S.E.2d 537 (W. Va. 2006).

65. *Bowman v. Barnes*, 282 S.E.2d 613, 618 (W. Va. 1981); *Bradley v. Appalachian Power Co.*, 256 S.E.2d 879, 885 (W. Va. 1979).

66. *King v. Kayak Mfg. Corp.*, 387 S.E.2d 511, 517-18 (W. Va. 1989).

67. *Yost v. Fuscaldo*, 408 S.E.2d 72, 77 (W. Va. 1991); *Goebel v. Dean & Assocs.*, 91 F. Supp. 2d 1268 at 28-29 (N.D. Iowa 2000).

68. *Eastern Steel Constructors, Inc. v. City of Salem*, 549 S.E.2d 266 at Syl. Pt. 8 (W. Va. 2001); (Questioned. See Note 58), *Taylor v. Ford Motor Co.*, 408 S.E.2d 270, 272 (W. Va. 1991); *Sewell v. Gregory*, 371 S.E.2d 82, 86 (W. Va. 1988); see generally *Dawson v. Canteen Corp.*, 212 S.E.2d 82, 83-4 (W. Va. 1975).

69. *Affholder Inc. v. N. Am. Drillers, Inc.*, 2005 US Dist. LEXIS 44076 (S.D. W. Va. Sept. 28, 2005).

70. *Affholder Inc.*, 2005 US Dist. LEXIS 44076.

71. W. Va. Code § 46-2-607(3)(a) (2013); *Hill v. Joseph T. Ryerson & Son, Inc.*, 268 S.E.2d 296, 305 (W. Va. 1980).

72. *Bower v. Westinghouse Elec. Corp*, 522 S.E.2d 424 at Syl. Pt. 2 (W. Va. 1999).

73. *Bower*, 522 S.E.2d 424 at Syl. 3.

74. *Davis v. Celotex Corp.*, 420 S.E.2d 557 (W. Va. 1992); *Rohrbough v. Wyeth Labs., Inc.*, 719 F. Supp. 470, 479 (N.D. W. Va. 1989) (dicta), *aff'd*, 916 F.2d 970 (4th Cir. 1990). But see *Perrine v. E.I. DuPont de Nemours & Co.*, 694 S.E.2d 815 at Syl. Pt. 5 (W. Va. 2010) (wherein the Supreme Court of Appeals of West Virginia held that "[p]unitive damages may not be awarded on a cause of action for medical monitoring.").

75. *Garnes v. Fleming Landfill, Inc.*, 413 S.E.2d 897 at Syl. Pt. 2 (W. Va. 1996).

76. *Ilosky v. Michelin Tire Corp.*, 307 S.E.2d 603, 619 (W. Va. 1983).

77. *Garnes*, 413 S.E.2d 815 at Syl. Pt. 3.

78. *Garnes*, 413 S.E.2d 815 at Syl. Pt. 4.

79. *Garnes*, 413 S.E.2d 815 at Syl. Pt. 5.

80. In reviewing such reward, the Supreme Court of Appeals of West Virginia should "first determine whether the amount of the punitive damages award is justified by aggravating evidence including, but not limited to: (1) the reprehensibility of the defendant's conduct; (2) whether the defendant profited from the wrongful conduct; (3) the financial position of the defendant; (4) the appropriateness of punitive damages to encourage fair and reasonable settlements when a clear wrong has been committed; and (5) the cost of litigation to the plaintiff." *Perrine*, 694 S.E.2d 815 at Syl. Pt. 7. "The court should then consider whether a reduction in the amount of the punitive damages should be permitted due to mitigating evidence including, but not limited to: (1) whether the punitive damages bear a reasonable

relationship to the harm that is likely to occur and/or has occurred as a result of the defendant's conduct; (2) whether punitive damages bear a reasonable relationship to compensatory damages; (3) the cost of litigation to the defendant; (4) any criminal sanctions imposed on the defendant for his conduct; (5) any other civil actions against the same defendant based upon the same conduct; (6) relevant information that was not available to the jury because it was unduly prejudicial to the defendant; and (7) additional relevant evidence." *Perrine*,694 S.E.2d 815 at Syl. Pt. 7.

81. W. Va. Code § 56-6-31 (2013).

82. 498 F. Supp. 629 (S.D. W. Va. 1980).

83. 288 S.E.2d 511 (W. Va. 1982).

84. *Blankenship v. Ethicon, Inc.*, 656 S.E.2d 451 (W. Va. 2007).

85. *Blankenship*, 656 S.E.2d at 451.

86. *Blankenship*, 656 S.E.2d at 451.

87. *In re State Pub. Bldg. Asbestos Litig.*, 454 S.E.2d 413, 424-25 (W. Va. 1994); *Davis*, 420 S.E.2d at 563.

88. *Davis*, 420 S.E.2d at 563.

89. *Davis*, 420 S.E.2d 557 at Syl. Pt. 4.

90. *See generally* W. Va. Code § 46A-6A-1 *et seq.* (2013); *Bostic v. Mallard Coach Co.*, 406 S.E.2d 725 (W. Va. 1991); *Adams v. Nissan Motor Corp.*, 387 S.E.2d 288 (W. Va. 1989).

91. W. Va. Code § 29-12A-1*et seq.* (2013).

92. W. Va. Code § 29-12A-5(a)(15) (2013).

93. *Kodym v. Frazier*, 412 S.E.2d 219 (W. Va. 1991).

94. *Kodym*, 412 S.E.2d 219; *Haynes v. City of Nitro*, 240 S.E.2d 544 (1977).

95. *Landis v. Hearthmark, LLC*, 750 S.E.2d 280, 289 (W. Va. 2013). In a product liability action brought for injury to a child, the parental immunity doctrine precludes a defendant from asserting a contribution claim against the parents of the child. *Id.* Nonetheless, "defendants may put on evidence calculated to establish intervening cause or the parents' comparative negligence" and misuse by the child's parents as a defense to liability. *Landis v. Jarden Corp.*, 2:11-CV-101, 2014 WL 186632 (N.D. W. Va. Jan. 15, 2014) (applying questions certified to West Virginia Supreme Court of Appeals).

96. *Smith v. Monongahela Power Co.*, 429 S.E.2d 643, 648 (W. Va. 1993).

97. *Smith v. Monongahela Power Co.*, 429 S.E.2d 643, 648.

98. *Smith v. Monongahela Power Co.*, 429 S.E.2d 643, 651-52.

99. *Addair v. Island Creek Coal Co.*, No. 12-0708, 2013 WL 1687833 (W. Va. Apr. 17, 2013) (unpublished) (requiring expert testimony in failure-to-warn claim when plaintiffs' claims "are all complex chemical exposure cases based on occupational exposure to 'float-sink' chemicals," holding that "both the illnesses claimed and the alleged proximate causation between the alleged illness and the chemical exposure were outside of the knowledge and experience of the average person.").

100. *See Wilt v. Buracker*, 443 S.E.2d 196, 203 (W. Va. 1993).

101. 526 U.S. 137, 119 S. Ct. 1167, 143 L. Ed. 2d 238 (1999).

102. *See West Virginia Div. of Highways v. Butler*, 516 S.E.2d 769, 774 (W. Va. 1999).

103. *Watson v. INCO Alloys Int'l, Inc.*, 545 S.E.2d 294, 301 (W. Va. 2001).

104. *Gentry v. Mangum*, 466 S.E.2d 171, 186 (W. Va. 1995).

105. *Jones v. Patterson Constr., Inc.*, 524 S.E.2d 915 at Syl. Pt. 6 (W. Va. 1999).

106. *Gentry*, 466 S.E.2d at 184.

107. *Gentry*, 466 S.E.2d at 184.

108. *Cargill v. Balloon Works, Inc.*, 405 S.E.2d 642, 646-47 (W. Va. 1991).

109. *Harris v. CSX Transp., Inc.*, 753 S.E.2d 275, Syl. Pt. 2 (W. Va. 2014).

110. *Morris v. Crown Equip. Corp.*, 633 S.E.2d 292 (W. Va. 2006).

111. W. Va. Code § 56-1-1a(a) (2013).

112. *Morris v. Crown Equip. Corp.*, 633 S.E.2d 292, 301.

113. *Morris v. Crown Equip. Corp.*, 633 S.E.2d 292, 301.

WISCONSIN

A. CAUSES OF ACTION

Strict liability and negligence constitute alternative theories of recovery for Wiscosin product liability claims.[1] When a plaintiff pleads a strict liability cause of action arising out of a product defect, the plaintiff should avoid pleading a corresponding warranty claim which could be subject to dismissal.[2] Absent asserting a strict liability claim for a product failure, a warranty cause of action may be pled, although such a claim would be subject to certain contractual defenses such as notice, privity, and limitations on available recovery.[3]

B. STATUTES OF LIMITATION

Causes of action for personal injury or wrongful death must be brought within three years after the cause of action accrues.[4] Causes of action for property damage must be brought within six years after the cause of action accrues.[5] For injuries that occur to minors, a cause of action shall be brought within two years after the minor reaches the age of majority.[6] A "borrowing statute" applies the shorter of the foreign statute of limitation or the Wisconsin statute of limitation to foreign causes of action brought in Wisconsin.[7] Wisconsin's "borrowing statute" applies equally to statutes of limitation and statutes of repose.[8]

Wisconsin has a statute of repose for product liability claims. A manufacturer is not liable for damages if the defective product was manufactured 15 years or more before the claim accrues, unless the manufacturer specifically represented that the product will last for more than 15 years.[9]

A separate statute of repose applies to actions arising out of improvements to real property. A cause of action for injuries arising out of an improvement to real property must be brought within ten years of "substantial completion" of the improvement.[10] This repose period does not apply to actions for injuries caused by defective material used in the property's improvement.[11] However, it is likely, although not decided, that the material may still be subject to a 15-year statute of repose generally applicable to product liability claims. Wisconsin recognizes a "discovery" rule for tort actions.[12] Under the discovery rule, the statute of limitations does not begin to run on a plaintiff's claim until the plaintiff's injury and cause of that injury are discovered, or in the exercise of reasonable diligence should have been discovered.[13]

C. STRICT LIABILITY

1. The Standard

A manufacturer will be liable if (1) its product is defective in design or manufacture or because of inadequate warnings or instructions; (2) the defective condition rendered the product unreasonably dangerous; (3) the defect existed when the product left the manufacturer's control; (4) the product reached the user without substantial change; and (5) the defective condition was a cause of the plaintiff's damages.[14]

Wisconsin does not require a plaintiff to prove that a product manufacturer could foresee a risk of harm to prove a strict liability claim.[15] Strict liability may also extend to include injuries to bystanders as well as to users or consumers.[16]

2. **Definition of "Defect"**

A product may be defective due to a design defect or manufacturing defect, or because the product contains inadequate warnings or instructions.[17]

As defined by statute, a product is defective in design if the foreseeable risks of harm that the product poses could have been decreased or prevented if a reasonable alternative design had been used by the manufacturer, and the failure to adopt this alternative design made the product not reasonably safe.[18]

A product that contains a manufacturing defect varies from the intended design of that product line, even though all possible care was exercised during the manufacturing process of the subject product.[19]

A product is defective due to a failure to warn or instruct when the foreseeable risks of harm that the product poses could have been decreased or prevented by providing reasonable instructions or warnings, and the omission of these reasonable instructions or warnings renders the product not reasonably safe.[20]

A defective design claim cannot be maintained where the alleged defect in the product's design is the presence of one of its ingredients, and that ingredient's very presence is a characteristic of the product itself.[21] This concept has now been codified in Wisconsin, as Wisconsin's statutes require a court to dismiss a case if the injury was caused by "an inherent characteristic of the product" that would be recognized by an ordinary person who uses the product.[22]

3. **Causation**

Generally, it is a plaintiff's burden to demonstrate that a product defect was a "substantial factor" in producing the plaintiff's injury.[23] The Wisconsin Supreme Court, however, has relaxed the burden of establishing causation in DES cases.[24] A DES plaintiff need only demonstrate "by a preponderance of the evidence that a defendant drug company produced or marketed the allegedly defective and unreasonably dangerous type of DES taken by the plaintiff's mother."[25]

A relaxed causation standard has also been applied in the context of a lead paint claim based on public nuisance.[26] The Wisconsin Court of Appeals found that the promotion of paint to the general public and through sales staff was enough to allow the case to go to the jury because the focus of a public nuisance suit is on the harm to the general public and not on individuals who have suffered specific harm.[27]

4. **Contributory Negligence/Assumption of Risk**

Assumption of risk has been abolished as a separate defense in Wisconsin.[28] Evidence of a plaintiff's contributory negligence is admissible and may bar recovery under certain circumstances, in either strict liability or negligence. Contributory negligence will bar recovery in negligence actions if the plaintiff is found to be more negligent, on a percentage basis, than the party from whom recovery is sought.[29] A plaintiff's negligence is measured separately against the negligence of each person or entity that is held to be causally negligent.[30]

In strict liability claims, the fact finder first determines what percentage of the total causal responsibility for the injury at issue resulted from the contributory negligence of a plaintiff, what percentage should be allocated to the defective condition of the product, and what percentage should be allocated to the contributory negligence of any other person or entity.[31] If the percent of causal responsibility allocated to a plaintiff is greater than the percentage of causal responsibility allocated to the defective condition of the product, the plaintiff may not recover damages on a strict liability claim from the product manufacturer, distributor, seller, or any other person or entity involved in placing the product into the stream of commerce.[32] If the percent of causal responsibility allocated to a plaintiff is equal to or less than the percentage allocated to the product, the plaintiff may recover damages, but such recovery is diminished by the percentage of causal responsibility allocated to the plaintiff.[33] A manufacturer, seller, or distributor's liability shall be reduced by the percent of causal responsibility allocated to a plaintiff for any misuse, alteration, or modification of the subject product.[34]

Wisconsin statutes also provide a defense relating to intoxication. If a plaintiff were found to be legally impaired due to drugs or alcohol, a jury is required to presume the plaintiff's intoxication caused the accident.[35] This presumption may only be rebutted with proof that the intoxication did not cause the accident.[36]

5. **Sale or Lease/Persons Liable**

Strict liability is imposed on product manufacturers.[37] Wisconsin courts previously held that commercial lessors may be subject to strict liability; however, no Wisconsin appellate court has ruled on whether commercial lessors may be subject to strict liability since the adoption of tort reform in Wisconsin in 2011.[38] A plaintiff's ability to proceed on a strict liability theory against product sellers and distributors is limited by statute.[39] A plaintiff must proceed against the manufacturer if possible.[40] Furthermore, a seller or distributor generally will not be liable if it receives the product in a sealed container and has no reasonable opportunity to test or inspect the product.[41]

The seller of a used product may be held liable for strict liability if the seller is engaged in the business of selling such products and the hidden defective condition of the used product arises out of the original manufacturing process.[42] A component part manufacturer may also be held liable for strict liability under certain circumstances.[43]

A reconditioner of a used product "who does not manufacture, distribute, or sell the product it reconditions is not liable in strict products liability for defects in the machines it reconditions."[44]

6. Inherently Dangerous Products

Wisconsin has not adopted comment k to Section 402A of the Restatement (Second) of Torts, which precludes the imposition of strict liability on sellers of "unavoidably unsafe" products. Sellers of inherently dangerous products may be found strictly liable for injuries resulting from the products.[45]

7. Successor Liability

A corporation purchasing the assets of another corporation will not succeed to the selling corporation's liability for products manufactured by the seller unless (1) the buyer expressly or impliedly agrees to assume the seller's liability; (2) the transaction amounts to a consolidation or merger of the buyer and seller; (3) the buyer is a mere continuation of the seller; or (4) the corporations fraudulently enter into the transaction in order to escape liability.[46] Wisconsin does not recognize the "product line" exception to the non-liability rule.[47] "Mere continuation" is proven through identity of ownership, management, and control rather than continuation of a particular product line.[48]

8. Market Share Liability/Enterprise Liability

In the context of DES-based litigation, Wisconsin has declined to apply either the "market share" doctrine adopted by the California Supreme Court in *Sindell v. Abbott Laboratories*[49] or the theory of "enterprise liability."[50] Instead, Wisconsin has adopted an alternative, burden-shifting theory of liability for DES cases.[51] A Wisconsin statute enacted in 2013 invalidated the expanded application of this "risk-contribution theory" to lead-paint manufacturers set forth in *Thomas ex rel. Gramling v. Mallet*, limiting the risk-contribution theory to the narrow application set forth by the Wisconsin Supreme Court in the DES case, *Collins v. Eli Lilly Co.*[52] The Wisconsin statute further limited the application of the risk-contribution theory to very narrow circumstances.[53] Generally speaking, it will only apply to those cases involving identically formulated products that cause the type of injury that is unique to the product and where the plaintiff is unable to identify exactly who sold the particular product that caused injury.[54] In addition, the plaintiff will need to name manufacturers who represent 80 percent of the geographic market where the injury occurred, and the product must have been sold no more than 25 years before the injury occurred.[55] Liability amongst the manufacturers, distributors, sellers, or promoters under this theory is several, not joint.[56]

In *Gibson v. American Cyanamid Co.*, the Seventh Circuit Court of Appeals held that this statute violates Wisconsin's due process clause as applied to cases that were already pending when the statute was enacted.[57] The court also held that Wisconsin's application of the risk contribution theory does not violate procedural or substantive due process.[58]

9. **Privity**

Privity is not required to state a cause of action for strict product liability in tort.[59]

10. **Failure to Warn**

The manufacturer, distributor, or retailer of an unreasonably dangerous product is required to warn the potential user of the danger. The duty arises if the entity has, or should have, knowledge of a dangerous use of the product.[60] The duty to warn is a duty to give a warning that is "adequate and appropriate" under the circumstances.[61] The plaintiff must prove that the absence of a warning was a proximate cause (or a substantial factor) of the alleged injuries. In some circumstances, a failure to warn constitutes negligence as a matter of law.[62]

A product is defective due to a failure to warn or instruct when the foreseeable risks of harm that the product poses could have been decreased or prevented by providing reasonable instructions or warnings, and the omission of these reasonable instructions or warnings renders the product not reasonably safe.[63] A defense to a failure to warn action is available when the plaintiff voluntarily confronted an open and obvious condition in the product if a reasonable person in the position of the plaintiff would recognize the condition and the risk that it presents.[64] This defense applies even when a reasonable person in the plaintiff's position would not appreciate the gravity of the harm threatened.[65] Wisconsin law is unsettled regarding whether the defense is an absolute defense to liability or merely an additional factor to consider in assessing the plaintiff's contributory negligence.[66]

11. **Post-Sale Duty to Warn and Remedial Measures**

Under limited circumstances, a manufacturer may be liable under a post-sale duty to warn.[67] Wisconsin does not recognize an absolute, continuing duty to warn of new safety devices that eliminate potential hazards. The post-sale duty to warn is most likely to be found where there is a limited market and number of products in existence. The post-sale duty to warn does not generally apply to mass-marketed manufactured goods that become increasingly safer with each new model.[68]

In a strict liability claim alleging a manufacturing defect, design defect, or failure to warn, evidence of remedial measures taken after a product's sale is not admissible to show that the product was defective.[69] Such evidence, however, still can be used to show that a reasonable alternative design existed at the time of sale.[70]

12. Learned Intermediary/Sophisticated User Doctrine

Wisconsin has adopted a sophisticated user defense, under which there is no duty to warn if the user knows, or should have known, of the potential danger, especially when the user is a professional who should be aware of the characteristics of the product.[71] This sophisticated user defense is premised on the well-established principle that "'there is no duty to warn members of a trade or profession about dangers generally known to the trade or profession.'"[72] While it is clear that the sophisticated user defense applies to negligence claims, it has not been definitively decided whether such a defense also applies to a strict liability claim based on an allegedly inadequate warning.[73]

The Supreme Court of Wisconsin has not yet determined whether the learned intermediary doctrine applies to drug manufacturers, and no Wisconsin appellate court has adopted it in this context.[74]

13. Substantial Alteration/Abnormal Use

A manufacturer is not responsible for injuries caused by a substantial change in the condition of the product occurring after the initial sale, or due to abnormal use, but the substantial change or abnormal use must be one that could not reasonably be foreseen or expected.[75]

Damages for which a manufacturer, seller, or distributor would be liable "shall be reduced by the percentage of causal responsibility for the claimant's harm attributable to the claimant's misuse, alteration, or modification of the product," and if the causal responsibility allocated to the plaintiff exceeds the causal responsibility allocated to the defective condition of the product, a plaintiff may not recover on a strict liability claim against the product's manufacturer, seller, or distributor.[76]

14. State of the Art

"State-of-the-art" evidence is admissible for the purpose of providing the jury with a basis to determine whether the design of the product was unreasonably dangerous.[77]

15. Malfunction

Where evidence rebuts the existence of other probable causes, evidence of malfunction may be considered evidence of defect.[78]

16. Standards and Government Regulations

Evidence of industry custom and safety standards is admissible on the question of reasonable safety or defect.[79] If a product complied with relevant governmental or agency standards or specifications, a rebuttable presumption is created that the product is not defective.[80]

17. **Other Accidents**

Evidence of other accidents may be admitted on the issues of notice, defect, or causation, but only where the other accidents are shown to have occurred under conditions and circumstances similar to those of the accident in question.[81]

18. **Misrepresentation**

Misrepresentation is an independent tort in Wisconsin.[82] Where a plaintiff sues under both strict product liability and misrepresentation, Wisconsin has evaluated misrepresentation as a contractual claim, not a tort claim.[83]

19. **Destruction or Loss of Product**

Wisconsin courts have the discretion to impose sanctions against parties if the product at issue has been altered, destroyed, or lost.[84] A party may obtain judgment as a matter of law as a sanction for destruction of evidence by showing that the opposing side engaged in egregious conduct, which "consists of a conscious attempt to affect the outcome of litigation or a flagrant knowing disregard of the judicial process."[85] As a lesser sanction, the jury may be permitted to draw a negative inference against the party that destroyed or fabricated evidence.[86]

20. **Crashworthiness**

The "crashworthiness" or "second collision" doctrine imposes liability upon a manufacturer for design defects that do not cause the initial accident or collision, but which are found to have caused additional or more severe injuries.[87]

Following Wisconsin law on strict product liability, the plaintiff must first prove that the product was in a defective condition and unreasonably dangerous when it entered the stream of commerce, and that the defect was a substantial factor in enhancing the plaintiff's injuries.[88] It then becomes the manufacturer's burden to demonstrate that the plaintiff's injuries were not enhanced by the defective and unreasonably dangerous condition of the product.[89] Under some circumstances, a jury may then be required to apportion the plaintiff's damages between what would be attributable to enhancement and what would be attributable to the initial accident.[90]

D. **NEGLIGENCE**

Wisconsin's Supreme Court has held that, "In Wisconsin, everyone has a duty of care to the whole world."[91] Wisconsin follows the broad duty concept articulated in the minority opinion of the seminal New York case, *Palsgraf v.*

Long Island Railroad Co.[92] This view directs that "nonliability be based on considerations of public policy rather than couched in terms of an absence of duty."[93]

A plaintiff may recover for negligence in designing, constructing, inspecting, or warning about a product.[94] Wisconsin's comparative fault statute diminishes the plaintiff's recovery in proportion to the plaintiff's negligence.[95] A plaintiff may not recover against a particular defendant if the plaintiff's negligence is greater than that of the particular defendant. The plaintiff's negligence is measured separately against the negligence of each person found to be causally negligent.[96]

E. BREACH OF WARRANTY

A warranty cause of action may be plead arising out of a product failure, although a warranty claim would be subject to certain defenses such as notice, privity, and limitations on available recovery.[97] Wisconsin recognizes the economic loss doctrine, which may limit claims arising out of a product failure to warranty claims.[98] Where a product failure causes damage to persons or other property, however, the economic loss doctrine will not apply and tort claims may be asserted.[99]

Wisconsin recognizes various exceptions to the economic loss doctrine. The "other property" exception to the economic loss doctrine allows a plaintiff to bring a tort claim where a product damages other property, which is evaluated based upon the so-called "integrated system" and "disappointed expectations" tests.[100] The "fraud in the inducement" exception to the economic loss rule allows tort claims in a narrow context and will apply only "where the fraud is extraneous to, rather than interwoven with, the contract."[101]

The economic loss doctrine may also apply to bar tort causes of action for claims arising out of mixed contracts for products and services. Wisconsin courts use the "predominant purpose" test to determine whether a mixed contract is predominantly for the sale of goods or of services. The economic loss doctrine's limitation on tort claims would not apply to contracts that are predominately for services.[102] The "integrated system" test also applies to contracts for services that provide component products "that have no independent value or use apart from their function as components of the product into which they were incorporated."[103]

F. PUNITIVE DAMAGES

Punitive damages are regulated by statute in Wisconsin.[104] To recover punitive damages, a plaintiff must show that a defendant acted maliciously toward him or her or in an intentional disregard of his or her rights.[105] The phrase "intentional disregard of the rights of the plaintiff" has been broadly construed and requires a plaintiff to show "that a defendant acted maliciously toward the plaintiff or intentionally disregarded the rights of the plaintiff, not that a defendant intended to cause harm or injury to the plaintiff."[106] Further, the defendant's conduct that gives rise to the punitive damages does not need to be directed at the specific plaintiff who is seeking punitive damages.[107] Punitive damages are not recoverable incident to damages for wrongful death under Wisconsin's wrongful death statute[108] and are not available without a recovery of compensatory damages.[109]

Punitive damages are limited and "may not exceed twice the amount of any compensatory damages recovered by the plaintiff or $200,000, whichever is greater."[110] This limitation does not apply to punitive damages awarded against drunk drivers.[111]

G. PRE- AND POST-JUDGMENT INTEREST

Unless there has been a statutory offer of settlement, pre-verdict interest is not recoverable in personal injury cases.[112] If a statutory offer of settlement is made (and not accepted) and the offering party later recovers a judgment greater than or equal to the amount of the offer, that party may collect interest at an annual rate of one percent plus the prime rate as of January 1 of the year the judgment is entered, "if the judgment is entered on or before June 30 of that year or in effect on July 1 of the year in which the judgment is entered if the judgment is entered after June 30 of that year, as reported by the federal reserve board," on the amount that is recovered from the date that the offer of settlement was made until the amount is paid.[113]

If a judgment is for the recovery of money, interest accrues at an annual rate of one percent plus the prime rate as of January 1 of the year the judgment is entered, "if the judgment is entered on or before June 30 of that year or in effect on July 1 of the year in which the judgment is entered if the judgment is entered after June 30 of that year, as reported by the federal reserve board," on the total amount of the money judgment from the time of the verdict, decision, or report until the time when the money judgment is entered.[114] In addition, a successful litigant is entitled to post-judgment interest, which accrues at an annual rate of one percent plus the prime rate as of January 1 of the year the judgment is entered, "if the judgment is entered on or before June 30 of that year or in effect on July 1 of the year in which the judgment is entered if the judgment is entered after June 30 of that year, as reported by the federal reserve board," on the amount recovered by the successful litigant from the date the judgment is entered until the date the judgment is paid.[115]

H. EMPLOYER IMMUNITY FROM SUIT

In most instances, Wisconsin's Worker's Compensation Statute provides the exclusive means for an employee injured by an employer's alleged negligence to obtain compensation from the employer and the corresponding compensation carrier.[116] Only if an employer possesses a second persona so completely independent from and unrelated to his or her status as employer can the employer become a third person, vulnerable to a tort suit by an employee notwithstanding the exclusivity provisions of the Worker's Compensation Statute.[117]

However, an employee may supplement any compensation received from the employer by bringing an action against any responsible third parties.[118]

Additionally, even though an employer is immune from liability, that employer may be included on a special verdict form for purposes of apportioning fault when an employee is injured in the course and scope of his or her employment.[119]

I. **STATUTES**

Wisconsin has passed several statutes that specifically regulate product liability actions brought in the state.[120]

Wisconsin's statutory age of majority is 18 years of age.[121] Under statute, a minor under the age of seven is conclusively presumed to be free of contributory negligence or of any negligence whatsoever.[122]

Wisconsin enacted tort reform legislation that took effect February 1, 2011. Wisconsin appellate courts have examined the revised standard for expert testimony stemming from this legislation and set forth in Wis. Stat. § 907.02 and held, in two non-product liability cases, that this revised standard is not applicable to cases commenced before the effective date of the tort reform legislation.[123] In addition, in *Gibson v. American Cyanamid Co.*, the Seventh Circuit Court of Appeals held that the retroactive application of Wis. Stat. § 895.046 to cases commenced prior to this statute taking effect violates Wisconsin's due process clause.[124]

J. **JOINT AND SEVERAL LIABILITY**

In strict liability actions, if the percentage of causal responsibility allocated to the plaintiff is less than the percentage of causal responsibility allocated to the defective condition of the product at issue, a plaintiff may recover against defendants responsible for the defective condition of the product.[125] If multiple defendants are alleged to be responsible for the condition of the product, the fact finder then determines the relative percentage of causal responsibility of each product defendant.[126] Wisconsin imposes joint and several liability on any product defendant whose causal responsibility is determined to be 51 percent or more of the total responsibility for damages to the plaintiff.[127] The liability of a product defendant whose causal responsibility is determined to be less than 51 percent of the total responsibility for damages to the plaintiff is limited to a percentage of the total damages equal to the percentage of fault allocated to that particular defendant.[128]

In negligence actions, Wisconsin law has a modified joint and several liability comparative negligence statute. Where previously there was unlimited joint and several liability,[129] there is now conditional joint and several liability. If a defendant's negligence is less than 51 percent, its liability is limited to its percentage of causal negligence. Defendants whose causal negligence is 51 percent or more are jointly and severally liable.[130] This statutory section does not apply to cases involving concerted action[131] or to strict product liability claims.[132]

A *Pierringer* release allows a plaintiff who has sued several defendants to settle with one and preserve its claims against the rest.[133] At trial, the jury apportions fault among all the parties, including the settling defendants. The plaintiff can only recover the percentage of damages the jury allocates to the non-settling defendants. A *Pierringer* release requires the plaintiff to indemnify the settling defendants from future contribution claims brought by the non-settling defendants.

Patrick S. Nolan
Eric W. Matzke
Quarles & Brady LLP
411 East Wisconsin Avenue
Milwaukee, Wisconsin 53202
(414) 277-5000
(Fax) (414) 271-3552

Endnotes - Wisconsin

1. *See, e.g., Vincer v. Esther Williams All-Aluminum Swimming Pool Co.*, 69 Wis. 2d 326, 330, 230 N.W.2d 794, 797 (1975).

2. *See Austin v. Ford Motor Co.*, 86 Wis. 2d 628, 644, 273 N.W.2d 233, 240 (1979).

3. *St. Paul Mercury Ins. Co.v. The Viking Corp.*, 539 F.3d 623, 626 (7thCir. 2008); *Paulson v. Olson Implement Co.*, 107 Wis. 2d 510, 319 N.W.2d 855 (1982).

4. *See* Wis. Stat. § 893.54 (2012).

5. *See* Wis. Stat. § 893.52.

6. *See* Wis. Stat. § 893.16.

7. *See* Wis. Stat. § 893.07.

8. *See Wenke v. Gehl Co.*, 2003 WI App 189, ¶20, 267 Wis. 2d 221, ¶20, 669 N.W.2d 789, ¶20, *aff'd*, 2004 WI 103, 274 Wis. 2d 220, 682 N.W.2d 405.

9. Wis. Stat. § 895.047(5).

10. Wis. Stat. § 893.89. *See also Kalahari Dev., LLC v. Iconica, Inc.*, 2012 WI App 34, 340 Wis. 2d 454, 811 N.W.2d 825; *Kohn v. Darlington Cmty. Schs.*, 2005 WI 99, 283 Wis. 2d 1, 698 N.W.2d 794.

11. Wis. Stat. § 893.89.

12. *See Hansen v. A. H. Robins, Inc.*, 113 Wis. 2d 550, 560, 335 N.W.2d 578, 583 (1983).

13. *See Doe v. Archdiocese of Milwaukee*, 211 Wis. 2d 312, 333, 565 N.W.2d 94 (1997).

14. Wis. Stat. § 895.047.

15. *See, e.g., Green v. Smith & Nephew AHP, Inc.*, 2001 WI 109, ¶70, 245 Wis. 2d 772, ¶70, 629 N.W.2d 727, ¶70.

16. *See Howes v. Hansen*, 56 Wis. 2d 247, 254, 201 N.W.2d 825, 828 (1972).

17. Wis. Stat. § 895.047(1)(a); *Gorton v. Am. Cyanamid Co.*, 194 Wis. 2d 203, 221-22, 533 N.W.2d 746, 754 (1995).

18. Wis. Stat. § 895.047(1)(a); *Gorton*, 194 Wis. 2d at 221-22, 533 N.W.2d at 754.

19. Wis. Stat. § 895.047(1)(a); *Gorton*, 194 Wis. 2d at 221-22, 533 N.W.2d at 754.

20. Wis. Stat. § 895.047(1)(a); *Gorton*, 194 Wis. 2d at 221-22, 533 N.W.2d at 754.

21. *Godoy ex rel. Gramling v. E. I. duPont de Nemours & Co.*, 2009 WI 78, 319 Wis. 2d 91, 768 N.W.2d 674.

22. Wis. Stat. § 895.047(3)(d).

23. *See Howes v. Deere & Co.*, 71 Wis. 2d 268, 273-74, 238 N.W.2d 76, 80 (1976).

24. *See Collins v. Eli Lilly Co.*, 116 Wis. 2d 166, 342 N.W.2d 37 (1984).

25. *Collins v. Eli Lilly Co.*, 116 Wis. 2d at 196, 342 N.W.2d at 51.

26. *City of Milwaukee v. NL Indus., Inc.*, 2005 WI App 7, 278 Wis. 2d 313, 691 N.W.2d 888.

27. *City of Milwaukee*, 2005 WI App 7, ¶¶15, 19, 278 Wis. 2d 313, ¶¶15, 19, 691 N.W.2d 888, ¶¶15, 19. Ultimately, this case was tried before a jury which returned a verdict in favor of NL Industries, Inc. that was affirmed on appeal after the court concluded that "the evidence was sufficient to support the jury's finding that NL Industries did not intentionally cause the public nuisance found by the jury." *City of Milwaukee v. NL Indus., Inc.*, 2008 WI 181, ¶2, 315 Wis. 2d 443, ¶2, 762 N.W.2d 757, ¶2, *pet. rev. denied*, 2009 WI 34, 316 Wis. 2d 719, 765 N.W.2d 579.

28. *See, e.g., Kubichek v. Kotecki*, 2011 WI App 32, 332 Wis. 2d 522, 796 N.W.2d 858 (citing *Moulas v. PBC Prods., Inc.*, 213 Wis. 2d 406, 418-19, 570 N.W.2d 739 (Ct. App. 1997), *aff'd*, 217 Wis. 2d 449, 576 N.W.2d 929 (1998)).

29. *See* Wis. Stat. § 895.045(1).

30. *See* Wis. Stat. § 895.045(1).

31. Wis. Stat. § 895.045(3).

32. Wis. Stat. § 895.045(3)(b).

33. Wis. Stat. § 895.045(3)(c).

34. Wis. Stat. § 895.045(3)(c).

35. Wis. Stat. § 895.047(3)(a).

36. Wis. Stat. § 895.047(3)(a).

37. Wis. Stat. § 895.047(1).

38. *See* Wis. Stat. § 895.047(2); *Kemp v. Miller*, 154 Wis. 2d 538, 554-58, 453 N.W.2d 872, 878-79 (1990).

39. Wis. Stat. § 895.047(2).

40. Wis. Stat. § 895.047(2).

41. Wis. Stat. § 895.047(3)(e).

42. *See, e.g., Nelson ex rel. Hibbard v. Nelson Hardware, Inc.*, 160 Wis. 2d 689, 467 N.W.2d 518 (1991); *see also* Wis. Stat. § 895.047(2) (limiting the circumstances under which a plaintiff may proceed against a product seller or distributor).

43. *See, e.g., Komanekin ex rel. Hausmann v. Inland Truck Parts*, 819 F. Supp. 802, 809 (E.D. Wis. 1993) (citing *Shawver v. Roberts Corp.*, 90 Wis. 2d 672, 685, 280 N.W.2d 226 (1979)); *Pomplun v. Rockwell Int'l Corp.*, 203 Wis. 2d 303, 309, 552 N.W.2d 632 (Ct. App. 1996); *see also DeSantis v. Parker Feeders, Inc.*, 547 F.2d 357, 361 (7th Cir. 1976) (citations omitted); *see also* Wis. Stat. § 895.047(2) (limiting the circumstances under which a plaintiff may proceed against a product seller or distributor).

44. *Rolph v. EBI Cos.*, 159 Wis. 2d 518, 524, 464 N.W.2d 667, 669 (1991); *see also Strasser v. Transtech Mobile Fleet Serv., Inc.*, 2000 WI 87, ¶41, 236 Wis. 2d 435, ¶41, 613 N.W.2d 142, ¶41 (nothing that a reconditioner "may, however, be held liable for negligence in its own work").

45. *See Collins*, 116 Wis. 2d at 196-97, 342 N.W.2d at 51-52.

46. *See Fish v. Amsted Indus., Inc.*, 126 Wis. 2d 293, 298, 376 N.W.2d 820, 823 (1985) (citation omitted).

47. *See Fish*, 126 Wis. 2d at 305, 376 N.W.2d at 826.

48. *See Fish*, 126 Wis. 2d at 301-02, 376 N.W.2d at 824.

49. *Sindell v. Abbott Labs.*, 26 Cal. 3d 588, 607 P.2d 924 (1980), *cert. denied*, 449 U.S. 912 (1980); *see Collins*, 116 Wis. 2d at 189, 342 N.W.2d at 48.

50. *See Collins*, 116 Wis. 2d at 186, 342 N.W.2d at 47.

51. *See Collins*, 116 Wis. 2d at 197-98, 342 N.W.2d at 52.

52. *See Collins*, 116 Wis. 2d at 197-98, 342 N.W.2d at 52; Wis. Stat. § 895.046.

53. Wis. Stat. § 895.046(4).

54. Wis. Stat. § 895.046(4).

55. Wis. Stat. § 895.046(4)-(5).

56. Wis. Stat. § 895.046(6).

57. *Gibson v. Am. Cyanamid Co.*, 2014 WL 3643353, at *4-6 (7th Cir. 2014).

58. *Id.*

59. *See Dippel v. Sciano*, 37 Wis. 2d 443, 459, 155 N.W.2d 55, 63 (1967).

60. *See Flaminio v. Honda Motor Co.*, 733 F.2d 463, 466 (7th Cir. 1984) (citation omitted).

61. *See Schuh v. Fox River Tractor Co.*, 63 Wis. 2d 728, 739, 218 N.W.2d 279, 285 (1974) (citation omitted).

62. *See, e.g., Anderson ex rel. Skow v. Alfa-Laval Agri, Inc.*, 209 Wis. 2d 337, 353, 564 N.W.2d 788, 795 (Ct. App. 1997).

63. Wis. Stat. § 895.047(1)(a).

64. *See Griebler v. Doughboy Recreational, Inc.*, 160 Wis. 2d 547, 558, 466 N.W.2d 897, 901 (1991); *Pagel v. Marcus Corp.*, 2008 WI App 110, 313 Wis. 2d 78, 756 N.W.2d 447.

65. *See Griebler*, 160 Wis. 2d at 558, 466 N.W.2d at 901; *Pagel*, 2008 WI App 110, ¶¶8, 18, 313 Wis. 2d 78, ¶¶8, 18, 756 N.W.2d 447, ¶¶8, 18.

66. *See Hansen v. New Holland N. Am., Inc.*, 215 Wis. 2d 655, 665-66, 574 N.W.2d 250, 254 (Ct. App. 1997).

67. *See, e.g., Sharp ex rel. Gordon v. Case Corp.*, 227 Wis. 2d 1, 26, 595 N.W.2d 380, 391 (1999).

68. *See Gracyalny v. Westinghouse Elec. Corp.*, 723 F.2d 1311, 1318-19 (7th Cir. 1983) (citation omitted); *Kozlowski v. John E. Smith's Sons Co.*, 87 Wis. 2d 882, 901, 275 N.W.2d 915, 923-24 (1979).

69. Wis. Stat. § 895.047(4).

70. Wis. Stat. § 895.047(4).

71. *See Haase v. Badger Mining Corp.*, 2003 WI App 192, ¶¶19-21, 266 Wis. 2d 970, ¶¶19-21, 669 N.W.2d 737, ¶¶19-21, *aff'd but criticized*, 2004 WI 97, 274 Wis. 2d 143, 682 N.W.2d 389.

72. *Haase*, 2003 WI App 192, ¶21, 266 Wis. 2d 970, 669 N.W.2d 737 (quoting *Shawver*, 90 Wis. 2d at 686).

73. *Mohr v. St. Paul Fire & Marine Ins. Co.*, 2004 WI App 5, ¶34, 269 Wis. 2d 302, ¶34, 674 N.W.2d 576, ¶34.

74. *Peters v. Astrazeneca, LP*, 417 F. Supp. 2d 1051, 1054 (W.D. Wis. 2006) (citing *Kurer v. Parke, Davis & Co.*, 2004 WI App 74, ¶21, 272 Wis. 2d 390, ¶21, 679 N.W.2d 867, ¶21).

75. *See Schuh*, 63 Wis. 2d at 742-43, 218 N.W.2d at 286-87; *Dippel*, 37 Wis. 2d at 460, 155 N.W.2d at 63-64.

76. Wis. Stats. §§ 895.047(3)(c); 895.045(3)(b).

77. *See D. L. ex rel. Friederichs v. Huebner*, 110 Wis. 2d 581, 595, 616-17, 329 N.W.2d 890, 906 (1983); *see also Wis. Elec. Power Co. v. Zallea Bros., Inc.*, 606 F.2d 697, 703 (7th Cir. 1979).

78. *See Sumnicht v. Toyota Motor Sales, U.S.A., Inc.*, 121 Wis. 2d 338, 373-74, 360 N.W.2d 2, 18 (1984).

79. *See Sumnicht*, 121 Wis. 2d at 372, 360 N.W.2d at 17; *Huebner*, 110 Wis. 2d at 595, 329 N.W.2d at 896; *Raim v. Ventura*, 16 Wis. 2d 67, 72-73, 113 N.W.2d 827, 830 (1962).

80. Wis. Stat. § 895.047(3)(b).

81. *See Farrell ex rel. Lehner v. John Deere Co.*, 151 Wis. 2d 45, 76, 443 N.W.2d 50, 61 (Ct. App. 1989) (citation omitted).

82. *See Lundin v. Shimanski*, 124 Wis. 2d 175, 184, 368 N.W.2d 676, 680-81 (1985).

83. *See, e.g., Wis. Power & Light Co. v. Westinghouse Elec. Corp.*, 645 F. Supp. 1129 (W.D. Wis. 1986), *aff'd*, 830 F.2d 1405 (7th Cir. 1987).

84. *See Milwaukee Constructors II v. Milwaukee Metro. Sewerage Dist.*, 177 Wis. 2d 523, 529, 502 N.W.2d 881, 883 (Ct. App. 1993).

85. *See Garfoot v. Fireman's Fund Ins. Co.*, 228 Wis. 2d 707, 724, 599 N.W.2d 411, 419 (Ct. App. 1999); *Sentry Ins. v. Royal Ins. Co. of Am.*, 196 Wis. 2d 907, 918-19, 539 N.W.2d 911, 915-16 (Ct. App. 1995); *Milwaukee Constructors II*, 177 Wis. 2d at 532-33, 502 N.W.2d at 884-85.

86. *See Jagmin v. Simonds Abrasive Co.*, 61 Wis. 2d 60, 80-81, 211 N.W.2d 810, 821 (1973).

87. *See Sumnicht*, 121 Wis. 2d at 348-49, 360 N.W.2d at 6.

88. *See Maskrey v. Volkswagenwerk Aktiengesellschaft*, 125 Wis. 2d 145, 156-58, 370 N.W.2d 815, 821-22 (Ct. App. 1985) (citing *Sumnicht*, 121 Wis. 2d at 357-58, 360 N.W.2d at 11); *see* Wis. Stat. § 895.047(1).

89. *See Farrell*, 151 Wis. 2d at 66-67, 443 N.W.2d at 57; *Maskrey*, 125 Wis. 2d at 158-59, 370 N.W.2d at 822 (citations omitted); *Johnson v. Heintz*, 73 Wis. 2d 286, 301-07, 243 N.W.2d 815, 825-28 (1976); *see also* Wisconsin Civil Jury Instruction 1723.

90. *See, e.g., Farrell*, 151 Wis. 2d at 66-67, 443 N.W.2d at 57.

91. *Miller v. Wal-Mart Stores, Inc.*, 219 Wis. 2d 250, 260, 580 N.W.2d 233, 238 (1998).

92. *Gritzner v. Michael R.*, 2000 WI 68, ¶20 n.3, 235 Wis. 2d 781, ¶20 n.3, 611 N.W.2d 906, ¶20 n.3 (citing *Palsgraf v. Long Island R.R. Co.*, 162 N.E. 99, 99-101 (N.Y. 1928)).

93. *Schilling v. Stockel*, 26 Wis. 2d 525, 532, 133 N.W.2d 335, 339 (1965).

94. *See, e.g., Kutsugeras v. AVCO Corp.*, 973 F.2d 1341 (7th Cir. 1992); *Smith v. Atco Co.*, 6 Wis. 2d 371, 94 N.W.2d 697 (1959); *Lemberger v. Honeywell Int'l, Inc.*, 2014 WI App 1, ¶¶18-19, 352 Wis.2d 245, 841 N.W.2d 580.

95. *See* Wis. Stat. § 895.045; *Delvaux v. VandenLangenberg*, 130 Wis. 2d 464, 497-98, 387 N.W.2d 751, 766 (1986).

96. *See* Wis. Stat. § 895.045(1).

97. *See Austin*, 86 Wis. 2d at 644, 273 N.W.2d at 240; *St. Paul Mercury Ins. Co.v. The Viking Corp.*, 539 F.3d 623, 626 (7th Cir. 2008); *Paulson v. Olson Implement Co.*, 107 Wis. 2d 510, 319 N.W.2d 855 (1982).

98. *See, e.g., Daanen & Janssen, Inc. v. Cedarapids, Inc.*, 216 Wis. 2d 395, 573 N.W.2d 842 (1998); *Wilson v. Tuxen*, 2008 WI App 94, 312 Wis. 2d 705, 754 N.W.2d 220.

99. *See Bay Breeze Condo. Ass'n, Inc. v. Norco Windows, Inc.*, 2002 WI App 205, ¶28, 257 Wis. 2d 511, ¶28, 651 N.W.2d 738, ¶28 (citation omitted).

100. *Grams v. Milk Prods., Inc.*, 2005 WI 112, ¶43, 283 Wis. 2d 511, ¶43, 699 N.W.2d 167, ¶43; *see also Foremost Farms USA Coop. v. Performance Process, Inc.*, 2006 WI App 246, 297 Wis. 2d 724, 726 N.W.2d 289 (discussing the two tests in further detail and noting that the inquiry starts with the "integrated system"

test and that the "disappointed expectations" test is applied "if the damaged property appears to be 'other property' under the 'integrated system' test").

101. *Kaloti Enters., Inc. v. Kellogg Sales Co.*, 2005 WI 111, ¶42, 283 Wis. 2d 555, ¶42, 699 N.W.2d 205, ¶42 (citation and internal quotation marks omitted); *see also Cerabio LLC v. Wright Med. Tech., Inc.*, 410 F.3d 981, 989 (7th Cir. 2005).

102. *Linden v. Cascade Stone Co.*, 2005 WI 113, ¶¶8, 32, 283 Wis. 2d 606, ¶¶8, 32, 699 N.W.2d 189, ¶¶8, 32.

103. *Linden*, 2005 WI 113, ¶32, 283 Wis. 2d 606, ¶32, 699 N.W.2d 189, ¶32.

104. Wis. Stat. § 895.043.

105. *See* Wis. Stat. § 895.043(3).

106. *Wischer v. Mitsubishi Heavy Indus. Am., Inc.*, 2005 WI 26, ¶61(1), 279 Wis. 2d 4, ¶61(1), 694 N.W.2d 320, ¶61(1), *reconsideration denied*, 2005 WI 134, 282 Wis. 2d 724, 700 N.W.2d 276; *see also Strenke v. Hogner*, 2005 WI 25, ¶36, 279 Wis. 2d 52, ¶36, 694 N.W.2d 296, ¶36, *cert. denied*, 549 U.S. 1251 (2007) (concluding that the statute "necessitates that the defendant act with a purpose to disregard the plaintiff's rights or be aware that his or her conduct is substantially certain to result in the plaintiff's rights being disregarded").

107. *Strenke*, 2005 WI 25, ¶51, 279 Wis. 2d 52, ¶51, 694 N.W.2d 296, ¶51.

108. *Wangen v. Ford Motor Co.*, 97 Wis. 2d 260, 314-15, 294 N.W.2d 437, 464-65 (1980). This case has been superseded by statute (895.85) with regard to the standard by which punitive damages may be awarded, not for its holding that punitive damages are not available incident to damages for wrongful death actions.

109. *See Tucker v. Marcus*, 142 Wis. 2d 425, 438-39, 418 N.W.2d 818, 823 (1988).

110. Wis. Stat. § 895.043(6).

111. Wis. Stat. § 895.043(6).

112. *See, e.g., Johnson v. Pearson Agri-Sys., Inc.*, 119 Wis. 2d 766, 350 N.W.2d 127 (1984).

113. *See* Wis. Stat. § 807.01(4).

114. *See* Wis. Stat. § 814.04(4).

115. *See* Wis. Stat. § 815.05(8); *Calaway v. Brown Cnty.*, 202 Wis. 2d 736, 756, 553 N.W.2d 809, 817 (Ct. App. 1996).

116. *See* Wis. Stat. § 102.03(2); *Mulder v. Acme-Cleveland Corp.*, 95 Wis. 2d 173, 290 N.W.2d 276 (1980); *see also Tatera v. FMC Corp.*, 2010 WI 90, 328 Wis. 2d 320, 786 N.W.2d 810 (discussing potential liability of brake manufacturer in the context of injuries arising out of work done by an employee at a machine shop that subcontracted with manufacturer to grind third-party asbestos-containing brake linings to fit manufacturer's brake assembly and finding that claims were barred).

117. *See Henning v. Gen. Motors Assembly Div.*, 143 Wis. 2d 1, 15, 419 N.W.2d 551, 556 (1988).

118. *See* Wis. Stat. § 102.29.

119. *See Connar v. W. Shore Equip. of Milwaukee, Inc.*, 68 Wis. 2d 42, 227 N.W.2d 660 (1975).

120. *See* Wis. Stats. §§ 895.045, 895.046, 895.047.

121. *See* Wis. Stat. § 990.01(3), (20). "[F]or purposes of investigating or prosecuting a person who is alleged to have violated any state or federal criminal law or any civil law or municipal ordinance," "adult" is a person who is 17 years old and a "minor" does not include persons who are 17 years old. Wis. Stat. § 990.01(3), (20).

122. *See* Wis. Stat. § 891.44.

123. *In re Commitment of Knipfer*, 2014 WI App 9, ¶2, 352 Wis. 2d 563, 566, 842 N.W.2d 526; *In re Commitment of Alger*, 2013 WI App 148, ¶2, 352 Wis. 2d 145, 149, 841 N.W.2d 329, 331; Wis. Stat. § 907.02.

124. *Gibson v. Am. Cyanamid Co.*, 2014 WL 3643353, at *4-6 (7thCir. 2014).

125. Wis. Stat. § 895.045(3)(c).

126. Wis. Stat. § 895.045(3)(d).

127. Wis. Stat. § 895.045(3)(d).

128. Wis. Stat. § 895.045(3)(d).

129. *See Fitzgerald v. Badger State Mut. Cas. Co.*, 67 Wis. 2d 321, 331-32, 227 N.W.2d 444, 449 (1975).

130. *See* Wis. Stat. § 895.045(1).

131. *See* Wis. Stat. § 895.045(2); *see also Richards v. Badger Mut. Ins. Co.*, 2008 WI 52, ¶¶2, 55, 309 Wis. 2d 541, ¶¶2, 55, 749 N.W.2d 581, ¶¶2, 55 (concluding that "895.045(2) is the legislative codification of the concerted action theory of liability").

132. *See* Wis. Stat. § 895.045(3), which defines joint and several liability in strict liability claims.

133. *See Pierringer v. Hoger*, 21 Wis. 2d 182, 124 N.W.2d 106 (1963).

WYOMING

A. CAUSES OF ACTION

Product liability claims may be premised on any or all of the following theories: negligence,[1] breach of express and implied warranty,[2] and strict liability.[3]

B. STATUTES OF LIMITATION

1. Negligence

Wyoming has a four-year statute of limitations for personal injury or property damage. Wyoming is a discovery state, which means that the cause of action, and thus the statute of limitations, "is triggered when the plaintiff knows or has reason to know the existence of the cause of action."[4] The plaintiff's lack of knowledge of the identity of the tortfeasor does not prevent the statute of limitations from running.[5]

Note that if the product defect resulted in a death, the applicable limitation period is two years pursuant to Wyo. Stat. § 1-38-102(d).

2. Breach of Warranty

The Wyoming legislature has adopted the official version of Uniform Commercial Code Section 2-725 (Wyo. Stat. § 34.1-2-725), and the statute of limitations therein has not been modified by other statutes of limitation. The statute of limitations is not more than four years after the cause of action has accrued, and can be less if the agreement of the parties reduces that period, but it cannot be reduced to less than one year. A cause of action accrues when the breach occurs, and, subject to certain exceptions in Wyoming Statutes Section 34.1-2-725, a breach of warranty occurs when tender of warrantied goods is delivered.[6]

3. Strict Liability

The personal injury/property damage four-year, and wrongful death two-year statutes apply. See Section B.1, *supra*. Actions based on strict product liability are tortious rather than contractual in nature.[7]

4. Exception for Improvements to Real Property

For manufacturers, suppliers, and others, no action can be brought in tort, contract, indemnity, or otherwise more than 10 years after substantial completion of an improvement to real property.[8] Whether a product constitutes an improvement to real property is a question of law, but its resolution is grounded in fact. Where there are insufficient facts regarding the use and permanency of the product, a question of fact exists and the fact finder must determine whether the product was an improvement.[9]

C. STRICT LIABILITY

1. The Standard

Wyoming adopted the standard set forth in Restatement (Second) of Torts Section 402A (1965) in *Ogle v. Caterpillar Tractor Co.*[10] In *Ogle*, the court stated that the Restatement definition formed "the best starting point from which the cause of action can evolve," pointing out that many of the "finer points" not explicitly covered in Section 402A and the official comments had already been considered and decided elsewhere.[11] Wyoming court's application of this standard will be governed by the public policy that product liability is intended to afford a cause of action against manufacturers or suppliers of defective mass-produced products in order to permit recovery by plaintiffs who would not recover under a negligence theory and distribute the damages among those most able to prevent future occurrences or who would pass on the loss to all customers.[12]

2. Definition of "Defect"

"A product is defective when, at the time of sale or distribution, it contains a manufacturing defect, is defective in design, or is defective because of inadequate instructions or warnings."[13]

A defective product may be defined as one that fails to match the average quality of like products; a product is defective when it fails to perform reasonably and safely the function for which it was intended.[14] A defective product is a product which is "not reasonably safe," or is "unreasonably dangerous" to the user or consumer. If a product is safe for normal handling and consumption, it is not defective.[15]

> A prima facie case that a product was defective and that the defect existed when it left the manufacturer's control is made by proof that in the absence of abnormal use or reasonable secondary causes the product failed "to perform in the manner reasonable to be expected in light of [its] nature and intended function."[16]

The erroneous choice of a product, however, is not a defective product for purposes of strict liability.[17] In *McLaughlin v. Michelin Tire Corp.*, tires installed on a scraper created severe bouncing and vibration problems and made the scraper hard to control resulting in an accident. Summary judgment was upheld for the defendant on the cause of action based on strict liability because plaintiff failed to show an actual defect. Still available to the plaintiff was a cause of action based on implied warranty of fitness for a particular purpose.[18]

Under present Wyoming law, in order to prove a design defect the plaintiff must show a reasonable alternative design. However, the Wyoming Supreme Court intimated in *Campbell ex rel. Campbell v. Studer*,

Inc. that it may be inclined to consider the arguments proposed by comments b and e to Rest. 3d. Torts § 2 against such a requirement in certain cases if the proper case were to present itself.[19]

If the product itself is not defective but may be unreasonably dangerous if it is used improperly, a plaintiff may show a "defect" by establishing that the manufacturer failed to warn about dangers associated with the product.[20]

The question of whether a product is defective because a safety device was not standard equipment or a recommended option depends on a balancing of various factors, including:

(1) the dangerousness of the product with the safety accessory including weighing the obviousness/unreasonableness of the danger, relevant safety standards, the presence of a warning, and the effectiveness of the safety device to prevent the risks of injury, and

(2) the relative positions of the manufacturer and the buyer, including industry custom, the buyer's awareness of the availability of safety accessories or of the danger of using the product without them, whether the manufacturer offered the safeguards and the buyer refused them, the feasibility of installing the safeguards, and/or the buyer's reliance on the manufacturer's expertise.[21]

Under these principles, a manufacturer may have a duty to design a product containing safety features to protect against outside hazards, for instance, against falling objects.[22]

3. **Causation**

"Proof of proximate cause is as necessary under warranty and strict liability causes of action as it is in a negligence action."[23] Recovery under theories of strict liability is barred regardless of a product's defective condition where the damages/injuries are determined to have been proximately caused by something other than the defect.[24] "However, the allegedly defective product need not necessarily be introduced into evidence in order to establish grounds for recovery. Circumstantial evidence can establish that a manufacturer's defective product caused a mishap and associated injuries."[25]

Wyoming applies the standard for admissibility of expert testimony consistent with the principles outlined in *Daubert v. Merrell Dow Pharmaceuticals, Inc.*[26] These requirements were applied to exclude expert causation opinions due to the failure to establish the necessary reliability criteria in *Hoy v. DRM, Inc.*,[27] and *Ronwin v. Bayer Corp.*[28]

4. **Contributory Negligence/Assumption of Risk**

Under Wyoming's Comparative Fault Statute, Wyo. Stat. § 1-1-109 (2013), in actions accruing after July 1, 1994, all culpable conduct, referred to as "fault," is subject to modified comparative principles.[29]

The comparative fault statute specifically identifies and requires application of comparative principles for all negligence, strict tort, or strict products liability, breach of warranty, assumption of risk and misuse or alteration of a product. Thus, all fault attributed to a plaintiff, including contributory negligence, assumption of risk, intentional conduct, and misuse or alteration, will reduce the plaintiff's recoverable damages and will bar recovery completely if the plaintiff's fault exceeds 50 percent of the total fault of all "actors."[30] Additionally, all actors who proximately caused any part of the plaintiff's damages, regardless of whether parties to the action or subject to suit, shall be included on the verdict form. A defendant is liable only to the extent of his individual fault, and shall bear no responsibility for damages caused by the fault of another.[31]

The Wyoming Supreme Court has held that under Wyoming's comparative fault statute, intentional misconduct must be compared to the negligent conduct of others, thereby reducing a negligent actor's liability by the intentional actor's percentage of fault.[32] The same rule would presumably apply to aid a strictly liable party where another party's intentional act is a cause of the plaintiff's injuries.

5. **Sale or Lease/Persons Liable**

An injured lessee can sue the manufacturer or another previous seller of the product prior to the lessor. (Comment 1 to Section 402A.) However, there are no Wyoming Supreme Court cases addressing whether the lessor may be strictly liable.[33] A "plain reading" of both Section 402A and the comments to that section would only include sellers of products.

While the Federal District Court for the District of Wyoming has not addressed the lessor issue, it has held that strict liability applies to bailments for mutual benefit, that "the mere fact that a person leases, rather than purchases, should not deny him the protection the law affords," and that "the Court cannot identify a legitimate reason why a person injured by a defective product should be deprived of [the] protection [of strict liability] simply because he was the bailee for mutual benefit and not the purchaser of a product."[34]

The Wyoming Supreme Court declined to extend product liability to a landlord of a leased residential dwelling, for injury caused by an integral component of the dwelling.[35]

6. **Inherently Dangerous Products**

The buyer of an inherently dangerous product, in particular, propane, need not prove it was in a defective condition when it left the hands of the seller.[36] Comment k to Restatement Second of Torts Section 402A would presumably apply. Electricity is not a product within the definition of Section 402A.[37] The Federal District Court for the District of Wyoming has stated that pharmaceutical drugs are unavoidably unsafe products.[38]

7. **Successor Liability**

No Wyoming cases discuss this issue.

8. **Market Share Liability/Enterprise Liability**

No Wyoming cases discuss either market share liability or, in the context of product liability, 'enterprise' liability. It is the opinion of these authors that Wyoming would follow the overwhelming majority of jurisdictions (at least with respect to asbestos claims) that have declined to adopt the market share liability theory. See *Becker v. Baron Bros.*[39]

9. **Privity**

While no Wyoming case specifically discusses privity in relationship to strict liability, the Supreme Court's embrace of Section 402A and its comments eliminate a privity requirement between buyer and seller. (See comment 1 to Section 402A.)[40]

10. **Failure to Warn**

Failure to warn is recognized as providing a cause of action based on a product defect. "If the product is not itself defective but may be unreasonably dangerous if it is used improperly, a plaintiff may show a 'defect' by establishing that the manufacturer failed to warn about dangers associated with the product. . . . Unlike traditional strict liability claims, a claim for failure to provide adequate warnings incorporates some negligence components in determining whether a warning is necessary and/or whether the warnings provided were adequate."[41]

The warning must be associated with the product itself. There is no requirement for a warning relating to dangers caused by outside dangers.[42]

Failure-to-warn cases have two separate requirements of causation: (1) the product for which there was no warning must be the cause of the injury complained of and (2) the plaintiff must show that a warning would have altered his behavior.[43]

While not officially adopted by the Wyoming Supreme Court, the Wyoming Civil Pattern Jury Instructions do set out a cause of action for failure to warn.[44]

11. **Post-Sale Duty to Warn and Remedial Measures**

No case explicitly adopts a post-sale duty to warn as a basis for strict liability.[45] There is no post-sale duty to warn of defects that cause damage only to the product itself. Where the claim is for pure economic loss arising from damage to the product itself, a claim based on a duty to warn—presumably pre- or post-sale—is not recognized and is better adjusted under contract than tort principles.[46]

With regard to post-sale remedial measures, the Wyoming Supreme Court adopted the majority rule that there is no post-sale duty to retrofit a product not defective when sold.[47] However, additional comments, clearly dicta, suggest that should post-sale injuries result from normal and expected use of the product, such a duty may arise.[48] In *Swank v. Zimmer, Inc.*, the United States District Court for the District of Wyoming ruled that subsequent remedial measures were inadmissible unless the evidence was used for the purposes enumerated in Wyoming (or Federal) Rules of Evidence 407 such as proving ownership, control, or feasibility of precautionary measures, if controverted, or impeachment.[49]

12. Learned Intermediary Doctrine

The Wyoming Supreme Court adopted the Learned Intermediary Doctrine in *Rohde v. Smiths Medical*, holding that pursuant to the learned intermediary rule the manufacturer and the distributor could not be strictly liable for the patient's injuries where the manufacturer specifically warned the patients physician of possible side effects.[50] In *Rohde*, the Supreme Court upheld summary judgment in favor of Smiths Medical, as plaintiff failed to present any testimony and evidence that the warnings provided to Rohde's treating physician were inadequate.

The rule was discussed by the Tenth Circuit Court of Appeals in a prescription drug claim that arose in Wyoming.[51] A drug manufacturer discharges its duty to consumers of its prescription drugs when it has reasonably informed prescribing physicians of the dangers of harm from the drug. In addition, a manufacturer can rebut the presumption that, if an adequate warning had been given, plaintiff would have heeded it, if it can prove that a different warning would not have made a difference in the actions of the physician.

13. Substantial Alteration/Abnormal Use

Comment g to Section 402A of the Restatement (Second) of Torts, which provides that plaintiffs must prove the product was defective when it left the seller's hands, was given approval in a 1988 Wyoming Supreme Court decision.[52] Plaintiffs, in a car that was on fire, suffered damages because a seatbelt buckle would not release. Adopting the "inference of defect" rule, the Wyoming Supreme Court upheld the directed verdict in favor of defendant, holding that the plaintiffs had failed to prove that there was no abnormal use and no reasonable secondary causes for the malfunction. Misuse or alteration of a product are specifically listed acts in Wyo. Stat. § 1-1-109 to which comparative fault principles apply. (See Section I, *infra*.)

14. State of the Art

"State of the art" is an area in which there is guidance from decisions that were tried on strict liability theories but that predated Wyoming's formal adoption of Section 402A. "There is no duty upon a manufacturer to adopt every possible new device which has been 'conceived or invented.'"⁵³ A "standard of conduct" by which to judge the defendant's product may be established by showing that other manufacturers have adopted a certain design.⁵⁴ Cases to date have not distinguished between "state of the art" and custom. See W.C.P.J.I. 3.08. See also, W.C.P.J.I. 12.02, entitled "Duty of Manufacturer—Product Design and Manufacture," which states that a "manufacturer is required to exercise reasonable care in the . . . design . . . of a product to insure that it is reasonably safe for an intended use or for a use which the manufacturer should reasonably anticipate."

15. **Malfunction**

While the Wyoming Supreme Court has at times used the terms "defect" and "malfunction" interchangeably, there is no defined separate cause of action arising from a product "malfunction." The more common, and accurate, use of the term "malfunction" is that a malfunction is the result of a product defect. As the court noted in *Rhode v. Smiths Medical*:

> In *Sims*, [*Cf* fn 52] we rejected the plaintiffs' contention that mere proof of a product malfunction was sufficient to create an inference that the product was defective. Instead, the plaintiff has the "additional burden to present evidence that there was no abnormal use and no reasonable secondary causes for the malfunction."⁵⁵

16. **Standards and Governmental Regulations**

No Wyoming case has discussed the violations of, or compliance with, standards or government regulations in conjunction with *strict liability*. Violations of or compliance with standards or governmental regulations is relevant with regard to claims of *negligence*.⁵⁶ Because of the Wyoming Supreme Court's inclination to adopt Restatement of Torts provisions, the authors believe that given the appropriate case, the court would permit evidence of compliance or non-compliance with standards and regulations in strict product liability litigation. *See* Comment d to Restatement (Second) of Torts, Section 286. Violation of statutes or regulations are also proper in considering punitive damages.⁵⁷

Wyoming's Recreational Safety Act, W.S. 1-1-122 does not apply to, and therefore does not protect, a seller of recreational equipment from a cause of action based upon a claim of defective design or manufacture. The Act does, however, protect the provider of the recreational activity, such as a ski lift operator, in a cause of action based on a claimed defect in the equipment being used by the provider, so long as the injury is the result of an "inherent risk" of the recreational activity.⁵⁸

17. **Other Accidents**

Evidence of other accidents or absence of other accidents is admissible, subject to the discretion of the judge as to reliability, authentication, probative value, and a host of other factors.⁵⁹

18. **Misrepresentation**

To date, Wyoming has not specifically adopted Restatement (Second) of Torts Section 402B. *Misrepresentation by Seller of Chattels to Consumer.* Note however that *Phillips v. Duro-Last Roofing*,[60] was tried in Federal District Court on various theories, including Section 402B. The federal court certified the case to the Wyoming Supreme Court on the question of the applicability of Wyoming's then existing comparative negligence statute.[61] While the question of whether Section 402B liability would be recognized in Wyoming was not an issue in that certification, the court gave no indication that Section 402B was not a valid cause of action.[62]

19. **Destruction or Loss of Product**

Recovery may still be had under the inference of defect rule where the product has been lost, destroyed, or is no longer available for examination or production at trial.[63] Reversing the trial court's dismissal of the plaintiffs' claims as a sanction for loss of evidence, and relying on 2 *Jones on Evidence, Civil and Criminal*,[64] and Richard E. Kaye, Annotation, *Effect of Spoliation of Evidence in Products Liability Action*,[65] the Wyoming Supreme Court in *Abraham v. Great Western Energy, LLC*, held that there were a range of sanctions that could be imposed, depending upon the circumstances of the loss of evidence. The court concluded that on remand, "it may be that a sanction less than summary judgment or dismissal of the complaint is appropriate, or even no sanction at all."[66]

20. **Economic Loss**

Wyoming follows the "economic loss rule" which bars recovery under theories of strict liability, negligence, and/or failure to warn where the plaintiff claims purely economic damages unaccompanied by physical injury to persons or other property (i.e., the damage is only to the defective product itself).[67] Recovery must be had under theories of breach of warranty, and/or breach of contract, not tort. The Wyoming Supreme Court reinforced its application of this rule and declined to recognize an exception where there is an absence of contractual privity between the parties.[68]

21. **Crashworthiness**

The "crashworthiness" or "second collision" doctrine is a viable cause of action in Wyoming:

> [A] manufacturer of an automobile is charged with anticipating that the automobile will be involved in collisions with other automobiles or objects while being used for the purpose for which it was intended. Such foreseeable collisions must be taken into account in determining whether the manufacturer has met his duty as a reasonable and prudent man in designing and constructing an automobile. The manufacturer's duty is to design and construct automobiles in a

reasonable and prudent manner so that failures of the parts of the automobile will not cause injuries to the occupants when a collision occurs.[69]

D. NEGLIGENCE

Negligence means the failure to use ordinary care.[70] The essential elements of a negligence claim are: (1) a duty; (2) a violation of the duty; (3) proximate causation; and (4) an injury.[71] For apportionment, see Section I., *infra*. In an action based upon negligent design or manufacture, there must be a demonstration of fault on the part of the manufacturer, designer, or distributor.[72]

The Wyoming Supreme Court has held that showing a defect is a required common element to every products liability case.[73] Based upon that holding, the Tenth Circuit Court of Appeals has ruled that a jury's finding that a product was not defective, but that the manufacturing defendant was negligent, was an inconsistent verdict. The jury verdict in favor of the plaintiff was remanded for a new trial.[74]

E. BREACH OF WARRANTY

Warranties covering goods are governed by Wyoming Statutes Sections 34.1-2-313, 314, 315, corresponding to the Uniform Commercial Code. Breach of these warranties is often alleged in the same complaint with the theories of negligence and strict liability. However, as described in Section B.2., *supra*, there is a difference as to when statutes of limitation will be deemed to be triggered. Also, certain damages may be recoverable only under contract or warranty theory, that is, when there is damage only to the product itself. (See Section C.20, *supra*.)

F. PUNITIVE DAMAGES

Punitive damages may be awarded if, and only if, a preponderance of the evidence shows that the defendant was guilty of willful and wanton misconduct. "Willful and wanton misconduct is the intentional doing of an act, or an intentional failure to do an act, in reckless disregard of the consequences, and under such circumstances and conditions that a reasonable person would know, or have reason to know, that such conduct would, in a high degree of probability, result in harm to another."[75]

Wyoming has established objective standards for the imposition of punitive damages. In *Farmers Insurance Exchange v. Shirley*,[76] the Wyoming Supreme Court adopted the seven factors articulated in *Green Oil Co. v. Hornsby*,[77] and approved by the U.S. Supreme Court in *Pacific Mutual Life Insurance Co. v. Haslip*.[78] These factors include:

(1) Punitive damages should bear a reasonable relationship to the harm that is likely to occur from the defendant's conduct as well as to the harm that actually has occurred.

(2) The degree of reprehensibility of the defendant's conduct.

(3) If the wrongful conduct was profitable to the defendant, the punitive damages should remove the profit and should be in excess of the profit, so that the defendant recognizes a loss.

(4) The financial position of the defendant.

(5) All the costs of litigation should be included, so as to encourage plaintiffs to bring wrongdoers to trial.

(6) If criminal sanctions have been imposed on the defendant for his conduct, this should be taken into account in mitigation of the punitive damages award.

(7) If there have been other civil actions against the same defendant, based on the same conduct, this should be taken into account in mitigation of the punitive damages award.

The Court also discussed the need for a reasonable ratio between the amount of actual damages and the amount of punitive damages.[79]

G. PRE- AND POST-JUDGMENT INTEREST

Pre-judgment interest is provided by rule of court under the doctrine of unjust enrichment.[80] It is meant to compensate the plaintiff not only for the amount by which he has suffered damages in the usual sense, but also for the loss of use of the money to which he is entitled.[81]

In order to recover pre-judgment interest, the plaintiff must show (1) the underlying claim was liquidated (no pre-judgment interest on unliquidated claim); and (2) that the debtor received notice of the amount due.[82] A claim is considered liquidated when it is readily computable by simple mathematical computations.[83] While a claim for prejudgment interest may not be based on opinion or discretion, a mere difference of opinion as to the amount due will not preclude pre-judgment interest nor do disputes as to liability.[84] An award of attorneys' fees was deemed liquidated so that prejudgment interest thereon was awarded.[85]

Pre-judgment interest will accrue from the date the claim becomes liquidated or the date the defendant receives notice of the amount due.[86] It will accrue at the rate of seven percent A.P.R. unless some other rate is called for under a contract or agreement between the parties.

Given that a cause of action under negligence or strict liability may not be had where the damages are purely economic, and that personal injury damages are largely the result of opinion/discretion by the fact-finder, it is questionable whether pre-judgment interest would ever be awarded in a product liability suit.

A plaintiff is entitled to post-judgment interest from the date of the verdict.[87] Such interest is calculated at the rate of ten percent, unless some other rate is called for under a contract or agreement between the parties, in which case the interest would be calculated at the agreed-upon rate.[88]

H. EMPLOYER IMMUNITY FROM SUIT

The Wyoming Worker's Compensation Act[89] grants statutory immunity to participating employers from common law wrongful death and personal injury torts in return for the employer's participation in a no-fault industrial insurance fund to provide "rapid and certain relief for work-related injuries and death...."[90] If an employee who is injured at work is covered by worker's compensation, and the employer is current on his contributions, recovery under the act is the "exclusive remedy" available to the employee.[91]

Third parties do not share this immunity.[92] Thus, an independent contractor, third-party supplier, or manufacturer could be held liable if at fault.[93] The third party may have an indemnity claim against the employer, from which the employer would not be immune.[94]

I. STATUTES

There is no title or chapter of the Wyoming Statutes specifically devoted to product liability. Relevant statutes have been cited above and in the endnotes, including breach of warranty, statutes of limitations, statute of repose, and perhaps most significantly, the comparative fault statute, Wyo. Stat. § 1-1-109 (1994).

Under the comparative fault statute, discussed above in C.4, negligence, intentional and willful and wanton conduct, strict tort, strict products liability, breach of warranty, assumption of risk, and misuse or alteration of a product are all subject to comparative fault principles. The comparative fault statute apportions fault among all actors in product liability cases, regardless of the legal basis of fault. A defendant is not entitled to credit for settlements made by other parties or actors.[95]

For the purpose of obtaining valid releases or other enforceable agreements, the age of majority in Wyoming is 18.[96]

J. JOINT AND SEVERAL LIABILITY

With the adoption of Wyo. Stat § 1-1-109, "Comparative fault," statutes relating to contribution among joint tortfeasors and joint and several liability (Wyo. Stat. §§ 1-1-110 through 1-1-113) were repealed.[97]

James C. Worthen
Murane & Bostwick, LLC
201 North Wolcott
Casper, Wyoming 82601
(307) 234-9345
(Fax) (307) 237-5110
E-mail: jcw@murane.com
Web site: www.murane.com

ENDNOTES - WYOMING

1. *Ford Motor Co. v. Arguello*, 382 P.2d 886 (Wyo. 1963); *Ogle v. Caterpillar Tractor Co.*, 716 P.2d 334 (Wyo. 1986).

2. For express warranty, see Wyo. Stat. § 34.1-2-313 (2013 Lexis); for implied warranty of merchantability, see Wyo. Stat. § 34.1-2-314 (2013 Lexis); for implied warranty of fitness for a particular purpose, see Wyo. Stat. § 34.1-2-315 (2013 Lexis).

3. *Ogle v. Caterpillar Tractor Co.*, 716 P.2d 334, 341.

4. Wyo. Stat. § 1-3-105(a)(iv)(C); *Olson v. A. H. Robins Co., Inc.*, 696 P.2d 1294, 1297 (Wyo. 1985).

5. *Nowotny v. L & B Contract Indus.*, 933 P.2d 452 (Wyo. 1997).

6. *Painter v. General Motors Corp.*, 974 P.2d 924, 927 (Wyo. 1999); *Ogle v. Caterpillar Tractor Co.*, 716 P.2d 334, 339 (Wyo. 1986).

7. *Ogle v. Caterpillar Tractor Co.*, 716 P.2d 334, 345.

8. Wyo. Stat. § 1-3-111. The constitutionality of this statute was upheld in Worden v. Village Homes, 821 P.2d 1291 (Wyo. 1991). The statute was termed a "statute of repose" in contrast to a statute of limitation. Claims for failure to inspect or maintain property in a safe condition, after substantial completion of the construction are controlled by the four-year statute of limitation, not Wyo. Stat. § 1-3-111. *Goodrich v. Seamands*, 870 P.2d 1061, 1063-64 (Wyo. 1994).

9. *Miner v. Jesse & Grace, LLC*, 317 P.3d 1124, 1132 (Wyo. 2014).

10. *Ogle v. Caterpillar Tractor Co.*, 716 P.2d 334, 341; see also *Estate of Coleman v. Casper Concrete*, 939 P.2d 233 (Wyo. 1997).

11. *Ogle v. Caterpillar Tractor Co.*, 716 P.2d 334, 342.

12. *Ortega v. Flaim*, 902 P.2d 199, 205 (Wyo. 1995); wherein the Wyoming Supreme Court declined to apply Restatement (Second) of Torts Section 402A to a claim brought by a social guest of a tenant against a landlord for a claim of a defective stair case.

13. *Campbell ex rel. Campbell v. Studer, Inc.*, 970 P.2d 389, 392 n.1 (Wyo. 1998). Section 2(b) of Restatement Third Torts, which defines a product "defect," was cited and quoted by the Wyoming Supreme Court in the course of its

discussion in *Campbell*. The court, however, found it unnecessary to specifically adopt or apply the Restatement definition. Based, however, upon the Wyoming Supreme Court's reliance upon Restatement Second Torts, the authors would predict that when presented with an issue that would call for the application of provisions of Restatement Third Torts, the same will be adopted.

14. *Valentine v. Ormsbee Exploration Corp.*, 665 P.2d 452, 461-62 (Wyo. 1983) (citing *Maxted v. Pacific Car & Foundry Co.*, 527 P.2d 832, 835 (Wyo. 1974); *Drier v. Perfection, Inc.*, 259 N.W.2d 496, 504 (S.D. 1977)).

15. *Campbell ex rel. Campbell*, 970 P.2d at 392; Wyoming Civil Pattern Jury Instruction 11.04.

16. *Rohde v. Smiths Med.*, 165 P.3d 433, 435, 2007 WY 134; *Sims v. Gen. Motors Corp.*, 751 P.2d 357, 361 (Wyo. 1988) (quoting *Tweedy v. Wright Ford Sales, Inc.*, 64 Ill. 2d 570, 2 Ill. Dec. 282, 285, 357 N.E.2d 449, 452 (1976)); *Valentine*, 665 P.2d at 462.

17. *Buckley v. Bell*, 703 P.2d 1089, 1095; *McLaughlin v. Michelin Tire Corp.*, 778 P.2d 59 (Wyo. 1989).

18. *McLaughlin*, 778 P.2d at 68.

19. *Campbell ex rel. Campbell*, 970 P.2d at 392 n.1.

20. *Rohde*, 165 P.3d at 441, 2007 WY 13.

21. *Loredo v. Solvay Am., Inc.*, 212 P.3d 614, 634, 2009 WY 93 (2009).

22. *Loredo*, 212 P.3d at 634, 2009 WY 93.

23. *Waggoner v. Gen. Motors Corp.*, 771 P.2d 1195, 1204 (Wyo. 1989); *O'Donnell v. City of Casper*, 696 P.2d 1278, 1287 (Wyo. 1985). *Lippincott v. State Indus.*, 145 F.3d 1346, 1347 (10th Cir. 1998).
See also *Ogle*, 716 P.2d at 345 ("Even if a product is defective, unmerchantable or negligently manufactured, the seller may not be liable for a plaintiff's injuries which are caused by unforeseeable alterations in the product rather than the original defects.").

24. *O'Donnell v. City of Casper*, 696 P.2d 1278, 1287 (Wyo. 1985) (citations omitted).

25. *O'Donnell*, 696 P.2d at 1287.

26. 509 U.S. 579, 113 S. Ct. 2786, 125 L. Ed. 2d 469 (1993), *cert denied*, 516 U.S. 869, 116 S. Ct. 189, 133 L. Ed. 2d 126 (1995). Among other Wyoming Supreme Court decisions, *see Bunting v. Jamieson*, 984 P.2d 467 (Wyo. 1999).

27. 114 P.3d 1268 (Wyo. 2005).

28. 332 Fed. Appx. 508, 2009 WL 1678198 (10th Cir. 2009).

29. "Fault" includes acts or omissions determined to be a proximate cause of death or injury to person or property. As originally enacted, § 1-1-109 did not specifically include intentional or willful or wanton misconduct, but did use the phrase, "in any manner negligent." In *Bd. of Cnty. Comm'rs of Teton Cnty. v. Bassett*, 8 P.3d 1079 (Wyo. 2000), the Wyoming Supreme Court held that this language required comparison of all species of culpable conduct.

30. "Actor" means a person or other entity, including the claimant, whose fault is determined to be a proximate cause of the death, injury or damage, whether or not the actor is a party to the litigation.

31. Wyo. Stat. § 1-1-109(d); *Haderlie v. Sondgeroth*, 866 P.2d 703, 708-709 (Wyo. 1993); Pinnacle Bank v. Villa, 100 P.3d 1287 (Wyo. 2004). However, a defendant may be liable to another defendant for contractual or implied equitable indemnity. *Diamond Surface, Inc. v. Cleveland*, 963 P.2d 996 (Wyo. 1998).

32. *Board of Comm'rs of Teton Cnty. v. Bassett*, 8 P.3d 1079, 1084 (Wyo. 2000).

33. In *Ortega v. Flaim*, 902 P.2d 199 (Wyo. 1995), the Wyoming Supreme Court refused to extend strict liability to a landlord for a leased residential dwelling, or to an integral component of the dwelling. *See also Waggoner v. Gen. Motors Corp.*, 771 P.2d 1195 (Wyo. 1989).

34. *Gray v. Snow King Resort*, 889 F. Supp. 1473, 1479 (D. Wyo. 1995).

35. *Ortega*, 902 P.2d at 205.

36. *Abraham v. Great W. Energy, LLC*, 101 P.3d 446, 456 (2004), *relying upon Van Hoose v. Blueflame Gas, Inc.*, 642 P.2d 36 (Colo. App. 1982).

37. *Wyrulec Co. v. Schutt*, 866 P.2d 756 (Wyo. 1993).

38. *Estates of Tobin by Tobin v. SmithKline Beecham Pharms.*, 164 F. Supp. 2d 1278, 1288 (D. Wyo. 2001).

39. 138 N.J. 145, 649 A.2d 613 (1994).

40. This exact issue is currently pending before the Wyoming district court in the case of *Corsi v. Jensen Farms*, 2:12-cv-00052-SWS (D. Wyo. 2013). A decision from the court is expected before the end of the year.

41. *Rohde*, 165 P.3d at 436 (citing *Jacobs v. Dista Prods. Co.*, 693 F. Supp. 1029, 1030 (D. Wyo. 1998)).

42. *Loredo v. Joy Techs., Inc.*, 212 P.3d 614, 632, 2009 WY 93.

43. *Abraham*, 101 P.3d at 456, *relying upon Tune v. Synergy Gas Corp.*, 883 S.W.2d 10, 14 (Mo. 1994).

44. W.C.P.J.I. 11.05: "A defective condition can include a defect . . . in the instructions or warnings reasonably necessary for the product's safe use."

45. *But see* W.C.P.J.I. 12.06. *See also Continental Ins. v. Page Eng'g Co.*, 783 P.2d 641, 664 (Wyo. 1989) (Urbigkit dissenting).

46. *Continental Ins.*, 783 P.2d 641; *United States Aviation Underwriters, Inc. v. Dassault Aviation*, 505 F. Supp. 2d 1252 (D. Wyo. 2007).

47. *Loredo*, 212 P.3d at 632, 2009 WY 93.

48. *Loredo*, 212 P.3d at 632, 2009 WY 93.

49. *Swank v. Zimmer, Inc.*, 2004 WL 5254312 (D. Wyo. Apr. 20, 2004).

50. *Rohde v. Smiths*, 165 P.3d 433, 436 (Wyo. 2007), citing *Jacobs*, 693 F. Supp. 1029.

51. *Thom v. Bristol-Myers Squibb Co.*, 353 F.3d 848 (10th Cir. 2003).

52. *Sims v. Gen. Motors Corp.*, 751 P.2d 357 (Wyo. 1988). *See also Rohde*, 165 P.3d at 437.

53. *Maxted v. Pacific Car & Foundry Co.*, 527 P.2d 832 (Wyo. 1974).

54. *Wells v. Jeep Corp.*, 532 P.2d 595 (Wyo. 1975).

55. 165 P.3d 433, 438. *See also, McLaughliin v. Michelin Tire Corp.*, 778 P.2d 59, 66-67 (Wyo. 1989).

56. In *Distad v. Cubin*, 633 P.2d 167 (Wyo. 1981), the Wyoming Supreme Court adopted the standards of the Restatement (Second) of Torts §§ 286, 287, 288, 288A, 288B, and 288C to govern the relevance of a violation of a statute, ordinance, or regulation as to questions of negligence. *See also Dubray v. Howshar*, 884 P.2d 23 (Wyo. 1994); *Pullman v. Outzen*, 924 P.2d 416 (Wyo. 1996).

57. *Farmers Ins. Exch. v. Shirley*, 958 P.2d 1040, 1053 (Wyo. 1998).

58. *Muller v. Jackson Hole Mountain Resort*, 139 P.3d 1162, 1166 (Wyo. 2006).

59. *Glenn v. Union Pac. R.R. Co.*, 262 P.3d 177, 2011 WY 124. *Cf. Caterpillar Tractor v. Donohue*, 674 P.2d 1276 (Wyo. 1983) (evidence admitted), with *Sims v.*

General Motors Corp., 751 P.2d 357 (Wyo. 1988); *see also Caldwell v. Yamaha Motor Co. Ltd.*, 648 P.2d 519 (Wyo. 1982).

60. *Phillips v. Duro-Last Roofing, Inc.*, 973 F.2d 869 (10th Cir. 1992).

61. The Court found that the then existing Wyo. Stat. § 1-1-109 did not apply to any action involving strict liability. *Phillips*, 806 P.2d at 837.

62. *Phillips*, 806 P.2d at 837-38.

63. *Valentine*, 665 P.2d at 461.

64. § 13:12 (1994 7th ed. and Supp. 2000).

65. 64 102 A.L.R.5th 99-100 (2002).

66. 65 2004 WY 145, 101 P.3d 446, 455-56.

67. *Continental Ins.*, 783 P.2d at 649; *United States Aviation Underwriters*, 505 F. Supp. 2d 1252.

68. *Excel Constr., Inc. v. HKM Eng'g, Inc.*, 228 P.3d 40, 2010 WY 34.

69. *Chrysler Corp. v. Todorovich*, 580 P.2d 1123, 1129-30 (Wyo. 1978). *See also Fox v. Ford Motor Co.*, 575 F.2d 774 (10th Cir. 1978); *Harvey By & Through Harvey v. General Motors Corp.*, 873 F.2d 1343 (10th Cir. 1989); and *O'Donnell*, 696 P.2d 1278.

70. *Wyoming Civil Pattern Jury Instruction 3.02*. "The concept of ordinary care accommodates all circumstances so that the degree of care varies with the circumstances." *Wyrulec Co. v. Schutt*, 866 P.2d 756, 762 (Wyo. 1993).

71. *Turcq v. Shanahan*, 905 P.2d 47 (Wyo. 1997).

72. *Loredo*, 212 P.3d at 630.

73. *McLaughlin v. Michelin*, 778 P.2d 59, 64 (Wyo. 1989).

74. *Bradley v. Gen. Motors Corp.*, 116 F.3d 1489 (10th Cir. 1997).

75. *Wyoming Pattern Jury Instruction 4.06*. For a discussion of willful and wanton misconduct, *see Danculovich v. Brown*, 593 P.2d 187 (Wyo. 1979) and *Loredo*, 212 P.3d at 633.

76. *Farmers Ins. Exch. v. Shirley*, 958 P.2d 1040 (Wyo. 1998).

77. 539 So. 2d 218, 223-24 (Ala. 1989).

78. 499 U.S. 1, 111 S. Ct. 1032, 113 L. Ed. 2d 1 (1991).

79. "After BMW, our jurisprudential approach in Wyoming would not pass muster before the Supreme Court of the United States in an instance such as this in which the punitive damage award is 234.375 times the actual damage award. 'When the ratio is a breathtaking 500 to 1, however, the award must surely 'raise a suspicious judicial eyebrow.' *TXO*, 509 U.S. at 482, 113 S. Ct. 2711, 125 L. Ed. 2d 366 (O'Conner, J., dissenting).' *BMW*, 517 U.S. at 583, 116 S. Ct. 1589. The Supreme Court would find the ratio in this case equally breathtaking, and our standards of review are totally subjective." *Farmers Ins. Exch.*, 958 P.2d at 1045.

80. *State v. BHP Petroleum Co., Inc.*, 804 P.2d 671, 673 (Wyo. 1991).

81. *Rissler & McMurry Co. v. Atlantic Richfield Co.*, 559 P.2d 25, 32 (Wyo. 1977).

82. *State v. BHP Petroleum Co., Inc.*, 804 P.2d 671, 673 (Wyo. 1991).

83. *BHP Petroleum Co., Inc.*, 804 P.2d at 673.

84. *Cargill, Inc. v. Mountain Cement Co.*, 891 P.2d 57, 66 (Wyo. 1995); *Dunn v. Rescon Tech. Corp.*, 884 P.2d 965, 968 (Wyo. 1994). ("'The fact that a skilled accounting may be necessary, involving a determination of amount of sales, prices received, and overhead expenses does not prevent the allowance of interest.'")

85. *Stewart Title Guar. Co. v. Tilden*, 181 P.3d 94 (Wyo. 2008).

86. *BHP Petroleum Co., Inc.*, 804 P.2d at 673.

87. Wyo. Stat. § 1-16-102.

88. Wyo. Stat. § 1-16-102(b).

89. Wyo. Stat. §§ 27-14-101 through 27-14-806.

90. *Harbel v. Wintermute*, 883 P.2d 359, 362-363 (Wyo. 1994) (quoting *Hamlin v. Transcon Lines*, 697 P.2d 606, 616, *reh'g denied with opinion*, 701 P.2d 1139, 1142 (Wyo. 1985).

91. Wyo. Stat. §§ 27-14-104(a). *See also Brebaugh v. Hales*, 788 P.2d 1128 (Wyo. 1990) (partner individually enjoys the same immunity as the partnership); *Pool v. Dravo Coal Co.*, 788 P.2d 1146 (Wyo. 1990); *Clark v. Industrial Co. of Steamboat Springs*, 818 P.2d 626 (Wyo. 1991).

92. With the exception of co-employees, who enjoy the same immunity as their employer except for intentional acts. Wyo. Stat. § 27-14-104(a).

93. *Pan Am. Petroleum Corp. v. Maddux Well Serv.*, 586 P.2d 1220 (Wyo. 1978).

94. *Pan Am. Petroleum Corp.*, 586 P.2d 1220; *Diamond Surface, Inc. v. Cleveland*, 963 P.2d 996 (Wyo. 1998).

95. *Haderlie v. Sondgeroth*, 866 P.2d 703 (Wyo. 1993).

96. Wyo. Stat. § 8-1-102(a).

97. Wyo. Stat. § 1-1-109(e).